The principles and practice of management

The principles and practice of management

Edited by
E F L Brech, BA, BSc(Econ), FBIM

James Bowie Medal.
Fellow of the International Academy of Management.
Chairman: INTEX in the United Kingdom.

Longman

London and New York

Longman Group Limited
London
*Associated companies, branches and representatives
throughout the world*

© Longman Group Limited 1975

First published 1953
Tenth impression 1961
Second edition 1963
Sixth impression 1968
Seventh impression 1970
Third edition 1975

ISBN 0 582 45039.X

Library of Congress Catalog Card Number 73-886 99

Set in 9D/11 Universe Medium 689
and printed in England
by J. W. Arrowsmith Ltd, Bristol BS3 2NT

Authors

Part One **Management in principle**
E F L Brech

Part Two **Marketing**
C G A Godley

Part Three **Manufacturing, supply and technical development**
Richard Field`

Part Four **Personnel: human resources management**
Norman Price

Part Five **The finance and control function**
H E Betham

Part Six **Computer management**
B G Maudsley

Part Seven **Organisational planning and management development**
N V Terry and E F L Brech

Contents

Preface

In an age which is not unfairly described as obsessed by management, there need be no impropriety over sentiments of pride and joy on the occasion of the re-launch of a favoured product in this market.

For over twenty years now, this volume in its earlier editions has, manifestly given satisfaction to its customers, and that is what business management is basically all about. Editor, Authors and Publishers can bask in the warmth of achievement through success in the market-place: for this volume has, indeed, persistently held its place. And, not only at home—for, in these last several years, very nearly half the sales have recurrently been abroad, a modest contribution to the nation's exporting accomplishments.

This Third Edition is the outcome of a thorough-going revision. Consideration was given to revision of the basic design and specification, as is appropriate for good marketing practice. The decision reached, however, was firmly in favour of retaining the fundamentals of concept and framework, a judgement that will now be tested anew in the market over the coming years. Major changes have been made on application and treatment; and, without disrespect to the previous contributors, in the team of Authors.

It is now again the hope of all concerned that the volume continues to afford a comprehensive and up-to-date presentation of the principles and practice of management, with regard paid realistically to the novelties that are worthy of endurance. Once again it has to be stressed that 'comprehensive' cannot mean 'all-inclusive': during the past decade advances in management practice have been too numerous and varied to enable all to be captured in a meaningful way in one volume claiming to stand as a serious and authoritative textbook. The significant trends *have* been captured.

The basic approach of Author's individuality has been preserved in regard to presentation of content and textual treatment, while editorial responsibility has ensured the absence of contradiction or inconsistency in substance. Some details of sectional layout differ, but not anything that is significant.

At an important point of time in Britain's industrial history this revised Third Edition is offered for the benefit of a new generation of up-and-coming managers, whose competence in professional service, as they advance to higher levels of responsibility, may well be the effective reassurance of the nation's continuing viability and, thereby, of the standard of living of its people.

Esher
January 1975

E. F. L. Brech
Editor

Acknowledgements

We are grateful to the following for permission to reproduce copyright material:

The Advertising Association for a table 'Advertising Expenditure 1973' from *Advertising Quarterly*, Summer 1974; British Institute of Management for an extract from 'Committees in Organization' by L. Urwick from *British Institute of Management Review*, Vol. III (1936) and an extract from *Management Abstracts, Digests and Reviews*, Vol. 13, No. 4 (1973); British Leyland for an extract from 'Further notes on Learning Curves' 2.11.67 by Work Study Co-ordination Department; British Overseas Trade Board for an extract from *Destination Europe, British Overseas Trade Board*, May 1973; British Standards Institution for an extract from *British Standards Year Book*, 1973; Centre for Interfirm Comparison Ltd for the table 'Pyramid of ratios', © 1974 Centre for Interfirm Comparison Ltd and the table 'The interfirm comparisons', © 1974 Centre for Interfirm Comparisons Ltd; Electronics Instrumentation & Production for an extract by S. Beer from *Love and The Computer*, 12 June 1963; The Grassland Research Institute for a table 'Composition for "Dry Sow" feed' from *The Composition of Compound Feedstuffs and U.K. and E.E.C. Conditions* by J. R. Crabtree, July 1972; United Kingdom Atomic Energy Authority and The Controller of Her Majesty's Stationery Office for an extract from 'A Systematic Approach to Group Technology' by D. Bennett from *Production Planning and Control*; The Controller of Her Majesty's Stationery Office for extracts from: *Training for the Management of Human Resources*; *Industrial Relations Code of Practice*; *Research Paper No. 3 Royal Commission on Trade Unions and Employers Associations*; *The Redundancy Payments Scheme, Seventh Revision* and *The Training and Development of Managers*; Harlech Television Ltd for the table 'Distribution of National Income'; The Institute of Chartered Accountants in England and Wales for 'Statements of Standard Accounting Practice from *The I.C.A. Handbook*, July 1973; Institute of Marketing for an extract from a brochure 'Marketing—The Concept and its application'; Institute of Personnel Management for an extract from *Organization and the Personnel Manager* by Adrian Cadbury, © 1970. Used with permission of the Institute of Personnel Management; British Institute of Management and Institute of Statisticians for an extract from Basic reference paper prepared by Ronald Brech for conference on 'Managing the Future' jointly sponsored by the British Institute of Management and the Institute of Statisticians; Joint Industry Committee for Television Advertising Research and Harlech Television Ltd for an extract from the *Jictar Establishment Survey Report* January 1973, which covers all the ITV areas. Reprinted by permission; Legion Publishing Company Ltd for an extract from 'Expenditure by Media 1969' from *Advertising Directory*; the author and Management Publications Ltd for an extract from *Managing for Revival* by E. F. L. Brech; Oxford

University Press for translation of 'Martial's epigram' from *The Oxford Dictionary of Quotations*; Times Newspapers Ltd for an extract and Table from a feature article 'Production' from *Sunday Times* 28 January 1973 and an extract from a feature article quoting data from an analytical study of the 1970/1 Census of Productions by Dr E. G. Wood from *The Sunday Times Business News*, January, 1973.

PART ONE Management in Principle

by E. F. L. Brech

1 Introduction

Another generation has come and gone since the American philosopher, James Burnham, with some critical insight into the affairs of our times, christened the epoch that of 'the managerial revolution'. He was seeking to identify the mainspring of economic and social progress in the tides of human living. For decades before him men had been content to see that mainspring in technological prowess and had written their history in the context of the mechanical advances that characterised the 'industrial revolution'. Right through to our own day technology has held its dominance of dominion over man's wellbeing, though the objectives and the methods have changed. In the years of the industrial revolution objectives lay in technology for manufacturing progress—textiles, metals, machine tools. For our own day, industrial advances are sought and found as the spin-off from the technology of nuclear power, of computer design, of space travel and of jaunts to the moon.

There can be no cavil with the significance of technology to the life and living of modern man. James Burnham, however, was putting his finger on a parallel to this significance: technology of itself has no inherent motive power for economic or social progress. This, man has to supply by personal skills in direction, coordination and control—personal skills of leadership and commercial acumen, the abilities of some men and women to impel progress by their influence on and over the activities of their fellow beings in the business of living.

These skills are of themselves simple and are applied at two different though interrelated levels: the one set comprises mental skills of deliberation, judgment and decision, the determination of objectives and goals, with the ways and means of effectively attaining them; the other set includes skills of attitude and behaviour, and the capacity to motivate fellow human beings to give of their best in the team effort towards the accomplishment of those objectives and goals. Loosely regarded, these two sets of skills can be thought of as respectively concerned with 'thinking' and 'doing' and, in brief, the combination of these two is what *management* itself is all about.

Few words in the human vocabulary have suffered as much confusion over the years as 'management'. Being a term in popular usage, it can be bandied about without specific concern for precision of meaning. To many people the term automatically connotes the entrepreneur, especially of the tycoon type, the men whose commercial acumen enables them to engage profitably in 'wheeling and dealing', often in a merchanting or property context rather than in manufacturing industry. By others again, management is held to mean financial manipulation, particularly at the capital level, and there is a widely common usage in personal terms, 'the management' meaning the body of men and women responsible for running the affairs of firms. This application can be seen as the obverse of the process itself in which those men and women engage—very simply, a process of 'arranging things and getting things done'. Whatever special leanings individuals may have, it is likely that pretty well everybody would concur in finding this description acceptable, even if somewhat oversimplified.

In the industrial and commercial setting of Britain, management has over recent years become commonplace in everyday discussion, largely because of the troubles and difficulties through which the nation has been passing. Yet there is little clarity of understanding as to how that management plays its part, or even whether it is effectively playing the right part. It could be argued that this is not a matter of any particular concern to the nation's citizens as a whole, but is rather a preserve for the professionals themselves, the directors and managers. There is much in Britain to suggest this argument being widely supported, and herein could be a source of much of the contemporary national weakness. 'Management is the affair of the managers—leave it to them to bother about' could be an acceptable philosophy, if the nation really did have confidence in those managers' skills and competence. The evidence for that would be continuously vigorous and profitable industry and commerce, something that Britain has certainly not seen for over twenty years.

In its industrial and commercial setting, management is *not* something that can be left to the managers themselves, that is of no concern to the citizens and to the community as a whole. Just the contrary: the community *must* be vitally concerned about the competence and effectiveness of management, because this is the source of its livelihood and the only foundation for progress in its standard of living. The directors and managers may not themselves see things quite like this because they are, understandably, caught up in the activities and interests of the firms to which they belong or by which they are employed. Their lack of recognition, however, makes no difference to the basic fact.

The economic setting

One truism is so much overlooked that it is worth stating explicitly: all wealth for the nation's life can come only from its industrial and commercial enterprise: and improvement in that life can come only from the betterment of enterprise. This, no less, is the responsibility that the nation's directors and managers are carrying.

They may not customarily, if ever, think of themselves in this role. They will be more conscious of their personal setting: as owners of the enterprise, as representatives of an owning family, or of the many hundreds of shareholders in a large public company. Yet, whether conscious of it or not, whether interested in it or not, the truth remains that the directors and managers are responsible for part of the mechanism of community living, their firm is inescapably a microcosm in the economic macrocosm. The progress of civilisation has turned the simple mechanism of exchange into the complex structure of the twentieth-century worldwide industrial and commercial system—the business system—with its innumerable manufacturing units of all sizes and kinds, and its legions of trading, transport and financial houses. This complex pattern of economic activities has two interrelated aims:
(*a*) Making goods and/or services available for purchase by members of the

community at home, or in other parts of the world; and (*b*) In the course of conducting such activities, providing the employment and the payment of wages and salaries, through which the people can buy their commodities and services.

Much of the activity in producing goods and services is of an intermediate character, that is to say, the production of equipment, tools, materials and other things (as well as many kinds of services) by means of which, at later stages, commodities are produced to meet the direct needs of the consumers at home and abroad. The intermediate products and services merely make the chain longer and more complex, but do not impair the objective. In the last analysis, it is only the consumers' expenditure in satisfying their needs or wants that motivates economic activity. There can be no other source of economic motivation. Nor is the difference between 'home' and 'abroad' more than marginally significant in terms of economic motivation, for both streams of purchasing stimulus give rise to claims on the nation's productive facilities.

In the same way, the incomes of people of the community at home—whether from wages, salaries, interest on loans, profits, or export sales of goods and services—are the only source of funds for supporting the purchasing stimulus, the other half of the balancing force in the gross domestic product. This is where the 'levels of earnings' and the 'levels of prices' interrelate as forces influencing the community's standard of living: this is why full employment interrelates with the economic health of the community and cannot be considered as a social objective in isolation.

Each and every firm is, in effect, a unit in the community's economic system, participating in both stimuli by providing goods or services to the market and by paying remuneration and profits to its workforce and shareholders. Each firm, thereby, has its share in the general economic activity, according to its selected purposes reflected in its marketing programme, from which, if successfully accomplished, the profits will be earned as the return on the capital invested. Directors and managers take up their place in the economic system through the formation of their marketing programme, which interprets the trading objectives that the firm has been founded to accomplish, that is, the goods or services that it proposes to supply to its market. From this, too, will stem the demands that it will make for manpower, material, machines, money; and it will spell out the returns it seeks to earn on the resources so invested.

Because of the firm's concern with supplying goods or services, the marketing programme will be a reflection in miniature of the community's pattern of consumer expenditure; and it is for this reason that the formation of that marketing programme will have necessitated some regard for the economic environment. Technological factors (and social influences like major unemployment in the 1920s and 1930s) have tended to overemphasise the 'producer' aspect of economic activity through firms. Neglect of the 'consumer' aspect lies at the root of much of the topsy-turvy economics of our time. The same people, broadly speaking, represent the two aspects, because they are both the producers and the consumers. The citizens of any community are 'producers' when regarded as employers, managers, shareholders, or employees and workers; but they are 'consumers' (in themselves and through their families) when they turn their attention to spending their earnings.

This fundamental economic role no firm can escape, and it puts into correct perspective the common business objective of 'making money'. That objective directors can achieve only through the satisfaction of the market. The directors of a car manufacturing firm, for example, are in business to make cars and to sell them at home and abroad to citizens wanting cars and prepared to choose their firm's products in the qualities and styles offered, at the prices quoted, and with the service facilities offered. If any of the features in this equation fails, then the consumers will not take the cars offered, but will choose somebody else's: the directors will see their own firm's business correspondingly flag. If they are, on the other hand, more successful in operating the equation, they will be earning their profits ('making their money') only because they have correctly diagnosed market requirements and have adequately met them.

Even if not seriously seen by citizens in this significant way for their own wellbeing, management in the present generation has been increasingly impressed on their consciousness. In part in the context of industrial troubles and crises, in part as a medium for television entertainment, management has forced an inroad in the national mind; and a third avenue to reinforce these two has been the long-standing daily or weekly display of vacancies for managerial appointments. The 'managerial revolution' has truly been made manifest; in an era of major technological advancement the nation has cause to find that its economic and social progress, reaping the harvests of technical prowess, is vitally dependent on the skills of management, whatever these may happen to be.

Those last few words are more important than a passing quip, for they point to one of the major weaknesses in the contemporary scene. There has indeed been substantial advancement in management practice, and a vast extension in the range, scope and depth of management studies: yet, curiously, there seems to be still no accepted understanding of the nature of the management role or of the skill it entails—no authorised version, as it were, of management principles or of the essential themes in the gospel that is preached. This is not to imply that the nature of management is not of itself understood; on the contrary, a clear analysis has been available as long as the earlier editions of the present volume, and before. There is, however, no *accepted,* universally adopted definition in the sense in which the scientist knows that all his confrères accept the one meaning for the one particular term. Not that this matters seriously, the differences are superficial rather than substantial, and in the event most managers appear to be doing much the same things in practice, whatever their theoretical understanding of their role. The drawback in this situation lies in the obstacles it creates to the advancement of knowledge and the pursuit of systematic studies. Where every man can claim to be his own authority, orderly cognitive argument is difficult; and management is now in the stage of development when it can benefit materially from the analytical review of experience and the constructive interchange of rationally based ideas. Like any body of knowledge, it can draw progress from disciplined comparative study.

In this respect, management suffers from the drawback inherent in its own setting: it is an employment undertaken and a skill practised by many thousands of persons in many different industrial and commercial communities—as well as in many other fields—within organisations of widely differing character and size, with numerous differences of objective and varieties of personal composition. It has evolved numerous techniques for more effective performance, yet these are 'tools' for carrying out a skill of which the real character is still imperfectly recognised. That there should be many controversies about the relative importance of various aspects of management is but a natural consequence of such a situation.

Career
patterns

Among the many persons who are occupationally engaged in management, most have qualified earlier in their industrial or commercial careers in specialised technical or professional fields—as engineers, chemists, accountants, company secretaries, and the like. They have risen to higher executive positions through years spent in the specialised practice of their profession or technology. Hence they tend, naturally enough, to have a bias or inclination to see management from a certain standpoint, and often lack the capacity to see it as a whole.

Ready illustrations of this tendency come to the mind of anyone with firsthand knowledge of the affairs of industry or commerce. To the engineers, for instance, management is primarily a matter of the design of product and the design of tools, associated with the layout of production flows and the field that has come to be labelled 'production engineering'; from these it is but a small step to questions of planning, rate-fixing, piecerate, bonus systems and other techniques that link up the technical operations with the daily activities of the operatives. To the accountant, management looms largely as a matter of figures; he is interested in the statistical data that record progress, usually couched in money terms; his interest is accordingly centred on procedures which enable him to 'control' expenditure and to identify the expenditure with its outcome and which show themselves in summary form in profit and loss statements and annual balance sheets. New lines of thought are less concerned with the recording of past financial history, the comparison of this year's progress with last year's, than with routines for the control of current expenditure against appropriate predetermined standards. If one turns to yet another branch of technical industry, to the chemist, management appears primarily as a matter of formulae and mixtures, the flow of semi-solids, liquids or gases through a series of plant in which given chemical changes are carried out, and in which the most important requirements are the control of temperatures and pressures, the control of ingredients, and of the quality of the emerging mixtures; the chemical manager's processes are running right if the readings are in accordance with the best standards, and if the samples at various stages of process come up to the formulae set.

To pick out the technical bias of managers in a technical field is not to imply criticism of such executives themselves. They have been trained and developed in a given atmosphere; their whole background has been concentrated on aspects of their technology, and in the absence of any guide as to what management is or means, one cannot rightly blame them if their rise into higher executive levels finds them unable to depart from the customary technological or professional standards to which they have for so long been subject.

Within the present generation a great deal of attention has been given to the 'human factor'—an interest arising out of the wartime need to secure a higher level of labour utilisation, emanating primarily from the shortage of manpower. Experience gained in those abnormal conditions taught industrial managers that the productivity of people at work is enhanced by improvements in the physical and social environment of their work and by the promotion of a sense of participation in its achievement, such participation being not only effective performance of the allotted job but, in addition, a sense that their contribution is of importance to major objectives and to the wellbeing of the organisation. Developments in this more human aspect of management have in their turn given rise to yet another specialist bias, this time in the direction of the human being. They have led many persons, erroneously, to the view that the specialist personnel aspect of management should dominate all others, and a new professional field of 'personnel management' has emerged to parallel the more factual approach of the engineer and the accountant.

The detached observer can see the true position, that each of these specialist aspects is but a part of management, that all have a contribution to make to the total. The true character of management must be seen as a process or skill compounded of several essential elements, many of which are steeped in the traditional technologies, and each of which has its own contribution to make to the effective working of that process as a whole.

2 The management process

Seen against the background and setting outlined in the foregoing introductory chapter, 'management' may well be found too simply described (on p. 4) as being just a matter of 'arranging things and getting them done'. Yet, however much more complicated it may have become by reason of modern practices and techniques, this in fact is really what it is basically about. Considerable misunderstanding has arisen from failure to appreciate the fundamental core of truth contained in that simple wording, and it will be well worth while to bring home explicitly the lesson implied here. Few would quarrel with the assertion that the purpose of 'management' is to ensure that some particular operations or activities *do* get carried out or performed. Many people would want at once to add the descriptive adverb 'efficiently', a notion that will call for some explanation a little later on. 'Management tasks' are thus widely recognised as centring on decisions for planning and guiding the operations that are going on in the enterprise towards a given accomplishment, and with the best practicable usage of the resources involved.

That this understanding is not always recognised so simply and so clearly is due to the fact that in most industrial and commercial activities 'management' is overshadowed by other factors—either the technicalities of operations or the demands of commercial achievement in the pursuit of expanding sales, or perhaps even the complications of the financial and other control routines. These latter may well be unavoidable accompaniments of modern business, but it is important to realise that they are in fact only the tools for the manager's job: they are not the job itself, nor do they really help to explain what that job is.

An illustration

The true nature of management can be more easily seen by analysis from a simple example; for instance, the building of half-a-dozen houses on a small site.

1. Obviously, the first requirement is to know what houses are to be built, how they are to be laid out on the site, the type of materials to be used, the dimensions, the style and quality, the fittings, and so on. These items may be regarded as the objectives and general policy of the particular building operation, and are provided by the architect's specifications and plans. In addition, there is the question of how to go about the work on the site—where to start, which way to proceed, whether to build one house through and then start the next, or whether to complete each stage on all six at once, how long to take and how many men to use. This may be regarded as formulating the

general programme of operations, and is fixed by the Master-builder, in agreement with the architect and tied in with the client's wishes.

2. On this operation the establishment of the 'authority' in charge of the job calls for little special arrangement: the Master-builder takes control—or a General Foreman is put in charge. As the job is comparatively small, will this 'manager' remain on the site full time? If not, arrangements are made to appoint one of the trades foremen to stand in as 'manager' probably always as a working foreman. His responsibilities for decision need to be defined—his relations with the architect's visiting representative, the limits to his powers of independent decision, and so on. Above all, his position as acting overall 'General Foreman' needs to be made clear to all tradesmen and labourers on the job; he may himself be a bricklayer or a carpenter, but what matters from the management standpoint is his position and responsibility as supervisor nominated to act in place of the boss.

3. The allocation of major jobs to the men is largely determined by their own trade skills. But many general jobs will arise for which men will need to be detailed by the Foreman: perhaps unloading lorries, or helping in certain other operations when their own is partially completed or temporarily held up. Certainly, from time to time, a 'human planning' or allocation of tasks will have to be carried out by the Foreman. The engagement of additional or general labour is another item that comes into consideration here.

4. A good deal of preparatory work will be done before any operations start on the site—ordering of materials, hire of equipment, and so on. As soon as the constructional activity starts (even at the stage of preliminary groundworks), the detailed planning becomes very important: how the equipment is to be used; the erection of scaffolding; the sequence of jobs; the layout of the materials on the site; where to unload supplies in relation to where they will be used; alterations to programme or planned methods because of weather difficulties or non-arrival of certain supplies and equipment. However much of the planning is done in advance, modifications are bound to occur, and so some continuous replanning activity will be called for. In a building operation, of course, much of the sequence of jobs is predetermined by the type and plan of house, but even here adjustments are bound to arise from circumstances.

5. To start the job off does not call for any issue of 'commands' in the military sense, but it is the Foreman's task to issue instructions as the work gets under way, and to keep up the working pace on the job. This is essentially a human task. It is in part concerned with attendance and time-keeping, with meal-breaks and tea-making; but it is in much larger measure a matter of keeping harmony and team spirit, and encouraging all the men to get on with the job with a sense of responsibility and enthusiasm. In other words, it is the task of keeping up morale and a consequential good performance of operations.

6. The actual building operations proceed according to the technical dictates of the specifications and plans, as interpreted through the various construction trades and in accordance with programme and plans. They are the activities around which management is weaving its pattern of planning, coordination and control, and they directly reflect the objectives of the project.

7. At many points, some at the outset and some later, the Master-builder and his Foreman will be required to make value decisions on various aspects of the

project and the activity. Some of these will have been made in relation to choice of materials, plant or method, determined by judgments on comparative costs; and these will have been enshrined in the initial specifications and programmes. Yet others will arise as work progresses: delays in delivery of some materials may suggest changes in sequence of operations or in methods of working, or perhaps a reference back to the architect for an alteration of specification. Economic judgment has to be exercised as a basis of decision, and it may occur, too, exclusively at the level of the Foreman when lesser issues are at stake, for example a minor change in plan because of depletion of a trade gang due to sickness absence.

8. As the job proceeds, the Foreman (as well as the architect's man and the Master-builder) will be keeping an eye on progress. He will be watching to see that all the work is done according to specification and plan, that the correct materials are used, that quality of workmanship is as laid down, that correct dimensions are followed, proper finishing touches given where necessary, no faults or errors left uncorrected, and so on. He is exercising a detailed supervision of work for quality, correctness and cost and a control of performance and progress in accordance with the pre-set programme. The time factor is taken into account, and the Master-builder keeps a continuous eye on overall actual costs as compared with the planned estimates.

9. Coordination of work is largely provided by the technical specifications and by the Master-builder's construction programme, but there is still a daily task for the Foreman to undertake. Perhaps at one stage the bricklayers are getting too far ahead of other trades; perhaps the carpenters are dropping too far behind and will shortly hold up the next operation. In a smaller way, the need for coordination will arise whenever a lorry arrives with supplies and has to be unloaded: the Foreman must decide which men to call off, where to put the materials, and so on.

10. Finally, the Master-builder and the Foreman will all the time be acquiring experience of how management and supervision are successfully applied on a building site. In any well organised contracting firm, charts and records would be used to keep note of progress measured against programme, and actual cost against estimate, and this information would be used subsequently as the basis of management decisions in settling future programmes. In an informal way, every manager and supervisor is acquiring and 'recording' in his own mind experience of the best ways of planning and of doing this and that. On the building site, the Foreman's keenness in observing and recording (remembering) the good and bad incidents in planning and in actual progress will make a big contribution to his effectiveness as a supervisor. So, this recording process may be regarded as the last essential feature of the whole management activity.

Looking back at these ten items, it will be noticed that only one of them (item 6) is the physical job of building the houses. The other nine are concerned with preparations, with review of progress, with judgment of economic values, with supervision and leadership of the working team, with coordination of jobs and men. In other words, these other nine are the 'management and supervising' activities associated with that operation of house-building.

**The
elements of
management**

Is it possible to reduce these 'managerial' tasks to any broad general classifications? Items 1, 2, 3 and 4 have a strong element of planning; they are concerned with predetermining the lines of operations, the methods, the equipment, the allocation of tasks, and so on. Item 3, in addition, contributes particularly to coordination.

Item 5 is primarily a process of inspiration, or leadership, but also has a strong element of coordination in it, by integrating the activities of the working group through the issue of commands, together with the constructive supervision of performance in quality and output. Items 8 and 10 are concerned with checking the quality, performance and costs, i.e. with control of the operations to ensure that progress is satisfactory and that the methods applied may be recommended for future use. Item 9 is entirely coordination. Item 7 is a special aspect of control in checking and deciding comparative values relative to possible changes of planning.

It would thus seem from this simple analysis that there are four broad classifications in this example of 'management':

Planning, i.e. determining the broad lines for carrying out the operations (the policy, the general programme, the overall plans, the costs, the organisation); preparing the appropriate methods for effective action (equipment, tools, material supplies, working instructions, techniques, working teams, etc.); and setting the targets of expected performance, cost and outcome (profitability).

Control, i.e. checking current performance against predetermined standards and targets contained in the plans, with a view to ensuring adequate progress and satisfactory performance, whether physical or financial; also contributing to decision in continuing or changing the plans, as well as recording the experience gained from the working of these plans as a guide to possible future operations.

Coordination, i.e. balancing and keeping the team together by ensuring a suitable allocation of working activities to the various members, and seeing that these are performed with due harmony among the members themselves, as well as in relation to plans and programmes.

Motivation (or inspiring morale), i.e. getting the members of the teams to pull their weight effectively, to give their loyalty to the group, and to the task, to carry out properly the activities allocated, and generally to play an effective part in the operations, services or tasks that the organisation has undertaken; with this general inspiration goes a process of supervision to ensure that the working teams are keeping to the plans and attaining an adequate level of effectiveness and economy of work. (This is the process popularly labelled 'leadership'.)

The important point to appreciate is that the building of houses *could not be* effectively or economically carried out without these management activities. The building itself could proceed, but there would be waste of skilled men's time and effort through many trials and errors, waste of material through absence of planning, and numerous delays and difficulties through faulty allocation of jobs and lack of coordination. This is the purpose and function of the management activity, to enable the building operation to be carried through smoothly, effectively and economically. The last of these three purposes means that the resources used in the operations will have been so deployed, in the judgment of the Manager or Foreman, as to attain the best possible outcome with the least necessary usage.

At the heart of the Manager's activity will have lain the consideration and judgment of the economic factors that could promote decisions appropriate to attaining such results through the medium of the groups of people engaged on the operations.

**Management
action**

Were it possible to look more closely into the detail of the management activities summarised in the simple illustration above, the manager(s) could be seen applying the four elements in a real life context. At times, one element would be active in isolation from the others: say, for instance, when the Master-builder is discussing with the architect an aspect of specification, or a change in timing because of non-availability of materials; or when he is working out his schedules and programme for the following week's work. Such activities are instances of the *planning* element, applied alone. Much of the management activity, however, will involve a natural combination of two, three or all the elements, so naturally combined that the manager is not himself aware of any differentiation. Say, for instance again, that the Master-builder has a weekly meeting in the site hut with the Foreman, the leading bricklayer and the concreting ganger; the purpose of the discussion is to review current performance and progress against the programmed targets, and to confirm or to refashion the work schedules for the following week in the light of the current achievement. In this very purpose there is an automatic combination of *planning, control* and *coordination; motivation* comes in at once when the Master-builder asks the Foreman and the leading workmen to work to the plans for the following week and perhaps to attain somewhat better progress than has recently been in evidence.

What kinds of activities are customarily thought of as pertinent to each of the four elements taken in isolation will shortly be considered. Broadly speaking, *planning* is the only one that occurs in real life situations in isolation to any serious extent; *control* and *coordination* invariably involve interassociation with each other and with *planning*. It could be argued that *motivation* occurs alone, for example, during a joint consultation session with representatives of the operatives; or, when the manager is giving a 'pep-talk' to his departmental supervisors. Yet in either of these cases there is pretty certain to be some inclusion of or reference to current performance or to expected targets and developments, i.e. an incursion of the *control* and *planning* elements. Moreover, the very action of bringing together representatives or foremen from different departments of the organisation implies a contribution to *coordination*.

The point at issue here is not worth pursuing any further, for, in everyday industrial life, the manager will be exercising a role characterised by the varying combinations of the four elements. His concern will always be to have resources and activities well organised (arranged) in relation to the performance that he wants or seeks to achieve (objectives and targets); and to direct or regulate the application of those resources so as to attain the best practicable progress of activities, the best attainable performance by the personnel engaged on them. In parallel, he will be concerned to maintain (to resort to a little jargon at this early stage) optimum cost-effectiveness; the best useful output in relation to the input committed. His own role is a recurrent interaction of 'thinking' and 'doing'. The thinking is, first, in the form of deliberation about resources, timings, targets, circumstances, influences, expectations, hindrances—all bearing on the activities over which his role is set and the objectives that he is committed to attain. In part, this thinking will be concerned with the short term, the current situation, but he knows he must always be taking account of the longer term implications. From such deliberations he will arrive at conclusions (= judgment) on the basis of which he will be ready to initiate action (= decision) either on his own part, or by those departments and personnel that lie under his jurisdiction. It is this interrelated combination of judgment and decision that constitutes the essence of management in action, the medium by which the four elements are applied in the realities of industrial and commercial life.

Responsibility and decision

There are people who place some importance on the distinction between the 'thinking' and 'doing' facets of the manager's role, but there is no real justification for this: the distinction is largely arbitrary, if not artificial. A very great deal of the manager's own tasks lies in the 'thinking' facet, because he is essentially always involved with what is being done and how that relates to what ought to be done, with performance and outcome and how these compare with targets and expectations. Much of his own 'doing' is an adjunct to his 'thinking'—in the study of figures, of charts, of criteria of performance and other control data, or in the preparation and writing of reports, revising plans and the like. The other aspect of his 'doing' is concerned with the human factor in his role, with consultation, with communication by the issue of instructions or by other modes. That he must at times be concerned with technical matters does not in any way invalidate this assessment, because in this field he will once again be primarily active on the 'thinking' plane. Should a manager occupy himself in technical 'doing' to any extent (for example, in laboratory research or in trying out machining operations) he can rightly be accused of neglecting his managerial role! Nor is this assessment gainsaid by recognising that the manager is held accountable for the accomplishment of the activities that are under his jurisdiction: on the contrary, for this is the essence of his role—'arranging things and getting things done'. It is for this reason that the notion of 'executive' comes into play as the commonly used alternative for 'manager', for the job of the 'executive' is literally to get things done. (In passing, it may be useful to note another common usage which is an extension of this same notion: the title 'Chief Executive' now commonplace as an alternative to 'Managing Director' or 'General Manager'.)

The important facet of the executive role that does call for some emphasis is that of the inherent *responsibility* for getting things done. If the managerial role is correctly seen as a combination of 'thinking' and 'doing' in the form of 'judgment and decision' leading to the attainment of effective performance, the significant feature of this role must lie in the 'accountability' that it entails. It is inescapably the manager who is *responsible* for arranging and getting done the things that are under his jurisdiction, and, thereby, for managing the activities of the personnel involved.

References to responsibility and accountability inevitably conjure up immediately the interrelated notion of 'authority' and the often alleged disparity between the two. A closer look into this allegation in more practical form will be pertinent in a later context: the need here is to look analytically at what is involved, so as to clear away something of a nonsensical confusion. The allegation is often heard from managers that they carry 'responsibility' but 'lack the necessary authority'. This statement, as it stands, is nonsense—but there must be something that gives rise to the commonly repeated impression. If the situation alleged is examined analytically in the context of the manager recounting this allegation, it will nearly always be found that in fact he *lacks responsibility* as well as authority. In other words, he holds a certain role by title (and is paid for holding it), and in broad terms he has some extent of understanding of what is expected of him in that role. What he lacks is a specific and clear understanding of the scope and scale (or depth) of the jurisdiction that the role carries for judgment and decision, and for the initiation of action stemming from that decision.

The simple explanation will always be found to lie in the absence of definition of responsibilities delegated. The delegation has been made only in broad terms, or only vaguely, or only by the implication of a title—certainly *not* in the form that will be referred to later (p. 45) when the requirements of effective delegation will be examined.

Accountability

Reverting to the wording used on page 14, the key word to fasten on in this situation is 'accountability', because this is the true core of the management process or the managerial role. The manager is *not* in that role just to do jobs; not to think of designs, nor to work out engineering methods, nor to sell products, nor to undertake any other of these practical activities of industry and commerce. His role is, by definition, to see that all these things get planned and done effectively—by the people employed under his jurisdiction for these very tasks and purposes. His role is, by definition, to think (especially to think ahead), so that from his deliberation will come judgment leading to decision as to programmes, plans, methods, standards and targets; and leading to the initiation of the activities from which the performance will ensue to attain the plans and targets. This is the very nature of *accountability,* for it inherently implies being accountable for performance and attainment.

'Accountable' and 'responsible' are identical in this implication, and it is instantly seen that the implication must be specific: a manager can be accountable or responsible *only for something.* To posit otherwise is meaningless. The immediate object of the accountability is a decision or series of decisions from which stem plans and targets, and activities working towards their fulfilment.

Accountability and decision belong together, the one the obverse of the other; together they form the essence of the managerial role, and together they beget authority—not in any vague or uncertain way, but in the natural consequential sense that a man or woman can only be accountable for something if it lies within their jurisdiction to form and make decisions about it. Again, not just meaningless or purposeless decisions, but decisions that bring about this performance which is the objective of the accountability.

All this is just another way of saying that 'responsibility (= accountability)' and 'authority (= decision)' inherently belong together. Analytically considered, 'responsibility without authority' (or conversely) is an inherent contradiction, for the one cannot exist without the other. Practically considered, in terms of the common allegations, the situations alleged as being the one without the other will be found in reality to be cases where *neither exist.* The manager alleging 'responsibility' but lamenting his 'lack of authority' is really confessing that he is lacking the responsibility as well: the jurisdiction of his role is deficient, because if he does not have the power to decide (= authority) he cannot be held accountable (responsibility). To have this relationship correct is the centre point of delegation and it will be re-examined in practical form in that setting.

The human facet

Nowhere does the nature of the managerial role, with its combination of 'thinking and doing' or 'judgment leading to decision' come out so clearly as in the exercise of jurisdiction over the personnel concerned in undertaking the activities of the enterprise. People form a natural part of the activities of industry and commerce in two different ways: as the consumers (= customers) of the products or services made and sold, and as the employees who bring about the manufacture and the sale of the products or services. Not, of course, the same people in the corresponding situations, but human elements in both levels, none the less. Just as the medieval philosophers could argue enjoyably over how many angels could dance on the point of a pin, their presentday counterparts can engage in dialectic as to whether (for instance) a fully automated computer-controlled production department—having no employed personnel at all—is strictly speaking a subject of 'management activity'. Let the argument be joined elsewhere! For this context, it can suffice that far and away the greater proportion of industrial and commercial activities involve employed personnel, to a greater or less extent. In the norm, therefore, management has this inherent human or social character; the executive has to take command of people as a natural feature of his responsibility—the element of 'motivation' is justified as essential.

This is not the place to go into the implications of the human facet of the managerial role, save only to stress its importance. To underline, particularly, the considerable extent to which the manager's skills of 'thinking and doing' and 'judgment and decision' are called into play on the human plane, whether from the customer standpoint or from that of the employee. The present generation is the first in Britain's industrial history to which the description 'fully articulate' could properly be applied: witness the combination of minimum school-leaving at sixteen years with legal majority at eighteen years; witness, too, the everyday involvement in the affairs of the times through the medium of the TV channels. It is, of course, from the standpoint of employee management that the major demands on the manager's skills will stem. In Britain at least, these demands have to be faced on two planes at once: at the individual level of personnel relations and man-management within each particular company, factory, office, depot or department; at the national level through policies and problems emerging from industrywide attitudes or deliberations. It has to be recognised that the latter often impinge intimately on the former, yet the individual manager seldom has any channel of support from the national or industry level. Within his own jurisdiction, and with the support of the colleagues who are his co-managers in the firm's organisation, he has to cope as well as possible with the human situations under his command.

His major concern must be the attainment of performance and the containment of cost. Motivation is his instrument. Social skill is his requirement:

without that, his chances of applying effectively the instrument of motivation are likely to be slender, perhaps even negligible or non-existent. A manager's human or social skills will enable him to take his people along with him in the pursuit of performance. These are not skills of bonhomie or camaraderie; he is not called on for jovial back-slapping and anecdotes in the canteen; nor even for the time-honoured allegory of 'knowing all the men by their first names' and remembering their birthdays. Nor does it have to be assumed that the skills for social accomplishment are rare inborn qualities gifted to only few men and women and never to be acquired by others less fortunately endowed. The basic human skill is a matter of principle—the genuine recognition that 'people matter'. On this recognition can be built an acquired attainment of 'taking people along', provided the necessary and appropriate effort of 'thinking and doing' is applied to it. Mostly, the 'thinking' is the more important facet, so that mature judgment has been formed before the decision is taken as to the action to be initiated. The annals of personnel management in any industrial milieu are replete with experience of human problems and conflicts stemming from inadequately considered initiatives. Between recognising that 'people matter' and successfully 'taking them along' in performance, the social skills required in the manager are quite simple—though their effectiveness in the real life situation will always turn on the underlying informed judgment. In summary, the simple requirement can be stated as follows:

1. Seeing the other person's point of view. In turn this involves recognising the emotional factor in human situations; an understanding by listening (especially to what is *not* being said).
2. Developing and fostering personal contact (with an individual or with members of a group) as a foundation for cooperation. This in turn calls for imparting appropriate information to the persons concerned; consulting with such persons in matters that bear on their own involvement; and by communicating and consulting, offsetting fears relating to impending changes, expected or unexpected.
3. Through these human reactions, promoting confidence in the leaders of the activities and self-confidence in the persons or teams participating.

This brief summary of a major aspect of management practice is further studied in Part Four.

Motivation

Within the industrial and commercial context, the manager's social skills are never applied in a vacuum, but always in the context of the activities, operations, problems, deficiencies or successes of the working situation. Much of the substance of the consultation and communication must inevitably be that of plans, targets, progress, performance, quality, cost, efficiency and profitability. Thus the three other elements (planning, control, coordination) play their part in the success of motivation. The manager who is supported by firm and effective information on planning and performance can go into consultations with higher confidence of successful communication and cooperation than the one who, not effectively and systematically informed, has to engage in consultations about unknowns, about ifs and buts, from which mistrust and conflict could be the natural outcome. Perhaps the construction industry in Britain has the best collection of archives to illustrate this point, especially among medium-sized firms. The commonly encountered paucity of planning and control system has caused many a confusion over targets and bonus earnings, and led drearily to many an unnecessary stoppage; or, at best, has played into the hands of willing agitators standing by for the opportunity to create the stoppage. Because of inadequate planning of operations, with interrelated availability of materials or equipment, men on the site have not been able to work in accordance with the intended norms, and thus have not earned the expected bonus. No fault or deficiency on their part, but the contracting firm has not taken such a philanthropic standpoint. So, no bonus earned, none paid—and the foundation is laid for friction and conflict on the job. The fault has recurrently lain in deficiencies of planning, the absence of systematic and reliable techniques concerned to provide for (= plan) and monitor (= control) the continuing progress of the operations.

The point being emphasised here is that, for the manager in industry and commerce, whether private enterprise or public corporation, motivation cannot be thought of as an isolated element, purely a matter of good human attitude. It is essentially and intimately involved with the overall application of management, that is to say, with the other three elements of planning, coordination and control as well. Not that this assertion in any way downgrades the importance of the 'motivation' factor in the manager's role, or gives him any excuse for neglecting it, whether accidentally or by disinclination. Once given that the people are required for job performance, the manager has the responsibility for taking them along in his own task of getting that job arranged and accomplished. While his human (or social) role can be exercised to some extent by effective consultation or communication in the planning stages (before or at the outset of the operations concerned), a great part of it will be applied through 'supervision' as the operations proceed. Supervision can be thought of as a human facet of the 'control' element. Some part of it, of course, is applied through techniques and data—using control information of comparison between 'actual performance' and 'target or standard', as in the case of many widely used systems of production control, budgetary control, and so on. Yet a large part of supervision remains human, in the form of direct oversight and contact with the men and women on the job. In any enterprise above the scale of very small workshops, depots or offices, much or most of this aspect of supervision will be delegated to 'supervisors'—foremen, chargehands, gangers—but the manager is *not* thereby relieved of *responsibility* for effective motivation. He has passed on to his subordinate supervisors a share in the day-to-day tasks of motivation, together with some participation of the overall responsibility for its effective application: he cannot shed the responsibility, he cannot cease being accountable for its outcome, in human terms or in performance terms. This is what gives the importance to 'supervisor training'—a requirement that must persistently confront every manager.

Such delegation adds another slant to the manager's human relations task, in the sense of the interplay between himself and the supervisors associated with him under his jurisdiction. It also brings in relationships with specialists in the firm's organisation, such as a Personnel Officer or a Safety Officer. While such relationships are in part a facet of the overall human pattern in a managerial role, and thus subject to much the same sort of social skills, they also raise considerations of 'organisation structure' as the framework of the delegation, a topic to which attention will be turned shortly.

A definition

Looking back on the simple illustration of management in action and the comments on the essential interrelated elements, it is now appropriate to fasten on the notion of 'responsibility' or 'accountability' to which reference has been made here and there. This is in effect the core of the managerial role: 'to arrange things and get them done effectively through the operations of people employed'—an implicit *responsibility* mandated to the manager. It is not he who will perform the operations; but it is he who is held accountable for ensuring that they are performed and that the performance is effective. Recognition of this basic notion enables a formal definition to be set down in, say, the following form, though many variations of wording could be used to express the essential features:

● *Management* is a social process entailing responsibility for the effective and economical planning and regulation of the operations of an enterprise, in fulfilment of given purposes or tasks, such responsibility involving:

(*a*) judgment and decision in determining plans and in using data to control performance and progress against plans;
(*b*) the guidance, integration, motivation and supervision of the personnel composing the enterprise and carrying out its operations.

The management activities that translate this process into effect in industrial and commercial enterprises form a complex pattern, as the contents of this present volume very well portrays. Various subdivisions and groupings of those activities depend on the operations and character of the enterprises, and some aspects of these subdivisions will be examined in the context of 'delegation' (see p. 45).

In the present context of seeking to attain a thoroughgoing understanding of management by means of an analytical review, there are three special facets of the overall process that can also be usefully identified by sub-definitions:

● *Direction*. That part of management which is concerned with the determination of objectives and policy and the checking of overall progress towards their fulfilment, leading to accountability for the vitality and profitability of the enterprise.

● *Organisation*. That part of management which is concerned with the determination of (*a*) the responsibilities by means of which the activities of the enterprise are delegated to or distributed among the (managerial, supervisory and specialist) personnel employed in its service; and (*b*) the formal interrelations established among the personnel by virtue of such responsibilities.

● *Administration*. That part of management which is concerned with the installation and carrying out of the procedures by which the programme, plans and targets are laid down and communicated, and the progress of activities regulated and checked against them.

Science v. art

It may seem to some people unusual to find management referred to as a 'process'; yet if thought is applied objectively to the contents of the past few pages, it must be recognised that this is about the most accurate description of it. A 'process' is something that is carried on or carried out, usually in a systematic way, sometimes in a predetermined way, and it may be either simple or complex. It does not have to be physical, nor necessarily involved with anything physical. This is precisely how the manager's role and tasks may be summarised; something that he does or carries out, by a combination of two interrelated phases of personal action:

- On the mental plane, judgment and decision concerned with the determination of objectives, of ways and means of working towards those objectives, of plans and targets, and concerned also with the review of performance and progress towards the required or expected accomplishment.

- On the behaviour plane, the exercise of attitudes and skills for getting effective cooperation and high performance from the men and women engaged on the operations under his command.

By no stretch of imagination can the overall combination of these personal actions be thought of as anything else but a 'process'. This is not to deny that a skill, a high skill, must underlie the exercise of that process. This is the skill described in the jargon as 'management competence'. It is not necessarily an inborn aptitude, specifically separating some people from others; it is a skill or competence largely made up of mental and personal factors, but there is a great deal to be gained in it by way of serious learning and self-development—the competent manager is rarely found readymade. There are managers who suffer delusions in this respect, believing or imagining that *they* have the 'management hunch' to a high degree of excellence: the personnel serving under them know how hollow this hunch rings.

The notion of 'hunch' or 'flair' in management also arises from confusion with 'business acumen', that is to say, an innate though rare capacity for swift evaluation of situations that can lead to commercial profit. It is found in many of the men who make comfortable livings out of buying and selling, even in the form of small-scale trading in street markets; it is found (and endorsed as more respectable) in the 'big names' of property business, share dealing or financing takeovers. The skill here is commercial acumen and not necessarily management competence at all; in fact some of these men could well prove to be poor managers in the true sense of that term.

There is, of course, an element of 'entrepreneurial acumen' in any higher management responsibility—in the sense that the manager has to form a judgment and make a decision as a consequence of his personal interpretation of the situation he is dealing with; however much information is given to him to assist judgment, he has personally to reach a conclusion and decision, of greater or less significance, according to circumstances. The differentiation implied in this foregoing sentence is sometimes pin-pointed as the distinction between *decision making* and *decision taking*—the former referring to the formulation of the judgment by the evaluation of the facts and figures, the latter implying the decision to direct or instruct consequential action and thus accepting accountability for the outcome.

It will not be amiss here to make a passing reference to what was once a passionately argued controversy: is management a science or an art? Echoes of the argument can still be heard, so it may be worth a few words to lay the ghost. To some extent the dispute raged over difference of approach, but to a much greater extent it was a confusion over terms rather than a serious conflict of opinion. Neither side troubled to make clear what they meant by the choice of respective label 'art' or 'science', and neither went to the length of seriously analysing the true nature of the thing about which they were arguing; had they done this, much of the force of their alleged differences would have disappeared. Those defending management as an *art* meant by their claim that it had in it a very large element of personal skill, such that mere learning of techniques would not lead automatically to competence. So much of this skill was centred on human judgment and human considerations of cooperation and morale that any mechanistic approach could not achieve success. In serious analysis this could not, and would not, be denied. On the contrary, it would be re-emphasised. Does this criterion constitute an 'art'? What resemblance would it have to the skills of the painter or the musician? The analogy used by the advocates was that of the medical doctor, pointing to his understanding of the psychological and emotional factor in therapy and to the significance of 'bedside manner' in his approach to the patient. All very true, and analogously relevant to the practice of management. Yet, how does this constitute an 'art', unless that label is being used in a very loose and general sense?

On the other side the advocates were more impressed with the significance of mature judgment as a factor in effective management. Without in any way denying the importance of 'the human factor in management', this view fought shy of emotion because of the danger of its degeneration into hunch, or uninformed and irrational decision; emphasis was laid on getting the relevant facts of a situation as the basis of deliberation and decision. Proceed, it was advocated, as the *scientist* does in his own realm: collect the facts and the data; study and analyse these as necessary; determine conclusions; check their validity; make the final decision; and again check its outcome. Such a 'scientific method' approach has a cold mechanistic ring about it, but that was never the intention of the protagonists favouring 'scientific management'. Human aspects and situations were always among the facts to be studied and considered. Perhaps the choice of label was as inaccurate and as unfortunate as that on the other side of the controversy; it was chosen as a slogan during a campaign in America in the early 1900s, when no doubt it served a local purpose well. The passing of decades, however, fogged the significance of the label, and so later advocates came to speak of 'the science of management'. That a systematic body of knowledge underlies the competent practice of management hardly anyone today would deny; and much of that knowledge lies in various fields which are of themselves academic disciplines. The summation of such parts cannot constitute a new 'science'. What the advocates really meant is that competence in management necessitates both an adequate basis of knowledge and a mature systematic approach; they did not mean that management is on all fours with nuclear physics.

Thus from both sides the controversy disappears into the thin air of terminological inexactitude. Putting the essential parts of the two sides together, the true view of management emerges as a skilled *process* entailing human considerations, requiring maturity of judgment, a systematic approach, a wide range of knowledge. Add to this a foundation of ethical standards, and one has all the makings of a profession; certainly neither a science nor an art, as these words are normally understood.

To the managers of today, it may well seem difficult to imagine that protagonists used seriously to engage in controversy and conflict over semantics. Fortunately, this kind of academic exercise has so fully disap-peared that even to recall historical anecdotes (some of them amusing) can now serve no purpose. *Management* has become an accepted name for the responsible process defined above, and is well on the way to being the international word as well. Witness the body that lived from 1924 to 1974 as CIOS (Conseil Internationale d'Organisation Scientifique), now renamed the 'World Council of Management' with exactly the same word (and spelling) in the official French version.

3 Management action

Up to this point the examination of the management process has been in analytical terms, abstracted from many of the realities of life and setting within which the individual manager has to express his role. Whether as owner-manager or as employed manager, his role is set in industry and commerce, in the business system, and he carries out that role within the confines of a given firm, a business establishment. In the older established industrial communities like Britain, business establishments tend to be thought of primarily in 'ownership' terms, particularly in the case of the medium or smaller firms still standing in personal or family ownership. The firm is to the owners the means of livelihood, the basis for building up capital wealth, the family heritage. Even in the larger enterprises, with impersonal ownership through large and scattered public shareholdings, the firm is still thought of in property terms as investment for earnings through dividends or as the source of capital gains by growth of asset value. Public shareholders reflect the attitude of family owners in *not* taking particular interest in the wider concept of the firm seen in its setting in the overall economic system—a cog in the mechanism of community living, a microcosm in the economic macrocosm.

Nor do shareholders consciously see the twofold interrelated economic objective which inescapably underlies all the activities of the firm whose shares they hold: the parallel purposes of supplying the goods and services that consumers need, and providing the means by which these consumers can purchase their goods and services. Looked at fundamentally, any and every unit (or firm) in this complex macrocosm of business enterprise takes its role from its setting and involvement therein, and it exists, in the last analysis, in order to provide something directly or indirectly for the benefit of the citizen-consumers. Each enterprise individually has, as it were, a specific share in those general purposes, according to what has been determined for it by its founders, or their successors in the presentday body of governors or directors.

As constituted under Company Law, the directors of a firm have a first responsibility in legal terms—to ensure that affairs are conducted in accordance with the company's constitution and with the law, and in fulfilment of objectives laid down in the Memorandum of Association. These objectives may be concerned with the manufacture and/or sale of commodities, or with the provision of services of one kind or another, or with the conduct of some other activities. Out of such operations the owners expect to reap remuneration on their investment or reward for their venture, in the form of profits.

The market setting

This latter derivative objective was implicit in the formation of the enterprise and figures prominently in the mandate entrusted by the owners to the directors. The directors accomplish this implicit objective by undertaking the much fuller responsibilities involved within the direction of the enterprise—all the activities that they will direct and control in the manufacture and sale of their products, or merchanting through wholesale channels for home and export trading, or the provision of services such as transport, electricity supply, banking, advertising, loans for house purchase, or amusement in the form of television or the theatre. They are thereby contributing to the living of the citizen members of the community through affording opportunities to purchase as consumers (customers) and through opportunities for earning as producers (wages, salaries, dividends). They have no choice in this objective as long as they keep their firm actively in business. The firm's very existence as a going concern makes it an integral part of the working economic fabric of the modern industrial society, though few directors overtly recognise their role in this form.

In this economic setting, the management of industry and commerce finds both the background and the substance of its role: to arrange the various things that will be required to meet these two objectives and to be responsible for ensuring that those things get done. Many contributing factors have to be combined among those 'things' of the economic activity: land and premises for manufacturing, distributive and administrative operations; materials to be acquired, whether used in the raw state direct from natural sources or as the outcome of synthetic processes; plant and equipment, machine tools, or, in the case of distribution, ships, rolling-stock and motor vehicles. Such factors of production and distribution are not of themselves productive—they need the skill and effort of man. Throughout the entire range of economic affairs, the dominant feature is the work of the men and women employed, the human effort in part directed to the manipulative and operative tasks and in part to the mental processes of designing, calculating, drafting, planning, corresponding, selling, deciding, managing. It is the pervasiveness of this human element that gives management its special character as a social process. However these human forces are employed they need to be unified, coordinated, welded into a team effort and directed effectively towards a given purpose. In this lies the role of management.

Some emphasis needs to be placed on the duality of aim in the basic principle of economics: the provision of goods and the maintenance of employment. The rise of a capitalist system in the eighteenth and nineteenth centuries and the emergence of large-scale unemployment earlier in the twentieth, have both tended in Britain to add weight to what might be called the 'producer' aspect, that is, to the interests of the personnel employed in the factories and depots. Not only has this indirectly encouraged and fostered the growth of a strong trade union movement, but it has also promoted a good deal of direct concern for the wellbeing of the workers. Much of the driving force behind the development of behavioural sciences in industry in recent years has stemmed from this source. No criticism is implied by this observation: all these developments are good things and they belong closely to the important element of motivation in management. Even taken at its narrowest interpretation, worker satisfaction is an important contributing influence to high performance on the job.

The consumer

Attention is drawn to this producer emphasis in order to contrast it with the long-standing neglect of the *consumer* aspect. Broadly speaking, of course, in any industrial community the same people are largely both the producers and the consumers: 'producers' when regarded in their employment context, as employers, managers, shareholders, employees in factory, depot, office, and the like; 'consumers' themselves and through their families in the conduct of their everyday living, by paying rent or mortgage dues, and spending on the needs and enjoyments of the household. The *consumer* aspect, however, does have another significance, and the long-standing neglect of it has been at the root of much of Britain's topsy-turvy economic policies and practices, as well as being the major influence causing the sluggish attitudes of enterprise and the consequential poor trends of growth. Too much preoccupation with producer interests has warped management views and led to wrongly slanted business objectives and policies.

Latterly some shift of the emphasis has been in evidence at governmental levels, with concern for the consumer being given an overt place in political programmes and propaganda. Yet, it is far more important that the directors and managers of business enterprises should take up this concern and set it in correct perspective in their own roles. *The consumer interest is the fundamental factor in industrial and commercial enterprise*: the economic activity of a community, of its very nature directed to the twofold objectives of providing goods and services and the wherewithal for acquiring them. But the motive power comes from the first of the two facets: it is the citizens seeking to satisfy needs and wants who wind up the economic system, providing the demand that producer activities will seek to satisfy. So fundamental is this principle that it could be fashioned into a slogan: 'Business has no meaning unless to serve and satisfy a customer (consumer).'

When a firm sees its activity correctly set in this perspective, it recognises at once the paramount importance of the *marketing* factor in management. Marketing starts with identifying the customers (consumers) the firm intends to serve and seeks to satisfy, so that they will continue to come to it for the supply of their needs. Marketing thus imposes on management a first responsibility to know and to understand the product or service it is offering and the market (consumers) to which it is offered. Correctly interrelating these two provides for the firm a *marketing programme* as the direct medium for fulfilling its objectives. This basic approach to the foundation of management in practice has been summed up in simple terms by urging on directors and managers the key question, 'What is your business?' If they could keep this always in the forefront of judgment and decision, accepting the obligation to provide the satisfactory answer, then they are well on the road to continuously effective management. And, put into the contemporary jargon, their management will be *market-oriented*.

The firm that sees its correct setting in the economic system answers this key question by fixing its location in the market(s) it is seeking to serve with the products or services it is offering, whether at home or abroad. Its customers may not be direct users as consumers, but, rather, other firms requiring that product or service as an intermediate for their own manufacture and supply of products and services with direct appeal to consumers at one or more stages removed. Whether as a supplier of final consumables or as an intermediary anywhere in the economic chain, an individual firm has unavoidably to make use of resources of manpower, of materials, of machines. It buys or hires these factors of production, paying for them in open market purchase; and it obtains the wherewithal to purchase the resources from the sales in turn of its products or services to consumers, supplementing the expenditure of the initial capital invested at its foundation or obtained by way of loans. This is where the profit objective emerges, for the conduct of the firm's trading activities has to result in overall earnings that will leave adequate returns on the investments made by its owners. Earnings that represent just the 'cost' of the capital (the equivalent norm of interest) are not adequate, because there must be reward for the assumption of the risk in the enterprise—the risk that the marketing may have been inappropriate, and, therefore, the product or service remains unsold or inadequately sold relative to the scale on which it has been produced, bringing failure of the capital invested rather than profit on its exploitation. With this risk to run, the lender will require a greater return as part of his safeguard and encouragement to invest, and it is the compensation for the risk undertaken that gives rise to the real significance of profit—described by one economist as 'the reward for uncertainty'.

Business forecasting

It is not uncommon for *risk* and *uncertainty* in the business world to be thought of as unusual features, perhaps even somewhat artificial and brought about by the influence of arbitrary external forces. Yet, nothing could be further from the truth. Risk and uncertainty are endemic to the business system on the free enterprise formula, natural concomitants of the setting from which business activity is generated. The natural basic objective has already been stated in the simple form—'to serve and satisfy a customer, at a profit'. In that statement the needs and wants of the customers (ultimately, those consumers who form the market) are the motivation, the driving force of business activity; and the first fundamental of marketing is to investigate, assess and evaluate those needs and wants. This is the purpose and scope of market research, the outcome of which leads to the computations from which the firm's marketing programme is built up.

In essence, then, a firm is formulating its programme for production, supply and sale *ahead of the realistic demand,* the demand which is supported by the consumers and customers willing to buy and having the wherewithal to pay for the purchases. There are, of course, situations and occasions when a known demand exists before there is any production to meet it; such instances are, relatively speaking, rare. The norm of business is to assess and evaluate demand ahead of manufacture and supply, at least in quantitative terms. This is implied by describing marketing and business management as 'future oriented', a feature confirmed in many firms by the annual ritual of the sales budget and in some others by longer forward-looking market programming. It is from this future-orientation of business that the factors of uncertainty and risk arise. However good the market research that a firm conducts or commissions, the essential determination of the marketing and manufacturing programme remains a matter of executive judgment from which uncertainty cannot be eliminated. Directors and managers do their best to be well-informed before they take their decisions on marketing programmes, manufacturing schedules and sales plans, but they can seldom expect or hope to have the assurances of certainty in evaluation. As wise executives they will endeavour to support their judgment by assessments of the extent of the uncertainty they are recognising—establishing the level of probability of their expected performance in the market within the parameters of the intended programme. The 'uncertainty' is thus converted into 'risk', recognised as the inevitable corollary of the marketing programme.

The marketing programme

What gives rise to the uncertainty of the business situation? Nothing very exotic or quixotic! Just the facts of life of the market and of the men, women and children composing it. As has already been noted, the market of any particular firm is a share in the economic and social life of the community, and the motive power of that life stems from the spending (or the saving and investment) of the citizens of the community as they go about their ordinary affairs. The 'market' of the complex modern business world is no different at all from the more readily visible and recognisable 'market' of the local town or the everyday 'markets' of Petticoat Lane and the Portobello Road. The uncertainties arise because no one knows who is going to come to the market and in what numbers, or what those who come will want to buy or have the wherewithal to pay for. No one knows how sparing consumers feel or how spendthrift, or how they can be persuaded from the one state to the other. Or how their readiness to purchase can be effectively stimulated to the point of handing over the price in payment for something needed or wanted. Add together all these intangible forces in hundreds and thousands of people, in relation to as many hundreds and thousands of goods and services on offer, and the extent of market uncertainty is no longer difficult to recognise.

Much of the uncertainty comes from the fact that the consumer citizens of the community (including, in the case of export markets, those of communities abroad) do not themselves know what they are going to want next week or next month, and still less next year. Yet in many a manufacturing firm quantitative decisions have to be taken certainly a year ahead (for example, for purchases of materials) and often two, three or more years ahead (for example, new production equipment or extensions of premises). A marketing programme has thus to be essentially forward-looking on a time-scale related to the periods of gestation for design, development and production. In the most effective form, the marketing programme will be drawn up on what may be usefully referred to as 'the rolling approach', cast some three or four years forward. For this to be realistic as distinct from fictional or imaginary, the firm must engage in some extent of economic forecasting, if only by making reference to economic projections offered or published by the national economic agencies. The forward-looking marketing programme can be formulated in a meaningful way *only* if it is related to best-possible judgments based on known assumptions regarding the forces that will bear upon the particular markets that the firm is seeking to serve within that programme. And among those 'forces' will be the expected trends of economic progress for the community as a whole: this is what the national institutes and agencies are seeking to assess and make known in their projections or forecasts, publishing alongside them the background facts and the assumptions on which their evaluations have been determined.

This is the edge of the important and complex subject of business forecasting; also a highly controversial one. Much of the controversy is due to misunderstanding; some, regrettably, can be attributed only to prejudice. To enter this controversy or to make any approach to elucidating it can serve no purpose in the present context. However, directors and managers wanting to be marketing oriented and effective in performance *must* go into the subject, whatever its complexity or difficulty. Not that they are required or expected themselves to engage in the business forecasting process, save in the sense of the inescapable engagement involved by the very actions of formulating a forward-looking marketing programme. The wider scope of economic forecasting, as the setting for business forecasts, is best left to the specialists; directors and managers should then consult with them to attain effective relevant interpretations of what the projections are heralding. To this extent, directors and managers need at least to understand what 'forecasting' entails and implies, so that they are the better able to lock into the economic and social framework within which their own marketing activities will have eventually to be conducted, and therefore within which their programme will need to be formulated. This will be required in quantitative terms, not just as general descriptions.

The nature of forecasting

The best help that can be given to directors and managers at this stage and in this context will be in guidance as to the true character of 'forecasting' in its economic or business setting. The first indicator is to emphasise that 'forecasting' does *not* mean 'prophesying': it is on this erroneous confusion that much of the misunderstanding rests, as well as most of the prejudice. The true orientation of forecasting in this context has been well summarised in the following paragraphs:

> Forecasting is the use of a numerate and logical system, incorporating judgment values, to evaluate the probabilities of future occurrences or outcomes. It is *not* a scientific method of prophesy, which implies knowing the future with certainty, no matter what actions are taken meanwhile. Forecasting has no part with prophecy: it identifies possible outcomes and assigns them their relative probabilities.
>
> The logic structure is based on the known relationships and past experience. It also incorporates an assessment of how people or events are likely to react as judged from that experience, after allowing for known or probable changes in the environment. Hence every forecast can be falsified: it could be argued that the purpose of a good forecast, revealing a possible outcome that is unwelcome, is to ensure that the appropriate corrective action is taken, so that a different outcome is achieved.
>
> The value of a forecast lies as much in its analysis of the operative factors in relation to the environment and in its indication of likely changes, together with their limits, as it does in assessing the probabilities of the likely outcomes. The analysis reveals the areas of concern: it identifies the problem, it can infer the type and degree of corrective action. But a forecast cannot say what should be done. It can test the options open to the decision taker; it cannot choose them.
>
> Uncertainty is the natural state of the world as we know it. It can never be totally eradicated. It can be understood and quantified (using either mathematics or judgment or both), and thereby converted into risk.
>
> Risk inevitably remains a personal assessment. No matter how sophisticated are the means used to measure uncertainty, there still remains the element of personal confidence in those means. This is conceptually equivalent to the statistician's confidence level—the inherent risk that has to be accepted. Hence the need for dialogue (between the specialists and the managers) and forecasting provides the opportunity for dialogue.[1]

[1] Extract from 'Managing our future' by R. J. Brech, a background paper prepared for the Joint Seminar of the British Institute of Management and the Institute of Statisticians in June 1973.

Correctly understood by the directors and manage[r] confirms their acceptance of the basic objective tha[t] fulfil—the service and satisfaction of customers, at a pr[o] looking assessment is helping them to understand the m[u] needs and wants and the personal endeavours towards filli[n] spending (or saving). This is true market orientation, the unce[ ] tion of the paramouncy of the consumer in economic motive p[o]

**The profit
objective**

Seeing this more fundamental role of firms in business—and it is a role n[ ] can escape—enables another cliché to be reinterpreted. Recalling a com[m] from an earlier context, it is a commonplace view that firms are in busine[ ] 'to make money' and therefore the 'earning of profits' is seen and quoted a[s] the primary objective. No one would sensibly seek to quarrel with the importance of that objective, but it does need to be interpreted in a correct perspective. 'What is your business?' would be answered meaninglessly by the response 'to make profits'; there must be another intervening answer that relates to the activities from which the profit-making will stem. To recall the instance previously used, British Leyland Motors have a business in design-ing, manufacturing and selling cars and trucks; to sell them at home and abroad is a primary objective, the customers being sought and found among citizens needing or wanting cars and prepared to choose that firm's designs in the quality and styles offered and at the prices quoted. Should any of these features in the equation fail, then the consumers will buy other firms' cars, and the British Leyland business will correspondingly fail. That firm makes its money through profits, only because it has correctly diagnosed market requirements and has been able to offer consumers what they want at the prices they are prepared to pay.

The slogan can now be rewritten 'business has no meaning, unless to serve and satisfy a customer—at a profit'. And the perspective can be correctly set: business firms earn their profits ('make their money') because and as long as they have served and satisfied their customers.

This reinterpretation of perspective has an important bearing on objectives in management. A great deal has been written and spoken on this topic in recent years, and an impression could well have been gained that something new has been discovered. 'Management by objectives' held sway in the nation's industrial circles for some years as the newly found mode of practice, but it really represented little more than a reintroduction of the wheel, with perhaps some advice on new and better ways of using it. Objectives are fundamental in management, however looked at: they start at the level of the firm in the statements set out in the Memorandum of Association that provide the first broad answer to 'What is your business?' Within the firm, a sound philosophy of management rests on the acceptance of objectives of profitabil-ity through successful performance in the market; only by continuous success in creating and maintaining customer satisfaction can the firm expect to survive in face of competition.

This basic objective will then be reflected by a 'marketing attitude of mind' in all the firm's managers and personnel, their activities mutually coordinated to serve and satisfy customers, thereby to earn profits for the firm and reassure their own continuity of employment and remuneration. At the working levels,

objectives will be reinterpreted into budgets, plans and targets,
to the various divisions of activity that make up the firm's
on. The objectives of individual managers will then lie in the
of the stated norms, not in isolation one from another, but as an
ed pattern of mutually-acknowledged responsibilities, so that the
important overall objectives of the firm as a whole can be automatically
ved through the effective operations of the individual managers in
cert.

Several times already, the phrase 'under their jurisdiction' has been used in
these pages in reference to the managers' role, indicating the delegation of
specific responsibility within the organisational framework. The significance
of this phrase is to be examined later, and the point will be made then that
delegation does not, and must not, create or encourage barriers. Whatever
jurisdiction is delegated to an individual manager, in terms of objectives
specific to his role, he retains an essential responsibility for coalescence into
the management process of the firm in total. Delegation is a mode of
convenience for fostering the better application of management competence;
it does not fragment the essential unity of the management process. Objectives individually allocated in divisions or sections of a firm are reflections of
those of the firm overall, and it must remain a fundamental principle with
every manager that his performance towards his own delegated objectives
includes contributing to those of the firm as a whole.

**Performance
objectives**

So far from 'objectives' in management being anything new, they simply
ensure that the managers are working to some purpose. If the spirit of the firm
is marketing-oriented, the managers will see their objectives also in terms of
the wider economic setting, thus ensuring continuing viability for the firm,
continuing service and satisfaction of its customers, continuing employment
for its personnel, and probably growth of scale for its own activities derived
from growth of profitability.

To ensure the coordination of objectives and to foster cooperation in their
attainment, there is a lot to be said for the practice of specifically making them
known to managers and personnel in the firm. This is a responsibility for the
Board of Directors and the Chief Executive. In the reality of industrial life this is
seldom done overtly, and perhaps a good deal of positive motivation is thus
lost. Managers and personnel can easily lose sight of their objectives in
serving and satisfying customers and in the repercussions of these in the
continuity of employment. Britain's industrial picture of the past twenty years
has shown innumerable instances of this truth—loss of employment because
of loss of trading through customers going elsewhere for better products or
service or better prices and delivery. Keeping managers and personnel alive to
the facts of economic life contributes to maintaining the firm's vitality.
Attention can be kept on quality, efficiency and performance as the guarantee
of continuing employment, because they are the means of maintaining
customer service and satisfaction.

Quality is a reflection of product design and policy, and is maintained
through specifications and standards, as well as through the vigilance of the
managers and supervisors in applying those standards. In one sense, quality
control can be seen as an aspect of managerial efficiency, or a reflection of it.

Efficiency is a bedrock of management competence, both as an objective and
... mind. As the simple illustration above showed, it could even
... efficiency of performance is the essential purpose of manage-
... operations of house building *could* proceed without manage-
... would then expect waste of materials and manpower, loss of
... efficiencies, poor progress, excess cost. The purpose of manage-
... iate such misuse of resources and loss of progress. Put another
... *nment of efficiency of performance and economy of operation is*
... *e management process.* A manager taking up his role automati-
... s this generic responsibility in respect of everything that falls
... isdiction. Mostly, no overt reference is made to this, even if the
... given a written statement of his terms of reference. One of the
... products of the 'management by objectives' technique was the
... sion of a 'job improvement' item in the schedules laid down for
... anagers, specifically calling on them to indicate where they could
... seek opportunities for improving efficiency. It ought not to be
... o remind managers of this, because they should see it as a normal
... heir professional expertise.

The environment (handwritten marginal note)

**Use of
resources**

There is a wider aspect to this thought, in terms of social responsibilities
vis-à-vis the community. No firm 'creates' its own manpower, its own
materials, its own resources. These things it obtains from what is available in
the community: it buys what it needs by paying wages and making purchases,
mostly with borrowed money. The money and the resources are available for
other firms as well: so, any firm which uses them wastefully through
inefficiency (poor management) is making the community suffer, because the
funds and resources could have been used to better advantage elsewhere. A
firm cannot escape its responsibilities to the community in which it is set,
whatever the form of its ownership or control: responsibility for the effective
use of human and other resources; responsibility for the quality and value of
products or services supplied; responsibility for continuing viability as the
basis of customer satisfaction and of employment. The better its performance
in these directions, the more worthy its contribution to the community and the
better, therefore, the claim of its owners to the profits of their enterprise.

It is on the managers (including the directors) that this wideranging
responsibility devolves, essentially by role, by profession.

A passing note on semantics may be in place here in reference to the terms
'efficient' and 'effective', for both are commonly bandied about in the jargon of
management discussion. In this volume both are used and no distinction is
drawn between them—the same idea of attaining the best possible performance of operations with the minimum use of resources, or at minimum
costs. Yet, there are some persons who do draw a distinction: 'efficiency' is
used in relation to physical or mechanical facets of operations, such as
machines, materials, man-hours; 'effective' is used of the non-tangibles, such
as policies and procedures. Another distinction has also sometimes been
drawn in the broad application of management, where 'effective' is held to
mean that the *right* judgments and decisions have been formed, while
'efficient' refers to the mode of carrying them out. Fortunately, semantics of
this kind are not very important, and both terms can be used as circumstances

or inclinations determine. The notion is the same in both, and the obligation on the managers remains, whatever the word.

Other terms have also come on the scene in recent times to highlight the manager's responsibility for getting things done well, and among the most useful might be 'the three Ps'—performance, productivity, profitability. Used together as a slogan, they have applied something of a dramatic force to strengthen the urge to managers to improve on what they are currently doing, and to bring home the message of the inescapable obligation to seek such improvement. Each of the three terms reflects an aspect of the management process:

● performance: to attain good output from economical application of re-sources; to maintain efficient operating in all activities and from all equipment and systems; to meet the requirements of targets, plans and budgets as laid down in a manufacturing or marketing programme.

● productivity: specifically to seek improvements in ways and means—in methods, equipment, use of materials, systems, procedures, manpower and so on; especially by the application of diagnostic and betterment techniques.

● profitability: sharing with all managers in the firm a genuine concern for cost-effectiveness, for vitality of outlook, for progressive advancement, for marketing-orientation, and thereby contributing to improving the firm's profitability through better overall service to customers.

Management activities

Rounding off this analytical examination of the process as a foundation for more serious study of its practice, management has been presented as the exercise of a deliberate and decisive responsibility combining four essential elements of *planning, motivation, coordination* and *control.* In practice, these elements do not appear in their simple elemental form, but are clothed partly in procedures or techniques and partly in the thinking and action of the manager. How they appear is, of course, the substance of the following Parts and chapters of this volume, subdivided into the four major activities that have long been characteristic of industrial/commercial enterprises: marketing, production, personnel, control. (A fifth major activity characterises many businesses—research and development—and this is dealt with specifically in Part Three.) If the practices of management within any of these major divisions are analysed, the validity of the four elements can be confirmed, for all the management activities can be classified to one or other of them. The elements do not, of course, all occur in management practice in the same form: *planning* and *control* tend to be found mostly in the garb of techniques and procedures, closely interrelated with each other to the extent of forming a 'feedback cycle' as shown in Fig. 1.3.1 opposite. *Motivation*, on the other hand, lies largely in personal action and attitude on the part of the manager, but many 'personnel techniques' are certainly a contributory part of this element in practice.

How the elements can be matched with management action (keeping still to the four main divisions used for this volume) is amply illustrated by the summary in the following pages.

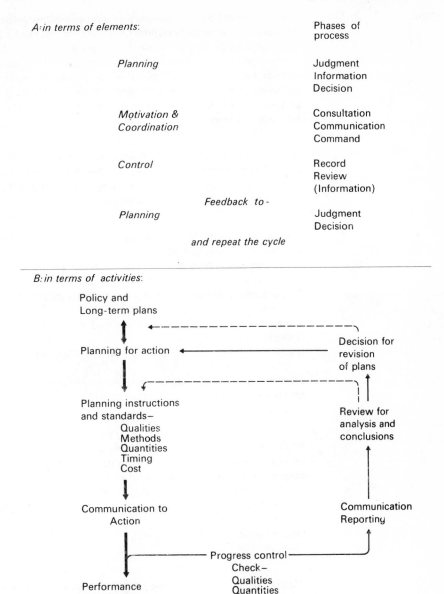

A: in terms of elements:

| | Phases of process |

Planning

Judgment
Information
Decision

Motivation &
Coordination

Consultation
Communication
Command

Control

Record
Review
(Information)

Feedback to -

Planning

Judgment
Decision

and repeat the cycle

B: in terms of activities:

Policy and
Long-term plans

Planning for action

Decision for
revision
of plans

Planning instructions
and standards—
   Qualities
   Methods
   Quantities
   Timing
   Cost

Review for
analysis and
conclusions

Communication to
Action

Communication
Reporting

Performance
and Results

Progress control
   Check—
   Qualities
   Quantities
   Timing
   Cost

(Solid lines represent normally expected flow ; broken lines represent periodic /possible alternative.)
The flow lines between the stages embody the human relations and actions (consultation, communication, motivation). Management judgment is exercised appropriately at all stages. The coordination flow of the whole process in the cycle reinforces the unity of management action.

Fig. 1.3.1

Planning

Policy. The primary management responsibility arising under the *planning* element is the determination of policy, i.e. laying down objectives and the general principles on the basis of which it will operate. This is required not only in a general sense, but also in relation to each of the major divisions. Without a known policy in respect of all its activities, an enterprise cannot function effectively, if at all. A well-defined policy relating to all aspects of an organisation can be of considerable value in promoting coordination and smooth working.

Organisation structure. A second general responsibility under *planning* is that of organisation structure, i.e. the arrangement of the managerial and supervisory responsibilities for delegation, and the formal relationships that will be fashioned by the delegation.

Production. Some of the management activities concerned with *planning* in the field of production are:
Link with marketing to ascertain forecast of sales requirements and so to establish a true (potential) programme of output.
Preparation of programme and breakdown into sections.
Technical layout of operations.
Analysis of operations for allocation of jobs and machines.
Materials specification.
Budget of material supplies; pre-purchasing; pre-allocation (linking up with 'control' element).
Methods and time study to determine operation times and rates.
Machine loading and production planning.
Inspection routines.

Marketing. Some *planning* activities are:
Economic forecasting and marketing intelligence.
Market research ('assessment of potentials').
Layout of sales territories and budgets.
Preparation of sales campaign, including advertising or other sales promotion.
Budget of stocks to be carried.
Transport programmes.

Financial management. The *planning* activities in this field are closely related to the 'control' element and are best considered there. Special features are: the provision of capital, the maintenance of working capital; cash-flow forecast and availability of funds; profit projection.

Personnel. Includes:
Planning of manpower requirements and supply; requisitions.
Selection and placement; forecasts for promotion.
Training and job instruction.
Working hours, holidays, substitute manpower, etc.
Cloakroom accommodation, canteen facilities and other amenities.
Management development programme.

Control

'Planning' lays down the programme to be followed and the standards or budgets to be attained. 'Control' watches to see that the programme and the standards or targets are adhered to, or brings to light the reasons why not. In most contemporary methods and systems of management the two elements are combined in one procedure.

Information. The Board of Directors has a general oversight of all the activities of the organisation and looks to the Managing Director or General Manager to bring forward the *control information* that will enable performance and cost to be checked against the policy, programme and targets laid down. In this sense, top management frequently uses the field of financial activities for providing the means of all 'control' in the form of *management information* derived from management accounting to reflect comparisons between 'target' and 'actual' so that decisions can be readily taken as to next steps.

Production. The usual management activities relating to observing the productive performance or the progress of output are:
Progress control (often called 'production control').
Utilisation of manpower, machine-hours, fuel, power.
Materials or stores control (to foresee and prevent shortages and waste of material).
Balance of components, work in progress, etc.
Quality control (perhaps by statistical methods).

Marketing. Stock control (quantities of goods in stock).
Sales progress control, broken down into territories, products, salesmen's quotas, or any other desirable subdivision.
Delivery control (to check for transport delays).

Financial management. Here the planning and control activities are interlinked. The whole management accountancy system of a business is a scheme of control, or recording and checking the expenditure, but certain aspects of it are more readily recognised as 'tools' of management; for instance:
Labour cost control (perhaps on the basis of work study standards).
Materials cost control.
Sales expense control.
Overhead expense control.
Standard costing systems.
Budgetary control (by which a complete plan of financial needs in relation to every aspect of production, distribution and personnel is prepared in advance and used for planning purposes and for subsequent continuous checking).
Higher control (a specialised system of preplanned expense control, on simpler lines than the 'budget').

Personnel. All forms of record and report, employee-rating, merit-rating, management appraisal and so on.

Coordination

Many of the procedures of planning and control contribute an inbuilt feature of *coordination*, but there are few specific techniques. Mostly coordination is sought and achieved by the active skill of the manager or supervisor himself, giving practical form to his personal attitude of constructive cooperation and sense of mutual responsibility. As already indicated, any form of planning system is a help to coordination. Committees can also be used for this purpose.

Motivation
(leadership)

This again is an element in which special techniques are not available, but in which the human skill of the manager and supervisor is called into play. The task is to fuse the varied individual human capacities and powers of the many people employed into a smoothly working team with high morale and high productivity. It is a task closely linked up with the element of coordination. It is an element in their responsibility of which managers and supervisors have hitherto too frequently been ignorant and negligent. There is a great deal to be said as to how this task can be carried out, but in brief the major points may be summarised as follows:

Securing interest, by keeping people informed of proposed developments and of progress.

Maintaining loyalty, by fairness in allocation of work, rates of pay, discipline, etc.

Maintaining personal keenness by fostering a sense of participation.

Promoting group harmony, by joint consultation.

Preventing frustration, by providing a sympathetic outlet for grievances and grumbles.

Preserving impartiality, by ensuring cooperative discipline and fairness in judgment.

Encouragement of responsibility in the affairs of the organisation.

4 Policy

The clear delineation and understanding of a firm's objectives provide the first and essential basis for the effective direction of its affairs, the more truly so if those objectives are being interpreted on the more meaningful lines that have been spelled out in earlier pages. Further, as has already been said, making those objectives, especially in their fuller connotation, explicitly known to the firm's managers adds to the strength of the foundation for the effective management of its operations and activities. Directors and managers can be more thoroughly at one in their respective contributions to what are well recognised as common objectives. Yet another major lead has to be given to the management team, in the sense of guidelines as to how affairs are to be conducted towards the fulfilment of the known objectives: such guidelines are commonly referred to as 'policies'.

Policy can be defined as the modes of thought and the body of principles laid down to underlie and to guide the activities of a firm (or other organisation) towards declared or known objectives. There could be an argument in favour of the view that 'objectives' form part of the policy and should therefore figure at the outset of the definition. Let that view be adopted if there is an inclination towards it, for the point is not one of substance: Policy finds its character just as truly if it is seen as the guidelines towards objectives. In the real life situation, moreover, it is more than likely that objectives and policy will be seen as so inevitably interrelated that the one will always be considered in the context of the other. There is the further point that both are in the province of 'direction', that is to say, they are the responsibility of those who have initiated the enterprise or who have provided the necessary finance to launch it. This responsibility rests at the level of overall business leadership and control: in the very small enterprises, with the one man or the small partnership coming together to start the business, with or without further financial support.

When larger-scale business activities are started up, the need for the greater financial support makes the 'company' the customary and appropriate legal form, and thereby the responsibility for objectives and policy can be more specifically pinpointed: in the Board of Directors established under the legal formalities to conduct that company's affairs in accordance with Memorandum and Articles of Association. The Board of Directors will be composed by agreement of the parties concerned—those initiating the project, those providing the finance, and others who may have been brought into the venture for specific reasons—and the size and composition of membership will reflect the agreed wishes of those parties. Thereafter responsibility for the conduct of the company's affairs will be delegated by the owners (i.e. the initiating and investing parties) to that Board of Directors, and they themselves will be able to exercise any jurisdiction only through the medium of a General Meeting of shareholders (owners) called and held in accordance with the Articles of Association. One advantageous byproduct of the legal form of the company lies in this very pinpointing of responsibility for direction, facilitating putting squarely on to the Board of Directors responsibility for determining and delineating objectives, for formulating policies, for governing affairs so as to ensure effective accomplishment, and for overall control of that accomplishment.

It is perhaps worth noting that a similar focus of direction and accountability is also established in the nationalised industry organisations and other similar public enterprise corporations where the normal company form is not used: there is a council or similar body to undertake the same role.

An important consideration needs to be stressed in this context: this responsibility for direction and overall control, whatever the organisation, belongs *corporately* to all the members of the Board of Directors or governing council. In law any one director is legally held accountable for the proper performance of the company's affairs; but in management practice the responsibility for determining objectives, for formulating policy, and for overall control must lie corporately with the Board of Directors as such, and not be usurped by any one member. An usurpation it certainly would be, if any one director took this line, even were he the Managing Director.

Objectives and policy

The link between objectives and policy can be seen to lie in a recognition of the three parties to whom the Board of Directors owe accountability in terms of the full objectives that their responsibility covers, once granted their place in the economic system. There could be argument about respective priorities of the three, and in practice the directors have recurrently to face problems of balancing these interests or priorities. Yet, the discussion in the foregoing pages will support the identification of all three, probably in the following order of priority for most practical purposes:

1. The customers to be served and satisfied; in the last analysis this means the body of citizen-consumers composing communities at home and abroad, and identified relevantly in the company's marketing programme.
2. The personnel employed on the company's affairs in various sectors of operation and activity; particularly in terms of stability of employment and remuneration as the counterpart to economic consumption.
3. The shareholders who have made available the finance for initiating and conducting the enterprise; in terms of return on their capital, safeguarding the investment and the promotion of asset value.

With objectives determined, a firm's policies guiding the efforts towards achieving them will need to be made up in a pattern of four interrelated facets:

1. What might be called the *ethical foundation* of the enterprise, made up of two aspects: (*a*) standards of fair trading: the basic principles upon which the firm proposes to conduct commercial relations with other firms and with persons outside of itself, for example, customers, suppliers, banks, the local officials, the general public; and (*b*) standards of good employment: the principles which the firm will observe in regard to conditions of employment and dealings with employed personnel, including their authorised representatives in trades unions.

2. The organisational and operational foundation underlying the structure and conduct of the firm's operations, again in two aspects: (a) channels and methods of trading, by wholesale, retail, export, direct sale, and so on; and (b) internal arrangements, planning, equipment, and management practice generally, i.e. policies underlying the effectiveness and efficiency of management or bearing on the firm's application of the 'three Ps'.

There is, in effect, an 'internal' and an 'external' aspect in each case, and the firm will thus have paid full regard to its guidelines in respect of both relations with the outside world and its own inside activities. Formulating its outlook and attitude on the two external facets would constitute the *general policy* of the firm, and these broad guidelines would reflect in the formulation of more detailed aspects called for in the two internal aspects. The latter would shape into 'sectional' policies, lining up with the main divisions of operations and the major functions of management activity: for example—marketing and selling; production and supply; research and development; personnel management and industrial relations. It will be important to ensure that sectional policies are not isolated, but stem from the main general policy and reflect it; these sectional policies are more likely to require changing from time to time, and this is where a danger can arise of changes inadvertently departing from (or even contradicting) a feature of general policy.

Contemporary trends of interest in Britain are bringing industry and commerce more and more into the life of the nation. This seems an odd thing to say, when regard is paid to the fact that the nation's life and living depend inescapably on that industry and commerce; all the wealth and remuneration of the community stem from the activities of industry and commerce, and all the needs of citizen-consumers can be met only through those same activities. There is no economic system separate from the collection of firms that make it up, and the nation has no 'product' other than what comes from this same collection of firms. It is perhaps this somewhat fundamental thought that has been gaining wider recognition within the nation, and especially among those groups of citizens whose own occupations or activities do not bring them at first hand within the industrial or commercial milieu. Regrettably, one of the first consequences of this widening interest is to bring industry more acutely into the cockpit of politics, but this will no doubt pass, especially if the nation's directors and managers exert more of their own professional influence. One way in which they can do this is to ensure that their firms' objectives and policies reflect their recognition of that essential role in the economic wellbeing of the community. Every firm might seriously consider adopting objectives in the following broad form and formulating policies that will honour these objectives in achievement:

● To contribute to the economic needs of the community by the manufacture and supply of the products which it is set up to produce, or by carrying out the particular lines of trade or service that it is designed to provide.

● To contribute to the economic and social wellbeing of the community by improvements in the quality and volume of the products made available, and by reductions in the price at which they are available; in other fields, by improving the service that is being offered and lowering the cost without impairment of quality. It is by reductions in cost of existing products and services that a community makes advances in its standards of life, because, by having to spend less money on known or admitted needs, consumers have a margin to spend on the satisfaction of further wants, investment for savings purposes, or the pursuit of educational or recreational amenities.

- To improve the standards of employment by raising the level of working conditions and by enhancing personal and social satisfactions at work.
- To respect, or contribute to the advancement of, the local amenities of the particular community in which the enterprise is physically set.
- To provide for the continuing pursuit of efficiency in all activities and for the promotion of vitality in ensuring the future stability and progress of the enterprise, in maintaining its profitability and in the sound employment of the capital invested.

Impending legislation in Britain (as well as in other countries of the European Community) is likely to give some force to objectives of these kinds, but the force may well be unbalanced, even wrongly slanted, unless there is a sound lead from the profession of management and direction. In particular, the requirement to nominate an employee representative to membership of the Board of Directors will yet further strengthen concern for the 'producer' interests. Legislation bearing on consumers is more concerned with 'protection' against trading malpractice. There is no feasible way in which consumer interests can be 'represented' in the thousands of Boards of Directors that make up the British economy. Nor should any such approach be necessary. If Boards of Directors are themselves *marketing oriented* and alive to the responsibilities reflected in the five 'social objectives' listed above, the consumer interests will be adequately and appropriately looked after. The slogan comes back here—'business has no meaning unless to serve and satisfy a customer'. To have that honoured in firms' policies and practice is the most effective way of fostering consumer interests and the viability of the firms themselves at the same time.

The formulation of policy

The clear formulation of policy, in general and in sections, and its announcement within and without the organisation in a written declaration, can be of the highest importance in promoting the effectiveness of management.

Policy is the basis of the structure of organisation needed for carrying on the affairs of the enterprise: unless policy is clearly defined, it is not possible to frame an organisation, because it is not possible adequately to determine the appropriate executive responsibilities and relationships; nor can the appointed managers carry out these responsibilities with effectiveness and coordination. The clear formulation of policy underlies planning, whether in relation to the capital and equipment required, the premises, the channels of trade, the levels of employment, the purchase of materials, or many other more detailed aspects of the programme for getting the enterprise into operation and keeping its activities moving. It is also important to appreciate that policy has a contribution to make to coordination, especially in the larger organisations, and to the maintenance of morale. Where policy is clearly defined, in its general and sectional aspects, the organisation is already a long way advanced towards ensuring that its managers will keep in step in the day-to-day discharge of their responsibilities.

The relevance of policy to morale is not often realised. Information as to objectives and policy is a known means of promoting and securing cooperation. In an organisation where managers keep all these things to themselves, and argue that workers or staff should get on with the job and 'do as they are told', morale is often low: ignorance breeds indifference and suspicion, moods which manifestly hinder cooperation and will to work. Clear policy is an aid to information. It removes the sense of aimlessness and promotes a sense of participation, besides inspiring in employees confidence in the soundness of management. They know what the company is trying to do; they know how plans are formulated for the attainment of the known objectives; they are aware of the standards of trading and employment that have been laid down. They have in this knowledge a lead towards cooperation and the response of good effort in the performance of their own part of the total job. This is of particular importance to managers and supervisors, for whom a clear understanding of the company's policy affords a firm basis for the daily practice of their responsibilities and the continuous promotion of sound employee relations.

Policy is also the basis on which the results of management can be assessed. The establishment of criteria of effectiveness and their use in assessing the achievements of the organisation is the other half of the responsibility of the Board of Directors, the higher level of management. It falls to them to ensure that the objectives of the enterprise are being attained and that the policies that have been laid down are being followed. They have then to ensure that all operations and activities are being carried out at an adequate level of effectiveness and economy: it is in this connection that the various types of control data and management information come into play. At the lower levels of control, the function of such data is to ensure that plans are being followed and reasons for departures known. In addition, the daily, weekly or monthly data are contributing to the overall periodic information which will enable 'top management', and the Board of Directors, to ensure that adequate standards of performance and profitability are being attained in accordance with the predetermined objectives.

Policy must be related to facts. In an industrial or commercial organisation this must mean that policies and programmes are based on forecasting, to ascertain market or production requirements and other fundamental factors of economic operation. Whether such forecasting is in the form of a systematic analysis based on techniques of market assessment, or whether it is a more formal review of economic conditions and expectations, is not of immediate moment in the present context. How the approach is made must largely be determined by the nature of the industry or trade, the type of product handled, and other specific circumstances of the company concerned. However attained, a factual basis is the first requirement in the formulation of programmes for implementing policy, and in this direction important contributions can be made by the executives and functional specialists below the level of the Board of Directors.

Responsibility for the formulation of policy necessarily and formally lies with the Board of Directors themselves, but this does not and should not preclude their obtaining substantial and valuable guidance from the members of the organisation below: in the first place these members' specialist knowledge can be the basis on which accurate and factual forecasts of markets and sales potentials are made. Their daily dealings with the problems of management afford them a more realistic appreciation of the circumstances in which trading has to be carried on—material supplies, machine capacity, manpower, and the many other factors that can so easily play havoc with even the best-sounding policy, if inadequately considered. They also have a closer view of the structure of management and so of the weaknesses and deficiencies that can be a bar to carrying a policy into effect. Apart from such positive contributions from the managers to the formulation of policy, there is another morale aspect here: if managers are to be expected to carry heavy responsibilities for the affairs of the organisation, they should be consulted on and invited to contribute to the fundamentals of that organisation, i.e. its policy. They cannot be expected to show a high level of cooperation, or to secure it from their subordinates, if their own superiors adopt the 'theirs not to reason why, theirs but to do or die' attitude in this all-important direction.

The channels of policy

In most cases these contributions to policy from the members of the organisation will be coordinated by and focused through the Managing Director, as the one-half of this two-way channel of contact. If there is to be effective interpretation of policy into instructions for executive action, there must be a single source of reference. This is the purpose of the office of Managing Director: the individual holding it is *at once* a director sharing in the corporate responsibility for determining objectives and policy, and the chief executive in command of the lines of management responsibility leading down to operations. He is the first channel through which the process of management will flow. Equally, he is the final stage in the flow of contributions back from within the organisation, and thereby a focal point for consideration and consolidation. In organisations where some of the executives or specialists are also members of the Board, certain difficulties could arise from this situation unless there is clear understanding of the specific role of the Managing Director as the sole 'chief executive' and thus the sole authoritative channel of interpretation and communication between the Board and the organisation below.

To convey policy from the Board of Directors to the members of the executive structure is a task *inherent* in the role of the Managing Director, for his responsibility can be summed up as the combination of the first and last stages in management, i.e. interpreting policy into programmes and operating instructions, and reporting back to the Board on the working of management. To him falls the responsibility for ensuring in the first instance that objectives and policy are known to all members of the organisation, and so to set the tone that will govern the level of morale through all subordinate ranks. In the smaller units, particularly in the case of single owners, this first stage is inextricably intermingled with policy formulation: as his own boss, the single owner lays down the policy and interprets it in the same breath. The same is largely true of the partnerships and the smaller companies, as well as of larger companies in which all the directors also hold full-time executive appointments: the few men concerned at the top are at one time a Board of Directors sitting round a table in formal array, but for the greater part of their time they are individual managers, with the Managing Director as their chief. To draw the distinction between their two capacities is not always easy in thought and frequently very difficult in action. But in principle the distinction is there.

The Managing
Director's role

In larger organisations, the position of the Managing Director is usually clearer in his relationship with the communication of policy. The Board as such may contain a number of persons who carry executive responsibilities within the organisation, and in addition other persons whose services to the company are restricted to the part-time duties required by attendance at Board Meetings. The Managing Director is specifically appointed and recognised as the executive head of the organisation, responsible to the Board for ensuring that policy is correctly interpreted and that there will ensue effective fulfilment of the policy, so as to achieve the objectives. This is not for one moment to suggest that human frailties will not give rise to complications; for instance, any of the directors also holding executive responsibilities for specific parts of the organisation may usurp the Managing Director's function and issue his own instructions which *purport* to be the sole interpretation of policy. Such bad practice does not vitiate the principle: *only* the Managing Director carries responsibility to the Board for the interpretation of policy; he alone holds the dual role of director-cum-executive. The other directors must be seen as exercising *two distinct functions* or living two different roles: they share the corporate responsibility of directors, as members of the Board, when sitting at Board Meetings; they return to their rather different position as executive subordinates to the Managing Director when they leave the board room to take up their responsibilities for specific parts of the organisation. The common habit of talking about 'a director in charge of', say, manufacturing or sales, involves a contradiction in terms.

In general discussion one frequently finds the 'formulation of policy' spoken of as though it were a deliberate non-recurrent activity. This is, of course, in some respects true: at the outset of a business or at many stages of its development, the Board of Directors will make concrete and specific decisions which constitute the basic objectives and lines of working of the enterprise, i.e. its policy. These will, however, be variously modified and added to time and time again as the business proceeds; and so they should be. Policy, as the foundation of a vital process of commercial action, has itself to be kept alive and in tune with the action required, and thus the adjustment is a byproduct of the serious review of performance and progress, in the light of new facts and changing circumstances. The important thing is that policy should not be vacillating, thereby producing an unstable foundation for executive action. This can be guarded against chiefly by the attitude of the directors themselves, recognising the significance of this point and ensuring that all their considerations of policy adjustments and formulation is mature and thorough.

Much is to be gained in this direction from 'formalising' the Board's corporate actions in policy deliberation and decision: if directors make it a practice to conduct their decisive policy deliberations within the formal framework of a Board meeting, with adequate explanatory documentation and record, experience has shown that a lot can be gained in the maturity with which policy is formulated. Naturally, more informal discussions and exchanges of view may well have preceded these final deliberations, but by this specific step the Board will have ensured that a definite policy decision has been taken. Moreover, the clear recording of that decision will also ensure that the decision is understood in the same way by all directors and will make possible a reliable communication of it to the other members of the organisation. For most businesses it is no burden to go to these lengths whenever a Board has (major) policy considerations and it could well be found that systematic treatment when such considerations do arise will not only reduce their recurrence, but—more important—obviate the necessity for the sorting out of trouble due to subsequent misunderstandings of policy.

Interpretation

For policy to exert its appropriate influence on the effectiveness of management below, it has to be 'interpreted' or reflected in executive instructions. In the Managing Director's two-way role, this interpretation is also a continuous or recurrent process, carried out through his meetings and discussions with his subordinate managers, or partly through the issue to them of budgets and programmes. Some 'interpretation' of policy occurs, too, in the form of his decisions on specific matters brought to him for consideration. It is an element in the skill of a Managing Director that he can make these decisions *ad hoc* in relation to the particular points while keeping true to the main pattern of policy laid down. Thus the task of interpreting policy is one readily recurring among the daily activities of the chief executive.

Further interpretation of policy has also to take place at lower levels, especially in the larger organisations. The broad lines of 'sectional' policy may have been laid down by the Board in formulating their general policy, or by the Managing Director in his major instructions. There will necessarily have to be some review and reinterpretation in the specialist terms appropriate to the various divisions of the enterprise: this is a natural item in the functional responsibilities of executives in charge of such divisions. In many instances this reinterpretation of policy at the lower levels merges into planning, and serves as the link between policy and programme of action. This is seen especially in the field of manufacturing: at the level of the Production or Factory Manager, policy is formulated in all the technical terms required for laying down the production plan or manufacturing programme. Similarly, in a firm using budgetary control, policy is translated in financial terms into the form of approved expense budgets and related standards of performance.

These aspects of policy show how it is woven into the fabric of management and bring out clearly the important features that policy must be flexible, capable of adaptation or reinterpretation in the light of changing circumstances. Yet, at the same time, it must be kept unified and consistent.

5 Organisation

As policy is the foundation of management in action, so *organisation* is its framework. It is another aspect of the planning element, this time concerned with determining and delineating the pattern of delegation of responsibilities for management. From time to time in the foregoing pages, the phrase 'under his jurisdiction' has been used in reference to a manager, pointing to the fact that some delegation has taken place. *Organisation* is concerned with establishing what this delegation is and to what extent it is to be or has been carried: it is essentially a matter of determining a framework for the orderly and coordinated exercise of the management process.

The term 'organisation' is sometimes used to refer to arrangements of a more general kind, as a reflection of the common verb, such as 'to organise' a children's outing: but, in the management context, there is no longer any dubiety about the restriction of the term to the pattern of delegation;[1] in other words, a static concept of framework within which an active process goes on.

That organisation is necessary is no more than a commonplace of clarification: the purpose is the very simple one of working out properly, and then making clear to all concerned, what responsibilities are being delegated to which managerial positions. Generally, the delegation and the delineation of it go beyond the managerial roles to include supervisory positions in charge of operating sections, and also to include specialist services established to assist and support executive management, such as personnel services or accounting. The substance of this working out is conveyed in descriptive definitions of the responsibilities delegated, with indication of the main relationships which are set up by that delegation. The full pattern of delegation is known as an 'organisation structure' and the skeleton of it may be portrayed on an organisation chart (called by some people in jargon an 'organogram').

The chart is *not* the organisation structure—it is no more than an outline illustration of the grouping of the responsibilities and of some of the authority relations that arise among those groups. Simply to draw lines from a chief executive to his subordinate executive colleagues, including diagonal lines to indicate functional or specialist relationships, may be a useful representation of certain facts in any given organisation, but it is only a pictorial presentation of specific relationships. Of itself it does not codify the responsibilities of the various executives or specialist posts concerned. This can be done by clear definitions of the scope and breakdown of such responsibilities, with indication of the official to whom the executive in question is to be held responsible,

---

[1] The only exception arises in connection with work study techniques applied in administrative (office) activities, where they go by the name 'O & M': the letters refer to 'organisation and methods', but it is common for practitioners to speak of 'organisation with a small o', because the word is really being used in its general sense concerned with the 'arrangement' or 'layout' of work.

who in turn is responsible to him, and the particular relations he needs to maintain with other executives not in his own direct sequence.

The 'relationships' are part of the planned pattern of the working of management, which is conducted from one section to another, not only through the senior position to which these sections are attached, but by means of lateral or functional relations directly subsisting among the sections, enabling them to cooperate in the pursuit of the common objectives and in the fulfilment of the common policy. This is readily seen at work, for instance, within a manufacturing unit where there is a Planning Manager and a Factory Manager, both responsible to a senior production executive. The one has responsibilities, for instance, for laying down the manufacturing plans, the other has responsibilities for ensuring that the plans are carried out. Lateral relations exist between these two executives to ensure continuous coordination and cooperation in the mutually shared task of translating policy into an agreed output programme and seeing that the programme is fulfilled.

Defining responsibilities

Similar illustrations can be drawn readily enough from the relations between, say, the Factory Manager and the Sales Manager within one organisation, or in the specialist relations between a Personnel Officer, responsible for recruitment, training, welfare and similar procedures, and a Factory Manager who carries full responsibility for the planning and attainment of production programmes. Schedules of responsibilities lay down in broad, general terms the field that these individual managers or specialists are called on to cover, that is to say, the extent of the responsibilities delegated and what kinds of interrelationships are called into play by that very action of delegating those responsibilities. Set out like this, the action of determining delegation sounds both complex and mysterious: in point of fact, it is neither. Working on the management of a given firm, and with the cooperation of the managers concerned, it is a simple and straightforward task to determine how responsibilities should best be delegated and what consequential interrelationships ensue. Usually there is more than one possible and practical arrangement: which is finally chosen will be arrived at by consultation and discussion with the managers concerned, weighing up the pros and cons as they bear on the effective working of the management process in that firm, given its current policies and circumstances. This is the only valid criterion, that the pattern of delegation should promote effective and coordinated management practice. The consequential interrelationships will be among the matters discussed and assessed, and will play their part in an evaluation of the alternatives towards the choice of the optimum arrangement.

That the subject of organisation has for some time been of considerable interest is due to the many deficiencies or weaknesses characteristic of the structure of management in industry and commerce, leading invariably to inefficiency and high costs of operating, as well as to many personal experiences of conflict and confusion. It is astonishing how frequently the same deficiencies or weaknesses recur, and how often they are due to the absence of definitions of respective responsibility. There is, of course, the further difficulty of lack of agreed or authoritative principles of organisation structure, from which a chief executive could draw guidance when he wants to set up a sound structure by defining the responsibilities and relationships of himself and his

subordinates. He may, perhaps, have some help from contemporary literature, but he has still to rely largely on his own judgment. If starting with a new
organisation, he is in a position to proceed analytically: to start with the
formulation of management aims and policy; then to group for his own
purposes the particular tasks that have to be undertaken; then deciding in
broad outline the planning and control techniques; thus eventually arriving at
groupings of responsibilities, duties and relations that will lead to a systematic
structure.

When trying to remodel an existing organisation the problem is more
complicated, because some regard must be paid to the present framework. In
this case the formulation of executive responsibilities can best be carried out
with the active cooperation of the managers, supervisors and specialists
themselves. Each can be asked to write down in broad outline the various tasks
and activities for which he regards himself responsible, and the lines along
which he proceeds to fulfil them. He can be asked to group these tasks under
certain major headings, which have perhaps been broadly formulated in
advance. Someone nominated as 'Organisation Secretary' (or 'Planner')
would collect these detailed documents, and after scrutiny take up with
individuals concerned amplification or clarification of obscure points. Note
should particularly be taken of items of duplication or omission that he can
recognise from his own more central standpoint. He would then proceed to
analyse the completed documents, in order to obtain a comprehensive picture
of how the total responsibilities of management are distributed, to ascertain
how they contribute to the fulfilment of policy, and to mark out the instances of
overlapping, duplication, deficiency or omission. The Chief Executive is then
in a position to examine with his subordinates the 'map' of the organisation
territory as at present laid out, and to agree with them the ways in which
certain fields or parts would be better regrouped, to ensure a higher degree of
coordination, a better cover of management responsibility, a closer fulfilment
of policy, a better distribution of load, or remedies to correct such deficiencies
and gaps as have been revealed. The review would be rounded off by writing
up the schedules.

What to call these documents presents something of a problem. For a very
long time the only title used was 'schedules of responsibilities', with possibly
the variation 'definitions of responsibilities'. Then different usages began to
appear, in the form of 'terms of reference' or 'mandates', and for quite a time
the American label 'position specifications' was common. In 1967–69 the
British Department of Employment and Productivity (as it was then called)
published some reports on management training and used in that context the
title 'management job description'. This has, in consequence, become the
most popular version and has customarily been abbreviated MJD: this form
will be used exclusively from now on in the present context.

**Organisation
structures**

As described above, the task of analysing and determining responsibilities
for systematic delegation may seem to be formidable, and may lend support
to the view that organisation is an aspect of management pertinent only to the
larger units. Nothing could be farther from the truth; even the smallest
organisation can gain from knowing exactly how its management works. As
soon as two or three managers and supervisors are brought into existence by

growth from the very small stage, the need for demarcation of responsibilities becomes not only valuable, but essential to good management; and such demarcation is nothing else than the determination and definition of responsibilities and relationships, i.e. setting up an organisation structure.[1]

It might be useful at this point to enter a warning against any search for 'a typical organisation'. There is, admittedly, a broad common pattern of organisation to be found in the average British companies. A Board of Directors represents the owners (shareholders) and carries a corporate responsibility for the objectives, the policy and the overall progress of the enterprise. Responsible to the Board is a chief executive (the Managing Director or General Manager) called on to translate policy into instructions for executive action, to initiate the whole process of management, and to answer to the Board for its effective operation throughout the enterprise. This responsibility is discharged by the processes of delegation, and is reported back to the Board through the medium of accounts, reports and statistics. Below the Managing Director come the hierarchy of senior, intermediate and junior managers, smaller or greater in number according to the size of the enterprise, and appropriately divided along varying lines according to the tasks to be undertaken, the prevailing needs and other factors. Some managers carry direct responsibility for the immediate operations of the enterprise; others hold appointments of specialist (functional) character. In either case the executives are sharing part of the total responsibility for the planning and regulation of the activities of the enterprise, according to the particular division of function allotted to them. To enable these executives or managers to carry out their responsibilities effectively, they are assisted at the working level by 'supervisors' whose responsibilities are less, if at all, concerned with planning, but mainly centre on the oversight of operations to ensure that plans are followed or departures from plan promptly reported to the responsible executive.

This rather characteristic general pattern is, however, only in a superficial sense 'typical'. The outward similarity of responsibilities at each major management level cloaks the very varied distribution or arrangement of them that will be found within even a small number of seemingly comparable organisations. It may broadly be said that there is no *general* pattern for the distribution of executive responsibilities; there would appear to be certain basic maxims of organisation structure commonly applicable, but with considerable differences in actual application. Paramount among these is the principle of the unity of management. Whatever the character, size or aims of an enterprise, the organisation structure represents from top to bottom the framework of a single process. Starting in 'direction' and moving right down to the immediate supervision of the routine activities of making, distributing or recording, the whole scheme of management responsibilities is an integrated pattern, designed to carry out effectively the planning and regulation of these activities and to ensure that the set objectives are fulfilled at the optimum level of operating efficiency and cost.

Types of organisation

The fallacy of referring to a 'typical' organisation is often paralleled in the error that there are 'types' of organisation, the three most commonly referred

---

[1] This is not the appropriate place to go into more detail of the methods and illustrations of defining responsibilities in forming an organisation structure. A full-length treatment is available in the companion to this volume, *Organisation—the Framework of Management* by E. F. L. Brech.

to being: the line or military type; the line and staff; and the functional. In the first, all responsibility is direct from subordinate to senior, and conversely; there are no specialist positions bringing to bear a subsidiary responsibility cutting crosswise into the up-and-down pattern. The second is described as a mixture of direct executive responsibilities with the specialist ancillary services, and is illustrated from widespread experience of everyday practice: the factory which has an executive in charge of production or manufacturing paralleled by a specialist (functional) personnel officer providing direct to the factory the numerous customary services. The third type is sometimes illustrated in the textbooks in chart form as a pattern of diagonal lines without up-and-down lines below the top level; its significance is said to be that each specialised activity has its own lines of responsibility for application reaching directly and specifically to the point of application. This is a concept difficult to understand in theory, and hardly capable of illustration from industrial practice; one may legitimately question whether, in the form in which it has been expounded, it has any validity at all.

From the descriptions of the practice of management that make up the later parts of this volume, it will be seen that, except in the very small enterprises, some form of specialist activity is nearly always present. This means that the pure (so-called) 'line' type is seldom found, while the 'line and staff' pattern, in simple or complex form, tends to be the commonplace one. The notion of 'types' of organisation is thus one that serves little useful purpose, and from analytical consideration may be definitely written off as a somewhat pointless concept that has been allowed to go unchallenged. In a number of quarters the term 'functional' is now commonly used as descriptive of an organisation with exactly the same meaning as 'line and staff'; and the phrase 'a normal functional pattern' is becoming increasingly widespread as an alternative reference to the notion comprised in the 'line and staff' structure.

Delegation

The primary purpose of organisation structure is to afford an effective framework for the delegation of management responsibilities, and for the continuing coordination of such responsibilities, though delegated. Of itself the *structure* does not carry major significance, for it is no more than a *framework,* a pattern of subdivision and correlation. Within that framework, the management process has to continue effectively and in coordination: the importance of coordination becomes emphasised, because the formation of any given organisation structure, as the means and framework of delegation, creates a grave danger of separatism and disparity. Delegation, through an organisation structure created by the determination and definition of responsibilities, means that the firm's managers, supervisors and specialists have had mandated to them *accountability* for specific activities, operations or services. The basis of that mandate lies, on the one hand, in the firm's requirements for maintaining effective direction and management, and, on the other, in the skills, knowledge and experience that the nominated managers and others can offer.

The danger of separatism arises because this very action of mandating specific responsibilities involves some unavoidable measure of fragmentation of the process of management. By the establishment of this organisation structure, the firm's overall management has, as it were, been subdivided: this is the purpose of the structure, the very meaning of delegation. The reason for it, of course, is to make for more effective management, by enabling the various facets of the management process in that firm to be more competently attended to: but the danger of the fragmentation lies inherent in the subdivision by which the delegation is carried out. Two different but interrelated aspects of delegation afford safeguards against this danger: the one is in the *medium* of delegation; the second is in the *personal* acceptance and application of that delegation.

As has already been stressed, delegation is effectively created and established only by the appropriate and clear delineation of the pattern of managerial and functional responsibilities, and by their definition into terms that are commonly or uniformly understood by all the managers and specialists to whom that delegation is made. What is being delegated to them is responsibility for activity or for service; the right to form and take decisions according to their best judgment, within the scope and scale of activities or services allotted to their jurisdiction. This last observation underlines the real significance of the delineation and definition of responsibilities in delegation—for this is the only way in which the expression 'under their jurisdiction' can have any real meaning. Such delineation and definition is the only way to make clear to all the managers and specialists what their respective scope and extent of delegation are and how these interrelate within the single overall process of management for that firm. It is therefore manifest that the delineation and definition of respective responsibilities, if competently and effectively carried out, is a major safeguard against disparity and separatism. This can be readily illustrated from real-life situations, but such illustration calls for close regard to the details of the delineation and goes beyond the type of examination that can be undertaken in the present context.[1]

While a great deal of support to management unity can be provided from effective definition of the pattern of delegation, another major contribution has to come from the competence, attitude and behaviour of the managers and specialists to whom the delegation is made. Management is not a process that goes along of itself; it is applied by men and women, and its effectiveness is therefore inseparable from the good or the bad of human attitude and behaviour. There is a lot to be said about this 'human feature' of management effectiveness throughout this study, but only one aspect need be taken up here, because it is immediately relevant to the definition of responsibilities by which delegation is established.

The intention of delegation is to mandate to managers and to specialists areas of jurisdiction within which to exercise judgment and decision: to them is delegated responsibility and authority for nominated activities and services, and the nature of the interrelationships among these respective areas of jurisdiction is also made clear. All the members of a particular organisation (the firm's managers and specialists) are thus clear about how they share in the single overall process of management of that firm's affairs. The framework provided (the organisation structure) ensures that unity is preserved by coordination within delegation: the managers and specialists themselves can confirm that unity within the given framework or they can thwart it, mar it. This may seem a curious thought to pose: it seems hardly reasonable to suppose that managers would thwart or mar effective management of their employing

---

[1] Practical illustration is provided in the 'case material' that forms the subject matter of chapters 7 and 8 of *Organisation—the Framework of Management*, see especially pp. 199–203.

firm's affairs. Consciously, maybe not; but, unconsciously, the danger is there. The only real safeguard, in terms of this personal attitude and behaviour, is for managers to be *always conscious of their own role* in maintaining the unity of the management process within the firm's organisation overall.

Two aspects

This can be easily attained if every manager and specialist will recognise that by delegation he acquires a *dual role of responsibility*: he has the specific area of jurisdiction for which he has been appointed to the post he holds; but he has *also his share in the overall process of management* within which his specific area is set. The two aspects are interrelated, and both are essential. The former may come more readily to mind, but the latter is no less inescapable. Every manager or functional specialist can see his place in the organisation structure correctly and adequately only if he recognises the duality of aspect, accepting equally responsibility for his respective area of jurisdiction as for his share in the nexus of managerial cooperation represented by that organisation structure. A very useful phrase has just been used, worth committing to memory as the reminder of the duality of role: 'the nexus of cooperation'; it belongs to every manager and to every functional specialist, and it is mandated to him by delegation just as fully as is his own specific role.

To be effective, delegation must clearly ensure a genuine and specific mandate of responsibility with authority for decision. *What* should be delegated and *to what extent* are the matters that have to be deliberated and determined specifically in each case concerned: that is what is meant by saying that a pattern of organisation needs to be 'tailormade', and hence that the search for a typical structure is vain. In broad outline, the substance delegated in the case of certain positions may well be similar from one enterprise to another; for example, the responsibilities of a Factory Manager, or of a Personnel Officer, or of a Chief Accountant, may be similar in a number of concerns. This is different from saying that a standard MJD could be prepared for these positions—as a basic working draft, maybe; but not in any form that could be definitively used unaltered. A correct and appropriate definition of responsibilities, as the medium of delegation, can be made only in terms of the circumstances and needs of the individual firm, and is best attained through a cooperative effort from the members of the firm's organisation.

It can be noted in passing that systems of management information assist delegation: for example, targets of performance, with an approved budget of related expenditure, correlate with the extent of decision delegated to the executive concerned; the absence of negative variances in his actual results shows the outcome of his application of that delegation. Through an integrated system of management information, authority to decide is seen to be effective in appropriate extent at various levels and in various sections of the organisation. Continuous review of the performance and progress of operations, and of their cost, feeds back to the managers the facts on which to exercise their judgment as the basis of ensuing decision—decision to keep things going as they are, or to make changes in plans or in the mode of their application. Delegation of authority and responsibility, supported by sound data for guidance, gives to all levels of management the effective framework for coordinated executive decision and, thus, for effective performance.

MJDs

The purpose and usage of MJDs for the planning of delegation within an organisation structure and for effective management development will be fully considered in the special context of Part Seven (see page 991). Some illustrations of MJDs in varying forms are also set out in the Appendices to Part Seven (see page 1040 onwards).

Relationships in organisation

In formulating an organisation structure, it has been indicated that relationships as well as responsibilities need to be defined; the explanatory label 'formal' is usually added to mean that it is those relationships that are in fact enshrined within the pattern of responsibilities laid down. Other relationships also arise, namely, 'informal' ones, which are the good (or bad) personal working relations generated among the holders of the various positions. Both kinds are important for the effective practice of management—but the latter, the informal personal relations—are *not* a question of organisation structure. They are a reflection of personal attitudes and a matter of management action relevant to a later section of this study.

The formal relationships are those that the chief executive or the Board of Directors intend to see occurring as part of their design for the effective working of the organisation pattern. These are, therefore, enshrined in the MJDs when correctly drawn up, and they fall into three broad categories, which can be conveniently described respectively as 'direct', 'lateral', and 'functional':

Direct (executive) relations

The relationship existing between a senior and his subordinates, and conversely. The senior may be a Managing Director or any other manager, and his subordinates the junior managers, supervisors and other grades down to the operative levels. The relations involved are those of instruction on the senior's part and compliance by the subordinates. (This is not to suggest an authoritarian approach, as obviously the element of motivation requires a proper human flavour to the instructions and appropriate consultation with subordinates.) In principle, the relationship is that of 'direct authority', in the customary sense in which a senior may give valid orders to subordinates within his jurisdiction: these relations are customarily described as 'direct', and are readily illustrated from the position of a Factory Manager, Chief Accountant, Supervisor and many other managerial or supervisory positions in industrial organisations vis-à-vis their immediate subordinates.

In the MJDs these *direct* relationships will be shown in two ways:

(a) at the head of any schedule there will occur the caption 'responsible to', with indication of the superior position to which this one reports as a direct subordinate under authority;

(b) at the end of the schedule there will (may) be shown the subordinates (whether lower managers, supervisors, or rank and file) over whom this position has executive authority (command).

Some writings have in the past described these direct relationships as 'line relations', borrowing an analogy from the notion of 'line and staff' used to describe management activities themselves. This is an erroneous usage in terms of its origin in naval and military parlance: the term 'line' specifically signifies *activities*, and by analogy it could be transferred to *responsibilities*, but not to the relations arising therefrom. In the context 'line and staff', both terms refer to activities or responsibilities, or to the persons performing them, but *not* to the relationships.

Lateral relations

The working relations between executives or supervisors at the same level of responsibility and holding parallel authority. In the exercise of management, two managers may both be responsible to a common senior for different sections of the activities of the enterprise; or they may be responsible to different seniors. The effective working of management calls for collaboration between them on points of mutual interest, without reference back to the common senior or to the respective seniors: the executive relationship thus set up between the two managers is described as 'lateral' and it can be variously shown in the MJDs, according to the pattern determined. For example, it may be required that one manager has to consult with another on a given matter *before* he takes a decision on this matter, even though the decision is one lying clearly in his jurisdiction; the definition would then begin with the wording 'In consultation with . . . , responsible for determining and deciding . . .'

Lateral relationships also exist in the more general sense that every manager has an inherent responsibility for serving the enterprise as a whole as well as looking after his own part or section; and thus he has an obligation to display a cooperative attitude towards all colleagues. In this sense, formal lateral relations merge into the informal relations mentioned above.

Functional relations

Those which arise in the case of a specialist position contributing a service to the managers and supervisors who compose the executive members of the organisation. The position and the service given arise primarily from specialised knowledge, i.e. within a certain field a body of knowledge and experience which is germane to the working and effectiveness of management in the organisation as a whole. Usually, it is only in the larger enterprises that such specialist services can be separated out into distinct positions, though the services themselves will arise in organisations of any size.

The specialist (or functional) officer has a responsibility for ensuring that the particular activities allocated to his jurisdiction are carried into effect throughout the organisation at a high level of effectiveness, a responsibility which has three aspects: the first is to assist in the formulation of the relevant sectional policy; the second is to advise his line colleagues and subordinate members of the organisation on the working of management in that particular regard; the third is to be answerable to his immediate senior, usually the Managing Director, for the effective conduct of the specialised activities concerned, i.e. he is responsible for advising and assisting the other managers and supervisors in carrying out those activities and for ensuring that their line instructions conform to the relevant specialist policy.

If a functional officer has subordinates or staff of his own, his relations with those persons are obviously of the direct type already described; similarly, his own relations with his immediate superior have the same character. But relations with other executives, supervisors and members of the organisation are of an indirect category, and are customarily labelled 'functional'. Illustrations can be drawn from the Personnel Manager or Officer responsible for ensuring that personnel policy is carried out by appropriate procedures and by an adequate standard of human relations at all levels of management and supervision; or from a Clerical Methods Manager, responsible for sanctioning routines and procedures, the design of forms, the purchase and the use of office equipment, etc., throughout the organisation. (Because of the considerable extent of confusions and difficulties that arise in practice over the delegation of these specialist, or functional, responsibilities, some further commentary will be made on them later.)

Whereas the three foregoing categories of relationship arise widely and frequently in most organisations, a fourth kind is sometimes encountered under the label 'staff relations'.

**Staff
relations**

A distinct relationship arising from the appointment of a (personal) assistant to an executive. The arrangement is not often found in industry, and occurs mainly in the top levels of the organisation, e.g. a Personal Assistant to the Managing Director. His terms of reference may be of general or specific character, but the nature of responsibility is clearly defined as assisting the executive to whom he is allocated. The Personal Assistant is, strictly speaking, not an executive at all, and certainly *of his own right carries no authority*; he is best regarded as an extension of the personality of the executive he serves, either for general or for specific purposes according to the terms of reference. In such a capacity he discharges his chief's responsibilities and dispenses his authority; he has no subordinates (except perhaps a secretary) and issues no instructions. Whatever he does within the organisation, he does on behalf of and with the authority of his chief. In consequence, it is only with his chief that he has any formal relations, and for these the description 'staff relations' is used. No label can be applied to his relations with other parts of the organisation because *of himself he has none*; his activities and his daily contacts with the managers are part of the working of management within the organisation, but the character of his responsibility is such that he can have *no formal relations*, direct or functional, with other members of the organisation, apart from his chief.

Of these four types of relationships the first and second are most frequently met. The 'direct' contact of senior and subordinate arises in even the smallest working unit of a man and a boy, or a plumber and his mate, or the village shopkeeper and her girl. The 'lateral' relationship can emerge only when there is more than one member in any one grade, for instance, two partners, both operating as principals, or two supervisors responsible to a Works Manager, each in charge of a separate department or section of the factory. The alternate Day Shift and Night Shift Managers of a department are related laterally, and many other illustrations can readily be quoted. Functional relationships develop as the unit begins to grow to larger size, though no numerical test can

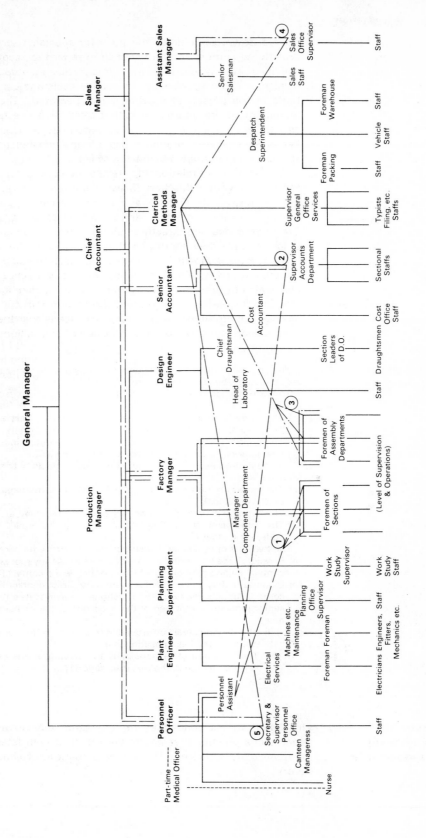

Fig. 1.5.1 Positions and relationships in an organisation

NB. The ringed numbers refer to notes on page 56.

be laid down. Sometimes the need for specialist service emerges early in growth, as is most commonly seen in regard to accounting and secretarial activities: even when still of quite small size, a manufacturing enterprise may need to engage specialist accountancy assistance, perhaps on a part-time basis in the person of a professional Secretary. The human problems of management are another field that often give rise to the need for expert assistance early in the growth of an enterprise, and the functional position of Personnel Officer is frequently brought into existence among the first of the specialist appointments below the Managing Director.

These groups of relationships give a meaning to an organisation chart and follow the layout of the chart. *Direct* relations are the verticals; *lateral* relations are the horizontals. *Functional* relations are customarily shown in dotted or broken form for distinction, and portrayed as diagonals from the specialist executive concerned directly to all other major points of relevant contact. In strict principle they should be shown parallel to the horizontal and vertical lines. The distinction is illustrated in Fig. 1.5.1: the dual portrayal there brings out the important point that, while in everyday practice a functional specialist will deal with subordinates of other executives on matters within his jurisdiction, in principle he is doing so with the concurrence of the immediate superior of such subordinates. In practice, this means that the functional specialist should keep that superior fully informed of instructions or decisions given to his subordinates.

Notes on the chart (Fig. 1.5.1)

The chart illustrates five functional relationships; in the organisation depicted there will, of course, be very many more.

The broken lines (— — —) show functional contacts between the Personnel Assistant and—

(1) The three Foremen of Component Manufacturing Sections (perhaps in regard to progress of apprentices or absence of some operatives);

(2) The Supervisor of the Accounts Department (perhaps in regard to recruitment of a new junior or a problem regarding one of the staff).

The dash-dot lines (—·—·—) show functional contacts between the Clerical Methods Manager and—

(3) The three Foremen of the Assembly Departments (perhaps in regard to Work Tickets or Stores Notes);

(4) The Supervisor of the Personnel Department Office (say, in regard to Record Cards);

(5) The Supervisor of the Sales Office (perhaps in regard to customer records or addressing of letters).

The two sets of broken and dash-dot lines show the functional relationships:

(a) Parallel to the horizontal and vertical relations, they represent the *formal* pattern of contact, i.e. the path along which *in principle* the contact flows;

(b) Diagonally they represent the *customary* direct contact between the parties concerned, though involving the functional specialist in a responsibility to keep the senior managers informed of the decisions or instructions given to their subordinates.

N.B. (i) The varying levels portrayed in this chart are for convenience of printing and not to be read as indicating status.

(ii) The omission of responsibility for 'Buying' in the organisation illustrated is commented on in the text (see page 61).

Specialist (functional) responsibilities

In regard to his colleagues on the same executive level as himself, a specialist's functional *relations* are identical with lateral relations, but his *responsibility* is different. The particular features of a functional responsibility are:

- it originates in expert knowledge of a given field, and exists in order to provide specialist service to the 'line' (operational) managers and supervisors;
- the functional specialist is always to be consulted before any decision is taken pertinent to his jurisdiction;
- he must ensure the attainment of the relevant sectional policy throughout those parts of the organisation where his jurisdiction extends;
- his decisions, rulings or instructions within the given field, and within the agreed policy, must be followed by the managers and supervisors, and cannot be gainsaid, overruled, or set aside except by his immediate senior executive;
- his responsibilities are mainly discharged by *other* executives and supervisors, and his 'instructions' therefore pass through the direct and lateral channels of the organisation.

With the increasing attention given in recent years to practical consideration and discussion of organisation structure, it is perhaps unfortunate that the notion of 'functional (or specialist) responsibilities and relationships' should have given rise to so much difficulty. As the foregoing comments indicate, the notion itself is simple and straightforward: it posits no more than that certain items in the process of management have been singled out for expert attention on the basis of an advisory and ancillary service to the managers who are carrying the main burden of executive operational responsibility. While some of the difficulties in practice have arisen because of lack of understanding of the notion or principle involved, by far the majority have arisen from three other sources:

1. absence of definition of the responsibilities respectively allocated and, therefore, of the relationships required;
2. failure to honour the natural requirement of cooperative attitude;
3. unfortunate personal preoccupation with (comparative) status, power or ambition.

No organisation approach can deal with the second and third items, and the first has been adequately covered in these pages. Some difficulty in practice may perchance have come from confusions in terminology, as well as from failure to understand, and it may be worth while to pursue these aspects a little further because of the widespread significance of the functional patterns in everyday management.

In all the difficulties and problems that arise in this context, the crux issue is always a variant of the one question—'Who has the authority to make the decisions and to issue the instructions embodying those decisions?' The parties to the difficulties are respectively the functional specialist(s) concerned and the executive manager(s) who use or apply those specialist activities. The question is thus translated into personal terms as: Does the specialist decide what is to be done and tell the executive to do it? Or does he *advise* the executive, leaving the latter free to decide for himself whether to accept that advice or not? In fact, of course, these two questions are not a correct antithesis; nor do they correctly express the true situation. They do, it is true, pose in a common and succinct form the almost perennial problem of 'the line *versus* the staff', but this very succinctness is the cause of the persisting trouble. More explicit posing of the true factors involved, representing clearer

understanding of the nature and significance of the 'functional responsibilities' as an item in the overall process of management, would remove the
problem by dint of mutual acceptance of a commonly shared role.[1]

Functional responsibilities (the 'staff') arise in specialisation of knowledge
or services, as was explained above. So it falls naturally to the specialist
concerned to determine the ways in which his part of the management
process ought to be made effective in practice—what methods, procedures,
operating instructions, and so on. Yet he is *not* the manager, and all his
specialist services will be made effective *within the jurisdiction of one or more
executive managers*; his services are in fact *their* tools, part of *their* exercise of
management responsibility. *Thus, it is reasonable that these managers should
be consulted before any such services or activities are applied among the
people and operations under their jurisdiction.* This does not gainsay the
specialist's expert knowledge, but it preserves the attitude of mutual cooperation; it enables the managers to develop and express confidence in the
specialist, because there is explanation and consultation, followed by understanding and acceptance. If there should be genuine disagreement that cannot
be resolved, the specialist is the expert authority, and he has no alternative but
to report to the (common) superior for a decision binding on both parties.

All this, of course, is an exercise in good human relations, not in organisation structure.

In the case of the larger and very large enterprises or establishments, a
particular difficulty emerges as a byproduct of size, because the functional
specialist activities are carried out by members of 'departments' often employing considerable numbers of personnel under the jurisdiction of a 'head
of department', who is the chief functional officer of the specialist activity
concerned. This pattern, and the scale of the activity within the department,
tends to mask the service or ancillary role which is the essential characteristic
of the functional specialisation. The head of department can more easily
appreciate this aspect of his position, as much of his time and energy is
dovoted to advice and guidance given to his colleagues, the executive
managers in the various operating departments—factories, sales offices,
depots, etc. It must rest with him to ensure that his subordinates (the
personnel within his department) also retain the correct appreciation of their
role and character.

This is particularly true in the case of those activities where the 'work' of the
department has, superficially, all the appearance of being a self-contained
activity. A good example is the accounting and costing department: the daily
routine tasks have all the appearance of a self-standing operation, which
builds up to a pattern of financial information belonging to the Chief Accountant or Financial Controller, and used by him to 'control' expenditure at top
management or Board level. If the department is large, the senior accountants
in charge can easily see themselves as 'executives', responsible for the
'management of routine operations'. And so, of course, in that perspective
they are; but for the department as such and, by implication, for all the
members of it, the correct perspective is better seen in relation to the
management process of the enterprise as a whole. In that context, their activity
is directed solely to providing the data and instruments of the control element
exercised   by   the   various   supervisors,   department   heads   and

[1] The fuller analysis and exposition will be found in chapter 3 of the reference cited in the footnote on
page 48 above.

managers—including those at the highest level linking with the Board of Directors. Thus, for example, cost data is the tool of control for the supervisors and managers of the manufacturing departments; sales statistics and turn-over revenue data are the tools of control of the sales managers and supervisors; and so on. At the level of the Managing Director, information for overall control is in the form of the periodic financial statements comparing the actual position with the budget forecasts. That the accounts and finance departments have large numbers of accountants and clerks does, indeed, involve various patterns of internal management in conducting their activities correctly and effectively, but *it does not alter the essentially functional role and relationship of these activities in the pattern of management conducted within the organisation overall.*

To round off these reflections on the functional principle in action, it may be useful to revert again to the problem of terminology, to the notion of 'line and staff' commonly used as the alternative title for the combination of executive management and functional specialisation which has become the common-place of most industrial and commercial organisations. It is the 'staff' item in this label from which the terminology confusion stems, largely because this one word has now come to be used with two different connotations, which may not always be explicit from their context. The two usages are mostly found embedded in the one descriptive title 'staff officer':

1. In the sense explained above, this position would refer to an 'assistant' accredited to a given executive of one kind or another, and authorised to take a range of decisions on his behalf. How far this authority extends is a matter of choice for the executive concerned, and one may assume that this has been (as it should be) clearly determined and indicated. In the common practice of industry, this position is largely exemplified by the so-called Personal Assis-tant with very limited scope of decision; but this is by no means inherent in the notion, and cases are not uncommon where a more senior and mature appointment is made, such that a large measure of responsibility and authority is exercised by such a staff officer. Here there is analogy with the 'General Staff Officer' widely known and applied in the Armed Services, though the analogy cannot be pressed too far because the industrial applica-tion is as yet relatively immature. Within the scope of the responsibilities carried by the superior, the 'staff officer's' jurisdiction is general, a full reflection of his superior's authority (unless for special reasons some items are specifically withheld); his relations with other managers and members of the organisation are, as described above, non-existent, for he is but an extension of his superior and has no responsibilities or relationships in his own right. There is no question of 'specialisation' or a functional responsibility arising in this use of the term.
2. In the second usage, the term 'staff officer' is but an alternative label for the functional specialist in the sense that has now been fully described—a label clearly reflecting the specialist services supporting the line activities or responsibilities. This usage is most commonly encountered in informal discussion situations, rather than as a title, though it can occasionally be met in that way within the larger public corporations, such as the nationalised industries. This second usage is clearly very different in connotation from the first, and an attempt is sometimes made to provide some protection against confusion by describing this second form as 'Specialist Staff Officer', in contradistinction to the 'General Staff Officer' of the Armed Services.

The significance of organisation

Reference was made earlier to a common view that organisation is one of the refinements of management, that the definition of responsibilities is all very well for the bigger and more ambitious enterprises, or those which like doing things with a sense of display. With the practical man, it is argued, there is no call for an organisation structure; he knows what his colleagues are doing, and they all get along quite well together by their mutual knowledge of each other and of the business as a whole. Experience has, unfortunately, proved this rather common view to be utterly erroneous, even in the case of quite small units. Again and again, difficulties in the operations or the management of a factory or a retail stores can be traced to weaknesses in organisation—either faults in the allocation of responsibilities and the determination of their relations or, more usually, to the absence of any real pattern of known responsibilities. Inevitably in such circumstances overlapping, duplication of effort, and misunderstandings occur, and many important things are omitted because no one seems to be responsible for them.

Such casualness in regard to organisation springs from failure to appreciate its position as the 'framework' of management: without a known and sound framework management cannot be effective. Organisation is closely related to policy, to planning, to control, to coordination and even to motivation. In the first place, as has already been said, the responsibilities that make up an organisation structure cannot be determined until policy is known, at least in outline. For the policy indicates what is going to be done, and in broad terms how: this alone makes it possible to draw up the proper framework for the necessary operations to achieve that policy. Conversely, of course, the existence of a stable and clear structure makes the dissemination and interpretation of policy easier, and enables its fulfilment to be more readily checked.

The framework of management practice

The known distribution of responsibilities provides a foundation for more detailed planning of operations, methods, lines of working, equipment, routines and the like. Obviously, it contributes enormously to coordination; the mere knowledge of who is doing what, and how the various responsibilities are interrelated, is in large measure a guarantee of coordination in the working of management. There is also a relevance to morale: much of the frustration that characterises so many of the executives and supervisors in Britain's industrial system springs from irritations due to lack of knowledge of their own and their colleagues' jurisdiction, from unfortunate experiences of wasted duplicated effort, or from a sense of despair due to lack of clarity as to limitations imposed on the exercise of responsibilities. The clear definition of responsibilities and relations contributes to better understanding, reflected in a greater measure of self-responsibility, of cooperation, of will to work, of effectiveness in daily action, and so of productivity. This is not to argue that organisation structure alone can achieve efficiency; that could not be so, because it is only one aspect of the process of management. But it is in a special sense a fundamental aspect, because it is the framework without which the process cannot be carried out.

The main practical task in forming an organisation structure lies in this definition of responsibilities and the consequent interrelationships—not on the basis of any standard form or pattern, but specifically designed to reflect the objectives, policy and intentions of top management and to coordinate with the procedures of planning and control that are being used. The design must seek to provide effective delegation of authority plus responsibility and so to create the framework for the full and effective exercise of the management initiative of the persons appointed to the positions—while preserving their overall coordination in common practice and purpose.

The point can be illustrated by reference to the chart in Fig. 1.5.1: the purpose of that chart is to illustrate certain relationships within the setting of a specific organisation. Like any organisation chart, it can do no more than display these interrelationships somewhat arbitrarily in a summary form; it tells nothing about the substance of the responsibilities allocated, except what is read into it from one's own interpretations of the titles used, and these could well be widely different for different people with different backgrounds of experience. It will be accepted from commonsense readings of obvious labels that this chart relates to an engineering concern of some kind, probably manufacturing a range of light assemblies, and of medium size in employment and turnover. It has many features which readers could, from their own personal standpoint of judgment, regard as 'odd', and they might be tempted to condemn these as 'wrong'. There could, however, be no *justification for such condemnation based on the chart alone.*

One special feature to mention is that the chart shows no Buyer or Purchasing Officer, though clearly someone must be responsible for this activity. All sorts of surmises are possible: perhaps the General Manager sees personally to purchasing as one of his own special responsibilities; or perhaps the Production Manager carries it; or perhaps the Planning Superintendent; cases have been known where this responsibility lies with the Chief Accountant. Suppose a position of Buyer is to be created, where should it figure on the chart? To whom should he be made responsible? There are persons to whom buying appeals as an activity of considerable commercial significance and who would without further reflection make the Buyer responsible to the General Manager, or perhaps even insist that he ought himself to be one of the directors. Much argument has been joined on this issue, but the problem need not be further pursued here: the one conclusion about which any definite stand can be taken is that *this illustrative chart affords absolutely no criteria at all for deciding where the position of Buyer should be inserted. That decision can be taken only after full consideration of relevant facts and circumstances, which a chart cannot possibly show.*[1]

The personality problem

A major problem that comes up in any consideration of forming an organisation structure is the question of 'personalities'. There has long been a controversy of 'personalities *versus* organisation', a conflict of view as to whether an organisation should be formulated according to an analytical review of policies, facts, procedures, etc., without any reference to personalities, or whether the grouping of responsibilities should be built around the available personalities.

[1] The responsibilities and activities of the Buyer are further dealt with in Part Three, chapter 4 (see p. 345); there is also a relevant comment in *Organisation—the Framework of Management*, see pages 215 and 258.

The controversy is easily resolved, by the answer that neither argument is entirely true. In smaller units it is often inevitable that the distribution of responsibilities should conform to certain personality requirements, while in the larger unit, experience suggests that it is safer for the structure to be built up independently of persons. In neither case can it be safely said either that principle should be disregarded or that the personal element should be entirely neglected. The wise line of procedure would seem to involve treating organisation as a technical issue and adopting the following steps:

1. Work from the known objectives and policy of the enterprise.
2. Define the responsibilities needed to secure fulfilment of this policy, and determine their appropriate groupings and relationships.
3. Determine from these definitions specifications of the qualities, qualifications and experience required to discharge the responsibilities effectively, i.e. prepare specifications for the various executive, supervisory and specialist appointments.
4. Select the persons to be appointed to the responsibilities in accordance with the specifications; or, if it is decided to appoint someone not exactly conforming, set down the known objective reasons for the departure from the specification.
5. Set the structure (responsibilities and relationships) to work according to the definitions, but if it is decided that certain departures should be countenanced, the known objective reasons for such departure should be set down; in every instance of departure it should be clear that basic principles are not being contravened.
6. The test as to the soundness or otherwise of such departure will lie in whether or not harmonious and balanced working of management is attained throughout the organisation, so that management is in fact ensuring true efficiency of operations and a high level of morale in the working teams.

One special aspect of the personal factor in organisation structure is that of the span of responsibility or supervision of a manager over subordinate managers or supervisors. The point arises with most significance where the activities of the subordinate sections are interrelated in their current working. A widely accepted notion is that the number of such subordinates should be 'limited to five or six', as though there were virtues in either figure. This notion originated from a Romanian management consultant working in Paris in the early 1930s; he calculated the combinations of reciprocal interrelationships that must arise in the course of contacts between a superior and increasing numbers of subordinates. With five subordinates, the total of relationships ('direct and cross' as he called them) is 100; with six, the total increases to 222, and with seven to 490. This last figure he regarded as beyond the range of expected competence of the average individual executive.

There is undoubtedly substance in the argument, and a clear conclusion can be derived that a definite limit is to be imposed on the span of responsibility (or 'span of control' as it is popularly but rather loosely called). Personal make-up and the specific character of the responsibilities covered and circumstances concerned must, however, be taken into account. Some men, in certain circumstances, might easily be overburdened with only four subordinates, whereas here and there an individual may well be able to carry eight or nine persons reporting to him. This again is a matter on which considerable thought is to be exercised before a decision is taken, and if there should be any uncertainty a sound management appraisal will always counsel choosing the lower number of subordinates, at the executive or supervisory levels, rather than the higher one.

Decentralisation

No commentary on aspects of organisation structure, however brief, can be complete without some reference to the problem of 'centralisation v. decentralisation'. Strictly speaking, this is not so much a problem as a notion round which a great deal of confusion and controversy has developed, much of it stemming from lack of precision in thought or in discussion. To review what is involved in this issue would virtually entail a recapitulation of all that has been said in foregoing pages, both about the process of management itself and about the purposes and means of delegating the responsibility that the process contains. For what can 'decentralisation' mean other than a general or a specific delegation of management responsibility? It is, in fact, confusion over words that mostly lies at the root of the controversy about the notion—confusion not only over the real significance of the term 'decentralisation', but also over the nature of 'operational' and 'functional' responsibilities, with both of which it has to be associated.

Without going deeply into the controversy, it may be useful to record here some observations to help in clarifying the subject. To begin with, a statement of what the terms can be held specifically to signify:

Decentralisation is best held to mean a state or pattern of organisation in which specific responsibilities have been 'delegated': the implication of this is that 'delegation' is the process and 'decentralisation' the resultant embodiment of it.

Centralisation can only mean reserving responsibilities to given units or sections of a central headquarters, but such units not necessarily of themselves carrying top management authority.

The delegation or subdivision of management responsibility can be made on either of two bases: (i) the whole of the process of command can be subdivided into the smaller self-contained units; or (ii) the process of command can be subdivided in such a way that there is concentration of specialist responsibilities established to serve the units of direct command. Naturally, the decentralised pattern reflects whichever basis has been used, the second being the one that gives rise to the combined pattern of 'operational' and 'functional' responsibilities. The distinction between these two in nature is the key to avoiding confusion in discussions of 'centralisation v. decentralisation'. Delegation of the 'operational' responsibilities involves the decentralisation of the process of command itself; the managers of the decentralised sections are thus the users of the services provided by the specialist or functional sections. These latter are by their very nature *ancillary* to the operational sections—not implying less importance, but specifically in character promoting the purposes of command and control, though without itself assuming any of that process of command and control.

Management can be effective when decentralised only when full provision is made for the integration of the delegated responsibilities of both categories. Neglect in this respect is the cause of most of the difficulties of 'decentralisation'. One could go so far as to say that in large-scale organisations there is often a deficiency in principle, because it is believed, erroneously, that the subdivided units of functional or specialist responsibility exist and function in their own right.

Turning now to the second term in the pair, taken literally 'centralisation' would mean that *all* management decision is reserved to the one point of command: in this sense, it is not encountered in practice outside the one-man business. In a more common form, 'centralisation' may be taken to mean that *responsibility for major management decision* is reserved to a group of (senior) executives at the headquarters. Once again, with an organisation of any size, this situation is unlikely to be met to any large extent—some powers of major decision must lie at lower levels, if the enterprise is not to be brought fairly soon to a standstill. In common practice today, 'centralisation' is understood to imply that major decision is reserved to senior executives at headquarters, and that, within a limited range (often not clearly specified or even known by the individuals concerned), day-to-day action is left for decision at the lower levels. Sometimes the term refers to the reservation of decision within functional or specialist responsibilities to headquarters departments: thus, for instance, in a manufacturing and trading concern, it may be arranged that all the accounting, cost accounting, and other control techniques are put into effect by a single system through all departments, with a Chief Accountant or Financial Controller responsible for the design and application of the system throughout. From the argument of foregoing pages it will be clear that such an arrangement is *not* correctly described as 'centralisation' unless responsibility for all *decisions* in respect of matters where financial and accounting aspects are pertinent is also reserved to this Financial Controller.

This whole discussion may be much assisted by recognising that 'centralisation' and 'decentralisation' are not clearcut alternative states existing in readymade form and applicable here or there, very much like taking one or other of alternative patent medicines. They go deeply into the process of management itself, and establishing the balance between them is part of the essential analytical task to be performed in determining an organisation structure. If there is any generalisation possible, it can be no more than advocating 'centralisation' to be applied in regard to policy and procedures, to ensure uniformity and balance of management action, whereas 'decentralisation' should be the principle for management responsibility in executive action. Even this wide generalisation might well be found open to question.

As is so frequently the case with aspects of management practice, understanding and sound action can be attained readily if there is clarity of thought in terms of the underlying analytical principles, and nowhere is this more true than in the juxtaposition of 'centralisation v. decentralisation'.

Looking to the future development of a firm, in the context of expansion of business, improvement of market or other aspects of progress, organisation as the framework and medium of delegation has also to be thought of ahead: consideration of 'organisation planning' will be found as a major subject in Part Seven (see page 923).

6 The theory of management

By whatever standards measured, it must be recognised that management is a very widely spread practice and in the past couple of decades its practitioners have built up a sizeable and impressive camaraderie. Many nations, large and small, now have national 'management institutes' and the three-yearly gathering of the World Council of Management (formerly CIOS) regularly musters several thousands of participants from a large number of these countries, no matter where the Congress is held (1969 in Tokyo, 1972 in Munich, 1975 in Caracas). The literature on the subject can only be described as vast: it must run to six figures in book-titles over the world as a whole, and is added to by a yearly output in the hundreds, not including the articles in various journals or magazines and the reproduction of conference proceedings.

A world scene with this extent of activity naturally prompts the question whether management should now be rightly seen as a 'profession', a topic that has already been much argued over the years in Britain without conclusive outcome.

Another question is even more poignantly stimulated, namely, whether there is an agreed body of principle and practice accepted in the main by these many and varied practitioners. Here a clear answer can be given—regrettably, in the negative. There is indeed a considerable amount of conformity in what the managers do and how they deal with specific objectives or operations: to this extent, there is a common corpus of practice, much of it fostered by cross-fertilisation of literature and by exchange of personal experiences in conferences and study programmes. Valuable as this commonality of practice may be, it does *not* constitute an agreed or commonly accepted body of knowledge that would be universally subscribed as essential. This goal has still to be reached, and, if ever management is to be recognised as a profession in its own right, the fundamental body of principles will have to be defined for broadbased acceptance.

Endeavours have been made consciously over many years to reach definitions of 'principles of management': these efforts have centred mainly in the USA and Britain, and have stemmed from a coalescence of basic contributions of the early pioneers of management practice, some going back to the beginning of the century, for example F. W. Taylor, the 'father' of 'scientific management'. In Britain, the search for principles was an active topic in the 1930s and 1940s, when it appeared as the subject matter of conferences or discussion evenings. These are episodes now of historical significance only, though one day the endeavours and the discussions may have to be resumed. As a matter of passing interest, one of the latest summaries of the 'principles' emerging from these earlier deliberations (dating around 1950) is reproduced here as Appendix II (p. 147), while some of the historical contributions are outlined in Appendix I (p. 132).

**The concept
of 'theory'**

Reverting to the narrower scene of management in Britain's industry and commerce, it is no less surprising to find no agreed cohesion about the fundamentals of either practice or principle, though, again, it would be true that in many firms over many industries there are large areas of common practice. Bearing in mind the extensive range of management studies in Britain's higher educational facilities, including the several postgraduate business schools or centres, it is the more surprising that an agreed set of principles has not yet emerged, still less an accepted theory of management. The main reason is undoubtedly the preoccupation with practice, and with ways and means of coping with practical situations and problems. Moreover, the past couple of decades (the period of the growth of the management studies facilities) have witnessed the emergence of numerous new or improved techniques, which have inevitably attracted attention in academic institutions—practices and techniques in marketing, in economic evaluation and forecasting, in long-range planning, in financial administration and management accounting, in data processing. Perhaps the one field in which anything like principles has been approached is that of motivation and personnel relations, where the incidence of the behavioural sciences has drawn guidelines for managers from research in social situations.

It can, of course, be argued with some strength that neither principles nor theory have any major significance for the practising manager, provided he is well trained in the fundamentals and the techniques of his management process. But this is exactly where the accepted body of basic knowledge would have its real value, in contributing the foundation of sound training for the up-and-coming practitioner. There is a ready analogy in many professions or fields of expertise that serve the community, and if management is ever going to gain recognition either as a science or as a profession this basic body of principles or theory will have to be developed.

The notion of 'theory' seems to be peculiarly unacceptable in the world of business management. Maybe because businessmen are wholly preoccupied with their short-term objectives of making money. Correctly interpreted, 'theory' means no more than a basic doctrine or body of knowledge in which are enshrined the essential features underlying effective practice and accomplishment; it is a thought process, an intellectual contribution underlying action, deduced from the systematic study and analysis of previous successful accomplishment. There is no reason at all why a theory of management should not be developed and purveyed as the common core or foundation of studies and training programmes. Yet this very thought seems to be anathema to most managers, especially the more senior and longer-established ones: to them it seems to connote the antithesis of practical success. As a term used in industrial discussions 'theory' frequently carries a derisive implication that the speaker regards himself as 'a practical man' enjoying a measure of success from his practice, and that accordingly he has no time for what he chooses to regard as doctrines or vague ideas. He christens these 'theories' because he is unable to relate them to any proof from his practice; he uses the term 'theoretical' to imply that to him an idea may sound good, but he is not able at the moment to find any convincing counterargument, nor does he want to admit the soundness of what is being offered. Frequently, too, this epithet masks ignorance, even if unwitting ignorance, and endorses instead a readiness to act 'off the cuff'.

In the present context, an exercise in long-range planning could be fully appropriate, and against the day when interest in the development and acceptance of a theory of management may become possible, some preliminary lines of approach will be in place. What is required of the theory is that it should summarise the essential features underlying effective practice and thus provide a body of principle which, if adopted as a foundation of training, will ensure that the trained practitioners have the first essentials for achieving success in that practice. So far as a theory of management is concerned, it must clearly be stated that 'success' does not necessarily mean making money for personal fortune: the criterion of accomplishment is not to be found in how much wealth the manager amasses to his own credit. The criterion must lie first and foremost in the basic objective of business management, namely, continuously to serve and satisfy customers at a profit to the firm.

A suggested outline

The essentials of the theory of management were spun out in the analytical examination earlier in this Part (p. 9), so that the presentation now is a recapitulation in different form. The following points could be held to constitute the basic theses of a coherent theory of management, from which by further review and analysis a corpus of principles could be deduced:

- Wherever applied, management is a *process of responsibility* for deploying resources to the accomplishment of a given objective or purpose: that is to say, for obtaining and arranging the resources and regulating their application through the medium of the personnel employed to accomplish that objective.
- For the given objective or purpose the *resources needed* will be a combination of manpower (the personnel employed) and physical resources (material and financial), all of which are available for a variety of applications to other objectives; the choice for the given objective thereby enjoins on management the responsibility for effective usage.
- Effective usage must imply conscious deployment of resources so as to attain the *optimum balance of input and output* in relation to the objective (=cost-effectiveness), the justification of usage for this objective rather than to others, and the readiness to seek improvement of the input/output ratio (=betterment of performance, productivity and profitability).
- The process of responsibility in deployment of resources is exercised as a combined pattern of *mental action and human behaviour* in relation to the given objective or purpose.
- The mental action is a process of deliberation leading to *judgment and decision* in respect of modes of deployment of resources and the continuing maintenance of good performance towards accomplishment of the objective.
- According to the scale and scope of the operations concerned, the process of responsible judgment and decision may have to be *subdivided by delegation*, implying the passing on to selected personnel of a given share in responsibility for judgment and decision over those operations.
- The operations ensuing from the decisions are carried out by the personnel employed to accomplish the objective and deployed under the command of the management team created by delegation: that team has an inherent

responsibility for *motivating the personnel employed* towards effective cooperation in the attainment of high performance, and in any efforts directed to the improvement of performance.

● The objective or purpose towards which the operations are directed predetermines the *main objective of management judgment and decision;* but management carries responsibility for interpreting this into subsidiary objectives promoting effective accomplishment, including objectives concerned with the improvement of performance.

● Judgment and decision can be applied effectively only if there is a *feedback process* showing achievement against intention, by means of techniques of information (tools of management).

● Effective deployment of resources requires periodic *review, confirmation* or *reinterpretation* of intentions (programmes, plans, targets) on the basis of the feedback of information showing actual performance and progress.

● In the exercise of this judgment, regard must be paid to the *future requirements* for accomplishing the objectives as much as to the current position, and adjustments of the latter can be effective only if made with due regard to the future position.

● The management process thus has an *essential economic character* in its concern for the usage of resources in the attainment of given ends, and must judge (balance) the economic factors against social demands that may arise from consideration of motivation (for example, the wellbeing of employed personnel).

The wording of the foregoing points may well seem arid, if not even stilted; that is unavoidable in an endeavour to set down major and complex principles in the minimum of text, and at the same time to give them an orientation for general application. Semantics, however, is not the object of the exercise. Attention should be given, rather, to the substance of these points, with their intention and implications. To attain a coherent theory of management cannot possibly be a one-shot affair, but will emerge only from a probably long-running exchange of views and experience contributed by persons sharing the same genuine intention.

The theory will then posit accepted basic concepts and will need to be interpreted into the principles that will form the guidelines to effective practice. Principles will, of course, be far more numerous than the handful of points that can state the essence of the theory: for, the principles will have to be fashioned in respect of several different facets of the overall management process. This is illustrated in the embryonic drafting preserved in Appendix II. It is also illustrated by the full content of this volume: concerned, as it is, with effective management practice, all that is set out for the guidance of directors and managers in the attainment of competent managerial action must be assumed to rest on a body of sound principles—even if such principles have as yet been neither commonly recognised nor identified. In the course of years, there is a groping towards accepted principles, if only because the exchange of experiences among managers is bringing them increasingly to realise the extent of common foundations for their own varied practice in the exercise of judgment, decision, motivation and control.

At the stage at which a body of principles is recognised by a majority, or even a goodly proportion of managers, management will have attained the standing and status of an acknowledged profession.

**Social
responsibilities**

Principles and theory are both reflected in practice, in the everyday exercise of the managerial role: this is why and how they are reflected in this volume. There is, however, one facet which does not usually get any extent of reflection in the real managerial life, or even recognition in any practical sense. Yet the trends of public opinion the world over are such as to bring it more and more into the focus of attention within industry and commerce. This is the facet that is customarily referred to as 'the social responsibilities of management', and it will be appropriate to give it some specific attention in this context.

The concept of social responsibilities is by no means new, whether in Britain or elsewhere, though it has always had a narrow connotation, referring exclusively to the wellbeing of the men and women employed in firms in industrial and commercial occupations, especially the former. It has not been seen commonly or readily as an aspect of the element of motivation, though this is where it should properly belong. Social responsibilities, where advocated at all, have been couched in terms of a supplementary humane consideration for wellbeing, rather than as a stimulus to performance. True, there has long been recognition of the fact that 'satisfied' or 'contented' workers (and employed personnel generally) can give a better output of work in quality and quantity than those employed in unsatisfactory conditions or under sufferings of grievance and conflict. As already noted earlier, concern for the 'wellbeing of the worker' has been a feature of Britain's industrial progress in the past thirty years and has tended to overemphasise producer aspects of industry, to the comparative neglect and detriment of the consumer aspects. It has even been argued that this overconcern with wellbeing and welfare of the producer section has caused the deterioration of the nation's economic vitality and brought the economy and standard of living to low levels in international comparisons.

This view of social responsibilities will be further considered in its proper setting in Part Four of this volume, but the concept has today to be acknowledged with wider and more farreaching connotations. Four can be readily identified, though three of them would not be usually thought of as 'social' as that description is commonly understood. Justification for their inclusion is that they concern the community in a very significant way, and this could hardly be regarded as stretching the description beyond reasonable acceptability.

(1) The consumer

The first aspect can be briefly dealt with because it has already figured to some extent overtly as well as by implication: it is the responsibility of management to the consumers, to the community seen as the body of citizens whose needs and wants can be satisfied only by and through the products and services of industry and commerce, and who are therefore in the last resort the customers of the firms. This responsibility is the bedrock objective of business management, which has no meaning unless to serve and satisfy its customers (at a profit). Overt acceptance of this responsibility is what characterises in management 'the marketing attitude of mind', and is the surest way by which the progressive vitality of firms, and of all industry, can be fostered. Whatever steps a government may take for customer/consumer protection, such an approach can achieve but little in contrast to what would be attained if only directors and managers recognised this responsibility and acted in accordance with its dictates.

(2) Resources

The second aspect is, again, one that has already figured in these pages, but it calls for some reiteration in the present context: this is the manager's responsibility for effective utilisation of the resources entrusted to him for the conduct of his operations, and the accomplishment of his objectives. Here, too, is a responsibility inherent in the management process, and which should reflect professional competence. The 'three Ps' (performance, productivity, profitability) must be seen as the manager's watchword, a responsibility not to be selected or rejected at choice, but inescapable. The professional attitude will be one of positive interest, an eagerness to seek improvement. Yet judgment must come maturely into play, for 'improvement' spells 'change', against which there is commonly a human antipathy, and possibly, fear. The manager's skills in human understanding and personnel relations will be his guide, for he has to attain a balance between the improvement he would like to attain and the fears of change that this would be likely to encounter. 'Taking people along' will be the measure of the challenge. In the human difficulties, however, there is no let-out from progress: this is where Britain's managers have failed so dismally in the past twenty years. Industry has needed improvement in almost every facet, but entrenched attitudes have woven widespread tacit impediment: to this challenge the managers have mostly failed to rise.

(3) Standard of living

The third aspect combines the previous two and projects beyond them. It is management's social responsibility for contribution to the betterment of the nation's standard of living. Coming down to bedrock realities, this is what economics and an economic system are all about—men and women going about the ordinary business of life, earning the wherewithal to maintain and to better that life by their spending. From this ordinary business of life and living stems a fundamental objective and responsibility of directors and managers, for they are at the focus of decision and leadership in the conduct of that activity; they are the means of balance between the input and the output—the application of resources through men and money to the continuing supply of goods and services. The process is a circle, or a cycle, a wheel in motion, and its progress is the pace of advancement in the people's standard of living. Crucial to any progress here at all is the skill of the directors and managers, their competence in achieving effective management through sound marketing decision and the efficient deployment of resources. Output always greater than input, the gain partly spent in better living, partly invested in better progress. The input-output formula poignantly reflects the basic principle of the economic system: 'Business has no meaning, unless to serve and satisfy a customer, at a profit.'

In the modern economy a living is earned through the input factor in the equation: by employment, manual or mental; by supplies, consumable or capital; by investment of funds for the conduct of enterprise. The input is directed by the skills of marketing and management to an output that is needed or wanted, something that firms or people are prepared to purchase or hire, that is to say, willing to pay for.

The implication of the formula is that everybody gains, or *should gain*: the skills of marketing and management can ensure that this natural gain *is* earned, and is real. The gain is the 'living'; the better the gain, the better the living. Improvement of the standard of living stems, in the first place, from better earnings and profits, such that the total volume of consumer spending can be increased. This is what an improvement in the standard of living means: more people spending more money on more things. Other contributions arise also from the more effective performance of industry and commerce through cost reductions, which can be applied to the lowering of prices to the consumer, or the freeing of resources for the production of other things, for quality improvements, for better service. An important contribution will come through public spending, national or local, on behalf of the citizen-consumer: public services, environmental improvement, culture, community amenity. Whether it be slum clearance, a new arts centre, a national theatre, or more widely available higher education, the community's desirable objectives can be attained only if its industry and commerce are producing the net wealth to sustain the costs involved.

A modern nation can have a standard of living, of service, of culture, as high as it wishes, with one simple proviso: that it also puts into its industry and commerce the extent of effort in brain and brawn to pay for it. Nobody owes us a living. Not even any contribution to our wished-for standard of living. Nobody? Well, the directors and managers of our industries and commerce do, because theirs is the professional obligation to direct and lead the wealth-producing activities. But let us be fair: this due they cannot render, unless the community gives them the proper support. Clearly, a mutual obligation exists. If the climate of support is created by the people and government, the professional responsibility of the directors and managers will owe the community its living . . . and give it.

Seen in this sense, management's 'social responsibilities' no longer have their age-long welfare connotation, but go right to the heart of the nation's wellbeing—a *primary* concern for the economic viability and vitality of the firm, the continuing service and satisfaction of customers, at a profit, with marketing as the motive force. Concern for the wellbeing of employed personnel is a derivative, part of the 'motivation' element in effective management. Concern for 'full employment' is of greater significance because it contributes to the focus on economic viability, in the effective utilisation of the nation's manpower resources and thus promoting the progress of the standard of living. A major feature in the skill of management must be seen to lie in the demands of balancing these considerations in objectives, economic and social, both on the narrower and on the wider scale. This will be recalled as a feature inherent in the management process (see the first item in the statement of the theory above: page 67).

(4) The environment

The fourth and final aspect of management's social responsibilities is one in which obligation is likely to overtake inclination, at least in Britain: it concerns the impact of industry on its physical environment. In this respect, British industry has a pretty lurid past to live down. Many of the more sordid relics of ugliness and despoliation in the older industrial districts have by now disappeared, and museums are the only places where the physical reminders live on. The emotional memories, however, are deeply ingrained in the nation's social structure and account for much of the bitterness that still bedevils industrial relations. Only sporadically have firms accepted any responsibility for their environment, and of these a few have attained international renown for their constructive contribution to social milieu: Cadbury at Bourneville, Lever Brothers at Port Sunlight, and some others. New standards in town planning and commercial architecture have done a great deal in the past twenty years to ensure a more attractive approach to factory premises and settings now newly building or rebuilt, and it is possible to assume that, in this respect of physical environment in terms of premises and layout, firms will customarily conform to the new standards of community elegance. The age of squalor is past.

There remains the problem of waste and effluent treatment, an area again in which industry's record has been shabby, to put it mildly. That a new approach will be taken is to be expected as the outcome of legislation, though a great deal of interim improvement can be expected from voluntary decisions, based on the expectation that clearing up the mess will be a good deal more costly later. Little purpose can be served by pursuing this point further, save only to pose the principle that the negligence of the past has meant the negation of a principle. The physical environment of productive enterprise is part of the community's resources for the benefit and enjoyments of its citizens: management carries an inherent social responsibility to respect that environment, on all fours with its responsibility to use other resources with good effect.

In this context of social responsibilities it may be felt that management is being looked at with a much wider area of concern than has customarily been taken. True, indeed. But this is only a matter of looking forward to what is likely to be commonplace in the course of a generation or two. Already, in most of the advanced industrial nations government legislation has imposed on management responsibilities and obligations that touch on many of the matters in this context; and the tendencies are towards increasing those developments. Influences in this direction may also be expected to infiltrate as a consequence of the increasing trade relations between the 'western' and 'eastern' countries. The wider spread of employee representation on Boards of Directors (a principle accepted in law in the EEC) will also bear influence the same way, though the emphasis is likely to be greater on matters concerned with employment conditions.

The pity in this situation is that, in the main, management is in the passive role, accepting what is enjoined on it by law or bowing to what is required of it by polite duress. There is no reason why management should not be the positive influence, in the lead. Once the directors and managers see their role and responsibilities aright, with the full rounding out of what these imply, they will realise how much the positive attitude can contribute to the accomplishment of their own objectives, including objectives of profitability. Nowhere is this more true than in their regard for the satisfaction of the consumer and for the productivity of performance. From these two sources the progressive vitality of business is born, and from that vitality, continuously maintained, will come the dual benefit of positive contribution to the community's standard of living and of increase of profit to the firm.

Seen against the backcloth that has been sketched out in this wide context of social responsibilities, the directors and managers of industrial and commercial firms are clearly being regarded as the focal forces for the nation's economic progress. Rightly so. This is how they should be seen and how they should see themselves, and this would truly make them into accredited members of a major profession.

The implications stemming from this view in relation to the training and development of managers and directors will be examined in Part Seven, as a topic of major significance (see page 991).

7 Criteria of performance

The underlying role of objectives in management has already been commented on in the earlier analysis (p. 38), and emphasis was placed on the artificiality of pulling 'objectives' into the forefront, as though something special or new. True, there can be value in calling on managers to pay closer heed to their objectives, or to delineate them more specifically, or to be more forthcoming in making them known to subordinates, or to use them more effectively in motivation by reinterpreting major objectives into subsidiary ones or into targets for individual operating sections. Perhaps the most important consideration in any advocacy of emphasising objectives is that of maintaining the integration of subsidiary objectives with the main ones of the enterprise. This was a danger inherent but latent in the 'MbO' campaigns of recent years, the danger of encouraging managers to find *their own* objectives in relation to their own roles—a danger that would be so very much greater and nearer in firms which have not formulated or made known the overall objectives towards which the Board of Directors are seeking to direct their firm's efforts.

For effective management in practice, this must always be a first consideration, a major fundamental: it can best be achieved by the formulation of a marketing programme for the firm, which will express the broad business strategy, the main targets of trading (products, markets, channels, scale), parameters of production or supply, and the expected outcome in profitability. The strategy and targets will have been based on an appropriate review of the economic and technological background to the firm's activities; and, if the directors really want to give effective guidance and motivation to their chief executive and his managerial team, they will have drawn up their marketing programme with a three- or four-year forward look, as well as the detail targets for the immediate first and second year ahead. The practices entailed are part of the subject matter of Part Two of this book.

Taking this lead from his Board of Directors, the Managing Director (chief executive) will use the marketing programme as the framework of the delegated operating objectives for the managers in charge of product development, production and supply, selling and sales promotion; and for the guidance and control of the personnel in charge of specialist services, such as research, employee services or management information. Along with the objectives and targets, the Managing Director will inculcate in all his team a 'marketing attitude of mind' such as to ensure their cooperation in effective and progressive management of all the firm's operations and activities. As long as he can sustain this attitude in his colleagues and subordinates he can feel assured of the continuing vitality of management practice and thereby of the wellbeing of the firm in the three main facets of service to customers, good employment for personnel, and profitability for the shareholders. And he will ensure that his own efforts in top management leadership will recurrently highlight this standpoint. A Managing Director could find a monthly or fortnightly meeting of his managers (at least those reporting directly to him) to be a valuable instrument for keeping alive the spirit of vitality and progress.

Performance and information

In fulfilment of the firm's objectives, as portrayed in the marketing programme, the individual objectives of each manager will centre primarily on performance, that is, on the effectiveness and efficiency of the operations and/or activities that lie by delegation within the jurisdiction of each manager under his command. It is here that the processes of judgment and decision will come most keenly into play, as the manager issues his instructions for action, and keeps his fingers on the pulse of response, to assess where and when changes of instructions may be called for or to decide what other steps should be taken. It is from here that the real motivation of the men and women employed will stem, and the burden taken of human difficulties that may arise from changing situations, or from misunderstandings, or from failures of communication. It is here that the balance of the economic and the human will be focused recurrently in the daily and weekly problems of the factory or office.

What is here required of the manager cannot be shortly summarised, because it is in effect a large amount of what is covered in all the following Parts. There is, however, one aspect that does claim specific mention, if only because it points to a deficiency commonly voiced by managers when discussing their own role and effectiveness: this is the question of management information.

Most managers in most firms have at hand some form of information about the operations and costs for which they are responsible. This may, in some instances, be figures the manager has prepared for himself, while in other cases there may be a supplement in the form of monthly or quarterly accounting data prepared by the firm's professional accountants. The significant features about management information in a firm are two: that data should be relevant and pertinent to the managerial roles as delegated; and that the system of data should be common or integrated, so that managers are not at variance through misunderstanding or misrepresentation. What the managers need is information that will enable them to see current performance and cost measured or assessed against the targets and plans laid down to reflect the objectives: this is how they can exercise the essential elements of their managerial process in an effectively coordinated way—control of performance against plan.

Performance directly reflects the disposition and utilisation of the resources under the manager's jurisdiction, and the outcome of decisions he has made in deployment and utilisation. Judgment and decision come most frequently and most significantly into play in this fundamental feature of the manager's role. To accomplish this judgment and decision soundly and reliably the manager needs correspondingly reliable information—the data showing the plans and targets stemming from the marketing programme, and in comparison the realistic figures, in physical and/or financial form, showing the periodic usage of resources (materials, manpower, machine-hours), the costs that this has incurred and the output that has been attained. The manager's attention will be focused particularly on the variances of 'actual' from plan or target, especially where these are negative or adverse. It is here that the notion of scientific method becomes relevant for the practice of management, namely, the sequential action of collating the relevant facts, considering and judging them, determining the conclusion to which that consideration leads, provisionally testing the conclusion, and finally issuing a firm decision in the light of the test. The latter becomes the plan, and, when the performance data show departure from the intended programme, then the new facts are considered so as to give rise to the new decision or the revised plan. The feedback cycle is thus complete (see page 33).

Because data are of the essence of this action and reaction, management information is commonly spoken of as among the 'tools' of the manager. Information 'tools' are needed differently in different parts or levels of an organisation, and data procedures have to be appropriately worked out to meet specific requirements. Management information is an essential feature of the management process, absorbed primarily in the elements of planning and control, with secondary contribution in coordination. Procedures designed to give effect to the information must be interrelated with the pattern of delegation. Information is the means by which the manager exercises his judgment in forming his decisions: the scope and extent of these are determined by the responsibility (defined) delegated or allocated to his role, and thus reflected by the divisions and levels of the organisation structure.

Of any manager's decisions some or many will be routine, pertinent to the daily and weekly activities under his jurisdiction: if errors of judgment occur here, they can normally be corrected without heavy cost. Other decisions will refer to major action and will be *ad hoc* to situations of importance, where errors of judgment could be capable of correction only at considerable cost. Sound principle would require that data availability should be appropriate to the significance of the decisions: where the costs of possible errors are high, more information is justified, even if it costs more to provide. Less information is justified where the error potential is insignificant. In terms of practice, statistical or mathematical techniques afford their true value to management in this respect, because they can facilitate the provision of minimum information pertinent to a given situation: for example, sampling and probabilities instead of fully worked out figures.

Developments in data processing by computer have emphasised the possibility of making more information available to management. Desirable as this object may at first sound, it could in fact be a *disservice* to management, and the claims so widely made in these terms may well mask a failure to understand the true nature of management information. What management *needs* is no more than the data *necessary* to guide, assist and promote correct decisions leading to effective operations. No matter how detailed the data, or how easily obtained, they can never substitute for the consideration and the decision of the manager. Automatic (or electronic) data processing can be recommended as a mechanism, if it can make correctly determined data available more quickly and presented more clearly, because then it can have two important consequences in management action:

1. It can reveal more promptly the variances of actual performance from targets set, thus enabling quicker remedial action to be taken by management and so prevent the loss or waste of resources.

2. It can more quickly make known changes in circumstances which would render the original targets inappropriate, and thus can assist management to review and change the targets more appropriately to the change in circumstances.

In both cases management is assisted in its basic task of securing optimum outcome from minimum application of resources.

Modern data processing techniques and equipment have made possible another important sector of information for management decision, namely, information about the future. For marketing decisions, and quite often for manufacturing decisions (for example, availability of materials or materials price trends), it is essential for the Managing Director to have reliable forecasts or expectations, and to be able to evaluate the implications of the changes or of the new conditions that are likely to pertain. These are factors bearing significantly on the formulation of strategy and of the forward marketing programme. Economic intelligence and market research can provide some or all of the input, and appropriately designed ADP (automatic data processing) programmes can process the evaluations. This possibility is perhaps the most valuable contribution that the computer has brought to management information.

Interfirm comparisons

The foregoing considerations of management information concern the managers and directors exercising their responsibility for the performance and profitability of their own firm, comparing their actual achievement, weekly, monthly or yearly, with what they set out to attain as reflected in the expectations consolidated into the marketing programme, the budgets, the plans, the targets. The internal data are being used to reflect and assess performance against objectives in the two interrelated aspects: in each area of operational or functional jurisdiction mandated to a given senior manager or specialist; and at the same time in the context of the objectives of the firm overall, as consolidated in the marketing programme or the operating budgets. These reviews are essential to effective management performance and are the prerequisite foundation for seeking any improvement of that performance.

Yet the internal data are inward-looking and may not always throw the most useful light on the firm's operations and achievements. Satisfaction with performance against one's own predetermined targets may mask opportunities for considerable enhancement of the targets, or may even mislead assessment of true effectiveness—inefficiencies not being spotted because of familiarities or because of being masked by successes elsewhere. Internal data cannot throw light on a firm's performance rating relative to its own industry or, in particular, relative to its competitors. This deficiency in management information can be made good only by objective comparisons with other firms in terms of key indicators of performance and profitability.

Interfirm comparisons enable those participating to have, in addition to their own control data and reviews, objective and factual assessments of their comparative standing with competitors or other firms in their appropriate sector of industry or trades, and thus to become aware of otherwise unsuspected weaknesses in policies, practices and performance. A firm may, of course, discover hitherto unrecognised strengths, which it can then translate into improvements of its marketing programme and commercial objectives.

Figures of other firms can be used as instruments of self diagnosis and as a basis for the revision of items in the marketing programme or in budgetary targets. They become available through 'interfirm comparisons' of management ratios. The term interfirm comparison (IFC) refers to an organised pooling among firms in an industry (or in a sector of industry) of certain business figures on an anonymous, voluntary, confidential and agreed uniform basis. To be effective, reliable and meaningful such pooling and comparison must be conducted by an independent and competent organisation, preferably specifically oriented to this objective. The best-known institution in Britain providing this service is the Centre for Interfirm Comparison, with some fifteen years of extensive experience now behind it.[1]

The Centre's main concern is with overall direction and control; accordingly, the configuration and collation of data for comparison are geared this way, and are converted into 'management ratios' by means of which participating firms can have a comprehensive review of their performance position comparatively with other firms known to be similar in scale and scope and often standing as competitors. Some of the main ratios usually covered are illustrated by Table 1.7.1. It is not possible to show by simple illustration the full range of data usually included in an IFC conducted by the Centre. These throw light on every major facet of a business, giving details relating not only to overall profitability (as shown in the example) but also to the productivity of different grades of labour, the structure of the labour force, utilisation of materials and of machines, degree of mechanisation, marketing, distribution and transport efficiency, financial structure and strength, and so on.

This pyramid of ratios (Table 1.7.1) provided the framework for an IFC scheme in which thirty-five light engineering firms were participating in a number of successive years. This outline was supplemented by further comparisons over all the participating firms: in all, some forty ratios were prepared and submitted to these firms, with a considerable amount of background information. The key ratios summarised in the pyramid illustrated formed the skeleton of the closer review, and the notes appended below the table show how and why they play this role.

Table 1.7.2 shows the substance of the comparison realistically, though again only a selection of the overall ratios issued are portrayed here. The final column picks out the relative position of one of the participating firms (firm E) in two successive years. This looks like a success story: return on assets (ratio 1) has gone up from $8 \cdot 7$ to $10 \cdot 8$ per cent due to a rise in both the firm's profit on sales (ratio 2) and its turnover of assets (ratio 3). The former has improved because the fall in the firm's production cost (ratio 4) has been greater than the rise in its marketing and distribution cost (ratio 5). Ratio 4 in turn has improved as a result of falls in the firm's material and works labour cost ratios 7 and 8.

[1] The Centre was founded in 1959, with the support of the British Institute of Management and the British Productivity Council, and its service is concentrated on anonymous and confidential comparisons, drawn from firsthand collection and analysis of data from the participating firms in the various sectors of industry. Some eighty industries have been covered over the years, and many thousands of firms have been participating, mostly for several successive years. The Centre, which is an independent, non-profit organisation, has long enjoyed the support of the Confederation of British Industry and of several of the NEDO Economic Development Committees. The Centre's services have recently been developed into the USA and some European countries, and it carries out several European interfirm comparison schemes through its associate organisation, the Centre for European Interfirm Comparison. Both organisations are located at Lincoln's Inn Chambers, Chancery Lane, London WC2A 1JB. The author wishes to thank Mr Herbert Ingham (Director of the Centre from its inception until March 1972) for his assistance by compiling the descriptive notes and illustrative tables in this chapter.

As to the firm's asset utilisation ratios, there has been an improvement on both the current and fixed asset sides (ratios 10 and 11). The rise in the debtors ratio 15 is more than off-set by falls in the materials stock, work in progress and finished stock ratios 12, 13 and 14. Furthermore, the two major fixed asset investment ratios 16 and 17 have improved.

The firm's illusion of success, however, was shattered when it compared its own ratios with those of other light engineering firms of its kind: the earlier columns of Table 1.7.2 (columns headed A–G) give the ratios of seven of the participating firms (out of the total of thirty-five). The selected firm (E) now

Table 1.7.1
'Pyramid' of ratios[1]

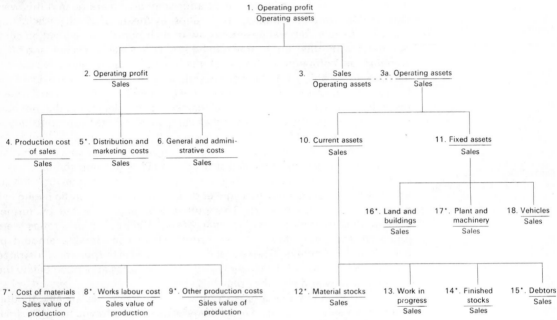

The ratio of *Operating profit/Operating assets* is selected as the primary ratio, because it reflects the earning power of the operations of a business. A favourable ratio will indicate that a company is using its resources effectively, and will put it into a strong competitive position.

The relationship between a firm's *Operating profit/Operating assets* depends first of all on two other important relationships (ratios) namely, that between its *Operating profit* and its *Sales*, and that between its *Sales* and its *Operating assets*.

Ratio 2 shows *what* profit margin has been earned on sales, whilst ratio 3 shows *how often* the margin has been earned on assets in the year. Ratio 3 shows how many times assets have been turned over in a year. Ratio 3a indicates the assets required per £1 000 of sales.

Thus the return on operating assets of a firm depends on the relationship between its ratios 2 and 3, and this in turn depends on the relationships between its sales and its profits (and therefore its costs), and between its sales and its assets.

* Additional ratios are provided to throw light on causes of differences in the 'starred' ratios above. These additional ratios are discribed in the Project Notes made available to the participating firms.

compares less well: this year, as the Table shows, the firm's profit on assets is well below that of four other firms and this is due to both its profit on sales (ratio 2) and turnover of assets (ratio 3) being relatively low. The firm's profit on sales (ratio 2) is relatively low mainly because both its production cost ratio 4 and its general and administrative cost ratio 6 are comparatively high, even though they compared well with the firm's previous year's figures. Firm E's

Table 1.7.2

The interfirm comparisons[1]

Ratios	A	B	C	D	E	F	G	Comparison Firm E Last year	This year
Return on assets									
1. Operating profit/Operating assets (%)	25·1	23·9	18·9	13·2	**10·8**	4·3	3·5	8·7	10·8
Profit margin on sales and turnover of assets									
2. Operating profit/Sales (%)	19·0	19·9	15·1	11·5	**10·7**	4·7	3·6	8·9	10·7
3. Sales/Operating assets (times per year)	1·32	1·20	1·25	1·15	**1·01**	0·92	0·98	0·97	1·01
Departmental costs (as a percentage of sales)									
4. Production cost of sales	62·8	63·5	71·1	71·9	**75·4**	80·2	80·9	77·4	75·4
5. Distribution and marketing costs	11·4	12·6	6·6	6·9	**4·9**	5·6	6·1	4·6	4·9
6. General and administrative costs	6·8	4·0	7·2	9·7	**9·0**	9·5	9·4	9·1	9·0
Production costs (as a percentage of sales value of production)									
7. Materials costs	32·0	28·7	32·9	31·6	**33·1**	35·8	33·8	34·7	33·1
8. Works labour costs	16·5	22·1	24·2	25·1	**26·8**	28·9	29·2	27·4	26·8
9. Other production costs	14·3	12·7	14·0	15·2	**15·5**	15·5	17·9	15·3	15·5
General asset utilisation (£'s per £1 000 of sales)									
3a. Operating assets	758	833	800	864	**990**	1 081	1 016	1 031	990
10. Current assets	465	481	412	474	**549**	608	543	582	549
11. Fixed assets	293	352	388	390	**441**	473	473	449	441
Current asset utilisation (£'s per £1 000 of sales)									
12. Material stocks	80	110	71	92	**100**	102	96	101	100
13. Work in progress	43	40	63	101	**188**	215	220	215	188
14. Finished stocks	132	102	57	75	**44**	67	19	53	44
15. Debtors	210	229	221	206	**217**	224	208	213	217
Fixed asset utilisation (£'s per £1 000 of sales)									
16. Land and buildings	130	158	194	174	**201**	244	241	206	201
17. Plant, machinery and works equipment	160	189	190	213	**233**	220	225	237	233
18. Vehicles	3	5	4	3	**7**	9	7	6	7

[1] The figures in the above table, though imaginary, are based upon actual IFC results. They are, of course, only an extract from the comparison, which covered many more ratios and firms. Copyright © 1974 Centre for Interfirm Comparison Limited.

distribution and marketing cost ratio 5 on the other hand, which had risen during the last year, is the lowest of all; this might reflect on insufficient marketing effort. The firm's production cost (ratio 4) is comparatively high, because, although its materials and works labour cost (ratios 7 and 8) have improved, it now turns out that both these ratios, and also its 'other production costs' ratio, are higher than those of firms A to D.

As to the utilisation of current asset investment, the firm's work in progress (ratio 13) is higher (i.e. less favourable) than those of firms A to D, even though it had improved in comparison with the previous period. Its finished stock investment (ratio 14) on the other hand, is almost the lowest of all; this however is not necessarily a favourable indication, since greater emphasis on stock production of standard products or components might help the firm to manufacture more economically.

The firm's fixed asset investment (ratio 11) is comparatively unfavourable, mainly because both its land and buildings ratio 16 and its plant investment ratio 17 (which had improved) are considerably higher than those of firms A to D.

In the actual IFC firm E received a detailed report relating to both the above ratios and the additional ratios mentioned at the foot of page 78, discussing the policy and performance factors underlying the firm's position in the IFC, highlighting its weaknesses and strengths, and indicating the directions in which improvements should be made.

How schemes work

The essential feature of an IFC scheme lies in the cooperation of the participating firms with the Centre. There is no similar 'cooperation' among the firms themselves, because there is not usually any contact among them; they do not even know each other, save by the accidental factor of personal acquaintance and conversation by individual directors or managers.

One of the Centre's major tasks is that of designing new IFC schemes suitable to the needs and circumstances of particular industries and trades. The first task is to bring together an adequate number of firms (there must be a minimum of five or six to make the comparisons useful) interested and willing to take part, preferably over at least two or three years, though no such commitment is initially asked for. Quite often a scheme has been started from the basis of a trade association; and, in more recent years, several have been set up in association with the Industrial Development Committees of the National Economic Development Council (NEDC).

Accepting the invitation to participate means that the firm will contribute figures confidentially to the Centre for analysis into the ratios referred to above, and into the comparative tables. (The Centre's expert staffs are often called on to assist firms in collating and preparing their data for suitable presentation.) Inevitably it takes weeks or months for all the figures to be gathered in from the participating firms in each yearly scheme: the compilation, checking and processing at the Centre is the speedier part of the task, though sometimes references back for clarification or fuller explanation are necessary. In due course, the comparative sets of ratios are complete for those firms in that particular scheme, for that year: these can now be compiled into the reporting document, which is sent confidentially to the Managing Director of each participating firm.

Under the letter codes these results can be compared, each firm being individually given its own identification. The firms are given advice on how to use the data reported for their own benefit, and arrangements can be made for more detailed individual reporting on the comparative interpretation of the results. This individual supplementary report discusses the firm's position, highlights points of weakness or strength shown up by the IFC, interprets differences between the firm's ratios and those of others, and indicates the directions in which improvements should be made. In many IFC schemes arrangements are made for the Centre's staff to discuss this report with the firm's directors and managers.

One thing that becomes quite clear is that IFC is not a statistical survey, but an important aid to self-diagnosis for each of the firms taking part. Its success turns as much on the cooperation of the firms as on the competence of the Centre's staff. This point has often been queried: will firms be willing to disclose such full performance and financial information to an outside organisation? Are they not afraid that this could do them harm? The first answer lies clearly in the Centre's successful experience and progress over fifteen years. Many thousands of firms in over eighty industries have readily contributed their figures for IFCs, manifestly without suffering any harm.

The crux of the cooperation lies in the confidence that the Centre and its staffs have generated in their own reliability: confidentiality and anonymity have been proven; the code-lettering in reporting has not been breached, and the only identification that occurs is what individual firms' directors choose to reveal to friends in other companies. Moreover, in the interests of confidentiality, the IFC ratios are made available only to the participating firms concerned.

International comparisons

The Centre has found that firms are increasingly interested in obtaining comparative yardsticks not only for their own country, but from abroad. This interest has been quickened by the expansion of the European Common Market. Accordingly, the Centre has set up a European interfirm comparison organisation (see footnote, p. 77) which prepares and conducts European IFC schemes by direct contact with firms and trade associations in Europe. So far ten different European countries have been involved. The Centre can also use its contacts with its associated organisation in the USA to develop European/American comparisons of key data.

Accounting comparability

Ratios do not disclose the actual figures of companies taking part: a company's sales may have been £100 000 with a capital of £50 000; another's sales may have been £20 000 with a capital of £10 000; in both cases the ratio of sales to capital will be 2:1 (or a capital turnover of twice a year). Furthermore, the ratios shown in IFC tables are unlikely to be the same as those which might be calculated from published accounts. Most of the information on which they are based is not given in published accounts, and such key items as figures for profit and assets (fixed and current) are defined in a special way: for example, current valuations of fixed assets are used, based on industry price ratios.

That leads to another question: are the figures of participating companies comparable? Will not the fact that they may use different bases—for, say, the valuation and depreciation of assets, the definitions of sales and items of cost—destroy the comparability of their figures? The answer is that in a properly conducted IFC all participants calculate their figures on uniform bases prepared after consultation by the conducting body. Figures given by individual companies are checked carefully and any query is discussed with the companies.

Even so, will the companies themselves not differ in, for example, size, stock policy, degree of mechanisation, marketing methods? Would such differences rule out IFC? The answer is that the object of IFC is not to compare companies but to reveal the effect on their performance of certain differences in their features and practices. In fact, if there were no differences between them they would learn nothing from the comparison.

Some major dissimilarities between companies (size, say) can be dealt with by grouping—by tabulating together the ratios of companies with a common major characteristic. But there are practical limits to such grouping if more than one or two dissimilarities have to be taken into account. They are best treated by interpreting the ratio differences individually, using background information from participants. Individual interpretation is essential to a successful IFC: the confidential reports given to each participant are the essence of the service.

Management information is thus put at the disposal of directors and managers in two interrelated modes, both of them objective in character: the one is the direct comparison with similar firms in ratio form; the other is the independent appraisal of and commentary on the firm's own performance as seen in management terms, at the level of direction and control. Interfirm comparisons are thus another aid to effective managerial performance; they do not do away with and replace a firm's own accounting and control data, rather they supplement the internal figures in a way that can make them more meaningful and useful.

Improving performance

This is the point at which to recall, in the context of managerial performance, the twofold role in which individual managers serve the firm employing them: the specific role of the executive or functional position to which each has been appointed and the supplementary role in the nexus of cooperation through which each manager contributes to the firm's performance overall. As has already been stressed, the two are intimately related: so much so that, if delegation is effectively made and management information systems appropriately integrated, the good performance by the individual manager in his specific role should automatically entail or produce the contribution to the overall firm performance. A key factor in attaining this correlation lies in the determination of objectives: the focus of responsibility for this is, of course, the Managing Director, who, as chief executive, must guide the formation of objectives for the firm's sectional operations and activities to ensure their consonance with the overall objectives mandated to him by the Board of Directors. The framework for this consonance of objectives, and of the operations and activities devoted to their accomplishment, is provided by the Managing Director by and through the marketing programme and the sectional plans and budgets into which that programme is interpreted, by coordinated deliberation among the (senior) managerial team.

This is the basic reason why so much emphasis is placed on the significance of consultation and cooperation among all the managers when objectives are being considered, reviewed or formulated. Again, as already mentioned elsewhere, a Managing Director can attain this intimate continuing consultation and cooperation among his managerial team by the medium of periodic or occasional gatherings, with agenda and documentation prepared in the interests of guiding deliberations and discussions towards consolidation.

Interfirm comparisons are primarily concerned with the firm's performance and position overall, and are therefore meaningful in the first place to the chief executive, the top management team, and the Board of Directors. They do, however, contribute to guidance in sectional performance: many of the ratios in Table 1.7.2 above (p. 79) clearly relate to achievements or failures of the managers in particular fields—manufacturing, purchasing, sales, maintenance. The specific supplementary reports also have much to say of relevance to individual managers in relation to their performance within the responsibility delegated. The summation of the plus and minus factors in these various sections finally adds up to the performance and profitability of the firm overall, wherein lies the primary concern of interfirm comparisons.

In this thought lies the answer to a comment sometimes heard—a curious comment, let it be said, probably born of superficial consideration of the managerial role: the observation is sometimes made that *managers individually* cannot be expected to show concern for the profitability of the firm overall because they are too deeply immersed in their own sectional responsibilities and too heavily absorbed in the accomplishment of their own objectives. The negation of this viewpoint does not now have to be specifically spelled out, for it is contained in all that has been written in the foregoing pages. Let it suffice just to recall that individual managerial objectives can have no meaning and no point, unless they are interrelated with, enmeshed with, the objectives of the firm itself: and the firm's objectives can be easily summed up in one word, profitability. To serve and satisfy customers at a profit, let it be said yet once again, is the reason for the firm's existence and activities—and, just as much, the reason for the manager holding his position.

'MbO'

This point does offer a useful opportunity for looking back again at the popularised version of the doctrine of 'management by objectives' (MbO). The basic principle in the doctrine is the natural and obvious one that managerial objectives are specifically determined in relation to the role concerned, as set out in a 'management job description'. The specified role carries two streams of objectives individually allocated to the job or position, the one inherent and the other imputed. The 'inherent' objectives relate to those activities prescribed for the job or position and are therefore concerned with current performance of the operations or services under the individual manager's jurisdiction. But these are set within the firm's marketing programme, and are interrelated among the various divisions or sectors of the firm's organisation by means of the budgeted plans and targets into which the marketing programme has been translated (or interpreted) as the framework for operations and activities. The 'inherent' responsibilities are, thus, essentially coordinated between the specific managerial role and the firm's objectives overall.

The same is true as well of the 'imputed' responsibility, so called because it is not spelled out in so many words, but tends to be taken for granted. The 'imputed' objectives relate to the *improvement* of performance by means of special efforts directed to the betterment of methods, of equipment, of organisation, of planning, and the like. It is, perhaps, artificial and misleading to refer to these as 'imputed' though this is convenient for purposes of distinction: the implication is that such objectives and efforts are not pre-scribed for any one particular managerial role, but are common to them all—inherent in the managerial role wherever exercised, and summed up in the slogan of 'the three Ps' (see p. 32).

The 'inherent' management objectives within a firm find their origin and first declaration in the marketing programme, setting out the trading performance and profitability objectives laid down by the Board of Directors, through the chief executive. Translated into operating objectives (the 'inherent' ones for the various divisional or sectional management positions) the marketing programme becomes spelled out systematically as the sales programmes (marketing programme targets), the manufacturing schedules, the purchasing specifications, and the various other forms of planning and budgeting procedures and documentation appropriate to the firm's system. Plans and targets provide the framework of control, enabling the chief executive in turn to provide the overall control of performance against that marketing pro-gramme. Through the systematic control thus exercised, all the managers responsible for the firm's trading operations are coordinated in their attention not only to performance, but also to profitability, in line with the firm's intended overall objectives. It is this standpoint that makes reasonable the identification of those additional 'imputed' objectives which are concerned with seeking for and striving to improve performance and profitability beyond or outside the predetermined plans and targets.

Herein lay one of the 'dangers' of MbO as enthusiastically propagandised, the danger of encouraging individual managers to seek or initiate changes intended to bring improvements that could have been at variance with the requirements of the common programme, or even inimical to good perfor-mance elsewhere outside the jurisdiction of the manager bringing in the change. The only safeguard against this danger can lie in the attitude of the managers at the higher levels—at once encouraging their subordinate man-agers to seek and to bring forward opportunities for improvement of perfor-mance and profitability, yet ensuring that there is appropriate recognition of implications elsewhere, thus coordinating the exploitation of such oppor-tunities and the initiation of the improvements. It is an essential responsibility for top management, for senior executives, to promote in subordinate managers this liveliness of mind for critical review of performance, progress and profitability, and for the attainment of management improvement; but, in parallel, to promote equal understanding of the unity of the management process, the interwoven nexus of cooperation which must characterise delegation.

In summary, each managerial role could be said to have three essential facets in terms of objectives: (1) effective performance in terms of specific responsibilities as set in plans and budgets reflecting the marketing pro-gramme; (2) seeking, and bringing forward for consideration and consulta-tion, opportunities for improvement of performance sectionally or overall; (3) contributing to maintaining the unity of management action and practice within the firm's organisation by means of which responsibilities are delegated—putting it into terms of jargon: respecting the nexus of coopera- tion inherent in the delegation of managerial roles. Underlying all three facets is the one major objective: striving for performance, productivity and profit- ability in the overall interests of serving and satisfying the firm's customers, at optimum profit to the firm.

In all three of these responsibilities for each manager individually, and for all of them together as the firm's management team, this same trinity or trilogy of objectives is also common and consistent—in all they think and do there must be the increasing concern for performance, productivity and profitability. Strictly speaking these three things are but different facets of the one process of *effective management:* hence, the apt description of trinity or trilogy in the sense of three things that can be considered separately but in essence belong together. And, whether thought of as 'inherent' or as 'imputed', they are inseparable from that process: how these objectives can be worked into 'management job descriptions' will be installed in Part Seven (Chapter 4: see page 953).

To ward off possibly spontaneous objections to the wording used in the foregoing eleven lines, let a cautionary sentence be promptly added. The spontaneous objections would stem from readers finding that wording apparently callous, inhuman, seeming to ignore the human character and social implications of the managerial role. Any such objection, raised in the present context, could only be unthinking, an instantaneous emotion, easily subdued; far too much has been said in the foregoing pages (and will be said in later ones) about the human factor in management to allow any such objection to claim validity. If objection were to be raised, it could rather go the other way round, in the context of Britain's industries over the past couple of decades—the concern for human wellbeing has overshadowed the signifi- cance of and the necessity for good performance and high productivity, as the only sound basis from which continuing concern for human wellbeing can realistically proceed. The 'three Ps' are *not* inhuman, they are not in antipathy to social obligations. Rather is the converse true: they are the only guarantee that management *can* show effective concern for social considerations.

Profitability

Looking at the activities of a firm overall (as is very well shown by the interfirm comparison procedures and reports), the three Ps can be validly reduced to the single objective 'profitability', in so far as it summarises and reflects the achievements, and the deficiencies, of the other two. 'Profit' is the normally accepted criterion of a firm's management success, but is a notion subject to a good deal of confusion, misunderstanding and controversy. Much of the argument is ill-founded, though it stems from understandable misconceptions in Britain's industrial history. This is argument about where the profits of industry go, crystallised in a somewhat artificial conflict between 'owners' (those receiving the profits) and 'workers' (those whose wages would eat into the profits). This conflict has now become deeply embedded in Britain's radical politics. The concept of the profitability of an enterprise as a criterion of success is seriously overshadowed by prejudices arising from social philosophy, professing to find unsavoury the idea of an unearned profit, accruing to (presumably wealthy) owners. The political concept attaching to such philosophy sees *all the outcome of industrial effort* as earned by the 'workers', and while there may be some allowance for legitimate interest on borrowed capital, this view holds that all further increment should belong to the 'workers' or to the 'community'—it should certainly not go just to the 'owners'.

In terms of the industrial scene up to the middle of the nineteenth century, there could have been some realism in these views, while the general pattern of industrial and commercial enterprise found its expression in the normal form of a one-man business or the small private company; in either case the capital and the impetus to progress coming from the one individual or the few in whom 'ownership' was vested. At any later period of Britain's economic history, however, such a concept could have little validity even on the political plane, because of the extent to which the continuing economic progress of society has been dependent on recurring investment of capital from wide sources, including much from the public purse. It is also relevant to stress the extent to which the earnings from industry have become dependent on the progress of mechanisation and technology as the fruit of capital expenditure devoted to knowledge, in no way related to the effort of labour. All antiprofit notions go back to earlier phases of the industrial revolution: the origins of consumers' cooperatives in the 1830s and 1840s were as much an antiprofit force as were the ideas and ideals on national ownership a hundred years later.

These radical views confuse the *earning of individual profit* with the *assessment of profitability* of the activity. This latter notion has to be admitted even in the enterprises which are themselves so organised that there is no individual profit motive—for example, the retail Co-operative Societies have to be 'profitable' so that they can not only finance their continuing growth but also pay a 'dividend' to their members. The nationalised industries are now required by government edict to earn profits from their operations at stated target levels.

Little purpose can be served by further pursuing these sociopolitical attitudes in the present context, though they are matters which should be adequately understood by managers, because of the influence which they exert in many aspects of industrial relations in contemporary British industry. That they are outmoded by the factual progress of society has, unfortunately, not entirely diminished their emotional significance among organised labour movements.

There is here a major educational programme to be undertaken, so that all citizens can have a full understanding and a right perspective of the profitability of industry and commerce. With understanding and perspective right, the nation's citizens will recognise that the only sufferers from anything that thwarts the promotion of industrial profitability are themselves, through a continuing fall in standard of living; and, of course, the citizens of the underprivileged countries for whom Britain would be unable to make any worthwhile contribution to development. Citizens on both political wings need to learn that the profits of the individual firms are the outcome of efficient operating, the added value that accrues when the input of resources is effectively deployed to attain a better return of output. Indeed, they can continue to argue how this additional margin can or shall be used, but not so to argue that they inhibit its being earned.

The disposition of profits	The basic principle of private enterprise is the constitution of a business directed to earning profit for the person or group of persons who have founded it, whether or not they participate actively in the conduct of the enterprise. Speaking in general terms, the profit earned from the enterprise can be regarded as a return in respect of one or more of the following things:

(a) Earnings on the capital invested, equivalent at least to what could be attained if that capital were invested in gilt-edged securities.

(b) Earnings from the mere fact of taking up participation in a venture which is not an investment in a gilt-edged situation, but inherently involves some element of venture or risk.

(c) Earnings which reflect the extent of risk, greater or less, over and above the mere act of taking a venture.

(d) Earnings reflecting application of the judgment or the flair of the entrepreneur in strict commercial terms.

(e) Earnings which can be seen as a reward for the managerial skills exercised in conducting the enterprise successfully.

(f) Earnings which are, in effect, payment for time and attention devoted to directing, conducting or actively participating in the enterprise.

The whole series of these six items would be applicable in the case of profits accruing to the owners only if they were *personally* engaged, with their private means and with their time, in the pursuit and conduct of the enterprise—for example, a small firm with two or three principals all engaged full-time or part-time as directors, managers or advisers in the firm, not paying themselves any other remuneration as part of the operating expense.

The principle of limited liability in joint stock enterprises has brought into the situation two major changes which would make the six above items *never* applicable in total. The first change is that the monetary liability of the investing shareholder is limited to the amount of capital which is represented by his purchase of shares and thus his profit is related only to items (a) and (c) in the above group. Secondly, shareholders who are active partners have their earnings in respect of items (b) and (c) limited to a return on the amount of capital of their investment, irrespective of the extent of the risk involved, because they no longer have the involvement of personal possessions outside the nominally invested capital. Items (d), (e) and (f) have no bearing at all on the shareholders as such; they apply only to owners who are employed as full-time or part-time managerial or advisory members (as well as to the professional managers and advisers themselves, apart from the shareholders): this remuneration is therefore regarded more correctly as a payment for services rendered or for skills supplied; the 'profit' element arises only if bonus arrangements are established related to the overall profit position.[1]

---

[1] The point has been made by some people that an employee in a business, whether he is employed as a manager or as an operative, in fact takes a greater degree of venture in accepting the post than does the shareholder; the latter ventures a certain sum of money (presumably related to what he is prepared to part with for the time being), whereas the man who takes employment in a business ventures his livelihood and his career, for the failure of the business may have very significant repercussions on the rest of his life, far beyond the mere fact of losing this particular employment.

It is also pertinent in this context to refer to the fact that an important element of 'profit' can accrue to owners of shares through capital appreciation attained in the form of the 'gains' from the sale of the shares at the enhanced values, as the venture thrives.

One of the major phenomena of the economic scene in any industrial country in recent years has been the widespread growth of companies with shares available for public purchase and the corresponding spectacular increase in share ownership as a normal medium of savings, replacing even in the middle strata of society the traditional thrift channels of savings banks, building societies, and government loans. (The 'unit trust' movement is for this purpose only an alternative form of share ownership.) This development has necessarily sharpened public interest in 'company results' to such an extent that the city pages of the national press have become popular reading. In this context, 'profits' and 'management success' have become uncritically interwoven: there is undoubtedly a factor of 'profitability' which is a sound criterion of management success, but this is not the 'profit' as shown as the outcome of the year in a company's Profit and Loss Account.

The latter is influenced by far too many extraneous facts: the attainment of profit *may* be a return for good judgment in the conduct of the enterprise, but it may equally be an accident of forces entirely outside the responsibility of the directors. It is the task of directors and management in a given trading business to apply resources to a programme of manufacturing and marketing: the prices which their product can earn are determined by the economic forces of the market, and the skill of management judgment lies in the endeavour to assess what these levels of price will be in relation to the type of product offered, its quality, its availability, etc. The prices and the overall sales values they can expect are *not* determined by the summation of their own costs, however skilfully they analyse the items of expenditure which they have to pay out to enable the product to be made available on the market. The sales revenues earned are determined by the market judgment of the community relative to other similar commodities offered by other suppliers, as well as relative to other ways of spending the equivalent money. In this sense, it would not be unrealistic to regard all expenditure or investment in the facilities of manufacturing and marketing products as 'fixed costs', to be employed to best marginal advantage. Management has then the task of seeking to keep these facilities employed to maximum advantage against minimum of expense, and to promote the outcome of the best possible continuing sales at the best possible prices, leaving a margin over and above the total expenditure in any given period. This is the margin known as 'profit'.

What the Board of Directors decide to do with the profits earned is an entirely different matter. They could pass these on to the consumer in the form of lower prices for the product or of special discounts, or perhaps in better quality, better pack, better service. They could, equally, pass profits on indirectly through the medium of expending them on better equipment or on more research and development, which will eventually lead to an improved range of products or services. Equally, the directors could decide to pass the profit on to all or to some of the personnel that the firm employs in different categories of occupation, either in the form of higher salaries and wages or in special bonuses. Again, they could, if they wished, divert the profit to communal ends, by paying out more in taxes or voting funds for local voluntary service purposes, for donations to universities, for charitable gifts to various institutions. Finally, the directors could use up these earned margins by paying them out to the owners of the business (perhaps, themselves) as profit-participations or as dividends to shareholders.

So far as 'profitability' is concerned as a criterion of management success, what is done with the profit earned is *not* the important feature. The more important point is: how does the profit arise? If it comes because of accidental and unexpected market or socio-economic forces, then management can regard itself as being 'lucky' rather than successful. The circumstances of the last few years in most European countries have seen many fortuitous circumstances of this kind, with large amounts of profits earned without any real judgment or skill on the part of management, other than the basic one of being in that kind of business at all. Even that may not be truly a matter of judgment, but a luck of inheritance or the windfall of chance, through an accidental and unexpected movement of public taste.

**The rewards
of success**

Profit can and does arise from true foresight or acumen in the decision to enter a particular industry about which there are deemed to be profitable expectations from serving customers, but which still entails a large measure of venture judgment in order to attain success. Commodities like ballpoint pens, certain semi-soft drinks, and a number of household appliances for kitchen use during the past decade or so are ready illustrations, a proportion of the success being fortuitous as a 'gamble', though possibly to be anticipated. At quite the other extreme, a Board of Directors and chief executive could take time and trouble to assess the economic situation in which they are working, to study the trends of social progress and consumer habits, to review technological factors, and, taking advantage of such known developments, effectively to lay down plans, skilfully directing operations to accomplish those plans. The profits arising from this set of circumstances could legitimately be described as *earned* by top management and the 'profitability' is thus a true criterion of management success. This would entail also effective internal planning and control action to ensure that the skills in market judgment have not been negatived by inefficiencies of operations, involving wasteful expenditure. Profitability as a criterion of success thus reflects the *combined skill of sound management (economic) judgment and effective management (executive) action.*

How much of the 'success' is to be ascribed to either facet of this combination is not in general terms important, though it could be important in specific cases. Where, for instance, raw material costs are high, the economic judgment factors in management's skill of purchasing could far outweigh all influence of internal executive action in attaining good profitability. Or again, where large-scale manufacturing equipment makes the fixed production expense high, the economic judgment experienced in competent marketing to maintain high volume, and consequently an effective utilisation of the plant, could be the critical factor assuring profitable outcome. So long as management is being looked at in terms of *individual* responsibilities, these specific facets of the process will predominate differently in different circumstances. Looking at the overall process of management, however, it is the *combinations of the facets* that need to be emphasised.

In differing degrees the two facets, economic judgment and effective executive action, are present in *all* managerial responsibilities, and skills in both are called for if management is to be competent and successful. Within the normal pattern of the organisation structure of an industrial or commercial company, the skills will be variously disposed in line with the delegation of responsibilities, and the major decisions leading to trading operations by the company will inevitably result from an integrated pattern of contributory decisions stemming from within the delegations. The profitable outcome attained—or the failure or losses, if that should be the result—is therefore the criterion of *achievement of all the contributing judgments.* At any one time or in any one situation, one phase or section of the management *may* have been more responsible for the result, but this may be difficult to assess comparatively and may certainly not be worth attempting to appraise on any such comparative basis beyond what the divisional or functional data show as performance against budget. The overall assessment of success can be attained through effective schemes of management information, as referred to above, and their design could be such as to give the essential minimum of guidance as to respective participation, in so far as this is needed.

Funds for progress

Quite apart from any reference to its significance as income to the owners of an enterprise, profit has a factual position in the economic system: it is one of the means of keeping an industrial or commercial activity in being, for it provides the wherewithal to 'plough back' resources for the furtherance of the activity. On a rough-and-ready definition, profit may be seen as the positive balance on the input/output ratio, the difference between the income from the activity in any given period and the expenses incurred in providing the activity in that period. (Such a generalisation begs a lot of very big questions, and can be reduced to nonsense by many accounting considerations; but it can suffice for the present purpose.) If the expenses outweigh the income, the outcome is, of course, negative—i.e. loss and not profit. With a positive profit, there are contributions available to plough back in maintaining the invested assets intact (though this could be legitimately regarded as an item among the 'expenses' of the activity) and in further developing the assets for better performance in future periods. The development could be technical, for example, by means of research to improve quality of products or to enhance the technological standards of the manufacturing equipment. The development could also be economic, for example, opening up new markets or improving channels of trading. It could be directly concerned with the advancement of management standards, for example, by the better training of managers for promotion. If resources to meet these objectives of progress and vitality are not earned from the current activity through profit, the existing business must remain stagnant, and improvements can be sought only on the basis of new capital added to pay for them.

There could be economic arguments to justify this approach, but they are valid only if an economic system is to be thought of as *essentially static.* Such a notion is probably wrong in principle, in so far as all human history has shown a seemingly inherent urge to the betterment of the society. The pattern of economic structure is probably correctly thought of as a rising spiral, such that the completion of one cycle of activity implies that the beginning of the next cycle is at a higher plane. The attainment of this upswing would thus be essentially dependent on the availability of resources to lift the activity from each notional cycle to the next. This is the essence of 'ploughing back earnings for maintaining vitality and progress'. It is also the essential justification for striving after profits. Perhaps it would be more accurate—in the light of the distinction drawn above—to say that it is the justification of 'profitability' as the objective of management.

Whichever term is used, the argument here can be supported by looking at the negative aspect. A business that is making 'losses' is so conducting its operations that (as expressed in monetary terms) its input of resources is greater than the values recovered for its output. In other words, it is wasting resources by using them to make available goods and services that the community (the consumers) is not prepared to take up at the prices asked. In the eyes of consumers, the resources would be better employed in the making and selling of other products and services—the ones where the support of demand enables profits to be earned, because customers are being served and satisfied.

This is a superficial treatment of a subject of considerable importance to managers, but any deeper pursuit would lead too far afield into a serious study of the principles of economics.

Productivity

While, in the broad approach, consideration of 'profitability' may be held validly to cover all the major aspects of the criteria of success for the operations of firms, some attention has to be given specifically to the other two Ps (performance and productivity), because they figure largely in the delegated responsibilities of individual managers. Fortunately, no further attention need be given to them here, because they are more appropriately dealt with in the other Parts of this book, where they are related to the specific context of the delegation—in manufacturing, purchasing, selling, or personnel management. All that is being advocated in those different contexts for effective management is directly aimed towards good performance (the 'inherent' responsibility and objective) and to improving that performance (productivity, the 'imputed' responsibility and objective). And it is the inherent responsibility of the Managing Director, as chief executive, to coalesce these many and varied efforts into the single stream of overall profitability for the firm, stemming from the better service and satisfaction of customers that these managers' efforts have made possible.

'Performance' does not give rise to particular problems of interpretation, because of its ready identification in the firm's management information system—in measurement against targets, budgets and plans consolidated into the marketing programme. 'Productivity', however, has been the subject of confusion and controversy: not so much in regard to ways and means of pursuing it, as in the context of measuring what has been achieved. The 'measurement of productivity' has long been a topic of argument and conflict, both in the cases pertinent to individual firms or in wider issues of the nation's economy. At the level of the firm, the topic will be looked at in the course of Part Three, and incidentally elsewhere in other Parts; on the wider plane some aspects can be briefly reviewed in so far as they could be (and, perhaps, should be) of professional interest to managers and directors.

The notion of productivity is easy to identify in broad terminology that most people would accept: the net outcome in a given period from a known input of resources (the factors of production). Therefore, an improvement of productivity will mean a betterment of the equation—either the same outcome from fewer resources used, or a higher outcome from the same input or usage of resources. This goes, of course, right to the core of what management is about, as has been repeatedly pointed out in these pages. From the first presentation in the simple illustration on p. 9, the management role has been portrayed as effective command over the disposition and utilisation of resources towards the accomplishment of known objectives; with the added rider of an inherent obligation to seek ways and means of improving effectiveness by the betterment of the output/input ratio.

In this principle lies the first justification for the need to *measure* productivity, so that the manager may know what results are accruing to his decisions and how soundly his judgment is being exercised. The measurement of productivity reveals that he is judging and deciding correctly, or shows that he is failing in some respects, or that circumstances are such as to frustrate the expected good outcome of his decisions. In this sense of *performance against plans, targets or cost standards,* productivity is measured by the control data shown in the firm's management information system, especially if sound principles of management accounting are being applied in such a way as to throw into relief the influence of fortuitous factors (a proper analysis of variances will do this). From performance deficiencies in the operating reports will come the pointers to opportunities for improvements, and here arises the second need for techniques of measurement—to ensure that the *increased productivity attained from an improvement programme* justifies the efforts and costs applied, another kind of cost-benefit equation.

Assessment of progress

Most of the factual studies so far carried out have been concerned with labour, in the assessment of the productivity of the manpower used in given manufacturing, handling and selling operations. The assessments are made over time to show the trend, and from one place to another, because usually there is more than one unit where the same activities are conducted. In some cases, studies have been industrywide, covering, for example, all the factories in the industry or within a certain region. Studies of even this seemingly simple order run into difficulties, because of variations in the range or design of product, or changes in materials used (affecting either the physical volume of output or the methods of manufacture), or because of differences in equipment available to operatives. Neutralising steps are taken to overcome these complexities, so that it has been possible to arrive at 'units per man-hour' which are directly comparable in terms of a notional 'standard product' as between one period and another, or one factory and another. The manpower included in such an index may be only that *directly* involved in the manufacturing operations or may be defined on a wider basis (specified).

The purpose of such comparison is to assess the effectiveness of the utilisation of labour or to ascertain whether there appears to be scope for improvements in operatives' methods, in layout and flow, or in equipment. Where the absorption of labour in manufacturing operations appears high, managements have sometimes derived from such productivity studies pointers to the need for changes in design of the product itself, or radical alterations in manufacturing process.

In similar physical terms, comparative productivity studies have been directed to space occupied for operations, assessed in terms of the notional 'unit of standard product'; also quantities of raw materials used, and, where technological processing is considerable, the consumption of fuel, steam and power. Other approaches have been made in financial rather than physical terms, and these have made possible a view of overall productivity of a factory or manufacturing department. On the financial approach, the neutralising of price changes has to be provided for, as well as of the other incidental changes of product or method. One study set up direct periodic comparisons of the productivity of factory units by taking the total values of output, materials, direct and other expenses, adjusting for changes in physical items and in prices or costs, and arriving at an index showing the true present cost of producing 100 units of 'standard product' as compared with last year's cost in directly comparable terms.

Added value

Where raw materials bulk large as an item in the manufacturing cost, productivity assessments can be arbitrarily influenced by price changes in the materials so that the whole comparison can be distorted, although there has been little other physical change. It has been argued that these cases can be best met by using the concept of 'added value': that is to say, excluding influences which are entirely determined outside of the firm itself, and taking into account only the total expenditures arising internally, plus the return to capital (depreciation and normal interest or cost of capital), set against the total value of sales. This gives a reflection of the productivity of the firm as a whole, concentrating on those items where its own jurisdiction runs, but with the full impact of customer reaction through volume and value of sales. The residual item in this sum is the net profitability which is top management's achievement attained by its judgments. Because of the interest likely to be taken in coming years in this approach to the assessment of performance and productivity, the matter is further reviewed in an especially contributed note set out in Appendix III (see page 154).

Over the different activities in a typical business concern the following are some of the main items that are recurrently watched to check performance and progress, and so contribute to an appreciation of changes in productivity. Each individual factor is assessed in terms of a 'notional standard unit of output':

- Changes in physical output—
    by operating section;
    by manufacturing department;
    by factory as a whole;
    by handling through warehouse.
- Labour costs (total or sectional).
- Materials costs.
- Capital costs (depreciation plus rate of interest).
- Selling prices (total or in product groups).
- Selling costs (total, regional, or otherwise subdivided).
- Advertising expenditure (total or subdivided).
- Changes in space occupancy (total and subdivided).
- Administrative or overhead expenditure.

Specific assessments of productivity can, of course, apply equally in other fields of management responsibility, for instance in marketing and selling. This is shown in some of the items listed in the interfirm comparison illustrations in Table 1.7.1 and 2 above. Selling costs and sales administration costs assessed per unit(s) of product sold, nationally or regionally, can give the same guidance to management as is gained in relation to manufacturing productivity.

Latterly, attempts have also been made to determine criteria by which the effectiveness of advertising can be assessed. The line of approach is a correlation of change in share of market in a certain year, with percentage of advertising expenditure for the given product group in the preceding year. This is necessarily a slow process of evaluation and will need several years of trial before an effective criterion of the productivity of advertising can be attained.

The simple conclusion that emerges from the consideration of these various approaches to the measurement of productivity is that there cannot be any single index or simple formula that will give managers an adequate appraisal of their own performance or of their endeavours to improve that performance. They will always have to make use of several components to get the overall picture of effectiveness and productivity, and these will need to be selected and determined in relation to their own requirements. Participation in inter-firm comparison studies will go a long way to assisting the determination of significant criteria or ratios for evaluation of comparative progress, but it may still be necessary to have other measures for purposes of internal guidance.

National productivity

It has been the theme of earlier chapters that the nation's economy is but the sum of the activities of the firms and corporations making up the totality of industry and commerce, together with the public sector activities and services. Added together, what is 'produced' by all these operations and services in the national economy as a whole is the 'gross domestic product' (GDP), reflecting the total of what is spent by the people and institutions on consumption and on investment. Add to this the capital and financial transactions going outside of the country, and the total now becomes the 'gross national product' (GNP). Both these concepts are familiar to directors and managers, because they figure readily in international economic reviews when portrayals of relative comparability are being made.

Using the GDP concept comparatively has enabled—however regrettable that this has to be so portrayed—Britain's relative decline in the past twenty-five years to be pinpointed. On the basis of comparable criteria of GDP per head of population among the fifteen or so advanced industrial nations, Britain has declined from third in 1945–50 to *fourteenth* at the latest date of assessment: of course, within the *same* list of countries. A pretty devastating reflection on the nation's productivity! Looked at another way, Britain at the earlier date (1949–50) had a GDP rating some *11·5 per cent above the average* of the fifteen nations of comparable industrial standing; by the early 1970s this had fallen to a level of over *22 per cent below that average*.

This is a sorry context in which to become familiar with the concept of GDP: but at least it helps to bring home the nature of the concept and its significance as an indicator of productivity. The stark comparative facts stated in the couple of sentences above indicate that Britain as an industrial nation has slid badly down the league table in the period of the past twenty to twenty-five years. Conditions within Britain itself might well seem to her own citizens not to have been too bad: after all, they could claim, it is not all that long ago that some of their political leaders were telling them 'You've never had it so good!' And, compared with longer memories, for example, the 1930s, things were indeed rosy! So, what does this 'comparative decline in GDP per head of population' mean? Is it just a fantasy notion, or a statistical nicety?

Far from either! The statement simply means that Britain's citizens have missed out in terms of what improving productivity could have given by way of advancement of the standard of living. At bedrock, that is what the GDP per head of population signifies. The other advanced industrial nations have taken advantage of improving technology and the betterment of managerial techniques to attain a corresponding progress in the level of productivity, and, thereby, in their standard of living. Britain has chosen not to do so. The comparable assessment of respective productivity merely reflects these facts in the useful indicator of GDP.[1]

The influence of technology

Whether on the national plane or for an individual business, one of the major complexities in determining true productivity is the problem of taking account of technological progress—new equipment installed to replace wornout machines, but the new having a higher level of efficiency and possibly a lower capital cost. The latter feature is not often met, for new equipment of a higher order of technological capacity can mostly be expected to be appreciably dearer than the items it is replacing, even allowing for changes in the value of money. Falling costs of equipment are, however, likely to be met with the progress of new inventions: it is already true of some items of electronic instrumentation and control gear.

The case of electricity generating reflects interestingly on this problem, for in recent years technological progress has supported the development of larger stations, but the capital cost is not proportionately larger. Doubling capacity may mean something only like one and three-quarters capital cost, and yet at the same time the running costs of the bigger, more advanced station could be some 2–3 per cent per annum lower. This curious economic phenomenon in a situation of progressive technology has enabled the traditional coal-fired generating station to fend off conquest by nuclear-powered stations: 'traditional' is perhaps a misnomer in this context, because the modern conventional generating unit has features which are technologically very advanced despite their lower cost.

These are thoughts at once sobering and stimulating to any director or manager, because, while they draw his attention to factors pertinent to his own role as an economic adjudicator, they also impress on him that there is no escape into easy criteria of adjudication, no escape from the depth of thought that must underlie his judgment and decision. This same conclusion is the dominant memory from any one of the many conferences, national and international, that have been held in the past years for deliberation on this topic. For it has been a popular topic in conference programmes, and there was even for many years a 'European Productivity Agency' to foster it. Many managers or directors could well have attended those gatherings in the

[1] This is not the appropriate context for any examination of the causes of the relative decline, even though those causes are highly significant to the profession and the practice of management. An attempt at examination is to be found in the author's specialist study, *Managing for Revival*, prepared and published for the British Institute of Management (1972).

expectation of coming home with pockets full of readymade productivity formulae, but they would have met with serious disappointment. Many aspects of productivity measurement have, indeed, been realistically and practically presented and discussed. Yet the outcome would have been little more than was voiced by the President of one international conference in his closing remarks: he could emphasise only that the benefit of the mutual exchanges lay chiefly in the challenge that each individual gained from re-examining his own criteria of productivity in the light of the others that he had observed or studied. Of these others, there will be some that he will want to adopt for himself, and some that he would like to try, with modification. He will continue to benefit from the recurrent comparisons with other managers and will therefore find some preference for common lines of approach. Yet he will acknowledge none the less that his measurements of productivity, his criteria of success, must be as individual to his management role as is his policy or his personal conduct.

Pay and productivity

There is some difficulty in attempting to comment on the relationship of earnings to improvements of productivity within firms or within national industrial corporations, because the guidelines to pay and prices policies are still in the process of being hammered out. There is, however, a basic principle that **increases in remuneration above a minimum norm must envisage the added remuneration being a consequence of, and therefore related to, improvements or increases of productivity.** The problem of the measurement or assessment of productivity will thus be recurrently raised as an issue of practical national significance. Opinion is moving in favour of an approach on the basis of the concept of 'added value' within the firm. A major merit of this approach is that it directly reflects the output/input equation.

From the standpoint of the individual firm, 'added value' means exactly what the two words say: it represents what the firm itself, by its own operations and activities, adds to the values of the materials, supplies and services that it has bought in from outside sources for the conduct of those operations and activities which in total make up the firm's own sales values, i.e. for, say, a year, its annual sales turnover in fulfilment of the objectives laid down in the marketing programme. It affords, therefore, a meaningful foundation upon which to measure progress in productivity. The concept can be portrayed in realistic terms as follows:

	£
Total value of sales turnover	A
Cost of raw materials and major bought-in components for £A turnover	B/1
Cost of other bought-in items, consumable stores, fuel and power, etc.	B/2
Cost of repairs to equipment, services contracted from outside sources, etc.	B/3
Cost of personnel employed in production, services, marketing and selling, administration, etc.: i.e. all activities of the firm	C/1
Cost of rent and other overhead items	C/2

Cost of depreciation on premises and equipment   C/3

Surplus earned for interest, taxes, dividends and retained profits   D

Value added by the firm is represented by the C and D items; the A item it receives from the market; the B items it pays out to suppliers; the C items represent its resources applied to production and selling operations, with supporting administration; the D item is its earnings from those operations.

Thus C+D = added value = A−B.

Productivity
objectives

Productivity can be loosely thought of as the continuing improvements of the firm's management performance in the use of resources within and through the operations it is conducting. It might at first seem arbitrary to reflect 'productivity' in 'improvement' rather than in current achievement, but this goes right to the core of objectives in management, as reviewed earlier. A basic objective lies in the effective and efficient usage of resources, and management must therefore *inherently* be always concerned to maintain and improve that usage. Maintaining the current standards or targets can be regarded as 'management performance'; any betterment on that can be taken as 'productivity', whether through achievement currently above standard or through the advancement of the standards set for future performance. (Hence the jargon phrase 'improving managerial performance'.)

The 'value added' concept enables productivity to be assessed in terms directly related to management activities and objectives, because the advancement will be seen as stemming from the areas over which the firm's managers exercise responsibility, i.e. all the activities covered by the C cost items in the above list. There is, of course, scope for productivity in the B items as well: better purchasing or negotiations resulting in better supplies or lower costs. Improvements from better *use* of materials and services would be reflected in the C items, because they are seen as the outcome of manufacturing or selling operations. Betterments in costs of materials or bought-in components due to the application of value analysis (or value engineering) techniques are a moot point, lying between the B and C categories: but, again, their occurrence will come through and within the production operations, so it is logical to see them reflected in the C items under managerial responsibilities.[1] (For the fuller consideration and illustration see Appendix III at page 155.)

The firm's objectives for productivity can be summarised in simple terms as increasing the value added by its operations:

1. the obvious first way will be by increasing selling prices, with all cost items remaining unchanged, and assuming that the volume of sales turnover is maintained (or not significantly reduced);
2. a similar result can come from increasing sales turnover at existing prices and costs, with no increase in overhead expenditures: this is meaningful only where the overhead items are at a significantly high level;

[1] These viewpoints have been disputed by some practitioners and writers; see for example E. J. Broster, *Planning Profit Strategies* (Longman, 1971), Chapter 5, 'Measuring Productivity'. The criticisms rest mainly on the significance of 'make v. buy' decisions in the supply of parts and components. In the context of manpower productivity, Broster favours a 'labour-weighted index' which he describes in that chapter.

3. the next opportunity arises from the point just made, i.e. from lower costs of materials, etc., through better purchasing, or from improvements in component/product design through value engineering;
4. better utilisation of materials, consumables, fuel and power, etc., is another source of adding value by management efficiency;
5. more effective and efficient use of the manpower represented by the costs in category C is the most obvious way of adding value through management actions, and quite often it can be the most rewarding, whether the effort be directed towards manpower in manufacturing, in services, in administration or (sometimes) in selling and sales promotion;
6. similarly, there are added values to be gained from improvements in the utilisation of machines, tools and other production equipment, in layout of processes and the organisation of working methods, in work handling, and the like; also with the corresponding approaches in the administrative systems and activities. (This category of improving productivity is, of course, closely allied with the foregoing one.)

These management actions represent what has been described in earlier pages as improving managerial performance, or enhancing overall efficiency. They are merely set now in a context of different terminology—that of 'adding value' instead of 'reducing cost': but the outcome is the same, 'increasing profitability'. (In passing, it can be noted from the foregoing observations how the 'three Ps' (p. 32) are intimately and inextricably interwoven.)

Productivity ratios

The value added approach, it was noted above, is the natural foundation for assessing productivity, because it directly reflects the input/output equation. The concept can thus be directly used for the measurement, recording and comparison of productivity within the firm from one period to another:

Manpower

Added value per employee is an indicator of manpower utilisation and profit—by total, by department or section, by project, for production personnel, or for those in other categories. Clearly, appropriate allowances and adjustments have to be made for changes in wage rates or for additional capital investment that may have been brought to bear, or additional overhead expenditure incurred in bettering the value added by manpower. Added value per 'manpower hour' could be a ratio facilitating employee bonus participation in production departments.

Overheads

Added value related to a given quantum of overhead expenditure can be an indicator of control as well as a reflection of vulnerability to fluctuations in sales turnover values. This kind of ratio can also be developed for application as a guide to the productivity of, say, research and development expenditure.

Capital

While not seeking to displace commonly accepted ratios (such as return on capital employed), a case can be made for an indicator drawn in terms of capital utilisation related to added value, reflecting the firm's capital intensity.

There is always a direct correlation between capital intensity and levels of employee remuneration deriving from the effective utilisation of the capital. Higher capitalisation implies that higher grade personnel are employed (for example, more skilled men and technicians, with fewer of the semiskilled operatives), and effective deployment of the superior technology (equipment + process + manpower) should afford the means of higher rewards, i.e. increased added value despite the greater remuneration and cost of personnel.

Interfirm

Added value ratios can provide an interesting mode of comparison among divisions or departments within one firm, as well as among firms in the same industry, if there is a mechanism for bringing the data into the light of day, however confidentially. (In this context, the services of the Centre for Interfirm Comparison (see p. 77) may be of relevance.)

This last consideration was used on a recent occasion to show how the added value approach can provide a more realistic portrayal of true productivity.[1] Using the conventional approach of 'output per head' in comparison with the index of 'added value per £ of personnel costs', the analysis showed the ranking of Britain's major industries as set out in the table below for a given year. The conventional portrayal (lefthand ranking)

Table 1.7.3

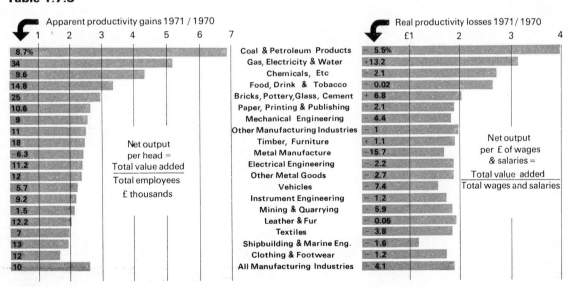

[1] This was a feature article in the *Sunday Times Business News* of January 1973, quoting data from an analytical study of the 1970/71 Census of Production carried out by Dr E. G. Wood, of the Centre for Innovation and Productivity at Sheffield Polytechnic. The quotation overleaf is from the same article.

showed a situation of reasonable progress in productivity—nothing really to write home about, but adequate to the somewhat complacent standards that Britain's industries have come to expect. On the 'added value/salaries and wages' formula, however, a very different picture is presented (righthand ranking): 'Not only are virtually all the (1971) figures absolutely low, but in sixteen out of nineteen major industries there was an actual *fall* in productivity'. Not even the poor expectations of Britain's directors and managers were really attained, when a factual assessment is made. This is the situation that has caused such a poor national standing for Britain in terms of GDP per head of population (see p. 94).

The added value approach to comparisons of performance, productivity and profitability may have one particular further advantage that really does deserve a mention. Because it reflects so poignantly the responsibilities and objectives of managers and directors, it can (and should) also stimulate the progressive attitude of mind inherent in the pursuit of the three Ps. And, as so many of the foregoing pages have laboured to underline, this is really what effective management is all about. Given an attitude receptive of and conducive to high performance and progress, managers and directors have ready at their hands all the means for accomplishing objectives of profitability in the interests of the firm and of the community.

8 Committees in management

No study of management in principle or in practice would be complete without some reference to the role of 'committees' as a medium or mechanism of communication and coordination. The word is used here for the moment as a generic reference for any gathering of two or more people brought together for a known or alleged purpose, other than social intercourse. Few managers are free from experience of committees in this sense; and, of course, all directors are by definition involved in the corporate sharing of a common responsibility through the committee known as the 'Board of Directors' holding periodic or occasional meetings.

It is a commonplace of experience to find managers and directors complaining of or ridiculing their own participation in committees—most experiences appear as ranging from 'poor' to 'downright bad'. Memories recur of long periods of discomfort with lengthy discussions on points of singularly irrelevant detail, or desultory exchanges of views on matters which are so important that no one dares to show a lead. Wanderings from the matter really in hand lead to boredom through the sessions, while participants have to listen to the inevitable talker who is the 'committee man' *par excellence.* Poor chairmanship, which makes all these deficiencies possible, is the last straw of irritation to any competent executive whose misfortune it is to be nominated to serve on an ineffective committee.

This dismal picture has been a joy to the cynics, and it has been the subject matter of lighthearted literature.[1] The topic has receded from popular managerial interest in more recent years, but the satire and the ridicule can still be found just below the surface. The earlier widespread discussion stemmed from management conferences and seminars, in which participants were involved from the larger companies and from the nationalised industries; for, in such organisations, committees were a customary mechanism for endeavours in communication and coordination. A lot of impetus came, too, from the development of 'joint consultation', for which the committee became the natural medium of bringing the two 'sides' together in cooperative discussion around a common table. As a matter of fact, experience often showed that such joint consultative committees brought more realism of progress and bred less stimulus to ridicule than most other gatherings within firms' organisations.

---

[1] The best-known satirical and humorous treatment is to be found in C. Northcote Parkinson, *Parkinson's Law (or The Pursuit of Progress),* (Murray), which originated in a series of articles written for *Punch.*

It is a pity that so few managers and directors, comparatively speaking, have enjoyed satisfactory performance in the committee medium, because this is an important medium. It could, and should, be a natural and effective mode of bringing interested parties together for deliberation on and discussion of topics of common interest, in respect of which they have interrelating responsibilities for cooperation. The committee or meeting *should* be the soundest medium of communication and coordination in the practice of management. This is not, of course, in any way to downgrade the personal strength and selfdependence of the individual manager: it is, rather, to offer him a medium for speedy and direct consultation for aiding his judgment, and for fostering effective decision in the knowledge that all relevant aspects of the matter or problem have been considered. Seen as a 'tool' of management action and coordination, the committee mechanism must be used and applied with the same degree of competence and skill as with any other technique or practice.

In itself the committee is a valuable framework of cooperative human effort, matching precisely the human facets of the management process—the need for common understanding (motivation through communication), the need for deliberation (consultation in the formation of judgment), and the need for unity of action (coordination in the exercise of decision). But, as a framework, the committee affords no more than the opportunity: the value of its contribution will depend entirely on the attitudes and skills of the persons (directors, managers or others) who seek to deliberate and discuss within that framework. Where there is among the participating members genuine desire and intention towards mutual consultation and cooperation, the committee framework can afford a most effective contribution: it needs to be supported by administrative efficiency and good practice, as referred to below. Few media could then match it for prompt, direct and unambiguous communication, or for efficacy in promoting coordination. In contrast, where attitudes are apathetic, superficial or negative, the scope that a committee offers for confusion and conflict is virtually boundless. This is where most of the 'poor' or 'downright bad' experiences have come from.

It is now some fifty years since Mary Follett, a wise educational psychologist, given an opportunity to observe industrial management practice, turned her shrewd and penetrating gaze on the attitudes and patterns of behaviour of directors and managers deliberating in committee. She had no wish to refute either the value of or the necessity for differences of outlook, of opinion, of objective, or of motivation, in the men meeting round the table, but she fastened on the powerful significance that such differences acquired when powered in committee discussion by attitudes of antipathy or by indifference to the common objective. Conflict she found healthy and valuable in cooperative effort, if directed by positive and constructive attitude: in this way, it could lead to excellent outcome through *integration* of viewpoint in deliberation and decision. From negative attitudes only negative results could ensue, or, at best, only compromise.[1] In her philosophy of cooperation in management, only *integration* could be of effective outcome to make the consultative deliberations worth the total man-hours devoted to the proceedings: from integration there could come a plus value, which was the direct antithesis of the negative solution implied in compromise. And the difference lies wholly in

[1] Mary P. Follett, *Creative Experience* (Longmans, 1924); see also her *Dynamic Administration* (London, Management Publications Trust, 1941).

the attitudes of the persons participating, fostered and supported by the guidance of competent chairmanship.

While the attitudes and intentions of the participating members are the major forces in the success or failure of committee accomplishment, the very character of the mechanism affords opportunity for weaknesses and deficiencies to overcome the good intentions. The role of the chairman acquires particular significance in this regard, for he is well placed to assess the balance of forces and to direct deliberations and discussions towards promoting the best outcome rather than the worst. He is also the focus of offsetting another major disadvantage from committee procedure, the loss of time taken up by overlong meetings: and this is expensive time when the participating members are senior executives, as is often the case.

Taking meetings as an useful and valuable tool to promote effective management action and coordination, endeavour should be made to learn positive and constructive lessons from the bad experiences and deficiencies of the past, such deficiencies as:

● The opportunity provided for the essential being clouded by the non-essential, and for extraneous points of view in any situation to be loaded into the deliberations.
● The temptation for those members who are unable or unwilling to shoulder responsibility in their own jurisdiction to allow points of decision to be taken over by their colleagues during the course of open deliberations.
● The opportunity for derogation from real responsibility over a wider area, because the committee is an amorphous body.
● The ready breeding ground for inefficiencies, because of the ease with which failures and deficiencies can be covered over when they are presented for discussion.
● The confusion which can result from a welter of discussion if this is not consistently and coherently directed; in such circumstances absence of information could be a better situation than incorrectly understood information.

Forms and purposes

Leaving aside the informal 'meetings' which take place day by day in respective offices among the executives and specialists serving in the organisation of a firm, the more formal gatherings for purposes of management through deliberation, communication and coordination can be summarised as follows:

Committee—a meeting which has a formal constitution and normally has formal proceedings, with sessions on a regular or periodic basis; it comprises a gathering of people representing different functions or spheres of knowledge, coming together to promote a common purpose or to fulfil a common task by the interchange of ideas: it is perhaps important to note that the different persons composing the committee, strictly speaking, represent differences of function, of experience, or of knowledge, and *not* differences of self-interest.

Meeting—any other systematically constituted meeting, in which the proceedings are not necessarily formalised nor regularly recurrent, and which has only a loosely established constitution; usually called *ad hoc* to consider specific matters, and not likely to have more than two or three subsequent sessions in the same context.

Conference—a large gathering of people brought together to hear an exposition of chosen subjects, followed by informal supplementary discussions and questionings by those in attendance; it could be such as to occur once only, or at long intervals if recurrent; proceedings may be formal or informal, and would be directed primarily to imparting information.

Working party—a small gathering of persons specifically selected to study a given subject or range of subjects, including problems or developments, with the expectation of outcome in the form of coordinated knowledge, recommendations, or programmes of proposed action; a 'working party' is commonly understood to use formal procedures of recording and documentation, as in a committee.

Seminar—an informal gathering of persons for the purpose of the advancement of knowledge and competence by mutual influence through the exchange of ideas, experience and criticism.

The purposes in the management field to which one or others of these gatherings can be directed may be summarised as follows:

Joint
consultation

This has the special characteristic of being a discussion among representatives, normally thought of as belonging to different 'sides'. Even here, there should *not be difference of self-interest,* since both parties concerned depend for their wellbeing on the soundness of the organisation in which they serve. Normally known as Joint Consultative Committee, Works Advisory Council, or some similar title, such bodies are formally established, with the representatives of management and employees nominated either within the one company, or on a regional basis. The purpose is, as the title suggests, consultation on matters of common interest in relation to industrial relations or employment policy and practice; some have the more specific objective of bargaining about contractual relationships, for example, the number of hours and shifts to be worked, job rates, overtime arrangements, bonus formulae, etc. Special cases of joint consultation are often found in relation to particular activities, for example, canteens, welfare services, or suggestion schemes.

Coordination
among
executives

This can be a formal or informal meeting among the managers and functional specialists in a company, designed to ensure coordination and balance in progress. A common illustration is for the coordination of a development project. Suppose there is a company which is increasing its output programme by means partly of additional shifts and partly of extensions to premises: while the programme is being formulated and initiated there are a number of executives who have major responsibilities in connection with it, each in his own field, and it is of importance that they should have a normal medium for thinking in unison as the programme and project get under way. Another instance is provided by the customary pre-contract planning meeting which is held by the bigger building and civil engineering contractors at the outset of any large contract; here managers, estimators, engineers, architects, contract supervisors, plant managers, buyers, and quantity surveyors come together to ensure uniform consideration of their individual specialist participation in the subsequent running of the constructional project.

Consultation among executives

This is comparable with the foregoing, with a slight difference of emphasis. Where a coordination purpose is served, the emphasis is particularly laid on enabling the individual executives to keep each other informed of what is going on, and to gain for themselves an appreciation of factors in other departments that will have a bearing on their own decisions. Where, however, a consultation purpose is the primary consideration, the emphasis lies on having the executives together to *interchange ideas* about the matter at issue, so that a variety of points of view can be considered before a decision is taken or action is initiated. Frequently, a committee or meeting of this kind is held by a senior executive with his subordinates and others, so that his own decisions can be formulated in the light of points of view expressed by these colleagues or subordinates.

Technical study

A group of persons to whom is entrusted a particular subject or proposition, which they are asked to consider from the various points of view that they represent and to report back appraisal or recommendations.

Uniform information

This would be a meeting or conference rather than a committee, and might well be held or called by a Managing Director to tell all his senior executives about new developments in policy and the implications of a new programme that will ensue. The more formal meeting that some companies hold daily in regard to the consideration of important incoming mail is of this character. So, too, is the sales conference held for the information of District or Branch Managers when a new product is being launched.

Advisory purpose

This is perhaps no more than a special aspect of the consultation purpose referred to above, where in this case the aim is, quite frankly, the securing of other people's points of view before a decision is come to. The advice sought may be on a wide scale, or may be confined to a specific technical or commercial aspect of a given subject.

Executive

This *must* mean that the power of decision is vested in the meeting or committee, although the description is often used loosely when the real purpose of meeting is initial information or advice among executive colleagues. As a management instrument, an executive committee raises some major issues, and these will have specific consideration in subsequent paragraphs. Outside normal industrial practice, *genuine* executive committees can be found where circumstances make a commonly shared decision imperative: for example, the management of funds in a superannuation fund or trust; or the conduct of the affairs of a sports club within a voluntary association; or the committee which adjudicates on and decides awards for ideas submitted under a suggestions scheme. Cases have been known in industry where the control of discipline has been delegated to a three-man representative committee with full decisive powers.

Management direction	In contemporary practice, a regular meeting of top executives (the heads of the main operating divisions and functional services in the organisation) is a common medium through which a chief executive (Managing Director) exerts his guidance and control, while preserving the essential reality of delegation. Perhaps held monthly on a given regular date, the meeting has a formal structure in the sense of dependence on agenda and supporting documents and of systematic chairmanship (by the chief executive); but proceedings are informal and are primarily directed to a combination of communication, coordination and consultation among the participating executives working towards a common objective. This objective is the fulfilment of the marketing programme, and the meeting is part of the chief executive's tools for planning and control within the programme; and for review or reformulation of that programme.
Formal governing committee	A normal pattern for the exercise of overall top responsibility for policy and direction is to be found in committee form—for example, a Board of Directors, the Council of any local authority, the Governing Body of a school, or hospital, and the Local Management Committee which is the customary governing authority in the Co-operative Society retail trading movement. It can be argued that this particular form of committee is an acceptable case of executive committee, the acceptability arising because of the value of several contributing minds in formulating the general directives that are to govern the affairs of the concern and in the exercise of an overall supervision of performance and progress. Such committees are 'executive' in the sense of being responsible for making decisions, directing general lines of activity and relevant financial authorisations, but they do *not* (or should not) *undertake the management decisions,* which initiate and control the executive action; those are more appropriately taken by the chief executive.
Educational	In the development of management training techniques in recent years, a 'meeting' form has been found very valuable as an aid to stimulation of thought and learning: various titles used are 'seminar', 'syndicate', 'case session', 'study group'. The essence of the arrangement is that a group of persons deliberate on and discuss in common specific subjects or problems,

in an endeavour to arrive at agreed conclusions or solutions. It is found that the mental exercise is the more valuable by reason of being conducted among a group, a good deal of the value coming from the immediate challenge and response inherent in the arrangement. Competent leadership and knowledgeable functional guidance are, of course, vitally important in ensuring successful application of the technique.

The 'executive committee'

While the whole subject of committees in management practice has become less and less a focus of interest and controversy with the passing of years, the one aspect of the so-called 'executive committee' remains a matter of lively argument. A Board of Directors, as mentioned above, is by definition a gathering of persons with a shared responsibility for decision: this is the essence of the corporate responsibility inherent in the role of the Board at the level of direction and overall control. *But nowhere else in the organisation is this corporate role repeated.* Meetings among executives, formal and informal, may be frequent and may play a large part as the medium for planning and control: the executive responsibility for decison remains by delegation with the executives participating. They are consulting each other in committee; they are communicating exchange of ideas and criticism; eventually they agree to a particular conclusion as a decision to do something, or to form a plan, or to submit a recommendation, or to reject a proposal. That agreement represents a concurrence of individual responsibilities, for none of the participating managers has transferred his own delegated juridisction to the committee.

The view is strongly held in some quarters that a committee *cannot* be 'executive' in character, and that any attempt to make it so or let it become so is an escape into irresponsibility. Instances can be and have been cited where a committee of managers does, to all intents and purposes, carry executive responsibility, but closer examination has always shown that this is an appearance only, for which no support can be found in substance.

What to the eye of the superficial observer is a 'committee decision' resulting in an executive instruction is in fact corporate recognition of decisions taken by the individual participating executives within their own responsibilities; having exchanged ideas and received the benefit of criticism and comment, the executives in session are forming their own relevant decisions while the committee's deliberations are in process. They are consulting with their colleagues, as they would necessarily have to do before final decision, but the consultations are taking place within a setting of coordination with those colleagues, instead of in the more isolated atmosphere of one-and-one discussions in their own rooms. The same holds for the meeting of a Managing Director with his senior operating and specialist executives; the illusion can be the stronger that this gathering is taking the executive decisions in its corporate capacity; the real process is that the Managing Director is taking the decisions within the corporate setting, but influenced by the contributions from his departmental and functional chiefs, who are deliberating with him.

The objections against so-called executive committees, so far as their role in industrial management is concerned, turn on the following considerations:

- Because of differences of personal outlook and attitude, the decision reached is likely to be a compromise based on the lowest common factor, rather than the best decision in the interests of a company. Such a result might be achieved particularly because of goodwill on the part of the members; if, for example, a normally cooperative individual feels that it will be impossible to secure true integration on the best decision, he may quietly withhold his objection to the compromise that is being pursued, so as not to impede promoting a common view, thus doing a disservice to the organisation because of the committee medium.
- The committee's decisions may be arrived at by the domination of one strong personality and may, in effect, be an agreement arrived at because of a fear of arguing.
- A committee cannot really exercise personal leadership over other persons who are not participating in it; this is perhaps the gravest objection to the use of an executive committee within the management framework. Even if the committee entrusts its chairman with the task of conveying in person the decisions emanating, there cannot be the same personal strength of inspiration that underlies the personal discharge of clear responsibilities by a good manager.
- There is the major weakness of avoiding issues, and consequently of arriving at decisions which are in themselves weak or which are not clearly formulated; they thus give rise to a situation in which management action at lower levels is made extremely difficult and, possibly, ineffective.
- There is also the element of instability that is produced by a committee, in so far as the attitudes of its members may well sway it in different directions on different occasions.

These main weaknesses were neatly summarised by Urwick more than twenty years ago in the following paragraph from a study that has remained the classic commentary on this subject:

A committee differs from an individual in three important respects. Its corporate personality is intermittent: it dies each time that a session closes. It is not available between meetings to make the detailed adjustments which are constantly necessary in translating policy into action. Being itself an organisation, it postulates activities of direction and leadership. But these activities are necessarily exercised by a chairman, whose authority is also intermittent and whose responsibility is not personal and specific, as would be the case with an individual. Its decisions can only be communicated to those responsible for acting on them in an impersonal form and, almost necessarily, in writing. Thus it cannot have the personal contact with subordinates enjoyed by an individual.[1]

Morale

There is a morale aspect in committee sessions among executives and specialists in an organisation structure which is worth taking into account. Any executive needs to be in frequent contact with his subordinate or colleague

[1] L. Urwick, 'Committees in organisation', *British Management Review*, **3** (1936), reprinted as a pamphlet in 1952 by the British Institute of Management.
  See also the findings of the research project described by Tom Burns and G. M. Stalker in *The Management of Innovation* (Tavistock Publications, 1961) especially chapter 5 on 'Management structures and systems', where an outline description is given of a firm 'dominated by management meetings', so arranged and conducted that they form a 'comprehensive system of communications' and provide the organisation structure. (This publication is a valuable study, particularly as a stimulus to serious analytical thought as to the relative significance of features in management practice.)

executives and officers, even if only by informal personal sessions. Periodic common gatherings can be a useful way of keeping in touch when pressing needs of a busy week make recurrent individual sessions difficult. A committee is not, however, a substitute for a suitable span of responsibility. Nor does it allow an executive latitude not to delegate. So, meetings designed to cover up such weaknesses should not be countenanced. The periodic formal meeting can assist ease of communication by an executive with the immediate members of his own team, and the members derive a benefit from the common personal contact—if one may assume that the meetings are well run. This morale value adds to the sense of participation and can be a major factor in promoting and maintaining cooperative attitude, as well as ensuring uniformity of information, i.e. 'keeping people in the picture'. Morale, coordination and effectiveness in an executive team are closely interwoven, and meetings or committees soundly based and well conducted can make important contributions to them all.

Effective practice

Most of the factors involved in ensuring that a committee or meeting is soundly based and well conducted are items of practical common sense, but it may be useful as a guide to effective practice to review the major items under four headings: role and purposes, membership, chairmanship, mechanics.

1. Role and purposes

Leaving aside any further consideration of executive committees, and recapitulating in summary form the details of earlier pages (103), a useful part can be played by a committee within an organisation in one or other of the following main capacities:

(a) as an advisory body, to assist an executive by bringing together for his guidance the knowledge and experience of various other members of the organisation, and getting them to deliberate on particular problems allotted to them;

(b) as a means of consultation, to ensure that the viewpoints of managers or functional specialists related to the matters in hand are adequately brought into consideration;

(c) as a coordinated channel of information, to ensure that all the interested persons receive the necessary information, receive the same information, and receive it in the same form, and at the same time;

(d) as a means for keeping harmony in development of progress, as well as of policy and action;

(e) as a medium for stimulating deliberation in the exchange of ideas for educational purposes.

Within any of these broad categories it is of the utmost importance that every committee or meeting should have a definite and clearly known purpose. To stress this may sound strange, because it is so obvious a point of common sense: even more strange is the fact of experience that many committees run on in such unsure circumstances that their original objectives have become obscured and *their real purpose is now not specifically clear.* When a committee is to have a continuing life, it is the more important to ensure that its role and its terms of reference are clearly stated, and currently kept in front of members. (A practical way of attaining this is to have the terms of reference reproduced inside the front cover of the folders in which each member's copies of the minutes are filed.) In effect, then, a committee has the equivalent of a 'definition of responsibilities', an MJD.

The basic feature of the formation of a committee or recurrent meeting is that the subject matter lends itself to development from the stimulus of many minds in unison and can be made more progressively effective by group deliberation: in other words, the committee treatment attains a level of accomplishment or progress that cannot be as well attained by individual discussions. There are, indeed, aspects of management practice in which this is true, particularly in the realms of formulating programmes and planning projects, or in the review of performance and progress.

An example

An outstanding illustration is provided by the short-term planning underlying the scheduling of civil aviation services ('short-term' as distinct from the forward forecasts concerned with the development or purchase of types of aircraft). Planning in this field is essentially a combination of facts from many sources, supplemented by calculations and computations—types of aircraft available, technical considerations of where they can be used, speeds, load capacity, fuel consumptions, etc. (operational facets); the timing of availability of aircraft in serviceable condition and number of flying hours before next scheduled overhaul (engineering or maintenance facets); the volume, type and location of passenger or freight traffic wanting air service or able to be obtained by commercial promotion, charter, agency arrangements, etc. (commercial or sales facets); the availability of air crews competent to operate the aircraft concerned over the routes to be followed, the crews being in fit medical condition, currently within their permitted quota of flying hours, and located at suitable bases or slip stations (personnel and medical facets); the economics of the proposed services in terms of revenues and costs, whether for *ad hoc* traffic or over a given season or period (financial facets); the provision of ground services and facilities, with adequate staff, to handle incoming/outgoing traffic at the proposed intermediate and terminal points, with any necessary technical servicing that may be due (overseas station facets); considerations of weather conditions, which may necessitate last-minute alterations to flight plans because of dangers in one area or another (another facet of 'operations', but covering also overseas stations, and technical services from outside agencies); the relevance of international air regulations, for there are stringent codes mutually agreed among countries with commercial air services (an international advisory facet).

Much of the information comes from current records and analyses being made as normal routines within the Operations, Sales, Engineering and other Departments of any airline—such as movements records, flight analyses, staff rosters, meteorological reports, sales forecasts, cost dissections, etc.—all of which can be coordinated and evaluated by computer as the basis for deliberation and decision. Scheduling or short-term planning in this field of civil aviation has to be fast-moving and flexible, which provides a strong argument for a properly constituted and efficient committee made up of a responsible member from each of the main departmental activities concerned and meeting regularly—so regularly that the members come to think in parallel and to develop a high sense of mutually cooperative responsibility for their important task. The chairman of this committee should be a non-departmental man, perhaps someone selected to represent the chief executive of the airline company; he would need to be experienced in operational and administrative affairs of his company, and his major responsibility in the sessions would be to ensure full contribution from each specialist point of view and to attain from these the achievement of the common objective in reliable and economic flight schedules or service plans.

2. Membership

It is essential that the constitution or terms of reference of any committee should contain a clear statement of the persons designated as members, and also arrangements in regard to co-option or the calling of persons to attend. The number of participants in the proceedings should be kept as small as possible: experience has shown that a committee of more than nine is normally too large. Members nominated to serve on a committee, and others selected for co-option, should be chosen on a basis of genuine relevance to the purposes which the committee has been established to serve. This is a matter on which comment may seem superfluous because it is such obvious common sense, but it is again a matter in which practice has seen common sense frequently flouted.

Questions of representation of interests, or prestige of departments can often be influential, and nominations to committees are often made in these terms, rather than on the basis of effective accomplishment of the objectives. Naturally the subject matter must determine which departments or activities are relevant and therefore whether they need representation. In a committee where uniformity of information, or some aspects of coordination, are the main purposes, then the factor of representation may be a determining point for membership. Where, however, there is deliberation to be accomplished to a degree that a positive outcome is called for, a more effective basis of choice should be sought in terms of ability to contribute realistically to the stated objectives. It is sometimes a good practice to list all the persons or representatives who *might* be selected for a given purpose, and then to rank them in order of priority on the basis of a criterion of effective contribution; if only four or five names are found, then a good quorum may have been reached; if, however, the list of 'possibles' goes longer, it may be found useful to limit the committee membership to, say, the first ranking seven or eight, leaving others to be available for co-option or attendance *ad hoc*.

A varying membership, in the sense of a small nucleus of standing members, supplemented by occasional different additional participants, may often prove a good practical way of forming a sound small working committee, coupled with adequate contribution of the varying relevant points of view. Calling for written contributions, or for 'witnesses' to attend once for a specific discussion, may again be found a useful approach to the same end.

Most experience goes to prove that a small committee attains more effective results more quickly than a larger one.

Whatever the composition of a committee, one of the most important factors for effective participation by its membership is the understanding and acceptance of the committee's terms of reference, a realisation of the deliberative and consultative nature of its role, and recognition of its objectives in effective outcome with economical performance. If members could apply a *budget control approach* to their committee's deliberations, they would be well on the way to sound membership as well as high achievement!

3. Chairmanship

Good chairmanship is almost the most essential prerequisite for a successful committee operation. Much of the widespread dissatisfaction with committees stems from recurrent experience of membership under poor chairmen. It has been argued that the qualities and pattern of behaviour of a good committee chairman are akin to those of the competent executive: there is indeed an analogy, even if the comparison cannot be pushed far. Awareness of objectives figures prominently in the chairman's role, coupled with an appreciation of the significance of, and the factors making for, effective and economical performance. It is in this respect that the analogy with good management holds closest.

He has, too, a task in human terms, in promoting a genuine sense of collaboration and a good team morale. He must have the ability to keep the committee's purposes alive in members' minds, while putting points for deliberation before them in such a way as to ensure a systematic approach to its tasks and to promote a full discussion of all relevant aspects. He must be able to hold off irrelevances and meanderings without giving offence, and while extracting the salient points from the discussion, to be alert for the important factors or facets that are being omitted. He must be prepared to make the occasional recapitulation in the interests of clarity of progress, and at times he must be able to gain attention for his own views without appearing to obtrude them. While concentrating on the matters being deliberated, he must generate response to his leadership in a brisk and effective performance by the committee, instilling into its members, without appearing pedagogical, a consciousness of the precepts of sound committee procedure. It is his duty to obtain from participants the requisite attitude of understanding, cooperation and responsibility which alone can ensure effective outcome.

No mean task! It has one consequence in suggesting that the chairman of a committee is often better placed when he is not an interested party in the matters with which he is dealing. Not everyone would agree with this point of view, and merit can be found in the argument that a committee performs its task better when the chairman 'knows what it is all about'. Perhaps a compromise solution is the right way out, provided it ensures that the member chosen as chairman does at least have personal, mental and behavioural capacity to attain the level of performance sketched above. The major difficulty confronting the man really knowledgeable in the subject is that of predetermined standpoint and thus the possibility of favouring certain of the points of view that will come under deliberation. It is primarily the chairman's role to get the best out of the knowledge and experience of the members of his committee, rather than to make his personal contributions. A major drawback to successful committee action is not infrequently met in a chairman of dominant personal make-up, especially if he is also voluble: that type of individual is mostly so prone to hold sway that he does not get useful participation from his members.

When a committee is used for coordination or consultation purposes within a management structure, another danger can be encountered from the executive standing of the chairman. It is not unusual in committees of this kind for the chair to be taken by the Managing Director, a situation which may tend to give the committee a spurious form of 'executive' role in the eyes of its members. The more so, if they are his immediate executive and specialist subordinates. In these circumstances a Managing Director (or other senior executive) presiding over a committee can be looked to by the members to give instantaneous decisions on matters raised, *ex cathedra* in his capacity as the chief or senior executive. The danger of this arrangement, which some people praise for its efficiency, lies in its destruction of that most valuable element in business committee procedure, the opportunity for detached and deliberation appraisal of a subject directed towards the submission of advice or recommendation to executive authority; this authority may then subsequently arbitrate without bias, having taken account of all other relevant factors, which may or may not be known to the committee.

All too often a Managing Director, serving as chairman of a committee, has to refuse to accept a decision reached by its members, because he knows of contradictory aspects of policy which he is not free to disclose; in consequence of an unexplained rejection, the members feel rebuffed, and confidence in the usefulness of the committee is inevitably shaken. If, on the other hand, the committee were to submit exactly the same conclusion as a 'recommendation' to an executive authority outside themselves, the effect would be the same without the ensuing emotional repercussions. Given enough time to prepare a reasoned reply, that executive can submit for the next meeting a constructive rejection of the recommendation, framing it in such a way that the members of the committee retain confidence in their own purpose.

This does not mean that a Managing Director or other senior executive should not serve as chairman of a committee, but that, if he does so, he must inevitably be a sort of 'Jekyll and Hyde', and separate his role as chairman from his executive position. From the chair he will have to submit to his executive self, with seriousness and conviction, a recommendation which he knows he will have to turn down. Any executive, serving as chairman or as member of a committee which has a role participating in management action, has sooner or later to face this problem: he can put forward arguments for or against a proposition during discussions, but he cannot accept from the committee instructions for executive action; these can come only from his own executive superior. In practice, a manager may often find it possible to carry out a course of action suggested by a committee on which he is serving, but only because he knows that it is in line with policy and general plans, that it comes within his jurisdiction, and that it would have his senior executive's support. In principle, therefore, this does *not* constitute accepting an executive instruction from the committee. Nor is the chairman of the committee held in an artificial executive capacity.

On the more detailed plane, another of the chairman's important functions is to ensure that there is good committee procedure, a matter in which he is materially aided by appointing a competent secretary.

4. Mechanics

Of first importance to the mechanics of any committee is the selection of a competent secretary, with a sound management approach to his administrative duties. He will be responsible for seeing that proceedings are adequately prepared in the form of notification of meetings, agenda and supporting papers—the latter distributed enough in advance to permit of some predigestion, and presented with adequate clarity and brevity to ensure absorption and understanding. How frequently have meetings gone adrift because members have become confused over page and paragraph references in a lengthy document which is the supposed basis of weighty deliberations! Again, a seemingly trivial point of practical common sense, but one in which experience has all too frequently and unfortunately necessitated emphasising the warning. As a main rule it can be said that agenda and supporting papers should be framed with a primary consideration for saving the committee's time and supporting the chairman's direction of its proceedings.

Much the same approach is called for in the other half of the secretary's documentation task: the preparation of the record or minutes of the meetings. Essentially these should be a brief and businesslike record of ground covered, major points considered, conclusions reached and recommendations decided. To attempt any record of what was *said* during the session can only result in lengthy documentation and much reduce the effectiveness of the minutes.

There are other important mechanics in regard to the timing and arrangement of meetings. Wherever possible, it is an advantage to preplan meetings on a quarterly or even a yearly basis, so that there can be plenty of advance notice. The danger of letting a meeting be held when there is no real business to transact must be recognised, particularly in the case of 'standing committees'. At all sessions proceedings should be kept down to limited duration consistent with adequate deliberation: lengthy sessions induce fatigue and staleness even among committee members. Two useful methods of preventing undue rambling are the issue of a 'timed' agenda (i.e. the chairman's suggestion of how long might be allotted to each item) or the tactful timing of a meeting at such an hour as will ensure a desire among members to bring proceedings to a close. Effective use of subcommittees for the predigestion of special items is important and can often be an effective means of reducing deliberations.

In the case of a standing or long-continuing committee provision should be made for change of membership to accord with any change of purpose, and when its task is completed, its existence should be formally discontinued or its proceedings suspended.

The physical environment of meetings can be important for successful working, especially the absence of extraneous noise or interruption, and the presence of plenty of good fresh air. 'Hot air' can be ruinous to a committee physically as well as metaphorically!

Apart from his general role of assisting the chairman and members to arrange and conduct their proceedings in the most effective and economical ways possible, the secretary also has certain specific responsibilities arising from his office. Two of these are particularly important to the pursuit of a committee's objectives:

1. In the first place, it is the secretary on whom falls the active responsibility for ensuring that 'action' or other 'follow up' from proceedings takes place as agreed. True, it is within the chairman's overall responsibility to be concerned about these as much as about other aspects of his committee's task, but he expects to rely on the secretary as his main *aide* in this matter.

'Follow up' may become a routine consideration in the preparation of agenda for ensuing meetings; if the secretary is normally systematic and methodical in the recording of proceedings, there is little special problem involved in pursuing items for which subsequent report and reference will be required. 'Action' to be taken on agreement in committee is similarly assisted: the secretary can have an 'action' note flagged in the margin of the minutes, with the name of the individual to whom responsibility has been entrusted.

This *aide-memoire* is of best practical value when minutes are issued promptly after meetings. In any case, the secretary will probably contact members, when preparing his papers for ensuing meetings, to ascertain whether completion of the action will be reported or whether reasons for delay may have to be offered. If a committee is one from which numerous items of action arise, being entrusted to various members, the secretary may see fit to have a further record of his own, in order to ensure continuing check on action remaining outstanding over perhaps lengthy periods: something as simple as a duplicate set of minutes in which each 'action' decision is consecutively numbered and crossed through in colour when reported completed; the secretary's own agenda papers would contain his personal reminder of items (numbers) outstanding at any one time.

2. The second matter to which the secretary must attend is the circulation of minutes or reports of a committee's deliberations to persons who are not members but are deemed by the committee as needing to be informed. A matter of principle or policy arises here to which the committee should have given attention as the basis of the instruction to the secretary to make the circulation. (An individual set of minutes need not be separately sent to each such outside person, but two or three sets marked for circulation on rota; location and other physical factors may have to determine what method is used.) In principle, the circulation of minutes or record to persons who are 'interested' but who are not members of a given committee can be a useful medium for restricting size of membership. Experience has repeatedly shown that persons are nominated to serve on some committees because their role requires them to be 'in the know', but may not necessarily make them specific contributors to the objectives of the committee. A mechanism for keeping such persons 'informed' of progress could obviate their active participation in normal membership, while leaving open a case for occasional attendance when particularly relevant.

Mechanics of committee procedure are often thought of as trivial; in fact, they can do much to hinder or promote effective committee performance and achievement.

The growing scale of industrial and business activity, with growing complexity, and increasing resort to specialisation of function within any organisation, makes the problems of coordination and communication increasingly difficult at the same time as it lays emphasis on their importance. Much can be done by means of circulated information—though very serious and expensive dangers are latent in this method—and some reliance can be placed on incidental individual contact.

There is no doubt at all about the fact that systematic meetings or committees can be a valuable instrument of coordination and communication in management, with a potentially high contribution to executive morale as well, if they are effectively constituted and conducted. No other mechanism can afford anything like the same opportunity for reciprocal relationships in deliberation or so ready a means of open and harmonious communication. It is a mistaken and shortsighted attitude to condemn committees as such solely by reason of unfortunate past experience. Training in the requirements of effective conduct can be as valuable a facet of 'management development' as any other.

9 Management consolidation

Any textbook on management must inevitably suffer from a malady of fragmentation: the subject cannot be expounded and commented on except in a piecemeal way by taking up for examination and illustration various aspects of it. With a subject so wideranging, the fragmentation of treatment virtually removes the study from reality, for in the real life situation fragmented is the one thing that management is not. (Those last words are, unfortunately, too often not true in the realities of real life!) Moreover, the presentation of the subject in this sectional and sequential form also masks the process of management itself, because the presentation has, again unavoidably, to be made through the medium of practices, procedures and techniques. This last aspect has been strongly in evidence in recent years, when there has been a very considerable initiation and development of techniques. These have been concerned mostly with the elements of planning and control, and have centred largely on the collation and presentation of data, 'management information'.

Regard has already been paid to the significance of such information as a 'tool' for the managers' judgment and decision in the exercise of planning and control. Yet the emphasis of interest given to these informational tools or aids too easily clouds the character of the management process within which they are applied. The essence of this process lies in decision and action: decisions about understanding and interpretation of the given objective, as well as about ways and means of accomplishing them; action in planning, motivating and controlling the operations directed to that accomplishment. The manager has, let it be repeated, first, a role of judging (determining) and deciding what to do and why, as well as how, who, where and when—all coordinated towards the known objectives by means of the subsidiary targets and plans; and, secondly, a role of securing from the employed personnel (at a variety of levels) the human performance and cooperation requisite for meeting targets, plans and objectives, with satisfaction in the job and contentment in the employment. The keynote of this role is in the responsibility for the effective combination of the two facets—putting them into contemporary jargon, respectively the *economic* and the *social* facets of management.

The manager has jurisdiction over resources of manpower, materials, machines and money; his decisions commit these to usage, irrevocably, and his judgment is the key to whether the outcome is advantageous or the opposite. Yet, his decisions are but fractionally carried out by himself—far and away the majority run through the teams of personnel under his command: assistant managers, supervisors, technicians, operatives skilled and unskilled, administrative staffs. From all these, in appropriate balance and unison, he has to secure a full measure of cooperation in effective and economically applied effort, yet keeping the contentment of working spirit without which his motivation would be fruitless. His own skill and attitude in the exercise of his managerial role are the only forces on which he can depend: perhaps, not just these alone, because he could and should have also the support of colleague managers alongside him in the organisation. This recognition reinforces the notion of the 'nexus of cooperation' which should characterise all management attitudes within an organisation.

Management unity

To each manager has gone by delegation (through the MJD—the management job description) the specific responsibilities appropriate to his position, and within this framework an understanding of the objectives and targets that belong to it. Yet, the delegation carries inherently this further responsibility—strictly speaking, two further responsibilities—the one, that he must always be on the alert for vitality of performance and progress, for the service of the 'three Ps'; the other that he is inherently inwoven in this network of managerial collaboration. Just by virtue of serving as a member of the organisation, by the medium of delegation through the firm's defined structure, he inherits the involvement in that collaboration. For, when all is said and done, the organisation structure is no more than an arbitrary—even when meticulously and skilfully drawn—arrangement for the interrelated fragmentation of an unified management process, fragmented into specific roles, so that the whole process can be more competently exercised in the interests of the firm overall, and thereby in the interests of its customers.

An individual manager takes individual responsibility, it is true, but not in isolation: perhaps not even in real isolation when he is the one and only manager. The little piece of jargon can be a useful reminder—the manager exercises his delegated responsibility within a nexus of (executive) cooperation. The reality of this truism is well borne home by the techniques of management, because they are mostly so fashioned as to be automatically integrated. The firm's objectives are set down in one marketing programme, pertinent equally to all its managers, whatever their place in the organisation. A production planning and control system runs commonly through all the manufacturing and supply sections, with specific relevance as appropriate to the sectional role. And management information systems today are customarily described as 'integrated', just because they are designed to cater within one system for all facets of management activity within the organisation.

The trouble with many of the contemporary techniques is that they provide and offer too much information, and too analytically presented—with the danger that they can cloud the manager's judgment rather than help his decision. As already noted, the sales promotion propaganda for data processing computers frequently blurbs about 'providing *more* information for managers': this could well be the worst possible recommendation. Less information could be a better aid to judgment and decision, if it is more appropriate information and better presented for clarity of understanding significant features, with ease of absorption. Techniques have another danger, that they can obtrude on the manager's human or social role, especially among his colleague managers and supervisors. No matter how excellently a firm's management information system provides to members of the organisation data for planning and control, the *human* exercise does not lose its significance. Not even perfect sheets of perfect figures, showing accurately where performance stands against target and plan, can relieve the manager of his responsibility for personal contact, communication and consultation with colleagues and subordinates: he must still talk with his fellow-managers and supervisors. Motivation is a human element and its force runs *within* the administrative elements of planning and control.

This line of argument has sometimes been crystallised as recognising the 'art' of management against the 'science'—the 'art' here referring to the human touch in communication and consultation, the 'science' being the data and the techniques. If such a juxtaposition helps to bring the point home, fine. It is a language that no longer has as much currency as formerly, but the point emphasised has lost none of its validity.

To see management in action in balance overall within a firm is wellnigh impossible, except over a long time scale; but perhaps there is an analogy with the jigsaw puzzle being tackled without a guiding picture. At first start, as with a newly appointed manager taking up his position within the firm, there are a number of self-evident pointers, like the edge-pieces to form the straight lines of the sides. Recognitions are gained from study of pieces, and fragments can be put together; just as the manager can deal with many matters and problems from the guidelines he has been given on initiation to the job. And so on, until a fuller grasp is gained of what the overall objectives are portraying as the appropriate lines of action. On the management scene, more guidance is given, naturally, from the firm's marketing programme, from the MJDs, from the periodic budgetary statements and the performance reports; and from the information gleaned in the discussions among colleague-managers during the monthly review meetings, or within whatever other form of collaborative framework happens to be provided.

As will be stressed in Part Seven, the importance imparted by a Board of Directors and a chief executive to organisation planning and management development can be counted as a major force for ensuring continuing unity of management action in practice.

Structures

It is possible, though, in broad terms to take a bird's-eye view of the management process in action in a glimpse at an average kind of manufacturing and marketing organisation. The first scene-setting that can be recognised is the tiered structure of three levels forming the framework of that management process—respectively, the Board of Directors, the Managing Director (chief executive) and the grouping of managers and supervisors.

1. Policy level

At the top layer, the Board of Directors are seen responsible, in corporate capacity, for the determination and delineation of business objectives (service to customers and profit targets), for the formulation of policy and for overall control in terms of reputation, performance, financial progress and profitability. The tasks falling to their role can be seen as: determining main objectives and giving guidelines for the major sectional objectives; forming lines of direction for overall policy and for reinterpretation into divisional or sectional aspects; economic appraisal of policy, projects and programmes; the provision of adequate financial means; schemes of control by which the activities and progress of the enterprise are to be assessed; the appointment of the executive authority designated to manage the concern (the Managing Director); provision for the legal responsibilities towards the community (in respect of the legal requirements of Company Law, the custody of property, and so on); plans and motivation for the continuing development and vitality of the enterprise. From among its number the Board elects a Chairman to preside over its deliberations. This Chairman is not as such an executive official of the company, but the president of the Directors, who holds office only at their formal deliberations and those of the shareholders.

2. Top executive

The second level is taken by the Managing Director who holds a dual office: as a member of the Board he shares the corporate responsibility of the other Directors, but his special position of chief executive he holds alone. It falls to him in this capacity to be the link between the Board and the rest of the organisation: to present the objectives and to interpret policy; to encourage participation in the formulation of policy; to issue the appropriate instructions that will set the organisation to work; and to maintain effective coordination and a high level of will to work. His responsibilities for morale are especially important, because it is from him that the 'tone' of the organisation is set—his attitude and outlook are likely to be reflected by the managers at lower levels, even down to the ranks of supervisors and operatives. Naturally enough, there will be certain differences in the detailed make-up of the responsibilities allocated to individual Managing Directors, but the character of such responsibilities will be broadly the same throughout.[1]

3. Operating executives

The third level is a complex of layers composing the executive organisation structure, in terms of divisions, departments or sections, within which are various managers and supervisors responsible to the Managing Director through a top line of senior executives. This is where all the differences in the size and character of enterprises come into prominence. A small trading unit may have only a Managing Director and half a dozen junior assistants: this chief executive is really an owner-manager, whose business is clothed in company form as a matter of legal convenience. A small manufacturing company may have a Chief Engineer serving as a technical executive to assist the Managing Director on matters concerned with design, plant, tools and quality, while an Accountant looks after the financial aspects and assists in selling, at the same time supervising such clerical routines as are carried out; the Managing Director may himself look after the factory and all general aspects of production, with the assistance of a Senior Foreman.

In the medium-sized and larger enterprises, whether in manufacturing or commerce, the total process of management within the organisation is split up among a hierarchy of managers and supervisors, whose scope and character are necessarily varied: this is where the definitions of responsibilities or MJDs come into play. According to the needs and circumstances of the enterprise,

[1] A comparative summary of the responsibilities of the Board of Directors and of the Managing Director is contained in chapter 8 of *Organisation—the Framework of Management*.

and in accordance with its objectives and policy, the total process of management under the Managing Director is divided into appropriate sections, groups or functional units, each with its responsibilities and relations determined as part of the whole. Each executive, specialist or supervisory post, in other words, is specifically set up to play a given role in the total pattern of management. Some of the tasks may be temporary ones—for instance, work of special technical development directed to bringing out a new product; or looking after a subsidiary factory evacuated for security purposes; or the building up and running of an Export Sales Department, for subsequent merging into the general sales activities. In such cases, a temporary executive appointment may well be made, with specific responsibilities which will be terminated or modified or merged in due course, as required.

Briefly, then, the organisation of any medium-sized or larger concern, whatever its field of economic activities, will consist of a complex of responsibilities and relations, determined by reference to the approved objectives and policy, and providing a framework within which the total process of management (including supervision at the operating level) can be effectively carried out in appropriate coordination.

What these managers (and supervisors) do, how they spend their working hours, is the subject matter of the following Parts of this study, and how the various aspects of activity fit into a coherent pattern is illustrated in Fig. 1.9.1. The core of the tasks performed by all the managers lies in the definition of management itself: to take responsibility for the planning and guidance of the sections of activities entrusted to them and for the motivation and cooperation of the persons entrusted to their jurisdiction. The human element in this task is very much the same in most managerial and supervisory posts, whatever their field of activity. Some differences of degree can be found, as between, say, a manager and foreman: the latter has a more circumscribed human job in the guidance and supervision of men and women at the working level, and in

Fig. 1.9.1

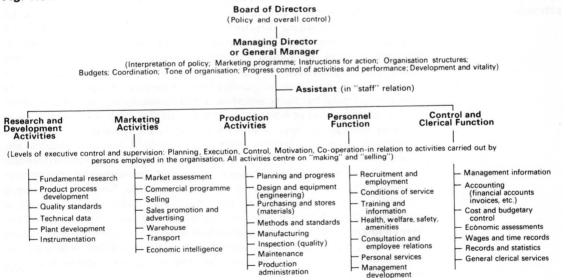

promoting a high sense of morale among them. The manager's personnel responsibility, on the other hand, may be more remote, directed to the supervisors themselves, getting a good team spirit among them, encouraging them and helping them in their own direct motivation task, thus setting the human tone of the department or section as a whole. Among themselves, managers may again find differences of emphasis due to particular circumstances: in highly technical manufacturing operations, largely process-controlled, the human responsibility may appear less prominent than the technical. Similarly, the character of the staff and work under the jurisdiction of, say, a Chief Accountant or a Retail Store Manager, may give rise to quite a different pattern of human relations and problems from that of the large-scale light engineering factory.

The techniques and procedures, by the medium of which judgment and decision are attained, exhibit more differences than similarities. These techniques, as the methods or 'tools' for carrying the management process into effect, necessarily reflect the policy and organisation of the enterprise and must therefore be to some extent specific to an individual enterprise. For instance, routines for production control may be differently worked out in two factories that have much the same product and layout, and work from the same fundamental principle of measured standard times. In this fact lies the weakness of the 'systems' that are sometimes offered to managers by firms specialising in the sale of a given type of office equipment. Superficially, the 'system' is widely applicable in a set way; but its application in that set way may cause serious weaknesses in the working of management in some organisations. The advances made in the study of management in recent years have led to the widespread use of common principles underlying techniques of control, though these will differ in detail application from factory to factory, or office to office.

Unity from attitude

The active pursuit and fostering of unity in management action within a firm's organisation is a role that falls in a peculiar and significant way to the chief executive (the Managing Director), and constitutes a major feature in the responsibility of general management. To him falls the responsibility for ensuring that the foundation and the framework of management (i.e. the policy and organisation of the enterprise) are determined with a clear recognition of the fundamental unity of the process of management itself. His own attitude must be characterised by a determination to preserve that unity. In this task the owner or manager of a small organisation has a big advantage; not only because in such a unit each man in the management structure customarily embraces tasks in more than one field, but also because the owner (or chief executive) is in a position to exercise closer unification through the smaller personal span that has to be covered. To some extent the smaller the size of the unit, the less the danger of separatism. There is, of course, a corresponding danger in these smaller units that the bias or the deficiency of a given individual at the top may lead to the overemphasis of some aspects of management or the neglect of others, thus leaving an imbalance which is not corrected by a compensating specialist in the particular fields neglected.

How the unity of management may be effected in practice can be shown by two illustrations.

Example 1

Take the case of a small firm manufacturing spectacle lenses, employing some seventy people all told. At its head there is a Managing Director, who is virtually the owner and is the technical brain behind product and processes. Because of the special requirements of the trade, his technical skill is of particular relevance to customers, and it is only natural therefore to find that he makes himself personally responsible for sales. In charge of the small factory he has established a Works Manager, a man who has been trained in this field and has grown up through the firm; latterly, he has been devoting time to learning something about factory organisation and management. The scope of his responsibilities is, of course, limited, and some of his friends from larger enterprises might well mentally classify him as 'a glorified foreman'. He is entrusted with full executive responsibility for production activities and carries out his tasks with the aid of three foremen: one looks after the tools and equipment, polishing heads, moulds and rough-lens stores, with a small staff working under him; a second looks after the processing operations, which for convenience are divided into four sections, each headed by a skilled working chargehand; the third foreman has responsibility for quality standards, for the inspection of lenses at intermediate and finished stages, for opinions on flaws and faults; he also maintains the stock of finished lenses and attends to despatch to customers, assisted by two girls for the packing and paperwork.

In the office, the Managing Director has a good-grade secretary with a small staff, to whom are entrusted the keeping of books and accounts, the payment of wages, the maintenance of personnel and wage records, the issue of customer invoices, and the other processes that go to make up the routines of a General Office. Included in the responsibility of this 'Secretary-cum-Office Manager' is the functional control of the two girls who, under the jurisdiction of the inspector, carry out the office routines in connection with stock records and despatch.

To the Works Manager fall, apart from the general oversight of the factory, the special tasks of planning and progress of production, the control of quality through the definition of standards and material specifications, and a general responsibility for the human aspects of management (the personnel function), even though he expects that the detailed contacts and activities will in the main be carried out by his three foremen.

Clearly the Managing Director is himself serving in three capacities—he is General Manager, Sales Manager and Technical Director or Manager.

This small organisation is representative of many thousands in British industry; perhaps its structure is more clearly defined than is customarily the case. The important point at issue is that there is no activity set out in this present volume that this little unit cannot carry into effect. Some of them, of course, may not be necessary in a formal way, the same purpose being attained by simpler means. Market research provides a useful instance: the Managing Director's personal contacts with the prescription houses (which are his wholesalers and his customers) enable him to keep track of new trends in customer demand, such as fashion in the shapes of frames and lenses. His participation in trade association discussions enables him to have advance information of possible lines of Social Security development that may have a bearing on his sales and manufacturing programme. Or again, in the case of budgetary control, the simplicity of the range of products makes the analysis of expenses less important; but not for one moment could it be suggested that the control of operating costs and expenses is not just as necessary in this tiny unit as in one ten or a hundred times its size. The same is true in regard to the planning of production or the control of progress through the sequence of operations. Naturally, the basis on which these activities are set up and the procedures by which they are carried into effect would be very much more simple than has been suggested in the relative chapters of this study, but the principles there set out to underlie such activities will apply in just the same way, and to a very large extent it may be possible to apply, with minor modifications, even the detailed routines suggested, if they are found to be justified.

In the personnel field a similar line of argument again applies; in matters of selection and training, in discipline, in consultation (especially of the informal kind), the principles described apply without variation; the techniques adopted will be much simpler and much less formal. Recruitment and training are, in fact, good examples because the skills entailed in spectacle-lens grinding and polishing are intricate, calling for a quasi-craft development.

The unity of management is clearly emphasised by the personal control of the single Managing Director, and by the continuous personal contact between himself and the Works Manager on production matters, himself and the Secretary-cum-Office Manager on control details. It is the attitude of this chief executive that can make or mar both the unity and the efficiency of the small organisation; this is no less true in the larger enterprises where it may be less obvious.

Example 2

The second illustration is drawn from a firm of considerably larger size, though again representative of the units which characterise certain industries. This is a garment manufacturing firm employing about 2300 people. Its organisation structure is something like the pattern represented in Fig. 1.5.1 (see page 55), with obvious modifications of the division shown under the Design Engineer. This firm is of sufficient size to warrant having a full range of the activities described in this volume: to portray the unity of management in action within such an organisation would mean little more than rewriting in specific form all that is set out in these pages. The point can be made equally well by selecting certain aspects for the purpose of illustration.

1. The Managing Director (who uses the title 'Director and General Manager') maintains coordination, and therefore provides the first basis of unity in management, by four particular features:

   (a) He has defined in writing the responsibilities of all his major and second-line executives, and a copy of the definitions (MJDs) has been issued to each of them. From the outset, therefore, they are clear as to who does what, and where their fields of responsibility begin and end. His own drafting of the schedule has ensured that there are no gaps and no duplication.

   (b) It is his practice to maintain daily individual contact with each of the top-line executives, and he has encouraged these in turn to follow the same practice with their own subordinates. In this way he and they keep a finger continuously on the pulses of the organisation, and are readily in a position to spot at the very earliest moment divergencies or deficiencies before they can become serious.

(*c*) In addition, he adopts the practice of a fortnightly 'Progress Meeting' of the senior executives, with the second-line men called in as pertinent. This meeting, while informal in character, follows a definite agenda, and is intended primarily for the purpose of coordination. There are occasions when the hour or so devoted to it represents more a social gathering than a serious management meeting, because there is nothing calling for major attention, but none of those attending feel that such occasions are a waste of time because of the considerable contribution that these regular contacts make to the unification of knowledge and thought on the affairs of the company.

(*d*) Within recent months the Managing Director has been instrumental in getting his colleagues in the Board of Directors to take seriously the establishment of a systematic 'marketing programme', in association with more effective control through a budgetary system. He has had a small project team of senior managers working out the lines of approach, taking initially a two-year view of the company's expected commercial activities and development. He has himself played a close and active part in discussion with the three members of this team, and he proposes to put a reasonably well formed one-year and two-year marketing programme before the Board of Directors shortly, instead of the more superficial form of 'Sales Forecast 1975' that he has hitherto prepared.

This will form a major force in management consolidation for the company, and will make the use of budgetary controls far more meaningful. While the marketing programme has been drawn up by the firm's own managerial resources (the project team serving as the focus and spearhead), the Managing Director expects to recommend to the Board the retaining of external consultant assistance for the design and initiation of the budgetary control system. When complete, this latter will add an immense measure of strength to the coordination of management action.

2. At a lower level, unity is illustrated by the attitude, for example, of the Production Manager in regard to the making-up sections of the factory and the maintenance of plant. Long before the marketing programme and budgetary control scheme had been mooted, the Production Manager had developed well-defined planning and scheduling in respect of current and future output, and had gone to the trouble of establishing a Planning Office, quite small, but effective. Thus, one of the common weaknesses of the larger manufacturing organisations in this industry has been overcome: by the integration of, for instance, the purchase of materials with the known forward making-up plans; by the coordination of maintenance requirements with pre-planned production operations; by the control of work-in-progress in relation to available man-hour and machine capacity. That this emphasis on coordination has made a serious contribution to the well-being of the manufacturing side of the organisation is evident from even a few minutes' conversation with the department heads and foremen.

3. Further illustrations can be drawn from the company's activities along functional lines:
(*a*) Plans have already been laid for determining the budgets on an annual and quarterly basis, with four-weekly statements. The basis of operation will be a regular meeting of the Sales Manager, the Production Manager and the Chief Accountant with the General Manager—of course, with

adequate consultation of subordinates at a lower level who have particular knowledge and information that may be required in framing the budgets.

(b) In regard to the records maintained within the jurisdiction of the Production Manager, for instance those of the Planning Office, there is close coordination with the requirements of the Accountant's Department, the more so now to meet the particular needs of the procedures for cost and budgetary controls. The introduction of a Clerical Methods Supervisor has been a useful means of coordinating the planning of procedures, to ensure that full advantage is obtained from such control schemes in relation to all the recording and communicating activities carried on throughout the organisation.

(c) The work of the Personnel Department is in turn tied in with all other activities. For instance, the absence records maintained in the Department are tied in with the time-recording and job-costing procedures carried out under the jurisdiction of the Accountant; in effect, the basic material for the Personnel Department's absence records is supplied from the Accountant's office, leaving the Personnel Department to deal with their peculiar part of this activity, i.e. the contact with the individuals concerned, as distinct from the gathering of the information. Similarly, in regard to recruitment of new personnel, there is close coordination with the Production Manager; in the first place, the Personnel Officer's participation in the General Manager's Progress Meetings keeps him informed of forward plans, and accordingly all recruitment and training programmes are based on known or estimated future trends of output. The actual technique of recruitment is based on close coordination between the Personnel Department and the managers and foremen in the cutting and making-up sections, in order to ensure not only that all accepted candidates conform to the general standards required by the company's policy, but also that they fit in with the individual supervisor's own assessment of his needs and are not likely to give rise later to incompatibilities on a personal basis. The same coordination is found in action in regard to the upgrading of juniors and lower-paid operatives whenever better jobs become available, as well as in regard to transfers between departments. Training required for most of the manufacturing and making-up departments is long; this forward view, coordinated with sales forecasts, has been an important factor in promoting efficient development in face of expanding trade.

In the early stages of the development of management within this organisation, it was the outlook and attitude of the General Manager himself that set the pace and determined the tone. But, gradually, as the organisation pattern became established, and as the various procedures were formulated, the growing sense of responsibility among the senior and lower executives prompted a ready response to the lead given in a wholehearted readiness to seek coordination as the natural corollary of everyday activities.

Systems

Unity of management practice can be appreciably assisted by soundly designed procedures of planning and control, with systems of management information. Data, whether in physical or financial terms, are essential media of effective management action. And *how* data are made available can materially affect the exercise of that action, for good or ill. The major contribution of contemporary practice in schemes of budget control and similar forms of management accounting lies in a twofold characteristic: alignment of data for decision and control with the pattern of delegation of responsibility; and design of the information procedures such as to ensure that the several specific elements form an integrated scheme, unifying overall information at the top levels of management.

Within such schemes any one departmental manager will receive daily, weekly, four-weekly, or other periodic figures portraying actual performance and expenditure against the targets, plans or budgets relevant to his own responsibility. He knows that he has made his own responsible contribution to formulating the targets and budgets (one aspect of decision), and that the 'variances' thrown out in the statements are matters on which he is expected to decide and initiate the corrective action (i.e. control interrelated with decision). This may be in a change of plan rather than a remedial step in the existing situation, and in this case he has to ensure reference to other managers who may be concerned. Above all else, he knows that the periodic information relevant to his own departmental responsibility is an integral part of a full scheme of 'management information' which reflects the objectives and policy of his company and parallels the structure of its organisation. With this knowledge, he can use these 'tools' with the full assurance of objectivity and the conviction of integration with colleagues sharing the role of management with him.

The most effective contribution to the unity of the management process overall in any firm comes from and through its marketing programme: this will be found described and discussed in Part Two, but a few preliminary observations will be in place at this point.

The properly prepared marketing programme is the first immediate portrayal of the firm's predetermined strategy for serving and satisfying its intended customers and thereby earning its projected or expected profits. This programme is, therefore, the expression of the firm's objectives overall. At the same time, because it enshrines and conveys the policies and intentions for the operational activities (for example, manufacturing and selling a given range of products through wholesale trading channels at home and abroad), it also delineates the objectives of the various sections of the firm's organisation and of the managers in charge of them. Thus, the marketing programme is the primary expression of 'management by objectives' for all directors and managers, and holds those objectives integrated in line with the major trading and profit targets that the Board of Directors are setting out to achieve. The delegation to divisional or sectional managers, made effective by the proper delineation of responsibilities (MJDs), ensures that they are aware of and alive to these specific objectives, to their own managerial role in achieving them, and to the opportunities for improving effectiveness in performance (the three Ps). Through translation or interpretation into operating budgets and plans, individual (sectional) managerial targets are determined, clarified and made known within the mechanism of the management information system. Realistic provision is thereby made for continuous coordination through the periodic review of performance and progress: the managerial 'feedback cycle' of planning and control is seen rolling, with the chief executive firmly in the lead of his team (see Fig. 1.3.1: see page 33).

Within a setting of this kind, all that may be thought of as the best in 'management principle' can be readily applied in practice, and the personal skills of the directors and managers themselves will have been harnessed constructively to sound motivation, to cooperation and to positive progress. Economic vitality will not be hindered or sapped by the obstacles of unnecessary confusion and conflict. This, in fact, is what *management* is really about, whether in principle or in practice.

10 Outline of Parts Two to Seven

The following five Parts of this volume propound the practice of management through the description and illustration of proven methods and techniques. It is not practicable to give at every turn the particular circumstances that characterised the evolution or development of the method put forward, but the techniques described are those which have been found capable of widespread and varied application. The purpose of the following Parts is to explain and illustrate how the process of management is carried into effect—and the reader should respond, if he wants to carry the techniques into practice, by analysing his own particular situation to see how each would be relevant, and how far these circumstances are sufficiently different to require some alteration in the treatment of the problem or the design of the techniques used. The easy accessibility of 'systems' in recent years has sometimes been an obstacle to better management, mainly because it has led managers away from making a critical appraisal of their own situations and of the methods of management best suited to them.

Parts Two and Three are devoted to management at work within the fields of marketing and manufacturing, the main branches of the economic system. In regard to marketing (Part Two) the emphasis is deliberately placed on those aspects that more closely concern the manufacturing company with products to sell to customers; less attention, and in only a more incidental way, is given to wholesale and retail trade and to transport. These latter form separate fields of activity for which specfic management techniques have been developed: the process and the elements of management there are similar, but it would take the present study too far out of balance between the Parts to have treated at length these specialist trading aspects.

Parts Four and Five are an examination of the two all-pervading aspects of management, as they are carried out within the fields of activity like marketing and manufacturing. The matter contained in them does not overlap with that of the preceding Parts, but should be studied alongside them. There is a danger in this method of presentation, in so far as it repeats the practice of industry in the separation of the aspects of the management process. The appointment of a specialist Personnel Officer or Financial Controller may often lead 'line' executives to feel relieved of responsibility for human relations in their domain or for the effective control of operating costs: such a mistaken notion can just as easily arise if these functions are separately studied. The gain from specialist treatment, bringing more authoritative knowledge to bear, must not be offset by any suggestion that 'Personnel' and 'Control' are outside management or outside the responsibility of the managers in Production and Marketing.

Part Six is a self-contained review of major aspects of the place of automatic data processing by computer as a means of service to all functions of management, with consideration of some features of the management of data processing itself as an internal activity.

Part Seven concentrates on the major topic of organisation planning and management development. In a sense, it does form something of a consolidation of the foregoing Parts, but its intention is rather to examine and portray how sound and effective management practice may be nurtured to become the norm of the nation's managers and directors.

Recommended titles for further reading are noted at the end of each part. Further details can be obtained from the library of the British Institute of Management which publishes detailed readings lists under selected headings.

Further reading

BAYNES, P. (Ed.) *Case Studies in Corporate Planning*, Pitman, 1973.

DRUCKER, PETER F., *The Practice of Management*, Heinemann, London, 1968.

HUMBLE, JOHN, *Management by Objectives in Action*, McGraw-Hill, in association with BIM, 1971.

REDDIN, W. J., *Effective MBO*, Management Publications Ltd, for BIM, 1971.

BRECH, E. F. L., *Managing for Revival*, Management Publications Ltd, for BIM, 1972.

CLAY, M. J. and WALLEY, B. H., *Performance & Profitability*, Management Studies Series, Longmans, 1965.

LINES, J., *Profit Improvement*, Business Books, 1973.

LOCK, DENNIS (Ed.), *Directors Guide to Management Techniques*, Gower Press Ltd, 1970.

ARGENTI, JOHN, *Corporate Planning*, Allen & Unwin, 1969.

DENNING, BASIL (Ed.), *Corporate Long-range Planning*, Longman, 1969.

BROOKE, M. Z. and REMMERS, H. LEE, *The Strategy of Multinational Enterprise*, Longman, 1970.

FOSTER, DOUGLAS, *Managing for Profit* (Vol. 1), *Managing for Growth* (Vol. 2), Longman Paperback, 1972.

BOYCE, R. O., *Integrated Managerial Controls*, Management Studies Series, Longmans, 1967.

AMEY, L. R., *Readings in Management Decision*, Business Series, Longman, 1973.

HAGUE, D. C., *Managerial Economics*, Business Series, Longman, 1973.

COPEMAN, GEORGE, *The Chief Executive and Business Growth*, Leviathan House Ltd, London, 1971.

PUCKEY, SIR WALTER, *The Board Room*, Hutchinson, 1969.

BRITISH INSTITUTE OF MANAGEMENT, 'The Board of Directors', Survey Report, No. 10, 1972.

JUDSON, A. S., *A Manager's Guide to Making Changes*, Wiley, 1966.

Measure of Productivity

FARADAY, J. E., *The Management of Productivity*, Management Publications Ltd, 1971.

GREENBERG, LEON, *A practical guide to productivity*, Bureau of National Affairs, Washington, 1973.

INSTITUTE OF PERSONNEL MANAGEMENT, Productivity measurement—a symposium for the Seventies, by the staff of Associated Industrial Consultants Ltd, London, 1971.

Committees and Meetings

DUN and BRADSTREET INC (Business Education Division), How to conduct a meeting, New York, 1969.

HEGARTY, EDWARD J., How to run better meetings, McGraw-Hill, New York, 1957.

LOBINGIER, JOHN L., *Business meetings that make business; a complete tactical guide to planning and organizing business meetings that produce positive results*, Collier–Macmillan, 1969.

SHACKLETON, FRANK, *The law and practice of meetings*, 5th edn, Sweet & Maxwell, 1967.

CURRY, T. P. E., *The Conduct of and Procedure at Public, Company and Local Government Meetings*, 20th edn, Jordan & Sons.

Appendix I An outline history of management literature and thought

The following is a brief review of the contributions to the evolution of modern knowledge of the principles and practice of management. For readers who may be interested, a more detailed review is to be found in:

1. Urwick, L. and Brech, E. F. L., *The Making of Scientific Management:* vol. I. *Thirteen Pioneers;* vol. II. *Management in British Industry;* vol. III. *The Hawthorne Investigations* (Pitman, 1945–50).
2. Child, John, *British Management Thought* (Allen & Unwin, 1969).

While in the course of Britain's industrial revolution during the nineteenth century, a certain amount of attention was given to the development of management techniques, it was only in the later decades of the century that this subject became one of any width of interest. The technical periodicals and journals began from about the 1870s onwards here and there to carry articles on certain aspects of production management, and the analysis of costs, and gradually in the following ten or twenty years there emerged a category of recurrent topics which would today be classified as 'management'. An odd book or two had been published bearing on this subject prior to 1870, but it can rightly be said that the first volume to aspire to a title as an outstanding nineteenth-century contribution to the British literature of management was Garcke and Fells, *Factory Accounting,* published in 1887. Here for the first time was the combination of the accountant and the engineer, representing the coordination of the two major aspects in management development at that period.

Early pioneers

In 1894, F. G. Burton began his occasional series of articles in *Engineering,* on the subject of engineers' estimates and cost accounts, two or three years later republishing some of them in the form of a small book. Just before the end of the century he brought out a full-length book of some merit: this was *The Commercial Management of Engineering Works* (1899). Its character was more that of an accounting and office handbook than a textbook of management in the presentday sense, though it has two or three very interesting chapters on the managers' responsibilities. (Burton was Secretary and General Manager of the Milford Haven Shipbuilding and Engineering Company.) Between his two publications, however, Burton lost a good deal of his pride of place when in 1896 J. Slater-Lewis published his historic study entitled *The Commercial Organisation of Factories.* This was a new work by a General

Manager, a highly qualified engineer, who had not previously written for the technical press. Here was a textbook of organisation and management in the best sense of the term, with many features that were astonishingly modern, decades ahead of their time—even an organisation chart, an illustration of the flow of documents, and interesting comments on the human aspects of management.

The next noteworthy contributor did not appear until 1908; this was a writer using the pseudonym 'A General Manager' for a long series of articles on 'Commercial Engineering'. His identity was revealed as A. J. Liversedge in 1912, when the series appeared in book form. Its content was even more a commercial handbook than Burton's, largely consisting of market information.

Apart from the articles in the periodicals, presumably written for the growing middle-class readership employed in industry, even greater interest in management was beginning to be taken among the professional ranks of the technical societies, such as the Institution of Mechanical Engineers and one or two of the local Engineering Associations, notably in Manchester. In the annals of such bodies one or two names figure prominently, particularly after the turn of the century, as the main exponents of the 'new' approach to management, and the first references to F. W. Taylor's pioneer work (published in the United States in 1895) began to appear.[1]

No further textbook of any note came on the market until 1914, when the first edition of *Factory Administration and Accounts* was brought out by Elbourne, assisted by two colleagues (Home-Morton and Maughling), once again representing the combination of accountant and engineer. This book is a review of the best features of contemporary management practice, though with a significant degree of pioneer thinking in its presentation. It is perhaps a tribute to the foresight of its authors that the book long remained one of the classics of production management under the revised title *Factory Administration and Cost Accounts*. Elbourne's other great work, *The Fundamentals of Industrial Administration*, appeared in 1934, specifically prepared as an interpretation of the principles and practice of management for the benefit of students pursuing elementary courses for professional qualifications in that field.

Another classic in early British management literature is *Engineers' Costs and Economical Workshop Production,* by Dempster-Smith and Pickworth (1914). Whereas it probably attracted more contemporary attention, as being of stronger practical appeal, it did not have the seeds of posterity within it, and disappeared with the passing of the years. It may be of interest to point out how frequently in the thirty years between 1885 and 1915 the subject matter of articles and textbooks centred on estimates and costs—a theme reflected in the practice of management in the considerable contemporary interest in premium bonus and similar incentive systems in the hands of Halsey, Weir, Rowan and others, following in the wake of Taylor.

Scientific management

While this general interest in management was emerging in Great Britain in the fifty years after 1870, the American scene was witnessing lively debate centring on the progress of *Scientific Management* under the direction of F. W.

[1] F. W. Taylor's main writings are available under the title, *The Principles of Scientific Management.*

Taylor and his associates. This little team of American pioneers—of whom the best known were Taylor, Gantt and Gilbreth—were more concerned with elaborating the techniques for the application of systematic management than with writing up their findings in literature; they did, however, each produce two or three volumes, all of which have lived down to our own times. Taylor and his associates were, broadly, concerned in the first place with diverting attention away from the struggles over the division of the proceeds of industry, to the need for a concerted effort to increase those proceeds for mutual benefit by better planning and a better will to work, supported by incentive methods and other forms of bonus technique. But much of their effort went into the elaboration and advancement of techniques for the planning and control of production, including such methods as time study, motion study, the division and definition of responsibilities, planning charts, job tickets, and many other of the features that are currently recognised as essential to production control systems. These three men, and Taylor in particular, come down through the years more by their contributions in these directions than by their more important fundamental contribution to the philosophy or principles of management applied in human terms. In their own country they gained, through accidental circumstances, a publicity that inevitably entailed increasing public interest in the more easily understood and the more pleasantly acceptable aspects of their work. In this country, the publicity engendered serious suspicion in the minds of the leaders of organised labour, and generated an emotional opposition that has persisted even to our own day.

It would not be unfair to describe the first ten to fifteen years of the twentieth century in Great Britain as a barren period in management literature, even though the technical press and the journals of the societies frequently published articles and papers, many of them devoted to the exposition of Taylor's teachings and methods. 'Barren' is a fair description, because of the superficial character of so much of this writing, and because of its failure to secure any serious acceptance among the industrial owners and managers. The outbreak of war in 1914 found British industry ignorant of contemporary advances in management thought and practice, save for such rare exceptions as Hans Renold Ltd, or the Cadbury organisation.[1]

H. Fayol

Overlapping on the one side with Taylor, and on the other with the First World War, was Henri Fayol, General Manager of a large French mining and metallurgical concern. Almost at the close of a long executive career, Fayol took the opportunity of a paper to a Congress of a Metallurgical Society in 1908 to review, as he saw them, the processes that went to make up his everyday practice as a chief executive; but it was some eight years later before this paper appeared in published form in the *Bulletin* of the Society, under the title, 'Administration industrielle et générale', and another ten years before it appeared in English. The text was reproduced exactly as given in 1908, even to the extent of the note which foreshadowed additional sections to follow, intended to elaborate the author's basic conception of management as a

---

[1] See *The Making of Scientific Management,* vol. ii, chapters 11 and 12.

process built up of the five elements: Planning, Organisation, Command, Coordination and Control. It is a matter of considerable regret that Fayol, despite his interest, did not see fit to complete the work or to add any further publication to his legacy in this field. It was only after his death in 1925 (then aged well over eighty) that his one and only paper on this subject secured wider recognition by its publication in book form, first in French and later translated into English. The importance of Fayol's contribution lay in two features: the first was his systematic analysis of the process of management; the second, his firm advocacy of the principle that management *can, and should, be taught*. Both were revolutionary lines of thought in 1908, and still little accepted even much later. The seemingly unedited and unfinished state of Fayol's matter makes the real value of his analysis difficult to appreciate at first reading. Confusion is the reader's main reaction to the juxtaposition of overlapping 'principles of administration' and 'administrative duties'. Yet in his simple deduction of the elements of the process of management, he reached a conception that has stood the test of time.

At the time of his own contribution (1908), or when this first appeared in an English version (1928), Fayol made virtually no impact on British management thought and practice. This came later, mainly through the advocacy of Fayol's approach widely propagated by Urwick in the 40s and 50s.[1] This advocacy was, in fact, to cause some confusion, because of Urwick's habitual reference to 'Fayol's *six* elements', whereas the Fayol text specified only the five cited above. Urwick felt that the first element was inadequately represented by the English word 'planning', because the Fayol, French word 'prévoir' also implied some 'forecasting' ahead of planning. This could be seen as little more than semantics; for, in any language, the concept of 'planning' must imply and entail some degree of 'foreseeing' or forecasting to have any validity at all.

Closer analysis suggests (see Part One, page 12) that Fayol's *five elements* should more correctly be reduced to *four*, by taking 'Organisation' as no more than a special aspect of *planning*. Fayol identified it separately and specifically probably because of his personal setting in a large-scale enterprise, where problems of hierarchy and of channels of delegation and communication loomed large. He was clearly—and rightly—impressed with the importance of 'organisation structure', but he was misled into regarding this as a specifically different element. 'Organising', even in Fayol's intended sense of establishing the correct pattern of delegated responsibilities, with consequent interrelationships and channels of cooperative communication, is manifestly an aspect of the element of 'planning': instead of methods or equipment or operational activities, what is being planned is the pattern of management activities themselves and certain modes of communication among them.

Mary Follett

To return to the observations of the earlier decades, throughout the 20s and 30s Mary Follett was coming to loom large on the management scene, both in America and in Britain. After some fifteen to twenty years in social and educational development, coupled with research in the industrial milieu, she was invited in 1924 to give a paper (her first) to a conference of the Bureau of Personnel Administration in the United States. Over the next four or five years

[1] A new English version and edition, freshly translated from the original French text, appeared in 1948 under the title *Industrial and General Management*.

she contributed the remarkable series of papers on the fundamentals of management, illustrated from practical events, that form such an outstanding addition to the literature of the subject (*Dynamic Administration*: collected papers reproduced from the Bureau's Conference). Mary Follett, broadly, was less interested in the practice of management than in the extent to which the everyday incidents and problems reflected the presence or absence of sound principle. She was chiefly concerned to teach principles in simple language, amply illustrated from everyday events—not the mechanics of management, but its special human character, its nature as a social process, deeply embedded in the emotions of man and in the interrelations to which the everyday working of industry necessarily gives rise—at manager levels, at worker levels, and, of course, between the two. Bearing in mind she was speaking of America in the early 1920s, her thinking can be described as little less than revolutionary, and certainly a generation ahead of its time. There is no evidence that Mary Follett ever had any contact with the persons who sponsored or conducted the Hawthorne Investigations, but the findings of those investigations, when they appeared in their full form in the 1930s, were a striking testimony to the soundness of her teaching. Again and again an incident described or a conclusion drawn from the Hawthorne studies can be recognised as reflecting a principle or a fundamental tenet that Mary Follett had advanced from her own observations of the industrial situation.

The progressive decades

In Great Britain the 1920s were marked by some publications of outstanding value that maintained a strong position of influence for many years, notably: John Lee's *Management: a study of industrial organisation* (1921); O. Sheldon's *Philosophy of Management* (1924); *Factory Organisation*, by Northcott, Urwick and Wardropper (1927); Urwick's *Organising a Sales Office* (1928); Powell's *Payment by Results* (1924). Perhaps, however, the really outstanding work of the decade was one that has become lost to posterity because its contemporary sales did not justify keeping it in print. This was the *Dictionary of Industrial Administration*, published by Pitman in 1927 as a collection of writings on the principles and practice of management by all the known authorities of the day under the editorship of John Lee.[1] It is a misfortune that this volume should have been born out of time, some decades ahead of the day when its full value would have been appreciated.

During these years the interest in costing was beginning to spread into its management aspects, and a few small publications were to be found, a notable one being Emsley and Loxham, *Factory Costs* (1924), later re-issued as *Factory Costing and Organisation*.

The corresponding period in the United States was considerably more fruitful, probably because a larger industrial population provided the publishers with the certainty of an adequate market. Again, many of the books published then went down to posterity in revised editions, as, for instance, Lamburgh's *Industrial Administration* (1923), the two classics in the personnel field: Tead and Metcalf's *Personnel Administration* (1920) and *Personnel Management*, by Scott, Clothier and others (1923). E. Schell's *The*

[1] This remarkable pioneer in British management literature has been unduly neglected. His contributions are now well recorded for posterity in John Child's *British Management Thought* (pp. 59–63, 132–3).

Technique of Executive Control also dates from 1924. The climax of these series of comprehensive studies was reached in America in 1931 in the first appearance of *The Handbook of Business Administration* followed by its more specific companion *The (Cost and) Production Handbook* (1934).

By this time, the subject of management had become, both in Britain and in America, one of considerable contemporary interest, supported by professional institutes; in the USA there was support as well by systematic studies at university level. The way was open for the great flow of textbooks and treatises that make it so difficult for the historian to pick and choose. Inevitably many of the studies were of a 'bread-and-butter' kind, concerned with the description and illustration of techniques for production management, for production control, for cost control, for sales management and stores control, for personnel practices, and the many other aspects of the day-to-day activities that go to make up the pattern of executive control in any medium or large-sized organisation. Inevitably also, many of such studies were short-lived, of passing interest only, because as practice developed, new techniques would be evolved and new textbooks called for. One can perhaps avoid the difficulty of selecting among this literature by refraining from specific mention, except to pay tribute to such pioneer British classics as T. H. Burnham's *Engineering Economics*, Elbourne's *Fundamentals of Industrial Administration*, and T. G. Rose's *Higher Control*—all dating from the 1930s.

The theory of management

Throughout these years there had been relatively little contribution to what might be termed the 'theory' of management, i.e. the systematic study of the principles upon which the everyday practice of the executive process rested. Outstanding in this field was L. Urwick's first major contribution to the literature of management, which appeared as a section of the *Dictionary* referred to above, under the title of 'Principles of Direction and Control', a systematic scheme of the fundamentals of management, obviously the product of farreaching and painstaking analytical thought, which even today has a valuable relevance to the study of the subject. (These 'Principles' are available to presentday readers in a reproduction in Elbourne's *Fundamentals*.) An equally useful American study was Webster Robinson's *Fundamentals of Business Administration*, first published in 1928. In 1931 came *Onward Industry* by Mooney and Reilley, an American classic in the study of organisation principles. This, not confining itself to industry, roamed over the whole field of organised human endeavour, in an attempt to find common principles that would serve to prescribe sound foundations for effective delegation. Subsequent editions appeared in 1939 and 1947 under the title *The Principles of Organisation* (with Mooney now as sole author). Historically, this book in its earlier edition may be regarded as the first systematic study of *organisation* on scientific lines. Though concerned with the static aspects of the structure of organisation and the formal lines of relationship, it had inevitably to deal with many aspects of an organisation at work, and so many 'dynamic' considerations came into the study: this gave rise to a shortlived fashion in the terminology of management—the use of 'organisation' as the name for the total process as well as for the structure of responsibilities.

In 1933 came Urwick's second book, *Management of To-morrow*, a combination of principle and practice, following largely on the lines of Mary

Follett in the endeavour to discuss effective management in action in simple terms of everyday life in the factory and the office, but at the same time attempting to lay down the fundamental principles upon which such effective management must rest. It followed Mooney and Reilley in the use of the term 'organisation' as the generic name, and brought out specifically for the first time the dual concept of the 'dynamic' and 'static' aspects. In spite of its limited issue, this book made a very important contribution to British literature and to the advancement of management thought: it was the equivalent in this country of its equally well-known contemporary in America, *Organisation Engineering*, by H. S. Dennison (1931).

By the mid-1930s the possibility of a 'science' of management was being canvassed, though by now the terminology tangle was already well to the fore. Many writers were using, not only the existing two terms 'management' and 'organisation', but beginning also to bring in the third member of the trilogy, 'administration'. This can be illustrated, for instance, by the joint Anglo-American publication (1937) of *Papers on the Science of Administration*, written and edited by Gulick and Urwick.

Apart from the two or three monumental works on the Hawthorne investigations, the last outstanding contribution to the literature of management before the outbreak of war in 1939 was Chester Barnard's *Functions of the Executive*, a penetrating analysis of the process of cooperation that is inherent in every aspect of management. Here the findings of the Hawthorne investigations were being used as an analytical instrument for examining the process of management, for the special purpose of throwing into relief its human or social character.

The postwar years

The two decades during and following the Second World War saw the literature of management enormously swollen in both Britain and the USA, as well as in other countries. Serious study of the subject was widely and vigorously extended, with the result that in almost every aspect there grew up a numerous and comprehensive bibliography. The American contributions far outweighed all others, even all others combined; this is an easy situation to explain, in so far as the United States have so many long-established colleges and university departments where management studies figure as a major item, and thus there exist substantial numbers of teaching and research staffs devoted to these subjects. The resulting literature is too considerable and extensive to permit of any sort of survey in short compass, as can be seen by reference to the catalogue or select lists of the Library of the British Institute of Management or other sources of bibliographical information.

While it is invidious to select individual titles, leave may be presumed at least for the mention of a recent special study by the sociologist W. H. Whyte called *The Organisation Man*: this presents perhaps the epitome of managerial development, reflecting the forecast of James Burnham's *Managerial Revolution*—for Whyte portrays and analyses, with almost frightening reality, the influences that the demands of large-scale management practice are exerting on the men and women of our day: a sociological and philosophical study, not a textbook, but of vital importance for every manager. Equally stimulating studies from a sociologist's hands, though with a more specific background of industrial investigation, have been the several books written by

Peter Drucker, stemming from his researches within the large American concern that was also the home of Mooney and Reilley (1931); for example, *The New Society* (1951) and *The Practice of Management* (1955).

New publications in the British literature of management were also numerous and, on the whole, of higher quality than those of previous decades. The war and immediate postwar years found interest centred largely in the fields of personal relations and industrial psychology, and a few references may serve to illustrate the trends. Books covering the human factor in management may be usefully represented by G. S. Walpole's *Management and Men* (1944), W. C. Puckey's *What is this Management?* (1944) and Brown and Raphael's *Managers, Men and Morale* (1948). Or among those with a more specialised approach: C. H. Northcott's *Personnel Management* (1945) and May Smith's *Introduction to Industrial Psychology* (1943). Techniques for production management also figured in a variety of publications, illustrated by two such different works as Willsmore's *Modern Production Control* (1946) and Vernon's *Manual of Industrial Management and Maintenance* (1946). Similar studies appeared in other fields, including those of Budgetary Control and the special applications devised by T. G. Rose under the title *Higher Control.* During the later years of the war (1944–45), the British Standards Institution brought out an interesting series of booklets on management methods called *Office Aids to the Factory,* and a similar contribution to the wider spreading of knowledge of management practice was made in 1947–48 by the Management Library in a series of *Letters to Foremen.*

An unusual study was Gillespie's *Free Expression in Industry* (1948), an interesting and original plea for recognition of the morale factor in human relations by the inclusion in the structure of management of freely elected 'morale leaders' parallel to the 'technical' executives and supervisors. Other contributions came from Britain's oldest teaching establishment in the field of management: the Manchester College of Technology founded its Department of Industrial Administration in 1918, but its first systematic publications appeared in 1946 as *The Manchester Monographs on Higher Management.*

In the more fundamental field of management principles, additions to British literature have been sparse, the only outstanding publication being L. Urwick's *Elements of Administration* (1945). A pioneer study was E. F. L. Brech's *Management: its nature and significance* (1946), an attempt to analyse the process of management into its basic elements and so reach the basis for a 'theory of management'. An American author, Alvin Brown, published two works, similarly endeavouring to expound the essential factors in the structure of organisation, virtually in logical line of succession from Mooney and Reilley. These two books are *Organisation—a formulation of principle* (1945) and *The Organisation of Industry* (1947). A parallel study from a background of American public service administration (though more concerned with the executive processes of delegation and decision than with organisation structure) is Simon's *Administrative Behaviour* (1947). Another important American addition to literature in the more practical field is Copeland and Towl's *The Board of Directors and Business Management* (1947), at that time the only study of its kind, systematically analysing the functions of the directors.

Two British studies later complemented this work: *The Company Director,* by Alfred Read (1953) and *Company Direction,* by J. W. Seymour (1954), together providing a full review of the legal and functional responsibilities of directors in public and private companies, and there have been subsequent specialist publications from the Institute of Directors. In the field of combined analytical and practical studies, a major pioneer work of later years was the specialist though comprehensive volume *Organisation—The Framework of Management*, by E. F. L. Brech (1957), which has remained unique as a study of organisation structure abstracted from the dynamics of the activities and personal relationships that are going on within it.

Management 'tools'

In the immediate postwar period in Britain an important trend was the growing recognition of accounting as a management tool rather than an historical record of progress. Wartime industrial experiences undoubtedly played a big part in stimulating this trend, initially focused on the Institute of Cost and Works Accountants (as then called, now renamed the Institute of Management Accounting). For some time the professional accountancy institutes stood aloof from this development, though individual members were becoming increasingly caught up. Three early works that gained widespread usage were: Warwick Dobson, *An Introduction to Cost Accountancy* (1954); Evans Hemming, *Cost Control for Management* (1952); Broad and Carmichael, *A Guide to Management Accounting* (1957). These can be seen as the precursors of the very considerable literature on management accounting and financial control that became available in the later decades.

In terms of management thought and literature related to practice, the scene of the past twenty years has been too generously and variously covered to make any synoptic observation easy, if indeed possible. Perhaps, the only useful way to set down the bird's-eye view will be by reference to a series of selected topics. The production of management books and articles in Britain and America can only be described as vast in numbers and comprehensive in scope, and there have been shifts of emphasis in subject matter, as different aspects of management practice have come into fashion and then dropped out again.

Throughout the postwar years, British studies of management practice have been assisted by numerous publications of the British Institute of Management (founded in 1947). A quarterly journal, *The British Management Review*, first appeared in the later 1930s, but was seriously interrupted by wartime difficulties and did not resume serious publication until 1946–47, continuing thereafter until merged into the monthly journal *The Manager* (now called *Management Today*) at a less serious level of treatment. Better known are the Institute's numerous pamphlets and booklets on a wide variety of selected subjects of specific studies of aspects of management practice. To supplement these aids to the practising manager interested to pursue serious professional development, the Institute has always maintained a reference and lending library service, plus a literature information service including monthly 'abstracts' of British and foreign publications.

The first major strand in the past twenty-five years could be seen as an overhang from the inevitable concern with production problems during the war years. As aids to manufacturing management, techniques that had emerged in embryo years before were brought up to date for active application. 'Work study' (dating back to F. W. Taylor in the 1890s and to Frank Gilbreth in the 1900s) is a ready illustration, enjoying a major lease of life in the return to peacetime industry and affording a significant opportunity for management consultant services, because of lack of training facilities outside of those professional establishments. Closely associated were techniques of production planning and control, again building from earlier initiatives (Gantt in the 1910s and Willsmore in the 1920s). Very soon a considerable specialist literature was beginning to develop covering these interrelated techniques: in the course of time for practical application they became consolidated into programmes for the betterment of production management, for quite a long time (starting around 1955) coordinated under the label 'improving managerial performance'.

The human factor

Similarly, as a byproduct of wartime influences, the field of personnel management and industrial relations drew an immense increase of attention, accompanied by an ever-growing literature. Throughout the 1950s and on into the 1960s, human relations in industry and many facets of behaviour and attitude dominated the British management scene. Primarily concerned with the human situation of the 'producer personnel' in factory, workshop and depot, there were also spins-off into supervisory roles and intermanagerial attitudes. A particularly interesting feature of this phenomenon was the extensive involvement of sociologists in these industrial milieux, often (perhaps mainly) through research projects or investigations from neighbouring University and Technical Colleges. Rarely would the sociologist be found in the full-time employ of the firm, unless incidentally because he/she was a member of staff of the Personnel Department, recruited for departmental duties rather than for sociology. The dominance of the interest in human and social factors in industry spilled over into the conference and seminar programmes: the easiest to get booked up for many years were those with a 'human' topic in the title or in the sessions. (One is, perhaps, allowed to make the wry comment that little good in real life terms seems to have come out of the euphoric effervescence of interest!) It has been argued by professionals from this field (Anthony and Crichton in *Industrial Relations and the Personnel Specialists*) that this dominance of human interest has been out of perspective and conducive to much of the malaise currently affecting Britain's industries.[1]

Inevitably, the literature, starting out in simple vein, soon became complex and sophisticated; and what was once happily accepted over long years as 'the human factor in industry' turned into the 'behavioural sciences'. In the context of the human facets of inter-managerial attitudes, this metamorphosis was well illustrated by Robert Blake's *Managerial Grid*.

One special project in the human relations field makes a topline impact in literature and discussion, but seems to have had correspondingly little influence in the real lives of other firms: this was the Glacier Project, a programme of very genuine development in the betterment of personal relationships and attitudes carried out internally in the Glacier Metal Co. Ltd, London. Radical changes in almost every aspect of management practice were worked out through consultation and put into effect through communication and cooperation. Widely discussed in conferences and seminars, the project produced a substantial literature, and was seen in many British circles as a

---

[1] The nature and extent of this dominating interest is well brought out in Child, *British Management Thought*, chapter 6, 'The challenge of social science'.

latterday version of the 'Hawthorne Investigations' (Western Electric Company, USA, 1927–32). Main titles in the series of publications are : E. Jaques, *The Changing Culture of a Factory* (1951) and *Measurement of Responsibility* (1956); W. Brown, *Exploration in Management* (1960), *Piecework Abandoned* (1962) and *Organisation* (1972).

O & M

Reverting to the thought of earlier paragraphs, another spin-off from wartime activities was on a more minor scale, though not without its own significance. Ever since 1919, H.M. Treasury has had a small 'investigations department', concerned with diagnostic studies for the improvement of paperwork design and office procedures. For wartime needs this small unit was expanded in 1941 as a medium for saving manpower by methods improvement, and the success of the service triggered off interest in local government, in the national industry organisations when these were set up about 1947 and in larger commercial concerns. The subject matter of the service was known as 'organisation and methods', the former word being used in the sense of the arrangement and layout of work, equipment and premises. Thus was born 'O and M' which can be conveniently described as work study applied in the office. Increasing application led in due course (about 1955) to the establishment of an 'O and M Training Council', so that many more firms and institutions could benefit from the application of skilled services. And the movement was supported by a major tutorial volume, C. E. Milward's *Organisation and Methods: a service to management* (1959), following hard on the heels of a smaller companion study by H. P. Cemach called *Work Study in the Office* (1958).

Office methods and procedures fell during the 1960s increasingly under the influence of developments in automated (electronic) data processing and became caught up in the emergence of *systems analysis* as a more comprehensive and penetrating form of O and M. Data-processing systems very soon became the centre of an extensive specialist literature.

It was about the mid-1950s that graduates began to be employed in general industrial and commercial occupations, as distinct from their hitherto traditional restriction to mainly scientific and technological roles. In the ten years on from the early 1950s the number of graduates entering first employment in industry and commerce went up at least four or fivefold. Many went into production supervision and service as distinct from research or technology, and increasing numbers (including Arts graduates) were going into administrative, commercial and marketing occupations. Later, the tide turned towards various forms of 'management services' including O and M, operational research, or systems analysis. By 1959 about half the graduates leaving universities were entering industry and commerce as first employment, a phenomenon sufficiently striking to justify a review by PEP, published in 1957 as *Graduates in Industry*. It also justified in the same year the commencement of a commercial periodical annual publication on *Opportunities for Graduates* (Labovitch for Cornmarket Press). It may well have been the surge of intake at better levels of intelligence and education that sparked off and fed the enormous expansion of management courses and seminars that characterised the ten years 1959–69. An equally prolific offering of educational opportunities had never before been seen in Britain, or elsewhere for that matter. In turn, the course attendance fever may have bred the contagion of the interest in *techniques*, which figured as another characteristic feature of the decade. Techniques were being sought and tried virtually as substitutes for the managers' own roles in judgment and decision, though many served only for diagnostic purposes.

Other techniques

Several endeavours were made to clarify the purpose and scope of management techniques, as distinct from data processing systems: the first, a study group under the auspices of the British Institute of Management (1961), which carried the label *Management Services* (see Part Seven, p. 1025). A compendium of techniques was compiled by Clay and Walley (1965) and published under the title *Performance and Profitability*. A spate of titles followed in the next four or five years, including: Perrigo, *Modern Managerial Techniques* (1968); Argenti, *Management Techniques* (1969); Lock and Taverner, *The Director's Guide to Management Techniques* (1970); McRae, *Analytical Management* (1971)—this last dealing more with the techniques in the direction of operational research, decision-theory and other fields where 'models' and mathematical aids are brought into use. An endeavour to provide a comprehensive review of how techniques and systems fit into the practice of management in the everyday situation was made by Paul Hanika in *New Thinking in Management* (1972).

'Organisation structure' was a topic sporadically claiming interest, particularly in courses and seminars, but it did not become at any time the subject of extensive literature. One reason for this could have been the popular habit of viewing 'organisation' mainly in dynamic terms, i.e. in relation to the personal attitudes of the men and women holding the organisational roles. Good illustrations of this were found in Burns and Stalker, *The Management of Innovation* (Edinburgh, 1961) and in Puckey, *Organisation in Business Management* (1963), the latter particularly concerned with the significance of 'group' attitudes and relationships among the people in the managerial and supervisory posts. As long as the personal or dynamic factor took precedence, writing would be more related to the overall setting of management practice than with organisation structure as such. One study combining the two aspects together was Barnes and Others, *Company Organisation: theory and practice* (1970), while a series of case studies following a theoretical introduction was offered by Sadler and Barry in *Organisational Development* (1970).

Management development

Of growing interest in this context came the subject of *promotion* in the managerial hierarchy, associated with the development of the skills and competence appropriate to promotion: again a topic that figured largely in conference and seminars, an early published study was sponsored by the Acton Society Trust (1955): *Management Succession,* a research project conducted by Rosemary Stewart into the recruitment and promotion policies and practices of some fifty-odd British companies employing over 10 000 personnel apiece. Two further complementary studies were published by George Copeman (1957): *Leaders of British Industry* and *Pay and Promotion for Executives.* And another was published in the the same year jointly by the

University of Manchester and the British Institute of Management as *Company Executive Development Schemes,* being an analytical and comparative review of management succession arrangements in a sample of about one hundred firms in north-west England.

From these beginnings, 'management development' became in the 1960s the major fashionable subject in Britain's industrial circles. It is not unfair to refer to it in this way, because the interest was very much more in discussion than in realistic action. Obviously, this interest tied up closely with the mushroom growth of courses, seminars and conferences: in these settings 'management development' figured prominently and recurrently. Nor can the interest be ascribed to stimulus of the Training Boards, for in most industries these Boards were hardly effectively established by the end of the decade, when the fashion of the topic was beginning to lose its glamour.

The Industrial Training Act 1964 had its purposes more in the fields of artisan and operative skills than in training for managerial roles, though it is possible that the needs of supervisory personnel may have been among the original objectives. With the setting up of some thirty Industrial Training Boards, it soon became evident that the furtherance of training for management could not and should not be entirely left out of attention, but that it would be folly to leave each ITB to deliberate and act independently in this direction. Accordingly the Central Training Council (of the then Department of Employment and Productivity) initiated a joint committee to review the subject comprehensively and to bring forward common guidelines from which individual ITBs could develop policies and practices appropriate to the industries in their scope. Two reports were produced by the Committee in fulfilment of its mandate: (1) *An Approach to the Training and Development of Managers* (HMSO, 1967); (2) *Further Proposals for Training and Development of Managers* (HMSO, 1969). This important topic thus acquired an official foundation to lend support to what had been going on from private initiatives in earlier years, which could be illustrated in a booklet by T. J. Roberts, *Developing Effective Managers,* published by the Institute of Personnel Management (1967).

A special slant from the earlier private initiatives was given by the emergence (early 1960s) of the recommended practice of 'management by objectives', associated with the name of John Humble. In the context of its time, this slant could be seen as an endeavour to frame a management philosophy into a technique (see Part One, p. 29). In substance MbO formed a followthrough from 'improving managerial performance' on to 'management development' picking up 'corporate planning' on the way—though this third concept really leapt into the forefront of fashion only late in the 1960s, mainly as an importation from America. As a concept it gained some hold in Britain on the basis of John Argenti's book *Corporate Planning: a practical guide* (1968), followed by a national conference on the subject held in London in February 1969. At this date there was already established a 'Society for Long-range Planning', which acted as a sponsor for the conference and for the publication of the proceedings edited by B. W. Denning under the title *Corporate Long-range Planning.* Yet the roots did not go deep in the realms of top management, and the subject drifted off into the hands (or minds) of the statisticians, the operational research specialists and the academic departments.

So true was this that by 1970 it was possible for a research investigation to find that only a small handful of leading firms had in practice anything that could be held remotely to resemble what the conference had been preaching.

Another special event in the broad field of management development was the appearance of R. W. Revan's book *Developing Effective Managers* (1971), described as 'a new approach to business education'. This was a report on the special project mounted and conducted by the Belgian institution 'La Fondation Industrie-Université'. The programme was a direct endeavour to bridge the gap between theory and practice, between learning and action, by a combination of educational studies in management with the carrying out of selected practical tasks in somebody else's firm. On a more sophisticated scale, this could be seen as another version of the use of 'management services' as a medium of 'management development' advocated by Brech (1972) in *Managing for Revival* (chapter 7).

Despite the discussions and literature, and despite the importance of the two subjects as contributions to managerial performance and progress, neither *corporate planning* nor *management development* have taken their rightful place in the real life situations of Britain's industries and commerce. And the nation suffers in consequence—though there is little or nothing that literature can do about that. The failure of these concepts to be understood, grasped and applied can almost certainly be ascribed to Britain's national apathy about marketing. British industries and commerce do not have an accepted philosophy of marketing, that is to say, the orientation of managerial objectives to the *earning* of profit *through the service and satisfaction of customers.* The lack is not new, for it has been a major feature of the British economy back over the past thirty years: 'producer' dominated, to the neglect of the consumer. Marketing has been seen primarily as market research, supplemented by sales promotion and advertising, rather than as the motivating force of profitable progress. Weakness in marketing must inevitably produce the rundown of momentum that has now become the commonplace experience of the nation: this note can form the appropriate swan song of this review of the national scene, for it has been fully recorded in *Managing for Revival* already cited.

The international management scene has already become too extensive and complex to admit of synopsis in a meaningful way. American literature is readily available and widely known in Britain, but language barriers have so far precluded anything more than passing acquaintance with literature from other countries. But there is a focus in the long-standing sessions of the International Council of Organisation (CIOS); starting in 1924, these have been held (except during the war years) every three years in different countries, and since 1935 papers and discussions have been published for sale as collected volumes of *Proceedings.* Over the years, the collections afford a very useful review of how thought and practice are tending in many parts of the world. Virtually every advanced country now has a 'national management institute' affiliated to CIOS, and participating in the triennial congress. (It is worth noting, in passing, that at the Congress of 1975 held in Caracas, the name of CIOS has been replaced by 'World Council of Management'.)

Since 1958 CIOS has been supplemented by a specialist offshoot in the form of the *International Academy of Management*, a forum for the more distinguished contributors to thought and practice. The Academy has produced no publications, but its Fellows meet regionally every two or three years. It would form the natural focus and medium for any endeavour to consolidate for international reference the best of management literature produced in the various sectors of the world.

In this final quarter of the twentieth century, it would not be untrue to claim that the practice of management is supported by a body of thought and a volume of literature not far below that of other branches of human endeavour. That much of the literature is as yet superficial is an inevitable byproduct of the early stage so far reached in the development of management skills—the signs are many that improving and expanding practice is promoting depth of thought, and the deepening of treatment in literature will in due course be a natural corollary. The evidence is already there in many of the studies emanating in recent years from both British and American sources. A recent trend in both countries has been the 'popularisation' of management literature through publication in paperback, thus providing easier access for the directors, managers and would-be managers in the smaller firms. It is not only the cost of the hardback volumes that is offputting (and costly many of them indeed are), but their very appearance as books, serious and weighty. If the paperbacks can help to increase reading and learning about improvement of management practice, this is all to the good of the nation and its standard of living.

Appendix II Principles of Management

Surprise was expressed in Part One (p. 65) that, despite the extensive scale of management studies and deliberations, national and international, no consensus had yet been attained as to what constitutes the theory of management or the fundamental principles from which its effective practice would stem. As there indicated, interest in this aspect of development has long been in evidence, and many attempts have been made over the decades to bring contributions forward, though mostly piecemeal in approach. Such interest has gained little support from the cadres of practising managers and directors, especially when given expression in the international gatherings. Five factors seem to explain this lack of support:

1. Managers have been too exclusively concerned with practical problems, which is to be found inborn in some individuals and missing from others. rather than to the managerial; accordingly they tend to be more concerned with detailed issues than with the principles that underlie such practice.
2. There is a long-standing tradition that management is a special aptitude, which is to be found inborn in some individuals and missing from others. Industrial developments in more recent times have proved this view to be fallacious, but its persistence has hindered recognition of underlying fundamental principles, common to management wherever it occurs and whoever is responsible for it.
3. The emergence and development of techniques and systems on a considerable scale in all countries have attracted attention to the means and methods by which the management process is applied in the real life of everyday activities, and have masked the basic features of that process itself; effective performance has been seen to stem from the combination of personal competence and sound procedure (or system), thus diverting recognition from anything more fundamental within or beneath the process.
4. In most industrial countries, and particularly in Great Britain, economic progress was made mainly on technological foundations; that is to say, the improvement of machines and equipment, the development of better methods of transport, the improvement of materials, and so on; it is only in comparatively recent times that management has been identified as contributing specifically to industrial and commercial progress.
5. The few writers or thinkers who have been attracted to the fundamental aspects of management, with a view to elucidating basic principles, have shown a marked tendency to approach their analytical task on an individual basis; they have not normally taken as their own starting-point the body of knowledge already existing as the result of contributions from earlier

writers. In consequence, their writings have tended to conflict, or to lead to confusions, instead of building up a cumulative 'knowledge' of management.

The nature of 'principle'

A 'principle' means a fundamental truth accepted as underlying reasoning or action; it is a primary axiom or a basic law from which effective practice can be developed. This is the sense in which the term is used in many branches of human activity, and in several professional fields accepted principles are the common foundation of expertise and success.

Principles of management will need to be developed one day in this same sense: they *could* be deduced by *a priori* analytical reasoning from the nature of the management process, but acceptability is more likely if they are determined from practice—say, from a comparative study of observed strengths and weaknesses. This approach, of course, would necessitate a very considerable scale of firsthand cooperative research, well beyond anything that has yet been thought of; yet, not beyond the combined resources of an international framework such as the World Council of Management.

Inevitably, principles of management would have to be couched in general terms, so as to be viable in different industries and commerce, as well as in organisations of varying size and character. Moreover, they must be so formulated as *not* to include or imply implementation by *specific methods*. 'Methods' are ways and means of applying principles: thus, any given principle could be carried into effect in different organisations, or by different managers, by different methods.

To be valid and appropriate a body of 'principles of management' must relate to all the essential facets of the management process in action, and so to the essential elements which constitute it—planning, control, motivation, coordination. As it happens, in management practice, once the organisation reaches any size above the minimal, a special facet of 'planning' has to be brought to bear in the form of delegation, leading to the formation of an organisation structure (see p. 45): a full body of principles must, therefore, include items in this direction.

Existing principles

For what they are worth, an early set of principles are preserved in this Appendix: they first appeared in earlier editions of this volume, and stemmed originally from study groups interested in this topic in Britain in the later 1940s and early 1950s (see the historical reference on p. 137). They were drawn up from some few existing contributions, supplemented by deductions from analytical study of the practical working of management in industrial firms, checked against observations of strengths and weaknesses. Their only realistic value on the contemporary scene is as a stimulus to further deliberation on this topic and as a starting-point for any more serious development that might be initiated. The full version was presented (in 1953 for the first time) under four headings:

A. Principles of management (general).
B. Planning and control.
C. Organisation structure.
D. Coordination and motivation.

A. *Principles of management (general)*

1. In economic affairs, the primary purpose of the enterprise, and so of management's responsibility, is the provision of goods and services in accordance with the requirements of the consumer.

   N.B. (i) This does not imply that the consumer requirements are to be the *sole* determinant of economic activity, without reference to other factors, such as the technical needs of production or design.

   (ii) In many enterprises the product handled is such as to contribute only indirectly to consumer needs: the ultimate purpose is still as stated, though one or more stages removed.

2. An essentially interrelated primary objective, inherent in the setting in the economic system, is the contribution to an overall effective level of employment at standards of earnings consistent with the socially accepted norms of 'fair wages'.

3. The interpretation of the purpose of an enterprise or organisation lies in the formulation of its policy. Sound policy, in relation both to overall purpose and to the activities of the various divisions or sections of the organisation, is the foundation of effective management.

4. The formulation of policy is the responsibility of the highest level of management; for instance, in a Limited Company, the responsibility of the Board of Directors acting on behalf of the owners (shareholders).

5. The formulation of policy, and the exercise of all aspects of management directed to achieving its fulfilment, must be based on adequate consideration of the relevant facts without and within the organisation.

6. The aim of management is, in achieving the purpose or task to which it is directed, to attain and maintain an optimum level of effectiveness and economy of operation in all the activities of the enterprise. Among the essential ways of attaining such effectiveness is the promotion of contentment and morale of the persons composing the organisation.

7. Management thus acquires a secondary social aim in the promotion of contentment and morale.

8. Because of its nature as a social (human) process, management responsibility must be carried into effect as a continuous and living activity on the part of the appointed manager(s), and cannot be replaced by techniques or systems designed for operation by subordinate personnel in the prolonged or recurrent absence of the manager(s).

9. Irrespective of the size of the organisation, or of the divisions into which its activities may in practice be divided, the process of management within that organisation is a unity, and its several parts or aspects must be recognised as related items in the one integral process.

10. The only reliable basis of approach to effective management in action is a systematic method based on: diagnosis of situation—ascertainment of facts—assessment and interpretation—decision and instruction—check results.

11. The criterion of management is to be sought in—(*a*) achievement of purpose; (*b*) the effectiveness of operations, measured usually in terms of productivity per man-hour employed or cost per unit of product produced or work performed; (*c*) the contentment of the members of the organisation. 'Profits' may be a convenient index of the first two criteria.

B. Planning and control

1. Ascertainment and assessment of all relevant facts, without and within the enterprise, are essential factors in sound planning and control.

   N.B. (i) These two elements are *essentially* interrelated, *control* being the obverse of *planning*.

   (ii) Both are largely carried into effect by means of techniques or procedures, and form the 'administrative' aspect of management. They provide 'tools' of management, and so are always *means, ends* in themselves.

   (iii) Apart from the techniques by which these elements are carried into effect, they are also to be reflected in the attitude of managers in discharging their responsibilities.

2. Two essential preliminary stages in the determination plans are:

   (a) the formulation and delineation of objectives and policy, overall as well as in appropriate sectional terms;

   (b) the laying down of the responsibilities or tasks allocated to the various members of the group or enterprise, and of the (formal) interrelations consequently arising among them.

3. Sound planning and control require the determination and setting down of appropriate standards of performance in respect of the various activities or operations of the enterprise, reflecting the stated objectives: these are to be determined by systematic analysis and assessment of the relevant facts.

4. The effectiveness and economy of activities or operations are controlled by a continuous comparison of actual achievements or results against these predetermined standards.

5. The selection of the personnel, equipment, materials, methods, processes, etc., to be used in carrying out the operations, should be based on a continuous review of all relevant factors, and determined on an analytical basis.

6. Effectiveness and economy of operations can be assisted by— specialisation, simplification and standardisation.

7. In striving for economy of operations, as the counterpart of effectiveness, it is important to keep a balance between long-term and short-term results or consequences.

8. In the application of techniques of planning and control, full regard must be paid to the human needs of members of the organisation: the techniques alone cannot secure effectiveness of operations, and neglect of human requirements inevitably militates against their successful application.

C. Organisation structure

1. Organisation is an aspect of planning, concerned with the definition of:

   (a) the responsibilities of the positions held by the managerial, supervisory and specialist personnel employed in the enterprise; and

   (b) the formal interrelations established by virtue of such responsibilities.

2. The structure of organisation of an enterprise is the framework for carrying out the responsibilities of management, for the delegation of such responsibilities, for the coordination of activities or operations, and

for the motivation of members; the design of the structure must be directed to promoting the effective working, at all levels, of the four elements of management.

3. The responsibilities or activities allocated or delegated to all managerial, supervisory and specialist positions held by the members of an enterprise, or of all its main and subsidiary divisions or sections, should be clearly defined, preferably in writing: the definition should also specify the (formal) relations of each particular member or section to any others with which there is to be active contact.

4. When the size of the enterprise necessitates subdivision of responsibilities, the most useful broad division is into specific primary groups, determined by specialisation of function or operation.

5. When the increasing size or activity of an enterprise (or any other factors) threatens to impair the effectiveness of management through the overloading of members, appropriate provision is to be made for the delegation of responsibilities to other positions in the direct line or to the specialist members: appropriate provision has then also to be made to ensure continuous effective coordination.

6. The definition of responsibilities and relationships forming an organisation structure should provide:

   (*a*) a single chief executive responsible to the policy-forming body for the effective conduct of all the operations of the enterprise;

   (*b*) adequate decentralisation of decision through the delegation of responsibility;

   (*c*) clear lines of responsibility linking the chief executive with the various points of decision or operation;

   (*d*) the span of responsibility or supervision of a superior limited to a reasonable number of (executive or supervisory) subordinates, if their activities are interrelated;

   (*e*) the integration of functional (specialist) sections in such a way as not to impair the clear lines of responsibility and command.

7. If responsibilities are properly defined, the delegation of responsibility, and its acceptance, automatically implies delegation of the corresponding authority to take decisions and to secure the carrying out of the appropriate activities. If limitations are intended to apply to any executive's responsibilities, they should be specifically mentioned in the definitions.

   N.B. When responsibilities are delegated, a superior is still to be held accountable for all the relevant activities of subordinates within his jurisdiction, whether he has issued specific instructions for such activities or not.

8. An organisation structure cannot be regarded as immutable; it must be flexible enough to admit of adjustment when required by changes in basic circumstances.

D. Coordination and motivation

1. The aims of management, in the achievement of a given purpose or task through effective and economical activities or operations of persons associated in an enterprise or organisation, can be attained only if there is willing cooperation from and coordinated activity among those persons.

2. However sound the framework provided by the policy, plans and organisation structure of the enterprise, effective management implies a responsibility for deliberate and continuous coordination, and specific mechanisms to this end may be required.

3. The effectiveness of operations and the maintenance of cooperation among members of an organisation are in part determined by the personal and social contentment derived by them from their participation in the tasks of the enterprise.

> *N.B.* (i) A person employed in any organisation necessarily goes into that employment as a 'total person', continuously subject to influences derived from temperament, background, domestic circumstances and many other factors external to the working situation.
>
> (ii) It is now becoming increasingly recognised that inherent in management as a social process is a *direct* responsibility for the promotion of personal and social satisfactions of the persons under its jurisdiction; the attainment of such satisfactions in a 'group situation' is one of the reasons for persons taking up employment.

4. Coordination of operations requires *balance* of activities as well as unification; it can be most effectively attained by direct continuous contact among the persons concerned, starting at an early stage of their activities, and proceeding with due regard to the relevant facts.

5. The issue of instructions (command) and the supervision of operations are among the channels through which the element of motivation is carried into effect.

6. Communications (instructions, etc.) should flow along the lines of responsibility and relationship set out in the organisation structure.

7. Willing cooperation, through high morale (will to work) among members of an organisation, is promoted by:

> (a) keeping them informed of matters concerning the activities of the organisation;
>
> (b) consulting them in regard to its regulation and further development;
>
> (c) fostering in them a sense of self-responsibility for the performance of their tasks;
>
> (d) affording them opportunities for self-development, compatible with the purpose and interests of the organisation;
>
> (e) encouraging them to contribute to its effectiveness and development apart from the performance of their allotted tasks;
>
> (f) fostering their responsible participation in its management.

8. High morale is in part determined by the confidence and respect felt by subordinates for their superiors; outstanding among the factors promoting such confidence and respect is an unquestioned basis of fairness and objectivity in dealings with subordinates.

9. Members of an organisation cannot be expected to develop a spirit of willing cooperation in its purposes and tasks, unless they are able to anticipate reasonable security of tenure of their membership of that organisation.

10. Discipline means acceptance of the necessary rules or regulations of the enterprise, and is the natural concomitant of high morale: the need for special provisions for 'the maintenance of discipline' is an indication that morale is not adequate.

11. Discipline, as a reflection of high morale, is best attained by fostering the sense of responsibility of subordinates—by enlisting their cooperation in the formulation of the code of regulations and by providing for independent review in cases of alleged grievance or dispute as to the application of that code.

12. However democratic its principles and structure, the level of morale of an organisation (its 'tone') is largely a reflection of the human attitude and outlook of its chief executive.

Appendix III Added value and its use to measure productivity[1]

The main potential uses of the added value indices are in relation to past changes in productivity and to future wage and salary increases. Forecasts can be made of:

1. Money available for future increases.
2. Productivity increases that must be obtained if future increases are to be covered.
3. Future demands for capital if productivity is to be raised to the required level.

Definition

Briefly, the added value for a firm, or for any other organisation, is the value added to materials by the process of production. It also includes the gross margin on any merchanted or factored goods sold.

The main constituents of a company's output and added value are shown in Table 1.III.1.

The added value makes up the fund from which is found wages, salaries, insurance, pensions, hire of plant and machinery, cost of repairs and maintenance, cost of operating road vehicles, rents, rates and taxes, selling expenses, depreciation, profit, and all other similar charges.

Calculation

Added value is obtained by taking:

1. The total value of sales and work done (including the value of merchanted goods sold and of canteen takings if the canteen is run by the firm).
2. Adding the value of stocks at the end of the year.
3. Subtracting: the value of stocks at the beginning of the year;
   the cost of materials and fuel purchased;
   the value of goods purchased for merchanting and for canteen supplies;
   payments for work given out to other firms;
   payments for transport.

An overall portrayal of added value is given in Table 1.III.1, while a possible sheet for determining it is suggested in Table 1.III.2 (opposite).

[1] This text has been prepared and written by R. S. K. Riddle: reproduced by permission of the Author and of Urwick, Orr and Partners.

Table 1.III.1

The concept of
added value

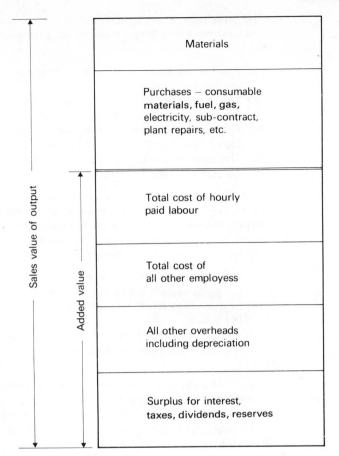

Table 1.III.2

The determination
of added value

Actual Sales	A	
Stock—opening	B	
closing	C	D
Stock to spares		E
TOTAL SALES—ACTUAL		F
Selling Price Variation		G
ADJUSTED SALES		H

(= B − C)

(= A + D + E)

(= F − G)

Purchases—at standard cost	J
(Direct materials, consumable,	
sub-contract, plant repairs	
by outside contract, bank	
interest, etc.)	
Purchase Price Variation	K
Works Expenses	L
Tooling	M
Accruals e.g. gas, telephone	N
TOTAL PURCHASES—ACTUAL	P
Purchase Price Variation	K
ADJUSTED PURCHASES	Q

(= J + ... + N)

(= P − K)

ADDED VALUE—ACTUAL   X   (= F − P)

ADDED VALUE—ADJUSTED   Y   (= H − Q)

Uses of the added value concept

The need for an effective and relatively simple overall measure of productivity has been generally felt for a long time. This need has grown due, for example, to:

(i) The limited application of Work Study schemes and doubts about their long-term stability.
(ii) The increasing number of operators whose pace of work is controlled by machine cycle times or by processes.
(iii) The wish to determine the relative overall productivity of, say, two factories within the same organisation.
(iv) The weakness of using Sales Value as a basis for comparative ratios e.g. Sales/Employee, Sales/Capital Employed.

The concept of added value, as it has been developed during the past few years, has contributed significantly to resolving these problems. It is now possible to review the overall productivity of a factory or of all employees in a more general and searching way, and also to determine its relationship to capital investment and to labour. For example, it becomes possible to:

(i) estimate the additional capital required to achieve a long-term sales programme with only a limited supply of labour;
(ii) forecast how much finance will be available for future wage and salary increases;
(iii) determine whether improvements in productivity are keeping pace with increases in wages and salaries.

Effect of capital intensity

Capital intensity is defined as the capital employed per employee.

In general the greater the capital intensity the greater the potential productivity; e.g. the better the tooling the greater the potential output.

An analysis of figures available from the engineering industry shows the trend that for each additional £1 000 of capital intensity the additional Added Value per Employee is about £300. For industry overall the figure is about £200.

Adjustments based on these figures should always be made if comparisons are required between *labour* productivity rather than between *factory* productivity.

There is no implication that merely injecting more capital will increase productivity. It must be invested in plant or equipment from which an adequate return is forecast. It is therefore essential that there is an effective procedure covering applications for capital expenditure. An element of this procedure should be a minimum level of return on investment.

Determination of productivity trends

A. Basic data required

The basic data required are annual figures of :

1. Added value (see Table 1.III.2).
2. Total number of employees (hourly paid and staff).
3. Total remuneration of all employees.
4. Total hours worked by all employees.
5. Capital employed.

In order to determine the general pattern of productivity development figures are preferably needed for the past four to five years.

B. Methods of
productivity
measurement

Possible measures of productivity using the added value concept are the
following (with further comments on page 159):

1. *Outline*

(a) Added value per employee.
(b) Added value per hour worked.
(c) OFPI (Overall Factory Productivity Index)
    This takes added value per hour worked for successive years, and relates it
    to a reference year value of 100.
(d) OLPI (Overall Labour Productivity Index)
    This is the OFPI adjusted for the effect of changes in Capital Employed from
    the reference year.
(e) FUVI (Factory Unit Value Index). This relates the OFPI to any changes in
    wage and salary levels in order to determine the change in 'net productiv-
    ity'. This index can be interpreted to answer the question, 'Are we giving
    away more in wages and salaries than we gain from *factory* increases in
    productivity?' (See Table 1.III.3.)
(f) LUVI (Labour Unit Value Index). This relates the OLPI to any changes in
    wage and salary levels. The corresponding question is: 'Are we giving
    away more in wages and salaries than we gain from *labour* increases in
    productivity?' (See Table 1.III.4.)

Table 1.III.3
Factory
productivity

I. *Introduction*

This Table contains a worked example of how to determine overall changes in
factory productivity, i.e. changes that take account of the total value of work done,
of the total wages and salaries paid to achieve this output, and of the productivity
that can come from investing more money in the business.

The productivity changes that arise from labour alone, i.e. excluding the effect of
increased investment, are covered in the next Table (Table 1.III.4).

II. *Added value*

	Year 1	Year 2	Year 3	Year 4
Added value (£000s)	2 032	1 921	2 274	2 652
No. of employees	1 655	1 625	1 570	1 490
Added value/employees	1 228	1 182	1 459	1 781

III. *Hourly pay*

	Year 1	Year 2	Year 3	Year 4
Total pay (£000s)	1 210	1 278	1 280	1 292
Total hours (000s)	2 357	2 310	2 234	2 121
Pay/hour (£/hr)	0·504	0·553	0·573	0·609

IV. *Productivity*

A. Overall Factory Productivity Index (OFPI)

The OFPI is based on the added value per man hour, i.e. Added value ÷ Total
hours in a particular reference year.

For example, for Year 1 above,

$$\text{AV/man hour} = \frac{2\,032}{2\,357} = 0·863$$

This can be used as the reference year by dividing into the corresponding figures
for subsequent years as follows:

	Year 1	Year 2	Year 3	Year 4
AV/man hour	0·863	0·832	1·018	1·250
OFPI	100	96	118	145

These figures indicate that after an initial setback productivity has improved
significantly.

B. Factory Unit Value Index (FUVI)

The FUVI sets out to relate the changes in added value to changes (increases) in wage and salary rates in order to determine whether the 'net productivity' (FUVI) which includes the effect of changes in capital employed, is improving or deteriorating.

$$FUVI = \frac{\text{Added value per employee}}{\text{Average hourly pay rate}}$$

compared with a reference year as follows:

	Year 1	Year 2	Year 3	Year 4
(AV/employee) ÷ (Average hourly rate)	2 437	2 138	2 547	2 925
FUVI	100	88	104	120

These figures show that the effect of increasing wages and salaries has been to halve the 'net' improvement in productivity of the factory.

But there has been an unknown—at this stage—contribution to improved productivity from capital investment. It is important to determine this contribution before deciding whether to increase wages and salaries further (see Table 1.III.4).

Table 1.III.4
Labour
productivity

This Table takes the figures used in Table 1.III.3 to determine changes in overall *factory* productivity and demonstrates how to determine changes in overall *labour* productivity.

Effect of capital employed

The effect of increasing the capital employed per employee by £1 000 is, on average in the engineering industry, to increase the added value per employee by about £300. Hence corresponding adjustments must be made to a company's annual figures of added value per employee and the capital employed changes in order to determine true changes in labour productivity. The figures in Table 1.III.3 must therefore be adjusted as follows:

	Year 1	Year 2	Year 3	Year 4
Capital employed (£000s)	4 470	4 612	4 910	5 300
Capital employed per employee (£)	2 700	2 840	3 130	3 560
Change since Year 1		140	430	860
Added value per employee (£)—original	1 228	1 182	1 459	1 781
Adjustment (− 0·3 of change in CE/employee since Year 1)		−42	−129	−258
Revised AV/employee	1 228	1 140	1 330	1 523

Labour Unit Value Index (LUVI)

The LUVI sets out to determine how overall *labour* productivity is changing in relation to changes in the overall pay rate.

$$LUVI = \frac{\text{Added value/employee adjusted for changes in CE}}{\text{Average hourly pay rate}}$$

compared with a reference period.

The example of Table 1.III.3 is reworked as follows:

	Year 1	Year 2	Year 3	Year 4
Adjusted AV/employee (£)	1 228	1 140	1 330	1 523
Average hourly pay rate (£/hr)	0·504	0·553	0·573	0·609
(AV/employee − (Hourly pay rate)	2 437	2 062	2 321	2 500
LUVI	100	85	95	103

These should be compared with the very much more optimistic figures of:

	Year 1	Year 2	Year 3	Year 4
OFPI	100	96	118	145
FUVI	100	88	104	120

2. Added value per employee	The added value, unadjusted for the effect of capital intensity, is divided by the total number of employees, hourly-paid and staff. It is an absolute figure that can be used to compare the productivities of different factories, organisations, or industries. This is an overall figure, and ignores the positive effect on productivity of increased capital intensity and the negative effect of increased wages and salaries. There can also be some distortion due to the effect of different working hours.
3. Added value per hour worked	The added value, unadjusted for the effect of capital intensity, is divided by the total number of hours worked. This is an absolute figure serving the same general purpose as added value per employee but taking account of the different hours worked. It therefore puts in a more realistic light the contribution to added value made by the hourly paid.
4. OFPI (Overall Factory Productivity Index)	OFPI for Year $N = \dfrac{\text{(Added value per hour worked} - \text{Year } N)}{\text{(Added value per hour worked} - \text{Year } 1)} \times 100$ The object of this index is to demonstrate relative changes of productivity *within* a factory or organisation. Comparisons between units will only demonstrate differences in rates of change of productivity. This is an overall figure incorporating the effects of changes in Capital Intensity and in wage and salary rates. An example is given in Table 1.III.3.
5. OLPI (Overall Labour Productivity Index)	This index is the OFPI adjusted for the effects of changes in capital intensity but not for changes in wage and salary rates. An example is given in Table 1.III.4.
6. FUVI (Factory Unit Value Index)	This relates Added Value per man hour to the average hourly rate. (FUVI for Year N) = (OFPI for Year N) $\times \dfrac{\text{(Average hourly rate} - \text{Year } 1)}{\text{(Average hourly rate} - \text{Year } N)} \times 100.$ The index therefore demonstrates whether the growth in *factory* productivity is keeping pace with the growth in wages and salaries. For example, if the index is over 100, the productivity growth is keeping ahead of the growth in wages and salaries. An example is given in Table 1.III.3.
7. LUVI (Labour Unit Value Index)	This index is the FUVI adjusted for the effects of changes in capital intensity. It is the best available indicator of changes in overall labour productivity. It brings together the contributions to productivity from everybody within the organisation. An example is given in Table 1.III.4.

PART TWO Marketing

by C. G. A. Godley

1 The marketing operation

The modern approach to marketing is a concept of business based on two aspects:

If a business is to exist, or to continue, it must identify and satisfy customer needs and do this profitably. From this view, the overall strategy proceeds to the point that this attitude involves the whole company, because everyone in the company is involved in selling and satisfying customers as well as in making the highest profit for the enterprise and using the resources of the company as efficiently as possible to this end. No one section can arrogate to itself this responsibility which is what all business is about. This concept of marketing is therefore a corporate affair and the philosophy behind it must be understood by management at all levels. In effect this means that marketing involves finance, production, research, development, distribution and selling procedures.

The second aspect of marketing is concerned with techniques and tools and with those activities expressly designed to satisfy the needs of a company operating correctly in accordance with the ideas described in the above statement on overall strategy. This study of the functional aspect of marketing will be considered in the following areas:

Marketing activities. These will include market research, product research, product planning, sales analysis, sales forecasting, sales promotion and distribution.

Marketing management. It is basic to marketing that all marketing considerations and all marketing activities must be integrated into the work of the company. The importance of marketing as a functional approach should be recognised by the company and this marketing attitude should be actively pursued. A company dare not passively wait to see what happens in its market.

Marketing techniques. There are four major types of technique used in marketing:

- Techniques used to inform a company about a market and about customer acceptance of its products. How all this statistical information is collected together and put into a meaningful form for the company is one of the tasks of market research.
- Techniques used to create an impact on a market, to inject demand for a product, to influence consumer awareness and demand. There is a constant

market/product relationship to be observed. These techniques include:
pricing
product planning
advertising
public relations
sales promotional techniques.

● Techniques used to analyse and interpret the results of marketing activities. These are very important in determining the marketing mix and price/volume relationships. Every aspect of the marketing activities followed should be examined in figures and facts so that advantage can be taken of successful moves or remedial action taken to avoid failures.

● Techniques based on practical skills both in market research in the field or sales promotional work in personal selling or advertising. A great deal of marketing technique of this kind is thus practical knowledge that comes from working with salesmen, copy writers, market analysts and so on.

These marketing activities and techniques are discussed at length in later chapters.

A definition

It is advantageous to have a definition of marketing and there is none better than that given by the Institute of Marketing:

> *Marketing is the management function which organises and directs all the business activities involved in assessing and converting customer purchasing power into effective demand for a specific product or service, and in moving the product or service to the final consumer or user so as to achieve the profit target or other objectives set by the company.*

Economic derivation

To understand clearly the essential nature of the marketing task it is helpful to turn momentarily to economics and particularly to see how modern macroeconomics have developed from ideas formerly held about the relation of production and consumption. The classic view based on the theories of Jean Baptiste Say held that supply always created its own demand. It was felt that the total production could always be absorbed by the market, so that overproduction and general unemployment were alike impossible. Both Keynes and the classicists proceeded from the view that the national product, as it is produced, itself gives rise to the creation of money that will buy the product.

The traditional approach to economics has been an enquiry into four aspects of society: production, distribution, exchange and consumption. Until the First World War production was held to be the critical factor in society and consumption was accorded a passive role in economic studies. The beginning of modern marketing thinking arrived with the realisation that mass production is of no practical interest unless modern production techniques can be matched by the possibility of large-scale consumption which depends on the ability to increase the marketability of the output.

Whether the market will in fact buy the goods it has created gives rise to new theories and it is here that old and new ideas of economics diverge. It is seen that consumption depends on the national income, the distribution of income (expenditure, savings), the quantity of money in the hands of households, and the amount of taxes. The consumer has a choice between spending and saving and a choice in how and where the money is spent. Similarly overinvestment in any particular industry is seen to produce more goods than the market could absorb in a multiplier effect because the equilibrium between the amount of goods and money produced had been disturbed. From a marketing point of view the conclusion is that to produce goods that do not correspond to market requirements either from the point of view of consumer needs or consumer ability to pay is disastrous and, in fact, antisocial. A company must discover what a market wants, and anticipate new tastes and habits. Before articles can be made for sale a closer examination of the market is required and this is the beginning of the present marketing attitude.

In the 1950s and the 1960s more countries became industrially developed and new giants in the commercial world, especially Japan and Russia, made their presence felt. A considerable part of the technological effort of all countries was directed towards the creation of machines to produce finished goods of all kinds faster, cheaper and, if possible, better. Industry sought for economy of scale. The old ideas of selling and advertising were not enough to sell goods that were already overproduced beyond the total market requirement. Not all the sales promotion in the world could make people eat more bread. But wheat in other forms, cereals in other presentations, ready-to-eat breakfast foods, these the market could take, and sales of these products rose dramatically.

It can be seen therefore that consumption begins with problems of choice for the consumer, firstly as to what he chooses to do with his money, whether to save or spend it and in what way to spend it. Secondly there is the choice of how to allocate the money spent, and this depends on what his needs are, how available products can satisfy his needs and what one product can do more than another, for the same price. This leads to the most important factor of product differential, or product plus as marketing men usually call it, around which sales promotional compaigns are built.

| Production *versus* consumption | There is a further consideration of this production and consumption view of marketing that has already been mentioned in Part One (see pages 24–6). Each company exists as a means of satisfying consumer demand on the one hand, and as a means of employment and a source of purchase money on the other hand. Its employees are both producers and consumers. At times when the needs of the market are overlooked in favour of the producers' demands, reactionary forces such as consumerism set in to emphasise a fact that all marketing men know to be true. A market will not long continue to take goods or services produced without heed to the market requirements solely to keep people in employment. |

| Industrial and consumer products | One other aspect of marketing must be mentioned here since it is of great importance. Marketing is falsely assumed in some quarters to be concerned solely with sales operations such as selling packets of corn flakes, or soap, and |

with commercial television. Nothing is further from the truth. Industrial products demand just as much painstaking study and preparation of market conditions and requirements as consumer products, especially in working out long-term strategic studies. This question of industrial marketing will be treated further later in this section.

The marketing process

Four important marketing activities are here briefly examined before a review of the whole marketing operation is made. Research into consumer habits and requirements is the beginning of the exercise, but this, in itself, is complicated and, at best, the examination of conditions that change as they are observed. Such analysis therefore must be continuous if trends and developments are to be recognised and correctly interpreted. The definition of a market and what marketing understands by the term is made in the next chapter. Here it is sufficient to say that markets may be considered as any group of buyers and sellers in reasonably close contact or communication.

Research into the market

1. Customer requirements, in goods, services, benefits. New demands thrown up by changing habits or new techniques.
2. Reasons for buying. What motivates people to buy new machinery, new consumer goods?
3. Segmentation and channels of distribution.
4. Long-term trends.

In analysing market changes and in trying to find market demands that are unsatisfied a company must primarily be concerned with goods within its scope of manufacture. A company mainly interested in the manufacture of large diameter welded steel piping for the flow of oil from one place to another would be deeply involved in the development of North Sea underwater fields and similar projects, but not interested in constructional jobs outside these areas. A company must be primarily concerned with goods for which it possesses adequate production facilities and technical experience.

Product management and strategy

These days it is accepted that all products live through phases of introduction, growth and aftermath. Profits on goods are eroded by the effect of competition, or the passage of time and managing a product range to give a company the highest profitability becomes an important task falling within the marketing ideas.

The system of distribution

In almost every country in Europe, and certainly in America, the costs of physical distribution have increased rapidly during the past ten years. The major cost in selling goods in America is not the cost of transporting goods from say, London to New York, but the cost of services required in bringing the goods from New York to the customer. Transportation, warehousing, merchandising, jobbing, selling, brokering all add their percentage to the final cost. Europe is fast developing in this pattern and the efficient management of distribution is obviously an area where profitability can be improved. It requires far more than transport management.

Profitability

Pricing strategy is obviously a key marketing function but marketing has a wider responsibility for profitability than that resulting from pricing policies. Formal profit planning is now accepted as a worthwhile exercise in companies that have the personnel resources to carry it out. Basic to profit planning on a long term company scale is a deep marketing involvement in supplying goods that the market needs which can be sold with the required profit margins, an efficient distribution system, and a product range using a company's manufacturing capacities to the full. But above all, and as a prerequisite to all other actions, it must seek to serve and satisfy customers.

Marketing today

At this point it can perhaps be restated clearly that the total marketing concept is concerned with the optimum use of the total resources of a company so that maximum profitability follows. It therefore demands continuing market sensitivity, maximum plant utilisation and an intelligent and persistent selling effort. How these factors are merged into one corporate effort is one of the tasks of top management. It is true that in some companies the term 'marketing' is used in the narrower sense of *activities within a market* directed to aid the selling side in its task, that is, packaging, presentation, advertising, merchandising. But clearly marketing is responsible for market intelligence; that is, the collection and processing of timely information about the market, and interpretation of these facts for the company. It is responsible for suggesting patterns of response from the company in the shape of estimates of what should be made and sold and at what price these goods should be sold and how they should be distributed. And it does all these things against a constantly changing background. Sometimes if the company is powerful enough, or introduces a new process far in advance of anyone else, the company itself changes the background. Note for example the introduction of a vegetable-based 'creamer' for use in tea and coffee instead of dairy cream, that has created a new industry overnight. (The company that began this industry in Buffalo, New York State, has 90 per cent of the market that has been built up in the last ten years. The company claims that the new product, a vegetable-based, non-dairy liquid creamer is a functionally superior replacement for cream.)

It is true that there has been a certain amount of overselling of the idea, and today reactions can be seen, in some cases quite strong, against the concept of marketing. These reactions stem largely from misunderstanding of what this concept really is, and in come cases against examples furnished by bad application of marketing ideas. In some companies there are two parallel systems, sales and marketing. The sales section deals with line management in selling, while marketing deals with market analysis, presentation, sales promotion and advertising.

Two possibilities will illustrate the position of marketing in some companies today. In many small to medium-sized companies there is no clearly defined marketing function. There is selling, there is new product development, and when somebody has the time there is a certain amount of market analysis. The company is usually so busy selling that no one has the time to examine the market critically and to realise that dramatic changes are taking place in habits and distribution. So when changes come, this type of company, while making excellent products and managing a first class sales force, is always several places behind its major competitors. Its new products tend to be 'me-too' products and when major distributive changes occur it joins in the new pattern several years late.

The other danger occurs at the opposite end of the scale, and the larger the companies the greater the danger. Management in a large company may become a highly specialised function and the larger the company the more specialised management functions may become. Specialisation is such that a feeling of isolation is part of the burden of the company man. In such large organisations there is always a danger that sales and marketing men may pursue different policies.

Sometimes sales people in such large organisations may actually mount sales campaigns not strictly in accordance with marketing ideas held by their colleagues in other parts of the company.

In the first case no one recognised the importance of the marketing aspects of a company and in the second case the marketing activities were not efficiently integrated in the work of the company.

The marketing operation	However, within these two extremes it is now generally accepted that this total marketing concept is essential to the successful conduct of business affairs today and the principle holds good for all businesses of any size and character although the application of the principles will differ according to the nature and development of the company concerned. There are five elements to the conduct of a marketing operation.
1. *Market research*	Market research will include, among other things: ● Research into the market, including questions of consumption and motivation; the segmentation of the market and the development of new markets; channels of distribution and major changes in buying patterns. ● Evaluation of the present product range. ● An estimation of future trends and requirements so that short term actions do not put the future at risk. ● Information on competitors activities, products, methods, and the impact of competitors on the market. *Note. Marketing research* endeavours to analyse the whole of the elements in the overall marketing operation; *market research* is the analysis of the market in all its aspects.
2. *Product development*	Evaluating the standing of existing products and identifying the need for new products. Assisting in the production of these new goods or services to meet customer requirements.

3. *Marketing planning*

This will include amongst other things:

● Assessment of market requirements.
● Survey of company resources especially with a view to long term development.
● Evaluation of a new product range.
● Projected profitability of range.

4. *Selling*

All those activities concerned with the actual sale of goods, pricing, selling, sales promotion, advertising, merchandising.

5. *Control*

Since marketing exists in order that the company should supply goods required by customers for sale at a profit, targets and objectives must be established and procedures for planning and control within the terms of the overall marketing scheme must be maintained. Control must provide a continuous feedback to the management centre of the company: this is but a specific instance of the "feedback cycle" inherent in the process of management (see Part One, page 33).

Marketing responsibilities

Marketing is obviously a top management responsibility and most companies would see top management structure built on this foundation:

BOARD OF DIRECTORS

Managing Director

Finance Executive   Marketing Executive   Production Executive

and indeed this is the classical foundation for most companies. The Marketing Executive must understand the following factors:

1. Markets and products. Control of the whole activity demands constant feedback and periodic appraisal of the totality of the marketing operation. The Marketing Executive will need this appraisal in order to consider matters such as new product development or product modifications and the development of marketing plans as they affect sales, advertising and sales promotion. In all this, in all that he does, he begins from a customer requirement, a customer service, and works backwards to his manufacturing plant.
2. He will live in the markets in which the company operates, he will know his customers and endeavour at least to follow continuously changes in taste, in distribution, or new customer trends.
3. The financial involvement of his company. He will know the targets and actual return on capital invested in the business. He will be aware of the present capital structure and the forecast capital requirements in the long term. He knows the liquid assets to current liabilities and knows, too, the future financial commitments towards which he must work. He is concerned with earnings per share and cash flow, and when shareholders can

complain that the company's money would give higher yields in the Post Office he must answer this too. In summary he carries a great deal of the responsibility to the company for adequate return on capital and the accretion of adequate financial resources.

4. The implications of production in terms of contribution and labour usage. He will be aware of the labour situation in his factory or factory units. He will seek a balance between labour and financial resources knowing that one of the worst areas for loss in a company is plant that is not fully utilised, or too high a production of scrap or faulty material.

The establishment of the system

In most companies, marketing activities have always existed, although they are sometimes not known as such and usually not assembled into one system. Sales analysis, pricing, product development, which are all marketing activities, are generally found under the headings of accounts, finance and production. The problem of altering the shape of the organisation and altering, in so doing, the pattern of personal relationships that have previously existed is a delicate task to be undertaken with care. A company must arrange a new pattern for distribution of responsibilities and also lay down clear procedures for planning and control. What it has to do is threefold:

to regroup present activities so that marketing functions come into a marketing system;

to add on to this base those marketing functions which are necessary but have not previously appeared;

then either to appoint senior and junior management to control these activities or train present management for these duties.

This can best be illustrated by a simple management diagram which is shown in Fig. 2.1.1 in two models, A and B. In both patterns the activities are precisely the same but whereas A is the usual pre-marketing pattern, B shows the disposition of the activities under the marketing concept.

These charts can be varied; some companies for example put R and D under marketing. Eventually sales analysis is replaced by market research (or rather added to the wider duties of market research embracing, amongst other things, sales analysis) and marketing also includes Financial Analysis and Long-term Planning. The company can add to the marketing list at will according to the nature of its work, for example, Packaging or Design, After-sales Service, Product Presentation and so on. But the diagrams will serve to show how a system concerned with marketing can be established within a company.

Delegation of responsibilities

The Marketing Executive is responsible for the overall thrust and direction of the whole marketing effort. This can only be accomplished efficiently by the delegation of marketing responsibilities to managers and by building the group concerned into an integrated team. The objective is a balanced group whose work is coordinated and conducted in such a manner that the overall marketing effort goes forward as one controlled operation.

There can be no standard pattern since each company will develop the structure most suitable to its needs, but delegation of responsibilities helps to create the structure specific to the company and provides a framework within

Fig. 2.1.1
Distribution
of management
responsibilities

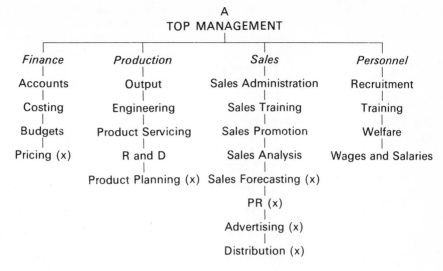

A
TOP MANAGEMENT

Finance	*Production*	*Sales*	*Personnel*
Accounts	Output	Sales Administration	Recruitment
Costing	Engineering	Sales Training	Training
Budgets	Product Servicing	Sales Promotion	Welfare
Pricing (x)	R and D	Sales Analysis	Wages and Salaries
	Product Planning (x)	Sales Forecasting (x)	
		PR (x)	
		Advertising (x)	
		Distribution (x)	

Activities marked (x) are placed under marketing in diagram B.

B
TOP MANAGEMENT

Finance	*Production*	Marketing		*Personnel*
Accounts	Output	*Marketing* Services	*Selling* Services	Recruitment
Costing	Engineering	Sales Analysis	Sales Administration	Training
Budgets	R and D	Sales Forecasting	Sales Training	Welfare
	Product Servicing	Product Planning	Sales Promotion	Wages and Salaries
		Pricing		
		Advertising		
		Public Relations		
		Distribution		

which the work can proceed. Firstly, therefore, in any company there must be delegation of responsibilities, by management job descriptions. The Marketing Executive must begin by defining what jobs need to be done and by whom they should be done.

It can be stated that in smaller firms it is the practice for market research to be centralised; in larger companies, it is usual to find separate research sections to cover the needs of different products or different company divisions. If however a start is made with a centralised research operation, the division of responsibilities can be seen. The division made here between various sections will vary from company to company but the principles of the job description are valid for any type of company.

The diagram (Fig. 2.1.2) shows the major responsibilities on the two chief sides of the marketing section of a company.

Fig. 2.1.2
Marketing
responsibilities

MARKETING EXECUTIVE

Marketing Services	*Sales Services*
Market Research	Sales Administration
Product Research	Sales Operations (Field)
Forecasting and Statistics	Head Office Sales
Financial Analysis (Pricing)	Sales Training
R and D	Merchandising
Advertising (Packaging)	Customer Technical Services
Sales Promotions	
Public Relations	
Distribution	

The fuller details of each part of the marketing responsibilities can now be considered. These groupings are not fixed and can be varied to suit the individual requirements of separate companies. A number of separate sections are suggested. In some companies these responsibilities will be found in fewer sections, or even in one or two sections only. Nevertheless, the principles underlying these responsibilities remain and build up the total marketing activity.

Market research

Staff will include statistician, librarian, market research supervisor, sales analyst, market analyst.

This section is responsible for market analysis in depth and interpretation of the analysis; this means constantly surveying market performance and potential and constant attention to market structure. Awareness of the emergence of new markets or new segments involves covering all necessary facets of market and consumer research. It also means endeavouring to quantify market potentials, or new products, and endeavouring to detect future prospects and the underlying reasons for observed trends.

Product research

Staff will include statistician, technical librarian, product research supervisor, technical members as required by the product.

This section is responsible for study and analysis of technical developments and, in conjunction with R and D, evaluating the use of new materials and new processes. It studies company and competitive products and competitive technical literature, and in some cases will use teardown methods. It also studies the product range performance as reported by the sales side and conducts a continuous study of customer complaints. As part of product planning it studies characteristics and performance of present and new products with a continuous evaluation of these factors. This entails field trials or placement tests of new products and a study of outlets for new products.

In some companies, it will also be concerned, in conjunction with advertising and distribution, in the technical side of packaging, the study of materials used for packing, film, wood, plastics, foam, to observe their performance, cost and suitability.

Research and development

In this section the staff will consist of technical people skilled in branches of knowledge required by the company, physicists, chemists, engineers, mathematicians and so on. The work usually proceeds in research laboratories where full experimental facilities are available and the work goes on in close association with the product research section. (In some companies the two sections are merged.)

The major responsibilities of this section are keeping up to date (a continuous process) with (1) new materials and processes; (2) new manufacturing techniques and product features. In conjunction with other marketing services sections, a continuous survey of

- Performances of present products.
- Modifications, improvements of present products.
- Performances and details of competitive products.
- Customer complaints.

This section is the clearing centre for the study of all suggestions and new ideas received from all sources, and all brain-storming ideas related to the company, its methods, its products or ideas widely divergent from these. It takes ideas from all sources and from all activities and acts as a screening process.

Forecasting and statistics

This section, when it exists, is really a statistical library, which in some companies is found as part of the section dealing with financial and cost analysis. The staff will include people trained in statistical method.

The major responsibility of this section is the maintenance of complete statistical records necessary for the marketing sections, including company statistics, national statistics, and industry statistics; details of customer requirements and buying patterns. The section will also provide data to help in forecasting sales and distribution patterns and to quantify market potentials. It works very closely with the market research section, and in so doing helps to set quotas or targets and suggests profitable areas for selling activities.

Financial analysis

Most of the staff of this section will be accountants trained in modern management accountancy methods.

The responsibilities of the section are twofold: a control activity (in conjunction with statistical section), and an activity which provides a financial measurement of all the marketing activities of the company. The section will study company costs and price records. It will study company and competitors' accounts (trading accounts and balance sheets). It is responsible for recognising and isolating profitable and unprofitable areas. It endeavours to assess the profitability of new ventures, or new products. It suggests action to improve the marketing mix.

It has a special responsibility to help the marketing executive in price fixing. Considerations of pricing/sales volume/profitability form a continuous study.

Distribution

The staff of this section will be transport executives and statisticians.

Responsibilities cover the study of distribution within a market (that is to say, analysis of market segments, market buying patterns) in conjunction with the market research section, and the study of physical distribution problems (warehouse location, storage methods, materials handling facilities, stock control and transportation).

The section is therefore responsible for a continuous study of markets to observe patterns of distribution and to define market segments not fully satisfied or new market avenues opening up. It is responsible for transport operating returns and reports and returns on stock levels and productivity (where multi-depot systems are involved).

Advertising, sales promotion and public relations

These sections are treated as one although in most companies they are split up, in different ways according to the nature of the company. They are, however, all concerned with one overriding responsibility: selling by impact on the market. The staff will be people trained in the many techniques that are concerned with the advertising and sales promotional world.

The responsibility of this section is the study and selection of the best methods of advertising and sales promotion. This includes the study of all company and competitive advertising methods and sales promotional aids, discount terms, selling rates, distributor allowances, and details of past sales campaigns. It includes selection of all special advertising and selling techniques, premiums, special gifts, dealer franchises; the selection of the media most suitable for the company, trade press, dailies, weeklies, monthlies, TV and so on.

In conjunction with the product research section it will be responsible for new packaging and new presentations as regards graphics, colour, style.

The overriding responsibility is to see that the advertising and sales promotional methods employed are not only the most productive for the company but are contained each year within the limits set down by the marketing budget.

Marketing objectives: a summary

A company which views its problems as part of an overall marketing operation, faces the future with positive action because it is *planning* for the future and not just drifting. Such a company is aware of the need for change and lives in an atmosphere that facilitates and welcomes the mechanism for change. This attitude demands and encourages freer communication between departments. This in turn helps in a freer interchange of ideas. Thorough planning, which is an essential part of marketing, demands and encourages higher standards, especially in a continuous effort to obtain the highest skills in management, particularly in long term planning techniques.

Mass production, *per se*, is not marketing. Because marketing takes into account the whole sum of all the activities of an enterprise, it constantly reverts to considerations of the totality of the effort, the maximum use of resources, the maximum profitability of the enterprise. It returns always to the key questions of service to customers and thence to maximum productivity and so to maximum profit.

Marketing serves to show the answers to four basic questions:

1. *What is the basic character of the company?* What are its strengths and weaknesses? Are top management, middle management and lower management soundly established, efficient, compatible with each other, and all agreeing with the long term plans for the company and the steps necessary to achieve these steps? If there are problems in management at some point or other (and usually in most companies, there always are) what plans has the company drawn up for dealing with these problems? Or do they just slide? Each company must work out its own salvation.

2. *How is top management control exercised?* How is the company run? There must be one chief executive and this man must know precisely what he is doing. There must be a framework of speedy decisions on problems that matter and not an atmosphere of notes and reports circulating endlessly from one department to another whilst nothing is decided.

3. *Where does the money come from?* Where is our real business? Are we shipbuilders or are we constructors in metal and wood? Could we make, instead of ships, offshore oil rigs, offshore terminals or submarine piping? Is all our money caught up in an industry that is dying and, if so, what can we do about it? Should we sell out and go into another industry, or another location?

A company must constantly examine its markets and its products and their relation and inter-reaction. A company can be making firstclass products for a market that has changed. Plastics have changed the nature of many markets previously using metals. Transistors and new electronic equipment have changed the size and shape of all electrical apparatus. Computer installations become progressively smaller.

4. *Is our management correct for our kind of company at its present stage of development?* The management structure needed for a company with a turnover of £400 million annually would be unnecessary for a company with a turnover of £40 million annually and probably disastrous for a company with a turnover of £4 million annually.

In summary, it can be seen therefore that marketing as it is now known has evolved as a consequence of social and commercial conditions during the last thirty years to become a specialist function of top management. It has been grossly misunderstood and confusion has followed discussion as to the actual meaning of the word. It has too often been construed superficially as the activities of selling, presentation and advertising, and indeed, sometimes the terms of advertising men and marketing men are held to be synonymous. But these activities are but a small, although important, part of the whole scheme. Marketing enables a company to adapt itself constantly to meet a changing background.

2 Marketing research

It has been seen that no management can move safely in a market without knowledge of the market and this means, in practical terms, that a company has to inform itself as precisely as possible on four major areas:

The general background of social and political events and economic trends. Government policy affecting taxation or money supply or industrial relations is particularly important.

The specific background of the market in which the company moves, its size, its composition and what is happening to it. Market trends and requirements. Market segmentation.

Product research including evaluation of present products and new product possibilities.

Distribution analysis—selling, advertising, promoting.

In this chapter an attempt is made in some detail to describe in a practical manner how these various tasks are tackled. It can be readily understood that the information just mentioned can reach a company in three ways, which constitute three basic avenues for source material:

1. Data derived from internal operations. This means quantitative information from the company sections, produced within the company:
   - financial intelligence on costs, profits, sales;
   - production intelligence on capacity, plant, utilisation, raw materials, storage and materials handling facilities, manpower;
   - market intelligence on selling organisation, distributive systems and warehousing, stock levels, terms, discounts, prices, sales promotional and advertising activities;
   - personnel intelligence on numbers, labour turnover, training, organisation.

   Since all this measurable information is produced within a company, all that is necessary is to establish what is required and to arrange for circulation of the information or collection by one central section or agency which would probably be the market research section.

2. Data derived from market research conducted outside the company. Sales and distribution records, consumer research or user research, sales promotional research and product research, warehouse location and distribution analysis. Some of this information will come from trade associations and published government statistics such as *Monthly Digest of Statistics* or from the *Census of Production and Distribution*. Some research will be

purchased data from market research agencies either to give market information on competing brands, stocks, sales, displays and so on or consumer information broken down by demographic details such as age, sex, location or consumer preferences.

The need for such outside research work would be discussed with the marketing manager or executive who would decide, probably in consultation with the company advertising agency, which research to undertake and the specialist research agency to employ.

3. Environmental studies of social, political, economic and business trends. This information comes from government publications, from bodies such as the *National Institute of Economic and Social Research,* from special government-sponsored committees, from financial, economic and statistical newspapers and so on.

It will speedily be acknowledged that a great deal of information, from sources inside and outside of the company, is available to the market research section, once the wheels have been set in motion and, generally speaking, no market research section has time to study and assimilate all of it. Selection of material and priority of tasks is therefore essential because from the great mass of information available the market research men have to provide the company with reports in meaningful form of immediate significance. This section is concerned to examine what is meaningful, how priorities should be established and how reports should be prepared.

The overall framework

Research into the total marketing environment and research into aspects of the market are carried on permanently.

This can be an enthralling and sometimes fascinating activity because conditions are always changing. A market that has, in total, been static for years, may have segments within it that show dramatic gains and losses. This therefore is the beginning of the task and this chapter will be concerned with the following divisions of the subject:

The overall pattern
- Market research
- Desk research
- Examples—A time scheme for market research
          A brand manager's work sheet
          Research report for Product A

Various aspects of research and research outside a company
- Field research
- Consumer goods
- Industrial products
- Quantitative methods
- Behavioural science

Presentation of reports
- Sources for information

Business models

Market research

Each company will need to examine, for itself, the following factors:

Research into the market

The composition of the market. The size of the market and market potentials. Customer requirements and how they may be met. Customer attitudes and characteristics. Competitors' shares and activities; as many facts as possible.

Research into the company response to the market

The selling pattern, the sales organisation and promotional methods. The marketing mix most suitable for the company, and this will be subject to change.

The product range

The company needs a separate evaluation of the present range and proposed new products. Some attempt should be made to ascertain how well the present range of products answers today's market requirement. The company should try to evaluate an ideal product for today and tomorrow even if no company so far has produced this.

The pricing policy

The pricing policy should be under constant review. There must be sufficient margins to satisfy the company needs for cash flow.

The system of distribution

As conditions within the market change, costs escalate and margins change, so that the pattern of selling and distribution must respond to the new costs. Distribution systems must therefore be under constant scrutiny.

Market research: costs

In practical terms, a great deal of the information just described can be obtained with no great expense and without special work commissioned from outside research agencies. (A list of sources of information is given in Table 2.2.2 on page 200.) For example, a company that makes biscuits can find out from its trade association the total market divided into varieties, and an annual record to show trends within the market. From the Ministry of Agriculture, Fisheries and Food it can observe figures for consumption of foodstuffs, by different regions, by households and by social class (National Food Survey).

From the Economist Intelligence Unit, periodical surveys can be purchased showing brand shares of the total market and discounting trends. So far very little has been spent but if the company wishes at this stage to do so, it can purchase from an agency such as Nielsen a comprehensive survey of the market showing brand shares and company shares in great detail.

Details of selling and marketing, and surveys of the product are all obtainable within the company and from company records. These details together with figures on distribution will all come from internal research. All that needs to be done is to gather the information, collect the facts into a report having meaning for the company, analysing the facts, with comments, where necessary.

Once reports have been submitted to management these can be studied in the marketing section and can be used by them as a base for the establishment of the marketing plan. This usually begins with sales forecasting (which is discussed in greater detail in chapter 4 of this Part) and forms part of a marketing programme for three or four years on a rolling basis. This means that the marketing programme is considered in its effect always over a period of three to four years by continuously adding on estimates for a further period to replace the period that has elapsed. (This point is taken further in chapter 4 dealing with overall marketing management.)

Market research:
scope and sources

Market research can now be examined in greater detail. Some market research is usually carried out in all companies although it is not always found grouped in one section. For example all companies possess sales records of various kinds, and records of customer complaints, or customer requests. Many companies have detailed analysis records of development ideas and what happened to them.

One of the first jobs of management in marketing is to collate this information into a system which fits into the market research pattern. Market research information falls broadly into two categories, and research is both internal and external:

1. Collection of facts. These are mostly figures of sales, agencies, service agreements, distribution facilities. Details of complaints.
2. Collection of opinions, attitudes, feelings.

(There is also a further use of research in connection with test launching of new products.)

Every business has a mine of information within its own records (usually sales, transport and distribution, and production) and within the records of its own industry. Research may, in fact, reveal gaps in these records. From the company's own records the following facts are assembled:

Distribution

Sales trends, sales costs, sales organisation.
Customer pattern and distribution system.
Profitability measured by product and by volume.
Delivery costs, depot systems.
Imbalance between production and selling, overloaded periods and low activity periods.

Production

Resources utilisation, manufacturing patterns.
Volume, capacity, limiting factors.
Manpower.
Storage facilities and materials handling ability.

Financial aspects   Profitability, product mix, selling and promotional costs. The overall task is to establish the following facts about the company:

- Product performance and profitability.
- The most lucrative areas of distribution. A record of the difference in volume and profit between the best and worst salesmen, areas and products.
- The most unfavourable aspects of sales; complaints of products, delivery, service.
- The biggest and most profitable customers.
- The least profitable customers (sometimes also the biggest).

In conjunction with the financial sections marketing will know therefore the product mix and contribution per product. This is required to know where money really comes from. The need is to have all these facts to see the business as it really is and to see how overheads and costs can be carried. It is asserted that market research first showed the newspaper world the financial facts of life and how a paper could have a daily circulation of over one million copies and still not pay its way.

Desk research   Market research is divided into two categories: *desk research*, which means information obtained from written or published sources both within and without the company; and *field research*, which usually means work within a market carried out for specific purposes.
    Desk research includes the following elements:

General background—from published sources, outside the company, industry figures; economic, social or political moves of consequence to the company.

Specific background—from sources within the company.

- Sales records, moving annual totals by areas, by salesmen, by distribution, by class of customer. Methods and channels of distribution. Market segmentation.
- Product complaints, service complaints, servicing records.
- Product records. Records in terms of profits and volume. Product mix.
- Production records. Labour demands and resources. Value analysis.

There is a great deal of vital information hidden in company records or available in published records easily obtainable by any company. Certainly all this desk work should be attempted before any effort is made to undertake outside original field work, which is highly specialised and very expensive.
    From the market analysis resulting from desk research a company should be able therefore to build up a picture of internal and external facts:

- Trends in the market. What is happening to the market and to the company share of the market.
- Competitors' activities. New moves and developments outside the company.
- The weaknesses and strengths of the company and the company products.
- Developments in the distribution system. Lapses in the company distribution system. Areas neglected or not adequately covered by the company.
- Contribution by line and by product mix.

The final profitability of the company depends on this knowledge and it will form an important part of the marketing mix when management is considering the overall maketing strategy.

Examples

Before looking at field research and the many forms of product and user research it is helpful to examine three examples to show the practical problems and attempted answers in market research work. After looking at these three practical examples it should, at least, be quite clear what marketing research is, how information is collected, and in what form it is presented.

1. A time scheme for market research

In most companies, in some form or other, and at all times, information along the lines so far discussed is available. It is desirable to establish some method in collecting, collating and circulating intelligence affecting the company. Some information arrives on the market research desk automatically, some has to be dug out of other departments, or collated from outside sources. Some information is collected daily, some weekly, and some is produced yearly. It is therefore desirable to follow a time pattern of a marketing section to see how the end results are built up.

Daily. The computer section (or accounts section) will provide daily figures of despatches to warehouses and customers, sales, credits. Production will provide daily figures of stock levels, production totals.

Weekly. The computer will probably provide weekly accumulator figures of sales by type, by area, in weight or units, and sterling. Production will provide similar records of output.

Monthly. From trade sources will be received figures for the industry as a whole and if the company subscribes to an outside research agency there will most probably be a monthly presentation showing what is happening in the market as a whole and what competitors are doing. There will be monthly returns on plant utilisation, scrap and stock levels. There will be the monthly examination of the year's budget and progress against budgeted estimates can be measured and variances observed. Most probably there will be monthly meetings of the departments concerned, at which new products or modifications to existing products will be examined. Special projects such as close examination of specific details affecting market ideas—as, for example, larger sized outers, or smaller individual packets, or light weight machines—will probably come up for discussion at monthly meetings. Complaints from customers received during the month are examined closely.

Periodically (quarterly or yearly). Summaries of results received during the year are prepared and examined against events for previous periods. Research and development programmes are examined in the light of previous meetings and progress in following up new ideas is critically examined. Most probably at quarterly meetings will take place discussions of special items of market research that take longer than a month to prepare, such as a study of warehouse locations, or new channels of distribution, or special requirements of overseas markets.

From all this information—and the background of economic and commercial information coming from daily, weekly and monthly newspapers—the essentials stand out; what the company is doing, measured in relation to what it has done, what the competition are doing, and what is happening in the market, and in particular, what is happening to the company products in the market. Are new products required?

Long-term strategic planning. Management is concerned with the business of change and since this necessarily extends into the future, embracing both problems and opportunities, more and more companies are engaged in long term formal strategic planning. Continuous analysis based on quantitative methods is used to form a framework by which qualitative assessments can be made. This is mentioned here since the economic background and the beginning of long term planning stem from these periodic market surveys. The subject is dealt with at greater length in chapter 4 and chapter 8 under the heading of Marketing Control (see pages 237 and 281).

2. A Brand Manager's worksheet

In many respects a Brand Manager represents a marketing manager in miniature since he is responsible for the efficient welfare of a brand. This means that he is constrained to see that the right products are produced in the first place and secondly that they are marketed as efficiently as possible. He constantly studies the product and the market and the relationship between the two.

A Brand Manager, as a marketing manager, must work on facts, not on hunches. These facts will be collected and assembled by the Brand Manager, who records them in a reference book or on work sheets or some other system. If an examination of a brand reference book is made it is easy to follow the close parallel to the marketing manager's task.

The brand reference book will usually have five main sections:

1. *Financial data.* Facts for this section will come from management accounting, costing and finance sections.
2. *Product data.* From production, research and development.
3. *Sales and distribution data.* Sales, packaging, distribution sections.
4. *Advertising, sales promotion, merchandising data.* Information from these three departments.
5. *Market data and miscellany.* From market research who would in most cases act as a source for much of this information required by the Brand Manager.

Financial data

(a) All details of product costs as given in supporting figures for the budget. That is, product cost, factory, administrative and selling overheads. The split between fixed, variable and semi-variable costs.
(b) All details of prices, trade discounts, wholesale and retail margins; promotional discounts and VAT charges.
(c) All details of sales for the last two to three years and current against budget estimates.

(d) All competitive information on prices and terms, especially sales promotional expenditures.

Product data

(a) All technical data required. For industrial products this would be quite considerable and should give product details from the company and from its main competitors.
(b) Projected product developments. Records of programmes outlined and promised.
(c) Customer complaints. Again for industrial products this could be one of the most important sections.

Sales and distribution data

(a) All sales data by product, by area, by distributor, or by salesman. Sales figures should be by moving annual totals so that trends are being constantly reviewed.
(b) All market distribution details, such as new outlets, new channels of distribution.

Advertising, sales promotion, merchandising data

(a) Information about current and previous advertising work will probably come from the advertising agency. It will show the media used, the type and weight of advertising employed and the results obtained—as measured by market research.
(b) Sales promotional schemes, sales bonuses, premium gifts, personal selling schemes will be recorded from sales department. Costs and results will also be recorded.
(c) Merchandising and merchandising promotions will be recorded by the merchandising department. Full details of methods, schemes, costs and results will be noted.

Market data and miscellany. In this section of the reference book all market information from outside the company is noted. This should show what is happening to the market, what is happening to the company product and what is happening to competitive products in the market.

The sources of this information will be published data such as *Monthly Digest of Statistics*, or *National Food Survey Reports* or information from purchased data such as Nielsen or Attwood.

3. Research report for Product A

It is now possible to consider a research report for Product A: suppose it to be a multi-purpose domestic appliance which can be used for washing clothes and crockery. A market research report follows: (The sources given are authentic; all figures are fictitious.)

The product

Product A is a multipurpose washing machine for domestic use and can be supplied as a top loader or a side loader. Washing, rinsing, drying of both hard and soft goods are automatic.

Introduction

From figures supplied by the British Electrical and Allied Manufacturers Association it can be seen that although sales of washing machines declined between 1963 and 1967, sales of electrical appliances, which are in any case very much affected by the level of purchase tax, showed a distinct rise in later years. Between 1970 and 1972 when the first multipurpose washing machines were introduced and purchase tax was reduced to be followed by a lower rate of VAT, sales showed marked improvement. Our new model therefore arrives on the market at an opportune time.

Market size

It is difficult to judge exactly the size of a market for a new product but it is estimated that the total washing machine market should be some 750 000 units representing a value of £34 million.

Market penetration

During the years 1970–72 ownership increased rapidly, but is growing slowly as against the ownership of ordinary washing machines. Ownership is now estimated at around 14 per cent as compared with over 60 per cent in USA, Sweden and Japan.

	Penetration per cent (households)
United Kingdom	14
Holland	18
United States	65
Canada	63
Japan	75
Germany	25
Italy	22

Source: BEAMA

Production

Production of multipurpose washing machines is slow. The machines are relatively expensive (twin tub washing machines range from £60 to £95; multipurpose machines from £185 to £250) and only two manufacturers so far are concerned.

UK production of multipurpose domestic washers

	Volume	Value (£)
1970	1 200	240 000
1971	5 000	1 000 000
1972	25 000	5 000 000
1973	57 000	13 000 000

Source: BEAMA

Imports

Very small imports of multipurpose domestic washers have so far been recorded, but as the EEC develops it is probable that larger imports from Italy will result.

UK imports by country of origin

	1972		1973	
	Units	%	Units	%
Italy	3 000	12	5 000	8·8
West Germany	1 000	4	1 000	1·75
Japan	1 000	4	2 000	3·5
Other	500	2	500	0·87

Source: Customs and Excise

Advertising

Because only two manufacturers have so far been concerned with these new machines advertising has been relatively modest and confined to press, almost entirely in women's magazines. No TV has so far been used.

	1972 Press	*1973 Press*
Company A	£300 000	£600 000
Company B	£400 000	£550 000

Source: Legion Publishing Company

Brand shares

Although Company A, producing Product A, was first in the market, Company B has overtaken it in volume of sales and the market at the moment is evenly divided between the two companies.

Prices and margins

The selling prices of the two companies are comparable varying in a range from £185 to £250. It is hoped that, as production and sales lift, these prices can be considerably reduced.

Outlook

Sales of domestic machines depend greatly on government restrictions on HP facilities. Price is obviously an important factor and it is confidently expected that prices can be reduced as production increases. The cheaper priced models from Italy represent a considerable danger that can increase as the UK goes further into the EEC. However sales of the company's Product A are expected to reach 100 000 units by 1975 with a value of some £18 million.

Various aspects of research

Field research

In many circumstances desk research on information readily available within the company and outside it will provide an almost complete picture. But there is a great deal of information available only from field research although in many cases this will not be necessary to the marketing plan. In the consumer trades there is a considerable background of fieldwork on tap from agencies such as Nielsen and Attwood. Such agencies supply shop and household information of a very definite character to subscribing clients in all the major consumer food, drink, tobacco and pharmaceutical industries. It is almost

Fig. 2.2.1
When is the
right time to enter
a growing market?

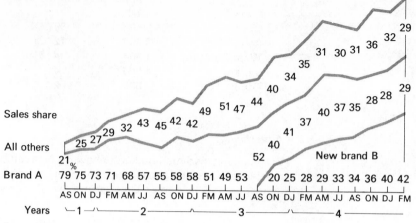

Sales share

All others

Brand A

Years

Source: Nielsen food index

impossible for any company in the consumer fields to stay seriously in the market without the help of background marketing intelligence as supplied by first class agencies. Not to have this information is to be moving blindfold in markets where competitors may know and use a much more precise picture. The information gives facts and shows trends. Here are a few samples from Nielsen to show market research in *action*.

When is the right time to enter a growing market? No manufacturer should plunge into a market without first attempting to obtain as much information as possible about it and after due observation of trends within the market.

A manufacturer produced a new product within a growing market. Instead of immediately launching the product the manufacturer proceeded by thorough market analysis on such things as competitive quality and price and distribution patterns to tailor his own product and marketing activity towards the point where all loose ends had been tied up. In this way his brand was launched in year 3 and became a brand leader in year 4.

Fig. 2.2.2
Why aren't chemists
purchasing enough
of my brand?

Consumer sales
Retailer purchases

Brand H

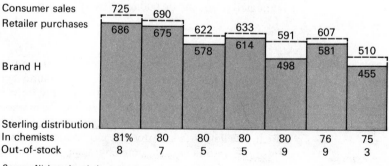

Sterling distribution
In chemists
Out-of-stock

Source: Nielsen drug index

Fig. 2.2.3
Turnover trends by
type of grocer in
Great Britain/
percentage

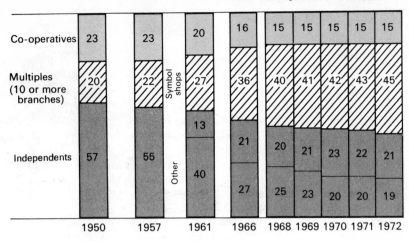

Source: D.T.I.& Nielsen food index

*Where is the
blockage?*

In this case distribution is good but the shops were selling from stock each month so that no build up of sales could follow. Market research showed the nature of the problem. Either the salesmen were not good enough or there were not enough salesmen. The answer was to engage more salesmen. Figure 2.2.3 shows dramatically the movement within the food trade in the UK between the years 1950 and 1972. This is precisely what market research must do, to follow these conditions that change continuously. No manufacturer in ignorance of these changes can supply a market adequately.

Figure 2.2.4 shows a national profile for the years 1967–72. Over these years food shops showed an increase of over 30 per cent which is higher than the average for all retail shops and reflects the improvements in food retailing resulting in greater efficiency and higher volume over a wider range of goods.

Fig. 2.2.4
The trend of
grocery turnover in
Great Britain

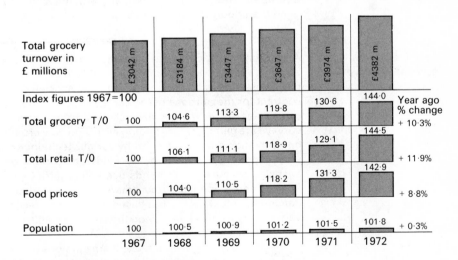

Source: Nielsen food index, D.T.I. & Registrars general

Fig. 2.2.5
Grocery turnover *v.*
Buying points in
Great Britain

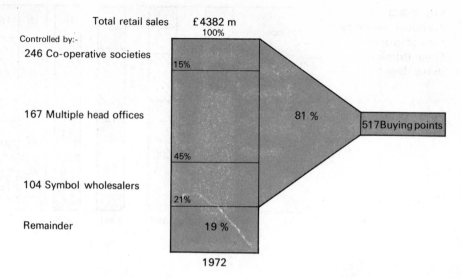

Source: Nielsen: C.W.S. Multiple directory

Concentration of
buying power

Figure 2.2.5 shows the concentration of buying power in fewer points. By 1972 some 517 buying points covered 81 per cent of the total grocery trade of the country. This emphasises the change in the marketing problem of those companies that work through the major outlets only. It means selling and advertising efforts can be channelled through those major outlets and with a minimum sales effort by high calibre people.

More important, these various diagrams represent the overall framework of market research because they show how markets change, and change continuously. They illustrate graphically how marketing intelligence is vital to a company and show that a company working without market research is like a blind man floundering in the desert.

Fact finding and
motivation surveys

Apart from the background of marketing intelligence already discussed there remains a great body of work in the field covering market research for specific purposes. This is usually carried out by specialist research agencies under contract for the purpose of the survey or sometimes, in the case of very large companies, by the market research department of the company. These special surveys are generally fact-finding efforts on new products or existing products or motivation surveys covered by various techniques. Unless the company is very experienced, this type of fieldwork should be entrusted to outside agencies because the methods used all require highly skilled expertise and field research conducted by amateurs in any other way is misleading and dangerous. Most research is based on sampling techniques and this depends very largely for its efficiency on the correct establishment of the universe and the random sample taken.

Special surveys are mounted to learn opinions on new products, or opinions on products compared with competitive products for quality and price. The manner in which the interviewing is carried out, and the forms of the questions are again highly technical and demand great expertise to obtain the most reliable answers. The investigators must be highly skilled and adequately controlled. The design of the questionnaire, if one is used, is most important and the subsequent analysis and interpretation of the answers requires a skilled professional effort.

Motivation surveys attempt to discover why people act or think in certain ways and to measure the area of such opinions. The two major methods are in-depth interviews and group discussions. In-depth interviews may be long interviews conducted by trained psychologists or more generally long interviews conducted by skilled investigators usually with carefully prepared questions. Only one person is interviewed at a time and the value of this technique lies in the skill in devising the pattern of questioning and the skill in

Table 2.2.1

Profile individuals

	Wales & West (HTV)				Wales & West (Severnside)				All Areas			
	All individuals		Individuals in ITV households		All individuals		Individuals in ITV households		All individuals		Individuals in ITV households	
	000's	%	000's	%	000's	%	000's	%	000's	%	000's	%
All individuals	4 680 (100%)	100	3 996 (85%)	100	3 947 (100%)	100	3 872 (98%)	100	54 297 (100%)	100	52 510 (97%)	100
Males: Total	2 284	49	1 962	49	1 926	49	1 898	49	26 266	48	25 506	49
Under 16 years	608	13	523	13	519	13	519	13	7 306	13	7 132	14
16–24	302	6	264	7	262	7	258	7	3 390	6	3 318	6
25–34	288	6	244	6	252	6	246	6	3 493	6	3 339	6
35–44	300	6	259	6	246	6	244	6	3 455	6	3 387	6
45–54	326	7	284	7	267	7	264	7	3 607	7	3 540	7
55 and over	460	10	338	10	380	10	367	9	5 015	9	4 790	9
Females: Total	2 396	51	2 034	51	2 021	51	1 974	51	28 031	52	27 034	51
Under 16 years	576	12	496	12	501	13	496	13	6 974	13	6 849	13
16–24	293	6	251	6	242	6	237	6	3 260	6	3 152	6
25–34	289	6	253	6	241	6	238	6	3 558	7	3 439	7
35–44	321	7	276	7	272	7	267	7	3 667	7	3 600	7
45–54	317	7	272	7	274	7	269	7	3 633	7	3 567	7
65 and over	600	13	486	12	491	12	467	12	6 939	13	6 427	12
Children Aged: 0–3 years	281	6	240	6	238	6	236	6	3 141	6	3 020	6
4–15	903	13	779	19	782	20	779	20	11 139	21	10 961	21
Adults Males:	1 676	36	1 439	36	1 407	36	1 379	36	18 960	35	18 374	35
Females:	1 820	39	1 538	38	1 520	39	1 478	38	21 057	39	20 185	38
Housewives:	1 500	33	1 271	32	1 307	33	1 245	32	18 473	34	17 191	33
Average size of household:	3·00		3·14		3·02		3·11		2·94		3·06	

Source: JICTAR Establishment Survey Report January 1973 covering all the ITV areas and reproduced with permission of JICTAR.

assessing the results. Market research is seeking to uncover these various opinions connected with the rejection or purchase of the product in question. Group discussions are conducted with panels made up of people brought together for this purpose. Both methods clearly depend upon the amount of preparation and the personal skill and experience of the investigator.

Consumer goods

Because marketing activities are usually found in consumer advertising and promotional activities in the consumer trades, consumer research has developed to an extent where it is an accepted part of the commercial landscape. Research into consumer habits and tastes by age, by sex and by social status is accepted as part of our life and we have already discussed the ways in which a company can go about measuring and analysing its own markets and their subdivisions. The pattern of work to be done is known and accepted; information about the company, the industry, and the markets in which it moves; information about the consumer customers, their habits, their opinions, their needs. All this work can be covered by known procedures within a company or from research agencies or advertising agencies employing marketing services. All that remains for any given company is to tailor the research effort to the needs and financial abilities of the organisation.

The task of the Marketing Manager is to keep his company informed through consumer research on those major points listed earlier in this chapter (see pages 178–9) and, in addition, to make sure of the following:

1. Specific monitoring tasks such as brand shares of an industry or the movement of sales and competition during periods of advertising or special sales pushes.
2. The reception of new products and the effect of their appearance into the market.
3. The composition of the market by classification of consumers.

Industrial products

Marketing is often assumed to be concerned primarily with consumer products. This is quite wrong and moreover lends a misleading character to the problem of market research. As a nation the UK produces three or four times as many industrial products in value as consumer goods, and the effect of good marketing and efficient market research on industrial products is of the greatest significance for the economy.

Industrial market research needs attention for its own sake and not as a poor cousin of consumer research. The principles are the same, but the two markets are essentially different and the application of those principles therefore also significantly different. A consumer product is bought to be consumed, an industrial product is bought to make money for the *buyer*. Herein lies a world of difference and perhaps explains why we should tackle the problem in a quite different manner. But the important thing is that it should be tackled. Market research is as vital for industrial products as it is for consumer goods.

Whereas the consumer researcher is concerned usually with a product of very short life and its effect on mass markets which can be analysed in many directions in depth, the industrial products researcher is concerned in many cases with highly complicated and sophisticated machinery with components and raw materials supplied to exact specifications, and his analysis must necessarily include examination of all the technical features of his machinery and similar machinery of his competitors. Since industrial products are used as part of a manufacturing process we are also concerned to analyse a derived demand. If a company builds mobile cranes for handling containers it is concerned to follow the construction of container ships and container handling terminals in all parts of the world.

Unless the company is newly formed, many sources of information are therefore, to begin with, internal and will consist of records of sales, servicing and particularly technical complaints. It will probably possess full documentation of former dealings with customers giving technical details of performances, load capacities, and criticisms. From the company industry it will probably obtain, or be able to obtain, information on the industry in home markets and abroad. When, however, the company moves outside to field research it approaches such a wide field that the first vital step must always be a precise statement of the problem. The brief, either to the research department or to an outside agency, must define precisely what the company is trying to measure.

Industrial products are found in four major categories:

1. Raw materials: goods purchased for use in the production of other goods and services, such as flour, fats and sugar for a biscuit manufacturer, or metal and paints for a motor car manufacturer.
2. Industrial equipment: goods purchased to fit and equip producing units such as ovens, conveying machinery, packing machines, materials handling facilities.
3. Industrial supplies: goods purchased for consumption of usage by production units such as industrial supplies of food, soap, paper, detergents.
4. Industrial services: services purchased to facilitate the production of goods, such as cleaning, security, fire protection, rodent destruction, building maintenance.

The market research department or agency in industrial products spheres is therefore concerned with all or some of the following:

- Materials used and their origins
- Machines or equipment; details of all available competitive makes, performances and prices.
- Applications of the product and the end products produced from them if they are components.
- Markets concerned, trends and estimates of future potential.
- Financing possibilities available for long term purchasing or leasing.
- Government regulations covering the markets.
- Distribution facilities and service possibilities.
- Resource allocation.

Illustration No. 1

If the company manufactures a range of *high speed packaging machines*, what is the information it should seek to obtain and record in its files for *any given customer*?

1. The company, its manufacturing units, its principal products. Its geographical location in regard to the market end distribution (for example, if it is situated in the south of England it might be able to sell to the Common Market

from its English factory). Its size in terms of employees, its position within its industry.

Does it sell on quality of the product or does it sell by price and discount? In the second case, cost of operation and initial purchasing facilities will be important.

2. The company's selling policy.

3. The company's principal customers and how they rank in its total market.

4. Where the company product fits into the customer's business. Is it providing a packaging machine for a major product that is already established, or a new line?

5. Details of customer machinery at present used. Details of other manufacturers' machinery, or machinery made by the company and previously bought by him. Details of specification, power supply, maintenance facilities. Has there previously been trouble with machinery supplied to this customer and why?

6. Details of credit facilities likely to be required. Details of government aid available if the company is dealing with foreign markets. Group buying arrangements.

Illustration No. 2

If the company is concerned with industrial market research into the development of a special market it would probably undertake this work in conjunction with an outside agency and endeavour to set as precise details as possible to define the subject of the survey and its purpose. What are the details required for *any given market?*

Market requirement: Submarine welded pipeline

The company manufactures submarine pipelines particularly for the oil industry and is especially interested in the development of the North Sea oil and gas fields for the years 1975–85. What form should the survey take?

Origin of the survey

There are three major source materials in the United Kingdom and of these coal with a production of 140 million tons annually represents some 37% of UK primary energy and natural gas about 12%. These two are home produced but the third source, petroleum, *is almost totally imported.* The annual volume of petroleum used in the UK is approximately 100 million tons which is about 47% of the UK energy requirement. The annual cost of 100 million tons of oil consumed in the UK prior to October 1973 was roughly £1 000 million. The effect of the new prices introduced by the Middle East groups was to multiply this cost by four. The development of the North Sea oil and gas fields is therefore an essential factor in the survival of the UK economy. It is hoped that by 1985, when all economically viable sources of North Sea energy will have been found and be in use—although what is economically viable depends on energy prices in world markets and on energy demand—the annual production available to UK producers will be some 200 million tons.

This development depends on the attitude of the British Government towards the question of financing and exploitation and also to the back up industries in the shape of manufacturers of offshore terminals, submarine pipelines, offshore rigs, pumping installations. The essential tools are ancillary pieces of marine engineering such as drill bits, halidé floodlight installations, derricks, mud pumps and so on. So far American knowledge is based on over a century of experience but it is also true that Italy, Holland and France have achieved great successes in pipe laying and submarine services.

Subject of the survey

The survey is concerned with the supply of automatically welded submarine large diameter steel pipelines (32 to 48 inches). The pipelines are concrete coated to help in the laying procedures and to give mechanical protection. The method envisaged is the use of lay barges for siting the pipelines, and sledge-drawn high pressure water jets for trench cutting operations.

Project

It is proposed to examine in detail the following points:

1. The product and its application.
2. The market and modes of sale; owners, rentals, finance houses, locations, competition. Probable sales methods; purchasing channels and credit facilities.
3. Government aid. The British government is already taking steps to help industry in this field and the various avenues for aid must be examined and evaluated.
4. Servicing requirements.
5. Production facilities.

The product

The marine pipeline will have a $\frac{3}{4}$-inch wall and be to ×65 specification. In general the pipeline will be 32 inches in diameter but this will vary according to the specific needs of different fields and varying depths. The submarine line will be covered in a 2-inch thickness of concrete and when laid it will be buried as far as possible to prevent damage from impact by anchors or trawls. The pipeline will be automatically welded and must be laid from a lay barge in depths between 300 and 400 ft.

The application

The use of thick wall pipeline is to enable the system to carry gas compressed in solution with crude oil to shore where it can be separated. The length of piping required varies from 100 to 250 miles.

The market

The market consists primarily of all those oil companies enjoying offshore area allocations. But the development of the whole area is controversial and neither the British Government nor the oil companies have agreed on satisfactory methods of financing operations of this magnitude, nor the terms under which the oil is to be brought to the market. The eventual rate of expansion which should be accelerated to help the British economy may be slowed down by what is financially desirable. The survey must therefore specify exactly those oil companies concerned and also make estimates, as far as is practicable, of possible development as it affects these companies.

Probable sales methods

All supplies for specific projects are the subject of tenders.

Servicing requirements

The company must establish by research the servicing requirements needed and location of spares and maintenance crews.

Production facilities

Since new machinery and equipment will probably be required on a very considerable scale, the long-term implications of financing the acquisition of additional production facilities must form a separate study.

Government aid

The British Government is seeking to help British manufacturers in various ways. The Ship and Marine Technology Requirements Board (now a part of the Department of Industry) is concerned with joint ventures on research and development relating to ships and offshore engineering. The Offshore Supplies Office (now part of the Department of Energy) is an agency concerned with the need to see that British suppliers receive full opportunities in the market for offshore activities. Because manufacturers from other countries have experience in this field not available to British companies, joint research and development must help British companies to compete on an equal footing.

Conduct of work

Information required

1. *Assessment of the market*

(*a*) Number and location of offshore area allocations.
(*b*) Number and location of drilling rigs.
(*c*) Number and location of onshore terminals and storage units.
(*d*) Estimate of the development of (*a*), (*b*) and (*c*) during the next five years.
(*e*) Dimensions and characteristics of submarine pipelines likely to be used and pipe laying techniques required.
(*f*) Main purchasing companies most likely to purchase from British sources.

2. *Competition.* Particulars of leading manufacturers' products, details and prices.
   United Kingdom
   United States of America
   Japan
   Germany
   Italy
   Other countries.

Method

1. Analysis of own records and customer histories.
2. Trade association.
3. Government publications.
4. Chambers of Commerce.
5. Purchased information services.
6. All other sources. (The oil companies themselves possess considerable records.)

What data does a marketing company need?

The basis on which all this work rests is the collection of data. In large organisations, where computer facilities exist, there is always the danger that too much data is assembled and no one knows what to do with it. In fact there is endless argument on this subject. There is always the search for that extra variable, previously overlooked, that will complete the model. There is also the danger of hoping that if only there is enough data, the model will solve itself.

The construction of the conceptual model and the collation of data to be employed are the same task and should be controlled throughout by the same person or authority. Some of the approaches usually tackled by quantitative methods are:

- Brand penetration
- Repeat purchasing rate
- Sales forecasting
- Stock handling and control
- Multiple warehouse siting
- Advertising media response and cost.

Quantitative methods in marketing

Here is the field of the mathematician and statistician and a certain degree of numeracy is required to understand the possibilities and dangers of this kind of analysis. Predicting trends by extrapolation carries its own particular dangers as demonstrated by those industries which have during the last five years extended their machine capacity to the point where the whole industry is overproducing. Whether this work is called operational research or quantitative method this is seeking ways to solve marketing problems or help in reaching marketing decisions based on known facts.

Faced with decisions to make, a person has a choice. There are decisions a person *should* make, and decisions a person *does* make. There is a choice, and whether a purchaser buys her old kind of toothpaste or a new brand that has just appeared rests on probabilities of choice. It is on the theory of probabilities—basically the work of Thomas Bayes and Andrei Markov—that decisions can be studied and applied to such factors as brand-switching, market penetration, sales forecasting, market share. Mathematical or logical models can be constructed, which are simplified versions of situations that could exist in real life. By manipulating the major variables the analyst is in fact experimenting with the model, as in real life. A model is an attempt to produce a real life situation in a structured pattern showing how the component factors interact one with another. These developments are quantified to produce conclusions or results. This outline review of the nature and use of "business models" is amplified later in the chapter (see page 199).

Observational studies

Observational studies attempt to find the pattern of interrelationships between data based on observation. The simplest and most common form is by analysis of cross-classification. This research can try to answer such questions as:

(a) How many chocolate biscuit eaters purchase supplies daily or weekly?
(b) How many chocolate biscuit eaters are under twelve, or over fifty?
(c) How many chocolate biscuit eaters are unmarried people living alone?

The risks inherent in this kind of work derive from the size of operation required and the complexity of the work and the need to be sure that all relevant factors have been taken into account. However, in the hands of experts, the method is valuable, especially in answering questions where sets of relevant variables are present.

Simulation studies

Such studies are based on the construction of models of some real operation or pattern and the manipulation of the models. This work is more complex than observational studies but can be used most completely in conjunction with computer programming in the creation of systems of great depth. The principal advantages of this method are as follows:

1. Simulation studies can take advantage of a large background of accumulated material from previous marketing sources and by including them in a general pattern obtain greater knowledge about each part. This is especially so for studies of complex products, such as the market for transformers in Europe or the market for Hydrocarbon Research systems.
2. Simulation studies may be used as bases for future activities, either in research and development or in selling or profitability targets.
3. Notional comparability can be observed through projection.

Heuristic
programming

This is a special branch of simulation studies based on 'rules of thumb' methods of problem solving. Instead of trying to evaluate from a large number of decisions the one decision that will give *optimum* results, the analyst attempts to find a *satisfactory* solution acceptable to the system. (Heuristic education is a system where the pupil is trained to find the best answers for himself.) It is a system that has been used on examinations of investment trusts and depot locations and materials handling.

We might endeavour to set up a flow chart for the question of factory siting for Europe. Will we be able to manufacture all we require for Europe from our factory in England or shall we need to establish factories or depots in Europe and if so where? This is perhaps the most important question for many companies to answer in the years 1980–90 and we perhaps see how we would begin to face up to the problem.

Flow chart

Stage 1

(a) Factory location. South: Evaluate higher costs for rent and labour. Midlands and North: Evaluate higher transport costs to the south.
(b) Distribution pattern suggested for Europe. Evaluate volume of trade estimated for France, Germany, Norway and Sweden, other countries. Which are the two major markets?
(c) Shipping and transport costs within major markets.
(d) Evaluate pattern of demand and product flow. Will delays caused by bad weather, dock strikes, interfere with trade? What effect will be produced by the channel tunnel?

Stage 2

Evaluate the costs savings to be expected from the siting of a separate factory either in or near the major markets. As, for example, in Hamburg, Frankfurt, Antwerp. Would this secondary factory remove warehousing requirements in some countries, and reduce transportation costs and distributors' services and commissions?

Stage 3

Evaluate the extra costs of production and the costs saving in distribution by the establishment of a group of smaller production units in three or four major markets. Evaluate the cost of one major production unit in England and a group of smaller assembly units in three or four major markets.

Stage 4 Evaluate as many combinations of Stage 2 or 3 as are possible to give the most satisfactory results balancing production costs against distribution charges.

Note. In all systems using quantitative methods it is essential that the work is carried out by experienced fully qualified operators. The penalty for having a little knowledge in this branch of research is considerable and this is no country for amateurs.

Behavioural science

Markets are composed of customers each of whom is an individual, or companies or corporations made up of individuals, reacting each in his own way. Marketing, as we have said, attempts to analyse customer requirements and the behavioural sciences attempt to analyse why people behave and think as they do. What makes people tick? When Mary Quant made a new kind of fashion for young people, she was selling not only clothes, but freedom, a new dimension in expression where each young person could seek to move in her own direction without the domination of grown-ups' style of dress and social conformity. When Rowntrees sell After Eight and Matchmakers they are selling not only chocolate, but elegance and social distinction, the suggestion of good living. When people buy a Rolls-Royce car, they buy more than a form of transport from point A to point B. Each manufacturer, indeed, has to try to discover the social function of his product.

This is certainly work that would have to be carried out by outside research agencies but we should understand the nature and significance of the activities. All markets are made up of people, existing in groups, interacting with each other and influencing each other's ideas and habits. Groups behave in certain ways according to norms established by the groups, which may be classified by age, by sex, by social positions, by geographical positions, by religion or many other categories. This ruling applies to all members of all groups, including customers, manufacturers, trade unions, supermarket operators, and so on. The two basic factors that most interest market researchers are the questions of learning and communication. How are ideas passed around in a group and what motivates people to change habits of thought and action? When a manufacturer considers that he has established what constitutes, for him, his major market he must still communicate with this market in a way that will be acceptable. For the message to be accepted, not only the correct medium, but the correct method of communication must be used.

Motivation, perception and learning are three basic factors for action resulting sometimes in the purchase of merchandise, and are three targets for advertising copy. The advertiser supplies reasons for benefits, or fear if the customer does not follow the advice offered, to motivate the reader or viewer into action. Cognition is the mental process of perceiving; a brand image can be readily seen as a powerful feature of cognition. Cognitive dissonance is the effort made by a person to achieve consistency between what he believes or knows and what he actually does. The cynic would say that cognitive dissonance arises when a customer makes a purchase and discovers afterwards that he has bought the wrong article.

A customer moves through many stages before he makes a decision to purchase. Market research attempts to measure these steps and suggests ways in which effective communication can be made to this customer. The two major methods to achieve this are in-depth interviews and group discussions, but observational studies are also widely used and there is an overlap here with quantitative methods. The aim of all this work is to give the Marketing Executive precise information about the nature and character of his markets, to isolate his major market, to recognise consumer behaviour patterns, and supply information on advertising activities that have taken place, followed with suggestions for future methods of work.

Presentation of reports

A market research department collects and collates information, from inside and outside sources and it has to do something with it. This is the preparation and presentation of timely factual reports. The reports should contain an exposition of facts as they are, sometimes with an assessment of the situation and sometimes with interpretation. The reports should never include decisions, opinions or suggestions for action; this is the responsibility of the Marketing Executive and his associates. The following precepts are helpful when providing report material:

1. The information should be presented in such form that it has immediate meaning and relevance to the company. It must be timely, since conditions are always changing.
2. It should provide material capable of serving as a starting point for new sales directions, or new tactics, or new products.
3. It should provide facts which will serve to evaluate past performances and to predict future possibilities. It should help in the task of forecasting and evaluation.
4. At all times, information must be relevant, practical and up-to-date. Research for the sake of research is not only a waste of time and money, it can also be dangerous.
5. Management's overall task is to make decisions on known facts; it has to decide how the objectives of the company can be met, by whom, and in what period of time. To do this, management must be provided with the most accurate information obtainable, so that adequate control and planning are possible.

Sources of information

In addition to those sources within the company that have been discussed earlier in this chapter there are a number of sources outside the company of which the most important are given below.

Within a given industry, and probably from its trade association, there is access to information for the whole industry so that comparisons can be drawn between what a particular firm is achieving and what is happening to the industry.

The chief sources of published information are (some detailed items are set out in Table 2.2.2 (see page 200):

- Government publications
- Embassies and consulates

- Specialist information agencies
- Press. Directories, year books, trade papers
- University research units
- Banks' commercial intelligence departments for home and overseas markets.

Business models

Earlier in this chapter reference was made to Bayes decision trees, models and simulation exercises. In the following chapter, dealing with product development, the text will be concerned at one point with Critical Path Method and network analysis. The application of some of these methods to business problems is discussed here in brief and the application of model building to marketing problems is described in greater detail. It will be realised that these techniques require a considerable background of knowledge and experience before they can be employed with confidence. (Books dealing with these techniques in detail are given in the reading list at the end of this Part.) It will also be realised that marketing control at this level is most productively employed by large companies who possess the computer facilities and staff to apply these techniques with the greatest advantage. A company covering 2 or 3 per cent of the market scarcely needs recourse to such methods.

Quantitative business planning techniques

Business management has developed in such a way that the marketing executive is called on to make decisions based on economic and quantitative business analyses. Figures are used to assess, evaluate, control, decide at all points. Most modern quantitative business planning techniques show relationships between facts about a business expressed in figures. In other words a marketing man must be numerate, since models and simulations are being used more widely by organisations as an aid to the understanding of strategic planning. Techniques alone do not solve problems, but they provide a framework on which judgments can be made. The most commonly used techniques are described below.

1. A model is an attempt to represent an actual real life situation in mathematical or diagrammatic form, although this is always a simplification. Figs. 2.2.6/7/8 show respectively 'models' of major motor routes and airports of Europe, a simplified flow diagram for ammonia synthesis for natural gas in the chemical industry, and a flow chart presenting the provision of new doctors in the United Kingdom (see pages 201–3).
2. Simulation means activating the model. When the variables contained in the model are altered or manipulated the result is a simulation of actual results which attempts to show what would result if specified assumed conditions occurred: see Fig. 2.2.9 (see page 204).
3. Systems showing the development of processes:
   (a) Network analysis is a diagram of an ordered set of activities and events. Each path in a network is unique inasmuch as it contains at least one activity different from the activity of other paths (see page 218).
   (b) Critical path method (CPM) shows the total job time for a given network which is of course the total sum of all activities along the longest path (see chapter 3, pp. 218–9).

Table 2.2.2
Government
publications
(HMSO)

Monthly Digest of Statistics: all aspects of our economy.
Annual Abstract of Statistics: a statistical analysis over a wide field.
Census of Population.
Census of Distribution: covering retail, wholesale and service trades.
National Income and Expenditure Blue Book.
Department of Employment Gazette.
Trade and Industry Journal.
Department of Trade and Industry: library and reports. (The library is one of
  the largest and most up to date in the UK.)
British Overseas Trade Board Export Handbooks.
Dept. of Trade—Trade and Navigation Accounts.
Dept. of Trade—Export List.

Useful addresses

Central Office of Information, Hercules Road, London SE1.
Department of Trade, Export Services Branch, Hillgate House, 35 Old Bailey,
  London EC4, or Regional Offices.

Embassies and
consulates

The commercial sections of British embassies and consulates contain a great
deal of local knowledge and staff to interpret this and help when required. The
service available for British industry is invaluable, but many companies seem
unaware of the magnitude and quality of the work that is provided.

Specialist
information
agencies

The Market Research Society Yearbook (obtainable from 51 Charles Street,
London W1X 7PA) is the quickest method to obtain information about
specialist agencies. There are over 100 member companies of the society.
Institute of Marketing, Moor Hall, Cookham, Berkshire.
Moody's Services Ltd: financial and statistical.
Exchange Telegraph Co. Ltd: financial and statistical.
Dun and Bradstreet: credit rating and capital structure.

Other sources

Aslib, 3 Belgrave Square, London SW1 (Association of Special Libraries and
Information Bureaux).
National Institute of Economic and Social Research, 2 Dean Trench Street,
London SW1.
Economic Intelligence Unit Ltd, Spencer House, 27 St James's Place, London
SW1 ALHG: special reports on UK and European Marketing.
The Times Business News includes the *London and Cambridge Economic
Bulletin* now published as a supplement.
Economist Weekly Newspaper, 25 St James's Street, London SW1 A1 HG.

(c) Programme evaluation and review technique (PERT) is an extension of CPM. CPM network is based on an estimate of time for each activity. PERT requires three estimates, minimum, most likely, maximum. These are weighted on a 1–4–1 basis so that the most probable time emerges (see p. 220).

4. Systems dealing with developments of complicated factors:

(a) *Bayesian analysis or decision trees.* This is a theory concerned with the course a decison-maker chooses in following a series of decisions. It is a procedure for evaluating the outcome of probabilities. A marketing executive could use this method to study what might happen to one of his products if he injected a powerful advertising programme for that product into his overall marketing scheme. A financial executive would use decision trees as a guide for making capital budget decisions (see p. 195).

Fig. 2.2.6
Major motor
routes and
airports of
Europe

Source: Financial
Times Management
Diary 1973

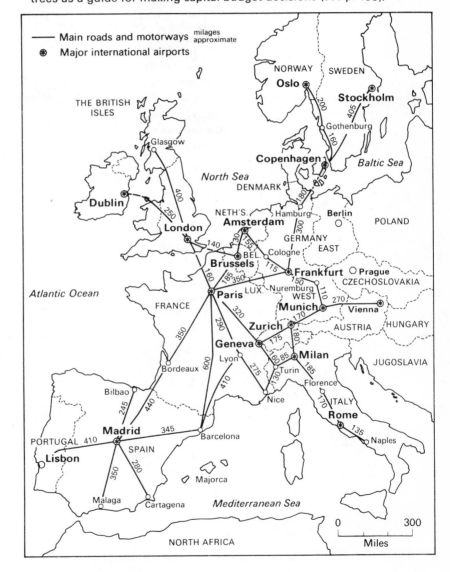

Fig. 2.2.7
Simplified flow
diagram for
ammonia synthesis
for natural gas
in the chemical
industry

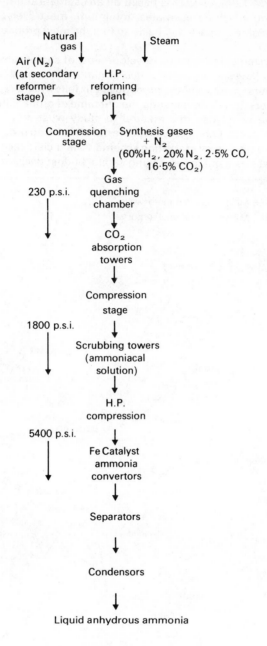

Natural
gas

Steam

Air (N_2)
(at secondary
reformer
stage) →

H.P.
reforming
plant

Compression
stage

Synthesis gases
+ N_2
(60% H_2, 20% N_2, 2·5% CO,
16·5% CO_2)

230 p.s.i.

Gas
quenching
chamber

CO_2
absorption
towers

Compression
stage

1800 p.s.i.

Scrubbing towers
(ammoniacal
solution)

H.P.
compression

5400 p.s.i.

Fe Catalyst
ammonia
convertors

Separators

Condensors

Liquid anhydrous ammonia

Source: British Gas Corporation from the Industry magazine *Flambeau*.

(*b*) *Heuristics* is a branch of simulation where solutions are sought by following acceptable solutions to each part of the problem (not the best, but an acceptable solution). This system can be used for warehouse or factory location problems (see p. 196).

(*c*) *Monte Carlo methods* are basically experimental sampling methods to consider processes that are based on probabilities or events closely allied to them. It has been used for governments to study the effects of economic policy on a country, and for doctors to study the effects of anti-drug measures.

5. Sundry mathematical techniques:

(*a*) *Risk analysis.* This is one of the most important and widely used techniques. It is a simulation used to assess the risks and advantages inherent in following alternative plans. It is a technique employed increasingly for problems of capital equipment, R and D projects, merger decisions. It is therefore pre-eminently a tool for long term strategic planning and it is used for long term corporate plans for diversification, new product proposals and acquisitions.

(*b*) *Econometric methods* comprise the systems used to analyse and measure the movements of economic variables. Basically this is done by a system of correlation and regression analysis and by variance analysis.

Fig. 2.2.8
Provision of
doctors in
the United
Kingdom

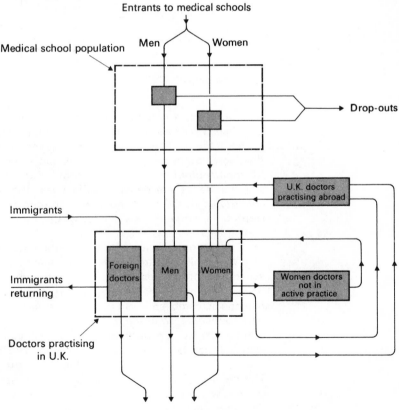

Source: CAS Occasional Paper 8—Operation Research Models and Government. Reproduced with permission of the Controller of HMSO.

Fig. 2.2.9
Simulation
and reality

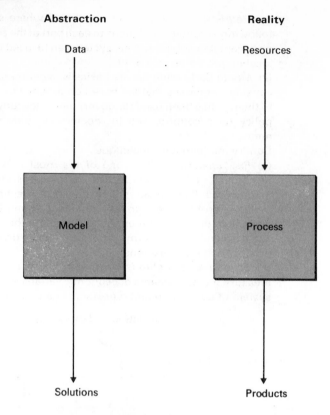

(see p. 214)

(c) *Correlation and regression analysis* is a system to determine the degree in which two or more variables may differ. Regression defines the exact shape of the relationship (a straight line) and correlation seeks to quantify the degree of the relationship (good, bad, indifferent).

(d) *Input/output analysis* is a system designed to show the interrelationship and hence interdependence between industries. For example the I/0 analysis would attempt to show what the effect would be for any industry to step up its demand for a service or commodity on the sales of all other industries.

(e) *Linear programming.* This is a method used to determine the optimum plan to be followed from several alternative courses. It is widely used for scheduling production, market forecasting and plant utilisation. It begins by defining the alternatives, computing an objective value for each alternative and so establishing an optimum value.

(f) *Exponential smoothing.* Once a product has taken its place in the normal marketing programme of a company, and once the initial growth stage has passed its future sales will depend on where it is in relation to the product life cycle (see p. 214) and to developments within the company. This means taking into account the sales forecast and deciding whether the product warrants continuation and how much support should be given to it. The most popular technique to deal with this situation is known as exponential smoothing. The technique seeks to develop control rules from historical data and measure them against the significance of possible future development. In other words, once the initial impetus of the selling-in period is over (which may be three months or three years) future sales depend on trends, whether the product is in a growth, levelling or decline stage, and need the development of weighting factors to achieve a reliable forecast.

Large-scale models

Having briefly surveyed the most popular techniques now used, it is time to consider the employment of large-scale models for planning techniques.

Scenarios. A scenario is a system of ordered procedure to pursue a sequence of future events both probable and possible and considering in terms as precise as possible the implications and complications of such developments. It is common these days for governments to have special committees consisting of sociopolitical and economic members whose task is to survey for the government various alternative policies and to predict the possible outcome of future events. Pollution, race relations, industrial relations, area development, full employment are all subjects for scenarios. Large corporations are equally concerned over long term developments. What courses are open to us, what courses are open to our competitors, what conditions shall we both be working in by 1980? Scenarios are models in words.

Fig. 2.2.10
A simple marketing model

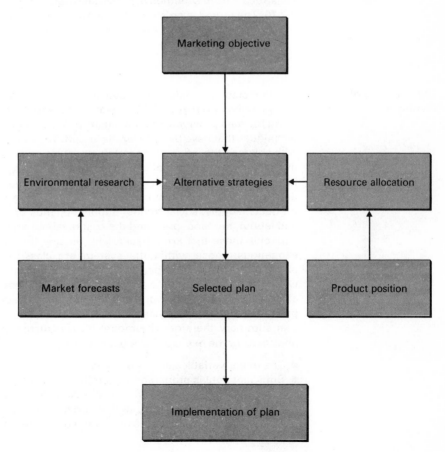

Corporate models. Models are used to show the effect of alternative courses to be followed by a company. They are used for such objectives as predicting cash flow, to forecast earnings and profit growth, to determine priorities in capital expenditure and to guide programme planning. Models are of course used to develop marketing programmes.

Marketing models. A marketing operation is concerned with the future activities of the company and because of this it embraces risks and advantages. The efficient use of marketing models can reduce areas of uncertainty. It also ensures that all management concerned is fully aware of all known and estimated risks and complications of any given plan of action. A model is of course a continuous reproduction of real life. It is never therefore completed but should be continuously brought up to date as changed circumstances require.

A model begins as a simple statement of things. Total costs are equal to fixed costs plus the variable costs per unit times the number of units sold:

$$a = b + cy$$

where a = total costs, b = fixed costs, c = variable costs and y = the volume in units. But from this extremely simple beginning a market model can be constructed from a method of processing data to provide information: see Fig. 2.2.10. The model is an attempt to show from data provided by the company the probable outcome of the activities concerned with the data provided.

The construction
of models

The first step is to define the objectives of the model. That done, a detailed analysis must be made of all relevant data, and the model is constructed by using the data provided, employing in so doing some or all of the quantitative techniques that have been so far discussed. The model is concerned basically with showing the influence of certain variables on other variables. A market is influenced by questions of price, demand and supply, amongst other things. Price depends on the cost of labour, materials, overheads, and the overall demand and supply position. Demand depends on price, price of competitive products, supply, social trends. Supply depends on availability of materials and labour, demand, price and the cost of labour and materials. Within these variables those that are independent, outside the system, are classified as exogenous: those within the system are classified as endogenous. For example exogenous independent variables are labour and material availability (in the UK we buy on a world market, so that the price of our meat for example is governed by world conditions) labour costs, material costs and the price of competing products.

In summary therefore the model is constructed in five stages, once the objectives of the exercise have been defined:

● The major variables are shown and their interaction is studied.
● Sufficient data is prepared to quantify the interactions.
● The model is assembled and it is checked, that is validated.
● The model is manipulated, so that variable relationships are computed.
● The relationships that have been computed experimentally are implemented.

Here are some of the key factors that would be required in the assembly of the model and used in the first printout:

1. Statistics on market size and growth.
2. Company sales by product type and by region and by price.
3. Number and classification of customers.
4. New government regulations, taxes, etc. affecting the market.
5. Competitive moves known or estimated.
6. Rate of market decline or growth.
7. Major segments within the market.
8. Existing product plan short term and long term.
9. New product plan short term and long term.
10. Forecast of total market consumption.
11. Forecast of trends by segments of the market.
12. Effect of competition within the enlarged European Economic Community.
13. Total cost of sales.
14. Total cost of sales promotional activities.
15. Forecast of estimated profit contribution on marketing operations.

The argument for a marketing model always returns to the same starting point. The management seek to understand the implications of changes in marketing mix, to assess the interrelationship of variables. What happens with a change of price, or the introduction of a new product, or the reduction of a sales force? How best does a company achieve maximum profitability in the years ahead?

It has been said that management's task is to use its resources of money, labour, materials that are available to the company as efficiently as possible. Also available to the company is information, growing up inside and outside the company and providing the company with data from which decisions can be made. Management has the task of taking all this information and using it as a basis for judging alternatives so that the greatest efficiency follows.

3 Product management

The product mix is basic to the marketing programme and therefore product management is of vital importance to the success of the enterprise. Managing the product line and new product development is the centre of the drive towards greater efficiency and greater profitability, although it is true that product management is interpreted in different ways in different parts of the company. Nevertheless the basic idea of a deliberate planning procedure concerned with present and new products means that management recognises that the business is constantly changing and that management is working towards a future objective.

To the production executive product management means essentially an operation directed towards maximum plant and labour utilisation with a minimum of unused overheads; to the sales executive it means products that give him maximum volume without increasing his selling costs so that the productivity of the sales force is high; to the financial executive it is a method of using the most favourable product mix so as to ensure that the maximum profitability follows. Although they start from different origins, these aims are not necessarily conflicting, and one task of the marketing executive is to attempt to bring harmony into these various activities.

This, in practical terms, means that a company is always concerned with a company/market/product relationship in which the company is continuously concerned with its relationship to its markets (sometimes it has to redefine its basic objectives) and the relationship between its markets and its products. How this is done is the subject of this chapter, which approaches the problem through three broad elements:

1. The meaning of product management.
2. The generation of new products.
3. New product launching.

First, it is advisable to realise the difference between a number of related terms:

Product item means the product itself, i.e. a certain motor car designated by power, size, style, performance: the unit product.

Product range or product line means the total range of products in one class, i.e. a range of cars, or a range of biscuits, or a range of meat products: a family of items offered for sale.

Product mix means the total production of all product ranges and the proportions in which they are sold. A large meat corporation might have a product range of meats in cans, and another of preserved meats, and another of processed chicken. The total mixture would be the product mix and would largely govern the profitability of the total enterprise.

The meaning of product management

If a product is to be successful it must answer as well as possible the requirements and standards of customers in all markets. This is true of all products a company makes and the company will always endeavour to have a range of products that each answers a customer/market need. Few companies can do this over the total range of products made and in practice some of the range are good sellers, some are average and some on the decline. Product management therefore begins with the overall task of supplying a range of goods or services that satisfy three basic requirements:

1. Market needs must be met as nearly as possible which results in a satisfactory volume of business and hence an impact on the market. From this follows a meaningful market share.
2. Profit results from this condition also because articles answering market needs do not require low prices to achieve sales volume.
3. Finally from these first two conditions growth must necessarily ensue, since growth results from constant attention to market needs.

However, products do not exist in a vacuum and are attacked by competitive moves as well as changed market needs. In addition the profitability attached to any product can be adversely affected by resources allocation resulting in plant limitations. Therefore the overall task of product management will depend very largely on the following factors:

- Number of products made and the need for rationalisation. Plant utilisation and the position of labour requirements.
- The variations and modifications of standard products required by different markets. This is especially true for overseas markets where various presentations of a standard product may be required.
- The price levels and effect on profitability of changes in prices of raw materials.
- The changes in post-production costs necessary to market certain products that alter the final profit picture in this way.

Therefore from the information collected by the market research section from the market and the information supplied within the company by the production departments a joint picture emerges of market needs, the company response to the market, and the resulting company image, or impact, on the market and final profitability. There are two extreme cases that can be considered here. Perhaps the most violently changing of all markets is that for popular records. Each week the market trends and tastes vary. A top selling popular record results in big business for the manufacturer (and large royalties for the artiste) but it is estimated that something like 25 per cent of all records produced are commercial flops. Each record manufacturer therefore has the extremely difficult task of spotting changes in market tastes and beating his competitors. This has given rise to rack jobbers who undertake to display only the best selling records at any given time, which makes innovation difficult and the manufacturers' task even harder. At the other extreme can be seen manufacturers like Rolls Royce and Volkswagen who maintained one model (or very nearly one model) for many years, whilst their competitors were changing, sometimes quite drastically, the shape and character of their products every three or four years. No doubt these companies did so for good marketing reasons although this point of view might be felt by some to be open to question.

The reasons for product management

The basic reasons underlying the need for product management can now be examined in detail.

Changing customer requirements

This is the first consideration: all other considerations stem from it. The requirements of customers and markets are always changing as a result of fashion, the interchange of ideas, government regulations or new movements.

Changing technology

Changes in the use of materials, the development of new materials, and the evolution of new processes all result in new products and new demands. This is especially true in industrial products and has been seen recently in microcircuits and the development of small calculating machines, the emergence of new materials and methods in construction industries, and the development of plastics in many fields. It is a continuous process.

Profit

This must be the next consideration for product management. The product mix determines very largely the final profit picture of the company. It is necessary therefore to establish clearly the profitability of each product so that the contribution that each line makes is known. Profit margins can be eroded by the actions of competitors, by the passage of time, by the increase in costs of raw materials. Marketing demands a product mix that ensures firstly the volume necessary to cover overheads, and secondly on top of this the maximum profitability. Obviously a wise mixture of products is required since it is not always possible to sell the highest profit margin lines in the greatest volume. On the other hand a company must avoid a situation where it is existing primarily on large volume low margin products. A first objective to such a company would be new lines, new products, or new markets offering larger profit margins, and these would have to be found if the company is to continue.

Survival and growth

The terms are synonymous since no company today can survive without growth. In an economic climate where costs increase yearly it is impossible to contain or satisfy these costs without growth. These are the ways a company usually grows:

● By development in the market: this means selling additional products, or modified products. Innovation can be of product, or packaging, or presentation, or methods of distribution, or methods of communication, that is changes in distributors or advertising. It also means selling in greater volume by more sales or more advertising effort.

- By development of other markets: this means selling existing products in new markets, new areas, overseas markets, or merely in areas in the home market not presently attacked. This involves constantly examining the channels of distribution and market segmentation.
- By diversification: this can happen in two ways: either by developing new products for new markets, or by joint venture which means carrying a product produced by another company but marketed and exploited by the first company.
- By mergers or acquisitions: this is really an extension of the previous factor but basically it means adding other products or markets to the range of the company to achieve growth.

Maximum utilisation of resources

As stated earlier in this chapter one major objective of product management must be the maximum employment of all company resources: maximum plant utilisation, full use of labour and management, minimum defective production or scrap, and maximum use of the company's capital resources. Every production manager is conscious of variances in labour overheads and plant utilisation and he knows how much more productive and profitable the enterprise would be if he could arrange a product line giving him the maximum use of his total resources. To do this completely is perhaps impossible except for short periods. Nevertheless one aspect of product management must be concerned with this factor.

Product planning

Planning the product line must clearly begin with an assessment of the present product range and an evaluation of the points made so far in this chapter. When this has been completed the need or desirability for new products can be considered. Obviously, this total effort is continuous and is conducted as a background to product management as a whole. In summary therefore management is concerned with the following:

Assessment of the product range

Market development. Is it possible to achieve wider sales for the present products by developing new markets—or new segments of present markets—and by so doing increase the volume and profit? Can this be augmented by other or newer sales methods?

Market penetration. Is it possible to improve present sales with the present range but with slight modifications, or by changes in packaging or presentation, or modifications in the products themselves to meet current demands? Market shares and customer acceptance must be evaluated.

Profitability. It is accepted that the product mix must be examined and the pattern of profit build-up known precisely. Contributions or margins change because of increased costs of raw materials, labour or distribution. Sales volume, *per se*, means little. What does matter is the maximum volume from those lines making the greatest contribution. Non-profit lines have to be considered for elimination.

Present product development. What changes can be considered to increase volume? What changes in distribution are possible? A product can be given an extension of life by changes in design, manufacture, presentation or pricing.

New technologies. What changes in materials or methods can be used in the present range or new ranges?

Performance rating. Is the range too large or too small? Is the company in danger of producing a large number of small margin products? Are any lines particularly valuable as image builders? What products are valuable as vehicles for growth? Which products give reason for sales and promotional support as a means to achieve growth?

Resources utilisation. The company must examine the range critically to see how each product fits into the overall capacity for labour and machinery. A company cannot afford products that demand disproportionate amounts of labour or machinery time. Unless the production units can achieve their standards for labour, costs and plant utilisation, the company cannot make its maximum profit.

Product planning responsibilities

The marketing executive will be responsible to the board of directors for long term product assessment but clearly this is a team effort that goes forward continuously. In many companies there will be a product group, or development group, under the chairmanship of the marketing executive, meeting at monthly intervals to maintain this study.

The group will have members from Planning, Research and Development, Production, Engineering, Personnel, Sales and Finance, because all are involved in new development work and all such work must be planned from the very beginning. Most companies use PERT or critical path charts to follow and illustrate the development of new ideas into the company. (These methods are discussed more fully in this chapter under the section dealing with new products.)

Where such a group (assisted and, in some cases, motivated by the Marketing Department staff) meets regularly, the work of product assessment, modification and development is a continuing task and methods can be evolved to achieve the desired objectives. New products then become the work of a team each responsible for a company activity. Without this method, new product development or even present product modification becomes a chance affair without any particular objective. With this method, product assessment and new product development becomes an accepted part of company procedure. A number of important points may be made:

(*a*) It is obvious that product planning must be a continuous process.
(*b*) It must begin always in terms of customers' needs or market requirements. The need for the intervention of the marketing staff in this respect is also obvious.
(*c*) New methods and new materials available must be considered.
(*d*) It is a team effort involving all those departments ultimately concerned.

The major objectives of such a group would be:

1. *Develop new markets for existing products.* This can be done by examination of the distribution pattern of the company and slight modifications of the product to meet the new market pattern. Thus, detergents sold in small attractive packets for individual consumers can be produced in large functional containers for industrial purposes.
2. *Remove products, or markets, or customers that are not profitable.* This is to remove clutter that makes little or no contribution.
3. *Develop new products that can be handled by the present sales pattern, to revive market share and profitability.* This is to maintain the company's attack on its market, to hold back competition, and to do so with an adequate profit margin.
4. *Develop byproducts, or reserve products* that could be sold through other channels if the company decide to do so.

The generation of new products

It seems certain that all products move through certain phases which constitute some pattern of life cycle, although some products appear to be suspended in a growth phase that is infinite. The sales line for products such as Nabisco Ritz Crackers, Johnnie Walker Red Label Whisky or Players cigarettes would be a straight line extending to infinity, rising slightly each year to cover the effect of annual increases in population. Nevertheless for most products there is a cycle of invention, development, introduction, growth, major period, declining or revitalisation and recycling period and it is helpful in product planning to bear these usual patterns in mind. This is so because a management considering its products in terms of a life cycle must proceed to an exact analysis of each product and its relation to the market which means in turn that it is examining its own position very clearly.

The product life cycle

The invention and development phase

This is one of preparation and of the utmost importance to the ultimate success of the product; to some extent the end result will depend on the thoroughness with which the preparatory steps are taken. If market requirements have been correctly observed, and if the product really is a new product and not a variant of a competitive product, its chances of success are much greater.

The introduction phase

This phase is also vital because in many cases the manner in which the new product is introduced can make or mar the newcomer. Timing of the introduction is important.

The growth phase

Once a company feels that the product is to be launched nationally the important thing here is to distribute and sell as widely and quickly as possible. Advertising and sales promotional work will probably be heavy.

The major selling phase

This phase which may last many years is the period when investment and introduction costs are paid off and the product makes its maximum contribution to the company.

Fig. 2.3.1
Product life
cycle

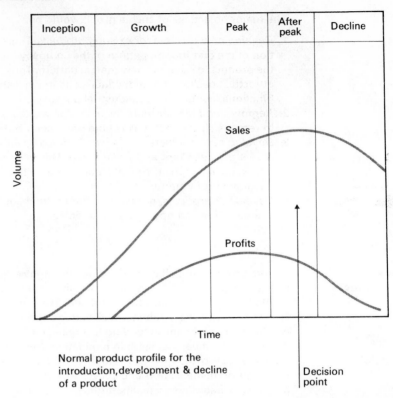

Inception	Growth	Peak	After peak	Decline

Normal product profile for the
introduction, development & decline
of a product

Decision
point

The final phase	Eventually most products reach a point where sales decline or can be maintained only by such heavy promotional expenditure that profit dwindles and may eventually disappear. Long before this ultimate end a wise product planning team would have replaced it or revived it in some way or other. It is the usual experience however that once a line has reached the point of decline the cost of upholding it in terms of selling effort and advertising expenditure becomes prohibitive. A typical product life cycle is shown in Fig. 2.3.1.
Reasons for new products	A company must have new products if it is to stay alive. As has been already demonstrated the first reason is to maintain the company's share of the market, or in other words its impact on the market. Without this the company would disappear. Secondly, new products enable a company to safeguard its profit margins and even to improve them. The conjunction of these two reasons produces the third reason for new products which is to achieve growth. But beyond this a company must consider new processes or new materials available so that it is not left behind when its competitors move into these new fields. There is here a vital link between R and D and marketing.
Basic requirements	Since new products are vital to the continuation of any company it must evolve a method through its product planning team to examine regularly all the

required factors concerning its products and markets. How this
not greatly matter except that the more decisions are based on
facts and figures the more reliable the final assessments will be.

Here is a preliminary list of basic requirements for new products:

1. The ideal new product would come within the company's manufa
   and technical resources.
2. The product must possess some advantages over present products.
   'product plus' is essential to break into the market.
3. It would use the company's present strength in distribution, to tak
   advantage of existing goodwill or reputation in directions for which the
   company is already accepted.
4. The market for the product should be large enough to give a required
   volume within two years. It must also be a market not totally dominated by
   one giant.
5. The product must be capable of sales volume at a price acceptable to the
   market which yet yields the company a sufficient margin of profit.
6. The product ideally should not require large capital investment in new
   machinery, or new selling methods. However if these are called for, the new
   product must be carefully evaluated and the financial implications of large
   capital investment, or new selling methods precisely evaluated. If the
   market projection justifies these new steps then the proposals for the new
   product can proceed.

New product strategies

The overall product planning effort concerned with old and new products and
old and new markets is obliged to take a total view, so that the need for new
products becomes obvious and the possible nature of these new products is
easier to recognise. The product planning team will then proceed through a
series of recognised stages:

1. Rationalisation of the present range means eliminating non-profitable
   products (and markets).
2. Developing the present range by modification or by additional selling
   activities.
3. Exploiting the present range by finding new markets at home or overseas.
4. Developing and introducing new products to meet new customer requirements.
5. Considering the company/market/product relationship in all its aspects.

Note. In considering product strategies the dual effect of changes in product
range as well as product mix (for definition of terms, see p. 208) must be
considered.

Where do new ideas come from?

The selection and development of new products involves the whole company
but the development group or planning group would probably evolve their
own method for gathering ideas. The major sources for ideas, which would
come initially in all sorts of shapes and sizes to be sifted by the marketing
section or the development group or both, are usually as follows:

marketing section itself. This should be the most reliable source of new because the section acts as a clearing house for ideas from all sources part of its routine function to evaluate new ideas against the marketing nd of known facts. Continuous study of the market suggests exploration by other sections.

ales department and field sales organisation. These people are in touch ith the market and in some respects are a first line of information. Where criticisms or complaints form a valuable source of product knowledge as in the provision of machines or specialised equipment, reports coming back from the field serve a useful starting point for ideas. However, information coming from sales people in the field must always be examined critically because they feel the full weight of the competitive effort so that ideas and requests from sales people have a habit of cataloguing competitive advantages that need to be copied and surpassed.

The research and development section. Usually this section, together with market research, produces most of the ideas that actually find their way into the factory. If, as is often the case, the research and development work is led by an energetic and intelligent man with drive, the happiest results follow. The essential is that a method is established for painstaking research and careful development of ideas moving through processes of evaluation and screening to the final assessment. R and D will often be the first source of knowledge of new materials available or new processes used.

Other sources. Many valuable ideas come from the factory floor and some from customers. It is important to consider all ideas, however unusual, and subject them to critical analysis. Many companies offer financial rewards and promotion to new ideas successfully adopted from the factory floor. Companies often find that new ideas all come from the same old source as has always been used (sometimes indeed from one man) and somehow they must find a way to tap new sources. Suggestion schemes can indeed be a most valuable source of new ideas. Careful analysis of customers' complaints often leads to minor improvements and sometimes to major developments.

Processing new ideas

New ideas can arrive from many sources and involve the entire organisation of the company before they take shape as a company product. So that this may be done efficiently with all sections concerned aware of the progress of the idea through the development processes a careful control must be maintained. It is equally important that all sections can see for themselves where the new idea has arrived at in time and development, and this means copies of network analysis or a central office where development charts or network analysis can be studied.

There are three similar methods to control this work. The common feature of all is a network, or diagram, or bar progression to show sequence and duration of different and separate activities that together make up the final result.

Critical path method (CPM)

In CPM each separate activity is listed and a possible time scale suggested. From this point estimated costs for each activity can be calculated so that at any given time the costs for proceeding or abandoning the idea can be measured. Thus:

		Marketing suggestion new product A Days
A.	Market research	55
B.	Opinion survey	40
C.	Sample materials	15
D.	New dies	25
E.	Trial manufacture	15
F.	Procure bulk materials	20
G.	Production planning	10
H.	Procure sample batch	75
I.	Distribution to selected depots	20
J.	Establishing selected agencies	30
K.	Recruiting extra salesmen	60
L.	Training salesmen	15
M.	Arrange press reception, PR work	30
N.	Advertising and initial brochures	40

Sequence

1/2	A and B begin the operation
3/4	C and D can be ordered together
5	E follows
	At this point the company decides to go ahead with a full scale batch manufacture and
6/7/8/9/10	F, G and H, J and K begin together
11	I follows when supplies are ready and at the same time
12/13	L, M, N can be prepared.

PERT: programme evaluation and review technique

In PERT each activity duration is given three estimates: *optimistic, pessimistic, most likely,* so that a weighted average can be obtained and the probable overall time can be calculated.

Bar charts

Both CPM and PERT require draughtsmen to produce and alter network analysis charts. There are a number of suppliers now who make multicoloured bar charts which can be assembled against a magnetic background (so that altering the charts can be simply done) and the use of colour strips enables the separate activities to be shown against the product idea. These multicoloured bar charts are an excellent variation of the network analysis system and much easier to assemble and modify.

All these systems seek to control three major factors, time, resources and costs, and do so usually by arrow diagrams (Fig. 2.3.2), bar charts (Fig. 2.3.3) or network analysis (Figs. 2.3.4 and 5). The manner in which this is done is as follows:

Stage 1. List all the separate activities that are concerned and estimate the duration of time and cost for each activity.

Fig. 2.3.2
Arrow diagram

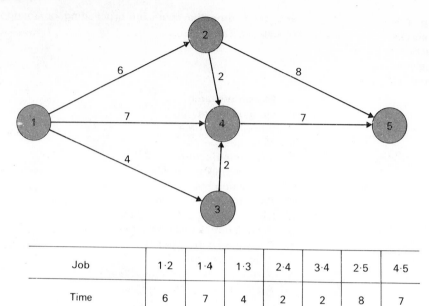

Job	1·2	1·4	1·3	2·4	3·4	2·5	4·5
Time	6	7	4	2	2	8	7

Fig. 2.3.3
Bar chart of
job sequence

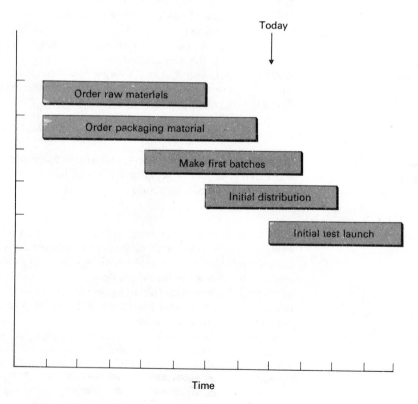

The indicator for today is moved
through the charts daily

Fig. 2.3.4
A simple
network
analysis of
three jobs.

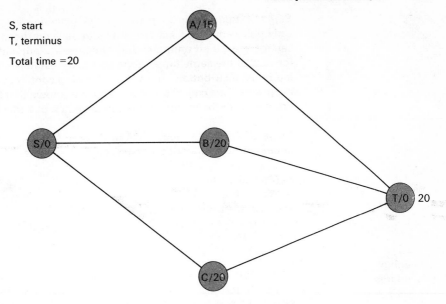

S, start
T, terminus

Total time =20

Fig. 2.3.5
A network
analysis of
seven jobs.
T = units of time

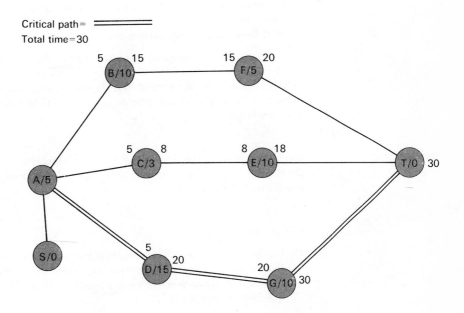

Critical path=
Total time=30

Stage 2. Endeavour to place all the activities in a job sequence. Some activities cannot be started until others have been completed (salesmen cannot be trained until they have been recruited) and other activities can go forward at the same time. Preparations for establishing agencies, for arranging initial distribution, for making shipping contracts, for arranging advertising promotions can all go ahead once it is known that the company is going to proceed with the manufacture and despatch of a trial batch.

Stage 3. Translate these facts to diagrams, bar charts or network analysis. Endeavour to work out the most reliable estimate of time taken thus:
1. Best time $= a$.
2. Most likely time $= b$.
3. Worst time $= c$.
The average time will then be $= \frac{1}{6} (a+4b+c)$.

Screening
procedures

It has been said many times that the reason most new products fail is lack of attention to detail in the development stages. This means that all new ideas have to be screened against a background of known facts. The desiderata for new products are known and can be specified. A product planning activity, which means making the most use of current products and finding new products to make the most use of resources, proceeds through a commercial specification as follows:

1. Maximise the present good products as long as possible. Where products are buoyant encourage and support them. Push in markets where the company is successful.
2. Endeavour to find extra distribution or extra markets for these current products that are successful. Push successful lines into other markets.
3. Find new products for present markets to supplement present successes or make up for declining products.
4. Find new products for new markets.

In most cases a company should proceed through these stages in order. Until stage (1) has been satisfied further steps are not desirable.

This said, it must be realised that screening procedures can be applied to an analysis of the market, the product, or indeed to the development process of the new idea.

New product
analysis

Every part of the development of a new product should be examined in great detail so as to make sure that nothing vital has been overlooked or given insufficient attention.

Preliminary steps

1. Define product exactly, enumerate the plus-points.
2. Examine the effect of the product on the present capacity of the company.
3. Establish a responsibility for the product; establish a new product team.
4. Establish a budget.

Product evaluation

1. Internal data (capacity, plant utilisation, cash flow).
2. Evaluation of market/product (see below).
3. Estimate trends (sales and market forecasts).
4. Draw up overall plans.

Detailed preliminary planning

1. Examine method of work in detail and establish priorities.
2. Examine time schedules and establish PERT or critical path charts for the venture.
3. Define requirements in personnel, material, money.
4. Examine in detail resources allocations.
5. Establish alternative plans.

Evaluation of market/product

The cardinal features that must be known and evaluated are profit and growth potential:

1. Define the market and the major segments. Segmentation is most important by (a) price; (b) type of customer or distribution channel; and (c) product types.
2. Size of the market in volume and value. What trends are apparent? Is it declining—static—growing—growing rapidly?
3. What is the special nature of the market, defined by age groups, by social classes? Can it be affected by external actions, such as government actions in the shape of economic regulations or new moves against pollution, or health scares?
4. Estimate the expected profit pattern of the new product.
5. How stable is the market? Is growth possible for this product at home or overseas?
6. Examine saleability. How well will this product fit into the existing sales picture?
7. Production. Define the task of fitting this new product into existing engineering, technical and production capabilities.

If desired, a formal analysis and rating system for each part of the problem can be made. Thus:

Market	Weight	Poor	Average	Good
Present size	3	£2–3 m	£3–5 m	£5–10 m
Growth	3	Static	Growing	Good growth
Nature	4	Sensitive	Resistant	Not sensitive
Peak periods	4	1 peak	Fluctuations	None

or in another way:

Market group	Factor	Weighting	Rating	Score
Size		3		
	£2–3 m		1	
	3–5 m		2	
	5–10 m		3	
Growth		3		
	Static		1	
	Growing		2	
	Good growth		3	

An analysis for each factor of market assessment or product in this way.

New product launching

Launching new products is an expensive procedure and the cost of failure can be high. Moreover in spite of all the time and trouble expended on new products and their introduction, experience shows that in some parts of industry, particularly in the consumer fields, the incidence of failure is very high, something over 60 per cent of all new products. Many preliminary tests have been evolved to reduce the risks. One danger lies in prolonging the test periods too long because this can present valuable information to competitors. This commercial intelligence is passed around quite unwittingly, often by suppliers, and no special spy system is required. A delay of more than 18 months between test marketing and final launch must present information to all the trade.

Launching procedure

By experience a pattern has been evolved for launching new products which usually follows this sequence:

- Market research
- Market evaluation
- Market appreciation
- Marketing plan
- Product testing
- Test marketing in one or two areas
  Panel tests
  Group tests
  Placement tests
- Reappraisal of marketing plan
- Area launch
- Complete launch

Some of these factors will be discussed later in detail.

Product testing

Industrial products will be tested at all stages of development for such factors as performance, output, durability, test-running. Similarly consumer goods

will be product tested during the developing stages for all consumer requirements such as taste, flavour, texture and so on. Machines of course can be
tested against known specifications and measured in performance against
competitive machinery or models. These can be tests of performance,
strength, flexibility.

Test marketing

Test marketing is used to find customer acceptance of the new product, to
evaluate the position of the new product in the ultimate overall marketing
plan, to estimate the pattern of distribution required for a complete launch and
to estimate the sales promotional effort required to send the new product
successfully on its way. Consumer goods use a whole battery of tests to
eliminate failure. Industrial products employ pre-marketing tests such as
simulation exercises, controlled pilot plant or customer application studies.

*Consumer goods
test marketing*

Before going to an area launch it is usual to carry out consumer acceptance
tests. The size and duration of these tests must depend upon the time and
money available and the controls laid down by the critical path analysis charts.
The chief methods are as follows:

Test panels. These will be selected groups of consumers who are faced with
the new product and products already on the market of a similar nature and
asked prepared questions that build up into a consumer picture of the product.
It is essential that the consumers invited to serve on the panel are a
representative sample of the whole market—that is to say, a selection of
consumers of differing age groups, social classes, occupations and so on. The
work is highly technical and is best done by agencies who specialise in this
work.

House to house questionnaires. This is a variant of the first method. Instead of
asking consumers to attend a meeting place such as a town hall, the
researchers conducting the test marketing call on households, again with
carefully prepared questionnaires and with samples.

Random interviews. These are interviews and questions with sampling
conducted at places where pedestrian traffic flow is heavy such as market-
places, fairs, supermarkets, and so on. All of these consumer tests depend
primarily on the knowledge and skill of the people conducting the tests and
their skill in framing the questions. Equally important is the choice of samples
offered as test products and control products.

Placement tests

These are tests where goods are actually placed on sale in carefully selected
and observed shops or, in the case of machinery or industrial products, placed
on trial for a given period with selected customers. These tests are usually
conducted over larger groups than can be covered by consumer panels and
indeed placement tests with some selected supermarkets will be almost
equivalent to area launches.

Area launches

Area launches are the last stop before complete launch and are based usually on TV areas or on selected marketing areas. For example for many years in the UK most marketing people have used the framework of the seven major conurbations of Greater London, Greater Manchester, West Midlands, Greater Glasgow, Merseyside, Tyneside, and the Leeds–Bradford area.

Within these densely populated areas lives something like 40 per cent of the population of the whole country accounting for some 43 per cent of the total retail trade of the whole area. Each area supplies the following advantages:

- A large population sufficient to give a cross section of age and income groups.
- The areas are so concentrated so that test selling is relatively inexpensive.
- A large variety of trades and crafts and a large variety of all kinds of shops.

If these areas are too large then a smaller beginning can be made by using test towns that present similar characteristics. The towns usually chosen come from this list: Aberdeen, Bournemouth, Chatham, Darlington, Exeter, Leicester, Norwich, Worcester, York.

Complete launch

Before a company goes to a complete launch it is essential to evaluate all the information that has been gathered so far from product testing, consumer tests, placement tests, and regional market tests and if necessary reappraise the overall marketing plan. By this time the company will know not only if the new product plan is to go ahead, but it will have further knowledge of the sales force's ability to handle the line, what chances of success are likely, what initial share of the market is possible and what price levels and promotional costs are required. The essentials for success are:

- Pre-selling market analysis of customer requirements.
- Adequate initial test marketing programme.
- Then speed in a successful follow-up with concentration on the new effort.

4 Overall marketing management

Overall management from a marketing point of view is concerned with fitting all the pieces together in such a way that the maximum benefit to the company ensues. It surveys the factors we have so far discussed and endeavours to mix them so that the highest profitability is obtained. It adds to these factors the operational activities of selling and sales promotional efforts of all kinds and it attempts to exercise a constant control (by means of feedback) of all the factors involved. This is commonly called the *marketing mix* and since this is the framework of marketing management we repeat it here. It will of course vary from company to company since each company endeavours to find the right combination of all these factors so as to arrive at the best final results. A high-margin low-volume company would proceed quite differently from a low-margin high-volume operation. What is important is that each company should recognise exactly what it is doing and follow the appropriate steps.

Marketing mix: major factors

Market research: Company research. Our markets are always changing; our customers are always changing. The company itself, and all its elements must be examined critically at stated periods.

The products made; the product range of the company. We must choose products the market wants; we must endeavour to choose products that give us maximum plant utilisation and the most favourable volume/profit ratio.

The presentation, packaging and image of the product range. The outward appearance, the design, the presentation of our goods must be under constant review.

The policy for pricing. We must carefully manage our pricing to yield the maximum advantage from Volume/Price/Cost relationships. This needs continuing attention and action.

The policy for discounting and trade terms. We have to decide how we deal with the trade to the maximum advantage. We cannot go against the current commercial practice in the marketplace but we must not lead it in overgenerous terms or extra discounts. Incentive buying terms that encourage trade are a most important marketing device.

The selling policy and method. Do we sell to a few large customers or distributors with a highly paid but small sales force or do we deal with 50 000 customers through a large sales force? We have to choose what is best for us in the long run, and this is not always doing what our competitors do. Do we sell goods under our own name or do we make goods for other people?

The sales organisation and operations to be followed. Do we have a highly structured sales force, with merchandising as well? Do we have highly skilled technical representation? Do we sell through personal effort and personal representation, or is our policy to achieve distribution and sell through advertising?

After-sales service, technical aid and complaints service. For many companies, especially those in the industrial field, the most important factor (and sometimes the most costly) is the after-sales service supplied. Japanese and German motor car manufacturers' selling programmes in the USA have been characterised by the most aggressive techniques employing lavish after-sales service as the 'product plus'.

The channels and method of distribution; stock maintenance and materials handling capacity. This is a factor of increasing importance for all companies and of overriding importance for some. This is one of the areas where major savings can be made, especially when stocks can be reduced by the use of computer control. Dead stock is money denied to the business and reduced stocks made possible by computer control represent, in many cases, one of the biggest areas of financial advantage from the use of computers. This is particularly true of stock dispersed throughout the country in many stock points, such as multidepot operations, or multiple shops.

The advertising and promotional policies: PR. This, for many companies, is the most important factor of all in the marketing mix. Indeed for some companies the advertising and sales promotional mix is, in fact, the marketing mix. How we advertise our goods, the means and the methods we use to do this, the money we spend on sales promotions and on public relations, must influence decisively our marketing results.

Here then, in a very brief summary, is a marketing blueprint for any company and, correctly employed together with financial control, it must help the company to higher productivity and profitability. The manner in which this marketing management is applied will, of course, influence the degree of success of the company, and we may perhaps examine a number of special aspects of the matter.

Planning for action

The basic selling plan for any company begins with the following steps:

1. The market situation supplied by market research. What we are doing, what our competitors are doing, what our industry is doing.
2. The sales forecasts.
3. The sales budget.
4. The Company budget.
5. Marketing plan with the establishment of separate targets for areas, customers or salesmen, broken down for markets and segments of the market, for products and for time periods.
6. Feedback and control.

Beyond this, marketing management will have already decided on the markets it will attack, and the product mix to be used. Likewise it will have something to say about channels of distribution and costs, especially in relation to the competition. What effects will these plans have on our resources allocation? And what advertising shall we use and in what form? All these questions must be satisfactorily answered both as short-term and long-term benefits. No doubt there will be during this stage of planning the closest collaboration with finance and production to make sure company targets are achievable, and if achievable, are going to be met.

In all these plans it is essential—

- to set precise targets;
- to set times to achieve these objectives;
- to ensure feedback for instant and continuous control;
- to modify plans to remain on target.

How do we attack the market?

We can talk about the market for motor-cars, or the market for transformers, or the market for crucibles but we are talking about total markets and only giant companies are concerned with frontal attacks over the whole line. Every company should be prepared to tailor its efforts so that the maximum success is possible under normal trading conditions. When Carl Duerr revived Jensen Motors Ltd he was not competing with the British Motor Corporation on a broad front. He was producing an efficient, high performance car designed for a limited but highly specialised market.

It is necessary to be selective, and for a company to select those markets which should provide them with the volume and profit required. Markets can be divided by geography, by type of trade, by type of usage, by social class, by technology. This is the old adage of concentrating on what the company can do best and selling it where the company can find the greatest acceptability. This may be because of product application, or specialities of any kind (sometimes service specialities developed by the firm) or resources and facilities available.

For example, when a food manufacturer looks at the food market in England he sees, among other things, the following market segments, all of them requiring slightly different treatment and some requiring conflicting services or packaging:

Grocery shops
Multiple and Co-operative shops
Symbol wholesale groups
Cash and carry wholesalers
Hypermarkets and discount stores
Industrial catering establishments
Traditional wholesalers
Transportation services

Markets can be examined and divided by trade groups, as above, by income and age groups, by occupation, by social class. Variations in demand caused by geography are also important, in some industries, especially in food and furniture, but this factor is becoming less important with the speed and spread of modern communications. The major market variables are:

Trade classification   Sex
Buyer motives   Geographical location
Age   Education
Income   Social class
Occupation

For most trades the first four are the most important. What really matters is that the company must examine the market carefully and select its area of attack. To mount a full scale assault along the whole length of the great wall of China can be suicide. There are many chinks in it which can be selected.

How do we improve profitability?

The management of marketing is intended to result in greater profitability and this can come about principally from three factors lying within the marketing area:

- more sales without undue increase in selling costs;
- reducing costs wherever possible;
- utilising all capital (in whatever form) to the utmost.

Of course, as we have already seen, most improvements in profitability can more readily be achieved by attempting a better balance amongst the factors that create profit. These can be briefly stated:

- Reduction in stocks, which usefully follows from efficient use of computer control but need not necessarily wait for this. Multidepot operations inevitably mean or require a precise stock control. Materials handling is also important. So many ways can be followed to handle stock more quickly, more efficiently—as for example mobile stacking in cargo ships which enables a high degree of mechanisation to be brought to this operation—and all this means less money tied up in stocks.
- Reduction in monies owing to the company which can and often does run into millions of pounds these days. In a period of expensive money it pays a company to employ elaborate schemes to activate the flow of money back to the company.
- Price increases. This factor must be used with caution because it can affect volume.
- Incentive schemes of all kinds aimed at higher production or higher sales, or maintained sales.
- Increased expenditure on advertising or sales promotions aimed at higher sales volume without a proportionate increase in other sales expenditure (for example, no additional staff).

Costs reductions begin with a critical examination of all the major marketing costs involved. This requires acceptable standards, in terms of time and performance, so that we can judge variances against a stated measure. Naturally, the highest profitability results from the highest volume of the largest margin lines that also give the company the maximum labour and plant utilisation so that unrecovered overheads are minimal. This situation is ideal and cannot be maintained without a sustained effort of control and correction. The major marketing costs are given in summary below and these should be studied in detail for comparative purposes. We should seek to separate those costs which vary directly with the volume of sales and those which are fixed.

Marketing costs analysis

Marketing costs are best considered under different headings according to their origins.

Development costs

Market research
Packaging and design
Dummy runs.

Product costs

Product design
Special export requirements, split runs, special packaging
Packing costs.

Sales costs

Sales force costs; salaries, expenses, transport discounts and allowances; trade discounts and long term incentive discounts
Advertising costs
Sales promotion costs. Below the line expenditure, premium schemes, sales incentives, co-operative advertising
Guarantees and warrants
Merchandising and exhibition expenditure.

Distribution costs

Transportation
Warehousing
Stock control, especially in multidepot operations
Returns
Distribution costs variance between different market segmentations.

Service and administrative costs

Receiving and processing orders
Complaints and after sales service
Credit facilities, especially in overseas markets
Invoicing and statements
Credit reduction, and debt collection.

The total expenditure of the company, which includes all marketing costs, is contained within the company budget, and this total expenditure is broken down into the various cost centres. But the expenditure of each centre must itself be examined constantly in great detail to make sure that all costs are necessary and are making their contribution to the final profitability of the enterprise.

How this is done will depend on the character of the company. Many consumer companies selling in volume endeavour to express sales promotion costs on a unit basis. But this clearly does not take account of the price/volume/margin relationship, and once fixed costs have been covered the margin of profit changes dramatically. Other companies include all expenses separately within their budget programmes and control expenditure by monthly breakdowns. Company global figures under such headings as sales promotion, merchandising, premium incentive schemes and so on can be broken down by marketing or sales into shares per area, or customer, or sales sections.

Pricing policy and product performance

This is a matter to be found at the centre of the control of marketing costs stemming from the company attitude towards pricing. We must first discuss how prices are fixed. For most products there exist two significant points:

1. A price above which the product will not sell;
2. A price below which no *extra* sales can be made.

Clearly between the medieval concept of a just price, and the modern idea of maximum profitability there is some divergence. Nevertheless pricing should not be left to chance and, once established, prices must be reviewed frequently. There are two major principles of price fixing; market value and cost plus pricing and both are difficult of exact definition.

Market value pricing

1. Value to the customer (this will vary according to the customer).
2. Alternative buying possibilities open to him; prices, values, performances (as soon as a product has any special features, or unique elements, this factor is difficult of appraisal).
3. Product differentials; is the product really different and in what way? Product differences that exist for a manufacturer may be non-existent to the customer.
4. The selling company's impact and reputation.
5. The buyer's attention to price as a factor.

Once the company has decided on the price at which it will sell—which is determined largely by its efforts to obtain the largest contribution to the profitability picture of the company, it is then faced with two questions:

● Will this price give it the maximum profit for the volume that will most probably ensue?
● Will the end result be a financial gain for the company?

Cost-plus pricing

This method of pricing is by establishing a cost estimate and adding a margin for profit. It is often the practice where a range of products is made to add the same margin for each product. The disadvantage of this method, which some call an arbitrary way of price fixing (since prices *in a market* have no relation to internal costs of any company—the company must conform to the market, not the market to the company) is that it produces a number of problems:

1. Allocated costs are hard to establish; how are costs spread over the product lines of a company? What do we mean when we talk about recovering

costs? (How can we recover costs in a company except by making an end profit, and to do this we may have to reduce our selling prices, or increase them?) This can result in overpricing some products and underpricing others.

2. No allowance is made for volume changes.
3. Demand is not taken into account; the market may be willing to pay a much higher price.
4. It is difficult to avoid costs that are out of date; so that, at best, our prices are based on estimated costs of raw materials and wages which in these days can be altered considerably within any twelve months.

Pricing decisions and marketing strategy

Under present-day conditions the time-span of products tends to be shorter than in the past. Since products can no longer look forward hopefully to an infinity of selling, there is much to be said for making the maximum profit as soon as possible and only reducing prices when competitors appear. On the other hand, many large companies today with a product commanding a considerable part of the market would still price the product low enough to afford maximum volume and, if possible, keep competitors out. The trouble with this policy in a period of inflation is that the company is operating its volume on a narrower margin, which can vanish overnight.

The important thing is to attempt some study of the profit–volume relationship by an endeavour to examine closely the various factors affecting the issue. It is necessary to distinguish clearly between *fixed costs* (those which remain constant over a certain period, e.g. rent, rates, salaries, depreciation) and *variable costs* (those which vary directly over the same period with the amount of business done, e.g. ingredient costs, transport costs). The difference between variable costs and sales revenue is called the *contribution*, because clearly this amount represents the contribution made by the sales effort to cover fixed costs and to provide a profit. *Breakeven point* is the point where the contribution is equal to fixed costs. From the breakeven point we can see the margin of safety which is the percentage that sales can drop before arriving at the breakeven point. For example:

	Company A	Company B
Sales revenue	£5 000 000	£10 000 000
Breakeven point	3 750 000	9 500 000
Safety margin	25%	5%

Let us assume the following conditions:

Sales	£5 000 000	
Variable costs	3 000 000	
Contribution	2 000 000	
Fixed costs	1 500 000	
Net profit	500 000	
Breakeven point	3 750 000	$\left(\text{Sales} \times \dfrac{\text{Fixed costs}}{\text{Contribution}} \right)$
Margin of safety	1 250 000 (25%)	(Sales—breakeven point)
Profit volume ratio	40%	$\left(\dfrac{\text{Contribution}}{\text{Sales}} \times 100 \right)$

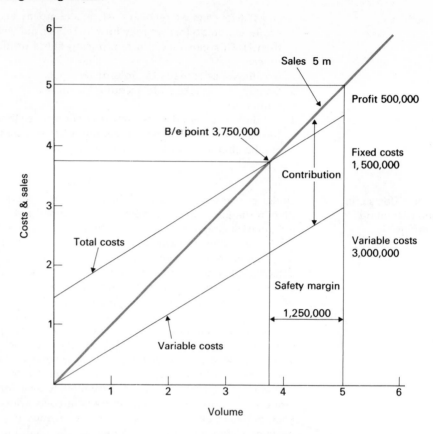

Fig. 2.4.1
Breakeven
chart

(*Note*. On this budget, with a sales estimate of £5m and a profit of £500 000 the rate of profit is 10 per cent. However, once fixed costs have been covered the profitability becomes much higher and is the ratio between contribution and sales which is 40 per cent.) This is shown in chart form in Fig. 2.4.1.

However marketing management has the choice of selecting varying prices at which a product can be sold and attempting to plot the estimated sales volume and profit from each price:

Selling price per unit	£8	£9	£10	£11	£12
Estimated sales volume	10 000	9 000	8 000	6 000	4 000
Variable costs £5 per unit					
Fixed costs £9000					
"Contribution"	30 000	36 000	40 000	36 000	28 000

The selling price of £10 per unit would probably be chosen to ensure the maximum profitability, so long as we were sure this price was not too high to invite competition. Sales volume is obviously affected by many factors of which price is often the most important. The elasticity of demand must be estimated and some sales and profit projection attempted. But this must be done with great caution in today's commercial atmosphere. No company moves in a vacuum.

Factors bearing on prices, costs and returns are fully reviewed in Part Five.

Distribution

Marketing is concerned with two aspects of distribution:

Distribution within a market. This means channels of distribution within a trade and segmentation of the market to ensure that distribution is effective and comprehensive.

Distribution between markets. Here basically we are concerned with materials handling facilities, transportation, warehousing, and distribution systems.

In recent years no aspect of marketing costs has shown greater increases than distribution and this is true for all countries and all sophisticated markets. It is equally true that in this area lies a fruitful field for costs reductions. We have already discussed earlier in this chapter (How do we attack the market?) the problem of market segmentation, and market channels. The market must be analysed constantly in precise detail to make sure that the products of the company are arriving at every possible outlet.

Physical distribution in the sense of moving the product from one place to another on its way to the ultimate customer is the area where costs escalate and can upset a marketing programme. Here the major costs are:

● Wages. Transport and crane drivers' wages have sharply increased.
● Machinery. Lorries and mobile cranes, stackers and all materials handling machinery becomes more sophisticated and more expensive. It is essential to see that they are fully employed.
● Maintenance and repair charges have also sharply increased.
● Warehousing costs have risen. It costs more to build and maintain warehouses in the 1970s.
● The sheer costs of stocks both of materials in progress and finished goods in transit can rise to frightening figures as the company grows and its distribution increases.

But we also have to consider still further the reduction in these costs made possible by regard to the following factors:

● Size and type of vehicles. Large vehicles for long distance hauling. Containers for overseas deliveries. Medium sized vehicles for town deliveries.
● Loading methods. Bulk loading or unit loading. Night and day facilities.
● Frequency of deliveries, altered according to size of customer and special requirements.
● Location of delivery points; built up area, depot area.
● Own transport, hired transport or both.
● Nature of transport. Container and groupage service; train, lorry, air, ship.

The Marketing Manager clearly has a duty to see that his marketing ideas do not push up his transport costs unduly. If he suddenly introduces a number of new products he greatly complicates the work of stackers and loaders in all his depots. If he suddenly introduces a product twice as heavy as anything previously handled without consideration of this factor he can cause chaos in the depots and probably a strike as well.

The key to management of distribution costs is a precise control of all elements of the costs involved and a continuing effort to find ways to reduce them. No costs should be taken for granted. A company must have timely and accurate cost information. It is here that the use of computer services can be most effective, especially in multidepot stock control.

Sales forecasting

Sales forecasting is the beginning of the operation to plan our marketing moves in the following year. We need sales forecasting to be as accurate as possible because on these forecasts we base our marketing plans and indeed our company budget in which we plan all our company activity for the coming year and our expected profitability.

We should first examine all external factors that will influence our markets:

- Government action. Government control of wages and prices. The effect of entrance into the Common Market, the introduction of Value Added Tax, the European restitution system. Actions of foreign governments that may affect our overseas markets.
- World market trends. Changes in world commodity prices, or government intervention in such world prices.
- Social changes in the market. The effect of the new Industrial Relations Act and equal pay for women. The effect of large scale unemployment.
- The competition. We must try to estimate what our competitors are likely to do in the near future.
- New materials, new products. We must try to evaluate the effects of new materials or new products on our company.

Then we should examine all internal factors:

- Plant capacity. Are our resources fully utilised, or is new plant being installed next year? What difference will this make to our sales volume?
- Labour facilities. Have we adequate labour for all branches of the company throughout the year? Do we have peaks and troughs?
- Are we introducing new lines?
- What will happen to our costs of ingredients and level of sales prices next year?
- If our sales and production increase do we have adequate materials handling facilities, or storage depots? Do we have alternative plans for overcoming this problem?

Having surveyed these background external and internal factors we can then proceed to a practical method of sales forecasting. It is said that it is difficult to use past figures to predict future business, but if careful records have been kept these form a reliable base from which to start. (If statistical methods are to be followed in great details there are many excellent books on the subject and names of some are given in the book list at the end of this section.) We would suggest a practical plan based on the following pattern, as already outlined in an earlier chapter:

1. *Analyse and process past sales figures.* We calculate sales for the last three years under products (a graph line for each product) and we prepare moving annual totals for each product. We show these figures in chart form. We project the trend for each product (longer than three years is not relevant).

2. *Internal changes.* We allow for changes due to
   price increases
   new channels of distribution
   additional sales staff
   advertising campaigns or sales promotions
   new lines, or new versions of present products.

3. *All other factors*, including
   competitors
   political changes (common market, taxes, new legislation)
   other contingencies.

Once the total sales estimates have been forecast by product line for the whole company these can be broken down by areas and by time periods to be agreed by the sales side and to form the basis for sales targets and sales plans for the following years.

The company budget

The marketing programme of any company is translated into financial terms by means of the company budget. This company budget embraces all the activities of the company but in the first place is built up on the sales forecast which states the volume of trade estimated for the following year. This section is concerned only with those items of the budget that are of direct interest and responsibility to the marketing section. (The company budget itself is fully covered in Part Five: see page 691).

The Marketing Manager is concerned with the following budget factors:

1. Total gross sales
2. Total trade discounts
3. Total net sales
4. Total marketing expenses
   (*a*) Selling expenses
   (*b*) Advertising
   (*c*) Sales promotions
   (*d*) Transportation and delivery
   (*e*) Public relations
   (*f*) Market research
   (*g*) New product development.

Each factor will have an individual separate analysis which will serve to build up the total budget and also to show variances as the year proceeds:

1. Total gross sales, made up by product, by areas, and by markets (Home, Overseas, etc.).
2. Total trade discounts: analysis of the amount and make up of trade discounts to be given.
3. Total net sales.
4. Total marketing expenses:
   (*a*) Selling expenses: salaries by divisions, home and overseas sales; expenses; bonuses; car expenses; insurances etc.
   (*b*) Advertising appropriations; appropriations by media and by product.
   (*c*) Sales promotions: all below the line expenses; long term bonuses; incentive premiums; sales promotions; dealer incentives.
   (*d*) Transportation and deliveries: cost of own transport; cost of hired transport; depot costs; personnel car costs; insurance; maintenance costs.
   (*e*) Public relations: cost of PR work through the press and personal contacts; summary of expense programme.
   (*f*) Market research: summary of suggested programmes.
   (*g*) New product development: summary of suggested programmes.

–   Once the final budget has been agreed and accepted the business plans for the following year are made and in the ensuing year checked at monthly intervals for variances from the standards laid down.

Marketing plans

The various factors we have surveyed so far in this chapter are the elements on which a company builds its marketing plans. The sales forecast and the company budget are drawn up to cover the company activities in the following twelve months but marketing plans will be constructed to cover three or four years in advance, always on a continuous planning process. In this way a company ensures that what it plans to do in the immediate future will not obstruct or put at risk its long term plans.

To do this a company has to ask itself continuously a number of questions.

1. Does the company know its market share and is it satisfied with this? How can the company grow and by what steps? Has the company fully examined the market, with its segmentation and diversification? Markets may be segmented by geography, by type of trade, by type of distribution. The rapid rise in air traffic alone means new segments of old markets opening up to all kinds of trade including the construction industries for new airports, new buildings, new runways.

2. Is the company overconcerned with production efficiency or customer satisfaction? Why should this be? A company whose directors were all engineers, where no one in top management had any connection with selling, would tend to see all its problems in terms of production.

3. Where is the company going? What new products, what new directions is it moving towards? Is diversification useful or a mirage? Are mergers desirable or necessary? This question is basic to all the others. A company has to answer, for itself, the following questions:

Present strategy. What is the business of the firm? How does it relate to the total market? What are the managers trying to do?

Alternative strategies. What alternatives are open to the business to improve its future potential? Joint ventures, mergers, expansion from within?

Future strategies. In considering the probable development of the economic background in general, and the industry in which the company is engaged in particular, what future strategies should the company consider?

4. What is the company strength? Is it the same now that it was ten to twenty years ago? Have competitors changed in scope and character? What happens to the company in the European Economic Community? This is really an extension of the previous point and begins with an analysis of the company. Changing total conditions in a market can radically alter the prospects of a company. The advantages a company previously enjoyed can disappear with changes in market patterns.

5. Is the company management and its control fully adequate to deal with the changes that lie ahead? Management grows older and business conditions grow more complicated. A policy for developing new managers is an essential requisite for survival, and more importantly and in most cases more painfully, a policy for integrating the new men in the management team must be carried out. Retiring managers are apt to be slow to relinquish power and quick to interfere with younger managers.

The marketing plans are of course part of the company overall plans and they must therefore work towards company objectives. These must number amongst the top priorities the following points:

- Profitability and growth. Profit measured as a percentage of sales and also as a return on assets invested in the company.
- Market penetration. However we regard the markets we serve and the segmentation of these markets, we seek for a position where the company has an influence, an impact on the scene.
- The accretion of physical and financial resources, thus allowing the company to grow and allowing personnel employed by the company to develop and grow also.

Long-term planning

Arising naturally from the concept that marketing plans must be based on a longer period than the next twelve months, the idea of longer term planning as a corporate activity is to be found in those forward-looking companies whose size and wealth demand the greater assurance of growth and survival. Forward planning on a long term basis has many advantages but of them all the most important benefit is that it engenders forward thinking about future activities, and forward planning.

Not to plan ahead in today's climate is to leave the future to chance, and at best means that good situations are not exploited and full use of company assets in money and personnel is not made.

Long-term corporate planning requires a detailed analysis of the present situation of the company, a clear statement of the objectives of the company and an examination of the means whereby these objectives can be met and alternative plans of action if they are not met. Clearly long-term planning involves the whole company, but the marketing side is heavily involved in the programmes and indeed in the formulation of long-term planning. This management operation has been very heavily criticised, and whenever a large company faces a difficult period the cynics immediately point to the long-range planners. This view, which is widely held, is most unhelpful. However difficult it is to engage in serious long-term planning there is one inescapable fact that every marketing man knows. To go forward into the future, in contemporary conditions, merely on the basis of day-to-day business, to manage a company on the basis of hope and courage without any forward planning whatsoever, is to put the company at risk. To plan a future, to take steps to provide for the future, to plan to meet the changes that the future must bring, at least means the company is prepared for storms and unlikely to be submerged by them.

By long-term planning we understand planning for three years or more. Some companies work to plans for ten years and beyond. In all cases the endeavour is to consider all aspects of an operation in terms of men, skills and plant, together with the money available, and to ensure by long term plans that clearly defined objectives are not only laid down, but made the target of planned activities within a measurable time scale.

The question of long-term planning is examined in greater detail in chapter 8 under the heading of Marketing Control.

5 The selling operation

The marketing executive of a company possesses two major factors by means of which he can seek to obtain sales volume profitability. One is *personal selling* and the other is *advertising*; the promotional efforts of these two factors will largely determine the overall drive of the company, its impact on the market, its efficiency and profitability. In this and the following chapters the selling efforts of a company are described in some detail.

The background of the industry in which a company moves dictates to a certain extent the kind of distributive pattern and hence the organisation of the sales force it employs. (One company will need a limited number of highly trained highly paid technical salesmen calling on head offices; another will require a force of 100 men with area and district managers calling on all branches of trade within an industry.)

Within this framework the task of personal selling can best be comprehended by considering the two basic phases of this activity. First a company has to build and maintain a sales force of the necessary calibre and then it has to employ this sales force to its utmost capacity. These two basic divisions will be examined in this way:

1. Selection and recruitment of the right kind of people.
   Induction and initial training in sales work.
   Motivation.
   Organisation, administration and development.
2. Control and management of a sales force.
   Stimulation and support.
   Continued training, especially in specific tasks.
   Fitting the sales effort to the marketing plan.
   Reducing sales costs.

Selection and recruitment of salesmen

In spite of all the selling aids available from advertising, sales promotional schemes, incentive sales programmes, the force of personal selling remains of the greatest importance in the marketing mix. Indeed some people would still maintain it is of the highest importance since no other factor in the marketing mix can produce such an influence on the sales volume. The Institute of Marketing and PA Management Consultants Limited published a joint report under the title of *Salesmen under the Microscope* which should be read and studied by every marketing man. The survey showed, among a comprehensive analysis of many aspects of the situation, that all companies, including those making industrial products as well as consumer goods, expected a considerable difference in performance—and in all cases the expectation was founded on experience—between the results of an average salesman and a good one. The margin, in fact, was over 25 per cent. This is a very considerable increase in turnover for a minimal increase in selling costs. A company must employ men of the highest calibre in the selling task.

The problem is how to recognise these men and where to find them. The selectors, the men who interview candidates for such jobs, must themselves be men of wide experience in selling and interviewing and men of discernment. It is easy to recognise the non-starter but difficult to spot the near-genius, who has never done any selling but will always be at the top of any sales competitive table. It is perhaps a good start to list the attributes of a successful salesman. A short list of the most important points is given:

● Enthusiasm, the most important attribute of all, without which no selling is possible.
● Confidence in himself and his company; this soon communicates itself to the buyer.
● Persistence, a refusal to accept a blank order sheet.
● Self-discipline, the self-imposed time and motion study.
● Integrity, which builds up confidence in the buyers.
● Command of language, necessary for persuasion and communication.
● Mental and physical energy.
● Understanding the value of good personal relationships and all that this means.
● Desire to make money. The source of continuous drive.

But a list of qualities is not sufficient, because in addition to being men of the right calibre the men chosen must come into selling for the right reasons; not as a stop-gap, not as a fill-in, but by choice, because the candidate understands the importance to a company of personal selling, understands equally what is required of him and believes that selling in these conditions and within the framework offered is the one job that he feels he can do supremely well.

The industrial salesman

The industrial salesman requires all these qualities but other things as well. He must possess technical qualifications required by his industry and a thorough product knowledge enabling him to describe his product not only in terms of his customer's business but also in terms of industry advantage. He must in other words possess a technical background relating not only to his own product but also to the products of his competitors. He must have a complete knowledge of his industry. At each call he has to present:

● his own company product or service;
● the application of his product or service, *in terms of his customer's business*;
● the picture of how his product will help his customer in the industry or trade the company serves;
● the advantages he offers over competitive products.

There is an additional role filled by salesmen that is of the utmost importance, especially to the industrial salesman. A salesman has to deal with complaints and, correctly handled, this is a valuable service not only for the customer but the supplier company. Consumer complaints correctly acted on can remove the cause of the complaints and enable a company to move nearer to the point of customer satisfaction.

In the case of the industrial salesman far more is at stake. The industrial salesman in dealing with complaints should, by correct advice, enable the customer to obtain better utilisation or perhaps to change to another model more adequate to the customer's purpose. In any case the salesman can help solve problems and suggest possible answers because he will already have seen the same complaint elsewhere. He probably discusses the same or similar problems with the technical staff of his customers and in fact can pool the special knowledge he acquires. In doing these things he builds up confidence in his company and creates goodwill for the future.

Recruitment methods

Each company will adopt its own methods for recruiting sales staff. These may include personal recommendations (especially from within the sales force), trade associations and newspaper advertising. Salesmen come from all walks of life and therefore it pays to set a very wide net ranging from university boards to the daily press. It is desirable to interview candidates at least two or three times and some companies commonly interview five or six times in order to screen off possible failures. The cost of a failure in a sales organisation can be high because not only does trade fall away but the competition can build on the failure.

Evaluation charts, or screening procedures, are common at such sales interviews although the value in their charts lies in the skill of the interviewers and their interpretation of the results. A suggested evaluation chart is shown as Fig. 2.5.1.

Induction and initial training

Since the difference in efficiency between one sales force and another may form the basis for the difference in performance between two companies, it pays to set up systems for recruiting the best men and then training them as efficiently as possible. This begins with a man's induction to a company and nothing is more important to a new recruit than an efficient introduction and training. The pattern of his whole career is set during the initial training.

If the new recruit has not sold before, he requires training in basic techniques. Assuming this is done, each man then requires training within the company along the following lines:

- Industry background.
- Company background.
- Product knowledge.
- Survey of competitive activities.
- Sales organisation of the company and territory maps.
- Management and control procedures.
- Administrative details. Procedures for orders, deliveries, customer complaints, service requirements, cash collection, reports, daily, weekly or periodically.
- Expense allocations and controls.
- Selling policies, selling aids, selling procedures.

Fig. 2.5.1
Evaluation
chart

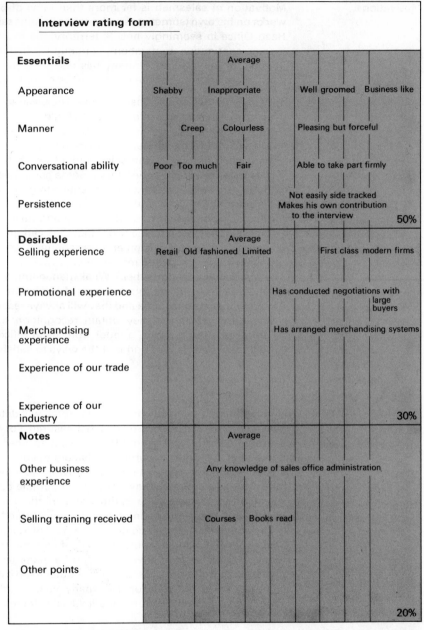

Interview rating form

Essentials						
		Average				
Appearance	Shabby	Inappropriate		Well groomed	Business like	
Manner	Creep	Colourless		Pleasing but forceful		
Conversational ability	Poor Too much	Fair		Able to take part firmly		
Persistence				Not easily side tracked Makes his own contribution to the interview		50%

Desirable						
Selling experience		Average				
	Retail Old fashioned Limited			First class modern firms		
Promotional experience				Has conducted negotiations with large buyers		
Merchandising experience				Has arranged merchandising systems		
Experience of our trade						
Experience of our industry						30%

Notes						
		Average				
Other business experience		Any knowledge of sales office administration				
Selling training received		Courses	Books read			
Other points						20%

This done (and such a programme can take three days or three weeks depending on the product knowledge required), the new man can go off for field training with an outside manager. Here he will learn to put into practice some of the things he has learnt at Head Office or in the company training centre, and will begin to build up his product knowledge—much of which can only come by seeing where his product fits into the businesses of his various customers. A suggested form, based on job analysis, is given in Fig. 2.5.2 to show checking procedures for standard selling jobs.

Motivation

Motivation of salesmen is far more than rates of pay. Because a salesman works on his own (sometimes in the case of export salesmen, miles away from Head Office in seemingly hostile territory), he must discipline himself. This means continuous motivation—continuous, that is, long after the initial impulse of joining the company has disappeared—is the key to the whole effort. Here are some of the main sources of motivation of a salesman:

1. Money in the form of basic income. The basic salary must be high enough to form a sensible base on which to build.
2. Money in the form of incentive bonuses. These bonuses come in many shapes and forms and are the extra reward for additional effort. They are controlled as part of the sales budget which the Sales Manager has to maintain for his marketing tasks. Some companies are of the opinion that good cars are a very powerful incentive to good salesmen:
3. Opportunity to grow with and in the company. Salesmen act and re-act on the basic policy that trade is growing and they are an integral part of the growth. They need to see proof that they can grow within their company.
4. The nature of supervision and management, conditions of service. Salesmen will support strong management in every endeavour so long as strong management supports them. Weak management is out of place in selling.
5. The challenge of the job; a sense of fulfilment. Salesmen, by their very nature, need a challenge and they will always respond so long as when they meet the challenge they obtain recognition for their efforts. A paragraph in a trade paper, a letter from head office, a note in some public relations material, are some of the ways to satisfy this requirement.

Organisation, administration and development

How men are organised within a sales force will determine very largely how efficiently they can be controlled and measured. For example it is desirable to set men to work in measured territories, measured that is to say in terms of population, weighted according to factors of communication, urban or rural areas, class of society purchasing power, so that as far as possible all territories in a company have nearly comparable buying power. In this way, selling efforts between one territory and another can be measured, and sales targets, and hence marketing plans, can be attacked methodically.

The administration and field management of a sales force calls for adequate field supervision and an efficient chain of command. It has been accepted for many years that six or seven men form a management load beyond which practical control is not possible. On the other hand it is essential to check that a company does not develop too many chiefs and not enough braves. A suggested scheme of control for a field sales force is shown in Fig. 2.5.3.

This means, in effect, that the company has 4 regional managers, 12 area managers and 72 territory salesmen, but of course added to this selling effort would undoubtedly be a number of national accounts executives, merchandising and display personnel and probably advertising people as well.

The day-to-day control of such a sales force would be effected by daily reports from the territory salesmen and weekly reports from the area managers. An example of a daily record sheet is shown at Fig. 2.5.4 (see p. 247). The point of major concern about these reports is the detailed analysis of each job.

Fig. 2.5.2
Job analysis
applied to
basic training
techniques

Performance rating											
Salesman											
Training officer					Area			Date			

	Lowest				Deciles				Highest		
	0	10	20	30	40	50	60	70	80	90	100
Distribution	•	•	•	•	•	•	•	•	•	•	•
Quotas met	•	•	•	•	•	•	•	•	•	•	•
Correct stock check	•	•	•	•	•	•	•	•	•	•	•
Merchandising arranged	•	•	•	•	•	•	•	•	•	•	•
Current sales promotions arranged	•	•	•	•	•	•	•	•	•	•	•
New lines introduced	•	•	•	•	•	•	•	•	•	•	•
Other	•	•	•	•	•	•	•	•	•	•	•

The highest performance is considered as 100%

In this way a central management can follow very closely how its selling tasks are being performed in the field and a clear picture can be built up in Head Office of the state of development of selling plans towards targets.

Control and management of a sales force

We have so far discussed the recruitment and induction of salesmen, their initial training and motivation and their organisation in a sales force. Many companies go no further than this and feel that from this point onwards a sales force must work out its own salvation. It is however at this point that a progressive company begins because a sales force that has been established with all the correct procedures needs to be stimulated, supported, activated and employed towards specific tasks required by the marketing executive. How all this is done is the subject of the remainder of this chapter.

Managing any activity means basically that we are planning certain actions and we must effectively stimulate and control what we are planning to do, which in this case means selling our products to the volume required by our sales plan with the selling costs allowed in our budget.

Plan

1. We have been given objectives by the marketing plan. Volume, product mix, marketing mix, sales promotional costs, discounts, incentives have all been allowed for.
2. We have agreed these objectives with our sales people and they have agreed that the objectives are reasonable and feasible. We have preliminary discussions with our sales people how we shall attain our objectives and what incentives are necessary to do this.

Fig. 2.5.3
A simple sales field management structure

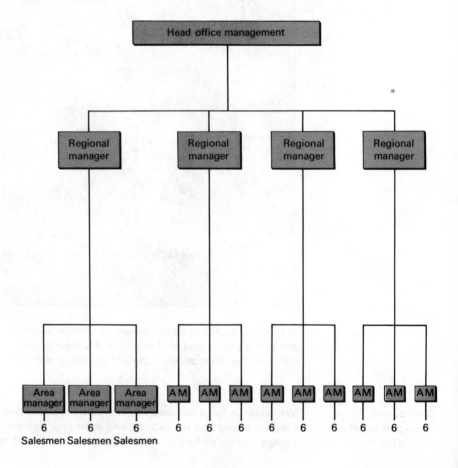

3. We set time scales for reaching objectives. It is useless waiting for the third quarter of a year to realise that sales targets cannot be met.

Work

1. The sales side receives the plans, agrees them, and digests them.
2. It begins the implementation of the plans.

Feedback

1. We check continuously, against a time pattern, and progress according to the plan.
2. We appraise the results and seek alternative action if necessary.

Analysis

From our controls we seek to answer the following questions.
1. What is going according to plan? We must have some plusses to compensate for failures elsewhere.
2. Where are we going wrong? Why are we going wrong?
3. Where is immediate remedial action possible?
4. What can we do better?

The essence of what we are doing is a precise and timely control of our selling efforts directed always towards the fulfilment of the sales part of the overall marketing plan. We must know when things are off-target so that we can take remedial action in time. The manager in the field is constantly asking himself the following questions:

● What am I trying to do?
● How am I trying to get there?
● Who or what is hampering the efforts of my team?
● How much time is left for my team to achieve the objective?
● How well or badly, in fact, are we doing?

Stimulation and support

A salesman is confronted with a standard set of objectives common to most companies:

1. To reach his own personal sales quotas.
2. To manage his territory and journey sequence so that he spends the maximum time with his customers and his costs are minimal.
3. To bring in new customers to allow for customers who disappear, or for growth.
4. To recognise customers capable of growth and develop his trade with them to the utmost. The essence of good selling is development and growth.

In order to achieve these objectives, year after year, he needs constant support from his head office in the shape of advertising, sales promotion, special schemes, public relations. In fact he needs all the ammunition, above and below the line, that his company can give him. Let us look at this in diagram form (Fig. 2.5.5).

The efficiency and the success of the field operations in all their aspects will depend very largely (once we have the right people, who have been adequately trained and are well organised) on the weight of support for the sales force coming from the stimulation efforts. And these must go on always renewing themselves in character and content for each marketing plan. Incentives on incentives, all strictly controlled within the sales plan, are necessary to maintain a continuing volume of sales. In addition to incentives given for specific selling tasks, such as attaining a target of sales volume, opening a given number of new accounts, arranging a given number of special displays or exhibitions, each man needs support in the following sales promotional areas:

- Displays and sales through special merchandising.
- Packaging. Presentation must be first class.
- Point of sale promotions.
- Trade shows, exhibitions, demonstrations.
- PR back-up.
- Consumer advertising.
- Special promotional schemes such as premium gifts, or incentive schemes, competitions.

In his day-to-day activities the salesman needs support by the provision of routine selling tools. These must include samples, brochures, visual sales aids, sample cases, and special requirements for his job according to the nature of the product he is selling.

Continued training, especially in specific tasks

Two factors are required to turn an average selling force into an above average condition. *One is an efficient management and the second is continuous training.* Nowhere is training more rewarding than in selling and it is training in specific tasks—specific that is to the company requirements—that can make a considerable difference in the final results. Business conditions change rapidly and continue to do so. A sales force must equally change its methods of approach constantly in order to meet these ever changing conditions. This demands constant in-company training in those specific tasks necessary to achieve the company objectives. The training must be in-company because only people within the company can realise the special needs of the company and analyse the methods necessary to supply the correct answer. A salesman therefore requires initial training in the mechanics of the job and the continuous coaching in sales methods designed to yield the best results. If this continuous training is coupled with adequate incentive schemes the result is a highly efficient selling force.

There will of course always be the need for training in outside establishments. The trainers have to be trained and a company must keep abreast with selling ideas from outside. But it is the permanent application of the training idea within a company that can produce the most notable results.

The objective in all this continuous training is to have a sales force that works as a total force concentrating on those marketing tasks demanded by the overall plan. The opposite is a large force where each part does what it finds to be the easiest jobs first and no overall plan for marketing mix or product mix can be truly efficient under these conditions. A sales force

Fig. 2.5.4
Daily recrod sheet

Daily record sheet

Name	District	Type of outlet				Display agreed			No. of cases merchandised			No. of cases for promotion						if applicable			Total cases
		c & c	S/M	S/C	C/S	Mass	D./B	Shelf	Mass	D/B	Shelf	1	2	3	4	5	6 S.C.	New A/C	Cour-tesy	Pio-neer	

No. _____

Date _____

Day's totals
Totals B/Fwd.
Totals to date

Total calls
Total orders

Complete on Friday
Non-productive calls
Average per order

Fig. 2.5.5
Support for
salesmen

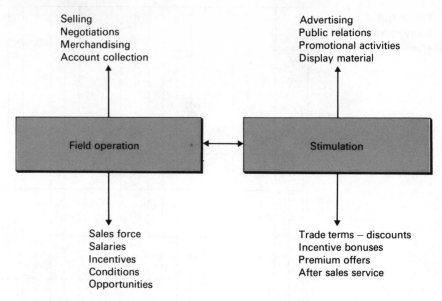

Selling
Negotiations
Merchandising
Account collection

Advertising
Public relations
Promotional activities
Display material

Sales force
Salaries
Incentives
Conditions
Opportunities

Trade terms – discounts
Incentive bonuses
Premium offers
After sales service

working as a total national force, specifically trained, actively stimulated, and closely controlled so that both drive and flexibility are maintained, can produce quite astonishing results.

Fitting the sales
effort to the
marketing plan

Without an overall control, fitted in most cases to a marketing plan, a sales force does the best it can to produce the maximum volume possible. But by working within a marketing plan, a sales force adequately controlled and stimulated attempts to accomplish three necessary tasks:

1. It has to sell a product or range of products in a volume as great or greater than the target set down in the marketing programme and to do this with the sales expenses allocated for that purpose. It must therefore be efficient.
2. It has to achieve this with the product mix and the marketing mix laid down by the marketing plan, if the company is to achieve the maximum profit. It must therefore be a sales force trained to achieve special objectives of the company.
3. It has to achieve these two first objectives in a carefully spaced time programme that avoids seasonal peaks and troughs. To do this the sales force must be closely controlled and the selling effort directed constantly towards the final objectives.

Sales management requires two control factors to help it achieve these three objectives. The first is the constant supply of information so that a complete picture is present of the state of the game at all times. The second is continuing supervision in the field when managers can discuss with their men weekly, monthly, periodically, the progress made. Among other things management must review:

● the record so far in order to see what help is needed and in what form;

- sales targets (If sales targets are not going to be met for some product, or some area, what aid could be used from head office? What are the reasons for failure? Competitive activity, price, delivery? In each case, what is the answer?);
- overall objectives as well as specific objectives.

A company therefore needs the right men to do the selling job and these men must be fully trained in this work and fully supported and stimulated in the field. The company also needs the right men to supervise the sales force, and the supervisors need a system of feedback so that remedial action can be taken in time. Information reaches management in a continuous stream and this must be collated, digested and acted upon. In particular warning systems must be set up:

- The sales plan sets up objectives.
- The selling team set up dates to reach their objectives.
- Control checks and rechecks as the plan proceeds.

Reducing sales costs

There are two major ways to approach the problem of reducing sales costs. One is by strictly controlling and checking all selling costs that are currently met in running a company. Salaries, bonuses, fringe benefits, holidays, sales meetings, training expenses, entertaining, car expenses are all costs that must be met but should be controlled. However, there is a limit to expense control of this type and undoubtedly selling and distribution costs take an ever greater percentage year by year out of the company budget.

The answer must be sought in supplying the sales force with additional volume so that the costs of selling and distribution are reduced in percentage of the greater volume resulting. This can be done by merging two or more companies within an industry or by adding to the products carried a range of complementary but not similar products. During the 1970s every marketing manager has sought an easy answer to this problem of how to obtain greater volume from the same expenditure in sales and distribution costs and it seems likely that more complementary sales patterns will ensue in the future. The cost of a highly organised sales force today selling and distributing on a national scale is so high that management must seek ways and means of reducing this ever growing burden. Adding extra products that will not reduce the primary product volume is the most obvious answer.

Sales brokers

In considering this problem of selling expense, there is a further solution which is more commonly found in America than in this country. Although manufacturing economies of scale are considerable, these efforts can be wasted by post-production costs. These distributing, warehousing, selling and merchandising costs can be very high indeed and each year some or all of these charges increase. Selling brokers therefore have been established by which a manufacturing company contracts out for its selling efforts and expenses which by this method are shared with other companies. Fully integrated sales brokers buy goods from manufacturers, store, sell, deliver and invoice the goods to the retail shop or store. Quite obviously a system for sharing delivery and selling costs must present certain advantages and in America quite large corporations exist selling only through outside brokers.

6 Advertising

Within the marketing programme, top management has the task of selling and promoting sales as efficiently as possible, always within the financial limits provided by the budget. Sales promotion, advertising and public relations are three activities designed to give greater sales volume, all within the framework of the overall marketing design. This chapter and the following one discuss advertising and public relations in this light.

Advertising, together with promotional activities implemented through advertising, constitutes a most important weapon available to the marketing executive. For some years total advertising expenditure in the UK has amounted to over £800 m annually and it is estimated that a further £250 m annually is spent on back-up material such as exhibitions, display materials, premium gifts and so on. The pattern by media is, broadly, as follows:

		£m
Press advertisements		625
National newspapers	161	
Regional newspapers	257	
Magazines and periodicals	72	
Trade and technical journals	72	
Others	63	
Television		210
Posters and transport		30
Cinema and radio		9
Total advertising expenditure		874
Percentage of gross national product		1·4%

(*Source*: Advertising Association: 1973 figures.)

Note. Amongst advertisers other than mass consumer goods are found:

Airlines	£5 226 064
Banks	3 400 546
Travel agents	3 334 945

(*Source:* Advertising directory of the Legion Publishing Co. Ltd., 1973 figures.)

Clearly, personal selling and advertising are part of a company's efforts to communicate with buyers or would-be buyers and the more successfully a company can do this, the stronger it can bring its products to the notice of its customers, stressing the advantages its products possess over those of its competitors, and so maintaining and widening its market share. This activity is so important it must ultimately be the responsibility of the marketing executive since the marketing mix employed will affect so drastically his final volume and profit.

A communications industry

This communication with a customer by a company should be clearly understood in all its aspects.

Personal selling

● Routine selling, by periods, by areas.
● Development selling, to open new territories and new customers.

Direct mail

● Letters, brochures, samples direct to consumers.

Showrooms and after-sales service units

● Showrooms to display products.
● Service units to supply after-sales service or deal with customer complaints.

Advertising

● Trade advertising to communicate with dealers.
● Long term advertising to create favourable brand image and reputation of products. Press, television, posters etc.
● Short term specific advertising for immediate response.

Sales promotional activities

● Packaging and presentation. This is always of the utmost importance and must be constantly reviewed, alike for consumer and industrial products.
● Merchandising and merchandising displays.
● Demonstrations, sampling.
● Exhibitions, trade shows, conventions.
● Point of sale promotions.
● Special personalised promotions.
● Premiums and incentive buying promotions.
● Sales brochures, slides or films (especially for industrial products).

To coordinate all these efforts in one marketing plan so as to arrive at the maximum volume with the lowest costs is a major task. The company has set itself a marketing budget and only by working towards the precise objective set down in the budget and within the costs framework allowed by the budget can the company reach its highest profit potential. This is the very stuff of marketing policy within the market place.

A useful beginning is to examine in some detail the work of an advertising agency, to see where this work fits into the marketing plans of a company and finally to see how personal selling, advertising, and promotional costs are slotted into the marketing plans of a company.

The purpose of advertising

Advertising is a relatively low cost method of communications with large numbers of potential customers. It does this in three ways:

- It informs customers of new products or services, or changes in existing products or services. It spreads information.
- It emphasises the advantages of benefits, the unique features of goods and services to customers at a profit to the manufacturer. It sells.
- It builds up knowledge and confidence in companies. It creates goodwill.

Advertising does these things against the background of the company's personal selling and distribution. This means it obtains recognition for the company and its salesmen, it pre-sells the service or product being offered and increases the company impact on the market. In this way effective advertising produces the following results:

- It increases sales.
- It develops and expands markets.
- It helps to build up brand goodwill.
- It serves as a guarantee of standards.
- It opens a wide choice of competitive products for consumers and so helps the function of a free market.
- It contributes to the company image and reputation.

A closed market, an artificially controlled market, means high prices and little choice. A free market with a wide choice inevitably means lower prices and better goods since competition forces out the second-rate and the unnecessarily expensive items. Advertising is essential to a free market. The cost of advertising, as the cost of distribution, is a necessary element, controlled within a marketing plan whose ultimate objective is higher volume, lower costs and greater profitability. Those responsible to marketing management must ensure that advertising is totally integrated in marketing plans and correctly controlled and timed for the maximum results.

The Advertising Department within the company

Within the company the advertising section has a vital role to play to enable the company's advertising and sales promotional efforts to be carried on efficiently. The main tasks and objectives of such a section are as follows:

coordinating all sales promotional efforts and advertising so that company efforts are not fragmented and lost;
ensuring that all such company promotional efforts move towards the objective laid down by the marketing programme;
feeding the advertising agency with ideas arising out of company background and constant contact with the selling department;
helping to spend the money allocated in the budget to the most efficient ends; that is, the the highest volume of sales for the lowest cost;
serving as a link between the technical men in the advertising agency and the sales department of the company;
ensuring that all design and presentation work undertaken by or for the company fits into the company scheme: this monitoring will apply to all display work and merchandising activity, and work undertaken by people such as distributors on behalf of the company.

**Client/agency
relationship**

To a certain extent a company will receive as much from an advertising agency as it puts in. The company has a great deal to give the agency in knowledge and experience of its market, its products and what has happened to it in the past and to its competitors. The agency for its part is a specialist in communication and marketing and in what should be best for the company in the circumstances. The company acts on two cardinal principles:

1. Effective campaigns are usually the work of an advertising agency.
2. The most successful results follow from close working relationships between the company and the agency. This is because the expertise of the company in its field of production or service is married to the expertise of the agency who provide men skilled in problems of coverage and cost effectiveness of various media and highly skilled copywriters, visualisers and men with knowledge of market resources.

In using a modern advertising agency a company has at its disposal a team of expensive highly skilled specialists and today most advertising agencies discuss the advertising problems of companies against the whole market background and not as an isolated job of newspaper space. To get the best out of this relationship the company should know the following:

- The organisation, facilities and method of work of the agency.

- The nature and scope of back-up services available (design, packaging, public relations, market research, merchandising).

- The basic principles behind the planning work carried out.

On the other hand the agency should know the following:

- Full information about the products and methods of distribution of the company. If there are grey areas of doubt, the agency might recommend the use of market research commissioned for the purpose.

- The precise objectives of the advertising campaign. This will serve to identify the target audience.

From this point onward the agency can recommend media plans and discuss coverage in national newspapers, television, magazines, posters, cinemas and so on. The campaign can be scheduled to appear in the right sized spaces with the necessary frequency at the most important consumer purchasing period. The agency, having absorbed the marketing background for the company's current selling task, attempts to produce an advertising concept to communicate the sales message in such a way as to achieve the maximum impact. As the campaign proceeds the agency and the company together study reaction in terms of sales and distribution in order to see what amendments need to be made.

**Selecting an
agency**

Because so much can depend on the effectiveness of advertising as an integral part of the marketing plan, it follows that the job of selecting an advertising agency is one of the highest priority. How should a company go about selecting an agency?

1. The company must first assess its own requirements and define the type of agency required, whether it should be local, national or international, and also an agency specialising in consumer goods, financial services or industrial products. Perhaps an agency having special skills is required.

2. The company must then consider the question of size. A large agency is one having a turnover of £10 million annually and, generally speaking, small companies do not choose to go to large agencies. Size of agency billings can be found from the Institute of Practitioners in Advertising, or the Advertising Association. Having found a number of agencies in selected categories the company should then examine the work these agencies are producing for current clients.

3. The next step is to visit selected agencies, to assess the people with whom the company will deal and to examine at first hand the services available.

4. Finally the company may ask one or two agencies to prepare outline proposals although many agencies would object that preparing proposals in the abstract does not reveal much. It should also be remembered that agencies usually make charges for anything other than simple preliminary reports.

The most important factors to ascertain about an agency are: For whom do they already work and what have they done? What is the calibre of the top and middle management? and What is the nature of the agency organisation?

Agency remuneration is normally based on commission, usually 10 to 15 per cent, allowed to recognised agencies by media owners. Although in England this is still the basic form of remuneration, there is a growing practice to pay by a yearly fee where client expenditure is below a certain level or where agencies perform a certain amount of work such as market research, display design or packaging that does not come within the media arrangements. This yearly fee is negotiable in advance.

Advertising industrial products

There are certain characteristics of industrial selling that differentiate the pattern of advertising from that of consumer products. The purpose of advertising industrial products is more complicated than the purpose of advertising consumer products, most of which is basically reminder advertising. For the consumer, the decision to buy is made by the individual who sees the advertisement, but the advertisement for an industrial product or service may have to appeal to, and be studied by, a group or a committee. The advertisement for an industrial product informs, advises and explains product characteristics in great detail. It is informative rather than emotional and will seek to emphasise the advantages of the product advertised.

There are basically four types of industrial advertising although some break these down into further subdivisions:

1. *Informative or catalogue*. This is a factual advertisement, with photographs or drawings showing the equipment, and giving complete specification as in a trade catalogue. This is an announcement to the press and usually carries little or no gloss in the shape of write-up.

2. *Product differential.* This is an extension of the first method but the product advantages and differential from other makes are emphasised. A factual advertisement to which is added the technical salesman's arguments.

3. *Repetitive.* A type of industrial advertisement relying on past successes and seeking to exploit them. 'Smith's electric sit-on rider fork lift trucks are found in 80 per cent of all car firms in the Midlands.'

4. *Prestige.* This type of advertisement is frequently seen in services or industrial undertakings (especially used by banks and insurance companies) where the prime object is to spread confidence in the companies concerned.

Note. Because industrial products are sold to a relatively small market (compared with the millions of the mass consumer markets) the use of direct mail advertising—including the use of technical brochures and supporting leaflets—is a very effective selling tool. Each company should build up its own direct mail list from sales, enquiries, representatives' reports and trade press sources.

Advertising in the marketing budget

It has already been seen that when the Marketing Director looks at his budget and at the expenditures after the gross margin has been established, he is faced with costs covering the following items: distribution, sales forces, sales promotion and advertising, after-sales service, and administration. How effectively he uses the money allowed for selling, sales promotions and advertising will very much influence his volume of fixed costs and hence his eventual profit. Obviously he must have control of the total amounts allocated to various sales promotional activities so as to arrive at the best marketing mix from this point of view. There are three major methods of selling and controlling advertising appropriation, although in practice a company would probably use a mixture of all methods:

Sales/Advertising. The amount allocated for sales promotions and advertising can be given a fixed percentage of the budgeted forecast. This enables control to check the total amount spent and also to vary the directions in which the money is spent between consumer advertising through the usual media and sales promotional efforts in other directions.

Case rate. This is the amount of advertising appropriation per unit of sales. This may be per case or per dozen for consumer articles or for each single product for consumer durables such as washing machines or television sets. This method is useful for companies concerned with growth, especially since the case rate can be scaled so as to include a further incentive for volume buying.

Specific task appropriation. Where a new product is being launched, especially a new machine or apparatus, the initial advertising and sales promotional allowance may have to be calculated as part of the cost of getting into the market. Here some consideration of the total market advertising and market share required by the product, with a consideration of what the major competitors are spending, may help to arrive at a meaningful figure.

Total marketing
costs

Now therefore the Marketing Manager can take his budget appropriations and begin to study his problem of how to spend the money to achieve his maximum profit. He is faced with the following requirements:

Sales costs	Retailers or distributors	Advertising
salaries	trade discounts	television
basic salaries	quarterly discounts	press
incentive bonuses	incentive bonuses	magazine
expenses	cooperative advertising	posters
travelling	promotional allowances	transportation
cars	displays	brochures
sampling	catalogues	direct mail
equipment	price lists	cinema
administration	trade seminars	radio
sales literature	trade shows	show rooms
sales aids		exhibits

Directed expressly to the ultimate consumers
Premium gifts
Price reductions as special offers
Competitions
Exhibitions and store demonstrations
After-sales service
Customer complaints service.

All these costs must be contained within his budget appropriations. The manner in which he spends his money between advertising and sales promotions will depend largely on the product sold. A fast turnover, volume consumer product in a mass market will need a constant injection of below-the-line promotions as opposed to direct consumer advertising. (*Below-the-line* expenditure is an omnibus term for promotional expenditure such as competitions, premium gifts, money-off deals and incentive bonuses to salesmen, dealers and distributors.)

**Marketing
objectives
and plans**

If a return is made to the budget, items of particular interest to the marketing management can now be examined in more detail and from these we can understand the marketing plan that arises from them. Special items are marked in boxes and in addition statements of the three most important items are also shown. These are distribution, sales promotion, and after-sales service.

The company in our hypothetical budget (shown below) manufactures a highly individual, high performance mains radio, designed and produced in a very modern style. The unit price is £50 but because the model involves a number of revolutionary features a fairly heavy allowance has been made for dealer service and after-sales service. A special feature of the company is the emphasis on special demonstrations and exhibitions and a moderately heavy (for this sized budget) appropriation for television and press advertising. The ratio of advertising to personal selling is approximately 3:2.

		£000	%
Budget	Gross sales revenue	5 000	100
	Trade discounts	300	6·0
	Net proceeds	4 700	94·0
	Raw materials	1 600	32·0
	Packing	520	10·4
	Direct labour	480	9·6
	Labour overheads	90	1·8
	Utilities	60	1·2
	Factory overheads	400	8·0
	Gross margin	1 150	31·0
	Distribution	190	3·8
	Sales force home	220	4·4
	Sales force export	70	1·4
	Sales promotion	305	6·1
	After sales service	150	3·0
	Administration	115	2·3
	Net profit	500	10·0

Units sold 100 000

		£	£
Distribution	*Despatch*		
	Wages, salaries	30 000	
	NHI and pensions	2 400	32 400
	Own fleet		
	drivers' wages	15 000	
	petrol/oil	4 000	
	repairs	11 000	
	road tax	1 500	
	leasing charges	12 500	44 000
	Hired transport		
	contracted transport	51 600	51 600
	Depot expenses		
	rent	52 000	
	salaries	8 000	
	insurance	2 000	62 000
			190 000

Cost per unit   £1·9

Percentage of gross revenue   3·8%

Sales promotion expenses		£
	Television	55 000
	Press dailies	28 000
	weeklies	30 000
	magazines	95 000
	Trade press	30 000
	Brochures	12 000
	Direct mail	20 000
	Demonstrations	10 000
	Special exhibitions	25 000
		305 000
	Cost per unit	£3·05
	Percentage of gross revenue	6·1%

After-sales service		£	£
	Showrooms		
	rent	45 000	
	salaries	22 000	
	overheads	15 000	82 000
	Distributors		
	agency agreements part		
	cost servicing contracts		40 000
	Transport		
	travel and accommodation		
	costs service engineers		28 000
			150 000
	Cost per unit		£1·5
	Percentage of gross revenue		3·0%

Market requirement

The company assess that there is a market requirement for a moderately priced mains radio of a modern individually styled design. On the one hand the market is supplied with standard factory process type models at a relatively low cost, or imported models answering most customers' requirements at an extremely high cost. To fit into modern living schemes and the quest for individuality most people would prefer to buy a piece of apparatus that enhanced their living space as well as being a satisfactory appliance in itself.

Strategy and main points

The model is not entirely new but a modification of a previous product. The company has the following objectives:

Sales. 5 per cent increase in unit sales; 15 per cent increase in gross revenue.

Distribution. It is planned to add on a further 100 special dealers.

Advertising. The company plans a 5 per cent increase in television and a 25 per cent increase in colour supplements and colour pages of weekly magazines. A direct mail campaign to all shops and dealers is also planned to fit into the promotional mix and to enhance the value of the special exhibitions planned for the next year. It is not intended to increase the sales force or distribution facilities.

Profit. There will be no extra charges in sales office administration or furnished goods inventories and it is planned by these means to increase the net profit by 20 per cent to the figure of £500 000 or 10 per cent of the gross revenue.

7 Public relations

For many years it has been customary for the section on PR (if there is one) to appear modestly towards the end of the book on marketing and this is characteristic of industry's approach to this all-important subject. Logically it should appear near or between the chapters on personal selling and advertising because PR is an extension of the effort at communication and contact between the source of the product and the consumer.

In the minds of the Board of Directors of any company exists a mental image of the company compounded between belief, hope and sophistry, and using a vocabulary of words such as progressive, efficient, forward-looking, flexible, one of the most modern in Europe. These same Directors see their products as articles of superior quality possessing features found only in these particular goods. In the minds of all the people who deal with this company might be found far different images and other descriptive words. The gap between what a company thinks of itself and what the distributors, or employees, or customers think may constitute a considerable barrier to trade and a major obstacle in the way of higher profits. No marketing man can afford to ignore this problem, although many companies do so. *Unless a company produces goods that are obviously superior to all others in that same class, the image the company reflects must be a considerable factor in its marketing efforts.* Having no image at all cannot help, because if a company is totally unknown, the public and traders always imagine the worst.

> 'I do not love thee, Dr Fell,
> The reason why I cannot tell;
> But this alone I know full well,
> I do not love thee, Dr Fell.'

When visitors remark after a visit to a company that they had no idea that the factory was so large, or modern, or efficient, that they had no inkling that the company was so well run, then it is high time for this company to concern itself with PR work. A company endeavours to present a favourable image of itself to its associates and customers. How well it does this will have an important bearing on its commercial success. Public relations is a continuing effort to represent the company, its aims, its methods, its activities, in the best light and to provide a permanent background of information freely available. It therefore requires an understanding and an ability to use the chief communications media in an effort at continuing relations with the public. It should be part of senior management. It should be part of a planned programme involving a deliberate action towards the creation of understanding and goodwill for the benefit of the company. PR cannot be turned on and off like a tap.

How is an image built up?

The public build up an image of a company or a society on many factors, on physical and intangible factors. Here are a few of these factors:

letter headings, stationery, cheques, envelopes, house style;
packaging, presentation, design;
commercial vehicles, private cars;
advertising, volume, style;
products, characteristics, qualities;
service, before, during and after sales;
conduct of all who are in or connected with the company;
reputation ('who steals my purse steals trash');
public announcements.

It is often claimed that it is possible to judge the character of a company by the people who work for it. It has been said that it is possible to judge the managing director from the behaviour of the lift attendant or the telephonist. It is absolutely certain that some companies acquire a reputation far beyond their commercial success but doubtless adding greatly to their triumph. Here are a number of names taken at random from varying socio-economic backgrounds:

Bowaters	Mitsubishi
Lufthansa	The Labour Party
Olivetti	The Conservative Party
Pan AM	The Liberal Party
The Times	Sotheby's
Rover	*The Economist*
Rolls Royce	Unilever
Borg Warner	Shell Mex
Volkswagen	Pirelli
Ford	Dunlop

Each one of these names has a distinct image, a reputation that has been built up in the public mind.

Does it matter?

The public will buy goods they can rely on from companies they can trust, and they build up their knowledge from all the various sources available to them. Untried goods from unknown companies face an almost impenetrable barrier. The trade also reflect this confidence in known and trusted products and will stock and display such products, believing that the presence of such goods in their shops enhances the tone of their own business and builds up an air of affluence and confidence.

Therefore it matters very much in terms of business and end profits that a company enjoys good relations with everyone inside and outside the business. It activates the flow of goods into and out of the shops, and this means profits to the manufacturer.

There is a second reason today why a company must be concerned with public relations. Every company exists as a full member of society and what it does and how it conducts itself is of great moment to the public. Society is concerned with economics and ecology, and concerned to see that companies behave as good citizens and good people to be with. A company therefore must be concerned with public opinion and what the public view is of the company, its services, its policies and its products. This is part of an overall effort to secure an acceptance for the company, to build up a favourable attitude to its aims and activities, which will be translated towards its goods or services.

How PR works

A company PR programme is charged to prepare material for dissemination through the press, radio and television. Material prepared for this purpose should have a news value which is offered by the company to the media concerned. Advertising is space which has been purchased. The PR function is to supply information, news or items of social interest. It seeks to do this in as many ways as possible. Apart from the main vehicle of the press there are trade and other magazines, women's clubs, technical schools, universities, schools, social clubs, local authorities. Beyond this will be exhibitions, films, brochures or specialised publications, and specific documents put out by the company of which the annual report is certainly important.

A typical PR programme will include something like the following:

News announcements

1. Each new product, or product modification, is announced with photographs and full details as widely as possible with all features.
2. Every significant move in manufacture, selling, distribution, advertising is announced in the press as widely as possible.
3. News features concerned with new processes, new methods and so on, especially discoveries or new ideas having a socio-economic interest are announced through the main media.
4. Company prestige announcements affecting the company or its top management are featured as widely as possible.

Special articles, books, brochures

The company constantly endeavours to produce or take part in production of special articles or other published work having some bearing on the company's activities in terms of the trade and the public.

Consumer relations

These will be many and varied, limited only by time and the company budget. They will include exhibitions, lectures to clubs, schools and so on. Recipes, promotions, hints on using company products alone or with related items. For example, motor-car manufacturers produce books on touring and hotel guides.

Trade relations

This will include distributors, retailers, stockists, agencies, and embrace conferences, seminars, visits and personal contacts. In all this the company hopes to create a favourable picture of the activities of the business and of the totality of the company, not just the products.

How PR
programmes can
be set up

A company has a choice of three directions:
1. It can set up its own public relations department within the company, but unless it has fully qualified personnel in the company, this solution would be most unsatisfactory.
2. It can use the public relations section of its own advertising agency, where this exists.
3. It can use the services of an outside public relations agency, and for most companies this is the most efficient solution.

PR work is a top management responsibility and any PR programme should be conducted on the basis of a five-year plan. It is therefore part of long-term planning: the PR Section should be brought in at an early planning stage to advise top management and help in the production of the long-term plan. PR is not a succession of stunts, nor is it merely a question of press 'mileage'. A journalistic background, however, is of great advantage since so much of the work is not only connected with the press, but consists in presenting items about a company in a form that the press will want to use. PR people will therefore try to cooperate with editors and feed them with newsworthy items. Sometimes this takes the form of press supplements and here again the PR people will endeavour to supply the press with the type of article they require. PR people endeavour to reflect the whole company, its local, national and international activities, its position in the industry as a whole, new developments in its building or organisation, movements of its staff.

It is usual for PR agencies to work on a fee basis, calculated on the time given by PR personnel used on the account. In addition there will be out of pocket expenses for travel, photographs, and sundry expenses. Generally fees are arranged annually and paid monthly. Most PR agencies require a contract for at least three years, because PR work is always long-term and immediate results are not to be counted on.

**What does a PR
agency expect
from a company?**

A PR agency, to give a company the best service, would ask for a full participation in and knowledge of the running and development of the company's business. Someone in the company, or some section, must have the responsibility of keeping the agency completely informed with all that is going on and helping to build up the PR programme in all its aspects. The PR agency will want to be given the chance to help with new designs, new recipes, new presentations; with trade conferences, with public visits, with exhibitions and public meetings. All this demands that the PR people have access to all the company news as it unfolds so that they can decide and make suggestions as to the best way to use this intelligence.

The PR people have to establish on behalf of the company working relations with that part of the press where the company will hope to be seen. The company should be accepted as a willing cooperator and as a source of information on its particular expertise. To do this, the PR people must move with authority and the knowledge of what the company is really doing. Without full cooperation from the company the outside public relations agency is attempting an impossible task. PR people should take part in company meetings, especially sales and advertising, but also in new product development and personnel, since these are rich areas for PR work. International news is helpful to build up a complete picture, and stories of successes or new ventures in overseas markets can be most welcome. The PR agency would therefore expect to be given a stated policy and an objective. The agency would endeavour to discover those areas of communication where the company was weak or at fault and to remedy the situation. The PR agency's job is to introduce the company to the world, to remove misconceptions, to transmute the everyday actions of the company into interesting newsworthy items. The PR work basically is to inform, to promote an understanding and so help to build up the reputation of the company and hence the public confidence in its work.

Methods

The agency, or the PR section of a company, would most probably prepare each year a suggested programme for the following twelve months having in mind the objectives outlined by the company and most likely by the marketing section. The work of the year will fall into certain categories according to the methods chosen. PR is certainly not just a question of press publicity. A judicious mixture of all PR methods should be employed.

Press, radio, television

It is important to establish good personal relations between the company and the various media concerned. Personal visits are valuable, especially when new ventures are going forward, new factories, new machinery and so on. A PR agency will help to do this to begin with, and the company must build on this and earn the right to enjoy these good relations. The people from press and radio can learn about the company, about the industry and its social problems and contributions. This is what life is about and it is part of the newspaper man's world. Good relations are of benefit both to the company and to the communications industry.

Another important factor is that material for the press and radio must be given to them in a form they can use, and here the value of journalistic training can be seen. This part of the job calls for experience, knowledge and skill.

Public contacts

This will include exhibitions, fairs, demonstrations and visits to special activities such as clubs, schools, societies, all having an interest in the company's operations. It is essential that all these activities receive the correct treatment, so that the work builds up into a continuous programme. Exhibitions can be well done or badly done and it is up to the PR people to see that the maximum is extracted from all trade fairs and exhibitions.

Films

Some companies, especially those making industrial products, can obtain great advantage from commercial films. It is obviously of great importance to see that the script and treatment of the film itself makes the most of the PR scene and also to see that when the film has been made, it reaches the right people in the right manner. A good commercial film is a first class PR job for a company but it must be fully exploited and given maximum showing.

Publications   These range from annual reports to books, and include brochures, leaflets and small treatises on special subjects. Annual reports have for some years been the subject of concern and attempts are being made to improve them by clearer presentation and modern layout. Awards are made for the best annual reports. The truth is that everything put out by a company reflects that company and its personality. (Lufthansa make a special point of using the very best kind of elastic band and prove the point that everything is important down to the smallest detail.)

Summary   PR is a most important marketing tool and it is a matter of some mystery why it has taken so long to be recognised as such in England. Nevertheless as anyone who has worked in marketing can testify, PR brings results, it is essential to the marketing mix, it is not expensive, and the work can be appreciated by all within a company.

8 Marketing control

At any given time the senior marketing executive of a company is concerned with at least three overlapping but separate time patterns. First with the short term twelve months plan that engages the company's current activities, then with the immediate future plans extending over the next two or three years, and finally with longer-term plans stretching forward for perhaps ten years. He lives always in these three layers of planning and must constantly adjust his ideas. Market assessment and product development are both continuing processes, but present activities must not jeopardise the future. In terms of management procedure this time plan resolves itself as follows:

Year 1

The budget: the financial expression of the marketing programme concerned with the immediate future. A control instrument for the following year with monthly meetings where actual performance is measured against budgeted figures.

Years 2–3

Short-term marketing plans. The marketing executive plans his marketing programme as a combination of short term and long term objectives. Years 2–3 are extensions of normal budgeting and the last year, that is year 3 or year 4, will consist of broad based objectives covering the major commercial requirements. The programme is constantly under review as a period of three- or four-year duration, with year 1 renewed each year to take its place as the year of the budget.

Years 4 onwards

Long-term marketing plans, also known as corporate or strategic planning. This is an endeavour to assess the future development of the environment and of the company within it. The importance of this approach has been stressed by E. F. L. Brech as follows: [1]

> The marketing programme will be, increasingly, the framework of progress and growth, and of more far-reaching improvements, such as diversification, overseas expansion, or management development. . . . Knowing products and potential markets available to it, the firm selects those opportunities which will enable it to afford the best possible supply and service to customers at optimum profit-levels for itself; it recognises the channels of trading for this supply, whether at home or abroad, and gets thereby

[1] *'Managing for Revival'* (Management Publications Ltd. 1972), chapter 3.

guidelines to the organisation of its selling and sales promotion efforts; strategic guidelines take account of the economic, technological and social environment within which the trading activities will be carried on; they take account also of the financial resources and physical facilities available to the firm, as the basis for determining the scale and range of its operations.

Managing has been defined as 'planning, motivating and regulating the activities of persons towards the effective and economical accomplishment of a given common task'. *Control* therefore begins with a clear statement of the common task, a precise definition of what is being attempted: and control must continue throughout the activities until the desired results have been achieved. However control is managed, it must check continuously two factors: (1) the planned performance and the variations from it, and (2) the time factors involved in the completion of the programme. To cover these two points control reports must therefore include (*a*) results to date and variances from plan with estimate of results over the remainder of the period; and (*b*) suggested remedial action or suggested action to exploit successes. Should plans be interrupted by external factors such as major strikes, currency movements of significant magnitude, or world disasters adversely affecting the supply or prices of raw materials, then control must estimate the effect of these factors on the plan and the required action necessary to attempt to restore the possibility of achieving the original objectives.

Variance analysis

Control of factors within the current twelve months' plans will certainly be undertaken within the framework of the yearly budget examined in detail in a monthly breakdown. The budget, as was seen earlier in chapter 4 on sales forecasts, begins with an estimate of sales, and it is on the estimated sales volume and product mix that the budget structure is established.

Control exercised through a budgetary procedure has the following advantages (among others):

- It establishes precise objectives and separates these common objectives by departments or sections of the business so that results for each section as well as the totality can be seen.
- By using variance factors control can easily recognise (*a*) variances in labour, material, and expenses; (*b*) changes in volume; and (*c*) changes in price.

Marketing management should therefore be able to notice unnecessary selling or sales promotional expenses or failure to reach expected levels of sales and to see where the failures are occurring. The overall marketing plan, which is an essential extension of the yearly budget and is developed in parallel with it and indeed supports it, clearly states two different major objectives:

1. It gives first of all a clear statement of marketing goals in terms of volume and money and states also how these goals are to be achieved.
2. In so doing it announces for the production side the product requirements in detail of kind and timing so that production activities and labour requirements can be foreseen.

The danger areas for marketing management to watch are:

- Failure to reach required volume.
- A product mix that reduces the expected profitability of the operations.
- An undue rise in selling costs, particularly (a) trade discounts; (b) sales promotional costs; (c) special promotional efforts.

Total senior management will proceed further to watch for labour variances due to operating inefficiency, machine shutdowns, and scrap variances due to material or operator defects.

Periodic marketing reports

In addition to the monthly examination of budgetary progress marketing will certainly require reports of much greater frequency to serve as a confirmation that all is well, or alternatively to act as danger signals. These will be:

Order analysis, daily and weekly. This will provide the first notice of sales falling away or increasing too quickly (so that production must be warned). But also it will provide information on size of orders (too many unprofitable orders require attention) and the make-up of the orders by type of product and type of customer. As the figures are built up this analysis can also show trends.

Order and despatch records, daily and weekly. It is desirable to check continuously the time taken to process orders and to deliver them, especially where many depots are concerned and especially for customers overseas. A reputation for poor delivery service does not help a company to grow.

Customer complaints records, monthly. Customers may complain of faulty products and it is essential to record all complaints and the manner in which they are dealt with. Apart from the product line itself customers may complain of any of the following and in each case marketing management should know:

- poor deliveries, as stated above, in terms of time;
- faulty deliveries, in terms of damage to the product;
- delays in invoicing or despatch of statements;
- insufficient or too long delayed after-sales service.

Longer term review factors

Beyond the controls inherent in working within a budget framework, marketing management must be concerned with a review built up to show trends and movements on a longer time basis:

- From analysis of the market, management must follow customer requirements, market changes, competitive actions and sales policies.
- From departmental heads will come reports and feasibility studies within the overall marketing programme on product planning, labour resources planning, investment and sales planning.
- Periodically the management activity must include a review of sales margins achieved, turnover rate and profitability.

Again, beyond this must be a system of periodic review of all those factors that have already been discussed previously (especially in the first two chapters of this Part) that provide the permanent background of the marketing executive. It is helpful to summarise what this background should be, and this has been attempted as a continuing process of preparation, processing and operation.

Preliminary

Economic environment

1. People. Demographic, psychological and sociological changes, especially changes due to the effect of continued inflation and the impact on money supply.
2. Technology. Innovation, availability of infrastructure, knowledge and its dissemination and application, process control and productivity.
3. Institutions. Political framework, trade unions, employers' federations, new supranational blocks such as the European Economic Community, 'the Establishment'.

Preparation

Market assessment

1. Industry and trade statistics.
2. Company statistics, by product line, by area, by type of customer.
3. Customer statistics, by types, size and size of orders.

Product assessment

1. Research and development.
2. Customer complaints.

Production activity

1. Plant utilisation.
2. Resources allocation.

Marketing activity

1. Sales promotional methods and costs—own and competitors.
2. Transportation statistics.
3. Competitive marketing activities.
4. Packaging and presentation analysis.

Financial conclusion

1. Costs, by function, by area, by salesmen.
2. Prices—own and competitors'.
3. Marketing expenses.
4. Trading accounts.
5. Budgetary statements.

Processing

Market assessment

1. Analysis of segmentation of markets.
2. Determining growth or decline factors.

3. Estimating sales of new product lines.
4. Moving annual totals, by products, areas, customers.
5. Survey of new markets.

Product assessment

1. New product preparations and modifications.
2. New product ideas, reception and selection.
3. Diversification to new products.

Production activity

1. Scrap or waste factors.
2. Overtime worked.
3. Changes in overheads.
4. Employees by numbers and changes in wage rates.
5. Engineering service charges.

Marketing activity

1. Advertising media, costs and results.
2. Sales promotional mix, cost effectiveness.
3. Changes in distribution desirable.
4. Modification of presentation or packaging required.

Financial conclusion

1. Establishment of contribution by products, by areas, by customers, by salesmen.
2. Establishment of the effect of product mix, marketing mix, incentive promotional mix.
3. Profits by function, by area, by salesmen.

Operational   *Market assessment*

1. The arrangement of targets and quotas.
2. Defining markets for action.
3. Effects of pricing on volume.

Product assessment

1. Feasibility studies for new developments.
2. Product range analysis.

Production activity

1. Low costs production.
2. Maximum plant utilisation.
3. Minimum wastage, scrap or defectives.
4. Efficient usage of materials.

Marketing activity

1. Optimum use of advertising media.
2. Aggressive, cumulative sales promotion.
3. Exploitation of major potential through product/market mix.
4. Optimisation of results.

Financial conclusion

1. Cost of money.
2. Cash flow priorities.
3. Sundry creditors.
4. Sundry debtors.
5. Stocks, finished goods, raw materials, work in progress.

Objectives and standards

From the background of marketing activities must naturally emerge a series of logical objectives and standards for any company wishing to grow and expand. These objectives will become or form part of long-term planning in due course, but they begin as immediate short-term objectives. Just as one of the tasks of market research must be to check the value of market research so one of the tasks of marketing management must be to check the operation and efficiency of all marketing activities within a company to make sure they are permanent and worth while.

Long-term planning

Long-term planning seeks to evaluate the future conditions under which the company will work and especially to define as precisely as possible three factors governing the future of the company: the risks inherent in certain developments and the risks inherent in avoiding such developments and the cash requirements that will form the financial framework to the company's probable future.

The objectives therefore of the company's long term plans will be formed round four major directives:

1. *Environmental research.* A constant surveillance to appreciate the changing environment in which the company will be operating.
2. *Statistical decision making.* An attempt to provide an understanding of the logic and limitations of forecasting and other mathematical aids.
3. *Risk analysis.* An attempt to show and evaluate risk in terms of probability analysis.
4. *Strategic conception.* A constant endeavour to reappraise, reformulate and evaluate present and alternative strategies and to offer a basis for selection of future strategy.

The case for long-term planning

The idea of controlling the operations of a company on the basis of a yearly budgetary system, divided precisely into functional sections showing detailed targets and standards is now commonly accepted although not everywhere practised. The idea of long-term planning, that is planning forward over a span of three to ten years, is not so widely accepted, and the question naturally arises as to the necessity or validity of so doing. Why should a business endeavour to plan ahead on a long term basis? An attempt should be made to state reasons clearly and precisely:

1. The business climate in sophisticated markets is such that running a business on an *ad hoc* basis—'some years we go up, some we go down'—is bound to lead to extinction or takeover. This is because at best opportunities may be missed, or at worst disasters are magnified.
2. The tempo of business has increased considerably (among other things, the computer has seen to this). Business ideas circulate freely on an international basis and although hard work can increase production, new ideas can shatter markets. There is no longer time for companies to realise that they are on the wrong track, to change direction, and start off again correctly.
3. Because of this constant interchange of ideas, and the constant ferment of business pressures, the whole process of business is not only more complex, but more competitive, and wrong decisions can be more dramatic in effect. There is a smaller margin for error. No business is as simple as it once was.
4. Business throughout the world lives in a climate of continuing inflation. (It has always done so but the pace has now increased considerably.) Therefore all the arguments so far advanced have added force, because inflation means that costs rise faster, margins decline faster, and investment becomes more expensive.
5. Long-term planning means two things of great significance to any company. First, it means that in planning for the future consideration must be given to all contingencies that may arise and if the company is wise, it will take timely action. (If its management structure is weak it will do something about this before it becomes a disaster area.) Secondly, in the process of planning, a company sets up targets and goes through the motions to reach these targets. This in itself must be better than drifting with bright hopes.
6. If a company wishes to continue to exist it must grow, and grow wisely. This means long-term planning.

Why growth?

Why should a company grow? What should be its aims? Of course there are many reasons but some common to all companies would surely include:

- profitability;
- market penetration;
- market impact;
- personnel development;
- physical and financial resources development.

Companies must tell themselves (if they didn't already know) where they think they ought to be at some future date and must then produce long-term plans to make sure they arrive there. It is certain that, without planning, their future arrival at the desired destination will be fortuitous.

What is meant by growth? Obviously growth can mean increase in the total size of operations, or growth in market share. More importantly it should mean growth in profits and marketing management could not be happy at a situation where a company doubled its volume of business and increased its profits marginally. Growth can also mean impact on the market, growth in excellence, in product superiority or product characteristics. Many companies achieve growth by being the leaders, or the best, in their chosen field. Jensen Motors, for example, achieved growth in this manner.

How is growth achieved? There are first of all three clearly perceptible methods to do this:

1. To exploit in every way possible the range of products at present made.
2. To modify, to augment, the range with similar products.
3. To move into new fields entirely fresh to the company.

But within these three major factors there are other steps that can lead to growth:

Enlarging the sales force. How many salesmen, agents or distributors to employ must be under constant review by the marketing section.

Improving or modifying the product line. There must be a continuous search in two ways. How to produce better products, how to produce these better products more cheaply. There is never finality in this task.

Altering the channels of distribution. When a market is characterised by segmentation—and most markets are—changing channels of distribution, or altering the emphasis given to certain channels, may considerably alter the volume of business achieved.

Selling to other markets. Instead of selling only to agricultural merchants, selling also to agricultural cooperatives and to farmers. Instead of selling only to the UK, selling also to other EEC countries.

Selling other products. This may mean innovation in terms of product, or presentation, or service, or even advertising and sales promotion.

These factors apply to growth within a company. There are ways to grow outside the company structure:

Joint venture; joint ownership. These are methods of pooling expertise from more than one company and following a commercial operation with the partners working at arms' length. This can be useful where the success of the operation depends on a merger of two special groups of knowledge or technical background. The disadvantage of this method, a disadvantage very obvious to accountants and financial managers, is the difficulty of conducting joint operations of this kind with an equitable sharing of costs and profits. The financial arrangements must cover a method of sharing investment costs, marketing, production and administrative costs and agreement on how profit is split.

Licensing agreements. These are usually agreements for overseas companies, either for marketing or manufacturing rights or both. An alternative form is a franchise agreement where arrangements are made for companies to exploit a product or service produced by another company. The great advantage of licensing and franchising is that the original company is not obliged to enter into heavy financial commitments of stockholding, marketing and administration in running this additional area or market.

Takeovers or mergers. If this policy is followed it must be followed with method and not as a spare time job for the Chairman or Managing Director. In an ideal situation there should be a senior executive charged with takeover progression. This man and his staff will be fully aware of the dangers, advantages and complications inherent in merger operations both in the initial stages of negotiation and the more difficult stages of integration. Unless there are demonstrably clear advantages to be obtained from a merger, in terms of management structure, production facilities, marketing strengths, market shares and financial resources, a merger should not be attempted. Volume for the sake of volume is commercial nonsense.

The appraisal of long-term plans

The long-term plans of a company should be established on the following desiderata:

A precise understanding of the end purpose of the business. This means the ultimate aim of the company, its scope, potential and character. If a company says that it makes breakfast foods it limits its markets: if it says it makes convenience foods it enlarges its market; if it says it makes foods it expands its potential still further. What can the company do better than other companies? What can belong to it, individually, that no other company can copy?

The possession or acquisition of the means by which it hopes to attain its end purpose. This embraces money, management, production facilities, distribution systems. It means above all the recruitment and retention of the right calibre of management at all levels.

The organisation and management structure necessary to achieve the company aims. Of course if the right people have joined the company, the correct organisation and management structure will be developed by them.

The ability to evolve an operational control required by the company. This means, amongst other things, the ability to recognise, isolate and eliminate limiting factors whatever they may be and usually in a management situation limiting factors are directly concerned with persons.

What are long-term plans?

Each company must postulate its own long-term plans, since each company exists within its own particular universe. Common to all companies however should be the following:

- Profit growth to give increased resources for investment.
- Increased earnings per share to attract new capital.

● A higher, or more successful, achievement of certain management ratios particularly:

(*a*) net profit to net sales (this indicates the competitive standing of the company, and is a most important marketing indicator, especially in relation to competitors if this can be seen from interfirm comparison figures);

(*b*) net profit to tangible net worth (this shows the return on money invested in the business: if the figure is low it can mean the money is invested in a stagnant or dying industry. What diversification steps should then be considered?)

(*c*) turnover rate of capital employed (a slow rate of turnover can mean that the company impact is small, its penetration of the market weak; too much money has been invested in plant and not enough money in marketing).

● Growth in sales and growth in market shares.
● Growth in reputation and impact and influence on the market.

Measurement of progress

Assuming that a company is completely aware of itself and its ultimate purpose (Thomas Tilling, which originally was concerned with transportation, is now engaged with building materials, textiles, insurance, vehicle distribution etc.; W. R. Grace, which originally was concerned with shipping throughout Latin America, is now operating in chemicals, fertilisers, consumer foodstuffs, packaging materials etc.), how does it measure its progress towards the future objectives? The traditional methods of appraising a company's worth, for investment or consultancy purposes, based on financial history may no longer be valid or adequate for modern purposes. A past history of success is no guarantee of future success along the same lines. These factors must be critically examined in order to produce a plan for long-term fulfilment:

Finance

Are the assets of the company represented in the accounts in a realistic manner? Are company assets fully employed?

Is there an efficient financial control exercised through budgetary control with monthly analysis statements?

Are all product contributions known precisely?

Are development schemes held up for money?

Has the company adequate financial resources for growth and development? If not, does the company know how it can obtain the funds necessary?

Given the funds necessary, has it the management structure to use them efficiently?

What is the company record over the past five years, and its estimated expectation, for the next five years, of these three factors:

(*a*) net profit/total assets (per cent)?

(*b*) net profit/total net sales (per cent)?

(*c*) total net annual sales/total assets (times per year)?

Management

Are the members of the management teams adequate in terms of experience, training, calibre and personality? Do they in fact constitute a balanced team? Are they trained in management techniques? Is succession assured?
Is there an adequate system for information or control data?
Are they energetic, aggressive, restless, ambitious?
What is their degree of professional competence? How well do they compare with management structures of the chief competitive houses?
What will be the age of each of the board directors in five years' time? Is management autocratic or by committee?

Production

Are the plant and machinery in good condition? What is the average age of the plant? Is it renewed or renewable on sound economic and financial measures? Are the plant and the site efficiently used? Is the site an expensive one in view of local labour costs or rates and services, and if so what advantages accrue from being there?
Is production effective, with maximum plant utilisation and minimum wastage?
How does the company produce new ideas for products? Are these found in laboratories or from customer research or both?
What disciplines are involved in the search for new products? Is it a team effort?
What is the company record for innovation over the last 5 years?

Distribution

Assuming that the company is aware of its share of the market and its distribution by areas, is it satisfied with their share and how will it go about to achieve more?
Is the company primarily concerned with production efficiency or customer satisfaction?
Why are the company products bought? (Practically every manufacturer would answer 'quality' to this question.)
Has the company a clearly defined and effective marketing and selling effort? Is the sales force effective? Are distribution facilities adequate?
If marketing and selling costs are too high has the company a clear idea of the next steps towards reducing the burden of these costs? If this means selling additional products that are not directly and immediately competitive, does the company know where to go for them?

Organisation
development

As part of long-term planning many companies are giving methodical attention to the development of the organisation of the company in order to fulfil long-term plans. This basically means defining objectives, analysing jobs and assessing personnel available. It can mean restructuring middle and top management and reorganising the pattern of management to meet the specific tasks laid down for the company. The overall task of organisation development is perhaps best undertaken by an outside consultancy effort since it is difficult for anyone within a company to be disengaged from routine duties long enough to see organisational problems in a clear perspective.

Management
development

Parallel with the development of organisation is the development of management and the one proceeds from the other. No sensible forward planning is possible unless the right men and women are developed and given the organisational structure in which to work. There must be a continuing systematic effort to provide a management team combining experience and drive, opportunities for advancement for good men within the company, and facilities for recruiting outside management material when greater or wider experience and expertise are required. These things must go on against an observed timetable so that management continuity is safeguarded.

These important topics of organisational planning and management development are appropriately dealt with in Part Seven (see page 919).

**Profit
improvement
programmes**

The purpose of long-term planning is to provide a rigorous but flexible framework for the formation of marketing and profitability strategies.

Planned programmes, then, for individual companies are attempts to provide tailormade schemes drawn up on the basis of the company's needs and facilities so that the long-term profitability of the company is achieved. However, it must be conceded that this usually cannot be done in the average company where all members are already fully committed to their several tasks. Such programmes demand the experience in training and method of specialists either within, or more usually, outside the company. The work consists in planning and understanding the nature of forecasting and the methods by which such forecasting can be evaluated and interpreted to the benefit of the company.

Although most companies that manage systematic budgetary control successfully are committed to containing or limiting costs within the budget framework, it is commonplace that from time to time companies feel the need (especially in inflationary periods) to mount special cost reduction or profit improvement programmes. The trouble is that unless these cost reduction efforts are properly controlled, expenses are saved in one part of the budget, to appear again in another area.

Profit improvement programmes require a systematic approach to performance improvements undertaken in such a way as to constitute a permanent feature of the company activities. One way to make more profit is to sell more volume under such conditions that the expense of the extra sales is more than covered by the selling price. A second way is to reduce expenses without cutting back sales or eliminating activities that do not contribute towards the production of profits. It is felt that the average manager does his best to live within his budget and his allocated costs. Beyond this he has not the time for concern.

The profit improvement schemes usually begin at this point and proceed to a study of the organisation and the establishment of sectional tasks for divisions of the company. These tasks, explained to group or sectional managers and agreed by them, are monitored and controlled by section managers usually working with a team of outside consultants, since here again the work of investigation and control requires people not immersed in the day-to-day running of the business. The work demands continuous application and training procedures for the company management staff appointed to the special task. It is therefore only applicable to companies having a managerial staff of some magnitude.

Appendix I EEC members and associates

The British Overseas Trade Board has published a summary showing the present EEC and its Associated States together with an outline of possible future arrangements concerning Commonwealth Countries.
This is a very useful summary.

Original six full members

Belgium
Federal Republic of Germany
France
Italy
Luxembourg
Netherlands

Acceding member states

Denmark
Irish Republic
United Kingdom

EFTA non-candidates (Special Relations Agreements-SRA)

Austria	—industrial free trade, with special arrangements for some sensitive products
Finland	—industrial free trade, with special arrangements for some sensitive products
Iceland	—industrial free trade, with special arrangements for some sensitive products; implementation of concessions on fish under this agreement depend on a satisfactory outcome to the present dispute on fishery limits.
Norway	—expected to sign Special Relations Agreement
Portugal	—industrial free trade, with special arrangements on a range of agricultural items
Sweden	—industrial free trade, with special arrangements for some sensitive products
Switzerland	—industrial free trade, with special arrangements for some sensitive products

Present EEC Associates and trade agreements in the Mediterranean

Greece	—association leading to full membership
Turkey	—association leading to full membership
Malta	—preferential agreement—should lead to eventual customs union and association
Spain	—preferential agreement
Israel	—preferential agreement
Arab Republic of Egypt	—preferential agreement
Cyprus	—preferential agreement
Lebanon	—preferential agreement
Morocco	—partially associated
Tunisia	—partially associated
Yugoslavia	—non-preferential trading agreement
Iran	—agreement easing EEC tariffs on imports from Iran

Yaounde Convention

Burundi
Cameroon
Central African Republic
Chad
Congo-Brazzaville
Dahomey
Gabon
Ivory Coast
Malagasy Republic
Mali
Mauritania
Mauritius
Niger
Rwanda
Senegal
Somalia
Togo
Upper Volta
Zaire

The Yaounde Convention provides for: the gradual formation of a free trade area between the Community and each of the nineteen; a highly flexible aid system; and political institutions in which the Community members and the nineteen cooperate on a basis of full equality.

Arusha Convention

Kenya
Tanzania
Uganda

The Arusha Convention basically provides for mutual trade preferences on a wide variety of products, but there is no provision for the granting of aid.

South America

Argentina	—non-preferential agreement
Uruguay	—negotiating for non-preferential agreement

Developed Commonwealth Preference states and South Africa

Australia	—Commonwealth preference to be phased out

Canada	—Commonwealth preference to be phased out
New Zealand	—Commonwealth preference to be phased out
South Africa	—preference to be phased out

Commonwealth states not offered association

India	Sri Lanka (Ceylon)
Pakistan	Malaysia
Bangladesh	Singapore

The EEC wishes to reinforce existing trade relations with these countries.

Hong Kong

The EEC has agreed to bring Hong Kong into the Generalised Preference Scheme.

Gibraltar

Not being included in the Customs territory of the enlarged EEC.

Independent Commonwealth countries who can seek association or a simple commercial agreement

Barbados	Malawi
Botswana	Nigeria
Fiji	Sierra Leone
The Gambia	Swaziland
Ghana	Trinidad and Tobago
Jamaica	Tonga
Lesotho	Western Samoa

Plus the three present Arusha States

Negotiations did not begin until the Autumn of 1973, but the above Commonwealth States are being asked to say whether they want to negotiate at all. Present trading arrangements continued until 31 January 1975 when the Yaounde Convention expired. Mauritius has signed the existing Yaounde Convention.

Dependent territories (other than Hong Kong and Gibraltar)

Bahamas	West Indies Associated States
Bermuda	(Antigua, Dominica, Grenada, St Lucia,
British Antarctic Territory	St Vincent, St Kitts-Nevis-Anguilla)
British Honduras	Cayman Islands
British Indian Ocean Territory	Central and Southern Line Islands
British Solomon	Falkland Islands and Dependencies
Islands Protectorate	Gilbert and Ellice Islands
British Virgin Islands	Montserrat
Brunei	New Hebrides
Seychelles	Pitcairn
Turks and Caicos Islands	St Helena and Dependencies

These territories will be offered association under Part IV of the Treaty of Rome (as will the Danish Possession of the Faroe Islands).

EEC-UNCTAD generalised preference scheme

The EEC operates a preference scheme under UNCTAD which allows most developing nations duty-free or preferential access for most industrial goods into the Community.

Further reading

BRITTAN, SAMUEL, *Steering the Economy*, Penguin Books, 1971.

GODLEY, C. AND CRACKNELL, D., *Marketing for Expansion and Europe*, Longman, 1971.

HOLMES, P. M., *Marketing Research; principles and readings*, Edward Arnold, 1966.

MORSE, STEPHEN, *The Practical Approach to Marketing Management*, McGraw-Hill, 1967.

PEN, J., *Modern Economics*, Penguin Books, 1970.

BRECH, R. J., *Planning prosperity*, Darton, Longman & Todd, 1964.

FOURRE, JAMES P., *Quantitative Business Planning Techniques*, American Management Association, 1970.

FRANK, R. E. AND GREEN, P. E., *Quantitative Methods in Marketing*, Prentice-Hall, 1967.

HENRY, HARRY, *Perspectives in Management, Marketing and Research*, Staples, 1971.

MILLER, ERNEST C., *Advanced Techniques for Strategic Planning*, American Management Association, 1971.

STACEY, N. A. H. AND WILSON, A., *Industrial Marketing Research*, Hutchinson, 1969.

WILLS, GORDON, *Sources of UK Marketing Information*, Nelson, 1969.

ZALTMAN, GERALD, *Marketing—Contributions from the Behavioural Sciences*, Harcourt Brace, 1965.

FOSTER, D. W., *Planning for Products and Markets*, Longman, 1972.

TIETJEN, K. H., *Organizing the Product Planning Function*, American Management Association, 1963.

WARD, PETER, *Dynamics of Planning*, Pergamon Press, 1970.

BUELL, V. P., *Marketing Management in Action*, McGraw-Hill, 1966.

CHAPMAN, R. A., *Marketing Today*, International Textbooks, 1971.

KOTLER, P., *Marketing Management*, Prentice-Hall, 1967.

SMALLBONE, D. W., *The Practice of Marketing*, Staples, 1972.

WILLIAMS, L. A., *Industrial Marketing; management and controls*, Longman, 1967.

WILSON, A., *The Marketing of Industrial Products*, Hutchinson, 1968.

DUXFIELD, D. B., *Management and Training of Technical Salesmen*, Gower Press, 1962.

GOLDMANN, HEINZ, *How to Win Customers*, Staples, 1969.

INSTITUTE OF MARKETING, *Salesmen under the Microscope*, IM, 1968.

ROWE, D. AND ALEXANDER, I., *Selling Industrial Products*, Hutchinson, 1968.

HOBSON, J. A., *Techniques in Modern Advertising*, Institute of Practitioners in Advertising.

PAINE, MICHAEL, *Advertising; the marketing approach*, Crosby Lockwood, 1968.

BOWMAN, P. AND ELLIS, N., *Manual of Public Relations*, Heinemann.

JEFKINS, *Public Relations Practice*, Intertext Books.

STEPHENSON, H., *Handbook of Public Relations*, McGraw-Hill, 1971.

BEER, STAFFORD, *Management Studies*, Aldus Books, 1968.

BRECH, E. F. L., *Managing for Revival*, Management Publications, 1972.

CANTOR, JERRY, *Pragmatic Forecasting*, American Management Association, 1971.

DENNING, B. W., *Corporate Long-term Planning*, Longman, 1970.

FOSTER, D. W., *Practical Management*, Longman, 1971.

MERRETT, A. J. and SYKES, A., *Capital Budgeting and Company Finance*, Longmans, 1966.

PROUT, T. P., *Industrial Market Research Workbook*, Gower Press, 1973.

PART THREE Manufacturing, supply and technical development

by Richard Field

1 Manufacturing

In Part One, the principles, theory and criteria on which management is both based and judged were spelt out. This Part concerns the practice of management as applied to the design and manufacture of goods or the supply of services. Again referring to Part One, the three Ps (Performance, Productivity and Profitability) were spelt out as aspects of the management process (p. 32). This Part brings the three Ps into focus in their practical application:

Performance
   —design, research and development to produce a product specification acceptable to the customer;
   —inspection and quality control to ensure he gets it.
   —output targets and costs.
Productivity
   —to seek improvements in the ways of making the product or providing the service, covered by production engineering, method study and work measurement or operations research, and to reduce costs of production or service.
Profitability
   —this covers all aspects of manufacture:
   designing the product the customer wants;
   production planning and control to ensure he gets it on time and will re-order with the same company when he needs more;
   making it at such a cost that the price the customer will pay leaves a satisfactory margin for profit.

This first chapter sets the scene by relating the design and manufacture of goods to the requirements of the customer through the activities of marketing, and then takes a bird's eye view of production industry in its widest sense. It is very easy for anyone in industry to be so involved with his own organisation as to be unaware that his company is not typical of industry as a whole. Indeed it would be pertinent to ask whether there is such a thing as a typical industry or typical company. One thing however is certain, the principles of management are common to all industries, and although the details of its practice may vary with the size of the company or type of commodity or service provided there will be few organisations where some or most of the practices outlined in this section will not be relevant.

The manufacturing function

The manufacturing function can be defined as 'the organised activity of transforming raw materials into finished products'. In this definition, raw materials can be anything from rough ore to a complex piece of electronic equipment, for the raw material of one organisation is the finished product of another. In this context too the manufacturing function also includes production activities which are not strictly in the category of manufacture. For instance many of the disciplines of production management are as applicable to horticulture as they are to engineering, food processing or the manufacture of chemicals.

The relationship between manufacturing and marketing will be constant, in that manufacture will always follow marketing, though manufacture may either precede or follow selling; even in the manufacture of similar products, one manufacturer may make for stock to be sold 'off the shelf', where another will only put in hand to cover specific customer's orders.

Within the manufacturing activities covered by this Part the activities will usually operate in the order, research—design—development—production. It is in this order that the Part is laid out, but the order of presentation is only relevant to the *practice* of managing aspects of the manufacturing activities, the principles of course underlie all the management functions. The principles must be sound. The man who adheres to them is less likely to run into difficulties of his own making than is the man who works by rule of thumb or instinct, or takes refuge in expedients which at best are temporary. Compromise and expediency lead at best to muddle, at worst to chaos and possibly complete failure. This does not mean that there is only one right answer to any one problem, or that any two companies making identical products must be identical in methods or organisation. Any organisation should reflect the personalities and abilities of the people who work for it. For as no two people are identical, it is even less likely that two organisations composed of many people will be identical.

Whenever a number of people get together with a common objective, someone takes the lead in directing the work of others. He may be as physically involved as his colleagues, for example the leader of a mountaineering expedition; likewise in industry, in a small organisation the 'boss' may still work at the bench, in addition to buying the raw materials and selling the product. As the organisation gets bigger, separate functions will be handled by a specialist. The leader or boss will direct the work of others and in this context will be a *manager*. Whether his title includes the word 'manager' or not may well be more a matter of choice than of activity. At the shop floor level the manager of the men is called a Chargehand, Foreman or Overseer. A Chief Inspector in one company may have duties identical with the Quality Control Manager in another. In the text that follows the term 'manager' will be used in this general sense and may refer to anyone whose function is to manage the work of others.

Activities covered

In dealing with the manufacturing function, all those activities are covered which are concerned directly with research, design and technical development and the production of goods or materials. Except perhaps for pure research, these activities are all linked to the product specification: this is perhaps best illustrated in a simple diagram below, Fig. 3.1.1.

The activities shown above are generally performed in the 'works', though many may argue that research or design is not a 'works' activity.

Fig. 3.1.1
Relation of
specification
to works
activities

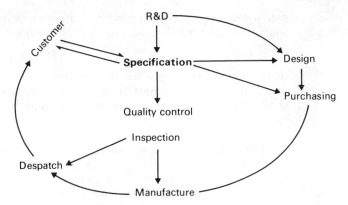

Not every student manager will find his job—or the job he may aspire to—described in detail, but most of the common activities normally carried out in a manufacturing unit are covered as far as it is possible to do so in a book of this kind.

The following activities are covered:

Research and
technical
development

This section covers *pure research*—which can be described as extending the frontiers of scientific knowledge; and *applied research*—which covers all activities that transform the market or customer requirements into working drawings or process specifications that can be used on the shop floor to produce the finished article. The activities will be those usually the responsibility of a Technical Director and will include those associated with the Chief Engineer, the Research Manager and the Chief Draughtsman in an engineering works, or the Chief Chemist in a process factory. The design of the company's product is included, both from the aspect of meeting foreseen market requirements, and for the translation of customers' specific requirements into specific solutions.

Supply

Supply is the responsibility of the *purchasing* function, frequently called the 'buying office'. The department is responsible for buying all materials required for production, and all other items and supplies not manufactured in the company's own plant. It is responsible for finding suppliers capable of meeting the specification for materials required, negotiating prices, and conditions of purchase, and placing orders; it is also responsible for ensuring that required delivery dates are met. In many companies, particularly in process industries which have a very high material content in cost of sales, this is a major activity headed by a senior executive.

Production
administration

This is dealt with in its specialised parts:

(*a*) *Production engineering*, which is responsible for deciding and specifying how work is to be done and covers the investigation of methods, the preparation of process specifications, ordering or design of plant, tools and equipment, and the measurement of work and establishment of time standards.

(*b*) *Production planning,* which decides and issues schedules for when work is to be done, and covers materials and stock records, preparation for long- and short-term manufacturing programmes, shop and machine loading and progress chasing.

(*c*) *Production control,* which is a specific application of the control function, and is concerned with recording results and correcting for deviations from programmes and variations from standards. Strictly speaking, inspection is a control activity, but as it is seldom, if ever, under the authority of those responsible for production administration and is very much a specialised activity, it is dealt with separately.

(*d*) *Operational research,* which provides management with a quantitative basis for decisions or the solution of specific problems through the ascertainment and measurement of facts, the probability of their accuracy or error, and the use of mathematical techniques and analogies for predicting results.

Ancillary services and departments

This section deals with works departments which are ancillary to production, i.e. they do not make any part of the product, but provide a service. They are dealt with under the following headings:

(*a*) *Storekeeping.*
(*b*) *Quality control and inspection.*
(*c*) *Works engineering,* covering buildings and services, plant and tools and maintenance.

Management in production

This is concerned with the organisation and supervision of the actual doing, i.e. with people more than paper. It is *general management* on a smaller scale. The activities are considered under the following headings: inspiration and coordination and the integration of supervision and skill; selection and promotion; training remuneration and incentives; performance; meetings and joint consultation.

Integration with marketing

It was shown in Part One (see page 25) that a primary responsibility of management is to know the product or service it is offering *and* to know the consumers or market to which it is offered, the correct interrelation of these two providing a foundation for a *marketing programme.* However, once the needs of the market have been established and the programme by which these needs are to be filled is fixed, then it is a *production* responsibility to see these are fulfilled. Production is integrated with the marketing or distribution activity by the General Manager or other chief executive, through the coordination and reconciliation of the sales forecasts and programmes with production programmes. Production is not self-sufficient, but it can be looked upon as the middle links in the chain of activities, starting from the obtaining of an order or receiving an enquiry and ending with the dispatch to customer or sale over the counter. Production policy, forming part of the general company policy, must tally with marketing policy. If the latter is to go for seasonal markets, production must be flexible enough to respond; if the policy is to keep production steady, stocks must be built up in preparation for the seasonal demand. Long-term production programmes must reflect long-term marketing or distribution plans, building up capacity of plant or sections of the works to meet changes in demand or emphasis in advertising. Technically too the policies must agree. Continual small modifications to design or product may prove disturbing to customers because of existing stocks; less frequent but more radical changes may be a better policy. Similarly, production must not place too much emphasis on quality with the consequent higher price if the sales policy is to go for a low-priced market where quality is not required.

There is often a tendency for sales and production staffs to be antagonistic. Certainly, ideal requirements for each do not always appear to coincide; to please the customer sometimes disrupts production. This antagonism is likely to develop in the very concerns where the production and sales divisions are well led by vigorous capable executives with a pride in their departments. The antagonism must be curbed and departmental prides related to a coordinated whole. The biggest factor in bringing this about is the general sharing in the formation of policy. When the Board, who are primarily makers of policy, and the top management clearly define the wider purpose of the business, insisting that a primary purpose is to serve its customers well and to make a profit in doing so, and when the chief executives concerned share in formulating the secondary policies required to achieve this purpose, then there is likely to be unity of outlook, and production men will recognise that they have a duty to serve the sales departments and through them the customer.

When the managers themselves are involved in identifying and agreeing their functional or departmental objectives, through the medium of contributing to and collaborating in the company's marketing programme—which is concerned with the whole organisation achieving the company objectives—the antagonism between functional departments will disappear. Goodnatured rivalry may be advantageous, but when departmental interest comes before company interest, the department is in jeopardy, for the department cannot exist without the company.

It is not always possible to explain to operators at the desk, bench or machine exactly why certain instructions or actions are necessary (and indeed these can often look senseless or useless), but it is possible to explain policies and the reason for them. Instructions and actions can then be seen as a part or an expression of these policies whereupon the need for them will be understood; and understanding is the first essential to correct performance.

Types of production

Production is a very wide term indeed, and it is not made much narrower through being qualified by the term 'industrial'. If it is assumed that all those persons engaged in the professions, central and local government service, and wholesale and retail distribution are not engaged in production, then according to the *Department of Employment Gazette* for November 1971, out of a total of 22 million persons employed, 10·24 million or 46·6 per cent are engaged in 'production'.

A classification of all the types of production thus segregated can be divided into four main groups:

		No. employed
1.	Mines and quarries	406 000
2.	Construction	1 243 000
3.	Public utilities	361 000
4.	Manufacture	8 234 000

Within each of these groups there are, broadly speaking, three types of production, or put it another way, production is carried on on three scales. They are: jobbing (usually small-scale); batch (usually medium scale); and flow or mass (usually large-scale).

Jobbing

Jobbing is concerned with the manufacture of single products to a customer's individual requirements, i.e. 'one-off'. Each job or order stands alone and is unlikely to be repeated. No two jobs are exactly alike and long runs on a single product are uncommon. Jobbing is carried on by a large proportion of the small manufacturing companies in Britain, and by many quite large companies. Because they are small and the proprietor so often discharges many or all of the executive functions it is usually considered that small companies cannot use or have no need of all the 'systems' and modern developments of systematic management. But the truth is that it is just in these small companies that the application of sound production management principles and the use of simple methods of production administration can effect so large an improvement in effectiveness.

Batch

Batch production operates in those companies where a batch or quantity of products or parts is made at a time, but where production of a part or product is not continuous. This occurs when there is a variety of products manufactured to stock and when orders are diverse, but for fairly large quantities and not for 'one-offs'. But perhaps the most common reason for batch production, and one which creates the complexities and many of the difficult problems of production administration, is the use of standard components in different products and models. This type of production is typical of industry, not only in Britain but in most industrial countries, including the United States. It calls for general purpose equipment and machine tools, flexibility in organisation, and a high standard of skill at the foreman and executive level. While the skill of all operators may not be as high as in factories on jobbing production, and tooling may not be so complex as on mass production, a high degree of skill is required in setting up tools and jobs and in deciding rapidly the most effective way to do a job. It is on this type of production in all industries that control is most difficult to secure and where badly designed and elaborate systems and paperwork can so easily clog the wheels and bog down production.

Mass production

Flow or mass production is limited in general to large-scale units, although continuous or flow operation is used frequently and with advantage for certain products or processes in factories mainly on batch production. In this type, products or parts of identical kind are in continuous production, going through exactly the same sequence of operations, and all processing units (machine, plant or operation) are always employed doing the same operation. Mass production has resulted in, and depends on, the development of the single-purpose type of machine. Frequently only one product, and one or perhaps two or three models or grades, are produced, and the production rate is high. Mass production reaches its most advanced stage in the large process industries like flour-milling and petrol-refining or in factories making such standard articles as domestic refrigerators, cars, and vacuum cleaners. Factories operating on a mass production scale are usually large, and employ thousands rather than hundreds. Many of the problems of management in this type of factory arise from the very size of the units and the consequent lack of contact between the higher management and operators, and the removal of skill from the jobs, resulting in lack of interest.

Effect on organisation

The above different types of production tend to give rise to different forms of organisation, and with the usual management problems appearing more significant in one than another. In *jobbing production* a high proportion of skilled technical people is required, the sales organisation is usually relatively small, and overheads are often low. Plant or production processes are varied and flexible but capital investment is small. Production planning is not usually a difficult problem, and management decisions are short term. Product cost is high.

On the other hand, *mass production* requires a highly organised marketing activity, accounting and commercial staff are large, and overheads high. Plant tends to be specialised and inflexible so that the emphasis in production is on maintaining a high and steady level of activity. Capital investment is high, and management decisions must be fairly long term. Unit cost is low.

Process

Process production goes to the extreme in inflexibility and capital investment and consequently the emphasis is on very long-term decisions and a marketing organisation that can maintain a steady flow of orders.

Batch production is midway between the extremes and calls perhaps for the greatest flexibility of management and emphasis on production planning and production (or industrial) engineering. It also needs the most balanced organisation. Unit costs can be higher or lower than in the other types, and total profits per £ of capital employed or per employee likewise.

Automation

Automation has been used in the highly developed process industries, particularly in the chemical industry, for some time. It is now in use in mass production plants and is being developed for smaller-scale use. It is unlikely to lead to a reduction in the total number of people employed, any more than the industrial revolution did. In fact the scarcity of persons available for production is forcing the development of automation. More skilled persons will be required and there will be fewer on direct production. The lack of skilled technical people and the need to train them is likely to retard the rate of application of automation and prevent a rapid 'revolution'.

Table 3.1.1 illustrates this diversity of type and scale and gives examples of each type of production for each group of industries.

The development of a factory from job production to batch production occurs naturally, and as a rule creates no major problems. It is usually the logical result of a gradual increase in volume of turnover, or of the application of standardisation of parts, as the business grows and its customers' needs become known. But it is the decision to apply mass production methods that is fraught with danger and has proved so disastrous in many cases. The premature application of such methods into the manufacture of domestic refrigerators in the USA, and of wireless sets in this country, are examples of the results to be expected. A factory laid out on mass production lines is a single-purpose machine in itself, and a change in fashion, inventions and radical improvements in design may make it obsolete almost overnight. The loss of profit entailed by a shutdown for a changeover can be expensive, as even Ford found out. It is dangerous to set up a factory for mass production for a product still in its early commercial stages, or when it is subject to fashion or public taste, or if the market potentialities are not definitely known. The decision to do so therefore must be a deliberate one and taken only by the Board of Directors as a matter of high policy.

Table 3.1.1

Examples of types of production

Industry	Type of production		
	Job	Batch	Flow
Mines and quarries	Quarries on special work for architecture	Normal mines	Oil wells
Agriculture and fishing	Normal mixed farm	Special stock and poultry farm Large market gardens	Whaling, herring, kippering and salmon canning
Building and civil engineering	Bridges Individual houses	Housing estates Public works maintenance	Modern road surfacing
Manufacture	Special-purpose machines Prototype work	All manufactured articles and most engineering and consumption industries	Cars, vacuum cleaners, telephones, electric lamps and motors, sugar-refining, flour-milling, paper-making
Transport	Furniture removal Plane chartered	All forms of transport	Public transport and special industries, e.g. milk

Size of factory

In order finally to get in perspective the average or typical size of a manufacturing unit in Great Britain, analysis of the following figures quoted in the *Ministry of Labour Gazette* in April 1962[1] reveals, for establishments employing more than ten people:

- well over half the number of factories employ less than 100 persons but account for only 20 per cent of the total number employed;
- at the other end of the scale just over one third of the total number employed work in factories employing more than 1 000 each, although the number of factories is only 2·1 per cent of the total.

Of the factories employing more than 11 persons each, 26 per cent are in the groups 100 to 1 000 and employ 45 per cent of those employed. This latter group is most typical of British industry and is the size with which we are most concerned in this study of production management.

Table 3.1.2
Number of employees
and establishments
related to firms
of a given size
range

Employees	Establishments		Employees	
	Number	Per cent of total	Number (000's)	Per cent of total
11–24	12 571	22·8	222	2·7
25–49	14 704	26·6	523	6·4
50–99	12 774	23·1	897	11·0
100–249	8 714	15·8	1 338	16·4
250–499	3 499	6·3	1 214	14·8
500–999	1 693	3·7	1 163	14·2
1 000–1 999	777	1·4	1 078	13·2
2 000–4 999	351	0·6	1 031	12·6
5 000 or more	78	0·1	712	8·6
Total with 11 or more employees	55 161	100	8 178	100

Organisation structure

The importance of effective management, of a sound organisation structure and of the understanding and application of its principles has been emphasised in Part One (see pages 45–48) and will be further considered in a different context in Part Seven (see page 923). In the present context it remains only to look briefly at the organisation structure needed for the Production Division. Frequently this division covers by far the largest number of persons and departments, and there is always the danger of having too many persons individually responsible to the head, i.e. the Works Manager, Production Manager, or whatever his title may be. This is a common fault, fifteen or even twenty people answerable directly to a Works Manager is no unusual situation and is a frequent cause of mediocrity, sluggishness and downright inefficiency in many of our factories today.

There are good reasons for thinking that the optimum size of a manufacturing unit is between 500 and 1 000 employees. In such a unit advantage can be

[1] This is the latest date for which this information is available. However the picture will not have changed significantly since that date.

taken of specialisation of activity and the use of production engineering and planning staff without losing the personal touch which comes from close contact between directors, executives and employees at all levels. This is recognised in the USA. The productivity report on Welding made by the team which visited the United States in 1950, and published by the Anglo-American Council on Productivity, stated (page 55): 'It is of interest that one major company had 125 separate works of which all but eleven employed fewer than 500 people. These smaller works were considered an advantage because they afford a closer contact between employers and labour, which resulted in a better relationship between the two.'

For a typical unit of any size between, say, 300 and 750 employees in the factory, the chart in Fig. 3.1.2 shows a typical structure for the Production Division, with suitable alternatives for the head of each department. (Titles of course are less important than definitions of responsibilities.)

The technical activity is clearly a production activity, and is treated as such in this book. It is, therefore, shown in the diagram as responsible to the executive in charge of production. In some concerns, however, particularly where it is closely tied up with the sales division or where there is a high technical content in the product the technical division is responsible directly to the Managing Director. In these cases Production Engineering and Planning may be separately responsible to the Works Manager. Or there may be two or three main operating divisions; for example, Processing, Packing and Storeroom in food manufacture, Printing and Binding in printing, Cutting, Making and Warehouse in clothing, and Machining and Assembly in engineering, each responsible to the Works Manager, without exceeding unduly the latter's span of control. On the other hand, if the technical activity is small and intimately bound up with works facilities, as is common in small jobbing businesses, it is often more satisfactory for one person to be responsible for the technical and administration activities. In a small factory of under a hundred people, one person might be responsible for the technical, planning and inspection activities, the Works Manager himself directly supervising the several foremen or chargehands.

In the medium-size factory employing 500–1 500 people, a more elaborate structure may be necessary. This may take the form shown in Fig. 3.1.3. On this chart departments are shown in panels with activities listed below. In still larger organisations, each of the second-line departments may be further divided. In all cases, however, the general form would remain the same, and the line of responsibility shown should not be departed from except in unusual circumstances. In factories in which a chemist is the technical executive, e.g. chemical processing and food factories, he is likely to be responsible for formulae and methods, and not the Production Engineer. He may also be responsible for factory inspection and test.

Production
organisation

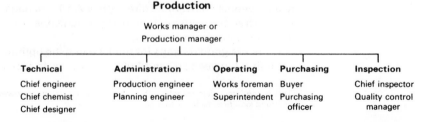

Fig. 3.1.3 Organisation structure for medium sized factory

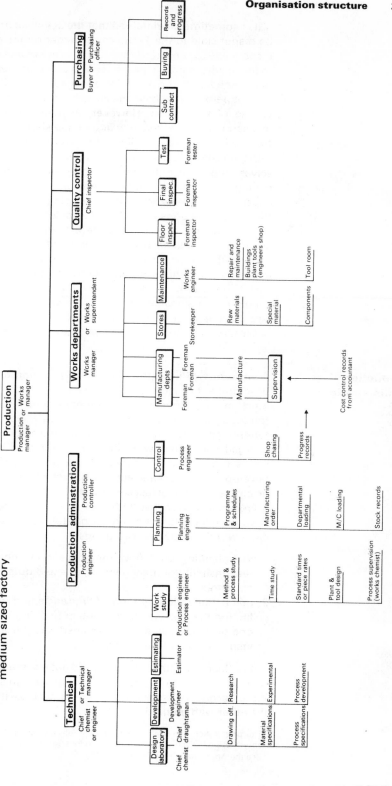

It is sometimes maintained that the activities of inspection and test should be responsible to the Technical Manager on the grounds that the personnel responsible for ensuring that quality is maintained should not be responsible to those whose activities are seen as being primarily to ensure that output is maintained. In fact companies engaged on work for the Ministry of Defence are not permitted to have the inspection function reporting to the manager in charge of production. However, in many concerns the large number of inspectors and checkers working on the shop floor justifies their supervision by, and hence responsibility to the works or production management.

Organisation charts, such as shown in Fig. 3.1.3, are insufficient by themselves, they can only indicate areas of responsibility. In order that each manager knows his detailed responsibilities, he should agree with his superiors a 'management job description' (MJD) which in addition to giving the areas of responsibility should also define the key tasks. Where formalised 'management by objectives' is operated there will also be agreed performance standards against each key task. In addition, each person should be given a copy of the MJDs for other supervisors in the form of a loose-leaf manual, including a copy of the organisation chart. Finally, it must be remembered that such organisation charts and definitions of duties soon get out of date; they should not be considered fixed and invariable for all time. As developments take place in company policy, size or personnel, amendments may become necessary, and these should be put into effect in a clear and definite manner.[1]

Production administration

A word or two is required as an introduction to what is a relatively recent development of industrial organisation—the delegation to specialists of that function of production management concerned with forms, figures and forethought. Not that there has not always been a lot of figures and forethought required in business. But the setting up of a central department charged specifically with the task of doing all the planning and issuing of works orders and of keeping check on progress is relatively new. It is a development associated with the growth of scientific management, which had its birth at the end of last century, and with large and complex organisations.

Frederick Taylor, the 'father of scientific management', back in the early days of this century, having set out to determine what precisely was a 'fair day's work', discovered two things:[2]

1. that planning, work flow, material supply and other factors, which are the responsibility of management, affected output in addition to the effort of operators;
2. that a tremendous amount of time and energy was wasted by skilled men in finding the best way to do a job or in doing it the wrong way, whereas the one best way could be determined scientifically and laid down in precise instructions for future repetition.

It is clear that although Taylor did not use the term 'production administration' as a function of management, he recognised its content, and what is more, recognised its two parts, one connected with work flow or planning, and the other with methods.

---

[1] The preparation and use of 'management job descriptions' (currently referred to widely in the abbreviation MJD) are fully considered in Part Seven (see page 953).
[2] See the Appendix to Part One (page 133).

Several common words have been pressed into service to describe the various activities of this branch of management, and most probably because it is not an exact science, but has developed in the solving of day-to-day problems, there is as yet no definition of their meaning. Terms such as planning, progress, production control, progress chasing, shop planner, progress clerk and so on, have been used with different meanings, or to refer to different activities in different organisations and textbooks. The word 'planning' is perhaps the most widely used. In some organisations it refers exclusively to the activities concerned with, and the department responsible for, determining the way in which a job is to be done, and the preparation of jigs and tools, operation time and so on. In others, particularly where there are few changes of method, and where new methods are not being continually studied, it is applied to the activity of preparing production programmes in relation to time, issuing shop schedules and generally steering work through the shops. In other organisations the term is used for the whole process of production administration, including methods, programmes, shop orders and progress.

There is indeed some justification for using the word 'planning' for all the activities covered by Fayol's *prevoyance*.[1] All forethought or work put into arranging beforehand how and when a job is to be done can be called *planning*, but with the need to specialise on the various activities of production administration, it is better in industry to be more specific and to use other terms for divisions of the activity. One of the earliest terms used, at least in England, for that activity of production administration dealing with pro- grammes, particularly on the shop floor, was 'progress'. It has been widened from its use in describing the work of the assistant to the foreman who looked after the clerical work attached to programmes in the shop (as a progress clerk or progress chaser) to include all the activities associated with preparing production programmes. There are many variations of these terms, and of others in use, evidence that there is no clear idea of what is meant by *production administration*, nor what are activities, duties and responsibilities. It may be thought that the technical characteristics of industry vary so widely that a common treatment of production administration, or a common ter- minology, is unlikely to be of any use.

Managers usually claim that their business is 'different', and with justifica- tion. No two businesses or organisations are exactly alike, any more than two persons are alike—and businesses are built up of persons. Nevertheless, not only the principles, but also the techniques of administration, and particularly of production administration, apply to all businesses. In this sense, businesses do not differ; production administration can be equally effective in them all, large or small, and whether they produce nylons or knitting machines, chemicals or cars. In order, therefore, that it can be discussed in relation to all industries, it is essential to define terms and to build up a commonly accepted use of such terms.

Definition of terms

There are three distinct, though related and sometime combined, activities concerned with getting production into stride and keeping check on its progress. They may be briefly described as follows:

[1] See page 134 in the Appendix to Part One.

1. Methods. Determining the most practical and economical way of doing a job, laying down standards for its performance, and designing the tools and equipment required. This can be best described as *production engineering*, sometimes referred to as *industrial engineering*. This term is valid whatever the industry; it is not specific to engineering, although the activities covered by production engineering have been developed rapidly and intensely in engineering. The study of methods and of the best way actually to do a job in a factory is an engineer's, or requires an engineer's training and outlook. The product may be pottery or chocolates, or even farming, but in this age of mechanisation and the application of power, the plant for producing and the best way to use it is an engineering problem. It is therefore a production engineering problem. The fact that there is a professional *Institution of Production Engineers* gives added force to the term.

2. Programmes. Arranging for what work shall be produced, and when. It is the activity concerned with the clerical routines, pre-planning production, preparing schedules of work to be done, the issue of works orders and control of stocks of materials and components. Since the word 'planning' is usually associated with this kind of activity, and is the most commonly used, the term *production planning* best describes it and will be used in this book.

3. Checking up on performance against standards and programmes. This activity can best be described as *production control*, in line with the analysis of management activities. It must not be confused with its frequent use for the whole process of production administration. It is concerned with comparing actual results with standards which have been laid down by either of the two other activities and the statistics are prepared and used by them or by the Accountant. Action is ultimately taken by supervision, i.e. managers or foremen, as a result of any differences that are revealed.

The terminology position may now be summarised:

'Production administration' consists of:
Production engineering—methods, tools, standards of quantity and time etc.
Production planning—programmes, works orders, production schedules, shop loads, material stocks.
Production control—recording results and performance, checking against programmes and standards, and pointing out corrective action required.

Production management involves the use of these activities, coupled with the human task of supervising the actual execution of the work to be done, ensuring good morale and coordinating the team.

There is one further term, 'tools', which requires explanation—having a special significance in engineering. The machines used for cutting and forming metal are called 'machine tools', and tools handled or put into the machines just 'tools'. But tools are used in all industries: moulds in potteries, lasts in boot and shoe manufacture, trowels and hods in building, formes in printing and boxmaking, and so on. In this book, therefore, the word 'tools' will be used to cover all such uses.

Systems and dangers   It is necessary to sound a note of warning against believing many of the claims made by 'systems', visible card records, movable bar or line charts, duplicating machines and so on, in particular that they 'control' production. They do nothing of the kind. Correctly designed, they make records rapidly available and present a mass of data in a simplified, easily comprehended form that can be grasped with a minimum of time or effort. They are 'tools' of production administration, and as such can be very effective tools indeed; but like all other tools, they have to be used by workmen and cannot work of themselves. A few such tools effectively used are more successful than elaborate systems. There is a tendency to measure the effectiveness of 'production control' systems by their complexity and by the amount of information that can be gathered from them. In this way small firms unwittingly encumber themselves with elaborate records and procedures and refinements of technique suitable only for the large-scale organisation, and even then of doubtful value. For this reason techniques and procedures described in chapter 5 of this Part will be kept simple and sufficient to illustrate principles only.

It is important to remember that what is wanted in production administration work is a firm grasp of principles and the methods of setting about a problem, and that the actual methods adopted and forms used may have to be fitted to the particular case, modified and certainly simplified if possible, as experience is gained and conditions change.

Persons engaged in the administration of production must be aware of dangers such as the following:

- Tendency to overrate the relative importance of production administration and to forget that it is only part of the total process of management—and never the most important. It appears increasingly important to persons who become wrapped up in it.
- Inclination to forget that production administration is a tool of management, and like all tools must not be allowed to become rusty, but must be kept sharp (or up to date).
- Losing sight of the fact that production engineering, production planning and production control in action all bear on people and inevitably create reactions, good or bad.
- Failure to realise that production administration is a service to supervision and not an end in itself. It supplies information to production but must not dictate to supervision.
- The recurring temptation to make manufacture fit production control 'systems', to compromise sound management principles for the sake of simpler production planning procedures, particularly when these have been in operation for some time. Systems must be flexible, adaptable and as simple as possible.

Supervision

When designs have been prepared, and drawings, specifications, or formulae issued, when methods of production and programmes have been worked out and the plant and tools provided, someone must still do the work or actually make the job. And when there are more than two or three persons jointly concerned with the doing, i.e. there is an organisation or a team, then someone must be responsible for generally overseeing the job, i.e. for supervision. If the team is larger than ten or a dozen a full-time manager is needed, and we have management in action on a small scale. As the team or organisation gets larger, management becomes a bigger job, detailed super-vision has to be delegated, and the title for persons performing the function changes, becoming Managing Director or General Manager at the highest level.

Whatever the position in the organisation, and whatever the title, the job of management involves supervision of people. Supervision is primarily and in the main a human problem—it is concerned with persons not forms. David Lilienthal, the man through whose leadership the great adventure in regional development in the USA, the Tennessee Valley Authority, was so successful, said 'making decisions from paper has a dehumanising effect, much of man's inhumanity to man is explained by it'. And persons differ, they are not all cast in the same mould. It is a fundamental law of mechanics that every action has an equal and opposite reaction. But in the realm of management, commands and actions of a supervisor must induce reactions in the same direction and not in an opposing one.

The *personnel* activity has developed in industry to advise and assist management in dealing with human problems. But just as on production matters a manager is advised by the technical department, planning, produc-tion engineers, chemists, inspectors and so on, but must remain responsible for ultimate action and what goes on in his department, so on personal problems he is responsible for their ultimate solution. There has been a tendency to look upon the person responsible for the personnel department as a Personnel Manager with authority to make decisions relating directly to problems of supervision in a department. This is a mistaken view of the personnel activity and a dangerous surrender of authority for a manager. A manager must always be responsible for all persons in his division of the organisation, and must therefore study the personnel or supervisory part of his job as keenly as he does the technical part; and the higher up the organisation structure he rises the more need there will be to deal with persons and situations instead of things. We have the technical knowledge today to raise productivity and with it our standard of life beyond all previous rates of increase; what is needed in addition is the ability to get people to work effectively and willingly together and as a coordinated enthusiastic team. The advice of the Personnel Officer should be sought whenever it might be helpful, but a manager must learn to deal with day-to-day problems himself. As in so many other cases, prevention is better than cure; it is better to prevent personnel problems by good management in day-to-day affairs.

The wider aspects of leadership, morale, welfare and what makes people willing to work are dealt with in Part Four. In chapter 7 of this Part we shall consider the problems to be faced by the manager in his own department. These cover such topics as: inspiration and coordination; selection, training and promotion; remuneration and incentives; performance; meetings and joint consultation.

Titles

A special problem calling for mention here is that of status and titles. Between the Managing Director and the chargehand in a manufacturing company there are many management grades. In a company employing some 7 000 people, there could be nine definite grades, and in a medium-size engineering firm employing 500–600 there often are seven. In all grades management is, or should be, actively in action, although the degree of responsibility involved and the proportion of time spent on the two functions of management, control and supervision, vary. Generally speaking, in each division of an organisation the grade varies with the number of individuals for whom a person is ultimately responsible, but this is not true as between different divisions. The rank or status of a manager depends on factors other than responsibility for the performance of those under his charge; for example, technical knowledge or skill, responsibility for money, information and goodwill. A Foreman in the works may have the same rank or status as the Chief Clerk in the general office or a section leader in the drawing office, though he may supervise many times more persons.

The proportion of time spent by managers on administrative work and on supervision varies with the grade, the chargehand spending almost all his time on actual supervision of persons and the Managing Director spending the greater portion of his time on administrative work. This can be illustrated as in Fig. 3.1.4. It is to be noted too that the amount of technical skill and managing ability required by a manager varies in the same way. A chargehand must himself be able to do all the jobs for which he is responsible and his management ability need not be of a high order. The reverse is true of the Managing Director.

There is much heartache suffered by those of small mental stature on account of supposed or imagined lack of status or inadequacy of title. Those who worry about their status have none to worry about. Although by many much store is set on the title of foreman or manager, it is not the title, but the duties that are covered by it which are important. A person's value to a company and hence to the community, and therefore to some extent his

Fig. 3.1.4

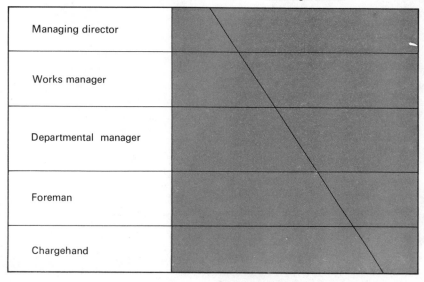

Administrative work
Managerial skill

Managing director

Works manager

Departmental manager

Foreman

Chargehand

Supervisory work
Technical skill

status, is measured by his grade, which carries a certain remuneration and certain privileges. A chief chemist may be on the same grade as a works manager, and the chief inspector may be in the foreman's grade and remunerated accordingly. But a person's status to a large extent, like the respect he receives, is earned by him and extended to him by those around him, of their own free choice—it cannot be handed out by order or proclamation. To have earned respect and the status due to him is the hall-mark of a good manager, whatever his status or title.

2 Research, design and technical development

Between the customer and the manufacturing unit there must always be a flow of information if the company is to stay in business. A company cannot live for ever on what Peter Drucker calls Today's Breadwinners.[1] There must be a design of new products, or development of existing ones or development of resources to meet changing customers' requirements. The relative position of these inputs in the information circle shown below (Fig. 3.2.1) will depend on whether the company makes for stock or makes to customer requirements, whichever is the case the information can be represented thus:

Fig. 3.2.1
Information flows

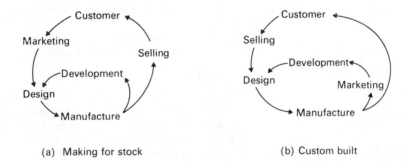

(a) Making for stock   (b) Custom built

The above diagrams represent the information flow loops in many companies; however in very large companies and a few small ones, there will be an additional information input arising from Research. In industry generally, this research is directed at expanding the range of the company's products or investigating problems allied to a particular branch of industry, but in research establishments, such as will be found in universities, the research is directed at extending the frontiers of man's knowledge, frequently without any clear idea of to what use the information so obtained may be put.

The scale of technical research today is such that many millions of pounds are spent annually by industry, the universities and research establishments. The pace of this technological development can be judged by reference to the aero-space industry. When the first edition of this book was published, single seat research aircraft were breaking the sound barrier in level flight; now passenger aircraft travel in excess of twice the speed of sound and man has made several landings on the moon. Before such changes become reality, a vast amount of money is spent on research and development. It is estimated that the expenditure on research in this country doubles

---

[1] P. F. Drucker, *Managing For Results*, chapter 4.

every ten years. On this basis the annual figure for the past few years has been approaching £800 million. Obtaining the best results from the expenditure of this amount of money is not solely a matter of technical excellence but also one of management. In effect the research and development activity in the UK can be likened to a large organisation with a purchasing power of £800 million and employing over 60 000 people.

From the standpoint of management practice, this vast and vigorous endeavour in scientific and technological advancement has consequences of particular importance. In the first place, research and development are today undoubtedly the mainspring for continuing industrial progress in individual companies as well as on the national scale; in many industries they are also the most likely sources of realistic improvement in effectiveness, because scientific and technical innovation can so often attain either a speedy or a dramatic reduction in cost, or increase of output, out of all proportion to what can be attained by changes in methods or rises in labour productivity. Research and development matter to management for an entirely different reason too—because they are such costly activities and, once initiated, can lead to a continuing expenditure which is difficult to keep in bounds. It has been estimated that the overall cost of employing a scientist on research work in an industrial establishment today is of the order of £10 000 per year. Even in a small enterprise serious research and development work cannot be contemplated unless some four or five scientists are working together; this entails a budget approaching £50 000 per year, and in any company above the 'small firm' category likely to be double that figure; nor are results customarily attained quickly.

The first decision to embark on scientific research work or serious technological development thus represents for management a matter of major importance. It is not just a question of finding a well-known and highly qualified professor from a neighbouring university, inviting him to forsake the quietude of academic paths for the challenging hurly-burly of industry and letting him loose in the company. A few firms have taken this line of approach, but there has seldom been any satisfactory achievement as a result. Some scientific or technical guidance can be acquired, but no serious work results. To embark on a research programme is a major decision, and while the advice of such a man at board level can be invaluable in assessing the situation and reaching the decision, the initiation of the programme calls for a clear understanding of the policy implications and of the financial consequence.

Research v. Development

It will be as well, first, to clear up a point of terminology, for a good deal of confusion arises over the use of the two terms 'research' and 'development', either separately or in association. No amount of analysis would enable a line of demarcation to be attained in detail, because the terms necessarily have different connotations in different technical settings. For all practical purposes it is sufficient to arrive at a working definition of each, and in many industries or enterprises it may be necessary to adopt a different management approach to each. Broadly speaking, the following difference has become commonly accepted:

Research is used to refer to basic scientific work leading to the acquisition of new knowledge, to the analysis of materials, or to the critical examination of the elements of process change; for example, the investigation of chemical structure or physical properties of materials, or the study of the influences on materials of treatment by given processes such as heating or dehydration, or the observation and analysis of the behaviour of any material or device in transient or steady state.

Development refers more to technical studies necessary to turn basic knowledge into product formulation, into methods of processing the formulation, the design of the equipment for the process, and other such phases of preparing for the translation of knowledge into production.

In practical life the line of demarcation is often blurred, and has to be resolved in individual cases by reference to the known circumstances being dealt with. Fortunately, it is frequently the case that no line of demarcation is called for, and the only practical issue that arises in this respect is whether the two activities should be combined into one laboratory under one head or should be separately dealt with—a question to which no general answer can be given. Quite often the answer has to be attained in terms of the very practical consideration of what the firm can afford; in many a small or medium-sized business, the scientific and technical requirements are known to be limited, even though important, and the Board of Directors may well decide that they can afford a small establishment staffed with a small number of skilled people, but nothing bigger. They can, therefore, rightly look to this unit to supply all that the firm requires in the way of its technical research and pre-production development, as well as the primary task of true scientific research on a limited scale. In recent years, there has been an increasing readiness on the part of educational institutions (especially the Universities of Technology and the major Polytechnics) to undertake R & D projects or tasks on commission from industrial firms; this has often proved to be a valuable and economical approach for the smaller or medium-sized firms.

In very big firms, there are known cases where two distinct laboratories exist within the same broad field, or at least two separate sections, the one devoted to 'fundamental research' and the other continuing on with the 'technical development'.

The more important issue interrelated with the distinction is the question of the functional head to whom the research and development activities report. In many engineering companies it has been customary for this work to be responsible to the production head, whether he be called Technical Director, Production Executive or Factory Manager. This has long been justified by the opinion that the research and development projects are closely interrelated with the everyday experience and requirements of the factory departments, particularly when considered in association with tool design, and that any separation at the top level might lead to an undesirable remoteness of the research and development work. Experience has proved, from the standpoint of development activities in the sense described above, that there is good logic in this argument; but it has proved also that there is a stronger case for the identification of research work with the product rather than its production, to avoid essential development being either neglected or recurrently impeded by the immediate demands of production. Where the research unit falls under the jurisdiction of an executive also responsible for manufacturing management, there is this ever-present danger of long-term research work being interrupted by 'trouble shooting', or of the pursuit of research projects being thwarted by the urgencies of *ad hoc* factory requirements, in addition to the cost of the distraction of expensive scientists by absorption into the solution of relatively inexpensive troubles. Experience has pointed also to the very different attitude and outlook of those engaged on research, from those involved with production, as well as to the importance of letting their tempo of work be dictated by the needs of the project that they are studying. There is, moreover, a significant difference in the cost items entailed in fundamental research as against pilot production and manufacturing, and the criteria of judgment of success or failure are quite different. Even in relation to contributions to existing manufacturing methods, there is the value that a research laboratory under separate top responsibility could take a more detached view and therefore give a more objective commentary. All things considered, the case seems to be strong for maintaining top management responsibility for research and development separate from that of manufacturing or production.

Organisation of research and development

Who then is the appropriate executive to whom research and development should be responsible? This, again, is an issue to which there is no easy general answer, because so much must depend on the circumstances of the company concerned or on the stage which its particular scientific developments have reached. What is involved here can perhaps be illustrated by the cases of three companies in different fields.

First illustration

The first is a medium-sized business in the textile industry with a long-standing successful history in traditional fibres. A family business, with rather more than 140 years of history reaching a point where the then young family member in charge as Managing Director felt that the economic situation ahead would be such as to make traditional fibres no longer as reliable a field of business as they had been in the past. He felt, therefore, compelled to take his company into the area of manmade fibres. There was no intention that the company should embark on the basic manufacture of the fibres, but that it should continue its normal activities of spinning and weaving, depending on outside suppliers for basic materials. This meant having an understanding of the scientific and technological factors involved in dealing with such materials, but not necessarily having a fullscale laboratory to go into the underlying fundamental knowledge. A greater part of this basic knowhow could be bought from outside by cooperating with companies who would supply the prepared materials. The Managing Director was himself not a technical man, but he felt, nonetheless, that it would be wise to keep the technical direction in his own hands, at least in the early stages. He therefore had to obtain technical support, and this he did by appointing as a personal assistant a young graduate scientist who had had some experience in the chemical development of manmade fibres. In the course of two or three years a small-scale laboratory was developed, but, throughout the whole successful accomplishment of the launching of yarns and cloths of manmade fibre construction, the scientific and technical support grew no bigger, nor was there any change away from the top responsibility resting in the hands of the Managing Director, acting as though in a secondary capacity of technical director. The problem of integration of the market potential with the selling of the yarns and cloths was thus easily attained because of the Sales Manager's responsibility to the Managing Director himself. At one stage consideration was given to the possibility of establishing a 'technical directorship' in its own right, but the Board were unanimous that more would be lost than would be gained, and so the original pattern remained. (It was changed only at a later stage of growth in the business, when it became necessary for the Managing Director to free himself as a person from this second responsibility in order to be able to concentrate more fully on the problems of direction in a period of complex growth.) In this case, there was clearly no true specific research work involved, but little more than a technical support to produce and process development.

Second illustration

Another example is provided by a small business in which three original founder partners formed the top management. By mutual agreement, one ran the business as General Manager, with a large interest on the sales side; another was in charge of manufacturing; and the third, with a junior assistant, took over the responsibility for engineering and technical development. The business was concerned with a specialised branch of light engineering in which intricacies of design were very important and involved two or three supplementary materials as well as metals. The small range of standard product was supplemented by a sizeable variety of special orders made in batch quantities. Accordingly, the technical development problems were very intimately bound up with the sales and manufacturing responsibilities, and, through a very definite phase of growth, the business was able to maintain its technical excellence by dint of the close interweaving of the technical direction with the top management.

Third illustration

The third case, on a rather different scale, concerns a large business in the chemicals field, where from an original standpoint of two or three products, economic considerations necessitated spreading into a number of different areas, some by diversification from the original group and others by the acquisition of new lines or the buying-in of business. After several years of development in this way, the company found itself in a position where it had two or three chemical laboratories situated in different plants, as well as an engineering design unit which was, to all intents and purposes, a laboratory for the design of chemical manufacturing processes and plant. Coordination of these various aspects of research and development was largely attained through the good personal relationships among the scientists in charge of the laboratories and the two or three managers responsible for the factories, themselves qualified technical men. Overseeing the coordination of research and development was a member of the Board with long service in one of the earlier constituent companies, a qualified chemist with a deep personal interest in research work. Highly respected for his knowledge of the company's areas of development, he was readily accepted by all those whose daily lives were spent in the fields of research and development, and thus an effective coordination was attained in a rather loose rough-and-ready way. With the growth of the business and a continuing increase in diversification, this form of coordination began to prove inadequate. For one thing, research staffs became difficult to get, as well as expensive, and at times the two or three laboratories found themselves in competition for the scarce manpower available. A major problem in organisation thus arose, as to how the coordination and direction of these multifarious activities should best be attained. On the one hand there was a need for fundamental research serving all the units in the group, and this might be an argument in favour of a single central basic scientific laboratory, separated in jurisdiction from any of the units and constituted under a Research Director. On the other hand, the laboratories had to give certain services to the manufacturing units in relation to quality specifications and control of process, and thus there had to be qualified scientific staffs available on the manufacturing locations. There was also the special problem of engineering design, as the company was one which did a good deal of pioneer work in the manufacturing methods for its own products. The situation provided an interesting case study and lent itself to many possible solutions. Foremost among the many factors influencing deliberation was the importance of systematic pursuit of fundamental knowledge and the ability to carry scientific personnel to this end. Taking into account the expected continued growth of the business, it was eventually decided to constitute a Technical Development Department into which were combined the scientific research and the engineering design. These were established in their own building at one of the major sites, but outside the jurisdiction of the local site management. They were responsible to a Technical Director, with whom lay the responsibility for the coordination of research and development policy with marketing potential, as well as the overall direction of the scientific research programme. Much of the 'engineering design' was of an experimental kind, interrelated with the findings from chemical research. In addition, this unit carried a functional responsibility for service to the manufacturing units, and at each of the latter there was established a small-scale working laboratory designed to serve the needs of local manufacturing control, each laboratory falling under local management but looking to the central laboratories for specialist scientific guidance. Through similar channels, the central laboratory was able to have engineering services provided to meet its needs in the construction of test plant at one or other of the factories.

Development and marketing

This third example throws into relief the problems of coordination at the levels of policy and top management, a problem which has different facets in different circumstances. If the Managing Director is himself scientifically or technically qualified, and is well supported by competent subordinate executives in other functions, there is usually close coordination in all the various aspects required. It is where the chief executive has a commercial or administrative mind and background that the problems of top coordination can emerge seriously; it is frequently alleged that in this case a Managing Director may not provide adequate technical understanding and support for those in charge of the research and development activities. To counter any unwitting habitual neglect it is important that he should make consciously deliberate endeavours to keep in mind his definite responsibility for the integration of scientific and technical thinking, along with those other aspects of the business which come more readily into his purview. He should ensure that he maintains good contacts with the director or other executives responsible for the research and technical services; he should ensure being in attendance at periodic discussions among the various executives concerned, and should so arrange activities that the scientific and technical members can in their turn participate in normal management meetings.

Common interest

A major facet of top management coordination, having particular bearing on the effective outcome of research and technical development operations, is that between research and marketing. A major issue comes into question here, for these are activities not commonly thought of together. All too frequently cooperation between these two aspects of management is superficial, and working liaison between them tends not to take place in any active way until the research or development units have 'something ready for the market'. It can then be found that the 'something that is ready' is out of line with true market needs, or that it gives rise to a conflict of interests between the technical and the marketing executives. It is of the utmost importance that the coordination between marketing and research should occur early in the formulation of a product or of a research programme and should be along the lines of cooperative thinking. Diagram (a) in Fig. 3.2.1 (p. 303) shows a continuing flow of information between design, development and manufacture, with a continual input from marketing of the changing requirements of existing and potential customers. In many products there is a 'design' factor which is fundamental to successful marketing, and this may well bring about automatic cooperation because neither side can pursue its own task without some briefing from the other. This would apply particularly in regard to purpose made engineering products (see Fig. 3.2.1*b*) where the design or formulation depends primarily on customers' specifications and may be carried out by a development unit rather than in a true research laboratory. There are, however, numerous fields of products—in manmade fibres, in prepared foodstuffs, in beverages, in cleansing agents, in chemical and pharmaceutical lines, in household materials, and so on—where new or improved formulation depends on the pursuit of fundamental research, or at least on deeply penetrating scientific investigations. This is the work carried out in the research organisations serving specific industries, and where lack of adequate liaison with marketing can result in truly expensive failures.

Coordination

Top management has the responsibility for seeing that the need for coordination of interest, outlook and activity is fully understood by marketing and research personnel, and honoured in everyday practice. The minds and natural attitude of the personnel in these two fields tend normally to be very different, almost antipathetic; communication may be found mutually difficult. There are, in other words, ready barriers to cooperation and equally ready inducements to go off down separate paths. Top management needs to be at hand with the recurrent reminder that both departments or units are serving the same business. The preparation of the research programme on the one side and the regular review of the marketing budget on the other can be timely occasions for this to be emphasised; there is no reason why both parties should not be made active participants in each other's mandate, so far as the forward aspects of development are concerned. Informal interim contact will also be necessary to ensure common interpretation of research findings, and to assess adjustments that may be necessary to expectations, because of the failure of some research experiments.

The market guidance to research is perhaps the more important aspect, because of the heavy cost of research work and the length of time required for the pursuit of any project that embodies basic scientific investigation. Research cannot be switched on and off at whim, and most experimental tasks calling for detailed analysis are time consuming before they field reliable results. Likewise the recruitment and training of the required specialist staff also requires much time and the flow of projects cannot be started and stopped in step with the short-term fortunes of the company. In point of fact, this requirement makes the customary annual basis of budgeting inadequate as far as research is concerned; a formal yearly review of progress and of expenditure on research can be valuable instruments of control, with the budget for an ensuing year serving as a useful directive. The research programme, however, needs to be seen in terms of longer cycles, say of three to five years, in which the yearly mandate is but one phase. It is in this longer-term directing of research effort that the close interrelation with marketing intentions has its major significance. The interaction is, of course, a process of twoway influence.

It can be assumed in this context that the top marketing management will be responsible for what might be described as the economics of new products or, in other words, the problems of cost determination and pricing. It will be their responsibility to obtain the necessary support of financial colleagues and the underlying marketing intelligence data on which to decide targets for the volume of production to be undertaken, the standards of quality to be attained, the likely price ranges for launching the product, the expenditures for a given scale of test and launching, and a calculation of projected profitability. It would be reasonable to expect that budgets should be prepared for these costs of launching the product and for market growth over a given period before the volume of sales is expected to reach the projected profitability, so as to attain the planned return on the total investment incurred. In this attainment the overall top management responsibility for coordination of research and marketing reaches its full fruition.

Quality control

Another aspect of coordination affecting research is that of providing for technical control of manufacturing activities, which can be particularly important in some industries. The problem can be illustrated by the example of a pharmaceutical company with a wide variety of products, many of them entailing formulations with complex processing and critical areas of treatment. To maintain the *quality control* in these circumstances it is necessary for a close degree of expert chemical supervision to be provided to the manufacturing departments, without impairing the normal production management responsibility. The company concerned was one of long establishment, and its manufacturing departments tended to be headed by men of long service who, while not having scientific training or qualifications, had gained a good deal of knowhow through experience over the years, often being active in the early days of initiating particular products. The whole of the manufacturing processes fell under the jurisdiction of a Works Manager, supported by these departmental heads or supervisors. For research purposes, the company had for some years been developing a full-scale laboratory staff with several well qualified chemists. Most of their interest lay in the search for new formulations and new avenues of product, but they were also required to serve the works departments in respect of test samples and quality control. The Chief Chemist, as head of the laboratory, was responsible to a Technical Director, the point of top coordination being the Managing Director, to whom the Works Manager was directly responsible. To maintain the control of quality in manufacturing, the Chief Chemist was required to work closely with the Works Manager, and he had an overriding jurisdiction to stop any production process on which quality was deteriorating from specification. To apply the control in practice an arrangement was made giving nominated qualified personnel from the laboratories areas of supervisory responsibility for the quality of specific product groups or departments. The arrangement ensured that each received, at intervals during the day, test samples drawn from stipulated stages of process within his product group. If tests showed quality deterioration, the chemist had the responsibility to order adjustments to process and to stop the manufacturing altogether when the checks proved that the processing was running seriously out of line with specification. Neither the Chief Chemist nor his nominated laboratory assistants had any other responsibility over the manufacturing departments than in respect of the quality control, and the clear understanding of the situation enabled very smooth working to be attained.

The above example is interesting from two points of view. First, it shows how the research laboratory can provide an effective quality control service to production. It also shows how the requirements of production can distract or disrupt a laboratory programme. For any research worker to have his attention distracted at random intervals, and have to stop what he is doing to perform some routine test, is to risk errors and failures in the research work. In the situation quoted above, it would have been preferable to have one or two technicians employed entirely on quality control and so enable the research staff to concentrate undistracted on their research work.

Board membership   The problem of responsibility for research and development often raises the question of the responsibility for these activities at Board level. Although there is no logical reason for difficulties in practice it is often stated that technical activities are not adequately represented by scientists or engineers on the Board of Directors. This view is borne out by the results of a recent survey[1] which showed that out of 380 Chief Engineers covered, only eight were directors, but of 323 Sales Managers, 169 were also directors.

[1] Inbucon Salary Survey, 1972.

The claim for such representation appears to be made either because it is felt necessary to further the interests of progress in technical matters in business, or because the scientists and engineers feel slighted that their intellectual capacity is not further used. However, in those companies which are technologically oriented it is usual to find at least one member of the Board carrying the responsibility for research, development or design as his main function. Indeed it is difficult to see how the Board of such a company could reach an informed decision without the presence of a director whose specific responsibility it is. The discussion about the atomic reactor and the bicycle shed is not so far from the truth on some occasions.[1] In spite of this there are many progressive technical enterprises which owe their vitality to a vigorous management mind at the top, able to harness the constructive contributions of able technical assistants, but in this there is a flair given to few. The problem is not one to which generalisations can be applied. The need for board representation will be governed by the activities of the company, some technologically oriented companies can justify both a Research Director and an Engineering Director, however in other companies the most technical man is the maintenance fitter.

The other aspect of Board membership for scientific personnel is the corollary of the Board's appreciation of technical matters, i.e. the scientist's appreciation of the impact of the technology on the business as a whole—in other words the most brilliant scientific mind in the company does not necessarily make the most effective technical member of the board. The only justification on the part of scientific personnel for admission to Board membership must lie in the same argument that is pertinent for any other groups of people, namely the ability to make effective contribution to the policies and progress of the business. There are, undoubtedly, a number of firms where the inclusion of a scientific member on the Board would be a definite advantage, but there are many others where the scientific background of a Board member would be as such a matter of indifference: even in the latter, the scientist would have his claim to consideration if he happened to be a person able to make a sound contribution to Board discussion and responsibility. There is probably a strong argument that the systematic training which a scientist has undergone should give him a level of mental ability that is of value to Board deliberations. Scientific and technical contributions to policy and progress can be made by means other than participation in the Board: for example, by the executive in charge of research and development activities being effectively constituted as a special adviser to the chief executive or to the Board as a whole.

Where the Board is mainly an executive one each of the main activities should be represented, i.e. heads of Marketing (or Sales), Production, Technical and Financial. In this context, the Technical Director should be competent to represent the interests of, and be responsible for, the policies of the scientific and technical staffs. Where such activities as export sales, research and development or purchasing are particularly vital in relation to the rest of the organisation, their interests and policies could well be represented in the Board room. If the Board is entirely or mainly non-executive it is important to ensure that it is composed of people who have a competent knowledge and experience of each of the company's organisational activities and if among

[1] C. Northcote Parkinson, *Parkinson's Law*, chapter 6.

these research or design is very important to the company's success, then at least one director should be qualified in the specific technology involved.

Nevertheless it must be remembered, particularly by executive directors, that all are of equal status and have equal overall responsibility for the direction, success or failure of the company. As executives they may have different levels of responsibility and status; they only operate as directors at Board meetings.

The management of research and development

This is perhaps a useful point at which to turn attention to the rather different topic of the application of management within the domain of research and development activities. Broadly speaking, all aspects of the management process are relevant, but the mode of their application is different in a number of respects, largely arising from the concentrated specialisation of work and from the generally high mental calibre of all the personnel concerned. Individual differences are also encountered, dependent upon the circumstances of the research and development activities in different laboratories. Some of the aspects of management practice within research may perhaps be worth comment in this context, but the problem is a big and complex one which requires on the part of the senior specialist executives responsible for research and development much fuller study than is proper for the present context. The aspects that will be taken up here are some of the broader ones that call for top management attention, whatever the scale on which research and development activities are established in an industrial enterprise. An interesting overall summary of the management problems is given in the columns of Table 3.2.1 overleaf.

Organisation structure

Taking first the question of organisation structure, this is an aspect relevant only in the larger laboratories: in the average run of medium or smaller businesses, the laboratory may be no more than a small team of scientists under a single head, and the only problem of internal organisation may arise through differences of discipline of the scientists concerned. Organisation problems begin to emerge only when the numbers of personnel in a laboratory are reaching into the twenties and thirties. In one large manufacturing concern there is a laboratory with over 100 qualified personnel: its work is broadly chemical in character, but it does have a number of supplementary scientists assisting the chemists. The organisation pattern is designed to secure the most effective work from the scientific teams and the fullest degree of effective coordination of the different activities. At the top there is a Laboratory Manager who is supported by three Divisional Managers, each responsible for a major section of the work of the laboratory. The line of demarcation for the divisions is that of the objectives towards which the research is orientated, broadly represented by consumer products, industrial products and plant design. Within each division the scientists are grouped into three or four sections, each containing anything from eight to twelve scientists. Here the basis of grouping differs, being sometimes that of an area of work, and sometimes that of the particular scientific skill employed. In this way it becomes possible to provide the higher grade specialist services, such as

Table 3.2.1

Management problems in a research and development organisation

	A. Technical work	B. Service work	C. Money	D. Facilities	E. Organisation and personnel
1. Basic policy decisions (re-examined occasionally, but not periodically)	1A. Scope, size and character of research and development work: areas to be investigated; proportion of work to be done inside the laboratory, elsewhere in the company and outside the company, patent and licence policy.	1B. Character and amount of service to be furnished research workers; location of service facilities; proportion and type of work to be done in decentralised shops, in centralised laboratory shops, and outside the laboratory.	1C. Determination of total amount to be spent on research and development; method of providing funds.	1D. Size and type of facilities; centralised v. decentralised research; location with respect to other departments of the company.	1E. Basic organisation structure; number, responsibilities, and relationships of supervisors, staff, research workers, etc.; relationship of laboratory to other parts of the company; methods of communication.
2. Planning for specific future periods	2A. What projects are to be worked on; how much emphasis should be devoted to each.	2B. Amount and kind of service work required to support technical programme (shops maintenance building service, procurement, public relations, legal, etc.)	2C. Preparation of financial budget; i.e translation of plans into financial terms.	2D. What items of equipment should be added, repaired or discarded; mechanism used for transmitting recommendations and decisions.	2E. Matching work to be done with abilities and interests of men available.
3. Operations	3A. Problems associated with actually doing research work; communication of ideas, progress, etc. within the laboratory and to others; coordination of related work; transition to development and production.	3B. Scheduling; relationships between technical organisation and service organisation; problems peculiar to each service function.	3C. Recording what is spent; various accounting problems; specific restrictions on the expenditure of funds.	3D. Responsibility for custody and use of equipment; loans, etc.; operation of equipment pools; assignment of space.	3E. Selection, promotion, dismissal, training; monetary and nonmonetary rewards; creation and maintenance of atmosphere; supervision and motivation.
4. Checking up	4A. Evaluation of rate of progress and probability of success; decisions to expand, contract, continue or stop work on a project; nature of the review process.	4B. Finding out whether service departments are providing proper service to technical departments; finding out whether service departments are operating efficiently.	4C. Use of financial information as a basis for checking performance.	4D. Methods of obtaining assurance that decisions are adhered to; appraising usefulness of various types of equipment.	4E. Measuring performance of individuals; finding out what they have been doing and how well they have been doing it.

Source. R. N. Anthony, *Management Controls in Industrial Research Organisations,* 1952.

spectroscopy and gas chromography, to be made available economically for the assistance of the various research sections that call for them. Obviously, at the level of the Divisional Managers, there has to be close coordination in the planning of work, so that the services of the specialised units can be deployed in a balanced way to meet the varying needs of the different sections. Attached to the Laboratory Manager are two staff units, one concerned with the equipment and personnel services, and the other with administrative and statistical services. Normal provisions are made for periodic meetings and other mechanisms for consultation and cooperation. From any close personal observation it soon becomes clear that the Laboratory Manager's own role is very much more that of management practice than of research activity.

Other aspects of research and development work in which organisation requirements emerge are those especially which relate to provision for test production, for pilot manufacturing, for transfer to normal manufacturing, and initial technical control in this last phase: these, however, are less matters for organisation structure within research than the planning of systematic arrangements between research and production management.

Planning and control

Within any laboratory or technical development unit, *planning* is a very important management element, and with it the associated element of *control*. As has already been stressed, most research and development projects absorb a considerable amount of time on the part of several experts and supporting staff, thus making any project correspondingly expensive. It is often argued that research and development activities, being brainwork or 'think work' cannot be planned, still less controlled. This may well be a misconception of the words, for it is unlikely that anyone would be willing to argue that such activities, and the sizeable expenditures which they inevitably incur, should be allowed to run without supervision or checking for performance. Planning and control, as elements of the management process, can be applied as effectively within research and development as they can elsewhere; there will be differences of application, and, in particular, planning must take account of the fact that attempts at forecasting of time required for projects are often unrealistic. Even this does not preclude the possibility of setting targets, the more so if this is done as part of the responsibility of those carrying out the project. Planning and control require, in the first place, an overall programme of projects to be undertaken, say for example, on an annual basis within a three-to-five year phasing. Without such a programme it would not be possible to determine the scientific manpower required or the way in which the research budget should be formulated. Within the annual programme it will be essential to plan at least in the sense of allocating priorities, or of indicating target dates for projects which call for specific completion, if they are to be of value. The allocation of such priorities and targets gives to the scientific teams guidance for their own working effort so that they can make the best use of time, particularly enabling them to decide when the stage is reached that it is wise to leave a project to simmer before further work is done on it. In any sizeable laboratory, it will be necessary to have a register giving some sort of progress review, so that the cost of projects to date can be assessed, and some indication drawn as to the advisability or otherwise of going on.

Progress records

There are laboratories where the planning and control techniques are carried to the extent that the scientific teams are required to record basic notes of work done, which become archives for later reference, thus preventing abortive repetition of work that is known to have produced negative results. In most laboratories it is customary for a scientific team setting out on a new project first to collect and examine the literature of the subject, and in a unit where the work is directed to a given product field, the literature should consist most usefully of such records of relevant past experimental work. It is normal management procedure to take steps to avoid unnecessary overlap of work, duplication of reading or research into previous work, repetition of abortive efforts and the waste of time that results from unsystematic approach to important discussions.

All this means nothing more than saying that it is as important to know as accurately as possible the true cost of research and development work as it is to know the cost of manufacturing a product. There is a widespread general idea that research and development are good activities in themselves, and that there is no need for their economic justification: nothing could be farther from the truth, and no Board of Directors could accept this standpoint as a valid principle. The Directors have every right to expect the same justification of their research and development expenditure as they have for all other activities and the same sense of urgency and respect for target dates as the organisation must have for customers' delivery dates.[1]

Cost and performance

The most effective way of controlling the cost and performance of research or development or other technical departments is through budgets—see Part Five, p. 755. First the Board should satisfy itself that the company is spending enough on research and development as such—a manufacturing company should have cause for concern if it is not spending (effectively) 2 per cent of its sales turnover (in some instances it is much more) on R and D. The Board should then authorise expenditure budgets and monitor actual expenditure.

For budgeting purposes, costs should be considered under the usual headings:

Capital expenditure.
Wages, salaries and associated expenses, National Insurance, pensions, etc.
Materials directly used in the projects.
Sundry consumable materials and services.

These costs should also be recorded and analysed under specific projects. Expenditure can then be compared, under the usual headings, with budgets for each accounting period. At the same time, expenditure on all projects should be reviewed to ensure that authorised expenditure is not being exceeded and, perhaps still more important, that the progress of each project can be compared with programme. It is often not realised by research and design staffs that time lost against programme can be more important and have more adverse effect on profits, than costs incurred, particularly when marketing programmes are tied to development or design.

---

[1] The subject of the planning and control of research activities is fully considered by Hiscocks in his book *Laboratory Administration*, two extracts from which are reproduced as Appendices A and B following this chapter. So far as the planning of detailed work in a laboratory is concerned, there is some administrative similarity with the situation in a technical design and drawing office: procedures in this context are referred to in chapter 3 below (see p. 329) and are also to be found in a pamphlet entitled *Drawing Office Organisation*, published by the British Institute of Management. In the case of very complex and large-scale research and development projects (for example, those contributing to national defence programmes or to space exploration) a number of highly sophisticated progress control techniques have been worked out, especially in the USA. One of these, with the codename PERT, was initiated by the well-known international management consultant group Booz-Allen and Hamilton (the code stands for Programme Evaluation and Review Technique). See below, pp. 384–9.

It is notoriously difficult to measure the performance of those engaged in creative or research work, but some attempt is worthwhile and can perhaps best be expressed as the return on capital expenditure in terms of profit on turnover (both expected and actually achieved) from the first year or say three years—for individual projects and for the whole department.

Group research

When companies combine or merge with other companies, a practice which is increasingly common in the industrial scene, then whereas each company by itself could not either afford or justify its own research establishment, frequently the combined needs and finances of the group make the setting up of a research unit a viable and rewarding proposition. In these circumstances the management of the unit will require considerable skill to ensure that research effort is given to each company according to its need, avoiding preferential treatment to one favoured company whose problems may be more academically interesting. The financing of the research unit in these conditions should be from consolidated group profits, not by means of a levy on each operating company within the group. In this way operating companies are prevented from making comparisons between the cost and the service required, particularly in years when little help is needed. This of course does not mean that the research unit is unaccountable for its expense. The manager responsible must satisfy the group board that the group as a whole is obtaining value for money.

Research at national level

So far, this chapter has dealt with technical development and research carried out by companies maintaining their own research establishments. However, for every firm that can justify its own research staff there are many which could never do so. This can be judged by Table 3.1.2 (p. 293) which gives the number of firms in each size bracket. Also, firms which do carry a small research or development staff may come across a problem which requires equipment or skills outside their own capability. To meet this need and the need of the small firm that only occasionally requires serious research effort there are some forty-one industrial Research Associations. The principles behind all these associations are the same: a cooperative effort by a group of firms interested in the field concerned. This effort is given permanence by the establishment of a laboratory with a small permanent staff whose job is to serve the members of the association. Finance for these Research Associations comes from three sources:

1. Annual subscription from member companies, usually on a *per capita* basis.
2. Sponsored projects, in which one or more companies sponsor a specific line of research and have sole right to the benefits therefrom.
3. Grant aid from a government department. The responsibility for the various associations was determined on the breakup of the Department of Scientific and Industrial Research (DSIR) in 1965, as follows:

The Department of Trade and Industry

Brush-making	Motor vehicles
Cast iron	Non-ferrous metals
Ceramics	Paint
Coke	Paper and board
Cotton, silk and manmade fibres	Production engineering
Cutlery	Rubber and plastics
Drop forging	Scientific instruments
Electrical	Ships
Furniture	Shoes
Glass	Springs
Hosiery	Steel castings
Hydromechanics	Tar
Lace	Welding
Laundering	Wool
Leather	Industrial psychology
Linen	Mycology
Machine tools	

The Ministry of Agriculture, Fisheries and Food

Flour-milling and baking	Fruit and vegetables
Food manufacturing industries	Toxicology (industrial biology)

The Department of the Environment

Construction	Timber
Heating and ventilating	Water

In addition to the laboratories run by the above associations there are some seventeen wholly government financed research laboratories whose activities and areas of responsibility are shown in Table 3.2.2.

Table 3.2.2
Titles of and responsibility for government research laboratories

Laboratory	Department responsible
Building Research Station	Department of Environment (DOE)
Computer Aided Design Centre	Department of Trade & Industry (DTI)
Fire Research Station	DOE
Forest Products Research Laboratory	DOE
Institute of Geological Sciences	National Environment Research Council
Hydraulics Research Station	DOE
Laboratory of the Government Chemist	DTI
National Engineering Laboratory	DTI
National Physical Laboratory	DTI
Radio and Space Research	Science Research Council
Road Research Laboratory	DOE
Safety in Mines Research Establishment	DTI
Torry Research Station	Ministry of Agriculture, Fisheries & Food
Tropical Products Institute	Overseas Development Administration of the Foreign and Commonwealth Office
Warren Spring Laboratory (Materials handling, Mineral extraction, processing, etc.)	DTI
Water Pollution Research Laboratory	DOE

Each Research Association employs on average some 120 personnel, making a total of about 5 000 of whom about a third will be graduates or have comparable qualifications. Each Association is governed by a council drawn mainly from the industries concerned, with the coopted support of university personnel or members of other relevant institutions. The Association's laboratory has its permanent head to ensure that stable programmes of work can be framed and pursued. The programmes of the Research Associations are essentially practical in outlook, concentrating on problems chosen by the members as being of the greatest industrial importance. Their work leads to more efficient production, to better quality products, and to economies in manpower and materials. This investment in brains is a business proposition likely to yield exceptional dividends.

The research programme of each Association will be geared to the needs of its members. It is the responsibility of each Research Association council to see that the best use is made of available resources, this being the day-to-day responsibility of the Director whose job is therefore one of managing research rather than carrying it out. There will always be plenty of worthwhile work to be done. The Director's main dilemma will be how to meet the requirement to use the resources to benefit the greatest number of members, without neglecting the needs of the small specialist firms.

The work of the Associations relates to materials, to processes, to products, as well as incorporating the appropriate fundamental research investigations. 'All information obtained by a Research Association is for the benefit of the members, and the results of investigations which may be of immediate practical application are communicated to them first. The Council may, however, decide to release the information for general publication, and this course is adopted for much of the basic research.' It is of interest to note that in recent years this national coverage of research activity has spread beyond the scientific and technical fields to embrace 'production economics' as well as some human and social problems. These have not been taken up in all industries, but a substantial amount of valuable work has been carried out by a few Research Associations which has afforded lessons to many industries, and has complemented studies made within more specifically sociological circles.

The existence of this wideflung network of industrial research activity on the national scale means that no company and no management need feel deprived of research and development facilities on grounds of size or cost. Many managements may not be aware of this framework and to that extent it could be of interest to record a reminder of the advantages of membership of a Research Association:

1. Members are the first to receive results of all investigations made on their behalf.
2. Results are the property of members and most of them may be freely used. Where the work has been covered by a Research Association patent, members receive preferential terms.
3. Members receive abstracts and surveys of the technical literature published in many countries, often with comments on the importance of new developments.
4. Books and periodicals may be borrowed from the specialised and comprehensive library maintained. The Staff is available for consultation on technical problems arising in the works of members.

5. The staffs of many Research Associations are trained to help member firms to raise productivity.
6. Members are kept in touch with technical developments of importance to the industry.
7. The staffs of member firms can often receive training from the research association in the latest techniques of control or of research.
8. The members decide the policy of the Research Association by electing the council and by serving on it or its committees.[1]

Government research

In addition to the Research Associations, generally set up to serve the interests of their own industry, there is a range of government-sponsored organisations with activities in the field of research and development:

● The Science Research Council supports work in universities and laboratories in a wide variety of fields such as control engineering, radio astronomy and nuclear physics in accordance with a policy of 'Selectivity and concentration in the support of research'.
● The National Research and Development Corporation engages in the commercial exploitation of patent rights for inventions derived from publicly supported research, for example at universities. The NRDC also provides financial support for the development of inventions in the public interest.
● A range of government financed research laboratories listed in Table 3.2.2.
● At selected universities organisations called University Industrial Centres were set up in 1968–70, each offering a consultancy service on the problems which industry could bring to them.

In the economic circumstances and tempo of this phase of twentieth-century industrial progress, there can be few companies which have not given some consideration to possibilities of technical developments, on however small a scale. Even in retail trading new automatic stock-room equipment has become available, and in one form (the Gompertz-Solartron automatic warehouse) affords a system of electronically controlled delivery to customers whose selection has been made from display samples and marked on instruction tickets. Serious long-term forecasting in presentday conditions almost invariably imposes on top management an obligation to take account of possible technological developments, and, behind them, to the outcome of advancing knowledge through research. The pursuit of continuing profitability begins widely to acquire a deep technological aspect, which in its own interests a firm cannot overlook. In this respect the individual business interest coincides with the national interest, and a company actively taking account of research and technical development is *ipso facto* contributing to national progress and thereby honouring its social obligation.

Social implications

The standard of living of the people and the position of the nation in worldwide economic competition both call for effective application of new knowledge,

[1] 'Combining for Research', published for the Dept. of Scientific and Industrial Research by H.M. Stationery Office, London, 1960.

and it is within the normal scope of industrial management responsibility to consider how best this is to be attained. There are, indeed, contributions to be made at governmental level, but these are largely supplementary in the context of a free enterprise system. It is unwise for managements to sit back and wait for a lead from the government of the day; or to content themselves with resolutions and speeches urging the government to 'do something' to promote technical progress through research and development. Such an attitude is tantamount to abnegation of the responsibility inherent in the management role. The government contribution—whatever the colour of the party in power in the Western formula of democracy—comes in background facilities: in the expenditure supporting national and industrial laboratories, and in the provision of adequate technical education facilities. The lead to make full and effective use of these, and to secure practical application from them, falls naturally to those holding top management responsibility.

What is required from the Boards of Directors of individual companies may be aptly described as making an investment in intellectual capacity. Neither the conduct of research and development work for individual purposes, nor the interpretation of scientific trends as the basis of policy, can be attained without an adequate supply of good brainpower, suitably trained in scientific and technological disciplines. Better educational provision to make the supply greater, or differently slanted, has been urged on the government and in some disciplines output of graduates now exceeds demand and it is probable that the more important issue in most industrial enterprises is that of the effective use of the brainpower already available. There is in British industry plenty of evidence of scientists inadequately employed—well qualified scientists engaged in firms whose requirements would be better met by technicians, or men of high calibre spending considerable proportions of their time on the details of projects which could easily be delegated to junior assistants. This is an issue on which management needs to be particularly judicious in considering its investment: buying in qualified scientific and technological brainpower, as an investment in intellectual capacity, requires the same careful deliberation as the purchase of manufacturing equipment. The broad decision is taken in terms of policy and objective, but the investment is effective only when the full scheme of ways and means of implementation has been assessed and approved. It is in this context that the question of 'technical representation at Board level' begins to have genuine pertinence, and sound argument would support the case for some scientific membership of the Board, if that is the best means by which top management responsibility for technical development can be determined and applied.

APPENDIX I. PROGRAMMING WORK IN A RESEARCH LABORATORY

The following is an extract from a paper by Sir Arnold Hall, FRS, Director of the Royal Aircraft Establishment, Farnborough, discussed at a seminar at the London School of Economics (quoted from E. S. Hiscocks, *Laboratory Administration*, chapter 9, 'Programming'.) The Royal Aircraft Establishment is the largest scientific institution in this country, and the extract gives an account of the system of technical programme planning and progressing employed there:

A separate programme of work is developed for each technical department of the Establishment. It arises from discussion between the Headquarters of the Ministry of Supply, other interested agencies, and the Establishment. The scientist and engineer is given every opportunity to express his opinions and advise on the programme. In forming the research programme full regard is had for advice from the Aeronautical Research Council and its Committees. Full weight is given to the views expressed by the industry, either directly, through its representation on research committees, or through the Society of British Aircraft Constructors.

A regular quarterly meeting is held in each technical department, at which all concerned with the programme of work and its progress meet together. This 'Programme Meeting' serves both as a means of discussing additions to the programme, and as an essential element in progressing.

We plan and progress our work in two ways. Parts which are suited to the treatment are time-planned, the task being broken down into technical phases, the overall date plan being built from the estimated time involved in these phases. The time plan is recorded in simple chart form, and a progress plot is superimposed at regular intervals. The analysis, and the estimate of progress, is made by the officer responsible for the work; a planning section is responsible for maintaining the record, and drawing the attention of the appropriate senior officer to any serious discrepancy between plan and achievement. A record of staff deployed on the work is also shown on the planning chart. The plan and its progress are reviewed regularly, and a re-plan or a re-deployment of staff is made if the situation requires it; should the forecast dates be changed, all concerned are informed of the adjustment.

In carrying out work involving well-known techniques a reasonably accurate assessment of the 'delivery date' can be expected from this process. It also highlights quickly any serious setback. But no scientist would expect such a system to be of any real value in the oversight of basic scientific work. Our work covers all shades from the basic research to the application of well-known techniques, though the latter is much the minor part. We use the planning and progressing system described fro the 'readily plannable' work, and extend its use some way into the less precise areas of activity. For the progressing of basic work, we use the medium of discussion, the state of the work being reviewed and discussed by those best qualified to judge it, at the regular programme meetings; the programme is then modified as may appear necessary. For the meeting, a document is drawn up setting out the position reached on each item of work and given a circulation which ensures that it receives a full measure of helpful and competent criticism.

We extend the application of the 'programme meeting' technique from the basic work towards the more 'plannable' work, so that every item is covered either by one method or the other, or both. There is no hard and fast rule on a matter of this kind, but there is this to say: it is folly to suppose that any routine planning system will be of much use on very fundamental work (because a discovery cannot be predicted by date) and it is equal folly to argue that time planning should not be employed on many items of applied research and project work. It is the greatest folly to suppose that any system can replace able leadership and clear decision.

APPENDIX II. CONTROL OF RESEARCH EXPENDITURE

The following recommendations are extracts from E. S. Hiscocks, *Laboratory Administration*, ch. 10, 'Evaluation'.

The discussions in this chapter will have made it obvious that the statistics obtainable in the field of laboratory administration are in a completely unorganised state. If a code of practice could be established so that true and immediately understandable comparisons could be made between the different collection of figures, the work would be more than repaid by the usefulness given by reliable figures and the correlations that might be perceived.

The following tabulation is put forward as the basis required for an assessment of the laboratory's progress in a number of different ways. If all laboratories were prepared to publish these figures, then valid comparisons could be made that might lead to significant improvements in the use of men and money. We need information on the following points:

A. *The total annual cost*

This should be broken down into:

(a) Salaries, Wages, and all costs directly attributable to staff such as pension contributions, National Health Insurance, etc.

(b) Capital Expenditure, i.e. on new buildings and major alterations to existing equipment costing more than £250 each, or any other agreed sum. (NB. £250 was the figure given in 1956. £600 is probably more realistic now.)

(c) Laboratory Apparatus and Materials, i.e. all running costs directly related to the research-work proper. Under this heading would also come maintenance and minor alterations.

(d) General Expenses (i.e. items not directly or easily related to specific researches), including travel, stationery, postage, library, cleaning, furniture, office equipment.

Detailed heads under any of the above major categories would be useful for minor purposes, but these four heads should be sufficient to give the major criteria, in conjunction with the staff figures also needed.

These are:

B. *Total staff employed*

This figure to be compiled of:

(e) Science or technology graduates, members of professional institutes with corresponding standards.
(f) Other scientific staff, i.e. sub-professional.
(g) Technicians.
(h) Clerical and executive staff.
(i) Other staff, e.g. labourers, porters, canteen staff, drivers, etc.

Finally, to obtain information relating to building-use, the following figures should be obtainable.

C. *Working space*

Total floor space.
Total working floor space, to include any addition made during the year under review. (The definition of working space to be that outlined earlier in this chapter.)

From these eleven figures a great assortment of measures can be compiled, which should answer many questions in the administrator's mind. For instance, A/B gives the crudest measure of cost to staff, but A/e gives the cost in terms of the qualified man only. The most valuable measures to be obtained from the above figures fall into three groups:

(i) the cost per unit of staff
(ii) the support ratio
(iii) the use of space ratio.

The most important ratios in the first category will undoubtedly be:

a/e i.e. total staff cost per qualified man;
a/B i.e. total staff cost per member of staff;
A/e i.e. total expenditure per qualified man;
A/B i.e. total expenditure per member of staff.

These will satisfy most general requirements, but on occasion the administrator will find it invaluable to work on cost figures related to total scientific staff, i.e. $(e + f)$ or scientists and technicians $(e + f + g)$. Alternatively, he may wish to know detailed costs in relation to numbers of staff, such as the capital cost per head, or the running cost per head, and these he can obtain by taking the relevant cost figure out of the Group A and forming his ratios with the required staff figures from group B.

The most important ratios in category (ii), the support ratio group, are given by:

f/e	i.e. ratio of sub-professional to professional staff;
g/e	i.e. ratio of technicians to professional staff;
$(f + g)/e$	i.e. technical support ratio to professional staff;
$(h + i)/(e + f + g)$	i.e. non-technical support ratio to technical staff.

Use of these ratios over a period or in comparison with similar ratios for other organisations will highlight staff deficiencies, and suggest possibilities of more economical uses of scarce categories of staff.

In the third group, the use of space ratio, the figures under the heading C can be combined with any combination of the staff figures under B to give a broad statistical picture of space utilisation. In addition, the ratio $k/1$ will show the architectural use of space, which is not dependent on the numbers of staff employed, but reveals the economy or otherwise of the basic lay-out.

3 Design for production

In the previous chapter we saw that there is a continual flow of information between marketing, research and development, and manufacture. We have looked at organisational and management aspects of research and development; now let us look at the practical aspects of preparing the working drawings or specifications which will give the necessary instructions to enable the production departments to manufacture the required product. The technical design of a product should always be recognised as a productive function, and therefore the planning and progressing of its output and the study of its effectiveness are just as important as for direct operations on the factory floor. The importance and extent of the product design function in comparison with the productive effort will vary. Many concerns sell technical expertise to solve specific problems, and as a result each customer's order has to be individually designed or formulae developed to produce the specific solution. Other companies produce large numbers of items to a few standard designs or specifications; the design activity in this case will be directed at producing the next generation of breadwinners. Whichever of these situations or the many possible gradations between them the design department has to fill, the basic guidelines for the control and management of the department will be the same. Deadlines for the production of new designs must be met, liaison with production departments will be equally necessary, and above all, designs or formulae, in addition to satisfying the needs of the customer, must also be related to production economics and not just to design office convenience.

The title of the head of 'design' function[1] will vary probably more than in any other area of industrial activity; for example a Chief Chemist in one firm may be the man responsible for all research and development, in another, the same title may be applied to the man responsible for preparing daily production process specifications. Whatever the title, his job will require, in addition to technical expertise in the particular sphere required, a wide knowledge and experience of the application of this expertise within his firm's industry. In some cases the title may indicate the craft from which the job came. For instance in the brewing industry the Chief Chemist may still be called the Head Brewer.

Whatever the title given in individual cases, the general responsibilities will be similar, the following list is typical of those that will be found:

- to interpret the Company's policy in relation to design of its own products and interpret customers' requirements in relation to their enquiries and orders;

[1] Wherever the term 'design' is used in this chapter, it should be taken to mean the activity, whatever it is called in an organisation, responsible for specifying or deciding exactly what the production departments must produce to give the customer what he wants.

- to translate these designs and requirements into clear and adequate working drawings, specifications, formulae or other instructions in a manner satisfactory to the Works Superintendent and to issue them to the production departments;
- to lay down and specify standards of quality and accuracy to maintain the Company's reputation and minimise production costs and to ensure standardisation and interchangeability as far as possible;
- to prepare estimates of the cost of producing a job to customers' requirements, and send to Sales Department for conversion into tenders to be submitted to customers, covering cost and the margin of profit laid down from time to time by the Managing Director; and to maintain such records as are necessary to enable this to be done quickly and accurately;
- to keep abreast of developments in the design, use and manufacture of the Company's products and carry out development, research and experimental work to this end;
- to keep and store safely and tidily accurate file records of all drawings, specifications and calculations;
- to supervise and coordinate work done and maintain discipline in the department, and to ensure that all members of the department are adequately trained in their duties and particularly that juniors and apprentices receive a good technical and practical training;
- to adhere to the Company's personnel policy.

Factors influencing design

Customers' exact requirements

A satisfied customer is one of the best salesmen a firm can have; he is a perpetual recommendation. It is essential therefore for designers to find out exactly what the customer really requires. When the product is a shelf product sold ultimately to the public, it is mainly a market research job, although even then the designer has to seek information which the marketing staff and even the customer may not realise affects the design. In the large number of firms which supply equipment and intermediate products to other companies it is usually left to the designer to ensure that he has all the information he requires. The salesman finds the markets and the customer and secures the order with a specification of requirements and conditions of service. But it is repeatedly found in practice that certain conditions and factors are taken for granted by the user and assumed by the designer, and when the product is put into service it is found to be faulty in some respects and that the fault is in the design. The designer therefore must ensure that he has all the information.

A good way to meet this point is for the designers to have by them a detailed and comprehensive questionnaire relating to the kind of products with which they deal. Whenever the designer tackles a new design, he should either fill in the answers himself, seeking from salesmen or customer those which he cannot supply, or submit the whole questionnaire in the first place. An alternative is to submit a detailed statement of the design before final acceptance, but a customer is less likely to check this accurately than to give correct answers to specific questions.

A product need not be better than the market for which it is intended. At the same time, however good a design may be, it fails to satisfy the user if maintenance is difficult or troublesome, or if it is inconvenient in use: for example, motor-cars and factory equipment which are difficult to get at for service and repair; machines which are inconvenient for the operator; containers, bottles and cartons which are difficult to open or use; furniture which is comfortable but heavy to move and difficult to clean; detergents which are harsh on hands; such products cannot be considered well designed and do not sell easily. This means that designers must have a commercial outlook and should see their products in use in all kinds of conditions as often as possible.

User

One of the factors too often ignored, more particularly with designers of machines, is the convenience and comfort of the operator or user. With the development of production engineering and work study techniques there has been much improvement in this respect in recent years, but one still meets plenty of glaring instances of neglect. Power presses are seldom comfortable to operate, and it is quite common for the working position and operation of wrapping, packing and weighing machines to be unnecessarily tiring, or to need an unnatural stance; for example, tables or delivery chutes of machines cause operators to bend over, yet are so obstructed below that the operators cannot sit with knees bent and feet supported. How many sink or kitchen units for the modern house have been designed with an eye to appearance, yet the user cannot stand with feet tucked under the sink or table and must therefore work with the body off balance, with the consequent strain on the back muscles? In other cases, operation handles require an unnatural stretch or action, or are hard to work.

Materials

It might be thought that all designers are aware that materials affect design. This is probably true, but it is worth emphasising that improvements and new materials are constantly being developed, and that there is a tendency always for busy designers to work in materials to which they are accustomed and of which they have had long experience, and to neglect the newer ones. To keep up-to-date involves a continual reading of technical and scientific journals, close collaboration with the buyer—and an open mind. It is always worth while making suppliers aware of new requirements; there are always some who are ready to consider new uses and needs—they are the designers of another product.

Works methods
and equipment

It is the general impression in most works departments that the designers have little idea of how a new product or part will be made, or could be made most economically. This is an indication of the lack of consideration given to the point by designers. Small modifications to designs can often result in considerable economies in production costs. This is a well-known fact to production engineers in engineering, but is often not realised in other industries. It can of course be overdone, and result in stereotyped design when improvement may be an asset. It is usual for engineering draughtsmen to spend some time in the works departments (it is ideal for them to go through every department), but it is by no means universal. There are so many processes in industry today that it is unusual for any one firm to employ a large proportion of them and impossible even then for technicians to have practical experience of them all. Chemists and other 'designers' or technicians often have scant knowledge of engineering or factory methods. Indeed, their profession is so specialised that it is difficult for them to gain such knowledge. It is important, therefore, to emphasise the need for the establishment of a routine or procedure which ensures that, where designers have not an intimate knowledge of production methods and techniques in their own works, the works staff or production engineers have an opportunity of scrutinising designs or specifications before their form is finally determined.

It is essential for designers in the first place to understand and take into account the plant available and methods used, and to design with the method of production in mind. A common fault is to leave too much information to be supplied by too many people. There is a temptation always for the design or technical department to leave manufacturing and process details which become general practice in a works—'old Spanish customs'—to foremen, operators or inspectors. This is dangerous. All goes well as long as there are no staff changes, but when there are changes, often unexpected and due to death, sudden resignation, or need for expansion, the new people on the job take some time before they pick up the knowhow, and mistakes occur. It is essential in specifications and on drawings to be specific and complete. For example, in process industries instructions such as 'heat', 'soak', 'dry', etc., should be defined as to degree, and in engineering the limits in dimensions should always be stated on drawings and not left to be remembered (or forgotten) in the production departments. All these factors can affect the quality and cost of the product. It should also be borne in mind that over specifying can be very costly, although it may be simpler for the draughtsmen to specify 'all machined dimensions $^{+0 \cdot 05}_{-0 \cdot 02}$ mm; analysis of the component may show that this is only required on a few dimensions, the rest can be as wide as $\pm 0 \cdot 2$ mm. Specifications and drawings must therefore be clearly, accurately and minutely defined.

Organisation of department

The purpose of the Design Department is to prepare and issue instructions to the Works Department to enable them to manufacture. This is done with the aid of some or all of the following documents:

Specification. A written description of the product (and its parts), process or formula.

Drawing. This may be a pencil sketch, carbon copy, tracing or print (blue or white), showing the object, usually in three views (plan, elevation and end view) with dimensions. It should include all information required in manufacture, such as materials, limits or dimensions, jigs and tools, etc.

Parts list or formula. A list of all parts or components of a product, with brief particulars of each.

Material schedule. Total material required, summarised under material headings.

Amendment note. A written statement of an amendment to either of the above.

Log of design. A classified record of designs or formula.

Register. A record, indexed, of drawings, specifications and formulae and a record of products or special orders on which 'own design' components have been used.

Specifications

Because technical people often have poor command of language, specifications are sometimes not as clear as they should be. They should be written, bearing in mind that they are most likely to be used by persons having less knowledge of the subject than the writer. Short sentences should be used, the matter set out in headed paragraphs, and illustrated where it is difficult to explain adequately in words.

Drawings

A drawing should be an accurate pictorial specification of exactly what the object it represents must be. It must be accurate and complete. It is important, therefore, that drawings should be fully dimensioned, and that every dimension should be accurately defined. This means that the variation permitted for each dimension is stated, and this is done by stating the tolerance permitted. An explanation of tolerances, fits and limits is given later, in chapter 6. It is important to remember that a dimension has no real meaning unless the permissible variation from it is known. A statement should therefore be included on all drawings giving the general tolerance on all dimensions which are not individually limited. The following is a good example from common practice:

> —Tolerances allowed—
> Unmachined surfaces ±2 mm
> Machined surfaces and CRS of machined holes ±0·5 mm
> unless otherwise stated.

The principle of 'one part one drawing' is now generally accepted for details and there is everything to be said for it. Drawings can be kept smaller; a great many parts can be satisfactorily reduced to a scale which enables 210 by 297 mm drawings to be used and, as this is a standard stationery size (A4) it simplifies filing. It also avoids the troubles and waste of time which occur in the works when several parts are shown on one drawing and more than one part is in production at the same time (a very frequent occurrence). It also enables drawings of similar components to be grouped or filed together—see under Group technology, pp. 481–2. This would be impossible to achieve where all details for one assembly are on the same drawing.

Parts lists

Parts lists vary from very brief lists of parts, most of which are illustrated by drawings, to fairly lengthy and adequate descriptions of many of the parts listed, including material specifications and post production processes such as heat treatment or plating. In practice a good deal of trouble is experienced with them because small items are omitted by oversight on the part of the person preparing the list. For this reason they should always be double-checked. To avoid the lengthy and expensive job of writing them out on tracings and printings, they can be run off on duplicators, or other reproduction equipment.

Material schedule

Since a parts list is prepared in a form to suit the works department, if it is necessary either to purchase or allocate material for each order then it is a great convenience to both the Stores Records and the Buyer to have a material collation list. This is a list of all material included on the parts list, material of the same kind and size being totalled and grouped and like materials being grouped together. It should be prepared by the Drawing Office and issued at the same time as the parts list. In a large Drawing Office a special clerical section can be used for this work.

Amendment and revisions

It is always difficult to keep specifications, drawings and parts lists up to date, to ensure that all copies are corrected when alterations are made, and that no old copies are in use. Failure to do so can result in work being done incorrectly, with consequent increase in costs. It is essential therefore to lay down a reliable procedure for dealing with the problem. Where it is impractical to withdraw and reissue a corrected document, a standard revision or amendment note should be issued by the originator of the document to be amended, and copies sent to all departments that receive the original document. It is unsafe, in practice, to issue copies only to the department which appears, at the time, to be affected. In normal circumstances certain departments may not need information which only concerns others; but unusual circumstances always arise, and it is then that all the information, including amendments, is required.

In the case of drawings, however careful the reissue of new drawings and the withdrawal of old ones, there are always wrong drawings left in existence. A simple and very safe method of issuing amended drawings is to differentiate between those which affect interchangeability and those which do not. For the former the drawings must be reissued with the part given a new number (if not the same as the drawing). When interchangeability is not affected, the number need not be changed, but a revision or issue number should be added, either in the drawing number itself or as a descriptive note or both.

Log or record of design

When there are many variations of design for various products continually being prepared, a log or record book should be kept, in which is entered every design, and against each, in headed columns, brief particulars of the various major parts of the design. It must be referred to before any new design is undertaken to ensure maximum standardisation. It is surprising how often such a record is referred to by the technical, production engineering and sales staff.

Sections and
specialisation

In line with the development of industry generally, designers and other technical men have become specialised, and in the larger firms the technical departments tend to be sectionalised, each section being headed by a senior man. Depending on whether there are many small designs or projects being dealt with at a time, or one large one, so sections either deal with all similar projects or all the same parts of each large project as it comes along. In either case persons become highly specialised in their own class of work, and as this means that they become very familiar with and memorise all the details, which are never very easy to record and index, work is dealt with quickly, and the maximum use can be made of standardisation and previous experience. There is, however, an element of danger in such specialisation, not to be overlooked. When specialised knowledge, and a memory of unrecorded detail, are suddenly removed, as must happen from time to time, there can be a serious loss. For this reason it is important for the head of the department to keep in touch with all jobs and all divisions of work in the department, to examine and talk over with his staff all the new work coming into the department, and to insist that all vital information and data are adequately recorded.

A good deal of design work involves intricate and advanced mathematical calculations, and a special section is often set up to deal with them for the whole of the department. Such problems as the stresses in parts of machines, the strength of materials required and the quantities for large projects are dealt with in such sections. The advantage of specialist skill has to be set off against the delay to which this arrangement almost inevitably gives rise, but in a large engineering drawing office, where it is impractical for all draughtsmen to have the requisite knowledge, it is essential.

A much less certain case can be made out for the frequent arrangement of a separate section for checking all designs, or work produced in a technical department, before use. The aim, of course, is to ensure that all work is absolutely correct when issued to the works; faults found afterwards (or not found) are always expensive. Nevertheless, in practice the tendency is always for the designers to rely on this check. It promotes a better sense of responsibility and a higher standard if each man is responsible for his own work, arranging for such checking as may be necessary with his senior. Where 100 per cent accuracy is vital, as for example in the aircraft industry, a final check is unavoidable.

In the same way parts lists, generally speaking, should be prepared by the man producing the design, since only he can be certain that everything is included, these being written legibly in a method best suited to the reproduction facilities in the office. Where, however, designs or projects incorporate standard designs or subassemblies, and material schedules are also required, a special clerical section to deal with lists, compiling the material lists and gathering together copies of the standard subassemblies, can be effective and economical. Such a section should be responsible also for the issue of work from the department, ensuring that copies of originals and revisions are circulated correctly and superseded copies withdrawn.

Work planning

The Design Department or Drawing Office is as much a production department as any in the works, it is in the direct line of manufacturing processes from receipt of an order to its despatch. That its cost is usually included in overheads does not alter the fact, and in some companies handling large projects the design and drawing time is included in the final price as a direct cost. It is just as important, therefore, to plan and measure work done in the Design Department as in a department of the works. To do this it is unnecessary to have time sheets or to clock on jobs, neither of which is popular or usual for office staff.

Since it is impossible to plan reliably without a measure of the time likely to be taken to do the work, let us first of all consider the problem of measurement. The usual reaction of designers and technical staff to any suggestion that their work should be measured is that it is impossible to say beforehand exactly how long it will take to think out a new design or solve an awkward designing problem. This may be so for completely novel designs never before attempted, but experience shows that in dealing with the normal run of work forming a company's regular production it is possible with practice to estimate the time normally taken within sufficient accuracy for it to be used for a measure of individual performance and for planning.

In a small office, the head of the department, and in a large one, the section leaders, should, when scanning each new job before allocating it to a designer or section, assess the standard time required for dealing with the job, i.e. the time which an average designer on that class of work in the department would take to deal with it, giving conscientious attention to it. Each job is allocated and the 'standard time' for it recorded. As each job is completed and issued to the works, the designer (or group) is credited with the 'standard time' on his weekly record. The total of the 'standard' hours produced for the week, or other period, is compared with actual hours worked, and the weekly figure and cumulative total are recorded for each man and the department as a whole. Experience at estimating the 'standard time' and in studying records of results enables the person doing so to become quite accurate. There is no need to use the times for any method of payment by results. If, however, results and doubts about probable times are discussed fully with the person concerned it can have a beneficial effect on output. When such a scheme is first introduced it will be found that the total standard hours produced in a period for each man and for the whole department is considerably less than the actual hours worked, but after a time, six months or so, performance improves (and estimates are made more accurately) and the standard hours agree closely with actual hours. Even if performance does not improve, the estimated time will at least adjust itself to actual time, so that planning can be accurate, but inevitably such a method of measuring and examining results has a beneficial effect on output.

Planning of work should then be dealt with in much the same way as it is dealt with for factory departments. Again in practice the most effective way is to show the length of standard time allowed each designer (or group) on a Gantt-type chart on a time base. A more flexible way is to mark the time along the edge of a card representing the job and place in pockets of a load board marked horizontally in weeks and months. In this way not only can the load on each designer be seen and overloading avoided, but the date for completion of each job and new jobs coming in can be given and the effects on existing promises of dealing with urgent orders out of turn can be assessed. To ask a designer to drop a job to take up a more urgent one is inimical to concentration; to do so repeatedly is to invite small and large errors, and too many of them. Planning can go a long way towards avoiding this.

Indexing and filing

The correct filing and indexing of technical documents, specifications, formulae and drawings is an important matter, but one often neglected. It is essential that there is no loss of time in finding them when they are required (and time so lost can be considerable), and that they are not damaged during storage or in the filing process. Moreover, it is even more essential that designers, whose time is valuable, can readily refer to data which has a bearing on a present problem when the filing number of the document containing it may not be known.

Safety

Dealing first with safety, it has been found that the most satisfactory method of filing all technical documents, except books, is a drawer-type metal filing cabinet. For a maximum protection of documents, care in use, and most rapid reference, the suspended-type folder should be used, and in general the A4 size is most satisfactory. The suspended folder method is also satisfactory for larger drawings if they are folded, although for very large drawings, drawers are not suitable and cabinets opening from the top should be used. If drawings are standardised on commercial stationery sizes, e.g. A4 (and this size is satisfactory for the majority of detail drawings), standard equipment can be used.

Protection against the hazard of fire should be given serious consideration; drawings, formulae, specifications and the like are extremely valuable documents, and in most cases it would be physically impossible to replace or remake them unless another copy existed. It is advisable, therefore, either to store all such documents in genuinely fireproof equipment (much so-called fireproof equipment is only partially so) or to store one copy of the document some distance away from, and certainly in another building from, the master copy, or as a safeguard against a general conflagration, to do both. An alternative to an exact copy is microfilm copies. These need special photographic equipment, but there are firms in most large towns who specialise in this service, and such copies have the great advantage of taking up very little space. Perhaps the most satisfactory way, if space is available, is to file the master copy (tracings of drawings) in a strong-room and have copies available in the department for reference purposes. This has the added advantage of preserving the master from damage and defacement in normal use.

Identification

In order to identify and file drawings and other documents, it is usual to give them an individual number. The simplest method, but one which has no other purpose than mere identification, is to number them from one up, i.e. start at number one and number each successive document made or filed with the next unused number in a register. It is possible, however, to devise a system or code which ensures that the documents are filed in some sort of useful order and which facilitates memorising and identification. Such a code involves the separation of the items into groups or categories and their classification which makes a code useful and effective. In technical departments where the data, including specifications, abstracts from technical journals etc., cover a very wide sphere, then the general classification used in public libraries in Britain can be used, and any public library will give detailed particulars or a demonstration. In general, however, the data or documents to be filed cover a limited field peculiar to the firm's activities or products. It is then necessary to build up a classification and code to suit this limited range. For specification and formulae dealing with processes, it will be found useful either to classify according to names of processes, subdividing for subsidiary processes, or according to products. For drawings there are in general two alternative methods of approach, either to classify according to product or according to type of part. Where it is possible to use standardised parts in different products (and this should be encouraged) classifying should be according to part. Drawings of like parts are then filed together.

In order that items can be identified individually and in classes, they must be given symbols, and the symbols and the method of allocating them must satisfy the following requirements: (*a*) provide a logical classification; (*b*) result in a simple and flexible index; (*c*) allow of easy insertion of new classes.

Several forms of symbolisation have been suggested, but generally either alphabetical or numerical ones or a combination of both are found most satisfactory. The following example used in the aircraft industry in this country, originally given in BS 1100 (p. 19), still illustrates a method suitable for a single product:

The number is VA521317 but each portion is thought of and spoken of independently, thus V.A5.21.317:
The first portion V indicates the firm
The second portion A5 indicates the product type
The third portion 21 indicates the sub-assembly
The fourth portion 317 is the part number.
The part number may be modified to indicate for example the hand of parts, odd numbers being used for lefthand parts and even numbers reserved for righthand parts.
Another example used an eight-figure code, all figures.
The number of the part is 61012314:
Figure 6 is the product category
The second two figures 10 indicate the model
The fourth and fifth two figures 12 indicate for example the tonnage in the code
The last three figures 314 indicate the part number of the model 61012.

Perhaps the best method of all, providing maximum simplification and standardisation, is a decimal classification. For example, where it is desired to file or store all like parts together, irrespective of the model for which they are used, in order to make reference to all such parts quick and complete, the class of part is coded in the first three figures, and the part number by figures following the decimal point, thus: 126·15 represents the 15th design of part 26 in group 1 of the firm's products.

If there are more than 99 parts to a group or product, three figures before the point must be used for parts and if the number of products of groups exceeds nine, the number before the point would become five figures, e.g. 1101·1, being the first design of part 1 of group or product 11.

Part numbers are allocated in a block to subassemblies. As drawings are filed in numerical order, all designs of the same part are filed together and all associated parts are filed adjacent to each other. From the drawing office point of view this is perhaps the most effective way of numbering drawings. In practice, it is found that a symbol built-up of numbers only is most satisfactory, it can be extremely flexible within wide limits, and leads to less confusion on the telephone than one containing letters, many of which sound similar.

A number of codes have been developed which aim to specify the form of the component and in some cases also the material from which it is made. Two well known examples of this approach are the Brisch and Opitz codes. While both these codes are designed to specify the component in terms of specific physical parameters, the Opitz code is designed to be universal, so that although it applies to machined parts only, identical components produced in different factories should have the same code number. The Brisch code, however, is tailored to meet the specific needs of each concern and therefore two companies producing identical parts may not necessarily give these parts identical code numbers. A more detailed description of these two approaches is given in *Techniques of Production Management* by Ray Wild (Holt, Rinehart and Winston, 1971).

Finally, it is good practice and generally accepted nowadays that part numbers and drawings numbers should be identical. This again simplifies identification, aids the memorising of frequently used parts, and saves space and writing on documents. It certainly avoids errors and confusion in the works.

Standardisation

Standardisation to some extent has become commonplace. Indeed, it is taken for granted, in industry and everyday life. Many objects in common use, the telephone, motor-car, cycle, household articles, boots and shoes, and even the readymade suit, would not be so cheap as they are were it not for the extensive and intensive use of standardisation. Yet a good deal more could be done to gain the advantage of standardisation both between different firms manufacturing the same product and within individual firms. The benefits of standardisation begin, and its application for the most part must be worked out in the design department. More could be done between firms that make or use intermediate products, e.g. water and steam valves, household plumbing and fittings, books, bottles and similar articles, to ensure the overall sizes which make for interchangeability between one brand and another are standardised. And within a firm it is quite usual to find different draughtsmen designing similar parts for different products with only small differences, when an identical part would be quite satisfactory for both cases. Or again, materials are specified which have to be purchased specially when, with a little thought, a standard material or size in stock could be used.

The advantages of standardisation are:

To the producer:

● bigger production batches and more continuous runs resulting in lower tooling and set-up costs;
● possibility of breaking down operations, of increasing mechanisation and of using special-purpose high-production plant;
● reduction in idle plant, tools and space;
● reduction in stocks of materials, components and finished products;
● reduction in overhead staff costs (drawing, design, planning and clerical);
● easier service and maintenance of products;
● possibility of concentrating marketing effort and costs on smaller range;
● generally, increased output and productivity and lower costs.

To the user:

- lower prices;
- interchangeability whatever the supplier;
- improved stocks and supplies, service and maintenance.

It is as well, however, to remember that there are disadvantages, or rather dangers, in standardisation. If carried too far, or adhered to too rigidly, it can sterilise design and make desirable or worthwhile changes slow in adoption until too late (until, for example, a market is lost: Henry Ford nearly ruined his business by hanging on to his Model T just a shade too long). Standardisation is possible for most articles, the design or performance of which satisfies all normal requirements, e.g. bolts, pipes, roller chain, electric plugs and water taps. It is unwise to standardise in a rapidly changing technology or to tie standardisation of dimensions to performance before performance of a product is reasonably established. Furthermore, however desirable it may be to standardise and mass produce certain articles, there is always a need for special design for a special purpose. But the firm that adopts as its policy mass production based on standardisation cannot economically deal with specials—in practice they do not mix—and it may well be that in this country with the accumulated skill and know-how of generations, with a high level of craftsmanship reinforced by general education, the special product for one factory and the mass produced for another will continue to be a good arrangement, and indeed the most suitable for British manufacturing industries, for a long time to come.

The objects of standardisation are to facilitate the interchangeability of parts and to reduce costs by limiting variations of material, nomenclature, set-up of process, as far as possible. It can most effectively be brought about by observing the following aspects of the principle:

Nomenclature. The sciences are built up on the application of defined terms. Similar precise definitions should be used in all technical work, and this applies particularly in the industrial Design and Techncial Departments, and in the case of drawings, specifications, and similar documents.

Dimensions. Standardisation of dimensions and their definition by limiting the variation has become almost universal. By the use of such standards and tolerances and the rejection of parts whose dimensions do not conform to them, interchangeability of parts has become possible. Whitworth started the good work on screw threads, and today most articles and materials in general use, such as sheet metal, wire, rolled-steel sections, commercial stationery, boots and shoes, electric plugs and sockets are standardised as to certain vital dimensions. The method of specifying the desired accuracy of dimensions is dealt with in chapter 6 under 'Inspection' (p. 498); see also *British Standards for Workshop Practice,* BS Handbook No. 2.

Quality. Only by the standardisation of quality of raw material can a manufacturer ensure a reliable performance of his product, and without reliability there would neither be the safety nor the freedom from trouble and inconvenience which we take so much for granted today. A standard quality is ensured by specifications laying down tests and performance.

Tooling. This is of special significance because without standardisation of tools, interchangeability of parts and standard times and performance would be impossible, and on this depends all planning in factories. It also ensures accuracy of dimensions in such cases as drills for holes and taps and dies for screw threads.

Performance. This again can be a special case of quality when applied to finished products. Standards for testing ensure that a product will do what it is designed or specified to do within prescribed limits. Standard times are a measure of performance for human operation (see p. 410).

Processes. There is usually a best way, and in certain industries such as the chemical industry, only one correct way, of doing a job. With standard materials, tools and specifications, methods can be standardised and a uniform product ensured.

Standardisation applied to industry in this country has been developed and organised by the British Standards Institution, which explores the need for, and issues British Standard Specifications in two technical divisions covering engineering, constructional, chemical, textile, general, service and consumer goods, and this widening interest can be expected to continue if the need is there. The activities of the Institution are briefly explained as follows: 'The principles observed in the preparation of British Standards are that they should be in accordance with the need of the economy, should meet a generally recognised demand and take into account the interests of producers and users' (*British Standards Year Book,* 1972).

Some 5 000 standards have been issued and in addition about 500 aircraft standards and lesser numbers of the automobile series and marine series of codes of practice.

The BSI also distributes international standards of the International Standards Organisation (ISO) and recommendations of the International Electrotechnical Commission (IEC) and standards of overseas countries.

Estimating and contracts

Nature of activity

Estimating the total cost of a product or a service before work starts is an activity which is carried on continuously only in those companies which manufacture to customers' special requirements or provide special services. It is not a continuous activity in companies whose products are completely standard and made for shelf or warehouse stock. This means that it is not usually found in factories manufacturing articles which are eventually bought by the general public, such as sewing machines, furniture, food, confectionery and readymade clothing, but is limited, by and large, to firms making (or repairing) plant and equipment to individual order or for civil engineering and public works contracting. Standard products can be costed accurately and the selling price determined for repeat sales, this being varied only according to the quantities ordered or the type of customer and the service he renders to the ultimate consumer. This adjustment of prices is a Sales Department function.

When it is necessary to quote a prospective customer a price for supplying an article, machine or plant before he is prepared to order (i.e. against an enquiry) some kind of an estimate of the ultimate costs has to be prepared.

This can vary from an extraction from previous costs of the cost of each part or item to what may be called 'guesstimating', or intelligent guessing. When preliminary designs are not prepared in detail, the accuracy of the estimate depends on the skill with which the estimator interpolates from records of previous costs. Obviously, the more complete the records and the more effectively they are indexed, the more accurate will be the estimate. It is possible, of course, to estimate each detail, piece by piece, and to build up a complete estimate, but in practice this generally takes too long and is too expensive, so that something between this and a pure guess is required.

The job of the estimator then is to arrive at as accurate a forecast as possible of the ultimate cost of a product or project before work on it commences or is authorised, and in the shortest time and at a minimum cost.

It is obvious that continually underestimating will involve the risk of a loss on the year's trading and ultimate financial failure. It is not always realised that overestimating can be equally serious. It not only loses individual orders, but, by thus limiting or reducing turnover, increases the burden of overheads and particularly of selling and estimating costs, since the costs of unfruitful quotations must be recovered in the overheads of other orders.

Methods and practice

As the accurate determination of the correct price to be charged for a standard product is decided from a study of figures prepared by the Cost Department from actually recorded costs, or from a study of the market, we shall deal here only with estimating as it must be carried on in firms which have to quote for special orders.

Customers' requirements

When dealing with an enquiry, the first and essential job is to find out exactly what the customer wants. This is not always as simple as might be thought. It is very easy for an estimator, experienced in his own firm's usual work and products, to make unwarranted assumptions. Also users of equipment may know what they want in general terms, but not be aware of the need to state certain working conditions or limiting factors. Furthermore, a customer may think he knows what he wants and ask for it, not knowing exactly what is available or what might be more satisfactory for his purpose.

It is very necessary for the estimator to scrutinise the enquiry in detail and with the greatest care, looking for any gaps in the information, and any doubtful requirements. If in doubt, or if there is any information lacking, he must ask for confirmation before proceeding with the estimate. If there is not time to do this the assumptions that are made should be noted and explained to the customer with the quotation for confirmation. If the estimator, from his knowledge of the trade or the customer, thinks that the customer really needs something different to fulfil the purpose he has in mind, then it should be suggested, even if it would mean a smaller order or no order at all. There is no sense in selling a customer something which he will later find he does not want, or which is inadequate; good advice given in this way establishes confidence and ensures future enquiries.

Certain standard information may always be required. For example, manufacturers of overhead travelling cranes always require to know, in addition to the weight to be lifted and the span across the track, the speed of lift required, the height, roof clearance, electric supply and atmospheric conditions (if in a foundry or chemical plant or similar situation). In such cases a standard data sheet should be printed, and either filled in by the salesman obtaining the enquiry, by the estimator before beginning his estimate, or sent to the customer immediately on receipt of the enquiry for him to fill in and return. The latter course is advisable if only for confirmation.

Data

The basis of an estimator's work is the cost data. In order to do his job effectively he must have available records of costs, recorded and filed in such a way that they can be referred to simply and rapidly, and of course updated. The best method of filing will depend on the kind and extent of the data recorded, but the loose-leaf ring binder is very satisfactory in practice.

It is sometimes suggested that very detailed data is required, such as for example the times to do operations, labour rates, and the cost of materials as bought. These details may be required in rare cases, but to build up estimates in such detail is expensive and usually unnecessary. What is wanted is costs of normal products or parts of them for each size or variation likely to occur, with some indication of extra costs incurred for additional special equipment. Standard costs (see Part Five, page 688) are a help with this problem, particularly when a detailed estimate is required.

If standard costs are not available, past costs of whole products (to take crane manufacturers, again, of whole crane) and of parts and normal materials (such as crabs, blocks, carriages, motors and girders) should be recorded. For the whole product and for major subassemblies the cost should be plotted on graph paper against the variable factor, horsepower, load, weight, or what-ever it is. If there are several variable factors, it will be necessary to plot several graphs. It is not necessary to plot the cost of each value of the variable factor; four or five points will indicate the nature of the curve, which can then be drawn in for other values with sufficient accuracy. The values of costs can be plotted as detailed estimates are made, or better still from previous actual costs. Gradually, a very comprehensive set of figures can be accumulated from which it is comparatively simple to find the cost for any set of factors, interpolating for values of a variable between those plotted.

Figure 3.3.1 is an example (figures not actual) of the kind of graph referred to. In this case it is assumed that there would be a graph for each major subassembly and a set of curves for each type of each subassembly. The important thing is to find the variable factors against which the cost varies in a uniform manner; in the case of structural steelwork of a standard design it may be weight, for packing-cases superficial area, for electric motors horse-power, and so on.

In addition to such records of costs, it is necessary to have recorded information concerning limiting factors of the plant capacity. The works will be able to handle production within a certain range without abnormal arrange-ments or equipment, but outside these limits usually above a certain size or weight, it is impossible to produce, or special arrangements have to be made. For example, the kinds of limiting factors often overlooked, with disturbing results in the factory, are the maximum lifting capacity of cranes (and subassemblies or parts of special machines may be above this capacity), the

Fig. 3.3.1
Cost chart
for estimating

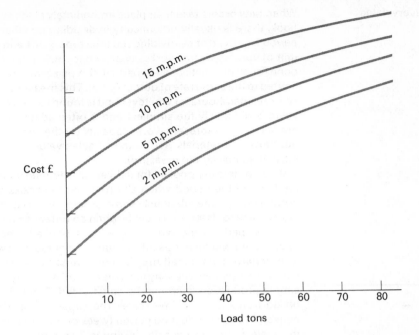

size of machine tools, particularly the swing of lathes or the table of boring machines, the size of doorways or exits from erecting shops. It is essential to note all such capacities, and whenever an estimate is being considered for something outside previous experience, all unusual features must be ex-amined for such snags.

Cooperation with other departments

It is most essential that when a new type of job or one outside previous experience is being considered special features should be referred to other departments interested if there is the least doubt in the estimator's mind as to whether he has accurate information. The Production or Methods Engineers should be consulted whenever there is any question of tooling or special processes, and the Drawing Office if the design is unusual in any way. If tools and drawings are included as a direct charge in the estimate and it has not been possible to plot costs for reference purposes, these departments should be asked for their estimate. If this is normal procedure a standard form can be used, relevant information being filled in by the estimator and sent to each department for completion and return. These departments should also be consulted on the delivery period to be quoted if special drawings, tools, or methods are required.

A close liaison must also be maintained with the sales department and technical engineers or representatives. They are likely to be able to interpret a customer's real requirements when these are stated ambiguously in the enquiry, and can decide the best way to approach the customer if it is considered desirable to suggest an alternative or modified product. In many cases correspondence and contacts of this nature with the customer must go through the sales channels.

Delivery dates

When new orders take their place immediately at the end of the queue or order book, there is usually no difficulty in deciding on what delivery to quote. The period is arrived at by dividing the total orders on hand measured in £ or some unit of volume by the works capacity per week in the same unit. This may be done for all products or each particular type according to whether each type is limited to the same rate of output or not. This measure can be in terms of value, volume, man-hours, or whatever unit is found to be sufficiently accurate; sales value is obviously the simplest and is often adequate, but it frequently does not accurately represent works capacity (or the varying proportion of bought-out parts or materials per pound of sales value and varying profit margins make it an inaccurate measure).

When orders are booked for delivery at a definite time and some of the dates are beyond the period when all orders on the books could be completed at normal output rate, obviously some orders can be completed earlier. It is then not so easy to determine exactly when an order can be delivered, i.e. to know for what periods the works capacity is booked. The Production Planning Department will have this information, of course, and will have to be referred to if departmental detail programmes must be consulted. If, however, it is possible to allocate capacity in terms of a unit (value or some unit of volume), a simple production chart can be constructed. Production periods are marked off horizontally on a time scale. The capacity absorbed by orders already booked in each production period (week or month) is marked off vertically on the scale of unit of capacity. A line is drawn horizontally at the level of the capacity absorbed (with steps for planned increases or decreases). This should be corrected weekly or monthly and will show at a glance in what periods capacity is available and how much.

Whatever method is adopted, it is essential for all delivery promises to be made in line with the Production Planning Department programmes, or on a basis agreed by them and confirmed periodically.

Final build-up
of estimate

The method of finally building up the estimate to include all charges, works overheads, administrative selling and profit margin, should be agreed with the accountant. Because the estimator cannot be expected to have the broad view of affairs and of sales policy in particular which is necessary in dealing with estimates, he is sometimes only permitted to build up to the total works cost, or perhaps total cost, but not selling price, the final margin being added either by the Sales or General Manager. In many cases, however, the estimator compiles the final selling prices. When the appropriate overhead expenses and profit margin have been added (if not already included in the synthetic cost data) to make the selling price, it is advisable in any case for the final estimate or tender to be confirmed either by the Sales Manager or General Manager. To reduce the work on senior executives which this may involve, small tenders below a stated value can be sent to customers without reference, those above a high value referred to the General Manager and those in between to the Sales Manager. In practice it is sometimes found necessary to vary the profit margin or the competitive strength of the price as a measure of selective selling. In times of depression, and when orders at normal prices for any reason do not fill the works to capacity, it may be sound management to take some work at little or no profit to help to carry the standing charges or overheads, using marginal costing technique. Too many orders at these levels will result in an overall loss, and in such times senior management must record and watch the cumulative effect as orders are received. On the other hand, because of inadequate plant, unwillingness to lock up a large part of works capacity, or for other commercial reasons, it may be desired to ward off certain orders unless an unusually high margin can be obtained to offset such considerations. Only the General Manager is in a position to decide such matters.

An effective method of adjusting the selling price to attract or repel orders according to their material or labour content is to add different profit margins to each element of total cost, adding a higher percentage to that element which is in short supply. If, for example, an average profit margin on cost of 15 per cent (13 per cent, on selling price) is required, material is on the average 70 per cent, and labour 30 per cent of total direct cost, and it is desired to attract orders with a low rather than a high proportion of labour content, the following differential margins could be used:

	Add %
Material	11
Labour	25
Overheads	15

This would yield 15·2 per cent on total cost when material and labour are in the normal proportion, since:

	%
11% of 70%	7·7
25% of 30%	7·5
	15·2

But when the labour content is high, say 50 per cent of direct cost, then the total margin would be:

	%
11% of 50%	5·5
25% of 50%	12·5
	18·0

which is higher than normal, and would tend to make such orders more uncompetitive. The total margin can be divided so as to attain the selection of orders desired.

Tenders

A tender or quotation is a written offer to do a certain amount of stated work or supply certain goods at a definite price and in accordance with stated conditions. Such a tender or quotation, when accepted by letter, note or order, constitutes a contract in law. It is clearly set out and conditions clearly defined. Such conditions should be reasonable in character and stated in terms as precise and unambiguous as possible to avoid dispute and legal action. Simple English should be used as far as possible, and the long sentence with too many qualifying phrases avoided. It is not possible to cover here all the information, terms and conditions which at times have to be covered, but the following are the more generally used. Model forms of contract and tender can be obtained from most trade associations and professional institutions.

Specification

The goods, work, or services to be supplied, should be precisely stated by the use of a standard form of specification where possible. Outline drawings may have to be included if certain overall dimensions have to be adhered to. The specification must include limiting figures for performance and duty.

Price

The net price must be stated and any discounts allowed. Terms of payment must also be stated; for large installations progress payments, part payment on delivery or during erection may be required.

During times when costs are fluctuating (particularly rising) rapidly, the right is claimed to adjust prices to costs ruling at the time of dispatch. It is not commercially sound practice in normal times.

Delivery

It should be made clear whether the delivery date is when it leaves the works or is delivered to the customer and exactly what, if any, penalties are involved for late delivery.

Inspection

The right or necessity for the customer to inspect may need to be specified.

Guarantee

Any actual or implied guarantee should be most clearly defined. This question is a prolific source of dispute. The responsibility for equipment included, but bought from other manufacturers, should be made clear. Often the final supplier disclaims responsibility. Service for a limited period is sometimes included in the contract price; if so, the precise nature or limitation of such service should be defined.

Penalties for non-fulfilment

If any penalty for the non-fulfilment of any part of the contract is accepted, it should be most precisely defined, as dispute can easily arise and legal action follow any non-fulfilment under penalty.

Conditions specified in order

Any conditions which have been stated or referred to by the customer in his enquiry or order must be specifically referred to in the tender, and such conditions must be either accepted or repudiated.

4 Supply

Responsibilities of the Buyer

The Purchaser, or Buyer as he is alternatively called, is responsible for the largest single item in the trading account of many businesses: the material content of total cost. It is more than the cost of wages and salaries combined, more than administrative overheads, more than taxation. Of course it can be quite a low percentage of sales value in service industries and for products for which sales and advertising costs are very high, as with personal luxury articles, but can be as high as 70 per cent in highly mechanised and process industries; in manufacturing industry generally it is around 40 to 45 per cent, and if the value of consumable stores, stationery and similar items normally reckoned as overheads, is included, the average figure for industry would be about 50 per cent. The Purchaser is not only responsible for signing orders, and hence committing the company to pay, for this large amount of money, but by his skill and effectiveness he can reduce the amount or increase the value received for outlay. Obviously therefore it is just as important that this activity of buying should be effectively performed as any other in an organisation; it ought not to be thought of lightly, nor staffed by persons without skill or training, nor should its responsibilities be left loose and undefined. The word 'effectively' is purposely used, because the measure of a Purchaser's value is not always the reduced prices at which he can obtain goods from time to time, but the success with which he can obtain satisfactory materials, find alternative better materials at an economic price, and at the same time obtain good *continuous* service from his suppliers. And continuous implies that a supplier is not forced out of business by unprofitable prices. The Buyer should at all times maintain a high standard of commercial morality and honourable practice in the conduct of his business. Fortunately, the professional body catering for buyers, the *Institute of Purchasing and Supply*, is doing a great deal to make 'management' aware of its responsibilities in the matter and to raise the standard of training and qualifications.

Integrity

In many respects the Buyer can be open to more pressure on his moral integrity than any other employee in an organisation. However much we deplore the practice, many companies will spend considerable sums in entertaining a Buyer or giving him expensive presents in an attempt to induce him to place particular orders or contracts with them. This is not the place to suggest which should be refused and which, if any, accepted; sufficient to say that the Buyer who accepts presents and subsequently finds that the provider of the present is *marginally* the better buy finds himself in a cleft stick. If he gives the order to this company he runs the risk of being accused of bribery. If he does not give the order to this company, he is not obtaining the best buy for the company. Obviously the Buyer who accepts no favours can act with complete freedom and need fear no accusations.

Position of the Buyer

The person to whom the Buyer is responsible and the activities for which he is responsible vary more perhaps than for any other executive in industry. Problems of status as well as of organisation structure are involved. This is because the function of a Buyer is not properly understood or is not considered of great importance, or simply because the relative importance of materials in the total build-up of cost varies so much. In flour milling and sugar refining, for example, there is one primary material, it represents a very large proportion of total cost, and market fluctuations of its cost can have a big influence on profits. The Buyer may then be a firstline executive and even a director. Wood case making, printing and weaving are similar though not such extreme cases. But in a large part of manufacturing industry many diverse materials are used, prices remain relatively stable, and large contracts for supplies are not frequent. In this more normal situation buying is a production activity following the designer and planner in the logical sequence of activities (though not necessarily lower in status). In a very small company it may be combined with other activities carried out for example by the Works Manager or the Secretary, but in most companies it is a specialist activity requiring a sizeable staff which should be under the authority of a skilled Purchasing Officer who should be responsible to either the Production Control Manager, Works Manager, or, if there are a few but important primary materials, then perhaps to the Managing Director.

Jurisdiction

For what is a Buyer responsible? It is often claimed that the Buyer should be responsible for stores records and even for Stores Departments. It is argued that as the Buyer needs to keep records of requisitions, orders, part deliveries and such running contracts as there are, he can just as easily (and perhaps on the same document) keep records of stocks, and since he is responsible for obtaining materials, he should be the custodian until they are required for production. But in developing a sound organisation structure it is important to group like activities and skill together in order to take advantage of specialist skills, and a Buyer's skill is, or should be, as an interviewer, negotiator and interpreter of markets and his company's requirements (similar to selling but in the opposite sense). *Stores records* are primarily a tool of those responsible for programmes (production planning); they more than anyone are most concerned with level of stocks, stock movements, allocations and replenishment, and in any case arrange for replenishment of finished and component stocks manufactured by their own company and must keep records of these. On the other hand the job of *storekeeping* is very much a works activity involving the active supervision of persons doing manual work on the shop floor, often well dispersed; it is not the kind of activity suitable for control from an office desk, the occupier of which must be available for interviewing suppliers' representatives for much of his day.

In the extractive and primary material industries (flour milling etc.), there may be a case for the Buyer to maintain materials records, but in normal manufacturing industry where (a) there is a wide variety of materials the demand for which varies with manufacturing programmes, and (b) storekeeping involves a good deal of dispersion and handling, then *stores records* should be a planning activity (see p. 368), and *storekeeping* should be responsible to the Works Manager (see p. 466). There may be instances where the persons who would normally be responsible for stores records or storekeeping are not capable of discharging this responsibility effectively, whereas the Buyer is a very capable person. In such cases the Buyer could no doubt absorb the responsibility of these activities, but such special cases should be recognised for what they are, expedients, and as not adhering to the general principles of correct organisation structure.

The following can therefore be taken as defining the job of a Purchasing Officer or Buyer:

Job specification
for Buyer

- Responsible to Production Manager
- Responsible for buying all materials and supplies
- Authority over Buying Department staff

Responsible for:

1. Buying all materials, supplies and equipment required by the Company; to this end he will:
   (a) study the commodity market and keep abreast of prices, price trends and deliveries;
   (b) maintain up-to-date records (including catalogues and trade literature) of sources of supply of materials, services, products and equipment likely to be required by the Company;
   (c) adhere to the Company's buying policy and interpret this policy to the staff under his authority.
2. Developing and maintaining an effective buying service; to this end he will:
   (a) interview suppliers' representatives, where advisable, in collaboration with an executive concerned;
   (b) advise departments concerned of any changes in price, availability or delivery likely to affect normal routine buying or replacement of stocks;
   (c) translate requisitions for supplies into orders or contracts on suppliers, ensuring that requisitions are duly authorised and within the limits laid down;
   (d) issue enquiries to alternative suppliers, collating all quotations and accepting the most suitable, where necessary in consultation with or reference to the technical executive concerned;
   (e) progress and follow up orders and call off contracts;
   (f) scrutinise and vouch for invoices received;
   (g) dispose of scrap, residues, surplus material and plant;
   (h) supervise and coordinate the work of those under his authority;
   (i) ensure the safety and good condition of records and equipment in the Department.
3. Developing and maintaining a high morale in the Buying Department; to this end he will:

(a) adhere to the Company's personnel policy; especially to ensure that members of his staff are doing the work most suited to their abilities and are provided with the opportunities of making the best and fullest use of their capabilities;

(b) instruct, train and guide all under his authority in the exercise of their duties effectively and in accordance with the policies, plans and programmes laid down;

(c) advise of the selection, appointment and promotion of all staff under his authority.

The Buyer will cooperate with:

Planning Engineers on deliveries of materials and supplies, required for execution of orders received.

Production Engineers on alternative methods of producing supplies required.

Design Office on forward ordering in relation to Company's stated delivery dates; and on specification of materials and quotations for special equipment.

Works Engineer on quotations for machine tools and plant required.

Estimating Office on price queries and delivery dates.

Accountant on checking of invoices and passing for payment; and on competitive prices for supplies.

Personnel Adviser on staff absence, vacancies, general welfare and employment conditions.

Buying is very much a specialist activity. It calls for commercial acumen as well as a wideranging knowledge of industries and materials. It is concerned with value for money as well as the technical suitability of materials bought and their arrival when required. Skill in the specialist activity can be taught, although buying is one of the occupations in industry where long experience in the job, in the particular industry or company, is especially valuable, buyers change their employer less often than most executives. There are so many alternative suppliers of most materials and articles, all of whom claim by advertisement or direct approach that their product is the most suitable or the best, that only experience enables a Buyer to decide, without testing each time an order is placed, which firms he can rely on to supply what he must have. In fact the Buyer's main responsibility is for buying materials and articles of the type and quality his colleagues (designers, plant engineers, office managers, etc.) require, in time for their needs, and at a price which secures for his company the best value for its money, choosing wisely from the many suppliers who tender their products. His colleagues state what they want and when (being the best judge), and the Buyer's job is to get it in time and at the best cost. His concern and experience is in commercial dealings and markets and to ensure a continuous, dependable and economical supply of the materials and articles his company needs.

Value for money

The best value for money is not always synonymous with low purchase price. It can be obtained several ways:

1. By getting a better article at the same cost. In this case the company will only derive benefit for the better value to the extent that it can make use of the better quality article. A higher quality that cannot be taken advantage of has no higher intrinsic value.

2. By getting the same article at a lower cost. There is obviously better value here but a Buyer must be on his guard to see that future consignments do not fall off in quality, that he does in fact get the same article.
3. By paying a higher price for a much higher quality article. This can be justified and yield better value if, in the design or in use, full advantage can be taken of the added quality, e.g. by using less of the article or if it results in less labour, maintenance or more production.
4. By paying much less for a lower quality article where this lower quality is adequate for the purpose in view. This is a case of overspecification, a very useful and usually overlooked source of reduced costs. It is most likely to be revealed by work study, particularly applied to product design or formulation, but the Buyer should be on the lookout for cases where too high a quality, standard of accuracy or of finish is being asked for; his colleagues may not be aware of it.

In looking at the above alternatives the Buyer must be concerned not with lowest initial cost but lowest total cost. For to save 6p per unit on the purchase price of a commodity which is bought in large quantities may seem a big saving, but if quality is poor, requiring higher goods inwards inspection or warranty costs, or delivery is poor thus holding up production and perhaps incurring additional expense of fitting at a later stage of production, then the total additional cost to the company may far exceed the 6p per component apparently saved. A similar approach should be made to the purchase of capital items, and indeed this thinking is not new, nearly a century ago John Ruskin wrote:

> It is unwise to pay too much—but it is unwise to pay too little. When you pay too much you lose a little money, that is all. When you pay too little, you sometimes lose everything because the thing you bought was incapable of doing the thing you bought it to do. The common law of business balance prohibits paying a little and getting a lot—it can't be done. If you deal with the lowest bidder, it is well to add something for the risk you run. And if you do that, you will have enough to pay for something better.

In his frequent and wideranging contacts with supplier industries, the Buyer is in a better position than his colleagues to know of alternative materials and products and of alternative methods of producing them. He is also in a position to get early information of new materials, processes and services. He has the responsibility of keeping abreast of these changes and of advising his colleagues of them.

Standardisation of design can result in a considerable reduction in the costs of production. This applies not only to the Buyer's own company, but to his suppliers too, and any standardisation should result in lower prices and better value.

Forward planning

Business conditions are never static. As the pressures of supply and demand vary, price and the availability of commodities vary too. The swings, from conditions of scarcity to conditions of surplus capacity and back again, are made more violent than they would otherwise be, because so many Buyers do not pay due regard to market trends and plan ahead; they react only when the conditions have already changed considerably, adding force to the swing. As a result they get caught short of supplies or get overstocked. It is a Buyer's responsibility to be acutely sensitive to the changes in market conditions and fully aware—so far as he can obtain the information from his colleagues—of his company's requirements into the future, so that, by forward planning, he can avoid the effects of short supply and high prices or of being left with too high stocks on a falling market. It calls for an ability to understand the implications of the statistics of commercial and industrial activity and to cooperate with and advise his colleagues on the preparation of long-term plans and programmes. To this end he will need to keep certain records and charts himself and must ensure that he is supplied with the necessary information from his own company.

Sources of supply

A Buyer has to build up dependable sources of supply; it is wasteful and unnecessary to send enquiries to all suppliers for every order. There must be mutual trust and fair dealing between buyer and supplier. This means that strictly ethical standards and methods are adopted by the Buyer, encouraging competition without taking unfair advantage of position and circumstances. The reception of suppliers' representatives should always be prompt, courteous and businesslike. It would be a good education and experience for a Buyer to become a salesman or representative for a time. It is fatally easy not to be interested in a new line, or a product competitive to one already giving satisfaction, and to miss opportunities of buying better or more economical materials through not being energetic enough to find out what is available. To tell a salesman that his price is high when it is low, to refer to imaginary competition, or otherwise to misrepresent directly or by implication in order to coax a lower price or an extra discount from a salesman induces instability into relations, is bound to lead to misrepresentation in return, and earns for the Company an unpleasant name. Such tactics belong to the past; they may succeed in isolated cases, but salesmen are quick to detect such methods and to use appropriate tactics themselves.

Fair dealing

Fair dealing requires that advantage will not be taken of an obviously incorrect quotation which will mean a loss to the supplier. If a price which will not produce a profit is deliberately quoted, and known to be so, that is a different matter, but in general the Buyer expects the seller to make an adequate profit. How else can the supplier continue in business and to give service? A fair price which enables a manufacturer to make a reasonable profit and supply competitive goods and adequate service, including a margin for development, is essential in modern industry, and is as much a matter of interest to the Buyer as to the seller. Fair dealing also requires the Buyer to state clearly for what reason he has to turn down a quotation. This does not mean that he must disclose the competitive prices, but it is not fair to competitors to give inaccurate reasons for uncompetitive prices.

There must obviously be confidence and cooperation between buyer and seller, and in the long run a dependable supplier is a worthy partner to the Buyer. Such confidence and cooperation cannot be built except on a basis of fair dealing.

Policies

A buying policy should be laid down clearly by the Board of Directors or by the Managing Director in line with company policy. It will be of course part of the production policy, or arise from it, and will be dictated by the kind of production programme adopted. For example, the programme may require much greater quantities at one time of the year than another, but the buying policy may be to take regular supplies over the whole year to suit the suppliers, and to take advantage of lower prices, stocking during the period of lower demand. It should not be left to the Buyer to operate as he thinks fit, with the risk of being reprimanded for what may be thought unwise use of discretion.

Three broad lines of policy are usual:

1. *To buy on a bargain basis.* This may be pursued in the case of staple commodities and for the major materials in process industries. It offers large profits on buying, with the consequence of large risks, and it is of a speculative nature. Speculation is an activity belonging to the Stock Exchange, and should not find its place in ordinary industrial activities. If it is pursued as a policy, it is usual for the buying to be under the control of a senior executive of the company.

2. *To buy on contract.* In this policy, contracts are given to suppliers for large amounts of future requirements, for a year, or for indefinite periods subject to review and cancellation with an appropriate period of notice. It has the advantage of avoiding the necessity for carrying stocks by the user and of giving a measure of stability to suppliers. It also gives the Buyer an assurance of continuity of supply and of service. Under mass-production conditions, this latter feature is most important and the policy may be well justified.

3. *To buy against current market conditions.* This is the more usual policy, giving the Buyer a wide discretion. Orders are placed for the minimum quantity required for the replacement of stock to meet particular demands, and alternative quotations are obtained, either for each order, or occasionally as a check.

Frequently, in normal industrial conditions a combination of the second and third policies is laid down, contracts being limited to certain major raw materials.

Subcontracting

It is not unusual for a company to arrange for other firms to manufacture some part or parts of its own products or carry out some of the necessary manufacturing processes to its own design and specification. The practice is widely used in the motor-car industry, where often as many as half of the components of a vehicle are produced by subcontractors to the designing and assembling firm. It is also used in other industries, chiefly when a company's capacity to meet its customers' requirements is temporarily insufficient. In the latter case, cost is not always a decisive factor, but for a permanent arrangement it must be cheaper to subcontract than to make. This can be so when advantage is taken of specialisation and of the lower overheads of small units. Small firms with specialised plant or techniques, e.g. gear-cutting, plastering, engraving, etc., can become highly skilled and efficient and their costs correspondingly low. Whether or not such subcontracting is employed is a matter of policy, balancing the cost, lower or higher, against such factors as avoiding purchase of additional buildings and plant, effective control of quality and delivery, interruption of supply due to causes not under the company's own control (strikes, etc.). Subcontracting is primarily a Buyer's responsibility though he may need the advice and assistance of Works departments for assessing the competence and capacity of the tendering companies. His main problem will be one of maintaining quality of product or servicing and maintaining regular and reliable delivery. He will also be involved in maintaining accurate records of contracts and deliveries; if these are not always up to date and accurate, considerable losses can accumulate. If subcontracting becomes permanent and a large proportion of the company's supplies it is advisable to set up a special department, staffed with suitably qualified persons, under the Buyer, to deal with it.

Limiting value of order

It is usual for a limit to be placed on the individual value of any one order. This value may vary with the type of commodity. Orders above these limits are referred to a senior executive or the Managing Director for final authority. This may be necessary to fit in with financial policy when liquid capital is strained, or when the coincidence of several large orders in a period may strain the company's arrangements for regular settlement of accounts.

Purchase of capital equipment

Purchase of capital equipment, additions to plant or buildings, or replacements thereto, should be dealt with in a special manner. Expenditure on such items does not arise as a matter of routine, and must in any case fit into any capital expenditure budgets or programme. It is, therefore, essential for all items above an agreed amount to be covered by a capital sanction authorised by the executive concerned. In a large concern it is advisable for certain executives only to be authorised to order capital equipment, and for the amount of capital expenditure per year and per period to be laid down for the executive concerned. In a period of expansion, it is possible without some such control, for a company to undertake commitments for the purchase of plant which it cannot meet.

Procedures and records

The type of order form and the procedure adopted for requisitioning and placing of orders vary widely. In all cases, however, it is strongly recommended that only the Buyer be authorised to place official orders on behalf of the firm. Works Engineers and Office Managers often contend that only they know what they require. This may be so, but the order should still go through the Buyer. Buying, and the associated records, are a specialised activity, and every use should be made of the specialised skill thus built up. In all cases, therefore, persons requiring materials should state their requirements to the Buyer on an official requisition. When the material or article must fulfil certain conditions, the requisition must be accompanied by a specification. When the source of supply or the particular brand or maker of the article required is not stated it is the Buyer's responsibility to buy where he can. At other times it may be necessary for technical departments to obtain all this information first and to determine by test or otherwise what is most suitable.

When samples or quotations are required the requisition form should be used in the same way, stating that an enquiry or quotation only is required in the first place, and that these are to be submitted to the department originating the requisition, or not as stated.

Although the Buyer is not responsible for storekeeping or inspection, but is required to check and sign for the validity and accuracy of invoices rendered by suppliers, he should insist on a proper advice of goods received and of an adequate examination or inspection. Practice with regard to inspection of goods received varies, from a detailed inspection of all consignments (which can be very costly indeed), to a cursory examination of identification and quality. If suppliers have a thorough and adequate final inspection of their own production, it should only be necessary for a receiving firm to check that goods received are as specified on the order. The Buyer should select and train his suppliers so that he can rely on them to maintain his specified standards; by doing so he will enable the cost of inspection of incoming goods to be greatly reduced. However, some spot checking at least is desirable, as a protection against carelessness or error in the suppliers' organisation.

Order forms

The layout of an order form suitable for normal requirements is shown in Fig. 3.4.1. All copies are made at one typing, and different colours are used to aid sorting and distribution.

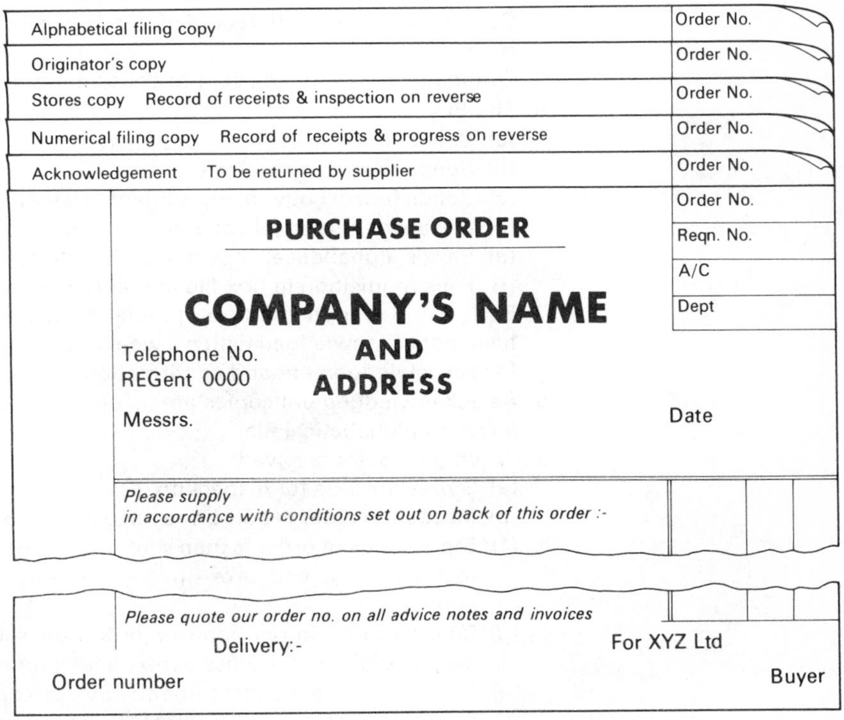

Alphabetical filing copy — Order No.
Originator's copy — Order No.
Stores copy — Record of receipts & inspection on reverse — Order No.
Numerical filing copy — Record of receipts & progress on reverse — Order No.
Acknowledgement — To be returned by supplier — Order No.

PURCHASE ORDER

Order No.
Reqn. No.
A/C
Dept

COMPANY'S NAME
AND
ADDRESS

Telephone No.
REGent 0000

Messrs.

Date

Please supply
in accordance with conditions set out on back of this order :-

Please quote our order no. on all advice notes and invoices

Delivery:-

For XYZ Ltd

Order number

Buyer

Fig. 3.4.1 Purchase Order set

The following example of standard practice instructions for the ordering of materials, supplies and outside services through the Buyer uses the minimum possible forms for adequate control, and can be taken as a basis from which to develop a satisfactory procedure for any particular company or set of conditions. For example, it may be necessary to obtain additional authority and signature for orders over certain amounts, or for certain materials, and central buying for associated or subsidiary companies would involve a modified routine.

1. All materials, supplies and services from outside contractors are to be ordered through a Buyer by sending to him a requisition setting out what is required.
2. When the originating department wants to see quotations before placing an order, a requisition form is to be used marked plainly in capitals ENQUIRY. Quotations when received are referred to the department concerned. The Buyer may at other times refer quotations obtained at his own discretion to the executive concerned for advice on selection of the most suitable.
3. A capital sanction authorisation is to be obtained by the originating department for all purchases of a capital nature above £100.
4. On receipt of a requisition, the Buyer translates the requisition into an order by typing out an official order set.
5. An official order set comprises:
   Purchase order (white) sent to supplier.
   Acknowledgement of order (pink), being an exact copy sent to supplier for signature and return.
   Buyer's copy (white) for numerical filing.
   Stores copy (buff), with record of goods received and inspection report on reverse.
   Originator's copy (blue), sent to department originating the requisition.
6. The Buyer:
   (a) Sends first two copies to supplier.
   (b) Sends third copy to Stores.
   (c) Sends fourth copy to department originating requisition.
   (d) Files own numerical copy in card index.
   (e) Places alphabetical copy in unacknowledged file.
   (f) Files requisition in box file in number sequence.
7. Each day Buyer checks through unacknowledged file, and to firms who have not acknowledged within a week, writes an appropriate letter asking for acknowledgement and confirmation.
8. As acknowledgement copies are received from suppliers, they are transferred to alphabetical file.
9. When goods are received:
   (a) Stores arrange for inspection.
   (b) Inspection enter report on reverse side of Stores copy of order.
   (c) Stores copy of order is then sent to Buying Office, who transfer record to their copy, and take up any discrepancy, and report rejects to suppliers.
   (d) Buyer sends Stores copy of order, on same day, to stock control section of Planning Office, who transfer information to stock records.
   (e) For single or last consignments, Stores copy of order is returned to Buyer. For part consignments, Stores copy of order is returned to Stores.

10. Invoices for goods received are submitted to Buyer for checking and authorisation.
11. The following departments are authorised to issue requisitions:
    Drawing Office: materials requiring long delivery periods.
    Stores Control: special materials and supplies.
    Stores: general consumable supplies and hardware.
    Production Engineers: plant, tools and equipment.
    Tool Stores: tool replacements.
    General Office: stationery.
    Pattern Shop: timber supplies and maintenance.

Records

It is essential for the Buyer to build up reliable records which will give him control of orders placed and comprehensive information regarding materials available and likely to be required, and standard and competitive prices. The extent of these records will depend on the size of the firm, but the following records are the minimum which are required for effective control.

Copies of orders

Two copies of the order should be filed, one filed under the company's order number numerically, and the other under the supplier's name alphabetically. It is essential that one copy is available for very rapid reference. It is usual for the order to be known internally by its order number, and therefore the numerical copy is filed under its order number for rapid reference. Using the order set on the previous page, the length of the form is made 10 mm shorter than A4, i.e. 210 by 287 mm. The numerical copy is folded to within 10 mm of the bottom, where the order number is repeated, making it 210 by 130 mm and suitable for inserting in a visible-edge cabinet, the quickest form of reference file. The top half of the back of the form, which is printed to received delivery records, is uppermost after folding and filing in the cabinet. The alphabetical copy is filed in whatever way is found most convenient, and forms a cross index with the order file.

Record of purchases

It is also necessary to keep a record of all purchases of each material or part. This is best done on a card file, with one card for each material or part. Each order placed should be entered with particulars of the supplier from whom ordered, the price and quantity. Suitable headings for such a card record are given at Fig. 3.4.2. It is not necessary to keep a record of the value or purchases made for each supplier. This information can always be obtained, if required, from the accounts department.

Fig. 3.4.2
Card headings

Standard price		Material			Code No.	
Supplier	Description		Price	Date	Order No.	Quantity

Catalogues

A library of catalogues of suppliers of material and equipment likely to be used is invaluable, and should be kept in good condition, up to date and adequately indexed. Because of the varying size of catalogues, it often proves to be a difficult job, and it is frequently found that the simplest way is to use box files. Because many suppliers have a wide range of products, it is usually found impossible to file according to the kind of product or associated products, and one must rely on a straightforward numerical or alphabetical filing with a cross index. These indices of catalogues can be broadened to include an index of suppliers of materials, whether catalogued or not. Although it may duplicate some of the information in trade directories, the latter can never be completely comprehensive.

Progress and follow-up

It is essential to progress orders on suppliers as it is to progress orders in the company's works. Continuity of supplies can be as important as cost. Indeed, in mass production it is the essential prerequisite. Those connected with manufacturing industry in the period following the Second World War had frequent and bitter experience of this. Running out of stock of odd items, often quite small, can result in products being held up in a half-finished or almost completed state for weeks on end. At such times very inflated prices are paid for supplies from alternative sources. Not only in mass production factories is the delay serious; the restriction on turnover and hence profitability in any factory can be very serious.

In difficult times, as in times of shortage, an outside progress man who visits suppliers regularly and can get on personal terms with the man who matters, Works Manager or Planning Engineer, can be most effective; he should be responsible to the Purchaser and when much work is subcontracted it is almost essential, and advisable when there are running contracts that have to be coordinated with flow production programmes which are subject to acceleration or modification.

Progress can only be measured against a predetermined requirement, and the requirement in this case is the delivery date, which forms part of the contract to supply, accepted by the supplier when he accepts the order. In order that progress can be 100 per cent effective, it is essential to know of every order not delivered to time. The simplest way of throwing up such orders is to keep the reverse of a Delivery Promise book, i.e. a Delivery Due book. Each order made out is entered in the Delivery Due book on the page for the day (or week) when delivery is due. Each day (or week) orders appearing as due should be checked with the order record, and if a delivery has not been received, follow-up action should be initiated.

Follow-up action will depend on circumstances, but usually starts with an 'urge' letter or reminder. Such letters must not appear casual or merely routine, and for this reason must be as carefully compiled as any other letter. Although a standard form of letter can be used, it is better to have several forms (which can be selected to suit the circumstances or the supplier), and individually typed letters are likely to command more attention than duplicated ones. Further promises given should be followed up with increasing pressure, and it is in difficult cases that the personal contact or outside progress man can be more effective.

Specifications and contracts

It is essential for the Buyer to make absolutely clear to the supplier exactly what is required, the tests, if any, to be passed, and the conditions attached to an order, which, when accepted, becomes a contract in law. In order to state clearly what is required, Buyers are strongly recommended to use specifications, and wherever possible to use those published by the British Standards Institution, since they are likely to avoid special production—and hence higher prices. If there is not a British Standards Specification applicable, or other recognised specification, I.S.O., A.S.M.E., DIN etc, a specification should be obtained from or drawn up in collaboration with Designers, Technical Chief, or Production Engineers. Such specifications can be made to cover general classes or particular goods, and do help to maintain uniform quality and avoid misunderstandings.

Conditions attached to the placing of an order and to which the supplier is to be held to comply should be drawn up in collaboration with the technical departments and the Accountant and checked with the appropriate trade association which often has standard forms. The following can be taken as typical, although much more detailed and complex conditions are sometimes laid down:

Official order. No goods will be paid for unless an official order can be produced if required. Any specifications, drawings, patterns, etc., supplied by us with reference to this order remain our property.

Rejections. Any article found to be defective, inferior in quality, or in excess of the quantity ordered, may be rejected and returned to you at your own risk and expense. A debit note will be sent informing you whether replacement is desired or not.

Suspension. In the event of strikes, accidents, or other unforeseen contingencies, delivery may be suspended at our request.

Cancellation. Undue delay in delivery or a continuation of defective supplies shall entitle us to cancel the order.

Advising. An advice note quoting our order number must accompany the goods or be sent by post same day as goods are despatched.

Invoicing. An invoice must be sent on same day as goods are despatched, and must quote our order number, failing which invoice may be returned.

Statements. Monthly statements of account to be received by us not later than the fifth of the month following invoice date, otherwise payment may be deferred a month beyond the ordinary due date.

Terms. Payment will be made during month following that in which goods are invoiced.

Liability for injury or damage. This order is subject to the condition that in so far as it relates to erection or other work to be carried out on our premises or elsewhere to our instructions, you accept liability for and will indemnify us against all claims, cost or expenses arising in connection with such work, whether at common law or under statute, as a result of injury to or death of any person, or to loss of or damage to any property unless such claim arises solely as a result of neglect, default, or omission by ourselves or our servants.

Delivery. To these works unless otherwise instructed. In case of overdue orders we shall be entitled to claim delivery by passenger train or other special transport at your expense.

Carriage. All goods to be delivered carried paid unless otherwise arranged.

Empties. No charge for any form of packing, including cases, barrels, etc., will be acknowledged except when expressly arranged, but every effort will be made to return such packages to you.

Just as a Buyer attaches conditions to his order, so also does a company usually attach conditions to its tender or quotation for the supply of goods. Some of these conditions may conflict with each other. As an order for the supply of goods is a contract in law, it is essential to resolve the conflict. The Buyer must either accept his supplier's conditions or obtain a written agreement to his own or to such modifications of the supplier's conditions as he requires. In particular, he should see that there is no clause in the conditions of sale, as sometimes occurs, which makes quite valueless any previously stated warranty or guarantee. It is also essential for an order to describe exactly what is being ordered or to ensure that the supplying firm's tender or quotation is exactly explicit. There are several ways in which the mention of some particular quality in goods may effect a contract for their sale, and confer on the Buyer rights for his protection or redress for errors. Words used in an order describing the goods becomes a condition of the contract and the Buyer should ensure that they correctly interpret his requirements. If a Buyer, in requesting an article from his supplier, uses certain words to describe it and the suppliers offers one as so described, the words become a definite part of the contract and the Buyer may reject or recover damages accordingly. But a personal warranty given by a salesman does not make a term of contract. To avoid any later trouble, important properties or description of an article to be purchased should be written into the order or contract.

There are two traps the Buyer must avoid: (1) placing unpriced orders; (2) giving an indefinite delivery requirement.

Unpriced orders probably originate more from the plant maintenance department than any other. The plant engineer will send a piece of equipment to either a breakdown repair service or the manufacturers and send a purchase requisition to the buying office probably saying in confirmation of a telephone conversation—'repair as necessary'. When the invoice is received the dismayed plant engineer finds it would have cost little more, and sometimes less to purchase a new unit. In these circumstances the Buyer must endorse the order—'advise price before commencing work'. Likewise an urgent order placed on an ASAP (*as soon as possible*) delivery puts no onus on the supplier to deliver within any particular time other than that which suits his own convenience. There are a number of ways of avoiding this difficulty, the Buyer can ask for the delivery required, e.g. seven days, and place the onus on the supplier to say he cannot meet the required delivery, or ask the supplier to advise his best delivery when confirming the order, but these are just palliatives, there is only one sure way, and that is to obtain price and delivery from all suppliers before placing any firm order.

5 Production administration

When F. W. Taylor was analysing the various roles of a foreman, he realised that in addition to directly controlling his labour force, which included hiring and firing, the foreman also determined how and when each job should be done (see p. 296 above). Because he was almost certainly a craftsman in the job he was supervising, he also knew how long the job should take. As the size of business grew the complexities and techniques necessary to make the most effective use of all the resources available, made it impossible for the foreman to be responsible for all these functions. Today there are specialist services to assist the first line supervisor and allowing him to concentrate on his prime functional responsibility for the men under his control. This chapter deals with the administrative functions of:

● Production planning, or planning ahead.
● Production engineering, or process planning.
● Production control, or Monitoring performance against plans.

Production planning

The object of a production policy is to ensure that the products (or services) are supplied in the required volume, of the required quality, at the time required, and at a minimum cost. This demands effective and flexible production planning; effective in meeting all the requirements, and flexible to do so in spite of sometimes rapidly changing requirements or conditions. Delivery promises can be broken if assessments of capacity are wrong, and congestion, bottlenecks, idle time and other excess production costs can arise if all supplies (including information) are not forthcoming when they are required. Guesswork is not good enough and memory is an unreliable servant. In all but the smallest organisation a person cannot carry all the details of delivery dates, supplies and capacities in his head without making mistakes or neglecting something. Waiting for work, instructions, or tools, is one of the biggest contributory causes of high costs—or at least of costs being higher than they should be, i.e. excess costs. Well thought out schemes of production planning substitute facts for guesswork and reduce waiting time considerably. Orders must be delivered to time, and for economical production there must be a minimum of interruption to flow due to lack of work or information, and in order to maintain steady employment a balanced load of work must be maintained between departments. The objects of production planning, therefore, can be stated as:

1. to relate orders and delivery promises or plans to capacities available or conversely to provide the capacity and production to meet agreed or accepted demand;

2. to ensure that material and components are available when and where required;
3. to produce a steady flow of work through all departments;
4. to preserve a balance of work between the various departments;
5. to preserve adequate manufacturing instructions to enable management and foremen to concentrate on supervision and production technique, and relieve them of detailed clerical work;
6. to provide management with information to correct for possible delays and difficulties before they arise or become serious.

It is sometimes objected that production planning increases clerical staff and involves a large increase in paper work. This is not usually true; it is more usual for there to be already a large amount of paperwork, often on scrap pads and memo books, spread throughout the organisation. Simple and effective systems of planning replace this scrappy paperwork with well designed forms, which ensure that the information required is recorded in a way most convenient to those who have to use it. A frequent objection, particularly from older and experienced managers, to planning or departmental loading is that his business is different, and there are so many day-to-day alterations to suit customers or suppliers that it just is not worth drawing up plans or programmes. Experience proves that good production planning inevitably reduces the frequency of change, and that in any case the existence of some plan reveals quickly the precise effect on production and promises already made which any new alteration will have. Too often factories flounder from one week to the next, attempting to meet the demands of pressing customers, nearly all of whom get their goods later than promised merely because too much has been promised.

Terminology

It is necessary to be clear about the meaning and use of certain terms used rather loosely in connection with production planning in industry. Certain words which are in common use in normal speech and writing have a specific use in industry, and others are used with different meanings in different places. The meanings which will be attached to such words in this text, therefore are set out below.

Production planning. The meaning and content of this term have been explained in chapter 1. It is used instead of the term 'Production control', as defined in British Standards Booklet BS1100, p. 2, 'the means by which a manufacturing plan is determined, information issued for its execution, and data collected and recorded, which will enable the plan to be controlled through all its stages'.

Planning department. The department charged with the responsibility of planning production in the above sense.

Schedules. Lists or charts setting out work to be produced in a period, or in order of priority or to stated dates. It is commonly used synonymously with programmes.

Capacity. The amount of production which can be done in a period with the labour and facilities available in assumed conditions.

Loading. The process of setting the amount of work to be done against the capacity available, for operator, machines, department or factory.

Stock control. The maintenance, usually by a system of records, of adequate stocks of materials and components to enable production to continue according to plans.

The tools

It will be obvious that the tools of the production planner are formed of figures and facts. For the tools to be effective the figures and facts must be accurate and available when required. It is understood that figures used by designers and accountants must be accurate, but not always recognised that they must be equally so for the planner. Too often the times for operations, or figures of output, are approximate within wide limits, and then there is surprise because plans do not turn out to be realistic.

The staff

The type of person employed on the work is also of importance. He must not only have a very good memory, but also must be logical and have an analytical type of mind, but not a single track mind. That is, he must be able to take a wide view of his field of operations and take in and memorise many details and keep several major jobs or problems alive in his mind together. At the same time he must be resourceful (and not merely in finding excuses) but not easily flustered. Quite a specification! It certainly cannot be fulfilled successfully by a shop clerk who may happen to have a good memory of the firm's products but is without training or experience.

Executives in small factories of say less than 100 persons (and we have seen that there are more factories in Britain smaller than this than there are larger) need not be apprehensive that planning involves expensive 'systems' and large clerical staffs. Planning is a mental process, the result of an attitude of mind, a determination to do things in an orderly way, and to do them in the light of facts and not of guesses. Simple records and schedules of weekly priorities with an accurate measure of capacity and demand can be as effective as the most elaborate systems.

The characteristics of effective planning are:

- it has a clearly defined objective in view;
- it is simple and flexible;
- provides for and uses accurate records and data;
- establishes standards for measurement of results and progress.

Responsibilities

The following can be taken as an example of the responsibilities of the head of a Production Planning Department:

- Carry out the Company's manufacturing policy in relation to production programmes.
- Determine capacity of all manufacturing departments and prepare long and short term loads.
- Translate orders received from the Sales Department (via Design or Drawing Office) into orders on the Works Departments.

- Prepare schedules of production for all departments and issue them in such a form, and at such a time, as to enable the departments concerned to produce the work required at the right time.
- Maintain progress records to show actual against planned production, and take necessary action to correct deviations as far as possible.
- Advise the Sales Department when it becomes known that delivery promises cannot be maintained.
- Answer enquiries from customers as to the progress of their orders, remembering that good delivery and the honouring of delivery promises is an important part of the Company's reputation and manufacturing policy.
- Maintain accurate records of all material and component stocks and movements in and out of stores in such a way as to anticipate future requirements and always to have material available for production to customers' requirements.
- Requisition from the buyer materials and supplies required, giving the necessary information, including the time when goods are required. Prepare schedule of requirements for suppliers and integrate with the Company's production programmes, progressing as required.
- Train staff in the effective performance of their duties.
- Adhere to the Company's personnel policy and ensure that subordinates do so.
- Keep abreast of developments in modern production planning and technique.

A word is required on the inclusion of stock records under the Planner's authority. Both in textbooks and in practice it is frequently put under the authority of either the Storekeeper or Buyer, on the misguided assumption that, because the Storekeeper is responsible for actual stocks and the Buyer for obtaining them, one or the other ought therefore to be responsible for records. The records are a tool and used mainly by the planners. The same records can be used once a year for stock valuation purposes, but their main purpose is to ensure that a proper production flow and balance between departments is facilitated by accurate stocks—and production flow and balance between departments is a planning department responsibility. It is fundamentally wrong for clerical work which can be done just as easily in an office, away from noise and under specialist supervision, to be done in a works department—and the stores is a works department. The Buyer's job, on the other hand, is to buy and is concerned primarily with external agencies—he should not be responsible for level of stocks or accuracy of records.

Organisation of department

The work of a Production Planning Department generally falls into three sections, dealing with three stages of the sequence of operations. They are:

1. Compiling and recording facts.
2. Developing plans.
3. Putting plans into operation and controlling results.

1. *Compiling the facts.* Information is gathered together, recorded and filed in a way which is suitable for use by planners, and so that reference to it is easy and rapid. The information is of three kinds, relating to:

- customers' orders and requirements;
- stocks of materials and components;
- plant available, capacities, operations and process times.

Unless the organisation is of such a size that each kind of information is dealt with in a separate section, it is advisable for all of it to be handled by one section under the supervision of a person skilled in the work. Its organisation is mainly a problem of filing and entering up figures or records from vouchers, i.e. transferring information and striking balances. It can usually be staffed with juniors, female, or relatively unskilled labour, but must be carefully supervised and checked by very reliable people. The absolute accuracy and double-checking required in banks is not essential, but inaccuracies can be troublesome and costly.

2. *Development of plans* comprises the vital part of planning. It is here that the effectiveness of results is ensured, and where the ability to scheme, think ahead and take all factors into account is so essential. It is a job mainly done on paper, juggling as it were with figures and charts. Sales budgets must be broken down into or integrated with long-term production plans, factory and departmental plans formulated, and weekly or daily or even hour-by-hour loads prepared. In small factories a few simple charts or schedules suffice, but in very large organisations a vast amount of detailed information, in the form of masses of figures, flows into the section, and must be rapidly and regularly collated and reissued for action. Extreme tidiness is essential, and if those concerned are not to be bogged down by a continuous stream of insistent enquiries demanding attention, much of the work must so be organised as to be dealt with in a routine manner by juniors.

3. *Putting plans into action* consists of translating the plans into shop instructions and can be mainly of a clerical nature. In practice, however, it is at this stage that a certain amount of decentralisation is advisable, and the hour-by-hour machine or operation loading and the actual issue of jobs to operators is done either in or adjacent to the foreman's office, or in a shop office. Progress work, that is, checking performances against plans and reporting results (with recommendations for corrective action and requests for urgent actions) to foremen or other supervisors, which is really an aspect of control, is frequently carried out from the same office and even by the same persons. These stages and the tools used are shown diagrammatically in Fig. 3.5.1 overleaf.

The complexity of an organisation structure for production planning depends on the type of industry or manufacture rather than its scale. In *mass production* and *continuous process manufacture*, production planning consists of balancing the flow of materials (or components) from outside or component manufacturing departments, with consumption by the factory or assembly departments. This applies particularly in the automobile or similar industries, where a good deal of preliminary work on materials is subcontracted, no large stock of materials is kept (or could be for the immense consumption rate) and a small interruption to production affects a large part of the factory and is very expensive. In factories engaged on *batch production* of partly standardised products (by far the greater number in Britain), there is the added complexity of setting up (time and cost) varying batch sizes, and the

Fig. 3.5.1

Production administration showing stages and tools used.

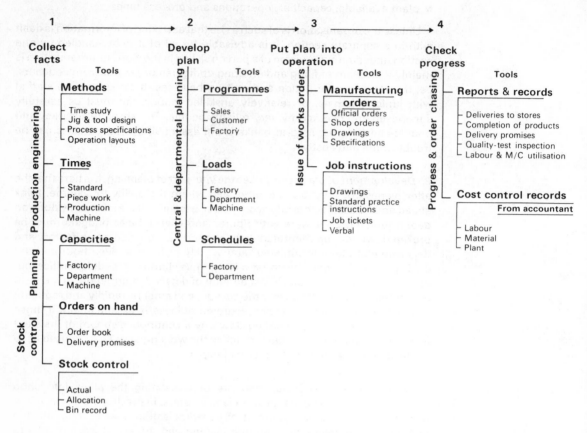

synchronisation of finishing dates for parts and subassemblies when batches vary so much. It is predominantly a question of continual adjustment in order to maintain balanced loads on departments and to correct for unforeseen delays. When the product is *designed to customers' requirements* the total process time is increased by the time required for design or preparation for each order; consequently the period over which planning must extend is greater, making the problem more complex. Production planning is most complex when the product is mainly to customers' requirements, but is designed to incorporate many standard parts kept in stock. When the number of orders exceeds something like fifty per week, the amount of information to be handled becomes large and the department correspondingly so. Computers or programme machines may then be an economical proposition.

Computers

Electronic computers have already made their impact on large organisations and groups of operating units. As they are made smaller and cheaper they will be increasingly used by the smaller and more typical organisations.

The kind of problem for which they are eminently suited occurs in a group of mills weaving cloth. The cloth is of different quality, weight, width, colour and design, the orders are for a different number of pieces, for one delivery or split deliveries, and for delivery at specified dates or to schedule; the looms differ, some being capable of weaving only plain and cheaper grades of cloth, others being versatile have a high capital value and should have the maximum time on the higher value material. Planning, therefore, is a complicated problem of determining the most profitable way of allocating production to available capacity. This is a problem which can be solved by 'linear programming', involving a large number of equations and 'unknowns', by an analogue computer; it can also be handled by a data-processing computer with the aid of punched cards. Similar problems have been solved in connection with minimising transport and depot costs and obtaining optimum results in oil refining.[1]

Installing production planning	The question often asked by those who become aware that they must do something about the need for an effective planning scheme is: How long will it take to put in? As usual, it all depends on the scheme, the job it has to do, and the limiting factors of the shortage of skilled staff, the continuity of sales programmes, market stability, and the delivery periods of stationery and special equipment. But unless all or most of these conditions are favourable, it is found in practice that it takes between one and two years to put in a complete scheme and to make it work effectively and permanently. The factor which most affects the time is the availability of skilled staff. But in whichever way it is tackled it takes time to get it running smoothly, and for everyone in the works, unaccustomed to 'systems', to understand and support it. One cannot graft on something new and expect immediate fruit. It is preferable first to prepare all process data and times, as these are seldom available in the form required. To plan on approximate data gives only approximate results—hit and miss—and the misses can be annoying, disturbing and discouraging to the works—but sometimes immediate results can be obtained with approximate figures and the Sales Department may be grateful for them.
Universality of technique	Experience has shown that the basic principles, techniques and procedures of production planning are common to and effective in all industries. Production planning is a universal activity, and the tools developed, systems, indices, forms, procedures, office machinery, and so on, are not peculiar to one industry. What follows in this section, therefore, can be taken to be of general application. Even though the illustrations relate to engineering, they serve their purpose by illustrating method and principle.[2]

[1] The role and significance of computers as an aid to production management is further considered in a later section: see page 442. In the overall context of data processing, computers form the subject-matter of Part Six (see page 861).

[2] A more detailed exposition of the practice of production planning is given in the booklets published originally by the British Standards Institution as BSS 1100 but now obtainable from the British Institute of Management: Part 1, *Principles of Production Control*; Part 2, *Production Control—The Small Factory*; Part 3, *Application of Production Control*.

Compiling and
recording the
facts

Production planning consists broadly of relating what is wanted to what is available, on a time basis. Obviously, this can only be done if all the facts are known: facts relating to what has to be produced and when, and facts relating to capacities and materials available. This in turn involves still more detailed facts of materials, stocks, plant, methods, labour, times, production, scrap, delays and amendments. To plan an operation like the erection of a bridge calls for the collection of all facts relating to that one operation only, but in a factory, production of one kind or another continues indefinitely, so that we have the added requirement that all the facts should always be available in a suitable form. One of the skills of production planning therefore is to be able to compile, record and index all the information required, so that it can be kept up to date, be speedily available and be readily and effectively used.

In the logical sequence of events, the orders from customers or sales requirements provide the first set of facts, but since we must consider a unit which is operating on a continuous basis, it will be more helpful if we consider first the permanent records which form the background as it were to all the planning operations. The first of these is stock records.

Stock records

In a very few large mass production units materials flow straight into production within a day or two of receipt, but nothing like this is possible in the majority of factories. In most factories some materials or components must be kept in stock against a probable or a known future requirement, and it is therefore essential to know what stocks are available, when they need replenishing, and when orders must be placed for further supplies. There are two rather different methods in use, one depending on a knowledge of the *actual* stock at any time, and the other on the amount of *free* stock, that is, the amount available and *not allocated* to or absorbed by future production. Which method to use depends on circumstances and the kind and extent of control required. The free stock method ensures that all future commitments are covered by orders, whereas the actual stock method only ensures that there is sufficient material in stock or on order to cover *normal* requirements with normal delivery periods from suppliers. It is difficult to be sure what will be normal, so that the actual stock method is dangerous and, when consumption is liable to fluctuate irregularly, often results in production stoppages owing to stocks becoming exhausted. For example, a stock equivalent to two months' normal demand of a material may be exhausted in two weeks if an unusual order absorbs an abnormal amount of this material; and it may not be possible to replace it in two weeks. The free stock method is almost essential in times of continually rising demand, but when production periods in the factory exceed the time for delivery of materials, excessive stocks may be created. This danger is severe if the company receives large orders for scheduled delivery over long periods. Neither method prevents stocks running out if suppliers take longer than expected or promised to deliver the goods.

Perhaps the simplest method of controlling actual stocks, and one quite suitable where demand and delivery periods are steady and actual quantity in stocks is only required to be known for annual stocktaking purposes (and is then counted), is to box or parcel the minimum stock quantity as described on p. 473 and known as the 'two bin' system. When in similar circumstances a clerical record of actual stock is also required, the bin card record of stock movement and balance is satisfactory. In practice a combination of stock control methods is usually the most appropriate. Analysis of the annual cost of components will usually show a 'Pareto' distribution—i.e. about 20 per cent of the items by number account for about 80 per cent of the annual cost. It is obviously this 20 per cent by number that requires the greatest control. A suggested guide as to which types of stock should be controlled by which method would be to arrange the stock items in descending order of cost of annual usage:

A The first 20 per cent by number, control by allocation.
B The items covered by the range 21 per cent to 60 per cent control by actual stock record.
C The final 40 per cent cover by 'two bin' control.

The two types of control, A and B, will have to be done clerically (with or without a computer) in which case the information which has to be utilised or recorded is:

Amount required (for allocating)
Amount ordered (for allocating)
Amount used (for actual)
Amount received (for actual)
Balance—free or actual
Date and job or order No. (for reference)
Specification of material or part (for re-ordering)
Minimum stock (safety margin)
Re-order quantity (normal batch)
Unit value (for stock-taking purposes).

Because rapid reference is essential, it is usual to do all recording on visible edge cards, and much ingenuity has been used in their design and the equipment for housing them. There are numerous types from which to choose to suit varying uses and commodities, and three only are illustrated:

1. for allocating future requirements from free stock;
2. for replacing stocks when actual stocks are reduced to a minimum figure and for recording orders placed;
3. for allocating from a free stock and at the same time revealing actual stock.

Illustrations

Illustrations of suitable forms are given in Figs. 3.5.2, 3 and 4, with a few typical entries shown.

Allocating from free stock (Fig. 3.5.2). This is the simplest form of record. The same columns and entries can be used for actual stocks, 'issues' replacing 'allocation' and 'receipts' replacing 'ordered', the 'balance' being actual stock and not free. To open such a record the total present known requirements are deducted from the total stock available (ordered, in progress and in stock) and entered as an opening 'free stock'. An opening figure of 15 is shown in the illustration (from which subsequent entries can be followed). A new order is placed, or batch put into production, either when 'free stock' is reduced to nil or a minimum reserve. The latter is only required if a very urgent order, using

Fig. 3.5.2
Stock card for
allocating
from free stock

Date /Job No	Alloc	Order-ed	Free	Date /Job No	Alloc	Order-ed	Free	Date /Job No	Alloc	Order-ed	Free
			15								
14·2·74	4	–	11								
3·5·74	12	–	−1								
AB	–	40	39								
5·5·74	5	–	34								
6·5·74	1 – Scrap (No3)	–	33								

Batch _____40_____   Patt No _____

Description _____Bush_____   Frame _____ Part No __/ 111_____

Fig. 3.5.3
Stock card
replacing
actual stock

	Receipts					Issues			
Date	Order No	Quant	Rec'd	Outstand		Date	Order No	Quant	Stock
									14
						4·5·74	BP	4	10
10·5·74	AA	40		40					
16·5·74	AA		20	20					30
						20·5·74	BQ	3	27
24·5·74	AA		20						47

Order Pt 10   Batch 40

Description   Part No / 111

this part or material, is likely to absorb any existing stock and is likely to be required immediately or before other orders booked.

Replacing actual stocks (Fig. 3.5.3). In this case further supplies are ordered or put into production when the actual quantity in stock falls to a predetermined minimum (order point). This minimum quantity must be sufficient to supply normal issues from stock over the period normally taken to obtain replacement. The lefthand half of the record deals with the orders for replacement, the righthand half with issues and actual stock balances. For methods of calculating re-order quantities see p. 371.

Fig. 3.5.4
Stock card
replacing free
stock and
recording actual

Date	Order No	Order-ed	Free	Alloc	Rec'd	Stock	Issued	Date	Order No	Order-ed	Free	Alloc	Rec'd	Stock	Issued
			4			14									
4·5·74	BP					10	4								
6·5·74	124		−1	5											
10·5·74	AA	40	39												
16·5·74	AA				20	30									
20·5·74	BQ					27	3								
22·5·74	125		32	7											
24·5·74	AA				20	47									

Description   Batch 40   Part No /111

Replacing free stock and recording actual (Fig. 3.5.4). This record is a combination of allocation and actual stock records. It could be made comprehensive by adding a column for balance-on-order as in the second illustration. For all normal purposes it gives all the information required for maintenance of stocks; in the few instances when the balance on order is required, it can be found by totalling receipts and setting off against the quantity ordered. It needs greater care and skill from clerks than the first two illustrations, but when accurately maintained and checked periodically, the record of actual stock can be accepted for stock-taking purposes to avoid the annual physical check and the problems this involves. It will be noticed that the free stock and actual stock entries and records are independent of each other, and that actual stock at any time may be more or less than the free stock.

It may sometimes happen that there are a few items of stock which, because of their importance to production, require to be specially watched. The basic materials in certain process industries, like grains in flour milling, flour, sugar, etc., in food and confectionery, and linseed oil, solvents, etc., in paint, are important in this way, and the head of the Planning Department or the Works Manager himself may wish to have a visible record or wall chart of stocks of these items. A simple chart can be constructed as illustrated in Fig. 3.5.5. It is corrected daily or weekly by the Stock Records clerks. There are similar moving bar charts available from office equipment manufacturers which show three facts on each bar.

Quantities to order

There are numerous means of determining the quantity of items to place on order, whether for outside purchase or in-plant manufacture. A number of approaches are given here together with a brief explanation of some of the terms used in stock control.[1]

[1] For more detailed theory behind stock replenishment and batch size policies the reader is recommended to study A. Battersby, *A Guide to Stock Control*, BIM, Pitman, 1962; and S. Eilon, *Elements of Production Planning and Control*, Collier–Macmillan, 1966.

Fig. 3.5.5
Movable
bar chart

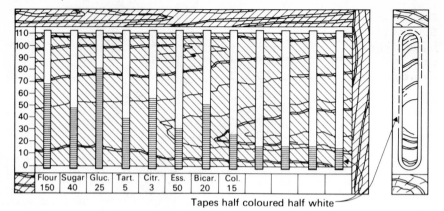

Tapes half coloured half white

When determining re-order policy the following factors must be taken into account:

- Rate of usage.
- Rate or lead time of production or delivery.
- Cost of initiating a batch—orders, job cards, set up.
- Cost of stock holding, cost of storage, interest on capital, etc.
- Type of call off, steady rate or random.
- Factory load balance.
- Acceptable risk of running out of stock.
- Economic batch quantity.

The theoretical approach to economic batch size is to consider the total ordering/set up costs against the cost of stock holding. As the batch size increases the 'set up' cost per item decreases, but the cost of stock holding increases. This relationship is shown in Fig. 3.5.6.

Fig. 3.5.6
Cost—Batch size
relationships

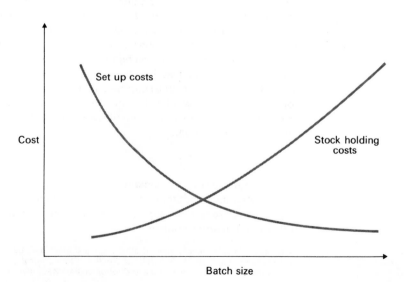

Readers with a mathematical turn of mind will recognise that the minimum total cost solution to this situation is not simple. If we take a straightforward situation with known constant demand and known constant production rate, then the economic batch quantity is given by:

$$Q = \frac{2CS}{I(I + \gamma) + 2B}$$

where

C = Consumption rate
S = Set up costs
I = Interest rates
γ = Ratio of consumption rates to production rates
B = Total storage costs per piece per unit time.

Frequently demand is neither known nor constant and the insertion of probability into this equation is rather beyond the scope of this book, other than to say that it considerably increases the complexity of the economic batch size equation. The disadvantage of using economic batch sizes is that the batch size is likely to be different for every component manufactured or purchased with consequent difficulties in scheduling.

Statistical method

If the production situation requires that the ability to meet random demand is of greater importance than obtaining the most economic batch size and customer's required delivery period is less than manufacturing lead time—this may be most relevant in fabrication shops where total set up costs are very low in any case—batch quantities can be determined which will ensure that, within specified confidence limits, components for a product ordered at random intervals by the customer can be met from stock. In this case the batch quantity will be given by:

$$Q = LD + t\sigma$$

where

L = the lead time (i.e. total production or delivery time)
D = Average expected delivery rate
σ = Standard deviation of demand intervals
t = Probability factor dependent on the degree of risk of running out of stock that is acceptable

values of t are: $1 \cdot 28$ for 10 per cent probability of stock out
$1 \cdot 65$ for 5 per cent probability of stock out
$1 \cdot 96$ for $2 \cdot 5$ per cent probability of stock out
$2 \cdot 33$ for 1 per cent probability of stock out
For a Poisson distribution $\sigma = \sqrt{LD}$.

'Duration controlled'
batches

It is a common practice in some manufacturing concerns to determine batch sizes on the basis that the batch should produce one week's work (or some other period) on the longest operation. This approach will have the same disadvantage as economic batch quantity without any of the justification, and can lead to dangerously high values of stock and work in progress.

Standard or period batch control

In companies making assemblies for stock, the component parts may either be issued in standard batches of say 100 sets of parts, repeat batches of the same size being raised when re-order levels are reached either on allocation or physical stock figures. This is known as standard batch control. Alternatively a batch of parts can be issued for manufacture at predetermined periods, the size of the batch is then determined on a forecast of how many will be required before the next batch is produced, taking into account any existing stocks. This is known as period batch control.

There is no such thing as the 'correct' method of determining batch size or frequency; each organisation must determine its own solution. The greater the volume of like products produced, the greater will be the likelihood that detailed economic batch theory will be relevant; for concerns in small batch manufacture, less sophisticated methods are likely to be more appropriate.

Records of times and capacities for process and operations

The second type of basic data which must be compiled and made available is that which has to do with processes and operations carried on in the factory.

It is essential to have readily available the operations, plant required and production times for all products, parts and assemblies. This can be done in the form of a standard practice manual, or process book, or stock catalogue, but some kind of card filing is more convenient. In engineering and general manufacture, where there are many parts, many of which are standard, the information is best set out on process layouts or master route cards. An example of such a process layout is given in the Appendix to this chapter, Fig. 3.5.38, Operation Master (see page 448).

In whatever way it is set out, the following information should be on one record:

● Description and reference number of product or part.
● Material and amount required for one unit.
● Normal production quantity, i.e. production batch.
● Operations or processes involved in manufacture.
● Plant or machine and tools required for each operation.
● Production time for each process and operation.

The production time is best expressed as standard time, though allowed time can be used if standard time is not available. To avoid a conversion to actual time for planning purposes, all charts and measures of capacity should be in terms of standard time. Thus, for a week of forty actual hours, the available standard hours in a factory, where the normal performance is say 95 per cent, would be $40 \times 0.95 = 38$ standard hours.

The Production Engineers will supply all the above information (set out on process layouts, when these are used), deciding the normal production batch in collaboration with the Production Planning Department.

It is also necessary to have an accurate record of the plant and labour force available and their capacity. This may sound obvious to those in factories where a few continuous processes are in operation, but in the many factories on batch production with general-purpose plant and machines, it is often neglected, plant being taken out of commission because of breakdown and new plant or equipment installed without the Production Planning Department being informed. The Production Planning Department, therefore, should have a copy of the plant register, or at least a list of all plant, should be advised of all changes, and should keep the record up to date, it being the duty of either the Foreman or Maintenance Department to inform them of changes. Similarly, either the Foreman or Personnel Officer should inform them of changes in labour force which will affect capacity.

Orders on hand

Finally, the Production Planning Department must know what has to be produced, and therefore must know of all orders on hand and delivery promises made. This again can be a simple or an elaborate job, depending on the type and number of orders. When customers are supplied from shelf stock, the Sales Department keep stock records of finished products and requisition (or order) on the Production Departments as free stock is absorbed. In other cases Production Planners are advised of the customer's actual order and requirements. In either case orders are recorded as received in the Production Planning Department, and marked off as completed. In most cases it will be found that the best way of doing this is on visible edge card records. The card must be designed to suit the kind of order and the information frequently required in connection with it, e.g. portion completed. Either one card can be used for one order (if there are always several items per order), or one line of the card for each order. The cards should be filed in some logical sequence, and it is of considerable help for reference purposes in the works and sales offices if it is arranged with the Sales Department for order numbers to be allocated to orders in the works in some code which designates the type of product. Orders are then filed in production groups and number sequence, providing a logical reference for planning purposes. It is important to log each order immediately it is received, to allocate a works order number immediately (if the sales order number is not used) and to cross off or enter the date immediately it is completed. Failure to do either of these things results in false computations of balance of work on hand and in neglect to produce, or in overproduction of orders.

Long-term plans or budgets

Production plans must, of course, be based on sales demand. When there is no positive sales programme, plans can only be based on trends. Normally there are sales programmes, both long-term and short-term, and broad or long-term production plans are developed from general conferences between all executives and the Managing Director when future sales programmes are discussed. In the case of the larger mass production factories, manufacturing consumption goods for the general public, such as cars and radios, proprietary foods, toilet preparations, etc., a definite sales programme is agreed on, and this must be broken down by the Production Planning Department in a preproduction programme for the new product or sales push. When such a programme involves drawings, special tools, or plant, and detail manufacture or assembly, it should be set out in chart form on a time basis, so that the interrelated completion dates for each stage or part can be seen. Such a chart is shown in Fig. 3.5.7, taken from BSS 1100, Part 3. Difficulties, ensuing for example, from lack of capacity to meet the programme, lack of equipment and need for special tooling, etc., are discussed by all concerned at the preproduction stage, and general agreement on all stages obtained before the programme is confirmed.

Fig. 3.5.7   Planning chart for production services

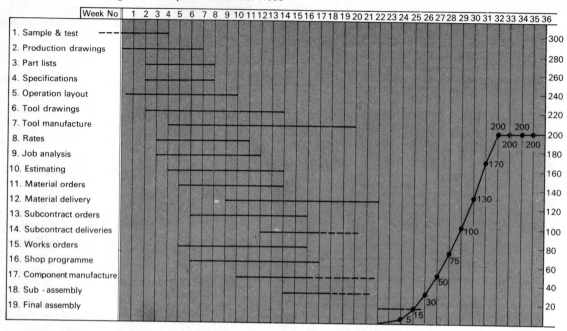

An important framework for continuing coordination of sales and production requirements and quantities is provided by the establishment and application of a systematic *marketing programme*, as described in Part One (see page 27) and Part Two (see page 236).

Interpreting the programme

Usually no radical departure from previous demands is planned or expected. A more or less continuous flow of orders for the company's products or services is received, varying in volume from time to time. But it is still necessary for the Production Planning Department to take a fairly long forward view and to develop long-term programmes. In the first place, it is essential to know what is the total load on the factory represented by all orders on the books, in order to know what delivery period can be promised to customers for manufacture to customer's order, or what finished stocks to carry when manufacturing to stock. It is also necessary to know whether this load will keep the departments or processes equally loaded. In this we encounter the problem which vexes all those interested in measuring overall output, planners, statisticians and economists: what measure of output to use in firms or industries manufacturing many different lines or products. A ton of cement is much the same wherever it is manufactured, but two yards of cloth may be very different in quality and in the amount of machine hours and man hours required for production, and two electric motors even of the same horsepower can be very different in design. The only accurate measure is machine hours or man hours, but the breakdown of every order into detailed man hours for long-term planning is impracticable. It is frequently sufficient to use man or machine hours for the process or department common to all products or otherwise controlling (total) output. If a simple measure of volume is not possible, it will usually be found that value in £p is adequate, if the spread of kinds of product remains fairly steady and corrections are made for appreciable variations. The total load divided by the factory capacity per week (actual or budgeted) gives the time in weeks it would take to manufacture everything on order, and therefore the delivery period.

If there is only one or a few very similar products, and orders are executed in strict rotation, then little more information on future load is required. More often, however, there are many dissimilar products, each absorbing different amounts of each department's capacity, or orders are taken for delivery at a specified time, and not merely in rotation, and sometimes both conditions apply.

In either case, orders must be taken for delivery according to capacity available, or capacity must be adjusted to suit orders received and delivery required, and in practice forward plans are made to reconcile these two alternatives. The problem resolves itself into a matter of setting off orders received against capacity, actual or budgeted. Taking first the case when orders are to be executed in rotation and not at a specified time, the period it would take to manufacture the total load (value, units, etc.) of orders on hand should be assessed periodically, weekly, or monthly. If the period varies, it must be decided either to adjust quoted delivery periods accordingly, adjust capacity, or (if the period is falling too rapidly) ask for more sales effort. When output measured in value or volume, does not reflect capacity proportionately, and the only accurate measure is hours (man hours or machine hours), then it is necessary to divide the products made into categories of like kinds (if they do not fall naturally into definite categories) and, for each category, to select the most representative unit, taking into account demand and hours capacity absorbed. Orders are then recorded and assessed for capacity in terms of these representative units. Capacity can be checked departmentally in this way without a great amount of statistical work (see Fig. 3.5.8). Since for a given

Fig. 3.5.8   Planning data for capacity assessment

Product	Load in equivalent units	Department 1		Department 2		Department 3		Department 4		Department 5	
		Per unit	Total	Per unit	Total	Per Unit	Total	Per unit	Total	Per unit	Total
A	258	0·16	41·28	0·25	64·50	0·19	49·02	0·27	69·66	0·42	108·36
B	9	0·13	1·20	0·01	0·09	0·16	1·44	0·60	5·40	2·13	19·17
C	200	1·50	300·00	1·52	304·00	27·00	5,400·00	30·00	6,000·00	30·50	6,100·00
D	12	0·75	9·00	0·30	3·60	1·20	14·40	2·00	24·00	3·50	42·00
E	147	2·00	294·00	2·50	367·50	3·00	441·00	3·50	514·40	4·00	588·00
F	57	0·65	37·05	0·93	53·01	0·30	17·10	2·00	114·00	2·50	142·50
G	132	0·27	35·64	0·49	64·68	0·65	85·80	0·92	121·44	1·20	158·40
H	70	1·76	123·20	3·00	210·00	0·75	52·50	0·90	63·00	1·40	98·00
I	435	2·00	870·00	2·50	1,087·60	3·00	1,305·00	3·50	1,522·50	4·00	1,740·00
J	69	0·51	35·19	0·75	51·75	0·86	59·34	0·97	66·93	1·10	75·90
K	77	0·49	37·73	1·17	90·09	1·01	77·77	1·10	84·70	1·30	100·10
L	112	0·50	56·00	0·65	72·80	1·20	134·40	2·50	280·00	2·55	285·60
M	68	0·17	11·56	0·40	27·20	0·90	61·20	1·30	88·40	1·27	86·36
Total std hrs		1,851·85		2,396·72		7,698·97		8,954·53		9,544·39	
Capacity		88		132		220		264		220	
Weeks		21		18		35		34		43	

overall volume of production definite financial and production facilities are required, it is necessary to budget total volume and allocate this to the various categories. An example of the build-up of such a production budget using typical average units for each category of product manufactured is given in Fig. 3.5.9.

Having established such production budgets, or assessed the capacity required to meet the demand reflected in all orders on hand, the effect on plant and labour requirements and material supply (long-term contracts and

Fig. 3.5.9

Sales and production budget based on 30 per cent increase on sales for financial year

		Sales			Average unit		Prelim. budget uniform increase for all categories		Final budget adjusted for present trends	
		Total sales value	No. of units	Average value	Unit taken as std.	Est. value of av. unit	Sales +30%	Est. prodn. in units	Est. total sales	No. of units at av. unit value
		£		£		£	£		£	
Group 1	A	51 786	45	1 150	5-ton	1 200	67 400	56	67 400	56
	B	56 178	35	1 585	5-ton	1 600	73 000	46	73 000	46
	C	15 201	89	171	2-ton	150	19 760	131	19 760	131
Total		123 115	—	—	—	—	160 160	—	160 160	—
Group 2	A	6 065	101	60	½-ton	77	7 880	102	11 470	149
	B	17 458	132	132	2-ton	115	22 700	105	14 470	125
	C	10 028	44	228	5-ton	175	13 040	75	18 542	106
Total		33 551	—	—	—	—	43 620	—	47 982	—
Group 3		23 287	—	—	—	—	30 250	—	30 250	—
Group 4	A	28 519	160	170	5-ton	150	37 020	247	34 500	223
	B	6 964	75	91	3-ton	90	8 870	98	11 390	126
Total		35 483	—	—	—	—	45 890	—	45 890	—
Group 5	A	17 285	906	19	2-ton	17	22 450	1 320	19 038	1 120
	B	6 105	211	29	2-ton	25	7 950	328	7 000	280
	C	3 580	288	12·4	2-ton	10	4 650	465	4 650	465
	D	3 780	88	42	1-ton	—	4 910	118	4 910	118
Total		30 980	—	—	—	—	40 190	—	36 826	—
Group 6		9 242	—	—	—	—	12 000	—	12 000	—
Group 7		7 371	—	—	—	—	9 580	—	9 580	—
Group 8		23 150	—	—	—	—	30 030	—	30 030	—
TOTAL		£286 179	—	—	—	—	£371 720	—	£371 720	—

minimum reserve stocks) must be assessed, and the information passed on to the appropriate department. Plant and labour requirements are not usually neglected, but the adjustment (particularly for a marked increase in output) of minimum stocks is also essential; it is frequently forgotten.

Factory loads

In the case of orders which are quoted for delivery at a specified date, or when it is necessary to build up a broad programme of the load on the works (or department) represented by orders to be produced, it is necessary to log orders as they are accepted or put into the programme in the week (or period) concerned. This can be done either graphically or by merely listing orders on a sheet for each period. Perhaps the simplest is to record the value in £p or other unit, of each order on a card in a visible edge system, one card for each week. If necessary, separate series of cards can be used for each department or process. A sliding coloured tab is slipped inside the visible edge of the card holder and is adjusted horizontally as each addition is made. The result at any time shows the load in each week, and, across all cards, the way the load varies. Alternatively, a wall chart can be used, being adjusted periodically. This can be done by small nails driven into a board in lines, vertically to represent the scale of units and horizontally in weeks (the nails in effect being at the points of intersection of lines on a graph). Coloured elastic is stretched round or through the nails to form a graph, separate colours representing budgeted and scheduled capacity. A similar result can be obtained by using squared paper blocking-in or crossing through squares as units of volume are absorbed or booked. Such charts show clearly where capacity is unabsorbed and available for new orders.

When the number of orders per week is small it is possible to plan orders into a load board. An effective way of doing this is to originate a card or ticket for each order, and to draw a line along the top edge to a scale equivalent to the number of hours or capacity absorbed by the order. These cards can then be slipped into horizontal pockets of the load board (see Fig. 3.5.10), behind each other and overlapping, with the load lines end to end, the board being marked with the same scale and divided into weeks. One pocket should be used for

Fig. 3.5.10
Load board

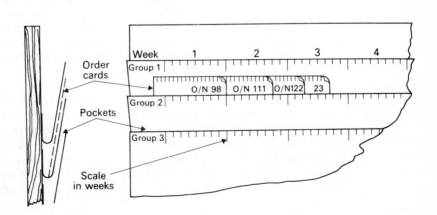

each unit of capacity (products, department, or group). In this way the load can be built up as far ahead as wished, it is readily visible, the completion date of existing or new orders can be seen, and it can be used for progress checking. The pockets can be made of metal or wood or even printed paper stuck on to a board, the ends wrapped round the edges of the board, the scale being printed on the face of each pocket.

Departments loads

Departmental loads—long-term. Unless all orders received absorb the same proportion of capacity for each department and thus preserve a balanced load between departments, it is necessary to check regularly forward loads on departments in order to preserve balance. To do this the procedure outlined above should be followed in a more detailed manner on a departmental basis. When output of the product is easily measured in terms of volume, this is not difficult, but when hours is the only measure because the individual jobs vary so much, the method of grouping into categories should be followed. All orders in hand should be analysed to find the number of units in each category. For each category the number is then multiplied by the hours required in each department and the figures for each department totalled and divided by capacity to find the load in weeks. Periodically (weekly or monthly) net differences in units for each category between orders received and despatches should be extended similarly and added to (or subtracted from) previous loads. These periodic loads should be plotted to reveal any trend. An illustration of the assessment of capacity absorbed, calculated in this way, is given in Fig. 3.5.8. In such a case the loading in departments is obviously not balanced, and either orders must be increased to correct the underloading, or capacity in the overloaded departments must be expanded.

Departmental and machine loads, short-term. Actual orders at some time have to be issued to the works for production. In process and mass production industries, where processes are in continuous operation on the same product (for example, cement, steel, margarine) this amounts to little more than instructions for starting and stopping. When different grades of the same product are made, as in paper-making, or glass container manufacturing, order of priority for each grade or kind must be determined. If each order takes its turn and there is no delivery period problem, no more need be done, but if it is required to know when orders will be completed, then the production scheduled must be measured and related to capacity. In most manufacturing industries a variety of different products, articles or components is manufactured in each department, and few departments, machines or operators make the same article continuously or permanently. It is then essential to issue instructions for production at the rate at which it can be completed. This means actually measuring the amount of work it is proposed to schedule for immediate production over a period. An approximate measure is no longer of any use, and if capacity and output cannot be measured accurately in some unit of volume, then man hours or machine hours must be used. Thus we get what is commonly called departmental or machine loading. When instructions for production are issued in the form of a list of jobs or orders to be done in a period or in order of priority, such lists are usually termed production schedules.

Batch planning

It is at this stage that the planning problems become complicated and the technique needs most skill. The methods and techniques in use are many and varied, and indeed must be so to suit the widely different types and scales of production. In a book of this kind it is impossible to refer to every one. As, however, the principles underlying them all are the same and can be applied to all industries, a few illustrations will serve for an understanding of how the problem is tackled. Planning for batch production for a variety of machines or processes is about the most difficult, and will therefore be referred to in any specific illustrations.

At the loading stage of planning there are always opposing forces to be kept in equilibrium, the desire to meet customers with urgent demands and the undesirability of disturbing existing programmes; the need to keep inventories low, and the preference of the works for large batches, and so on. All such factors have to be remembered and allowed for when building up programmes or loads prior to issuing production schedules.

This detailed loading can either be made directly to machine or operator, or in two stages, first to department or group, and then to individuals. If all machines are exactly the same and there is absolutely no difference in operator skill or aptitude, then loading immediately to machines or individuals is permissible. But where there are operator differences or idiosyncrasies, it is far better not to lose the personal touch and to arrange for the production supervisor to have some or the last say in job allocation. This can be arranged by first loading to department or group in the production planning department, and then either the foreman or planning clerk in the department loading to individual or machine. The importance of this personal touch at the final stage of planning at the point of impact on the man or woman cannot be overemphasised, and is too little appreciated. With Shakespeare,

> We fortify in paper and in figures,
> Using the names of men instead of men,
> Like one that draws the model of a house,
> Beyond his powers to build it,

dehumanising administration just where it most requires the personal touch. This accounts not a little for the indifference and even hostility to 'systems' and to operators 'leaving it to the planner', when a word or suggestion at the right time could do so much to help the job along.

The simplest form of scheduling—it is hardly 'loading'—is by priority, keeping supervision informed at least several jobs ahead, and as far ahead as possible of the order of priority of each job. In its simplest form this is a written list. If a graphic or visual method is preferred, job tickets can be hung on hooks, one hook for each machine or operator, the next job always being uppermost.

A more comprehensive planning board consists of a series of four pockets for each machine and operator. The top two pockets each hold one job card, the lower two several. Into the top pocket is placed the job in production, in the second the next to be started, in the third jobs ready for production in order of priority, and in the fourth jobs waiting for materials, tools, or completion of a previous operation.

Loading to capacity can be done by list, graphically or on a load board. If a list is used there should be three columns in which are entered respectively: job reference (name or number), capacity absorbed (hours, quantity, etc.), and the cumulative capacity.

Fig. 3.5.11
Gantt chart for
planning

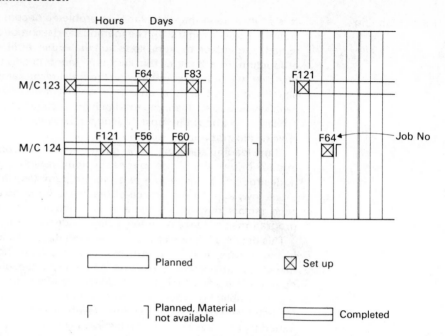

Perhaps the most widely used graphic method is the Gantt chart. It suffers from the one defect that it is not easily modified, rubbing out and redrawing lines being a time-absorbing occupation. When loads can be built up simply and are unlikely to be altered, the Gantt chart can be extremely useful and can be used to indicate progress. There are many variations, and illustrations are given in most books dealing with charts or production planning (e.g. *Management Handbook,* Ronald Press). Figure 3.5.11 is an illustration of a simple version showing the loading for two machines. The lines are drawn horizontally on paper specially printed, or on graph paper.

There are several methods of building a load board from materials likely to be available in any factory. They are usually made to take cards or strips of cardboard which are used to indicate the load. Perhaps the simplest is a board built-up of pockets as illustrated on p. 377. To avoid preparing special cards, one of the cards used in connection with the issue of jobs, for example the job or time card, should be used, marking along the top edge a line representing the time required to do the job. It facilitates drawing the line to have a scale printed along the top as shown in the illustration of a Move Note in the Appendix to this chapter (Fig. 3.5.43). If the boards are large, the pockets can be made of metal, but for small ones they can be made of strips of strong paper with the scale printed on each strip, which is folded backwards and gummed to a backing board. A portable board can be made in this manner for chargehands and foremen of small sections by using a piece of stiff cardboard as the backing board. There are of course several types of planning boards sold under proprietary names by office equipment suppliers.

Planning problems

So much for the tools of loading; the technique can only be learnt by practice, but there are several precepts which are generally applicable. The first essential is to use an accurate measure. It cannot be too strongly emphasised that the accuracy of planning varies directly with the accuracy of the information and measurement of capacity and performance. However much skill is used in loading, if the figures used are not accurate, departments will sometimes be overloaded and at other times short of work, resulting in overtime and idle capacity alternating violently, to the extreme annoyance of the foremen and operators, and engendering a hostility to the planning engineers when cooperation is required. Furthermore, promises given to customers or the sales department are not kept, resulting in urgent action to retrieve the position, adding further disturbances in the shops and incurring excess costs due to 'breaking down' jobs which are running to put in the urgent ones. In extreme cases the jobs superseded themselves become urgent, and eventually there are more urgent than normal jobs and planning becomes a continuous purge and a discredited instrument.

It is also important to allow for plant breakdown and maintenance and for absence of operators. For normal conditions this can best be done by loading to the normal standard hours produced per week as revealed in weekly labour control reports. This allows then for the average performance of operators. But over and above this the Planning Department must take steps to see that it is informed of any unusual breakdowns or absence likely seriously to affect plans, so that any necessary readjustments can be made. It is always advisable to schedule below capacity by a definite margin, which can then be filled up in the current period by urgent or rush orders.

In factories on batch production it will be found that a week is the optimum period for planning and shop loading purposes. Longer periods are apt to need too frequent revision, and a day is not long enough for collecting like batches together and for balancing up between machines and groups. Weekly schedules should be issued to departments long enough ahead for them to be given adequate consideration and preparation. The schedules themselves should be prepared far enough ahead by the planning engineers to enable their effect to be seen on work-in-progress and over- or underloading of certain machines in sections.

Batch problems

In factories on batch production of components for assembly into machines or units, the aim is to arrange for all components to be completed as nearly as possible together and in time for assembly to be completed by due date. For continuous assembly of one product or assembly of a special order, it is ideal to arrange for delivery of components to the job or to work station or layby in the assembly shop at the rate required, or just in time for assembly. In other cases components are delivered to a component stores, and if manufacture of components is not synchronised reasonably well with assembly, the stores will have to be larger than it need be. In assessing the production time for components (that is, the total time it takes to get them from the raw material stores to the finished part stores), it is not sufficient to add up the time taken in each process or operation. In continuous-flow production, where conveyor assembly is in use, this may be nearly so, but in intermittent or batch production, where batch sizes differ, all parts do not need the same operations, and operator times vary, there must always be a float of work behind each machine or operator, and this fluctuates. In addition, some kind of inspection or checking and some transport are required after each operation, so that a job seldom moves to the next operation immediately the previous one is finished. This in-between operation time is frequently longer than the direct operation time.

The relationship between the arrival of job to a machine, the length of time to machine each batch, the queue length and machine utilisation can be described using *queuing theory*. It can be shown that to ensure adequate machine utilisation, given random arrival of jobs and varying operation times, an average of two jobs in the queue will be required. However, increasing the average length of the queue beyond two does not substantially increase the machine utilisation. In most practical situations however, experience is the best guide to the relationship between operation time and queuing time for each activity.

There is a limit to the volume of figures and the number of factors which a normal staff can handle in a reasonable time with traditional methods. Electronic computers, however, make it possible to solve planning problems which involve a large number of factors, and their application to such problems is now being developed. For example, a technique has been developed for using a computer to solve the kind of problem in which it is necessary to obtain the optimum conditions for operating a series of activities with a certain number of (linear) restrictions. Manufacture of different products, stocking of different items of commodities, physical properties of different components of a blend are examples of such 'activities', and maximum plant capacity, maximum warehouse capacity, minimum cost of blend are respective 'restrictions' (see also pp. 444–5).

Example of
procedure

This example is once again taken from engineering, but the procedure is not restricted to it. It is in engineering that this detail planning technique has been most highly developed. Nevertheless, this procedure (and the documents illustrated on p. 392) can be used, with suitable modifications, wherever batch production exists. It is an example of a procedure pruned to a minimum of red tape and paperwork consistent with control and flexibility.

In order to illustrate the method of applying these planning techniques and to show how they hang together in practice, an actual example is described briefly below. The factory concerned manufactures products to delivery dates. The products all require an assembly stage and a variety of components, some of which are standard and others designed and manufactured for a particular order.

Works orders. Copies of all works orders, which are identified by a number coded to indicate type of product, are sent to all departments concerned. The orders give the customer's name, a certain amount of technical data needed by the various departments, and state the delivery date promised. This date is in line with the general delivery period agreed with the Production Planning Department, and with the appearance of the sales load board (see page 377) kept up to date for the sales department by the Production Planning Department. The Production Engineers' and Production Planning copies go via the drawing office, where with reference to their own planning board the date by which drawings will be ready is entered. The planning card used by the Production Planning Department is produced at the same time as the copies of the order and is attached to Production Planning copy.

Records. As orders are received daily by the Production Planning Department they are recorded by the Records Section in the visible edge card record, one per line on cards filed in numerical order which automatically divides them into groups. Vertical columns of the card are used for indicating progress of main stages of the order. At the same time the number of units in each group on the order is added to the weekly list of orders received and despatched, to be added to the cumulative total of units on order (despatches are deducted).

Forward load. The copies then go to the forward load section, where each order is scrutinised for special features which will affect planning and any notes of these are entered on the planning card. The measure of the capacity of the factory absorbed by the order is entered on the card and the card is filed into the appropriate week nearest the week indicated by the delivery date, according to existing load and budgeted capacity for each group of products. Each week is numbered, and the week number into which the card is filed is entered on the order record for cross-reference purposes. The week number is entered on the Production Engineers' copy of order to tell them (after allowing for normal production time) by when process information and tools will be required. The copy of the order is then filed.

The load (factory capacity and asembly capacity) is transferred periodically from the planning card file to a visible edge card index book, one card for each week, a coloured tab indicating the load. This reveals the distribution of load as far as orders are booked, and is used as a reference for scheduling, building of planning card load and keeping sales load board up to date.

Production engineering. As soon as the Production Engineers receive their copy of the order they examine it and any drawings attached, decide on the method of production of the whole and each part, and prepare process layouts, including standard times for each operation (calculated from standard data). All tools required are listed and any new ones noted for designing. The draft process layout is typed as a master, and is then available for use by Production Planning whenever they decide to initiate production. When tools have been designed, a tool manufacturing requisition is raised, giving the date the tools are required, and a process layout is prepared for these so that Production Planning will have documents for planning and control.

Draft schedule. Each week, and at a date some ten or twelve weeks ahead (time for the manufacture of components, assembly and test, and for planning routine) of the week to which it will apply, a provisional assembly schedule is prepared from orders in the planning card file. Slight adjustments may be made at this stage to allow for changes in capacity or urgency of orders, or other special circumstances. This provisional schedule is passed on to the Stores Record section.

Stores. The Stores Record section takes the parts list for each order listed and allocates all materials and components on free-stock records, throwing up requisitions for new manufacturing orders or buying orders on which is stated the week number by when delivery must be made. Special parts are not allocated, but a requisition to manufacture is raised for them. The requisitions to manufacture are sent to the document printing section, who run off all works documents. These, in sets, are returned to the component planning section of the Production Planning Department, where they are filed under the week number first entered on the requisition for manufacture. This file, in week numbers, forms the provisional schedules for component manufacturing departments.

Final schedules. Final schedules for the assembly departments are prepared and issued one full week before the week to which they apply, and copies are given to Stores and Test sections. At this stage certain orders included on provisional schedules may have to be deleted because of non-delivery of special material, or delay in component manufacture. At some time it may be necessary to bring forward other orders to meet urgent demands for customers (after checking material and component position) or to balance the assembly capacity.

Final schedules for component manufacturing are built up by component planners at least two to four weeks earlier than the completion week to which they apply, using standard times on the production documents as a measure of load. This involves a good deal of juggling and skill to ensure that each section in each department is fully loaded, but not overloaded. Loading to machines and operations is done in the department.

When building up loads, consideration has to be given to the following factors:

Urgent orders.
Special parts or tools.
Availability of raw materials (suppliers may have to be chased).
Need for subcontracting to cope with overloads.
Effect of change in demand on capacity of certain plant.
Excessive illness of operators, or breakdown of plant.
That maximum flexibility is provided for at each stage.

A department schedule is only made final just before it must be issued, and even then is just short of capacity for the department to allow for additions during the current week. This flexibility is of the utmost importance, especially in those factories on batch production and working to customers' orders. A production planning system which cannot respond quickly to urgent orders, changes in demand and difficulties with suppliers is not doing its job properly.

Network planning

The type of forward plans discussed above, are excellent for production units where the workload created by each order or unit of output is a relatively small proportion of the total and throughput times are measured in weeks, but in some industries such as shipbuilding and the construction industry the work load is created by a small number of large projects each one consisting of many individual activities frequently using many different trades and disciplines, with a total time from start to finish measured in months or even years. In such instances the use of 'networks' can make a significant reduction in the overall project time. *Network analysis* first establishes the logical sequence of performing operations, and then identifies those operations which directly affect the overall time of the project.

It is less than twenty years since the two well known branches of Network Planning PERT (Programme Evaluation and Review Technique) and CPM

(Critical Path Method) were first used in the USA. Now these techniques are almost universally used in the planning and control of large projects, such as shipbuilding—PERT started with nuclear submarine building—civil engineering, chemical engineering and projects of this type. Network Planning is a term which covers PERT, CPM and a whole series of techniques which have developed along the same lines, and new developments are still being made in the field of networks. The real advance of these techniques has only been practical with the increased availability of high speed digital computers, as the solving of a complex network by manual methods would be a practical impossibility. There are two commonly used notations in network analysis: the technique will be described here using the 'Circle and Link' notation in which each job is denoted by a circle and the logic of sequence is denoted by an arrow:

Activity B follows activity A

The alternative notation is the 'Arrow Diagram' in which the arrow represents an activity and the circle (or square) represents an event, i.e. a point in time when an activity starts or finishes. The above two activities would be represented thus:

Event 1 = Start of activity A
Event 2 = Finish of activity A − Start of activity B
Event 3 = Finish of activity B

Sequence

The first step in producing a network diagram is to define the logic and sequence of every job to be covered and then construct a sequence diagram. A simple method of doing this is:

(i) List all the individual activities required to complete the job in hand, and give each one an identity, i.e. either a number or a letter.
(ii) Against each activity indicate:
  (a) The expected time necessary to complete it.
  (b) Any jobs which must be completed before it can start.
(iii) Draw a rough sequence diagram which conforms to the logic required by the above.
(iv) Check for any paradoxical situations, and recheck the logic if any are found.
(v) Redraw the network to eliminate as many crossovers as possible.

A simple example of step (iv) would be:

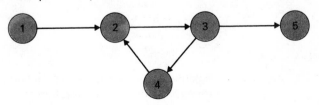

There are two paths through this network:

(a) 1–2–3–5
(b) 1–2–3–4–2–3–4–2– – – – – – –

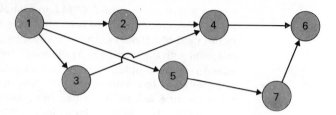

The network would then be redrawn (= step v) as follows:

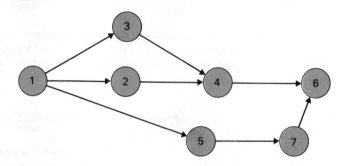

It will rarely be possible to eliminate all crossovers, but the fewer there are, the easier will be the analysis.

Critical path

Let us consider a simple job with eight activities. The sequence diagram being thus: the letter giving the identity of each activity, the number giving its duration:

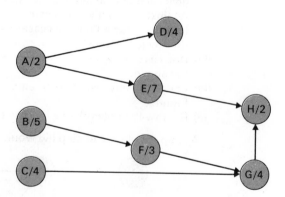

In order to carry out the scheduling process it is necessary to create two dummy activities of zero duration at the start and finish:

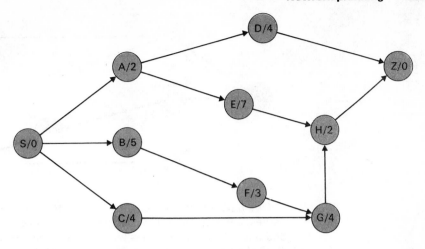

It is now necessary to calculate the earliest start time and the earliest finish time for each activity. These times are shown on either side of the activity circle:

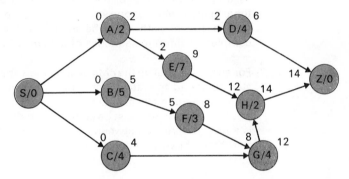

The next step is to work from the last dummy activity and show the latest start and finish time for each activity:

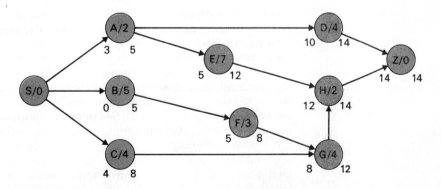

If the earliest start and finish and the latest start and finish are now shown on the one diagram it will be seen that one set of activities have the same earliest and latest start and finish times:

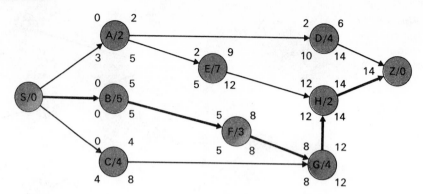

If we now look at the activities B–F–G–H it will be seen that the times of the earliest and latest start times are the same, as of course also will be the earliest and latest finish times. Jobs with the same earliest and latest start times are *Critical* jobs, and the succession of Critical jobs is known as the *critical path*. Reduction in the time taken to complete any one of the jobs on the critical path will reduce the total time necessary to complete the project. This makes the assumption that none of the 'non-critical' jobs take more than the expected time. In the event that one such job does exceed its anticipated time, the effect on the critical path must be analysed, for under these circumstances a completely different sequence of jobs may form a new critical path.

Float

For all the jobs not on the critical path, there is a difference between the earliest start time and the latest start time. The job may start at any time over this period and not make any subsequent jobs critical, this difference is known as *total float*. If one job must be completed before two others can start, and there is a time difference between the earliest finish time of job A and the earliest start time of two dependent jobs B and C then this difference is known as *free float*.

Resource allocation

In planning the labour requirements of a large project it is most important to achieve as near as possible an even buildup of work, a steady level during the major volume of work, and an even rundown at the end. This pattern should be repeated for each trade, although the timing of the buildup and rundown of the requirements for each trade will be different. Resource scheduling, using the information from the critical path network on a bar chart for each major resource can help to make the most economical use of the labour available and pinpoint critical areas where extra outside help might be required. By systematically adjusting the activities within the allowable limits of total float the best balance of resource requirements can be found. This aspect of network planning is usually carried out on a computer, as the time necessary to analyse even a relatively simple network manually would be prohibitive.

A simple case of eight activities on a bar chart with their respective resource requirements shown in Fig. 3.5.12. By delaying the start of activity C by the total float available the resource requirement becomes an even buildup followed by an even fall. In the first arrangement six men are required for weeks two and three and then two men must be found alternative work for weeks 4 and 5 before being required again in week 6, followed by a sudden reduction to two men for weeks 7 to 9.

Fig. 3.5.12
Bar chart of
resource
requirements

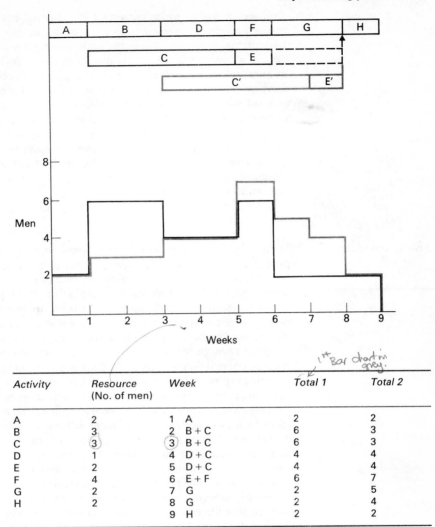

Activity	Resource (No. of men)	Week		Total 1	Total 2
A	2	1	A	2	2
B	3	2	B + C	6	3
C	3	3	B + C	6	3
D	1	4	D + C	4	4
E	2	5	D + C	4	4
F	4	6	E + F	6	7
G	2	7	G	2	5
H	2	8	G	2	4
		9	H	2	2

It is not the intention of this book to give full coverage to the subject of network analysis, the intending practitioner is advised to read one of the many textbooks on the subject.[1] However, anyone practising management to-day should be able to understand and interpret a network or critical path diagram produced by other persons.

Implementing plans

Having decided when work shall be produced, authority must be given for it to start and instructions given to get material on the move and actually to do the work. Methods for doing this vary from a copy of the customers' order, to a detailed specification with part list and drawings and detailed manufacturing instructions, with all supporting documents for each part. Procedures are

[1] e.g. A. Battersby, *Network Analysis*, Macmillan, 1970.

simplest at the opposite extremes of industrial organisations, i.e. the small business with a working proprietor who can give verbal instructions and personal supervision, and in the continuous flow mass production factories where all work moves automatically through an established standard sequence of operations so that planning instructions are almost limited to starting the right amount of material at the first process. In between are the intermittent flow or batch production units, and it is in these that paper work becomes more complicated and where consequently there is most need to find ways of reducing the work involved. Where personal supervision is adequate, there is no need to impose unnecessary or complicated systems. This is possible in small process units and in those factories where it has been possible to arrange for conveyors (either power or gravity) to control operators and the flow of work.

Forms and records

In most industrial situations the managers, supervisors and operators must be provided with written instructions, and in their turn must render written records. It may appear a truism to say that paper work and systems must be simple in order to get all the information to all the departments requiring it promptly, accurately and regularly. But there are many executives who readily recognise this, yet only consider one form at a time and neglect to work out a coordinated system or procedure. Odd scraps of paper and memo books may be good enough for occasional use, but they are not effective vehicles for regular information and records. Specially printed forms should be designed for the purpose. The preparation and movement of forms should be considered as a coordinated whole, just as production is. Foremen, storekeepers, checkers and other works personnel should not be allowed to start their own records and design their own forms without reference to a master plan and design, and it is advisable for one person to be made responsible for designing and authorising all new forms. The chief production planning executive should be competent to do so and authorised accordingly.

Wherever possible, forms should be made to serve more than one purpose or record, and steps should be taken to ensure that they are promptly dealt with so that the last person to use a form is not unduly delayed. This means that the design and layout of forms must be well thought out, providing for all the essential information and displaying it in a way that enables those who have to use particular information to recognise it quickly. For most purposes it will be found that forms are most effective when designed with headed panels for each item of information, the same information, such as Job No., appearing on all forms in the same place, heavy lines drawing attention to significant information. The Appendix to this chapter contains examples of well-designed forms. When forms are to be used on a typewriter, spacing of information or panels should suit typewritten spacing—on normal machines ten per inch horizontally (2·5 mm per letter) and six per inch vertically (4·2 mm per line).

Works order

A manufacturing or works order is the executive authority to the works or department for production to start. In the simplest cases this may be a copy of the customer's order on the firm, but in companies manufacturing proprietary lines to warehouse stock the works may never see a customer's order or know a customer's name. In most manufacturing units the order as received from the customer has to be translated into shop language with a good deal more information than is given by the customer. This is usually done by the Order Department or Contracts Department. Even when a customer's order is accompanied by a complete specification, there is usually much more technical information required in the way of formulae instructions or drawings, which have to be prepared. This is given on the documents described in chapter 3, p. 330. In most cases, of course, from shoes to ships and toys to telephones, this involves instructions for the manufacture of individual components, and for their assembly. The manufacturing order for the whole product, and the kind of information it gives, varies widely according to the product and industry, and it would be of limited interest to describe a specific case, but in batch production at least, one component is very like another so far as arranging for its production is concerned. Material for it must be drawn from stores, it is subjected to one or more operations, delivered into a component or finished part stores, and is subsequently reissued with others for assembly. It will be sufficient therefore if we understand the principles and procedure for putting previously prepared plans into operation as they apply to a component, knowing that they will apply to subassemblies and final assemblies by treating these as a unit.

Production documents

Figure 3.5.13 shows in the simplest form the order routine and documents used for production of a component. Information is required to authorise and record:

The movement of material from stores to a production point.
The identity of material as it is processed.
The preparation of machine and/or tools in readiness for work to be done.
Actual start of work, where and when.
The time allowed and actually taken to do the work.
Date when completed, and quantity good and scrapped.

In addition to the Production Engineers' and Production Planning Departments, this information is needed by some or all of the following departments:

The manufacturing department concerned—Foreman or shop planner or progress clerk and time clerk.
The Inspector in the department.
Stores Department—material and finished.
Wages Department.
Accounts Department or Cost Office.

The following documents are required, at least:

Process layout (master route card or operation instruction) describing the method of production: for each component.
Indentity label: for each part.
Material release note (requisition) for obtaining material: for each part.
Job card (time card)—describing and authorising operation: one for each operation.

Fig. 3.5.13
Documents
for production
planning

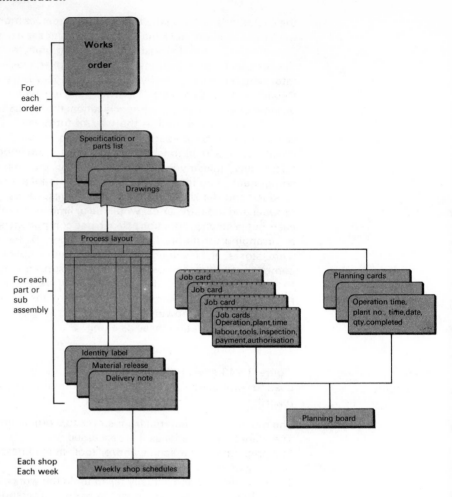

Planning card (move note or delivery note), for planning and progress information (the job card can sometimes be used): one for each operation.
Cost card, for calculating or recording cost (standard or actual): one for each part.

In many systems in operation more documents than this are in use, particularly for each operation, and while this may be justified in certain cases, the same results can usually be obtained with a smaller number. Certainly supervision must be better and the work and documents must be dealt with more quickly after operations are completed, but this is a strong argument in favour of the smaller number of documents. It cannot be too strongly emphasised that paperwork and the appearance of paperwork must be kept to a minimum in an organisation, and on the shop floor especially. It is disliked by operators and foremen alike. As far as possible all writing and paperwork of any kind should be done in offices by trained personnel and not on the shop floor by operators at the machine or bench.

This is one of the two compelling reasons for the development and widespread use of preprinted documents. The other is that they reduce to an absolute minimum the risk of errors due to transcription and recording of information. By preprinted documents is meant production planning documents which are prepared, and bear, in printed or some variety of duplicated form, all information pertaining to a job or operation which is known before it is issued (e.g. job number, drawing number, tools required, etc.). There are two principal forms, one using a special carbon impression on chromo-surface (or ordinary) paper as a master, and the other using a stencil. Both have their advantages and adherents. In some cases they can make a substantial reduction in the amount of clerical work and labour required in the works.

Illustration (Appendix)

Since generalities are not very helpful when studying planning in action, or devising procedures for the use of the documents involved, a specimen set of instructions and of all documents used is given as an Appendix to this chapter (see page 447). It covers the use of preprinted documents, but these are not essential, and only the instructions dealing with the operation of preprinting would be affected if handwritten documents were used; more information, of course, would have to be written in the shops. The instructions describe in detail how each document is used for authorising work to commence, recording work done and when, and the time taken and hence payment to be made. It is emphasised again though this particular set of documents was obviously prepared for an engineeering factory, the same documents of substantially the same design can be used in any factory making piece parts.

Documents for each part (or operation) should be sent to the department concerned with the weekly (or daily) schedule on which they are listed. A bundle of documents can, of course, constitute a schedule, but there is a risk of loss or misplacement which makes this inadvisable. Schedules should be sent to departments in time for the latter to make their own plans with ancillary departments, e.g. material and tool stores, so that everything is ready when the operator requires it.

Availability of tools, etc.

The availability of tools, or their equivalent, formers, templates, etc., is frequently a problem in factories on job or batch production, particularly when these have to be manufactured specially for each order. When the tools have already been made previously, the problem is one of getting information to the tool stores in time for them to have the tools ready when they are required by the operators. In this case it is advisable for the tool stores to be supplied with a daily or weekly schedule, or worksheet, as far in advance as it is necessary for them to prepare tools. If possible this should be limited to one day, and the schedule can then be given to the tool stores by the planning clerk in the shop concerned. The tool stores are then able to prepare the kit of tools, including drawings or other instructions, for each job, ready to be handed to the operator immediately it is asked for. When new tools have to be made for a job a suitable routine procedure must be worked out to ensure that tools are available when they are required. This procedure must be adhered to strictly in practice; there is often a tendency to allow such procedures, which involve ancillary departments like the toolroom, to go by default.

Although the procedure has been covered in the instructions given in the Appendix to this chapter, it is a problem peculiar to itself, and the following additional notes may be helpful.

The drawing office or whatever the technical department is termed, must discuss tooling and special manufacturing methods with the Production Engineers during the design stage to enable special measures or tools which will take an unusually long time to produce, to be dealt with. A copy of the works order or part list, with any drawings and other technical information, is sent to the Planning Engineers, who enter on it the date when tools must be ready and send it on to the Production Engineers. The latter prepare process and operation layouts, and decide what tools are required, sending a list of the tools, or the documents for each tool, whichever is more convenient to the Planning Engineers. The Production Engineers should then record all drawings which have to be prepared and the date by which they have to be completed, in order to enable tools to be prepared for when they are required. The Planning Engineers plan and schedule and progress the production of tools in the same way as they do production, including them on the normal production schedules when they are made or dealt with at all in production departments, to ensure that they receive the same attention as other work (they are one-offs, and production departments are very inclined to neglect one-offs and special work). If tool production is left entirely to the toolroom and not controlled by the Planning Department, there are bound to be instances when tools are not ready when they are required, particularly when plans are revised, or jobs brought forward, as they must be at times.

Unless jobs are planned to individual machines by the Production Planning Department centrally, departmental schedules must be broken down into machine or operator loads in the Department Foreman's office or shop planning office. The same technique is used as already explained for departmental planning (p. 378), but more use is likely to be made of load boards. The one chosen will depend on the nature of the work and the complexity of operations. A board which helps to accumulate and reveal the load on a machine or operator, and when jobs are due to start and finish, is more useful. The move note (Fig. 3.5.43) has been designed so that it can be used in this way.

Production engineering, or process planning

The old type of foreman is apt to think that the appointment of a production engineer, process engineer, or chemist, reduces his usefulness, his value to the company, or his status. It does nothing of the kind, of course. It is true that, before the development of production engineering, and the use of chemists in the works as well as in the analytical laboratory, the Works Manager and his foreman supplied the production knowhow and decided how a job should be done. But it is now recognised that the training and supervising of persons is a much more complex job than it once was, and to relieve a foreman of a large amount of administrative work makes a higher general performance possible and his job more valuable, not less. It is essential to separate planning from doing, administration from execution.

When a new material is developed, or a new product designed, the method of production is obviously either known or worked out. But from then onwards all is change. Better methods of production are being discovered continually. Furthermore, in many factories, particularly those engaged in engineering, the detailed method of production for each part to be manufactured, the machines to be used and equipment required, is decided subsequent to design. The task of deciding the best method of production, of saying how a job shall be produced, and of finding new and better ways of doing so, should be the responsibility of a *Methods or Production Engineering Department*. In a company where the technical knowledge is supplied by chemists, production methods would be the responsibility of the works laboratory.

In deciding the most practical and economical way of doing a job, the production engineer or chemist must have regard for the costs of production, and therefore for the time to do the job. He must have some say also in new tools or equipment required. These are the four divisions into which the activities of the production or methods engineer usually fall—that is to say, method study, work measurement, tool or equipment design, and shop and factory layout.

These four aspects all call for close collaboration with the Technical and Works Departments. The design of jigs and tools might be thought to be a logical development of the Design or Drawing Office work and in some companies it is done in the Drawing Office. But it cannot be effectively developed without detailed study of methods and work being done in the factory, and, as will be shown later, this study forms the basis of standards for time, and hence for payment by results, production planning and costs. This study work called for a specialised technique and training quite different from Drawing Office work. The outlook required is different too. It is more successful in practice, therefore, if it is recognised as a separate activity, and combined with the design of tools and equipment. To avoid it becoming too remote from or independent of the Drawing Office, Design Department or Technical Department, new drawings, designs or technical developments should always be referred to, and discussed with, the Production Engineers before final issue.

The development of production engineering as a special skill and the extensive use of the specially designed tools and equipment have contributed largely to the very much greater output per man-hour in the USA than in this country. There is no doubt that it is through such development, adding horsepower to manpower, and taking out the manual effort from jobs, that the way lies to reduce manpower requirements:

> The records of the United States and the United Kingdom have demonstrated that over a period of many years productivity in industry bears an important relationship to the amount of energy which is available per employee. In the USA the figure is approximately twice that in the UK. This fact, in our opinion, accounts in large measure for the greater output per man-hour in many industries in the US. (First Report of the Anglo-American Council on Productivity.)

Because Production Engineers tend to get machine- or gadget-minded there is a danger that they will forget or neglect the human factor. Men should not be made into robots. The foremen may have something to say if the division of labour, for example, is carried too far, or if new methods are forced on them without consultation. Continued and close cooperation between the production engineers and works departments is absolutely essential.

Functions

Broadly, then, the function of the Production Engineering or Methods Department is to determine, in collaboration with the Design and Works Departments, the most effective, economical and suitable methods of production, to lay down standards for material and time, and to design special tools and equipment required.

The following can be taken as typical of the responsibilities of the head of the Department:

1. Scientifically investigate processes and operations in order to:
   (a) establish the correct way of carrying out processes and of performing operations;
   (b) eliminate unnecessary and ineffectual operations;
   (c) reduce operator's fatigue to a minimum.
2. Obtain or if necessary prepare drawings for all jigs, tools and inspection equipment.
3. Carry out studies to determine the amount of work involved in operations.
4. Establish standard times, which, when used as a wage incentive, will enable an average qualified operator, working well within his or her capacity, to earn at least the standard amount of bonus agreed between the operators and management, including an appropriate allowance for rest and fatigue.
5. Collect, collate and file data relating to operation times to enable standard times to be rapidly and easily prepared.
6. Investigate and report when required on all forms of excess cost.
7. Establish and cultivate mutual confidence between the department's staff and supervisors and operators.
8. Adhere to the Company's personnel policy and see that subordinates do so.
9. Train staff in the effective performance of their duties.
10. Keep abreast of modern developments in manufacturing methods of all kinds, but particularly where related to the manufacture of the Company's products. In particular, recommend to the management the purchase of modern or improved designs of machines which will improve production or reduce costs.

Work study

Man has always been interested in better or easier ways of doing things since he first thought of the wheel and cart to help him carry loads. The present industrial civilisation is the result of finding easier and quicker ways of doing work. Until a comparatively few years ago, however, man mainly concentrated on designing equipment and mechanism to save hard work. It is only in recent years that men, chiefly engineers, have studied the ways men do the jobs that men, and not machines, must do. F. W. Taylor, who established and popularised the scientific approach to this matter, began his studies into better methods of doing work in the Midvale Steel Works in the 1880s. Taylor was appointed, at an early age of twenty-four or so, chargehand of the lathe operators in the factory. He soon realised the men were not giving an output that he knew was reasonable and easily attainable, and at first he had to use the disciplinary methods customary in those days (and for many years since). He discovered, however (and Taylor was a searcher for facts and reasons), that the difficulty and disagreements generally encountered lay in different ideas, rather abstract ideas, which everyone had of what constituted a 'fair day's work'. No one really knew what did constitute a fair day's work. He realised that if it were possible to find a way of measuring this abstract value in terms which had a basis in fact and could be understood, then most of the bitterness and mistrust would be eliminated. He determined to find a way, and adopted the scientific approach to the problem. He began a series of carefully controlled and recorded experiments on lathes, and started on his career of work study and scientific management:

> Taylor started with an individual worker at a lathe, started, as the trained research worker starts, to find out all about it, to observe what he was doing and leaving undone, to analyse and to measure every factor in his task which could be made susceptible to measurement. In short, he began to build up a 'science' of cutting metals on a lathe. Gradually he isolated the various elements and set to work to improve the factors which made for high performance, to eliminate causes of delay and interruption, to reduce the craft of the tradesman to precise and detailed written instructions.[1]

In addition to discovering exactly what the work content of a job on the lathe was, he discovered that there were certain factors which affected total output. The method adopted by different operators for doing the same job varied—there was no one best way—and operators lost a good deal of time experimenting and trying out various ways themselves. In addition, planning of work and flow of material was uncertain, and caused a good deal of waste of time. Both these factors are management's problems; they are in fact, the major part of management's administrative task.

It is a long time since Taylor made this approach to the study of the work content of a job and of factors affecting it, and today there can be no doubt that the scientific approach and the establishment of the one best way under correct conditions is essential to obtain a measure that is factual and will be accepted by the operators concerned of what constitutes a 'fair day's work'.

Analysis of operations

It is possible to say with reasonable accuracy exactly how many parts an automatic machine will produce per hour, the designer or machine-setter can state precisely the rate of output of, e.g. a cigarette-making machine, an automatic machine producing screws, a printing machine, or an automatic loom on a given weave. But how many articles will be produced in a day or a week in a given factory; how many looms or automatic screw machines can an operator look after, and how many cigarettes can be made by hand per hour, chocolates wrapped, orders packed, or customers served in a department store? You will notice that the question is, how many *can be,* not how many are. The answer to these questions can only be obtained with any degree of accuracy by studying the work being done, at the time it is done, the effort required and the skill of the operators, and including in the study the conditions under which it is or may be done, and any delays that may occur. It is not sufficient to take an average of past performance, to ask the operator or the Foreman, or to take a spot check. That may tell us how many are being done, but it will not tell us how many can be done. Only *work study* can do that.

[1] Urwick and Brech, *The Making of Scientific Management*, vol. 1, p. 30.

Furthermore, there are few methods of doing jobs which cannot be improved on, however much they have been developed and however well they are being done today. New materials, new techniques, new equipment are being developed continually. Filling powder by scoop or shute was a slow as well as a dusty job until someone studying the dust problems remembered that fluids are filled by vacuum; insulation materials were cut by hand with scissors until someone studying how to increase production remembered how printers cut paper and cardboard to shape. Unexpected, and often substantial, improvements in output can frequently be obtained by objectively studying the way work is done with the aim of finding out what is the best and quickest way to do it. It applies equally as well in the offices as in the works.

Gilbreth, the pioneer of *motion study*, who devoted the greater part of his career to the search for 'the one best way to do work', was able quite early in his search to eliminate unnecessary movement and effort from bricklaying in the USA, and obtained outputs, without undue fatigue, which skilled brick-layers in England consider impossible nearly fifty years later:[1]

> Even in his very early days the results that Gilbreth achieved were remarkable. Thus, for instance, the work of bricklaying was so simplified that the eighteen motions formerly thought necessary to place a brick were reduced to four or five, and, indeed, in one case, to two. Those which remained were made as simple and effective as thorough study could make them. The final result was that Gilbreth's men, who had formerly worked to their limit to lay 1 000 bricks per day, were able, after a short period of instruction, to reach a daily output of 2 700.

The daily approved output in England today is somewhere between 400 and 800.

Terminology

There has been a considerable lack of uniformity in terminology used in the field of work study and this has led to much misunderstanding. To avoid this it is necessary to define certain of the more frequently used terms. The following are definitions of terms as used and understood by authoritative workers in the field; they accord closely with the British Standard *Glossary of Terms in Work Study* (BS 3138: 1969):

Work study. Work study is a tool or technique of management involving the analytical study of a job or operation for one or both of the following purposes:

(*a*) the determination of what exactly has to be done; what are the optimum conditions—methods, layout, batch size and equipment, and what cause of ineffective work can be removed;

(*b*) the measurement of the work content of the job for use in planning, costing, wage payment (incentive) and control.

Work study is defined in BS 3138 as:

> A management service based on those techniques, particularly method study and work measurement, which are used in the examination of human work in all its contexts, and which lead to the systematic investigation of all the resources and factors which affect the efficiency and economy of the situation being reviewed, in order to effect improvement.

[1] Urwick and Brech, *op cit.*, vol. 1, p. 138. See also the historical Appendix to Part One of this volume, page 132.

Method study. The systematic recording and critical examination of the factors and resources involved in existing and proposed ways of doing work, as a means of developing and applying easier and more effective methods and reducing costs.

Work measurement. The application of techniques designed to establish the time for a qualified worker to carry out a specified job at a defined level of performance.

Time study. A work measurement technique for recording the times and rates of working for the elements of a specified job carried out under specified conditions, and for analysing the data so as to determine the time necessary for carrying out the job at a defined level of performance.

Rate fixing. Rate fixing is a term used for the rougher approximate or workshop method of setting a time or piece-rate for a job. It aims at setting a task or rate for a job as it is currently being performed with only an approximate allowance for ignorance to cover all factors likely to affect the actual time (including delays which should be prevented from occurring).

Rating. A method of assessing a worker's rate of working relative to the observer's concept of the rate corresponding to *standard* rating. The observer may take into account, separately or in combination, one or more factors necessary to the carrying out of the job, such as speed of movement, effort, dexterity, consistency.

Rating scales. The series of numerical indices given to various rates of working. The scale is linear. The three most commonly used scales start at zero and take 80, 100 and 133 respectively as the numerical value of standard rating. The British Standard recommended scale is the 0–100, where 0 corresponds to no activity and 100 is *standard* rating.

Standard performance. The rate of output which qualified workers will naturally achieve without over-exertion as an average over the working day or shift provided they adhere to the specified method and provided they are motivated to apply themselves to their work.

Standard rating. The rating corresponding to the average rate at which qualified workers will naturally work at a job, provided they adhere to the specified method and provided they are motivated to apply themselves to their work. If the standard rating is maintained and the appropriate relaxation is taken, a worker will achieve standard performance over the working day or shift.

Standard time. The total time in which a job should be completed at standard performance, i.e. work content (total), delay contingency allowance, unoccupied time and interference time, where applicable.

Job evaluation. A generic term covering methods of determining the relative worth of jobs.

Merit rating. Systematic and as far as possible objective, relative assessment of the behaviour, quality or value of employees by an analysis of classified characteristics, e.g. reliability, versatility, etc.

The need for work study

If you ask any Production Supervisor to list his six greatest problems at any point in time, it is probable that his list will include some or all of the following:

Production bottlenecks—usually specific ones.
Availability of tools.
Availability of materials.
Work flow within his department.
Condition of the machines or equipment.
Balancing work load between sections.
Availability of the right calibre of labour to do his 'special' type of work.

In each of the above problem areas one or other of the various techniques covered by the term 'work study' will be able to help a supervisor ease, if not solve, his problems.

In the years just after the Second World War, work study was known, understood and practised by relatively few 'enlightened' managements. The years since that time have seen an evergrowing acceptance and widespread practice of work study in all its facets. Most manufacturing companies employing over 100 or so direct operators now have a work study section. This does not mean however, that all work has been studied and the need for work study will decrease; in fact with the constant change in products and production techniques available and the ever present need to make the greatest possible use of available resources, work study is as important now as it ever was.

There are two main branches of work study, these are method study and work measurement. The BS 3138 definition of these terms is given above, but they can briefly be defined thus:

Method study answers the questions: What? How? Where? Who? Why?
Work measurement answers the questions: How long? and hence, When?

These are simplified definitions, but they serve to clarify the difference between the two. Thus we see that work study provides the basic data which management must have in order to plan ahead, load its resources, organise production, cost the activities, and if appropriate, provide the basis for a realistic payment by results system.

Benefits

We can now return to our supervisor and his problems. How can work study help?

Production bottlenecks. A 'production study' of the problem job or section will enable an overall review and diagnosis to be made to establish what is wrong and why. This may focus attention on specific areas as those below.

Availability of tools and materials. Method analysis of a job at the planning stage will show how the job is done and therefore what tools will be required, the feed-back of work measurement data will enable production control to determine when these tools and the raw materials will be required.

Work flow. One of method study's basic techniques is the study of the flow of materials or components. Analysis of this information and, where possible, the elimination or reduction of movement seldom fails to find some improvement that can be made.

Conditions of machines. While work study of itself cannot improve a machine tool or other piece of equipment, analysis of the operations performed on it when compared with the same operations performed on a similar machine in good condition, reveals the cost of operating substandard equipment. This usually leads to justification of appropriate remedial action: repair, overhaul or even a new machine.

Work load balance. By combining method study and work measurement the work content of a series of grouped operations can be ascertained. Analysis of this information will usually show where simplification, combination or redistribution of work will enable each operation to carry the same work content and thus arrive at a balanced work load.

The right labour. Most Supervisors are convinced that the work undertaken in their shop is different from any other and requires special skills and long training. But many such jobs when subjected to detail method study can be simplified and taught much more rapidly than many supervisors would expect. Gilbreth's experience with the bricklayers was quoted at the beginning of this chapter, this approach to the training of operators has been developed into a field of its own—*skills analysis and systematic operator training.*

Work study can therefore help the Production Supervisor to solve or ease many of his day to day problems; thus there is a present and continuing need for work study in all its aspects at shop supervisor level. The need for work study does not however stop at the shop floor. Work study can and does provide the means to improve the practice of management throughout the organisation. The following list shows where various aspects of work study can help in many aspects of management concern:

Cost reduction. By analysis of method and materials, it can lead to a reduction in the content of both in the final product, whether directly (i.e. direct labour and materials) or indirectly in the use of indirect labour, materials or services, or reduction in levels of stock and work in progress.

Increased output. This is not always synonymous with cost reduction. In a situation where increased output, albeit at slightly increased unit cost, can lead to increased total profit, work study can show the least cost by way of achieving the desired result.

Standardisation. Standardisation and simplification of components at the design stage by the use of value engineering can, in addition to the benefits listed above of cost and work in progress reduction, also improve the product's acceptability to the customer and thus secure repeat business.

Time standards. The establishment of accurate time standards, through systematic work measurement, provides management with its most universal tool. Time is the basic measurement for—estimating, planning, scheduling, performance measurement, incentive, and costing. These aspects of management action can only be as accurate as the information they use.

Productivity. Without trying to define productivity at this point (see chapter 7 below and Part One, page 32) 'productivity improvement' is a two word summary of both the need for and the aims of work study. By whatever technique it is achieved increased productivity means increasing the ratio of value of goods or services supplied to total resources employed in supplying them, and this is the sphere of activity called Work Study.

Method study

Method study is the first stage of work study. It aims, by systematic analysis of existing and proposed methods of performing work, to find the most effective and economical way of performing a task. The techniques are not only of benefit to manufacturing industry, they have been successfully applied to such varied operations as retail trade, building, catering, hospital work and farming. In manufacturing industry method study should always be applied before a new design is put into production. In this way the most economic production is established from the start and before ineffective methods have had time to become a habit. The most effective time to apply work study is at the drawing board stage; in this way designs can be formalised which are best suited to the facilities available to produce them. This approach is the basis of 'value engineering'.

The techniques involved in method study for an existing job, or a product at the design stage, are basically:

- Select and define the job to be studied.
- Observe and record the existing or suggested method.
- Analyse critically.
- Develop a new method.
- Install the new method and train the operator.
- Maintain the new method.

Select and define

A method investigation may be requested for any number of reasons but it is essential for the study man to know why the study has been requested; if the objective is to reduce cost, a new method that reduces time but uses very expensive equipment may not be acceptable. However in a different situation reduction of operation time to remove a bottleneck may justify an increase in the cost of that specific operation.

It is also important to set defined limits to the investigation.

Method study investigations frequently reveal scope for savings in areas outside the immediate objective; the temptation to be immediately side-tracked must be resisted but any areas indicating scope for substantial improvement should be noted and made the subject of a separate study.

The manager requesting the study should also define the scope of the investigation in terms of the required end result; for example, a batch production shop is required to produce 100 units per week of a certain product.

To achieve this, one section is having to work excessive overtime to keep pace with the rest of the department. The investigation is to reduce the work content of the bottleneck operation to eliminate the overtime requirement. Under these conditions the method study man who comes up with a solution that enables 2 500 units a week to be produced on this one operation but requires £10 000 worth of equipment to do it, is unlikely to win any medals.

Observe and record   Observation is usually by eye and recording is usually by hand using and 'shorthand' in the form of symbols for each type of activity.[1] The most commonly used are those embodied in BS 3138 which are shown below:

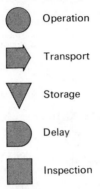

Operation

Transport

Storage

Delay

Inspection

These symbols together with short explanations are used to form a 'process chart' which is *a means of visualising a process for the purpose of improving it.* A typical example of a material flow process chart for an old and revised method is shown in Fig. 3.5.14. It will be noticed that the symbol for *delay* or *temporary storage* used in the example Fig. 3.5.14 is not the same as that shown above and recommended in B.S.3138. Some practitioners prefer the double triangle symbol as the D when written quickly can be mistaken for an O.

It is important for the studyman to be clear in his recording to chart the movement of one only of the following in any one chart:

Operator
Machine
Material

Mixing these will hinder the subsequent analysis. There are several charting techniques available to the work study practitioner, e.g.

String diagrams—for recording distance moved (see Figs. 3.5.15 and 16).
Two handed process charts—for recording movement of each hand.
Multiple activity charts—for recording the inter-relation of two or more men or machines.

These and others will be detailed in any textbook on Work Study. It is not the aim of this book to provide a textbook for work study students but to provide managers and students of management a quick view of the tools of the trade and their uses.

[1] Other methods of recording and charting are detailed in the ILO handbook: *Introduction to Work Study, 1969.*

Fig. 3.5.14
Material process
chart. Cutting,
weighing and
packing tobacco

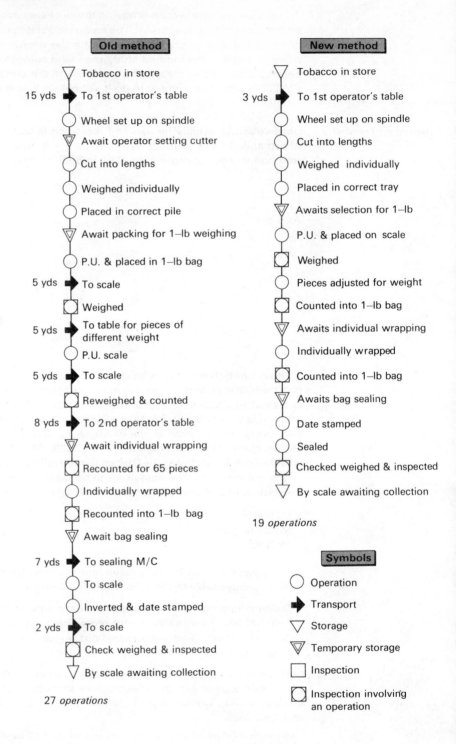

Old method		New method
▽ Tobacco in store		▽ Tobacco in store
15 yds ➤ To 1st operator's table	3 yds ➤	To 1st operator's table
◯ Wheel set up on spindle		◯ Wheel set up on spindle
▽ Await operator setting cutter		◯ Cut into lengths
◯ Cut into lengths		◯ Weighed individually
◯ Weighed individually		◯ Placed in correct tray
◯ Placed in correct pile		▽ Awaits selection for 1–lb
▽ Await packing for 1–lb weighing		◯ P.U. & placed on scale
◯ P.U. & placed in 1–lb bag		◻ Weighed
5 yds ➤ To scale		◯ Pieces adjusted for weight
◻ Weighed		◯ Counted into 1–lb bag
5 yds ➤ To table for pieces of different weight		▽ Awaits individual wrapping
◯ P.U. scale		◯ Individually wrapped
5 yds ➤ To scale		◯ Counted into 1–lb bag
◻ Reweighed & counted		▽ Awaits bag sealing
8 yds ➤ To 2nd operator's table		◯ Date stamped
▽ Await individual wrapping		◯ Sealed
◻ Recounted for 65 pieces		◻ Checked weighed & inspected
◯ Individually wrapped		▽ By scale awaiting collection
◻ Recounted into 1–lb bag		
▽ Await bag sealing		*19 operations*
7 yds ➤ To sealing M/C		
◯ To scale		**Symbols**
◯ Inverted & date stamped		◯ Operation
2 yds ➤ To scale		➤ Transport
◻ Check weighed & inspected		▽ Storage
▽ By scale awaiting collection		▽ Temporary storage
		◻ Inspection
27 operations		◻ Inspection involving an operation

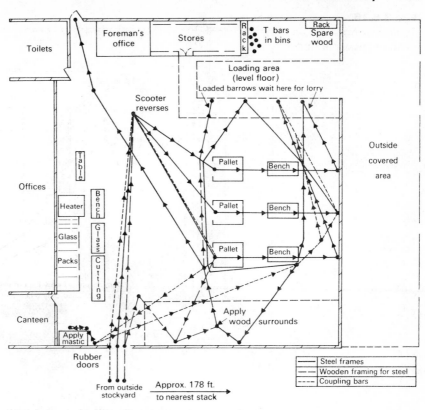

Toilets

Foreman's office

Stores

R a c k

T bars in bins

Rack Spare wood

Loading area
(level floor)
Loaded barrows wait here for lorry

Scooter reverses

Outside
covered
area

Offices

Table

Heater

Bench Glass Cutting

Glass

Packs

Pallet   Bench

Pallet   Bench

Pallet   Bench

Canteen

Apply
mastic

Apply wood surrounds

Rubber doors

From outside
stockyard

Approx. 178 ft.
to nearest stack

	Steel frames
	Wooden framing for steel
	Coupling bars

Fig. 3.5.15
Illustration of
typical string
diagram, old method.
Diagram shows
paths of movement
of steel frames,
wood surrounds
and coupling bars

The purpose of work study is to *analyse* the old method and *develop* an improved method.

In analysing the present method, a well constructed chart shows its value, the operations incurring expense can be separated from those adding value.

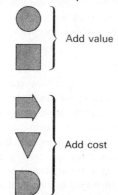

Add value

Add cost

Elimination or reduction of the cost adding elements and simplification of the value adding elements will usually be the objective in developing a new method. During this phase of the study the following questions must be examined and answered. What is done and when? Who does it? Where is it done? How and why? Answers should yield the first clues to improving the method.

Fig. 3.5.16
Typical string
diagram, new method

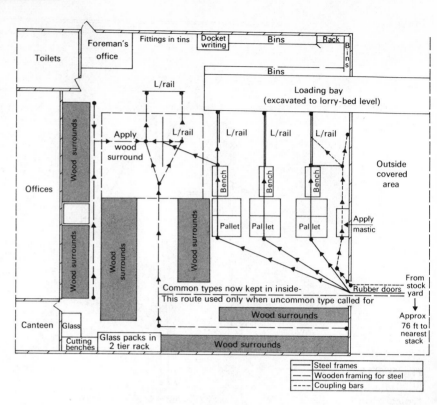

During the whole development phase it is important to take the operators and their supervisors along with the developing method and obtain their ideas and suggestions. A new method developed in isolation has less chance of succeeding than one developed with the cooperation of the people who will have to perform and supervise it. It is useful to have an informal working party through which the work study engineer can meet the representatives of operators and supervisors, to explain and discuss what is involved.[1]

*Installing a
new method*

Installing a new method is an exercise in human relations; the majority of people are resistant to change, experience has shown that it is always wise to conduct some systematic training whenever a change in method is introduced. Depending on individual circumstances and plant custom, this training may be carried out by the work study man, the supervisor or a training officer and may be done in the department where the operator usually works, or in a separate section away from the production shop. This 'off the job' training is particularly valuable when the process requires the operator to keep pace with others, this situation may not exist until the operator has had considerable practice. When the operator is fully conversant with the revised method, the appropriate time standard should then be set (for methods of setting time standards, see Work Measurement, p.409).

[1] This is the context where major considerations of human relations, consultation and cooperation arise: these are fully studied in Part Four (see page 621).

Maintain

It is not sufficient to complete a method investigation and then leave the operator and the shop supervisor to their own devices. We must ensure that the method and time are adhered·to and that old habits are completely forgotten. To this end an operation layout or process specification is compiled which lays down the method in as much detail as is required to enable the operator or a subsequent operator to follow the correct method. It should detail any special tools, jigs or fixtures that will be required and also contain as much information about what is and what is not in the job concerned, to enable subsequent queries to be answered should the performance compared with the standard drift appreciably. This information is as necessary in a day

Fig. 3.5.17
Operation layout

Layout No	Operation No		Operation layout					Part	No
1	2							Body	X X X X

Drg No	Material	Batch qy	Dept	M/C or group	Grade of labour	Operation		
1072/1	GM CSTG		CAPST	1	MF2	Bore face & tap		

No	Operation	Station	Travel	Cuts	Feed	R.P.M.	Jigs and tools
1	Chuck feed to stop & true	T1			H80		3 jaw chuck & stop
2	Rough & finish face	RP	·64	2	H120	750	H81
3	Rough bore for $1\frac{1}{2}$ " gas	T2	·75	1	A80	465	FS cutter
4	Finish ditto	T3	·87	1	H120	"	E91
5	Chamfer for tap	T4	·14	1	"	"	FS cutter
6	Tap $1\frac{1}{2}$ "	T5	·87			74	$1\frac{1}{2}$" taper gas tap NH STD

Gauging procedure			*Note*: Spigot in chuck to suit bore in 1st end to prevent crushing
Detail	Guage	Frequ	
$1\frac{1}{2}$" thrd	$1\frac{1}{2}$" taper gas N :	1/10	
			Authorised
			Time allowed
			Set-up	Per 100
Prepared by	Date		
	30·8·45	Date 30·8·74	2·00	5·85
			Hours	Hours

rate shop as it is in a piecework one, for production control and costing can only be based on factual time standards. Figures 3.5.17 and 3.5.18 show examples respectively of an operation layout and a process specification.

Fig. 3.5.18
Process specification

PROCESS SPECIFICATION
Welding Shop—Profile Cutter

1. Process
This specification covers gas cutting in the Welding Department procuring plate (assisted by crane operators where necessary), the disposal of 'off-cuts' and scrap, but not the disposal of waste and slag from under the profile machines.

2. Operation
(i) Procure raw material (plate) from stock area and position on work table.
(ii) Procure template.
(iii) Position template to ensure most economical use of material.
(iv) Position burners to give correct spacing of component to be cut.
(v) Cut profile in accordance with maker's recommended procedure.
(vi) Check first off with inspector.
(vii) Stamp or otherwise mark components for identification.
(viii) Chip off slag from component.
(ix) Book on and off job.

3. Time standards
The standard (or allowed) time covers all the operations included in this specification. If for any reason an additional operation appears necessary it must be reported to the foreman. If the foreman agrees the necessity of the additional operation he will contact the Time Study department for either a revised time or a special allowance. Allowances will not be made for additional work not reported at the time.

Operators must book off immediately a job is completed and on to the next job at the same time. Waiting time if necessary must be booked to the appropriate cause.

Training for
work study

The application of systematic work study is not feared by operators anything like as much as it was twenty to thirty years ago. This is because it is much more widely practised and therefore much better known—fear is usually of the unknown. Among many trade unions it is accepted to such an extent that they have their own work study experts. This acceptance has come about from a realisation that when correctly applied the results benefit their members as well as management. In enabling the operator to work more efficiently—not harder—and in revealing weaknesses in the management areas of material and tool supply, production control and scheduling, servicing and so on, the operator is able to spend more time on production work and hence, in a piecework situation, earn a higher wage.

The practice of work study involves constant contact with personnel at all levels in an industrial organisation—managers, supervisors, operators and trade union representatives. Consequently the work study practitioner must have a personality acceptable to all these groups. On the other hand he must be critical, taking nothing for granted without confirmation, and tactful; it requires a considerable degree of tact to get a skilled craftsman to accept that an outsider can devise a better way of doing the job he has been doing for years. In addition to the above personal qualities, the work study man will be required to work with figures and write reports, consequently he must have ability in numeracy and literacy.

It is desirable that the potential work study man should have some practical background experience of the type of industry concerned and this may be a formal trade apprenticeship or shop floor experience allied to a higher qualification such as National or Higher National Certification. The actual training in work study practice should be a combination of formal off-the-job training, preferably at an establishment away from the work environment, followed by guided application of the techniques under a trained practitioner. During the guided application phase of work measurement training, the trainee's work should not be used for setting time standards until his team leader or departmental head is satisfied that his work is both accurate and consistent. During the guided application the trainee should have specific projects to undertake which should, as far as possible, include elements of method study and work measurement.

Detailed recommendations for work study training from Assistant Practitioner to Team Leader are contained in *Training for Work Study Practice*, HMSO 1971, SBM/11/360359/2, a report prepared by the Joint Committee of Industrial Training Boards. Appendices to this report suggest job descriptions, syllabuses and supervised projects for this training. This report should be required reading for managers whose responsibility encompasses the work study function.

Work measurement

The need for standards of work content

If we can establish a standard measure of work or output independent of the type of work performed, then it will be possible to compare actual performance against this standard. This performance comparison may be made between individuals in one department, between departments or even between factories. We can also compare the actual work expended in producing a given article, with the standard or expected content, any difference between the two being a measure of the efficiency of converting raw material into product. So we have:

1. The standard cost (work content plus material content) which should be used per unit of product.
2. The excess cost, if any, above this standard.

Obtaining a measurement of the work content of all production jobs within the factory will enable production to be planned to a time table and also give (a) the number of units to be produced; (b) the time standard for each unit on each production facility; and (c) the performance of operators or machines against the standards. It will be possible to determine how long a job will take with the existing facilities, or conversely, what facilities will be required to ensure the product is completed in a given number of production hours.

Finally, a measurement of the work content of a job and the operator's performance against the standard will provide a sound basis for a payment by results incentive. The problem has always been, what is a fair day's work on which to base the standard? Method study fixes the method of performing a specific task, work measurement allied to that method, fixes the work content. Rate fixing, which was a means of arriving at an acceptable time by barter, usually took no specific account of:

The skill and experience of the operator other than his negotiating skill.
The speed, effort and attention during an observed performance if any.
The conditions under which the operation is carried out and the fatigue resulting from them.
The actual method adopted to perform the task.

The first two factors are taken account of by a rating factor which is a subjective judgment on the part of a trained observer. The third is covered by a relaxation allowance dependent on the job, requirements and conditions under which it is applied,[1] and the fourth is laid down by method study.

Measurement of work content is essential, if the following four functions are to be carried out with any degree of meaning:

● Management control, assessment of performance against standards.
● Production control—preplanning, resource loading, etc.
● Costing.
● Payment by results incentives.

Units of measurement

The practice of paying a pieceworker a price per piece completed was universal in the nineteenth century and continued well into the twentieth, although labour costing became more complicated as guaranteed base rates were established with a superimposed bonus price per piece. Measurement by units of price per piece are acceptable for piecework bonus schemes and costing, but it is not a useful measure for either management control, production control or resource loading. The only useful common unit is time, which is applied as a time per operation or as the reciprocal in units of production per hour. This latter form is more applicable in process industries where production performance can only be measured as a rate through all processes, e.g. 10 000 gallons of product X per day. Measurement of the standard output from process plant is usually relatively straightforward. In ideal circumstances it will be the design rate, or at worst a statistical analysis of actual throughputs under varying conditions. However, the determination of a standard of work output from that very variable machine, the human operator, is a different proposition.

There are a large number of work measurement techniques now available to suit varying conditions and situations most of which are derived at some stage from rated time sudy which is taken here as the base from which to develop the other methods.

Time study

The basis of time study is that an operation performed by a trained and competent operator is observed by a trained observer, each work element is

---

[1] See table of fatigue allowances, ILO *Handbook*, quoted above, (p. 403).

recorded and the actual time taken to perform each element is measured by stop watch and recorded against the element description; simultaneously the observer makes an assessment of the operator's performance in comparison with his concept of *standard performance*. This 'rating' is also recorded against each element so that after the study is completed the time for each element can be related to the standard performance.

Rating. It has been recognised for a long time that a man on incentive will work faster than a man paid a flat day-rate. Early experiments indicated that the value of this increase was about one-third. From this result the concept was born of standard performance as being that of the daywork operator producing sixty minutes' worth of work in one hour and the piecework operator producing (at 'incentive performance') one-third more, i.e. eighty minutes' worth of work in one hour. This led to rating scales that recognised two specific points one being one third more than the others, i.e. 60–80 or 100–133 and all times were related to the standard (or expected) time at daywork performance. However if we expect our operators to work at incentive performance there is no logic in setting a time standard that you expect to be bettered by about 30 per cent. The British Standard *Glossary of Terms in Work Study* (BSS 3138, 1969) defines standard time as 'the total time in which a job should be completed at standard performance, i.e. work content, contingency allowance for delay, unoccupied time and interference allowance, where applicable'. The rating corresponding to this performance level is given an arbitrary notation of 100 and the BS recommended rating scale is taken as 0–100.

Most companies in the UK now use the 0–100 rating scale although there are enough companies still using either the 60–80 or the 100–133 scales for it to be necessary when discussing time standards, to ensure that the same reference of standard performance is being used.

The ability to put a rating value on an observed performance can only be gained with training and practice and under no circumstances should untrained personnel be permitted to carry out time study on the shop floor without this training.

Timing. The standard measuring instrument for time study is the decimal stop watch, however there are two distinct approaches to timing, 'flyback' and 'continuous'. In *flyback* timing the watch is returned to zero at the end of each element, so each time recorded is the actual time taken for that element. *Continuous timing* leaves the watch running for the full duration of the study and the watch reading is recorded at the end of each element. This means that the difference between consecutive watch readings has to be taken to arrive at the elemental time taken. Flyback timing is used most widely but is particularly relevant for short repetitive cycle work, continuous timing is most commonly used where long non-repetitive operations are carried out. A sample study sheet for each type of time study is shown in Figs. 3.5.19 and 20.

A detailed description of procedure in making a time study, element description, break points between elements and so forth is not relevant here. The student of work measurement should refer to a textbook on the subject.[1] However, a brief description of the procedure by which actual time is converted to standard time taking into account rating, fatigue, contingency allowance is appropriate.

[1] E.g. ILO *Handbook*, or R. M. Currie, *Work Study*, Pitman, 1960.

Fig. 3.5.19
Work study
sheet:
flyback timing

		Time study sheet											

Time off _____ Total ineffective _____ Time study No _____
Time on _____ Total effective _____ Sheet No _____
Study time _____ Total recorded _____
(from separate watch)

Code & El No	Element description	R	Min	R	Min	R	Min	R	Min	R	Min	Sel't'd basic min and freq	Relaxation allowance
	Check time	Basic min		Basic min		Basic min		Basic min		Basic min			Elemental standard minutes
												Total B/f
												Elemental standard minutes C/f

Standard time. The time study will record: the workplace layout, the description of each element, and the time taken and rating against each. In addition facts relating to the operator, the equipment and so forth are recorded on a front sheet which forms part of the completed study (see Fig. 3.5.21).

From the information on the study sheet, the standard time is calculated as follows:

1. Convert actual time to basic time, i.e. time at standard performance (100), by multiplying the observed time by the observed rating and dividing by the standard rating:

$$\text{Basic time} = \frac{\text{observed time} \times \text{observed rating}}{\text{standard rating}}$$

e.g. Actual time 0·50 min.

Rating 90

$$\text{Basic time} \quad = \frac{0·50 \times 90}{100} = 0·45 \text{ min.}$$

2. Calculate the average basic time for each element.
3. Determine the appropriate relaxation allowance for each element.

This allowance is to compensate the operator not only for the amount of physical effort required to do the job, e.g. the lifting of a heavy weight, but also for such factors as eye strain, unnatural position, heat, fumes, noise and so on, and of course, man's natural needs of tea breaks and toilet. A typical table of fatigue allowances is shown in Fig. 3.5.22.

Fig. 3.5.20
Work study sheet: continuous timing

Time study sheet			

Operator

Job number

Operation number

Study number

Date

Observer

Sheet of sheets

Element	R.	W.R.	O.T.	B.T.	Element	R.	W.R.	O.T.	B.T.

Fig. 3.5.21
Time study
front sheet

Time study sheet

Sheet No   of   Study No:
Date: Observed by:
                                                         Calculated by:

Operator(s)name: Nos: Job No:
                                                  Drg.No:
Department: Part No:
Section or area: Operation No:

Location and / or set up description: Study finished: Total effective:

                                         Study started: Total inneffective:

                                         Total elapsed time: Total recorded:

                                              % error:

Operation description: Component description:

Jigs /fixtures /special tools: 0-100
                                              Rating   60- 80
                                                        100-133

Machine details:

Sketch of workplace /component:

Remarks:

Fig. 3.5.22
Typical table
of fatigue
allowances

Percent	Example of job
8–10	Light work Good conditions Operator seated
10–12½	Bench work with use of small hand tools Operator seated
12½–15	Hand press, small power press, spraying
15–17½	Medium power press Metal filing Free hand grinding
17½–20	Power riveting Some viewing Heavy presswork
20–25	Some foundry jobs Heavy welding Trucking heavy loads by hand

Very short cycle +2½%

4. Add the relaxation allowance to the average basic time for each element. If the allowance in the above instance totalled 15 per cent—
then 0·45 min + 15% = 0·516 min.
This is known as STANDARD TIME.

5. In some circumstances agreements have been made between management and trade unions that a standard performance should yield a given level of bonus, in which case a 'policy allowance' is added to give an 'allowed time'. This practice is to be discouraged as far as possible, as it defeats one of the main advantages of issuing a standard time. The standard time is that time which you expect the trained operator actually to achieve over the full working day, taking full account of relaxation needs and so forth, thus it gives the piecework operator a direct target figure, not one that he has to beat by so much per cent to earn bonus. It is also an immediately realistic figure for planning, estimating and production control purposes.

Contingency allowance. When the standard time has been calculated it is sometimes necessary to add a contingency allowance to cover occasional factors which are largely uncontrollable in their incidence. Tool wear in a machine shop, occasional waiting for an overhead crane in a heavy assembly shop, are two typical examples covered by a contingency allowance. If this allowance is greater than 5 per cent or so then steps must be taken by management to improve the situation; the allowance should only cover the residual items which would cost more to control than the benefits so obtained. The incidence of these factors can usually be determined from analysis of the whole series of studies taken in each department. Alternatively they may be determined by a sampling technique known as *activity sampling*, otherwise known as *ratio delay study*. This technique is also very useful as a means of determining the percentage of any activity taking place, particularly in group work, without the need to conduct a continuous study over all the operators in the group.

Activity
sampling

Activity sampling is a technique which makes use of the statistical relationship between:

the percentage of the total time for each activity under observation;
the allowable tolerance in the result;
the degree of confidence we can accept that the result is a true representation of the facts;
the number of observations taken in the sample.

Understanding of the statistical principles on which the technique is based is not necessary in order to be able to carry out a satisfactory study.[1]

Activity sampling has a number of distinct advantages and a few disadvantages when compared with time study:

Advantages
1. The number of man hours required to achieve the same accuracy of result is less.
2. One observer can cover many operators, machines or activities.
3. Observation period can span a number of weeks to cover any cyclical pattern without occupying excessive man hours of study time.
4. The study being less obtrusive than a time study, operators tend to relax to their normal behaviour patterns.
5. Trained time study observers are not required.
6. Results are not affected by interruptions.
7. No stop watch or other accurate timing device is required.

Disadvantages
1. It is unsuitable for short cycle repetitive operations.
2. Detail of operator's method is not possible, and therefore it is rarely possible to use the results for the prime determination of operation basic time.
3. Being a statistical method it may well be less understood by the operators.
4. Danger that observations may not be truly random.

Method. Having explained the purpose and technique of the study to all the personnel involved, the first task is to make a short pilot survey to determine:

(*a*) the factors to be recorded in order to provide the required information;
(*b*) the approximate percentage of total time in each activity;
(*c*) the time necessary to make one round of observations.

In addition it will be necessary for the observer to decide on:

(*d*) the acceptable tolerance of the answer;
(*e*) the degrees of confidence in the result.

From this information the number of observations necessary can be calculated:

---

[1] The basis of statistical sampling is given in M. J. Morony, *Facts from Figures*, Penguin Books 1956, ch. 10.

If N = number of observations required

P = percentage of the activity under study as a proportion of the total time

E = percentage error (tolerance) acceptable

K = a constant, dependent on the required confidence level.

For a 68 per cent level $K = 1$
a 95 per cent level $K = 4$
a 98 per cent level $K = 9$.

Then
$$N = \frac{KP(100 - P)}{E^2}.$$

This relationship can also be read direct from a nomograph (see Fig. 3.5.23).

For example if we take a simple case in which the pilot study shows a machine working about 70 per cent and not working 30 per cent with an acceptable error of 5 per cent at 95 per cent confidence:

$$N = \frac{4 \cdot 70(30)}{25} = 336 \text{ observations.}$$

The next step is to determine the duration of the study and the observation intervals. The duration of the study should cover a whole number of natural work cycles, for example a machine shop may clean machines on a Friday afternoon, or a despatch warehouse may have a quiet day on Monday. The average interval will be the number of working hours in the study duration divided by the number of observations. The minimum interval is the time for one circuit of the observation points and hence knowing these the maximum interval can be calculated.

The actual time intervals between observations are taken from a table of random numbers using all those that fall between the minimum and maximum determined above. At the end of the study the percentage of each activity is calculated from the number of observations of that activity occurring and the total number of observations. Taking the example above, if there were 336 observations and the machine was found to be working 245 times that would give 73 per cent working. The percentage error can then be recalculated from the formula:

$$336 = \frac{4 \times 73 \times 27}{E^2}$$

or

$$E = \sqrt{\frac{7860}{336}}$$

$$= \sqrt{23 \cdot 4} \quad \text{or} \quad \pm 4 \cdot 8 \text{ per cent.}$$

Thus we find that the true percentage activity lies between 68·2 and 77·8 per cent. However if the error is greater than the acceptable error more observations must be taken to reduce it.

Standard data. One valuable advantage of scientific work measurement over ordinary rate-fixing, in factories engaged on batch or jobbing production, i.e.

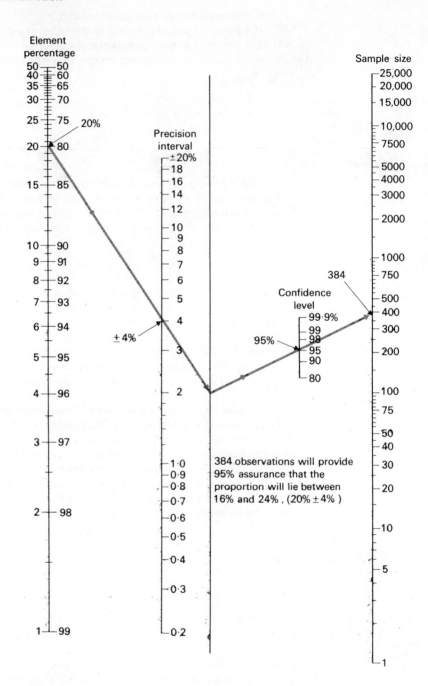

Fig. 3.5.23
A nomograph
for activity
sampling

384 observations will provide
95% assurance that the
proportion will lie between
16% and 24% , (20% ±4%)

where machines or operators are not continuously engaged on the same job, is that standard times can be established for operations or elements which are combined in different ways for different jobs. In such circumstances, quite a large staff of time study men are required if every job is to be studied whilst it is running, but if basic data for each likely operation is first established, then a much smaller staff is adequate for preparing standard times.

From a large range of studies of all types of work and operations, and for all operators, standard times for each element are recorded. From a study of these, with rechecks when necessary, one standard time is selected as an average or mean. Once the process or operations required are decided and laid down, the total standard time for a job can be built up by merely selecting and adding together the appropriate times for elements. To reduce clerical work, groups of elements which are frequently found in combination are summarised. Examples of this technique for machine operations are given in Figs. 3.5.24 and 25, overleaf.

It is frequently found that the time varies with certain factors, such as weight, size, shape and accuracy. Time can be saved in determining the time for each variation, and a valuable check on results made, by finding the factor which controls the variation in time and plotting against this factor the standard times from a few studies along the range of variation. If the correct factor has been found, the results will lie approximately along a straight line or regular curve. If they do not, either the factor is wrong, the studies inaccurate, or there are unknown variations occurring during the studies: see example in Fig. 3.5.26, page 422. Such curves also form a valuable means of averaging results and of checking the accuracy of results. A curve (or straight line) drawn through plotted results indicates the mean result and should be used for reading off standard times for values of the variable factor. Points which lie some way off the line are suspect, and should either be ignored or better still checked up.

Unfortunately this method is as yet little known or practised and those to whom it is new usually doubt whether it is practicable or even possible. The author, however, has found it completely successful, effective, and economical, and the method is included in the curriculum for training Work Study Engineers at the Department of Work Study and Staff Training of the Engineering Employers' Federation, Bristol, and is used by ICI[1] and other large companies.

Predetermined motion time systems (PMTS)

A number of approaches have been made to the problem of determining standard time values for all operations. The principle behind these approaches is to determine the basic motions from which all others are built up. Then determine the standard time value for each of these basic motions. With a time value for every movement it is theoretically possible to determine the standard time for any job regardless of its duration. However, due to the time taken to build up the time standard for each minute of work from basic methods, second and third order systems have been developed which identify commonly occurring motion patterns so that bigger units of time are used to build the standard. This does of course affect the accuracy of the overall result, but it is usual to apply the order of data applicable to the accuracy with which it is possible or practical to define the work.

[1] R. M. Currie, 'Development and scope of work study', *Proceedings of IME*, 168 no. 25 (1954).

Early work on PMTS was undertaken by Quick, Spear and Koeler in the USA between 1934 and 1938 and published in 1945. The system is known as 'Work Factor' and was obtained by time studies using stop watches reading in 1/1000th of a minute and cine cameras. The units of time in which each of the motions is measured are 1/10 000th of a minute.

There are three developed forms of work factor to reduce the time necessary to apply the technique:

● *Simplified work factor* combines certain of the elements and hence is quicker to apply.
● *Ready work factor* is a modified version of the simplified work factor; the time units are in milliminutes (1/1000th of a minute).
● *Abbreviated work factor* is the quickest to apply but loses some of the accuracy—within plus 12 per cent of times prepared using detailed work factor; the time units are in 5/1000th of a minute.

Fig. 3.5.24

Basic times for time standards:
Manipulative elements—No. 4 Herbert Capstan lathe

No.	Element	Selected Standard Time	Study number							
			1	2	3	4	5	6	7	8
1	Start machine	0·020	0·019	0·016	0·015	0·023	0·010	0·019	0·016	—
2	Stop machine	0·060	0·068	0·050	0·050	0·080	0·063	0·060	0·056	—
	Pick up and load:									
3	A. Simple location	0·150	0·106	0·073	0·184	0·176	0·161	0·153	0·165	0·133
4	B. Difficult location	0·250	0·365	0·209	0·291	0·250	0·327	0·233	0·223	0·300
5	Load bar	0·300	0·380	0·250	0·123	0·365	0·300	0·150	—	—
6	Feed bar to stop (including turret up)	0·300	0·364	0·253	0·460	0·360	0·154	0·300	0·232	0·310
	True up:									
7	A. Bar work	0·150	0·140	0·160	0·175	0·153	0·195	0·148	—	—
8	B. Chuck work	0·300	0·199	0·324	0·355	0·330	0·274	0·225	0·350	0·320
	Unload and put down:									
	A. from chuck:									
9	(i) Light work, easy to remove or finish unimportant	0·180	0·162	0·165	0·185	0·197	0·129	0·188	0·171	0·172
10	(ii) Heavy work, difficult to remove or easily damaged	0·260	0·206	0·308	0·273	0·219	0·262	0·290	0·315	0·358
11	B. from collet	0·070	0·059	0·059	0·069	0·064	0·100	0·078	0·056	0·087
	Tighten down:									
12	A. Small effort	0·140	0·117	0·147	0·185	0·111	0·140	0·190	0·157	0·137
13	B. Great effort	0·300	0·287	0·277	0·287	0·300	0·300	0·295	0·320	0·410
14	Turret up	0·070	0·061	0·066	0·067	0·062	0·068	0·065	0·079	0·096
15	Turret away to stop	0·065	0·058	0·066	0·062	0·056	0·064	0·064	0·056	0·048
16	Turret away	0·050	0·070	0·058	0·050	0·058	0·057	0·057	0·040	0·030
17	Index turret (away, index and up)	0·095	0·077	0·108	0·107	0·094	0·097	0·088	0·096	0·089
18	Index front tool post	0·095	0·096	0·096	0·070	0·084	0·145	0·083	0·078	0·080
19	Rear tool post up ⎫ Front tool post up ⎭	0·090	0·073	0·075	0·086	0·093	0·084	0·072	0·081	0·086

Fig. 3.5.25a

Groups of elements for time standards
No. 4 Herbert Capstan lathe

Constant elements	S.M.s	S.M.s	S.M.s	S.M.s	S.M.s	S.M.s	S.M.s	S.M.s
Start machine	0·020	0·020	0·020	0·020	0·020	0·020	0·020	0·020
Stop machine	0·060	0·060	0·060	0·060	0·060	0·060	0·060	0·060
Pick up and load								
A. Simple location	0·150	0·150	0·150	0·150	—	—	—	—
B. Difficult location	—	—	—	—	0·250	0·250	0·250	0·250
Tighten down								
A. Small effort	0·140	0·140	—	—	0·140	0·140	—	—
B. Great effort	—	—	0·300	0·300	—	—	0·300	0·300
Unload and put down								
A. Light work, easy to remove or finish unimportant	0·180	—	0·180	—	0·180	—	0·180	—
B. Heavy work, difficult to remove or easily damaged	—	0·260	—	0·260	—	0·260	—	0·260
Totals	0·550	0·630	0·710	0·790	0·650	0·730	0·810	0·890

Figure 3.5.25a can be summarised as shown in Fig. 3.5.25b.

Fig. 3.5.25b

Summary of manipulative elements

No. 4 Herbert Capstan lathe

Constant elements depending on type of article	Light work easy to remove or finish unimportant S.M.s	Heavy work difficult to remove or easily damaged S.M.s
Easy to locate, small effort to tighten	0·550	0·630
Easy to locate, great effort to tighten	0·710	0·790
Difficult to locate, small effort to tighten	0·650	0·730
Difficult to locate, great effort to tighten	0·810	0·890

There are a number of other PMT systems, but the one which is probably the most used, and of which there are the most variants is Methods—Time—Measurement (MTM), developed by Maynard, Stegmarten and Schwab (early 1940's). The data were collected from ciné film analysis and the units for each basic motion are expressed in Time Measurement Units (TMU), where 1 TMU = 0·00001 hours (0·036 seconds).

MTM recognises nine basic movements thus:

Reach
Grasp
Move
Turn
Apply pressure
Position
Release
Eye control
Leg and body movement.

Fig. 3.5.26
Standard time
from studies
plotted against
variable factor

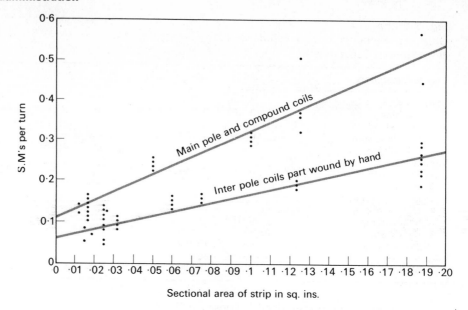

Each of these has from 2 to 19 subdivisions giving 66 indentifiable classes of movement. Each movement has a code, for example: $= {}_mR10\,B$ means 'reach 10 inches for an object whose position changes slightly at each cycle, the hand being in motion at the start but stationary at the end'.

One of the significant points in favour of PMTS is that, in order to obtain the correct motion patterns, the method must be analysed in detail, thus providing a simultaneous critical examination of the method. However, this detailed analysis raises one of its disadvantages, that is the time taken for an analyst to build up each minute's worth of time values. To make the application of PMTS a realistic proposition in a wider range of situations than would justify the time and detail of MTM, second and third generation MTM-based systems have been developed both by the MTM Association and independently by other workers, a brief summary is given below:

1. Master Standard Data, developed by Crossen & Nance of the Sirge A. Birn Co. Inc. All time values are combinations of basic MTM motions.
2. Primary Standard Data, developed by F. J. Neale of Urwick, Orr and Partners. In addition to simplifying the number of motions from 66 to 16 the data were converted from Westinghouse levelled to basic time in milliminutes at 100 on the BSI scale.
3. Simplified PMTS, developed by ICI Ltd. In depth of detail this lies between MTM and Primary Standard Data. Again the units are in milliminutes at 100 BS.
4. MTM II is a developed form of MTM.
5. Primary Standard Data II was developed from PSD in 1968 in an attempt to devise a PMTS of sufficient simplicity and speed of application to be applicable to maintenance work and certain 'one off' type jobs. The number of basic motions is reduced to 6 and only 24 time values.

In order to put some of these in perspective, it can take in excess of one hour to build up one minute of work value by MTM; about 20–30 minutes for one minute of work by Primary Standard Data and 5 minutes by PSD II.

Accuracy in work measurement should never be made an end in itself to the extent that the cost of obtaining the data exceeds the value to be derived from its use. The accuracy to be applied in any situation should reflect the cost involved and the accuracy with which it is practical to define the method to be employed, whether the time is to be used for control, planning, costing or incentive purposes. For example it would be uneconomic to use MTM to produce an assembly time for say a giant printing press, which is usually designed to fit a given space and so in its final configuration is a 'one off' with an assembly time probably running in excess of 1 000 man hours. A number of techniques are available for the jobbing industry where the basic function of the products may be similar, though differing greatly in size, detail design and layout. One of these is comparative estimating.

Comparative estimating

Comparative estimating basically consists of comparing the new job, or elements of the new job, whichever is applicable, with known and accurately measured 'benchmark' jobs. Knowing the times of the reference benchmark jobs, the next step is to estimate the time for the new job. For example, two reference jobs A and B have reference times 10 and 15 hours respectively. A new job X has a work content greater than A but less than B; however, it is judged to be closer to A, so that the reference value of 10 hours is allocated to it. The Comparative Estimating technique makes use of the following facts:

1. An estimator's ability to make an accurate comparison with a benchmark is increased if the time values for successive benchmarks are in geometric progression.
2. When several estimates, each subject to error, are added together, the percentage error of the total is less than that of the individual errors, this is because the total error of a number of estimates is equal to the square root of the sum of the squares of the individual errors. Using this fact we can see that it will be possible to control the accuracy of the final result by choosing the number of estimates in the control period in relation to the maximum possible error of each individual estimate.

Comparative estimating consists therefore of choosing a series of time bands covering the range of jobs to be considered. The mid point of each band has a time value known as the reference value and a small number of reference jobs which have been accurately measured represent typical jobs round each reference value.

Terms used. Explanation of the terms used and the formulae connecting them is best made by reference to a diagram thus:

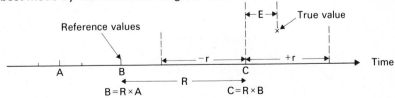

A, B, C, etc., are the reference values in geometric progression.

$R =$ the multiplier so $B = R \times A$, $C = R \times B$ etc.

$\pm r =$ the range, so the upper limit of the A band is $A + (A \times r)$ and the lower limit is $A - (A \times r)$

r is usually expressed as a percentage, i.e. $\pm 20\%$

$E =$ the error between the true value and the reference value.

$$\text{Total error} = \sqrt{\Sigma E^2}.$$

$$\text{Relative error} = \frac{\text{Total error}}{\text{Total job time}}.$$

So if $n =$ the number of jobs,

and $m_a =$ the average job time, then

the total job time $= m_a n$,

and the individual error $= m_a r$.

Then, the relative error $= \dfrac{\sqrt{n} \times (m_a r)^2}{m_a n} = \dfrac{r}{\sqrt{n}}$.

Application. In order to set up the series it is first necessary to determine the spread of work values; note the shortest and longest encountered. The series can then be determined by:

1. The number of reference values required.
2. The range of accuracy to each value.

   Only one of these can be the independent variable.

1. Number of reference values:
   (a) Determine the ratio of highest to lowest reference values H/L.
   (b) If n is the number of values required, then the multiplier

$$R = (n-1)\sqrt{\frac{H}{L}}$$

Example

   If the highest reference value is   50
        lowest reference value is   10

   And the desired number of values is 5,

   Then $R = 4\sqrt{\dfrac{50}{10}} = 1 \cdot 495$

   or practically $1 \cdot 5$, so the series of values would be 10, 15, 22·5, 33·7, 50·5.

2. Range of accuracy:
   (a) Determine the range of accuracy required.
   (b) Express this as a decimal e.g. $\pm 20\%$ would be $0 \cdot 2$ (i.e. the error).
   (c) Calculate the multiplier $R = \dfrac{1 + r}{1 - r}$.
   (d) Use R to determine series.

Example

   Using the figures from the previous example:

   Highest mid point $= 50$

   Lowest mid point $= 10$

   and a required range of 20%, i.e. $r = 0 \cdot 2$

   The $R = \dfrac{1 + 0 \cdot 2}{1 - 0 \cdot 2} = \dfrac{1 \cdot 2}{0 \cdot 8} = 1 \cdot 5$

So the series is again:
$$10, 15, 22 \cdot 5, 33 \cdot 7, 50 \cdot 5.$$
In practical terms whole numbers would be used
$$10, 15, 23, 34, 51.$$

All that remains is to determine the number of jobs required to give the required degree of accuracy in the final result.

We know that the relative error is $\dfrac{r}{\sqrt{n}}$.

So,
$$n = \left(\frac{\text{range}}{\text{relative error}}\right)^2$$

If in our previous example we want an overall accuracy of ±5 per cent from an individual accuracy of 20 per cent, then the number of jobs

$$= \left(\frac{20}{5}\right)^2 = 16$$

This technique is suitable for shop loading, planning and certain incentive purposes. However it cannot be used in an incentive scheme where each job stands to earn or lose bonus on its own; in the above example sixteen jobs would be required for each bonus assessment.

Learning curves

In the previous section a number of techniques available to management are outlined in which the work content of any job can be measured within an accuracy of say ±5 per cent. Yet anyone who has been involved in production management for any period of time will be aware that even with well measured standards, operator performance tends to drift upwards without any relaxing of the standard times. This phenomenon is a result of the continuance of the learning process, which goes on to some degree indefinitely, so we have the apparent contradiction that there is no such thing as a standard time for doing a job. If we understand the learning process we are in a better position to tackle the problems and take advantage of the opportunities associated with it.

History

Before the 1939–45 war the American aircraft industry had become aware that the total number of man hours required to build each successive aircraft of a particular design reduced as the number of aircraft built increased, and this reduction followed a regular and predictable pattern.

With the outbreak of war the US airforce commissioned research into this phenomenon. The research was carried out at Stamford in cooperation with the Martin Company at Omaha. The result of this research showed that in that particular situation, each time the cumulative number of aircraft built was doubled, the total man hours required on each aircraft was reduced to 80 per cent of the previous figure. Thus the second aircraft would take only 80 per cent as much direct labour as the first, and the 200th would take only 80 per cent as much direct labour as the 100th. This is known as an 80 per cent learning curve. A series of learning curves on linear scales is shown in Fig. 3.5.27. If these curves are plotted on log-log scales they approximate to a straight line (see Fig. 3.5.28). These curves can be expressed mathematically that the average cycle time taken for x cycles follows a law of the general type:

$$T_x = AX^{-n}$$

Fig. 3.5.27

80 per cent learning curve on linear scales

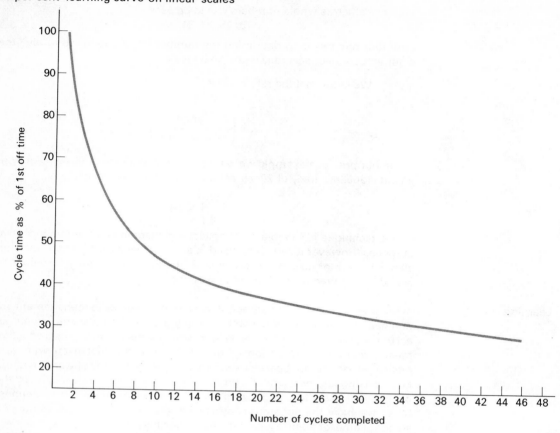

where x is the number of cycles completed and A and n are constants. It will be seen that when $x = 1$, $T_x = A$; so A is the time for the first off.

In the early days of research into learning curves, it was thought that for relatively short cycle operations the cycle time would reduce to a standard and then remain constant. However in experiments on short cycle work (less than 0·1 minutes) of 500 cycles per day 5 days a week for 5 weeks[1] reduced cycle times were still noticeable after 8 000 to 10 000 cycles. It should be noted that the learning curve can only take place on manipulative (i.e. not machine controlled) operations.

Why does it happen?

As an operator learns to undertake an operation, he will have to think less about what he has to do, in other words his movements will become automatic. In addition to the learning of a set pattern there is the much greater effect of change in method pattern. Reporting on analysis of learning in Pressed Steel Fisher, the Work Study Coordination Group wrote:

[1] R. M. Barnes and J. S. Perkins, 'A study of the development of skill during performance of a factory operation presented at the American Society of Mechanical Engineers Annual Meeting, New York, December 2–6, 1940'.

Fig. 3.5.28
80 per cent
learning curve
on log–log
scales

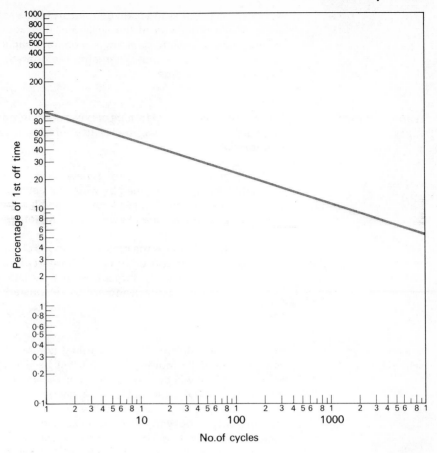

It is true to say that we can measure and record a standard time for a given method, but we are unable to define that method closely enough for people to see the minute changes in motion pattern which take place in the process of learning; and it is these minute changes in learning together with the many changes in the services to the operators which create the phenomenon of 'Learning'. A practical example of this was noted when the job of girls packing biscuits was studied, expressly to discover how study was related to learning. When the study was first made, one particular motion pattern concerned a complicated 'pick'. When the expert in MTM who made this study first saw the job, he could not believe, when the job was studied some 20 000 cycles later, that this complicated 'pick' had become a 'pick' of the simplest type.

The writer of this note makes a very significant point in his statement of 'changes in the services to the operator'. In the Author's experience using learning curves in the analysis of labour costs for new products, rather than individual operations, the whole organisation, from material procurement and production planning and control to the operator on the shop floor, is subject to the learning effect. Although the only measure of the learning effect is direct labour hours booked to a particular job, it is the Author's experience that many excess hours of direct labour incurred in the early stages of a new product are due to organisational and management problems as well as operator inexperience. At the other end of the scale learning does flatten off due to slight modification to design, or change in operators in a gang, or acceptance of a standard 'norm' of output. Thereafter the operator completes the job more easily in the same time.

Learning curves in practice

Having discovered that learning curves apparently make nonsense of our time standards, how can we make use of the knowledge of the learning phenomenon?

1. *Estimating.* In estimating for a new range of products, the steady state conditions will be determined by whatever estimating techniques are in use. Application of learning curve knowledge will enable the additional start up costs to be estimated and allowed for in the total pricing of the job.

2. *Forecasting.* Perhaps the most obvious use of learning curves is in forecasting labour requirements or output at the start of a new product. Either output per unit of time can be forecast with a constant labour force or labour requirements can be forecast to achieve a constant or specified output rate.

Incentive schemes

Because time reduction due to learning is related to the number of cycles completed and the completion rate will be accelerated if an incentive is applied, the two will be cumulative, if an incentive can be applied early on in the life of a new product without the danger of runaway or loose standards after the job has been running some months. This can be done by applying learning curve knowledge to the measured time after a known number of cycles; a reducing target or standard time can be set to cover the steep part of the learning period. The Author has applied this approach with satisfactory results, thus providing an incentive in the early days of a new product and a realistic standard for piecework after the learning has taken place. Theoretically the learning process will continue *ad infinitum*, but changes in the composition of the group concerned, the effect of slight changes in material, plus the effect of the machine controlled part of the operation, effectively flatten the learning curve in most practical situations.

Production control: monitoring performance against plans

In this chapter on production administration we have so far discussed preparing and establishing standards for operations and time plans for carrying them out. Supervision, that is managers and foremen, then take over the execution of the plans. But no matter how accurate the standards, or how perfect the plans, since human nature is fallible and not all the factors affecting production are under the control of management, there are in practice mistakes and failures to achieve standards of performance.

To enable corrective action to be taken to limit and reduce the effect of these mistakes and failures and to prevent their recurrence there must be some means of measuring deviations from plans and shortcomings in performance. This is an activity of control discussed in detail in Part Five, of which

production ce...
control in which...

1. The control of \...
   industry today as...
2. The control of m...
   excess costs of pro...
   concerned with *mate...*
3. The control of quality of...
   since it is a highly techniu...
   processes and skills in the...
   inspectors and testers, and th...
   chapter 6. It is significant tha...
   quantity and process productio...
4. The control of *machine utilisation*...
   of machines in terms of machine h...
5. *Automatic control* more generally cal...
   of continuous-flow production, centrali...   ...ime
   machines or computers.

It is pertinent to point out that there is a scien...   ...in the nature of
control in all its forms; it is known as 'cybe...   ...workers in several
branches of science—electronics, mathematics, e...   ...nics, psychology, biol-
ogy and others—in studying complicated 'systems' which exhibit a degree of
feedback of information and self-regulation, have found principles which
appear to be common to all. The self-sensing and self-regulating circuits and
systems in electronics are used for the automatic machine tool. Physiological
control in the animal body involves a system of feedback of information to the
controlling organ, the brain. General theories that are being, or will be,
developed in this new science are likely to be of use to management, and the
new science will help to take scientific management a great deal further along
the road to making decisions on a quantitative instead of a subjective basis. It
is already finding an answer to problems in extremely complex situations
which are generally beyond the scope of operational research (out of which
the new science has grown), in industry at least. This subject is dealt with at
some length in chapter 8 below.

Progress

It will be recognised at once that controlling variations from production plans,
or progressing, can be done only from a detailed knowledge of plans and
results, and in any but the smallest organisations this means *records of
results*. Since in practice it is usually found advisable, and is in fact recommended, to appoint special men as progress men or chasers, there is a danger
that duplicate records are set up. The Planning Engineers must have records of
results to keep their plans up to date and to adjust for them in future plans. If
planning and progress are not integrated nor production planning documents
and procedures designed to cater for both activities, each will have its own
system of recording results. It is not unknown for the Planning Engineers to
spend a good proportion of their time frantically adjusting their plans, after the
progress men have made theirs. Planning schemes introduced by inexperienced persons have been held to scorn and failed on this account. It is

happen when progress men have been operating before ... called or are appointed by or are responsible to foremen of ...s.

...e first place, therefore, it is essential for progress to be a responsibility ...f the Production Planning Department, and for the progress men to be under the authority of the head of this Department. Secondly, all planning and production documents and procedures should be designed to incorporate records which the progress men will require. This has been done in the documents included in the Appendix to this chapter. Thirdly, it is important to choose and train the right type of person. Because a progress man is likely to be frequently changing programmes or asking for urgent action, he must enlist the ready cooperation of supervisors. It is essential for him to have a cheerful and friendly disposition, and yet be determined. If he is too assertive and overbearing, he will get little cooperation from supervisors; if he is too easygoing, he will not get the results required. A retentive memory for detail is also essential and an extensive knowledge of the firm's products is advisable.

Progress can be organised in two ways:

- each progress man responsible for a section or department;
- each progress man responsible for one product or group of components.

In the larger units both methods may be seen in operation.

If it is laid down and clearly understood that a production schedule is an assignment which it is the foreman's duty to complete, then the former method is likely to be most satisfactory. Even then it may be found advisable to have one man responsible for the progress of customers' or urgent orders, throughout the factory, in addition to departmental progress men. What must be guarded against is a progress man building up so much authority that he wrecks planned schedules in his enthusiasm for short-term results.

The progress man's main 'standards of reference' are the production schedules, weekly or daily, and lists of orders promised. It is one of the advantages of departmental production schedules that they are a department's assignment for completion by a given date. If work is crossed off as completed, work not completed, and therefore behind programme, can be immediately seen by the progress men. It is even better of course to know what jobs have been started late or are running behind programme. This means a record of when jobs started, in addition to a record of when jobs are completed. It is not usually justified if most jobs do not last for longer than one day. In either case in factories or departments on batch production the best way of keeping an eye on whether jobs have started or finished to time is by using a planning or load board provided with a scale of time. Normally, however, sufficient control is obtained by checking jobs finished against the weekly or daily schedule, and it requires far less paper and clerical work.

Delivery promises

Another aspect of progress work which is important is respect for delivery promises to customers. There is an unfortunate tendency in industry, more prevalent in a seller's market, to assume that a slight lateness on delivery promised is not very serious, and that to get orders by quoting a better delivery than it is possible to maintain is good business. Both are bad business, bad for planning in the customer's factory and damaging to a firm's reputation, however good that might otherwise be. Broken promises of delivery should be looked on like any other broken promise—it is just 'not done'. The incidence of broken promises is sufficiently important for a special report to be made weekly to the Works Manager. This should at least show the number of deliveries made overdue and its percentage of all deliveries. The incidence should be so small that the Works Manager should be able to see and deal either daily or weekly with a list of all orders promised and not delivered to time. Each order should be recorded at the time the promise is made on a weekly (or daily) promise sheet. At the end of each week (or day) orders delivered should be crossed off, leaving broken promises. Prevention being better than cure, a duplicate of the promise sheet should be given to a progress man some time before the due date—time enough to check progress and take urging action if necessary.

Tooling

It is important for tools to be completed on time, since tools not ready when required will throw production programmes out of gear. Therefore, tool orders must also be progressed, and the record recommended above for dealing with delivery promises by recording and throwing up deliveries due is effective, since it directs attention to jobs likely to be held up, in time for corrective action to be taken.

Shortages

Shortage lists for raw materials and components should be prepared regularly by the progress men for urgent action by either the Buyer or component-producing departments. These can be collected from the stores or thrown up automatically by return of requisitions or material release notes. It is useful for stores, particularly component stores, to post up on a blackboard or wall chart all items out of stock. There are always some items or aspects of production which senior executives need to keep an eye on personally. Charts, wall-boards, or special forms are useful for this purpose if, and only if, their number and the numbers of items on them are few and the items which need attention 'hit the eye'. In process factories stocks of scarce materials may need special attention, in others output of important products or the load on departments may need watching from time to time. Charts are most convenient for the purpose, lines being drawn vertically to a quantity scale for each item listed horizontally. In practice the weakness is that whilst a line can always be extended, it must be rubbed out to be shortened. A simple homemade board which provides adjustable lines is shown in Fig. 3.5.5 (p. 370). If it is desired to keep an eye on the progress of a few important orders in a factory with a limited number of processes, as in printing, a chart can be used (as in Fig. 3.5.29); a circle or diagonal line can indicate that the process is required, and a tick or an opposite diagonal line that the process is completed. If a board is used, cardboard discs can be hung on hooks and removed as the process is completed. Dates written on the discs add a time element to the control.

Suppliers of office equipment can provide very ingenious adjustable visible charts or boards for progress work. Keen and impressionable planning and progress men sometimes see in them a cure-all for progress problems. It is assumed that they work. They do not: they are tools, and as such must be operated by people who must be trained to be skilful and reliable in their use. It is unwise to use visible boards when the number of items is large, hundreds or

Fig. 3.5.29
Order progress
board

Customer	Comps.	Engrs.	Platen	Wharfe.	Miehle	C. & C.	Bind.
212 B. Jones	Ø		Ø				O
215 Smith & Wells		O		O	O		
216 Bl. Eng.	Ø	Ø			Ø	O	O

more; just as good results can be obtained by cards or paper and at less cost in labour or space. But for a small number of items they can be most effective.

'Line of
balance'

It is worth while at this point to mention a technique for monitoring the progress of batch orders required on a scheduled delivery. This technique known as the 'line of balance' has been described as 'a crystal ball that really works'. Although it has been developed to quite a sophisticated management tool in the construction industry[1] in its simplest form it can help the production controller to foresee troubles before they become critical, or alternatively ascertain very quickly the effect of programme changes. The Author has used the line of balance technique to monitor the production of a running contract in a jobbing/small batch manufacturing concern, and found it extremely helpful.

The first step in the process is to construct a network of the important stages in the manufacturing (or construction) process. This network (using the arrow diagram notation) must then be drawn on a time scale with the completion or dispatch activity at the lefthand side of the diagram as in Fig. 3.5.30.

The next step is to plot, on the same time scale, a cumulative graph of the required delivery of the finished products. For deliveries required at a constant weekly rate this will be a straight line, but frequently companies require scheduled deliveries which are not constant. Fig. 3.5.31 shows a typical requirement for the product in Fig. 3.5.30.

The third step is to construct a histogram of the cumulative number of items that have passed each identified stage of the network. This histogram should have the same vertical scale as the graph of customers' required deliveries. The graph (Fig. 3.5.31) assumes that deliveries are due to commence the following week.

Finally all three figures are combined on one sheet in such a way that the respective time scales and the quantity scales are coincident (see Fig. 3.5.33).

If we now project from each event to the due delivery line and thence to the work in progress histogram (dotted line on Fig. 3.5.33) we shall see the number of components that must be at each stage in order that the required delivery rate will be maintained. If we look at Fig. 3.5.33, we see that the number of machined frame castings (event 12) is less than is required (this could be machining problems, or casting supply). A crosscheck with 8 (castings delivered) shows an even more serious shortfall, although 1 (castings on order) shows a surplus. The problem is obviously with the supplier of castings.

The *line of balance* chart can be used to give a rapid answer when the question of altered delivery schedules arises. If the customer asks 'how soon after the holiday period can you increase deliveries to 30 per week?' a quick

[1] Philip Lumsden, *The Line of Balance Method*, Pergamon Press, 1968.

Fig. 3.5.30
Network for
motor
manufacture
(line of
balance

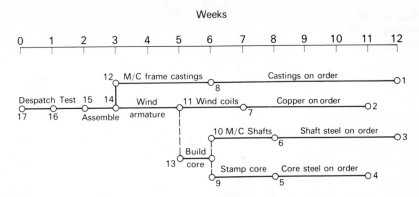

projection shows that with the exception of the castings there are no problems. So effort is then concentrated on establishing how soon the casting supplier can increase his rate of output, or perhaps finding an alternative supplier. The prime advantage of this approach to project control is the simplicity of the principle and the speed with which the effect of a new set of circumstances such as a changed delivery schedule can be assessed.

Cost control

Meeting the term cost control in this section dealing with production may cause the reader to pause and think—'but this is an Accountant's job'. True, the accountant is responsible for calculating and accounting for all costs, but *only the person immediately responsible for actual expenditure can control the cost*—and that means the man on the shop floor, the operator and the foreman. And for a supervisor to be in control of the costs for which he is responsible, he must know what costs should be and what they actually are, so that he can take action to reduce or entirely avoid differences, i.e. excess costs.

Fig. 3.5.31
Cumulative
requirement
graph

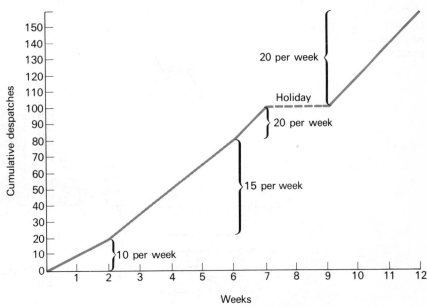

Fig. 3.5.32
Histogram of
completions

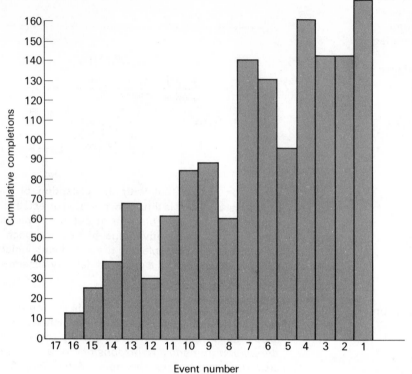

Fig. 3.5.33
Combined line
of balance
chart to
show
production
position

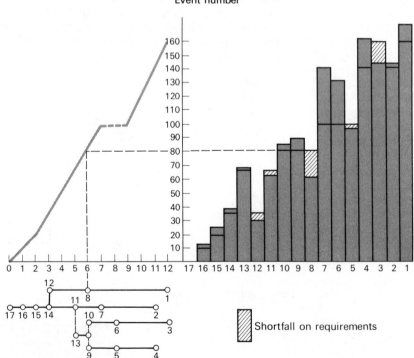

A supervisor has neither the time nor the facilities to record and calculate his own costs, so that he must be provided with the information; that is, he must be provided with another administrative service, just as he is by the Planning and Progress Engineers on programmes and deviations from them for controlling production flow. For controlling costs the accountant supplies the information in the form of cost control reports showing:

● for material—the cost of material used in excess of standard with an analysis of the causes of such excess;
● labour—the cost of labour used in excess of standard analysed in the same way as for material, the effective performance of each operator and department, and the total cost per unit of production.

The supply of these reports and their interpretation is a production administrative activity and, as such, is dealt with here.

It may be necessary first to distinguish clearly between the terms 'cost control' and 'costing', lest they should be confused or assumed to be synonymous. *Costing*, as normally practised, is the computation of the total actual cost of a production or process after manufacture. *Cost control*, in the modern sense, is the control of all items of expenditure by regular and frequent comparison of actual expenditure with predetermined standards or budgets, so that undesirable trends away from standard can be detected and corrected at an early stage.

The former is historical, and while comparisons can be made between total cost and selling price of a product to reveal the profit or loss, little can be done about any excess cost except to deduct it from any total profit for the period, since the cause of the excess is not known. Even if the cause can be found for any particular product or component, its incidence cannot easily be detected, so that little can be done about it. On the other hand, well-designed cost control techniques reveal the actual cause of all excess costs in some detail, their magnitude, and their trend, i.e. increasing or decreasing. They are revealed too, immediately after the event, so that foremen and all concerned are aware of cause and effect and can take immediate steps to improve unsatisfactory results. In this chapter we shall deal only with direct material and direct labour costs. Overhead expenses, which are controlled by comparisons with budgets, are dealt with in Part Five. Suffice to say here that supervisors must be presented with reports of actual expenditure, preferably compared with budget, regularly and immediately after the period to which they refer. Supervisors must be held accountable for all the expenses over which they have authority and control (e.g. loose tools, but not heating).

It has been explained earlier how the Production Engineers determine the correct material for use on a process or on a job, and the standard time for doing it. In practice, more material is used and more time spent over a period (e.g. a week) than the standard necessary for the total production for the period. The excess, of either labour or material, on any job usually has nothing to do with the job itself, but is due to such causes as careless operating and waiting for tools. What is wanted, therefore, to control these excesses is a record of them, not by job but by cause. And since the absolute cost of such excesses for a department is likely to increase with production, to get a true measure of performance it is necessary to know the relative cost and therefore to express the incidence of total excess costs as a percentage of total costs.

Finally, it will be appreciated that cost control figures must be presented to the persons responsible for the expenditure; that is, to the foreman or supervisor of the department. And to enable effective action to be taken, the reports must be rendered immediately after the end of the period to which they refer, e.g. by Tuesday of the following week. To be fully effective they must be broken down to sections of a department where this is appropriate. In order to avoid duplicating work and extra operations in the accounts or wages office, the preparation of these reports should be integrated with the preparation of the payroll and operating accounts.

Material cost control

Excess material cost is revealed either as scrap or as an excess withdrawal from stock compared with standard for the amount of finished product manufactured. The most effective way of controlling scrapped material is to prevent the disposal of such scrap by anyone except an authorised person, and then only to a stated receiving depot, e.g. stores, against a document, such as a scrap note stating the cause and signed by an inspector or foreman. The scrap notes can then be valued and summarised either daily or weekly in the form of a report showing the cost under each cause heading compared with previous average and budget. Since it is usually impossible to prevent all waste or scrap, it is not enough to record actual scrap and its value; it must be compared with some standard (previous average or best or a budget) so that differences on the wrong side are immediately apparent. A suitable form for this purpose is illustrated in Fig. 3.5.34. Other headings by cause can be used according to the type of product or process. For example, in a foundry they would be: Total melt, cupola, risers, moulding, fettling, Total.

Fig. 3.5.34
Excess material cost sheet

Excess material cost

Week	Total material or labour			Due to operator			Due to machine			Faulty material			Other causes			Total			Remarks
	Amount £	p	%	Amount £	p	%	Amount £	p	%	Amount £	p	%	Amount £	p	%	Amount £	p	%	
Budget			100																
1																			
2																			
3																			
4																			
5																			
6																			
7																			
8																			
9																			
10																			
11																			
12																			
13																			
Total																			

It is usual for the Accounts Department to provide an overall control as a check on whether all material is accounted for as a good product or scrap. (In the absence of such a check, there is a tendency for scrap to be understated or 'Lost'.) Such control is effected by comparison of standard amounts (as laid down in process layouts) with amounts actually used. It will relate to each material used and apply to each department or process. The difference should be accounted for by the scrap recorded; where it does not, steps should be taken to explain the discrepancy; it may reveal unsuspected waste.

When material is issued in bulk from stores or drawn on as required by operators in the department, and scrap, waste, or overusage is not identified as such, as e.g. in industries using materials in sheets (press work) or reels (wire) or planks (casemaking), etc., it is impossible to issue only the correct amount for a job, and so to control usage in that way. A control can still be provided, however, by the Accounts Department rendering periodical reports showing the standard amount which should have been used for the products completed compared with actual bulk issues for the period. In any one period there will be slight differences due to variations in the amount of material in progress in the department, but over a period the difference should remain substantially constant (for a constant proportion of scrap) and a gradual improvement or deterioration will be revealed.

Labour cost control

Excess labour cost can arise from the following causes:

Waiting time paid to operators for periods when they are not able to work on jobs.
Low effectiveness where a guaranteed minimum rate is paid.
Premium payments, e.g. overtime, learning, etc.
Wrong grade of labour.
Unused capacity, i.e. low output for some indirect operators.
Excess piecework payment or excess time spent due to faulty material or faulty equipment.

Only excesses under the first heading are brought to the foreman's notice immediately and in detail, and only then when he personally signs or scrutinises each record of waiting time. Immersed as he is in the day-to-day problems of shop management, he cannot watch the incidence of each cause of excess cost, far less the total cost or its trend. It is necessary, therefore, to provide him with a weekly statement, his *weekly operating statement* as it were. Very detailed ones are often recommended, and daily reports are even used, but these involve the Wages Department (or some other department) in a considerable amount of extra work and the foreman in an interpretation which is too detailed for him to give to it the necessary thought and attention. Of the several methods of presenting the essential information which the foreman must have, the form shown in Fig. 3.5.35 is a good example. It is not suggested that this form covers all cases or includes all causes of excess costs or indices of performance that may be required, but it will serve as a basis for preparing a suitable form for any specific need, and it is one which with slight modifications only has been used in industry and proved most effective, giving the foreman the picture he requires of his labour costs and the necessary control.

Fig. 3.5.35
Memorandum on excess cost

Quarter ending _____   Department _____

Labour cost control

Wages analysis

Week ending	Direct wages			Total direct (actual)	Total excess		Charge-hands and setters			Indirect wages — Others			Tool setting by operators		Total indirect (actual)	Grand total (actual wages)	Transfers
	Measured work at standard	Unmeasured work			Actual (as over)	% of total direct	Standard	Actual	% excess	Standard	Actual	% excess					
		Actual	% of total														
Average bt.fwd.																	
1																	
2																	
3																	
4																	
5																	
6																	
7																	
8																	
9																	
10																	
11																	
12																	
13																	
Average carried fwd.																	

Memorandum

Week ending	Cost per unit	Output per op. hr.	Hrs. earned	Hrs. on Stds.	% bonus on Std.	Atten-dance hours	% bonus on attend	Avail. m/c hours	% m/c effective	Actual m/c hours	% Signature
Average bt. fwd.											
1											
2											
3											
4											
5											
6											
7											
8											
9											
10											
11											
12											
13											
Average carried fwd.											

(Front)

Memorandum on excess cost

Quarter ending ____

Foreman's responsibility

Week ending	To equal P.W guarantee	Waiting for job	Waiting for set-up	Waiting for tools & drgs	Tool attention	Faulty labour	Learning	Wrong grade	Total	Faulty labour other depts.	Total excess cost	Foreman's bonus % on total wages	Bonus
Aver. bt. fwd													
1													
2													
3													
4													
5													
6													
7													
8													
9													
10													
11													
12													
13													
Aver. car. fwd													

Management's responsibility

Week ending	Policy	Faulty material	Faulty equipment	Plant failure	Planning	Drawing office	Design office	First aid and meetings	Cleaning down	Overtime	Total
Aver. bt. fwd											
1											
2											
3											
4											
5											
6											
7											
8											
9											
10											
11											
12											
13											
Aver. car. fwd											

(Reverse)

The form covers a thirteen-week period, and is entered up weekly by the wages clerks, sent to the Works Manager, and thence to the foreman for information and action, and report back to the Works Manager if requested. It is returned to the Wages Office in time for the next week's entries to be made. The average figures for the previous quarter (or budget figures if preferred) are entered as the opening line, so that continuity is preserved, and, as each week's results are added, trends are revealed.

The top portion of the front of the form brings home to a foreman the total costs for which he is responsible and their make-up. It is an analysis of the payroll for the department rapidly summarised by the wages clerks from the different classes of time or job cards. The total excess costs are shown and expressed as a percentage of the relevant figure. The unmeasured labour cost, i.e. the amount paid on day-work, is shown, as this can be considered uncontrolled, and should be kept to a minimum. The difference between standard and actual wages is the total excess labour cost and is analysed by cause on the back of the form.

The standard for indirect wages is arrived at by agreeing on the number and therefore weekly cost of supervisors and labourers for a given number of operators. This number of operators can be expected to produce a normal number of standard hours per week. The total cost of supervision divided by the normal total standard hours gives a cost per standard hour for supervision, which, multiplied by the total standard hours recorded for the week, gives the standard cost for supervision for that week.

The bottom portion of the front of the form is used for remarks by wages clerks, Works Manager, or foreman, and for indices of performance. The total hours earned divided by total hours on standard (on piecework) expressed as a percentage is the index of piecework performance. If work measurement is done correctly, as recommended earlier, this figure is a true measure of performance, and can be used for comparisons between departments. Dividing the earned hours by total clock hours (including daywork hours in both figures) gives the overall effective performance of the department.

Excess costs

The cost per unit is the total wages costs of the department divided by the total hours earned or tons produced or other unit of production, and shows the trend of the true effectiveness of the department. The cost per unit goes up if piecework performance goes down, excess costs go up, or the total output goes down with the same supervision and other indirect wages cost.

Excess costs are analysed on the back of the form under two headings, those for which the foreman of the department can be held responsible, and those for which other members of the management team are responsible. The Works Manager may have to deal with the latter, but the foreman is expected to act on the former. The analysis of waiting time is picked up from the reason given on the time card record and the headings are self-explanatory; others can be used to suit circumstances. The item 'To equal P. W. guarantee' is the amount which has to be paid to pieceworkers over and above their piecework earnings when these are below the minimum guaranteed. Such operators are working below a satisfactory standard and well below normal. The cost of using a wrong grade of labour is picked up by the wages clerk from the job card when the grade of operator who does a job is different from that laid down by the Production Engineers and appearing in the standard data on the job card. It is ineffective use of labour by supervision. Excess cost due to faults in other departments is transferred out and vice versa.

In practice, when excess costs due to one or more causes are high or begin to rise, it is wise for the foreman to arrange to investigate personally over a limited period for each incident recorded for these causes immediately it is reported. He is then able to find quickly the exact cause and to take effective remedial action. The report points to where such close attention is required, and it throws up the bad spots. To those unaccustomed to such reports, it is surprising how effective they are in drawing the attention of senior executives to increasing costs and deteriorating performance.

It is noted that in the example, provision is made for assessing a foreman's bonus, on the basis of his success in controlling excess costs in his department. The particular method used will depend on circumstances but the report does reveal a measure which can be used in this way.

Machine utilisation	At one time machine utilisation was considered to be one of the most important shop floor statistics, more important even than labour utilisation. There are now many situations brought about by (*a*) the increased cost of direct labour, and (*b*) new thinking on the overall cost of production including the cost of work in progress. Where maximum machine utilisation is not always the lowest total cost situation (see under Group Technology, p. 481) it is still necessary to keep an eye on it. This is particularly so where the overall capacity of the factory is dependent on the output from a group of machines, whether the group be a complete machine shop, a batch of automatic machines, or a continuous production or process plant where a delay on one machine can affect the output from the whole plant.

Where, as in most cases, machines are attended or operated by individuals, the overall machine utilisation of a department can be calculated from operators' job cards by the wages office and included in the labour cost control. Provision has been made for this on the form referred to above (Fig. 3.5.35). When this report, or other information, reveals that utilisation is unsatisfactory, it may be necessary to have a more detailed analysis for each machine. As with excess labour costs, this is best done by recording the actual loss at source, that is the delay or machine down time, at the time it occurs, with a note of cause. The simplest method is to provide a daily log sheet for each machine, preferably fixed on a board or holder, on which the operator or attendant can enter the time machines stop or start, and the cause. The principal causes of machine delays are mechanical breakdowns, setting-up troubles and unsatisfactory material. The first can be reduced by an effective scheme of preventive maintenance (see p. 491), the second by a great deal more attention to the training of setters and to the design of tooling (particularly important in specialists and short-run production so common in Britain), and the last either by better inspection of incoming material, or by more attention to regularity from previous processes or operations.

For machine shops with a large number of high production machines it is now possible to purchase proprietary systems which will record, at some remote point, the duration of running on each machine, also by the operator dialling or punching a code on a panel near his machine, the cause of every type of stoppage is automatically logged and analysed. As with most 'systems' it ultimately relies on the human element, in this case the operator who must remember to punch the correct code at the correct time.

Computers in production management

In previous sections reference has been made to the use of computers as an integral part of the process of production management, namely in the solving and updating of PERT networks for major projects (see pages 384–388). In addition to this rather specific case, computers are able to provide quicker and fuller information to the Production Manager in such areas as:

Stock control
Raw material mix for minimum production cost
Shop loading and progress
Departmental and operator performance
Machine utilisation
Excess cost analysis.

The computer is able to provide as much or as little information as the situation demands, and it is true to say that whatever management information is provided by present manual/clerical methods, it can be produced more rapidly, more fully and more accurately by computer—but not necessarily more cheaply. Rarely does the translation of manual systems on to a computer reduce the direct cost, but this is not to say that the exercise is not worth while, for the benefits to be obtained from the three improvements mentioned may justify the expense.

Two illustrations of typical procedures of production control in which the computer plays a large part may serve better here than a number of generalities.

First illustration

The first example is taken from engineering, the company concerned making large capital process plant, each one a special in itself but comprising many standard components. The procedure has of necessity been abbreviated; should the reader require a full system, any of the large computer manufacturers will provide one, probably filling a large number of A4 ring binders.

On receipt of a customer's order, general capacity is reserved in each department on the basis of the labour hours used in the preparation of the estimate and the agreed delivery date. When the parts lists, with new drawings where necessary, are issued they are fed into the computer, which holds a storage memory of the process layouts, complete with allowed times, for every existing component. (There is a procedure for eliminating obsolete items.) With this information and the due delivery date, the computer then:

1. Calculates the batch time for each operation of each component.
2. Calculates the week that each operation is due to be completed—rules are written in for the relationship between operation time and queue time between operations.
3. Loads each production facility with the calculated number of batch hours for the appropriate week.

4. Calculates total raw material requirements of each type and allocates from the 'free stock'. If re-order levels are reached as a result of this a signal to re-order is produced.
5. Prints a job card for each operation, a material release note, stores, delivery note and identity label for each component or batch.

At the end of each week a summation of all the hours loaded on each production facility for each of the weeks ahead is produced (see Fig. 3.5.36). This weekly forward load summary takes into account not only the new jobs loaded to a factory during the past week but also the reduction in load due to operations completed during the week. As operations are completed all job cards are passed through the computer and the following returns are computed and printed out:

Operator wage and performance
Gross hours, standard hours and excess hours on each job card
Operator and departmental excess cost analysis
Standard hours 'off loaded' from each facility
Production capacity on each facility. This is computed from the total hours worked on any machine group and the total standard hours produced.

This data is fed back to the forward load printout so that the Production Controller can tell quickly what sections, if any, are overloaded and can then make arrangements for either alternative methods or subcontracting to achieve the required completion date. The work content of all jobs subcontracted is subsequently subtracted from the load file.

Fig. 3.5.36
Computer printout of shopload

	0/D	15	16	17	18	19	20	21-25	26-30	31+
								WORKS	19-05-72	
156	54	156	130	113	52	35	15	30	21	12
158	62	180	151	108	64	42	18	42	17	2
161	172	1240	1184	972	884	621	533	503	320	530
162	206	2286	2001	1784	1242	1063	984	1106	848	720
163	198	2124	1989	1524	1097	998	842	874	701	504
165	182	2029	1122	1021	984	917	707	661	434	286
166	177	2540	2244	2004	1876	1212	971	820	591	300
167	221	2186	211	1824	1989	1129	1060	911	724	682
210	82	984	721	598	306	221	132	100	102	91
212	151	862	887	661	612	584	419	440	382	121
214	199	1054	922	881	703	627	513	521	446	302
215	118	821	718	612	533	483	361	424	208	97
220	81	602	412	306	241	133	92	146	87	14
230	24	310	242	166	103	91	32	66	72	20
244	39	286	251	233	154	131	101	78	61	13
245	39	392	311	290	213	191	137	130	92	7
246	52	404	302	211	201	147	98	120	86	28
310	11	152	98	67	21	7	12	17	6	0
315	8	204	166	134	121	92	61	58	34	2
320	6	161	155	101	56	31	12	0	2	0

LOAD SUMMARY

Second
illustration

The second example comes from the manufacture of foodstuffs for cattle. The products are made and sold to a specific minimum nutritional formula. An example of such a formula for a pig food is:[1]

	%
Protein	12·0
Oil	2·1–6·0
Fibre	3·5–7·0
Calcium	0·9–1·1
Phosphorus	0·6–0·8
Lysine	0·65
Methionine	0·25
Methionine+Cystine	0·47
Total digestible energy	68

However, the many possible raw materials from which these products are made are subject to availability, price changes, and to variability in their composition; for example, the weather during the ripening period can have a marked effect on the composition of any cereals used in the mix, or the oil content of groundnuts, which are a common ingredient. The company's aim is not only to obtain the guaranteed formula at the minimum cost, taking into account the various cost and composition combinations of the constituents, but also to obtain this minimum cost for the total output of the production period—usually one month. To do this calculation manually for one product would be a long and difficult exercise in linear programming; to do it for the whole range of products scheduled for any one month's production schedule would be impossible without the help of a computer. The computer is so programmed that when the monthly figures of

production requirements (quantity and formulae)
material composition
material costs
material availability

are supplied, it calculates the least cost formulation of each product which also gives the least total cost for the month. In addition printouts can be provided showing the amount of each raw material remaining unallocated at the end of the programme. This information will be vital for determining purchasing requirements for the coming month. Figure 3.5.37 shows part of a typical computer printout giving raw material usage, value of unallocated stock, product ingredients, product formulae and cost of ingredients against product codes 01 to 09.[2]

Reliability of
input

It must be remembered that however good a computer-aided production control system is, it can only be as accurate as the information fed in, and as good as the personnel running it. Blind belief in the infallibility of a computer printout can lead the believer very much astray. A healthy scepticism and an occasional crosscheck by manual means can prevent the manager being led astray by false figures.

[1] Figures taken from J. R. Crabtree, *The Composition of Compound Feedstuffs under UK and EEC Conditions*, Grassland Research Institute, Report no. 11 July 1972.
[2] Reproduced by courtesy of Crosfields Farm Foods Ltd, Bristol.

Fig. 3.5.37

Computer printout of feed linear programme

RAW MATERIAL PLANNING MODEL2 FOR HAILSHAM MILL FOR DEC 1972,RUN ON 02 NOV 1972

TABLE 1.

RAW MATERIAL	DELIVRS IN MONTH	01	02	TOTAL RAW MATERIAL USAGE BY RATION 03	04	05	06	07	08	09	DUMMY RATION	TOTAL USAGE	PURCHASE OR STOCK	STOCK BFWD	PURCHAS COST
HERRG	67.0	.	.	6.2	.9	.	3.0	.0	.	.	13.0	23.2	-43.8		184.00
MB55.	47.0	.	.	5.1	1.9	.	16.5	18.0	8.3	7.3	13.0	70.0	23.0		84.00
									.	.	4.0	5.0	-1.0		82.70
GNTXT	25.0	.	4.5	7.9	.4	.	18.5	9.2	4.8	24.9	5.0	75.2	50.2		71.60
SYA45	53.0	.	.	3.3	3.7	6.1	2.0	29.0	9.0	.	7.0	60.0	7.0		76.60
GUAR.	23.0	13.0	10.0	.	.	.	.	.	.	.	7.0	30.0	7.0		39.10
LINXP	10.0	.	.	.	.	.	.	.	.	.	.	.	-10.0		70.50
MGL24	62.0	43.7	2.3	14.9	1.0	.	.	.	.	.	8.0	70.0	8.0		36.60

TABLE 2

RAW MATERIAL	PURCHASE COST	LIMITED SUPPLY	01	02	VALUE OF MATERIALS NOT USED IN RATIONS 03	04	05	06	07	08	09
HERRG	184.00	.	115.11	115.96	.	.	180.00	.	180.00	180.00	180.00
MB55.	84.00	102.51	.	.	.	.	101.71	.	.	.	.
GNTXP	82.70	.	.	78.69	78.57	78.10	73.12	77.94	77.77	77.94	77.72
GNTXT	71.60	.	71.45	.	.	.	70.48	.	.	.	.
SYA45	76.60	.	68.76	69.04	.	.	.	.	.	.	76.05
GUAR.	39.10	66.64	.	.	61.38	.	.	57.68	58.39	57.68	58.30
LINXP	70.50	.	62.44	62.14	.	.	.	.	.	.	.
MGL24	36.60	46.27	.	.	.	.	44.12	45.57	45.57	45.57	45.53

TABLE 3

RAW MATERIAL	01	02	RATION FORMULAE (PERCENT) 03	04	05	06	07	08	09	DUMMY RATION
HERRG	.	.	2.50	1.50	.	1.25	.	.	.	11.93
MB55.	.	.	2.03	3.21	.	6.85	2.50	4.61	2.50	11.93
GNTXP	.29	.	.	.	.	.	.	.	.	3.67
GNTXT	.	2.24	3.15	.70	.	7.71	1.28	2.65	8.57	4.59
SYA45	.	.	1.30	6.11	5.10	.81	4.03	4.99	.	6.42
GUAR.	3.71	5.00	.	.	.	.	.	.	.	6.42

TABLE 4

CONSTRNT NAME	01	02	03	RATION ANALYSES 04	05	06	07	08	09
OIL..	3.75	2.60	3.00	2.50	2.08	3.00	2.50	2.50	2.50
PROT.	15.50	15.50	15.50	16.30	13.80	16.80	15.80	15.80	16.50
FIBRE	2.50	9.00	5.48	4.49	4.88	2.71	3.04	3.07	3.76
AVLYS	.	.	.65	.73	.62	.64	.61	.61	.61
METH.	.	.	.22	.33	.26	.31	.27	.27	.27

TABLE 5

CONSTRNT NAME	01 UNIT	TOTAL	02 UNIT	TOTAL	03 UNIT	TOTAL	04 UNIT	TOTAL	05 UNIT	TOTAL	06 UNIT	TOTAL	07 UNIT	TOTAL	08 UNIT	TOTAL	09 UNIT	TOTAL
OIL..	.964	3.62	1.070	2.78	.767	2.30	.615	1.54	.	.	.474	1.42	.440	1.10	.474	1.18	.427	1.07
PROT	1.182	18.32	1.212	18.79	.882	13.67	.825	13.45	.759	10.47	.819	13.76	.855	13.51	.819	12.94	.855	14.11
FIBRE	-.497	-3.72	-.524	-4.72														
AVLYS	.	.	.	.	7.292	4.74	7.603	5.55	8.114	5.03	8.096	5.18	8.084	4.93	8.096	4.94	8.086	4.93
METH.	.	.	.	.	4.323	.95	.	.	.	.	.	.	4.391	1.19	.	.	4.392	1.19
M.C..							4.387	2.54	4.79	2.15	4.428	2.48	.318		4.428	2.30	.	.
CALK.	-.168	-.20	-.247	-.30	.173	.14	.261	.29	.138	.14	.356	1.14	.318	.95	.356	1.07	.321	.96
PHOS.	2.475	1.49	2.412	1.45	2.334	1.40	2.748	1.92	1.153	.69	2.875	2.01	2.845	1.99	2.875	2.01	2.848	1.99
RSALT					.160	.06	.190	.07	.143	.05	.226	.08	.211	.07	.226	.08	.213	.07
S.E..	.064	4.14	.	.							.	.	.	.	.	.	.	.
M.E.A	.	.	.	.	.012	14.27	.014	17.66	.13	15.31	.017	22.07	.016	20.40	.017	21.06	.016	20.55
YUNIT	.	.	.	.	.	.	.	.	.	.	.001	.03	.005	.09	.001	.02	.004	.13
FLRNE	-4.775	-.05	-4.575	-.05	-4.138	-.08	-5.695	-.23	.	.	-6.118	-.24	-6.022	-.24	-6.118	-.24	-6.031	-.24
MINMT	.	.	.	.	.	.	.	.	.	.	.	.	.	.	.	.	.	.
MOIST	.	.	.	.	.	.	.	.	.	.	.	.	.	.	.	.	.	.

In the first application of a computer to production control as outlined above, the computer is replacing office manual functions and by so doing may have hidden the real advantage of the computer. Existing systems are as they are because of the limited capacity of the human brain and human 'communication'. The computer was devised to circumvent these shortcomings, yet we end up just speeding up the system which is devised on this basis of human limitations. Stafford Beer has made the point.

Some of those who boast of their firm's and their own foresight and adaptability are indeed embracing change, but they are unwittingly making sure that it is artificial; it is a change in which nothing actually alters. Most of our applications of computers are worth while and certainly they should have been undertaken, but this does not mean to say that we have really done anything much. These applications are indeed 'but dressings of a former sight'.[1]

A few companies have made a more fundamental change and have taken the computer right to the shop floor, providing terminals at strategic points where the operator dials the information normally found on a job card, direct to the computer. A few pioneering firms have even linked the computer direct to numerically controlled machine tools into one integrated system. But it will be a long time before this approach is ever likely to be common practice. In the meantime we can expect to see increasing use of computers to aid a more conventional approach to production control, probably with smaller companies using a direct link to a central computer rather than possessing their own. Whatever the outcome along these lines the computer will only assist the Production Manager, it will help him make better decisions, or the right decisions sooner, it can never do the job of managing. Managing involves making decisions. The computer can never make a decision. It can take a number of predetermined courses in a number of different situations but without the 'feel' of the situation it is likely to make the mistake of the computer that was programmed to translate from English into a variety of other languages. On being given the expression 'out of sight out of mind' the translation became 'blind idiot'.

Production administration principles

As in everyday life, so also in the particular activity of management, experience proves that as a basis for all conduct it is wise to adhere as closely as possible to sound fundamental principles. The more one departs from principles, the more necessity there is for hasty decisions and expedient action to meet awkward situations which ought not to have arisen. One cannot always be certain of where some decisions are likely to lead, but if they are made in accordance with proved principles, then they are certain to lead in the right direction and to satisfactory results in the long run. It is useful, therefore, to have a body of principles, if only of limited application, in this relatively new science of management.

From experience and the study of the operation of the administrative activities discussed in this chapter, the following principles emerge:

1. Planning is a function of management to be distinguished from doing; In the structure of an organisation the two should be separated and those persons responsible for doing (executives and foremen) should be supported by administrative staff whose duty is to supply information on how and when work is to be done, standards of measurement, and reports on results compared with standards.
2. There are three divisions of the administrative activities:
   production engineering (concerned with methods and standards);
   production planning (concerned with programmes or time plans);

[1] Stafford Beer, 'Love and the Computer', Address at symposium, 'Electronics, Instrumentation and Production', at Bristol College of Science and Technology 12 June 1963.

production control (comparing results with standards and plans).
Each should be separately recognised and its specialised technique developed.

3. To reduce human effort to a minimum and to increase output per man-hour, work must be studied scientifically.

4. Work can be measured in a common unit and the work content of a job assessed. Standard times, expressed in a unit based on the rating of speed, effort, attention and skill, with a due allowance for relaxation, provide an accurate measure.

5. Standards to be used as a basis for planning and control for the material and labour content of production can be established.

6. The most satisfactory basis for payment by results is an accurate measure of the work content of a job.

7. Production planning is impossible without reliable information; and accuracy of results (given constant performance by supervision and operators) varies directly with accuracy of information.

8. The more the information which has to be transmitted, the less effective the results of planning are likely to be.

9. As far as possible paper work must be done in offices by trained personnel and not on the shop floor by operators at machine or bench.

10. To be effective, planning must be simple, flexible and balanced; be based on accurate measurement, and provide means for measuring performance against plans.

11. For production control to be effective, results must be compared with standards (of performance, cost or programme) in reports which reveal the extent and cause of any discrepancy. Such reports must be rendered promptly, and corrective action must be taken immediately.

APPENDIX: Production planning documents

Description of forms

This instruction describes a method of preparing and using Production Planning Documents which makes use of modern techniques and duplicating machines for preparing pre-printed documents for use on Planning, Production and Cost Accounting. The main purpose of pre-printed forms is to ensure that as much information as possible is entered on works production documents before they are issued to the works, and that such information, after careful check of original entries, is automatically transferred to all copies from a *Master Document*. The method adopted has three important advantages; it prevents transcription errors, prepares all documents rapidly and economically, and reduces the amount of clerical work in the shops to a minimum.

Master document

A master document is prepared for each component and each machine to be manufactured. This master is in two parts:

1. A permanent master (Fig. 3.5.38), on which is entered all permanent information relevant to production of the component or machine, including a summary of each operation in list form (i.e. process layout or master route card), and in the case of the technical design documents, design data required in all works.

Fig. 3.5.38
Permanent
master document
with variable
heading

Order heading master							

Customer		Quant	Description		Part No		Job or mach No
Stock		40	Shaft		140.2		342.E

Date iss	Material release	Special instructions					Date due
10/8	40 billets						Wk.35

Layout iss	Material spec & quan per		Patt No	Description			Part No
1	M. 152.9 2⅛" D21.7/16" L			Shaft 70 R A1			140.2

Route	Dept	1 9	2 9	3 9	4 9	5 9	6 3A	7	8	9	10	11	12
	M/C or group	527	42	61	527	54							

Operation master	Op No	Dept	Mach or group	Operation	Jigs tools and gauges	Labour grade O head ref	Time allowed	
							Set up	Hours per
Type on dotted line only	1	9	527	Centre face turn		M7 C	.25	.5
	2	9	42	Grind		M7 D	.2	.48
	3	9	61	Key seat		M5 C	.2	.18
	4	9	527	Screw		M6 C	.2	.16
	5	9	54	Drill peg hole		M1 C	.05	.01
				(These times are purely imaginary)				

2. A variable heading, on which is entered information relating to the particular order or batch to be manufactured.

The two portions married together form a complete master document for the particular batch.

Production documents

From the *component master* the following documents are prepared immediately an order is created:

1. *Material release note* (Figs. 3.5.39, 3.5.40), specifying type and quantity of material required for 100 units and for the batch. Only the total amount of material specified is 'released' in the first instance, and more can only be obtained by presenting an excess material requisition. After materials are issued it is returned to Planning, who adjust stock and progress records. It is then sent to Accounts, who debit and credit appropriate inventory accounts.
2. *Identity label* (Fig. 3.5.41), used for identifying a batch and specifying each operation and the department where performed, i.e. the route. This label accompanies the work throughout all operations, and on it is recorded details of scrap and good work produced.
3. *Job card* (Fig. 3.5.42), one for each operation as specified on the master, giving the time allowed for the operation, and the jigs, tools and gauges required. On this is recorded the operator's name and check number and the number to be paid for. It is later used for wages computation.
4. *Move note* (Fig. 3.5.43), one for each operation specified on the master. On this is recorded the quantity passed forward, scrapped and to be rectified. It is returned to Planning Office when the operation is completed, where it is used for progress records.
5. *Delivery note* (Fig. 3.5.44), for the final operation only. On this is recorded the quantity finally delivered to Stores. The information is checked by Stores and entered on progress and stock records by Planning Office. It is then sent to Accounts, who debit and credit appropriate accounts.

Fig. 3.5.39
Material release note—fabrications

Material release note–fabrications

Customer		Quant: 10	Description: Bracket CE/OB/FV		Part No: 120.25	Job or mach No: 350.B
Date iss: 22/8	Mat,l release: 10 sets	Special instructions				Date due: Wk.50
Required by	Layout iss: 1	From stores: 3 11	Sht. 1 of 1	Drg No: 120.25	Description: Bracket CE/OB/FV	Part No: 120.25

Stores control	Quan per part	Material code No	Material description	Wt./part	Total	Quan this batch	Value
	1	M190-4	18″ × 18″ temp 1	46 lbs			
	1	M190-3	14″ × 14″ temp 2	21			
	1	M190-1	6$\frac{1}{2}$″ × 18″ temp 3	8.9			
	2	M190-3	8″ × 13$\frac{1}{2}$″ temp 5	25.5			
	2	M190-1	6$\frac{1}{2}$″ × 8$\frac{1}{2}$″ temp 4	8	109.4		
	1	M181-76	1″ × 2$\frac{3}{4}$″ × 4$\frac{3}{4}$″	3.2			
	4	M181-11	3$\frac{1}{2}$″ × 3/16″ × 1$\frac{1}{8}$″	1			
	12	M181-8	1$\frac{3}{4}$″ × 3/16″ × $\frac{5}{8}$″	2.2			
	2	M181-8	1$\frac{3}{4}$″ × 3/16″ × $\frac{3}{4}$″	.4			
	4	M181-6	7/16″ × 5/16″ × 1″	1.34	81.4		
	Cut	Issued	Stores sig			Total cost	

Fig. 3.5.40
Material release
note

Material release note					
Customer		Quan	Description	Part No	Job or mach No
		40	Shaft	140.2	342.B
Required by	Date iss 10/8	Material release 40 billets	Special insructions		Date due Wk.35
Progress	Layout iss 1	Mat spec & quan per Steel M 152.9 2⅛"dia.21.7/16" long	Patt No	Description Shaft 70R A1	Part No 140.2
Stores control	Stores sign	Date issued	Weight cwts | qrs | lbs | ozs	Rate	Value

6. *Progress envelope* (Fig. 3.5.45), in which all works documents are kept until issued and after use, and on which is recorded the progress of the job (quantity and date) through the works.
7. *Cost card* (Fig. 3.5.46), a facsimile of the complete master, with additional columns for Cost Account purposes.
8. *Tool requisition* (Fig. 3.5.47), advice of tools required and receipt for tools taken from tool stores.

From the *technical specification master* the following documents are prepared:

9. *Official order record.* This is a complete copy of the master, and includes all information, technical and commercial, relating to the order, i.e. customer, machines and spares orders, prices, delivery instructions and design data.
10. *Technical specification*: a complete copy, as in 9, but omitting price details.
11. *Invoice order*: a copy of the commercial portion of the master, including delivery details and prices of all items.
12. *Despatch instructions*: a copy of the commercial portion of the master, omitting prices, but including data required for nameplates, etc.
13. *Instruction card*: one for each assembly operation and for certain components. This card will give the operator all the technical data required at this operation.
14. *Planning card*: one for each order. This will have only a brief description of the order as given at the head of the master, but will have planning data added, and be used for building the forward master load on the works.

Fig. 3.5.41
Identity label

Identity label											
Customer				Quan	Description			Part No		Job or mach No	
				40	Shaft			140.2		342.B	
Date iss 10/8	Matl release 40 billets			Special instructions						Date due Wk.35	
Layout iss 1	Matl spec & amount M. 152.9 2⅛" D 21.7/16" L			Patt No	Description Shaft 70R A1			Part No 140.2			
1 9	2 9	3 9	4 9	5 9	6 3A	7	8	9	10	11	12
527	42	61	527	54							

Fig. 3.5.42
Job card

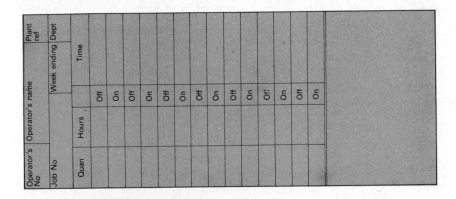

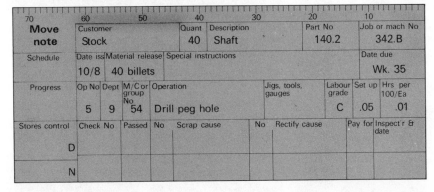

Fig. 3.5.43
Move note
(progress advice)

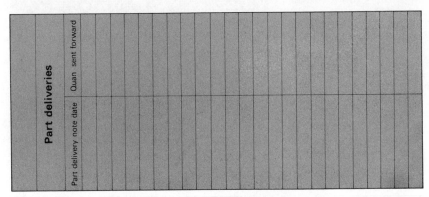

Fig. 3.5.44
Delivery note

70 60 50 40 30 20 10

Delivery note	Customer	Quant	Description	Part No	Job or mach No
	Stock	40	Shaft	140.2	342.B

Schedule	Date iss	Material release	Special instructions	Date due
	10/8	40 billets		Wk.35

Progress	Op No	Dept	M/C or group No	Operation	Jigs, tools, gauges	Labour grade	Time allowed: Set up	Time allowed: Hrs per 100/Ea
	5	9	54	Drill peg hole		C	.05	.01

Stores control	Operator's name	Quantity passed and sent forward	Rectifications: No	Rectifications: Cause	Inspector	
	Check No		Scrap: No	Scrap: Cause	No to pay for	Date

Part deliveries																			
Quant sent forward																		Delete as necessary	Date
Part delivery note date																		Deliver to: Stores / Assembly / Despatch	Received

Fig. 3.5.45
Progress envelope

Progress envelope	Customer	Quan	Description	Part No	Job or mach No
	Stock	40	Shaft	140.2	342.B

	Date iss	Matl release	Special instructions	Date due
	10/8	40 billets		Wk.35

	Layout iss	Mat spec & quantity per	Patt No	Description	Part No
	1	Steel M 152.9 2⅛″diam. 21.7/16″L.		Shaft 70R A1	140·2

Schedule		1	2	3	4	5	6	7	8	9	10	11	12
	Dept	9	9	9	9	9	3A						
	M/C or group	527	42	61	527	54							
Order part list	Start												
	Finish												
	Oprs No												
	No good												
	No scrap												

Fig. 3.5.46
Cost card

Cost card	Customer Stock		Quan 40	Description Shaft		Part No 140.2		Job or mach No 342.B		Material	
										%	
										Labour	
	Date iss 10/8	Material release 40 billets		Special instructions				Date due Wk. 35		A	
										B	
	Layout iss 1	Material spec & quan per 2⅛″ D	M 152.9 21.7/16″ L	Patt No	Description Shaft 70R A1			Part No 140.2		C	
										D	
Route	Dept 1	9 2 9 3 9 4 9 5 9 6 3A 7 8 9 10 11 12								E	
	M/C or group 527	42 61 527 54								Total cost	

Op No	Dept	Mach or group	Operation	Jigs, tools, and gauges	Labour grade O head ref.	Time allowed Set up	Hours per	Std rate	Labour cost		
1	9	527	Centre face turn		M7 C	.25	.5				
2	9	42	Grind		M7 C	.2	.48				
3	9	61	Key seat		M5 C	.2	.18				
4	9	527	Screw		M6 C	.2	.16				
5	9	54	Drill peg hole		M1 C	.05	.01				
			(These times are purely imaginary)								
									Total		

Fig. 3.5.47
Tool requisition

Part No.	Opn. No.	Clock No.
Date issued	Date reqd	
Remarks:—		Total tools received
Tool requisition	Received tools & drwgs to this reference	
	Date	Signed

**Procedure
for use of
documents for
component orders**

In the following procedure it is assumed that each person hands on a document to the person dealing with the next subsequent operation. The procedure is illustrated in the flow chart, Fig. 3.5.48.

1. Originate orders

By *standard components* is meant those parts which are made against job numbers through a stock control routine.

*Standard
components*

Stock Records Clerk
(a) Originate order when order point on stock of a component is broken, by writing out a requisition for manufacture.
(b) Calculate quantity of material to be released (i.e. length of bar or number of castings, etc.), and enter on requisition for manufacture.
(c) Enter on requisition for manufacture the actual stock of castings or fabrications.

Shop Schedules Clerk
Receive requisition for manufacture from Stock Records Clerk, and scrutinise and amend batch quantity if circumstances call for this.

Typist
Type component order heading master from information on requisition for manufacture.

Duplicating Machine Operator
(a) Take operation master for component from file.
(b) Marry order heading master and operation master, and run off documents on duplicating machine, thus:
1 Material release note (for fabrications two notes are usually required—one for bar stores and one for plate stores).
1 Job card for each operation.
1 Move note for each operation.
1 Delivery note (in lieu of move note for last operation).
1 Identity label.
1 Progress envelope.
1 Cost card.
(The cost card is only necessary for the initial issue of a master operation layout, and for standard items to be run off without component order heading master.)
(c) Refile master, and scrap order heading master and requisition for manufacture.

Shop Schedules Clerk
(a) Receive progress envelope containing all documents. Draw load line on all planning tickets and replace tickets in envelopes.
(b) File in the appropriate section of the 'standard' waiting file under machine size sequence.
(c) Send cost card for new components to Cost Office.

*Special
components*

By *special components* is meant those parts which are made only to special order numbers, and not to minimum and maximum stock requirements.

Forward Load Planner
(a) Scrutinise order parts list of machines on assembly schedule for availability of material.
(b) For machines where material is not available, write out appropriate urge notes and pass to Buying Department.
(c) Where all material is available, raise requisition for manufacture for each special part on the order parts list.
(d) Obtain operation master copy and calculate quantity of material to be released, and enter on requisition for manufacture.
(e) Send requisition for manufacture to typist.

Typist
Type component order master heading from information on requisition for manufacture.

Duplicating Machine Operator
(a) Take operation master from file (or obtain from Production Engineers).
(b) Marry order heading master and operation master and run off documents as for standard components.
(c) File master, and scrap order heading master and requisition for manufacture.

Shop Schedules Clerk
(a) Receive progress envelopes containing all documents. Draw load line on all planning tickets and replace tickets in envelopes.
(b) File in the appropriate section on the 'special' waiting file under machine size sequence.
(c) Send cost card for components to Cost Office.

2. Build component manufacturing load

Shop Schedules Clerk
(a) Each week, when departmental assembly schedules are built, scrutinise all jobs in both standard and special component waiting files, and build up a load on each department in priority order (i.e. according to date due on headings). Write out draft schedules of loads.
(b) Should special circumstances warrant reduction of size of batch, arrange for duplicate documents for the second half of the batch.

Typist. Type departmental schedules from drafts.

Forward Load Planner
Record on order parts list week number of schedules for any special parts that have been scheduled.

3. Issue schedules

Shop Schedules Clerk
(a) Issue schedules to Shop Planners of department concerned one week ahead of the scheduled week.
(b) With the schedule, issue move notes and job cards to the department in which operations are performed, and send material release notes and identity labels to the department in which the first operation is performed.

4. Manufacture

Shop Planner

(a) Build up load on planning board with move notes for each section.

(b) Send all material release notes to Stores concerned, as requisition for raw material, and to enable Stores to prepare all the material in advance of requirements, stating day on which material will be required.

(c) On day previous to when job is to commence, send identity label to Stores marked with the machine number or operator to which the material is to be delivered, and the time by when it will be required.

(d) On day previous to when an operation is to commence, make out tool requisition and send to Tool Stores.

Tool Stores

On receipt of tool requisition put up kits of tools for job operation specified, and place requisition with tools.

Foreman or Chargehand

As instruction for commencement of job, hand Move Note to operator.

Operator

(a) Take move note for new job and identity label for job finished to Time Clerk. Having been clocked on, retain move note for new job, and refix identity label to finished job.

(b) Present move note to Tool Stores for drawing, jigs, tools and gauges (retain move note). Enter clock number on tool requisition and sign.

Time Clerk

(a) Clock the time on job cards of new job and job finished.

(b) Enter operator's name and department, with the week number, on the new job card and place in current job tray.

Inspector

(a) After operator has completed the job, make a final inspection, and make out scrap note for any scrap. If there is any faulty work which can be rectified, arrange for rectification, if possible, by the operator responsible.

(b) Enter on move note the quantity passed forward, the number to pay for, and, if any, the number scrapped. Date and sign move note.

(c) If batch must be passed forward before rectification, enter quantity to be rectified, and complete move note, and make out new move note and job card for this operation, and identity label, by hand. The foreman to arrange for completion of batch and any further documents, if required. If operator is to be paid for any scrap or rectifications not sent forward (fault lying elsewhere), enter quantity to be paid for in panel of move note.

(d) Enter on identity label number of parts passed forward.

(e) Hand move note to Time Clerk.

(f) Sign move note each time a check inspection is made.

(g) For a final operation, on receipt of delivery note from Time Clerk, arrange for immediate transfer of batch to destination.

(h) If part deliveries are made from a batch, make out a part delivery note for any partial delivery with the part delivery note number.

Time Clerk

(a) When job is 'clocked off' transfer job card to 'completed' tray.

(b) When move note is received from Inspector, transfer quantity to be paid for from move note to job card.

(c) Extend actual hours for job and enter on front of job card in panel immediately at right of 'Actual hours at nat. bonus'.

(d) At the end of week write out new job cards when operator has to be paid for work done on a job not completed in that week.

(e) Enter on front of new job card the quantity previously paid for and actual hours for this quantity in panel 'Previous actual hours'.

(f) When completing a carried forward job card, deduct the quantity previously paid for, as shown on move note, to leave quantity to pay for on this card.

(g) Send job card to Cost Office, and hand move notes to Shop Planner.

(h) For a delivery note of a final operation, mark off schedule and hand delivery note immediately to inspection.

Storekeeper

(a) On receipt of material release notes, prepare material, castings or components, ready for issue.

(b) Enter on material release note for raw materials the quantity (or weight) of material for batch to be issued.

(c) On receipt of identity label claiming the material, enter date issued, and sign material release note. Send material to machine or operator indicated on identity label, at, or before, time specified.

(d) Send all completed material release notes to Planning Office once daily.

(e) On receipt of finished components from a manufacturing department, check description and quantity of goods with identity label and delivery note. Sign back of delivery note, with the date, and send to Planning Office. See that identity label is firmly fixed to special batches, and where necessary to standard batches.

Progress Record Clerk (Planning Office)

(a) On receipt of move notes, record completion of operation on progress envelope, file move notes in envelope.

(b) On receipt of delivery note for all components, mark off office copy of shop schedule, and hand delivery note for standard components to Stock Record Clerk.

(c) For specials, in addition to marking off final operation on progress envelope, enter on order parts lists that manufacture of component is complete. Send delivery note to Cost Office.

(d) File progress envelope in 'orders completed' file.

(e) For weldings delivered to casting stores, mark progress envelope for machine shop batch 'Weldings ready'.

Stock Records Clerk

(a) On receipt of material release and delivery note for standard components, record receipts and issues on stock record cards.

(b) Sign material release and delivery notes and send to Cost Office once daily.

Procedure for use of documents for assembly orders

Forward Load Planner

(a) At the time requisitions for manufacture are raised for special components (see p. 456), write out in pencil with carbon the variable heading for assembly master; see that any special instructions of general interest are included in the variable heading.

1. Originate orders

   (*b*) At this stage, when there is more than one machine on an order, decide on the number of machines to be put through as a batch, and make out the variable heading for each batch quantity.

   (*c*) Send variable heading to duplicating machine operator.

Duplicating Machine Operator

   (*a*) Take operation master for assembly from file (or obtain from Production Engineers).

   (*b*) Marry order heading and operation masters and run off documents as follows:

     1 Move note for each operation for each batch or machine.

     1 Job card for each operation (except test) for each batch or machine.

     1 Delivery note in lieu of move note for finishing and for machine painting operation.

     1 Identity label for each machine.

     1 Progress envelope for each batch.

     1 Cost card for each order.

   (*c*) Refile master and order heading master until advised that order is complete.

Shop Schedules Clerk

   (*a*) Receive progress envelope containing all documents. Draw load line on all planning tickets and replace tickets in envelope.

   (*b*) File in waiting file under machine number sequence.

   (*c*) Send cost card to Cost Office.

2. Build assembly load

Shop Schedules Clerk

   (*a*) Each week build up assembly load from load in waiting file. Adjust, if necessary, to preserve as near as possible a uniform load through all Assembly sections.

   (*b*) Write out draft schedules of load.

Typist

   (*a*) Type departmental schedules from drafts.

   (*b*) Record scheduled week number on order book card index.

3. Issue schedules

Shop Schedules Clerk

   (*a*) Issue schedules to Shop Planners of department concerned one week ahead of the schedules week.

   (*b*) With the schedule, issue move notes and job cards to the department in which operations are performed, and send material release, assembly notes and identity labels to the department in which the first operation is performed.

   (*c*) With the schedule, issue job instruction cards.

4. Manufacture

Shop Planner

   (*a*) Build up load on planning board with move notes for each section.

   (*b*) Send material release and assembly notes to Stores concerned two days previous to when machine is to be built, to enable Stores to prepare material in advance.

(c) In assembly shop, components for building will be put out on stillage platforms and parked by stores inside assembly shop, identified by a handwritten tie-on label. Assembly shop labourer will collect and move platforms to fitter.

Foreman or Chargehand
As instruction for commencement of job, hand move note to operator.

Operator. Take move note for new job and identity label for job finished to Time Clerk. Having been clocked on, retain move note for new job, and refix identity label to finished job.

Time Clerk
(a) Clock the time on job cards of new job and job finished.
(b) Enter operator's name and department, with the week number, on the new job card and place in current job tray.

Inspector
(a) After operator has completed job, make a final inspection. If there is any faulty work which can be rectified, arrange for rectification, if possible, by the operator responsible.
(b) For sub-assemblies, enter on move note the quantity passed forward, the number to pay for, and, if any, the number scrapped. Date and sign move note.
(c) For dealing with rectification in detail assembly, see p. 458, *Inspector.*
(d) Hand move note to Time Clerk.

Time Clerk
(a) When job is 'clocked off', transfer job card to 'completed' tray.
(b) When move note is received from Inspector, transfer quantity to be paid for from move note to job card.
(c) Extend actual hours for job, and enter on front of job card in panel immediately at right of 'Actual hours at nat. bonus'.
(d) At end of week make out new job card for uncompleted jobs, and mark 'Brought forward'. On job card to be closed mark 'continued'.
(e) Send completed job card to Cost Office, and hand move notes to Shop Planner.
(f) For delivery note of a final operation mark off schedules and hand delivery note immediately to Inspection.

Storekeeper
(a) On receipt of material release to Assembly Notes, prepare material ready for issue.
(b) Mark off parts lists for items issued. Send parts lists to Cost Office when all materials on the order have been issued.
(c) Sign material release to assembly notes and send to Planning office daily.
(d) Assembly Stores. Gather together all parts required, put up on stillage platform, write machine number on manilla label, tie on batch and park in Assembly Shop.
   For sub-assemblies follow same procedure, using trays and Identity Labels supplied.

Progress Record Clerk (Planning Office)
(a) On receipt of move notes, file in progress envelope, and mark off progress on envelope.

(b) On receipt of delivery note, mark off order book card index.

(c) When delivery note on last machine is received, transfer progress envelope to orders completed file.

Stock Records Clerk

(a) On receipt of Material Release to Assembly Notes, adjust records.

(b) Sign Material Release to Assembly Notes and send to Cost Office once daily.

Procedure for use of ancillary documents

1. General

The following ancillary documents are to be used in conjunction with the preprinted documents, and are to be filled in by hand when required:

Excess time card
Excess material requisition
Stores credit
Waiting time card
Scrap note.

With the exception of the Stores credit, these documents all record excess costs, i.e. money spent on either material or labour in excess of what should have been spent. It is vitally important, therefore, not only that they are accurately made out, but are authorised by a foreman, so that the head of the department is aware of the excess costs in his department.

If either of the material documents, i.e. Stores credit or excess material requisition, or scrap note, are spoilt, they must not be thrown away, but must be marked across the face 'cancelled', and sent forward with the other completed documents.

2. Excess time card (Fig. 3.5.49)

1. This is to be used whenever extra standard time is allowed on a job because of some unusual cause, i.e. when, because of some temporary condition in the shop more time will be required to do a job and the extra time can be assessed.

It is not to be used when standard times are permanently adjusted.

2. It is only to be made out and authorised by a Work Study Engineer.

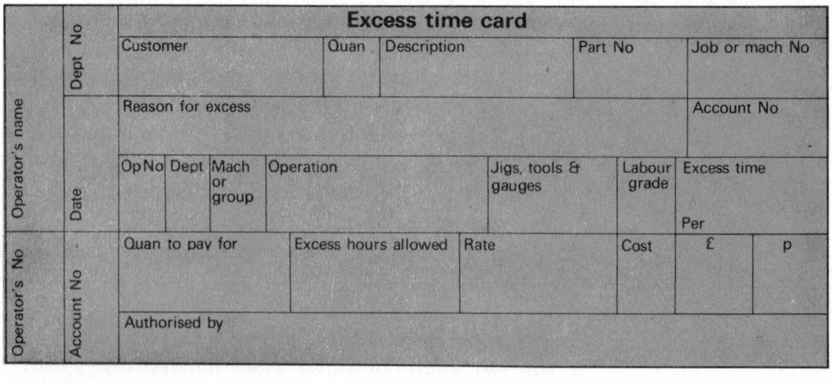

Fig. 3.5.49
Excess time card

Fig. 3.5.50
Excess material
requisition

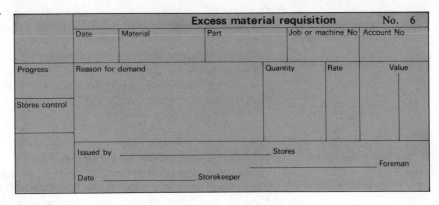

3. It is important to give the account number on which the excess cost is to be charged, and to state the exact reason for the excess, particularly showing the responsibility.
4. Excess time cards are to be attached to the job card to which they relate, and sent to the Wages Department.

3. Excess material requisition (Fig. 3.5.50)

1. This is to be used when an extra issue of material is required, because it will be impossible to finish the job with the amount of material available, due to scrap, loss, or shortage on original requisition.
2. Normally it will only be used when the amount of scrap is unknown, or material has been cut to waste.
3. Under 'Reason for demand' the exact details and the reason excess material is required must be shown.
4. Excess material will only be issued against the signature of a Foreman or some higher authority.
5. The Material Requisition is to be forwarded to the Planning Office with Material Release Notes.
   Note: See Scrap Note for replacement of scrap.

Fig. 3.5.51
Stores credit card

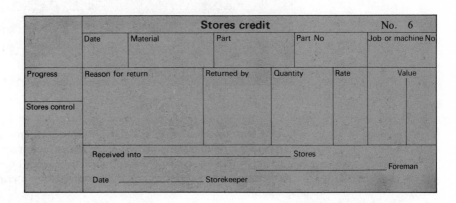

4. Stores credit (Fig. 3.5.51)	1. This is to be used when, for any reason, job cancelled or material found to be surplus to requirements, material or components have to be returned to Stores.
	2. It must be signed by the Foreman of the Department returning the materials or components.
	3. Stores credit notes are to be forwarded to the Planning Department with material release notes.

5. Waiting time card (Fig. 3.5.52)	1. This is to be used whenever an operator has to be paid for waiting time, i.e. the operator is prevented from, or delayed in, doing work.
	2. It is to be made out in total by the Foreman or Chargehand, including the 'time on' and 'time off'. Because operators can, and might be tempted to, claim more waiting time than has actually occurred in order artificially to increase bonus earnings, it is most important that the exact time when waiting commenced and finished shall be known and checked by the supervisor responsible. It also gives the supervisor the opportunity to investigate the cause, and to take steps to prevent its recurrence. It will be advisable for one card to be used for each incident. One card must never be used for waiting time on different account numbers.
	3. The exact cause for lost time must be stated, indicating the responsibility. When the responsibility is considered to belong to another department, a card should preferably be countersigned by the Foreman of the other department on the day the card is completed, in order that he can be made immediately aware of the lost time and excess cost, and take steps to prevent its recurrence.
	4. Waiting time cards are to be handed in to the Time Clerk, who will confirm that all time in the day is accounted for.

Fig. 3.5.52
Waiting time
card

| 6. Scrap note (Fig. 3.5.53) | 1. This is to be used to record components completely rejected as scrap. |
| | 2. It is to be made out by the Inspector rejecting the work, and the cause of the scrap must be clearly stated, and the account number indicating the responsibility entered, consulting the Foreman concerned if there is any doubt. |

Fig. 3.5.53
Scrap note

Scrap note					No. 3101	
Date	Part			Part No	Job or M/C No	Account No
Dept	Check No	Name		Operation at which scrapped		
				No	Description	
Cause of scrap				No scrapped		Cost
					Mat	
					Lab	
Re-issue of material authorised		Inspected by			O'hd	
		Foreman		Inspector	Total	
Material reqd		Amount	Issued		Date	

3. A Scrap Note is to be used for each job and operation, i.e. the scrap from several operations or different jobs must not be included on one scrap note.

4. Should it be necessary to replace the component scrapped, and therefore obtain further material, as may occasionally happen on the first operation of a special part, the material required may be drawn from the Stores by completing the bottom of the scrap note, and using the Note as a requisition instead of using an excess material requisition. It is the Inspector's responsibility to find out whether it will be necessary to replace the material at this stage.

When replacement of scrap must be put through separately and cannot go with the original batch, the scrap note must not be used as a material requisition, but a new set of documents must be issued from the Planning Office. The Planning Office will decide whether to issue a replace order on receipt of a scrap note for which replace material has not been drawn. It will help the Planning Office, in the case of urgent jobs, if the Inspector refers the scrap note immediately to the Progress Engineer or Planning Office direct.

5. After summarising by Inspection Department, scrap notes are to be forwarded to the Planning Office, who will forward on to Cost Office.

6 Ancillary services or departments

Storekeeping

The importance of storekeeping in modern industry is not always appreciated as it should be. Whilst the production departments are well equipped, the storekeepers are hidden away in cramped quarters, ill-equipped and with poor lighting conditions, and are generally underpaid in comparison with operators on production. It is not to be wondered at that loss of stock, wrong issues, unexpected running out of stock, and incorrect vouchers are a continual source of delay to production and of worry to production staff. To see the issue in its right perspective, it is only necessary to realise that the few persons in the Stores are responsible for, and handle at one stage or another, the whole of the material used by production. This may be worth 50 per cent or more of the total sales value of production; the value of receipts into, plus issues from Stores in a factory is greater than the total works cost, and at any time there is likely to be in stock material, components and finished products worth a quarter of the annual turnover, yet frequently unskilled labourers are expected to be Storekeepers. The truth is that storekeeping is more than a labouring job, and should be remunerated as such in order to attract and retain the necessary quality of personnel.

It may be said in answer that card indexes, stock control systems and goods bins take much of the skill out of the job. But card indexes are no substitutes for good storekeeping; they do not work of themselves, but must be *used*. A good Storekeepr can have an amazingly comprehensive and detailed knowledge of a firm's products, which can be used by him rapidly and in a fraction of the time it takes to refer to an index or other record. Theirs is one of the few occupations in which a man's value to the company arises more from his experience with the company than from his technical or practical ability.

Persons should be selected for storekeeping who are tidyminded and neat and tidy in their habits, and have a good memory. Tidiness can be taught, but while a person's memory can be improved, there are some who start with a big advantage by having a naturally good memory. It is essential also for a Storekeeper to be good at figures, or at least not bad at them. Whilst it may not be necessary for the ordinary Storekeeper to enter up records, and it is in fact unwise for this to be necessary, he must be able to count, and count accurately without checking. It is surprising how often persons are selected for storekeeping who are constitutionally unable to concentrate sufficiently to count up to reasonably large numbers. Far more care than is usually exercised should be taken in selecting persons who have either the right training or the right aptitude.

Kinds of stores

Stores are places where material is kept and the kinds of stores fall into five broad classifications as follows:

Raw material
Component or piece-part
General supplies or indirect materials
Finished product or warehouse
Tools.

To some extent the kind of stores influences organisation and activities, but, broadly speaking, the principles and methods of storekeeping, layout and records recommended in this section will be found generally applicable to all types.

Raw material stores

These are of two kinds, those requiring bulk storage so frequent in the extractive and processing industries, and the ordinary kind of stores in which a range of raw materials is kept in bins or rooms. Stores for bulk storage are usually specially designed for their purpose—for example, silos for the storage of grain and bunkers for coal—and are in reality a stage in the manufacturing process and should be dealt with as such. Handling these is a mechanical problem. In the case too of certain materials which are subject to excise duty, such as tobacco, cocoa, tea, etc., there is the need for a bonded side of the stores under the close check and inspection of a representative of the Customs and Excise Department of the Government, from which material cannot be withdrawn until appropriate duty has been paid or vouched for. Similarly cold storage in certain food processing industries, or in some aspects of horticultural enterprises, presents special problems.

The layout and organisation of the ordinary kind of raw material store varies widely with the industry and size of factory, though principles are still generally applicable. In engineering, pig iron for the foundry and rough castings and rolled-steel sections for the machine shops are frequently stored outside, as they are relatively unaffected by climatic conditions. In large factories a separate store for each material, or similar kind of material, is justified. In large food factories the main ingredients, colours and essences, and packing materials, are stored in separate stores; in textile factories the different types of fabric are kept separate; in printing, the paper sundries and inks are kept in different stores. In large factories, each main shop may have its own raw material stores supplied from the main stores.

In all cases it is advisable, and essential for smooth production flow, for the raw material stores to be at the input end of the factory. Unless production flow is arranged in the form of a U, this means that the raw material stores must be separate from the component and finished product stores.

Component stores

Component stores, and here we are not concerned with process factories, are of four kinds:

1. Standard stock used in a variety of assemblies or finished products: (*a*) made on the premises; (*b*) bought out.
2. Made to order, or specials required only for one order or too infrequently to justify carrying stocks: (*a*) made on the premises; (*b*) bought out.

These stores employ the majority of storekeepers in manufacturing industry, present the most diverse problems and require the greatest skill and ingenuity to render first class service. Layout invariably involves racks or bins, and adequate space is always a problem.

General stores

For a variety of reasons it is often found advisable for all or most of the consumable (indirect or expense) materials, those which do not go directly into the product, to be stored on their own. Oils, greases, paint and rags are messy, and soon make a stores dirty and untidy. Furthermore, when the component Stores is organised on a preselection and accumulation basis for assembly, it diverts the Storekeeper's mind from his job to have to attend to individual wants for small supplies like files, emery cloth, wipers and so on.

Responsibilities

There are conflicting opinions and a good deal of loose thinking as to what a Storekeeper's responsibilities should include, and to whom he should be responsible. It is maintained by some that, in addition to looking after stores, he should keep all stock records and be responsible for ordering material. It is also maintained that the Head Storekeeper should be responsible to the Buyer, or to the Secretary, or to the Accountant, or to Production Control, or for sections of stores to be responsible to departmental foremen, and all these arrangements can be met with in practice. A Storekeeper's job is to keep stocks, to receive and issue them, and in between to store them tidily in a minimum of space with the minimum of labour. It is a physical job. It is not his job to keep records; that is part of stock recording, which in turn is part of production planning. To function effectively, production planning must have up-to-date information of stocks, and must be able to refer to stock records immediately in building up production programmes. This cannot be done if the records are not in the Production Planning Office, and duplication should be avoided both on the score of cost and of accuracy.

As was made clear in chapter 5, the head of Production Planning is a specialist in the compilation and use of records: a Storekeeper is not, but he must be a specialist in the physical handling and storing of materials. It is wrong therefore to ask him to maintain records, or to expect this to be done as accurately in the works as in an office staffed with persons trained in the work. This does not mean that the Storekeeper can forget all about stocks held; he can, by suitable technique, act as a backstop on the need for stock replacement or adjustment.

In spite of the above statement, there can be special stores where the size of the enterprise does not justify dividing the storekeeping and stores records responsibilities; for example the tool stores of a small company: in this situation it is right to expect the Storekeeper to maintain both the stores physically and also the relevant records, raising requisitions for replacement stock on the buying office as required. In these circumstances, however, the initiation of new stock, and the fixing of minimum stock and re-order levels should be the responsibility of a more senior manager.

Since the storing of material is clearly a physical job, the Stores should be considered a works department, and storekeeping a works job, the Storekeeper therefore should be responsible to the Works Manager or Superintendent. As it is a specialist's job, all stores should be under the supervision of one person, the Head Storekeeper (or alternative title). The Foreman or Head Storekeeper is then able to coordinate the activities of the various stores and economise in labour. He is able to call on other sections of the stores when any one is suddenly overloaded, as frequently happens when large consignments of materials arrive, and in times of illness.

In view of the above, the following can be taken as the duties of a Head Storekeeper:

1. Generally, to:

   - supervise the work of storekeepers, and to instruct and guide them in carrying out their duties, ensuring that they are effectively performed;
   - ensure cleanliness and tidiness in the Stores;
   - cooperate closely with the Buyer, Chief Planning Engineer, Inspection Department, and with production Foremen generally;
   - adhere to the Company's personnel policy, and ensure that subordinates do so;
   - ensure that any records required are promptly and accurately made;
   - provide a prompt and efficient stores service to all departments.

2. Specifically, to:

   - receive goods from outside suppliers, check-count and arrange for inspection of quality; report to Buyer deviation from specification of order;
   - receive components produced in the works, and check-count;
   - store all material and components safely and tidily, and in a manner in which they are immediately available;
   - check actual stock of every item, preferably once every three months, but at least every six months, and advise Stores Control of any corrections required;
   - issue materials and components called for on receipt of appropriate release instructions; issue surplus to original requisitions only against excess material requisition, and receive back materials in excess of requirements only against material returned to stores note;
   - record accurately:
     (a) receipt of all outside supplies on back copy of order arranging for inspection report on each consignment;
     (b) receipt of parts manufactured in works on delivery to stores note;
     (c) issue of material against material release note;
     (d) issue of finished parts against parts list.

Storekeeping methods

More 'systems' have been sold to industry for storekeeping and stock control than for any other business activity. What are really offered are tools, and these are mostly to do with stock records already dealt with in chapter 5. In this section we are concerned with the use of such tools and with methods of actually storing the goods and materials.

The first fundamental principle of good storekeeping is the old maxim for good housekeeping, 'a place for everything and everything in its place'. To which should be added, 'and know where it is'! Nowhere else in a factory is tidiness more important. Whether or not bins or shelves are used, materials and parts should be neatly arranged, and the whole stores should present an orderly appearance. If goods have to be stored on the floor, as they may be, it is essential to arrange them in bays with gangways and to keep them as tidy as if in bins.

*Equipment and
layout*

The equipment now available is so varied, and most of it so well known, that it is unnecessary to deal with it in detail here; a study of catalogues is a fruitful way of getting new ideas to meet specific problems. However, there are certain precepts, modern developments and pitfalls which should be generally known.

In the first place, it should be remembered that it is false economy not to have adequate space and adequate bins or racks (with a margin for growth). Since floor area is expensive, this means that the maximum use has to be made of height. When the goods to be stored stack easily and the quantities are large, equipment for stacking should be used. Stacking trucks with forks which can be raised by power, and wooden or steel platforms or pallets, answer the problem. When the goods do not stack, or the quantities are small, shelves or bins should be used, and again to economise in floor space these should be as high as possible. Bins up to 4 or even 5 metres high are quite satisfactory provided that light parts only are stood in the top half and that safe, convenient and easily moved steps can be provided. A modern design makes the maximum use of floor space by building the racks or bins in short self-contained sections, and erecting these on rollers which ride on rails let into the floor. Rows of these sections are placed close together, and in each row there is one section missing, so that any section can be uncovered in any row as illustrated at Fig. 3.6.1.

Long bars or tube, or lengths of timber, should be stacked on end in racks which can be built up inexpensively from angle iron. Rods or stays are fixed to a horizontal back rail, so that they stand forward from the rails to act as divisions or compartments for the different sections of material, Fig. 3.6.2. Very heavy bars must be stored horizontally for safety, Fig. 3.6.3.

Fig. 3.6.1
Roller binning
system
(plan view)

Fig. 3.6.2
Racks for
storing bars
vertically

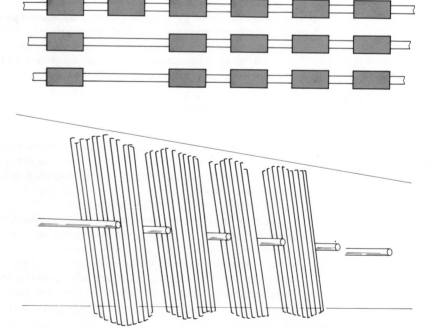

Fig. 3.6.3
Horizontal
storage racks

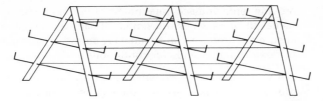

In general, metal racks or bins are preferable to wooden ones; they take up less space for the same load and are more easily erected and adjusted afterwards. There are several manufacturers who supply standard equipment which is so made that it can be adjusted to suit the particular requirements of the stores.

Stores should be arranged so that goods are not received through the same entrance as that from which they are issued. Gangways should be sufficient to allow trolleys to pass and slopes or different levels should be avoided if at all possible. In Component Stores supplying an Assembly or Packing Department, the goods should be so stored that it is possible to work from one end of the store to the other, gradually accumulating components for an order or requisition in the sequence stated on the requisition. When a Store serves more than one department, each requiring substantially different materials or parts, the ideal layout is for the stores to be arranged past the end of each department and the goods to be stored as near as possible adjacent to the department issuing them, thus:

Fig. 3.6.4
Arrangement of
stores for more
than one
department

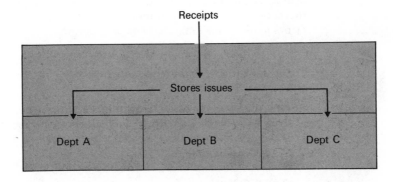

Classification

It is important that all materials and items stored should be identified by some simple, clear and logical system of classification. An effective system not only simplifies the Storekeeper's job and identification throughout the organisation, but it also assures a minimum of duplication and variety. The introduction of such a system in a company using a large range of materials and components can lead to a quite amazing reduction both in variety and in total inventory cost. Some notes on classification, using Brisch or Opitz codes, were given in chapter 3.

For components which form part of the final product and which are made to a drawing, the method of classification must serve an overriding purpose in the Drawing Office (see p. 335). In general however, a system of classification to be effective must:

provide rapid and accurate means of finding an item;
reveal all items which are similar or can be used alternatively;
ensure that items are automatically stored in their correct place;
be flexible and provide for continuous additions.

A very satisfactory system is a code which uses numbers only to identify groups or classes of articles, the characteristics of classes being arranged so that identification proceeds from the general to the particular. An item is known by a number and all items have the same number of digits. The size of the code (number of digits) depends on the variety of items involved; in manufacturing industry it is found that a seven- or eight-figure code is adequate to include all materials, components, tools and plant.

The following two examples illustrate the technique:

Class	Code	Class	Code
Materials	1.......	Tools	4.......
Copper	13......	Gauge	43......
Strip	131.....	Caliper	435.....
Covered	1312....	Stores	4357....
Stores (Elect)	13124...	Size 150 mm	43576...
Size 20 mm × 2 mm	1312407.		

Insulated copper strip 20 mm × 2 mm in the Electrical Stores—1312407

A 150 mm caliper-type gauge in the Tool Stores—43576

It is advisable to start classification as soon as possible and once established to insist that it is kept up to date. The results of the classification should of course be set out in a catalogue. In practice it is found that the logical form of the code greatly assists in memorising the numbers of items and reduces errors in identification, reference and storing.

Storing and locating

There are broadly three alternative methods of storing a mixed variety of articles in a Store:

1. When consignments are large or bulky, to carry the bulk stock in a reserved store and a small quantity of each article in the active store.
2. To keep the whole stock of each article together, all articles of a like kind being stored together.
3. As 2, but articles stored, irrespective of kind, in the order in which required in a normal list.

The second is usual and more satisfactory in practice. It makes for neatness and orderliness so vital in Stores, and Storekeepers find it easier to memorise where everything is when articles of a like kind are stored together. Although there must be a record of where everything is, it would be obviously a very slow job if a Storekeeper had to go to an index for many items. A person who knows where everything is is a treasure (and not such an uncommon one) and everything possible should be done to enable a Storekeeper to become one.

A logical system of numbering items or parts is a further aid to memory, both for identity of a part and for location. If the part can be given a number according to its location in the Stores, it simplifies matters considerably for the Storekeeper, but this is not recommended for general use. Almost invariably there are overriding demands from other departments for a system of code numbers which classifies parts or materials strictly according to kind and size, or to product or model and so on. A code of numbering for parts and materials which is built up according to kind and size is easier to remember than one built up according to location. However, it is essential to have in the Stores an index of location, and this should be based on a code built up logically, and flexibly for expansion, as illustrated in Fig. 3.6.5:

Fig. 3.6.5
Numbering of
stores bins

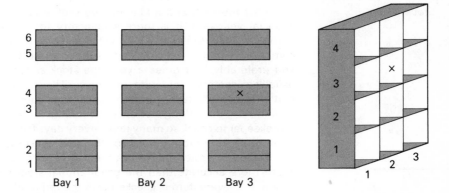

Number each bay or section of racks from 0 to 9 or 99.
Number each row of racks 0 to 9.
Number horizontal rows of bins or shelves in each rack 0 to 9.
Number vertical rows of bins in divisions or shelves in each rack 0 to 9.
Therefore, bin x is referenced as 3423.

As stated earlier, recording of stock in the Stores is not in general recommended, and requisitioning for replacement of stocks is not normally therefore a Storekeeper's duty. However, there are certain classes of material and articles which have a general-purpose use and which, in normal times, can be obtained at relatively short notice so that minimum stocks are small. Storekeepers can be made responsible for maintaining stocks of these without having to keep records. The minimum quantity for each item is first calculated and authorised. This is the quantity necessary to supply normal demand (with a margin of safety) through the period required for obtaining a further supply. This minimum quantity is then boxed, wrapped, or placed at the bottom of the bin and covered with a piece of cardboard, wood or sheet metal, and the remaining stock placed on top. When the loose stock has all been used, it indicates that the re-ordering point has been reached and a requisition is placed on the Buyer for further supplies. When new supplies are received, the minimum quantity is again boxed or covered. This is known as the 'two-bin' system of stock control. (This method can also be used as a danger signal on those items for which Stores Control are responsible for requisitioning.)

If it is found impracticable physically to identify the minimum stock or if for other reasons it is decided to keep a record of stock balances in the Stores, the bin stock card is the simplest method. This card is hung on the front of or placed inside the bin to which it refers, and is entered up and the balance struck at the time stock is put in or taken out. This ensures promptness of records. The simplest design of card has rulings on one side for recording quantities received and issued, and on the reverse details of the item, its stock number, description, location, order quantity and minimum stock quantity. It can be originated by the Buyer and used as an advice of order placed and to be received. It is useful to print one side red, so that it can be turned this side uppermost when stocks are low as a visible reminder of the fact to the storekeepers.

Stock-taking

To avoid the rush and additional work of stock-taking once a year at the financial year end, it is more satisfactory to arrange for what is termed perpetual inventory check. Provided each item in stock is checked and compared with stock records, and the latter corrected if necessary at least once and preferably four times a year, the stock as recorded at the year end is usually acceptable for audit purposes. The simplest effective alternative methods for making this perpetual check are either for independent staff to be appointed to do nothing else but go round the Stores checking stock, or for the Storekeeper to check so many items every day. The former, if more regular, is likely to be very monotonous for the staff concerned; the latter gives each Storekeeper a vested interest in the accuracy of his stock. Either method is much more accurate than the usual annual stock-taking. In either case, to ensure that every item is checked with the required frequency, Stock Control should issue a daily list of items to be checked.

Receipts and issue

A sound principle to observe in dealing with the receipt and issue of Stores materials is that nothing is received and nothing issued without a written authority and signature for receipt. If this is not faithfully adhered to, it will be found too often in practice that verbal arrangements and memory are very unreliable. This means that a *goods received note* or its equivalent must be made out by the Stores for all consignments received from outside suppliers, and an *internal delivery note* accompany all deliveries from works departments. All goods received from outside suppliers should be against an *order* from the Buyer, and the procedure can be used as outlined in chapter 4 (see p. 354). If a consignment is received which has not been authorised by a written order, as occasionally happens when senior executives give verbal orders and forget to confirm by official order, then a *goods received note* should be written out immediately to notify Buyer, Stock Control and Accounts. Then if so desired and to keep records tidy, an official order set can be made out to cover the consignment.

It is important also to ensure that every consignment is checked and inspected, and it is preferable to do this independently of the supplier's consignment note—knowledge of what is stated on the consignment note is apt to lead to only cursory examination of the consignment, on the lazy assumption that what is stated must be correct. Inspection should be prompt, so that appropriate action can be taken without delay with the supplier, in case of discrepancy or fault. Goods received from internal departments will have been inspected, but count must be verified before signing the delivery note: the signature indicates responsibility for quantity and therefore records.

In order to link up planning procedures and to give the Stores an opportunity of preparing materials to be issued in advance of requirements and so avoid waiting time, requirements should be stated as far as possible, not on requisitions written by operators, but on *release notes*, issued by the Planning Office. Such notes are likely to be more legible and accurate, particularly if preprinted. Also, since only the correct (standard) amount of material required will have been stated, more can only be obtained on presentation of another requisition or preferably an *excess requisition*, and thus there is provided an automatic check and record of excess usage, and therefore of excess cost.

If a list of materials or parts is required, a copy of the material or part list should be used, covered, if necessary, by a *material release note* quoting the material or part list. Requisitions for long lists of parts, written out by works departments, always lead to inaccuracies. This copy of the material or part list is a Stores 'tool', and therefore should be designed with this in mind, i.e. it shoud be set out in such a way as to minimise work in the Stores. Materials or parts which are stored together, e.g. nuts, bolts and small hardware, should be grouped together. Also if part issues of large batches are usual, provision should be made for this, with an extension margin for marking off each issue. The essential thing to bear in mind is to keep paper work in the works to a minimum—it is seldom expertly done outside an office properly equipped.

Works engineering

For production executives or those aspiring to such positions, information on the factors affecting the choice of site for a new factory or buildings is apt to be more than a little theoretical. It is given to few of us to have the opportunity of building a new factory from virgin ground—and being able to choose the ground. Even when it is decided to put up new buildings their design is quite rightly the function of a specialist, the architect, who is (or should be) well aware of all the factors involved. Nevertheless, the production man must know of certain factors which vitally affect the production unit and the effectiveness of work done, and see to it that they are given due consideration when a new factory is built, or an existing one extended; some of them are insufficiently understood by the technical specialist.

Factory site and buildings

A dominating factor affecting the choice of site for a new factory is the availability of labour and its type or characteristics. The material factors, such as access to various means of transport, availability of services such as electricity, gas and water, drainage and foundation problems, can all be readily assessed by the technical experts, but the human factor is not so easy to assess. There has always been a tendency for industries to develop in certain towns or localities, as much because of local skill as for any other reason, e.g. needle manufacture at Redditch, chain-making in the Black Country, and furniture-making at High Wycombe. There is more engineering skill and tradition in Birmingham than in Hereford, but there is more competition for it. Those who have tried to develop new industries in country districts or towns where the special skills which are required are not indigenous, have sometimes paid for the experience. Workers are not so mobile as one might expect, so that if local skill is not available, production methods must be deskilled. It can and has succeeded in many cases, but the warning is that it is always more difficult, and takes longer, than is expected.

Another point to remember is that people do not like to travel far to work, so that there is likely to be more labour available in or near a residential area or housing estate than in a heavily industrialised area. It has been known for a firm to build a factory and then find it just cannot get labour at all.

Another factor often miscalculated is the room required for expansion—it will almost always be more than predicted. Adequate room for expansion is always a good investment.

Type of building and site layout

The type of building and layout of site necessarily affect each other but both should be considered functionally, i.e. in relation to the work being done, and the best way to do it. In process factories, extraction and chemical industries, the buildings must be built round the processes. For example, in sugar-refining and flour-milling advantage is taken of gravity flow resulting in tall many-floored buildings. In the more normal type of factory, just as much attention should be given to production flow. This should be in one direction only.

The following is an outstanding example of how buildings can be designed round the process. The major factors which had to be taken into account in designing the new factory were:

● A large number of items of packing materials, cartons, labels etc., had to be kept in stock, thus requiring a great deal of room.
● An equally large number of items had to be kept in finished shelf stock, thus taking up even more room.
● A small space required for process work, preferably on the ground floor.
● Many different lines to be in production at the same time with relatively small runs.

The ultimate layout adopted is shown schematically in Fig. 3.6.6. The actual filling, wrapping, packing, boxing etc., is performed on conveyor belts, of which there are many, each constituting a unit, running in parallel lines across the central part of the building. Packing materials are fed mostly by chute and delivered to stock floor by continuous elevators. The administrative departments form a block across one end of the building. This may appear a little unorthodox but a little study will reveal its many advantages and how functionally successful it is. Equally successful results can be obtained if trouble is taken to analyse the functional requirements of production in the same way.

Fig. 3.6.6
Functional layout of building

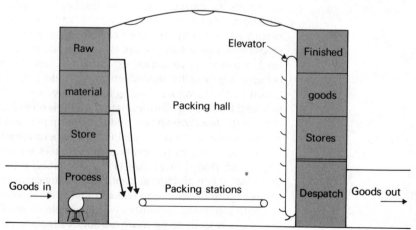

Fig. 3.6.7
Functional
construction
of building
and layout

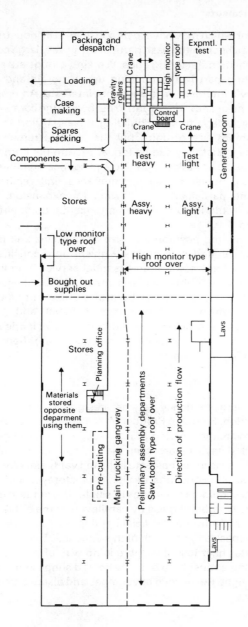

Another example is given in Fig. 3.6.7. In this case there was in existence a traditional saw-tooth roof type of building which was too small for requirements; the roof was too low and the structure not strong enough to carry the size of cranes required for some of the activities and the site was restricted. In the solution adopted two end bays of the old building were removed, one of which was re-erected at the opposite end. An extension was built using the 'monitor roof' type of construction which provided, economically, the height and span required and still enabled large cranes to be carried on the steel building structure. The form of structure used was in fact fitted round the layout which had emerged from detailed work study.

A factor which may have to be considered in industry more in the future than it ever has been in the past, particularly in very large concerns, is the size of the individual manufacturing units. Working groups are social groups, and play a dominating part in the building up of morale and of loyalty to either the company's interests or to sectional interests. An employee is more likely to feel that he or she matters and to be loyal to the company in a small unit than in a very large department or building. Research work is needed to throw light on the optimum size of units, but the point to remember with the design of buildings is that they can be too large from the human point of view.

The position of administrative and service buildings, the laboratory, drawing office, power house, maintenance and repair department is always important, particularly in allowing for expansion. What can be the right position in the factory at one time may be quite wrong when the factory is extended.

Similarly, the position and size of canteens and parking areas for cycles, motor-cycles and cars must be given more consideration than used to be necessary. Canteens are an essential service in industry today, and a good deal of their undoubted value is offset if the buildings and conditions are very unsatisfactory, as they can be if of a makeshift nature. With the increasing distances which employees need to travel, and the consequent growing popularity of motor vehicles, adequate provision is required for parking. To many companies this problem is acute today; there is no need to invite the problem in the future.

Single v. multi-storey

The modern tendency in the design of buildings is for single-storey construction. From the Production Manager's point of view this obviously has many advantages, giving greater scope for rearrangement and avoiding the transport delays inherent in the multistoreyed buildings. A single-storey building also is much easier to light and ventilate. When, because of the cost of floor area or restrictions of site, multistoreyed buildings have to be used, windows should be as large as possible. The modern tendency is for the whole of the walls to be of glass by cantilevering the outside edge of the buildings from the main frame. Artificial lighting is expensive; the maximum possible window space avoids much of this expense. The expense is partially offset by the greater heat loss, but there is no way of compensating for the dull and depressing atmosphere of badly lighted shops, nor for continually working in artificial light. Respective advantages and disadvantages may be summarised as follows:

Single-storey

Rearrangement of production and departments easier than in multistorey.
General supervision facilitated.
Good and uniform distribution of natural lighting.
Transport cheaper, quicker and easier.
Fire risks less than in multistorey.
Window maintenance less (but roof maintenance more).
Heavy machinery can be installed anywhere.

Multistorey

Departments are self-contained units and tend to better group feeling.

Factory more compact, and high-speed lifts are quicker than walking long distances.

Services (pipes and cables) shorter.

Gravity transport can be used for certain materials.

Less roof space and maintenance (gutters, coverings, etc.).

Lavatory blocks more conveniently situated.

Good ventilation not so easily arranged.

Serious restriction on use of heavy machinery.

If there are strong reasons for having wide shops with a large floor area unobstructed, the lattice-girder type of construction can be used. These have been frequently used for aeroplane construction, where extremely wide shops with no roof supports at all are required; spans exceeding 30 metres have been built. For roofs which have to carry additional loads like cranes the 'monitor type' should be used.

Conditions

Adequate artificial illumination, heating and ventilation are an essential prerequisite of effective production and accepted without reservation by modern managements. These aspects of factory services and working conditions are dealt with in chapter 4 of Part Four. Keeping up good standards is a continuing responsibility of factory management; for example, the painting of factory buildings and workshops, like window cleaning, is frequently neglected. There is ample evidence of the psychological effects, beneficial and otherwise, of colour schemes and general appearances of the places in which people work. The colour scheme must be chosen with as much care as the materials of which the buildings are made, and emphatically should not be a drab brown. It is true that no colour scheme can be everyone's choice, but there are some that will please most and others that can only be described depressing; a bright and cheerful one is a good investment. The Factories Act lays down that workshops must either be painted at least once every seven years and washed every fourteen months, or limewashed every fourteen months. It is today almost as cheap to put on a coloured distemper or emulsion paint every year, and thus always to preserve a cheerful atmosphere, as only to wash down.

The following are other problems which may arise, and which should be given full consideration in advance, when planning new buildings:

- If there are many piped services in multistorey buildings, e.g. hydraulic power, gas, compressed air, oxygen, in addition to the normal water and electric supply, the mains should as far as possible be taken up the building through a common shaft, like a lift shaft. This is a great convenience to the Maintenance Department.
- Certain processes give off fumes or a great deal of heat. It may be advisable to site these so that they do not affect other departments. Effective extraction arrangements are necessary in any case.
- High levels of vibration and noise can be minimised or insulated. It may be advisable to segregate departments in which vibration or noise cannot be avoided. The problem is accentuated if such are on upper storeys.

● When it is essential to divide a building into departments, standardised steel partitions, which can be ceiling height or lower as required, and can be solid, half-glass or expanded metal, are most effective, and are easily moved when rearrangement makes this necessary. Brick walls are a great deterrent to schemes of rearrangement.

● The increasing moves against environmental pollution will make it necessary for all waste to be carefully controlled. This may require elimination of solid or gaseous waste from chimneys and extraction ducts; treatment and purification of all waste water before being put into public drains or sewers, and possibly facilities may be required for storage and removal in bulk of toxic waste that cannot safely be treated. It is no longer acceptable to pour all waste down the nearest drain.

Layout

The one fundamental principle to which all good factory or departmental layouts must conform is that production generally must flow in one direction, and must never retrace its path in the opposite direction. Flow production reaches its ultimate perfection, of course, in the mass production layouts on the conveyor belts in the automobile industry. But the same principle of unidirectional flow should be adhered to whatever the product or process. This applies to the factory as a whole, to units of it, departments and to sections, although it cannot apply in detail in departments doing jobbing work. In continuous process industries especially, such as food, chemicals, metallurgical, etc., the products usually pass through a fixed sequence of machines or operations; although there are exceptions, as in bulk processing, when some of the materials, having reached one stage, are fed back to an earlier stage. But in the fabricating industries, such a fixed sequence is not usually inherent in the manufacturing methods, and as the factory develops and methods are altered, often the layout, like Topsy, just grows, and flow production is forgotten until reorganisation becomes essential.

An illustration of how a slight rearrangement of layout can greatly simplify production flow is shown at Fig. 3.6.8.

Types of layout. There are two commonly used approaches to plant layout and one less common approach which is showing distinct advantages in certain circumstances:

1. Group layout, which is common in most jobbing factories, machines or operations of a like type are grouped together as for example in a machine shop where all centre lathes would be grouped together, all milling machines together, all capstans grouped together, and so on.
2. Line layout, where machines are arranged according to the sequence of operations usually on a specific component.
3. Group technology, which is a special case of line layout using many of the advantages of line layout to cover families of components rather than specific ones.

In most manufacturing industries a mixture of 1 and 2 will be found, for these are purely arrangements of the machines and equipment. *Group technology* however, requires a reappraisal of components right back to the drawing office.

Fig. 3.6.8
Factory layout,
old and new

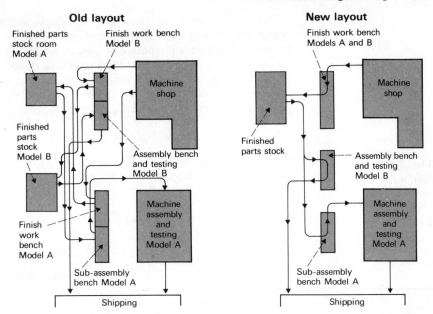

Old layout

Finished parts
stock room
Model A

Finish work bench
Model B

Machine
shop

Finished
parts
stock
Model B

Assembly bench
and testing
Model B

Finish
work
bench
Model A

Machine
assembly
and
testing
Model A

Sub-assembly
bench Model A

Shipping

New layout

Finish work bench
Models A and B

Machine
shop

Finished
parts stock

Assembly bench
and testing
Model B

Machine
assembly
and
testing
Model A

Sub-assembly
bench Model A

Shipping

Group layout has its major advantages in terms of supervision and administration. A group layout permits the supervision of each type of operation by a person who is, or becomes, a specialist. In machine shops where one setter services a number of similar or identical machines this has obvious advantages.

Production Engineers have long been aware that the most economic way of producing an item, or a range of items, is mass or flow production where each machine is tailored to perform the specific but limited range of operations required. By careful design of the line, operations are so balanced that each operation takes very nearly the same time as each other and so ineffective time is kept to a minimum. By arranging these machines in a line of consecutive operations transport is kept to a minimum. Line production is taken to the limit in the mass production motor car industry.

In most engineering organisations, the ideal of balanced operations on a line producing only one or two components is unobtainable, the total demand for any one component does not justify its own special line, so components are produced in batches, either to meet specific orders or on an economic batch size basis. The result however is frequently high investment in both finished stocks and work in progress.

Group technology

Group technology is an approach to the production of a variety of components required in small batches which goes some way to achieving the economics that flow line production achieves. However to achieve this, two of the rules which have guided Production Engineers for many years have to be subjugated. These are:

1. maximum machine utilisation;
2. factory layout on a machine group basis, i.e. grouping all machines of a similar type together.

The group technology approach is to analyse all the components produced within the factory into families of components, which have a similarity of shape and hence will require a similar series of processes on machine operations. It is essential that the analysis be done by critical analysis of the *shape* and not the name, function, product or other such attribute of the component. Figure 3.6.9 shows three components all of which have a similar overall shape but all have vastly different functions. The breakdown of each

Fig. 3.6.9
Similar
components
identified
by group
technology

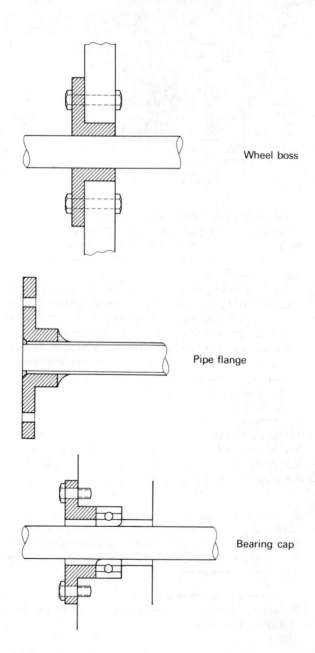

Wheel boss

Pipe flange

Bearing cap

component can be on a numerical code classification (see also p. 336). However in group technology classification the levels of classification would be:

General geometric definition of shape.
Additional features, e.g. holes, keyways, slots, etc.
Raw material form—bar, casting, plate, etc.
Raw material type—steel, brass, aluminium, etc.
General overall size.

Let us look at a typical example:

Shape—cylindrical, parallel, solid.
Additional features—none.
Raw material form—round bar.
Raw material type—steel.
Size—10 mm to 20 mm diameter, 50 mm to 100 mm long.

This description, while defining fairly closely the final product, could still cover the following: plain shaft, gudgeon pin, dowel, stop pin, and hinge pin. No doubt the reader can add many more to this list. One additional quality may still need to be added—the final tolerance of the component.

When the range of components has been classified into groups on this basis the next step is to determine what load the demand of each group creates on the various machines required to produce that group. At this stage it may be possible to achieve an improvement in utilisation of some specific machines by making slight adjustments to group boundaries. Likewise by considering the total load and realising that it now becomes a large batch of similar components, some change in production technology may be appropriate. When the machine requirements and tooling requirements have been ascertained then the machines required to produce each group of components can be physically grouped on the factory floor into a flow line.

The immediate effect of this change will be dramatically to reduce the set up times between components, for each one is so like others following the same route that only minimal changes in setting are required. With a reduction in set up time total throughput time will be reduced with its consequent reduction of work in progress and the need for high stocks of finished parts.

Once the analysis of the existing components has been completed, the information should be made available in such a way that a draughtsman producing a new component can mentally or actually sketch what he requires, then search the records of existing components that conform to the same basic shape and in so doing may well identify one that although performing a completely unrelated function may be so close to his requirements as to require little or no modification to suit the new function.

The effects of applying group technology can be very significant. One company who applied this principle to the whole of its operations recorded the following benefits:[1]

Finished stock—reduced by 44 per cent or £550 000.
Average manufacturing time—reduced from twelve weeks to four weeks.
Value of despatches per employee—up from £2 220 to £3 105.
Average income/employee—up 35 per cent.

[1] Figures from Group Technology Centre, UKAEA Report, *A Systematic Approach to Group Technology.*

Layout modelling

When the arrangement of a layout is being worked out on the drawing board, a great deal of time can be spent on redrawing the various possible arrangements. It will be found that cardboard templates cut to represent each machine, bench or other equipment, are a great help. Before cutting out they are drawn in outline, showing principal features, to the same scale as that of the outline drawing of the building or department. If there are moving portions of a machine, e.g. traversing tables, these are shown at the fully extended and closed position, and operating levers and the position taken by the operator are indicated. These templates can then be moved about the drawings until the most satisfactory layout is found; it is then drawn in and dimensioned.

It is always difficult to visualise the relative positions of plant on the floors of multistorey buildings. A good model of the building can be made as follows. Stick on to plywood or perspex a plan of each floor, and cut round the outline of the building. Assemble the plans in correct sequence on vertical steel bars about 6 mm diameter, separating each floor by distance-pieces long enough to enable the middle of the floor to be seen. This vertical distance will normally be more than would be correct for true to scale, but this does not in any way spoil the general effect nor the help the model can be in studying overall layout, transport and services. Coloured tapes can be used to indicate the path of various products, components, or services.

In factories where component or material stores and services departments, such as the toolroom in engineering factories, or the maintenance department in others, serve several production departments, it is always a problem to know where best to site them. The shape of the building may allow of no alternative, but when it is a single-storey rectangular building, so common in modern industry, a successful solution is to place the service departments along the outside walls, arranging the production departments at right angles to them across the shop. The sketch at Fig. 3.6.10 illustrates this for an engineering factory and shows how production is made to flow in one direction.

An illustration

An example of layout which emerged from detailed work study investigations was given in Fig. 3.6.7. It will be noted that the stores are sited the full length of the building and parallel with the production shops, and that materials are stored opposite the department which uses them, reducing transport and facilitating communications. Although there are ten fairly self-contained departments dealing with sections of production, one way flow is provided. Limitations of site forced a change of direction at rightangles from the Test Department to the Packing and Despatch Department where, in both departments, handling has to be done by crane. The change in direction was facilitated without involving a handling problem of putting-down and picking-up again unnecessarily, by arranging the intermediate operation of painting to be done on roller conveyors linking the two main departments.

At one time problems associated with countershafting made rearrangements of layout as production developed and methods changed almost impossible, or at the least expensive. Individual motor drive provides the necessary flexibility (in addition to the important psychological benefits of an unobstructed view in the shop), and there is little excuse today for not rearranging for economical production.

Unfortunately, too little attention is paid by machine designers to the correct working height for operators at machines. The working height appears to

Fig. 3.6.10
Layout for
(*a*) separate shops;
(*b*) one shop

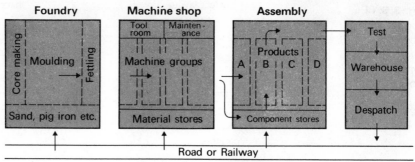

Layout for separate shops

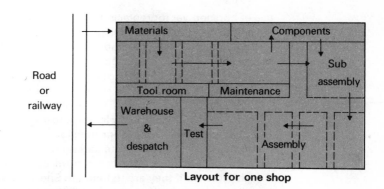

Layout for one shop

result from constructional requirements of the machine instead of effective operating and minimum fatigue for operators. The Works Manager or Engineer of the factory using the machines, therefore, must watch this point and correct for it.

Machines should be elevated, or sunk, to make the operating height correct. This is essential if machines are to be linked up with conveyors—why should it not be for operators?

In planning a layout, a frequent fault is not to allow sufficient or any room for work stations, i.e. areas where work can be kept tidily in between operations. It is useful to have one for each machine group, and certainly one for each department, preferably at the incoming end. Such stations are a great help to progress men; they are easier to control than work left around sections or machines where it so easily gets mislaid or forgotten.

When arranging for work to be performed along conveyors, it is better to provide each operator with a small table at rightangles to the conveyor and for the operator to sit facing the travel of the belt, than for the operators to sit along and facing the conveyor. The operators do not have so far to reach the belt and can more readily keep an eye on work travelling down it. This is illustrated in Fig. 3.6.11.

Plant and
equipment

The astonishing increases in production per man-hour obtained in many American factories (and some British ones) in the 1950s were chiefly due to the

Fig. 3.6.11
Correct and
incorrect
layout for
conveyor
work

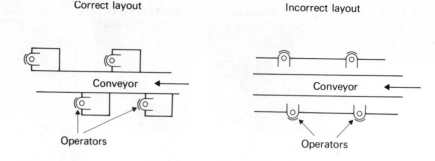

use of horsepower for replacing manpower, putting machines to do the heavy work and men to do the designing, minding and maintaining. Among the conclusions that were common to almost all the reports of the productivity teams from Britain who visited the United States in the 1950s, the greater use of tooling and power for lifting and handling was given as a primary reason for the American superiority in output per man-hour.

Evidently output is largely a matter of machinery and horse-power. If this is so, plant and tooling are likely to be more important than ever in the future. It is true that the larger scale of production possible in the USA with her huge home market makes elaborate tooling more economical than it can possibly be in Britain, yet much more can and will have to be done in the medium-sized British factories if they are to flourish. Special assembly jigs and mechanical handling equipment (conveyors, forklift trucks, stillage trolleys and such like) as well as special-purpose machines can effect considerable improvements in productivity.

It is not always easy to decide on when to buy new machines or to replace old ones. Formulae can be used; several are given and discussed in the literature of this subject.[1] In principle these set off the annual value of savings resulting from installation of the new machinery against the capital outlay and the profit the capital could earn in the business (or outside) if differently employed. Generally speaking, it is sound to err on the side of buying new plant; in the long run it pays to have modern plant. It is wise to reserve a substantial portion of annual profits for the express purpose of replacing old and buying new plant. In doing so it must be remembered that due to inflation depreciation reserved in the accounts is unlikely to match replacement cost when plant has to be renewed.

In general, there are two types of machines:

1. Special-purpose, designed for a specific purpose for one article or product.
2. General-purpose, capable of dealing with many sizes and types of work.

The special-purpose type of machine is common enough in process factories, and is much used in engineering factories on large-scale mass production. It usually enables a much higher output to be obtained than is possible on the equivalent general-purpose machine, and ensures absolute uniformity and standardisation of work turned out. It is high in capital cost, requires better

[1] See, for example: T. H. Burnham 'Engineering Economics' volume II, or sections in The Production Management Handbook.

toolroom service, is expensive in set-up and idle time, is soon made obsolete, and has a small secondhand value. On the other hand, the general-purpose machine is much more flexible (particularly important in times of slack trade), is cheaper to buy and maintain (spares are more likely to be available), and requires less special tooling. It may require higher skill on the part of the operators, but this is likely to be an advantage in the future. Bridging these two extremes is the range of *numerically controlled* (NC) machines. These are usually high in capital cost, but are much more versatile in their use than special-purpose machines, indeed batch sizes as low as two can be economic on some NC machines. It must not be thought that NC machines are confined to engineering; there are now for example, computer-linked knitting machines which will produce a sample of knitted cloth direct from a coloured drawing using a special probe. The sequence is shown diagrammatically in Fig. 3.6.12.

In purchasing machines the following points should be borne in mind:

1. If more than one machine of a given type and size are required, machines of the same capacity and output rate should be installed. This much simplifies machine loading, enabling Planning Department to load to a group instead of to individual machines.

2. Reliability is important—and valuable—particularly to Planning. Breakdowns not only involve maintenance costs and perhaps idle labour costs, but reduce turnover, a much more expensive matter.

3. Simplicity of set-up and of operating reduces idle time and human effort, expensive factors.

4. Automatic lubrication and totally enclosed features reduce maintenance and ensure continual operation. Too little attention is paid by designers to the need for protecting vital parts of a machine and enclosing as much of a machine as possible to protect it from dust and foreign matter. (If machines had aprons to the floor, operators could not use them for dumping rubbish underneath.)

5. Repeatability and reliability of the product produced can be as important as the rate of output.

Fig. 3.6.12
Diagrammatic computer-aided Knitting machine

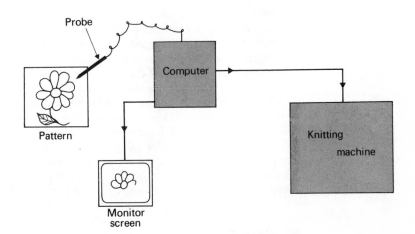

Tools and
toolroom

It is in the engineering industry that the modern toolroom and its technique have been developed to their present high standard, partly because of the influence and enthusiasm of the youngest branch of engineering, Production Engineers. But all industries use tools, and most of them can learn from the engineering industry of the advantages of tooling and of highclass toolroom service. In many industries the provision of small tool equipment is usually just one activity of the Maintenance Department, Carpenter or even of the Works Manager, and no attempt is made to develop the rather specialised outlook and skill required. What follows therefore deals, so far as current practice is concerned, mainly with engineering shops, but managers in other industries are strongly urged to take a leaf out of the book of experience of the engineering industry and to devote time and attention to developing a firstclass toolroom service wherever possible.

The production of tools (and in this context tools include jigs, gauges, patterns, templates, etc., and what applies to the toolroom applies to the pattern shop) has grown from an offshoot of the machine shop or production departments to a highly skilled expensively equipped department. Its importance is greatest in those engineering factories engaged on high quality production, or on large quantity repetitive production.

Experience has shown that most of the filing and fitting together of parts during assembly can be avoided by the provision of well-designed jigs, fixtures and tools, for use during the machining or fabricating stages, to ensure absolute uniformity and interchangeability. Really high quality work to fine limits can only be executed on a production basis with the aid of specially designed tools and holding fixtures. All craftsmen believe that it is as important to hold and secure the part or article being worked as to hold the tool correctly.

Because tools and jigs must be made to finer limits than the parts with which they are used, a toolroom or pattern shop must in general be equipped with high grade and accurate machinery and tools, and staffed with highly skilled men. In very large factories it is true that manufacture of tools can with success be put on a production basis, many of the operations being simplified and deskilled so that they can be produced on standard machines and by semiskilled labour, but in the small and medium-size factories, which constitute a majority of engineering factories, the need for flexibility places the emphasis on all-round skill.

When beginning to develop a toolroom, it is a common mistake to underestimate both the capital cost of equipment that is ultimately required and justified, and the room required. Because it is not a production department in the narrow sense, there is a danger of squeezing it into unsatisfactory premises or denying it the space it requires to use effectively the valuable equipment with which it is provided. With the associated tool stores, one-tenth or more of the space taken up by the shop it serves may be required by the toolroom. The layout of the toolroom in relation to the tool stores is important too. Even in large factories, where the stores can have its own tool repair section, it is advisable for the stores and toolroom to be adjacent. Tools that are returned to the stores should without fail be examined before they are put away, being reground, reset and repaired as necessary. It is usual for this to be done in the toolroom in a section set apart for the purpose, which should be under the authority of the toolroom Foreman, and located immediately adjacent to the stores.

Integration with manufacturing programme

It is vitally important to integrate tool production with works manufacturing programmes. Failure to do so inevitably results in either jobs waiting while tools or jigs are rushed through, or manufacture commencing without them, with the consequent inaccuracy and increase in costs. If it is not possible to assign a completion date to a tool when its design is first decided upon, then the toolroom must be given the tool requirements for production schedules sufficiently far ahead to enable them to make the tools in time for requirements—and tools, gauges, or patterns, and so on, are not made in a day or two. Because of this need to integrate the work of the toolroom with production, it is advisable in engineering factories for the toolroom to be under the authority of the Works Manager or Works Superintendent. In non-engineering factories tool production, or its equivalent, is normally the responsibility of the Works Engineer.

Tool stores

The organisation of tool issue, receipt and storage depends on the number of tools stored and handled, and the number of tools required per job. The simplest method, and one quite adequate for small tool stores in engineering and other factories, is the check system. The operator asks for the tool he requires, either by description or number, and in exchange for the tools hands in a metal or plastic disc on which is stamped his own name and number. This disc is hung or placed on the hook or space occupied by the tool. Normally an operator is only allowed a small number of discs, five usually being adequate. When, however, this results in too much waiting time at the stores serving hatch, or the jigs, tools or gauges required for jobs are numerous and complex, other methods are adopted for tool issue. The Production Department notifies the Toolroom a day or two ahead of jobs which will require tools (a copy of production schedules is often sufficient). The Toolroom has an indexed record of the tools used for each job, and from this the Storekeeper collects the set of tools in advance. Each tool number is entered on a *tool receipt*, which the operator requiring the tools signs before being allowed to take them away. From this receipt the operator's check number is transferred to the tool record card, so that at all times there is a record of where every tool is. The tool receipt is cancelled when the tools are returned and the entry on the tool record is cancelled.

Maintenance

The need in all industries, manufacture, mines, docks, or transport for the efficient upkeep of buildings, plant and equipment is, one would think, too self-evident to need emphasising, yet its importance is not always realised. Most firms know the total cost of their maintenance staff, but few could say what is the excess cost of production due to plant failure and other production delays due to poor maintenance. It can be surprisingly high, up to 5 per cent, and even 10 per cent on the total cost of direct labour, and with only 200 operators (male and female) on direct production at an average of say £30 per week, that is an excess cost of between £15 000 and £25 000 per annum. In certain types of industries, for example glass-making, and similar process industries with a high capital investment in plant, the Maintenance Department is nearly as important and has nearly as many employees as the Production Departments. In many companies in all industries, the controllable expenditure in overhead cost on buildings, plant and equipment, e.g. on repairs, renewals, services (heat, power), etc., may be equivalent to anything up to 25 per cent of the cost of direct labour on production.

In large firms the Maintenance Department includes most of the skilled trades, each perhaps with its own department; a small firm is likely to need only one or two men in each of several trades, usually millwrights, electricians and carpenters. In medium-size firms, particularly those not engaged in skilled engineering, there are likely to be upwards of ten or twenty, and it may be found that each trade has its own foreman, each responsible to the Works Manager. This is wrong. Unless the skilled trades are also production departments, as happens in general engineering, all maintenance men should be in one department responsible to one person, who is in turn responsible to the Works Manager (or similar executive). Even in general engineering there is everything to be said for keeping maintenance apart from production and responsible to a Maintenance Foreman. Maintenance then is much more likely to be planned, and production executives, particularly the Works Manager, released from the disproportionate amount of time which breakdown problems absorb.

Responsibilities

What should such a Maintenance Foreman's responsibilities be? The following can be taken as typical:

- Maintain all property, buildings, plant and machinery in good working order and ensure continuous supply of power, water, gas and air supplies and the efficient working of the sewage system.
- Periodically inspect and overhaul as necessary all such property, buildings, plant and machinery.
- Attend to breakdowns and other repair work promptly, so as to minimise to the utmost production delays or interferences with services.
- Supervise and control all personnel working in the section.
- Maintain discipline in the department.
- Adhere to the Company's personnel policy and ensure that subordinates do so.
- Establish and encourage among personnel in the department a spirit of service to production departments.
- Ensure that care is taken of tools and equipment used by the department.
- Ensure that operators make accurately any records required of them (e.g. time spent, work done).
- Continually watch all forms of excess costs (particularly waste of power) and reduce to a minimum.

In larger firms these duties would need to be shared by operators or sections in the following manner:

Millwrights' or Mechanics' Department. Responsible for installations, upkeep and repair of all mechanical plant. It may have its own machine tools, and would be likely to include millwrights (who are skilled in moving and installing plant and machines), machinists, fitters, pipe-fitters and sheet-metal men. If the factory produces its own power, or steam, for process it will be responsible for the boilers and engines. Likewise, if the company has a large fleet of vehicles, vehicle maintenance will be a responsibility of this section.

Electricians' Department. Responsible for electrical plant, motors, wiring, lighting, substation and switchboard, and if the factory produces its own power the generating equipment. In most factories it is now necessary to include an electronics technician in addition to other electricians.

Carpenters' and Building Department. Responsible for upkeep and repair, and small extensions of all buildings and furniture. It would include plumbers, bricklayers and painters as well as carpenters.

When it is necessary to design special plant and machinery for the Company's own use, or to rearrange plant frequently, a small Drawing Office is needed. In addition, there may be a small 'outside' staff responsible for gounds, cleaning windows, lavatories and so on.

It is essential to have in the Maintenance Departments men who can work with little supervision and have a large amount of initiative, because by the very nature of the work, they must at times work on their own, frequently outside normal working hours, and in conditions of emergency when just the right tackle or materials may not be available. It is necessary, too, to imbue the department with the idea of 'service to production'. Wage incentives for maintenance operators, which depend on overall effectiveness of performance of the departments they serve, are useful in this connection, though they cannot succeed if the attitude of prompt and ungrudging service is not always shown by the foreman and executives in Maintenance Departments.

Preventive maintenance

The effectiveness of a Maintenance Department is indicated, not so much by the speed with which it does a repair, as by the way it keeps a plant running and free from any breakdowns and delays. It cannot of course be held responsible for neglect or misuse by operators; that is a major responsibility of supervision. But a well devised scheme of preventive maintenance strictly adhered to is the soundest way of ensuring the minimum trouble from plant breakdowns. Such a scheme is based on the regular periodic inspection of every item of plant likely to give trouble, from boilers and large machines to steam traps and portable tools. It is often maintained that there is no time, or the staff is not available to carry out the necessary inspection; the truth is more often that the staff who should be doing preventive work are absorbed in 'shutting the stable door'. Once a system of routine inspection and of planned overhaul and repair has been running for some time, there is a net saving in time and labour.

1. A plant inventory (if one does not exist) must be prepared, and, what is not usually included, the inventory details of parts of the equipment which are subject to wear, unexpected breakdown or neglect must be recorded. A suitable form for use in visible-edge binders as an inventory book is shown in Fig. 3.6.13.
2. Determine the frequency of inspection and of lubrication or other service, if this is to be done at the same time, for each item of plant and machinery.
3. Prepare inspection schedules in terms of location of plant and frequency of inspection.
4. Assess standard times for the work; if in large works, routine maintenance work can be done on piecework.
5. Prepare schedule of regular overhauls for equipment which needs them whatever its condition, e.g. boilers.

It may not be possible at the start to define exactly all parts and points on a machine that require inspection, but as experience is gained the information can be recorded. It is useful to prepare an inspection sheet or card for each item of plant, listing vertically each inspection point, with vertical columns in which the maintenance inspector can insert a mark as he inspects each point. He should enter on a report sheet only items which require attention, with comments. The report should be scrutinised by the maintenance foreman for decisions, in consultation with production staff on when necessary work is to be done.

Inspection routines

To prepare the inspection schedule the items of plant are set out in a time chart arranged with items vertically and each day (or week) of year horizontally. Plant should be grouped either departmentally or according to type, and the type of inspection or service indicated by symbols, as for example:

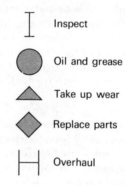

I	Inspect
●	Oil and grease
▲	Take up wear
◆	Replace parts
⊢⊣	Overhaul

All inspections etc., falling on each day (or week) can then be brought on to a daily (or weekly) tour or tours depending on the size of plant and number of maintenance inspectors required. The tours must be so arranged as to minimise walking time, take advantage of specialisation on certain types of plant if the quantity makes it possible, and to provide a certain amount of spare time for exceptional difficulties which may be encountered. It may be necessary, of course, to arrange for some of this work to be done outside normal production times. It is also important to attach to each tour, or to give to each inspector an exact definition of the duties to be covered.

Preventive maintenance cannot be said to be effectively under control unless, in addition to the routine inspection, there is also a record of breakdowns, which brings to the attention of management the frequency and causes of such breakdowns, and management do something about the evidence thus presented. Such records would need to classify breakdowns under the following headings, which show where the responsibility lies:

● faulty or insufficient maintenance;
● faulty design;
● faulty operator;
● unknown causes.

Fig. 3.6.13
Plant record
card

Plant and machinery record (mechanical)	Location		Description		Inspect	Number	
	Maker and description of plant					Maker's number	

				Floor space	Weight	Date delivered	Date in operation
Supplier							

Method of holding work	Coolant	Lubricant	Drive		H P	Amps	
			Type	Size of pulley		No load	Full load

Capacity		Alterations	
		Date	Details

Accessories, alterations or remarks	Parts or details for routine inspection

Front view

Repairs			**Overhauls**		
Date	Details of running repairs	Repair order No	Date	Details of major overhauls	Repair order No

Back view

To collect and present the facts, the production supervision of the department or section in which the breakdown delaying production for an appreciable period, say a quarter of an hour, occurs, should record the breakdown on a Breakdown Report and send it to the Cost Office, via the Maintenance Engineer, giving the following information:

- plant affected;
- cause of breakdown;
- period of breakdown;
- loss of production;
- urgency.

The Maintenance Engineer should add his comments and ensure that the report number is quoted on the job cards of the men doing the repair, or alternatively record the hours and names of mechanics in the report. The Cost Office can then calculate the cost of the breakdown, and render a summary report to both Works Management and Maintenance Management showing the cost under responsibility, as illustrated at Fig. 3.6.14. Such a report brings home to those responsible, not only cost of repairing, but the value of the production lost; both are excess costs, reducing potentially available profit.

Fig. 3.6.14

Weekly report on cost of plant breakdowns

Department	Responsibility and cost										
	Maintenance		Operator		Design		Unknown		Total	
	Produc-tion loss	Repair cost	Produc-tion loss	Repair cost	Produc-tion loss	Repair cost	Produc-tion loss	Repair cost	Produc-tion loss	Repair cost
Total										

In the very small firm an elaborate scheme of preventive maintenance is not required, and it is always more important to get a repair done than to record its cost. Excessive repair costs will be evident to manager or engineer. Nevertheless, preventive inspection should be practised, and it ensures that it will get the attention it requires if the person responsible is methodical, and this involves some simple form of inspection routine or schedule, perhaps one machine a day, which is rigidly adhered to.

Quality control and inspection

Quality control used to be the name given to a specific approach to the maintenance of quality by statistical methods; however it is now accepted as a much more general term and is defined in BS.3138 as 'procedure and means (including sampling methods based on statistical principles) of measuring and maintaining the quality of products'. Thus the current concept of quality control is not confined to manufacturing industry; services will also be included and will cover such diverse activities as chemical analysis of a steel casting, measurement of small machine parts, running tests on a large diesel, moisture checks in a roll of paper from the mill, size, texture and flavour of peas in a can and bacterial checks in the kitchen of a large restaurant.

Inspection to ensure that the quality of the product is maintained will occur at many stages in the production of the finished article, whether this be a piece of engineering, a volume of some liquid chemical or even a grown product such as a mushroom. At any of the stages, statistical quality control methods may be employed, consequently we look at defineable types of inspection, and then examine the principles of statistical methods. However, before we can inspect any item, material or product, we must know the specification against which it is being produced. This specification might cover dimensions and surface finish, performance, chemical composition, or physical properties. Whatever the parameter being checked, the specification must show the design condition and the *acceptable deviation* from that condition.

Aims and
objectives

The primary aim of the Quality Control department is to control the standard of the Company's product. This standard is implicit in the Company's Sales policy and is interpreted in turn by the Managing Director, Works Manager and Chief Inspector or Quality Control Manager. The quality of the finished product must be in accordance with the specification, conversely there must be for all products a quality specification which is a reflection of Company policy, without such a specification, Sales staff and designers want the highest quality obtainable—for a given price a high quality product is easier to sell than a lower quality one—but production and works departments find a lower quality—synonymous with wider production tolerances—easier to meet, hence greater output and less scrap are obtained for a given cost.

To specify the quality of the finished article is not always easy, but should be attempted, agreed at board level and adhered to by all departments. Quality related to price is a commercial decision, for it is just as easy for a Company to go out of business selling too high a quality product at too low a price, as it is trying to sell too low a quality product at too high a price. Thus the quality specification should give a quality band not just the minimum quality requirements; for there are many ways in which over zealous or under confident inspectors can raise the acceptance standard until they are 'inspecting the Company out of business'.

In order to maintain the specified standard of quality the first objective of the Inspection Department is usually to prevent faulty work passing forward either to subsequent operations or to finished parts stores. This is essentially a negative operation, an equally important and more positive function is to prevent faulty work occurring, one aspect of this is discussed in detail below under *statistical quality control*, but in general the Quality Control staff should aim to be always on the look out for ways of preventing work falling below standard, and for areas where production methods can be altered, to take advantage of wider tolerance in the quality specification. These aspects will be apparent to inspectors by their observations of the nature and cause of faults or by being aware that advantage is being taken of only a part of the available production tolerance.

In order that the inspection staff shall not be overridden by the production departments, the Chief Inspector should be independent of production, and responsible therefore either to the Chief Engineer or Chemist, or to the Works Manager (if he is also responsible for the technical and production administration departments). In pharmaceutical industry the Chief Inspector has to be a qualified analytical chemist or pharmacist, and is always independent of production. This is most important. It does not mean that in status the Chief Inspector is necessarily on the same level as the head of the Production or Technical Departments, but it does mean that he has direct access to an executive at that or a higher level who is not primarily concerned with output. Strictly speaking, he represents the customer for quality of the final product, and the assembly departments for the quality of products from component manufacturing departments. He must be quite free from undue influence. He must of course use his discretion, and to do this wisely in a company manufacturing to customer's order he must be in close contact with the Sales Department. Although an Inspector has no responsibility for the quality of work produced, he is responsible for what is accepted, and in order to prevent waste production it may be customary to authorise inspectors to stop production which is continuing to fall below standard, insisting that the foreman responsible is immediately informed. Alternatively, there may be standing orders to those in charge of operating personnel, for production to be suspended if rejects have exceeded a given figure.

Need for inspection

Inspection these days is taken for granted, but it is pertinent to ask why inspection is necessary. It is as nearly non-productive as any department or function in a factory can be, and to that extent can be considered an excess cost—and one of the aims of management is to reduce excess costs to a minimum. Then why inspection? The 'Inspector' can be regarded as the customer's representative in the factory and hence he is there to ensure that the specification that the customer is buying against, as set out in chapter 1, is being maintained in the product. In this respect, the inspection or quality control activity becomes part of 'marketing' in that it is a control in the factory for ensuring that the firm's marketing strategy (i.e. to serve and satisfy the customers' needs) is being fulfilled in practice. However, one can still come across factories where there is no inspection department. In these it is usually found that either the Foremen fulfil the function or else the employees are craftsmen skilled in their particular job, the works relatively small, and all employees, operators, supervision and administration distinctly above average. It is a human problem. The truth is that inspection is necessary because human beings are fallible, and unless each person is a craftsman concerned only with producing a perfect article bad work is likely to be passed off as good, particularly if there is anything to be gained by it. That is the reason, of course, why payment by results, quantity results, can tend to lower the quality standard. (Payment by results can include a factor for quality and entirely successful schemes on process work have been applied which pay a maximum bonus when standard quality and output is attained, bonus decreasing when output is higher and quality consequently lower.)

All this does not mean that a lot of inspection is essential. It does mean that it is, or the extent of its need is, primarily a management problem. The higher the morale, quality and type of work, and the better the management, the less the need for inspection (and the less there are of all other excess costs as well, of course). But human nature being what it is, some inspection is always necessary. It is necessary to maintain standards of quality and interchangeability of component. This latter has had the biggest influence on the growth of the inspection function. Interchangeability (that is, every repeat of a component being identical, within narrowly prescribed limits, in size or vital dimensions) by eliminating all fitting and matching, reduces production time enormously. Without interchangeability the modern assembly-belt method would be impossible. Similarly, the repetition of process in say textiles or foodstuffs would be impossible without reliance on the quality of materials used, and this is only ensured by inspection during manufacture of the materials. And the make-up sections of the textile industry, as in the finishing sections of all industries, must depend on earlier processes for reliable standards of quality to avoid matching problems and to maintain production flow.

Responsibilities

The responsibilities of a Chief Inspector are normally to:

● organise and supervise the work of inspectors, testers and viewers;

- instruct and train staff in carrying out their duties and ensure that they are effectively performed;
- adhere to the Company's personnel policy and ensure that subordinates do so;
- give effect to the Company's policy relating to quality of products and standards of finish and performance;
- inspect first-offs and finished components and products and carry out periodic check inspection during production; report to operator and supervisor when processes or operations are departing from standard; reject work not up to standard;
- carry out final running or proof tests on finished products; record results on official test sheets and pass for delivery only those up to the Company's standard; refer back for rectification products not up to standard;
- render reports on work inspected, recommending corrections to methods and equipment where such may be necessary to maintain standards of finish and performance or to increase productivity;
- advise Foremen on methods of gauging and inspection carried out by operators;
- ensure that care is taken of tools, gauges and other equipment used in the Inspection Department;
- inspect consignments received of bought out materials and parts when requested by Stores, and render a report to the Stores and Buying Department on quality and adherence to specification of order;
- record work passed, rejected and to be rectified, arranging with the foreman for rectification where necessary;
- count and vouch for work passed forward and to be paid for;
- keep abreast of developments in methods of inspection and collaborate with the production departments to improvements to current practice.

These duties call for persons with special characteristics, developed spontaneously or by training, in addition to skill in the technique of inspection. An Inspector must, above all, be absolutely impartial at all times, and must always be able to make a decision which is unpleasant to workers who may be his friends. There can be no compromise with the facts and his judgment of them. This is much easier of course when the Inspector is not responsible to the production staff, but he still has to live and work with his workmates and some can be very unpleasant if they disagree with a decision, of if their wages are considerably affected by it. An Inspector cannot afford to be persuaded against his judgment, nor to alter a decision against the facts; it is the kind of precedent of which operators always take advantage, and quality always suffers. Then too, sound judgment is called for, that is, the ability to review quickly the various facts and factors which affect the suitability or adequacy of a job in borderline cases. When there are dimensional limits a decision is easy, but when the standard relates to finish or appearance, the standard must be carried in the mind yet not vary from day to day. Even in the case of dimensions, there can be a combination of borderline results which has to be set against the value of an expensive component scrapped or delay in delivery if it has to be remade. This is partly skill, but a person who is capable of sound judgment on any issue makes the more skilful Inspector. Lastly, the kind of person who, as a rule, does not make a good Inspector is the very fast skilled worker. Inspection work proves too slow for him and does not provide the opportunity for rapid rhythmic work and higher earnings for extra effort to satisfy his ambition.

If it is desired to pay Inspectors on an incentive scheme, and this is often justified and can be successful when the kind of inspection is of a routine nature and not highly skilled, there must always be a second overriding check, quite independent of the first. The person making this second check must not be paid on an incentive scheme based on output. Associated with this check must be a severe penalty for any work passed which should not have been, e.g. loss of bonus for the whole of the week.

Limits

It will be realised, from what has already been said, that quality, accuracy and finish are relative; there is, in a practical manufacturing sense, no absolute measurement. To an engineer 'dead size' means as accurate as he can measure with his micrometer, e.g. to a hundredth part of a millimetre (0·01 mm). In setting up any standard, therefore, it is not sufficient to state a single unit (of length, degrees of temperature etc.), but to express the standard as a permissible variation between upper and lower limits, unless the accuracy obtainable with instruments normally in use is good enough, e.g. metre rule, or commercial scales for weight. When other than commercial accuracy is required, limits are essential, and the standard is specified as a unit with a variation 'higher or lower' or 'up and down' not to exceed given amounts. In engineering this is expressed thus: 50 mm plus or minus 0·01 mm (50 mm ± 0·01 mm) meaning a dimension of 50 mm plus or minus 1 hundredth, or between the limits of 50·01 mm and 49·99 mm.

In the British Standards and other standards of limits frequently used in industry, the following terms are used:

Limits. Limits for a dimension or other unit of measurement are the two extreme permissible sizes (measurements) for that dimension (unit).

Tolerance. The tolerance on a dimension (measurement) is the difference between the high and low limits of size for that dimension (measurement); it is the variation tolerated in the size of that dimension (measurement), to cover reasonable imperfection in workmanship. In connection with the fit of a part into another, e.g. a shaft into a hole or bore, the following further terms are used:

Allowances. The allowance is the prescribed difference between the high limit for a shaft and the low limit for a hole to provide a certain class of fit.

Fit. The fit between two mating parts is the relationship existing between them with respect to the amount of play or interference which is present when they are assembled together. In general shop terms, a fit can vary between a 'heavy drive' to a 'coarse clearance', and British Standards list fourteen such fits, including various classes of push and running fits.

A full, but simple explanation of *Limits and Fits for Engineering* is given in BSS 1916: Part 1. A much more comprehensive analysis of standards, tolerances and fits, as used in engineering design and manufacture is given in *British Standards for Workshop Practice,* BSI Handbook No. 2.

Organisation

In order that the function of inspection shall not be negative only, it is essential to recognise that its task is to control the quality of production. Applying the principles of 'control' there must be:

- standards of quality laid down;
- records of deviation from standards, i.e. records, not only of rejects, but also evidence of frequency and importance or rejects and where occurring;
- action to prevent recurrence as far as possible or to minimise frequency and to rectify if possible work rejected.

Standards should be laid down in writing in specifications or on drawings, and on the latter it is important to remember that a dimension has no meaning if not associated with a tolerance. It is essential that it is clearly understood in a shop, and stated on all drawings, that dimensions to which no tolerance is specifically given, i.e. open dimensions, are to be a standard tolerance. In practice, dimensions relating to rough castings and other non-machined parts of a component are required to be to a tolerance of 2 mm (± 1 mm) and open dimensions of machined surfaces to a tolerance of four tenths of a millimetre ($\pm 0 \cdot 2$ mm).

The actual organisation of the work of inspecting, recording and taking of corrective action must obviously vary widely with the type of product, process and scale of manufacture. With armament and aeroplane manufacture, 100 per cent inspection at all stages and operations is usually called for. In the manufacture of barrows, agricultural machinery, etc., a much less rigid inspection is required, and in the chemical process industries a different type of inspection altogether is required. The first and major factor affecting the organisation of the work is whether 100 per cent inspection or only sampling is necessary. This is mainly an economic question, although as in the case of armament and aeroplane manufacture, absolute reliability is an overriding factor. The fact that 100 per cent inspection results in a high proportion of inspectors ('non-producers') to operators, as high even as 1 in 3, and the fact that sample or check inspection which does reveal errors is usually sufficient to maintain a reasonably satisfactory standard, suggests that sample inspection is usually adequate, and in practice this is so. When, however, work which slips through sample checks creates serious assembly delays or expensive reactions from customers, then 100 per cent inspection may justify its cost.

When sample inspection is adopted, it is essential for firsts-off a run or set-up to be inspected thoroughly. Thereafter, not only must samples be taken at a frequency to assure an adequate percentage check as indicated by experience but there should also be random checks at irregular periods and of the batch. Although not foolproof, this usually reveals persistent faults and really bad work. The frequency of sample inspection must be laid down as part of the standard of each operator or process. A method of doing this for machining operation is illustrated on the specimen operation layout shown in Fig. 3.5.17 (see p. 407). It remains then to decide on either centralised or floor inspection. In the former all work from a department is sent to the Inspection Department or made to pass through an inspection crib before passing on to the next operation. In the latter method inspectors go on to the floor and inspect work at the machine or bench. Only a study of the conditions on the spot can reveal which of these methods will give the best or cheapest results. In considering which to adopt, the following advantages of each should be borne in mind:

Advantages of centralised inspection

● Easier and better supervision.
● Division of labour possible, permitting employment of less skilled labour.
● More thorough and less liable to interruption.
● Tidier shops, and therefore easier to control flow of work.
● More accurate checking for wage payment, and less chance of falsification.
● Easier to progress.
● Losses from lost or stolen work and hidden scrap at a minimum.

Advantages of floor inspection

● Far less handling (in the case of very large components, transport to inspection crib is prohibitive).
● Less delay due to time lag in Inspection Department.
● Less work in progress.
● Shorter production cycle time.
● Faults can often be rectified immediately and by operator responsible.
● Patrol Inspectors can operate control charts to prevent faulty work occurring.

It is not proposed to illustrate all the kinds of records that should be made of the results of inspection, since these vary so widely, and obviously must be designed to suit the product and the organisation. As a help in the design of a scrap note, a suitable form is illustrated in Fig. 3.5.53 (see p. 456). Certain principles, however, must be adhered to if the amount of faulty work is to be controlled and steps taken to minimise what does occur. These are:

1. Records must be rendered as soon after the event as possible and preferably during the manufacture (see *Statistical Quality Control* on page 503) and to the person first able to do something about it.
2. To this end the Foreman should be supplied with a report item by item on the rejects in his department daily (or weekly or monthly). He should sign this and indicate action taken, and send on to the Works Manager (or other senior production executive). If he can scrutinise each scrap note, so much the better.
3. The cost of scrap (material and labour) should be rendered to foremen on weekly cost control reports.
4. Only Inspectors should be allowed to reject or scrap any work, and scrap should not be received by Reclaiming or Stores Departments without a covering note signed by an inspector.
5. Inspectors should be responsible for documents, arranging for the reprocessing or rectification of faulty work, and ensuring that the need for so doing is brought to the attention of Production Planning.

In a small firm, where personal contact between the higher management and the operator at the bench is both intimate and frequent and operators consequently are more aware of the significance of their work and can be made more aware of the need for quality, few, if any, inspectors are required. Except for a final inspection of the completed product, it is likely to be more successful to put the onus of passing forward only good work on the operator. It cannot be done, however, if any slackness or slipshod work is allowed to pass unnoticed and uncorrected. There must be pride in maintaining a definite standard. By and large, workmen prefer to do good work and will do so if put on their honour and if the general standard is set by example.

Types of
inspection

*Raw materials
and goods inwards
inspection*

One company's product is another's raw material. All goods received into any organisation should have some inspection. The very least acceptable is a visual check that the goods are as described on the order and the quantity received agrees with the quantity advised. In many cases it will be necessary to put the goods through a dimensional, functional, chemical or other more basic test, before accepting the consignment. As with all inspection procedures these tests may be on a 100 per cent or sample basis (see page 504).

*Work in progress:
inspection of
piece parts and
assemblies*

This covers the whole range of inspection techniques in most engineering factories. Parts or assemblies are checked to whatever degree of accuracy is called for; these tests will cover dimensions, form, surface finish, balance, electrical tests of all kinds, and a wide range of checking instruments and skills will be required.

*Work in progress:
process industries*

Inspection of process conditions is required during the production of chemicals, food, either during growth or processing, paper, glass and similar manufacturing and post manufacture processes. The correct conditions at all stages in the process have to be ascertained, usually by experiment or analysis. It is then necessary to ensure that these conditions are being maintained and so either continuous or intermittent checks are made on the process. These checks are usually recorded on control charts which show the change in conditions with the passage of time. Figures 3.6.15 and 16 show two control charts from widely different industries. Fig. 3.6.15 shows the temperature of a furnace and its load during a stress relieving cycle, and Fig. 3.6.16 shows the temperature of the hottest and coldest of eight test boxes of mushroom compost during the spawn running cycle, compared with the control limits. It is interesting to note in this case, that the natural variability between boxes was greater than the desirable control limits. As the heat is generated within the box by biochemical action, the process is not so easily controlled as an electric resistance furnace.

*Running or
service tests*

When the end product is a machine, it is usual to make tests in conditions as similar as possible to those in which the machine will be working in service. Motor-cars have road tests, electric motors and generators, cranes, special machine tools and machinery designed to a customer's requirements are run on a test bed, often in the presence of the customer or his representative, or tested on site before acceptance. In many instances, tests cannot exactly reproduce working conditions and in these circumstances a test of known severity, which exceeds the operating conditions, is applied. The amount by which conditions are more severe than normal is a factor of safety (or more strictly, of ignorance, since it is an acknowledgement that occasionally conditions may be worse than normal by an amount not precisely known). Typical examples of this sort of test would be pressure testing a heat exchanger or proof loading a lifting beam.

Fig. 3.6.15
Control chart:
stress relieving

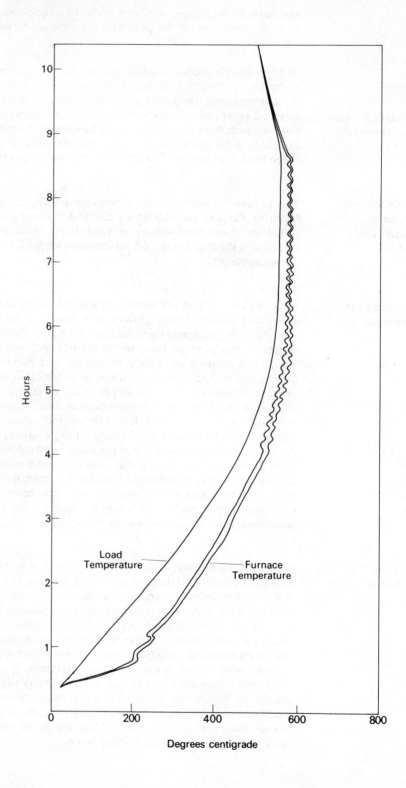

Load
Temperature

Furnace
Temperature

Hours

Degrees centigrade

Fig. 3.6.16
Control chart: bed
temperatures in
mushroom spawn run

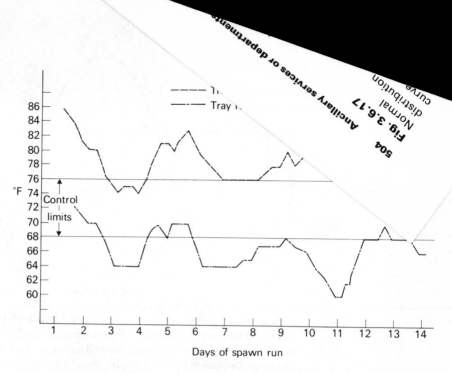

Days of spawn run

In all the above inspections a choice has to be made whether to inspect or check every feature of every item or only some features of some items. If we choose the latter we must know how many to check, and what the accuracy will be in the final result. In other words how closely does the sample conform to the whole batch. Determination of these facts is the basis of statistical quality control.

Statistical
quality control

The principle of statistical analysis of the features of a product, is based on the fact that however accurate the machine or process, not all the items produced will be identical, most of them will be very close to the set conditions and a few of them will be some distance from these conditions and even fewer will be a long way off. The pattern formed by these varying results will form the 'normal' distribution curve shown in Fig. 3.6.17.

The overall spread of the results will depend on the inherent accuracy of the equipment or process being used. If we take an example of two automatic lathes producing a component 25 mm in diameter, one is a much worn production machine, the other a new precision machine. Both are set to produce 25 mm diameter. The actual dimensions of the components produced on each machine might be as shown in Fig. 3.6.18.

The spread of the actual dimensions is known as the *process precision* and it is essential to know this figure for each type of equipment being used. For if we require our machine to produce a tolerance of ±0·01 mm and we produce the part on M/c No. 1, we shall reject about three-quarters of its total production. On the other hand, if we produce the part on M/c No. 2 we shall expect to get less than two faulty components per thousand produced.

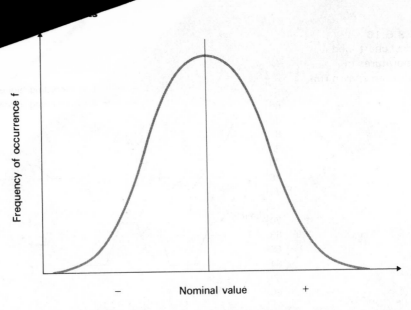

One more statistical concept should be introduced at this point, the Standard Deviation (Symbol σ). This is a measure of the spread of the curve; its importance in quality control is that 68 per cent of all values will fall within ±1 Standard Deviation from the mean, 95 per cent within ±2 Standard Deviations, and 99·7 per cent within ±3 Standard Deviations (see also p. 533). The use of this measure will become apparent later in this section. For a more detailed explanation of standard deviation see chapter 8, pages 532 onwards.

Control charts

In order to reduce the cost of inspection which would occur if every item was inspected at every stage in its manufacture a certain number of samples are inspected; from these samples it is possible to be fairly confident that the

Fig. 3.6.18
Process precision graphs: new and worn lathes

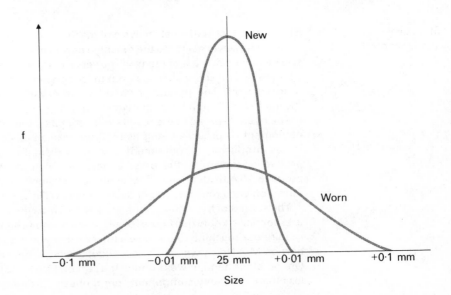

Fig. 3.6.19
Relation of
standard deviations
to normal
distribution curves

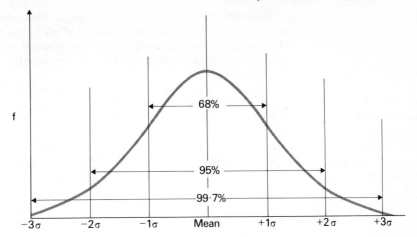

whole batch is like the sample. We say 'fairly confident' as it is possible to adjust the degree of 'confidence' by adjusting the sample size. However although one isolated sample may not tell us all about the quality of the product, samples taken at intervals will show if there is any change taking place in the mean position and therefore whether quality is being maintained or is drifting. The succession of points when plotted on a control chart will give a cumulative indication of what change is taking place.

The concept of an Inspector as someone who decides whether a component or product is to be accepted or rejected is now out of date for many applications. With the addition of a pencil and graph paper to his usual measuring instruments the Inspector can detect that rejects will occur if no corrective action is taken, while the process is still producing acceptable products, i.e. he can actually prevent rejects from being produced. In the control chart shown in Fig. 3.6.20, there are just two limits, the upper and the lower; these are the tolerances given for the product. The spread of actual values is well within this band, which leads to the conclusion that the process precision is well within the design limits. If we have the more usual situation when the process precision is of the same order of magnitude as the design tolerance and the machine is running accurately, we might expect a control chart to appear as in Fig. 3.6.21 (overleaf).

Fig. 3.6.20
Control chart:
upper and
lower limits,
showing drift

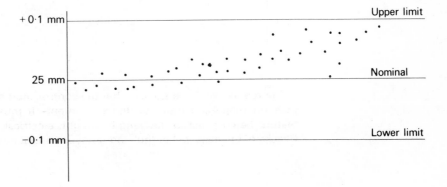

The chart in Fig. 3.6.20 shows results of dimensional checks on a product with nominal size 25 mm and tolerance of ±0·1 mm. While the process is *now* producing acceptable components, the upward drift (if not corrected) will soon cause oversize components to be produced.

Fig. 3.6.21
Control chart:
upper and
lower limits,
showing normal
distribution

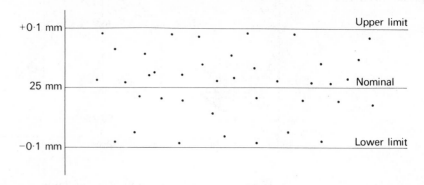

If we now use the knowledge that 95 per cent of our results will be within ±2σ of the mean, we can expect that only one in every forty checked will be above the dimension given by this figure. We draw on our control chart a 'warning limit' at this position. If there is one sample which is above this limit, it could be within the normal results expected, or it may be a sign that the process is starting to drift. In this case additional samples are taken to ascertain which is the case. We also know that we would expect only one sample in a thousand to be above the figure given by ±3σ. So we set action limits at this figure. Although there is a one in a thousand chance of a sample falling outside this band, we shall be so suspicious that action should be taken to check the process and reset the machine if necessary. Fig. 3.6.22 shows the pattern of the final control chart.

Fig. 3.6.22
Control chart
with warning
and action limits

The reader will have noticed that the control chart approach to inspection puts on major-constraint on the equipment—it must measure the actual feature being checked, i.e. length, weight, electrical resistance and so on. Checks of the pass–fail or 'go'–'no-go' type cannot be used.

7 Production management

Supervision:
a human
problem

Production management is concerned with getting things made or done. The technical function of this management is primarily concerned with material things, designs, processes and machines; the *administrative function* is concerned with facts and figures. The *actual doing*, execution of plans and supervision of the persons involved, is a *human problem*. It is concerned with people, who have emotions as well as abilities, rights as well as duties, free will as well as good will, and reactions that cannot be predicted with the accuracy of machine movements. It is a problem at least as old as civilisation; what makes it still so little understood and so difficult to solve today is that conditions have changed, and changed rapidly in the comparatively short industrial era. The Manager's job, or the Supervisor's, consists mainly of creating by word and action, by decision and example, by orders and organisation, an atmosphere within which people are motivated to work willingly, effectively, with continuous high effort; it is a job of *leadership*. Although a new type of leadership must permeate management from top to bottom (no section, department, works or organisation can be better than the man at the top), it is at the lower level of management, the level of 'supervision' as it is commonly called, as exercised by the Foreman, that serious lack of leadership causes most unrest and most reduces individual effectiveness. The Foreman or Supervisor, alone of the management hierarchy, is in constant daily touch with operators, and is most frequently giving direct orders and making personal decisions. Today he is often the weakest link in the chain of command.

The reasons and the difficulties are not far to seek. During the past few decades, the responsibilities of managers of all grades (including Supervisors in this broad classification) have been steadily reduced or changed. Certainly their power 'over' people has been reduced, even if their effective power is more. Specialists are now employed to do much of the work which, in the earlier days of the industrial era, occupied a Foreman's time. Processes and methods are laid down by technicians and Production Engineers, the order of production is decided by planning clerks, piece rates are worked out by ratefixers, costs and performances calculated by accountants, and even engaging and discharging and trade union negotiations are largely performed by (though not the ultimate responsibility of) the Personnel Office. Frequently, the Foreman is not on or represented on Works Councils, Joint Production Committees, or other consultative bodies, and he is often obstructed by shop stewards. Furthermore, wage trends have reduced the differential between his earnings and those of his skilled subordinates, reducing the incentives to acceptance of the supervisory role, for all its status. Finally, Foremen and other Managers are often promoted from the ranks because of proficiency as operators and not for abilities as leaders of men and receive no training for the job of supervision or management. All this has a depressing effect on the standard of management as a whole.

One solution is to select Supervisors and Managers mainly for their abilities even if latent, as leaders, and not only for their operating or technical skill, and then to train them specifically for the job of supervision. In addition to knowing something of the technical work being done by subordinates and associated specialists, the supervisory role consists of putting the right man in the right place, seeing that he is suitably rewarded for his efforts, giving him all the information he needs or should have, making decisions on the innumerable occasions which are not covered by standard practice, instructions and procedures, and continuously inspiring all his team to work willingly and well.

This is the point at which the role of Managers and Supervisors becomes inextricably woven in with that of their specialist colleagues in the field of 'personnel management'—a subject that is dealt with at length in the following Part. The point will be stressed that the Personnel Officer is an adviser to all Managers and Supervisors: he can help them to be more effective in the performances of their human tasks, but he cannot—and certainly must not attempt to—take these tasks over. His role is essentially ancillary; to the Managers and Supervisors themselves must belong the role of managing the men and women at work. To consider what this entails, however, inevitably necessitates referring to a number of activities which are customarily thought of in the context of the 'personnel function of management'; to go into such activities in this chapter would involve unavoidable overlap of subject and a great deal of duplication of text. Proper consideration of these activities is therefore left to Part Four, which should be read as an integral contribution to the consideration of the role of Managers and Supervisors in the management of production. It must suffice here to comment briefly on some selected aspects which more immediately arise within the purview of management and supervision in the factory.

Motivation

Inspiring leadership in everyday work can have astonishing results in raising men's efforts much above the ordinary level. To attain this managers must show by their enthusiasm and example that they have faith in the purpose of the job in hand and in the company's product or business, and are loyal to the company's policies, to their own seniors and to all their subordinates. It is not enough to show this on important occasions, it must be shown always in every small decision and action, in giving orders and receiving unpleasant ones, in reprimands and in commendation, in attempting the impossible and carrying out the routine jobs, in dealing with disputes and correcting or reporting grievances, in setting tasks and ensuring reward. To inspire his team and maintain a high morale, the Manager must set himself a high standard and live up to it. Respect, like authority, cannot be handed out or ordered, it must be earned. Men on the shop floor have a pretty accurate assessment of their boss's character; they know him at least as well as he knows himself, and usually better. He has presumably been chosen for his superiority, and they therefore tend to set their own standard of behaviour by his.

Inspiration, then, is the essence of leadership. Loyalty is a principal ingredient—loyalty to subordinates, to management and to the purpose of the enterprise. Others are keenness, which is infectious; absolute honesty in all things, but especially in discussions; interest in and liking for people, resulting in personal sympathy and understanding; readiness to face awkward situations and to accept responsibility, but unwillingness to ask others to do anything one would not do oneself; an ability to make prompt and resolute decisions, however unpleasant; and finally a sense of humour.

Discipline

Discipline on the shop floor is important, not only to prevent complete chaos developing, but in most industrial situations, adherence to rules and regulations is vital to the maintenance of safety. There must be rules defining where people may and may not go, where and how materials must and must not be stored and handled, certain machines must be guarded, goggles must be worn for specific operations; there are many such rules for all employees to adhere to as well as organisational rules such as starting and finishing times and so forth. The most effective precursor to good discipline is the example of the supervisor or departmental head; discipline based on the principle of 'don't do as I do, do as I say' will soon lead to chaos and may well lead to serious injury. Most people respect a strict but fair disciplinarian, but very few are really happy under a lax management, for laxness in administrative rules is usually matched by laxness in safety rules and someone eventually gets hurt.

One important ingredient of discipline is consistency, you cannot jump on the relatively new employee who is five minutes late, and ignore the shop steward who ambles in twenty minutes late without explanation. Likewise you cannot let standards gradually slide for eleven months of the year, and then have sudden 'purges' of discipline once a year. Everyone likes to know where they stand. Any rules should be fully explained so that all employees know:

- what the rules are;
- why these rules exist;
- what will happen if they break these rules.

If the rules are applied equally to all employees the discipline will not only be fair, but also respected.

Wider aspects of discipline, in the context of industrial relations, are considered in Part Four, chapter 5 (see page 608).

Communication

Communication is a vital tool of management, probably more today than it has ever been. There are two aspects to the problem of communication. The first is the manager's expertise in transmitting ideas, or instructions to another person or group of people in such a way as to ensure that the recipient of the information knows exactly what is happening or what he is intended to do. Long ago Confucius noted:

'If language is not correct, then what is said is not what is meant; if what is said is not what is meant, then what ought to be done remains undone.'

Not everyone in a supervisory position is necessarily good at expressing himself either verbally or in writing and so it is important to make sure by checking. Random checks can be undertaken by:

- asking the recipient to repeat his instructions in detail;
- asking the man on the shop floor his understanding of some information given to his supervisor.

All too frequently the only cross check is when a post mortem into an incorrectly carried out instruction reveals a misunderstanding in the initial communication. One large company investigated thirty-five unofficial stoppages of work, and found that eighteen of them were directly attributable to misunderstandings. In each of these cases when the true situation was explained the men returned to work at once, but, even so, many man hours had been lost.

The second facet of communication which management must take positive steps to achieve is the communication that replaces secrecy. Often this secrecy is unintentional; busy managers intent on their immediate problems may not find time to stop the department, call everyone together, and pass on the latest information on what is happening and why. However, most companies have formal Trade Union–Management meetings at specified intervals (see 'Joint consultation' below), at these meetings the union representatives are given much information that is of general interest. This information is then relayed by the representatives to their workmates, but with the possibility of changes of emphasis if not of content. There are three dangers of this means of downward communication:

1. If they do the job well, the Union representatives become the advocates of change, and so become management men and lose their office.
2. If they do not do the job well, the wrong information gets transmitted.
3. The shop steward becomes the main communicator and hence the leader; this destroys the authority of the shop foreman.

Shop stewards and other workers' representatives should be used for upward communication; downward communication going directly to departmental heads and foremen for relaying on to staff and operators. One approach to this problem which is proving successful is the use of briefing groups.

A briefing group is a periodic assembly of the whole department with the departmental head, be he Foreman, Manager or Director, to enable the boss to pass on to his subordinates what is happening and why, and to give an opportunity for general discussion on what needs to be done and how everyone can best contribute. To be effective briefing groups must be at regular intervals, not held only when there is some bad news to impart, or a rush job to get out. At departmental head level, once a month following publication of the monthly statistics is a good time; then all concerned can be kept alive to the fortunes and prospects of the company and so identify themselves much more with its continued success.

Finally, as communication is between people it is essential to present facts and get reactions, that is to communicate, as personally as possible. A few minutes' talk is worth more than pages of notices, and even in the talking, warmth and a sense of humour are more effective than a cold impersonal speech, however perfectly phrased.

Joint consultation

A large part of a Manager's time is necessarily spent in dealing with people, but little of it should be spent in actually giving instructions. For most of the time a Manager should be passing on or receiving information as a result of which subordinates take action, if action is necessary. In doing so he should provide reasonable opportunity for the other persons to express their opinions, even if they have to be corrected or rejected. In this way all subordinates, and the rank and file, are made to feel that their opinions count for something and that 'they matter'. The larger an organisation becomes the more difficult it is to do this; information along the channels of communication, up and down, does not move very freely and decisions made high up may appear arbitrary. Resistance may be met with instead of ready cooperation. More formal means of ensuring the flow of information becomes necessary and we have what is called 'joint consultation', a subject move fully reviewed in Part Four, chapter 5 (see page 620).

To the Manager, joint consultation committees and other formal means of consultation are apt to appear unwieldy and time consuming, and to undermine his prestige and authority. They can do just this if the Manager sits back and lets the committee do his work for him. But he must be continually alert to ensure that people turn first to their immediate superior for information or advice, and that information affecting people gets down to them from above quickly and sympathetically. This leaves the formal committee to deal with the inevitable grumbler and cases which go off the rails, usually due to personalities, and to act as a safety valve. All too frequently the communication channel is from senior production management to shop floor via shop stewards at a joint consultation meeting. It is rarely practical to have all foremen or other line managers present at the (monthly) JC meeting, but it is essential that these supervisors are given the same information before the works people responsible to them. There is little that undermines a foreman's position more than being told 'what's going on' by his subordinates. In addition, if a particular point has been either intentionally or unintentionally misrepresented in the telling, then the foreman must be in a position to correct it in the minds of his men.

Decision

Decision is another important element of leadership, and the nice balance between the impetuous hasty decision and a hesitant or procrastinating one has to be cultivated. There are some people who find great difficulty in making up their minds and sticking to a decision. Highly skilled technical persons and those trained in research often do not make successful managers for this reason; they have been so used to looking all round a question in every detail that they are unable to make a decision rapidly. Although it is essential to be able to make a decision, it must not be thought that it is possible to do so without a knowledge of the facts, and without a good deal of thought. A manager must not always be forcing his ideas; he must be a good listener as well as a good talker, and above all he must be able to get others to contribute their ideas and facts, and as far as possible, to share, or feel they share, in the decision. Sharing of decisions adheres to what Mary Follet called the 'law of situation'.[1] When all the facts of a situation are found (the law discovered), all concerned, supervisors and operators, obey the law; there is not the same feeling as when obeying orders. Authority can still be exercised, but it is the authority of the facts of a situation.

[1] In Metcalf and Urwick, eds, *Dynamic Administration*, Management Publications Trust, 1945, p. 58.

Cooperation, coordination and integration

These are elements of the technique of organising action. Cooperation is really a state of mind that can exist only on a basis of knowledge and appreciation of a common purpose that is understood by all. Likewise, coordination needs all concerned to have all the information necessary at the time common effort is required. Integration requires a pooling or gathering together of all the facts and ideas for the purpose of arriving at the best solution of a problem, one which is likely to be better than any one person's solution. In each case a sharing of information is required. In practice it means that there must be frequent meetings between those concerned, not necessarily large or formal meetings, but at least some opportunity to exchange views, ideas and facts. Under wise leaders this cooperation, coordination and integration ensures harmony, progress and effectiveness of the whole team. This is not a plea for formal meetings or committees; far from it. The atmosphere of committee rooms is apt to be deadening and sterile. But it does mean that the practice of bringing together those whose activities interlock is a good one and should take place at all levels. (This was more fully reviewed in Part One, chapter 8; see page 101 above.)

Selection and development

Because selection and training schemes are matters in which the Personnel Officer advises and undertakes a good deal of the work, this does not mean that they are no longer the line executive's responsibility. Ultimately the head of a department is responsible for the people he has working for him, and he must retain the final right of decision about people added to his staff, retained or promoted. He has the duty of requesting and considering the advice of the Personnel Officer, but he himself must make the final decision.

The skill of choosing subordinates is one which the young or newly promoted manager must learn, if he is to be successful. Many reorganisations would not have been necessary, and many unhappy organisations would not be so, had the executive at the head been skilled in the choice of men. Few persons remain what they are at an early age. All are susceptible to training—particularly good and stimulating training. So this is equally important; and it makes for more stability and loyalty than introducing persons into an organisation from outside at a high level. To choose good material at an early age and then to train means that each promotion is also a selection, so that selection, training and promotion, vital elements in management, form as it were a triangle thus:

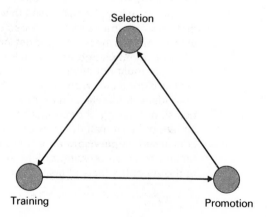

Skill in selection of staff demands of executives that they shall be good listeners and better observers. Dominant men usually get 'yes men' round them. To learn of a man's abilities and potentialities one must draw him out and encourage expression of views and abilities; this can only be done by giving him his head as far as possible. Although much improved techniques have been developed to aid selection by interview and test, they are not sufficient by themselves, and personal evaluation, particularly of character and personality, has still to be relied on. Such evaluation should be continually practised if it is to be reliable. For it to be practised only in the case of important appointments and for the inevitable mistakes to be made is expensive and wasteful. But it can be practised without actual appointments being involved by studying the behaviour of people one meets and checking one's judgment later. It will be found, except in rare cases, that a conscious effort of evaluation has to be made, otherwise the decision will be affected too much by emotional reactions and personal likes and dislikes.

It is a good practice for the manager to have a list of all his direct subordinates who would be contenders for his position if he himself were promoted. Against each he should record proficiency in the technical skills required for his job and also points on the personal qualities required. Analysis of the chart will frequently show a few 'contenders' each with various shortcomings, in technical knowledge, experience, or personal qualities. The manager should then take steps to initiate a training programme to make good those weaknesses. To do this it is not always necessary to let the men concerned know that they are in the running. The manager should know his subordinates well enough to know whether silence or knowledge will get the best results.

Again, this major subject is fully treated elsewhere in this volume: see Part Seven, chapter 6 (page 991).

Motivation and remuneration

The 1972 Contract of Employment Act makes it mandatory to each employee to have a contract which states either the level of his remuneration or the basis on which it will be calculated, therefore remuneration forms part of a legal contract between the employer and employee. It is thus every Manager's responsibility to know exactly the basis on which his subordinates' pay is calculated. For this reason, methods of remuneration likely to be encountered in Production Management are outlined here, even though the subject is dealt with in detail in Part Four.

Over the past ten years or so there has been much said and written on the subject of what makes a man work, what satisfaction he looks for in his work, why does he stay in any particular job and so on. In fact a complete science has been built up which has taken the name of behavioural science. The behavioural scientists have finally buried the theory that the financial motive is the strongest reason for staying in a job. However, as it is still a basic and very important subject for all of us, it is worth considering some of the bases on which wages are calculated. (The findings of the behavioural scientists are discussed in Part Four: see chapter 5, page 621.)

Bases for remuneration

At one time it could be said that there were two types of payment—daywork and piecework—daywork being paid by attendance hours, day or week, piecework being payment by the number of pieces produced in a given time. This simple division is no longer valid. There are many hybrid systems which are part daywork and part piecework. A few examples will be discussed later in this section. In addition to deciding on the basis of payment, it is also necessary to determine the relative worth of different jobs within the same organisation. So, although two men may each be paid by the hour (or week), if they are performing different tasks with different responsibilities they should probably be paid different rates per hour worked. The determination of the relative positions of a number of jobs has been given the name 'Job evaluation'. Correctly applied job evaluation ensures that there is a sound, logical wage-rate structure for all jobs and all grades of labour.

Job evaluation

Today there is a strong case for a national objective assessment of the relative worth of all jobs. For example should a mine worker earn as much or more pay than an electrical power station worker; if more, how much more? In theory if this could be done the perpetual spiral of wage inflation, with one group of workers trying to catch up with another, could be reduced to an annual national review. Or could it? On such a job evaluation where would the pop star or actor come? Surely the final arbiter of any person's worth is what the community is prepared, or forced by scarcity, to pay for his services. But it is possible to determine a fair and logical assessment of all jobs within either one factory or one group under the same management. For example it would be possible to produce a scale of all jobs in say one of the large motor manufacturers, whether they be in one central factory or in factories in many parts of the country.

There are a number of recognised techniques of job evaluation, from non-analytical methods such as ranking and grading, to analytical methods such as 'points rating', 'factor comparison' and 'profile' methods.[1]

Ranking

This is the simplest type of job evaluation. It is usually carried out by a panel of management and worker's representatives placing all jobs in order of importance on a 'felt fair' basis, and then assigning a rate to each position, as in Fig. 3.7.1.

Ranking has the advantage of being easily understood, but it can too easily perpetuate existing positions without challenge.

Grading

Grading is similar to ranking except that assessment starts by deciding on the number of grades and grade descriptions. Jobs are then matched against the grade description and slotted into the appropriate grade.

Analytical methods have varying degrees of complexity, and suffer the disadvantage of being less easy to understand. However the major advantage is that they indicate not only that one job is more difficult than another, but also

---

[1] The fuller treatment in Part Four will be found in chapter 4 (see page 586).

Fig. 3.7.1
Job evaluation
ranking

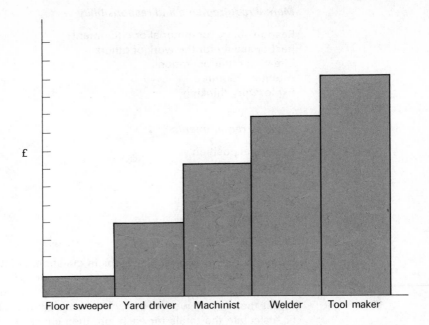

£

Floor sweeper   Yard driver   Machinist   Welder   Tool maker

how much more difficult. It is appropriate to outline one method here, points rating, which is the most commonly used method of job evaluation.[1]

Points rating

The analytical approaches to job evaluation all recognise that each job has a number of basic divisions of job content:

● Skill and experience
● Mental requirements and responsibility
● Physical requirements
● Working conditions

It must be remembered that these are the requirements of the job, not the particular attributes of the present man in the job. These factors are present to some degree or other in all jobs and each of these factors can be broken down to produce a range of subcharacteristics under each main heading, thus:

Skill and experience

Training and previous experience
Reasoning ability
Operation or job complexity
Dexterity

[1] Survey by the Prices and Incomes Board published as *PIB Report Job Evaluation*, September 1968; results: 47 per cent using Points rating, 28 per cent Grading, 20 per cent Ranking, 5 per cent Factor comparison.

Mental requirements and responsibility

Responsibility for material or equipment
Responsibility for the work of others
Effect on other operations
Attention required
Exploratory thinking

Physical requirements

Abnormal position
Abnormal effort

Working conditions

Degree of unpleasantness
Degree of danger

From a survey of the range of jobs in question, points are assigned to each characteristic, and then broken down to give points for each subcharacteristic. At this stage in the evaluation it is wise to take a number of well defined jobs across the range of work to be assessed, assign points to each subcharacteristic, calculate the totals for each job, then critically review the effects of the distribution of points to ensure the result gives a 'felt fair' balance. It will usually be found that some slight adjustment is necessary to the distribution of points between the factors and subfactors.

Rating

When the allocation of points to the factors is established, the panel of assessors take one subcharacteristic at a time and allocate points, within the agreed scale, to each of the jobs to be assessed. It is essential for all assessors to record their assessment before comparing notes, when agreed points rating has been arrived at for each subfactor of each job, the points are totalled and this total becomes the points value for a job or occupation.

Due to the change in accent of work content between manual and staff or managerial jobs, the assigned points to each subfactor will vary. Consequently it is not possible to use one scheme of points weighting to cover the complete range of jobs in a company.

Assessment panel

It is important that the panel of assessors should have the confidence of the personnel whose jobs are being evaluated. A panel consisting of equal numbers of shop floor and management representatives would be advisable for the evaluation of manual jobs. The chairman should be seen to be and accepted as impartial. The Personnel Officer is a usual choice. If the job evaluation is being undertaken by outside consultants, the resident consultant is the obvious choice, readily accepted as impartial.

Wage rates

In order to assign appropriate wage rates to each grade, notice must be taken of current maximum and minimum rates in the industry concerned and in the particular company. It is usual to fix the highest and lowest grade to be coincident with current wage rates and fix all intermediate grades on a pro rata basis. It is advisable to limit the number of grades, and although no hard and fast rule can be given, five to seven grades usually give an adequate number of steps while maintaining a sufficient differential between grades.

Piecework or daywork?

Job evaluation is neither a piecework nor a daywork system: it seeks to provide a logical job grading. Even after carefully evaluating the jobs, the decision must be made whether to pay work people within any one grade different weekly wages dependent on the quantity of work produced in the week, i.e. piecework, or to pay a flat rate of £x per hour regardless of the volume of goods or services produced or provided. Wilfred Brown (now Lord Brown) puts forward a strong case for the abolition of piecework and the substitution of other payment by results systems.[1] There are however guidelines to help management look at the suitability of various forms of payment to different types of production:

1. The presence of the following will indicate the possibility that piecework will be applicable:
   - ability of operators directly to affect quantity and/or quality of work produced;
   - operation cycle times measured in minutes and hours rather than days and weeks;
   - some repeatability of operation;
   - unmeasured work can be kept to less than 10 per cent of hours worked in each piecework department.

2. The following points will indicate that if payment by results is to be operated, a less direct form than piecework will have to be used:
   - rate of output independent of operator control, e.g. assembly lines in the motor industry;
   - very long operation cycle times, when the cycle time is greater than the normal pay period, usually one week;
   - little or no repeatability of operations, e.g. some toolroom work or breakdown repair work.

While it is possible to devise piecework schemes for most of the situations in this second situation, the scheme should not become an end in itself, lest the cost of running it exceeds the possible benefits to be gained.

Direct piecework

Direct piecework is probably the oldest form of industrial payment. Originally it was paid as so many pence per piece produced, starting at zero, and thus payment for a given number of hours worked would depend solely on the number of items produced, as shown in Fig. 3.7.2.

Piecework targets are now usually expressed in hours per piece or operation completed, this gives the same result as a price per piece but has the following advantages:

1. It encourages respect for the value of time and as such is good management. In modern conditions one contracts to buy so much time. Workers always convert their prices to the time required to do the job.

---

[1] See *Piecework Abandoned* (Heinemann Educational, 1962).

Fig. 3.7.2
Graph of direct
piecework with
no fallback
guarantee

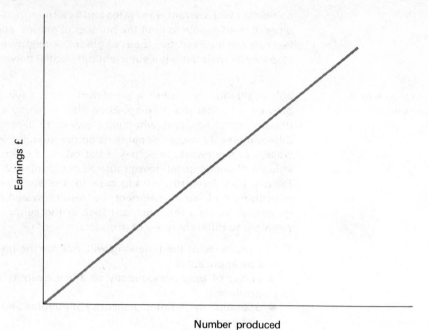

Earnings £

Number produced

2. Since work content of a job must first be measured in time, it is an added calculation to then convert to a price.
3. Wage rates may be changed without changing piecework times allowed, and a time allowed is the same whatever the hourly rate of the operator; piece price must be altered whenever basic wages rates are changed and different prices fixed for operators doing the same job on different rates of pay.
4. Work study, which is becoming increasingly important, is based on measurement of time taken, and effectiveness of work study depends on records based on time.
5. Comparison between the true costs of production are not invalidated by wage changes. One hour of work today is equivalent to one hour of work in the past or future, so that whatever changes there are in the value of money or wage levels, comparisons of the effectiveness of production and other indices of productivity remain relevant and true for a long period. This is most important.
6. Piecework earnings based on time can be expressed and worked out by the workers simply as a percentage. Furthermore, when they are based on the standard hour, the unit used in modern work study, the percentage bonus is the standard measurement of performance which can be used for comparing results between operators and department, between one period and another, and for the assessment of overall efficiencies for the payment of indirect operators.
7. Shop loading and programme planning, and the control of waiting time and other forms of excess costs, as well as the modern form of standard costing depend upon the accurate measurement of a job on a time basis.

The fact that piecework targets expressed in terms of *time allowed* per piece instead of *price* per piece give the same result is shown below.

Two factories produce similar articles. Time/piece is paid in one, price/piece in the other. In each factory there is a bonus paid on output. In factory A the bonus is 5p for a particular item, in factory B the bonus is 30p per standard hour produced, and the same item as in A has a standard time of 10 minutes each. An operator in A produces 7 components in one hour so his payment is $7 \times 5p = 35p$ bonus per hour.

In factory B the operator still produces 7 components in one hour, so his payment is 7×10 minutes (or 1·166 hours) at 30p per standard hour: $1·166 \times 30 = 35p$ bonus earned per hour.

In the idealised situation shown in Fig. 3.7.2 earnings increase directly with output, and direct labour cost per item is constant. However, in most of industry today there is a guaranteed minimum weekly earnings level for the standard working week, and a bonus rate that is less than the hourly time rate. Thus a piece worker's wage will consist of attendance hours × time rate + bonus earned × bonus rate. For example: in 40 hours worked, with a base rate of 95p per hour, a worker with a bonus rate of 30p per hour produces 120 items with an allowed time of 0·5 hours each. Then the week's earnings will be calculated thus:

$$40 \text{ hours} \times 95p = £38·00$$

plus bonus as follows:

$$120 \text{ items at } 0·5 \text{ hours each} = 60 \text{ hours}$$

$$\text{Bonus is calculated as } \frac{\text{Time saved}}{\text{Time taken}} = \frac{60-40}{40} \times 100 = \frac{20}{40}100 = 50 \text{ per cent}$$

$$\text{Alternatively } \frac{\text{Allowed time}}{\text{Actual time}} = \frac{60}{40} = 1·5$$

i.e. Allowed time is 50 per cent above actual time taken and bonus is 50 per cent. 50 per cent of bonus earnings of 30p = 15p per hour worked

$$15p \times 40 = £6·00$$

$$\text{Total earnings} = £38·00 + £6·00 = £44·00$$

The earnings/output and cost/output graphs for this situation are shown below (Fig. 3.7.3 *a* and *b*).

Fig. 3.7.3
Output
compared with
earnings/costs

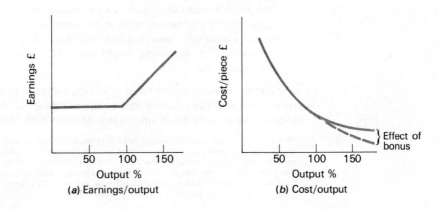

(a) Earnings/output (b) Cost/output

Piecework on
standard time

If piecework times are issued at 'standard' (for definitions see p. 399) and a rate is paid per standard hour earned then the calculation of performance, cost and earnings is much simplified.

In the above case the operator produces 120 items with a standard time of 20 minutes (0·33 hr) each. His consolidated rate is £1 per hour.[1]

$$\text{Earnings} = 120 \times 0 \cdot 33 \times 100\text{p} = £40 \cdot 00$$

$$\text{Performance} = \frac{120 \times 0 \cdot 33 \times 100}{40} = 100 \text{ per cent}$$

If he produced 130 items his earnings would be:

$$130 \times 0 \cdot 33 \times 100\text{p} = £43 \cdot 30$$

and his performance

$$\frac{130 \times 0 \cdot 03 \times 100}{40} = 108 \text{ per cent}$$

This approach has the following advantages and disadvantages:

Advantages

- Ease of calculation.
- Realistic target times for operators.
- True times and performances for scheduling and control.
- Constant labour cost per item produced above minimum guarantee.
- A strong incentive is provided to improve real performance.

Disadvantages

- Danger of runaway earnings if times are not very accurately controlled (this should be accepted as a discipline by management).
- Possibility of large fluctuations in weekly earnings.

Other systems
of 'payments
by results'

Over the past ten or fifteen years there has been a considerable disenchantment among managers and work people with direct piecework. This is usually based on the following reasons, which, with the possible exception of the first, are symptomatic of badly set up or poorly administered systems:

(i) Desire by operators to have less fluctuation in weekly earnings.
(ii) Wide disparity of bonus earnings between departments, and unrealistically high bonus earnings in some departments.
(iii) Wide disparity between earning potential of different jobs performed by any one operator, resulting in banking of job cards, artificial ceilings on earnings, and deliberate falsification of the start and finish time on individual jobs.

However, managements have still been aware of the necessity to measure performance for the purpose of management control. As a result a number of systems have developed under the general title Measured Daywork. The

---

[1] These rates are arbitrary. The variety of base rates, time rates and minimum earnings levels in the whole of British industry make it pointless to have sample calculations on rates applicable in any one specific firm or industry. Reference back to chapter 5 (p. 399) will remind the reader that standard time is the actual time a trained operator will take while working on incentive. Consequently standard time is usually less than 'allowed time', hence the rate per standard hour is greater than the corresponding rate per allowed hour.

principle behind these systems is that the operator is paid an hourly rate for all hours worked in a given period. This may be as long as six months, but usually one, two or three months. During this time his output is measured just as it would be if he was on direct piecework. At the end of the period a new hourly rate is calculated from performance over the previous period, and this is paid for all hours worked in the next period. In this way weekly fluctuations in net earnings are eliminated and the worker has only to adjust to a change in earnings say once in each six months. In another system[1] the operator contracts to produce a given level of output and is paid at that level until he or she either consistently achieves the next higher level and then contracts for that level, or constantly fails to achieve the contracted level and so—with due in-built safeguards—drops back to a lower level.

Group bonus schemes

There is no intrinsic difference between an individual and a group bonus scheme. A group bonus can be paid directly for the week worked or indirectly as in measured daywork. The only requirement is that all the productive hours of the group are set against the standard time for the unit of performance, then all the operators will earn the same percentage bonus. These schemes are particularly suitable for large assembly operations requiring a number of men to work as a team and when operators are on different rates. The writer has also found a group bonus to be useful in multishift assembly work. In a particular case it was found that with two shifts combined into one bonus earning team, arguments that the night shift did all the easy jobs leaving the awkward ones for the day shift ceased and greater flexibility of working was established throughout the team.

Profit sharing

The popularity of profit-sharing schemes ebbs and flows according to the general level of prosperity. They are popular with employees when there is profit to share, but become suspect and lose their savour when profits, and therefore remuneration, decline. Such schemes are more in the nature of sentimental attempts to meet the complaint of those who maintain that workers (as distinct from owners) do not get a fair share of increasing profits or prosperity, than deliberate financial incentives. Nevertheless they are usually looked on as forms of payment according to results—incentives to think of the company prosperity and work accordingly. As incentives to individual effort they fail in their purpose, and the mortality of such schemes is evidence that there is something unsound about them. There is no doubt that in certain circumstances particular forms of profit sharing can be effective, but success in a specific case is no guarantee, nor can it be expected to be, of success in other cases or in general. Such schemes are more likely to be effective or permanent in very small organisations where owner and employees work closely together, and business problems, as distinct from workshop problems, are apparent and can be understood and appreciated. They are likely to fail in general and in large concerns for two reasons:

- they are based on false premises—in particular that profits can be shared but not risks;
- as incentives they are too remote and lack power—reward is too remote from effort.

[1] Philips Premium Pay Plan.

An arrangement which gives to persons a share in the profits of investment, without any sharing of risks is unbalanced and bound to be unsound. Profit-sharing schemes do not usually incorporate any sharing in losses: there is no deduction from current or future earnings if the company makes a loss or less than a normal profit. Employees' earnings are 'guaranteed', but earnings of ordinary shareholders are not—dividend is paid for the loan of capital and for the risk involved. Furthermore, in steady years most employees come to look upon their share of profits, whether paid monthly or yearly, as normal, and to adjust their standard of living accordingly. The expected share out is often actually mortgaged in advance. When the first lean year arrives, as it so frequently does, there is much disappointment, disillusion and bitterness. The slump in morale then appears to far outweigh the advantages, and in fact this is likely to be true.

As an incentive to individual effort, schemes of profit-sharing, which depend on yearly results and on the actions of high executives who by single errors (like faulty buying of a major material, faulty decisions on sales policy, or bad design) can wipe out any efforts of the body of employees, have little direct effect. They are too remote from individual effort except to the few top executives who can see the effects of their own individual actions. Operators on the bench cannot see the cumulative effect of their individual efforts; indeed they are swamped, or may be negatived, by the efforts or lack of effort elsewhere.

One type of profit-sharing scheme which has attracted a certain amount of attention recently goes some way to meet this last weakness but does not appear to have been tried in companies where the make-up of total cost as between labour and material may vary appreciably from year to year. In process and mass production 'shelf goods' industries it may have some success. It is the scheme originated in America by the Nunn Bush Co. and its development, the Rucker Plan. A wages fund, out of which all employees are paid, is credited with a fixed percentage of gross sales, so that employees as a whole benefit by all of any increase in the productivity of their labour. They are guaranteed fifty-two weekly wage payments, and are paid on account until the final results of the year are known.

If it is thought that company loyalty and cooperation should be engendered or bolstered by financial methods, then some form of co-partnership or purchase of shares in the company may be successful, and there are several schemes now in operation (the Imperial Chemical Industries inaugurated a scheme in 1954 which sets a high standard). Certainly, for executives, senior and long-service employees, a stake in their company's assets should foster a feeling of joint ownership and responsibility.

Installation of payment by results scheme

Payment by results does not automatically ensure worker satisfaction, higher output or less labour trouble. A scheme, however good in itself, will fail or cause friction and trouble if management is ineffective and its relations with labour are bad; under really effective management any scheme succeeds to a degree. For a scheme really to succeed, other conditions must exist:

● Everything possible must have been done to improve and standardise methods of production, tooling, layout and organisation. Failing this all kinds of difficulties will arise, changes will have to be made which will give rise to argument and negotiation, and confidence will be shaken and be difficult to revive.

● The schemes must be fair, and this will depend most on the accuracy of measurement of work content. Inaccuracy of measurement leads to rewards which are not equitable between operatives, fears of rate cutting, and restriction of output. This will stifle many expected benefits from a financial incentive. Calculations must be simple and results paid quickly. Complicated systems are looked on with much suspicion, and the longer the period between effort and payment the less the incentive.

It is also essential, however simple the scheme, to give a detailed explanation of it to everyone concerned, Foremen as well as operatives. The writer has found that the ability of operatives in industry to grasp completely and understand the calculations and implications of the simplest and most direct schemes is unbelievably low. One is apt to forget that what looks simple to the initiated is a bit mysterious to people who left school long ago and are conditioned to their existing method of payment. And what appears mysterious is suspect. Furthermore, both Foremen and representatives of the operatives will understand quite clearly themselves, yet be quite unable to convey the facts to operatives or to convince them of the fairness of the scheme.

For this reason it is essential to take trouble to ensure that all the main body of operatives do understand what is involved and exactly how their efforts will be rewarded. It will require a great deal of patience. The first essential, of course, is an introductory meeting, either with all operatives or their elected representatives, and an agreement on principles. This should be followed by smaller meetings of departments, sections and groups with explanations and illustrations in full. Finally, but most important, Foremen and other Managers must be completely 'sold' on the scheme. It is to court certain trouble to put in any scheme against the wishes of or with the least doubts of the Supervisors concerned. They must be 100 per cent behind the scheme and show real enthusiasm for it. It helps considerably to give Supervisors and a shop steward or other representative some training in the methods of calculation and interpretation of results.

Before the scheme is finally installed, there should be a trial period during which any changes in organisation or methods can be tried out, difficulties can be resolved and operatives can see the possibilities of the schemes and its effects upon them.

Performance

Measurement

Most of us like to know how well we are doing. In industrial activity it is essential. A company must render an account at least once a year of its financial results. But the trading account is the results of the individual and collective actions of all employees from day to day in discharging their task, whatever it may be, and it is equally necessary for an account to be rendered on the results of their work, that is, of their performance. This is done for operators on piecework, since their output is measured. One of the very real advantages of measuring piecework on a time basis (page 517), is that the percentage bonus is a measure of performance which can be used for comparing individual and collective or departmental results.

Managers are responsible for the work, and hence the performance, individual and collective, of all employees under their authority. The total bonus percentage of a department is obviously one measure of departmental performance for which the Foreman can be held responsible. But there are other performances, often not measured or not measured accurately. Perhaps the most important of these are: total overall costs per unit of production (for example, per standard hour), and excess costs (see p.438). In some cases machine utilisation is equally important, as in transport and process industries. Although the quality of the product is usually checked if not controlled by the Inspector, the Production Manager is responsible for results. All managers must see to it that they have accurate reports of all such measures of performance relating to their department and take energetic steps to improve performance continually.

Labour

Whether a company operates piecework or measured daywork there will be a weekly calculation of each operator's individual performance. Each shop supervisor should receive a copy of the figures relevant to his department, a suggested format is shown in Fig. 3.7.4, and the production or works manager should have at least a summary showing shop averages and factory average.

Fig. 3.7.4
Weekly shop
performance return

Clock no.	Name	Total hours	OT	Hours on incentive	Performance %
100	A. Smith	46	6	44	106
102	B. Jones	40	0	40	102
104	C. Green	46	6	39	110
		454	46	436	105

The shop supervisor should scrutinise the figures weekly, particularly good performances should be complimented—'an ounce of appreciation is worth a ton of reprimand'. This also applies to good departmental performances. Poor performance, particularly when out of character, should be investigated, not so much to administer a reprimand, though this many sometimes be necessary, but to determine whether poor performance highlights a training need, equipment shortcomings, or perhaps personal worries about situations outside the workplace. In this case help from the personnel department may be required. With labour performance figures it is the significant change rather than the general level that is important.

Foremen should also be trained to understand and take action on the labour cost return (see Fig. 3.5.35 on pages 438/9) for their department. The most important measure is the cost per unit of output, a significant rise in this figure is cause for immediate investigation. Other sections of the report will indicate the areas requiring investigation, e.g. waiting time, rectification, excessive setting and so on.

Machines

Machine utilisation for the department as a whole is revealed in the *labour cost control report*, and this normally is an adequate index. If results are unsatisfactory, or performance begins to fall, it may be necessary, until the cause is found, to arrange temporarily for a detailed record of down-time (idle machine time) on each or certain machines. Such detailed records should not be continued beyond their usefulness if they involve any clerical labour away from the machine or which affects an operator's output. At all times records which are not used bring themselves and their originators into disrepute.

It is sometimes recommended that detailed records of maintenance and repair costs for each machine should be made. If such costs are heavy it is necessary, but it is clerical work which can be avoided except when the comparative maintenance costs of similar machines are, or are likely to be, in question. If the difference is appreciable, a Foreman knows without records; if there is doubt, detailed records must be kept for a period until costs are established.

Material or product

The performance of finished machines or parts, or the quality of products, are other aspects of performance. It is often thought that this is the Inspector's responsibility. It is not. Quality of product is the Supervisor's (Manager's or Foreman's) responsibility; the Inspector is really the representative of the customer (or Assembly Department or Sales Department), and is employed as *a guardian of quality*. The Production Supervisor must, in the end, produce a good quality article, and it is for him therefore to get and use reports on the performance, or quality, of his product. As with labour, he must look for incidence of cause and follow up in an endeavour to cure the cause. Nor is it right to assume that there must always be some waste or scrap, or that a normal figure needs no further efforts to reduce it. It is surprising to how low a figure scrap and faulty work can be reduced if the effort is made.

For process and continuous production work there is no better index of performance and guide to cause than the statistical method of quality control (referred to in chapter 6, see page 503).

Productivity

During the past ten to fifteen years there has been much stress laid on productivity. Not only has increased industrial productivity been a sufficient aim in itself, but for a period it was also the only means of obtaining government approval for wage increases during a statutory wages and incomes freeze. It is of course a very important index; however, its importance is not matched by its ease of measurement. Output per man hour is an index of productivity which can be measured in one factory or plant in one year, using value of sales and labour hours. This will give a false picture of productivity improvement if selling prices are increased without a change in labour hours. There is a similar problem when relating productivity in a firm mass producing washing machines or motor-cars to one making handpainted pottery, for example. Even the use of the productivity ratio *standard hours produced/actual hours worked* ignores the use of capital in the enterprise and thus prevents meaningful comparison between companies. One index of productivity that enables these points to be taken into account is *added value per employee* related to the company's capital intensity. The concept of added value is now familiar to most people, but its relation to hours worked, number of employees, or capital employed has not had a wide recognition as a productivity index. The subject has been further considered in Part One, chapter 7 (see page 91), and is supplemented there by a detailed review in Appendix III (see page 154).

Whether a company uses the ratio of standard hours produced to actual hours worked, or one of the added value based indices, it should be remembered that it is better to have an imperfect measurement of productivity within the establishment than none at all.

Control in action

The manager of a production unit, Production Manager, Works Manager, Foreman, or whatever his status title, must spend quite a large part of his time 'controlling' the activities for which he is responsible, that is, checking performance against programme or standards and taking action to correct errors or undesirable trends. The higher a manager's position in the organisation, the more he will have to judge results from reports and other documents (such documents should therefore be designed to make deviations, shortages, excess costs, overdue items, etc., stand out from the mass of figures).

Cost control reports, presenting performance figures and analysing excess costs according to cause (described in detail on pp. 437 and 440, should be used down to Foreman level, the Production Manager scrutinising them first, and discussing with his subordinates significant items, they in turn taking up in more detail with their assistants.

The Production Manager will examine other manufacturing expenditure by comparing with his budget (see Party Five, chapter 6, page 724). He will have discussed this with his managers before it was agreed and will likewise discuss results with them when they are known, usually at monthly intervals. Time should not be wasted in going through every item, but thought should be given to items in excess about which something can be done. The Production Manager will also need to check output, preferably weekly, against the Planning Department's programme, and, if manufacturing to customer's delivery requirements, overdue deliveries. Failures here may involve re-arrangement of production facilities, overtime or extra shifts, or additional labour, and conferences with the managers concerned. He will also watch earnings not only as an index of performance but in order to forestall possible trouble. (Preventive action where labour relations are concerned, and especially involving earnings, is much easier than the usual lengthy and unhappy process of negotiation.) Reports on stock levels and items (purchased or finished) out-of-stock will need to be discussed with the Buyer, Storekeeper and possibly Planning Manager, and again production plans or purchasing programmes may have to be adjusted with changes in material supply. Likewise, reports from the Personnel Department on absenteeism and turn-over may indicate action, either in the organisation or in respect of labour recruitment.

There will be other control reports used by a particular company. The important thing is that the Production Manager should not just receive, read and file reports, but should at least frequently, if not regularly, discuss doubtful or unsatisfactory, as well as good, results with the persons responsible. In this way the reports are kept alive, and those responsible for results are concerned to do something about them. Production is under control.

This concept is the background and basis of *management by objectives*, in which the management control process of:

determine targets
operate
check performance

has been formalised to a regular, say six monthly, pattern. As was pointed out in Part One, chapter 3 (see page 83) the principles of management by objectives are not new; indeed they are just good management in action. The need for management by objectives, however, is that in many organisations and for many people this does not happen unless it is programmed, introduced by an 'expert', or given a new fancy name. But whether it is done formally under such a title or informally as good production management, it must be done. Then the manager will be in control, he will be managing, and he will be achieving the objectives of his position as Production Manager.

8 Management decision-making: the operational research approach

It is no accident that progress in management has coincided with the growing use of measurements. However, due to the innate uncertainty of business, the figures which are produced by these measurements are in many cases so bedevilled with fluctuations that it is difficult to get a sensible message from them. It was uncertainty in figures which led to the development of statistical methods. In particular, the statistical approach is not to understand and respond to *ad hoc* random fluctuations but to determine the statistical pattern they form as a group and to draw a decision based on that pattern.[1]

By contrast, progress in science, although closely linked with measurements, was not faced with such a degree of uncertainty and this enabled scientists to formulate the laws of the situation much more precisely, very often in mathematical terms. For example, the laws of gravity and of magnetism are precise. It is reputed that they were developed by Newton from a simple model based on an apple and the earth, a model which he was able to express in mathematical terms.

The statistical approach and the use of models are the principal features in the operational research approach to solving management problems. *Operational research*, or 'management science' as it is sometimes called, arose out of inviting scientists of various disciplines to tackle management problems. It was inevitable that they formulated these problems in the form of models, perhaps built from mathematical equations. It was equally inevitable that the unpredictability of the management situation and of the measurements that those scientists wished to use led them to thinking in statistical terms, so that they could measure the uncertainty and the variability and take them into account.

The major fields of application of operational research have been in the management of stocks and of distribution systems. Every company holds stocks, in some form or other, but few have given a sufficient degree of analytical thought to the basic decisions of when to replenish them and by how much. Reductions in stock levels of 25 to 35 per cent are common achievements of the operational research approach, often accompanied by a higher level of service from the stocks.

Sales and distribution organisations have often grown in an unplanned manner, taking advantage of chance opportunities—perhaps out of a merger designed to give production economies. The study and improvement of such systems is ideally suited to examination by the mathematical models of operational research. Savings of over £500 000 have been made on annual production and distribution costs by redesigning the distribution system to

[1] This chapter has been especially written for this volume by C. J. Anson, to whom the Editor and Authors wish to express grateful acknowledgement.

relate the siting and capacities of production facilities, warehouses and depots to the location and delivery requirements of customers. These savings were more than twenty times the cost of the investigation.

Steps in the OR approach to management problems

The application of scientific method to tackling management problems has required, in principle, the following steps:

Definition of the problem

The first step may seem trivial, but it is essential to formulate the problem in a manner which will allow a mathematical model to be used. Furthermore the yardstick with which improvements will be measured as a result of any change should reflect the improvement to the company as a whole and not a narrow departmental point of view. However it is important not to tackle too big a problem. Limit the scope of the problem, for example by looking only at finished goods stocks rather than at all the stock-holding points in the company. In this way practical results can be achieved in a reasonable time, before the time or the funds allocated for improvement are absorbed.

Available data

Unless data relevant to all the significant features of the situation can be made available in the right form the OR approach cannot be applied. In one instance, no demand data was available for the individual stock items at the individual shops of a retail drapery chain. In consequence the OR approach to stock control could not be applied at the shops, but had to be restricted to the central warehouse where the demand data was adequate. Once data availability is secure, a preliminary analysis of the existing figures will determine the statistical patterns in them as a basis for building the mathematical models.

Mathematical model

The OR approach now formulates the laws of the situation in mathematical terms: it constructs a mathematical model of the situation. Once constructed, the model is tested against past history, perhaps on a section of the problem area. At this stage the availability of the data would be rechecked to ensure that the needs of the model can be met. One outcome may be to revise the model to take account of the limited data or calculation facilities. A further check to ensure that the implications of management policy are correctly built into the model would be made before applying it to solve the problem. The key features in this process are, on the one hand, to construct the simplest model which will solve the problem at issue, but on the other, to match the model to the problem, not the other way round.

Implementation

Operational research, like method study, inevitably results in changes and a need to persuade senior management of the benefits of such changes. However, unless the climate for change is favourable, OR may well become abortive at the implementation stage, even if the resulting benefits in capital reduction, cost saving or profit increase, security and service to customers, far outweigh the cost of the changes. Implementation of the changes often incorporates impersonal procedures to make routine decisions, and these replace a cherished personal involvement. Contributions to winning acceptance are: the development of simple rules such as fixed re-order levels and re-order quantities for each stock item, the writing of comprehensive manuals, and the training of staff—no matter how sophisticated the mathematical model chosen for solving the problem.

Monitoring

The management problems tackled by OR arise in a dynamic environment. It is imperative to monitor the basic data used in the mathematical models to ensure that the rules are changed whenever there is a significantly large change in the basic data. Moreover, there is an element of research and development in all operational research investigations and consequently the actual outcome of the proposed changes may differ appreciably from the estimates of the mathematical model. Consequently, the practical outcome of the proposed procedures also needs to be monitored. For instance in stock control, do the stock levels fall in value, and does the service provided by the stocks match that estimated by the model? If not, a review is needed to rectify the anomalies.

Techniques for OR

The kitbag of tools described in this section is by no means comprehensive, nor can the description of each tool be more than an outline. The tools have been chosen because of the important part they play in OR and more detailed descriptions are given in the recommended reading list following this Part (see page 550).

Statistical method

As mentioned previously, the measurements in management are usually bedevilled with unpredictable fluctuations and consequently many of the mathematical models of operational research rely on the statistical approach which has been developed to handle uncertainty in figures. Management figures are treated in a manner similar to the way an insurance company treats the uncertainty in human life. The individual outcome is unpredictable, but nevertheless, a management policy can be based on the statistical pattern these outcomes form as a group.

In the simplest instance, the variability or uncertainty in the figures is attributed to a large number of relatively small causes and the pattern of the group can be summarised by means of a frequency diagram.

Frequency diagrams

The amount demanded during the delivery time of a replenishment order for a particular stock item, extracted from stock and purchase order records, for each of the last thirty replenishment orders could take the following values:

17	19	12	15	13
18	19	17	16	17
19	17	15	17	15
20	18	14	16	17
13	15	16	17	13
16	16	13	15	15

The statistical approach is to disregard individual instances, in particular not to try to find out why the amount demanded was 17 on the first occasion, 19 on the second, and only 12 on the third. Instead the pattern as a whole is determined by concentrating on the frequency with which each value occurred.

If these frequencies are expressed as a frequency diagram, a bar chart in which the height of each bar is made proportionate to the appropriate frequency, the visual impact is immediate. The individual observation is lost in the group, the pattern of which is clearly shown. In this instance, the diagram in Fig. 3.8.1 shows that the unpredictable fluctuations make the figures scatter around a central value of about 16 and, moreover, there are no freaks or abnormalities in the data calling for special investigation.

The frequency diagram is the fundamental tool of statistical analysis. It enables situations as a whole to be summarised and used conceptually in building management policies. It is clear, just by looking at a frequency diagram that the average of a set of management figures is not enough. The variability in the figures has to be taken into account. Variability can seldom be eliminated, but it can be measured and used to plan the policies.

The simplest measure of variability is the *range*, which is the difference between the largest and the smallest of the observations. It is, however, an inefficient measure since it ignores all the observations except the extreme values. Consequently it is customary to use an alternative measure, the

Fig. 3.8.1
Frequency diagram

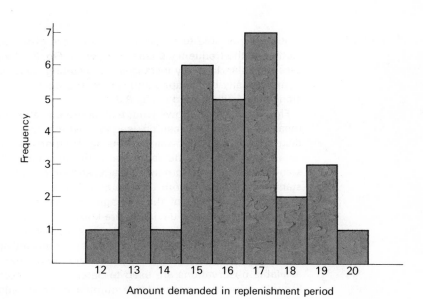

Amount demanded in replenishment period

standard deviation, which is calculated from the deviations of each of the observations about their average. If $X_1, X_2, \ldots X_n$, denote n observations and $\bar{X}$ denotes the arithmetic average, then the standard deviation (usually denoted by σ) of these observations is:

$$\frac{(X_1 - \bar{X})^2 + (X_2 - \bar{X})^2 + \cdots (X_n - \bar{X})^2}{n}$$

Thus in a simple example of 10 observations ($n = 10$)

X	$X - \bar{X}$ $= X - 9$	$(X - \bar{X})^2$
2	-7	49
3	-6	36
5	-4	16
7	-2	4
8	-1	1
9	0	0
11	2	4
13	4	16
15	6	36
17	8	64
90		226

Arithmetic Average $\bar{X} = \dfrac{90}{10} = 9$

$\Sigma (X - \bar{X})^2 = 226$

So
$$\sigma = \sqrt{\frac{226}{10}} = \sqrt{22 \cdot 6} = 4 \cdot 75$$

Normal distribution

If it were possible to obtain more and more observations on demand, the outline of the frequency diagram shown in Fig. 3.8.1 would become less and less irregular. In many instances the resulting frequency diagram would be symmetrically bell-shaped and can be approximated by the normal distribution which is illustrated in Fig. 3.8.2.

Figure 3.8.2 also shows what a standard deviation looks like and how this measure of variability can be used to illustrate the proportions of the normal distribution. About two-thirds of the observations in a normal distribution fall within one standard deviation from the average; 95 per cent within two standard deviations from the average, and almost all of them are within three standard deviations from the average. These proportions remain the same whatever the values of the average and standard deviation. So once the average and standard deviation are known the specific normal distribution, out of myriad possibilities, is completely specified (see also chapter 6, p. 505).

It is seldom practical to obtain the several thousand observations needed to produce a normal distribution. The average and standard deviation of the available observations are used to determine the normal distribution most likely to arise from such a large number of observations. For example, the average of the demands shown in Fig. 3.8.1 is sixteen and the standard deviation approximately two. These values would be used to determine the most likely normal distribution which is shown in Fig. 3.8.3.

Fig. 3.8.2
Normal frequency
distribution

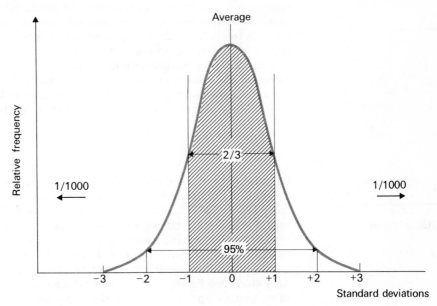

Amount demanded in replenisment period

Fig. 3.8.3
Normal distribution
estimated from
thirty observations

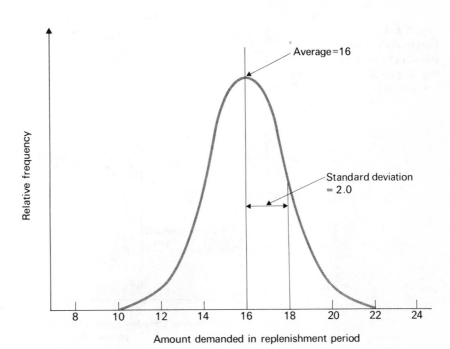

Amount demanded in replenishment period

Asymmetrical frequency distributions

It is usual to expect that the normal distribution will be a good approximation when data are collected by *measurement* (times, speeds, lengths, etc.). When data are collected by *counting* (number of stoppages per day, number of faults per length of carpet, etc.) it follows a distribution which may be quite asymmetrical, called the Poisson distribution. Tables of the Poisson distribution show the proportion of occasions on which different values of the count occur for a wide range of average values of the count. In practice, if the average count is ten or more the frequency diagram is sufficiently symmetrical to be approximated by the normal distribution.

In addition, in some stock control situations and in reliability studies the data collected can also form asymmetrical frequency diagrams. It is always desirable to plot a frequency diagram for the collected data, and if necessary to choose the most appropriate frequency distribution from a number of alternatives.

Pareto's Law: The important few and the trivial many

Pareto noted at the end of the nineteenth century that the bulk of the wealth in Italy was in the hands of 10 per cent of the population. Pareto's observations apply equally well in management situations where 'wealth' is being measured. For example, if items are listed in descending order of value, the top 20 per cent of a company's products, or the top 20 per cent of its customers, account for 80 per cent of the sales by value; the top 20 per cent of its purchase items account for about 80 per cent of the annual purchase expenditure. Figure 3.8.4 illustrates Pareto's law. It shows the cumulative percentage of the total sales plotted against the cumulative percentage of the total number of products, taking the products in descending order of their annual turnover.

Fig. 3.8.4
Pareto distribution: the significance of the 'important few'

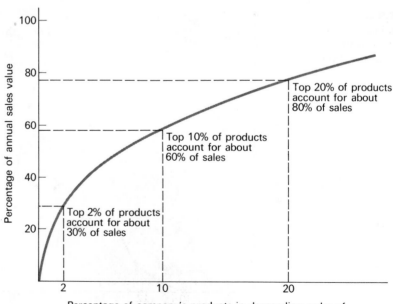

Percentage of company's products in descending order of annual sales

The practical import of Pareto's law is the recognition of the existence of the important few and the virtue of according them special treatment. For example, in production and stock control the replenishment of the important *few* components representing approximately 80 per cent of total inventory cost (Class A) could be made the personal responsibility of individual members of the purchase department. Class B items could be controlled impersonally through a computer or stock record card system. The trivial many (Class C) could be controlled through a very simple two-bin system without keeping formal records of stock levels.[1]

Wherever there is only one system there is a possibility that the important few are being neglected and the trivial many wastefully cosseted.

Adaptive techniques

The statistical approach to handling uncertainty is to regard variation as inevitable and to design buffers to accommodate it as cheaply as possible. On the other hand there are instances where it is possible to take stock of a situation as things develop. If the uncertainty can be compensated for after it has happened then adaptive techniques can be brought to bear. In practice it is useful to combine the statistical and the adaptive approach.

Project planning

Project network analysis, using critical path methods, is an adaptive planning technique, which has been described in some detail in chapter 5 (page 385). There are however two main steps:

1. Drawing a sequence diagram to ensure that a feasible sequence of operations is planned. At this stage the length of time to complete the operations is ignored. The sequence diagram takes the form of a network and from this the term 'Project network analysis' was derived.

Fig. 3.8.5
Project network analysis

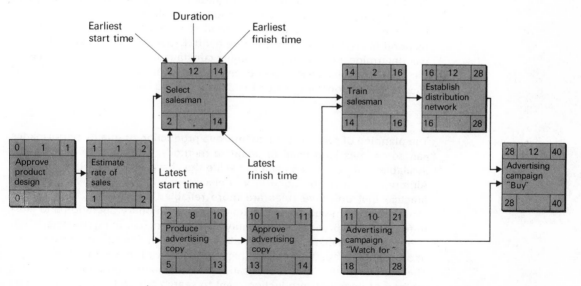

[1] R. Harrison, 'Selective stock control', *Work Study and Management Services,* March 1968, pp. 156–63.

2. Scheduling the operations to define the programme of work against a time scale. The earliest time at which each operation can start and the latest time at which it can start without delaying the completion of the project are determined by taking account of the sequence diagram and the length of time each operation takes. From this analysis, the operations to which priority must be given are identified: often the unsuspected operation is critical. Fig. 3.8.5 shows a sequence diagram with the appropriate scheduling calculations.

Should major revisions to the project be needed, they can be incorporated in revised plans without much difficulty because the sequence diagram can be modified separately from the scheduling of the project. In addition to this adaptive facility, network analysis has the facility to identify and measure the size of the buffers of spare time, the float, in the project so that the planner can assess whether there is sufficient to accommodate the uncertain delays when they actually arise.

Exponential smoothing

When forecasts of demand are being made on the basis of weekly or monthly figures it is clearly desirable to revise these forecasts when each new figure becomes available. The technique known as exponential smoothing provides a simple means of adapting the forecasts to keep them up to date. In its simplest form, it maintains a running average but in such a way that extra weight is given to the more recent figures.

The calculation routine is very straightforward. Suppose that the average weekly sales for a particular product line was 62, this figure would be used as the forecast for next week's demand. If this week's sales turn out to be 72, the revised forecast is 62 + 20 per cent of the difference (72 − 62), namely 64. The factor 20 per cent has been called the smoothing constant and experience suggests that the value of the smoothing constant should be somewhere between 10 and 30 per cent to smooth out random fluctuations and yet respond to significant changes in demand. Experience within each industry will determine whether the smoothing constant should be nearer 30 than 20 per cent—in which case recent events have rather more significance than in cases where a constant nearer 10 per cent gives a better forecast.

Process trials

The planning of process trials to improve production or quality performance can sometimes lend itself to adaptive methods. The result of each trial, if available in time, can be used to decide the characteristics of the next trial. Although this may be done in a subjective manner, it has been found in practice that objective rules are more reliable. For instance the adaptive sequence determined by the technique of evolutionary operation and illustrated in Fig. 3.8.6, will quickly identify the best set of operating characteristics.

Furthermore where raw materials change from season to season in an unpredictable way, the process characteristics need to react to this change. The continued use of trials based on evolutionary operation provides a method of operating production plant to search out and maintain the most profitable operating conditions.

Fig. 3.8.6
Technique for
evaluating
process trials

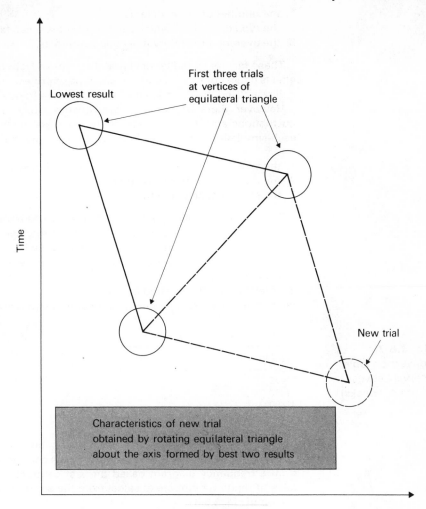

Model building:
use of simulation

In some instances the structure of the management problem is too complex to be tackled by straightforward mathematical or statistical methods, and the cost, time scale and complexity of the problem make it inappropriate to use adaptive operational trials. It is, however, often possible to tackle these complex problems by constructing a mathematical model of the situation and to carry out an exercise on paper, called *simulation,* to see just what would happen. The advantage of this approach is that it can be done without risk and several years' experience collected in a few days.

As with process improvement trials, certain characteristics are held constant throughout a simulation run, and deliberately changed before the next simulation run in order to assess the effect of such changes. These are characteristics which can in practice be held constant, for example when examining the service provided and the efficient utilisation of the project teams of a small company they could be:

1. the number of project teams;
2. the type of contract which each project team can tackle; and,
3. the average time interval between contracts.

These factors would be deliberately changed from run to run to assess the effects of changes in the number and type of project teams; in management's policy in using them; and in the impact of more frequent or longer contracts.

However there are other characteristics which are subject to random fluctuations and these random fluctuations are deliberately introduced into each simulation run. In the above small company they could be:

1. the time at which each contract is required to start;
2. the duration of the contract; and,
3. the specific type of contract.

These characteristics are specified in terms of a frequency diagram and are made to vary in an unpredictable (random) manner by selecting an appropriate value for the characteristic, rather like drawing raffle tickets out of a hat. The time at which a contract is required to start will be built up by random selections from a frequency diagram of intervals between contracts. These intervals would be extracted from past records and a conversion table relating random numbers to the intervals prepared, as shown in Fig. 3.8.7.

Fig. 3.8.7
Conversion table:
interval between
contracts (weeks)

Random number	Interval
01–70	0
71–90	1
91–00	2

Tables of random numbers would then be used to select successive intervals from this table. The duration of each contract would also be selected from a frequency diagram based on past contract durations, again using a table of random numbers to select from the appropriate conversion table, as shown in Fig. 3.8.8.

Fig. 3.8.8
Conversion table:
duration of
contracts (weeks)

Random number	Duration	Random number	Duration	Random number	Duration
00–16	1	69–72	10	91–92	19
17–26	2	73–75	11	93	20
27–35	3	75–78	12	94	21
36–42	4	79–80	13	95	22
43–49	5	81–83	14	96	25
50–55	6	84–85	15	97	27
56–60	7	86–87	16	98	33
61–64	8	88–89	17	99	52
65–68	9	90–	18		

If there is a restriction on the type of contract which each project team can tackle, a similar conversion table, Fig. 3.8.9, would be used to select the contract type.

Fig. 3.8.9
Conversion table:
class of contract

Random number	Class of contract
01–20	Industrial
21–26	Process Control
27–52	Feed Mechanism
53–72	General
73–82	Communication
83–92	Display
93–00	Power

Fig. 3.8.10
Contract record
sheet

Arrival interval		Date start reqd.	Duration		Contract type		Team No.	Date actual start	Date ended	Delay on start
(35)	0	0	(33)	3	(00)	I	4	1	4	1
(28)	0	0	(17)	2	(75)	C	15	3	5	3
(62)	0	0	(19)	2	(67)	G	14	3	5	3
(84)	1	1	(05)	1	(65)	G	13	3	4	2
(91)	2	3	(64)	1	(01)	I	10	3	4	0
Weeks work sold				9				Maximum delay		3
(95)	2	5	(95)	22	(71)	G	12	5	27	0
(48)	2	5	(48)	5	(65)	G	10	5	10	0
(82)	1	6	(06)	1	(45)	F	9	6	7	0
(91)	1	7	(74)	11	(11)	I	8	7	18	0
(44)	0	7	(69)	10	(32)	F	5	7	17	0
(60)	0	7	(71)	10	(25)	PR	13	7	17	0
Weeks work sold				59				Maximum delay		0
(75)	1	8	(65)	9	(49)	F	6	8	17	0
(67)	0	8	(45)	5	(31)	F	4	8	13	0
(65)	0	8	(11)	1	(42)	F	9	8	9	0
(21)	0	8	(22)	2	(31)	F	1	8	10	0
(17)	0	8	(66)	9	(48)	F	9	9	18	1
(69)	0	8	(59)	7	(27)	F	1	10	17	2
(61)	0	8	(16)	1	(45)	F	10	10	11	2
(56)	0	8	(28)	3	(47)	F	10	11	14	3
(95)	2	10	(58)	6	(44)	F	7	12	18	2
(04)	0	10	(76)	12	(55)	G	14	10	22	0
(25)	0	10	(25)	2	(98)	Po	15	10	12	0
(22)	0	10	(56)	7	(70)	G	11	10	17	0
(89)	1	11	(05)	1	(01)	I	7	12	13	1
Weeks work sold				65				Maximum delay		3

Fig. 3.8.10 shows a twelve-week contract record sheet for such a simulation run and Fig. 3.8.11 the related project team availability record. It deals with
an instance in which fifteen project teams of different levels of versatility were
available. Subsequent runs could examine for instance what would happen if
all teams could tackle all types of project; if the average number of contracts a
week increased, by changing the conversion table shown in Fig. 3.8.7; or if the
average length of contracts increased, by changing the conversion table
shown in Fig. 3.8.8.

It is clear that an investigation of this kind involves a series of runs simulating different operating conditions and strategies. To make fair comparisons between these operating conditions and strategies, measures of performance are needed. These measures will depend on the objective and form of the simulation. In the case of our small company they could be:

- the service provided to the company's clients, measured by the maximum delay in each month before starting a contract; and
- the costs resulting both from the number of project teams and from providing teams trained to different levels of versatility.

Simulation is a means of bringing the experimental approach to bear on management decision making and it is usually desirable to apply the principles of experimental design such as to ensure that the trials are planned and analysed efficiently. In this way the risk of repeating the simulation runs more than is needed, or of stopping before a satisfactory level of precision has been achieved, can be minimised.

Fig. 3.8.11
Team availability
record

Team		First week of period			
No.	Avoid contracts	0	4	8	12
1	PR	8	8	8; 10; 17	17
2	I, D	12	12	12	12
3	I, D	12	12	12; 18	18
4	PR, D	1; 4	4 (4)	8; 13	13
5	PR, D	4	72		
6	PR, D	5	5 (3)	8; 17	17
7	PR, D	12	12	12; 13	13
8	PR, D	3 (1)	4 (3) 18	18	18
9	PR, D	3 (1)	4 (2) 7 (1)	8; 9; 18	18
10	PR, D	3; 4	4 (1) 10	10; 11; 14	14
11	F, D	6	6 (2)	8 (2) 17	17
12	I, PR, D	3 (1)	4 (1) 27	27	27
13	I, F, D	3; 4	4 (3) 17	17	17
14	I, F, D	3; 5	5 (3)	8 (2) 22	22
15	I, PR, F, G	3; 5	5 (3)	8 (2) 12	12
Lost team weeks		(3)	(29)	(6)	
Weeks worked		57	31	54	
Utilisation, %		95	52	90	
Forward load (weeks)		81	33	61	72

Mathematical
methods

Mathematical methods in operational research are concerned with optimisation, for example with finding the *best* sequence of production or with making the *best* use of limited resources. In practical application, they involve a considerable degree of computation and would not have become feasible without the use of computers.

Best production
sequence

This type of problem arises where there is a multiplicity of choice and it would be completely impractical to evaluate all possible alternatives. Fig. 3.8.12

shows a matrix of the relative costs which are incurred when changing over production equipment currently making one product to manufacture another product in the current product range. A specific instance would be a large press making a number of different types of bumper bar. What is the sequence of production which will minimise the changeover cost and yet would enable all the products to be manufactured?

Fig. 3.8.12
Matrix of
changeover costs

Changeover cost to product

	A	B	C	D	E	F	G
A	—	1	11	5	5	2	20
B	4	—	8	3	27	3	9
C	6	48	—	2	12	8	56
D	1	8	10	—	60	8	40
E	1	4	6	24	—	2	12
F	3	9	3	9	2	—	4
G	4	8	1	1	5	5	—

From product (label at left of rows D)

Example: To changeover from Product B to Product E has a relative cost of 27 units.

To evaluate all the alternatives would require 7! (7! factorial = $7 \times 6 \times 5 \times 4 \times 3 \times 2$) namely 5 040 additions and would take merely five seconds on a computer: but if there were nineteen products in the sequence complete evaluation would take 50 000 years. Fortunately, by simple manipulation it is possible to change the matrix shown in Fig. 3.8.12 into another matrix which has the same optimum sequence and yet is more readily analysed. This matrix is shown in Fig. 3.8.13.

Fig. 3.8.13
Matrix of values
with same optimum
sequence

To product

	A	B	C	D	E	F	G
A	—	0	10	4	4	1	17
B	1	—	5	0	24	0	4
C	4	46	—	0	10	6	52
D	0	7	9	—	59	7	37
E	0	3	5	23	—	1	9
F	1	7	1	8	0	—	0
G	3	7	0	0	4	4	—

From product (label at left of row D)

Clearly the changeovers with zero cost are the ones which should be used to build up the optimum changeover sequence. The routes of zero cost changeovers are shown diagrammatically in Fig. 3.8.14 and the optimum sequence appears as A, B, F, G, C, D, A. This omits product E. In order to determine where E should go in the sequence, the cost of all the alternative positions for E are evaluated. The calculations at the foot of Fig. 3.8.14 show that the sequence of minimum changeover cost is A, E, B, F, G, C, D, A. If any other sequence is used then the extra cost of changeover can be calculated and the justification for its use assessed.

Fig. 3.8.14
Selection of
optimum sequence

Routes of zero cost changeovers

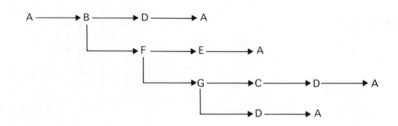

Longest route:	A,B,F,G,C,D,A

Missing product: E

Alternative positions:	*Changeover cost*
A,E,B	4+ 3= 7
B,E,F	24+ 1=25
F,E,G	0+ 9= 9
G,E,D	4+23=27
D,E,A	59+ 0=59

Optimum route: A,E,B,F,G,C,D,A

Making the best use of limited resources

The type of problem can be illustrated by the experience of one of the Gas Boards. It has several coking plants each with a maximum demand for coal, and is supplied by several pits each with a maximum output of coal. The coal can be carried either by road, rail or water, at different costs per ton and with different maximum throughputs. How do you choose which colliery should supply which plant and which method of transporting the coal should be adopted?

The mathematical technique for solving this type of problem is called *linear programming*. The basic approach is to define a set of feasible solutions, to select one feasible solution and then to select better feasible solutions in turn until the optimum solution is found. In many instances the restrictions and the resources are not permanent and most of the appropriate computer programs identify which restrictions have the greatest effect on limiting the company's throughput or profit.[1]

The problems are complex and although experience and manual allocation routines will be developed by the manager responsible, the power of a mathematical routine aided by a computer will inevitably produce a better solution. The oil industry use linear programming to optimise their use of the

[1] An example of the use of a computer for the solution of linear programming problems in the production of animal feedstuffs is given in chapter 5, pp. 444–5.

limited supply of different quality crude oils to meet the forecast demand for different end uses such as petrol, crude oil, petrochemicals; to optimise the use of the restricted production resources at their command in the refinery; and to minimise the cost of distribution from storage depots with limited resources to sales points with maximum demands. The savings have been massive.

Role of computers

Computers can provide fast, reliable and economic means of doing the calculations associated with operational research. Clearly computers are not essential since good work was done before they became available but nevertheless they are a tool which enables larger and more complex problems to be tackled, so adding to the practical usefulness of OR.

In some of the simpler mathematical models program packages have been constructed by computer manufacturers and computer bureaux and these allow the computer to be used with a minimum amount of prior preparation. Certain techniques, such as statistical analysis, linear programming or network planning, are much more precisely defined than others and in consequence more suited to program packages.

Statistical analysis

One straightforward program package deals with the statistical technique of *multiple regression analysis* which calculates the best relationship between one characteristic and several other characteristics. As an illustration, consider an investigation into the factors affecting the project and the sales of a food manufacturer. Results were determined for each of fifteen product groups, for each of four selling regions, and for each of four years, making a total of 240 figures. Corresponding to each result, the following information was collected:

- number of salesmen per million in population;
- percentage of product sold direct to retail outlets;
- number of lines in product group;
- population (millions) in selling region;
- advertising expenditure on product group.

These factors were first related to profit, and the standard computer package calculated the following equation:

Profit contribution (£) = 20 000 + 250 per salesman
  − 40 (percentage retail) + 90 per line
  − 100 (per million population)
  − 350 (per £1 000 advertising).

By careful study of this equation, strategies for improving profitability were determined. The effect that the changes in policy would have on turnover were assessed from the following equation which related the factors to turnover:

Turnover (£) = 15 000 + 1 300 per salesman
  − 200 (percentage retail) + 400 per line
  − 600 (per million population)
  + 500 (per £1 000 advertising)

Once the basic data had been calculated and the program package specified to produce the results in the required form, the computer made the routine calculations.

Linear programming

The calculations associated with linear programming are both complex and repetitive and consequently ideally suited to evaluation by computer. In practice the solution of any problem of worthwhile size is only feasible on a large computer, and even then special calculation routines have been devised to handle them. Computer packages are available from computer bureaux and from specialist computer consultants who will advise on their use. Once the problem has been structured so that the technique of linear programming can be used, and the computer packing appropriately specified to match, the computation is routine. Since only a small amount of data has to be introduced into the computer, the calculations lend themselves readily to access through a data terminal to a time sharing computer.

Simulation

The problems tackled by simulation are so dissimilar that computer package programs are completely inappropriate and a computer program has to be written specifically for each model. Special 'high level' languages have been designed to simplify the writing of such a program and to take advantage of the features which are common to different situations. Such languages tend to use a computer inefficiently, and on large scale simulations repeated a number of times, could result in excessive computer costs. Nevertheless they reduce the level of computer programming still required and also the number of programming man hours needed to get the simulation under way.

Constructing a mathematical model of an operating system in a suitable form for computer simulation is not a simple task.[1] Technical assistance will be needed in formulating the model, in formulating a program of simulation trials and in writing and running the computer program. In many instances there will be an equally large program of work to collect the relevant data and costs which must not be overlooked. The manager asking the questions needs to be involved throughout the whole exercise and the best results have almost certainly been achieved when he himself has led and coordinated the team of specialists.

Management problems

Some of the management problems to which OR techniques have been applied have been indicated during the description of the techniques in the previous paragraphs. In this section we have selected the 'important few' problem areas which account for the major part of operational research applications, and examine how the approach is applied.

Define the problem

The problems in the 'important few' category themselves fall into two major categories, those problems which arise from the apparently opposing requirements of different sections within an organisation, and those which require the use of mathematical manipulation of historical facts to forecast future requirements.

Stock control is a typical example of the first of these problems. The problem of balancing the production and sales preference for large stocks (large

[1] See J. W. Harling and S. J. Walter, 'Using computers to explore the Company's future', *The Director*, January 1967.

batches for production, ex-stock delivery for the salesmen) against the financial preference for small stock holding (obsolescence risk and use of working capital) has been mentioned elsewhere in this book.

Transport and distribution is a second example, where the desirability of few warehouses of large capacity has to be weighed with the alternative of many small warehouses, both of which must be cross related to the effects of siting in relation to both factory and customer. Other examples of this problem already covered elsewhere in this chapter and in chapter 5 are:

- allocation of materials to produce the most economic mix of end products;
- allocation of alternative production facilities to products;
- sequence of changeover of production facilities when changeover costs depend on sequence chosen.

Production and *sales forecasting* are examples of the second major area of OR activity and are very similar to each other. In each case the requirement is to determine how many, of what, and when. It is also important to decide in what form, scale and detail the information is required. Do we want to know the total plant capacity required over a period, or the specific capacity of a particular piece of plant in a given month? Likewise do we want sales forecast for next year in order to prepare this year's manufacturing program, or do we need a five-year forecast in order to determine our capital investment requirements?

Availability of data

The availability of data can be divided into three broad categories:

1. Readily available facts. These will come from existing company records or nationally available statistics. These might be units sold by the company, material used in a given time, supplier's delivery periods, or the location and capacity of existing warehouses.
2. Facts requiring investigation or calculation. Into this group would come total national or worldwide market for a particular product and any seasonal variation in the demand, transport and distribution costs by different classes of vehicle, shop capacities and throughput times, or the cost of stockholding.
3. The most difficult information to obtain is that requiring a considerable amount of interpolation, such as the cost of being 'out of stock', the future market for a product, likely future legislation and its effects, or the growth or change in living standards and pattern of spending.

It will be obvious from the above, that if an OR project requires data in categories 2 and 3, it will be longer and more costly than if the data were in category 1; however, the chances are that the possible gain is also greater.

Mathematical models

Most of the more important mathematical approaches to management problem solving have already been described in this chapter. It is, however, worth while to summarise under each major model approach a number of 'typical' situations or problems in which each might be employed.

Linear programming

● Least cost solution for a production period to achieve a specified product when the constituents, availability and cost of the raw materials vary.

● The routing of vehicles and the decisions on which warehouse should supply which depot. In this form of problem the model most commonly used assumes initially that each vehicle makes only one drop. Journeys are then combined so as to save the maximum journey mileage until each vehicle is loaded to the limit of weight, volume or journey hours.

Simulation

● To examine the service provided to a set of happenings, usually random, by fixed and controllable facilities—for example the service provided to lorries arriving at random time intervals at one or a number of loading bays. The number of bays, unloading teams and men in each team can be varied to determine the optimum solution.

Matrix analysis

● The least changeover cost described previously (page 541) is a typical example, where by mathematical manipulation of a matrix of possible alternative changeover costs the best cost solution can be quickly found.

● The solution to the travelling salesman's dilemma in what order to call on a known number of sites in order to minimise travelling distance, and hence time, can be solved using this approach.

Statistical methods

● Frequency diagrams are used to deduce information about the pattern of demand and usage of a particular item. This is particularly valuable for determination of re-order levels and re-order quantities to give a controlled chance of running out of stock.

● Graphical representation of the interdependence of delivery performance, stock levels and equipment utilisation as shown in Fig. 3.8.15 can provide guidance for the manager to arrive at a better balance of these factors.

Demand forecasting

In short-term forecasting it is usually possible to ignore the effect of economic influences and to use simple mathematical techniques such as exponential smoothing. For medium-term forecasts, however, the model needs to take account of systematic changes in demand either due to seasonality or to a drift in sales level. In addition, unpredictable major changes in competitive or governmental policy need to be assessed by experienced commercial executives and their effect on demand estimated by judgment, and used to modify the mathematical predictions.

In both short- and medium-term forecasting it is essential to try out the chosen model on past data, and by this means to assess the reliability which can be achieved.

Economic influences play a dominant rolè in the preparation of long-term forecasts of demand. The simplest model is concerned solely with identifying the dominant economic factors and measuring the degree of their influence on the sectors of industry sales most appropriate to the company. This is usually done by examining past historical figures and calculating the best equation linking the selected factors to past demand. For instance, the demand for domestic electrical appliances has been linked to the number of houses built, the availability of credit, tax rates, personal disposable income and product life. Subsequently, a more sophisticated model of the factors affecting

Fig. 3.8.15
Interdependence at customer delivery stocks and equipment utilisation

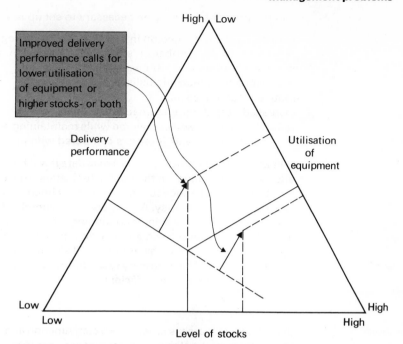

demand could be built, based on the initial analysis coupled with economic theory. The market for domestic electrical appliances could be subdivided into initial purchases and replacements, and each market examined separately. The factors affecting households making initial purchases almost certainly differ from those affecting replacement purchases which could well be dominated by the influence of product life.

Implementation

As with the institution of any change, the implementation of the OR investigation itself and later the implementation of any changes arising from it, requires careful handling and probably a high level of management involvement. Changes in procedure always involve altering the accustomed way people do things, hence the effect on the personnel in the organisation must be taken into account so that those involved know the reasons behind the change as well as the mechanics of it. Where the implementation of the OR solution requires major modifications to facilities such as re-layout of a production unit or relocation of warehouses, the change should be so organised to eliminate or at least minimise both temporary cost increases and reduced levels of service to the customer. The implementation itself may require to be controlled by the use of PERT or similar programming techniques.

Monitoring

Following any change such as those outlined above, the situation must be continually monitored to ensure that (a) the benefits predicted have in fact been achieved; and (b) the basic data on which the new situation is based are still valid.

In the case of (*a*), it may be necessary to set up new controls to check:

reductions in capital tied up in stocks, or work in progress;
reductions in the number of 'stock out' occasions or an improvement in the number of orders met 'off the shelf';
improvement in machine utilisation;
reduced material costs;
increased output per unit (machine or man hour);
reduction in vehicle miles covered while maintaining customer service levels;
improvements of sales forecasts compared with actual events.

In assessing the validity of the basic data it will be necessary to monitor the effects of any changes in the model, for instance the effect of amalgamations and takeovers, changes in legislation, tax changes and so on, that effect the way people spend money. A recent typical example of this was Britain's entry into the EEC which is having a continuing effect on patterns of sales and costs, as tariffs, quotas and so on are phased into our pattern of national trading.

Management must be aware of the likely changes and their time scale. In one instance it will be necessary to run the model every month, in another case an annual 're-run' will be sufficient.

Action plan

Choose the right place in the organisation

Operational research is essentially a staff function and in the larger company it should form a part of the management services team, alongside computer, O and M, and work study services. In the medium and smaller companies it is a service to be obtained from consultants, universities or colleges, unless one member of the senior executive has a special interest and aptitude.

Choose the right kind of man

The techniques and skills of operational research are not something which can be picked up from a two-week course. They call for a specialist of university graduate standard who has a flair for tackling management problems and implementing practical solutions. It will be fortunate if he can be recruited 'ready-made' and management must be prepared to provide considerable guidance and assistance to develop his skill to meet the company's specific needs.

Establish a programme of work

Clearly there should be a sufficient degree of need identified before contemplating either an appointment or consultancy assistance. This can be established either by an in-company investigation in depth of the problems involved, or by means of a consultancy survey. Once he is appointed, the OR specialist should become involved in preparing his future programme of work since he should have experience of the problem areas most suited to the operational research approach.

Establish a project team for each major problem

Operational research is concerned with management problems and its objective is to improve company performance. An operational research specialist cannot be expected to work in a vacuum—he needs the full cooperation, and the involvement of management. The most effective way to achieve a successful operational research application is to establish a project team for each major problem. The OR specialist will provide the necessary expertise. The line manager, or the chief executive if it is a companywide problem, should ensure that he gets a practical solution to his problem.

Further reading

Production management

BATTERSBY, A., *A Guide to Stock Control,* 2nd edn, Pitman for BIM, 1970.
BROWN, R. G., *Statistical Forecasting for Inventory Control,* McGraw-Hill, 1959.
CORKE, D. K., *Production Control,* British Productivity Council, 1965.
COUTIE, G. A., DAVIES, O. L., HOSSELL, C. H., MILLAR, D. W. G. P. and MORRELL, A. J. H., *Short Term Forecasting,* Oliver & Boyd, 1964.
CURRIE, R. M., *The Measurement of Work,* Management Publications Ltd for BIM, 1965.
DRUCKER, PETER F., *Managing for Results,* Pan Books, 1964.
HULL, J. F., *The Control of Manufacturing,* Gower Press, 1973.
INTERNATIONAL LABOUR OFFICE, *Introduction to Work Study,* 2nd edn, ILO, 1969.
KAY, F., for the Purchasing Officers' Association, *Purchasing,* Pitman, 1963.
LUMSDEN, PHILIP, *The Line of Balance Method,* Pergamon Press, 1968.
MAGEE, J. F. and BOODMAN, D. M., *Production Planning and Inventory Control,* 2nd edn., McGraw-Hill, 1967.
SEYMOUR, W. D., *Industrial Training for Manual Operations,* Pitman, 1954; and *Operator Training in Industry,* Institute of Personnel Management, 1964.
SINGER, E. J. and RAMSDEN, J., *Practical Approach to Skills Analysis,* McGraw-Hill, 1969.
WILD, RAY, *The Techniques of Production Management,* Holt, Rinehart & Winston, 1971.

Research and development

Among many publications on this subject, the following (established classics and some recent titles) are of special interest:
ANTHONY, R. N., *Management Controls in Industrial Research Organisations,* Harvard University Press, 1952. An American book which covers in some detail the whole field of research and development.
Britain 1972, HMSO, chapter 14, 'Promotion of the sciences'. This chapter gives a good overall picture in some twenty pages of the scope and activity of and expenditure on Scientific Research in Great Britain.
HISCOCKS, E. S., *Laboratory Administration,* Macmillan, 1956. A long-standing British classic, excerpts of which are quoted in the appendices to this chapter.
Industrial Research in Britain, 7th edn, Francis Hodgson Ltd 1972. This book provides an exhaustive directory of organisations engaged in industrial research in Great Britain; it covers Government departments, industrial firms, universities and colleges, professional bodies and computer services, as well as comprehensive coverage of libraries and publications devoted to technical and research subjects.
Department of Trade and Industry, *Technical Services for Industry,* HMSO, 1970. A directory of Technical Information and other services available from Government departments and associated organisations.

Operational research

Statistical methods

ANSON, C. J., *Profit from Figures—A manager's guide to statistical methods,* McGraw-Hill, 1971.
DAVIES, O. L. ed., *Statistical Methods in Research and Production,* 3rd edn., Oliver & Boyd, 1957.
MORONEY, M. J., *Facts from Figures,* Penguin Books, 1956.

Operational research

ACKOFF, R. L. and RIVETT, B. H. P., *A Manager's Guide to Operational Research,* Wiley, 1963.
BEER, S., *Decision and Control,* Wiley, 1967.
FLETCHER, A. and CLARKE, G., *Management and Mathematics,* Business Publications, 1964.
SASIENI, M., YASPAN, A. and FRIEDMAN, L., *Operations Research: methods and problems,* Wiley, 1959.

Linear programming

CATCHPOLE, A. R., 'The applications of linear programming to integrated supply problems in the oil industry', *Operational Research Quarterly,* **13** (1962), 161–70.
JONES, W. G. and ROPE, C. M., 'Linear programming applied to Production Planning—a case study', *Operational Research Quarterly,* **15** (1964), 292–302.
VAJDA, S., *Readings in Linear Programming,* Pitman, 1958.
VAJDA, S., *The Theory of Games and Linear Programming,* Methuen, 1956.

Network analysis   BATTERSBY, A., *Network Analysis*, Third Edition (Macmillan 1971).
LOCKYER, K. G., *An Introduction to Critical Path Analysis*, 3rd edn., Pitman, 1969.

Simulation   HOLLINGDALE, S. H., *Digital Simulation*, English Universities Press, 1965.
TOCHER, K. D., *The Art of Simulation*, English Universities Press, 1963.

PART FOUR Personnel: Human resources management

by Norman Price

1 The personnel function

Human resources management

The personnel function is the management of human resources and 'is concerned with the optimum deployment and development of people within an organisation in order that the objectives of the organisation may be met and effectively adapted to changing circumstances'.[1] This definition in a recent Department of Employment report marks the culmination of four major stages in the development of the personnel function.

First stage

The first stage was one of classifying the various elements which went to make up the total function, classified by Moxon[2] into six categories:

Employment
Wages
Joint consultation
Health and safety
Welfare; employee services
Education and training.

How these activities were carried out in practice formed the basis of the personnel function in many companies through the 1950s and into the 1960s. The essential concept at this stage of the development of the function was an acceptance that personnel management had a role of guiding and advising management rather than being an essential part of the executive operation of the organisation.

Second stage

Studies of the behavioural scientists in terms of both individual and group behaviour have posed the question: What sort of organisation is the industrial enterprise? This has led to an extension of the activities of the function into a second stage of development in which the operation of the personnel function has been seen to include such matters as corporate planning, organisation structure, manpower planning, remuneration and employee relations. This represents a second stage in the development of the above classifications.

Third stage

Recent studies have suggested that the function is concerned with the development of change within an organisation and Mumford has suggested

[1] Department of Employment, *Training for the Management of Human Resources*, HMSO, 1972.
[2] G. R. Moxon, *Functions of a Personnel Department*, IPM, 1951.

that Personnel Managers should be seen as 'change agents' as a result of studies on the social aspects of technical change in relation to the introduction of the computer and the need to develop a sociotechnical approach to change within an organisation.[1]

Fourth stage

The fourth and to date the latest stage of development is in the relationship between the 'line and staff' concept of the personnel role becoming less rigid and the recognition that the whole personnel function is changing to one that is seen as being concerned with the management of the human resources of the organisation.

Recent trends

Megginson has claimed that the environment for the performance of the personnel function has changed and suggests that there are certain trends which are affecting the total concept of the function.[2] He lists these as:

The improving economic position of the employees in an organisation.
The expanding role of government in the area of commerce and industry.
The growing power of the trade unions.
The rapid growth of technology.
The increasing complexity of business organisations.
The development of the behavioural sciences.
The changing role of management within companies.

All these factors are having an affect in the place which human resources management plays in the total operation of the organisation.

We have seen in recent years an increased emphasis on employee relations as a result of the measures provided under the terms of the industrial legislation of the past decade. Manpower planning has become an integral part of the personnel function and has become involved in the organisational analysis of the structure of the company. The essential weakness has been the inability of the personnel function to put a monetary value on its activities and this has been perhaps the largest factor inhibiting its acceptance as one of the essential elements in the company's profit-making decisions.

One of the failures of the studies by the behavioural scientists in their examination of the changing role of the personnal function over the last decade has been the ignoring of the economic, political, technical and consumer environments in presenting an analysis of the particular situations related to the management of the human resources. The emergence of the sociotechnical approach as defined in the studies of Mumford and Megginson may have made some contribution to remedying this defect.

Two aspects

It is now recognised that there are in fact two aspects of the personnel function in its concern with the management of the human resources of the

[1] Enid Mumford—Computers, Planning and Personnel Management, IPM, 1969.
[2] L. Megginson—*Personnel: a behavioural approach to administration*, Irwin, 1972.

organisation. The first is the process of analysing the existing conditions and resources in the light of the requirements of the organisation, followed by the diagnosing and defining of the problems and then the designing and carrying out of the necessary action to bring about change. This can be defined as the creative aspect of the personnel function.

The second is the administrative aspect required to execute an established policy and to provide the means of solution of the day-to-day problems as they occur and to provide the various personnel services required by the organisation, such as recruitment, induction training and the 'fire fighting' aspects of industrial relations. This second aspect is regarded in many organisations as the more important part of the function, although it is less exacting and less critical than the first.

In management of the human resources of the organisation, it is often the creative aspect that is still largely missing. While many Personnel Departments are adequately staffed to fulfil the administrative duties required, there is often no provision for carrying out the creative aspects of the function. This is a particular shortcoming of many organisations which are facing an increasing degree of organisational complexity. Personnel Departments should have some staff who are not exclusive specialists, but who come from and return to other management roles in the organisation.

Because personnel policies are in the interests of and affect managers in all the other management groups within an organisation, it is essential for Personnel Managers to recognise and practice an effective system of consultation and communication in the fullest possible sense.

The often unrealised danger to the personnel function in many organisations is that it becomes increasingly involved in the daily 'fire fighting' role, to the detriment of planning and the long-term requirements of the organisation. In the following chapter, in discussing the integration of the function in the corporate planning activities of the organisation, an attempt will be made to show that the planning and long-term requirements of the organisation need to use these aspects of the role of an effective profit-orientated personnel function in the successful human resources management of the enterprise in the present decade.

It can also be argued that while many behavioural scientists have complained that the business organisation has neglected the human and social effects of change within their organisations, equally many have ignored the importance of the economic, political, technical and consumer aspects of the environment within which the organisation has to operate. The concept of the sociotechnical approach may have the effect of changing this in relation to the work of the personnel function within the organisation. Over recent years a great deal of theory has been developed on the subject of organisation and structure and the Personnel Manager has to decide what part of the theory is of use when reviewing the management organisation and structure of his own company.

Areas of authority and responsibility

From the standpoint of the personnel function in assisting in the organisational structure and development of a company, there is the requirement to achieve coordination between the line and staff functions of the organisation, whatever type of structure is used in a particular company. This is a matter which has given rise to a great deal of confusion in defining the precise meaning to these definitions. Adrian Cadbury has attempted to clarify the situation:

> The fundamental reason why the labels of 'line' and 'staff' are misleading is that they are usually applied to people or positions. This is confusing because, to take a practical example, a pure staff job should not exist in a business since this would imply no direct control over anyone in the organisation and no relationships at all where advice carried some commitment to its acceptance. What the terms do distinguish are the different elements within a given job and the different relationships that apply between one person in an organisation and the others with whom he deals. If we use 'line' and 'staff' to analyse elements of a job and specific relations, confusion can be avoided. This may seem academic, but I believe that organisational difficulties are real enough without adding to them through loose terminology and one of the contributions which Personnel could make in taking charge of organisation planning is to stick to operational definitions.[1]

One of the great changes in modern industrial society has been that the great majority of people work either for or in some formal organisation and are therefore subject to the constraints, the rules and the hierarchies which are demanded by the formal organisation. In determining the areas of authority and responsibility for the personnel function within the organisation, regard has to be taken of the forces at work in determining the organisational structure of a company and their effect on the human resources. For example, the widening of the product range in a company with the consequent increase in sales volume calls for a more precise method of allocating resources and a greater degree of forward planning. This in turn is reflected in a new organisational relationship between the central services operating on an overall group basis (which may include the personnel function) and the operating units of the organisation which may be structured on a decentralised divisional basis.

The continuing trend in recent years of mergers and acquisition, and on occasions the disinvestment from existing and often long established activities, bring their own particular organisational problems for the personnel function in having to deal with the duplication of human resources which can arise from a merger, together with the need to deal with the differences in company background and philosophy between the existing organisation and the one that is acquired. The growth of the international and the multinational organisation with a wide geographical spread, either in one country or often in a number of countries, creates further problems in determining the requisite areas of authority and responsibility. In the personnel function it has to be decided what kind of group service is required and how it should operate in order to back up national or international geographical differences in managing the human resources of an organisation which often in the past has only operated in one national or international geographical location.

Superimposed on these developments, we have seen over the last two decades the increasing momentum of technological change and the effects of changes on the human resources of the enterprise, to which must be added the relationships which were shown to exist between technology and organ-

---

[1] Adrian Cadbury, *Organisation and the Personnel Manager*, IPM, 1970. See also Part One of the present volume, chapter 5 (page 45).

isation by Woodward in her now classic study of industrial organisation in 1965.[1]

What, then, is the responsibility of the personnel function in the planning required to create the organisational structure of the enterprise?

Firstly, there is the responsibility for the development of the human resources and from this the relationship of the individuals within the organisation, both with each other and with the enterprise as a whole; these relationships have to be reflected in the total organisational structure.

Secondly, there is the responsibility for supplying and updating the body of knowledge available on individual and group behaviour which has to be taken into account in the organisational planning process.

Thirdly, the function has a role in reviewing the structure so as to ensure that, in meeting the corporate aims of the enterprise, there is no waste of what is now the most expensive asset of most companies—the human resources.

Work organisation

The work organisation of the personnel function is one of applying the particular methods which are needed to suit the particular industry or activity of the enterprise. The various activities of work do, however, fall into certain ranges which should in general be part of all organisations. The following represents the sequence in which the operation of the function might be structured with a logical progression from each activity to the next:

Organisation structure. Responsibility for the efficiency of the organisation structure and for defining the areas of authority, responsibility and accountability with requisite job descriptions, development programmes and organisational reviews. (See Part One, chapter 5, page 45, and Part Seven, chapter 3, page 935.)

Corporate planning. Providing the personnel contribution to the corporate objectives and plans of the organisation. The integration of the personnel function in the corporate plan of the organisation.

Manpower planning. Assisting in the development of the manpower strategy of the organisation with the development of manpower forecasts and manpower models.

Remuneration. Responsibility for the wage and salary structure of the organisation. The development of job evaluation, merit rating and bonus schemes. The conditions of employment within the organisation.

Employee relations. The operation of the Code of Industrial Relations Practice. Trade union recognition and relationships within the organisation. The operation of consultative machinery and negotiating procedures. All employee services within the organisation.

Labour law. Responsibility for advising on all matters concerning the law of employment and the effect of labour legislation on the operation of the

[1] Joan Woodward, *Industrial Organisation Theory and Practice*, Oxford University Press, 1965.

enterprise with particular regard to the legislation covering redundancy, equal pay, industrial relations and contracts of employment.

Training. Responsibility for quantifying the training needs at all levels within the organisation. Developing the policy and plans for training to meet the needs. Allocating sufficient resources to implement the training plans of the organisation.

Employee services. Responsibility for advising on all matters concerned with working conditions and on statutory requirements covering health and safety. Employment benefit policies covering sick pay schemes, pension schemes and other employee benefits.

2 Corporate strategy and manpower planning

The concept of corporate planning requires the use and understanding of certain terminology in order to assist in the communication process within a company. The following definitions are ones often used in the corporate planning process:

Planning. This is defined as thought in advance of action, resulting in a method or scheme of action to include the identification of strengths and weaknesses within the company, the clarification of the company's objectives and the selection of the most advantageous course of action in terms of strategy and operating programmes. (See Part One, chapters 3 and 4.)

Formal planning. This is the means of carrying out the necessary processes of planning in a systematic and logical order and expressing the assumptions and conclusions associated with each process in a written record which is the formal plan.

Plan. The plan is a forecast of future accomplishment and is a written statement of what should be done, the way it should be done and a statement of what will result from this action with a specified time period—this may be from one to five years.

Divisional plan. In an organisation with a divisional structure, this is the plan drawn up and agreed by the Head of the Division, but which still has to be agreed and approved as acceptable by the Group Board of the Company.

Group plan. This is the total plan incorporating the divisional and functional management plans which has received the approval of the Group Board.

Corporate plan. This is the overall plan which includes the regular review of the environment within which the organisation is operating and determines what is the essential purpose of the Company and how well equipped it is to pursue it. The corporate plan establishes quantitative and qualitative objectives which can be realistically achieved within the period of the plan and which will reflect and blend the interests of shareholders, customers and employees. The overall concept of a corporate plan covers resource planning such as manpower planning, production planning and financial planning. The corporate planning function covers all activities of the business and acts as a catalyst and coordinator of the detailed plans proposed by the divisions and the functional management of the company.

Planning cycle. This is a timetable of the various events covering a review, a revision and a re-statement of all the factors, assumptions, objectives and goals that make up the plan and is usually carried out over a period of twelve months for each planning period.

Chief Executive's statement. This is a written statement at the beginning of each planning period setting out the chief executive's views and assumptions on the following factors, as incorporated in the marketing programme:

● environmental factors
● objectives of the company
● strategies of the company
● goals to be achieved.

Annual planning cycle. The following is an example of a typical twelve-month planning cycle:

Month	Action	Action by
January	First stage of corporate appraisal	Departmental Managers
February	Second stage of corporate appraisal	Departmental Planning Team
March	Preparation of divisional planning guidance notes	Corporate Planner
April/May	Preparation of divisional strategic plans	Divisional Planning Team
June	Presentation of divisional strategic plans	Divisional Planning Team
July	Preparation of Group strategic plan	Group Planning Team
August	Review of Group strategic plan	Group Planning Team
October	Preparation of divisional operational plans	Divisional Team
November	Presentation of divisional operational plans	Divisional Planning Team
December	Approval of Group strategic and operational plan	Group Board

Checklist for preparation of corporate appraisal

In relation to the involvement of the Personnel Manager in the corporate planning cycle, the checklist of a corporate appraisal could take the following form:

Personnel. For each designated unit in a company answers to the following questions should be discussed between the line managers responsible and the personnel officer of the unit.

Management

β 1. What are the ages and experience of your managers?
2. What is the realistic assessment of your senior managers' capabilities (by the standard of the industry and generally)?
3. Who will and who will not be able to grow as the company expands?
4. Do you have succession problems?
5. Are you satisfied with your performance review system?
6. What is the basis of your promotion policy and is this generally understood?
7. If you have lost managers in the past year whom you would have liked to retain, have you analysed the reasons and has this resulted in any change?
8. How do your managers perceive the company, their present job and future prospects?
9. In overall terms, what weighting do you feel is presently given to salary, fringe benefits, job satisfaction in the motivation of managers in your unit?
10. Is management development a concept which has any real meaning in your unit?
11. Is management training fully supported?
12. What is the attitude of your managers to white-collar unionism?

Manpower   *Manpower Supply*

δ 1. What is the age and structure of your manpower?
2. What implications does this structure hold with regard to forthcoming retirement rates, equal pay agreements?
3. What is and will be the availability of appropriate manpower groups in the localities of your unit?
4. How effective is your communication with the shop floor on proposed changes?
5. What is your strike record and what will affect it in the future?
6. Have you analysed the reasons for past strikes and/or lack of cooperation and if so has this resulted in change?
7. How good are your relations with the various levels of trade union hierarchy?
8. What changes in unionisation do you foresee occurring in your unit?
9. Do you have an effective grievance procedure?
10. Do you have job-enrichment programmes?
11. How do your pay and conditions compare with other comparable local employers?
12. What is your labour turnover and what are the main reasons for turnover?
13. Is absenteeism a problem and have you analysed the reasons for it?
14. What weight of pressure is felt for increased wages, fringe benefits, better working conditions?

Organisation

ε 1. Is your present organisation structure correctly reflected in the latest organisation charts?
2. Does this structure take due account of the objectives of the organisation?
3. Are job descriptions used and do these adequately define responsibility and authority?

4. Are all costs incurred being monitored at the right level?

The attempt to answer all these questions should enable those concerned to prepare a very brief statement on the strengths/weaknesses on the manpower and organisation fronts.[1]

Personnel:
(1) management

Please append a brief note on the strengths/weaknesses on the manpower and organisation points.

Management

1. Classification of management by age group:

Number by age group

	20–30	31–40	41–50	51–60	60+	Total
Sales						
Production						
Finance						
Administration						

2. How many of the above managers are (insert numbers):

Suitable for promotion without further experience/training?	
Suitable for promotion with further experience/training?	
Not suitable for promotion?	
Not suitable for his/her present position?	

The totals in these two tables should agree.

3. Do you have succession problems? If YES, state their nature.
4. Are you satisfied with your performance review system? If NO, state why.

---

[1] See the specimen check-list set out in Part Seven of the present volume (chapter 2, page 927); also chapters 6 and 12 of *"Organisation: the Framework of Management"* by E. F. L. Brech.

5. What is the basis of your promotion policy and is this generally understood in your unit? If *not* understood state why.
6. If you lost managers in the past year whom you would have liked to retain have you analysed the reasons and has this resulted in any change?
7. How do your managers perceive the company?

A growth company	YES/POSSIBLY/NO
A leader in its industry	YES/POSSIBLY/NO
A technologically advanced company	YES/POSSIBLY/NO
A company with good public image	YES/POSSIBLY/NO
Financially sound company	YES/POSSIBLY/NO

8. In overall terms what weighting do you feel is presently given to salary, fringe benefits, achievement, job satisfaction in the motivation of managers in your unit? Do you agree or disagree with this weighting? Give reasons.
9. Is management development a concept which has any real meaning in your unit?
10. Is management training fully supported?
11. What is the attitude of managers to white-collar unionism?

Personnel:
(2) sales manpower

1. What is the age structure of your sales force?

Age	20/30	31/40	41/50	51/60	60+	TOTAL
Number						

2. How many of the above are (insert numbers):

Suitable for promotion without further experience/training?	
Suitable for promotion with further experience/training?	
Not suitable for promotion?	
Not suitable for his/her present position?	

The totals in these two tables should agree.

3. Do you have an acceptable/unacceptable* (delete as relevant) turnover in sales staff? State your reasons,
   (a) for having an acceptable* turnover;
   (b) for having an unacceptable* turnover.
   * Whichever is relevant.
4. Are your sales staff paid and do they have working conditions—
   * better than immediate competitors?
   * same as immediate competitors?
   * worse than immediate competitors?
   (* delete those which are inapplicable. Please add any comment below.)
5. In overall terms what weighting do you feel is presently given to salary, fringe benefits, job satisfaction in the motivation of sales staff in your unit? Do you agree or disagree with this weighting? Give reasons.

Personnel:
(3) factory and office

1. What is the age and sex structure of your factory and office staff?

Age		18/30	31/40	41/50	60+	TOTAL
Male	Factory					
	Office					
Female	Factory					
	Office					

2. What implications does this structure hold with regard to forthcoming retirement rates, equal pay agreements?
3. What is and will be the availability of appropriate manpower groups in the localities of your units?
4. How effective is your communication with the shop floor on proposed changes?
5. What is your strike record and what will affect it in the future?
6. Have you analysed the reasons for past strikes and/or lack of cooperation and if so, has this resulted in changes?
7. How good are your relations with the various levels of trade union hierarchy?
8. Do you have an effective grievance procedure?
9. Do you have job-enrichment programmes?
10. How do your pay and conditions compare with other comparable local employers?
11. What is your labour turnover and what are the main reasons for termination?
12. Is absenteeism a problem and have you analysed the reasons for it?
13. What weight of pressure is felt for increased wages, fringe benefits, shorter hours, better working conditions?

Organisation
review

1. Is your present organisation structure correctly reflected in the latest organisation charts? If not, please explain.
2. Does this structure take due account of the objectives of your organisation?
3. Are job descriptions used and do these adequately define responsibility and authority?

The integration of the personnel function in corporate planning

From its involvement in the preparation of the annual corporate appraisal, the personnel function becomes integrated in the overall corporate planning cycle of the organisation.

From the corporate appraisal it is then possible to ascertain the situation that exists in each unit of the company covering the management in relation to the age and experience pattern of the existing staff, the effectiveness or otherwise of the management development and succession plans within each unit and how the managers perceive the company in relation to its future development related to their own job prospects. The appraisal also highlights the managers' attitudes to employment policies, training and development as it affects them. Similarly, in relation to the manpower of each unit, the corporate appraisal shows the age and structure of the present manpower, highlighting retirement rates as an indication of the replacement rate which exists linked to the availability situation in respect of the various manpower groups which make up each unit of the Company. The appraisal also reveals the general employee relations situation of each unit in relation to trade union organisation and its effectiveness in regard to certain quantifiable indices. The corporate appraisal also highlights the effectiveness of the existing organisation structure of each unit and shows whether the job descriptions currently in use reflect the correct assessment of the authority, responsibility and accountability of the management in the particular unit. Because the corporate planning cycle is related to the profit objectives of the enterprise, the appraisal also ensures that information is available on whether the cost incurred by the total human resources of each unit are being monitored at the right level.

If the personnel function is fully integrated in these corporate planning activities, it is possible to ensure that there is a constant and up to date supply of the necessary control information leading to the development of the required forecasting and budgeting techniques. If the enterprise is planning for any changes in its product mix or in any marketing developments which may call for an expansion or contraction of production capacity, the personnel function can be concerned and involved at the correct stage in making the revised forecasts of the manpower requirements, the manpower availability in a particular unit or locality and the necessary amendments to the wage and salary budgets.

The integration of the personnel function in the total corporate planning activity leading to the annual strategic and operational plan over the total planning period of the enterprise enables provision to be made for the appropriate personnel service to meet the long term requirements. If for example, new production units are part of the long term plan, the necessary recruitment and training of the manpower required can be organised over the period provided in the corporate plan.

What is manpower planning?

The corporate activity of an organisation generates its own demand for human skills. Therefore, those concerned with the management of the human resources of an organisation have three requirements to meet:

1. They must identify correctly the skills which are required, that is those which are in line with the objectives and goals of the organisation.
2. They must make the skills required available in the context of the changing requirements over a period of time.
3. They must utilise the skills acquired to the best possible advantage of both the organisation and the employee, both of whose respective expectations are changing over time.

The extent to which these three objectives are achieved can be influenced by the manpower policies which are adopted by the organisation. The manpower policies may embrace recruitment (including selection), discharge (including retirement and redundancy), training and development, remuneration (in all the forms it can take), employee relations and the performance and profitability of the organisation.

Manpower policies are therefore seen to operate in the day-to-day operations of the organisation.

Manpower policies formulated together become the integrated manpower strategy and this strategy has to be designed taking into account three factors:

1. The corporate objectives of the organisation generating requirements for certain manpower skills.
2. The external market situation for the manpower requirements.
3. The characteristics of the manpower within the organisation.

All these three factors may change from time to time or any one of them may be in a state of change at any one time so that the manpower strategy of the organisation at any one point may not always remain unchanged. Therefore, the success of any manpower planning exercise depends on the extent to which changes in strategy are identified and acted upon in revising the manpower policies and programmes. It is therefore essential to regard any form of manpower planning as a flow of information. This information must be available to ensure that there is a continuously up to date picture of the likely future manpower demand and supply. Manpower planning can be used to integrate the total activities of the human resources, management of the organisation and in the operation of personnel management within a particular company.

Depending on the areas in which change may originate, manpower planning has three streams of information: First, the estimated manpower requirements, which also incorporates the expectations of manpower utilisation; second, an analysis of the external market situation for manpower in the organisation. Both streams of information lead to an estimate of manpower availability.

Manpower strategy

Integrated manpower strategy comprises four interrelated factors:

1. Information: divided into *demand* and *supply*.
2. Strategic assessment of requirements.

● an indication of the importance of understanding the total manpower system and the influences acting on it.

The real objectives of the manpower model are the insight and awareness it produces rather than merely the mathematical solution.

3 Training

Establishing the training function

The training function is a management activity in which the Personnel Department provides the necessary specialist knowledge and usually carries out in addition the administrative requirements so that the function operates effectively within the organisation. There are four basic stages in establishing a training function:

1. to find out the training needs of the particular company at all levels;
2. to formulate a training policy which will meet the needs;
3. to evaluate the resources both financial and material which will be required to meet the needs;
4. to provide the necessary specialist training officers who will be responsible for implementing both the training policy and the training plan.

Training needs

A training need can be said to exist when there is a gap between the existing performance of an employee (or group of employees) and the desired performance. To assess whether such a gap exists requires a 'skills analysis' to be made. The analysis has five steps:

1. to analyse and determine the main requirements of the particular job;
2. to identify the tasks required to be undertaken to meet the job requirements;
3. to understand the procedures required to perform each of the job tasks;
4. to analyse the knowledge and skills required to perform the procedures;
5. to identify any special problems of the job and to analyse any particular skill required to meet the problem.

If we are considering a situation where no training function exists in the organisation, the skills analysis should be undertaken initially of those jobs or areas which appear to present the most urgent training need and this can be followed up by a skills analysis of all jobs when the training function has been established.

Training policy

Following the analysis referred to above, a training policy emerges from considering these basic elements of training needs. First, the training of the new employee, second, the training of existing employees, and third, the training required on the promotion or transfer of an employee.

These elements call for different requirements in formulating a training policy. New entrant training is to impart knowledge of the Company and its products as well as specific job knowledge, while the training of existing employees is usually to meet a requirement to improve the job performance and for employees who have been transferred or promoted, and the requirement is for training in those aspects of their new job of which they do not have the required knowledge.

The training plan to meet these various policy requirements has items which are common to all these training needs. The plan should therefore include:

- The content of the particular training.
- The performance target required.
- Where and how will the training be carried out.
- Who is responsible for seeing the training is carried out.
- The priority of the particular training requirement.
- The method to be used in assessing the results of the training.

Training cost

The Industrial Training Act 1964 has established over the last decade the hard fact that training (in any form) is an essential cost exercise for any organisation regardless of its size or the particular industry in which it operates.

Training costs money which can be quantified in terms of the waste of materials, time and human resources if it is not well organised and the Industrial Training Boards have attempted by their grant/levy provisions (which have been modified in recent years as the ITBs have developed) to emphasise the cost factor in training at all levels within an organisation. In determining the training costs, the following factors should be taken into account:

- The cost of staff to carry out the training plan: training officers and instructors.
- The accommodation costs in the areas where training is carried out.
- The cost of training materials and equipment, visual aids, etc. The cost of managing the training function in terms of staff, accommodation, secretarial assistance.
- The cost of using external courses in course fees, accommodation and travelling expenses.

The most effective cost control is to decide, in the light of the training policy, what training is required and then allocate the resources required in the form of an annual training budget rather than allocating a sum of money for 'training' and then hope that one will get results.

Training staff

The Industrial Training Act clearly stimulated the demand for training, with a consequent growth of the training specialist over the last ten years. In any organisation a senior executive should have the responsibility for training. In the smaller organisation this may be the chief executive himself. In larger organisations, the responsibility is usually part of the total personnel function and the Training Manager may be part of the staff of the Personnel Manager or Personnel Director. Whatever the size of the training organisation, there will always be the need for direct instruction and a great deal of the detailed application of the training plan should rest with the line managers themselves to their subordinates.

The continued training and development of instructors should be one of the more important responsibilities of the Training Executive.

This is an outline of basic steps in establishing the training function; the following Appendix gives the outline of a company training policy which might be followed in a typical organisation.

In so far as management training and development are concerned, full consideration is given in Part Seven, chapter 6 (see page 991).

APPENDIX. COMPANY TRAINING POLICY

The purpose of the statement of training policy

The purpose of the statement of training policy is to provide the framework within which training and development will be planned and operated within the Company. It is recognised that particular situations and specialised activities will require special consideration. It is not the intention to restrict the forms or methods of training, but to ensure that there is a systematic approach in all aspects of the Company's activities.

Industrial Training Act 1964

All Company operations in England, Scotland and Wales come under the jurisdiction of the appropriate Industry Training Board. Each Industrial Training Board imposes a levy upon the company it covers and may return some or all the levy in the form of grants to those companies which undertake training and development to a required standard.

It is not Company policy to train simply to meet the requirements laid down by the appropriate Industrial Training Board, nor to train for the sake of training. However, the Company does have the objective of maximising the grants available where such training is consistent with Company needs. To achieve this objective, there must be a systematic analysis of needs and the effective implementation of the Company training policy at all levels.

Objective of training

The objective of training policy is to ensure that every employee is provided with the opportunity and means to obtain the knowledge and skill required to perform his or her work efficiently and to be able to develop his or her abilities to the full within the areas which are relevant to the Company. It is Company policy to conduct or to undertake to provide appropriate forms of training to fit people for their work within the Company.

Responsibility for training

The responsibility for ensuring that Company training policy is followed and for ensuring that individuals are equipped with the requisite knowledge and skill, lies with Managers and Supervisors. The responsibility for providing advice on the most appropriate forms of training and for the administration of training activities lies with the Training Officers.

Measurement of the effectiveness of training

The measurement of the effectiveness of training is in the application of what has been learned by the individual on the job. The purpose of any training activity is to improve performance or promotion potential. It is an important part of the Manager or Supervisor's role to encourage and supervise the application of the methods and techniques which have been taught and to advise the Training Officer where the techniques or methods appear inappropriate.

Cost of training

There are two financial considerations: the cost of the Industrial Training Board levy and the direct cost of training. The levy can be recovered only if there is an efficient training system. The direct cost of training can be recovered only if the individual who has been under instruction performs more efficiently as a result of his training.

The penalties for lack of planned training and effective application are many, the most obvious being: failure to meet job requirements, poor quality product or service, waste of time, material and effort, inefficient communications, poor morale; all these directly affect both the reputation and the profitability of the Company.

Documentation

For every appointment in the Company there will be:

A job definition, stating the authority, responsibility and main duties of the job holder and defining the required level of performance.

A training specification, stating the knowledge and skills required for the satisfactory performance of the job and indicating how the knowledge and skills are obtained.

A training plan, stating the training time and the order in which the stages of instruction and experience will be given.

A copy of each of these documents will be retained by the Training officer.

Training pattern

The pattern of training for every new entrant will be:

Induction, to provide information about the Company's organisation and products, terms and conditions of employment, Company rules including safety, security and hygiene.

Job training, to provide the knowledge and skills required to perform the work for which the individual has been engaged at a required level of efficiency, and to define and explain to the individual what is recognised as the required level of performance.

Follow-up or refresher training, to reinforce the instruction given in the job training period and to remedy any weaknesses which have become apparent during this time.

In each case there must be 'direct instruction' by a trained instructor using an approved instruction manual. The 'job training' element must conform to the pattern defined in the training specification and training plan, both of which should be explained to the new entrant during the induction period.

Probationary employment period

During this period, the new entrant will undertake induction and job training which will include some work experience. There will be a regular appraisal of performance and 'follow-up' instruction on the job by both the instructor and the Supervisor of the section or department in which the new entrant is working. At the end of the probationary period, the new entrant should be able to perform the job at a predetermined level of efficiency.

Development and retraining

Changes in job requirements and the need to improve skills or to further the development abilities is a constant factor in the majority of jobs, and there must be a continuing review of the individual's training needs.

It is the responsibility of Managers and Supervisors to assess the individual's needs and in consultation with the Training Officer either to arrange for suitable training to be given or to provide the necessary training and experience within the Department. The requirement and action proposed or needed must be reported to the appropriate Training Officer and to the employee concerned.

Promotion or job changes

An employee who is promoted or who changes his job will undertake or continue with the training specified in the Training Specification and Training Plan and standards of performance required will be defined to him by the Manager and Supervisor to whom he will be responsible.

Operator training

Each employee joining the Company as an unskilled, semiskilled or skilled operator in the Production, Engineering or Distribution Departments will undertake an Induction course to provide:

(i) information about Company and Departmental organisation;
(ii) information about Company products;
(iii) terms and conditions of employment with the Company including safety, security and hygiene.

According to the work they undertake and according to the level of job knowledge and skill they possess, they will undertake a job training programme which will include:

● a statement of the responsibilities and duties in the job for which they have been selected;
● instruction by a trained instructor in the correct performance of the job;
● a statement of the required standards of performance.

The Supervisor of the section in which the new entrant is employed will be responsible for ensuring that the induction and training programme is published and has been satisfactorily conducted by a trained instructor, and that successful completion is noted on the employee's records.

Secretarial/clerical training

Every employee engaged in a secretarial or clerical job must be equipped to fulfil his or her role in terms of the knowledge and skills required for the satisfactory performance of the job as indicated in the appropriate job description.

Some new entrants to the Company will have already received job training and experience elsewhere and will require little if any initial job training. However, all entrants will undertake a programme laid down and maintained for each section by the Supervisor concerned and conducted by him or someone nominated and trained for the task. The programme will include:

- details of Company and Departmental organisation;
- information about Company products;
- conditions of employment with the Company;
- a statement of the duties and responsibilities of the individual;
- instruction on the correct performance of the tasks involved in the job;
- a statement of the required standard of performance.

The Supervisor of the section in which the new entrant is working is responsible for ensuring (a) that the programme is carried out according to the published programme by a trained instructor, and (b) that satisfactory completion of the training programme is noted on the individual's records and notified to the appropriate Training Officer concerned.

Career development plan

Graduate entrants

Graduates and those with equivalent qualifications are recruited to provide for management succession and to fulfil specialist roles. They are recruited either as: *Direct Entry*, to fill known or planned vacancies in departments for which their qualifications fit them, or as *Indirect Entry*, to undertake general training leading to appointments where specialist qualifications are not essential and where extended internal training is required.

Induction

Both types of entrant will undertake an induction course covering:

(a) Company organisation and policy in respect of their employment.
(b) The organisation and operation of manufacturing, marketing, finance (including management services) and personnel divisions.
(c) Company products.

Job training (direct entry)

At the end of the induction course, direct entrants will join the Department for which they were selected. They will be given the appropriate job definition and instructed on Company operation as well as on the correct performance of the tasks involved in their job.

Process
familiarisation
(indirect entry)

At the end of the induction period, indirect entrants will undertake a period of process familiarisation in which through a series of projects they will become familiar with all the manufacturing operation. During this period, the trainee will be given a written statement of the aims of each project, the areas they will cover, and the information they are required to obtain. At the end of the allotted period, their performance will be appraised by the appropriate Training Officer and the Heads of the Departments concerned.

Job training
(indirect entry)

At the end of the process familiarisation period, the trainees will join the department for which they are judged to be the best qualified at the time. In this function they will undertake job training which will include formal instruction in the appropriate techniques by a trained instructor, project work involving some responsibility, and experience in each of the major areas of activity within that Department. During this period, the trainees' progress and performance will be reviewed monthly by the Departmental Manager and the appropriate Training Officer. When the trainees have had six months' experience of responsibility, the Director concerned and the Training and Development Manager will review the appraisal forms and decide whether trainees should continue in the Department or be moved to a different or related Department to obtain broader experience. This decision will be based on:

(a) Progress and performance in the present department as indicated on the appraisal forms.
(b) The opportunities for relevant and worthwhile experience within the department.
(c) The anticipated succession requirements in all departments.
(d) The opportunity of obtaining suitable experience in a related department.

Second stage
training

If the trainees move to a second department they will undertake a programme of job training following a pattern similar to that outlined for the first period.

Direct entrants (and employees who are not graduates but who are judged by their Managers to be of equivalent ability and have similar potential to that of indirect graduate entrants) will be considered by the Training and Development Manager for inclusion in this stage of the Career Development Plan.

At each stage the trainee will undertake the training programme established for the level of work involved.

**Manager and
Supervisor
assessment**

Each year, the performance, promotion potential and training requirement of each member of management and supervision will be formally reviewed and recorded. The review will be made by the individual's immediate superior and endorsed by the Director and/or Manager in charge of the Department or function.

The assessment recorded on the appropriate form will be discussed with the individual by the assessor. Where it is felt that further training and experience is needed, this will be noted and used as the basis for planning departmental training activity.

Supervisory training

Before assuming supervisory responsibility the individual will be given the appropriate job definition and training programme, including instruction on:

- Supervisory duties (general and specific)
- Communication Procedures (general and specific)
- Company and Departmental Rules and Regulations
- Factory and Office Premises Legislation
- Personnel Procedures.

In addition, before or within three months of assuming supervisory responsibility, he will undertake a Supervisory Training Course of not less than one week's duration either at the Company Management Centre or at an institute or college selected by the Company.

The Manager of the Department in which the Supervisor-elect will work is responsible for advising the appropriate Training Officer of the training required for the individual and for agreeing the training programme planned. The Training Officer will be responsible for making the necessary alternative arrangements.

Supervisory development

It is the responsibility of the Manager to appraise the performance of those responsible to him, and he will note the training and development requirements on the appraisal form. In consultation with the Training Officer he will also make the necessary arrangements for attendance at the appropriate courses of instruction.

All courses of instruction and training attended by a Supervisor-elect will be noted on his personal record.

Manager training

Before taking up his management appointments, the individual will be given the appropriate job definition and training programme. He will also be given the following instruction before assuming full responsibility in the job:

- Managerial duties (general and specific)
- Communication procedures (general and specific)
- Company and departmental rules
- Departmental methods and procedures
- Work of departments with which as a Manager he will have direct contact.

In addition, before or within three months of assuming managerial responsibility, he will attend a management training course of not less than one week's duration at the Company Management Centre including instruction on: decision-taking; delegation of responsibility; communication; financial aspects of management; human relations. The Head of the Department in which the Manager-elect will work is responsible for advising the Training Officer of the training required for the individual and for agreeing with him the training programme planned. The Training Officer will be responsible for making the necessary administrative arrangements.

Manager development

It is important that every Manager keeps pace with changes and developments in his field of management and in business activity. The education, training and development of Managers is a continuing process, necessary to maintain progress and keep up with change; therefore no Manager can be regarded at any time as having fully completed his training. When the performance of a Manager is appraised, recommendations for further training, either by attendance at courses or by planned experience in another department, should be noted and discussed with the individual by the Head of Department together with the Training Officer. All courses in instruction and training attended by a Manager will be noted on his personal record.

Management entrants

From time to time the Company will recruit managers with training and experience in other companies. Such individuals are recruited because their training and experience are needed by, but not currently available within the Company. These entrants will be provided with the appropriate job definition and will undertake an induction programme which includes:

- Company organisation and policy;
- information about Company products;
- the organisation of the major Departments;
- visits to the Company units in the UK.

The programme for induction will be drawn up by the Personnel Director in consultation with the Director of the Division in which the Manager has been recruited.

Commercial training

Sales Division. Recruits to the Sales Division will undertake:

(a) A new entrants course, to include instructions on Company organisation and policy; communication procedures; the manufacturing process; company products; principles of marketing; techniques of salesmanship.

(b) A period of sales instruction and experience under the supervision of a Field Sales Trainer.

(c) Not more than eight weeks after the new entrants course, a refresher course including instruction on Company products; merchandising; advertising; techniques of salesmanship; organisation of work.

Throughout his/her period of training and experience, the trainee's performance will be assessed, and this assessment notified to the Sales Training Manager.

Marketing Division. After their induction course, those recruited as marketing trainees will follow a programme of planned movement and experience through the various sections of the Marketing Division and where appropriate will undertake a course leading to a relevant professional qualification at an approved college.

Finance Division. After their induction course, those recruited as accountancy trainees will follow a programme of planned movement and experience through the various sections of the Finance Division and will undertake a course leading to the appropriate professional qualification at an approved college.

**Engineering/
technical
training**

Engineering training. Each man employed in the Engineering Department must be equipped to fulfil his role in terms of the technical knowledge and skills required for the satisfactory performance of the job, as indicated in the appropriate Job Description.

Most new entrants to the Engineering Department will already have received job training and experience elsewhere and will only require familiarisation with the Company's plant and equipment. However, all new entrants will undertake a programme laid down and maintained for each section by the appropriate Supervisor and conducted by him or someone nominated and trained for the purpose. The programme will be divided into two parts. The first will cover induction as outlined above. The second will include:

(*a*) a statement of the responsibilities and duties in the job for which they have been selected;
(*b*) a statement of the required standards of performance;
(*c*) instruction by a trained instructor in the correct performance of the job.

The Supervisor will be responsible for ensuring that the programme is carried out by a trained instructor and according to the published programme and that the satisfactory completion of the programme is noted on the individual's record.

Research technologists. Most new entrants to the Research Division will have already received job training and experience elsewhere and will require little job training. However, all new entrants to the Research Division will undertake a programme laid down and maintained for each section by the Section Head and conducted by him or someone nominated by him and trained for the purpose. The programme will include:

● details of Company and departmental organisation;
● conditions of employment, Company and departmental rules;
● a statement of duties and responsibilities of the individual;
● instructions on the correct performance of the tasks involved in the job;
● a statement of the required standard of performance.

The Section Head of the section in which the employee is working is responsible for ensuring that the programme laid down is satisfactorily completed, is noted on the employee's records and is notified to the Training Officer.

Entrants to the Research Division are entitled to day release facilities, subject to the conditions outlined below.

Further education

Day release

Employees under the age of eighteen are entitled to be absent from their normal place of work for one day a week during the academic year to attend a course of study on relevant subjects at an institute of further education or technical or commercial college approved by the Company. Where the Company directs an employee to attend a course, attendance is obligatory and failure to attend will be regarded in the same light as absence from work.

Employees over the age of eighteen may attend courses with permission of their Departmental Manager and the appropriate Training Officer. This permission will normally be given where:

- the course is a continuation of a course begun before the age of eighteen, leading to a recognised and relevant qualification;
- the content of the course and the resultant qualification are required for the employee's satisfactory performance in his appointment;
- the employee is attending at least one evening class on the course where such a class is available;
- the employee has not failed or had to repeat an earlier stage of the course;
- in the preceding session, allowing for absence with prior permission or for certified sickness, the employee has attended 60 per cent of the evening classes and all the day classes.

Permission to attend such courses will be reviewed at the end of each academic year.

Block release

Employees will be given block release, i.e. a period of days of full time attendance at a course at a Technical or Commercial College, where such a course is an integral part of an overall training programme and where it is arranged by the Company in conjunction with the College. During the period of block release, the employee will receive his normal rate of pay.

Sandwich courses

Selected employees may be sponsored by the Company for sandwich courses, i.e. courses in which approximately six months of the year are spent in full time education and six months in obtaining related work experience. Sponsorship on such courses is at the sole discretion of the Company.

Full-time courses

Selected employees may attend full-time courses at universities, colleges of technology, or similar institutes at the Company's request, during which period the employee may be paid full salary or a proportion of his salary.

In all the above cases where the course is being undertaken at the Company's request, tuition and registration fees will be paid by the Company. If the course is being taken at the request of the employee, tuition and registration fees will be reimbursed by the Company at the end of each session, provided:

- the course is relevant to the employee's job or profession;
- the employee has a satisfactory record of attendance;
- the employee passes the terminal examinations and has a satisfactory record of classwork and homework.

Communication

Responsibility for the implementation of Company training policy and the effective adoption of schemes of training lies with Managers and Supervisors. The role of the Training Officers is to provide expert advice and instruction.

4 Remuneration

Wage and salary policy

It is the prime duty of those responsible for the human resources of the organisation to ensure that the wage and salary policy is an integral part of the personnel function of the organisation and is linked to the total corporate objectives as defined in the corporate plan of the company and related to the manpower and development policies of the particular enterprise. A wage and salary policy must be aimed at attracting, retaining and motivating employees at all levels, so that the organisation retains its employees and is able to make the optimum use of their respective abilities.

With the increasing cost of the human resources in relation to the total operating costs of the organisation, it has become necessary in recent years to have an effective method of control built into any wage and salary policy to ensure the most effective return for this major element of expenditure. There is therefore the need to ensure that any policy allows for a systematic approach to ensure that all employees are remunerated in a logical and equitable way for the particular work that they perform. Having determined a wage and salary policy to meet the requirements of the organisation, it is necessary to consider the various types of wage and salary structure which should be applied to meet the requirements of the particular policy which is to be followed.

Types of wage and salary structure

Dealing first with a typical wage structure, it is often necessary to take account of the requirement to arrive at the appropriate structure as the result of the application of a collective agreement arrived at by a process of negotiation between a trade union or group of trade unions representing the employees concerned and a company or group of companies within a particular industry. Therefore the wage structure for many manual grades and clerical grades is based on the concept of the 'rate for the job'; such a structure consists of a number of single wage rates for a series of particular jobs and is often termed the *single rate structure*.

Single rate structure

The concept of the single rate wage structure assumes that there is often a single level of performance for a relatively simple job performance with little room for variation between the low performer and the high performer in a particular grade of job. Often the only additional reward which can be built into this type of wage structure is some form of small additional payment based on length of service in a particular grade of job or service in a particular organisation or industry, in the form of an additional long service payment.

General wage adjustments under this type of structure are in the main confined to wage increases related to national or locally negotiated wage increases, often related to movements in the cost of living or to the movement in the market value (either national or local) of a particular grade or type of job.

Another development of a single rate wage structure is to link this concept with a particular rate for a job or group of jobs related to the age of the particular individual employee. This linking of age to the rate for a job, or group of jobs, is often the basis of wage structures in the Civil Service and public authorities, although it has often been used particularly in clerical and junior management jobs in certain industries such as banking, insurance and similar commercial organisations. Whilst there are certain advantages of linking age to the rate for the job, particularly up to a certain upper age limit, it has the limitation of implying that a further year in a job and an additional year of age should produce a better job performance by the employee concerned. This has been shown not to be the case in practice, despite the fact that many organisations have constructed their salary structures to the concept that one year more of experience plus one more year of age equals a salary increase. The ultimate development of this concept of salary structure is shown in the *incremental salary scale*, which is still a feature of all salary structures (except for the most senior jobs) in the public service and nationalised industries.

Incremental structure

The basic feature of an incremental salary structure is to reject the concept of increases based on individual performance and merit for one of granting an equal increase to all employees in the same grade of job related in the main to another year of service with the organisation. In recent years, to meet the needs of the above average performer, organisations which follow the incremental salary structure have introduced the concept of the 'double increment' for good performance, but this has obvious limitations because of the overall rigidity of this type of salary structure. With the increasing need for the motivation of good achievement in many types of managerial and supervisory jobs, most organisations in industry and commerce have adopted the *merit salary structure* as the type most suited to their needs.

Merit structure

The merit salary structure differs from other forms of remuneration systems in that it does not rely on a formal structure related to fixed increments, rates conditioned by age and service. The basis of progression through this type of salary structure rests on the individual performance of the particular employee within the particular salary range which is established for a particular job grade. The structure can take a number of forms to meet the special requirements of the organisation, but there are certain basic principles which are usually applied to this type of salary structure:

1. The relationship between the salary ranges in the various grades of the structure follow a fixed percentage progression which is calculated on the *mid point* of each of the salary ranges. The most common percentage progression adopted is usually between 15 and 20 per cent, thus the mid point salary of one salary range will be 15 to 20 per cent higher than the corresponding figure in the salary ranges above and below.
2. The *spread* of the salary range in each grade between minimum and maximum varies according to job level. For senior jobs the spread is usually 40 to 50 per cent, for junior jobs the spread can be between 20 to 25 per cent.

The number of grades in this type of structure can range from five or six to up to twenty or more grades, and it is usual for the salary range of one job grade to overlap with the salary range of the next grade to correspond with the particular job grading of the organisation. The salaries applicable to the particular job grade can be determined from the information obtained from salary surveys giving the salaries and ranges used by similar organisations who have employees carrying out comparable jobs.

Fig. 4.4.1 shows a typical merit salary structure. It has five grades with a total salary spread from £1 250 to £3 800. There is a 50 per cent spread in each grade and each salary band has a 50 per cent overlap with the next band.

The progression of an individual employee through the particular salary range of his or her job grade can be determined in a number of ways. Salary progression can be related to the annual performance appraisal with a salary increase related to a range of performance from below average through average to above average and outstanding for the 'high flyer'. The salary structure can be geared so that the various points in the salary range from minimum through the first quartile to mid point then to the third quartile with the salary maximum being reserved for the consistently above average performance appraisal. Progression through a salary range can be related to a period of years in the particular job grade. For example, an average performance may mean that the mid point is reached in four to five years, whilst the

Fig. 4.4.1
Merit salary
structure

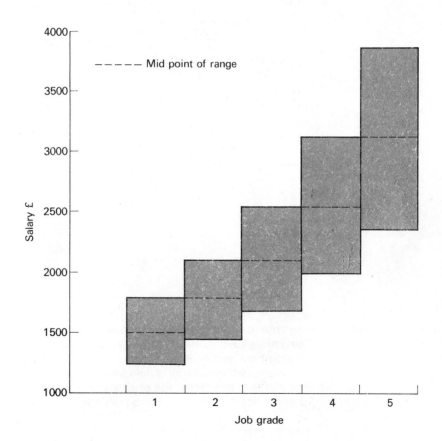

outstanding performer may reach it in three years, moving on to the third quartile, then being promoted to a job in a higher grade. A below average performer may not progress beyond the mid point of the particular job grade salary range. Fig. 4.4.2 shows how progression through a salary range can be determined by the relative performance of the employee concerned. If a merit salary structure is used the form of the structure can remain unchanged. The only adjustments required are changes in the salary values of each range, perhaps every two years to meet changes in the cost of living and external factors on job values which can be determined from the periodic salary surveys described earlier.

Fig. 4.4.2
Salary
progression
curves

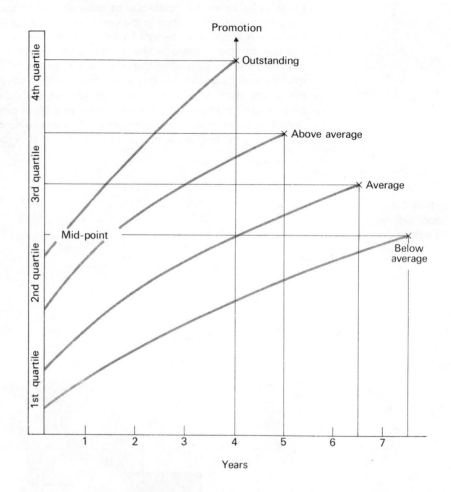

Job evaluation

All organisations have some form of wage or salary structure, but many such structures have formed without any systematic approach or accurate assessment of the worth of the various jobs which go to make up the particular structure. *Job evaluation* is therefore basically a set of methods which can be used to help produce wage or salary structures within an organisation. The process of job evaluation can be defined as a procedure for examining and analysing a number of jobs and establishing their relationship to one another; it follows that once the relationship has been determined, the evaluation can form the basis for determining the appropriate wage or salary structure. Job evaluation methods help in the establishment of one important element in any wage or salary structure, that is the element which is concerned with differentials. This is the central theme of the whole purpose of any job evaluation exercise and in times of national concern with differentials as the main event in matters of wages and salaries it emphasises the value of job evaluation as an aid to a greater acceptance of viable wage and salary structures as part of any incomes policy.

There is no single method of job evaluation and the systems can be generally divided into quantitative and non-quantitative methods.

Quantitative methods

Points rating. The first step is to determine all the factors which affect the jobs which are to be evaluated. The number of factors may vary considerably, although it is usual to reduce them to five or six main factors:

● Training and experience required
● Mental application required
● Physical effort needed
● Responsibility
● Working conditions.

Each of the factors used is then given a points rating according to the relative value of that particular factor to the total job being evaluated. The value of this method is that it provides the opportunity to analyse the job in a number of small factors, all of which together go to make up the total job. The total points value of each can be obtained and a predetermined formula is then applied to change the points value of each job into money values which then form the basis of the wage or salary structure.

Factor comparison. This method of job evaluation is an extension of the points rating method. Usually the maximum number of factors used are five:

● Mental effort required
● Physical effort required
● Skill required
● Responsibility
● Working conditions.

The basis of the factor comparison method is to select a number of key jobs at each level within the existing wage or salary structure. Each job is then analysed to determine what proportion of the total value of the wage or salary rate is paid for each of the five factors. This enables *factor scales* to be established so that all the jobs which are being evaluated can then be compared with other jobs, factor by factor, so as to give a ranking order for all the jobs, hence the name factor comparison. As the initial comparison is done in money terms, the final interpolation gives the job rate in terms of wage or salary for all the jobs which have been evaluated. The method is essentially similar to the points rating method, but often appears more complex when being explained to and understood by the employees concerned.

Non-quantitative methods

The two main non-quantitative methods of job evaluation are *whole job ranking* and *job classification*.

Whole job ranking. This method treats each job as a whole and ranks the job in importance relative to all the other jobs in the organisation. As with the other methods, the duties, responsibilities and qualifications are set out for each job. After this has been done, jobs are then ranked together in terms of value and responsibility until a number of similar jobs have been ranked together. A grade can then be given to the jobs of equal value until a grade structure has been built up. The final stage is to apply a wage or salary rate to each grade. This is a relatively simple method to apply and one which is easy to understand and to administer. It is often used in small organisations or for the introduction of job evaluation to a salary structure which may have previously consisted of a number of individual salary rates.

Job classification. This method is a development of the job ranking system. At the first stage a number of grades are determined and a wage or salary level is established for each grade. The next stage is to select a number of *bench mark* jobs and a full description is then prepared for each of the bench mark jobs, so that they can then be fitted in at the appropriate level to the predetermined grades and wage or salary rates. The final stage is to fit the remainder of the jobs being evaluated into the appropriate grade having regard to the position of the bench mark jobs. This should produce a finer distinction between the value of individual jobs than is produced by the whole job ranking method. Both these non-quantitative methods rely on ranking jobs in broad categories often in organisations where no systematic system had previously existed.

The use of job evaluation methods is increasing and it is useful to consider both management and trade union attitudes to its use.

Management attitudes

These should be considered: the practical value which job evaluation gives to an organisation and the following are among reasons given from a management viewpoint:

● It replaces the chaotic anomalies which often exist in wage and salary structures as a result of haggling by a rational structure based on job content.
● It produces a wage or salary structure which is equitable, if one accepts that rewards for work performed should be related to the content of the job.
● It permits greater flexibility in wage and salary payments, particularly when governmental intervention in the form of legislation on these matters as in 1966 and 1972/74 appears to deny the opportunity for the employers and trade unions to bargain effectively.
● It provides a firm base on which to effect changes in wage and salary structures when changes in job content occur.

Trade union attitudes

Trade unions on the whole now accept the purpose of job evaluation as being acceptable, but there is often a great deal of suspicion on the methods used by managements in introducing job evaluation in their organisations. Whilst the trade unions expect the introduction to be initiated by the employer, they expect also to be involved at the various stages on a joint basis.

The main trade union views on job evaluation are:

1. It may be taken out of the framework of normal wage negotiations and thus allow management judgments to replace bargaining as the basis of wage and salary rates.
2. Management will define, describe and assess jobs without adequate reference to the trade unions.
3. There will be confusion between the 'rate for the job' and the 'rate for the ability to do the job'.
4. It may lead to an averaging of the existing wage or salary bill without yielding an overall increase in rates.

The following are two examples of job evaluation methods:

1. Job ranking method

Starting with the job description for each of the jobs which have to be ranked, each description is studied and then the jobs are listed in descending order of value. For example, in the Sales Department of a company, the order might be:

Rank	Job description
1	General Sales Manager
2	Regional Sales Manager
3	Area Sales Manager
4	{ Sales Supervisor / Sales Trainer
5	Salesman
6	Trainee Salesman

A similar ranking exercise is carried out in the other departments of the company so that an across the board ranking exercise can be completed to establish the relative job values of all the jobs in a managerial and supervisory level in the company. The result may be:

Rank	Sales	Production	Finance	Personnel
1	General Sales Manager	Works Manager	Chief Accountant	Chief Personnel Officer
2	Regional Sales Manager	Chief Planner	Financial Accountant	—
3	Area Sales Manager	—	Cost Accountant	Industrial Relations Officer
4	{ Sales Supervisor / Sales Trainer	Departmental Manager	—	{ Training Officer / Staff Officer
5	Salesman	Senior Foreman	Project Accountant	Personnel Officer
6	Trainee Salesman	Foreman	Trainee Accountant	Personnel Assistant

The job ranking can be extended to cover various levels of jobs in the company so that the required number of levels are arrived at to determine the job grading structure for the total organisation. Similar job ranking can cover clerical and related jobs and specialist departments covering: purchasing, work study, research and development, etc.

2. Factor comparison method

In this method use is made of the basic ranking process, but instead of the whole job being used, a series of factors are used in arriving at the ranking for each job. In a series of clerical jobs, the following five factors might be used with a rating of 1–4 for each factor:

Educational standard required.
Training and experience required.
Relative importance of decisions to be made.
Confidential nature of the job.
Any supervisory responsibility.

A factor comparison ranking of four clerical jobs might produce the following ranking:

Job	*Factor comparison*				
	Education	*Training*	*Decision*	*Confidentiality*	*Supervisory*
Secretary	2	1	2	2	1
Typing Pool Supervisor	3	2	3	2	3
Invoice Clerk	1	1	2	1	1
Machine Operator	1	2	2	1	1

This would give a job ranking of:

1. Typing Pool Supervisor
2. Secretary
3. Machine Operator
4. Invoice Clerk.

This factor comparison method, like the whole job ranking method, can be applied to a series of jobs in the various departments within the company.

Merit rating

Merit rating is generally considered as a refinement of certain forms of wage structures and is used principally to provide an additional incentive to the employee by means of additional payments when a more detailed measurement cannot be arrived at by means of job evaluation. The practice of merit rating is in general applied to manual and clerical jobs.

An example of a merit rating system applied to a number of jobs in say an engineering company could take the following form:

A number of wage rates are established under the single wage rate structure covering the various trades, e.g. fitter, electrician, welder, etc. Each category of employee is then rated for 'merit' by means of a number of factors to which a total number of points are available. The factors cover the performance or merit of the employee such as skill, rate of work and quality of work. Additional factors cover timekeeping, attendance and reliability.

Under such a system of merit rating it is the responsibility of the Supervisor for rewarding the employee according to his skills and his work effectiveness.

Merit rating schemes are usually operated on the basis of six or twelve month intervals when the assessment is made to operate during the next period before the next assessment. Merit rating is often attacked by trade unions as leading to favouritism and 'blue-eyed boys'. The safeguard against this accusation is to have a small merit rating committee with the shop steward as a member and also with provision for appeals against the merit rating given to an employee if it is thought to be an unfair or inaccurate rating.

A similar type of merit rating scheme as the one described can be adapted for use in groups of clerical jobs, but merit rating is rarely used in supervisory or managerial jobs.

Bonus payments

Any form of bonus is in effect a supplementary form of remuneration which is paid in *addition* to the normal remuneration of an employee, and is usually ex-gratia and non-contractual in relation to the employee's contract of employment.

Bonus payments have extended in recent years and in some companies cover all employees, although the percentage of senior staff receiving some form of bonus is generally much higher than the percentage of manual and clerical employees who receive a bonus (excluding payments made under merit rating schemes). There are generally three types of bonus payments, the most common is the *traditional or Christmas bonus*. This is usually a payment which is not related in any way to the employee's performance or the financial performance of the company. The amount of bonus payment is often small in relation to the total remuneration of the employee and is usually a week's wage or salary or 1 to 2 per cent of the emplcyee's annual remuneration. This type of bonus payment is often associated with the paternalistic type of organisation where the cynical employee would say that it was the company's appreciation of the employee putting up with low wages and salaries.

A variation of the traditional bonus is the *good service bonus* which, as the name implies, is related to the continued service of the employee with his or her company. The payment is not usually paid on an annual basis. Payments are normally made at intervals of between two and five years although the average period for this type of bonus is to pay it every three years. Its best use is when it is applied to employees close to retirement who have reached the maximum of their salary range and are not likely to be promoted to a higher salary grade. A typical amount for the good service bonus paid on a three-yearly basis would be an amount equal to three annual salary increases which the employee would have received under the appropriate salary range.

The most effective and growing form of bonus payment is the *merit or performance bonus*. This type of bonus is a means of giving additional remuneration to an employee based on individual performance. This system is often part of the 'remuneration package' for directors and senior executives and the bonus payment can vary from year to year according to the profitability of the organisation over the previous year. The size of this type of bonus payment varies from company to company, 5 per cent of salary is usually the minimum level of payment and it can be as high as 20 to 25 per cent of salary. It is essential, if this type of bonus payment is used, that the individual performance can be correctly measured and assessed.

This subject is more fully considered, within the production management context, in Part Three, chapter 7 (see page 520).

Employee services

**Working conditions:
health and safety**

One of the most important functions of industrial management is that of maintaining safe working conditions within the undertaking, with a continuous effort to prevent accidents when and wherever possible. Accidents to employees are a serious drain on production, and consequently, like medical practice and treatment, 'accident prevention' has made good progress. Enquiries into high accident rates reveal all-too-frequent physical or mechanical causes. Accident prevention is the responsibility of management, and in a number of undertakings this responsibility rests with the Personnel Department. In some, however, depending on the size of the undertaking and type of plant installed, the carrying out of this function is delegated to a specialist known as the Safety Officer, Accident Prevention Officer, or Safety Engineer.

Under the Building (Safety, Health and Welfare) Regulations 1948, an employer employing more than fifty persons on building work is required to nominate a safety officer or 'competent person'. Thus, for the first time such person was given an official status, but in other industries it still remains the prerogative of the owner of the undertaking to decide how his accident prevention policy shall be put into effect and by whom. Opinion may differ as to the line of responsibility of such an officer, whether full-time or part-time. There is a good case to be made out for his being responsible to either the Personnel Manager or the Works Manager. The stronger argument is on the side of the latter—pinning on to the executive manager clear responsibility for safe working, with the specialist assistance provided. In the larger process plants, such as chemical works, steel works and so on, there is an equal case for 'line' responsibility to the Chief Engineer, with functional liaison with the Personnel Manager.

Safety

The Safety Officer should be a man of qualities rather than qualifications; his efficiency and sincerity of purpose should be above question, and he should possess moral courage to a high degree, and so command the respect of those with whom he comes into contact. Technically, he must have had good experience of the industry in which he is employed, with an aptitude for approaching all his problems with a detached, impersonal and commonsense attitude.

The size of the undertaking and the nature of the process will determine whether he shall be a full-time Safety Officer or one who carries out safety work in conjunction with other responsibilities. Where there exists a well developed Personnel Department, the need for a full-time safety specialist is often reduced.

Broadly, the functions of the Safety Officer may be described as the prevention of accidents by:

● routine inspection of plant, buildings, gangways, materials, etc;
● creating an active interest in safe working by means of propaganda;
● training employees and advising members of the Supervisory Staff in methods of safe working;

- the supervision of works employees in respect of protective equipment and clothing, and compliance with works safety regulations;
- advice, from the safety standpoint, on plant, layouts of shops, working methods, conditions, etc;
- analysis of accidents and keeping historical (statistical) records.

Naturally, many of his activities have a direct relation to the requirements of the Factories Act 1961 and the Factory Orders, together with any special regulations for safety issued from time to time by the Minister; it is therefore highly important that he should have a comprehensive and up-to-date knowledge of them to a standard where he is in a position to advise management. Responsibility for compliance with legal requirements rests clearly on management, and it cannot be passed on to, or usurped by, the Safety Officer.

The important obligation of maintaining good relations between a company and HM Factories Inspectorate should be a particular feature of the Safety Officer's duties by reason of his knowledge of the Acts, his specific industrial experience, as well as his intimate knowledge of the reasons for any accident that may occasion an investigation by HM District Inspector.

His association with the Personnel Department facilitates the routines attaching to his work, such as attending to insurance claims and making reports to HM District Inspector of Factories. This functional contact will also be of value in cases where legal proceedings ensue or where an accident gives rise to any strong feelings among employees. There is a further advantage. Strictly speaking, the Safety Officer is a technical man whose particular qualifications lie in his knowledge of the plant and equipment and of the regulations; but there is a large human element, both in the cause of accidents and in the promotion of accident prevention: this is a fact on which the Personnel Manager is much better able to be the source of knowledge and advice. A safety scheme should never overlook the possibility of 'accident-proneness' or other factors in the personal make-up of some individual employees who may sustain injury in circumstances which may have left other individuals unharmed. The investigation of any accident should always include, on the initiative of the Personnel Manager, reference to the purely human aspect.

In regard to the official requirement and procedures under factory and insurance legislation, the most desirable arrangement would appear to be:

- primary responsibility vested in the Personnel Manager;
- detailed work managed by the Safety Officer, where appointed;
- liaison with factory and technical executives, as safety is part of their normal 'human responsibilities'.

The keeping of statistical records is important, especially in the form of graphs and charts, so that the appropriate steps are taken to investigate and correct any adverse trends at the earliest opportunity.

Liaison with the Medical Department is an important factor in the human aspect of safety. The doctor or nurse may often be well placed to collaborate with the Safety Officer in the approach to the individual cases of recurrent accidents, having features which suggest that the cause lies in the human element instead of in the mechanical.

Accident prevention

The efficiency of a safety or accident prevention scheme depends on the cooperation of employees as well as on the skill of the Safety Officer. This is often a matter of training. Some companies incorporate training in safe working with their training schemes; others use the discussion group method. None of these methods can be more effective than informal talks to employees on the job, and instructive discussions with supervisors. A short informal talk to new entrants is useful to point out the specific hazards associated with the work upon which the employees are to be engaged, but not in a manner to give rise to fear, as this would defeat the object of the talk.

The investigation of accidents is an extremely important part of the Safety Officer's work. The investigation should be made as soon as possible after the occurrence, and should be approached with an open mind, free from any preconceived conceptions of a hypothetical nature. The plant should be examined for material evidence, and statements taken from witnesses and from the injured person, if possible. A conclusion should be arrived at only after careful consideration of the evidence in all its aspects, and great care should be taken to see that one does not become confused between the cause of the accident and the cause of the injury.

Providing the Safety Officer has the necessary experience and/or training, he should be given facilities for examining layouts in the initial stages, for the purpose of advising on any special measure he might consider should be taken into account to make the plant safe and, perhaps, to bring it into line with the requirements of the Factories Act. The first 'initial stage' lies in the Drawing Office, otherwise it may be too late to remedy an unsafe condition once drawings have been passed.

The development of protective gear has been an encouraging feature·in the past decade. Each industry has its own hazards, and these require the use of specific protective equipment, such as goggles, eyeshields, protective foot-wear, gloves, aprons, protective suits, respirators and breathing apparatus. In some industries, e.g. the chemical industry, the occupier or owner of the factory is by law required to supply protective equipment, and the employee himself has a legal obligation to wear it if there is risk of injury. Human beings are, however, often perverse about such matters, and many do their best to avoid wearing the equipment. These are the persons for whom the Safety Officer will always have to be on the alert.

The knowledge required, either in the Safety Officer himself, or in the combination of personnel and technical persons, sitting as an expert safety panel, may be summarised as follows:

- full acquaintance with the site and plant of their own factory;
- general knowledge of electrical circuits and good 'earthing';
- elementary hydraulics and an understanding of the term 'pressure';
- elementary principles of engineering in so far as it relates to the particular industry;
- outline of the production processes used;
- Factories Acts and special regulations;
- National Insurance requirements and official procedures;
- the human factors in accident causation;
- how to keep records and compile simple statistics.

Sick pay schemes have tended to develop on a two-tier system with provision for full salary (less any state benefit) for staff employees if they are absent due to sickness, and a more limited provision of some form of payment to augment the state benefit for weekly and hourly paid employees.

Analysis of sickness absence in many organisations has produced figures which show that the great majority of employees at all levels are absent for less than two weeks in a year due to sickness. It is therefore the problem of trying to control the short-term sick absence of one or two days at a time, or the 'annual' sick absence of a week or ten days each year which presents the greatest difficulty in attempting to operate an equitable sick pay scheme for all grades of employees.

Most sick pay schemes are still related to length of service in determining the amount of entitlement which the individual employee may have in the event of sickness, but a number of organisations are trying to introduce more flexible policies so as to avoid the cases where some employees regard their sick pay entitlement when based on 'length of service' scheme as something which should be taken each year. The general trend is to grant some form of payment for the first two weeks of sick absence each year on an almost automatic basis and then to operate schemes for the longer-term sick absence record and the employee's domestic circumstances, e.g. married, single, family, etc.

Many companies also make some provision for payment for absence for *domestic reasons*—this can cover such matters as the funeral of an immediate relative or the sudden sickness of a dependent relative such as wife, husband or child, or some other personal emergency which necessitates absence from work. Most companies have some form of rules to cover these eventualities and which make provision for payment for up to three days in any one year.

With the general improvement in the level of state sickness benefit which is now maintained on an annual basis many organisations are becoming increasingly aware of the cost of the various sick pay schemes which they operate. It should be recognised that the cost of five days sickness or domestic absence paid for each year represents an additional 2 per cent of the remuneration cost, often for a benefit which is now often seen as an accepted if somewhat unappreciated privilege.

The major change on pension schemes will be effected by the Social Security Act 1973 which comes into operation in April 1975. The new contribution structure will have proposed contribution rates of 5·25 per cent by employees and 7·5 per cent by employers payable on earnings up to a ceiling of about 1·5 times national average earnings.[1]

The Government is hoping that pension provision to supplement flat rate benefits will be made so far as possible through occupational schemes. The Government proposes to operate a fully funded Reserve Scheme, membership of which will be compulsory for all employees over age twenty-one whose employers are unwilling to operate their own recognised plans conforming to specified minimum requirements. The main condition for recognition will be that the pension accruing at age sixty-five (men) or sixty

[1] *At the time of going to press, this legislation was still subject to possible policy changes.*

(women) must not be less than 1 per cent of total taxable earnings up to the social security ceiling for each year of membership after April 1975. If the guarantee is at this minimum level the employer must also accept an obligation to provide cost of living increases, but he may obtain exemption from this obligation by guaranteeing a higher level of initial pension.

New conditions for the approval of company pension schemes by the tax authorities were introduced in 1970. The new regulations unify and simplify the conditions for approval that were previously contained in two separate codes. The new code will apply compulsorily to all schemes introduced after April 1973 and to all schemes that are substantially modified after that date. By 1980 all schemes will have to be approved under the new code.

The main limitation imposed by the tax authorities is that pensions provided through 'approved' schemes may not exceed two-thirds of final salary including any pension rights preserved from previous employment.

One major change in the new code is that it will now be possible to provide tax free lump sum retirement benefits through all approved schemes. The maximum lump sum will be $1\frac{1}{2}$ years' final pay scaled down for service of less than twenty years. If lump sum benefits are provided, the pension must be scaled down so that the overall benefits do not exceed the equivalent of a pension of two-thirds final pay.

Future trends in company pension schemes

Funding. The great majority of company pension schemes are funded, and relatively little use is made of book reserve arrangements. Funded schemes may be either self-administered or insured, the tendency being for the larger schemes to be self-administered, and the smaller ones insured. In the private sector of industry about 60 per cent of pensionable employees are in insured schemes. The size and flexibility of the stock market and freedom from official controls have encouraged active investment policies. Some of the larger self-administered funds have 70 per cent or more of their assets invested in ordinary shares and property. In recent years there has been a trend amongst insurance companies to compete for pension business by adding to their conventional tariffs the alternative of 'managed funds' for their larger clients. These are basically investment trusts managed by the insurance companies, the proceeds being used to purchase annuities at the time of retirement.

Contributions. About two-thirds of the members of company pension schemes are required to make some contribution towards the cost of their pension. In those schemes where employees are required to contribute, the average level of contribution is around 5 per cent of pensionable pay.

Pension calculation methods. The retirement pension for a full career is usually in the range of 50 to 66 per cent of pensionable pay including the state pension. Pension schemes for 'white collar' employees increasingly provide pensions near the top of this range, but pension levels for blue collar employees tend to be appreciably lower. Some companies now operate the same pension system for 'white collar' and 'blue collar' employees. Normal retirement age is usually sixty-five for men and sixty for women. There is no discernible trend towards reducing the 'normal retirement ages' on which pension schemes benefits are based.

Cost of living increases. Inflation has focused attention on the need to protect the purchasing power of pensions. Most large companies now review pensions regularly, and make ad hoc adjustments aimed at roughly restoring purchasing power.

Trade union attitudes. Trade unions have been unusually slow to interest themselves in pension planning, because their official policy was for many years to press for a major extension of social security rather than for improvements in employer schemes. There has, however, been a growing realisation that in taking this line, they have not been reflecting the preferences of much of their membership. There have been indications that attitudes are changing and trade unions are likely to display a rapidly growing determination to become closely involved in the planning process. In the last decade 'white collar' unionisation has been making rapid strides in certain industries, covering all grades from clerical to middle management. One of the main reasons for their success is undoubtedly the fears of redundancy, early retirement or damaged promotional prospects resulting from the growing wave of mergers and other industrial reorganisations. In this climate pension conditions are receiving much closer attention than in the past from employees and from the unions who represent them.

Other employee benefits

Medical benefits. In addition to the medical services provided in the work situation under the general requirements of the Factories Act and Office and Shops legislation covering health and safety, many organisations now have arrangements for certain groups of employees to have regular medical checks to ensure that all is well. These benefits can be provided for a marginal cost to the organisation and are generally appreciated by the employees concerned. Another type of medical benefit which is available in an increasing number of organisations is to provide arrangements through the various private health insurance schemes, e.g. BUPA, HSA and Western Provident, so that employees can insure against the cost of private specialist medical treatment if required. The company usually pays all or part of the premium required.

Food services. Nearly all organisations make some provision for their employees to obtain meals or refreshments at work or provide subsidised vouchers for obtaining a meal. Catering services are usually subsidised in some way. The company usually provides the accomodation and equipment required and the cost to the employee in the form of the charges for the meal are limited to the cost of the food and labour.

Provision of cars. This is a benefit which has grown rapidly in recent years and now features as an employee benefit in many United Kingdom companies, although it is operated to a much more limited extent in other EEC countries. This is probably the most substantial single benefit given to an employee because the cost of providing a medium-sized car taxed and insured, maintained and supplied with petrol, costs about £1,000 a year per car. The company will probably recover a proportion of this in the form of an 'operating charge' of 10 to 15 per cent of the cost collected from the employee and which meets the Inland Revenue requirements on the benefit provided to the employee for the private use of the car. Many organisations now make this type of car provision available to most of their management staff. Another category of employees, mainly sales staff and certain service grades, are often provided with a 'free' company car as a condition of their employment, with a small charge made for private use at weekends and on holiday. A third arrangement in relation to cars is to pay various forms of mileage allowance to employees who use their cars on company business. Some large organisations have this arrangement rather than incurring the large capital commitment in running a fleet of company cars.

Other benefits. There are numerous other employee benefits which vary from company to company and often meet particular needs. These benefits include the provision of company houses or subsidised loans to assist in house purchase. Most organisations producing any form of consumer product make some benefit available to their employees in allowing some form of discount on staff purchases. Companies also operate savings schemes, make interest free loans for short periods, operate friendly societies and give assistance in the form of educational allowances. The one benefit which is disappearing is the provision of sports and social clubs subsidised by the company. They now have little attraction to the majority of employees, so the subsidy benefits only a small group of employees who use them.

Conditions of employment

While remuneration is only part of the overall conditions of employment, it remains a major part of the conditions of employment for all employees from Chief Executive to Canteen Assistant. Various types of remuneration systems have been outlined and to give a total picture of the conditions of employment in a typical company, it perhaps can be best illustrated and explained by detailing the various conditions which form an employee's handbook.

By way of illustration, the following Appendix gives details of the conditions in an employee handbook, covering all the various conditions which apply to form the total employment conditions for all the employees within an organisation.

Section 1

APPENDIX. EMPLOYEE HANDBOOK

1. Establishments

Recommended departmental establishments are prepared during November each year for agreement by the Board. Once the Board have agreed the establishments for the financial year commencing 1 January, Managers will be informed of their agreed establishment. Should there be any necessity to alter a departmental establishment during the year an 'X' form will be prepared. This will state the proposed establishment against the current establishment together with an explanation for the change. The 'X' form will be sent to the Group Personnel Manager who will obtain authority for the increase from the Personnel Director. Once the change has been authorised the 'X' form will be returned to the Departmental Head as his authority to proceed with recruitment.

2. Recruitment

(a) Internal

Company policy is to recruit from within where possible. When a vacancy occurs it will be reported to the appropriate Personnel Department who will advertise the vacancy on the internal notice boards, having first checked the vacancy against the budgeted establishment. A short list of suitable candidates is drawn from the applicants and interviews are then arranged. Once the selection is made, the selected candidate and those not selected are informed without delay. Arrangements should be made between the receiving Departmental Manager and the existing Departmental Manager as to the date of transfer. Transfer should take no longer than one month to effect. There may be the odd exception to this where the transferee has not been replaced in the original Department.

(b) External

(i) *Weekly paid staff.* In general all weekly paid vacancies recruited externally are done by the Personnel Department at the lowest graded job. Internal promotion policy means that intake is principally at this level. Applicants are interviewed by the appropriate Personnel Officer and those suitable are passed to the Medical Department for examination. If this is satisfactory they will be allocated to Departments, after induction, according to need.

(ii) *Management, supervisory, specialist vacancies.* The appropriate Personnel Officer or Manager will prepare the necessary advertisement in conjunction with the Departmental Manager. For vacancies in management grades, a short list will be made for the Head of the Division and the Personnel Director—or his nominee—who will then make the selection.

3. Selection

Selection of both internal and external candidates is by interview or interview and tests. Interviews follow a basic pattern and are based on the NIIP seven point plan:

(a) *Physical make-up.* Has the candidate any defects of health or physique that may be of occupational importance? Is his appearance, demeanour and speech suitable for the position?

(b) *Attainments.* What are his educational achievements? What training and experience has he already had? How well has he progressed occupationally?

(c) *General intelligence.* What is the level of his general intelligence? How much general intelligence does he normally display?

(d) *Special aptitudes.* Has he any marked aptitude, dexterity, facility in the use of words or figures, etc.?

(e) *Interests.* To what extent are his interests intellectual, practical, physically active, social, artistic?

(f) *Disposition.* How acceptable does he make himself to other people? Does he influence others? Is he dependable? Is he self-reliant?

(g) Are there any domestic or special circumstances in relation to the candidate?

The aim of such a procedure of interview is to provide for a defensible assessment of potentialities. The questions under the headings are principally for the interviewer to ask himself in relation to the candidate.

4. Induction

(a) *Weekly paid staff.* All new weekly paid staff during their first week in the Company pass through the induction course.

(b) *Management and supervisory staff.* Induction programmes will be prepared for management and supervisory staff in accordance with the appropriate circumstances. The type of induction will be discussed with the employing Departmental Manager by the appropriate Personnel Manager. The necessary programme will be drawn up and issued to the new employee before starting and to all Heads of receiving Departments. Managers are asked to conform to the programme as closely as possible bearing in mind the importance of the first impression gained by the new employee and the fact that this may be the new employee's only opportunity to gather the necessary information which will be helpful to him in his new job. It is always difficult for Managers to find time for induction programmes, but a high priority should be given to this task.

5. Documentation

(a) *Weekly paid and supervisory staff.* Documentation is completed at the commencement of the induction course. New employees should hand over a P.45 tax form, National Insurance card and birth certificate.

(b) *Management.* Documentation is completed by the Pensions and Salaries Manager during the first week of employment. New employees should produce a P.45 tax form, National Insurance card and birth certificate.

6. Probationary period

(a) *Weekly paid staff.* New employees serve a probationary period of twelve weeks which may be extended by the Head of Department if he considers it necessary.

In the case of males, a new employee over twenty-one years of age will be required to pay Pension Fund contributions on his consolidated pay rate after his first twelve weeks service. In the case of females, entry to the Pension Fund (if eligible) will date from the completion of three years' service with the Company.

Any employee who, after leaving the service of the Company, is re-engaged will be treated as a new entrant. The Company, however, reserves the right to give consideration to the rate paid and the effective service date in special cases.

A formal written warning should be given during the probationary period if a new employee is not coming up to standard.

(b) *Supervisory staff.* The probationary period is three months. This can be extended if the Head of Department requires it. Termination can take place at any time during the period but the new employee should have a formal warning during the probationary period that he or she is not up to standard. Formal progress reports are issued by the appropriate Personnel Department before the three-month period is completed.

(c) *Management staff.* The probationary period is six months. This period can be extended if necessary. Termination can take place during the period, but the new employee should previously be warned that he is not up to standard. Progress reports are issued by the Personnel Director before the six-month period is completed.

7. Termination

(a) *Weekly paid and supervisory staff.* When it becomes necessary to terminate an employee a recommendation will be made to the appropriate Personnel Department. The grounds of dismissal will be discussed and if accepted a decision will be made as to the terms of dismissal. The employee will then be sent for and asked if he wishes to be represented by his trade union representative who will be present if required. Termination will be carried out by the Departmental Manager at this meeting. Full period of notice will be given or payment in lieu of notice, except in cases of misconduct where dismissal will be instant.

(b) *Management staff.* A recommendation will be made to the Group Personnel Manager for dismissal of those employees in Job Grades 1–6. In the case of Job Grades 7–12 the recommendation will be made to the Personnel Director. Either full notice will be given or payment in lieu of notice. Payment for loss of office will be discretionary and approved by the Personnel Director. In the case of misconduct, termination will be instant.

(c) *Statutory forms in relation to termination.* Any statutory form required in connection with dismissal will be completed in the appropriate Personnel Department.

Section 2

1. Remuneration

Weekly paid staff
Supervisory staff
Management staff

All current wage and salary rates are set out in the Wages Structure Manual issued by the Wages Department. This contains rules covering overtime, upgrading, downgrading, shift payment and holiday entitlement.

(i) *Salary structure.* The Management salary structure is a twelve-grade structure with a measure of overlap between each grade. Jobs within the Management salary structure are ranked according to the scope and skill of the individual job.

(ii) *Salary survey.* The company undertakes a Management salary survey every two years in which selected bench mark jobs are compared in considerable detail with equivalent jobs in twenty other similar companies. The aim is for management salaries to compare with the mid point of the salaries obtained in the survey. Each Manager should be told in which job grade his own job is ranked and which is indicated on the salary review sheets each year.

(iii) *Management salary progression:* (a) *Promotion.* It is company policy to promote from within where possible. On promotion it is usual to grant a salary increase which will normally take the Manager to the minimum level of the new salary grade.

(b) *Annual review.* Following the annual appraisal procedure individual management salaries are determined. Increases are related to performance and earned by merit. Increases take effect from 1 April each year and will be notified to individual Managers by the Head of Department. Copies of such notification will be sent to the Personnel Director. Each Manager should receive a formal counselling interview at this time.

2. Christmas gift

A week's salary or wages will be paid to all employees who have been in the Company's employ from the beginning of the current financial year and who are still employed at the time of payment in December. Those joining the Company after 1 January each year will receive a payment proportionate to service. This qualification will be announced at the time of the award. Those who leave before this date forfeit any right to the Christmas gift. This payment is subject to income tax deductions under PAYE.

3. Pension schemes

The Rules Booklet of the Pension Scheme can be obtained from the Salaries and Pensions Manager.

Section 3

Employee benefits

1. *Company cars*

Company cars are allocated to certain Managers and to certain Sales employees. The allocation of Company cars is made by the Personnel Director who will control the scale on which cars are issued which are based on job grades.

The cost of operating Company cars (except to Sales staff) is apportioned between the Company and the Manager on an agreed percentage basis. The principles which are followed in aggregating the cost are:

(a) Depreciation of 12 per cent per annum on the original cost of the car.
(b) Road fund tax.
(c) Insurance.
(d) Petrol and oil (with the exception of that used on annual holiday).

These items are totalled and the cost apportioned at the agreed percentage basis.

The Finance Division will send a monthly account to recover the individual contribution to expenses. During the month any expenses incurred should be submitted on the normal claim for expenses and these will be taken into account for the monthly computation. Repairs and maintenance will be paid by the Company but garaging will be the direct responsibility of the employee concerned.

2. *Life assurance*

Every member of the Pension Fund is covered from the date of joining the Fund for the payment of a benefit to his or her dependants should death occur from any cause whatsoever whilst in the employment of the Company. The amount of the benefit is defined by the Rules of the Fund.

3. *Company sick pay scheme*

A. *Weekly paid staff*

The Sickness Payment Scheme provides for payments to weekly paid staff during illness and is based on the following principles:

1. To give employees a feeling of security during illness, or incapacity through accident.
2. To have a system which is easily understood, gives uniform benefits to all and avoids the necessity for enquiry into employees' personal circumstances.

The Company bears the financial responsibility for the scheme and it applies to all weekly paid staff.

Entitlement periods. Employees are entitled to receive benefits according to the following table:

Continuous service	Sickness schedule rate
Under 3 months	No pay
3 months and under 6 months	1 week
6 months and under 1 year	2 weeks
1 year and under 3 years	5 weeks
3 years and under 6 years	10 weeks
6 years and under 9 years	15 weeks
9 years and under 12 years	20 weeks
12 years and over	26 weeks

Sickness payment year. The sickness payment year will commence on 1 January each year. Employees absent immediately prior to 1 January will not commence their entitlements for the new year until they resume work but the interpretation of the rules of the Sickness Payment Scheme shall provide a maximum of two weeks' benefit during the first year of service with the Company.

Reviews. In the event of an employee with one year's service or more exhausting his sickness benefit, a careful review of his case will be made. One year's service shall be interpreted for the purpose of the Sickness Payment Scheme as being twelve months continuous service including any period of absence not exceeding twenty-eight days.

Medical Department. Employees sent home by the Medical Department will receive full pay for that day and it is not counted as part of the Sickness Payment entitlement. For the purpose of this scheme, Sickness Absence will include:

(a) Certified illness.
(b) Time lost through contact with infectious diseases where such absence has been authorised by the Company's Medical Officer.
(c) Time spent on convalescence approved by the Company's Medical Officer, irrespective of the home or place of convalescence.

All payments will be made subject to:

(a) Reporting to the Medical Department.
(b) Receipt of medical certificate during the first three days of absence and weekly certificates thereafter. In their own interest, employees must send

these promptly to the Medical Department as payment is automatically stopped when a certificate is overdue.

(c) The Company's Medical Officer being satisfied that the length of absence is justified. (Should the Company's Medical Officer state that in his opinion an employee is fit to resume work, sickness payments will cease, but the employee has the normal right to appeal.)

(d) The Company seeking further medical advice and taking any action deemed necessary in the case of employees having frequent and prolonged absence from work.

(e) The discretion of the Company to make such amendments and variations as circumstances may warrant.

Other absence

Hospital visits. Employees with more than three months' service attending hospital and those with less than three months' service attending hospital at the instigation of the Medical Department will receive full pay if their absence is approved by the Medical Department and it is not of more than four hours' duration.

Accidents. In the event of loss of working time through accidents at work this scheme will not apply. Provided, however, that there has been no disregard of safety rules or supervisory instructions, the Personnel Manager may recommend that payment be granted by the Company. Such payment will normally make up the difference between the Industrial Injuries Benefit paid under the National Insurance (Industrial Injuries) Acts and the full consolidated pay rate. Payments are subject to regular review.

Absence for reasons other than certified sickness. Payment for absence for reasons other than certified sickness is made at the discretion of the Head of Department. It is by no means automatic and when paid, is counted as part of the Sickness Payment entitlement.

B. *Supervisory staff*

Sick absence is paid for in full, less the amount received in respect of National Insurance Benefit. The length of time for which this is paid is subject to review on an individual basis. Medical certificates are required after three days.

C. *Management staff*

Full salary is paid for sick absence to Management staff subject to the Company's review on length of time. A medical certificate is required after three days' illness. However, all National Insurance Benefits received whilst sick should be repaid to the Company's Pensions and Salaries Manager.

4. *BUPA*

The Company offers enrolment in the British United Provident Association to Management staff and pays the relevant subscription on their behalf. The subscription provides benefits at various levels which are reviewed from time to time.

When enrolled a Manager may include his dependants in his registration and he may opt for a higher scale of benefits provided he pays the additional subscription costs. In these cases the costs will be deducted from salary monthly.

BUPA benefits are intended to meet the costs of private accommodation in hospital and specialists' fees incurred for treatment given on the recommendation of the Manager's own doctor.

5. *Holidays*

(a) *Weekly paid and supervisory staff.* This is given in detail in the Wages Structure Manual.

(b) *Management staff.* The basic holiday entitlement is four weeks with the exception of managers earning under £2 500 per annum, whose basic entitlement is three weeks.

Additional service holiday entitlements are as follows:
After 3 years' service —1 day's additional holiday p.a.
After 5 years' service —3 days' additional holiday p.a.
After 10 years' service—5 days' additional holiday p.a.

6. *Expenses*

(a) *Weekly paid and supervisory staff.* Weekly paid and supervisory staff will be informed by their Head of Department of the commencing date of any period away from their normal place of work, probable length of stay, accommodation address, travelling arrangements and where to report, etc. Prior to leaving an expenses float may be obtained on written authority of the Head of Department. The amount will vary according to the place and duration of stay. On return to base, weekly paid and supervisory staff will be required to account for the expenditure of the expenses float.

Use of expenses float

(i) *Travelling.* If the journey is of over fifty miles, arrangement would be made to obtain rail or air tickets and these should be collected in advance from the appropriate Personnel Department. For shorter journeys, fares should be paid from the expenses float and claimed on an expenses form.

(ii) *Expenses claims.* Reimbursement is made for expenses incurred on the Company's behalf, i.e. travelling, hotel or other accommodation.

Hotel bills should be paid weekly unless otherwise agreed and the receipted bill should accompany the expenses claim. A claim for expenses form, together with all supporting bills, should be forwarded each week to the Head of Department who will authorise the payment.

The first and final expenses claim form should include details of travelling time outside normal working hours which will be paid at time rate and which is subject to income tax.

(b) *Management staff.* The Company will reimburse Management staff for actual expenses incurred on Company business. Expenses must be authorised by the Head of Department and all relevant bills must be attached.

7. *Air travel*

All Company employees with the exception of main Board and Divisional Directors will travel tourist class by air. However, Management staff flying on unbroken flights exceeding eight hours' flying time may travel first class. Also those travelling on business in company with a main Board or Divisional Director may travel first class.

8. *Rail travel*

All employees will travel second class rail with the exception of those Management staff whose salary is £2 750 or above who will travel first class rail. Employees travelling with another who is entitled to first class rail may travel first class.

9. *Car mileage allowance*

For employees using their own cars on Company business a mileage allowance of 6*p* per mile may be claimed on the Claim for Expenses form. For distances over fifty miles, travel by an employee's car should be approved by the Head of Department who should decide on the circumstances whether car or rail travel is the cheapest or most convenient. All employees travelling on Company business should ensure that they are covered by Class II car insurance. Most insurance companies will indemnify for limited journeys on Company business but where this is not possible Class II insurance should be taken out and will be reimbursed by the Company.

Section 4

Miscellaneous

1. *Telephones*

(*a*) *Home.* In certain necessary and authorised circumstances the Company will reimburse managers for telephone rental charges. This will be exceptional and only where it is necessary because of the nature of the job that the manager should be on call at home.

(*b*) *Business.* Company telephones are only to be used for private calls in cases of emergency. All other calls must be stated as private calls to the switchboard supervisor and the employee will be invoiced on a monthly basis. Private incoming calls should only be taken if they are urgent. Guidelines for telephoning are as follows:

(i) Calls are charged on a time basis. Therefore conversations should be kept brief.
(ii) Give priority to external calls as internal calls bear no charge.
(iii) Don't book calls and then leave the office—cancel the call first.
(iv) Telex or letter is more economical if possible.

2. *Food service*

In all locations, where possible, accommodation is provided for meals. The Company subsidises the catering operation and provides reasonable meals during working hours. No food should be consumed in the factory or office.

3. *Medical service*

The Company employs part time Medical Officers and nursing staff including a Sister in Charge at each major unit. All new entrants must undergo a full medical examination. The Medical Department offer a comprehensive service covering shift working and can be consulted by all employees on any medical problem.

4. *Fire precautions*

It is essential that Managers should brief all employees on fire precautions and procedures. These instructions are detailed in all localities by notice and memoranda.

5. *Housing transfer allowances*

When an employee is transferred at the request of the Company certain allowances are made. The administration of these allowances is the responsibility of the Group Personnel Manager through the appropriate Personnel Managers. Company policy is intended to meet the principle that an employee should not suffer financially as a result of moving home at the request of the Company. Before applying any of the scheduled benefits the Group Personnel Manager will discuss with the Director concerned that the change in residence which gave rise to the claim for benefit is made with his knowledge and agreement. Details of the schedules applicable in individual cases may be obtained from the appropriate Personnel Manager whilst questions on the administration of the scheme should be referred to the Group Personnel Manager.

6. *Security*

It is every Manager's responsibility to see that all classified information is kept secure. Classified documents should not be left unattended whilst out of the office. Drawers and filing cabinets should be locked each evening. Subordinates must be trained to treat classified documents and information with the security required.

Disciplinary action will be taken if classified documents are not treated with the strictest security.

5 Employee relations

A *Code of Industrial Relations Practice* became operative at the same time as the main provisions of the *Industrial Relations Act* on 28 February 1972. The purpose of the *Code* was advice and guidance for promoting good employee relations; its provisions were valid as evidence in proceedings before Industrial Tribunals on matters arising from the Act: i.e. Tribunals have to take account of relevant provisions of the Code in determining any matters that may come before them. The *Code* is often quoted in relation to questions of unfair dismissal when these matters are being considered by an Industrial Tribunal.

The Code of Practice

The Code covers seven main areas of responsibility in employee relations matters:

1. Responsibilities

The responsibilities of management, trade unions, employers' associations and the individual employee in promoting and maintaining good industrial relations. For management the Code says:

> The principal aim of management is to conduct the business of the undertaking successfully. Good industrial relations need to be developed within the framework of an efficient organisation and they will in turn help management to achieve this aim.

For the trade unions the advice is:

> The principal aim of trade unions is to promote their members' interests. They can do this only if the undertakings in which their members are employed prosper. They therefore have an interest in the success of those undertakings and an essential contribution to make to it by cooperating in measures to promote efficiency. They also share with management the responsibility for good industrial relations.

For the individual employee it suggests:

> The individual employee has obligations to his employer, to his trade union if he belongs to one, and to his fellow employees. He shares responsibility for the state of industrial relations in the establishment where he works and his attitudes and conduct can have a decisive influence on them.

2. Employment policies

The need for employment policies in which clear and comprehensive policies are suggested to be a pre-requisite to good industrial relations. Such policies should cover the planning and use of manpower, recruitment and selection, payment systems and status and security for all employees.

Paragraph 42 gives some useful views on a trend towards the equalisation of conditions of employment and job status by stating:

Differences in the conditions of employment and status of different categories of employee and in the facilities available to them should be based on the requirements of the job. The aim should be progressively to reduce and ultimately to remove differences which are not so based. Management, employees and their representatives and trade unions should cooperate in working towards this objective.

3. Consultation

Communication and consultation are suggested by the Code as being essential in all types of organisations irrespective of the size. Communication is the passing on through all levels of the organisation of the necessary information on the policies and intentions of the enterprise. The Contracts of Employment Act (see chapter 6) requires all employees to be given certain information on the terms and conditions of their employment. Consultation is providing the means for the joint examination and discussion of problems that concern both management and employees within the organisation.

4. Collective bargaining

On collective bargaining the Code suggests that this should be a joint activity which establishes the relationship between management and employees. This involves the question of the recognition of trade unions which will be dealt with later in this chapter.

5. Representation

The Code recommends a pattern which should be followed in the operation of employee representatives at the place of work and the terms which should cover the function and appointment of shop stewards and the facilities that should be given to them to enable them to carry out their duties.

6. Grievances

The Contracts of Employment Act requires employers to give details of the procedure that exists to enable any employee to raise any grievance that might exist. The Code suggests methods that should be established in organisations to deal with individual grievances and also procedures for dealing with collective disputes covering groups of employees.

7. Discipline

The Code recommends that management should have fair and effective arrangements for dealing with all disciplinary matters. This is particularly important in relation to any disciplinary action that may lead to dismissal, having regard to the 'unfair dismissal' provisions of the Trade Union and Labour Relations Act of 1974 (see chapter 6 page 639).

The following is an example of a typical disciplinary policy that may operate in a company.

Disciplinary policy

In normal circumstances any employee joining the company will anticipate continued employment provided that the conditions are satisfactory and the required performance maintained. It is therefore of extreme importance that during the initial period of employment an objective assessment is made of a new employee's performance. This is the responsibility of management who would then formally confirm that the individual concerned is a satisfactory employee.

Subsequently, there may be in some cases a deterioration in performance or attitude which management will endeavour to improve as an essential part of their normal function.

There will, however, inevitably be occasional situations where the application of disciplinary arrangements, including dismissal, is a necessary feature of employment conditions. The intention is to have disciplinary arrangements that are both fair and effective. It follows that employees should understand that misconduct and/or lack of ability to carry out expected job requirements could result in disciplinary action being taken. The action will depend on the nature of the individual case and could include warnings, transfer to other work, suspension or dismissal.

It is not possible to state every type of misconduct and/or inability to meet required standards. Some of the more obvious ones are:

Poor timekeeping.

Unauthorised absence from work.

Unreasonable absence from work.

Injury to other persons and/or Company property.

Disregard of Company rules and regulations including normal operating instructions.

Falsification of Company records.

Theft from the Company or other employees or unauthorised possession of the Company's or other employees' property.

General misconduct, which may involve other employees, or arise out of contact/association with the Company's customers, which makes continued employment with the Company impossible.

Failure to carry out the job in accordance with established job functions and requirements.

Application of disciplinary arrangements

In certain areas of the Company disciplinary arrangements will be contained in a procedure agreed with trade unions or other representative bodies. These will be based on general principles as indicated below which it is the responsibility of Management to administer:

(a) In all except the most serious breaches of discipline a sequence of warnings will be given. For comparatively minor offences an informal warning will be appropriate which will mean the employee concerned being given a clear indication of his shortcomings.

(b) In respect of more serious offences, e.g. failure to attend work regularly, or failure to meet the normal requirements of the job—a *formal warning* will be given. This will consist of an interview conducted by the appropriate manager who will: (i) state the reason for the disciplinary interview; (ii) give an appropriate warning; and (iii) if the circumstances warrant, make it very clear that a consequence of further disciplinary action could be dismissal.

In these cases a period of time, e.g. three months, will be fixed at the end of which the employee's performance record will be reviewed.

The factors stated above will be incorporated in a letter to the employee and representative if one is involved.

(c) The employee being warned should be given the opportunity of having a colleague or representative present at the interview.

(d) In addition to a formal warning, it may be necessary to impose additional disciplinary action such as a transfer to other work and/or suspension from work without pay.

It is important that a consistent approach is taken in the application of disciplinary action. Where warning of possible termination or suspension without pay is contemplated, prior discussion will take place with the appropriate member of the Personnel Department, and only in exceptional instances will this advice not be followed.

Serious breaches of discipline

In cases of serious breaches of discipline as, for example, theft or falsification of records, dismissal may be applied without recourse to warnings.

Dismissals[1]

As dismissal is the ultimate sanction on employees its use will be confined to exceptional cases. Dismissal will normally be applied where (a) an employee's record does not show reasonable improvement after formal warnings have been given; (b) a single offence makes continued employment with the Company impossible.

Thus no employee will be dismissed for a comparatively minor offence or for a first breach of discipline unless classified as serious. Nor will anyone be dismissed for inability to fulfil the requirements of the job unless a formal warning has been given.

In accepting that dismissal is the most severe penalty that can be applied all the circumstances of the case in question should be carefully considered and discussed with the appropriate member of the Personnel Department before such a decision is made. This would include a recognition of past service in terms of time and performance.

Authority to dismiss

Those who have supervisory responsibility over other employees *do not* have the authority to dismiss their immediate subordinates. Thus no Foreman has authority to dismiss. Similarly an Area Field Sales Manager cannot dismiss a Salesman; nor can a Plant Manager dismiss a Foreman.

Those who have supervisory responsibility will make the recommendation in any case involving the dismissal of an immediate subordinate; such recommendation will require confirmation by the next level of management.

In any cases involving management appointments in Grade 7 or above the prior agreement of the Group Managing Director is required before any dismissal action is taken.

Dismissal in writing

The decision and reason(s) for a dismissal will be given to the employee at a formal interview and confirmed in writing.

Nature of dismissal

Dismissal will be:

(a) immediate summary dismissal, i.e. without notice;
(b) with notice due under the employee's contract of employment; or
(c) with pay in lieu of notice.

---

[1] See p.640 for definitions of dismissal under terms of Trade Union and Labour Relations Act 1974.

Appeals

Employees have the right of appeal against disciplinary action. The appeal will be heard at a higher level of management which has not been directly involved in the application of the disciplinary action which is the subject of appeal. At appeal the employee may be accompanied by a colleague/representative who may also act independently on his behalf.

Use of
documentation

It is essential that adequate documentation be kept of relevant information on the employee's record.

Where appraisals are made any comments on lack of required performance or other failings should be clearly indicated.

Job requirements, particularly performance targets, should be clearly established and understood by the employees concerned. Above all, it is imperative that employees understand what is required of them in the job they hold. Accordingly they should be told of any shortcomings they have related to their performance or attitudes which are likely to lead to disciplinary action being taken.

General note

The underlying principles in this disciplinary policy are to codify a number of existing practices within the group so that a uniform and consistent policy is applied so far as this is possible.

The action to be taken is based on the relevant requirements of the Trade Union and Labour Relations Act 1974 in relation to unfair dismissal and the recommendations of the Code of Practice. Account has also been taken of a number of decisions of Industrial Tribunals in determining cases alleging unfair dismissal. The following are two examples of the written warnings that might be given.

A warning letter

Dear ....

I am writing to you following the meeting we had in my office on (date) when we discussed the matter concerning your (e.g. timekeeping, performance, general attitude).

During the meeting I pointed out to you that there was room for improvement and look forward to this being achieved.

I very much hope that the Company will have no need to take any further action on this matter.

Yours sincerely,

c.c. Personnel Officer
Representative/Shop Steward.

Final warning letter

Dear ....

Final Warning

1. I am writing to confirm the points made to you at the meeting at.................(place), on.................(date).
2. [A paragraph referring to the main points made at the meeting with details supporting factual evidence, e.g. performance figures, timekeeping or conduct as appropriate.]
3. At that meeting I made it clear to you, and now confirm that if there is not a significant and sustained improvement in your performance (timekeeping—conduct) the outcome will be the termination of your employment with the Company.
4. Your position will be reviewed again on ....(date). (Suggest three months after date of warning.)

Yours sincerely,

c.c. Personnel Officer
Representative/Shop Steward.

Trade union recognition and relationships

The claim for recognition from a trade union can come either where the Company has already agreed to some form of bargaining arrangement with other trade unions or where no arrangements exist at all. When a Company is faced with a claim for recognition there are a number of matters which should be considered:

1. First, what is the extent to which the claim for recognition is supported by the employees concerned and does the trade union represent the majority of employees in that particular work group?
2. If the company grants recognition, what will be the effect on any existing bargaining arrangements with other trade unions?
3. Whether or not the recognition, if granted, should extend to all employees in the work group—for example, should supervisors and the employees they supervise (if in the same work group) be in the same trade union or same section of a trade union to which recognition is granted?

In facing a claim for recognition from a trade union a company is entitled to know on a numerical basis the number of their employees in the particular work group who are members of the union making the claim for recognition. If the extent of the membership cannot be agreed between the employer and the trade union making the claim the services of the Department of Employment can often be used, for example, in conducting a secret ballot among the work group concerned.

There are a lot of different views on the level of membership which the trade union making the claim for recognition should establish before the company grants recognition. It is generally accepted that a simple majority of the employees concerned should be sufficient to at least grant recognition (if not the right to a collective agreement) that is anything that is 50 per cent plus of the total employees in the work group concerned.

After recognition the relations between the company and the trade union concerned move to the question of a negotiating procedure which is recommended in the Code of Practice as being based on 'agreed procedures which provide a clear set of rules and a sound basis for resolving conflicts of interest'. This last sentiment is a recognition of the 'pluralistic structure' which is becoming increasingly recognised as existing in our industrial organisations and which is dealt with in a later section of this chapter.

Collective agreements

Collective agreements can be in two parts: they can deal with matters of procedure or with matters of substance between the company and its employees, or they can deal with both. In general such collective agreements are in writing and are usually signed by both parties to the agreement.

Procedural agreements deal as the name implies with procedural items covering:

- the matters to be dealt with between the two parties to the agreement;
- arrangements for negotiating terms and conditions of employment for the employees covered by the agreement;
- facilities given to the trade union and its local officials including shop stewards;
- the procedure for settling any disputes that might arise.

Substantive agreements are concerned with detailed matters on terms and conditions of employment and may cover such items as:

- wage rates, overtime rates, piecework and other payments related to performance;
- hours of work, overtime and shiftworking arrangements, holidays and holiday pay.

Some such agreements also deal with:

- procedures in the event of redundancy or short time working;
- guaranteed pay arrangements, sick pay and pension schemes (the latter is still rare in agreements in the United Kingdom but not in some EEC countries);
- arrangements for the deduction by the company of trade union contributions from employees who are members of the trade union which is party to the agreement—the 'check off system'.

The following are two examples of typical agreements: the first for 'blue collar' personnel, covering both substance and procedure; the second for 'white collar' employees (supervisors and others), concerned mainly with procedure:

First example: 'blue collar'

An agreement made between 'X' Company Limited on the One Part and 'Y' Union on the Other Part.

1. *Introduction*

This agreement is made between 'X' Company Limited and 'Y' Union and applies to the hourly paid employees at Blanktown. (The Agreement also covers rates of pay and other conditions contained in Schedules attached to this Agreement.)

2. *Recognition*

The Company recognises that the 'Y' Union will represent the employees concerned in discussion on any matters related to rates of pay and other relevant conditions of employment.

In giving this recognition the 'Y' Union accepts that employees are free to join or not to join the Union. The Company will encourage its employees to belong to the Union although Union membership is not a condition of employment. Facilities will be offered for the deduction of Union dues from wages on terms agreed between the two parties.

3. *Representation*

(a) Members of the Union may elect six Shop Stewards for the men and for the women employees to act on their behalf in accordance with this Agreement, provided that they shall not be under 18 years of age or have less than twelve months' service with the Company.

(b) The Union shall inform the Company in writing of the Shop Stewards elected.

(c) The Union shall notify the Company in writing when a Shop Steward resigns or is relieved of office.

(d) Reasonable facilities shall be granted for the Shop Stewards to deal with questions raised within the framework of this Agreement in the section they represent. A Shop Steward shall be allowed to leave the section on Union duties with the prior permission of the Supervisor/Manager, and such permission shall not be withheld unreasonably. A Shop Steward shall not, however, be entitled to payment for time spent on Union business unrelated to the Company away from the department in which he/she is employed.

(e) Shop Stewards shall be subject to the control of the Union in respect of their Union duties and shall take all necessary steps to prevent any breach of this and any future Agreement between the Company and the Union.

(f) Actions taken in good faith by Shop Stewards in pursuance of their duties, as defined herein, shall not affect their employment with the Company in any way.

(g) At the same time, Shop Stewards shall be subject to the same working conditions as other employees and shall be subject to and comply with all rules and regulations of the Company.

4. *Procedures for the avoidance of disputes*

(a) It is not the intention of the parties to prevent or discourage employees from continuing to have direct contact with management. It is accepted by all that the most satisfactory solution to a problem results when agreement is reached between the individual and his or her Foreman. The procedure for avoiding disputes is available for use in the event of these parties being unable to agree.

(b) The following procedure shall be followed in order to settle any disputes and grievances concerning an employee:

    (i) An employee or employees wishing to raise a question shall in the first instance discuss the matter with their immediate supervisor.

(ii) If the problem cannot be satisfactorily resolved, then the matter may be referred to the Shop Steward who can take it up with the appropriate supervisor.

(iii) Failing satisfaction at this level, the question should be referred to the Manager for consideration.

(iv) If it is not resolved at this stage, it shall be discussed between the Manager, a representative of the Group Personnel Department, and the appropriate full-time official of the Union.

(v) If the matter is not resolved at this stage it can be discussed by the Managing Director of the Company, the Group Employee Relations Manager and the appropriate full-time official of the Union.

(vi) It is recognised that an issue which cannot be resolved by these means may be taken to arbitration. This would not, however, be regarded as a normal means of negotiation and would only be used in exceptional cases.

(vii) Every effort shall be made to resolve an outstanding issue at each stage and until this procedure has been completed and the result known, there should be no partial or general stoppage of work or any unconstitutional action or lock-out.

(viii) Pending settlement of any dispute, the same conditions that obtained prior to the dispute shall continue.

5. *Meetings*

(*a*) Meetings between representatives of the Company and the Union will normally be held during working hours and on the Company's premises.

(*b*) The Company recognises that on certain occasions Union meetings can with advantage be held on the Company's premises either outside or during working hours.

Permission to hold such a meeting must be obtained in advance from the Manager or his nominee.

6. *Notice boards*

Notice boards will be made available for Union announcements. Before publication, the contents of the notices will be agreed with the Manager or his nominee.

7. *Amendment to or variation of the agreement*

Should either party to this Agreement wish at any time to alter or revise any of its terms, one month's notice of intention shall be given. On receipt of this notice a meeting will be arranged as soon as possible.

8. *Termination of agreement*

Either the Company or the Union may terminate this Agreement by giving six months' notice in writing.

9. *Status of agreement*

This Agreement is not legally enforceable, but the parties clearly intend it to be binding in honour.

Signed for and on behalf of
X Company Limited...

Signed for and on behalf of
Y Union...

This is an example of an agreement made after the Industrial Relations Act 1971 had come into operation and clause 9 is included because the trade union did not wish the agreement to be binding in law under the Act, which would have been the case had this 'disclaimer' clause not been included in the agreement.

Second example: 'white collar'

An Agreement made between 'A' Limited and the 'B' Association representing their members who are employees of the Company.

1. *Preamble*

It is the spirit and intention of this Agreement to maintain and further the best possible relationships between 'A' Limited and those members of the Company's Supervisory Staff who are members of 'B' Association and towards this end the Company affirm the freedom of any of its employees in the Company's Supervisory Staff to join the Association.

2. *Definitions*

In this Agreement:

(a) 'A' Limited shall be referred to as 'the Company' and this Agreement shall apply to its plants and offices situate at X, Y and Z.
(b) The 'B' Association shall be referred to as 'the Association'.
(c) The following shall be referred to as 'Employees' Members of the Association employed in the Company's Supervisory Staff other than those covered by agreements with other unions.

3. *General principles*

(a) The Company recognises the right of the Association to exercise its function within the terms of this Agreement and the need to provide reasonable facilities for its officers.
(b) The Association recognises the right of the Company to manage its plants and offices and agrees on the need to achieve efficient operations by all reasonable means.
(c) The Company and the Association do not consider themselves called upon to observe any Agreement or Procedure in respect of Employees other than as provided for in this Agreement.

(d) The Company and the Association recognise that membership of the Association is not a condition of employment with the Company neither is it a prerequisite of employment with the Company that a prospective employee shall declare whether or not he or she is a member of the Association or is willing to become a member. However, facilities shall be given to the Branch Secretary of the Association to approach any new employee in Supervisory Staff on the question of membership of the Association and this facility will neither be unduly pursued or withheld.

(e) Arising from Clause 3(d) the Association undertakes that its members employed by the Company will not object to working with non-members of the Association.

(f) Deduction of Association subscriptions from salaries will be undertaken provided that the Association distributes and collects authorisation forms and passes these to the Company. The Company will not undertake the collection of any arrears or the refund of any subscriptions.

(g) Matters arising for discussion affecting the terms and conditions of employment of employees shall be dealt with in accordance with the procedures as established by Clause 5 hereof and shall be settled at plant or office level wherever practicable.

(h) Without departing in any way from the principles embodied in Clause 3(a), (b) and (g) the parties emphasise the value of consultations in both the successful operation of the procedure as set out in this Agreement and in the avoidance of disputes.

(i) The parties agree that at each stage of the procedure as set out in this Agreement every attempt will be made to resolve issues raised and that until such procedure has been exhausted there shall be no stoppage of work or lock out either of a partial or general character or other unconstitutional action.

4. *Representation*

(a) The Company recognise the right of employees to elect from their number representatives to act on their behalf in accordance with the terms of this Agreement. The number of such representatives and the area of representation shall be determined on a departmental basis and shall be agreed between the full time official of the Association and the authorised Company Manager who will normally be the Industrial Relations Manager.

(b) The representatives shall be known as 'B' Association Representatives and must be employees with at least two years' continuous service with the Company in the Supervisory Staff structure. This service qualification will not apply to representatives existing as at the date of the signing of this Agreement.

(c) The appointment of 'B' Association Representatives shall be determined by the Association; their names and the areas they represent shall be ratified officially and in writing by the Association to the Company. The Association also undertakes to advise the Company in writing when a Representative resigns or is relieved of office.

(d) All Representatives shall conform to the conditions of employment and regulations of the Company but shall be afforded reasonable facilities to carry out their functions within the framework of this Agreement in the areas they represent. Each Representative shall act as such only within the area for which he or she is appointed.

(*e*) Before raising any matter on behalf of an individual member or a number of members the Representative should obtain permission of his or her immediate superior before leaving their working area.

(*f*) Actions taken by any Representative in good faith in pursuance of his or her duties as defined in this Agreement shall not in any way affect their employment with the Company.

(*g*) Each Representative shall be subject to the control of the Association and shall act in accordance with the Rules and Regulations of the Association and with the provisions of this Agreement.

5. *Procedure*

Issues affecting individual employees.

(*a*) Any employee who wishes to raise an individual matter shall first discuss it with his or her immediate superior.

(*b*) If the matter is not settled to the satisfaction of the employee he or she may refer it to his or her Representative who shall discuss it with the Manager concerned.

Note. Issues of a Collective Nature. The procedure commences at stage (*c*).

(*c*) Failing settlement under Clause 5(*b*) the Representative concerned together with the Branch Secretary shall discuss the matter with the Industrial Relations Manager and the Manager concerned.

(*d*) Failing settlement under Clause 5(*c*) the Branch Secretary shall submit the matter to the Divisional Officer of the Association. In the event of subsequent discussions between the Divisional Organiser and the nominated official of the Company the Branch Secretary should be present.

(*e*) If the matter remains unresolved it will be referred to a meeting embodying the ultimate negotiating authorities in the Association and in the Company.

(*f*) Failing settlement under Clause 5(*e*) the matter shall be pursued by any means as may be agreed ending if necessary with:

(i) reference to the Conciliation Officer of the Department of Employment; or

(ii) reference to an independent arbitrator as agreed between the Company and the Association.

6. *Variation and termination*

(*a*) Any variation to this Agreement required as a result of circumstances which may arise and which are fundamentally different from those existing at the time of the negotiation of this Agreement or for any other reasons shall be negotiated only between the Company and the national officials of the Association.

(*b*) This Agreement shall only be terminated upon three months' notice in writing given by either party to the other.

Signed for and on behalf of 'A' Limited ....

Signed for and on behalf of 'B' Association..

This second example of a collective agreement has no clause on legal enforceability as it was an agreement made before the Industrial Relations Act existed and when all such agreements had no legal enforcement.

Consultative machinery

Besides the formal arrangements made under collective agreements there is often a need for some form of consultative machinery in a company.

The Code of Practice defines consultation as 'jointly examining and discussing problems of concern to both management and employees. It involves seeking mutually acceptable solutions through a genuine exchange of views and information'.

The Code further recommends that in all units where there are more than 250 employees there should be arrangements for management representatives and employee representatives to meet on a regular basis. If joint consultative arrangements are either being established for the first time or being revised the following points should be considered by the management of the unit:

- the arrangements provide opportunities for employees to express their views on proposed changes which affect them and encourage discussion of matters associated with the work situation;
- employee representatives have all the information they require to enable them to participate effectively in discussions;
- managers take an active part in the proceedings;
- the arrangements include effective means of reporting back to employees.

In setting up any consultative committee both management and employee representatives should discuss and agree the following matters:

1. The objectives, functions and membership of the committee and any sectional committees.
2. The arrangements and procedures for electing the members.
3. The rules and procedures for meetings.
4. The range of matters to be discussed.

The basis of the constitution of a Joint Consultative Committee might be as follows:

Structure

The consultative machinery will consist of a Committee composed of representatives of management and employees.

Terms of reference

The Committee should have as its terms of reference all matters affecting the employee during the continuance of his employment, except questions of wages where these are covered by collective agreements.

Where special Committees are thought desirable for deliberation on specific issues, they should take the form of Subcommittees of the main Committee, with the right to co-opt persons with special knowledge or experience of the issues under deliberation.

Constitution of committee

(a) Employee representatives should be elected; those of Management should be nominated. The Personnel Executive should be an *ex officio* member.

(b) All employees should have the right to vote for representation.

(c) Eligibility for election to membership of the Committee should be restricted to employees with a minimum of twelve months' service in the enterprise, but there should be equal eligibility as between members and non-members of the trade unions.

(d) The establishment of the 'constituencies' for representation purposes should provide for adequate representation of the technical and administrative (including clerical) staffs.

(e) All elected or nominated members of the committee should serve for a period of two years, with the proviso that there shall be an annual nomination or election of half the members in each category.

Employee relations

In this context employee relations are defined as the place of the personnel function in the employee relations aspects of the company's activities.

Twenty years ago the personnel function was regarded as some sort of buffer between a predatory management on one side and groups of unwilling and ungrateful employees on the other side. It is interesting that if we look at Moxon in his *Functions of a Personnel Department* originally published in 1943, revised in 1951, we find in the introduction a discussion of the different job titles associated with the personnel function, with various arguments put forward as to why the term 'Manager' should not be applied because those concerned with the personnel function must primarily be advisers to management and not part of management itself. Developing this further, Moxon's six divisions of the personnel function, ranging from Employment through Joint Consultation to Education and Training, Health and Safety and finally Welfare, implied an acceptance that the personnel function had a role of guiding and advising rather than being an essential part of the executive operation of his company.

Recent studies in terms of both individual and group behaviour have posed the question: What sort of organisation is the industrial enterprise? and it is suggested that a great deal of our views and attitudes depends on whether we view it as a *unitary* or as a *pluralist* structure. Are we defining the organisation as a team unified by a common purpose, or is it more correctly seen as a coalition of interests, a miniature of the society in which we live where there are many different groups with divergent interests over which the 'government' that is the management tries to maintain some kind of positive balance?

Unitary basis

If we examine the industrial organisation as a *unitary system*, it is well defined in Alan Fox's research paper to the Royal Commission on Trade Unions and Employers' Associations in 1968 as:

A unitary system has one source of authority and one focus of loyalty, which is why it suggests the team analogy. What pattern of behaviour do we expect from the members of a successful and healthily-functioning team? We expect them to strive jointly towards a common objective, each pulling his weight to the best of his ability. Each accepting his place in his function gladly, following the leadership of the one so appointed. There are no oppositionary groups or factions, and therefore no rival leaders within the team. Nor are there any outside it; the team stands alone, its members owing allegiance to their own leaders but to no others. If the members have an obligation of loyalty towards the leader, the obligation is certainly reciprocated, for it is the duty of the leader to act in such ways as to inspire the loyalty he demands. Morale and success are closely connected and rest heavily upon personal relationships.

Pluralistic basis

Relating this concept to the personnel function it represents a view which is held by many employers as to what an organisation ought to be like. Recent work by the behavioural scientists has shown how many industrial organisations actually operate. Fox describes the pluralistic system as follows:

> The organisation as a plural society, containing many related but separate interests and objectives which must be maintained in some kind of equilibrium. In place of a corporate unity reflected in a single focus of authority and loyalty, we have to accept the existence of rival sources of leadership and attachment. They need to be accepted, above all, by whoever is ruling the plural society in question. The problem of government of a plural society is not to unify, integrate or liquidate sectional groups and their special interests in the name of some over-riding corporate existence, but to control and balance the activities of constituent groups so as to provide for the maximum degree of freedom of association and action for sectional and group purposes consistent with the general interest of the society as conceived, with the support of public opinion, by those responsible for its government.

From this definition we accept that a company is made up of various groups with divergent interests; therefore the degree of common purpose which we can expect to find will be very limited, and this brings us again to the personnel function. Many personnel executives have been conditioned to the view that the whole function is centred on a regard for the people within it, on the other hand, the management of a company has to face many other considerations. It has to consider the technical resources, the shareholders, the customers, the government and in many cases the local community. An effective management must maintain some concern for all these divergent interests and cannot administer entirely in the interest of any one of them.

Peter Drucker has said:

> The main function and purpose of a business is the production of goods not the governance of men. Its authority over men must always be subordinated to its economic performance and responsibility . . . hence it can never be discharged primarily in the interests of those over whom the business rules.

Clearly the management of a company must sometimes act against the interests of its employees and this is obviously incompatible with the whole concept of common purpose.

A practical example of how the pluralist theory might be accepted within the context of the personnel function is to consider the place of the trade unions in a company. For this we have to consider that the relationship between the employer and the employee has two distinct aspects, firstly 'market relations' and secondly 'managerial relations'.

Market aspects

Market relations are concerned with terms and conditions of employment and are therefore economic in character. Managerial relations arise out of what the Company seeks to do with its employees having engaged them on certain terms and conditions. They therefore have to do with the exercise of authority.

The market relationship goes back to the beginning of the Industrial Revolution when the concept that this relationship must be established on an individual basis was expressed in the employer's view that if the employee did not like what he was offered he was free to go elsewhere, and this developed into the managerial relationship, particularly when applied as a defence against the growth of collective bargaining: 'Can I not do what I like with my own employees?'

Therefore with the development of trade unions, public opinion tended to accept trade unionism in terms of 'market relations' because it was often moved by seeing the effects upon people of an uncontrolled labour market. On the other hand, public opinion has not yet today come to accept fully trade union organisation in the context of 'managerial relations', it accepts the right to organise but is extremely unwilling to accept the results of such organisation.

Summarising the concept of the pluralist system, organisations have to face the fact that there are other sources of leadership, other centres of loyalty within the organisation and that it is with this situation that management must share its decision-making. If we see a growing acceptance of this theory, then personnel executives in the future will be forced to accept a completely new thinking in their approach to the traditional areas which have become established as the personnel function.

What perhaps has been the worst effect of this failure to accept change has been that whilst organisations recognised change they have preserved the pretence of maintaining their prerogative, and at the same time have connived at the extension of unilateral action by groups within the organisation, and because this has not been met by management it is perhaps the greatest loss of managerial control that has marked recent years. It is the process by which systematic overtime, overmanning and other manifestations of working group control have thrived.

Many organisations still operate on a unitary system, having little regard for the forces at work within their operations. In many of the areas in which the personnel function operates a real understanding of employee relations might be based firmly on a view of the organisation as a pluralist system which has a coalition of common interests and that if this is accepted the day-to-day problems that arise will have to be approached in the light of these arguments.

The human factor

The personnel executive whether he or she accepts the concept of the unitary or the pluralist system as developed by Alan Fox has to recognise that the behaviour of each employee and each group of employees in any organisation is influenced by the combination of a number of factors which have been studied by the behavioural scientists of the last two decades in great depth. They are:

● The personality of the individual.
● The part the individual has to play within the organisation.

- The expectations of other individuals who are in the same working group, about the behaviour of that individual.
- Any factors which are particular to that organisation.
- The standards of behaviour which are expected by the organisation and by the formal and informal groups to which the individual belongs.

'Hierarchy of needs'

The behavioural scientists have examined the organisation in terms of both individual and group needs in which all the elements are interdependent.

On individual needs, the most popular theory of motivation is that developed by Maslow[1], who explains human behaviour in terms of a 'hierarchy of needs'. His argument is that an individual is at any time in a state of deprivation and therefore the individual has to expend energy in driving towards the satisfaction of the needs. Maslow's hierarchy has five levels, to be satisfied in the following order:

1. Physiological needs: food, drink, etc.
2. Safety needs: freedom from pain, discomfort and threatening circumstances.
3. Needs for love, affection and of belonging.
4. Needs for esteem: desire for a stable firmly based high personal evaluation both in relation to self-esteem and the esteem of others within the organisation.
5. Needs for self-actualisation: desire for the capability to become whatever one is capable of, through personal growth and development within the organisation.

In our present level of industrial and economic development both in the United Kingdom and the other countries of the EEC, it can be argued that the majority of individuals are satisfied in the basic needs of Maslow's hierarchy, that is 1 to 3, although with diminishing satisfaction in the higher needs, 4 and 5, of esteem and self-actualisation.

'Theory X'

On the question of group motivation within an organisation, the work of Douglas McGregor[2] has given us the two concepts of management, Theory X and Theory Y. Theory X is based on three propositions:

1. Management is responsible for organising the enterprise with capital, materials, equipment and people in the interest of economic ends.
2. In respect of the people in an enterprise the process required is to direct their efforts, motivate them, control their actions and behaviour to meet the needs of the organisation.
3. Without the intervention of management people would be resistant to the needs of the organisation. People must be persuaded, controlled, rewarded or punished. Their activities must be directed, which is the task of management.

[1] Maslow, *Motivation and Personality*, Harper, 1954.
[2] D. McGregor, *The Human Side of Enterprise*, McGraw-Hill, 1960.

'Theory Y'

McGregor went on to argue that with the improvement in working conditions and in standards of living, certain basic needs are satisfied so that people look to the fulfilment of greater social and egoistic needs. He therefore suggests that the style of management needed to meet these requirements is not Theory X but Theory Y, which has also three propositions:

1. People are *not* innately passive or resistant to the needs of the organisation. They have become so as a result of their experience in organisations.
2. The motivation, potential for development and capacity for assuming responsibility are all present in people—they are not put there by management. It is therefore the responsibility of management to make it possible for people to recognise and develop these characteristics for themselves.
3. The task of management is to arrange and structure the organisation and its methods of operation so that people can achieve their goals by directing their own efforts towards the organisational objectives.

Personnel Managers in their responsibility for maximising the effectiveness of the human resources of the organisation might well consider the effects of the application of the pluralist system as defined by Fox with the organisational concept of Theory Y, as defined by McGregor.

Group motivation

In the study of people within an organisation, the reaction of the individual is often different within the same working environment. Hertzberg, in his studies of a group of professional men—engineers and accountants—found that this type of employee expected to be given good pay and fringe benefits and to be provided with an attractive place to work and were upset when there was any disturbance to their pay, security or working conditions. Hertzberg has defined these as the 'hygiene' factors of work which prevent loss of morale and efficiency but do *not* lead to any positive improvement in performance. For the professional men studied by him, the main motivation was opportunities to do their work well and to be judged by the results. Once the individual felt secure by reason of the employment conditions, recognition, autonomy and achievement became the *chief* motivators. This linked with McGregor's concepts points to the managerial style of the organisation in achieving the objectives of the enterprise with a motivational pattern of employee relations which best satisfies its particular employees. The total concept of employee relations is to meet the needs of change by studying human behaviour, technology and the social system.

The concept of overall change is illustrated by Likert[1] 'when an organisation seeks to apply the results of research dealing with leadership, management and organisational performance, the application must involve total systems modification and not an atomistic modification'. This advice of a behavioural scientist might well be adopted as a basic criterion for the study of the employee relations within an organisation by all managers, not least those responsible for the management of the human resources of the organisation.

[1] R. Likert, *The Human Organisation*, McGraw-Hill, 1967.

6 Labour law

The law of employment

The law of employment has developed in the United Kingdom in a three tier structure.

Rights and duties

The first level is the series of rights and duties which have been agreed between the employer and the individual employee and which together form the contract of employment. The development of these rights and duties so far as the law has affected them has not been achieved by a series of Acts of Parliament (at least until the legislation of the last decade) but by a series of judicial decisions in the courts, so that the basic law of employment has been made up of a series of *common law* decisions which have formed the basis of the contract between the employer and the individual employee.

However, certainly in the past seventy years there has been the development of a 'third party' which has had a growing effect on the individual employer–employee relationship: this has been the *intervention of the trade union* representing the interests of the employee from the shop floor through the local to the national level. In the years since the end of the 1939–45 war, the relationship between the individual employee and his employer has been to a greater extent affected by the negotiations with the trade unions (representing groups of employees) than by the decisions of any court on matters concerning the law of employment.

Statutory intervention

The second level in the development of the law of employment has been in a series of Acts of Parliament on a number of matters covering various aspects of employment conditions.

For nearly 150 years the only employment matters specifically covered by statutes were those of minimum safety and working conditions, covered by the legislation on these matters in the Factories Acts of the nineteenth century, culminating in the Health and Safety at Work Act 1974. The statute law providing for compensation for injury at work rested on the Workman's Compensation Act 1897 until this was superseded by the National Insurance (Industrial Injuries) Act 1946 as part of the postwar legislation on social security matters.

In the legislative area concerning conditions of employment, the United Kingdom lagged behind many other European countries in the post-1945 period, until the last decade, when we have seen a spate of legislation giving statutory backing to a number of factors governing the law of employment. The Contracts of Employment Act 1963 (now the Contracts of Employment Act

1972) gave to employees the legal right to minimum periods of notice to terminate the contract of employment and the right to written particulars of certain terms in the contract of employment.

The Redundancy Payments Act 1965 set up a scheme for statutory compensation for the loss of employment by reason of redundancy, which had not previously been provided for in the common law matters covering the law of employment.

The common characteristic of this second level in the development of the law of employment from the Factories Act of 1802 to the Contracts of Employment Act 1972 has been that Parliament has laid down by statute the *minimum* standards, which an employer can improve on but which outside special and limited circumstances cannot be reduced below the minimum laid down by statute.

Collective bargaining

The third level in the development of the law of employment is in the area of collective matters which have been developed on a concept by both employers and employees of 'free collective bargaining'. In the industrial history of the past 100 years, only the regulations at the time of the 1914–18 and 1939–45 wars have ever introduced the concept of the state's intervention in the collective bargaining situation until the Industrial Relations Act 1971: this has considerably influenced the second and third levels in the structure of the law of employment.

On the question of statutory intervention, the Industrial Relations Act 1971 made considerable modification and extension on matters of the minimum period of notice and the written particulars of employment which are now incorporated in the Contracts of Employment Act 1972. New Statutory rights were provided for the first time in statute law for employees who are unfairly dismissed and new rights were given to employees in relation to trade union membership.

On the question of collective bargaining within the framework of statutory provision, the Industrial Relations Act 1971 marked an important shift in the role of law in this field so that where the law had been minimal in the past, the new Act was equipped with a battery of new legal concepts for application in the area of employee relations. The purpose of this chapter is not to attempt to justify the success or otherwise of this statutory legal intervention, but to deal with and explain the effect of the five Acts concerned—Redundancy Payments Act 1965, Equal Pay Act 1970, Industrial Relations Act 1971, Contracts of Employment Act 1972 and Trade Union and Labour Relations Act 1974, in so far as they relate to labour law and the total operation of employee relations in the human resources of the organisation.

Because of its historical significance, the Industrial Relations Act of 1971 is outlined and reviewed in an Appendix to this chapter (see page 644).

Redundancy Payments Act 1965

The Act requires employers to make lump sum compensation payments, called 'redundancy payments', to employees who are dismissed because of redundancy. It also requires these payments to be made in certain circumstances to employees who have been laid off or kept on short time for a substantial period. The amount of the payments is related to pay, length of service and age.

The Act also established a Redundancy Fund, financed by contributions collected with the employer's flat-rate National Insurance contribution. Employers who have to make redundancy payments as required by the Act may claim a rebate of 50 per cent of the cost from the Fund (Redundancy Rebates Act 1969).

The Act provides for disputes about entitlement to redundancy payments or about claims for rebate from the Fund to be settled by Industrial Tribunals.

Nearly all classes and types of employee are covered. The Act defines an employee as 'an individual who has entered into or works under . . . a contract with an employer, whether the contract is for manual labour, clerical work or otherwise, is express or implied, oral or in writing, and whether it is a contract of service or of apprenticeship'. The Act therefore covers all employees in all kinds of employment. However, people who work in partnership or as independent contractors or freelance agents as well as others who work under contracts for services (as distinct from contracts of service) are not covered. Employees not covered by the Act are:

- employees with less than 104 weeks' continuous employment with their employer;
- employees who are normally employed for less than twenty-one hours weekly and have no contract which normally involves employment for twenty-one hours and more weekly;
- employees whose reckonable service ends on or after their sixty-fifth birthday (men) sixtieth birthday (women);
- registered dock workers engaged on dock work;
- share fishermen who are paid solely by a share of the catch;
- certain merchant seamen;
- crown servants and employees in the National Health Service;
- certain employees with fixed term contracts;
- employees who are husbands or wives of their employer;
- domestic servants who are close relatives of their employer.

If a dispute arises as to whether or not an employee's employment was continuous or not and the dispute cannot be settled between the two parties, it will be settled by an industrial tribunal and at the tribunal hearing the onus of proof will be on the employer to establish that the employment was not continuous.

The definition of dismissal because of redundancy is complex, but in general a payment has to be made to an employee who is dismissed because of redundancy where the whole or main reason for his dismissal is that his employer's need for employees to do work of a particular kind in a place where he is employed has diminished or ceased. It makes no difference as to the reason why the employer needs fewer employees—he may be closing a particular factory or office, there may be a trade recession in his particular type of business or there may be a change in production requirements due to technological developments. In all these cases, if the result is that the employer needs fewer employees, then any employees who are dimissed will have been dismissed because of redundancy.

Any dispute about the cause of dismissal will then have to be settled by the tribunal. In any tribunal hearing on such a dispute, the onus of proof will be on the employer to establish that the employee was not redundant.

Dismissal has a particular meaning under the Redundancy Payments Act: that the employee's contract of employment is terminated by the employer. It is immaterial for purposes of entitlement to redundancy payment whether the contract has been terminated by notice or not. For example, if an employee loses his employment because his employer closes his factory without formally dismissing him at all, he is not disentitled to a redundancy payment. Except where a lockout occurs an employee may also be taken to be dismissed if he leaves without notice, being legally entitled to do so because of his employer's conduct. Special considerations arise when an employer dies. However, there is no dismissal when an employee accepts a properly made offer of alternative employment with the same employer or a new owner of the business.

Redundancy situations

There may be occasions where a redundant employee is offered work by the same employer on the same terms and conditions after being given notice as being redundant. The following provisions then apply:

The request by the employer need not be in writing. Provided the offer is to take effect without any break in employment and is accepted by the employee, he is not entitled to a payment but employment would be continuous. If the employee refuses it and if he has no reasonable grounds for refusing—again he is not entitled to a payment. The sort of grounds for refusing which might be held to be reasonable might be if the employee, on the strength of being given notice, had arranged to sell his house and move to another area. If there were a dispute about whether the employee's refusal was resonable, it would be for the tribunal to settle. A more common situation is where the employer offers alternative work on terms and conditions which are different to the previous ones. The offer must be in writing. If the employee refuses the offer he is not entitled to redundancy payment provided certain conditions apply. The conditions are as follows:

1. The offer must be made to the employee before the due date of termination of the job in which he is about to become redundant.
2. The offer must be in writing. It should contain enough particulars to give a clear idea of what is being offered—e.g. what the work is, where it is, rates of pay and any other terms and conditions which are different from those under which the employee has been working up to then.
3. The new contract must take effect either without a break in employment or, if there is a break, it must not exceed four weeks. (In cases where the previous contract terminates on Friday, Saturday or Sunday, the new contract must take effect not later than the fifth Monday following that date).
4. The employment offered must be suitable in relation to the employee.
5. The employee must have acted unreasonably in refusing the offer.

The definition of what is 'suitable' when an offer of alternative work is made is one of the most common cases coming before the industrial tribunals. The Act does not define what sort of alternative work would be 'suitable'. If there is a dispute about this it is for the tribunal to settle. They can be expected to have regard to such things as the skills of the employee, the nature of his previous work and the earnings in the new job compared with his previous earnings, and, where the new job is in a different place, the difficulties which this might cause for the employee; and also to what has usually been acceptable as alternative in the industry or the particular occupation of the employee.

If the offer is properly made and the new job itself is suitable but the employee still refuses it, the employer must decide whether he has reasonable grounds for doing so. If there is a dispute it is for the tribunal to settle. They will have to look at any individual circumstances which the employee claims makes it difficult or impossible for him to accept the offer. They will also have regard to the need for offers of employment on different terms to be made in writing. In certain circumstances the absence of a proper written offer might entitle the employee to a payment, whether the offer is accepted or not.

The alternative work offered by the employer must be work in his own business. An offer of work with some other business does not relieve the employer of his obligation to make a redundancy payment (unless the other business is a parent company or subsidiary or a subsidiary of a common parent company or there is a change of ownership of the business).

Dismissal for any reason other than redundancy does not give an employee any right to a redundancy payment. For example, if the dismissal is wholly or mainly due to inefficiency, unsuitability or for health reasons there is no entitlement to any payment. However, if an employee has been given notice because of redundancy but is dismissed during the period of notice because of his conduct, he does not necessarily lose all his entitlement to a redundancy payment. He may go to a tribunal who may award the full amount of redundancy payment or part of it, or no payment at all, depending on the circumstances.

The other situation which may arise under the Act is where an employee is offered employment by the new owner of a business. Where there is a change in the ownership of a business, but the employee continues to work for the new owner on the same terms as before with no break in employment or accepts re-engagement on different terms, the employee is not entitled to any redundancy payment. The change of ownership does not break the employee's continuity of employment, so that if at some later date he is dismissed by the new owner so as to qualify for a redundancy payment, the payment (which will all be due from the new owner) will be based on the whole of the employee's continuous service with the business, including service with the old owner as well as the new.

Other provisions

The Act also makes provision for situations which may arise in relation to eligibility for redundancy payment if an employee goes on strike during the period of notice which has been given to him as required by the terms of his contract of employment. It also makes provision for situations where an employee has been laid off or kept on short time for a substantial period and wishes to terminate his employment.

Calculation of redundancy payments

The calculation of redundancy payments is based essentially on how long the employee has been continuously employed by his employer. Payments are related to the number of complete years up to a maximum of twenty years of employment.

There is also a maximum pay limit of £80 per week and for each year of employment from age eighteen to twenty-one, half a week's pay is made, for employment from age twenty-two to forty, one week's pay is made, for employment from age forty-one to sixty-five for men (sixty for women) one and a half weeks' pay is made, with a reduction if the redundant employee is aged sixty-four for men or fifty-nine for women. The calculation of payment is on the basis of age, length of service with an employer and weekly earnings (normally excluding overtime premium), with a limit of £80 per week, with a maximum service of twenty years. The basis of payment is as follows (a 'ready reckoner' is set out overleaf):

(a) for each complete year of service after the forty-first
    birthday $1\frac{1}{2}$ week's pay

(b) for each complete year of service (apart from those
    covered by (a), after the twenty-second birthday   1 week's pay

(c) for each complete year of service (apart from those
    covered by (a) and (b), after the week which began
    before the eighteenth birthday $\frac{1}{2}$ week's pay

If a man is past his sixty-fourth birthday (fifty-ninth for a woman) the redundancy payment is reduced by one-twelfth for every complete month which has elapsed between that birthday and the Saturday of the week in which employment ceases.

The Redundancy Fund

Employers are required to make weekly contributions to the Redundancy Fund in respect of all employees aged eighteen and over. These contributions are collected with the National Insurance contributions. In return, any employer who makes any redundancy payment as required by the Act can claim a rebate from the Redundancy Fund of 50 per cent of the cost of the redundancy payments made.

Equal Pay Act 1970

This Act which was passed in 1970 comes into force on 29 December 1975 and its purpose is to eliminate any discrimination between men and women in regard to pay and any conditions of employment. The elimination of any discrimination is to be achieved by:

● Establishing the right of any woman to equal treatment when in employment if the work she performs is the same as or of a broadly similar nature to that of men or is in a job which, although different from those of men, has been given equal value to men's jobs by a job evaluation exercise.

● Providing the means for the Industrial Court to remove any discrimination in collective agreements, pay structures and statutory wage orders which contain any provisions which apply to men only or women only and which have been referred to the Industrial Court. If there is any dispute on the question of equal treatment between an employer and an individual woman employee the matter can be referred to an Industrial Tribunal for a decision.

Ready reckoner for redundancy payments

(Reproduced by permission of the Department of Employment)

To use the table: Read off employee's age and number of complete years' service; any week which began before the employee attained the age of 18 does not count. The table will then show *how many weeks' pay* the employee is entitled to.

Age (years) †	2	3	4	5	6	7	8	9	10	11	12	13	14	15	16	17	18	19	20
20	1	1	1	1	—														
21	1	1½	1½	1½	1½	—													
22	1	1½	2	2	2	2													
23	1½	2	2½	3	3	3	3	—											
24	2	2½	3	3½	4	4	4	4	—										
25	2	3	3½	4	4½	5	5	5	5	—									
26	2	3	4	4½	5	5½	6	6	6	6	—								
27	2	3	4	5	5½	6	6½	7	7	7	7	—							
28	2	3	4	5	6	6½	7	7½	8	8	8	8	—						
29	2	3	4	5	6	7	7½	8	8½	9	9	9	9	—					
30	2	3	4	5	6	7	8	8½	9	9½	10	10	10	10	—				
31	2	3	4	5	6	7	8	9	9½	10	10½	11	11	11	11	—			
32	2	3	4	5	6	7	8	9	10	10½	11	11½	12	12	12	12	—		
33	2	3	4	5	6	7	8	9	10	11	11½	12	12½	13	13	13	13	—	
34	2	3	4	5	6	7	8	9	10	11	12	12½	13	13½	14	14	14	14	—
35	2	3	4	5	6	7	8	9	10	11	12	13	13½	14	14½	15	15	15	15
36	2	3	4	5	6	7	8	9	10	11	12	13	14	14½	15	15½	16	16	16
37	2	3	4	5	6	7	8	9	10	11	12	13	14	15	15½	16	16½	17	17
38	2	3	4	5	6	7	8	9	10	11	12	13	14	15	16	16½	17	17½	18
39	2	3	4	5	6	7	8	9	10	11	12	13	14	15	16	17	17½	18	18½
40	2	3	4	5	6	7	8	9	10	11	12	13	14	15	16	17	18	18½	19
41	2	3	4	5	6	7	8	9	10	11	12	13	14	15	16	17	18	19	19½
42	2½	3½	4½	5½	6½	7½	8½	9½	10½	11½	12½	13½	14½	15½	16½	17½	18½	19½	20½
43	3	4	5	6	7	8	9	10	11	12	13	14	15	16	17	18	19	20	21
44	3	4½	5½	6½	7½	8½	9½	10½	11½	12½	13½	14½	15½	16½	17½	18½	19½	20½	21½
45	3	4½	6	7	8	9	10	11	12	13	14	15	16	17	18	19	20	21	22
46	3	4½	6	7½	8½	9½	10½	11½	12½	13½	14½	15½	16½	17½	18½	19½	20½	21½	22½
47	3	4½	6	7½	9	10	11	12	13	14	15	16	17	18	19	20	21	22	23
48	3	4½	6	7½	9	10½	11½	12½	13½	14½	15½	16½	17½	18½	19½	20½	21½	22½	23½
49	3	4½	6	7½	9	10½	12	13	14	15	16	17	18	19	20	21	22	23	24
50	3	4½	6	7½	9	10½	12	13½	14½	15½	16½	17½	18½	19½	20½	21½	22½	23½	24½
51	3	4½	6	7½	9	10½	12	13½	15	16	17	18	19	20	21	22	23	24	25
52	3	4½	6	7½	9	10½	12	13½	15	16½	17½	18½	19½	20½	21½	22½	23½	24½	25½
53	3	4½	6	7½	9	10½	12	13½	15	16½	18	19	20	21	22	23	24	25	26
54	3	4½	6	7½	9	10½	12	13½	15	16½	18	19½	20½	21½	22½	23½	24½	25½	26½
55	3	4½	6	7½	9	10½	12	13½	15	16½	18	19½	21	22	23	24	25	26	27
56	3	4½	6	7½	9	10½	12	13½	15	16½	18	19½	21	22½	23½	24½	25½	26½	27½
57	3	4½	6	7½	9	10½	12	13½	15	16½	18	19½	21	22½	24	25	26	27	28
58	3	4½	6	7½	9	10½	12	13½	15	16½	18	19½	21	22½	24	25½	26½	27½	28½
59*	3	4½	6	7½	9	10½	12	13½	15	16½	18	19½	21	22½	24	25½	27	28	29
60	3	4½	6	7½	9	10½	12	13½	15	16½	18	19½	21	22½	24	25½	27	28½	29½
men only 61	3	4½	6	7½	9	10½	12	13½	15	16½	18	19½	21	22½	24	25½	27	28½	30
62	3	4½	6	7½	9	10½	12	13½	15	16½	18	19½	21	22½	24	25½	27	28½	30
63	3	4½	6	7½	9	10½	12	13½	15	16½	18	19½	21	22½	24	25½	27	28½	30
64*	3	4½	6	7½	9	10½	12	13½	15	16½	18	19½	21	22½	24	25½	27	28½	30

Weeks of pay

* For women aged between 59 and 60, and men aged between 64 and 65, the cash amount due is to be reduced by 1/12th for every complete month by which the age exceeds 59 or 64 respectively.

† Exceptionally, employees whose 20th birthday falls within a few days of the Saturday of the week in which their employment has terminated may have the necessary 104 weeks' qualifying service after the week which began before they attained the age of 18.

Rights of
individual women

An individual woman has a right to equal treatment with men when she is employed on like work, i.e. work of the same or a broadly similar nature to that of men, or in a job which, though different from those of men, has been given an equal value to men's jobs under a job evaluation exercise.

The comparisons which a woman may draw with men or with men's jobs are limited to men employed by her employer or an associated employer. Two employers are associated if one is a company of which the other (directly or indirectly) has control, or both are companies of which a third person (directly or indirectly) has control.

In considering whether a woman is employed on work of a broadly similar nature to that of men, regard must be had to the frequency or otherwise with which differences between her work and the work of the men occur in practice, as well as to the nature and extent of the differences. Moreover, the work is broadly similar only if the differences are not of practical importance in relation to the terms and conditions of employment. The question of jobs which have been the subject of job evaluation arises when the following action has been taken:

(*a*) job evaluation has been carried out;

(*b*) the terms and conditions of employment are based on job evaluation;

(*c*) a job carried out by women has been given an equal value with jobs carried out by men.

It follows that the men and women concerned must have the same terms and conditions of employment.

Job evaluation is defined as being a study undertaken with a view to evaluating, in terms of the demand made on an employee under various headings (e.g. effort, skill, decision), the jobs to be done by all or any of the employees in an organisation. There is no requirement in the Act to undertake job evaluation, but where job evaluation has been carried out before the Act comes into operation (or afterwards) women may, as a result, have a right to equal treatment with men.[1]

In general, the Act takes the results of a job evaluation exercise as they stand and is directed to requiring the equalisation of the terms and conditions of employment which are based on the valuation. But, in one respect, the Act goes further than this in requiring the equalisation of the terms and conditions where a job carried out by women and a job carried out by men have not been given an equal value under a job evaluation exercise, but would have been 'but for the evaluation being made on a system setting different values for men and women on the same demand under any heading'. The presumption in the Act is that jobs of different content are evaluated in terms of the demand which they make on an employee under such headings as effort, skill, etc. There may be discrimination on grounds of sex in the process of evaluation, if two jobs making the same demand in terms of effort are nevertheless valued differently because one job is carried out by women and the other by men. In such a case the results of the exercise must be adjusted so that, to the extent that the two jobs make the same demand on the employee, they are valued equally.

Reference to an
industrial tribunal

A woman who believes she has a right to equal treatment with men because she is engaged on the same or broadly similar work, or on work which has

---

[1] This procedure, and other related ones, are further dealt with on pages 514 and 586 above.

been rated as equivalent under a job evaluation exercise, but whose employer does not agree with her, may, from 29 December 1975 onwards, refer her claim for equal treatment to an industrial tribunal for a decision. Alternatively, the employer concerned may make the reference to the tribunal. Other persons or bodies (for example a trade union or an employers' association) may act on behalf of the woman or the employer in making the reference. The Secretary of State for Employment may also make a reference to a tribunal where it appears to him that a woman has a claim to equal treatment, but that it is not reasonable to expect her to take steps to make the reference herself. A reference to an industrial tribunal may be made within six months of the date of termination of the employment to which the claim relates, as well as during the period of the employment. A woman may claim arrears of remuneration, but not for a period longer than two years before the date on which she refers her claim to a tribunal. Where it has been established that a woman has a right to equal treatment with a man, either by agreement between her and her employer, or by decision of a tribunal, it may be that the man is still being paid more than the woman or enjoys some other advantage in terms and conditions of employment. In such a case, the employer will have to show that the advantage enjoyed by the man is 'genuinely due to a material difference (other than the difference of sex)' between the woman's case and the man's case. Thus an employer may have a system of additional payments based, for example, on length of service or level of output or degree of merit. Provided the system of payment distinguishes between one individual employee and another, irrespective of the sex of the employee concerned, the Act does not prevent a man receiving higher pay than a woman as a result of such a system. On the other hand, the system must allow a woman to be paid more than a man if, for example, her length of service, her level of output or her degree of merit exceeds his. The system of payment must not distinguish between men as a class of employees and women as a class, and a difference of pay between a man and a woman must be genuinely due to a material difference between the man's case and the woman's case.

Collective agreements

A collective agreement which, on or after 29 December 1975, contains any provision 'applying specifically to men only or to women only' may be referred to the Industrial Court for amendment with a view to removing the discrimination between men and women. The amendments which the court may make are specified in the Act. The court must first amend the agreement to extend to both men and women any provision applying specifically to men only, or to women only. For example, an agreement may lay down a men's rate of pay and a women's rate of pay (which is lower) for the same category of work. In such a case, the effect of the court's first amendment would be that the category of work in question would have attached to it two different rates of pay both applying to men and women. The court must then eliminate the duplication by striking out the lower rate. The final result would therefore be a single rate of pay for the category of work in question, applicable to all the employees concerned irrespective of sex, and equal in amount to the former men's rate of pay.

An example of how this might work in practice is as follows:

Assume a collective agreement between Company X and Trade Union Y provides for:

Skilled male rate	£35·00 per week
Semiskilled male rate	£30·00 per week
Unskilled male rate	£27·50 per week
Women's rate (all classes of work)	£25·00 per week

The court would amend the collective agreement so that, irrespective of the sex of the employee, the rates would be:

Skilled work rate	£35·00 per week
Semiskilled work rate	£30·00 per week
Unskilled work rate	£27·50 per week

The women's rate would disappear.

An agreement may lay down a rate of pay for women employees in a particular category and make no provision for men in the same category. The court cannot extend the scope of a collective agreement to cover men (or women) not already covered by the agreement. In such cases, therefore, a rate 'applying specifically to women only' continues to be required. In these circumstances, the court is required to raise the rate of pay concerned to the level of the lowest men's rate in the agreement. An example of this in practice is as follows:

Collective agreement as above, except that only the male skilled rate at £35·00 per week, the male unskilled rate at £27·50 per week and a women's rate (for all classes of work) at £25·00 per week exist. The court would amend the collective agreement so that irrespective of sex, all skilled work was paid at £35·00 per week and all unskilled work was paid at £27·50 per week.

The original women's rate 'applying specifically to women only' would be still required for women employed on semiskilled work because there was no category for semiskilled men in the agreement. But the court would amend the women's rate which had to be retained to £27·50 per week, that is the lowest men's rate in the agreement.

The court is required to make similar amendments to collective agreements referred to it which lay down terms and conditions of employment other than rates of pay and which discriminate between men and women. A reference to the Industrial Court for a declaration of any amendments which may need to be made to a collective agreement can be made by any party to the agreement or by the Secretary of State for Employment.

Pay structures

The provisions of the Act relating to collective agreements apply also to pay structures, except that references to the Industrial Court are to be made by the employer concerned or by the Secretary of State for Employment. A pay structure is defined as meaning any arrangements adopted by an employer 'which fix common terms and conditions of employment for his employees or any class of his employees, and of which the provisions are generally known or are open to be known by the employees concerned'.

Statutory
wage orders

Statutory wage orders made under Section 11 of the Wages Councils Act 1959 may also be referred to the Industrial Court for a declaration of the amendments which may need to be made to an order to remove discrimination between men and women. The amendments which can be made by the Industrial Court are the same as those for collective agreements.

Persons covered
by the Act

The rights of individual employees to equal treatment extend to all persons employed under a contract of service or of apprenticeship. Exceptions are persons employed wholly or mainly outside Great Britain or, in the case of employment on aircraft, hovercraft or ships registered in Great Britain, persons employed wholly outside Great Britain. The provisions of the Act relating to collective agreements and pay structures affect all persons employed under a contract of service or of apprenticeship to the extent that their terms and conditions are dependent on collective agreements or pay structures. The provisions about statutory wages orders extend to all persons within the scope of such orders as laid down in the Wages Councils Act 1959 and the Agricultural Wages Acts. The Act applies to employees irrespective of age and to Crown employees (except the Armed Forces).

Employment matters
covered by the Act

The Act extends to all terms and conditions of employment. A woman having a right to equal treatment with a man on the grounds that she is doing the same or broadly similar work is entitled to a contract of employment which is in every respect the same as the man's. A woman having a right to equal treatment with a man on the grounds that she is doing work rated as equivalent under a job evaluation exercise has a similar entitlement to the extent that the terms and conditions of both are determined by the rating of their work under the job evaluation. Each separate provision in a collective agreement, a pay structure, or a statutory wages order may be amended by the Industrial Court to remove any discrimination between men and women in that provision. Certain matters are excepted from the general requirement of the Act that there should be no discrimination between men and women in regard to the terms and conditions of a woman's employment. So far as the terms and conditions of a woman's employment are affected by compliance with the law regulating the employment of women (for example, Part VI of the Factories Act 1961) the Act does not require the equal treatment of men and women. For example, men might have a right under their contracts of employment to work a certain number of hours of overtime. A woman could not claim the same right by comparison with the men if she was prohibited by the law regulating the employment of women from working the number of hours in question.

**Contracts of
Employment Act
1972**

The law of employment in relation to period of notice and written particulars was codified by the Contracts of Employment Act 1963. The Industrial Relations Act 1971 modified and extended these provisions and the present position is contained in the Contracts of Employment Act 1972. The Act covers two basic matters concerning employment:

1. the rights of employers and employees to certain minimum periods of notice;
2. the right of employees to certain particulars of the terms and conditions of employment and to any changes in the terms and conditions.

Who is covered?

All employees are covered by the Act which means any individual who has entered into or works under a contract with an employer for any type of work and where the contract of employment (either expressed or implied) is in either an oral or written form.

Who is not covered?

The Act does not apply to:

- registered dock workers engaged on dock work;
- seamen and fishermen covered by the Merchant Shipping Act;
- an employee who is the father, mother, husband, wife, son or daughter of the employer;
- part time employees who normally work less than twenty-one hours per week for their employer.

The notice required to be given by an *employer* to terminate the contract of employment of an employee who has been continuously employed for thirteen weeks or more is:

(*a*) If the period of employment is less than two years   one week's notice

(*b*) If the period of employment is more than two years but less than five years   two weeks' notice

(*c*) If the period of employment is more than five years but less than ten years   four weeks' notice

(*d*) If the period of employment is more than ten years but less than fifteen years   six weeks' notice

(*e*) If the period of employment is more than fifteen years   eight weeks' notice

The notice required to be given by an *employee* to terminate his contract of employment with an employer is a minimum of one week's notice after he or she has been employed continuously for thirteen weeks or more. This period does not increase with longer service as the employer's requirement does to the employee. In practice, however, the employer and the employee may mutually agree to give and receive longer periods of notice provided they are not less than the minimum required by the Act.

Minimum period of notice

The terms agreed between an employer and an employee are in many cases part of a collective agreement made in a particular company or industry. The Act does not alter these in any way except in the case of the minimum periods of notice which have to be given.

Written statement of terms of employment

The written details which an employer has to give the employee is essentially a record of the important parts of the contract of employment between them. The details have to be given not later than thirteen weeks after the employment has commenced. If any changes are made in the conditions the details of any changes have to be given not later than one month *after* the changes take place.

Details of all the conditions do not have to be given in the written statement but the employee must be referred to, and have reasonable access to, the documents which contain all the relevant details which might be in a company handbook or works rule book, or booklets on a company's sick pay scheme, pension scheme, etc.

An example of a typical company booklet detailing terms and conditions of employment is given in chapter 5 (see page 598).

What does the statement have to cover?

Under the Act the written statement has to give the names of the employer and the employee, the date when employment commenced and the following particulars:

1. The scale or rate of remuneration and the method of calculating it, covering if applicable, details of piece rates and overtime, etc.
2. The intervals at which remuneration is paid: weekly, monthly, or some other period.
3. The terms and conditions relating to hours of work.
4. The entitlement to holidays (including public holidays) and details of holiday pay, including any accrued holiday pay due on the termination of employment.
5. Any conditions applicable when an employee is unable to work due to sickness or injury and any provisions for sick pay.
6. The details of any pension or pension scheme.
7. The length of notice of termination which an employee is required to give and is entitled to receive.

The Contracts of Employment Act 1972 requires additional information to be given to employees, which was not contained in the 1963 Act namely:

1. The person to whom the employee can apply if he or she has any grievance about his or her employment and how any application should be made.
2. The steps in any grievance procedure which may be available to the employee.

How is the Act enforced?

If an employee is dissatisfied because no particulars have been given to him or her, the matter can be referred to an industrial tribunal. The tribunals have the power to determine what particulars are required in order to comply with the Act and may require an amendment to be made to the details or to substitute other particulars if it decides that this is necessary.

Although the 1963 Act made provision that if the requirements of a tribunal were not met with by an employer within one week of the request, the employer could be prosecuted, and if convicted, be liable to a fine of up to £20 for the first offence and up to £100 for any subsequent offence, this rarely happened. The 1972 Act, which completely repeals the 1963 Act, does not contain any provision for criminal prosecution and relies on the order made by an industrial tribunal being complied with by the employer.

Trade Union and Labour Relations Act 1974

The basic aim of the Act of 1974 was to repeal the Industrial Relations Act of 1971, while re-enacting the unfair dismissal provisions with some additional provisions. The Act provided for the abolition of the National Industrial Relations Court and of the Commission on Industrial Relations, with the Registry of Trade Unions and Employers' Associations. (The main features of the 1971 Act are recorded in the Appendix at page 644.)

The main features of the Act

There are seven main features of the 1974 Act:

1. It lays down provisions concerning the status and regulation of Trade Unions and Employers' Associations. It also gives protection to employees against arbitrary exclusion from Trade Union membership and provides that every member of a Trade Union has the right to terminate membership on reasonable conditions.
2. It provides legal immunities for those carrying out certain acts in either the contemplation or furtherance of an industrial dispute.
3. It abolishes the concept of 'unfair industrial practice' and restores the legal immunities concerning industrial disputes to the position that existed before the 1971 Act.
4. It provides for employees to be protected from dismissal for belonging to a Trade Union or taking part in its activities, and this protection is extended to members of an independent Trade Union.
5. It repeals the right not to belong to a Trade Union and the closed shop is made legal.
6. It repeals the provisions dealing with procedure agreements, agency shops, recognition disputes and the disclosure of information by employers, which were all provisions of the 1971 Act.
7. It repeals the registration provisions for Trade Unions and Employers' Associations, but all Unions and Employers' Associations have to conform to certain requirements concerning their rules.

The Code of Industrial Relations Practice established under the 1971 Act is also retained (see page 608).

Unfair dismissal

The Act extends the legal right which existed in the 1971 Act for employees not to be unfairly dismissed and the right of complaint to an industrial tribunal for any one who felt this right had been infringed. This Act makes a number of additional definitions of dismissal which are dealt with below.

Who is covered?

Under the Act the unfair dismissal provisions apply to all employees in all kinds of employment except the following:

Who is not covered?

The unfair dismissal provisions do not apply to:

● employees with less than 52 weeks continuous service with their employer (reducing to 26 weeks six months after the Act comes into operation);

- employment in an undertaking where, immediately before dismissal, fewer than four employees including the dismissed employee had been continuously employed for thirteen weeks or more either at the same place or at different places;
- registered dock workers engaged on dock work;
- share fisherman who are paid solely by a share in the profits or gross earnings of a fishing vessel;
- teachers in Scotland covered by section 85 of the Education (Scotland) Act 1962 which affords protection against unfair dismissal;
- Part-time employees who normally work less than twenty-one hours a week for their employer;
- an employee who is the husband, wife or a close relative of their employer—'close relative' meaning father, mother, grandfather, grandmother, stepfather, stepmother, son, daughter, grandson, granddaughter, stepson, stepdaughter, brother, sister, half-brother, or half-sister;
- employees who before the effective date of termination of their employment had reached the age of sixty-five (men) or sixty (women), or who had reached the normal retiring age for their employment;
- employees who under their contract of employment ordinarily work outside Great Britain. An individual employed on board a ship registered in Great Britain is regarded as ordinarily working in Great Britain unless the employment is wholly outside Great Britain of the individual does not ordinarily live in Great Britain;
- employment under certain fixed-term contracts.

What is fair dismissal and what is unfair dismissal?

The Act lays down a number of reasons which are fair in the case of dismissal. These are:

1. Dismissal on the grounds of the capability or qualifications of the employee for the job for which he or she was employed. 'Capability' is assessed by reference to skill, aptitude, health or any other physical or mental quality; and 'qualifications' means any degree, diploma or other academic technical or professional qualification relevant to the position which the employee held.
2. Dismissal because of the conduct of the employee.
3. Dismissal because of redundancy. Redundancy has the meaning given to it by the Redundancy Payments Act 1965. Accordingly an employee is regarded as having been dismissed because of redundancy where the reason or principal reason for his dismissal is that his employer's need for employees to do work of a particular kind has ceased or diminished or is expected to cease or diminish.
4. Dismissal where the continued employment of the employees in a particular job would result in either he or the employer contravening a duty or restriction imposed by law.

The Act introduces several new concepts of unfair dismissal in that 'constructive dismissal' is now explicitly covered in the definition of dismissal; it is unfair to dismiss an employee for joining or belonging to or taking part in the activities of an independent union, or for refusing to join an independent union but it makes it fair where a union membership agreement is in force to dismiss an employee who is not a member of the specified union or who refuses to join or threatens to resign from such a union except in the case of a person who objects on grounds of religious belief to joining any union, or who has any reasonable grounds for refusing to belong to a union. In cases of this kind the dismissal could be held to be fair.

Complaints to an industrial tribumal

Any employee who thinks that he or she has been unfairly dismissed has the right to complain to an industrial tribunal.

An application must be made by the individual against whom the action complained of is taken and the time limit for making the complaint has increased to three months with discretion for tribunals to hear complaints made outside this time limit where they consider that it was not reasonably practicable for the complaint to have been made earlier.

The operation of a tribunal hearing a claim for unfair dismissal continues under the Act in the same way as described below (see page 643), but the overall limit of compensation is raised. This limit is now 104 weeks pay for the employee concerned up to a maximum of £50 per week: this gives a maximum for any one award of £5,200.

Conciliation

The conciliation provisions which played an important part in the working of the unfair dismissal provisions of the 1971 Act are re-enacted in the Trade Union and Labour Relations Act 1974 so that it is likely that as with the previous legislation, a considerable number of unfair dismissal claims will be settled by conciliation before reaching the stage of a tribunal hearing.

Legal immunities

The general effect of this Act on legal immunities for industrial action is to return to the position which existed before the 1971 Act but with some amendments.

The provisions which are substantially unchanged compared with the position under the 1971 Act are:

1. The protection given against action for civil conspiracy.
2. The protection given for peaceful picketing.
3. The provision which prohibits any court from ordering those taking part in industrial action to return to work.

The provisions which are substantially amended are:

1. The immunity which existed before the 1971 Act for persons inducing breaches of contracts of employment in contemplation of the furtherance of an industrial dispute is restored.
2. The prohibition of actions for tort against Trade Unions and Employers' Associations is restored and extended to future actions, and in the case of Trade Unions the immunity is unrestricted.
3. No injunction may be granted without the presence of the defendant in a trade dispute unless all reasonable steps have been taken to notify the organisation or person against whom the injunction is sought and an opportunity given to them to make representations.

Collective
agreements

The Act reverses the position established by the 1971 Act when Collective Agreements were presumed to be legally enforceable, unless the parties specifically provided otherwise. Under this new Act, Collective Agreements will be presumed not to be legally enforceable, unless they are in writing and contain a provision to that effect in the Agreement.

Under the Act there are provisions for the incorporation of disputes procedures into individual contracts of employment. The Act also provides that in the terms of any Collective Agreement a restriction on the right of employees to engage in industrial action cannot be incorporated into an individual contract of employment unless the agreement is in writing and contains a provision specifically authorising the inclusion of such a clause and is an agreement to which no Trade Union other than an independent Trade Union is party to the agreement.

The Act gives rights to employees who are excluded from membership of Trade Unions whether by way of expulsion or by refusal of admission to membership. Any employee who considers that they have been excluded may complain to an industrial tribunal and every member of a Trade Union also has a right to give reasonable notice to terminate their membership of a Trade Union.

With the abolition of the National Industrial Relations Court, the Act makes transitional arrangements to deal with cases which were pending before the N.I.R.C. before its abolition (see the Appendix at page 651). Where cases were started before 30 April 1974 (the date on which the Act was published as a Bill) the cases are transferred to the High Court, but for any cases where the action was started after 30 April 1974 the cases are regarded as closed, if they were not completed before the abolition of the N.I.R.C. in July 1974.

**The industrial
tribunals**

The *industrial tribunals* have existed for over a decade, having been first established under section 12 of the Industrial Training Act 1964. Originally they had only one function, namely to consider appeals against levies made under the provisions of the Industrial Training Act. However, in 1965 with the coming into operation of the Redundancy Payments Act of that year, their work was considerably increased as the tribunals were made the authority for determining all cases that arose under the provisions of the Redundancy Payments Act, and they were given further responsibility in any matters which arose from the Contracts of Employment Act 1963.

Since 1965, various other duties and responsibilities were given to the tribunals in respect of certain provisions of the Docks and Harbours Act 1966 and the Selective Employment Act 1966, and the application of the Equal Pay Act 1970 will add to the duties and responsibilities of the tribunals.

In practice, during the period from June 1965 until the provisions of the Industrial Relations Act 1971 came into force on 28 February 1972, over 90 per cent of the cases which came before the tribunals were redundancy cases under the 1965 Act.

Until 1971 the tribunals had consisted of a Chairman who was either a barrister or a solicitor of 'not less than seven years standing', who was appointed to the panel of chairmen by the Lord Chancellor. The chairmen are either full-time or part-time and are paid fees for their services.

The President of the Industrial Tribunals who is responsible for the Central

Office of the Industrial Tribunals (which is a Government Department financed by the state) designates from the panel of chairmen various persons who then act as chairmen of particular local tribunals.

The other two members who, with the chairman, form a particular tribunal are appointed by the Secretary of State for Employment usually for three-year periods (which can be renewed) and are drawn from lists which broadly represent both employers and employees, so that some members are managers and executives in companies and others are, in the main, local trade union officials.[1]

Members of tribunals are all part-time and sit as required, according to the workload of the tribunal in their area. They are paid fees when they attend and travelling and subsistence expenses.

The main type of work undertaken by tribunals is determining cases concerning the rights of individual employees and cases of unfair dismissal.

How does a tribunal operate?

The operation of tribunals is covered by a statutory instrument—the Industrial Tribunals (Industrial Relations) Regulations 1972. The essence of the work and operation of tribunals is to ensure that they are *accessible* to all who need to use them and that they operate in an *informal* manner (although they are in effect courts dealing with important civil matters). The following is an outline of the procedures, both in making an application to a tribunal and in the hearing of a particular case.

The applicant has to apply in writing to the Central Office of the Tribunals providing name and address and the names and addresses of the person or persons against whom the complaint is made (usually the employer if a claim for redundancy payment or unfair dismissal is being made). There is a time limit of four weeks *after* the dismissal in the case of a claim for unfair dismissal or six months *after* the dismissal in the case of a claim for redundancy payment.

After receiving the application, the Secretary of the Tribunals enters the details in a register and sends a copy to the other party known as the respondent (usually the last employer of the applicant). The respondent has fourteen days after receiving the details to 'enter an appearance' which is the legal expression for giving a reply. This reply, which must also be in writing, must give the name and address of the respondent and must also indicate whether he intends to contest the application, and if so, the reasons. The details of the respondent's reply are then sent to the applicant.

In all applications under the Redundancy Payments Act 1965 details of all documents, etc. are sent to the Department of Employment (whether they are a party to the proceedings or not) because if the claim is successful the

---

[1] With the extension of the work of the tribunals under the Industrial Relations Act 1971 it was necessary to increase the number of tribunals so that now there is a tribunal sitting in every major area of population in the United Kingdom and many additional members were needed to make up the three required for each sitting of a tribunal. However, with the opposition of most trade unions to the provisions of the Industrial Relations Act, it became clear that trade union officials would not be prepared to serve as members. As a result, in October 1971 the regulations were amended by a statutory instrument so that members could be appointed by the Secretary of State for Employment 'from a panel of persons appearing to the Secretary of State to have knowledge or experience of employment in industry or commerce appointed by the Secretary of State, after consultation with such organisations representative of employers or of employed persons as the Secretary of State considers to be appropriate'.

employer will be entitled to claim half the cost of any redundancy payment awarded by the tribunal from the Redundancy Fund (see page 628 for details).

The Secretary of the Tribunals will then send the relevant papers to the local office in the town nearest to where the applicant lives and a date will be set for the hearing of the case of which both applicant and respondent have to be given at least fourteen days' notice.

All tribunal cases are heard in public unless they concern any matter which would be against the interests of national security for the evidence to be given in public. If either the applicant or the respondent wish to make any representations in writing, this can be done not less than seven days before the date set for hearing the claim and copies must be sent to the other party in the case.

At a Tribunal hearing any person entitled to appear can:

(*a*) make an opening statement;
(*b*) call any witnesses;
(*c*) cross examine any witness called by the other party;
(*d*) address the Tribunal before they give their decision.

The tribunal can require anybody giving evidence to give their evidence on oath or affirmation.

The tribunals do not normally award costs to either party whatever the outcome of the case, but allowances for attending for applicants, respondents, and witnesses can be claimed whether the party is successful or not and would normally cover fares incurred in attending the Tribunal and any loss of pay, etc.

To allow all applicants and respondents a hearing, they can either present their case themselves or be represented by a barrister or solicitor, or by a representative of a trade union or an employers' association or by any other person acting on their behalf.

The decision of the tribunal may be either unanimous or a majority of the members making up the tribunal. The decision and the reasons are set out in a document signed by the chairman and after being entered in the Register, a copy is sent to each of the parties (usually the applicant and the respondent).

Although most of the cases concerning claims for redundancy payments and unfair dismissals end with the decision of an industrial tribunal, appeals on questions of law could be heard by the National Industrial Relations Court during its lifetime, and a number of important 'appeal decisions' have been given on both these matters by the NIRC.

APPENDIX   The Industrial Relations Act 1971

In the industrial and social history of modern Britain the Industrial Relations Act of 1971 can be expected to figure as one of the major events of the period, despite its short life. In spite of good intentions for national benefit, few statutes have generated such widespread hostility and opposition. Indirectly, the 1971 Act underlay the miners' strike of early 1974 and was thus a contributory cause to the General Election of February 1974, unexpectedly bringing down an established Conservative government. Against this background, and because of influences on present and future patterns of industrial relations that have stemmed from this item of legislation, and the episode in which it was set, it seems pertinent to retain in this volume an outline of its intentions, provisions and procedures.

The basic aim of the 1971 Act was to improve industrial relations, in the setting of two or three years of strikes and unrest, especially unofficial action. The intention was to create and establish an orderly framework, with new standards for conduct in a number of employment matters, by providing new ways of settling disputes and grievances, by extending the existing system of collective bargaining and by giving a wider role to the conciliation services of the Department of Employment and the Commission on Industrial Relations. The Act also created a new judicial institution, the National Industrial Relations Court (NIRC) and extended the work of the Industrial Tribunals.

The main features of the Act

There were six main features of the Act:

1. A Code of Industrial Relations Practice. This code set standards and gave guidance about industrial relations. It was designed to be the principal means of raising the standards of conduct in industry.
2. New rights and protection for individual employees.
3. A new concept of 'unfair industrial practice'.
4. New methods of settling 'recognition disputes', and bargaining rights for trade unions.
5. A new system of registration for trade unions and employers' associations.
6. A new system of informal judicial institutions—the Industrial Court (known as the National Industrial Relations Court)—and an extended system of Industrial Tribunals. These institutions upheld the new standards and individual rights defined in the Act and heard complaints of unfair industrial practice.

All the provisions of the Act (except two concerned with information to be given to employees and trade unions on the affairs of companies) came into operation on 28 February 1972 and remained until the repeal of the Act on 31 July 1974.

In dealing with the labour law as it affected individual employees, the Act laid down the following rights:

1. To belong to a registered trade union without interference from the employer and to take part in its activities.
2. To refuse to belong to a registered trade union or an unregistered organisation (subject to certain exceptions).
3. To complain to an industrial tribunal against unfair dismissal.
4. To complain to an industrial tribunal or the Registrar of Trade Unions and Employers' Associations against unfair treatment by a trade union or an unregistered organisation.

Unfair dismissal

The Act established for employees in most classes of employment the right not to be unfairly dismissed and made it an unfair industrial practice for an employer to dismiss an employee unfairly.

Who was covered?

Under the Act an employee was 'an individual who has entered into or works under a contract of employment'. A contract of employment was a 'contract of service or of apprenticeship, whether oral or in writing'. The unfair dismissal provisions therefore applied to all employees in all kinds of employment except those listed in the following paragraph.

Who was not covered?

The unfair dismissal provisions did *not* apply to:

- employees with less than 104 weeks' continuous service with their employer;
- employment in an undertaking where, immediately before dismissal, fewer than four employees (including the dismissed employee) had been continuously employed for thirteen weeks or more either at the same place or at different places;
- registered dock workers engaged on dock work;
- share fishermen paid solely by a share in the profits or gross earnings of a fishing vessel;
- teachers in Scotland covered by section 85 of the Education (Scotland) Act 1962 which affords protection against unfair dismissal;
- part-time employees normally working less than twenty-one hours a week for their employer;
- an employee being the husband, wife or a close relative of their employer—'close relative' meaning father, mother, grandfather, grandmother, stepfather, stepmother, son, daughter, grandson, granddaughter, stepson, stepdaughter, brother, sister, half-brother, or half-sister;
- employees who before the effective date of termination of their employment had reached the age of sixty-five (men) or sixty (women), or who had reached the normal retiring age for their employment;
- employees who under their contract of employment ordinarily worked outside Great Britain. (An individual employed on board a ship registered in Great Britain is regarded as ordinarily working in Great Britain unless the employment is wholly outside Great Britain or the individual does not ordinarily live in Great Britain);
- employment under certain fixed-term contracts;
- employees covered by a voluntary dismissal appeals procedure which had been exempted from the unfair dismissals provisions of the Industrial Relations Act by an order of the Industrial Court.

How was dismissal defined?

Under the Act 'dismissal' meant the termination of an employee's contract of employment by his employer, whether with or without notice.

The Act provided specially for the employee who was given notice by his employer, but who wanted to leave before the notice expired. If, in these circumstances, the employee gave notice in writing to terminate his contract (the length of notice being that required under the contract) on a date earlier than specified in the employer's notice, he was still regarded as being dismissed as though the employer's notice had taken effect. The reason for dismissal in a case of this kind is that for which the employer originally gave notice. This special provision applied only during the period of notice which the employer was obliged to give under the contract and not during any additional period which he may have given voluntarily. If, for example, an employee were entitled to four weeks' notice under his contract, but was in fact given six weeks' notice, the special provision would apply when the employee gave in his notice during the last four of the six weeks.

For employees on fixed term contracts there were special provisions. If there was a contract and the term expired without the contract being renewed, the employee would be regarded as being dismissed within the meaning of the Act. However, a complaint of unfair dismissal could not be made by an employee if:

(a) the fixed term contract was for a period of *two years* or more and was made before 28 February 1972 and was not a contract of apprenticeship;

(b) it was a fixed term contract of two years or more made at any time if before the contract expired the employee agreed in writing to forego the rights on unfair dismissal when the contract expired.

What is fair dismissal and unfair dismissal?

The Act set out a number of reasons which were *fair* in the case of dismissal. These were:

1. Dismissal on the grounds of the capability of qualifications of the employee for the job for which he or she was employed. 'Capability' was assessed by reference to skill, aptitude, health or any other physical or mental quality; and 'qualifications' meant any degree, diploma or other academic technical or professional qualification relevant to the position which the employee held.
2. Dismissal because of the conduct of the employee.
3. Dismissal because of redundancy. *Redundancy* had the meaning given to it by the Redundancy Payments Act 1965. Accordingly an employee was regarded as having been dismissed because of redundancy where the reason or principal reason for his dismissal was that his employer's need for employees to do work of a particular kind had ceased or diminished or was expected to cease or diminish.
4. Dismissal where the continued employment of the employee in a particular job would result in either he or the employer contravening a duty or restriction imposed by law.
5. Dismissal for some other substantial reason which would justify the dismissal of the employee from his job.

Rights on trade union membership

The Act gave every employee in employment or seeking employment the right between himself and his employer or prospective employer:

1. to belong to a registered trade union of his or her choice;
2. to take part in the activities of a registered trade union;
3. to seek and hold office in a registered trade union;
4. to not belong to a registered trade union or an unregistered organisation of workers subject to certain requirements if an agency shop or approved closed shop agreement exists.

It was unfair industrial practice for any employer to infringe an employee's rights to any of the above.

Agency shop and closed shop agreements

It followed from the rights of employees that no employer could insist, as a condition of employment or continued employment, that an employee must belong to a registered trade union or unregistered organisation of workers, or to a particular registered trade union or unregistered organisation of workers. The Act therefore made 'closed' shop agreements unenforceable. It explicitly made void any agreement which precluded the engagement of an employee because he was not a member of a registered trade union or unregistered organisation of workers—that is, a 'pre-entry' closed shop agreement. An employee who had reason to believe that an employer had refused to engage him because of a provision in an agreement which had the effect of preventing the engagement of employees who were not members of or had not been recommended for engagement by a registered trade union or an unregistered organisation of workers, could apply to the Industrial Court for an order declaring the provision void. This meant that both 'pre-entry' and 'post-entry' closed shop agreements were made invalid by the Act.

It was however open to an employer, a group of employers, or a registered employers' association to replace closed shop agreements by agency shop agreements with one or more registered trade unions.

An 'agency shop' agreement made it a condition of employment for those covered by it (a) to belong to the registered trade union concerned; or (b) to make an appropriate contribution to the union, unless they had a conscientious objection both to belonging to the union and to contributing to it.

Under an agency shop agreement, therefore, an employee retained his right to choose not to belong to the union. This was the basic difference between an agency shop agreement and an approved closed shop agreement, for under an approved closed shop agreement an employee (unless, exceptionally, he was a conscientious objector) was denied the exercise of this right.

An employer could dismiss or discriminate against an employee who, in the absence of any conscientious objection, refused or failed either to join or make an appropriate contribution to the registered union designated by an agency shop agreement. An employer could also refuse to engage an employee who indicated that he was either unwilling to become a member of a union designated by an agency shop agreement, or to pay appropriate contributions to it in lieu of membership.

Approved closed shop agreements

The right of every employee not to belong to a registered trade union or unregistered organisation of workers made closed shop agreements unenforceable. But the Act provided one exception: the approved post-entry closed shop agreement. The Industrial Court could give approval only in the exceptional circumstances when the Commission on Industrial Relations was satisfied that a number of stringent conditions were fulfilled and an agency shop agreement would not meet the situation satisfactorily. The basic difference between an approved post-entry closed shop agreement and an agency shop agreement was that under the former an employee could not (unless, exceptionally, he was a conscientious objector) exercise his right to choose not to belong to the union which was party to the agreement. Where a post-entry closed shop agreement had been approved by an order of the Industrial Court, the employer could refuse to engage, dismiss, or penalise an employee who, in the absence of a conscientious objection, refused to belong to the registered trade union. Only a few approved closed shop agreements were authorised by the NIRC, covering merchant seamen and actors.

The position of conscientious objectors

Under an agency shop agreement any employee who conscientiously objected both to joining a registered trade union and to contributing to its funds could offer to pay an equivalent contribution to a charity. But under an approved closed shop agreement, employees could be exempted from the requirement to belong to the union provided that they agreed to pay an appropriate contribution to a charity agreed with the union. Any dispute with the union under either type of agreement could be referred to an Industrial Tribunal to settle:

(*a*) whether the employee's conscientious objection was genuine;
(*b*) which charity should receive the employee's contribution;
(*c*) the amount which should be paid.

Complaints to an industrial tribunal

Any employee who thought that he or she had been unfairly dismissed had the right to complain to an industrial tribunal. Any employee who believed that the employer or prospective employer had infringed his or her rights in relation to trade union membership also had the right to complain to an industrial tribunal.

An application had to be made by the individual against whom the action complained of was taken. It could not be made by anyone on his behalf. It had to be made within four weeks of the effective date of termination of employment where the complaint concerned dismissal. Otherwise it had to be made within four weeks of the date of the action complained of, or if the action occurred on more than one occasion, within four weeks of the latest date on which it took place. The Act defined 'the effective date of termination' as meaning:

(*a*) the date on which the notice expired, where the employment was terminated by notice, whether given by the employer or the employee;
(*b*) the date on which termination took effect, where the employment was terminated without notice;
(*c*) the date on which a fixed-term contract expired, where dismissal related to the expiry of a fixed-term contract without its being renewed.

Before an industrial tribunal heard a complaint of unfair dismissal or infringement of individual rights in relation to trade union membership, an opportunity had to be given for resolving it by conciliation. Copies of all complaints were therefore forwarded by the Industrial Tribunals' Office to a Conciliation Officer.

Where an industrial tribunal was satisfied that a complaint concerning dismissal had been substantiated, it had to first consider whether it was practicable and equitable for the applicant to be re-engaged. If so, it recommended re-engagement, stating the terms on which it considered re-engagement to be reasonable. It could recommend re-engagement by the employer or by an associated employer. It could also recommend re-engagement in the job from which the applicant had been dismissed or in another job which the tribunal considered suitable. It would consider the alternative remedy of compensation only if satisfied that re-engagement was not practicable or where a recommendation for re-engagement had not been complied with.

If an industrial tribunal found a complaint of infringement of trade union membership rights well founded other than one concerning dismissal, it could make an order determining the employee's rights or it could award compensation to be paid by the employer, or grant both of these remedies.

In assessing compensation the industrial tribunal would apply the same general principles as those applied in the ordinary courts. The Industrial Relations Act required that awards should be just and equitable, having regard to the loss sustained by the complainant because of the action complained of, taking into account any reasonable expenses necessarily incurred because of the action and any loss of expectations arising from it. An industrial tribunal could reduce the amount of compensation where the complainant provoked the action or contributed to it, or where the employee had not tried to keep his or her loss to a minimum, for example by attempting to find further employment.

Where compensation was awarded following the unreasonable refusal of either the employer or employee to comply with a recommendation for re-engagement, the industrial tribunal could increase or reduce the amount of compensation.

Compensation assessed in accordance with the principles outlined was subject to an overall limit. This limit was 104 weeks' pay for the employee concerned up to a maximum of £40 per week; this gave a maximum for any one award of £4 160.

Conciliation

The question of conciliation played an important part in the working of the Industrial Relations Act so as to give both parties in any dispute the chance of reaching a settlement without the need for the matter in dispute going to an industrial tribunal.

On receiving a complaint, the Office of the Tribunal notified a Conciliation Officer in the area, to let the complainant and the employer know of the services of the Conciliation Officer available to them. The Conciliation Officer would try to promote a settlement if asked to do so by the complainant and employer concerned, or if he considered that he could act with a reasonable prospect of success. Where employment had been terminated, the Conciliation Officer's primary aim under the Act was to try, in appropriate cases, to promote a settlement by way of re-engagement. Where this was not possible he could assist the parties to reach agreement on a financial settlement, if both agreed to this course.

The Conciliation Officer would normally act after a complaint had been referred to him by an industrial tribunal, but his services would be available at the request of either of or both the parties where a complaint of unfair dismissal or infringement of trade union rights could be made, but before such a complaint had in fact been made.

For conciliation to be successful, employers and employees had to be able to talk frankly and fully with the Conciliation Officer without fear that the information they gave might prejudice their case in a subsequent hearing by an industrial tribunal if conciliation failed. The Act therefore provided that information given to a Conciliation Officer in the course of his duty must be treated as confidential. It must not be divulged to the industrial tribunal without the consent of the individual who gave it.

Industrial tribunals

The Industrial Tribunals had a period of just over two and a half years in dealing with claims for unfair dismissal as provided for under the provisions of the Industrial Relations Act 1971.

At the time the 1971 Act was passing through Parliament, observers of the labour law situation considered that the restrictions of the Act in requiring 104 weeks of continuous employment with an employer (reduced to 26 weeks in March 1975 by the provisions of the Trade Union and Labour Relations Act 1974) and the requirement to lodge claims within 28 days from the date of dismissal (extended to three months by the 1974 Act) were deliberate restrictions advised by the Secretary of State for Employment in order to limit the number of claims likely to be made by employees.

A Department of Employment estimate made after the 1971 Act came into operation was for 10 000 claims for unfair dismissal being made in 1972, rising to 20 000 claims in 1973 and in subsequent years. Department of Employment statistics given for the period from 1 February 1972 to 31 December 1973 showed that in fact 14 547 claims were made by employees alleging unfair dismissal as determined under the 1971 Act. Of these claims about 50 per cent were either withdrawn or were settled by the conciliation provisions before reaching the stage of an industrial tribunal hearing. Of the 7 000 or so claims that resulted in a tribunal hearing during the two year period about 35 per cent were 'successful' in that the tribunal found that the dismissal was unfair within the meaning of the Act.

An analysis of the 2 450 claims that succeeded showed that about two-thirds resulted in compensation being awarded to the applicant. The re-engagement provisions of the Act were rarely used by the tribunals and only some 5 per cent of the decisions had a re-engagement recommendation. The average compensation awarded in cases of unfair dismissal rose from £175 in 1972 to £200 in 1973 and only ten applicants from the 7 000 that resulted in a tribunal hearing were awarded the maximum compensation under the 1971 Act of 104 weeks pay $\times$ £40 = £4 160 although it was indicated that a further five applicants received compensation 'in excess of £4 000' as agreed compensation in cases settled by conciliation before reaching the stage of a tribunal hearing.

The National Industrial Relations Court

The *National Industrial Relations Court* was a new legal institution and did not exist in the United Kingdom before the passing of the Industrial Relations Act of 1971. As already explained, this Act marked an important shift in the role of law in the field of employee relations and the Act provided a number of new legal concepts for which the National Industrial Relations Court was the legal institution to which various matters could be referred.

There were seven main matters which could be dealt with by the NIRC:

1. To consider applications for and against an agency shop agreement and to make the necessary reference to the Commission on Industrial Relations. To make any orders in relation to agency shop agreements.
2. To consider applications for and against the setting up of a sole bargaining agency and to make the necessary reference to the Commission on Industrial Relations. To make any orders in relation to sole bargaining agencies.
3. To consider any applications to remedy a procedural agreement.

4. To hear all claims of unfair industrial practices other than those under Section 5 of the Act (relating to trade union membership and activities) and under Section 22 of the Act (concerning unfair dismissal). These were dealt with by the industrial tribunals.
5. To hear complaints against an employer who had entered into an agency shop agreement and was in breach of such an agreement.
6. To hear complaints brought by the Registrar of Trade Unions and employers' associations relating to breaches of the rules of either of these bodies.
7. To hear appeals on points of law on decisions of industrial tribunals on matters of unfair dismissal and redundancy claims. To act as the 'appeal court' on these matters.

In practice, the majority of trade unions in existence at the time of the passing of the Act deregistered and became in law 'organisations of workers', the matters covered by 1, 2, 3 and 5 did not become a large part of the NIRC operation.

Matters under item 5 on unfair industrial practices formed part of the NIRC operation during its operation and in several cases substantial damages were awarded against 'organisations of workers', not for the unfair industrial practice which had been alleged, but for contempt of the Court in failing to answer the allegations made against them, notably in the case of the Amalgamated Union of Engineering Workers which refused to recognise the NIRC and did not answer the charges brought against them in the Court.

The NIRC ranked as one of the High Courts in the United Kingdom judicial hierarchy and when sitting had a judge of the High Court or the Court of Appeal as its chairman if sitting in England and Wales, or a judge of the Court of Session if sitting in Scotland. The chairman sat with not less than two other lay members of the court, so that like the industrial tribunals there were generally three people making up the court, although there could be more lay members and for some important cases the total number was five, including the chairman. In practice there was a permanent chairman for the court which sat in London and a chairman for the court which sat in Glasgow.

The lay members who had equal status in the court to the chairman, were appointed by the Lord Chancellor and the Secretary of State for Employment as persons 'appearing to have special knowledge or experience of industrial relations'. Some twenty were appointed, a number were retired Personnel Directors and there were, for the same reasons as in the industrial tribunals, no trade union officials who served as lay members of the NIRC.

How did the National Industrial Relations Court operate?

Like the industrial tribunals, the NIRC operated under the provisions of a Statutory Instrument—the Industrial Court Rules 1971, which came into operation on 1 December 1971, which was the date the Court was operative under the 1971 Act, until the Court was abolished on 26 July 1974.

Again, as in the operation of the tribunals, the emphasis was on the NIRC being *accessible* to all persons who wanted to use it, and its proceedings were *informal* compared with normal procedures of a High Court. For example, the chairman did not wear his High Court judge's regalia and barristers appearing for the parties in a case did not dress in the formal High Court dress.

However, in relation to the attendance and examination of witnesses, the production and inspection of any documents and in other judicial matters, rights, privileges and authority existed as in any High Court in England and Wales and as in the Court of Session in Scotland. These included the right to take action for any *contempt* of the Court, hence the fines which were imposed against parties involved in actions who do not obey its decisions, but like the tribunals, the NIRC was concerned with civil matters and not criminal matters and any fines were for contempt of the NIRC and were *not* similar to fines imposed by any court dealing with criminal offences.

The procedures were basically similar to those of the industrial tribunals with the position of the applicant and the respondent being similar in the proceedings except that the applicant could be an individual or a company or a trade union or organisation of workers and in certain cases could be the Secretary of State for Employment (as in the case of the application for a ballot during the dispute between the Railways Board and the trade unions representing railway employees in the 1972 dispute). Equally, the respondent could be an individual or a company or a trade union or organisation of workers. As the NIRC was a High Court, legal aid was available for the parties taking part in the hearing, but like the tribunals, the NIRC did not normally award costs at the end of cases except where the costs incurred by one of the parties to the proceedings were incurred by reason of the proceedings being 'unnecessary, improper or vexatious'. This was to prevent somebody incurring costs because of a frivolous or improper application being made which they have to answer and incur expenses in so doing. Costs could also be awarded if there has been an unreasonable delay or other 'unreasonable conduct in bringing or conducting the proceedings'. Although the NIRC acted as an appeal court on certain decisions made in industrial tribunals, either party could appeal against a decision given by the NIRC to the Court of Appeal or the Judicial Committee of the House of Lords as the highest court in the United Kingdom. In the first year of operation a decision of an industrial tribunal on a matter of an unfair industrial practice did go through all these stages until a final decision was given by the Judicial Committee of the House of Lords, which had the effect of changing the law on the responsibility of a trade union for the action of its members (in this case shop stewards in dispute with an employer).

*A review of
NIRC*

When the 'life' of the NIRC came to an end on 26 July 1974, after an existence of just over two and a half years, few people mourned its passing. As an attempt to deal with industrial disputes within the framework of the law as provided under the Industrial Relations Act of 1971, it failed; but in matters of individual disputes concerning individual employees, either in relation to redundancy payments or in cases of unfair dismissal, it performed excellent work in numerous decisions when acting as an appeal court in relation to decisions made by industrial tribunals.

A general assessment of the Court's work would appear to lead to the conclusion that either the labour law in the United Kingdom is inherently unsuited for the legal processes of a formal court or that the time had not yet arrived for employers and trade unions to act in a sufficiently mature way in dealing with their respective causes to accept the intervention of lawyers and the formal processes of the law which the NIRC had to follow. Even if both employers and trade unions claimed that they were amenable to a judicial interposition in respect of their rival claims, it might be that the courts themselves (in this case a new court in the form of the NIRC) might not have been seen to be sufficiently neutral during the changes being undergone in the development of a modern social democracy, such as are being experienced in the United Kingdom during the 1970s.

In retrospect, the NIRC was never given an opportunity during its short existence of convincing all its users of its impartiality. It was created by an Act of Parliament, which was bitterly opposed throughout its passage through Parliament as few Acts have been opposed in the twentieth century, finally to the point where some trade unions actually refused to accept the existence of the legislation which was the basis of the NIRC's operation and led to the boycotting of the Court, notably by the Amalgamated Union of Engineering Workers.

Despite its problems, there is much that can be usefully learnt from the short life of the Court. The informality of its proceedings and its deliberate aim to project its image with the public, by facilitating the reporting of its proceedings and its decisions and explaining its role, were all worthy features so often still absent in relation to the operation of the law in other contexts; and most of all was the desire of the NIRC to provide speedy justice, by being available at short notice to hear the parties in dispute, by sitting on occasions late at night, during the law vacations and even on occasions at weekends.

The NIRC is unlikely ever to be re-created in the form that it existed in from 1 December 1971 to 26 July 1974, but one may see at some time in the future a legal institution performing a role in the operation of labour law, but learning from the mistakes of the 1971 Act which created the NIRC.

Further reading

Barber, David, *The Practice of Personnel Management,* Institute of Personnel Management, 1970.

Bell, D. J., *Planning Corporate Manpower,* Longman, 1974.

Contracts of Employment Act 1972, HMSO.

Dale, Ernest, *Organisation,* American Management Association, 1967.

Drucker, Peter, *The Practice of Management,* Mercury Books, 1961.

Employment, Department of, *Training for the Management of Human Resources,* HMSO, 1972.

Employment, Department of, *A Guide to the Industrial Relations Act 1971,* HMSO, 1972.

Employment, Department of, *Code of Industrial Relations Practice,* HMSO, 1972.

Equal Pay Act 1970, HMSO.

Industrial Relations Act 1971, HMSO.

Likert, Rennis, *The Human Organisation,* McGraw-Hill, 1967.

Lupton, Tom, *Industrial Behaviour and Personnel Management,* Institute of Personnel Management, 1964.

Lynch, J. J., *Making Manpower Effective,* Pan Books, 1968.

Margerison, C. J. and Ashton, D., *Planning for Human Resources,* Longman, 1974.

McBeath, G. and Rands, D. N., *Salary Administration,* Business Publications, 1969.

McGregor, Douglas, *The Human Side of Enterprise,* McGraw-Hill, 1960.

Megginson, Leon, *Personnel: a behavioural approach to administration,* Irwin, 1972.

Miller, E. J. and Rice, A. K., *Systems of Organisation,* Tavistock, 1967.

Niven, M. M., *Personnel Management 1913–1963,* Institute of Personnel Management, 1964.

North, D. T. and Buckingham, G. T., *Productivity Agreements and Wage Systems,* Cahners, 1969.

Pardoe, Alan, *A Practical Guide for Employer and Employee to the Industrial Relations Act 1971,* Jordans, 1972.

Pigors, Paul and Myers, C. A., *Personnel Administration: a point of view and a method,* 6th edn, McGraw-Hill, 1969.

Political and Economic Planning, *Joint Consultation—Chocolate and Sugar Confectionary Industry,* NEDO, 1968.

Redundancy Payments Act 1965, HMSO.

Trade Union and Industrial Relations Act 1974, HMSO.

Woodward, Joan, *Industrial Organisation Theory and Practice,* Oxford University Press, 1965.

PART FIVE The finance and control function

by H. E. Betham

1 Management control—an overall survey

Recent years have witnessed a number of major changes in the basic conditions governing the earning of company profits in this country, or elsewhere. Some of these changes have come about through government action, others through the pressures of public opinion: their combined effect has been so significant that most businesses have undoubtedly had to rethink their overall objectives and policies. Some of these changed conditions call for comment here at the outset:

- There has been a marked increase in the view that public companies have an obligation to the public at large and to their employees, rather than looking solely at growth and increased profitability. Some company chairmen will be well aware that these opinions are frequently expressed quite forcibly at annual general meetings.
- The change to the 'imputation system' of taxation and the introduction of Value Added Tax have caused many UK companies to review and amend their marketing and financial plans and policies.
- Government 'counter-inflation' policies are without question the chief factors that have led to boards of directors having completely to rethink their company's growth targets and marketing strategies. There can be little doubt that a prices and incomes policy—whether enforced by legislation or social contract—will be here to stay for quite a while. With selling prices and profit margins controlled, management attention is being increasingly directed to new ways of controlling and, more important, reducing costs.

In addition to the problems created by these developments, many companies had already found that business life was becoming increasingly complex and that the combined effects of inflation and high interest rates could threaten the continued existence of even the largest company. Some companies managed to get back on to an even keel, others did not, and the unlucky shareholders are no doubt still waiting for a return on their capital.

All these aspects of economic life have highlighted the vital importance of the *finance and control function* in modern company management, and in the pages that follow an attempt has been made to illustrate some of the ways in which this function can contribute to the overall development and growth of the company, while at the same time taking into account the influential factors outlined above.

In doing this, with the inevitable choice needed on what to include and what to leave out, the author has decided to write about those matters on which a newly appointed financial director might be called to give policy decisions during his first year of office.

Assessment of costs and resources

Mention has already been made of the problems facing the majority of businesses today, with ever-increasing inflation on one hand, and rigid controls on prices and margins on the other. In these circumstances a newly appointed financial director is likely to find that before he has been at his desk for five minutes he is being asked by other members of the Board for his views on improving the company's control procedures, so that costs can be kept in check.

He will probably agree with them that the control of costs is of vital importance, and he may even remind them of Mr Edward Heath's remarks to the Institute of Management Consultants, when he declared that 'most needed in British industry today is effective financial control of costs', or of Sir John Partridge's remarks as President of the Confederation of British Industry, that 'growth, in real terms, will rest on our capacity to control costs'.

Before taking any action on cost control, it is probable the financial director will have a talk with his accountant. Discussions will not proceed very far before it becomes clear that it is useless to try to control costs in isolation, because costs incurred are a reflection of activities carried out and resources used. There is a need to review these activities so that an assessment can be made of their effect on the growth and profitability of the business. In other words, it is necessary to look at *the overall control of the business and not just at the costs.*

A reason why he will probably agree to make the subject of control in its widest sense his first priority is that it is capable of producing useful results in the short term. There may be other aspects of the business which are in urgent need of improvement, such as the capacity and efficiency of the plant, the personal qualities and technical skills of the management and staff, the reputation of the company with the general public, the quality, range and variety of its products, but these are all factors which, if judged to be inadequate, may take a number of years to put right.

At this point the new financial director may decide that it will be useful to turn over in his mind the various aspects of management control procedures that are common to any business. Then, after he has obtained more knowledge and experience of the business he has joined, he can decide which particular control procedures to recommend. From previous experience, he is perhaps well aware of the utter futility of trying to force the management of his company to accept a control system, however appropriate, that is thought to be unsuitable.

The nature of control

A business of any kind needs two different but interlinked types of control: operational and financial. Looked at as a combined management function, the term 'overall control', or 'management control', or even 'control' can be used.

Control in a nutshell means setting up an objective, deciding how to get there, and then making sure the goal is achieved. A more formal definition is *'Guiding and regulating the resources and activities of a business or any of its parts by means of management judgment, decision and action with the purpose of attaining agreed objectives'.*[1]

[1] This definition is in line with the one given analytically in chapter 2 of Part One of this volume (see pp. 12 and 35).

Reverting to the twin aspects of overall control, an example of operational control in a simplified background is provided by a man filling a bath, who wants to ensure that, when the bath is full, the water is at the right temperature. His actions can be analysed as follows:

Objectives. He decides mentally on his 'objectives', e.g. he wants a full bath, just comfortably hot.
Operating plan. In order to achieve these objectives, he decides on his 'operating plan', e.g. turning the hot tap fully on and the cold tap half on.
Control comparison. After a suitable interval—say when the bath is one-third full—he tries out the temperature of the water. He finds it too hot, so has to decide on corrective action.
Corrective action. His decision is then to turn the cold tap full on also.

His subsequent action will be to repeat the test when the bath is about two-thirds full. If he now finds that the water temperature is just right, he knows that further corrective action is needed, otherwise the bath will be over-cooled when full. Accordingly he turns off the cold tap one-quarter turn. A final test when the bath is nearly full confirms that this decision was a correct one.

Thus, in a simple process of filling a bath, three separate cycles of control are necessary, each cycle consisting of planning, comparing, deciding on corrective action. The interesting feature to emerge from this analogy is that corrective action is based either on a comparison of actual results already achieved with the corresponding expected results, or on a forward assessment of how the final results will compare with target if no further action is taken (see Fig. 5.1.1, A man and his bath).

On the shop floor, the foremen and supervisors will be exercising control in this sense in seeing that the work is running smoothly, that work orders are completed on time, that machine breakdowns are avoided by adequate maintenance, that material wastage is minimised, and so on.

Turning now to financial control, a man with money to spend can do several different things with it:

Fig. 5.1.1
A man and
his bath

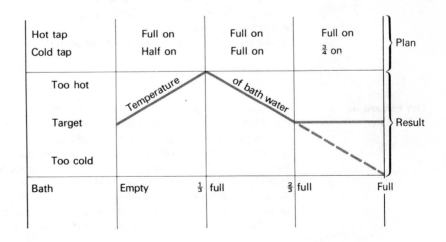

- He can leave it in the bank.
- He can spend it, e.g. on a world cruise or on repairing his car.
- He can invest it so as to produce an income by way of interest, dividends, or an annuity.
- He can buy something tangible, either to keep or for eventual resale, e.g. a motor car or a house.
- He can lend the money to someone else, either at a fixed rate of interest, or with a right to a share of profits.

Clearly, a man with a wide range of interests in life and with a limited amount of money available needs to exercise careful financial control if he is to get maximum benefit from it.

If the same man happens to be the proprietor of a manufacturing business he will find that his managers will be spending or investing his money for him, on materials, wages and salaries, plant and machinery, etc. Superimposed then on the need for operational control in the business is the need for financial control, to make sure that operations are carried out not only efficiently, but also at a profit; otherwise all financial resources would soon disappear and there would be little hope of obtaining any further funds from outside sources.

Translated into practical terms, this need to take financial control into account in carrying on the various activities in the business usually means carrying them out at the lowest reasonable cost while at the same time making the maximum use of the firm's available resources. Stated in this way, the problem of achieving overall control sounds reasonably straightforward, but unfortunately the decisions needed to maximise growth and profitability opportunities for the business as a whole may affect different functions in different ways. For example, the all-in cost of a product can be reduced by using cheaper raw materials and cheaper packaging, but if marketing management consider that these changes will have a harmful effect on sales the overall result may be a decline rather than an increase in profits.

There is therefore a need to control the various activities, transactions and resources of a business from the operational and financial aspects, from the point of view of the manager concerned, and from the point of view of the business as a whole. The ways in which all these aims can be achieved and coordinated are explained in later chapters.

An appropriate starting point for a survey of the various control procedures available to management is to examine in rather more detail the objectives of a business, so far as these can be expressed in general terms.

The nature of objectives

The overall objectives of a business may be briefly described as prosperity, growth and continued life. It is true that these somewhat materialistic aims do not paint the whole picture, and in many instances the management of a business might consider that these are purely subsidiary goals. For example, the directors of an aircraft manufacturing company might consider that their primary aim was achievement—achievement in building the world's best aircraft. In another case, the overall objective might be to provide services giving maximum value for money to the general public, and so on. Nevertheless, however valid these objectives may be, they cannot be used as the starting point for control because progress in attaining them must of necessity be a matter of opinion rather than fact. For control to operate effectively it is essential to be able to measure progress towards specific targets in factual terms, and the objectives outlined above comply with this condition.[1]

Prosperity

Taking the three objectives in order, the prosperity of a business can be measured in several ways. Leaving aside for the moment the nationalised industries, the general aim will be to earn a satisfactory annual profit, having regard to the expected return on the capital employed in the business. By *capital employed* is meant the total funds received from or belonging to shareholders and loan creditors, which will have been used either to acquire fixed assets or to provide the funds needed for working capital.

A get-rich-quick speculator operating entirely on his own will no doubt do all he can to *maximise* his profits and his ratio of profits to capital. He will be awake at night thinking of ways and means of increasing both. In the average business of today, however, it would be more accurate to state that the overall aim is to earn a *satisfactory* return. The directors or proprietors will decide what they consider to be a reasonable return, having regard to all the circumstances, and they will not worry unduly so long as this rate is actually achieved. Only in one respect will they be continually seeking to maximise profits, and that is in the maximisation of operating efficiency. Factors to be taken into account in assessing the target rate of return on capital will be the general level of interest ruling at the time, the economic climate, competitors' activities, and, in particular, the extent to which the company is expanding. This leads on to the consideration of the second basic objective—growth.

Growth

A young and expanding business will naturally consider that growth of turnover is the primary objective. All eyes will be on the trend of the total market, and on the share of the market which the business can secure and retain. It is true that profits are also important, because if sales were achieved only at a loss, working capital would soon be dissipated. Nevertheless, it is probable that the owners will be content with a lower return than they would hope to secure in the future. Profits ploughed back now by way of improvements to product or plants, or profits 'foregone' through reducing sales prices or increasing advertising expenditure, may be of critical importance in strengthening the hands of the management *vis-à-vis* the firm's competitors. The net result may therefore be an increase in immediate turnover, combined with an increase in profit of *future* years.

Over a period of years, the primary objectives of a business may change in emphasis. After a period of rapid expansion, the management may decide to consolidate the position won. The emphasis will then be on maximising profit through paying increasing attention to economy and efficiency. Later, when working capital has been replenished, the management may embark on a further period of expansion, with the emphasis on spending money to obtain more and more sales.

[1] These comments reflect, in terms of the practical business situation, the analytical presentation of the 'planning-control' cycle described and illustrated in Part One of this volume: see page 33 (and Fig. 1.3.1).

In view of the likelihood of this alternation of emphasis occurring from time to time, it is evident that one of the key points in any effective system of control is to ensure that everyone in the management team knows what the current objectives and policies are.

Continued life

Coming now to the third objective of 'continued life', it might be thought at first sight that so long as a business was prosperous and growing, this would automatically ensure continued life. However, it is always possible for a hitherto successful business to enter into a sudden decline, and there have been numerous examples of this during the last few decades. A major cause is lack of financial wisdom and control, caused perhaps by over-optimism leading to heavy purchases of materials or plant immediately prior to a severe slump in both activity and prices. Other causes are lack of care in providing for management succession, or inadequate planning ahead in the fields of research and development. These, however, are management rather than control problems, and in this Part we shall be concerned only with the financial control aspects.

All the remarks above apply equally to a nationalised undertaking, except that instead of aiming at earning a profit, they would hope to earn a satisfactory 'trading surplus'. The earning of such a surplus would then strengthen their hands against competitive undertakings because it could be used to finance additional capital expenditure without incurring additional interest charges.

Planning to attain objectives

There can be very little doubt that in the world today there is only one certain way of attaining objectives, and that is to draw up a carefully thought out plan detailing the decisions that have to be made and the steps that have to be taken to ensure success. In this context an interesting comparison can be made between the methods employed by a professional investment manager, looking after a wide-ranging portfolio of stocks and shares, and the method—or lack of method—employed by the average private investor. The professional investment manager will know that he is expected to build up the size and value of the invested funds under his control, and that he must demonstrate growth in both market value and income year by year. His whole future career may depend on his performance here. The way in which he will plan to attain his objectives is to agree in advance with his superiors the policy to be adopted, such as the proportions to be invested in fixed interest stocks, properties, ordinary shares and so on, and then to prepare a detailed plan how to carry out this policy, e.g. to build up over a period of months a 5 per cent stake in the XYZ Co. By way of contrast, consider the approach of the average private investor. He has no policy, no plan, and he usually buys a share after he has watched it rising strongly over a lengthy period, probably encouraged by newspaper tips or the comments of his knowledgeable friends. Unfortunately, large purchases of 'small lots' is frequently the signal to professional investors to realise their holdings, and inevitably the private investor finds that the price of the share he has bought is beginning to fall. After watching a steady diminution in value, he becomes discouraged and sells out all his shares, only to learn some months later that he sold out at the market bottom.

The marketing plan

Planning is just as necessary for the firm making and selling goods as for the professional investment manager. However, the question immediately comes to mind, who should draw up the plans? Can it be left to the managing director? It is hardly likely that he will want to be involved in the detailed work involved. If production management is asked to draw up the operating plans for next year, there will be a tendency for them to suggest a continuation of last year's pattern, with the maximum number of long runs and the minimum number of products. Unfortunately this may not result in optimising either sales or profits. With the majority of companies, there can be only one answer: marketing management must draw up a provisional marketing plan, and this is then discussed with production and financial management, and profitability of various alternatives assessed. When the marketing plan (further discussed in chapter 7) has been finally agreed, this becomes the cornerstone round which the firm's annual budgets are built up. Acting on these recommendations, the directors will have established a comprehensive 'marketing programme' in accordance with a fundamental principle of management in action (see Part One of this volume, pages 27–28).

Annual budgeting

The marketing plan may give quantitative targets, but it may also be expressed to some extent as written policies, courses of action and general aims. The next step is to build up a series of budgets which quantify the marketing objectives and the corresponding production requirements, both in physical and financial terms. The sales budget will enumerate the quantity and value of anticipated sales, the production budget will detail the output needed to meet these sales, and various expense budgets will show what the cost of all these activities will be. A summary budget will bring all the budgets together and highlight the resulting profit and loss.

A budget has been defined as 'a financial and/or quantitative statement, prepared and approved prior to a defined period of time, of the policy to be pursued during that period, for the purpose of attaining a given objective. It may include income, expenditure, and the employment of capital.[1]

In practical terms, the budget for a particular department will specify the quantity of output the department will be expected to produce during the year ahead, and the resources that management will need to produce this output—details of materials, man-hours, machine hours, power, steam, supervision and so on. To enable this departmental budget to be fitted into the overall picture, each of these resources will be costed out at the price or rates expected to be paid during the period.

It is important to note that the budget, even if subsequently broken down into months ('phasing' as it is called), is not intended to be carried out to the letter. It is merely the best possible estimate that can be made at the time of the policy that will be pursued during the forthcoming year or other budget period. As such, it serves several useful purposes over and above the normal benefits obtained from advance planning.

It provides a means of coordination of the activities of the business as a whole, it acts as a convenient means of communicating policy proposals and policy decisions and it provides a basis for subsequent control.

[1] *Terminology of Cost Accountancy*, Institute of Cost and Management Accountants, 1966.

Coordination

Dealing with each of these in turn, coordination is possible because for a brief period while the budgets are being prepared, everyone is prepared to look ahead and put down on paper what they are planning to do. Then while there is still plenty of time, a reasonable balance can be achieved between sales and production volumes, or between costs and profits. There will probably be no similar opportunity for complete coordination until budget time comes round again next year.

The whole exercise will of course be useless unless the budgets are soundly based. This means that in addition to basing the budgets on the marketing plan, full use will be made of economic forecasts, estimates of material price trends, wage rates, etc. Wherever work study engineers have been able to arrive at suitable standards of performance for factory or distribution operations, these will be built into the budgets.

Communication

Regarding the use of budgets for communicating policy proposals and policy decisions, there is in fact a two-way flow. Proposals usually start their life in the various departments which make up the scene of operations—at the coal face, to use a popular expression—and are then summarised, with the help of the accountants, as they pass up the management pyramid until they finally portray the overall effect of the detailed proposals. Top management may or may not make certain modifications in addition to the normal give and take necessary to achieve coordination; and the rubber-stamped proposals are then sent down the line again back to their originators. It is to be hoped that any significant amendments will be explained to those concerned, so that they have an opportunity to express agreement before the final decisions are taken. This will help to ensure that the budgets are attained.

Control

The way in which budgets are used as a basis for control is explained in chapter 3.

Short-term operating plans

Because so many factors have to be considered, the preparation of annual budgets usually has to be started several months before the year begins. As a result it may well happen that the budget is out of date by the time it comes into operation. In order not to reduce the value of the annual budget as a control base, it is often advisable to keep the original budget unchanged and to deal with the changed situation by establishing short-term operating plans, perhaps covering a period of three or four months. Thus the budget might have been drawn up on the assumption that selling prices would remain unchanged, but if the intensity of competition is suddenly stepped up, it may be necessary to make a drastic revision in policy, including a reduction in price and an increase in advertising. The effect of both these changes and of any revised ideas on future demand would be incorporated in the short-term plans.

In drawing up these plans one of the key factors to be taken into account is the *trend* of recent results, costs, etc. As illustrated in the example of filling a bath, the cumulative position to date may be in line with target, but the final result may be disappointing unless some immediate action is taken. In order to highlight the way things are going, it may be useful to recalculate from time to time the expected overall result for the year, basing such calculations on the sum of:

(a) results achieved to date—e.g. January to March;

(b) short-term plan for next three months—e.g. April to June;

(c) original budget figures for remainder of year (unless it would be more appropriate to project (b)).

Weekly or daily planning

The plans which have been considered above, annual and short-term, are aimed at establishing objectives and specifying policies to be pursued. They set the strategies and point out the routes to be followed. It is usually essential to supplement this planning with weekly or daily 'activity planning'. These plans will cover all the main activities: sales, production, maintenance, etc. Since they are prepared for the purpose of getting the job done rather than weighing up the financial aspects they will be expressed in physical terms, and they will be far more detailed than the longer-term plans. They point out the tactics to be followed and show just how far along the road one is to travel each day. They will be based on an assessment of the current order and stock position, or on short-term forecasts of future demand, and on expected production capacity. These plans should of course be drawn up within the framework of the annual budgets or short-term plans. In this way, the policies agreed by top management will find expression in the more detailed plans lower down the line.

The regulating function of control

Management, having agreed on annual budget and short-term plans, need to exercise the regulating function of control to ensure either that these plans are carried out or that they are appropriately modified where circumstances warrant it. In the last resort, where it becomes apparent that the original objectives cannot be attained during the period under review, then it is the job of the control function to point out the probable extent of the deficit at the earliest possible moment. The man looking forward to a hot bath does not want to wait until the bath is full before discovering that the hot water supply has run cold.

Assuming that the directors or proprietors of a business are dissatisfied with their existing methods of control and that they begin to seek advice on possible improvements, it is quite likely that they will be faced with a dilemma. They will find that there are a number of alternative methods, and a choice must be made as to the most suitable. Comments on some of the basic types of control are now given.

Visual control

In earlier days the head of a business might make a point of walking round on a tour of inspection each day. He would be relying on visual control for assurance that everything was going according to plan. Nowadays there are two distinct types of visual control: supervision of operator performance by foremen and supervisors, and control of mechanised operations through frequent inspection of a control panel. In recent years there has been a tendency in some quarters to suggest that top management ought to spend more time seeing what is happening on the shop floor or on the road, and less time looking at paperwork. It may be that the best answer in such cases is to reorganise and streamline the paperwork so as to improve its effectiveness for control purposes and to require less management time for its comprehension. This is one of the objects of the 'control by exception' techniques, as explained below.

On the other hand, there have been many instances where the visual control exercised by foremen and supervisors has been strengthened by suitable control reports in which actual performance is evaluated and compared with a standard. Control by instrumentation is more usually concerned with technical or quality considerations, but there are numerous examples of control instruments being used primarily for cost reduction. Examples are meters recording usage of power or steam in production operations, and machines recording machine stopped time. The information obtained from these instruments will subsequently be recorded in control reports and compared with standards, so that they are really a part of the measurement process in 'control by exception'.

| Control by exception (comparison with plans, budgets and standards) | The distinguishing features of this approach are frequent measurement and evaluation of actual progress, and comparison with the appropriate target figures. Management is called upon to make a decision on future action only if this comparison reveals an actual or expected divergence or 'variance'. This is the technique used by the man filling the bath, who used his hand as a measuring instrument. It is the technique employed in piloting an aircraft when flying by instruments rather than by eyesight. |

In measuring progress towards operational or 'growth' objectives (e.g. sales turnover or production output) comparison is made of results achieved to date with the planned results for the same period. On the other hand, when measuring progress towards the financial or economic objectives (e.g. trading profit for the period) control must be exercised both over the values earned (e.g. sales turnover or production output valued at predetermined unit costs) and over the costs incurred in achieving the sales or production outputs. This is necessary because profits cannot be attained directly in the same way that one can make a given quantity of finished products—they are the residue left over after all the costs of making and selling goods have been matched up with the corresponding revenue obtained from customers.

In practice, control by exception means comparing: (*a*) actual performance with expected performance, and (*b*) actual costs with target costs, in such a way that suitable corrective action can be taken if things go wrong. One of the first essentials is to break down the overall budgets into component parts, each part usually relating to a separate function or division of management. This procedure lends itself to delegation of authority and immediate responsibility. The head of each such function or division knows what his own particular objectives are, and he is given the means of checking up at frequent intervals to ensure that everything is going according to plan. Similarly, the overall control problem is simplified, because general management can look at a comparatively few grouped totals instead of at a mass of detail. They only need to delve into detail if one or more of the grouped results begin to get out of line with expectation, and the functional management concerned are unable to satisfy the central control that the position is being remedied.

Control by exception depends for its effectiveness upon a number of factors, for example:

- The validity of the target figures. Unless plans and control standards are soundly based, comparison with actual results may reveal little more than that the target figures were wrong.
- Both targets and actual results must be linked with managerial responsibilities—otherwise it will be difficult to make corrective action effective.
- Control reports must be issued sufficiently quickly and frequently to enable corrective action to be taken before it is too late. The general rule is that speed of presentation is more important than precise accuracy of detail.

Pre-control

Corrective action during a control period is sometimes impracticable, for example in the case of a firm unwilling to get rid of employees temporarily surplus to requirements. Where these circumstances are likely to arise, control action must be exercised during the budgeting stage rather than subsequently. For example, the best opportunity for making reductions in the cost of maintenance labour may be at the time the maintenance budget is agreed rather than later. In other words, it is easier to reduce costs if advance notice is given. Men can be switched to other work, or natural wastage can be used to effect reductions. Annual charges of all kinds must also be controlled before the commitments are entered into, because no subsequent control comparisons can lead to a reduction in these costs.

Control through motivation

It is important to remember that no method of control will prove effective unless the firm's employees are motivated in some way to achieve good results. If management is slack and apparently uninterested in achievement the operatives and staff will soon follow suit and work at the slowest possible rate.

Motivation is usually encouraged if everyone in the management team has an opportunity of taking part in deciding on target levels, and of subsequently being supplied frequently and promptly with the appropriate control results. Any attempt by top management to impose targets without any prior discussions with those concerned may have the reverse effect, and result in everyone trying to prove that the targets were wrong. This is the reason why so many early examples of budgetary control came into disfavour—lack of attention to motivation.

Control by *ad hoc* decisions

However detailed the annual and short-term planning, examples will always occur of unplanned incidents calling for management decisions during the year. These will usually be projects of one kind or another, such as a sudden request to acquire some new equipment which was not foreseen at the time the annual budget was prepared. This is another instance where control must be exercised before the commitment is agreed to and the contract placed. Control is in essence a check that the project being suggested represents the best way of investing the necessary funds.

Internal controls to guard against pilferage, theft and fraud

This is a specialised aspect of control upon which guidance can be obtained from those concerned with the audit of a firm's activities and transactions.

Corrective action

It has been shown (p. 661) that corrective action can be taken either when a divergence from plan has occurred, or when it looks as if a divergence will occur unless action is taken now. In order to establish the latter possibility, it is essential to report control results by successive periods as well as for the cumulative position to date. Only if this is done can trends be disclosed, and then projected to show estimated future positions. Corrective action may involve:

operational action, e.g. getting rid of operatives whose performance is below standard;

financial action, e.g. increasing the selling prices of certain products;

modifications to future plans, e.g. bringing forward a sales promotional scheme, deciding to step up production of a profitable line of products, etc.

Follow-up

Managers who have initiated corrective action of one kind or another will usually wish to check whether their decisions have been implemented, and whether the action has had the desired effect.

There is a further aspect of 'follow-up' to be considered—long-term improvements. Even if current performance is in line with budgets, management must be continually on the lookout for ways of effecting long-term improvements in productivity. If this is not done, a business may subsequently be at a disadvantage compared with competitors who have been more successful in this respect. In other words, for any given volume of saleable output, management should have their eyes firmly fixed on a downward trend over the years in the usage of resources, whether man hours or machine time, materials or power consumption, management time or clerical effort.

Technical research, statistical analysis, operational research and work study all have a part to play in effecting such improvements.

Long-range planning

The planning and control procedures outlined above are all related to a period of a year or less. Many companies, however, are finding that to an increasing extent they need to plan ahead for several years—three years, five years or even longer in capital intensive industries. This need can arise from purely marketing considerations, such as a proposal to build up export markets over a period of years; or from the essential need to plan well in advance if future demand is likely to call for factory extensions; or from the financial angle where advance knowledge of the years in which large capital outlays may be required can play a vital role in deciding whether to lock up surplus funds at a higher rate of return than can be obtained from short term deposits.

When first introduced long-range planning consisted of little more than a series of forecasts of sales and profits based on a projection of existing trends, but in recent years it has been found by many companies to be well worth while to draw up long-range plans in considerable detail. Each factor likely to affect future growth and profits is studied in depth, and the whole process of long-range planning (discussed in greater detail in chapter 9) becomes very similar to the compilation of annual marketing plans and budget, only extended over a longer period of time. The ultimate aim of most long-range planners is to be able to produce the annual plans and budgets as a byproduct from the longer-range plans, and the planning and control cycle will then appear as shown in Fig. 5.1.2, a specific representation of the overall cycle seen in chapter 3 of Part One (see page 33). When extended to cover the business as a whole, long-range planning is often referred to as 'corporate planning'.

Fig. 5.1.2
The planning and
control cycle

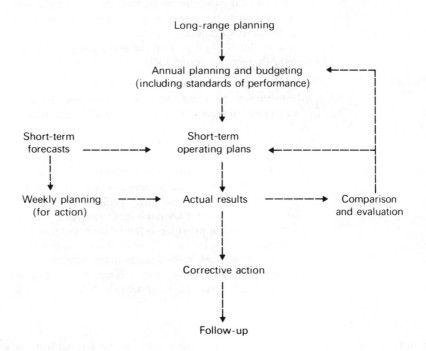

2 Organising for control and management information systems

Types of business firms

Having briefly surveyed the various kinds of control procedures, the newly appointed Financial Director will now wish to have a look at the basic characteristics of the business he has joined, so that he can decide what special points need attention in drawing up appropriate cost control procedures. He will also wish to look at other organisational matters, including his own role in the business.

First, with regard to the nature of the business, he can clearly recognise at least three distinct types of firms that sell goods:

an engineering firm, carrying out work to customers' orders, with prices based on cost plus profit, or agreed in advance on the basis of cost estimates;
a retailing firm, operating on a straight mark-up of products bought from a number of suppliers;
a manufacturing firm, making and selling standard products on the basis of a list price issued periodically.

He decides that it will be worth while to jot down on paper what *sort* of cost information he would have to collect and circulate to management, taking each type of company in turn, so that he can profit by the comparison.

Engineering firm

The Financial Director recalls from previous experience that the cost control system must be closely linked with the cost estimating system. Skilled estimators will work out how much material and how many machine hours etc. will be required for each job, and these will have to be turned into cost estimates by applying predetermined cost rates. Actual job costs will be compared with these estimates, either at the end of the job, or at various stages of the work in the case of major jobs, and these reviews may in turn be used to modify future cost estimates, or as pointers for finding cheaper methods of carrying out the work in future.

Retail firm

The cost of each article sold will be known from reference to the suppliers, invoices, and the mark-up will be based on these costs. Losses may occur as the result of pilferage by customers or staff, and these hidden costs will be reported to management as a byproduct of an effective stock control system. Selling, distribution and administrative costs will be collected by departments, and controlled by comparison with previous years' figures, or with previously agreed budgets.

Manufacturing firm

The Financial Director has already had a quick look round the company he has joined, and has seen a number of departments, each turning out a different product, with significant fluctuations in the volume of output each day. He has also examined the price lists at which these products are sold, and soon realises that the basis for any satisfactory control over production costs must be a link of costs with volume of output—in other words expressing the costs on a per unit of output basis, so that these can in turn be compared with selling prices, and the resulting gross margins assessed.

He realises that many costs in the factory and elsewhere in the business cannot be controlled in this way. The costs of maintaining the factory grounds, or of paying office salaries will in no way be affected by fluctuations in the daily volume of output. He is aware that, as is the case with the retail company's similar expenditure, the usual method of controlling such costs is to compare this year's expenditure with last year, or with a previously agreed budget, but he can see that further analysis will be needed, if he is to satisfy his Board that no excess expenditure is being incurred.

Size and structure

Having reviewed these three basic types of industry, the Financial Director now finds he needs to answer another set of questions before he can frame any recommendations for cost control:

- How large is the business? small family firm? medium size public company? multinational?
- How is it organised from a management structure and profit reporting point of view? by function? by product group? by region?

Size is a question of fact that should present no difficulty in answering. The size of the firm can affect the methods used in collecting and reporting cost and other management information. Obviously the use of a computer is more likely to be considered in the larger organisations. The size of the firm also has an effect on the way in which it is organised, and this aspect is considered below.

Management structure and profit reporting

In deciding to look at the company's management and profit reporting structure, the financial director is aware already from his preliminary review of control procedures that the only satisfactory way of controlling costs is to compare actual costs with predetermined target costs levels, whether in the form of budgets or standard costs. He is also aware that in setting these target cost-levels, it is not just a question of reducing costs to their lowest possible level, but is more a matter of eliminating unnecessary costs that could be avoided without prejudicing the marketability of the company's products or the goodwill of its labour force. He knows from his previous experience of the conflicts of interest that can occur between different functions of management, and how this causes difficulties in agreeing appropriate cost targets. For example, production management may point out the economies that would result from using less elaborate packaging, or reducing the number of varieties, while marketing management might strongly resist either of these moves, if they consider the changes would mean accepting lower selling prices or market shares.

Who then can resolve these conflicts of interest, and set the appropriate cost targets? There can only be one answer—whoever is directly responsible for the profitability of that part of the business. In the case of a small business, this means the owner or proprietor, but in the medium sized public company which the Financial Director has joined, some means of dividing up profit responsibility over the senior directors and executives becomes essential, otherwise the Chairman or Managing Director would be overwhelmed with decision making.

It is probable that more discussions have taken place in board rooms about the best way of dividing up profit responsibility than about any other comparable topic. There can be no general answer, and each company must be considered on its merits.

Single product companies

Taking first the case of a single product company, the management structure is likely to be on functional lines, e.g. as illustrated in Fig. 5.2.7 (see page 679). If the company is mainly dependent on its marketing management for keeping abreast of competitors and fostering the growth of the company, it may be reasonable to regard marketing management as profit responsible, and to look to production management to supply the required output at agreed target prices (Fig. 5.2.1). Any excess of actual production costs over these target figures would be regarded as a charge on the company profits and not as a deduction from profits on marketing.

If on the other hand access to raw materials or skill in manufacture is the key to the company's prosperity, then it may be appropriate to regard production management as profit responsible, and to set a target cost level to cover the costs of marketing and selling (Fig. 5.2.2).

Fig. 5.2.1
Marketing-oriented company

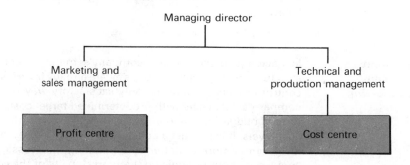

Multiproduct companies

The alternative approaches become rather wider when considering a larger company making several groups of products, and either possessing several factories or selling in different geographical markets.

If the company is organised functionally (Fig. 5.2.3), then the same considerations apply as set out above.

Fig. 5.2.2
Production-
oriented
company

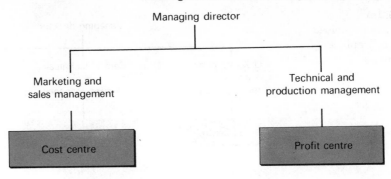

Fig. 5.2.3
Company organised
functionally

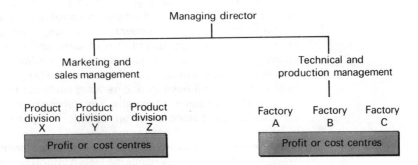

Where organisation is by product division the manager of each division will be held responsible for profits (Fig. 5.2.4).

A third approach arises when organisation is on a geographical sales basis (Fig. 5.2.5).

A variation of this organisation structure is sometimes seen when marketing management is divided up, not by geographical regions, but by type of sales outlets.

Fig. 5.2.4
Company organised
by product division

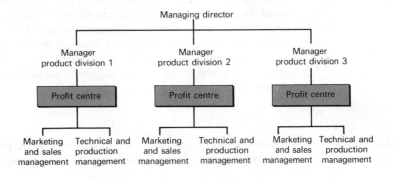

Fig. 5.2.5
Company organised
on a geographical
sales basis

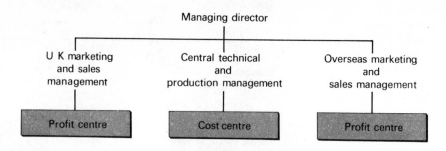

Management information

The financial director has now reviewed the various concepts of control, and given thought to the ways in which the company can be organised so as to pinpoint profit responsibility, and thus provide the basis for setting cost targets. By now he realises that the proposed cost control system will be part of a wider system of management information, which will give details not only of costs and cost targets, but also of sales and production volumes, sales prices, profit margins, and last but not least, profits—all arranged to coincide with the management structure that is eventually agreed for his company. At a later stage, he will have to decide what methods to use to produce all this information, whether manually, by accounting machines, by 'mini-computers', by having time on outside computers, or by installing the company's own main frame computer.

Before reaching this stage, he has to design the system in outline, but again drawing on previous experience, he feels it important to set down on paper the desirable characteristics of an effective system of management information—characteristics which lead to such a system being *used* by management, rather than being nothing more than an accountant's plaything. Here are some of the guide lines he recorded.

Simplicity of presentation

The first essential is to find out the kind of information which the key executives of the business expect to receive. A highly sophisticated system of management information with a mass of data circulated at frequent intervals is unlikely to be welcomed by a Board of Directors that prefers to manage the business by watching a few key figures. Simplicity in presentation should always be the aim, and in practical terms a compromise has to be struck between giving too much information on the one hand, and too little on the other. In the first case, important facts may be lost sight of through a natural disinclination to wade through page after page of figures. In the second case, if only a few figures are presented, these of necessity become averages, and once again important trends affecting only part of the business may be missed. The use of 'control by exception' as described in chapter 1, helps to simplify reporting procedures.

Method of presentation

The actual method of presentation is important. At one time, the chief debate was whether to present figures to the Board in a columnar form or whether to make a greater impact by plotting them on charts. Nowadays management of all kinds are gradually getting used to receiving much more information about the activities under their control, and with the growing use of computers, a computer printout is gradually becoming the more usual method of presentation.

Timing of information reports

Detailed information supplied to shareholders of a company in any year usually relates to the previous year, with comparative figures for the preceding year.

Information for management needs to cover a wider time span, and to be available at a much earlier date, and at more frequent intervals. To an increasing extent, company managements are studying the figures relating to:

(a) the probable outcome of the current year, i.e. a continuous updating of the latest forecast as to the year's sales, costs and profits:
(b) next year's plans and objectives (budgets);
(c) provisional plans for future years—particularly where capital expenditure on extensions, additions, etc. is likely to be spread over several years.

At the same time, comparison with previous years is still important because only in this way can long-term trends affecting the business be determined.

Management information reports

Anyone who has ever investigated and written down a comprehensive list of all management information reports circulating in a business, will know that management is invariably surprised at the number and variety of reports circulating on a regular basis. It is usually necessary to carry out a ruthless pruning exercise, to limit the circulation of reports to those who can make use of the information, and to cut out duplicated or overlapping reports. In other words, there should be a systematic review of the need for information, and of the best way of filling these needs. The introduction of computers in a business will lead to studies by systems analysts, but the management of the business must still decide which information they really need.

Fig. 5.2.6
Pyramid of control

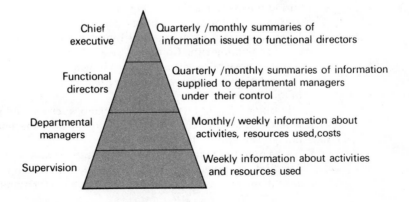

Chief executive — Quarterly /monthly summaries of information issued to functional directors

Functional directors — Quarterly /monthly summaries of information supplied to departmental managers under their control

Departmental managers — Monthly/ weekly information about activities, resources used, costs

Supervision — Weekly information about activities and resources used

Pyramid of
control

One of the long established concepts in building up a system of management information is known as the 'Pyramid of Control' (Fig. 5.2.6). By summarising information in this way, those at the top can avoid being issued with too much detailed information, but if key figures show that some aspects of the company's operations are getting out of line, it is always possible to obtain further information from the lower levels of management.

Responsibility
accounting

Full use should be made of the concept of 'responsibility accounting', which states that there is little merit in regularly issuing cost information to management unless the same management accepts responsibility for these costs and is in a position to take corrective action if they get out of line with target. This means that any cost document that contains a number of apportionments may be useful in showing up the cost of products, but may be useless as an instrument of control, since it will automatically relate to a mixture of management responsibilities.

The role of the
Financial Director

The words 'Finance and control function' used as a title to this Part are short titles covering the whole range of functions that the top financial man in a business may look after. Usually the function includes accounting and costing, annual budgeting and long range planning, data processing and administrative services, as well as the management of finance.

In the UK the term 'Financial Director' is probably used most frequently to describe the man at the top of this function, and will be used as such in this Part, although in some companies or countries, other titles such as Controller, Administrative Director, Commercial Director, may be used instead.

It is nowadays unlikely that whoever holds this post in any particular instance will have obtained experience in all the functions under his control on the way to the top. He may have worked his way up in the firm initially as the cost accountant and subsequently the management accountant. It is equally possible that he may have joined the business from the world of finance, or that his background may be economics, statistics, or operational research. Ideally any gaps or weaknesses in his experience will need to be compensated by making sure that his supporting staff supply the necessary expertise.

A typical organisation structure for this function in a medium sized manufacturing business is shown in Fig. 5.2.7.

Many variations on this pattern will of course be found in practice. In some firms, corporate planning may report direct to the chairman, and in large public companies the Company Secretary will also report direct to the Board. Another possibility is for the chief buyer to report to the Financial Director, particularly where the value of raw materials forms a relatively low proportion of total costs.

In other types of business undertaking, such as trading or agency concerns where the production function is non-existent, the financial role will in the main be similar to that set out above.

As a member of the Board of Directors the Financial Director plays his part in deciding on objectives and policies and exercising control. As a senior executive of the company he has responsibility for managing the departments

Fig. 5.2.7
Structure of
Structure for
financial control

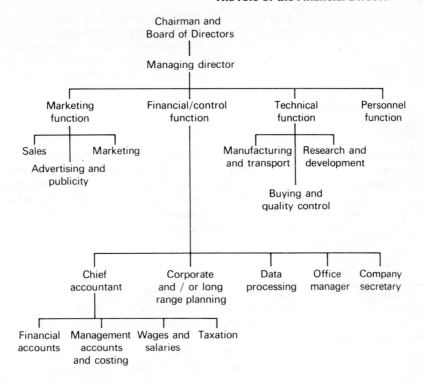

under his control—their organisation, staffing and activities. His staff will look to him to guide them in determining their objectives, in defining and agreeing the methods they should use, and in allocating to them adequate resources to carry out their tasks. Like any other manager, he must learn how to lead and direct them, to motivate and control.

Turning now to the functional rather than the management aspects of his job, primary responsibilities can be grouped under nine headings, as set out in the following paragraphs:

1. Reporting on results

The traditional role of the financial/accounting function has always been the reporting in financial terms of results achieved for the previous year, or other period. Money is the one common denominator applying to all business transactions, and the accountant by recording, classifying and summarising is able to work out the value of total sales turnover, and the costs incurred in achieving these. By matching costs with values, after taking into account the value of unfinished work at the beginning and end of the period, the key figure of profit achieved is arrived at.

2. Reporting on funds and their deployment

This covers reporting on the relationship between the various kinds of funds obtained by the business (shareholders' funds, loan capital, credit from suppliers, etc.) and the way in which these funds have been deployed (in buying land, buildings or plant, or in providing working capital for use in running the business). Since this relationship is constantly changing as sales are made or cash is received or spent, this relationship must of necessity be reported at a specific date, and the 'balance sheet' will invariably be prepared as at the last day of the year or other period for which profits have been calculated.

3. Providing information to management

To an increasing extent the financial/accounting function provides assistance to all levels of management in supplying quantitative and/or financial data, either at regular intervals or on an ad hoc basis, as aids to planning, decision making and control. The growing use of computers has played an important part in meeting these requirements and this function will usually be part of the financial director's responsibilities.

4. Assisting in the development of overall planning and control

One of the primary reasons for low profitability and static or limited growth in British industry during recent decades has been the tendency for the various functions of the business to operate as far as possible independently of each other. Marketing decisions will be taken with a view to maximising sales, without prior consultation with production people, and production decisions will be taken on the assumption that there should be no difficulty in selling new products regardless of cost. Similarly the administrative function may decide that information called for by other sides of the business is too costly or troublesome to produce, regardless of the influence which such information might have on the overall growth of the business.

One of the first steps taken to remedy these weaknesses was the introduction of budgetary planning and control. Annual budgets covering all sides of the business can be drawn up, setting the objectives to be achieved and detailing the costs and resources required to achieve them. As these budgets are prepared well in advance of their implementation, there is time to ensure that functional objectives are integrated in such a way as to optimise the overall development of the business. Overall control is similarly obtained by comparison of actual results against budgets.

Further developments in recent years have been the introduction of corporate (or long-range) planning, in which the objectives and strategies of the business are worked out in relation to resources available for periods of five years ahead or longer. This detailed look at the future becomes particularly important where heavy capital expenditure spread over two or three years will be needed before results can be obtained.

The need to plan for optimum profits while at the same time conserving the resources employed in earning these profits has been recognised by the stock exchange, the professional accountancy bodies, and the more enlightened public companies by highlighting the trend of earnings per share. Budgets, overall control, long-range plans, earnings per share, are the responsibility of the Board as a whole, but the financial/accounting function should normally take the lead in setting up the procedures and in coordinating the figures involved.

5. Drawing the attention of the Board to problem areas

During his attendance at Board meetings, the Financial Director may be called upon from time to time to give specialist advice on matters falling within his particular expertise. He should also be continually on the lookout for information, derived either from external sources or from the firm's own management information system, which will enable him to alert the Board to possible problems ahead. Similarly he may have to sound a warning note if decisions are taken either by the Government or by his own management which in his view will lead to future difficulties. An example of this is the need to work out detailed requirements for new taxation, such as Value Added Tax.

6. Management of finance

The Financial Director will be expected to advise, or know where to obtain specialised advice, on all matters in the financial field. These might include raising additional capital, investing surplus funds, or warding off takeover bids.

At all times but particularly during periods either of trade depression or of excessive expansion, he must keep a watchful eye on *liquidity*. He must alert his colleagues immediately if he considers there is a risk of liquidity problems arising, i.e. difficulties in meeting liabilities without recourse to selling assets. It is to be hoped that he never has to warn them of possible insolvency, where liabilities cannot be met even by selling assets.

7. Statutory and other requirements

Due attention must be given to the various requirements affecting the preparation of annual accounts and other returns. Some of these requirements are statutory, e.g. commitments under the Companies Act, others are imposed by the Stock Exchange, or the Accounting Standards Steering Committee (a joint committee set up by the major professional accounting bodies to establish standard accounting practice for reporting published results).

8. Taxation

Significant contributions to the net profits available for distribution as dividends or retention within the business can be made by ensuring that policy decisions taken by the company do not lead to a disproportionate increase in taxation. This is particularly important in view of recent legislation, or where taxation computations are complex due to the existence of subsidiary companies or of overseas branches.

9. Administrative duties

While some of the functions outlined above may rank as the highest priority, the need to keep administrative procedure running smoothly and economically should not be underestimated. The term 'administrative' is used here to include all the usual administrative accounting and clerical services, and it also includes such important matters as safeguarding the company's assets.

3 Costing, standard costing and budgetary control

The newly appointed Financial Director has carried out a broad survey of control methods, and he has looked at some of the ways of organising for cost control and management information systems. He now decides that it is essential for him to sharpen up his knowledge of the actual methods of costing available, with particular reference to standard and marginal costing. He also wants to remind himself of the steps to be taken in introducing budgetary control, and of the way in which budgeting links up with standard costing.

As indicated in chapter 2, the Financial Director's previous experience with costing methods has been in connection with engineering firms and their 'job costing' procedures. Accordingly he decides to start his investigation by comparing these procedures with the 'process costing' he expects to find necessary in his new employment.

Job costing

This is the basic costing method used by firms that make and sell something or provide a service as and when an order is received from a customer. In each case the price may be negotiated in advance, or based on the actual cost incurred with an addition for profits. Since any one order is likely to differ from all other orders received, the basic requirement of the system is to be able to identify the cost of *each order*. This makes it an expensive system to operate.

A typical example of a firm needing to use job costing is that of a jobbing builder or decorator. Customers may agree to pay for the work done after the job has been completed, on the basis of the time taken, or alternatively they may ask for an advance estimate of the price of the work, which they agree to pay (and the builder agrees to accept) whatever the actual cost of the job turns out to be. In either case it is clearly essential for the builder to be able to work out accurately the actual cost of each job, either as a basis for charging the customer, or as a check that the estimate was reasonable. Many small businesses have been forced into bankruptcy through using unreliable costing methods that have resulted in cost estimates and contract prices being fixed below the cost of carrying out the work. On the other hand, there is an equal danger of being forced out of business by overestimating costs and so being undercut by competitors with better costing systems.

The calculation of job costs involves two separate operations:

1. Identifying and collecting the 'out-of-pocket' costs directly incurred on the job. These will include labour costs of the men employed to carry out the work, materials used and expenses directly incurred on the job. The total of these payments (*direct labour, direct materials, direct expenses*) is often described as the 'prime-cost' of the job.

2. Adding to the prime cost an appropriate proportion of the firm's overhead expenses, including supervision, maintenance and depreciation of plant, administrative costs, etc. The method usually adopted for doing this is to express the total overhead costs as a percentage of the direct labour costs or alternatively to work it out as a cost per direct labour hour:

Last year

Total direct labour hours worked	10 500 hours
Total direct wages paid	£7 500
Total overhead expenses	£5 250

Overheads represent 50*p* per direct labour hour worked or 70 per cent addition to cost of direct labour.

Cost estimating

In practice, it is necessary to estimate in advance both the overhead charges and the total direct labour figures, since it is clearly impracticable to await the year end before sending out any estimates or bills for work done. It will rarely happen that these advance estimates coincide with the actual costs when eventually determined, and as a result the use during the year of these predetermined overhead rates will inevitably give rise to an over- or under-recovery of costs.

In the above example, the owner of the business decided that a reasonable estimate for next year would be:

Total direct labour hours to be worked	12 000 hours
Total direct labour wages to be paid	£9 000
Total overhead expenses	£6 480

and he accordingly works out that next year he should recover all overhead costs by allowing 54*p* per direct labour hour, or adding 72 per cent to the direct labour cost. He in fact decides to use the latter ratio and also to add a further 28 per cent for profit, making a total addition of 100 per cent. At the year end he finds that the actual results are:

Total direct wages paid (for 10 667 hours)	£8 000
Total overhead expenses	£6 750
Total charges for overheads and profit included on customers' bills £8 000 × 100 per cent	£8 000

Looking at these results from the profit angle, he finds the comparative outcome as follows:

Expected profit: £2 520 (£9 000 × 28%).
Realised profit: £1 250 (£8 000–£6 750).
The explanation for this drop of £1 270 is:

(*a*) Actual overheads exceeded estimate by	£270
(*b*) On the basis of £8 000 total wages, the percentage addition for overheads of £6 480 should have been 81 per cent, so that there has been an under-recovery of £8 000 × 9 per cent	£720

(c) As the work done during the year (as measured by the direct labour cost) was £1 000 less than expected, he has lost the profit margin on this amount £1 000 × 28 per cent   £280

                        £1 270

Where a firm using job costing is using plant or machinery to a considerable extent, a more equitable method of allocating overheads may be to express them as a rate per machine hour instead of the direct labour hour, and to charge them out to jobs according to the machine time required. The same problems of over- or under-recovery of overheads will of course occur.

Process costing

This is the costing system used by firms that do not wait to get orders from customers but decide in advance what products to make and at what prices to sell them.

In a process-type business, the typical manufacturing pattern is for a flow of material to pass from one department to another and, after going through various processes, finally to emerge as a finished product, or as one of a number of finished products. In view of the nature of the flow—either continuous as in the case of a sheet glass manufacturer, or in batches, as in the case of a bakery—it is clearly impossible to cost out individual units of product, and the method adopted is:

(a) to measure the output in appropriate units;
(b) to measure the costs incurred in producing this output;
(c) to divide (a) by (b) to arrive at the cost per unit.

In the case of a single production unit making only one product, this is all that needs to be done, but in the majority of cases there will be several products, each undergoing different processes and perhaps passing through different departments. A simplified example of this is shown in Fig. 5.3.1.

Fig. 5.3.1
Plan of production processes for products A and B

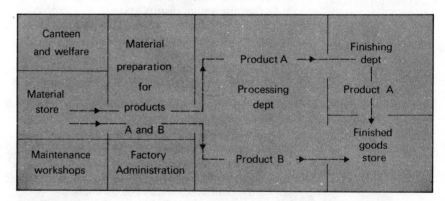

It will be appreciated from examining this diagram that the same approach to building up product costs can be adopted as was the case in building up job costs. Certain costs (e.g. direct labour) can be positively identified with the two products made, while other costs, such as factory administration, will have to be allocated on an appropriate basis. However, it is usually possible to allocate directly to products a wider range of costs than is possible with a job costing system. In the example, it is quite practicable to identify *direct expenses*, such as maintenance and repair costs of the production lines involved in making each product. Having identified them, the cost allocation for the year can be worked out, and as already mentioned, divided by the volume of production to give the cost per unit of product. This means that the only costs which need to be allocated to products on a pro rata basis (like the allocation of overheads in a job costing system) are the *indirect expenses*, such as factory administration, general cleaning, welfare, etc. In view of the large volume of products being manufactured in a typical mass production industry this greater accuracy in costing is clearly important, as the result of making an error would be magnified many times over.

Cost centres

In the above example, it may be imagined that the Cost Accountant has been asked to set up a costing system that will enable management to keep watch on the manufacturing costs of the two products, or more specifically the 'conversion costs', i.e. the cost of converting raw material into finished products. The procedure which the Cost Accountant will follow is to decide on 'cost centres', in respect of which he will measure output and costs. In some cases the cost centre will correspond with the department; in the example in Fig. 5.3.1 the work on material preparation is the same for each product, so all he needs to do here is to count total output of material and the cost of preparing it. In the processing department he finds that making product B is much more costly than making product A, so he needs to set up two cost centres in this department, with separate counts for the output of each product and a subdivision of costs. Finishing Department which deals only with product A comes under separate management, so is also treated as a separate cost centre (otherwise it could have been included in the Processing Department Product A cost centre).

Cost allocations

During the selected period, the Cost Accountant establishes that the weekly production output and direct conversion costs are as shown below in the first two columns. He then calculates the direct conversion cost as shown in the two end columns.

| | | Weekly costs (direct labour and expenses) | Direct conversion cost per tonne | |
| | | | Product A | Product B |
Department	Weekly output			
		£	£	£
Preparation	1 200 tonnes of material	240	0·20	0·20
Processing	1 000 tonnes of product A	320	0·32	
	200 tonnes of product B	200		1·00
Finishing (product A)	As for Processing Dept.	440	0·44	
		£1 200	£0·96	£1·20

The direct costs of conversion have been allocated to the two products on a factual basis and some means must now be found for allocating the indirect expenses to products. They may be allocated in proportion to:

(a) direct materials cost
(b) direct labour hours or costs
(c) machine hours
(d) direct conversion costs or
(e) total direct costs (a + d).

If in the above example, indirect expenses amount to £600 per week, and it is decided to allocate these in proportion to direct conversion costs, the appropriate percentage addition is

$$\frac{600 \times 100}{1\,200} = 50 \text{ per cent,}$$

and the total conversion costs become £1·44 and £1·80 per tonne respectively.

Product costs

At this point, someone in the company may query the need for calculating product costs at all. Why spend money in working out product costs in a firm that sells its products at prices determined by market conditions? Marketing management will form a view as to the pricing policy to adopt, and if they are first in the field with a new product likely to catch the public eye, selling prices will almost certainly be fixed well above cost in order to maximise profits before competitors catch up. Later on, when they have to compete with others, selling prices will once again be fixed by market considerations rather than being based on any figures produced by the Cost Accountant. In fact, management may take the view that the only time they need to have product costs calculated is in order to value the inventories of goods on hand at the year end for the purpose of preparing the annual accounts.

However, most manufacturing firms of any size have long since realised that an effective product costing system is an essential part of an information system designed to help management in making policy decisions and in exercising control. The determination of product costs will help to ensure that profits arising from the sales of profitable lines are not being masked by losses on sales of unprofitable ones. The calculation of profit margins on each product, by deducting product costs from average selling prices, is useful to marketing management for directing their marketing and selling activities. It provides an indication of the margin available for advertising and promotion expenses. It is the basis for preparing management information reports showing what profit has been earned in different sales regions. It is also a first step in calculating the relative profitability of different sales outlets by class of trade.

The effect of volume changes on product costs

It has already been shown in the job costing example that an unexpected fall in volume can lead to an under-recovery of overhead costs and a more than proportionate fall in profits. A similar effect occurs in process costing, except that the occurrence of over- or under-recovery is applicable to some of the direct costs as well as to indirect expenses. Since in a process type industry selling prices have to be determined before the products are sold, and since it is never possible to forecast exactly the volume of sales to be achieved in any given future period, it becomes important to work out in advance the effect on product costs of a range of possible sales volumes. Before this can be done it is necessary to study the *cost behaviour* of each element of cost, i.e. to study the extent to which costs will vary directly with volume of throughput, or remain fixed.

In the above example, the Cost Accountant worked out the conversion costs of the two products on the basis of the current levels of throughput and costs. It may be supposed that marketing management are contemplating boosting the sales of each product and that they enquire from the accounts department what the effect on product costs will be if sales of product A rise by 10 per cent and of product B by 20 per cent.

Before the Cost Accountant can work out these estimates, he will have to go and talk to factory management and find out:

(a) Is there adequate plant capacity to cover the anticipated increases of 10 per cent and 20 per cent, or will capital have to be spent on increasing capacity?
(b) Which costs can be expected to increase in direct proportion to the increase in volume of production? (e.g. direct labour)
(c) Which costs will rise to some extent, but less than the proportional increase visualised in (b)? (e.g. cleaning costs)
(d) Which costs will remain unaltered? (e.g. Manager's salary)

Armed with this information, including the knowledge that there is adequate plant capacity, the Cost Accountant is able to re-analyse the direct weekly costs of £1 200 as follows, according to their variability:

	Total	Product A	Product B
	£	£	£
Variable (i.e. with the volume of production)	850	710	140
Partly variable—say £50 fixed, £50 variable	100	100	—
Fixed	250	150	100
	1 200	960	240

and the indirect expenses of £600 per week are regarded as all fixed. The Cost Accountant is now in a position to estimate the revised conversion costs for the increased output, and he starts by calculating the variable cost per tonne from the existing data, after re-allocating the partly variable costs:

Product cost estimates

	Product A	Product B
Variable costs per tonne (inc. proportion of semivariable)	£0·76	£0·70
Revised weekly output (tonnes)	1 100	240

Revised direct conversion costs:		
Variable	836	168
Fixed (inc. ppn of semifixed)	200	100
	1 036	268
Indirect expenses £600 per week allocated pro rata to direct conversions costs	477	123
	£1 513	£391
Revised conversion cost per tonne	£1·37	£1·63
(Original conversion cost per tonne)	(£1·44)	(£1·80)

In carrying out the above calculations, the Cost Accountant has introduced an estimating procedure that enables him to provide answers to ad hoc enquiries. He will almost certainly then find it useful to prepare product cost estimates regularly for the year ahead in support of the company's marketing plans. He could continue to base these estimates on enquiries made from departmental managers, but he would be well advised to decide instead to introduce a full system of standard costing linked with budgetary control.

Standard costing   The underlying idea behind standard costing is to remove the guesswork to the maximum extent possible from these predetermined cost figures. This is done, as the name implies, by building up standard product costs from the following data:

—Standard specifications of the quantities and qualities of each material making up the finished product, the standard times required for each direct labour-operation, standards of machine efficiency, power usage, etc.

—Budgeted or standard material prices, wage rates, etc.

—Budgeted levels of indirect expenses.

—Budgeted or standard levels of output.

Standards for material usage, direct labour times etc. can be established by work study engineers, and if these standards are in fact being achieved, then the data built into the products costs will provide a reliable basis for calculating overall costs. If however factory performance levels are unsatisfactory for any reason and standards are not being reached, then the standard product costs will understate the true cost to this extent. One of the advantages of standard costing over the type of cost estimating outlined above is that the costs attributable to unsatisfactory performance can be isolated from the 'intrinsic' costs of the product, and management can decide whether to accept the position and add on a temporary allowance to this standard cost, or whether to base marketing plans on the eventual attainment of standard performance.

With regard to material prices, wage rates, etc., most companies will be unable to predict with accuracy the cost levels that will have to be paid next year, and product costs will have to be built up from the budget estimates. However if a company is in a position to enter into annual contracts for material supplies or wage rate payments, then the contract prices or wage rates can be used as standards in building up the product costs.

One of the key questions to be answered before standard costs can be calculated is the output target. It could be:

(*a*) *Budgeted output for next year.* This is probably the most frequently used basis, as the standard costs are then 100 per cent tied in to the budgetary control system. Any variations of actual output or expenditure compared with budget will provide a signal whether standard costs in total are being exceeded or otherwise. However, this method does have one major disadvantage where standard costs are being used as a basis for determining selling prices. If, say due to exceptional activity by a competitor, the sales volume of a product begins to fall, next year's budgeted output for this product may well be set at a still lower figure. Owing to the impact of fixed costs, this will increase the standard cost of the product, which if reflected in higher selling prices, could result in a still lower volume of sales. The resulting profit may then be less than if the selling price had been unaltered. Considerations like this lead many company managements to prefer to base standard costs on standard output targets, which in turn may be interpreted in either of the following ways:

(*b*) *the expected average annual throughput*, based on long-range plans, and taking the good years with the bad. This method overcomes the above problem and is particularly suitable for those companies making staple products such as bricks or steel girders for which there is a continuous demand unaffected by the vagaries of fashion.

(*c*) *the maximum possible volume of production*, i.e. assuming that the firm could sell the entire production output of the plant, based either on the number of shifts usually worked, or on the maximum possible. This method gives rise to the calculation of an 'ideal' standard cost, to act as a 'carrot', compared with the attainable standard costs derived in (*a*) and (*b*) above.

The important point is that management should be fully aware of the alternative that has been selected, and of the chances of attaining the standard.

Standard costs then are a method of building up predetermined product (or process) costs brick by brick from a series of agreed objectives and based on specific assumptions. When first introduced standard costing met considerable opposition from those who preferred to base all their decisions on last year's 'actual' costs. They forgot that last year's 'actual' conditions were unlikely to be repeated in the year ahead. In the long run, using a railway timetable is a better guide to catching a train and making a railway journey than basing one's plans on previous personal experience.

When building up standard costs, it is usual to classify the various cost elements according to whether they are regarded as being variable, semivariable or fixed in relation to changes in the volume of production. This will facilitate the calculation of various cost estimates for use by marketing management when evaluating marketing policies, as described earlier in this chapter. It also provides the basis for the control procedures known as *flexible budgetary control* (see p. 695).

Worked example of
standard costing

The worked example given in chapter 12 (p. 840) illustrates the calculation of standard product costs based on the budgeted output for the year (method (*a*) above), budgeted expenditure, and various standards of performance. The example also illustrates the way in which the standard costs form the basis for control.

Full costing

The product costing systems so far considered (actual, estimated and standard) are usually known as 'full' systems, since all costs are fully allocated to products.

Companies will naturally differ in their requirements for product costing purposes, and some will be content with merely allocating all factory direct expenses to products (as in the chapter 12 worked example). Some will decide to allocate all factory expenses, including indirects, others will also allocate selling, marketing and administration expenses. Much will depend on the company's requirements for valuing year end stocks for balance sheet purposes (see chapter 4, p. 707). As has been shown above, full costing systems are not particularly suitable for assessing the effect of various changes in the level of outputs. This is because, unlike variable costs which remain the same per unit of product for any level of output, fixed costs will give rise to a different 'per unit' calculation every time a different level of output is being assumed.

Marginal costing

Many businesses are now getting over this difficulty by making use of marginal costing for their assessment of various short term courses of action, while still adhering to full costing for long term considerations and balance sheet calculations. The underlying idea of marginal costing is to express only the variable items of cost as a per unit cost and by calculating the variable cost of sales and deducting this from sales turnover, arriving at what is known as 'variable profit', or 'contribution', out of which the various categories of fixed costs must be deducted before arriving at the final profit.

It will be appreciated that marginal costing procedures lead to very simple calculations when working out the costs of alternative volumes, i.e.

(new volume of output × variable cost per unit) + fixed costs.

Marginal costing has a further advantage: when expressed on a per unit basis, deduction of the variable cost from the selling price leaves the 'variable margin' or 'contributory margin'. This provides an indication of the scope for price cutting if perhaps marketing management wish to make special arrangements for bulk supplies at a very much reduced price, or if severe competition makes this necessary. Without a knowledge of this margin, firms might be tempted to reduce their prices below the out-of-pocket costs incurred, and very soon find themselves bankrupt. On the other hand, in the long run the business must be able to cover its full product costs, otherwise there would be no money in hand to pay for replacement of plant when this became necessary. In other words, management should have available both the marginal and full standard costs of their products. Considerable controversy has arisen among accountants over the years as to the merits of using the marginal costing approach for valuing year end stocks when preparing the annual accounts. This aspect is further considered in chapter 4.

The worked example in chapter 12 illustrates the use of marginal costing in arriving at marketing policy decisions.

Budgetary control and standard costing procedures

Reference has been made above to the link between budgetary control and standard costing, and this link is further examined here. Assuming that the marketing plan has been approved, and sales and production targets agreed, one of the first steps to be taken is how to communicate these decisions on objectives and policies to those who will be carrying out the day to day operations.

Decisions on budgeted objectives and policies tend to be taken in terms of products, markets, type of outlets, etc., whereas the operations necessary to achieve these objectives and policies are organised by departments, sections, sales regions etc., thus cutting across the product grouping and in effect involving a kind of matrix in which the product requirements (production and sales targets by brands) are recorded in a horizontal direction, and the corresponding output requirements and work load, by departments, regions, etc., are accumulated in a vertical direction (see Fig. 5.3.2).

Fig. 5.3.2
Product requirements and their effect on departmental or regional work loads

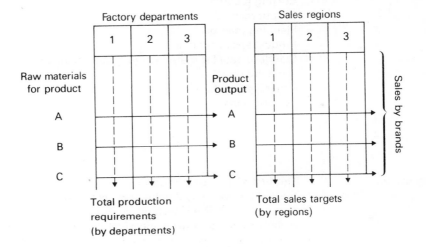

The same formation holds good if costs are inserted in the matrix representing the physical activities. Put differently, the manufacturing objectives of the company may be expressed either as making x tonnes of product A at a unit cost of £y, etc., or of Department 1 preparing m tonnes of material for products A, B and C at a cost of £n per tonne, etc. Or in other words, the departmental and material budgets are complementary to the standard costs, and the most effective way of obtaining cost savings in the latter is to make sure that budgets are effectively prepared, discussed with, and finally communicated to departmental managers.

Preparation
of budgets

The application of budgetary control procedures to the manufacturing and marketing sides of the business is considered in detail in chapters 6 and 7. The remainder of this chapter consists of a stage by stage account of the steps to be taken in installing a system of budgetary control in a business as a whole.

The first steps will be to decide on the team to introduce the system. If no one in the company has had any prior experience of *successful* applications, it may be decided to call in management consultants to carry out the task. If the Financial Director is in a position to guide the installation, then it may be decided to appoint a steering committee, consisting of say the financial, marketing and production directors plus the chief accountant, and to set up a working committee to carry out the installation, possibly consisting of members of the accounting, costing and work study departments, supplemented by one or two selected members of the sales and production sides of the business. Terms of reference will be agreed with the chief executive, and a target set for the completion of the installation.

General lines of approach, a detailed programme with target dates, and progress achieved, will be discussed and agreed at meetings of the two committees held periodically.

The working committee's first task will be to review the information that already exists and which is likely to help in the preparation of standard costs and budgets. This may consist of:

Accounting records
Costing records
Output records
Planning records
Product specifications
Standard data for manufacturing operations (man hours per unit of throughput etc.)
Organisation charts
Factory plans

Key factors

The first step in preparing the budgets will be to decide the period to which they will relate—usually the next accounting year—and the other key factors round which they will be built, such as production capacity or marketing plan. It may be necessary to decide which of these key factors is the limiting factor; if a company makes a specialist product for which there is keen demand, then next year's sales will be limited in quantity to the maximum output of which the factory is capable. If the products are made by skilled craftsmen of whom there is a shortage, then the maximum sales target must be based on the output which they can produce rather than on the maximum capacity of the plant. On the other hand, if there is spare capacity, or if it is possible to buy in any shortfall, then the marketing plan must be based on the capacity of the sales force to sell the company's products, or alternatively be geared to the amount it is proposed to spend on advertising and promotion. In practice the limiting factors may be of one kind for some products and of a different kind for others, and give and take is necessary before attainable sales and production targets can be set for all the company's products.

Having decided on the limiting factors and on the basis on which the budgets for the year ahead will be built up, marketing management will then prepare a provisional marketing plan specifying the quantities to be sold, the expected selling prices, and the proposed expenditure on marketing support. This will be passed to production management who, after taking into account any planned variations in stocks on hand of finished products, will arrive at the corresponding production targets for each product.

The next step is to examine what effect carrying out this production programme will have in terms of throughput in each department, and each manager will be asked to agree his budgeted output. He will have to make sure that his plant and labour force are capable of producing the planned output, based on previous experience of efficiencies, performance levels, and plant breakdowns.

Direct costs

The direct costs of processing in each department are then calculated from these throughput targets in terms of direct labour and direct expenses. In any one department, the direct labour cost will be budgeted volume of throughput (in units) × standard man hours per unit × budgeted wage rate per hour, plus a reasonable allowance to cover an acceptable level of non-productive time.

Direct expenses in each department will tend to be unaffected by changes in the volume of throughput, and can usually be budgeted after an examination of previous accounting records and a discussion with the departmental manager. They will include such items as supervision, depreciation and repair of plant, machinery and equipment. Some direct expenses may be variable in nature, such as supplies; other items such as power or ancillary labour may be partly variable and partly fixed. The total direct expenses for each department are then divided by the throughput to arrive at the budgeted cost per unit. These departmental costs are then accumulated for each product to arrive at the conversion cost per unit of product.

The material costs relating to each product (raw materials, packaging materials) are arrived at from an evaluation of the product formula or specification. For each material, the material content of a unit of product (plus a reasonable allowance for wastage) × the expected price of the material will give the standard cost of that material per unit of product, and when repeated for each material, will give the total standard cost of materials. This is added to the budgeted conversion cost to arrive at the standard direct cost per unit of product. As a cross check at this stage, the standard direct cost of all the products to be manufactured in the period ahead should exactly equal the total of all the departmental budgets for direct expenses plus the budgeted cost of materials to be used in production.

This matrix effect, which has already been referred to, is the key to one of the main advantages of the system. If actual costs of materials or departmental expenses begin to rise above budgeted levels, or if output drops below the agreed targets, then management is immediately warned that actual product costs are rising above standard, and appropriate corrective action can be set on foot.

Indirect expenses

Separate budgets are prepared for factory indirect expenses, selling, marketing and distribution expenses; and administration expenses. These budgets will have to be agreed with the managers concerned, and will be based in the first instance on previous actual costs. They should be built up in detail (salaries, wages, travelling, rent, rates, depreciation and so on), and provision should be made for any known increases, such as merit increases or cost of living adjustments. The opportunity should be taken periodically of carrying out detailed reviews or cost reduction programmes, to ensure that the budgets are not perpetuating inefficiencies.

If the budgeted sales or production volumes are significantly different from the previous year, then it may be appropriate to make adjustments to the indirect expense budgets, although any such adjustment would not be fully proportionate, since so many of the expenses are 100 per cent fixed.

The budgeted indirect expenses are apportioned over the budgeted production output or sales volume, in order to arrive at the standard indirect cost for each unit of product, and by addition to the standard direct cost, the product standard cost. Deduction of this cost from the standard selling price gives the standard profit margin.

Confirming the budgets

The budgets and standard costs have been based on policy decisions previously taken by management, and on the sales objectives built in to the provisional marketing plan. There now remains the important task of confirming that the target profits and profit margins disclosed by the budgetary process are acceptable to the top management of the company, having regard to the capital employed, and to the company's expectation of growth. If the profits are not acceptable—they may be thought too small, or perhaps unrealistically high—then the plans and budgets will have to be referred back to the two committees and rediscussed with departmental management. When the budgets have been finally approved, copies of the appropriate parts of the whole should be issued to those concerned, thus indicating to them their agreed performance and cost objectives for the year.

Control against budgets

Mention has already been made in chapter 1 of the 'pre-control' which is obtained when budgets are prepared and agreed. If there is no budgeting, and managers are able to obtain approval to increases of staff, additional equipment etc. on an *ad hoc* basis, it is very likely that costs will rise steadily and profit margins will be eroded. The need to work out how many men and what other resources are required *for the year ahead* prevents this piecemeal approach, and provides an opportunity for the budget committee to query the need for additional expenses if these do not look to be justified. However, it is still necessary to ensure that agreed budgets are adhered to, and the comparison of actual results with budget is an essential part of the system as a whole. How often should this comparison be made? Obviously this must depend on the company, but in general it is useful to make monthly and/or quarterly comparisons.

As indicated by the definition of a budget given in chapter 1, budgetary control may relate to income, expenditure, or the employment of capital. Budgetary control of expenditure may consist of a simple comparison of actual with budgeted costs—as in the case of branch office expenses—where the object is to see that authorised limits are not exceeded—or it may be designed to take into account fluctuations in the volume of work being done, as in a processing department where the output varies from week to week. Here the object of the comparison would be to see whether the costs incurred in producing the actual output are within budget limits, after taking into account the fact that some costs can be expected to rise directly with output, other costs to remain fixed, and some to fall somewhere between these two extremes. The technique which enables these comparisons to be made, and which provides an analysis of any 'variances' from budget by cause, is known as 'Flexible Budgetary Control'.

Flexible budgetary control

The idea underlying this technique is to be able to work out in advance the 'budget allowance' for each item of cost for all probable levels of output. For variable costs this means agreeing on a standard cost per unit of output; the allowance is calculated by multiplying out actual output by the standard cost. For fixed costs, unaffected by changes in volume, the budget allowance will be the same as the budget figure. With partly variable expenses, it may be possible to break them down into their fixed and variable elements, but otherwise it may be necessary to draw up a schedule of allowances at varying levels of output, based on detailed studies.

At the end of the month or other period, actual costs are compared with the budget allowances, and the resulting 'variances' analysed by cause as described below.

Variances

Efficiency variance. If the factory operations have been carried out less efficiently than was visualised when the budget was prepared, whether due to such causes as poor performance from the operatives, or excess wastage of materials, then costs incurred in producing a given output will be higher than anticipated and the excess will be known as an 'unfavourable efficiency variance'. If performance exceeds expectations then the variance is 'favourable'.

Price or wage rate variance. If the prices paid for raw materials differ from budgeted prices, then the increased (or decreased) cost of materials used due to this factor is known as a 'price variance'. The increased labour cost due to paying higher than anticipated wage rates may also be included under this heading.

Mix variances. A change in the proportion of raw materials going to make up a product may give rise to a *cost variance*, and this can be described either as a mix variance, or formulation variance. A similar type of variance arises on the marketing side, when actual profits may differ from budgeted profits, due to a change in the proportions of each product in total sales compared with budget. This is known as a *sales mix variance*.

When these variances have been determined, the final step in the process of control will be to work out the standard cost of the actual output (volume of output x standard cost per unit) and then to compare this with the total budget allowances. If actual output is the same as the budgeted output used to calculate standard costs, the two figures will be the same. If not, a 'volume variance' will be thrown up:

Volume variance. In building up the standard costs of a company's products, assumptions have had to be made about the volume of output, in order to be able to allocate the fixed expenses. If actual output turns out to be substantially lower than budget, and assuming that fixed expenses remain thoroughly fixed, then only part of the fixed expenses will be recovered in the standard cost of the actual output and the unrecovered proportion is described as an unfavourable volume variance. An over-recovery, or favourable variance, will occur if actual output is higher than budget. The determination of a volume variance is explained in the worked example in chapter 12.

| Phasing of budgets | Where a marked seasonal pattern exists, or where for any other reason the sales and production volumes are expected to vary between quarters, it is convenient to phase the budget accordingly. Phasing is further described in chapters 7 and 8, and is illustrated in the worked example (see chapter 12). |

| Budget revision | Long-range plans, by their very nature, are bound to be modified with the passage of time, depending as they do on so many assumptions about the environment and numerous external factors over which the company has no control. As the years go by, each long-range plan for a particular year eventually becomes the annual budget for next year, and will be supported by much more quantitative detail than was possible when the plan for that year was first formulated. Just as the various parts of the business interlock, so do the budgets with their supporting data, together with the standard costs derived from them, interlock with each other and with the summary budget which shows the picture of the company as a whole. It is sound management practice to keep the annual budget unchanged once it has been agreed, unless circumstances alter so much that some kind of revision becomes imperative. |

It has been pointed out in chapter 1 that budgets often get out of date because they have to be prepared well in advance of the year to which they relate. This difficulty is overcome by making use of short term operating plans to supplement the budget, plans which bring up to date management's ideas on marketing and sales objectives and policies, and on the corresponding production targets. The original budget and the standard costs derived from it are retained unchanged, to provide bench marks against which to judge actual performance.

However, if as the year progresses, some significant event occurs affecting the company's fortunes which makes it virtually certain that the original objectives will not be met, then there would be good reason for introducing a revised budget based on the new circumstances and conditions. Such a change would call for re-calculation of standard costs, of profit margins, of sales and profits, and of future cash balances and will naturally lead to a complete rethinking by all functional management of their aims and policies.

The one type of planning that is normally never altered, once agreed, is the operational planning on a weekly or daily basis that determines what shall be produced, on which machines, or which calls a salesman will make, etc. The relative degree of flexibility in planning is shown in Fig. 5.3.3.

Fig. 5.3.3
Flexibility of
planning

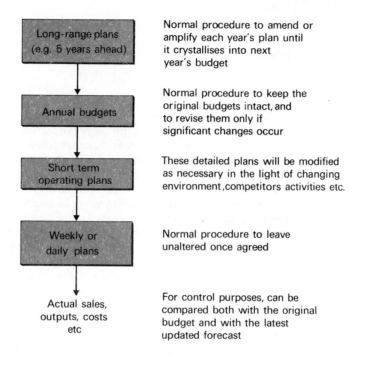

Long-range plans
(e.g. 5 years ahead)

Normal procedure to amend or amplify each year's plan until it crystallises into next year's budget

Annual budgets

Normal procedure to keep the original budgets intact, and to revise them only if significant changes occur

Short term
operating plans

These detailed plans will be modified as necessary in the light of changing environment, competitors activities etc.

Weekly or
daily plans

Normal procedure to leave unaltered once agreed

Actual sales,
outputs, costs
etc

For control purposes, can be compared both with the original budget and with the latest updated forecast

Making budgetary
control effective

Budgetary control and standard costing can be effective aids to the attainment of growth and profit objectives, or they can be a useless waste of management time. Much depends on the attitude of top management, and for maximum effectiveness it is essential that they are seen by all levels of staff to be giving the system their full support.

Other important points which have already been referred to in preceding pages include making sure that the system has been designed to meet the particular needs of the business; that there is an upward as well as a downward flow of communications, so that all managers can participate in the preparation and agreement of budgets; and that control reports are not over-complex, and cluttered up with cost details over which the recipients of the information have no control.

4 Profit and loss statements and balance sheets

The newly appointed Financial Director was asked by his Board to give priority to making recommendations for improved cost control, and he has now carried out his preliminary studies. Points that have struck him forcibly are that before cost control can become really effective, target levels of costs have to be agreed by reference either to the total profit being earned by the business or by a part of it, or to the profit margins earned on individual products or product groups. With these thoughts still in mind, he is called in to the Board room for urgent discussions on the latest Government counter-inflation proposals for limiting the profit margins which can be earned on home sales.

He can see clearly that the calculation of profit breakdowns and profit margins is not just a question of management information to be circulated to the Board and functional management for internal discussions and review, as used to be the case. These same figures will continue to be vital to the company if in future it wishes to adjust selling prices as part of its policy of growth and prosperity, and it will be essential to be able to produce them as part of the general accounting routines.

On his return from the Board room he is visited by the Accountant, who has called in to remind him that the annual accounts and balance sheet are due for completion, and that these will of course have to be drawn up in compliance with Companies Acts requirements. Also, if they are to avoid qualifications in the auditor's certificate, they will have to comply with the various accounting standards issued by the accounting bodies through the Accounting Standards Steering Committee.

The Financial Director decides that taking all these matters into account, it is essential for him to clarify his thoughts on the various ways of calculating profitability, and on the various requirements in preparing annual accounts referred to by the accountant. Bearing in mind Britain's continuing membership of the European Economic Community, he has also to be prepared for possible international requirements.

Methods of calculating profit

There are three basic ways of calculating profits earned by a business during any given period and these are described below.

1. Balance Sheet method

This method compares the *net worth* of the business at the end of the period with that at the beginning, the net worth being calculated in each case by subtracting liabilities from assets. Assuming that no funds have been injected into or withdrawn from the business by the proprietors during the period, the increase in net worth will represent the total profit earned. No guidance can be obtained from these figures as to *how* the profit has been earned. The example below relates to a small jobbing firm, and ignores taxation.

THE XYZ JOBBING CO

Period 1   3 months to 31 March

Net worth, 1 January		*Net worth, 31 March*	
	£		£
Value of buildings and plant at cost less depreciation written off	51 000	Value of buildings and plant at cost less depreciation written off—as at 1 January	51 000
		Additions during period	+7 200
		Depreciation for period	(−4 000)
		Balance 31 March	54 200
Total fixed assets	51 000	Total fixed assets	54 200
Work in progress:		Work in progress	
Job no. 38	3 100	Job no. 38 9 400	
		Job no. 52 8 000	
Stock of material on hand	7 500		17 400
Trade debtors	35 300	Stock of material on hand	9 100
		Trade debtors	30 200
Cash at bank and in hand	1 700	Cash at bank and in hand	1 200
Total current assets	47 600	Total current assets	57 900
Less creditors	18 100	Less creditors	22 000
Net current assets	29 500	Net current assets	35 900
Total net assets	80 500	Total net assets	90 100

Period 1: Increase in net worth £9 600

2. Profit and Loss Account method

If accountants are asked to prepare a statement on the above lines, they will always wish to check it by using the 'Profit and Loss Account' method. In this method, all expenditure is first listed under appropriate headings, regardless of whether or not the invoices have been paid. The next step is to list the sales made to customers during the period, again ignoring the question whether or not customers have paid their bills. The final step is to match the expenditure with the sales, make appropriate adjustments where they do not correspond, and find the profit or loss by deduction of one total from the other. In the jobbing firm example, material had been bought for stock and then issued to each job as necessary. This means that in order to match up with the sales, the appropriate figure is 'materials used' rather than 'materials bought', and this is obtained by adjusting for any net increase or decrease in stock over the period. In the same way, the firm knows that there are always one or two uncompleted contracts at the end of each period, and that it would be misleading to charge up the expenditure incurred on these contracts in the current period, since there would be no corresponding sales credit. As will be seen from the example, this expenditure is carried forward as 'work in progress' to the next period.

THE XYZ JOBBING CO

Profit and Loss Statement

Period No. 1

3 Months to 31 March

Expenditure	£	£
Salaries and wages		23 000
Materials bought	14 700	
Add materials in stock 1 January	+7 500	
Less materials in stock 31 March	−9 100	
		13 100
Supplies and services		9 100
Repairs		8 300
Depreciation of buildings and plant		4 000
Sundries		4 500
		62 000
Less increase in work in progress during period:[1]		
as at 31 March	17 400	
as at 1 January	3 100	14 300
Total expenditure to be matched with sales		47 700

Sales during period	£
Job no. 41	10 500
44	14 200
50	8 800
51	23 800
Total sales	57 300

Net profit £57 300 − 47 700 = £9 600

Although method 2 gives more information than method 1 about how the profit has been earned, it still does not show the relative profitability of each contract, and this can only be seen from method 3.

---

[1] In a manufacturing or trading business, similar adjustments would be necessary for stocks of finished products.

3. Costing method

With this method the costs incurred on each job are recorded and accumulated, and then agreed in total with the total costs charged in the Profit and Loss Account. Details for the jobbing firm are:

	Costs incurred:			Sales	Profit
	Previous periods	This period	Total to date	this period	or (loss)
	£	£	£	£	£
Job no. 38	3 100	6 300	9 400	—	—
41	—	8 200	8 200	10 500	2 300
44	—	9 500	9 500	14 200	4 700
50	—	9 400	9 400	8 800	(600)
51	—	20 600	20 600	23 800	3 200
52	—	8 000	8 000	—	—
	3 100	62 000	65 100	57 300	9 600

The purpose of the above example is to compare the different methods available, and for this reason no attempt has been made to illustrate the complications that can arise when it is desired to take credit for profit on jobs that have only been partially completed, such a procedure being necessary when considering major projects, e.g. building motorways or ships.

At this point it should be noted that some of the figures are factual, and some a matter of opinion. In the balance sheet, *cash at bank or in hand* is factual, and so are *creditors*, but the value of *trade debtors* may be open to doubt if customers are slow at paying up and there is a risk of bad debts being incurred. Perhaps the greatest room for differing views arises with the valuation of *stocks on hand* and *work in progress* (these figures appear in both balance sheet and profit and loss account). Valuing these at cost may be misleading if prices have fallen sharply since the balance sheet date or if a contract is going to result in a loss, and there is always the question of obsolete material. With regard to *fixed assets*, it is usually the case that balance sheet values do not represent current market values, and from time to time the directors may decide to revalue these assets. If the balance sheet figures are maintained at original cost, then it is virtually certain that the depreciation charged in the Profit and Loss Account will be insufficient to provide enough cash to replace the assets as and when necessary, and it will be prudent to make supplementary allocations from profit for this purpose.

The same three methods of calculating profits are applicable to process type industries, but instead of calculating the profit earned on each job or contract, management will wish to know what profit is being earned on each product or product group. The standard costing procedure described in earlier chapters is very suitable for this procedure, since it provides an appropriate means of calculating these costs in advance.

The fact must now be faced that it is seldom possible to talk about the profit earned by a product or group of products without a number of qualifying statements. This is due to the practice of striking profits at different stages in the business, depending on the purpose for which the profit figures are needed. This is best explained through an example.

Example

A manufacturing and trading company makes and sells two groups of products. Sales during the first month of the year are as follows (and for simplicity in this example it has been assumed there are no opening or closing stocks of raw materials, work in progress or finished stocks):

	Product Group ABC	Product Group DEF
Sales (000 kg)	1 210	870
Sales turnover @ £5·50 per kg	£6 655	@ £10 per kg £8 700

Certain costs incurred in achieving these sales are regarded by management as being fully variable with the volume of output, e.g. the costs of raw materials and packaging, and of direct labour costs paid according to the amount of output achieved. These variable costs amount to £3·20 and £6 per kg, so that after deducting these costs of £3 872 and £5 220 respectively, one is left with

Variable profit   £2 783   and   £3 480.

As referred to in chapter 3, these figures are of value to marketing management in deciding on the scope for cutting selling prices to secure marginal business, but they do not reflect the profit being earned in the long term, since they take no account of any fixed expenses. The next stage is to allocate the remaining departmental expenses in the factory to the two product groups, so far as they can be positively allocated. These expenses will include salaries and wages paid out on a fixed weekly basis regardless of fluctuations in output, maintenance and repairs, depreciation of plant, services. After deducting these factory direct expenses amounting to £1 620 and £1 850 respectively, the resulting profit figure is usually referred to as 'gross profit':

Gross profit   £1 163   £1 630

and it represents the profit earned on each product group before deducting the factory indirect expenses (such as welfare and security) and all the expenses of marketing, selling, distribution and administration. These expenses amount to £2 400 in all, and it is decided that an appropriate allocation to the two product groups is £1 050 and £1 350 respectively. This leaves

Trading profit   £113 + £280 = £393.

The company has some investment income, and has to pay debenture interest, and after allowing for these, the *profit before taxation* is £520.

After deducting the appropriate charges for taxation, the *net profit after taxation* is £360.

The newly appointed Financial Director somewhat grudgingly agrees with his Accountant that all the profit figures shown above will have to be calculated for internal control purposes and the last three will have to be declared in the annual accounts.

Published accounts requirements

The Financial Director and his Accountant now start to consider the various requirements which now have to be met before the firm's balance sheets and accounts can be issued to shareholders. Some of these requirements arise out of the Companies Acts, others from the recommendations of the Accounting Standards Steering Committee. For Companies whose shares are listed on the Stock Exchange, there are yet other requirements imposed by the Stock Exchange Council. Some of the more important requirements are described in the remainder of this chapter.

Turnover and profit analysis

Up to the passing of the 1967 Companies Act, very little information was provided by the majority of companies about the way in which profits had been achieved. Very few companies gave details of turnover or breakdowns of profit by class of business. The 1967 Act has changed all this by requiring companies to disclose the amount of turnover and the method of arriving at it; also to provide in the Directors' report an analysis of turnover and pre-tax profits by class of business (where in the *opinion of the Directors* the company carries on two or more classes of business that differ substantially). The above requirements of the 1967 Act as modified by the Companies (Accounts) Regulations 1971 do not apply to companies which are not holding or subsidiary companies, if their turnover does not exceed £250 000. Companies listed on the Stock Exchange with overseas interests are required to give a breakdown of turnover and trading profits on a geographical basis as illustrated in the following example from an agency business:

Extract from published accounts

Turnover

	Percentage Group turnover	Pre-tax profits (losses) £
By class of business		
Agents and traders	87·7	243 017
Cotton textiles	4·5	(28 507)
Insurance brokers	·3	(1 750)
Confirming, clearing and forwarding	7·5	359 838
	100·0%	572 598
Geographically:		
Asia	16·6	144 709
Africa	32·8	130 737
Canada and USA	22·0	(22 534)
Australia and New Zealand	2·9	163 568
United Kingdom	25·7	156 118
	100·0%	572 598
Investment income		97 632
		670 230

Companies selling commodities or products must state the values of items exported (with the usual exemptions for smaller firms).

Accounting policies   Accountants have traditionally adopted certain basic principles when preparing balance sheets and accounts, although in the past these have never been spelt out for the benefit of shareholders. One of the first Accounting Standards to be approved ('Disclosure of accounting policies', issued in November 1971) requires the Directors to disclose to shareholders any departure from the four basic concepts underlying the preparation of accounts which have been traditionally followed by accountants for many years.

The going concern concept   The assumption is always made that the business will carry on indefinitely, and assets and liabilities are valued for the balance sheet accordingly. For example, fixed assets such as plant and machinery are depreciated over the period of their expected life; their realisable value if the business were forced to close down at the year end would almost certainly be far less than the book values arrived at on this basis.

The accruals concept   In preparing accounts, it is traditional to work out the extent to which outgoings for payments due in the future had accrued due at the balance sheet date, and to charge this amount to profit and loss. As the same principle applied at the end of the previous year, no more than one full year's charge would normally be charged to profits, but the balance sheet would include as a liability the accrued expenses.

The consistency concept   As indicated earlier in this chapter, there are many different views on the way in which certain items should be valued in preparing accounts. For example, some companies may value their stock-in-trade at marginal cost, others at direct cost, or at direct cost plus a proportion of indirects, and so on. The important thing from the point of view of a particular company is that the method of valuation should be consistent from year to year, otherwise the results could be totally misleading. An apparent change from a loss in year 1 to a profit in year 2 might be due merely to a sudden decision to include a higher proportion of overheads in the stock valuations.

Occasionally, it may be necessary to change the basis on which accounts are prepared, but if this occurs, the Companies Act requires the change in basis to be reported.

The prudence concept   It has always been an accounting maxim to anticipate a loss but not a profit, on the grounds of financial prudence. For example, if through delay in preparing the accounts of a company that has had a good year, it becomes known that a large sum due from a customer at the balance sheet date proved irrecoverable, it is sound policy to provide for this bad debt when preparing the accounts. If this were not done the directors might be tempted to declare an increased dividend this year, only to find that a cut would have to be made next year, and this is against the general aim of a growing company to build up a gradual but steady increase in its rate of distribution without any setbacks.

It is not so easy to defend the principle of not anticipating profits until they arise. Numerous insurance companies now allocate to with-profit policy holders a proportion of the appreciation in the market value of investments held by the Life Fund, even although such increase in value may not have been realised. This is to ensure more equitable treatment between the policy holders now contributing to the life funds, and future generations of policy holders who will be entitled to the income from the fund. Another contentious point of principle relates to companies engaging in long term contracts. If a company enters into a three-year contract to build a motorway, is it correct to wait until year 3 before bringing in any profit? The directors will have to decide whether to include in each year's accounts a proportion of the anticipated total profit attributable to each year. The draft Accounting Standard ED6 on Stocks and Work in Progress referred to below, makes it clear that the directors in such a case should report on the method they have adopted.

The vast majority of companies will adopt these four basic concepts in preparing their accounts so that no comment in the directors' report will be necessary. The directors however *are* required to comment on the accounting policies adopted in dealing with some of the major items affecting the results of the company and its financial position. Many companies now collate such items into a consolidated statement, instead of adding series of notes; this practice is admirably illustrated in the example cited as Table 5.4.1 below, reproduced from the 1973 Report and Accounts.

Table 5.4.1
British Leyland
Motor Corporation
Limited Accounting
Policies

Consolidation
The consolidated profit and loss account and balance sheet include the accounts of the parent company and all its subsidiaries made up to the end of the financial year. Internal sales and profits are eliminated on consolidation and all sales and profit figures relate to external transactions only.

Acquisitions
When subisdiary companies are acquired any difference between the consideration price and the net tangible assets at the date of acquisition is taken to capital reserves.

Fixed assets
Depreciation of the net cost of fixed assets (less any investment grants) is provided at the following annual rates on a straight-line basis, to write off the assets over their useful lives.
Freehold land—nil.
Freehold buildings—$2\frac{1}{2}$%.
Leasehold land and buildings—$2\frac{1}{2}$% or by equal annual instalments over the period of the lease, whichever is the greater.
Computers—20%.
Fixed plant and major equipment including presses, cranes etc—10%.
Machine tools (including installation costs)—$12\frac{1}{2}$%.
Office equipment and furniture—$12\frac{1}{2}$%.
Works equipment, conveyors and racks—25%.
Profits and losses on the sales of fixed assets are included in trading profits. Regional Development Grants are included in creditors pending their release to trading profits on a straight-line basis over the useful lives of the assets concerned.

Special tools, dies and jigs
Amortisation of the net cost of special tools, dies and jigs (less any investment grants) is provided in annual instalments over the shorter of either their useful lives or a conservative estimate of the production run of the models to which they relate.

Trade investments
Trade investments comprise all interests in companies which are not subsidiaries of the Corporation. Income from these investments is accounted for only as received and losses are provided for as incurred. Full consolidation of attributable results would not materially affect the Corporation's results.

Deferred taxation

Provision is made for future taxation on the excess of the net book value of the fixed assets and special tools ranking for taxation allowances over the corresponding written down value for taxation purposes. Provision is also made for taxation on capital gains deferred under the provisions of Section 33, Finance Act 1965. Account is taken of any items charged against trading profits which will not be allowed for tax purposes until future years.

Repairs and renewals

All repairs and renewals are written off as incurred.

Research and development

All research and development expenditure, including the design and production of prototypes, is written off as incurred. Similarly, all expenditure in respect of patents and trade marks is written off as incurred.

Stocks and work in progress

The basis of valuation of stocks and work in progress is the lower of cost or estimated net realisable value. Current production stocks including finished vehicles and work in progress are valued at cost of labour and materials with additions for appropriate factory overheads.

Stocks of service parts in excess of the estimated requirements for the next two years are fully written off.

Warranty liability

Provision is made for the Corporation's estimated liability on all products still under warranty, including claims already received. This is charged against trading profits and is included in creditors.

Extraordinary items

All expenditures and income arising in the course of the Corporation's normal business are taken into account in arriving at the profit before taxation. Any significant prior year adjustments or major unusual items are noted in the accounts or the Report of the Directors as appropriate. Only expenditures and income which are completely outside the normal current trading operations of the Corporation are treated as extraordinary items charged or credited directly against earnings.

Rates of exchange

Realised profits on exchange, together with all losses on exchange, whether realised or unrealised, which arise on settlement of overseas liabilities are included in trading profits. Assets and liabilities in foreign currencies are converted into sterling at rates of exchange ruling at the end of the financial year.

Profits and losses arising on the conversion into sterling of the balance sheets of overseas subsidiaries and foreign currency loans held by UK companies are included in extraordinary items. In 1973 the net gain so included was transferred to deferred exchange in the balance sheet. From that year the policy is that gains and losses are similarly transferred to meet fluctuations in rates of exchange and any losses in excess of the reserve are written off as extraordinary items in the usual way.

Stocks and work in progress

As mentioned above, companies have adopted many different ways of valuing stocks and work in progress and the important point has always been to maintain consistency from year to year. Apart from other reasons, a change in the basis of valuing stocks could have unfortunate effects on taxation liabilities.

In May 1972 the *Accounting Standards Steering Committee* issued exposure draft ED6 on Stocks and Work in Progress and it contained the following comment: 'No area of accounting has produced wider differences in practice then the computation of the amount at which stocks and work in progress are stated in financial accounts.' In view of the significant effect that changes in the basis of valuing stocks can have on reported profits, it is already clear that this standard will continue to give rise to a certain amount of controversy until it is agreed, and that when finally approved and issued, it will repay considerable study by financial management. As the draft stands at the present time (early 1975) two recommendations in particular are likely to give rise to changes in the accounting treatment for the majority of firms:

1. At present it is general practice to value stocks at cost and at realisable value, and to substitute the latter for cost only if the total value of stock at realisable value is less than total cost. Under the exposure draft, it is proposed that this comparison should be made for each separate item of stock, or for each group of similar stock items.
2. The cost at which stocks and work in progress should be valued is at present interpreted in many different ways by different companies, but under the draft Standard it will have to be interpreted in only one way, viz: 'all that expenditure which has been incurred in bringing the product or service to its present location and condition. This expenditure should include, in addition to cost of purchase, such costs of conversion (including related overheads) as are appropriate to that location and condition.' This definition implies the use of a fully apportioned system of costing and will be a blow to those who had hoped to see marginal costing given greater opportunities in financial reporting. It is understood that a final draft will not be issued until appropriate discussions have taken place with the taxation authorities.

Meanwhile, the provisions of the 1967 Companies Act still apply: the manner in which stock in trade or work in progress is computed should be shown in the accounts if the amount is substantial.

For many years prior to the issue of this exposure draft, some accountants had been debating whether to recommend to their Board that stocks and work in progress should be valued at marginal rather than full cost. Their argument went as follows:

> Would it not be more realistic to value such stocks on the basis of the variable (or marginal) costs incurred, rather than following the traditional procedure of including an appropriate proportion of fixed costs? In other words, if sales of the company's products suddenly decline towards the end of the financial year, with the result that stocks on hand rise dramatically, what is the point in carrying forward to next year's Profit and Loss Account a large proportion of this year's fixed costs such as management salaries, depreciation of plant, etc? (This is the effect of including them in stock values.) Would it not be better to write them off as incurred even if it means knocking this year's reported profit figure?

It was always realised that there would be tax problems, but it is now widely appreciated that if the above Exposure Draft becomes accepted as an accounting standard, there is little point in giving any further thought to the marginal approach.

Reserves and provisions

The layman is usually baffled when he looks at a balance sheet containing the statement 'General Reserve £3 000 000', or perhaps showing several reserves, all differently described. He probably forms the opinion that the words mean that there is an equivalent amount of cash lying around waiting to be spent, at the discretion of the directors. It is a shock to him when it is explained perhaps that the reserve was built up from profits earned in previous years but not distributed as dividend, and that the cash representing these reserves has already been spent either in financing extensions to the manufacturing capacity, or in buying up new acquisitions.

Some companies have made it easier for the average shareholder to understand the accounts by grouping all reserves together and including them under the general heading of Ordinary Shareholders' Funds. Thus Unilever's balance sheet shows an item 'Profits retained and other reserves' added to 'Ordinary capital' to arrive at a total for 'Ordinary Shareholders' Funds' with supporting details attached in the accounts.

At one time companies were required to show capital and revenue reserves separately in the accounts but this is no longer necessary. Apart from the need to show separately any share premium accounts or capital redemption reserve funds created on redeeming preference shares, the only requirement of the 1967 Act is to classify reserves, provisions, liabilities and assets under headings appropriate to the company's business. Ever since the passing of the 1948 Companies Act, there has been a requirement to distinguish provisions from reserves. Provisions are defined in the Act, and include:

(a) Amounts written off or retained to provide for depreciation, renewals, or diminution in value of assets.

(b) Amounts retained to provide for any known liability where the amount cannot be determined with substantial accuracy.

Reserves are defined in a somewhat negative way as being amounts set aside that are neither provisions, nor (1967 Act) for the purpose of preventing undue fluctuations in the tax charge. Particulars of any movements in reserves during the year must be given in the Profit and Loss account or other statement.

The requirement to show reserves separately from provisions stems from the days when directors were able to conceal the existence of accumulated profits which they did not wish to distribute by describing them as 'provisions' or 'sundry creditors' and including them under the company's liabilities.

Fixed assets

As indicated above, the Companies Act 1967 requires companies to classify assets under headings appropriate to the company's business; fixed assets, current assets and 'neither fixed nor current' assets must be separately identified and the method of arriving at the amount of fixed assets under each heading must be stated. The term 'Fixed assets' can cover physical things like land, buildings, plant etc., or it may refer to other assets which it is intended to hold for more than a year, such as trade investments, investments in subsidiary companies, or payments for goodwill, patents and trade marks. The comments below refer to the 'physical' fixed assets.

With the exception of assets held before 1948, or those dealt with on a renewals basis, companies have to show for each fixed asset heading the aggregate of the following amounts:

(i) cost or valuation;

(ii) provision for depreciation since acquisition or valuation;

(iii) the difference between (i) and (ii).

They must also give particulars of additions and disposals of fixed assets during the year or period.

There is as yet no other guidance as to the precise meaning of these requirements, and as would be expected, different companies interpret them in different ways. Some companies take the view that there is no need to distinguish between the various kinds of fixed assets, except interests in land, where there is a specific requirement to analyse these between freehold, long leaseholds (i.e. over fifty years) and short leaseholds. In these cases land and buildings will be shown under one heading, analysed as above, and other fixed assets would be grouped together under some such heading as 'Plant, machinery, vehicles, furniture and equipment'. Other companies take the view that it is desirable to have separate headings for each class of fixed asset. Again, different interpretations are given to the requirement to disclose details of additions and disposals, and it may be that many companies are consciously giving more information than is legally necessary.

Where assets have been included in the accounts at a valuation, the year end amounts of the valuations must be shown. For assets valued during the year, the names of the valuers (or their qualifications) and the basis of valuation must be shown.

One other point to be noted; that the requirement to give the previous year's comparative figures for all items in the balance sheet does not now apply to additions and disposals of fixed assets (Companies (Accounts) Regulations 1970).

Earnings per share

Two of the key ratios that the management of any company find useful are the ratio of *net profit to sales*, and the ratio of *net profit to capital employed*. However, from the point of view of an actual or potential investor in the company neither of these ratios is as useful as knowing how profitable the company is when expressed as a ratio of *net profits to the total ordinary share capital*—in other words, in knowing the *earnings per share*, which can then be compared with the dividend declared by the company on each share, with the corresponding earnings for previous years, and with other companies' earnings per share.

Earnings per share may be affected by changes in 'gearing' (see page 833), as illustrated in the following example:

Two companies of equal size operating in the same industry have both been earning 20 per cent before tax on their capital employed, and they both now decide to increase the scope of their operations by 50 per cent through the raising of additional capital. Company A decided to make a rights issue to existing shareholders on a 1 for 1 basis at par (one new share at £1 for every £1 share held). This will bring in £500 000 additional capital. Company B decide to raise the additional capital through the issue of £500 000 Convertible Loan Stock, carrying interest at 8 per cent per annum and the right to convert into ordinary shares at par in ten years time. In the table below, it is assumed that both companies continue to earn 20 per cent on their enlarged capital employed in the following year, but whereas earnings per share in Company A have fallen from 20p to 15p because of the doubled equity, the earnings per share in Company B have risen from 20p to 26p because of the 'gearing' effect of the Loan Stock issue.

The directors of a company accordingly need to keep a close watch on earnings per share, and be continually looking for ways in which these can be maximised. If they don't, then it may not be long before a takeover offer is made and the directors find themselves out of a job.

Company A	This Year £000	Next Year £000	Company B	This Year £000	Next Year £000
Ord. share capital (£1 shares)	500	1 000	Ord. share capital (£1 shares)	500	500
Reserves	500	500	Reserves	500	500
			Convertible Loan Stock (8%)	—	500
Capital employed	1 000	1 500		1 000	1 500
Total assets: (Buildings, Plant, Working Capital)	1 000	1 500	Total assets: (as Company A)	1 000	1 500
Profit before tax	200	300	Profit before tax	200	300
Less tax	100	150	Less loan interest	—	40
				200	260
			Less tax	100	130
Net profit	100	150	Net profit	100	130
Earnings per share	20p	15p	Earnings per share	20p	26p

An accounting standard was issued in February 1972 (applying to quoted companies) and prescribed a standard method of calculating earnings per share. The definition is 'the profit in pence attributable to each equity share, based on the consolidated profit of the period after tax and after deducting minority interests and preference dividends, but before taking into account extraordinary items, divided by the number of equity shares in issue and ranking for dividend in respect of the period'. This standard was revised in August 1974 to clarify treatment of tax under the 'Imputation' system. One of the requirements of the standard applies to companies like Company B above, where the share capital may be enlarged at some future date through the exercise of option or conversion rights. Such companies have to indicate the 'fully diluted' earnings per share which would have resulted if all these rights had been exercised in the year under review. Thus the fully diluted earnings for 'Next year' for Company B are 15p per share, the same as Company A. (Profit 300 000 less tax 150 000 divided by 1 000 000).

Extraordinary items   In previous years when a 'windfall' profit occurred, such as a profit arising from exchange adjustments, or when an unusual loss occurred, there has been a tendency for companies to keep these items out of the Profit and Loss account, and show them instead in Reserve Accounts. The accounting professions now consider that this practice of 'reserve accounting' should be discontinued. An accounting standard (No. 6) was issued in April 1974, recommending that all extraordinary and prior year items (with certain specified exceptions) should be accounted for through the Profit and Loss Account of the year, and not through reserves. Some companies have followed this practice for many years.

Investments in subsidiary companies

For many years, limited companies were able to carry out operations through the means of subsidiary companies, in which they might own a major share or all the ordinary share capital, without having to report the results of these activities to the shareholders of the parent company, apart from recording the cost of the investment and the receipt of any dividends from these companies. This was seen to provide unscrupulous directors with a means of concealing the true value of their investment from shareholders in the parent company, and in the 1929 Companies Act legislation was introduced distinguishing between holding companies and subsidiary companies.

If Company A owns more than 50 per cent of the issued ordinary share capital of Company B, or if it holds shares in B that give it the right to control the composition of B's Board of Directors, then A is known as the holding company, and B a subsidiary of A. Once a company becomes a subsidiary of another, subject to certain special cases, it can no longer hold shares in its holding company, and any shares already held will have to be sold.

The Companies Acts lay down that a holding company must prepare a consolidated profit and loss account and balance sheet covering all subsidiaries, and has to submit its own balance sheet, but not a separate profit and loss statement. In certain circumstances subsidiaries accounts need not be consolidated, but in this case the reason for not consolidating has to be stated.

The holding company is required to show separately in its own balance sheet shares in and aggregate amounts owing from subsidiaries, also aggregate amounts owing to subsidiaries, including loans in each case. Other information that has to be shown, by way of note or otherwise, is a list of all subsidiaries, giving the country in which incorporated or registered, and the proportion of shares held (and whether directly or through another subsidiary). There are relieving provisions in certain circumstances; for example, it may be permissible to list only the principal subsidiaries.

Investments in associated companies

The general adoption of the Accounting Standard No 1, issued in January 1971 and revised in August 1974, has led to a major change in profit reporting by UK companies. Before this standard came into force on 1 January 1972 companies holding investments in associated companies (up to 49·9 per cent of the equity) were under no obligation to shareholders to make any report on the profitability or balance sheet value of these same companies. Investors would accordingly have to rely entirely on the valuation placed on these holdings by the directors, or by reference to the dividends received from them. This meant that the true value of such investments could easily be concealed from investors, as it had become increasingly realised that the Board of the investing company could in many cases effectively control the dividend policy of such associated companies even although they owned less than 50 per cent of the ordinary share capital.

From now on, if an investing group or company participates in the commercial and financial policy decisions of another company (including decisions on the distribution of profits), and if its interest in that company is that of a partner in a joint venture or consortium, or is for the long term and represents between 20 and 50 per cent of the equity voting rights and conveys the right to exercise a significant influence over that company, then the investment is described as an investment in an 'associated company' and the requirements of the Accounting Standard apply. These include giving the names of and interests in companies treated as associated companies, and of any other companies in which the holding is not less than 20 per cent of the equity voting rights, but which are not treated as associated companies.

Amounts to be included in the Profit and Loss account of the investing company or group are the attributable share of the associated companies profits and taxation, and in the Balance Sheet, the attributable share of the associated companies' reserves, as well as details of the cost and valuation of the share holdings.

The adoption of this standard by many companies has aroused considerable interest in the figure disclosed for the first time of profits earned by associated companies. At the same time it should be noted that several companies with large holdings of 49 per cent in other companies have decided not to regard the investment as being an investment in an associated company, on the grounds that even though they had common directors, they did not in any way influence the activities of that company.

Other investments

The Companies Act 1967 also lays down the particulars which have to be given in the accounts when an investing company holds in excess of one-tenth of any class of equity share capital of another company. The information required covering names of company, country of incorporation or registration, and the proportion of shares held, is similar to that required for subsidiary companies, and relieving provisions also apply in certain instances. It should be noted that unlike the accounting standard on Associated companies, there is no group requirement to give this information and if the investments of more than 10 per cent are made by another subsidiary, there is no need to refer to this in the holding company's accounts.

Other requirements of the Companies Acts refer to all investments other than investments in subsidiary companies, and the information to be given depends on whether the shares are quoted or unquoted. The aggregate amounts of quoted and unquoted investments respectively must be shown under separate headings; in the case of quoted investments the market value must be given, also the split of the aggregate amount between investments quoted on a recognised stock exchange in Great Britain and those quoted on a stock exchange of repute outside Great Britain. In the case of unquoted investments, the directors' valuation is one of the requirements. The income from investments included in the profit and loss account must distinguish between quoted and unquoted investments.

The format of the balance sheet

Ever since the year 1900 an audited balance sheet has had to be laid before the shareholders at the annual general meeting, but not until the passing of the 1948 Companies Act was it made clear that auditors also had to vouch for the profit and loss account.

In earlier years, the balance sheet was invariably prepared in horizontal form, with *Liabilities* on the lefthand side and *Assets* on the right. The layman might have been forgiven for not understanding why the money he had subscribed for shares and the profits accumulated by the business and not distributed were included among the liabilities. Nowadays most companies of any size show the balance sheet in two halves arranged vertically, the top half described perhaps as *Funds employed* or *Capital employed*, listing the various funds injected into the business from shareholders and other sources, and the bottom half possibly described as *Net assets employed*, showing how these funds were used *on the balance sheet date*, i.e. partly invested in fixed assets such as buildings, plant and machinery, partly in trade or realisable investments, and the balance in financing working capital requirements—stocks, debtors, cash etc., less amounts owing to trade creditors. Sometimes the order is reversed, with net assets shown at the top.

It is important to appreciate that the balance sheet is not a financial summary of the company's total resources; for example, unless there has been a purchase of one business by another, there will normally be nothing included in the balance sheet to cover the firm's accumulated skills, knowhow, experience and profit-making abilities—in other words its goodwill. If a business is acquired, then the excess of the purchase price over the value of the tangible assets taken over (fixed assets plus net current assets) can be regarded as payment for this goodwill, and will appear as such in the balance sheet. This confirms that the balance sheet is a record of the way in which capital available to the company has been used—goodwill only appears in the balance sheet when it has been purchased. Another example of this aspect is seen with property acquired under a lease. A firm may be lucky in using for its head office a building in a strategic position acquired many years ago on long lease on very favourable terms judged by modern values. The rent paid will be charged to profit and loss account but nothing will be included in the balance sheet to represent the value to the business of the building because no capital sum was paid for it. (In recent years, many instances have occurred where management were able to release capital for other purposes by selling the freehold of a property owned by the business to a finance company, and at the same time leasing it back from them at an agreed rental.)

The example of a vertically arranged balance sheet (pp. 712–13) shows how both company and consolidated balance sheet figures can be combined in one statement.

Inflation

The Accounting Standards Steering Committee issued an exposure draft on accounting for inflation in January 1973, but in July 1973 a government-appointed Committee of Enquiry was set up to consider the various methods of adjusting company accounts to allow for changes in costs and prices. In view of the time that would be needed before this committee could report, the ASSC decided to issue in May 1974 a provisional standard on 'Accounting for changes in the purchasing power of money' and it is hoped that companies will decide to follow the recommendations. The main features of the standard are:

(*a*) companies will continue to keep their records and present their basic annual accounts in historical pounds, i.e. in terms of the value of the pound at the time of each transaction or revaluation;

(*b*) in addition all listed companies should present to their shareholders a supplementary statement in terms of the value of the pound at the end of the period to which the accounts relate;

(*c*) the conversion of the figures in the basic accounts into the figures in the supplementary statements should be by means of a general index of the purchasing power of the pound;

(*d*) the standard requires the directors to provide in a note to the supplementary statement an explanation of the basis on which it has been prepared and it is desirable that directors should comment on the significance of the figures.

Further comments on inflation are given in chapter 11, together with illustrations of how to calculate the figures for the supplementary statement.

Other requirements for disclosure

The more important requirements noted in this chapter have nearly all needed policy decisions by the financial director as to their interpretation. The Companies Acts also call for the disclosure of much other information, mainly of a factual nature such as the remuneration of directors. For a full list of Companies Acts or other requirements, reference must be made to the appropriate authorities. Accounting Standards relating to the treatment of taxation in published accounts have also been issued recently.

**Illustration
of balance sheet
in vertical form**

Source: James
Finlay & Company,
Limited

**Balance Sheet
as at 31st December, 1973**

	Note	Group 1973 £	Group 1972 £	Company 1973 £	Company 1972 £
CURRENT ASSETS					
Stock		3,778,649	3,465,772	764,279	560,217
Debtors		7,261,327	4,994,127	1,847,323	1,893,083
Deposits Receivable		10,744,941	—	—	—
Bills Receivable		5,139,442	3,588,250	—	—
General Investments	10	277,154	1,332,888	277,154	1,310,802
Bank Money at Call and Cash		10,778,385	2,196,518	667,535	900,980
		37,979,898	15,577,555	3,556,291	4,665,082
CURRENT LIABILITES					
Depositors		17,884,060	312,313	275,466	312,313
Bank Overdrafts and Loans	8	8,770.342	5,916,079	1,091,487	657,646
Bills Payable		931,043	639,821	100,000	363,190
Creditors		5,229,729	4,315,086	1,625,178	1,492,782
Taxation		1,110,368	517,266	526,992	177,415
Dividends		325,200	368,700	325,200	368,700
		34,250,742	12,069,265	3,944,323	3,372,046
NET CURRENT ASSETS		3,729,156	3,508,290	(388,032)	1,293,036
FIXED ASSETS	9	3,790,766	2,504,154	1,104,364	877,287
ASSETS NATIONALISED		259,226	—	—	—
ASSOCIATED COMPANIES	11	17,729,266	16,097,510	4,036,588	3,975,163
TRADE INVESTMENTS	10	617,597	515,467	512,308	514,877
SUBSIDIARY COMPANIES	12	22,739	—	5,286,697	2,506,778
		26,148,750	22,625,421	10,551,925	9,167,141
Financed by:					
SHARE CAPITAL	13	3,500,000	3,500,000	3,500,000	3,500,000
RESERVES	14	22,470,788	18,976,213	7,051,925	5,667,141
		25,970,788	22,476,213	10,551,925	9,167,141
MINORITY INTERESTS IN SUBSIDIARIES		177,962	149,208	—	—
		26,148,750	22,625,421	10,551,925	9,167,141

Signed on behalf of the Board,

J. H. Muir, *Director*
C. M. Campbell, *Director*
R. W. McCracken, *Secretary*

5 Making use of profit information

The Financial Director has discussed with his colleagues some of the ways in which the management structure of the company can be framed so as to break down profit responsibility over the senior executives of the company. He has pointed out how these profit figures provide the key for setting target cost levels, which in turn will form the basis for cost control. He has also discussed with his Accountant the various ways of calculating profits, and also the more important matters which have to be considered when drawing up the firm's published accounts.

Profit figures will always be eagerly examined by the management, shareholders, and prospective investors, and the Financial Director considers it important to be able to explain to his colleagues the more important ways of supplementing this profit information through the calculation of margins, ratios, and other means. Accordingly, he notes the possibilities covered in the following paragraphs.

Profit on sales

Many companies publish this percentage in their annual accounts, usually as part of a ten-year record of salient features. It is probable that one of the main reasons for highlighting this percentage in this way is to show the world what a very small percentage of sales value is represented by profit, and for this reason the profit figure chosen is usually the final net profit, either before or after taxation. For internal management control purposes, it is usually better to take a profit figure before taking non-trading or purely financial items into account, so that the most useful ratio will probably be:

$$\frac{\text{Trading profit}}{\text{Net sales value}} \quad \text{expressed as a percentage.}$$

The management of many UK companies were painfully aware of the importance of this ratio when they read in the Government counter-inflation proposals that in respect of home sales there will be a restriction of net trading profits operated at the level of the whole enterprise, or of approved major subdivisions. These profits, expressed as a ratio of profits before tax to sales or turnover would be held to the average of the best two of the previous five years. If these margins are exceeded, then prices will have to be reduced.

There was no upper limit on the profit margin on export sales and, on home sales, provided the target margin was not exceeded, there was no restriction on total profits. In other words, there was an incentive for companies:

● to increase their export sales and export profit margins;
● to increase the volume of home sales at constant margins;

● to incur additional marketing expenses—with the object of increasing home sales at higher selling prices, but with no increase in margins;

● to incur additional capital expenditure on new plant etc. with the same object of increasing sales, since the additional depreciation can be used to keep margins constant.

If and when it becomes clear that inflation has been brought under control, these restrictions will probably disappear, but meanwhile the watch on margins will continue.

Profit to capital employed

The profits earned by a business come through the use of resources, such as fixed assets and working capital, which have been financed out of shareholders' funds or loan capital, or such as the use of factory operatives or salaried staff, which are virtually paid for as used out of revenues derived from sales. Reliance by management solely on the percentage of profit to sales as a management tool would thus ignore the value of resources financed by shareholders and others.

Taking as an example two companies operating in the same industry:

	Company A	Company B
Sales turnover	£2 000 000	£1 000 000
Profit before tax	100 000	60 000
Profit/Sales %	5·0	6·0

It would appear from these figures that Company B is rather more efficient, although A is twice as large as B. However, the relevant figures for the capital employed in each company are:

	Company A	Company B
Fixed assets	£600 000	£300 000
Net current assets	400 000	500 000
Total capital employed	£1 000 000	£800 000

By calculating the percentage of sales to capital employed, it will be seen that Company A obtains a higher return on capital employed than Company B:

	Company A	Company B
Profit/Capital employed	10%	7½%

This example illustrates the importance of working out these two percentages and from making comparisons, either between different units or divisions in the same company, or on an inter-company basis where the relevant information is available, for example, through the Centre for Inter-Firm Comparison, as described in Part One (see chapter 7, page 76).

The kind of questions which a comparison of these two sets of percentages will raise—such as why should Company B earn a higher percentage return on sales than A and yet achieve a lower return on capital employed—should lead to an investigation which will attempt to decide whether there are certain built-in advantages and disadvantages in each company which cause these differences, or whether management action can be taken to narrow down the differences. For instance, such an investigation may show that Company A is using a long established raw material for its product, while Company B has discovered a cheaper raw material which in no way affects marketability. If Company A decides to switch to this cheaper material, this would increase profits by £20 000 per annum, and eliminate the difference of 1 per cent in the ratio of profit to sales. Further investigation may then show that the management of Company B have been far too slack in preventing stocks of raw materials and finished goods from becoming excessive while at the same time they have allowed customers to take far too long in settling their bills. Tightening up under both heads will reduce working capital requirements by £300 000. Both companies will then be able to report a return on capital employed of 12 per cent.

In order to highlight the importance of keeping capital employed at a minimum for any given level of sales, many companies will supplement the above ratios with a third one—the ratio of sales value to capital employed. Thus in the above example, this ratio was originally 2 to 1 for Company A and 1·25 to 1 for Company B, but after the latter company had reduced its working capital by £300 000, both companies would show the new ratio of 2 to 1.

A point that needs watching here is that, if the management of different parts of a business are judged on their performance in raising the return on capital employed, there will be an incentive for them to improve the yield by eliminating as far as possible any new capital expenditure which is unlikely to bring in an immediate high return, by renting new plant and equipment instead of buying it, or by sale and lease back arrangements for some of the company's buildings. These actions may or may not be in the company's long-term interests.

A practical difficulty that can arise in making extensive use of the return on capital employed percentage is the method of arriving at the value of capital employed. For the business as a whole it may be agreed to take balance sheet values, or alternatively to adopt a policy of valuing fixed assets at current replacement values, reduced proportionally as each asset nears the end of its expected life (e.g. a similar method to that used by insurance companies in dealing with claims).

For sections of the business the accountants will have to work out separate figures of capital employed for each section, so that in total they agree with the balance sheet.

Consideration of *earnings per share* has been dealt with in the previous chapter (see page 711).

Profit margins per unit of product	Retail concerns selling goods at a standard mark-up will clearly be able to calculate their gross margins on each product, but manufacturing firms selling a series of standard products on the basis of previously issued price lists will need to be continually on the watch for fluctuations in the profit margins earned on these products.

Margin calculation is dependent on knowing the average net selling price of each product as well as the unit cost, and cases have frequently occurred where trading firms have been unaware of the true selling prices obtained, owing to laxity in controlling discounts granted to big customers. The advantage of using standard costs rather than actual or estimated costs for product costing have already been noted in chapter 3.

The determination of product profit margins is a major tool for use by marketing management in deciding on pricing policy, and this function is outlined further in chapter 7.

Breakeven analysis

Profit and loss statements show the profit earned in a given period, and they may be supported by schedules of profit breakdown by product groups or regions. Having examined these statements, management will often want to work out the effect on profits of various alterations in performance or conditions, e.g. the effect on profits of an increase in sales volume of 10 per cent and the vulnerability of the company if there is a sudden drop in demand. Breakeven analysis provides a convenient graphical way of showing a whole range of possibilities for the company as a whole on one sheet of paper.

This mode of presentation is illustrated in the two examples set out in Figs. 5.5.1(a) and (b) below and overleaf, and with fuller information in Fig. 5.5.2 (see page 722).

Fig. 5.5.1(a)
Breakeven chart (low)
Company A

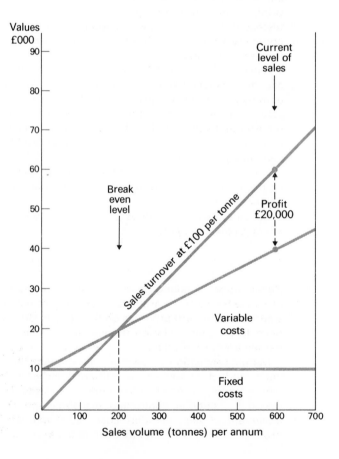

Fig. 5.5.1(b)
Breakeven chart (high)
Company B

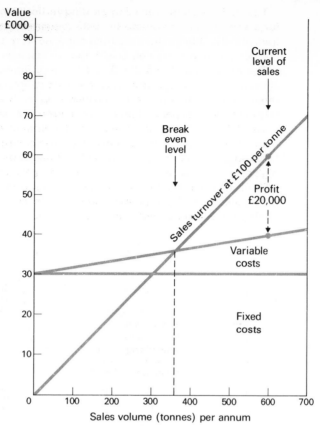

Breakeven charts provide a convenient way of expressing the characteristics of a business in graphical terms. They provide in simplified form the means of reading off profit levels at different sales volumes, and they show the sales level at which operating costs wholly absorb the revenue from sales, i.e. the breakeven point. Two basic assumptions are made in these simplified breakeven charts.

(i) That the sales 'mix' i.e. the proportion of each product or product group in total sales remains constant at all levels of sales.

(ii) That costs can be broken down into fixed and variable elements. The fixed costs will remain fixed at all levels of sales, and the variable costs will vary in direct proportion to the volume of output. It is always possible to prepare more elaborate charts that take into account departures from these two basic assumptions, but they will usually involve drawing curves rather than straight lines. However the straight line charts will usually suffice to illustrate the effect of limited variations on either side of the current or budgeted level of sales.

The charts are constructed by plotting vertically the values of sales and costs for a selected sales volume (usually the current or budgeted level) plotted horizontally. Other values are then obtained from the chart by drawing in the lines connecting these points with the vertical axis as shown in Figs 5.5.1–2.

The breakeven charts illustrated in these figures have been designed to show the effect of high, low and intermediate breakeven points. They relate to three similar companies, each of which is currently selling its production at the rate of 600 tonnes per annum and earning an annual profit of £20 000, but each of which has a different breakeven point. Company A is concerned mainly with manual operations, and fixed costs are low. Hence it has a low breakeven point (200 tonnes per annum). Company B is a highly mechanised business, with a high proportion of fixed costs, and consequently it has a high breakeven point (360 tonnes per annum). Company C is in an intermediate position, but it differs also from the other two companies by charging more for its products, relying heavily on advertising and promotions to boost its sales. The chart

Fig. 5.5.2
Intermediate
breakeven points
Company C

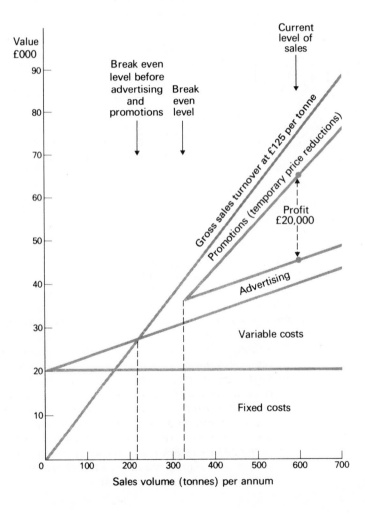

shows two breakeven points, one at 333 tonnes per annum if sales drop off and no cuts are made in the level of advertising or promotions, a second one at 220 tonnes per annum if all advertising and promotional expenditure is eliminated.

A breakeven chart can show also the influence of official 'counter-inflation' restrictions on the profitability of the company: see Fig. 5.5.3 reproduced from *The Financial Times* of 30 January 1973.

Fig. 5.5.3
What 'Phase Two
could do to
profits

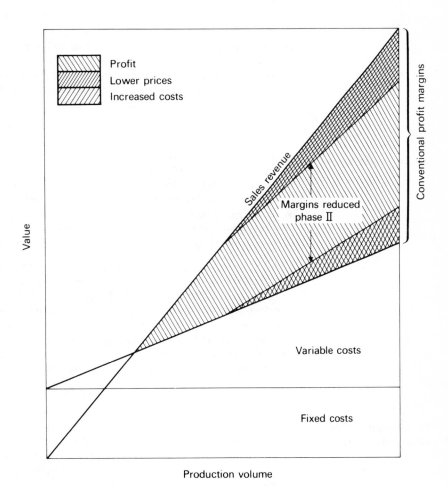

Summary

The new Financial Director has now completed his preliminary review of matters affecting the company as a whole, and he decides it is time to make a start on the more detailed studies before considering his own responsibilities for office management, taxation and financial control. There topics are dealt with in turn in chapters 6–11. (In Part Six the subject of data processing by computer as a means of preparing and presenting of management information is reviewed in outline: see page 885.)

6 Cost control in the factory

Anyone faced with a request to introduce or improve cost control procedures in a factory will readily appreciate that the principal aims are to achieve the desired output and to exercise control over the manufacturing costs *per unit of product,* so that profit margins are not eroded. Reductions in the cost per unit of product can come about through:

- achieving cost savings, such as employing cheaper labour, or using cheaper materials, or reducing material losses;
- improving the performance or productivity of labour, so that a given labour force produces a higher output;
- spreading the incidence of fixed costs over a higher volume of throughput, through reducing machine breakdowns, or improving layout, etc.;
- incurring capital expenditure, such as installing improved machinery or equipment, or extending capacity, provided the benefits of the increased throughput more than outweigh the additional depreciation incurred.

With the growing feeling that government controls on prices and profit margins are here to stay for some time, many companies now feel that the only way to achieve major profit growth in future will be to carry out a concentrated attack on cost reduction each year based on the four approaches set out above. In order to emphasise the fact that this overall cost reduction can come about either by improving performance, increasing throughput or by reducing costs, some companies have decided to call the whole operation a programme for *improving cost performance.*

Plant availability and utilisation

This chapter describes some of the management information reports necessary to achieve this aim, making use of budgetary control and standard costs. It starts with a review of control information associated with plant and machinery.[1] As industry becomes increasingly mechanised and the cost of replacing buildings, plant and machinery rises at an alarming rate every year, it becomes increasingly urgent for factory management to make sure that plant capacity is used to the maximum extent. In machine-controlled operations this means working the maximum number of shifts, and making the fullest possible use of plant availability during each shift. Standing charges

---

[1] This chapter needs to be read in conjunction with chapters 3 and 5 of Part Three, where the manufacturing and maintenance activities are considered from the standpoint of the physical aspects rather than the financial. The two aspects are, of course, closely interrelated: financial considerations are equally important to the Factory Managers and the Manufacturing Department Heads as to the Financial Controllers or Cost Accountants.

such as rent, rates, depreciation, interest etc. will be unaffected by changes in the volume of production put through the plant, so that to increase plant utilisation by 10 per cent will in effect mean a 10 per cent reduction in the fixed cost content of each product.

Control information designed to help factory management achieve these objectives should provide answers to the following questions:

● What is the maximum productive capacity?
● To what extent was this capacity made available?
● How was this availability utilised?

There are two ways of answering these questions—one in terms of machine time, and the other in terms of output. Each is considered in turn in the following paragraphs.

Machine time analysis

Where demand for a product is heavy, output may be limited only by the capacity of the factory to produce. In such circumstances every piece of plant and equipment will be operated to the maximum extent. This maximum, in the case of continuous operation, could be as high as 168 hours a week—but sooner or later a period of overhaul would be required, which would put the item of plant out of action for some time. Continuous working of this nature may be necessary in some industries due to the nature of the process. Thus a glass factory operates a furnace continuously for 168 hours a week for the best part of a year, but eventually the furnace has to be taken out of action and the walls relined, over a period of several weeks or months. In other industries plant may be operated twenty-four hours a day, but the necessary maintenance would be carried out at weekends. In all cases where plant is being operated on a maximum basis, some reduction must be made from the theoretical maximum in arriving at the number of hours per week that would be available for actual production over a period. Where there is operating on a single or double shift basis, the theoretical maximum working corresponds to hours of attendance, but a reduction must be made for hours needed for maintenance. With overtime working outside the normal shift hours, the time available for production will be correspondingly increased. This 'machine available time', as it is appropriately called, is an important figure to determine in advance, because it provides the basis for calculating the plant capacity—in

Fig. 5.6.1
Machine available time

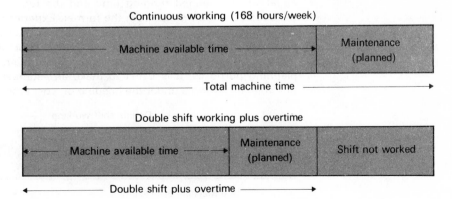

Continuous working (168 hours/week)

| Machine available time | Maintenance (planned) |

← Total machine time →

Double shift working plus overtime

| Machine available time | Maintenance (planned) | Shift not worked |

← Double shift plus overtime →

terms of potential output—in any period. It also indicates the planned division of the total machine time between production and maintenance. It is preferable to have this decided in advance, than left for discussion on an *ad hoc* basis each time the question of overhaul is considered (see Fig. 5.6.1).

One of the purposes of calculating the 'machine available time' is to provide a yardstick against which actual use of the plant can be compared. The object of this comparison is to spotlight unplanned stoppages, or excessive changeover time, etc. In order to distinguish between these factors and idle machine time caused by lack of orders, it is usual to deduct the latter from the machine available time before taking it as a base. It would also be necessary to make a deduction for any time during which it is planned to test the plant on experimental production:

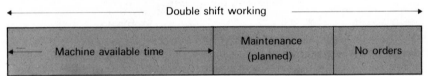

In order to arrive at the time during which it is hoped the plant will be actually used for normal production, deductions must be made for four further kinds of planned stoppages ('ancillary time'): tea and meal breaks, cleaning, changeover, starting and stopping time. After making these deductions, the maximum running time is arrived at—the time for which it will be planned to man up the machine and produce output:

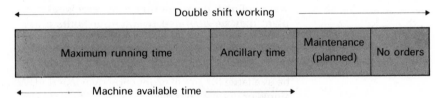

Up to this point, the breakdown of the total machine time has been assumed to have been worked out in advance as a basis for calculating the expected production requirements. If the analysis is repeated for each item of plant in the factory, it is possible to calculate the total plant running hours, and from this to deduce the requirements for labour, power and steam, etc. But before equating the planned running time and the required output, one further deduction must be made from the former. Experience shows that however carefully the work is planned, some unforeseen breakdowns or hold-ups will occur: for example, mechanical and electrical breakdowns, waiting time (waiting for materials, operators, supervisor, repairs, etc. and so on). For planning purposes, it is usual to make an estimated allowance for these possible occurrences under the heading of 'Lost time'.

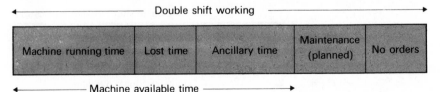

For control purposes, it is necessary to record the actual allocation of total time between the various items described above. It may be practicable to obtain a record of actual running time by automatic methods. The next step is to calculate the length of time the machine should have run, based on the actual output achieved (see Fig. 5.6.2). The standard machine performance in terms of output per minute or per hour of continuous running must be ascertained, and by applying these standards to the actual output, the standard or theoretical machine running time can be calculated. Any excess of actual over standard running time may be due to faulty production not included in the production count, to non-recording of stopped time, or to mechanical defects causing the rate of machine operation to slow down.

Fig. 5.6.2

Machine running time: planned and actual

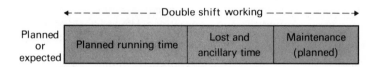

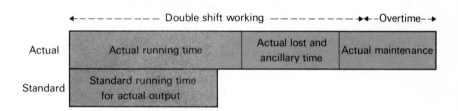

Control could be exercised by comparing actual running time with standard, actual lost time with expected, actual ancillary time with planned, and so on. However, owing to the possibility of the actual machine available time differing from the corresponding planned figure (e.g. due to a sudden influx of orders causing overtime to be worked as illustrated in Fig. 5.6.2), it is preferable to make use of control ratios. Control ratios which have proved useful are:

Machine availability $\quad = \dfrac{\text{Machine available time}}{\text{Total machine time}} \times 100$

Machine utilisation $\quad = \dfrac{\text{Actual running time}}{\text{Machine available time}} \times 100$

Machine efficiency $\quad = \dfrac{\text{Standard running time}}{\text{Actual running time}} \times 100$

Machine effective utilisation $= \dfrac{\text{Standard running time}}{\text{Machine available time}} \times 100$

Comparison can then be made between the planned utilisation or efficiency index and the corresponding actual indices.

A continuous watch over these indices for each of the major plant items, combined with investigation of unfavourable trends or tendencies, should help to ensure that maximum use is made of the potential capacity of the plant.

Maximum capacity
(output)

Reference has been made above to the utilisation of individual plant items in terms of time. One of the primary tasks of production management is to review the productive capacity of the plant as a whole in terms of volume, weight or unit quantities of output.

The first step in establishing a pattern of control is to determine the maximum output that *could* be obtained from the plant, assuming that demand for this output existed. Before this question can be answered, it is necessary to obtain a ruling on the number of shifts to be worked. The business may be in the habit of working single shift, plus overtime when necessary. Double shift working would only be contemplated if demand should justify it. In this case, the maximum capacity would probably be based on double shift working, since it is improbable that any higher rate of working would be practicable. Each case would have to be considered on its merits, and in some circumstances it might be reasonable to base the maximum on round-the-clock operations. Having decided on the number of shifts, the next step is to calculate the output that is theoretically possible during these hours. If a factory is divided into separate divisions or sections operating in parallel, each producing its own group of finished products, then it will be necessary to work out separate output figures for each section. If the factory is divided into a series or chain of processes or operations through which the raw materials or work in progress pass in turn before finally emerging as finished products, then it will be possible to establish a single output figure, expressing the overall capacity.

In the latter case it will usually be found that each 'link' of the chain has a different maximum capacity, and the overall capacity is limited by the link with the lowest potential throughput. The ascertainment of this potential bottleneck is of major importance from the point of view of plant design, as well as operational control. In control terms, the output of this section of the plant is referred to as the *key factor*, since it sets the limit on the overall output. It will be appreciated that one of the objectives of the plant engineers will be to step up the potential output of the weakest link in the chain, in which case another link will automatically become the key factor. It is unlikely that a whole series of operations will ever be completely in balance from an output point of view.

The desirability of establishing the key factor in a series of operations is particularly important when a number of different products are being manufactured in batches. If only one product is being produced, the maximum output can be clearly established as so many tonnes (or other units of quantity) per week. This figure would be obtained from technical data or systematic studies. If several different products are produced, and each product passes through the key factor process at a different rate per hour, then it is no longer possible to talk about a maximum tonnage unless the product mix is specified. This is illustrated in Fig. 5.6.3.

The figures shown relate to maximum capacities. The maximum capacity of the whole process is 12 tonnes per hour.

Fig. 5.6.3
Unmatched
production
capacities

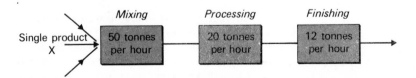

If a new product Y is then produced alternately with X, in equal quantities, and if this product has to pass through the finishing stage twice, then the maximum output of the plant is reduced to an average of 8 tonnes per hour (Product X 4 tonnes, Product Y 4 tonnes put through twice). On the other hand, if product Y has to pass through the processing stage twice, and only once through the finishing stage, the maximum output will remain unaltered at 12 tonnes per hour, since the capacity of the processing stage is more than adequate (6 tonnes X *plus* 12 tonnes Y = 18 tonnes per hour).

*Measuring
output*

One of the objects of establishing the maximum capacity is to use this figure as a control base against which to compare actual throughputs. It would create obvious difficulties if one had to state that the maximum capacity was 8 to 12 tonnes according to circumstances, i.e. the product used. There are two ways in which it is possible to arrive at a common denominator for measuring the output of a machine-controlled operation; one is to make use of the notion 'unit tonnes' and the other 'standard machine hours'. Thus in the first example above one could give factors of 1 and 2 to products X and Y respectively, and then describe the maximum output as 12 unit tonnes per hour. Assuming that the plant is capable of 70 'running hours' per week (see above) the maximum capacity could be expressed as 840 unit tonnes per week. Alternatively, this output could be described simply as '70 standard machine hours per week'. This is a more straightforward way of describing total output where there is a large variety of different products. The above information would be accompanied by a list of 'standard output rates per machine hour for each product', e.g. X 12 tonnes per hour, Y 6 tonnes per hour, etc.

*Manually
controlled operations*

Turning now to the case of a factory organised in parallel, it may happen that a section of the factory is allocated to the manufacture of a group of products by manual methods. It is possible that mechanical equipment is used to supplement these operations, but it will be assumed that the volume of output is determined primarily by the number of operators and the efficiency with which they work. In circumstances such as these it is equally valuable to be able to calculate a maximum output figure for use as a control base, but rather more assumptions have to be made in establishing it than are necessary in the case of machine-controlled activities. In addition to deciding on shift hours, it is necessary to determine what number of operators should be taken as the practical maximum, and at what level of performance they can be expected to work. The former figure can be based on the maximum number of employees that have been employed in the past at any time, or that are likely to be employed in the immediate future. The latter point is dealt with by assuming that the operatives will be working at 'standard performance' (see Part Three, chapter 5, page 399).

From this point onwards, the procedure is similar to that described above for machine-controlled operations. If only one product is being manufactured, the work study department will be asked to establish the standard times for the various operations, so that the maximum output can be established. Owing to the flexibility of labour a 'key factor' will probably not be relevant. An example is given below (based on single shift working):

Maximum number of operators 20.

Attendance hours 45.

Hours available for work 40 hours/week.

Standard times per case of finished product:

Preparing: Product P 20 mins., Product Q 40 mins.

All products—Finishing 15 mins. Labelling and Packing 5 mins.

Totals: Product P 40 mins.   Product Q 60 mins.

Calculation of maximum output per week (assuming operators work at standard performance):

Operator-hours available for work 800.

Output achievable: $800 \times \dfrac{60}{40} = 1\,200$ cases of Product P

or 800 cases of Product Q,

or 600 of P, 400 of Q, etc.

In view of the variability of the product mix, the maximum output would be described as 800 standard hours (or 48 000 Standard Minutes) and both planned and actual output would be measured in the same terms.

Planned utilisation of capacity	When policy plans are being prepared at the beginning of each financial year, one of the key questions to be considered is the extent to which it is proposed to make use of available capacity. Those firms that are in the fortunate position of supplying products for which there is a large unsatisfied demand will, of course, aim at making use of maximum capacity. Other firms less favourably placed will have to decide what quantity of products they think they can sell in the forthcoming year, and then work out what this means in terms of productive capacity. The typical experience of a developing business is to be short of capacity in early years but as capacity is gradually expanded and demand levels off, a state of equilibrium is reached. At this stage, the management will probably aim to make use of 80–90 per cent of their maximum capacity for most of the year, with a higher utilisation during peak periods.

This 'capacity usage' ratio, as shown on page 838, is an important figure to watch. If, when the operating plans have been prepared for a part of the factory, it is found that this index has dropped by some 10–20 per cent compared with the previous year, it is a clear indication to management that the fixed charges associated with that part of the factory will have to be absorbed by a correspondingly lower volume of output. This is likely to have a harmful effect on profit margins unless selling prices can be increased, but in this case the effect may be to reduce the level of demand, and thus lead to a still lower utilisation of productive capacity. In other words a vicious circle is created.

Consideration of these factors emphasises the importance of close collaboration between the marketing and production sides of the business. If marketing management are put in the picture regarding the difficulties caused by underutilisation of capacity, they may be stimulated to develop new products or make some other arrangements for utilising the spare capacity.

Plant maintenance   Having reviewed the importance of making maximum use of productive capacity, it is appropriate next to consider the cost of maintaining the plant at optimum levels of efficiency. One of the benefits obtained from keeping a detailed record of plant running time and plant stopped time is the information provided as to the incidence of maintenance and repair work. For example, the records may show that some machines, on which extensive planned maintenance work is carried out at regular intervals, never break down or require repair during the periods when they are being used for production. On the other hand, other items of plant on which very little routine maintenance is carried out may be breaking down at frequent intervals, necessitating the transfer of operators to other machines.

Consideration of these two extremes immediately raises the query as to how important it is to avoid breakdowns. It is only when this question is answered that it becomes possible to estimate how much planned maintenance work is required, or to attempt to exercise control over maintenance costs. An airline company provides an obvious example where breakdowns must be avoided at all costs, hence maintenance inspections and overhauls will be carried out at frequent and regular intervals, as prescribed by statutory regulations. Such a company cannot save money by reducing the frequency of maintenance attention, and any savings will come principally from increasing the efficiency with which the work is carried out. There is then a double benefit: any saving of time in carrying out the necessary maintenance jobs will not only cut down on maintenance costs, it will also increase the time available for carrying profitable payloads. On the other hand, a company making durable consumer products with plenty of spare capacity, may decide that planned maintenance should be reduced to a minimum, since a breakdown will involve no loss of production. Indeed, the only advantage obtained from overhauling plant before it actually breaks down may be that by so doing the total maintenance cost is less over a period, on the 'stitch in time saves nine' principle. In the majority of instances it is probable that a compromise between these two extremes is desirable.

Most businesses will normally be working somewhere near their maximum capacity, so that a serious breakdown will lead not only to a repair bill, but also to lost labour hours, as well as subsequent overtime working to make good the lost production. Where the maximum hours are already being worked, a breakdown will lead to loss of turnover and profits. If the breakdown is prolonged, there may be a loss of customers as well.

It is clear that the first essentials in drawing up the maintenance policy plans for the year are a knowledge of (a) the relationship between the frequency and extent of inspection and the frequency and extent of plant breakdowns; and (b) representative costs of inspections, overhauls, breakdowns, making good production lost through breakdown.

The basic difficulties inherent in trying to provide factual evidence for conclusions reached in this field are that data can only be built up over a lengthy period, and in the meanwhile general conditions may have changed. Despite the difficulties, it seems possible that future economies in the days of automation will come from studies such as these rather than from savings in direct labour or materials.

Maintenance costs budgeting

Assuming that maintenance policy has been agreed for each major group of machinery or plant, the next step required in the control of maintenance costs is the preparation of a maintenance budget. In the past, maintenance costs have been regarded by accountants as an expense which requires budgeting in the same way as rent, or depreciation, i.e. the total cost must be assessed and included in the budget of general manufacturing costs and expenses. It is not unknown for this figure to be obtained by difference, i.e. by deducting all other items of expense (which can be estimated with reasonable accuracy), together with the hoped-for profit, from the anticipated sales figure and thus arriving at a balancing figure of maintenance and repairs which the engineer is advised must not be exceeded. Such a hit-and-miss method of arriving at an allowable overall cost of maintenance will probably understate the effort required and so will lead to either a complete disregard of the budget by the engineers, or alternatively, if the budget is followed, a gradual deterioration in the efficiency of the plant.

The modern concept of a maintenance budget is a document which will set out in some detail the agreed maintenance policy for the year. Like all budgets, it does not pretend to be a blue-print for action. The actual maintenance effort will depend on many factors which can only be resolved as the year progresses: the volume of production, the type of product being manufactured, the type of material being processed, the extent of overtime working, the incidence of breakdowns, etc.

Fortunately for engineering (or maintenance) management, it is usually possible to provide some flexibility in planning the actual work load. Thus if an unexpectedly high number of emergency repairs have to be carried out in any one week, planned overhauls due to be carried out can be deferred until conditions become normal. If the maintenance staff looks like being unexpectedly slack, planned overhauls can be brought forward, or men allocated to standby capital work. In theory, the working of overtime when necessary should contribute to flexibility, but in practice overtime working is often regarded as a regular feature, however deplorable, for which work has to be found.

*—Budgeting for
labour*

The net result of the above factors is that it is often quite a simple matter to budget for the total cost of the *maintenance staff* during the forthcoming year. This total is found by projecting forwards the average number of men employed in the previous year, allowing for any planned increases or decreases, and multiplying the result by 52 times the average weekly pay (including overtime). In other words, owing to the importance attached nowadays to retaining skilled operators, it may be assumed that the total cost of maintenance staff will remain relatively stable from week to week.

What is not so simple to budget—and this is where the real object of control lies—is the *work* which the men will do during the year. If control is slack, the work will be allowed to accumulate, until eventually a case is made out for working longer overtime hours, or taking on more staff. To be effective as a means of subsequent control, the maintenance budget must be built up from certain basic assumptions, which will be clearly specified. Then if subsequent events show that actual conditions differ from expectation, the necessary adjustments can be made when comparing actual costs with budget. This is very similar to the procedure that is followed when a budget is prepared for the production activities of a business. Labour costs are budgeted on the basis of achieving a specified volume of production; if the actual volume of production differs from budget, then a corresponding adjustment is made when comparing actual labour costs with budgeted costs. The only real difference is that, in the case of maintenance, it is much more difficult to find out to what extent the actual work load differs from that visualised when the budget was prepared.

In the absence of recognised procedures, the following principles can form the foundation for drawing up the maintenance budget in such a way that basic assumptions are made clear:

1. Budget for the total number of man-hours that will be available for engineering or maintenance work (proposed number of men × number of weeks × average hours worked per week).
2. Allocate this total time over the different categories of work which it is proposed to carry out, e.g.
   (*a*) periodic lubrication, cleaning, adjustments, change-overs, etc.;
   (*b*) planned inspections;
   (*c*) planned overhauls;
   (*d*) repairing breakdowns or defects reported by departments;
   (*e*) alterations and improvements;
   (*f*) capital projects.
3. List the major items which it is expected will be carried out under headings (*b*), (*c*), also (*e*) and (*f*) so far as these are known. Insert the expected total times for each of these major items, and reconcile with the total time allocated. ('Plant history' cards on which details of maintenance hours booked on each item of plant over a number of years have been recorded will provide a valuable aid in arriving at these estimated times, although it must be remembered that they will not indicate whether previous experience was efficient or otherwise. The position can only be clarified if the work involved is studied systematically as described in Part Three: see p. 489.)
4. Specify the expected level of production on which the above calculations have been based, particularly as it affects the incidence of breakdowns (*d*).
5. Evaluate the budget in terms of £*p* (see p. 735 below).

Carrying out the above procedure will obviously entail a lot of work, but if it leads to a reduction in the cost of maintenance without reducing operating efficiency, it will be work worth doing.

A further important benefit obtained from budgeting maintenance activities in detail is the opportunity offered for coordination with production activities well in advance of actual requirements. At the same time, the budget will provide the accountant with a reliable basis for calculating maintenance costs for the forthcoming year for inclusion in product cost estimates required for profit planning purposes.

Maintenance control

Owing to the irregular nature of the work carried out, the maintenance budget provides little help in controlling the work done on a week to week basis. As the year proceeds, however, it should be possible to compare actual cost with budgeted cost, and actual work carried out with budgeted work—assuming that actual work done is analysed in the same way as that suggested for drawing up the budget, and that comparison is made with the appropriate proportion of the budget, depending on the length of the period being compared.

It should be noted that if the firm employs planner-estimators to assess the time required on each major job before it is begun, information will be available to indicate the efficiency with which actual jobs are carried out. In the absence of such estimates, the actual time taken on such major jobs will be compared with the allowed time included in the budget. If the actual time is in excess of budget, it will be difficult to pinpoint the reasons for the excess.

Labour cost

As indicated in the preceding section, it is comparatively simple to budget for the total cost of the firm's engineering staff—covering both maintenance and capital work. If it is considered that economies are possible, then one of the most effective ways of achieving them may be simply to reduce the budgeted number of men by one or two each year, and to allow natural wastage to reduce the effective numbers on the payroll in the same proportion. This procedure would be carried on for a year or so until a state of balance had been achieved. An increase in budget would only be permitted where a good case could be made out for an additional work load.

Summing up the ideas underlying the control of maintenance costs through detailed budgeting:

(*a*) The first step is to agree on maintenance policy, e.g. to decide to what extent planned inspections and planned overhauls should be undertaken, having regard to an agreed permissible frequency of plant breakdowns.

(*b*) Next, both budgets and actual maintenance data should be classified according to the type of job, e.g. routine maintenance, emergency repairs, planned maintenance, alterations or additions, etc.

(*c*) Statements should be attached to the budget giving details of the major jobs that are planned to be carried out during the year, or specifying basic assumptions made, e.g. an assumed frequency of breakdowns.

(*d*) Records should be kept of actual time spent on jobs during the year, and, if possible, these times should be compared with predetermined estimates of time required. Comparison should be made with budget, after adjusting for differences in basic assumptions.

(*e*) Budgets and control statements will be prepared primarily in quantitative terms, but will also be evaluated in money terms.

(*f*) The main benefits obtained from budgeting are in the opportunities afforded for long-term reduction of maintenance costs, for more effective coordination with production activities, and for providing a more accurate advance assessment of maintenance costs for profit planning purposes.

Spare parts and materials

Control of spare parts and materials used in maintenance and repair work is of necessity closely associated with the control of maintenance labour. Policy decisions will be taken concerning the frequency of planned inspections, and supplementary decisions made regarding the extent to which parts should be replaced before they are completely worn out. When the necessary policy decisions have been made, a maintenance materials budget can be built up, divided into the same categories as the maintenance labour budget. In order to avoid going into too much detail, it is usual to list separately the major items and to cover the smallest items by a percentage addition to the budgeted maintenance labour cost.

Plant history cards, on which a record is kept over a number of years of maintenance attention in the form of man-hours worked and jobs done, can also be made to indicate the usage of major items of materials or spare parts. These cards will then provide a useful aid to the preparation of maintenance material budgets. The cost of these major items will be evaluated as suggested below.

Control of actual usage of materials and spare parts can be carried out in several ways. In most instances it will be possible for maintenance management to approve the details of items required before they are issued from stores. However, in order to guard against duplicated withdrawals from store, it will also be essential to record actual usage of all major items and to compare this usage with the corresponding items included in the maintenance budget—or against previously approved detailed estimates if such are prepared.

The plant history cards already referred to are a useful aid to control. Certain plant items may require replacement at irregular intervals and it is useful to be able to look back over several years in order to check on frequency.

Evaluation of maintenance costs

From the previous comments, it will be realised that quantities, whether of man-hours or material items, form the basis of maintenance budgets and maintenance control. Only in the case of material items of low value is it necessary to control in terms of money, and then only for the reason of avoiding unnecessary detail.

There are several reasons why it is preferable to control labour costs and major items of materials in quantitative terms in the first place. Basic records must of necessity be kept in these terms, to avoid unnecessary clerical work in evaluating these quantities. If comparison is made only in financial terms, and an excess cost is disclosed, no corrective action is possible until the underlying quantitative reasons for the excess have been uncovered. Furthermore, because the true incidence of maintenance can only be assessed over a lengthy period, it is essential to be able to make valid comparisons over a period of years. This comparison is vitiated if made in financial terms, owing to the effect of changing price levels. At the same time, in order to get a perspective view of operating costs as a whole, and to estimate the incidence of maintenance costs on product cost estimates and profit margins, it is necessary to evaluate *total* maintenance costs in money terms. It may also be necessary to arrive at an *approximate* cost of *detailed* maintenance operations, in order to be able to consider the total cost of maintenance labour, materials and overheads for any job in relation to other factors.

Following these requirements, various shortcut methods have been established for evaluating maintenance budgets and actual costs. For example, it is usually adequate to use an average rate per hour for evaluating labour costs, based on the average earnings of the entire maintenance staff. If maintenance costs form a relatively high proportion of total costs it may be advisable to distinguish between two or three categories of labour, but little purpose will be served in trying to be more exact. If overtime is accepted as a regular feature of maintenance working, then the overtime premium can be included in arriving at the average rate. There is no point in spreading the premium over those jobs which happen to have been actually carried out during overtime periods. If overtime is only worked occasionally, then it may be better policy to use the normal rate for evaluating labour costs, and to throw up the cost of overtime premiums as a separate excess cost whenever it occurs.

With regard to maintenance materials, it is becoming standard practice not to charge out separately the cost of low-value items. A convenient procedure is to apportion costs to jobs on a suitable *pro rata* basis, usually as a percentage on maintenance labour. A labour-saving method of pricing out materials of higher value is to decide on standard prices which will remain constant for several years. When a quantity of any given material is purchased, any variation between actual cost and standard cost is transferred to a price adjustment account. All issues of the material are then charged out to jobs at the standard price, and this procedure can make a considerable saving in clerical work. Any balance on the price adjustment account at the year end is included in general factory overheads, and dealt with accordingly.

The allocation of maintenance costs

The analysis of maintenance costs by type of job, and by individual jobs, has already been considered. It is now necessary to consider the allocation of these costs to processes and products.

In many firms it is the practice to allocate all maintenance costs to production departments. Materials used and time worked for jobs carried out in any department would be charged out to that department at cost, plus a percentage addition (perhaps as high as 150–200 per cent) to cover the overhead charges of the maintenance department. The theory behind this allocation is that the production manager is primarily responsible for maintenance costs, because maintenance is caused by use of the plant for production. It also seems to be considered that the production manager will help to improve maintenance efficiency, because he will resent being charged with an excessive cost for this service.

There is a body of opinion which considers that this procedure falls between two stools. The chief engineer cannot be expected to worry unduly about reducing costs, because the whole of the costs of the department and staff are charged to other managers. The production managers are in no position to criticise the maintenance costs—in all probability if they make too much fuss they will have difficulty in getting any maintenance work done at all for them in future years—and even if the departmental maintenance costs do seem to be excessive, they can always blame the maintenance department. The position is in no way improved if production management is given an advance estimate of the expected cost of each major job. There is usually no alternative but to accept.

There seems much to be said for placing responsibility for maintenance costs fairly and squarely on the shoulders of the maintenance management. The fragmentation caused by spreading these costs over numerous production departments is then avoided, and they can be looked at as a unified total, analysed by type of cost and type of machine. The balance between capital work and maintenance jobs can be more clearly seen, and the long-term trends more easily traced. However it is the production manager who is in the best position to judge the effect on overall operating costs of more or less maintenance, and current opinion favours decentralising part of the maintenance responsibility to production management.

The apportionment of maintenance costs to products for *costing* purposes—rather than for control purposes—can still be achieved independently during the budgeting stage, as illustrated in the example set out in chapter 12 of this Part (see p. 840).

Output budgets

Having dealt with control information associated with the *provision* of productive capacity, it is logical to continue with the *use* of such capacity and with the control of production costs related thereto. The first step is the consideration of the proposed *volume of production* to be attained from the capacity provided. The level of production that is finally agreed with marketing management for inclusion in the annual plans is usually formalised in the production budget as explained in chapter 3. This will indicate the proposed utilisation of capacity for each section of the factory, and will specify the anticipated volume of output—either in detail for each product or in total for each product group. The production budget serves several purposes. It forms part of the integrated plans for the year, and is thus an instrument of coordination. It acts as a means of communication to all levels of production management regarding the proposed work load for the forthcoming year. It is the starting point for working out what production resources will be required. Finally, it acts as a convenient base against which to assess actual performance during the year, i.e. performance in achieving the desired output targets.

Its usefulness in achieving the last two objectives is increased if the budget is 'phased' as suggested in chapter 3. A phased budget will show the expected level of output in each month or other short-term period, taking into account expected seasonal peaks and troughs. Phasing is usually carried out by superimposing on the budget the pattern of previous years' production experience. The sales budget will be similarly phased, and the two budgets will have to be fitted in with each other, after taking into account proposed stock build-ups or run-downs. Phasing is of course unnecessary where the variations that have occurred have followed a random pattern rather than showing any pronounced seasonal trend.

Short-term production planning

Companies making durable goods that can be stored without fear of deterioration may be able to adhere rigidly to their production budget, particularly if it is phased to take into account expected seasonal variations. If actual sales exceed expectation the excess demand can be met from buffer stocks built up in previous periods. If sales fall away the unwanted production can be stored until required. Only if there is a really major divergence from plan, or a serious difficulty in obtaining raw materials, etc., will it be necessary to depart from the original yearly or half-yearly plan.

Other companies may find that it is impracticable to follow the budget precisely, and they may have to supplement the budget with short-term planning. Such companies would include those with limited storage facilities and those making perishable goods. Short-term plans would show both the proposed output, and the methods and resources needed to achieve it. The procedures are described in detail in Part Three (see chapter 5, page 365). The proposed output would be decided on after taking into account the original budget proposals, the up-to-date stock positions, orders on hand (if any), and the latest short-term forecast of current demand. As soon as the actual production for the day or week is known, comparison will be made with the short-term production plans, item by item. Any difference will be noted, and steps then taken to correct the position during the next period.

Comparison of actual with budgeted output

Of equal importance is the comparison of actual with budgeted output. In some cases, as has already been noted, the budget is intended to be followed precisely, and a continuous check against budget is then of obvious importance. In other cases, where actual production is based on short-term plans, it is important to keep a check on the relationship with budget. If the level of actual production (and of the short-term plans) begins to vary to a significant extent from the budgeted level, then it may be necessary to re-assess the overall position, and to decide what corrective action can be taken. If this is not done, opportunities may be lost for retrieving an unfavourable profit trend.

The comparison of actual with budgeted output is often expressed as a percentage, usually known as the 'activity' index. The two indices 'capacity usage' and 'activity' can be plotted in graphical form over a period of years, and provide a useful guide to long-term trends. The following example shows how these indices are calculated in the case of companies making use of phased budgets:

Quarter ended	Maximum capacity (tonnes)	Budgeted output (tonnes)	Capacity usage (%)	Actual output (tonnes)	Activity (%) Plan	Activity (%) Actual
March	1 200	1 200	100	1 100	120	110
June	1 200	800	67	800	80	80
Sept.	1 200	900	75	800	90	80
Dec.	1 200	1 100	91	900	110	90
Total	4 800	4 000	83	3 600	100	90

It will be seen that whereas the maximum capacity is 1 200 tonnes per quarter, the production budget is set at an average of 1 000 tonnes per quarter. This average budgeted output per quarter is taken as the base for working out both planned and actual activity. This method of calculating the activity index is helpful in arriving at the appropriate flexible budget allowance for semivariable expenses (see chapter 3). The indices will be worked out for departments and for sections of the factory.

As already stated, where more than one product is being handled in the same department, the output must be measured in a suitable denominator, such as unit tonnes, standard machine or labour hours.

Direct materials

The overall procedures for budgeting the costs of production have been explained in chapter 4, and it is now proposed to discuss some of the more detailed aspects relating to each of the main cost elements. In many industries, the most important element of cost consists of direct materials.

Direct materials include raw materials forming part of the product, and containers or packing material that can be directly associated with individual products. Materials that are used in too small a quantity to be worth identifying with individual products, e.g. glue or string, are usually described as 'supplies' or 'indirect materials' and are included in departmental or factory overheads.

In budgeting for direct material costs, it is necessary to consider separately the quantities, qualities, varieties and unit prices of the materials to be used. The first three of these factors will be provided by the technical specifications or formulae, which will usually set out the quantities, qualities and varieties of materials to be used in making a specified quantity of each finished product. The total quantities of each material necessary to produce the budgeted output can then be worked out by simple calculation.

The next task will be to decide on a suitable price to use in evaluating the budgeted usage. If forward contracts have been placed for the principal materials, these will provide the necessary prices. If materials are bought on a day-to-day or week-to-week basis, an attempt must be made to predict the average price that will have to be paid for each material over the budget period. The object is to arrive at representative prices which can be used as a foundation on which to build the policy of the company in terms of selling prices, profit margins, etc.

A difficulty sometimes experienced is that the product specification may be expressed in one measurement, e.g. length or volume, while the price may be expressed by reference to another measurement, e.g. weight. In this case it will be necessary to establish standard conversion factors from examination of previous results, or detailed studies.

Choice of materials

Part of the function of production planning, as described in Part Three (see chapter 5, page 365) is to make sure that suitable raw materials are on hand when required. Other functions are to see that the correct quantities are issued from store, and where there is a choice of materials, to see that the right choice is made. This is an aspect of material control that is receiving increasing attention, partly owing to the ever-growing number of materials becoming available. In many cases it is not just a question of substituting one raw material for another. There may be alternative combinations of raw materials, so arranged that whichever combination is selected, the requisite quality conditions will be satisfied.

When this sort of position arises, there are two ways of selecting the combination of materials that gives the lowest overall cost. One way is to sit down with a piece of paper and try out different combinations until one giving a lower cost than other selections seems a likely choice. (If there are many possible combinations, it may be impracticable to try out every alternative.) The other way is to make use of *linear programming*, a mathematical technique which can be used to select the combination with the lowest cost, as the result of systematic searching (see p. 544).

Control information for material usage

Unless adequate control is maintained over the usage of direct materials, avoidable losses can be incurred in several ways. One aspect of this control is to make sure that the agreed plan has in fact been followed, and that the correct materials have been used. There may be a tendency for operators to use excessive quantities of relatively expensive easily worked materials and to compensate for this by using too little of the relatively cheap difficult-to-work material.

Losses may occur at any stage during actual processing, through evaporation, seepage, spoilage, breakages, etc. Humidity may be an important factor during storage, and deterioration may occur if humidity is too great. On the other hand, if goods are sold by weight, losses will arise if the finished products contain less than their normal moisture content. Similar losses will occur if containers are overfilled, or if products are overweight. (A textile firm selling cloth at a nominal weight per square yard can lose money if this weight is fractionally exceeded, since the yarn is bought by weight and the cloth is sold by the yard.)

For these reasons, a continuous check on the actual usage of materials compared with target is usually an important feature of factory control procedures. This control is particularly important when materials form a high proportion of the total cost.

Control of usage is established by:

(a) measurement of the quantity of each material used;
(b) counting or measuring the quantity or volume of output, by products, and multiplying by standard quantities of raw material per unit (from product formulae or specifications);
(c) calculating the budgeted or standard usage of materials from (b), and comparing with actual usage. (Comments are given below of the procedure necessary when variations in formulae are permitted.)

Measurement of usage

Although it is usually possible to obtain an accurate count of completed production, it is frequently very difficult to measure the quantities of materials used; particularly in continuous process industries. Where materials are being issued almost continuously, it may be possible to record approximate weight or volume by means of a measuring gauge, but the accuracy will seldom be good enough to provide data for control purposes. Another method is to measure the quantity of material in store at the end of every control period and to calculate the usage from the 'deliveries into stock' figure, by adjusting for increases or decreases in stock. Here again it may be difficult to measure the stock sufficiently accurately to give suitably reliable figures for a short-term control. The only real solution in these difficult cases seems to be to make the comparison over a comparatively long period, and to select for the stocktaking date the time when stocks are low.

In the case of engineering and similar industries, the measurement of direct materials is usually a matter of accurate recording by the stores clerk. A useful procedure to facilitate pinpointing excess issues is to record the standard issue of materials or parts on one type or colour of form, and to record any additional issues on a different kind of form.

Another practical difficulty met with in trying to compare actual and theoretical usage of materials is the existence of work in progress at the end of the control period. There is no short cut—the work in progress must be measured, and its material content assessed. The best solution once again is to arrange whenever possible for work in progress to be at a minimum on the closing date of the control period.

If management is successful in obtaining an accurate count of production and work in progress and an accurate measurement of materials used, it is possible to compare actual with standard usage, and to assess the extent of any losses. Each business will know what percentage of overall process loss is considered reasonable, and only if actual losses start to exceed the accepted percentage will investigations be set on foot.

With batch production, it may be possible to measure out precisely the quantities of materials issued for each batch. In these circumstances systematic recording of surplus material returned to store or transferred to other jobs will be necessary, and it should then be possible to make a straightforward comparison of actual and theoretical usage as each batch is completed. In this way control can be exercised on a short-term basis without the complication caused by evaluation of raw material stocks or work in progress. Stocktaking will only be necessary at, say, quarterly or half-yearly intervals, when an overall reconciliation of material usage can be made as a check on the individual batch results.

The price factor

Variations in the prices at which raw materials are acquired can have a bigger effect on profit margins than variations in efficiency of use. Although this statement is generally true, it does not follow that management can do very much about it. Nevertheless, it emphasises the importance of keeping a close watch on the prices at which materials are actually purchased, or at which they could be purchased at current market rates. There can be no doubt that good buying can make an important contribution to the profitability of a business. It must be remembered, however, that competitors can be expected to have good buyers also. The object of control, so far as material prices are concerned, is to ensure so far as possible that opportunities for profit obtained through good buying are not frittered away through faulty planning, or lack of knowledge about the effect on prices and profit margins of material fluctuations. Faulty planning could mean requesting, when prices are high, a purchase of a large quantity of materials that could have been deferred until later in the year when prices were lower. Or it could mean failing to substitute a cheaper for a dearer material where various alternatives or combinations are permissible. Lack of knowledge of the effect of price variations could lead to failure to raise or lower selling prices in line with competitors, and thus result in a loss of turnover and/or profits.

Material cost
control reports

The purpose of a material cost control report is to provide management with information which pinpoints the reasons for actual cost differing from budgeted or expected cost. One aspect of this control—comparison of actual with standard usage—has been considered above, and in the material cost control report, the resulting usage variance is expressed in appropriate money values. Another aspect of control is to show up the effect on material costs of changes in material prices since the budgets were prepared. The usual way of doing this can be illustrated by considering one material (out of a number) used in the manufacture of a single product.

The first step is to calculate the standard usage, multiply this by the budgeted price, and so arrive at the expected or 'standard' cost. This is compared with the actual cost to give the total variance. In order to break this down into its components parts, the 'price variance' is established by multiplying the *actual* usage by the excess price. The 'usage variance' is then found by multiplying excess usage by the *standard (budgeted)* price:[1]

e.g. Standard cost 25 litres at £1·20 = £30
Actual cost 28 litres at £1·25 = £35

£5
─────

Analysed as:
Price variance   28 × £0·05 = £1·40
Usage variance   3 × £1·20 = £3·60

Excess cost   £5·00
─────

If several different products are made from the same material, it may not be practicable to record the issue of materials separately for each product. In this case, the standard material usage for each product will be calculated separately, then accumulated, and finally compared with the total actual usage. This makes it possible to calculate the total *usage variance,* and the total *price variance* for each material. If during the course of operations the usage variance shows a tendency to increase, steps might have to be taken to record issues of material for each product over a short period, in order to find out which one was getting out of line.

Alternative materials

The use of more than one material in a product does not of itself create any special difficulties; the standard usage for each material is calculated in the normal way. Complications can arise, however, where one material can be used as a substitute for another, thus in the following example, an alternative formula is used whenever the relative level of prices makes this an economical proposition.

Standard formula	*Standard price*	*Standard cost*
2 kgs of A	£5	£10
3 kgs of B	£6	£18
—		—
5		£28
—		—

Alternative formula (to be used only if total cost based on current prices is cheaper than cost of standard formula)

3 kgs of A	£5	£15
2 kgs of C	£7	£14
—		—
5		£29
—		—

[1] As an alternative the calculations can be as follows: price variance: *standard* usage multiplied by *excess* price; usage variance: *excess* usage multiplied by *actual* price.

Assuming that actual prices in week 23 are A £5, B £7, C £7·50, comparison of these formulae gives the following result:

	Standard formula	Alternative formula
A	£10	£15
B	£21	
C		£15
	———	———
	£31	£30
	———	———

The alternative formula will accordingly be used and assuming that actual usage is the same as standard, there will be a net variance from standard per 5 kgs unit of £2 (£30–£28), due to the combined effect of increased price and changed formula.

It may be more informative to management in cases of this nature to subdivide the net variance and show separately the favourable variance due to changing the formula, and the unfavourable variance due to the price increases.

In the above example this would give:

(a) price variance (£31–£28)	£3
Less (b) formula variance (£31–£30)	£1
	——
Net excess cost	£2
	——

Degraded materials

Another type of variance which may be thrown up in some factories is a reflection of 'degrading' of materials. If spoilage or breakage occurs, expensive materials may be returned for re-use, but because they have become mixed with cheaper materials, they can only be used as substitutes for such materials or as 'fillers'. No physical loss has occurred, only a loss in value and of effort already expended, which may frequently go unrecorded. It is often worthwhile to conduct a special investigation to find out the extent of such losses. If significant, it may be necessary to introduce routine control procedures which will disclose losses of this nature as a regular feature.

Budgeting and control of labour costs

Production labour for control purposes is usually considered under three headings—*direct, ancillary* and *indirect*.

Direct labour is the term given to describe labour that can be associated directly with the products being made. Direct labour is usually regarded as a variable cost for control purposes. In the case of unrestricted manual work there can be no doubt about this, because the output is entirely dependent on the number of operators allocated to the job, and the efficiency with which they work. In the case of machine-controlled work the variability may sometimes be questioned, partly because of the restriction imposed by the machine, and partly because of the lack of flexibility. Nevertheless there is usually scope for flexibility in the time worked on the job—if output rises, overtime will be worked—if output drops, operatives can be switched to other work for part of the day.

Arguments are sometimes put forward by management that labour should be treated as a fixed cost, because the firm has decided not to discharge any men who are surplus to immediate requirements—either because they have agreed to a 'no redundancy' policy, or because they wish to hold on to skilled operators who might be difficult to attract back again when conditions improve. Despite these reasons, it is probably better to treat the direct labour costs as variable, and to throw up where necessary the excess cost attributable to such a policy.

Ancillary labour is the term used to identify those operatives who are not working directly on the process, but who are nevertheless engaged on productive work. For example, in a textile weaving shed the loom operators would be classified as 'direct labour' because they are working directly on the product being made. The attendants who clean down the looms in between weaving operations are a necessary part of the production effort, but they do not work directly on the products as the loom operators do. They would therefore be classified as 'ancillary workers'. By contrast, the timekeeper who records the attendance hours of the factory employees is only *indirectly* associated with the weaving shed or with any other productive process, and he would therefore be classified as *indirect labour*.

The key to the difference between the three types of labour is the extent to which the cost of labour can be directly allocated to products, process cost centres, or departments. *Direct labour* can be wholly allocated to a product or process cost centre. *Ancillary labour* can be wholly allocated to the department in which the products are made or the process is carried on. *Indirect labour* cannot be so allocated, and for costing purposes it would be necessary to spread the cost ('apportion' as distinct from 'allocate') over the departments or products on some previously agreed basis.

The different classifications of labour are shown in the diagram at Fig. 5.6.4, of a factory manufacturing one product W in a series of operations, and three products X, Y and Z by parallel operations.

Direct labour

Having classified the total labour establishment into appropriate categories, the first step in building up the budgeted direct labour requirements for the year will be to examine the output budget, and to take particular note of the range or 'swing' of output between the several peaks and troughs. This information will be provided by the phased budget described in previous pages. When the proposed level of output has been noted, it is possible to arrive at an approximate assessment of direct labour requirements by comparing budgeted output with last year's actual output, and then budgeting for a corresponding increase or decrease in the existing labour establishment. However, such a procedure can only give a very approximate guide, and it has the great disadvantage of automatically perpetuating past inefficiencies without disclosing their extent. Also, if the firm makes a number of products and there is a considerable variation in the product mix from year to year, the estimate of requirements may be very wide of the mark.

There is only one satisfactory way of budgeting for precise labour requirements and establishing the basis for subsequent control, and that is by building up the labour budget from the output budget through the media of *labour standards* established for each product. There are two ways of arriving

Fig. 5.6.4
Classification
of labour

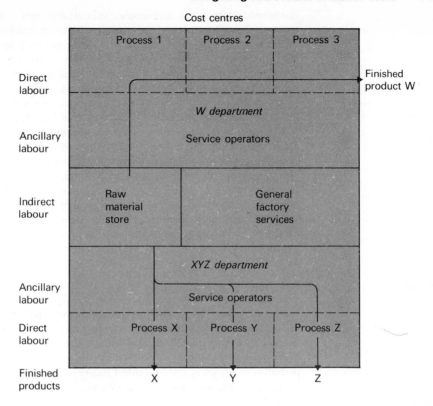

at these standards and each will be considered in turn—'managerial estimates' and 'work study standards'.

*Managerial
estimates*

Although it is generally recognised that standards obtained through work
measurement provide the most satisfactory basis for control, it frequently
happens that management are anxious to introduce control over labour costs
before the work study department has had time to establish these standards.
This position often arises because work study men must spend time in
studying the methods before they measure the time required for each job.

In these circumstances, departmental management will be asked to estimate the man-hours needed in each cost centre for each product. The
estimates will usually be based on examination of previous production
records. When the output budget is evaluated in terms of these standards, a
reasonably accurate assessment of future requirements will be obtained, but
once again the extent of 'built-in' inefficiencies will not be known. The
standards will represent average achievement over a working day after
allowing for breakdowns and other causes of stopped work.

*Work study
standards*

Standards are obtained from work study of processes and operations; they
specify the time required by a fully trained operator to carry out each
operation, assuming that the operator is working under normal conditions and

is motivated to work efficiently. This motivation can arise from effective management control, or from the operation of a suitable incentive scheme. The standard times will include full allowances for relaxation time, tea breaks, etc., and for unavoidable waiting time due to the nature of the process. No allowance, however, will be made for unplanned waiting time such as that caused by breakdown, waiting for materials, etc. (Procedures and terms used by production management and the work study specialists for these purposes are described and illustrated in chapter 5 of Part Three: see page 396.)

It follows from the above that a good team of operators should be able to attain the average level of output corresponding to the appropriate standards, providing that management and organisation are equally effective. If management control becomes weak and ineffective, if breakdowns and hold-ups become frequent, and if the rate of operator performance drops, all these factors will act to reduce the average level of output attained. The extent of the shortfall in output—or what comes to the same thing, the excess time taken for the output actually achieved—can be measured precisely by comparison of actual with standard.

Budgeting for direct labour

The accurate budgeting of labour costs will only be possible after some experience has been gained of comparing actual hours worked with the appropriate standards. The budget is supposed to indicate the costs which it is anticipated will be incurred if the policy of the company, as expressed in the annual operating plan, is carried out. It is in no sense a collection of cost targets that could only be attained if nothing ever went wrong. For this reason it is not possible to arrive at the budgeted hours of labour merely by multiplying the budgeted output by the appropriate work study standards. Some allowance must be included in the budget to recognise the fact that operator performance in recent experience has settled down below standard. Again, if the budget is to be realistic, some allowance must be included to cover 'reasonable' waiting time, again based on a study of past experience. When the budgeted hours have been determined, the budgeted cost would be calculated by evaluating the hours at the expected average wage rates payable during the budget period.

It must not be thought that the inclusion of these allowances weakens the effectiveness of the budget in helping to control costs. The reverse is actually the case. Departmental management are usually relieved to find that they have not been set an impossible task in doing as well as, or improving on, budget. Once they become convinced of its value, they will often take the initiative themselves to find ways and means of reducing costs, through the progressive reduction from year to year of the allowances originally included for substandard performance or non-productive time.

Example of direct labour control

The example below of the two methods of using these standards, firstly for control, and secondly for budgeting purposes, is based on the situation outlined in the factory diagram above (Fig. 5.6.4).

Factory management are anxious to obtain better control over the labour costs of the four products they manufacture, because profit margins are dwindling, and marketing management is pressing for a reduction in costs per unit. The work study staff establish the following standard times for product W, expressed in 'standard minutes' (SMs):

Process 1—20 SMs
Process 2—12 SMs
Process 3—18 SMs

In order to introduce a provisional form of control over product X, pending the establishment of measured standards, the departmental manager states that the overall rate of performance should be 2 tonnes per man-hour.

Production data for week 1 is:

W: 240 tonnes output. 250 hours worked in the three processes, plus 30 hours waiting time recorded.
X: 150 tonnes output. 80 hours worked in all.

Control data is worked out from the above, details as shown below. In this example 'hours' means 'man-hours'.

Product W
Output 240 tonnes. Total SMs per tonne 50.

Output expressed in standard hours $= 240 \times \dfrac{50}{60} = 200$

This output in fact took 250 hours, so that the rate of performance was only $\dfrac{200}{250} \times 100$ per cent of the standard expected from a good team of operators.

$\dfrac{200}{250} \times 100$ per cent $= 80$.

For convenience, this is referred to as an '80 performance', on the basis that standard performance (achieving the specified output in the standard time) is described as '100 performance'.

Operator performance

One of the advantages of expressing the results achieved by operators in producing output as a 'performance index' is that, regardless of the volume or variety of work undertaken, it is possible to compare these indices from week to week, and to draw conclusions from the comparisons.

The next step taken by management would probably be to calculate the performance separately for each of the three processes. This would indicate whether the poor overall performance was being caused by a bottleneck in one of the three cost centres. At the same time the reasons for the 30 hours' waiting time would be investigated to see whether this could be reduced in future. There would also be the possibility to be considered that unrecorded waiting time might have contributed to the poor performance figures. In some cases, particularly where incentive schemes are in operation, it may be possible to calculate separate indices for each operator.

Overall performance

Another useful index figure, which supplements the 'operator performance index' described above, is the 'overall performance' index. The two indices are similar, except that in the latter waiting time is included in the actual hours figure. Thus in the above example the 'overall performance' index for product W is:

$$\frac{\text{Output in standard hours (200)}}{\text{Total time worked on production (280)}} \times 100.$$

This works out at 71, compared with the operator performance index 80. These two indices, plotted from week to week in chart form, give an extremely concise bird's-eye view of the overall efficiency of labour operations.

Product X

A simple calculation shows that 150 tonnes of actual output compares with a theoretical output of 160 tonnes (80 hours × 2). The weakness of this form of control is that no one can be certain whether the original estimate was optimistic.

Multi-product control

In the example of a factory labour control given above, only one product was shown passing through each process. It would be quite possible in some businesses for several products to pass through the same chain of operations in batches, or to pass through *some* of the processes. For example, product W1 might pass through processes 1 and 3, W2 through 1, 2 and 3, while W3 might pass through 2 and 3, and so on. Under these conditions it is usually impracticable, or unnecessary, to record the time actually worked on each product. The production record will, of course, give details of the quantities of each product passing through the process, and by multiplying up these quantities by the appropriate standard times, it is possible to calculate the total 'standard hour equivalent' of the output. Actual hours worked, either including or excluding waiting time, are then compared with this total, and usually no attempt will be made to break down any excess over the products themselves. For example, waiting time may have occurred as the result of the foreman forgetting to order up the necessary containers for the product, or may be due to a machine breakdown. These costs are much better treated as departmental overheads than as specific charges to a particular product.

If it is found that poor performance is always obtained when a particular product is being worked on, then it is possible that the standard has been assessed at too low a figure. In this case it may be correct to allocate the estimated excess cost to the product until such time as the standard can be reviewed.

Labour control reporting

It will be appreciated that the above control over direct labour operations has been obtained entirely in physical terms without introducing the money factor. Even overtime working can be dealt with in the same way, the premium rates being expressed as extra hours paid for over and above the attendance hours actually worked. In addition to calculating the performance indices just described, it is usual to report in a 'labour cost control report' the details of standard hours, actual hours and the variance between the two. There will be a separate report for each departmental manager, and a periodic summary for the factory manager. There are many advantages from controlling labour costs in this way. Control data is expressed in terms that everyone on the shop floor understands—hours of work. The underlying reasons for excess costs are clearly highlighted without having to be searched for, and much clerical work in turning recorded hours into money is avoided. Furthermore the trends from year to year can be followed without having to make adjustments for changes in wage rates.

On the other hand, the totals of the weekly labour control reports should be converted into £p, in order to facilitate reconciliation with the weekly payroll, and to allow for the incorporation of the control data in an operating statement (see the illustration in the worked example in chapter 12, page 856). Where there is a risk of highly paid operatives being allocated to jobs which are normally carried out by lower grades of labour, it may be necessary to record money values in the detailed labour controls. Again if wage rates have risen during the year, it will be necessary to show separately the excess cost attributable to this factor. In these circumstances the procedure will be similar to that described for the control of direct materials. The 'labour wage rate variance' will first be obtained by multiplying total hours worked by the average increase in rates, and then the 'efficiency variance' established by multiplying out actual and standard hours at the budgeted wage rates. Ancillary and indirect labour (see below) will also be included.

Overtime control

Overtime working provides another example of an excess cost which is usually better treated as a departmental overhead. It may be purely fortuitous that product X is made during overtime, while product Y is not. The control of overtime working is a complex matter that calls for considerable care. One of the purposes of preparing a phased budget is to enable both operating and control management to calculate in advance precisely how much overtime will have to be worked during peak periods. It sometimes comes as a considerable shock to management when the total overtime premium payable over the year is collected together as one figure, and included as such in the annual budget. Sometimes overtime is unavoidable, as when it forms part of an arrangement to provide continuous working. In other cases, it may be due to seasonal peaks in demand, or to pressures to finish contracts on time, or to the desire to make up weekly wages to an acceptable figure. There seems to be a good case for considering the two categories separately to enable management to concentrate on reducing the 'avoidable' overtime.

The first opportunity open to management for reducing overtime is during the budgeting stage. They may decide it is possible to enrol part-time workers during the peak periods instead of working overtime. Or it may be preferable to work an extra shift for part of the year. The next opportunity is during the production planning stage. If systematic sales forecasting techniques are employed, it may be possible to predict with some accuracy the probable demand over the next few weeks or months. If storage space is available this will mean that production can be planned so as to smooth out the work load, and so avoid the overtime working that would have been unavoidable had planning been entirely on a day-to-day basis.

Control reports can show what overtime premium hours (or costs) have been incurred, but it is not so easy to arrive at a suitable yardstick for comparison. There is no difficulty in the case of regular unavoidable overtime—comparison will be with the budgeted figure. It is the intermittent overtime that causes the difficulty. For example, the budget may show that peak production during one month in the year will cause overtime working costing £1 300 in extra rates. Some managers will say this is equal to £25 a week, and suggest this figure be shown in the weekly labour control as the 'allowance' for overtime premium. This hardly seems an effective treatment as it appears to encourage overtime working when it is not necessary, and to give a totally inadequate allowance when it is. The position is not improved by treating it as a fully variable cost, which it clearly is not. Another method sometimes suggested is to give the allowance included in the budget for the particular period shown. The difficulty here is that the peak period may come earlier or later than anticipated, or be split into several peaks. Again, the volume of actual demand may differ considerably from expectation.

In view of these difficulties a recommended method is to build up in advance a schedule showing the authorised overtime premium hours for given levels of weekly or monthly production, based on a specified labour complement. Each time a labour control report is prepared, the appropriate overtime premium figure is read off from the schedule. No allowance will be given by this method for sudden pressures of work, and it will be assumed that the work load is evenly spread during the period. By this method any excess shown will represent a cost that could have been saved by careful planning. The schedule will provide the information needed for assessing the total overtime cost to be included in the annual budget. The procedure outlined above for reading off an allowance based on the actual level of output (as indicated by the 'Activity' index) is an example of *flexible budgetary control* as described in chapter 3 (see page 695).

Ancillary and indirect labour

The control of ancillary labour cannot normally be based on the measurement of the work load, since the duties carried out may be of an intermittent nature. The loom cleaner may spend a considerable part of his time waiting for looms to become ready for cleaning. Nevertheless it may be desirable to employ a number of such cleaners, because chance may decide that several looms become free at the same time, and it would be uneconomic to hold up fresh work while waiting for one man to deal with each loom in turn.

The usual method of achieving control is to decide on an agreed *allocation* of men, or of man hours, at varying levels of output or activity. These allocations would be based on the recommendations of the work study department, and would be agreed by the departmental management. Next, they would be set out as a 'flexible budget', in a similar way to that described for dealing with overtime premiums. Alternatively the information could be set out in graphical form, either in the form of a 'stepped' line (Fig. 5.6.5), or as a straight line (Fig. 5.6.6), the straight line being so arranged that it bisects the stepped line. The stepped chart shows that, if actual production is equal to the average budgeted level (taken as 100 per cent activity), three service operators

Fig. 5.6.5
Budget allowances:
service operations (1)

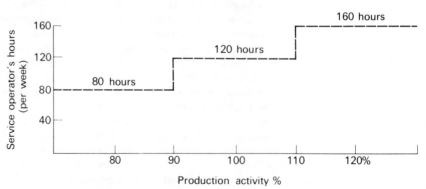

Fig. 5.6.6
Budget allowances:
service operations (2)

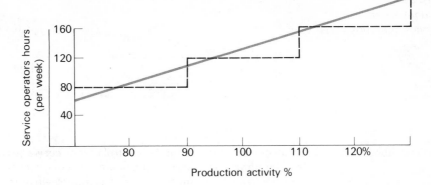

working a forty-hour week will be required. If production should rise by 10 per cent, an extra man will be needed, and if it falls to the same extent, only two men will be required. In the straightline chart these variations are smoothed out. It might be thought that the stepped line would be more effective than the straightline chart as a means of control, but this is not necessarily so. The reason for this is that if production in the above example fluctuates from week to week around one of the activity levels at which an extra man is needed and use is made of the stepped chart, the following position may be shown:

	Activity %	Service operators' hours		
		Allowed	Actual	Variance
Week 24	88	80	85	5
25	90	120	88	32
26	87	80	80	–

whereas if the straightline graph is used, the sudden jump either way is avoided. The use of the latter implies that there may be some way of providing extra assistance short of providing an additional man, and this is usually true.

In some cases, the total allowable cost for ancillary labour can be broken down into a fixed and variable element, and shown either graphically (Fig. 5.6.7), or expressed as a formula. Thus in the above example, the total service operator hours allowed for any tonnage of output would be given by the formula: 80 plus (1·6 × tonnage) hours. In budgeting for ancillary labour use is made of these schedules or charts to establish the budgeted hours corresponding to budgeted output or activity. Both budgets and control statements will be converted into £p as described for direct labour.

Criticism is sometimes raised that the preparation of flexible budget charts takes up a lot of time each year. If many charts have to be prepared it is sometimes possible to make them last for a number of years by gearing them to the percentage utilisation of maximum capacity, rather than to the planned activity for the year.

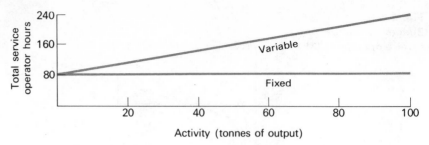

Fig. 5.6.7
Budget allowances:
service operations (3)

Indirect labour

Little need be said about the control of *indirect wages* because it will follow a similar pattern to that of ancillary labour, except for the fact that the allowed hours will be the same as the budgeted hours—in other words the cost is likely to remain constant regardless of fluctuations in the volume of output.

To conclude these comments on the control of labour costs, it is worth noting that the term 'ancillary labour' is of particular value in process industries, which will normally be using 'process costing' as distinct from 'job costing'. Under *process costing* all labour employed in a process department is treated as a 'direct expense' as explained in chapter 3. The labour charged directly to processes in this way can then be split up into direct and ancillary labour, depending on the variability with output as already described.

In a jobbing firm, such as jobbing engineers or jobbing printers, such a distinction is unnecessary. *All* labour other than that working directly on the job in hand is treated as indirect labour, and is included in departmental or factory overheads.

Power control

From time to time views are expressed that when automation becomes more universally applied management controls as we know them today will become unnecessary. All excess costs will then be eliminated because of the corrective action taken on the spot by automatic means. This may be a long way off, but many firms employ at least one semi-automatic procedure for preventing excess power costs being incurred, and perhaps this must be regarded as a step in the right direction. Reference is made here to the automatic warning bell that sounds the alarm if the demand for current during the previous ten minutes has exceeded the previously agreed limit. If, under a 'maximum demand' clause, the surcharge on the whole of the current consumed during the month or quarter is to be avoided, instant action must be taken to reduce the load during the remainder of the thirty-minute control period.

The usual treatment of *power charges* for control purposes is to allocate to each production and service department a proportion of the total cost, according to the metered or estimated usage. While it is perfectly logical to do this, it does have the effect of preventing the make-up of the total cost being seen, unless steps are taken to show the total position in a comprehensive report such as that shown in Fig. 5.6.8.

Although control information would be shown in this way, it would still be possible to allocate the total cost to departments if desired. Alternatively, only the cost of the current actually consumed would be so allocated and the fixed charge, maximum demand charge, mains losses and lighting charges would be allocated to factory overheads.

Fig. 5.6.8
Power control

Power control				Month _____		
Cost per kW hr	kW hours			Cost		
_____ p	Std	Act	V'ce	Allwd	Act	V'ce
Department A	Based					
Department B	on					
Department C	actual					
Lighting	output					
Mains losses						
Maximum demand charge						
Fixed charge						
Total cost			£			

The effective control of the power consumed means separate metering for each section of the factory taking current, or for those sections that are the principal users. It also means systematic reading of meters, say once a week, after the production activities have ceased, and the calculation of weekly usage. Metering should as far as possible coincide with departmental responsibilities. If this is not possible, it means that apportionments will have to be made, in order to arrive at the correct charge to be included in the departmental operating statements. The amount of interest displayed in power control reports by departmental management will be considerably reduced if a high percentage of the total cost is represented by arbitrary apportionments.

The next step would be to establish through technical studies the 'standard usage' of power, under varying conditions and with different kinds of throughput. It may be found that the power consumption should vary in direct proportion to the tonnage of throughput—or to the length of time the plant was running. Alternatively, in such operations as grinding it may be found that the consumption will depend on the particular raw material being ground. Power used for lighting purposes would be compared with a fixed budget figure.

Effect of
control

Experience has shown that, where the power costs in a business amount to a significant total, a control on these lines is well worth while. It might be thought perhaps that the introduction of such a control could have little effect on the quantity of current consumed, and that the clerical effort involved was therefore a waste of time. In practice, the introduction of such a scheme usually has the effect of increasing 'cost consciousness'. This leads to cutting down wastage of power, and to more energetic reporting of defects that should be put right. Thus, in one example where power costs were brought under control, it was found that conveyor belts and motors were switched off when not in use, whereas previously they had been left running. Defects, such as slipping clutches, were immediately reported. All this was achieved because the control report was prepared in such a way as to show up cost variances by departmental responsibilities. A cost report which merely compared the total usage of power with the standard usage would be unlikely to have any effect on reducing waste, because no one manager would be able to trace the result of any action taken.

If the control is to be really effective, it is important to make sure that the standards really do reflect the power consumption that should have occurred in the particular circumstances. Otherwise variances thrown up on a control report may be due to different conditions, or different materials passing through the process, rather than being caused by inefficiency. The annual power budget, for inclusion with the budget of other factory expenses, would be built up from detailed consideration of the budgeted activities in each department, by applying the appropriate standards, and evaluating the total usage at the estimated rate per unit. Separate figures would then be included for maximum demand charges, fixed charges, mains losses, lighting, etc., based on managerial or technical estimates.

The 'allowed' cost included in the specimen power control given above would be obtained by multiplying standard usage by budgeted rate. If the actual rate per unit differed from the budgeted rate, this would be included in the departmental variances, and the KWh figures would then give a better guide to comparative efficiency.

Steam control

Although the main savings in steam consumption and steam production will come from technical studies, experience has shown that substantial further economies are possible if suitable cost control procedures are introduced.

For control purposes, the boiler plant producing steam is virtually treated as a separate business activity, whose object is to supply the needs of the producing departments in the most economical way. The costs of steam production are controlled by reference to the activity of the boiler plant, as indicated by the quantity of steam distributed. The cost of fuel consumed would usually be regarded as being directly variable with the weight of steam produced, while labour costs would tend to be constant. Standards for steam usage in the production departments would be established by technical studies.

The weight of steam produced can be obtained by measuring the weight of water evaporated, while the actual usage of steam can be measured by steam meters at the outlet points. There will inevitably be mains losses due to condensation and leakage, and it is usually advisable to throw up this figure as a separate item on the control report. This is better than apportioning it over the users of steam; it means firstly that the departments using steam will be charged with the exact quantities shown by the steam meters rather than with an inflated figure, and, secondly, it directs the attention of management more forcibly to the full cost of the lost steam.

The steam distributed to production departments will usually be charged out to them at a predetermined price per kgm of steam, so that if the actual output at the end of the period is less than anticipated, the boiler plant costs may not be fully recovered, in which case the unrecovered amount will have to be charged as a general factory overhead.

In other instances, steam usage is charged out to production departments by the boiler plant at the end of each month or quarter at the actual cost per kgm, so that if activity slackens off, the cost per kgm of steam will be correspondingly raised. This system avoids complications but it obscures the fact that part of the actual cost of the steam is due to under-utilisation of boiler capacity, and it upsets the long-term comparison of steam costs in the user departments.

Considerable complications can occur where different qualities of steam are produced, or where power is generated as part of the steam-producing process. In the latter case, an equitable way has to be found for apportioning the cost of production to the two end products; in fact there are several ways, depending on one's point of view, but each method gives a different set of unit costs.

Control of other factory activities

The control of other factory activities follows a similar pattern to procedures already described. Generally speaking, budgets will be prepared to show the expected activities in some detail, together with the anticipated cost. Variations in production output will normally have no effect on these activities, so that control will be effected by a straightforward comparison of actual costs with budgeted costs.

Research and development

Many industrial firms find it necessary to spend considerable sums of money on *research and development*. Indeed, as competition at home and abroad increases in intensity, the importance of this function as a major contributory factor in attaining overall objectives of growth and profitability becomes increasingly emphasised as the years go by.[1] The first step to be taken in deciding how research and development costs can be controlled is to examine what sort of activities will usually be carried out, to consider whether these can be classified under broad general headings, and to note what kind of costs will be incurred. Although it is obvious that experience will vary considerably according to the particular industry, or, by reason of size and type of firm, it will usually be found that certain features of the work are the same in each instance—it is for this reason that it becomes possible to write about the *control* of research and development cost in a general sense. For example, it will usually be found that the activities carried out can be divided into the following categories:

Improvements to existing products. Efforts may be made to improve the 'sales appeal' of the product through better appearance, texture, flavour, aroma, lasting qualities, effectiveness in operation, etc.

Reduction in cost of existing products. Activities may consist of finding cheaper but equally suitable raw materials, or devising cheaper methods of processing. In either case, the lower cost may lead to selling-price reductions, and an increased volume of sales.

Creation of new products. Here the object is either to follow up suggestions made by marketing people regarding desirable new products, or to develop new products 'out of the blue'. (An example of the latter is the creation of selective weed-killers, which were discovered accidentally during research into plant fertilisers.)

[1] From the standpoint of the management of the technical activities involved, this subject is considered at length in Part Three, chapter 2, see p. 303.

Fundamental, basic, or exploratory research. In many cases, research workers in industry find that there is a need to undertake work not specifically connected with products. It may be necessary to find out certain facts, or to establish patterns of behaviour, either with regard to raw materials, or to the conditions under which the products will be used. Finding the answers may then subsequently open the way to improvements in specific products, etc.

Consideration of the type of cost likely to be incurred in carrying out the above four groups of activities shows that in nearly all cases the bulk of the expenditure will consist of salaries and laboratory upkeep, and that a relatively small proportion of the total will be spent on materials and supplies. In other words, a major portion of the total will be 'fixed' in the short term, and only in the long term will there be any significant variations in the levels of expenditure. There are, of course, laboratories where considerable amounts of expensive equipment have to be installed as essential to their work.

Control
procedures

Looked at from a purely financial point of view, research and development costs can be covered by normal budgetary control procedures. A budget can be prepared, based on the existing or proposed numbers of personnel, the expected average salaries, the expected outlay for equipment and supplies, and other expenses. Comparison of subsequent actual costs will show whether or not the budget is being adhered to, but, as indicated above, it is unlikely that variances will prove to be of any great significance in the short period, or even within one year.

However, if management are to exercise *effective* control over research and development costs, some means must be found of controlling the *work being carried out* as well as the total cost of the activity. In some respects, the problem is similar to that of the control of maintenance costs. Furthermore, since the work is nearly always non-repetitive in nature (unlike maintenance work), the whole emphasis is on 'pre-control', rather than on post-mortems of expenditure already incurred. Bearing these points in mind, a suggested method of exercising control over research and development activities is as follows:

1. Within the policies approved by the Board of Directors, prepare a programme of long-term research, together with appropriate development projects anticipated; allow for incidental reference studies required by other departments (if this is the company's practice).

2. Draw up long-term and annual budgets—showing total allocation of funds for research and development (in comparison with similar allocations for advertising and sales promotion, and with the expected overall profit).

3. Break down annual budget into short-term periods (e.g. quarterly) and give quantities and cost for each item (man-hours, total salaries, depreciation, etc.).

4. For the period immediately ahead (e.g. for the next three months), prepare schedule of projects to be undertaken, with list of priorities, and estimated man-hours to be spent on each project. For that part of the budget (e.g. the last nine months) for which it is not possible to foresee in any detail what projects will be undertaken, prepare estimates of total time to be spent on each of the four main groups of work.

5. Reconcile with total budget figures.
6. Introduce an effective system of project control. This will involve frequent review of the progress achieved on each project, with a positive decision taken on each occasion whether to continue or terminate. Compare the total time (and money) spent on projects with the budget figures.
7. Draw up detailed schedule of projects planned for the following quarter, having regard to the experience of previous quarter, and to expected future benefits.
8. Reconcile with budget totals for period, but where this is not possible, decide whether to amend or postpone one or more projects, or whether to press for a revision of the total budget figure.

The forms for presenting and reviewing data are illustrated in Fig. 5.6.9.

Fig. 5.6.9
Research and development control
19....
A. Man-hours

Total staff: Budget=10 Actual=	Details of project	31 March		30 June		30 Sept.		31 Dec.	
		Budget	Actual	Budget	Actual	Budget	Actual	Budget	Actual
		Hours	Hours	Hours	Hours	Hours	Hours	Hours	Hours
Product improvement Project 121 Project 122		1 400 1 000							
		2 400		2 300		1 800		2 300	
Cost reduction Project 35 Project 37 Project 49		800 300 100							
		1 200		1 200		900		1 000	
New products Project 153		500		700		700		900	
Basic research Project 74		600		800		600		800	
Total man-hours (ex.holidays)		4 700		5 000		4 000		5 000	

B. Expenditure

Total staff: Budget=10 Actual=	31 March		30 June		30 Sept.		31 Dec.	
	Budget	Actual	Budget	Actual	Budget	Actual	Budget	Actual
	£	£	£	£	£	£	£	£
Total salaries (inc. holidays)	9 000		9 000		10 000		10 000	
Other costs Supplies Maintenance and equipment Heat and light Cleaning, etc. Management, admin, etc.	1 500 1 000 400 300 2 500		1 500 1 000 300 300 2 500		1 200 1 000 200 240 2 500		1 500 1 000 400 300 2 500	
Total research and development costs	14 700		14 600		15 140		15 700	
Budget revisions								
£								

Note The figures inserted in the above control report are the budget figures agreed with the management of the research and development department just prior to the year's commencement.
At the end of each quarter details would be inserted of actual man-hours and costs, also details of projects for the following quarter together with budget ammendments if applicable.

7 Marketing, selling and distribution management information

The marketing programme

The marketing and selling activities of a company have to be looked at from two different standpoints. In one respect they are comparable with the production activities: in this sense, they form a function of management practice with their own specialist expertise and personnel, and in the majority of companies these activities will form a self-identified division or department in the organisation structure. Thereby, marketing and selling parallel the activities of manufacturing, processing, supply, development, maintenance services, and such like, which, taken all together, comprise the production function, represented by the kinds of department (factories, works, etc.) which have been the focus of interest in the preceding chapter.

Marketing and selling must, however, be seen also in the wider context that has been described above in Part One (see chapter 3, page 27) and in Part Two (see chapter 1, page 235). In this sense, 'marketing' has been posed as an all-embracing concern of the management of the firm's operations, the foundation and framework of its activities and efforts in fulfilment of objectives. The functional specialists naturally remain as the focus, but they are more correctly then to be seen as advisory leaders in the concerted management action, themselves closely tied in with the chief executive. It is in this sense that the fundamental significance of a company's *marketing programme* is confirmed (see pages 83 and 236): it forms the consolidating medium for all the managerial efforts of the team working with the chief executive and under his command.

Management information has to reflect this duality of setting. The information procedures and data for the company overall can make this reflection easily enough, if they are designed as an *integrated system*, of planning and control, with common principles and common modes of presentation, appropriately and adequately understood by all members of the managerial and supervisory team, including the functional specialists. As a matter of fact, the contemporary jargon uses for this approach the label, *integrated management information system*—cumbersome mouthful, indeed, but at least having the merit of specifically indentifying the essential characteristics of the concept. A company's marketing programme is, obviously, at the heart of any such system of information for integrated planning and control. Within that co-ordinated framework of information, the needs of the marketing and selling division or department will be provided for as part of the structure, taking their proper setting as reflecting the objectives of the marketing programme. It is this latter aspect that forms the subject-matter of the present chapter.

The preceding chapter demonstrated and reviewed information procedures for planning and control of the physical operations of the production and related departments, together with corresponding procedures for control of performance and cost.

The objectives being served were those reflecting the company's marketing programme in terms of quality, volume, delivery, reliability and cost of required output or service. In this present chapter those same objectives are considered from the standpoint of relations with the customer: assessing his needs, promoting his buying interest, selling him product, supplying and delivering that product, and maintaining continuing customer loyalty. These are the specific responsibilities of the marketing and sales functions: *their* needs in terms of information for planning and control of performance and cost will now be examined, with proposed procedures or system being demonstrated.

Coincidentally, regard will be paid to some aspects of management information needs towards the wider objectives of growth of business and improvement of profitability for the firm overall.

The annual marketing plan	Whereas the marketing programme stands as an integral presentation of the company's objectives and intentions into a limited (perhaps reasonably foreseeable) future, it cannot realistically serve as an operating management "tool" for practical control purposes. To serve in that way, it has to be broken into suitable sections or periods; this may often be an in-built feature, if the programme is drawn up on the 'rolling' formula (see chapter 3 of Part One, page 27). Convention has long since established the twelve-month period (calendar or other) as the convenient 'trading year', and the marketing programme can thus be readily sectioned into the year immediately ahead—presented now in the form of an *annual marketing plan*, which may incorporate or supplement the *annual sales budget*. This marketing plan or budget, for a defined and immediate period ahead, can take many forms, but, broadly, they all concur in presenting in some detail what the company's marketing management, supported by the chief executive, wish to see achieved during the coming year, in terms of the volume and value of sales, and of marketing support expenditure such as advertising and promotions. It will highlight any projected changes in product or pricing policy, any major new product launches, and any alterations in sales territories.

Much preliminary work will have to be carried out if the marketing plan is to be something other than a series of hopes or guesses, and financial management should be able to play a part in carrying out this work, particularly in helping to evaluate the effect of alternative courses of of action.

The kind of questions that need asking are:

- What level of sales can be expected next year if no changes are made in pricing or promotional policy, and if the level of competition remains unaltered?
- What would be the effect on sales if changes *are* made? (A whole series of calculations here.)
- What new products can be introduced next year, in what volume, and at what price?
- What changes are visualised in the sales force activities, and what new markets will be opened up?
- What opportunities could there be for price reductions from improvements in performance in factories or depots? Or in sales effectiveness?

Annual sales
forecasts

As has already been noted, the annual marketing plan will be built up after a number of alternative courses of action have been investigated, but the starting point will be a straight sales forecast of the level of sales in the year ahead, assuming no changes are made by the company or by competitors.

One way of arriving at a sales forecast is to look at the way the total market is likely to behave, and assess the share of this market that it is hoped to obtain or retain.

Another way is to build up the total forecast from much more detailed forecasts applying either to sales areas or to individual products. These forecasts must obviously be developed within the business—it is not possible to look at a 'total market' position for individual products, because no two manufacturers will make exactly the same product. There is always the possibility that the total market for a group of products may be declining, and yet a firm may sell one or two products within that group whose sales are rising progressively from year to year. It is necessary to look at the detailed position as well as the overall position. There is a close analogy here to the behaviour of the share markets. An individual share may continue to move for some years against the trend set by the shares of other companies in the same industrial group.

Forecast by
areas

The usual method of building up a sales forecast by areas is to ask the various managers to submit estimates of sales in their area for the forthcoming year or other budget periods. These area forecasts would be made on the assumption that no changes are made in existing marketing arrangements, either of product variety, prices, advertising and sales promotion activities, or of sales staff. If changes in any of these are actually planned, it will be better to make a separate adjustment for them later. In drawing up the forecasts, the area managers will discuss the current sales trends with branch managers and sales representatives. This discussion will include a detailed review of sales to the principal customers. It may be known that some of these are likely to be lost, while there may be prospects of others coming in. An advantage of building up an area forecast in this way is that it can be used later as a basis for comparison with actual area sales. Variations from target can then be associated directly with the management responsibilities concerned. When the area forecasts are complete, they are summarised and reconciled in total with the forecasts prepared in other ways. It may first be necessary to make adjustments in the case of areas in which previous estimates have proved to be either consistently optimistic or the reverse.

Forecast by
products

Sales forecasts by individual products will be built up in the first place by brand managers or their equivalents. These managers will have a special knowledge of developments affecting the products for which they are responsible—increased production, changes in design or price, etc. They are accordingly in a good position to decide whether there is likely to be any variation in the trend of recent sales of each product.

In the absence of any special developments, the sales forecast for each product or group of products will usually be determined by forward projection of recent trends. It will be assumed that if sales have risen by 5 per cent during each of the last three years they will go on rising at this rate, if they have fallen by this amount they will go on falling, and so on. It should be noted that this forward projection of past results could not be expected to serve any useful purpose in the case of fashion goods. (Each year would have to be considered on its own merits.)

The above procedure may give useful results for a number of years—in fact for as long as the trend continues. Eventually the time will come when an upward trend will suddenly be reversed, whereas the forecasts were probably making provision for the usual increase. There is of course no sure way of knowing in advance when an established trend is about to be reversed. A man walking up an undulating mountain road on a foggy day cannot tell how near he is to the summit. He only knows that he has not reached the top because he is walking uphill for longer periods than he goes downhill. Eventually he finds that he is beginning to descend for longer periods than he rises, and he then knows that he is past the summit. In exactly the same way, business management can only be reasonably certain of a change of trend after the change has first been detected and then confirmed.

It is thus vitally important to be able to detect a change of trend immediately it has occurred, and as soon as confirmation is received, to take immediate corrective action. It is surprising how frequently a sudden reversal of the trend of sales is allowed to go unnoticed for many weeks, until the warehouses are overflowing with unsold stocks. It may be wishful thinking on the part of the management, who are hoping that each week will bring a recovery that never comes.

Moving annual total

Sometimes the position is obscured by random fluctuations and seasonal peaks and troughs. In these circumstances several techniques can be used to smooth out the fluctuations, and thus to show the overall trend. The best known of these is the calculation and comparison of the 'moving annual total'. The 'moving annual sales total' is in fact the last twelve months' sales, no matter when the figure is compiled. Thus if the total is taken out during the month of September, the twelve months' total would cover the twelve months to 31 August. Next month a new total would be calculated, this time the twelve months to 30 September. Each new total is most easily obtained by adding in the latest month and dropping off the earliest month. Because the total always covers a year, the effects of random and seasonal factors are entirely eliminated. If the total is plotted each month in graphical form, the trend of sales can easily be seen.

Returning to the forecasting of next year's sales by areas and products, the various forecasts will be assembled and compared, and a compromise will be agreed on if the totals differ. Suitable adjustments will then be made in respect of new developments, etc., as already described, and the sales forecasts agreed.

Profitability estimates

At various stages in the preparation of the marketing plan, it is usually essential for marketing management to hold a series of discussions with other functional management. This stage will usually first be reached when preliminary ideas have been formulated about the products to be sold next year and sales forecasts have been prepared to indicate probable quantities. Discussions with production and financial management will centre round the estimated costs of making and selling these quantities of products, the prices at which they should be sold, and the profit contribution obtainable from them.

Use of product costs

In the period between the two world wars, when cost accounting was struggling to be recognised as an essential management tool, it was often possible to listen to heated discussions between the cost accountant and the marketing manager about the need for product costs. The cost accountant would say that the marketing manager *ought* to base his selling prices on these costs, the marketing manager in turn would declare that what the products actually cost was not of the slightest interest to him and that selling prices were based on a careful assessment of what the market would bear or on what competitors were charging, or on pure 'hunch'. Since those years, marketing management have found increasing use for information about the cost of the products they sell. Brand management need all the cost information they can get about the products they are interested in, and marketing management generally show an increasing interest in profitability of products, outlets, markets, regions, etc., instead of being merely concerned with the volume and value of sales.

In deciding on marketing policy for future periods there will certainly be discussion on the possibility of selling more of the products on which the highest margins are being earned, with a corresponding reduction in the least profitable lines. Assuming that there are no production problems in making a switch, it may be merely a matter of redirecting the sales force's efforts, or reallocating the advertising budget. However, before any positive action is taken to make changes, it is essential for marketing and financial management to thrash out the following points.

Cost allocations

First, how have the product costs and profit margins been arrived at? In particular, have the costs of selling and advertising been allocated to products and if so, on what basis? The point here is that, if this margin is struck after charging advertising to it on a factual basis, one heavily advertised product may have high sales and a low margin of profit per unit sold, while another product which is advertised only occasionally may show a high margin but a low sales volume there could well be no advantage in switching advertising from the first product to the second merely because the latter appears to have a higher profit margin. The correct course of action would be to compare profit margins before charging advertising, and the amounts spent on advertising on each product, and then take a view on whether a switch from one to the other would be profitable.

It is probably more usual for selling costs to be allocated to products on a uniform *pro rata* basis, but in this case a comparison of the resulting profit margins as a means of determining future sales policy would not be valid if the sales effort required to sell the company's products varied considerably between product groups.

Second, how will changes in the future level of sales affect unit product costs and profit margins? Accountants in the past have often prided themselves on the accuracy with which they are able to calculate the total cost of each major product, after allocating and apportioning costs from one department to another, and from each department to the products passing through them. Unfortunately in going to all this trouble to allocate or apportion both the variable and the fixed costs, they have destroyed the usefulness of the final totals in providing answers to the kind of questions listed above, because the costs per unit of product so calculated are valid only for the volume of sales or production throughput prevailing in the period to which the costs relate. To arrive at the unit costs which would apply to other levels of sales or production means very extensive recalculation.

Use of marginal costs

For these reasons, marketing management find that the marginal costing system, in which only variable costs are allocated to products, is very much more useful to them in working out future marketing strategies. Various courses of action can be considered and assumptions made about the effect these actions will have on sales volume. Then a simple calculation enables the marginal cost of each alternative to be assessed, and in this way the approach likely to lead to maximisation of profits can be pinpointed. The course of action referred to might be altering the sales or raising or lowering selling prices, or increasing or decreasing the amount to be spent on advertising and promotions.

In any discussion about the use of marginal costs by marketing management, someone on the accounting side may well put forward the view that it is dangerous to provide these figures to management. They point out that marginal costs do not reflect the 'true' cost of the product because they do not take into account an adequate proportion of fixed costs such as plant depreciation, management salaries, standing charges and so on. They are convinced that if marginal costs are publicised the marketing side of the business will be tempted to cut selling prices to just above these costs, and the business will soon find itself on the rocks because there is insufficient margin of profit to cover the fixed charges, quite apart from paying a dividend to shareholders.

To avoid difficulties of this kind it is important to maintain an adequate dialogue between the marketing and financial sides of the business, particularly on the purposes for which costs are required. As has been pointed out, marginal costs are of considerable value when it comes to assessing the many alternative courses of action open to management. Future policy can only be decided, first, by making assumptions about a large number of external variables—the economic climate, government action, the course of raw material prices, competitors' activities, etc., and second, by working out the effect on profits of making changes in what may be called the 'internal variables'—the effect of production changes, or redirecting the sales force, of increasing or decreasing advertising and promotional expenditure, of altering selling prices. Any attempt to work out a programme of action which will have the best chance of maximising profits becomes hopelessly complicated if the product costs also have to be regarded as a variable item, rising or falling with every change in the levels of sales and output.

Although the use of marginal costs will simplify these calculations, at the same time the limits within which they apply must be understood. If volumes rise beyond a certain point, extra production capacity may have to be installed or double shift working introduced, and the sales force may need augmenting. Estimates can be made of the additional fixed costs per annum likely to be incurred at various levels of output, and these will have to be taken into account in evaluating the expected results.

Use of full costs

The most useful costs to be used as an aid to pricing new products will almost certainly be the full cost rather than the marginal cost, but even here it may be helpful to know what the marginal cost is as well. Pricing policy will probably be based on a number of factors of which cost is only one. If the company is first in the field, it can be expected to fix selling prices at a high level, in order to take maximum advantage of the lead over competitors. On the other hand, it may be decided to fix prices initially at little more than marginal cost, in order to deter competitors from coming in. In the long run, management should make certain that prices are fixed above the full cost, and that the margin over this cost provides an adequate return on capital employed.

The cost and profitability studies described above will be equally necessary during the progress of the year, as conditions change and new products are brought out.

The sales budget

When all alternative courses of action have been evaluated, decisions will finally be taken on those most likely to result in the company attaining its growth and profit objectives for the coming year. The marketing plan will be circulated to and agreed by the Board, and the quantities and values of the products to be sold will be incorporated in the sales budget.

As has been pointed out in chapters 1 and 3, annual budgets are prepared well in advance of the year to which they relate, and it is entirely possible that as the year progresses, sales management may become increasingly convinced that the targets originally set will prove to be wide of the mark. In this situation, many companies will decide to maintain the original budget unaltered, and to supplement this with short term operating plans and revised forecasts of the year end results. Actual sales and profits would then be compared with both original budget and the short term plans and forecasts.

Phasing of sales budgets

Phasing of sales budgets to take account of seasonal influences often prove advantageous. It will be easier to tell whether the underlying trend of sales is altering if comparison of actual sales is made with a phased budget. The planning of marketing activities, sales journeys, etc., will also be achieved more effectively if the expected swing in sales demand is clearly set out in advance. Another benefit obtained from phasing applies to the planning of stock cover and storage facilities. The agreed aim may be to hold say four weeks' cover at all times. If sales are subject to seasonal fluctuations, this will mean that production will have to be stepped up to meet both the increase in demand and the increase in stock cover. Arrangements will also have to be made to provide the additional storage space required immediately prior to peak periods. The phasing of sales and production budgets will provide the basic information required for these purposes. An example of a phased budget is as follows (opposite):

Month	Unphased sales budget	Seasonal pattern*	Phased sales budget
	£000		£000
January	2 000	1/20	1 200
February	2 000	1/20	1 200
March	2 000	1/12	2 000
April	2 000	1/12	2 000
May	2 000	1/8	3 000
June	2 000	1/8	3 000
July	2 000	1/12	2 000
August	2 000	1/20	1 200
September	2 000	1/20	1 200
October	2 000	1/20	1 200
November	2 000	1/12	2 000
December	2 000	1/6	4 000
	24 000		24 000

* Based on average sales pattern in previous years.

Sales control information

Sales control, in the sense of comparison of actual with target sales, can be carried out in several ways. It is often necessary to make use of all three methods shown below at different stages of control.

Comparison with corresponding period in previous year

This is a well-tried method of reporting sales data, usually showing the results for the current week or month, and the cumulative figures from the beginning of the year. The figures relating to product group totals will be of particular interest to the Board and the general management of a company, because they will provide an indication as the year progresses of the report that will eventually be made to shareholders. Shareholders are, of course, not interested in achievement against budgets or other standards—they look more for a progressive increase from year to year in both sales and profit. In a smaller business the figures will be of equal interest to the sole proprietor or partners. Marketing management will naturally be interested in the same figures, but they will expect to be supplied with rather more detail, usually by individual products and by territories (areas, regions, branches, etc.). In some cases they may decide it is worth while to keep analysed records of sales to principal customers, or by classes of customer, e.g. chemists, grocers, wholesalers, etc. These records would usually give an analysis by product groups.

The degree of detail provided will depend to a great extent on the ratio between the cost of providing such an analysis and the average value of sales turnover for the units selected. Thus if the average customer spends £1 000 a month on the firm's products, such an analysis may be well worth while. If he only spends £10 a month, then an analysed sales record by customers would probably be uneconomic. *Total* sales by customers will be obtainable without difficulty from the sales ledger records. A useful compromise can often be made by deciding to rely on sampling techniques. By this means, a reasonably reliable analysis can be made with a minimum of clerical effort.

Comparison with
immediately
preceding periods

The importance of detecting a change in trend as soon as possible has already
been noted. Comparison with previous years either on an actual or cumulative
basis will not necessarily provide sufficient indication, because the fluctuation
that can occur in the previous year's figures may help to mask a change of
trend this year. For this reason it is usually advisable to compare actual sales
for the week or month with two or three immediately preceding periods as well
as with the previous year's figures. A better way is to plot the key figures in
chart form; this will show both the trend and the comparison with the previous
year (and, if desired, with budget) in a form that can be easily assimilated.

Comparison with
sales budget

In businesses that have to contend with seasonal peaks and troughs, the
comparison with last week or last month suggested above may not disclose a
change in trend. An increase sustained over two or three weeks may be merely
representing the beginning of the peak season. It is usually true that a better
guide to the underlying trend can be obtained by comparison with a phased
budget. Such a budget incorporates all that is known about total sales
expectation for the year, having regard to any new developments affecting
this year but not previous years. It also incorporates past experience on
seasonal fluctuations, by phasing the budget on the basis of this experience.
Any major divergence from this budget is therefore likely to indicate some
unforeseen trend or tendency concerning which it may be necessary to take
action.

Comparison against budget is of particular value when used in the control of
sales performance in each sales territory. The budgets will have been agreed
in the first instance by regional management as targets that should be
attainable if there is no major change in external conditions. This results in
their having a natural interest in the subsequent comparisons of actual sales
with the budget they helped to prepare. Each salesman will either be supplied
with figures showing the sales and target figures for his own district, or will
have an opportunity of examining these at regional offices. The total effect will
be considerable motivation towards beating budgets, particularly if it is made
clear that higher levels of management are very interested in the comparisons.
Alternatively, where incentive schemes are preferred, the scheme can be
based on such comparisons.

A further reason for comparing actual sales with budget is frequently
overlooked. The whole structure of the company's operating policy for the
year is usually expressed in the sales budget, which in turn is based on certain
assumptions regarding external conditions. The first warning that some of
these assumptions may prove incorrect is when actual sales begin to diverge
from budget. The divergence *may* be due to slackness or inefficiency on the
part of the sales staff, but it is just as likely that the divergence is caused by
changing external conditions. Whatever the reason, a clear warning is given to
management that policy and plans for the year call for review.

In those cases where sales budgets are supplemented by short term
operating plans and forecasts, it will be useful to include these targets on the
control statement.

Sales control data

Reference has already been made to the desirability of preparing sales
budgets in quantitative terms as well as in money values. The original records

of actual sales to customers will usually indicate quantity, price and value—the exceptions being in the case of retail establishments, where it is possible that either no record is made at all or that only total value is recorded. The summarisation of the actual sales figures for inclusion in sales control reports will normally follow the method adopted for preparing the budget. Sometimes money values for product groups will be included in the budget and in control statements, the latter being supplemented by quantity records for sales of individual products.

Orders received or deliveries invoiced?

A question which is sometimes difficult to answer is whether summarised control returns should be built up from sales orders received, or from deliveries invoiced to customers.

A summary of sales values, i.e. deliveries invoiced, is essential to the preparation of the periodic financial accounts, but the extent to which these sales figures are analysed either by product groups and products, or by areas and regions, is a matter of choice. Some such analyses will be essential if it is desired to compute profit margins earned by products or areas, etc.

The analysis of sales values by products may not be available, however, until a week or so after the end of the period to which they relate, and it is usually considered worth while to find a quicker way of establishing the trend of sales. In some cases the analysis of sales deliveries by quantities may be obtainable more quickly, and the same figures can then be used for stock control purposes and for the information of management. However, in the case of a company that accepts orders from customers, as distinct from a merchandising business that sells goods off the shelf for cash or credit, the earliest indication of sales trends by products is obtained from an analysis of orders received. Quite apart from the value which management place on an early indication of a change in trend, the efficient operation of a production planning system often depends on early knowledge of actual demand.

In deciding whether to undertake the analysis of orders received as well as sales deliveries, the advantages of earlier knowledge will have to be weighed against the cost of the additional clerical effort.

Orders on hand

In some businesses, particularly those in which production is based on orders in hand, it is vitally necessary to know what the unfulfilled orders on hand amount to. For example, a glass-making factory needs to keep a close watch on the outstanding order position, so as to be able to plan well in advance when to close down or start up a furnace. To start up a furnace and then find there was insufficient demand to keep it in continuous production over a reasonably long period would be a very costly procedure. In these circumstances it is usual to keep a running record of the balance of orders outstanding by posting to this record the daily or weekly total of orders received and deliveries made in satisfaction of orders—analysed in each case according to requirements. Provision must also be made for making deductions from the outstanding balance where orders are cancelled. Periodically, individual orders actually outstanding would be listed, and the totals agreed with the balances shown on a record as follows:

Unit = 100 kgm		Record of orders outstanding			30 June
Product	Orders b/f 23 June	Orders for week ended 30 June	Orders fulfilled (deliveries)	Cancel- lations	Orders c/f 30 June
PZ 1	105·2	28	24	—	109·2
2	27·6	—	7·60	3	17·0
etc.					

Sales control forms

Where some of the orders are for forward delivery, it will be advisable to analyse the balance according to months when delivery is due.

Examples of other Sales Control Report forms are given in Figs. 5.7.2–7 (see opposite and following pages).

Retail sales

A manufacturing and marketing business can obtain the requisite sales statistics by analysing orders received, delivery notes or invoices sent to customers, according to particular requirements. A retail business selling to the public on a cash basis may not be so favourably placed. For example, in shops which sell groceries or other foodstuffs; hardware, and other general goods; and in all self-service shops and supermarkets, there is usually no time in which to write out a written record of the goods which the customer has selected. This means that no reliable analysis by products or product groups can be obtained at the time of sale.

Sometimes a broad analysis is possible by segregating the categories of goods sold—for example in a chemist's shop toilet preparations would be on one counter, drugs and medicines on another. Then by installing separate cash registers on each counter, a sectional sales total is theoretically possible. In practice, it may be found that little reliance can be placed on this analysis because some customers may insist on obtaining their total requirements at one counter.

Other methods may therefore have to be found to obtain a suitable breakdown of total cash sales. One method applicable to fixed price articles is to maintain accurate quantity records of articles sent to the shops, and to arrange for a weekly (or four-weekly, etc.) stock check at each shop. By adjusting for differences in opening and closing stocks, the delivery figures for each article are converted into quantities sold. These totals are then multiplied out by the appropriate selling prices, and the total compared with the actual cash received total. Any differences will include losses through wastage, deterioration, breakages, pilferage and clerical errors.

Where the shop sells very many articles, the above method would be somewhat cumbersome. In these circumstances, where selling prices are fixed for reasonably long periods, it may be possible to use the 'selling price control' method. Under this procedure, all issues of goods to the shops are charged up at selling price. At the end of each control period, stocks are taken and also valued at selling prices. Reconciliation should then be possible with the total cash sales, and since deliveries to the shops can be analysed, the analysed cash sales can be obtained. This is illustrated in Fig. 5.7.1. opposite.

Fig. 5.7.1
Selling price control
and analysis

Period No 37   W/e _____

Deliveries to shop	(at selling prices)	
Product group	23	£505
Product group	31	£320
Product group	59	£875

Stocks at S.P.		Opening	Closing
Product group	23	£360	£620
Product group	31	£310	£280
Product group	59	£125	£520

Total cash sales   £1 050

Reconciliation	Total	Product group		
		23	31	59
	£	£	£	£
Opening stock	795	360	310	125
Deliveries	1 700	505	320	875
	2 495	865	630	1 000
Closing stock	1 420	620	280	520
Theoretical sales	£1 075	£245	£350	£480
Actual sales	£1 050	?	?	?
Pro rata analysis	£1 050	£239	£342	£469

Apart from the opportunity of analysis which this method gives, it is an extremely effective check against stock losses due to pilferage, errors, etc. The system would not be suitable where selling prices are frequently changed.

Fig. 5.7.2
Customer statistics

Month	This year				Last year				Previous years		
	Total	Product groups			Total	Product groups			Total	Total	Total
		A	B	C		A	B	C			
Jan											
Feb											
Mar											
April											
May											
June											
July											
Aug											
Sept											
Oct											
Nov											
Dec											
Total											

(These statistics would usually be kept in £ d)

Fig. 5.7.3
Weekly summary of
sales orders

	Unit of quantity ____ Dozen cans W/e 17th March,19____					
Product	Orders received			11 weeks to date		
	This week	Last week	Previous week	This year	Budget	Last year
Product group A A1 A2 A3, etc						
Total						
Product group B B1 B2, etc						
Total						
Product group C C1 C2, etc						
Total						
Grand total						

Fig. 5.7.4
Monthly summary of
product sales
(deliveries)

	Sales (deliveries)			6 months to date		
Product	This month	Budget	Last month	This year	Budget	Last year
	Qty £	Qty £	Qty £	Qty £	Qty £	Qty £
Product group A A1 A2 A3, etc						
Total						
Product group B B1 B2, etc						
Total						
Product group C C1 C2, etc						
Total						
Grand total £						

Note An alternative is to summarise by 4-weekly periods

Fig. 5.7.5
Monthly summary
of area sales
(deliveries)

Areas	Sales (deliveries)			6 months to date		
	This month	Budget	Last month	This year	Budget	Last year
	Qty £	Qty £	Qty £	Qty £	Qty £	Qty £

Area N
  District N1
    N2, etc						

Total						

Area SE
  District SE1
    SE2, etc						

Total						

Area SW
  District SW1
    SW2, etc						

Total						
Grand total £						

Fig. 5.7.6
Monthly sales
summary

Sales	Sales (deliveries)			6 months to date		
	This month	Budget	Last month	This year	Budget	Last year
	Qty £	Qty £	Qty £	Qty £	Qty £	Qty £
Product group A Product group B Product group C						
Total						
Area N Area SE Area SW						
Total						
Previous years						

Performance and cost control

The sum of money which a company is prepared to spend on marketing and selling costs is usually decided by Board policy. The objective of marketing and selling management is then to use this money as effectively as possible by building up goodwill, stimulating demand and obtaining maximum sales turnover at agreed selling prices. In the case of distribution, the objective of management is to anticipate as accurately as possible where and when to send the firm's products, in what quantities and in what varieties. Having

Fig. 5.7.7
Monthly Sales
summary

District N1	January		February		March	
	Actual	Target	Actual	Target	Actual	Target
Salesman 1						
Salesman 2						
Salesman 3						
Salesman 4						

decided this, the next task is to send the goods to their ultimate destination, or to store them as cheaply and effectively as possible until they are required.

When these two sets of objectives are considered from the point of view of cost control it will be seen that there is a basic difference in outlook. Marketing and selling management are not necessarily trying to cut down expenditure—they are trying to make the sums they spend more effective in achieving turnover. Distribution management on the other hand can be considered as an extension of production management, i.e. moving the goods one stage nearer the customer. Like production management, their objective is to carry out prescribed tasks at the least cost.

Check on effectiveness

Until comparatively recent times it was thought that the only control possible with marketing and selling costs was to compare actual costs with a previously agreed budget figure. This comparison is, of course, an essential part of the overall financial and management control; a company would soon run into difficulties if it plunged into a heavy advertising campaign or increased its sales force in disregard of previously agreed plans. Orders might come pouring in, but the diminution in funds available to meet production requirements and the limits set by existing production capacity might prevent these orders being fulfilled.

Something more than comparison of actual performance with budget is needed, however, if management is to exercise effective control. The something extra is a check on the *effectiveness* of the marketing or selling effort. This means that an attempt has to be made to compare the 'input', e.g. money spent on advertising, time spent by salesmen in calling on customers, etc., with the 'output', e.g. sales orders received. There are many reasons why it is extremely difficult to make an effective comparison, and to draw worthwhile conclusions. Nevertheless a considerable amount of research and investigation is being undertaken in this field at the present time, because the rewards for more effective control are very great.

Some of the factors which make it difficult to draw logical conclusions from comparisons are the activities of competitors, changes in the economic background, unaccountable changes in public taste, the ratio of selling price to prices charged by competitors, complications caused by policy decisions of customers with multiple branches, and so on. Some of the techniques which are being used to throw light on these problems are mathematical or statistical. The usual aim is to try and hold constant some of the factors which can affect the end result, allow other factors to fluctuate, and then to observe what effect these fluctuations have had.

Cost analysis

The more traditional techniques include performance and cost analyses, followed by analytical studies of physical operations. Such analysis can play a part in determining the effectiveness of advertising. For example, comparative estimates can be made of the number of potential customers who will receive an advertising message, if a given advertising allocation is spent in various ways. On the other hand, this analysis will not show up the different *impacts* which the various methods of advertising will make on the public, nor will it provide any clue as to the *amount* of advertising that is economically justifiable. Management judgment, aided by market research and statistical analysis, provides the only answer to these problems.

With selling expenses, it is usually possible to build up worthwhile controls over performance and effectiveness. Many companies arrange for salesmen to keep a record of the number of calls they make in a week. It is usual to draw up a rota of sales journeys, arranged in such a way that the salesmen call on every customer once in every cycle. The performance of salesmen, in terms of calls, can then be found by comparing actual calls with plan.

This, however, is only part of the story, and further analysis is necessary to find out what proportion of calls resulted in orders from customers. This percentage can be compared with a target figure. The real effectiveness of the salesman can only be judged, however, if the *quantities* of each variety ordered by the customers are examined and compared with some sort of yardstick—usually the previously agreed sales budget.

These checks on salesmen's performance can at best be only a guide to their effectiveness. Conditions change so quickly that to achieve only 80 per cent of target in the current period may represent a far better performance than 100 per cent achievement in the last period. Fluctuation of one kind or another will tend to average out over a period, so that a better guide to salesman's performance and capabilities will be attained by looking at the trends over a reasonable period of time.

Complaints are sometimes received from salesmen that certain journeys or areas are easier than others, and that a comparison of relative performance is therefore unfair. Or they may complain that the introduction of a new product has meant they have inadequate time in which to deal with orders for the other products. In cases of this nature, some companies have sent trained observers round with the salesmen, to find out what an average workload amounts to in terms of time. Studies are taken of the time needed for travelling, for talking to customers, for writing up reports, etc. When the total 'standard times' for each journey have been established, comparison can be made with actual performance by salesmen, and the scope for economy and/or redistribution of the workload determined.

Distribution costs

For many years company managements have tended to ignore distribution costs when reviewing ways and means of keeping costs under control. The reason for this is perhaps that there is no easy way of comparing money spent on distribution with a corresponding end result. Increased expenditure in the factory will be reflected in increased output, so that management can work to 'per unit of output' standard. Spending money on the marketing and selling sides of the business can be expected to result in increased sales, so that once again a yardstick can be established. With distribution however it is a different story. If the company makes use of a fleet of transport vehicles to carry out its distribution policy, then it is probable that these vehicles will undertake a wide range of tasks, sometimes bringing in raw materials, sometimes taking finished products to depots, and more frequently, distributing finished products to customers up and down the country. If the company makes use of third party transport, then monies will be paid out for similar tasks. In either case, the distribution manager will often be faced with some difficult problems when asked to authorise a marginal journey, such as sending a small quantity of goods a very long way in the shortest possible time.

Experience has shown that collaboration with financial management can be extremely useful, for example in establishing a series of costing rates for each vehicle, based on the mileage and number of drops. This makes it possible to calculate the true costs of carrying out a series of regular tasks, and policy decisions can then be taken on whether or not to accept similar requests in future.

It is also becoming increasingly recognised that distribution costs cannot be looked at in isolation, but must be reviewed in relation to the company's stock control policies.

8 Office management

The Board of Directors of a company will usually spend much of their time considering the operating and the financial objectives of the company, and what progress they are making in achieving these objectives. In relation to his own specific area of function responsibility, individual directors will each be looking at the performance and costs of his own sector of the business—marketing, technical, personnel, financial, research and so on. Collectively they will be reviewing the progress made by the company as a whole. Until a decade or so ago, it could be taken for granted that the one aspect of the business to which directors gave hardly a thought was the management of their various office departments; the general view being that office procedures were a necessary evil, eating away part of the company's profits, but thank goodness they could rely on old what's-his-name, the office manager, to make sure that the office costs did not get out of hand! Every now and again one of the directors would complain that the secretarial service was deteriorating, or that he was getting too much paperwork on his desk, or that he was not getting enough useful information, and the financial director would be asked to look into these problems. Perhaps the only times when really serious attention was paid by the Board to the question of office costs as a whole were periods of trade depression, when it became clear that the company must reduce all its costs if it wished to survive, and the office seemed to be a good place in which to make a start.

Cutting costs

Greater interest was aroused postwar in the Civil Service and larger concerns by the introduction of *Organisation and Methods Departments* whose function it was to streamline office systems, reduce paperwork and introduce mechanisation with the object of cutting costs. Additionally the advent of computers has provided further impetus to management in large and medium companies to review office activities. Directors have been attracted by the idea of making use of computers in their business, and very soon realised that one of the surest ways of justifying a computer would be to convince the Board that a computer would pay for itself in savings on office costs. As a result, investigations into office procedures have been launched in many companies, usually with the twin aims of providing better management information or a better service, combined with a lower overall cost. In many cases the result of such investigations has been to demonstrate that improvements can be made, and costs can be reduced, but not necessarily by introducing a computer into the business. The desired benefits can be obtained by the application of modern management techniques to clerical functions, and by the use of new ideas and new equipment to improve administrative services. These approaches to office activities are considered in this chapter.

Relative cost of office services

Assuming that the financial director of a company has been asked to carry through such a programme of improvement, his first task should be to agree with his colleagues precisely which areas of the business are being covered. The term 'office' is rather a vague one, and in the case of a manufacturing/marketing company, it is necessary to clarify whether the review is to cover only those activities carried out in the 'office block', or whether it is to embrace all clerical functions wherever they are carried out, including, for example, factory offices, sales depot offices and even the clerical work carried out by salesmen on their rounds.

His next task will be to make an assessment of the total annual cost of running the office services, and for this purpose if the offices are housed in freehold premises, he should include a notional figure to cover the cost of accommodation. This total cost should then be looked at in relation to the company's main operating costs excluding materials (the costs of converting raw materials into finished products and of selling and distributing them to customers). If raw materials form a high proportion of the total cost of a product, it may be misleading to work out the percentage of clerical costs to total costs, since the company is usually unable to do anything about reducing the material content of its products:

Example

	Total costs		Operating costs	
	£'000	%	£'000	%
Raw materials contained in finished product	1 250	83·4	—	—
Factory conversion costs (labour, expenses, overheads)	120	8·0	120	48·0
Selling and distribution expenses	80	5·3	80	32·0
Clerical costs	50	3·3	50	20·0
	1 500	100·0	250	100·0

It will be seen that looked at in relation to total costs the company's clerical costs seem insignificant at 3·3 per cent, but, when compared with other costs about which the company can take positive action to reduce, it is apparent that, at 20 per cent, the clerical costs represent a significant proportion of the total. With figures of this sort on the table, it becomes possible to assess how much it would be reasonable to spend on improving the effectiveness or reducing the cost of office services, in relation to the costs being incurred for the same kind of purposes in the marketing and technical fields.

**Programme
for survey**

Having made an assessment of how much time or money it is reasonable to allocate to an improvement programme, the way is now clear to make a detailed survey of the office departments, but it is first necessary to decide who shall do this. Neither the financial director nor the accountant nor the office manager is likely to have the necessary time to make this survey, because experience has shown that making suggestions for any real improvements in office procedures can be a time-consuming affair. In production departments, an experienced manager or consultant can gain from even quick and short observations valuable hints or guides to opportunities for improving efficiencies or for reducing costs. The average run of offices and administrative work do not lend themselves to any comparable results from broad-glance scrutiny. It usually takes days, or even weeks, to understand what jobs are being done, what methods and systems used, and how much time is really needed for these jobs. Anyone walking through a large general office may get the impression that everyone is busy, with some writing hard, others making long telephone calls, and others engaged in face to face discussions. The only way of finding out whether all this is necessary may well be to spend a day or more with each member of the department, finding out what is said and done.

Effecting improvements in office procedures after terms of reference have been agreed thus calls for the following decisions to be made on the organisation of the work:

Manpower

Who shall carry out the survey and implement the recommendations?
Assuming that the firm does not already possess an O and M department, or a fully trained O and M officer, there are a number of choices open:

(*a*) In the smaller firm, this is a task that could be given to a management trainee, who would work full time on the assignment for the necessary period, under expert supervision.

(*b*) If management is willing to wait, a useful alternative is to nominate a member of the office staff to become fully trained in Organisation and Methods work, so that after receiving this training he would be capable of carrying out quite complex assignments. In the larger firms, it will usually be found that it pays to keep such a man continuously on O and M work, so that all departments can be reviewed in turn and new methods introduced as they become known. Suitable courses for providing full training are run by the *Organisation and Methods Training Council*, and by various firms of management consultants.

(*c*) Another approach that can be considered is to hire the services of a fully trained specialist in O and M work from one of the employment agencies who provide these facilities. Such a specialist would be hired for an agreed period of time and would cost much less than making use of full consultancy services referred to in (*d*). He would work under the guidance and supervision of the financial director or his nominee.

(*d*) Finally, where the sums involved are large, it may prove the best course to invite a firm of specialist consultants to carry out the work, particularly where it is known that they are experts in some new technique likely to bring good results. The firm's accountants or auditors will usually be able to recommend suitable firms, or alternatively suggestions can be obtained from the *Institute of Management Consultants*.

In some circumstances, it may be appropriate to employ outside specialists to undertake the survey, and to use the company's own staff to carry through the recommendations.

<table>
<tr><td>Scope</td><td>

Which departments shall be studied, and in which order? Before deciding on the departments to be studied, it may be useful to classify them under two headings: those that are in the nature of 'paperwork factories', and those that are not. In the first group will be placed all those departments that work more or less continuously on the conversion of the 'input' in the form of raw data into the 'output' provided by the department, whatever this may be. Examples are:

</td></tr>
</table>

(*a*) Wages offices, where input in the form of clock cards, output records and tax tables is converted first into wage and bonus calculations, locational labour costs and lastly into take home pay.

(*b*) A sales routine office, converting the input of sales orders and price data into sales invoices and customers' statements.

(*c*) Many of the clerical functions carried out in banks, insurance companies and stockbroking firms.

The features which distinguish all such departments from other office activities is both the repetitive nature of the work and the ability to measure 'output', thus providing opportunities for measurement and control similar to those available to factory management when seeking to improve the efficiency of repetitive production processes.

Accordingly these departments are likely to be first on the list for study, particularly if the department contains a large number of clerical staff all carrying out similar operations. Generally speaking, the whole emphasis of the review in these departments will be to find ways of reducing the costs of preparation, since there is usually little scope of 'improving' the output. However, in some cases there may be a case for improving the quality of the output in the sense of making fewer mistakes.

Those office departments that do not fall under the heading of 'paperwork factories' can be broadly regarded as providing support services to management. Some of these services provide aids to management in communicating, e.g. secretarial or telephone services; others provide help to management in planning and controlling the activities of the company. Examples of these would be a planning department, or an accounts department providing management information. In the case of these departments, the review should not merely be confined to finding ways and means of reducing the cost of the service provided, but should also look at the service itself. Is it really necessary? What would happen if it were eliminated or reduced in scope? On the other hand, can the service be improved so as to have a greater impact on achievement of company objectives? An example of the latter is seen in the development of long range planning departments. At first these were regarded as being nothing more than guessing at the future, then they were seen to have some value in helping to define future objectives, and now they have suddenly come to be regarded as providing all the data for building up financial models of the company's activities. Having established the formula that profit equals sales volume multiplied by selling price less variable cost per unit, less fixed expenses, management is able to work out precisely what effect on future profits various policy changes will have. How shortsighted it would have been to stifle development of this sort by reducing the cost of the planning department by one clerk (the clerk who went on to develop this model building).

Consultation

Who will agree the recommendations made as result of the survey and what arrangements should be made to control progress? It is important that the management of the department being studied should have an opportunity of agreeing the recommendations made and supporting the subsequent implementation of changes. A useful way of ensuring agreement and keeping check on progress is to set up a Steering Committee, to include the financial director and departmental management as required. The Steering Committee should be provided with the terms of reference of each project, a programme of target dates for each stage of the work, and also progress reports recording achievement to date.

Making the survey

Those companies deciding to carry out their own surveys will usually find it expedient to make use of the following aids.

Job specifications

A job specification should be prepared for each post in the department, setting out responsibilities and providing details of all jobs undertaken. Job specifications are frequently used in companies to provide a basis for job grading, in which jobs are graded in order of importance and monetary value. If so used, the job specifications should contain details of special qualities required for the job, the range and number of internal and external contacts. When all job specifications have been completed for all departments, an examination of the detail may well reveal duplication of effort or unnecessary checking.

Work diaries

As a further guide to finding out what work is done in the office, each assistant should be asked to keep a diary for a week or so, listing all the different tasks undertaken and telephone calls made. For convenience, this can be in columnar form:

Time	Per-sonal	Taking dicta-tion	Typing	Filing	Tele-phone	Face to face discus-sions	Miscel-laneous (with details)
8.45 9.00	10	—	—	5	—	—	—
9.15 9.30	—	20	—	—	5	—	5 (travel arrange-ments)
9.45 10.00 etc.	—	—	20	—	—	10	—

Flow charting

The various examples of paperwork circulating within a company may well pass through some departments several times, so that careful charting of the flow of each document is necessary in order to provide a full picture of what is happening. It is customary to record the movement of documents and the operations carried out on them in a conventional way, and when all the flow diagrams have been completed it should be possible to reconcile the various operations recorded on them with the corresponding details given in the job specifications or work diaries.

			↓		
Carrying out an operation	Checking or inspection	Temporary storage	Transportation from one place to another	Storage	End of the road (document destroyed or action ceased)

Example

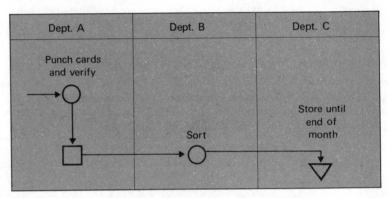

A flow chart need not be restricted to flow of documents; in the example shown (Fig. 5.8.1) telephone calls are included. This example combines a diagrammatic form of presentation with the conventional symbol for transport (→). (See also chapter 5 of Part Three, page 403.)

Procedures manual

Many companies find it useful to keep an up to date procedures manual covering all regular duties, and if this is available, it will save a lot of fact finding during the course of the survey.

When all the facts have been analysed the survey report will be prepared setting out recommendations for achieving improvements or cost savings. These benefits will often be obtainable either through the introduction of new or more suitable equipment. Comments on some aspects of these are given at the end of this chapter.

Diagnostic techniques

In addition to those already touched on, the following techniques or approaches are available to management, where it is desired to improve overall performance and/or to reduce costs in the administrative field. Fuller treatment of such diagnostic techniques is covered in Part Seven (chapter 8, see page 1025) and Part Three (chapter 5, see page 396).

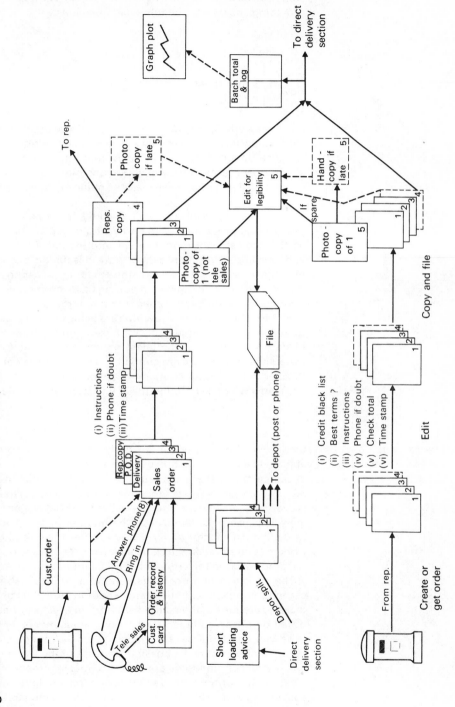

Fig. 5.8.1　Flow chart of sales control (Direct Deliveries)

Method study

Method study is just as applicable to the office as it is in the factory. Method study can be described in a nutshell: a systematic way of analysing the facts by providing answers to the following questions:

What is done?
Who does it?
Where ⎫
When ⎪
How ⎬ is it done?
Why ⎭

and then working out ways of simplifying the work by challenging the need for each stage in the process and so eliminating unnecessary steps, reducing distance travelled and so on. Answers to the first three questions will have already been provided by observations made during the survey procedure, and detailed enquiries will have to be made to provide the answers to the other three.

Method study in this way will be partly concerned with office routines such as invoicing procedures, and partly with management support services, such as the provision of management information. Clearly an O and M officer engaged in such a survey cannot work in isolation, but must work closely with his colleagues who specialise in the accounting, costing or planning functions, and carry them with him when putting up recommendations say to reduce the frequency of a series of management reports.

When he has found out how jobs are being done at present, he will be unable to make effective suggestions for making improvements unless he has an up to date knowledge of the latest equipment available, or unless he makes exhaustive enquiries from suppliers. It is nowadays equally essential for him to keep in touch with computer developments so that he can recognise the occasions when a computer feasibility study may be desirable.

Clerical work measurement

Clerical work measurement must of necessity differ from work measurement applied to a production process in a factory because of the inherent variability of clerical work. There is no reason why assembling one electric plug should take any longer than assembling all the other plugs of the same type, but there is every reason why the time needed to work out wages may vary from man to man, because of differences in the number of deductions, queries on clock cards, etc. This factor of variability applies to all office tasks and means that work measurement in the clerical field must be based on an overall average of the time required to carry out a particular task.

The objective of work measurement is to establish a 'standard time' for carrying out each operation, after method study has been applied to reduce these operations to their simplest forms. In a factory, these standard times are based on observed times after making adjustments for the rate at which the observed operators were working (known as 'rating'). In an office, the use of rating is often not really possible because of the variability of the work load, and in practice standards are based on measurement of actual output over a given period of time, or even by asking the employee what output he or she considers reasonable in say one hour. Such standards may not seem very demanding, but experience has shown that they provide a useful tool for planning work loads and/or allocating staff to particular jobs, and if applied as a control measure, they give an opportunity for job satisfaction by showing that the standards can be beaten.

Another more precise way of establishing standard times is by breaking down each job into a number of elements, the standard times for which have been predetermined as the result of prolonged observations. This system obviously calls for much more detailed work in administering it, but the various firms of consultants who market such systems are able to claim considerable economies through introducing this approach.

Value analysis of management practices

Value analysis is a well established technique for cheapening the cost of a firm's products. A small team is built up to include expertise from the purchasing, technical, marketing and financial functions, and they together question each component of the product and its packaging. As a result, it is often possible to substitute much cheaper materials without affecting the marketability of the product.

In a similar way, some consultants have been applying the same principles to administrative functions, and questioning the need for carrying them out in their present form. These investigations have often resulted in substantial savings.

For many years, accountants and office managers have been following the same general principles of cutting out unnecessary operations, although this action has usually been taken sporadically, rather than as part of a formalised approach to making a number of savings.

Examples of some of these steps to save money are:

1. Some firms that used to consider it essential to make an accurate stock-taking at the year end would close their offices on 1 January to allow this to be done. This cost the firm considerable sums in lost production and/or overtime. It is now often considered cheaper to keep an accurate stock recording system, and to extract the year end stocks from these cards; this is a simple listing operation. Physical stock-taking would be carried out section by section at intervals during the year. What was questioned was the need to take physical stock all at once on the same day.
2. At one time, auditors used to check all entries in a firm's books and all additions—now it is general practice to rely on test checking, thus reducing the cost of the audit. The need for complete checking was questioned.

Performance improvement programme

This is another recently developed approach to achieving savings in the administrative fields, particularly useful where it is desired to achieve prompt results and cover a number of departments. Results can always be achieved quickly be employing outside consultants, but this can be expensive and many firms are being attracted by the do-it-yourself advantages of improving managerial methods and performance. As was explained in Part One (see chapter 7, page 82), this can be a valuable basis for incidental 'management development' accompanying the methods improvement.

The underlying idea is to set up a working group, preferably (but not necessarily) led by someone with consulting experience, and including a departmental manager and perhaps someone with an accounting background. A programme is drawn up with target dates, for each department to be studied, and the departmental manager will be changed from time to time, so that no manager ever studies his own department. While engaged on the review, a manager will be working on it full time, so a deputy must be found to run his department in his absence.

The team interviews representative members from each department, examines what they are doing and how they are doing it, and discusses with them possible ways of simplification. Eventually they will arrive at a set of recommendations, will agree these with top management, and it is to be hoped, with the manager of the department, and will then be given the task of implementing their recommendations.

In summary, it can be emphasised that "the three Ps" have as much relevance and significance in the office as in the factory or depot (see page 32).

| Planning and control procedures | Most administrative work consists of a mixture of jobs, some of which occur at regular intervals, e.g. weekly management meetings; others occurring at different times during the year, with known dead lines to be met, e.g. submission of the annual budget; others arising out of the blue, perhaps in the form of an urgent request for special information required by the chairman; and fortunately, a number of jobs which are not particularly urgent, such as updating a procedures manual, can be used to fill in the slacker periods. |

If maximum advantage is to be gained from the varying degrees of urgency of these jobs, it is essential for an appropriate system of planning and control to be introduced, to enable the work load to be evenly spread. A Gantt chart will often provide a suitable basis for such a system.

Office accommodation

Any company with offices in London or other big cities will be only too well aware of the sky-rocketing cost of office accommodation in recent years. This factor has led many companies to reduce their administrative costs by moving either the whole or a major portion of their office services out of such high cost areas into regions where costs are much lower. Some have merely moved out into the suburbs, others have moved themselves lock stock and barrel well away from London. It is claimed that in almost every case the moves have not only saved the firms considerable sums of money, but have been appreciated so much by the staff that no one would ever consider moving back to the more densely populated areas. The principal reasons given are pleasanter working surroundings, healthier conditions, and the reduction in travelling time leading to more opportunities for sport and recreation. Any firm deciding to make a move of this kind would naturally need to make sure that the expected cost savings would not be lost through a considerable increase in travelling costs between the main place of business and the decentralised office, or be offset by a falling off in sales due to poorer communications.

Space standards

Other ways in which the costs of office accomodation can be reduced will include savings in space arising as the result of surveys into office procedures.

There is of course a limit to the savings that can be made through bringing desks and people closer together, and most firms will have established their own space standards. These standards will probably be graded, so that a manager of a department is allowed more space than his staff. This is reasonable, as he may have to call together small groups of people in his office for discussions. A minimum space standard is prescribed by the Offices, Shops and Railways Premises Act 1963: 40 square feet of floor space where the ceiling is 10 feet high or more, rising to 50 square feet if the ceiling is only 8 feet high (i.e. 400 cubic feet of space).

Other requirements of this Act (which should of course be consulted by those responsible for the design and layout of offices) relate to temperature, ventilation, lighting, sanitary conveniences, washing facilities, drinking water, accommodation for clothes, first aid and fire precautions, etc.

Open plan offices

Another way in which it is claimed that considerable savings can be made is through the provision of *open-plan* or *landscaped* offices. It is probably true that a considerable number of managers are prejudiced against the idea of an open-plan office, because the words bring to their minds a vision of the old style general office, filled with raised desks or benches, and numerous clerks sitting on stools. In actual fact a modern open-plan office that has been properly 'landscaped' looks more like the reception lounge of a luxury hotel, fitted with carpets, full length curtains, screens, potted plants and elegant office furniture. The underlying idea is that the advantages and savings in cost of an open-plan office are so great that the firm can afford to provide more luxurious fittings than they would otherwise have done; and practically all the items listed above serve a purpose in helping to deaden the sounds made by the occupants of the room. This is the major disadvantage of course: even with accoustic ceilings and sound muffling fittings, it is never entirely possible to shut out the sounds of other people's voices. The most that can be hoped for is that the general hubbub will be far less distracting than having to share a room with one other occupant and listening all day only to his voice. Exponents of open-planning attach very great importance to the need to have the offices properly landscaped, and they will claim that in those cases where companies have tried out open-planning and then reverted to offices separated by partitions, the reasons for failure have nearly always been an initial reluctance to spend enough money on the all-important fittings and decorations. The savings claimed for open-plan offices arise in the following ways:

- partitioned offices are frequently too large for one man but not large enough for two, and this waste of space is avoided if the partitions are removed;
- maintenance costs are reduced (fewer walls to decorate);
- frequent alterations in the positioning of partitions is avoided.

In addition, there will be a general increase in efficiency in the administrative procedures being carried out. Wasted journeys up the corridor will be avoided because Mr X can *see* that Mr Y is not at his desk, or is busy on the telephone.

The most successful landscaped offices are those that are planned during the design stage of a new building, as the room used in this way needs to be correctly proportioned. A long narrow room will never make a satisfactory open-plan office. Desks and screens can be used as integral parts with modular construction so that the effect of partitioning can be obtained in open and landscaped offices but with greater flexibility and lower costs.

Office furniture

Considerable advances have been made in recent years in designing office desks, and there has been a tendency to move away from the old-fashioned and very heavy desks that are such a barrier to flexibility on rearranging staff. One type of desk has the drawers contained in a separate pedestal that can easily be wheeled from room to room if the owner of the desk needs to make a temporary change (perhaps in order to work in close association with a colleague). Much attention has been paid to the design of desks and chairs in order to provide maximum comfort. British Standards covering the design of a general clerk's, typist's and machine operator's chair (BSS 2582) have been available since 1955.

Personnel policy

One of the findings arising from a survey of office procedures initiated as the result of complaints about the poor quality of the service provided may well be the need to establish a clearly defined personnel policy for office staff. Some of the points which need to be taken into account in drawing up or revising such a policy are noted below: they can be seen as specific instances of the broader policies and practices covered in Part Four.

Job specifications and job grading

Job specifications and grading have already been considered (p. 586), but one aspect which needs careful attention under the heading of policy is the extent to which jobs should be specialised on flow production lines. At first sight it would seem more efficient in a large office to reduce each job to the smallest number of components, so that each member of the office could become proficient in doing a limited number of tasks over and over again. In practice it has been found better to define jobs so that they include a reasonable variety of work; otherwise the constant repetition of one or two tasks becomes so boring that the staff decide to leave. In a busy consultant's office it was at first thought that everyone would be much happier if some of the jobs which seem to interfere with normal secretarial duties, such as having to ring up hotels and arrange travel details for other members of the department, were taken away from the secretaries and passed to a 'travel specialist' who would concentrate on this work. This idea was very quickly scrapped when it was discovered that the girls enjoyed being interrupted in this way, as it gave them a sense of 'belonging' to the department.

Job enrichment

The concept of making jobs more interesting and satisfying to perform while at the same time improving overall efficiency has received considerable attention recently under the title of *job enrichment*. The general idea is to get away from the situation in which a man in an office is only doing work because he knows he has to without really understanding what it is all about, and to make him feel more like a man who has an important role to play in ensuring that his company continues to flourish. Job enrichment also has the objective of more motivation for the employee, which in turn can lead to higher productivity and consequent lower office costs.

Salary policy

A firm is more likely to attract and keep its office staff if it has established a carefully worked out salary policy in which a range of salaries is allocated to each job grade and revised periodically in the light of changes in the cost of living and taking account of any government pronouncements on what increases are permissible. Annual increases of salary are then awarded within these ranges as the result of year end 'merit rating' assessments by supervisors or managers, but for junior staff under the age of twenty-one it is customary to give increases on birthdays rather than at the year end. Guidance on salary rates will be found in the *Clerical Salaries Analysis* published every two years by the *Institute of Administrative Management*, but of course actual salaries paid will have to be based on local conditions of demand and supply, and on the most recent government pronouncements on permissible increases.

Clerical trade unions

In government and local government offices, the majority of clerical staff have for some years belonged to one or other of the clerical trade unions, but in the case of limited companies and private firms, only a small proportion of clerical staff belong to unions. Nevertheless, there has been a significant increase in the membership of three unions (APEX: the Association of Professional, Executive, Clerical and Computer Staff; ATCS: the Association of Technical, Clerical and Supervisory Staff; and ASTMS: the Association of Scientific, Technical and Managerial Staff). In 1972 total membership was around 500 000, although of course not all these members are clerical workers. The clerical trade unions first attracted public notice shortly after the end of the Second World War when they were able to persuade a number of the larger firms in industry to abolish working on Saturday mornings. It is not possible to predict whether the proportion of office staff belonging to unions will continue to increase, or whether as some experts think, it will stabilise at around the present percentage.

The extent of unionisation must obviously be kept well in mind by those in charge of a survey of office procedures, and it is highly important that the unions concerned are kept fully informed about the objectives of the review, and of the recommendations when these are agreed.

Industrial Relations
Acts 1971 and 1974

Most companies that pride themselves on good management practices will already be following good codes of practice, but recent legislation has introduced important new provisions, especially in regard to 'unfair dismissal'. Where there is a possibility of reducing staff numbers following a survey of office organisation and procedures it is important for managers to be knowledgeable about the provisions of the recent Acts: see Part Four, page 639.

It is considered unfair practice to dismiss an employee without giving him a reason, or without warning him (in writing) where his performance is found to be unsatisfactory. However, it is recognised that with new recruits mistakes in selection may have been made, and no charge of unfairness can be brought if an employee is found to be unsatisfactory and a decision is taken to terminate his service with the company, provided this is done within twelve months of his appointment. An employee can claim to be unfairly dismissed if he can prove that he was not given clear instructions on the nature of his duties, so that training schemes now play an increasingly important part in personnel policy.

Training and development

Enlightened firms have always made sure that adequate training is provided for their administrative staff, but the setting up of the Industrial Training Boards in 1964 gave an added impetus to systematic training in clerical functions. Under the Industrial Training Act, all firms within a particular industry were required to make a contribution (a percentage of pay roll) to a central Training Board, and were then entitled to recover these contributions if they could prove that systematic training schemes were in operation for their employees. Further grants were made by the Training Boards when a company incurred certain specified training expenditure, such as employing a full-time training officer.

When an employee has been fully trained for a particular post, there is no reason why he should stay in that job for the rest of his working life, and management development schemes aimed at broadening an employee's experience and fitting him or her for more important work are just as appropriate on the administrative side of the business as in other functions.

Communications

Communications of one form or another take up a high percentage of total time available, not only in the office block but throughout the company as a whole, and it is clear that an approach to communications by means of 'value analysis' (see page 783) should prove useful in all but the smallest firms. It should be possible to classify the time taken up in making communications into:

- day to day routine communications essential to the running of the business such as sending out invoices, writing to customers with overdue accounts;
- communications in support of the decision making, planning and control activities of management;
- miscellaneous communications.

Communications will usually mean two-way communication, and will include the various ways in which the management and staff of a business communicate with each other and with their customers and suppliers: in face-to-face discussions, by telephone or telex, or through written or typed communications.

In addition to the above, communications solely within the business can occur through an inter-com system, or through a Post Office private automatic branch exchange (PABX) (which of course also gives facilities for outside calls), or during the course of internal meetings and presentations. Sometimes communications can be regarded as flowing outward only, e.g. information displayed on closed-circuit television screens in airport lounges or betting shops, or when training films are displayed. Information received by the business in the form of articles in newspapers or periodicals, or in letters from wouldbe suppliers can also be regarded as one-way communication —inwards.

Looking at communications from the point of view of cost, it is clear that as indicated above, the payments made for secretarial and typing services and for telephones, etc. form only a proportion of the total. The real cost should include the cost of managers and staff time spent in communicating, and in cases where firms have been worried about the high cost of administrative services, it has been found that excessive communicating, mainly in the form of committee meetings of one kind or another, has been the primary cause. A useful way of reducing the time taken in meetings was devised by a consultant, and consisted of getting a special clock made, that would tick away the cost of the meeting as measured by the total salaries of those present!

The allocation of a secretary to a manager is increasingly becoming a luxury which few firms can afford, and various alternatives have been and are being tried. Sharing a secretary with two or more managers can cause problems when both have peak demands at the same time, unless the secretary is trained in audio-typing rather than taking down shorthand. With audio systems, both managers can dictate their letters onto dictating machines at the same time and the secretary is able to type out the letters from the tapes one after the other without interruption. An alternative method with shorthand secretaries is to make use of a typing pool, but most managers prefer to work with a girl they know rather than being allocated a different girl each time they wish to dictate.

It is a well known fact of business life that some managers seem to spend their entire working day writing memos, or letters, or notes of meetings, while others seem to get by without ever putting pen to paper. Probably the happy medium is to use the telephone within reason, but to follow up a conversation with a written memo when some decision has been reached which it is important should not be overlooked or misunderstood. In some cases a telephone call cannot be made, e.g. if it would interrupt a meeting, and in these cases sending a handwritten note may be all that is necessary. It may be noted that handwriting is becoming increasingly accepted for internal business communications nowadays, and this can achieve a very real saving of secretaries' time.

The handling of inward mail is an important link in the chain of efficient communications, because there is a tendency in offices generally to await the arrival of the mail before getting down to real work. If the mail arrives up to an hour later than it should do, this virtually means cutting the time available for work by up to 12·5 per cent.

Office machines

The efficiency of office activities can be increased by an appropriate use of office machines, but in view of the wide range of equipment now available, it is becoming increasingly difficult to be certain one has made the right choice. A visit to one of the Business Efficiency Exhibitions held in London and other large cities can become a bewildering experience for anyone who has allowed himself to get out of touch with current developments.

There have been notable developments of office machines in recent years.

Typewriters

Electric typewriters have advantages over other kinds as keyboard operation is easier, and a perfect impression is obtained, no matter how erratically the keys are depressed. Apart from appearance, this has advantages in obtaining a large number of carbon copies. Variable type machines have been developed, particularly useful in typing high quality reports or letters from chief executives, etc. These machines automatically adjust the horizontal travel of the carriage to suit the width of the letter being depressed, so that a printed appearance is provided.

Automatic typewriters are used where it is desired to send out a large number of letters conveying the same message but without the appearance of having been duplicated. The original letters are typed on the machine and the result is stored on punched paper tape, magnetic tapes in cassettes, or magnetic cards. By recycling the tapes or cards the machine can turn out letters at a very high speed, with names and addresses individually typed in at the same time.

'Noiseless' typewriters have been developed which muffle the sound of the operation, and are particularly useful when the secretary sits in the same room as the manager to whom she reports.

In recent years the work of typing complicated documents such as reports or lengthy agreements, where two or more drafts may be required before the final document is agreed, has been made easier. The underlying idea is to be able to hold the complete draft as typed, in machine storage, and then to be able to make erasures, amendments or additions as necessary, without having to retype the remainder of the document. This idea has been further extended to normal correspondence work, where the problems of error corrections, amendments, etc., have been eliminated, and claims of up to 100 per cent increase in typing productivity have been made.

Dictating machines

Comparable to the growth of television has been the development of sound recording machines, from the prewar wax cylinder dictating machines to the bulky magnetic tape recorders, and on to the modern compact electronic equipment, including cassette recorders for general purposes and the more specialised dictating machines for office or portable use, with the recording medium either an engraved disc or belt, wire or tape. The use of portable dictating machines which can easily be slipped into a brief-case has been a tremendous boon to the busy executive who spends a large amount of time travelling, or to those who have to visit outdoor sites, such as builders, architects, engineers, etc. Minicassette tapes are the most modern development.

In the case of the larger office deciding to make use of audio-typing, it may pay to set up a centralised installation, with microphones in managers' offices, wired to a central pool of dictating machines situated in the typing pool. An alternative possibility now available is to make use of an existing PABX telephone system instead of having to install separate microphones.

Duplicating and copying machines

The word 'duplicating' has always been used to describe the process by which a master copy of a document is made, which is then used to run off as many copies as may be required. The principal methods used are:

Spirit duplicating, or hectograph method. The copy paper, dampened with spirit, is pressed against the typed, hand written or photo master copy by means of a rotating drum. It is a cheap and useful method for getting up to 100 or more copies and can be used to reproduce colours simultaneously by using the same 'master' but with different coloured carbon paper at the back of it.

Stencil duplicating. The stencil is made with a typewriter or hand stylus, or by electronic means, on a plastic coated sheet, and up to 1 000 copies or more can be run off on duplicating paper. If colours are required, it is necessary to prepare a separate stencil for each colour.

Offset litho machines. These are really office printing machines, of principal use where it is desired to run off a large number of copies going into thousands. Different colours can be obtained, but this calls for a separate inking for each colour. Large firms or institutions that have installed these machines have found a considerable saving in comparison with outside printing costs. One further point: once a machine is installed, parchment masters can be used economically for short runs. In recent years very cheap photo masters can be made on photocopying machines enabling the litho system to be used economically for short run work, producing high grade printed copies for all manner of office requirements.

Copying is the term used to describe making one or more copies of an existing document, and the traditional method is of course obtaining one or more carbon copies at the same time as the original document. The disadvantages of this method of copying are well known: carbon papers are messy, no one likes receiving an almost illegible bottom copy, alterations made after the original document has been typed usually need to be typed in separately because of the difficulty of re-alignment. Accordingly it is not surprising that one of the most spectacular growth industries has been the development of photocopying, now enabling an unlimited number of copies of the original to be made on plain or coated paper. At the present time, the following copying processes are on the market:

- Diffusion transfer, operating on a principle similar to that of the Polaroid camera—not now extensively used.
- Dyeline process—reproduces copies on special paper from translucent masters. Originally the process was used only for reproducing drawings and plans.
- Reflex photographic process—uses traditional photo methods, i.e. negative and subsequent prints. It is not now extensively used.

● Electrostatic processes:

   (*a*) copying on to sensitised paper with a special coating;

   (*b*) copying on to plain paper.

The big growth has been in the electrostatic processes, but the snag from the point of view of the user is the cost. If a plain paper machine is rented (few are available to purchase) usage is metered and a periodic charge is made according to the number of copies run off, in addition to the rent of the machine. If a coated paper machine is bought (and some can be bought quite cheaply), then the cost of the paper has to be taken into account. Another decision to be made is whether to get a machine capable of copying from a sheet of paper, or to get a flat bed machine which can make copies from the pages of a book.

Addressing machines are a specialised form of duplicating, only instead of printing many copies from one master, the machine is designed to print single copies (or sometimes several copies) from a large number of masters. The machines use either metal plates, film stencils, or masters made of art paper for use with the spirit process. Much of the work of addressing machines has now been taken over by computers. Some examples are invoice addressing and the billing from local authorities and public utilities.

Adding, calculating and accounting machines

Accounting machines have three separate origins—they all started life either as adding machines, as typewriters or as cash registers. So many improvements have been made over the years as the result of competition that they are now mostly capable of providing the same facilities: preparing invoices and statements, entering up ledgers, bringing down balances, working out the payroll and so on. The main advantage of accounting machines over manual methods are their speed and elimination of errors through their ability to enter up several documents or records at the same time. However, it should not be overlooked that for the smaller firm the same facilities are provided at very much less cost by specially designed writing boards. For example, it is possible to prepare pay slip, earnings record and payroll at the same time by clamping together the three specially printed sheets with carbon backing. Dramatic developments have taken place in the last decade. Practically all the accounting machines and calculators now have solid state electronics. They are mostly silent, extremely fast and simple to operate and increasingly cheaper in cost. Many have large internal and external storage facilities, and are programmable for a whole variety of tasks taking on work that was only considered possible for large computers a few years ago.

A development of the last few years has been the 'pocket' calculator, on sale in a wide variety of models, often at very moderate prices. It has today become no uncommon sight to see almost any fellow or girl in the office using a mini-calculator rather than the pencil and scrap-pad or the 'ready reckoner'.

Analytical equipment

For analysis of data under different headings, several types of office aids are available. For the smaller office much can be done with peg-boards, which make it possible, by overlapping a number of forms, to reveal only the figures which need totalling. This is likely to be much more accurate than copying the figures on to analysis sheets before totalling. Another simple system which can be used for analysing recorded data is to enter the information in coded form on a series of cards which have holes punched around the edges. The desired information is inserted on these cards by cutting away the edge of the card adjoining the hole, so that when a long needle is passed through a particular hole in a pack of cards and then raised, all cards remain in the pack except those in which the hole has been slotted in this way, thus segregating the selected cards. A slightly more sophisticated version of this idea needing special equipment uses cards punched with holes in rows covering the entire area of the card, and information is recorded by slotting out two adjoining holes.

For more extensive analytical needs, the choice for many years lay between a cash register type of analysis machine, an accounting machine which is fitted with 198 adding registers so that analysis under 198 categories is possible, and the well known punched card systems, entailing preparation of punching documents, punching, verifying, sorting and tabulating. Nowadays there is of course the further possibility of making use of an electronic computer, but this is a story on its own and is dealt with at some length in Part Six (see page 859).

Filing

In most offices, controversy is likely to occur at one time or another about the best methods of filing. The usual topics for discussion centre round filing organisation, physical location, and method. A newly appointed financial director may well find this to be an area where improvements can be made in administrative efficiency combined with a reduction in space and cost.

Organisation and location

A decision will be needed on whether to allow individual managers to retain their own filing—either in their own rooms or in their secretaries' offices, or whether to insist on all files being held in a single central office. Central filing has certain distinct advantages, perhaps the greatest of these being that perusal of a particular file reveals the action taken by all the managers in the firm, and so provides a valuable means of communication within the firm, minimising the risk of uncoordinated or duplicated action, and saving a lot of management time in hunting through files when it is desired to obtain a total picture of a situation. Against these advantages must be set the extra administrative cost of transporting all files to a central location and processing them there instead of keeping all relevant documents close to the people primarily using them, and the irritation caused by the considerable likelihood of finding that a file is 'out'. Another point to be considered is that if a central filing system is introduced, managers will tend to keep all current correspondence in their own desks as 'work in progress' rather than have letters lost to sight in a general filing system; if this is allowed to happen the principal advantage of central filing of inter-firm communications about current happenings will be lost.

A decision will also be needed on the length of time for which filing records should be maintained, and experience alone will give a guide here. A useful compromise is to arrange for all files and records more than a specified number of years old to be parcelled up and labelled with details of originating department, subject matter and dates covered, and then stored for another specific period of years in the company's archives which can be situated in any suitable low cost accommodation.

Method and equipment

It is now reasonably well known and accepted that filing a large number of records in four-drawer filing cabinets placed round the walls of the room is not efficient from the point of view of space utilisation. The same room will house many more records if fitted up with floor to ceiling partitions in which the files can be stored laterally along shelves, or hanging from rails in pockets. Filing cabinets are, however, still in demand for use in individual offices where the main need is to have readily available a limited number of files. An essential part of an efficient filing system is an appropriate coding system.

Where space is at a premium, as in the centre of large cities, and there are a large number of records to be stored, any one of which may be required for inspection at short notice, the use of *microfilm* should be considered. The records are photographed on to this film and when required are displayed on screens or photocopied. There are many systems of microfilming and methods of retrieval, available from manufacturers.

Forms

Forms can be broadly divided into the following groups:

- forms relating to individual transactions, such as invoices, petty cash dockets, cheques;
- forms circulated at regular intervals containing information for management, etc.

What exactly is a form? Most people would regard a form as being a piece of paper on which certain information is recorded under specified headings, so that when completed, one or more copies of the form can be sent to the people or departments concerned. This definition will include:

1. Forms relating to individual transactions or activities, such as sales invoices, purchase orders, cheque requisitions, etc.

A very large number of these forms will be used in the course of a year so that even minor improvements in design, aimed at simplifying them or reducing their cost can have a marked effect on administrative efficiency by the end of a year. Form design will be used to review:

- the size and quality of paper work (a reasonable compromise between cost and acceptability must be found);
- the ease with which data can be entered, e.g. in logical order, or extracted, for example making use of a column down the right hand edge of the paper if peg-boarding is to be used for summarising;
- the number of copies required, and the different costs of making these copies, e.g. carbon-backed paper as compared with inserted carbon paper;
- the clarity of the wording on the form, so that the risk of errors in filling them in is minimised;
- arrangements for numbering the forms so that they can be identified.

2. Forms filled in for the purpose of circulating information to management and staff, usually at regular intervals, e.g. accident reports, cost reports, budget statements, etc.

Here the main emphasis for form design is firstly on whether the form is needed at all; for example, does it merely duplicate information supplied in some other way; secondly, does it convey the information in the best way, i.e. does it have maximum impact on the recipient with the fewest possible figures to be studied?

One of the major grumbles of businessmen everywhere is the increasing amount of paperwork circulating on their desks. Some of this paperwork may be unavoidable, but there can be no doubt that unless firm steps are taken to exercise control, there is a tendency for the number of forms circulating internally to grow year by year. It is always easy to start a new form, but most people are reluctant to suppress an existing one. It is accordingly a sound idea to introduce a system of forms control, under which all forms circulating in a business are reviewed say every two or three years. The object of the review will be to see whether a need for each form still exists, whether the circulation list is appropriate, and to examine the design of each form in the light of the changing requirements of the business, and the systems used in it.

Organisation

An example of an organisation structure for the administrative side of the business is given in chapter 2, but this should be regarded as only one of many ways in which the function can be organised. So much depends on the nature and size of the business, on the way in which the operational functions of the business are organised, and on the extent to which some of the newer functions such as long range planning, operational planning, computer department, report independently to top management.

It would take many pages to set out all the major alternatives, and the best guidance that can be given to any reader is to examine the way in which businesses similar to his own are organised. This information can sometimes be obtained from Chairmen's reports, or articles in the technical, or financial press, or even by a direct approach to the company itself.

9 Long-range planning and project evaluation

It is a fairly normal procedure for the owners or managers of a successful business to scoff at any new development in the management field. When management consultancy first began to take root in this country, many a consultant will remember the typical reception handed out by owner-managers of long established family businesses when first approached. 'You really expect us to believe, Mr X, that after a brief look round the factory you will be able to suggest ways in which we can improve our business and our profits? After all, my brother and I don't know all the answers yet, and we've only been here twenty-five years?' Yet a decade or so later, when threats from overseas competitors were increasing and profits falling, those same two brothers would probably be anxious to obtain outside advice.

When it comes to management techniques, some new developments —such as network analysis (critical path scheduling)—have been generally accepted almost immediately, while others seem to face continuous lack of interest or even active opposition. Long-range planning is one of these and even today a comparatively small proportion of firms in this country have introduced formal systems of long-range planning. This is probably due to a reluctance to spend valuable time and money on building up a form of planning which management feel has no particular relevance to their type of business. 'In our industry and our business it is impossible to know what is going to happen next year, so what is the point in trying to look further ahead?' they say. What they fail to appreciate is that the same comment could be justifiably made by every business in the country, yet in an increasing number of go-ahead concerns not particularly noted for wasting money, top management are devoting a large part of their time considering alternative strategies, and in agreeing on objectives to be built into the formalised long-range plans. These same companies also think it worth while to allocate one or more people full-time to set up the appropriate planning procedures and to keep the plans under constant review. The main reason why they are prepared to do this is undoubtedly the fact that with competition from home and abroad increasing every year, the only certain way of keeping ahead of competitors is to start planning for new developments at the earliest possible moment in time. Even when new ideas have been crystallised, the possibility of shortages occurring in vital materials or skilled labour will mean that the orders for new construction work or major alterations will have to be placed long before the new facilities are needed. Long-range plans provide a formalised structure for linking together all the tasks that have to be thought out and set in motion well ahead of the time when the new products start coming off the production lines—or the sales force start opening up new markets.

Introduction of long-range planning

Assuming that a business has established the need for long-range planning and taken a decision to introduce it, management will then have to decide how to approach the task. A normal procedure would be to work through the following steps:

1. Set up the planning organisation

The Board will probably want to maintain close contact with the development of the plans without getting too involved in the detail. A way of achieving this is to appoint a small working team, to include representation from the marketing, production and financial sides of the business. This team will decide what needs to be done, prepare the first set of plans, and keep the Board informed through regular meetings. Later, when the procedure has settled down, a decision can be taken whether to set up a separate department to carry out the work on a continuous basis, or whether to carry on with the part-time services of the working team.

2. Decide on the range and scope of the plans

Industries that are highly mechanised or making very sophisticated products, or working to long term contracts, will clearly need to plan ahead for a considerable number of years. The majority of firms engaged in relatively simple manufacturing operations will find it beneficial to plan ahead for five years, although during the introductory stage it may be sensible to start with three and extend to five when experience has been gained.

Companies with experience of annual budgeting will know that the budgets will be based on marketing and production plans that specify what volume of each product will be made and sold and at what unit cost and price. With long-range planning it is obviously not possible to do this for a period say five years ahead, since many of the products that will be sold then are at present non-existent. Hence the only way of quantifying the longer-range plans is usually in financial terms, and at the same time it is obviously important to know what financial resources will be needed to develop these plans. In other words, there is a vital need to take a corporate view and look at all aspects of the business, its activities and resources. It is for this reason that some people prefer to talk about 'corporate planning'.

3. Decide on the objectives

There are two ways in which long-range plans may be drawn up. First, the Board might decide that what was needed was a long-range *forecast* of the growth of the business, and they would ask the planners to examine existing trends of sales, costs and profits, capital employed etc. and then make forecasts of the corresponding figures in say five years time. These forecasts would be informative, but the Board would to some extent be missing out on one of the opportunities provided by the technique of assessing the gap between what *may* happen and what *could* happen. With the second approach, the Board itself examines the trends disclosed by the planners' investigations into current activities, and then decides what the objectives should be. These objectives may be expressed in terms of market share, sales turnover, production capacity, operating profit, return on capital, or earnings per share. At the same time, the Board must give some guidance as to their views about the strategies and policies to be followed in attaining these objectives. They may state that they see no reason to change existing patterns, or they may specify changes in certain directions.

In this context it will be important for the directors to be clearly aware of the character of business forecasting: this is a process of evaluation of facts, factors, influences and probabilities, with a view to arriving at a rational and reasoned judgement of expected objectives. Forecasting is a process a long way removed from 'prophecy' (see chapter 3 of Part One, page 26).

4. Assess the gap

Assuming that the Board has adopted the second approach outlined above, the planning team must now prepare their forecasts of probable results during each of the planning years, taking into account the Board's decisions on strategies and policies, and any expected changes in external conditions. The usual starting point for these forecasts is an inspection of the trends established in recent years and a forward projection of these trends on the assumption that policies remain unchanged. Corrections are then superimposed on these projections to reflect the estimated effect of expected changes. This projection technique is particularly appropriate when applied to the forecasting of future sales. Life would be easy for planners if it were possible to do the same with profits, which are after all the main end product of the whole planning process. Unfortunately any attempt to predict future profits by straightline projection is likely to be so wide of the mark that the whole exercise is pointless. This is because profits are residual in nature and are determined by matching revenue with costs, and quite small percentage changes in each can have a major impact on profits—perhaps turning a profit into a loss (cf. breakeven charts, chapter 5). This means that no short cuts are possible, and before the forecast profit can be determined, planners must first make their forecasts for all the factors likely to affect these profits.

When the various forecasts of costs are being prepared, planning teams should be able to obtain help from studies into cost behaviour that are frequently carried out in support of annual budgeting procedures or of capital expenditure proposals. They will certainly need to have an accurate knowledge of the limitations imposed by factory capacities. As mentioned above, long-range plans should be fully comprehensive, and in addition to forecasting the sales and profit figures, forecasts should be made for cash flow, capital expenditure and capital employed.

When all these forecasts have been prepared, they are compared with the Board's objectives and the various 'gaps' assessed by deduction.

5. Quantify the uncertainty

It is evident that the farther ahead one plans, the greater the likelihood of actual results differing from forecast. Many companies find it useful to quantify the probable range of uncertainty. A convenient way of doing this is to include upper and lower limits in the long-range plans, with the target figures in between:

Operating profit	Year	1	2	3	4	5
Maximum		105	127	135	165	320
Target		100	110	125	150	200
Minimum		90	97	105	128	160

6. Review the plans	The planning team has now prepared forecasts covering all the main factors described above, with upper and lower limits for the key figures of sales and profits. The Board must now decide whether to accept these figures as the official long-range plans of the company, even if they differ from their original objectives. If there are gaps which they feel are unacceptable, then functional management will be called in to study the problems further and to suggest ways of closing the gaps. Fortunately the problems are being studied several years before they actually arise, and this of course is one of the major advantages of introducing long-range planning.

7. Communicate the plans	After these further studies have been completed and decisions taken on any necessary amendments to the plans, the plans are approved by the Board and communicated to those managers who will be concerned with their implementation.

8. Monitor the results and revise the plans	As the years pass, it will gradually be discovered whether the original set of long-range plans were realistic. Continuous comparison of actual with planned results and investigations into differences will all help in making future plans more reliable. Once a year, at least, the forward plans should be reviewed and revised where necessary. There is no point in trying to stick to a plan that has become outdated due to a major change in external conditions.

Example of long-range planning	A medium sized company making and selling foodstuffs decides to introduce five-year planning to supplement the firm's annual budgeting procedure. The actual results for the last four years and the budget figures for the current year (likely to be close to actual) are as follows:

£000	Four years ago	Three years ago	Two years ago	Last year	This year
Capital employed	775	827	869	997	1 031
Sales	1 689	1 822	1 893	2 022	2 306
Operating costs	1 569	1 705	1 772	1 877	2 134
Operating profit	120	117	121	145	172

The directors are encouraged by the sharp rise in sales and profits this year as compared with last year. Based on this trend, they decide on the objectives for the next few years. The targets for year five are:

Capital employed	£1 250 000
Sales	£3 850 000
Operating profit	£400 000

The planning team that has been set up to develop these long-range plans decides to project the five-year trends of the factors shown above, and then compare with objectives. For this purpose they decide to use logarithmic paper which will show any item which increases in value each year by a constant percentage (i.e. in geometric progression) as a straight line. The result of this work is shown in Fig. 5.9.1 and it will be seen that if these forecasts prove correct, the directors' targets will not be met by a considerable margin. The comparative figures are as set out below:

Year 5

	£000	
	Forecast	Target
Capital employed	1 400	1 250
Sales	3 200	3 850
Operating costs	2 900	3 450
Operating profit	300	400

It will be noted that although the directors gave a profit objective, the planning team made no attempt to project the profit figures shown on the chart for the last five years. Instead they worked out the cost objective set by the directors, projected the five years' actual costs, and found the profit by deduction.

The forecast results shown by this exercise give rise to considerable discussion within the company, and after various alternatives have been investigated, the directors decide that several improvements can be made in company policies, including the introduction of more profitable products, and they decide to leave the objectives unaltered. Operating management are kept fully informed of the gaps that need filling if these objectives are to be attained, and they take early steps to introduce improvements.

The directors watch the gradual implementation of these plans with great interest, and, at the end of each year, they call for a comprehensive review of results achieved. By the end of year five they find that although none of their own objectives have been met (see Fig. 5.9.2 overleaf), sales for year 5 are ten per cent above the original forecast, but profits fourteen per cent below. They attribute these somewhat disappointing results to the effect of price controls and inflated costs. The results are summarised below:

Year 5

	£000	Forecast	Actual[1]	Target
Capital employed		1 400	1 366	1 250
Sales		3 200	3 545	3 850
Operating costs		2 900	3 288	3 450
Operating profit		300	257	400

Whereas in the foregoing example the company and its objectives and forecasts are imaginary, the *actual figures* plotted in Fig. 5.9.2 (overleaf) are

Fig. 5.9.1
Projected results

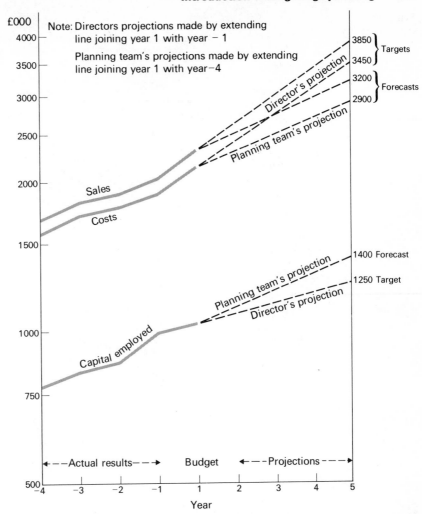

realistic, being reflected from the published results of a major British company.[1]

In the foregoing example, the long-term forecasts have been made by extrapolation of recent trends. Such forecasts are of course always liable to prove wide of the mark if a fundamental change in the trend occurs. In recent years forecasting techniques have been developed that are based more on a study of the fundamentals that can affect demand, and which should therefore be able to detect a change in trend before it occurs. (The original decision to develop Maplin as an airport was based on forecasts of air travel demand obtained by extrapolating earlier trends; the eventual decision to cancel the proposal was based on more sophisticated forecasts, that pointed to a slowing up in demand.)

[1] The data comes from the Unilever Group for the years 1964–72 (divided by 1 000): acknowledgement and appreciation are expressed to the Group by the Author.

Fig. 5.9.2
Actual results

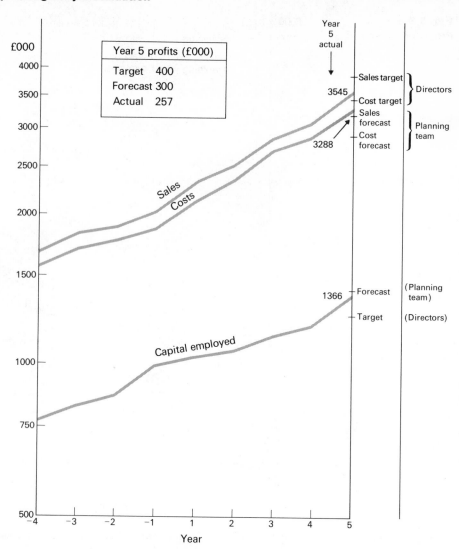

Project evaluation   At the time when long-range or annual plans are being prepared, management will frequently have to make a choice between alternative courses of action. The same need to evaluate alternatives will also arise when it looks as if current plans will result in objectives being missed. The decisions that have to be made during this process of evaluation can be divided into three categories:

1. Current operational decisions   Operating problems likely to recur at intervals during the year will involve such decisions as whether to vary the advertising allocation, or expand the sales force, or reduce selling prices, or to alter the product formula and so on. An illustration of this type of evaluation is given in the worked example in chapter 12 (see page 845).

2. Least cost action

Typical examples of choosing the course of action involving the least cost are: whether to manufacture or to buy-in a component needed in a finished product; whether to carry out certain engineering or maintenance work in the company's own workshops or to put the work out to contract.

The guiding principle to be observed in arriving at the decision is to include on the comparative statement prepared for the purpose only those values and costs that will be influenced by the decision. All past expenditures and all future costs which will continue to be incurred but which will be unaffected by the decision, must be ignored. Thus in arriving at the total cost of carrying out work in the company's workshops it would be wrong to include those general overheads—such as head office administrative charges—which would not vary whichever way the decision went.

The question often arises whether floor space should be included in the costs of alternative courses of action. This is a similar problem to the treatment of administration costs. If there is no alternative use for the space, then the cost should be excluded. If the space can be used for other profitable purposes, then the 'opportunity cost' should be taken into account.

'Opportunity costs'

By this title is meant the cost of a lost opportunity, rather than the actual cost incurred. For example, take the case of a firm owning two houses for use of its area management—a small house on the south coast and a larger house in a nearby market town. The smaller house costs £300 p.a. in rates and maintenance charges, the larger one £900 p.a. A decision is made to reduce overheads by using only the smaller house, and to let the other. Both houses are equally suitable for the company's purpose. It is subsequently realised that this was the wrong decision. In view of its situation the smaller house could have been let for £1 800 p.a. whereas the larger house was actually let for only £600 p.a. (tenants paying all charges in each case).

The 'opportunity cost' of choosing to occupy the smaller house is:

Rent lost (£1 800 − £600)	£1 200
Less saving in maintenance charges etc. (£900 − £300)	£600
	£600 p.a.

The actual cost of the house occupied (£300 per annum) is irrelevant, and so is the comparison of annual charges without taking into account potential income.

The question of alternative uses for money crops up when decisions have to be taken whether to make or buy a particular article, or whether to rent or buy a building. The latter is a particularly complex problem. Factors to be reviewed include:

- the percentage of the cost obtainable on mortgage, and the interest payable;
- the amount of marginal capital needed to complete the purchase or erection of the building, and the alternative uses to which it could be put;
- the comparison of the 'opportunity costs' of each alternative;
- the probable long-term trend of property values.

*Utilisation of
alternative capacity*

Another example of an alternative choice problem can arise when the policy to be adopted in allocating production levels between two or more similar factories has to be decided. For example, in a manufacturing business the firm's sole product is made at Factory A and Factory B. For a number of years, the latter factory has produced 60 per cent of the total output. The directors regularly keep an eye on the all-in costs at each factory, and for the current year, the planned utilisation and the estimated costs are as follows:

	Factory A	*Factory B*
Planned output per week	80 tonnes	120 tonnes
Cost per tonne	£33	£36

It is quite possible that the directors may consider taking advantage of the cheaper 'all-in' cost of Factory A by switching to it some of the tonnage produced at Factory B. In order to review the possibilities they call for a statement of *maximum* weekly capacity at each factory, which is found to be as follows:

Factory A 100 tonnes   *Factory B* 125 tonnes.

Accordingly, they may decide to make use of the maximum capacity at Factory A by switching 20 tonnes per week to it, even though this will leave Factory B operating at only 80 per cent capacity. However, before issuing the instructions to make this transfer, they discuss the situation with the accountant, who points out that the figures used may be misleading as a basis for deciding on alternative courses of action. He explains that it is necessary to work out the *additional* costs incurred in Factory A and compare these with the costs *saved* in Factory B. He then compares the variable costs in each factory and finds that the costs per tonne in A are £4 higher than in B. This means that switching 20 tonnes from B to A will increase variable costs by £80 per week, with fixed costs in each factory remaining virtually unchanged. The directors now realise that the most sensible course of action is to transfer 5 tonnes per week from A to B.

The conclusions reached from this example are that 'all-in' costs per unit can be misleading when it comes to choosing a course of action, and that the only real guide is provided by a comparison of variable costs applicable to each alternative. Furthermore, no meaningful conclusions can be drawn from an inter-factory comparison of unit costs unless accompanied by analyses of plant capacities and cost variability.

3. Capital project
decisions

Project decisions of the type considered above can usually be reversed if necessary, because there has been no investment of capital funds. With capital project decisions there is rarely the same opportunity to correct mistakes. If the new factory proves to be much more costly to operate than was contemplated when it was at the drawing board stage, very little can be done about it. It is evident that the only cost information that is likely to be of any value in helping to arrive at a correct decision is a careful assessment of what *future* costs are likely to amount to, in the particular circumstances envisaged. (This provides another example of the growing emphasis placed nowadays on forward or 'projected' information for control purposes. No amount of subsequent cost control can make good a faulty decision based on an inaccurate forward assessment of operating costs or capital expenditure.)

A capital project decision is frequently made on a provisional basis during the planning or budgeting stage, leaving the precise details to be settled nearer the time of starting work on the project. It is essential for those endeavouring to plan and control the cash resources of the business to receive advance information of such projects. If this is not done, surplus cash balances may be allocated to other purposes, and then if a request is received for urgent capital expenditure, the need may arise to sell securities only recently acquired, or even to postpone other projects considered less urgent.

Where the business is largely decentralised, a useful way of encouraging local management to submit their plans for capital projects well in advance is to introduce differentials in the sanctions required. Thus local management may be authorised to carry out capital work up to £10 000 without reference to head office, but if the outline of the project is first included in the annual budget statement, the sanction would be increased to say £20 000.

Capital project decisions invariably mean choosing between alternatives. If no alternative is available, no decision will be required. This means that a comparison must be made between the pros and cons of each method. It is usually found that some of these pros and cons can be expressed in quantitative terms, others cannot. An example of this is seen when a decision has to be taken whether to increase productive capacity in anticipation of selling a new range of products. Estimates can be made of the additional income and the additional costs resulting from this action, but the decision may be influenced by other factors, e.g. whether it will be regarded by other manufacturers as an intrusion into their fields, and will thus lead to retaliatory action. In such circumstances, the method of approach is to make the best assessment possible of the effect of measurable factors, and for management then to make the decision in the light of all the known facts.

Replacement decisions

The optional replacement of a piece of plant can be regarded as an investment of funds to be compared with other opportunities. If a certain capital sum is available, the question may arise whether it should be used to replace some of the existing outmoded plant by more up-to-date equipment and thus save on operating costs, or should it be used for building up additional capacity?

In this case the comparison will be between savings made on the one hand, and additional income on the other.

Confusion is sometimes caused over the question of depreciation charges on the asset which it is proposed to replace. It is sometimes thought that money will be saved by scrapping an existing machine on which there is a heavy annual depreciation charge, and by substituting a newer and cheaper machine, with a correspondingly lower annual depreciation cost. Unless a machine has a high resale value, which is unlikely, it is never possible to 'save' on depreciation; the actual cost of the machine was incurred in the year in which it was installed, and it is only a convenient accountancy arrangement to spread this cost over the life of the machine. The real comparison in the above instance would be to see what return would be obtained over the expected life of the new machine by way of savings in 'out-of-pocket' costs such as wages and power charges, etc.

Sometimes there is a reluctance to consider replacing a relatively new machine that has proved unsatisfactory in use because by so doing a heavy book loss would be incurred. This is analogous to the feelings of an investor who when faced with the need to realise capital decides to sell his most promising shares (which have risen and are likely to go on rising) rather than face a heavy loss by selling shares which have fallen well below the purchase price (and are likely to go on falling).

Project evaluation techniques

In the case of projects that result in the full benefit being obtained during the year when the cost is incurred, there is no particular problem in selecting the best alternative—it is just a matter of comparing the results shown by the evaluation. In many cases, however, a decision to undertake a particular project may involve the expenditure of capital sums on, say, new plant and equipment or on new distribution facilities, the benefits from which in terms of profit will not be realised until future years. The larger the capital outlay the longer it may be before an adequate return is received. Sometimes the project may consist of the introduction of a new range of products in the face of fierce competition, so that it will be necessary to sell them below cost for the first year or so in order to achieve a foothold. Eventually it is hoped to more than recoup these losses in future years. In these circumstances how can these alternatives where the benefit is deferred be compared with other projects where the benefit is more immediate? The answer is to make use of one or other of the various recognised approaches and techniques for assessing future benefits and comparing them with present or future outlays. There are four basic approaches, as illustrated in the example on pages 809–812.

'Pay-back' method

In this method, the additional income or expected savings per annum are compared with the net outlay by dividing the latter by the former to arrive at the 'pay-back' period, and then in turn comparing this result with the agreed criterion. For example, the factory manager may wish to scrap an existing machine and substitute a more up-to-date model at a cost of £10 000, with expected savings in manufacturing costs of £3 000 per annum. At the same time administrative management is seeking to obtain approval to install a mini-computer at a cost of £5 000 which, it is claimed, will save £1 000 per annum in clerical costs. If the agreed cutoff point is paying back the net outlay within four years, then the factory manager's project will go forward, but the computer project will not (unless the administrative manager can sell the project on grounds other than cost).

Although this method has the advantage of simplicity and ease of working out, it has the basic disadvantage of being too crude for all but relatively small outlays. It cannot distinguish between two apparently equal projects where in one case the saving is all achieved in the first year and in the other in the final year of the pay-back period. The method should accordingly not be used where the sums involved are relatively large.

Sometimes a degree of refinement can be brought to this method where there is adequate available capital, and each case can be judged on its merits. In this case, the rule might be to permit any project to be implemented where the net outlay was repaid within half the expected life of the asset purchased. Thus if experience shows that office machinery has an average life of five years and certain process machinery an average life of ten years, then the criteria for assessing the validity of new capital expenditure proposals might be pay-back within two and a half and five years respectively.

If the pay-back method is used, it should be noted that in calculating the cost savings, no account has to be taken of depreciation on the asset acquired, because the method itself takes care of this. For example, in the example first quoted above, where the pay-back criterion was four years, the rule can be interpreted as saying that if savings are equal to or exceed depreciation on the outlay calculated at 25 per cent p.a. on a straightline basis $(100 \div 4)$, then the project can go forward. Any capital allowances for taxation purposes on the other hand should be taken into account before calculating the pay-back period because these may vary according to the type of asset being acquired.

Return on Investment (ROI) method

With this method the return expected from the project is compared with some predetermined target rate. Only if the expected return is in excess of these rates will the project be permitted. The target rate may have been fixed at a level roughly equivalent to the average return on capital employed in the business, or it may have been decided on some purely arbitrary basis. A case can be made for varying this target figure from year to year according to the level of interest rates applicable to borrowed money. In periods of cheap money, when loans can be raised at 6 per cent or less, it may seem short sighted to deny a capital project expected to bring in 10 per cent or 11 per cent p.a. merely because this is less than a long established $12 \cdot 5$ per cent target. In periods of dear money when 10 per cent or more has to be paid to raise fresh capital, it would seem advisable to raise the minimum return to say 15 per cent.

In calculating ROI the usual method is:

- to estimate the additional profits to be earned, or the savings to be achieved, during the life of the project or for an agreed period of years;
- to deduct from this the depreciation applicable to the total time period (i.e. initial cost less residual or disposal value);
- to divide the answer by the total number of years and compare with the net outlay, to obtain an average annual percentage return on the project expenditure.

This is a more refined method of evaluation than the pay-back method because it does take some account of the time involved, but it still does not distinguish between cash benefits received early in the life of the project and those received towards the end of its life. With interest rates currently running at high levels, the length of time needed to wait for benefits to be received could have a considerable impact in making a time comparison of one project with another.

The two remaining methods of evaluation described below represent alternative ways of giving weight to the impact of timing. Both methods recognise the fact that £100 received in five years' time is less valuable than

£100 received today, and that the extent of this diminution in value can be calculated from tables if the prevailing rate of interest is known.

The preparatory steps for each method are the same: decide on the number of years to be included in the evaluation, and then prepare a cash flow statement, listing the cash disbursements and the cash receipts in each year, and the residual value (if any) at the end of the agreed number of years. In a typical capital project, expenditure on buildings, plant and machinery (including installation costs) will be incurred in Year 1, and a regional development grant may be received in Year 2. Further working capital may be needed for the project when it becomes operational, and will be entered on the sheet in the appropriate year. The items to be included on the receipts side of the statement will include any capital allowances for taxation purposes, together with any regional development grants receivable, the cash profit arising in each year after deducting corporation tax, and in the final year the residual value, if any. It should be noted that as corporation tax is payable in the year following the year in which the profits are earned, there will always be a time lag of one year (see example below).

Present value method

The basic idea of this approach is to find the present values of the cash flows in and the cash flows out by discounting them at an agreed rate of interest, and then to compare the answers and so by deduction arrive at the net present value of the project. If the discounted cash inflow is greater than the discounted cash outflow, then the net present value is favourable. If there are a number of possible projects to be considered, management will discard the ones where the net present value is unfavourable and then decide which of the others to select. In making this choice management will wish to look at the maximum sum invested and the size of the net benefit obtainable on each project.

In deciding on the rate of interest to use, there are generally several alternatives. One is to calculate the average cost to the company of capital employed in its business. This is a fairly straightforward calculation: divide the total dividends paid to shareholders and total interest paid on loans and debentures etc. by the total of shareholders funds (share capital plus retained profits) and loan capital. Such a calculation may not however provide a meaningful yardstick for comparing with future project opportunities because some of the loan capital for example may have been raised many years ago when ruling interest rates were very different. A more useful yardstick would be the marginal cost of capital: what rate of interest will have to be paid to raise fresh capital today?

Another approach is to use the rate of interest obtainable from investing in undated government securities at the time, since there is very little point in undertaking a new project with all the risks and uncertainty attaching to the prospects of success if the same income can be obtained from investing in risk-free securities. This rate of interest will normally be slightly lower than the marginal cost of raising additional capital.

Discounted cash flow method (DCF)

With the DCF method, instead of discounting the cash flow at an agreed rate of interest, they are discounted at a rate that results in the present values of both cash flows being exactly equal. For example, an investment of £614 today may bring in an income of £100 per annum for ten years and then nothing more, with no residual value. By trial and error, it is found from the tables that the ten-year cash flow has to be discounted at a rate of 10 per cent if the present values of these flows are to exactly equal the present value of the cash out, viz. £614. The DCF rate of return calculated in this way is a measure of the profitability of the project after giving weight to the timing of the cash flows, and enables management to list a series of projects in order of merit. To those managers who are not fully conversant with discounting techniques, the present value approach may seem easier to follow and understand than the DCF method. (This calculation is the sum of the factors in the 10 per cent column, years 1–10, multiplied by 100: see p. 812.)

Example of project evaluation methods

A company is considering a number of projects designed to improve profitability, and is prepared to invest up to £25 000 for this purpose. The accountant is asked to evaluate each project in turn, and for the first project detailed below to use all four methods of evaluation so that the Board can decide which method they prefer.

Project no. 1. Saving labour costs by purchase of specialised equipment. The evaluation is to be based on the following assumptions:

1. The equipment will cost £20 000 plus £880 installation costs.
2. The expected life of the equipment is five years, and there will be no residual value.
3. Staff costs are rising at the rate of 10 per cent per annum, and the saving in the first year will be £8 000.
4. Additional operating costs will be £1 200 per annum, rising by 5 per cent each year.
5. Corporation tax will be at a rate of 50 per cent.

The accountant prepares the following cash flow statement:

Year	Initial capital cost	Annual operating costs	Annual saving in labour costs	Corporation tax @ 50%	Total cash flow
		£	£	£	£
Installation year	(£20 880)	—	—	—	(20 880)
Operating year 1		(1 200)	8 000	10 440*	17 240
Operating year 2		(1 260)	8 800	(3 400)†	4 140
Operating year 3		(1 323)	9 680	(3 770)	4 587
Operating year 4		(1 389)	10 648	(4 178)	5 081
Operating year 5		(1 458)	11 713	(4 630)	5 625
Year 6				(5 127)	(5 127)

* 'First year' allowance of 100 per cent on the capital cost of the equipment. If this allowance had been less than 100 per cent, as in the case of industrial buildings, a 'writing down' allowance would be granted on the balance of expenditure and would reduce the corporation tax payable in each of the operating years.

† 50 per cent on year 1 income, £8 000 less £1 200. (Outward cash flow in brackets.)

Evaluation (a)   Pay-back method

Initial outlay	£20 880
Cash benefits	

	£
Year 1	17 240
Year 2	4 140
	———
	21 380
	———

Pay-back period two years.

Evaluation (b)   Return on investment method

Amount invested:

	£
Initial outlay	20 880
Tax allowance	10 440
	———
Net	10 440
	———

Benefits receivable during five years:

	£
Labour	48 841
Operating costs	6 630
	———
	42 211
Less tax @ 50%	21 105
	———
	21 106
	———

Average benefit p.a.   4 221

Less depreciation:

20% of £10 440   2 088   leaving   2 133 net

$$\text{Return on investment} = \frac{2\,133}{10\,440} \times 100 = 20 \cdot 5\%$$

Evaluation (c) Present value method

The rate of discount to be taken as 10 per cent.

Cash paid out	Amount £	Discount factor (p. 812)	Present Value £
Initial outlay	20 880	—	20 880
Year 6	5 127	0·5645	2 899
			23 779

Cash received			
Year 1	17 240	0·9091	15 671
Year 2	4 140	0·8264	3 421
Year 3	4 587	0·7513	3 441
Year 4	5 081	0·6830	3 470
Year 5	5 625	0·6209	3 492
			29 495

Net present value of savings		5 716
Maximum sum invested		20 880

Evaluation (d) DCF method

Various rates of discount are tried out until it is found that the two sides of the equation balance at a rate of 27 per cent (found from tables overleaf by taking the midway point between 26 and 28 per cent).

Cash out		Discount factor at 27%	Present value £
Initial outlay	£20 880	—	20 880
Year 6	5 127	0·238	1 220
			22 100

Cash in			
Year 1	17 240	0·787	13 567
Year 2	4 140	0·620	2 567
Year 3	4 587	0·488	2 260
Year 4	5 081	0·384	1 951
Year 5	5 625	0·303	1 704
DCF return = 27%.			22 049

The accountant points out that in evaluations of this type involving the writing off of capital expenditure over a number of years, the DCF method always gives a higher rate of return than the ROI method, and managers who are more used to the latter method should have their attention drawn to this. After due consideration, the directors decide to use the present value method, and the accountant is asked to evaluate the other projects on this basis so that a choice can be made.

Present value of £1 at interest rates up to 30% for 1 to 20 years

Year	1%	2%	3%	4%	5%	6%	7%	8%	9%	10%	11%	12%
1	0·9901	0·9804	0·9709	0·9615	0·9524	0·9434	0·9346	0·9259	0·9174	0·9091	0·9009	0·8929
2	0·9803	0·9612	0·9426	0·9246	0·9070	0·8900	0·8734	0·8573	0·8417	0·8264	0·8116	0·7972
3	0·9706	0·9423	0·9151	0·8890	0·8638	0·8396	0·8163	0·7938	0·7722	0·7513	0·7312	0·7118
4	0·9610	0·9238	0·8885	0·8548	0·8227	0·7921	0·7629	0·7350	0·7084	0·6830	0·6587	0·6355
5	0·9515	0·9057	0·8626	0·8219	0·7835	0·7473	0·7130	0·6806	0·6499	0·6209	0·5935	0·5674
6	0·9420	0·8880	0·8375	0·7903	0·7462	0·7050	0·6663	0·6302	0·5963	0·5645	0·5346	0·5066
7	0·9327	0·8706	0·8131	0·7599	0·7107	0·6651	0·6227	0·5835	0·5470	0·5132	0·4817	0·4523
8	0·9235	0·8535	0·7894	0·7307	0·6768	0·6274	0·5820	0·5403	0·5019	0·4665	0·4339	0·4039
9	0·9143	0·8368	0·7664	0·7026	0·6446	0·5919	0·5439	0·5002	0·4604	0·4241	0·3909	0·3606
10	0·9053	0·8203	0·7441	0·6756	0·6139	0·5584	0·5083	0·4632	0·4224	0·3855	0·3522	0·3220
11	0·8963	0·8045	0·7224	0·6496	0·5847	0·5268	0·4751	0·4829	0·3875	0·3505	0·3173	0·2875
12	0·8874	0·7885	0·7014	0·6246	0·5568	0·4970	0·4440	0·3971	0·3555	0·3186	0·2855	0·2567
13	0·8787	0·7730	0·6810	0·6006	0·5303	0·4688	0·4150	0·3677	0·3262	0·2897	0·2575	0·2292
14	0·8700	0·7579	0·6611	0·5775	0·5051	0·4423	0·3878	0·3405	0·2992	0·2633	0·2320	0·2046
15	0·8613	0·7430	0·6419	0·5553	0·4810	0·4173	0·3624	0·3152	0·2745	0·2394	0·2090	0·1827
16	0·8528	0·7284	0·6232	0·5339	0·4581	0·3936	0·3387	0·2919	0·2519	0·2176	0·1883	0·1631
17	0·8444	0·7142	0·6050	0·5134	0·4363	0·3714	0·3166	0·2703	0·2311	0·1978	0·1696	0·1456
18	0·8360	0·7002	0·5874	0·4936	0·4155	0·3505	0·2959	0·2502	0·2120	0·1799	0·1528	0·1300
19	0·8277	0·6864	0·5703	0·4746	0·3957	0·3305	0·2765	0·2317	0·1945	0·1635	0·1377	0·1161
20	0·8195	0·6730	0·5537	0·4564	0·3769	0·3118	0·2584	0·2145	0·1784	0·1486	0·1240	0·1037

Year	13%	14%	15%	16%	17%	18%	20%	22%	24%	26%	28%	30%
1	0·8850	0·8772	0·8696	0·8621	0·8547	0·8475	0·8333	0·8197	0·8065	0·7937	0·7813	0·7692
2	0·7831	0·7695	0·7561	0·7432	0·7305	0·7182	0·6944	0·6719	0·6504	0·6299	0·6104	0·5917
3	0·6931	0·6750	0·6575	0·6407	0·6244	0·6086	0·5787	0·5507	0·5245	0·4999	0·4768	0·4552
4	0·6133	0·5921	0·5718	0·5523	0·5337	0·5158	0·4823	0·4514	0·4230	0·3968	0·3725	0·3501
5	0·5428	0·5194	0·4972	0·4761	0·4561	0·4371	0·4019	0·3700	0·3411	0·3149	0·2910	0·2693
6	0·4803	0·4556	0·4323	0·4104	0·3898	0·3704	0·3349	0·3033	0·2751	0·2499	0·2274	0·2072
7	0·4251	0·3996	0·3759	0·3538	0·3332	0·3139	0·2791	0·2486	0·2218	0·1983	0·1776	0·1594
8	0·3762	0·3506	0·3269	0·3050	0·2848	0·2660	0·2326	0·2038	0·1789	0·1574	0·1388	0·1226
9	0·3329	0·3075	0·2843	0·2630	0·2434	0·2255	0·1938	0·1670	0·1443	0·1249	0·1084	0·0943
10	0·2946	0·2679	0·2472	0·2267	0·2080	0·1911	0·1615	0·1369	0·1164	0·0992	0·0847	0·0725
11	0·2607	0·2366	0·2149	0·1954	0·1778	0·1619	0·1346	0·1122	0·0938	0·0787	0·0662	0·0558
12	0·2307	0·2076	0·1869	0·1685	0·1520	0·1372	0·1122	0·0920	0·0757	0·0625	0·0517	0·0429
13	0·2042	0·1821	0·1625	0·1452	0·1299	0·1163	0·1042	0·0754	0·0610	0·0496	0·0404	0·0330
14	0·1807	0·1597	0·1413	0·1252	0·1110	0·0985	0·0779	0·0618	0·0492	0·0393	0·0316	0·0254
15	0·1599	0·1401	0·1229	0·1079	0·0949	0·0835	0·0649	0·0507	0·0397	0·0312	0·0247	0·0195
16	0·1415	0·1229	0·1069	0·0930	0·0811	0·0708	0·0541	0·0415	0·0320	0·0248	0·0193	0·0150
17	0·1252	0·1078	0·0929	0·0802	0·0693	0·0600	0·0451	0·0340	0·0258	0·0197	0·0150	0·0116
18	0·1108	0·0946	0·0808	0·0691	0·0592	0·0508	0·0376	0·0297	0·0208	0·0156	0·0118	0·0089
19	0·0981	0·0829	0·0703	0·0596	0·0506	0·0431	0·0313	0·0229	0·0168	0·0124	0·0092	0·0068
20	0·0868	0·0728	0·0611	0·0514	0·0433	0·0365	0·0261	0·0187	0·0135	0·0098	0·0072	0·0053

10 Recent developments in taxation

The new imputation system of taxation was introduced by the Finance Act 1972 and came into operation on 1 April 1973. In order to appreciate the full effect of the change made by this legislation and the implications for company strategy, it is necessary to consider some of the main features of the system of corporation tax which had been in existence in the UK since April 1964. The basic principle underlying the assessment of corporation tax during this period was that companies were charged at the agreed rate (varying from 40 to 45 per cent) on their profits after deducting various charges coming out of these profits, such as debenture interest. Dividends paid to preference or ordinary shareholders are not a charge on profits, but are in the nature of an appropriation of profits, and such payments did not reduce the liability to corporation tax.

One effect of the corporation tax legislation was to make preference shares relatively more expensive than an issue of debentures carrying the same rate of interest and as a result very few issues of preference shares were made to the general public after 1965, companies preferring to issue either straight debentures or debentures carrying conversion rights into ordinary shares.

Companies thus paid corporation tax on their chargeable profits but this did not in any way absolve the shareholders from also paying income tax, and possibly surtax, on the dividends they received from companies. Companies were required to deduct tax at the standard rate from all dividends paid, and to hand over this tax to the Inland Revenue as a separate item. The only exception to this rule was if the company had itself received a dividend under deduction of tax from some other UK company, known as 'franked investment income'. The tax on the latter could then be offset and only the net balance was remittable. Shareholders were separately assessed for surtax on the gross amount of the dividends received if their taxable incomes brought them into the range of this tax.

It will no doubt be appreciated that the overall effect of this system of taxation was to provide an incentive to distribute as little as possible by way of dividend because this course of action would minimise the total tax sum paid over. Eventually the government at the time decided that the double taxation of profits was inequitable and they agreed to introduce a system of taxation similar to that being used in some continental countries, that would mean that the total tax collected by the Inland Revenue from a company would remain the same regardless of the company's dividend policy.

The imputation system of taxation

After considering an alternative approach, it was decided to introduce the *imputation system*. Under this system a company will calculate the charge for corporation tax and will then decide whether to retain the remaining net profit, or whether to pay all or part of the balance to shareholders as dividend. If a dividend is paid, there is no longer a question of deducting income tax from a 'gross' dividend because the cash paid out to shareholders is the net dividend; the company has paid corporation tax on its profits and no further tax is due. If all shareholders were liable to pay tax at the new basic rate of 30 per cent on all their taxable income, then the scheme outlined above would be adequate in fulfilling the Government's intention of removing previous anomalies. But in practice, some shareholders with large incomes are due to pay higher rates of tax on various slices of their income, while others with low incomes are entitled to be repaid any tax suffered. The method adopted to take these factors into account is reflected in the name given to the new system and is based on 'imputing' to each shareholder an amount of tax equal to three-sevenths of the net dividend he receives. His dividend warrant will show the net amount paid and the tax imputed to him, known as a 'tax credit'. It will be seen that this tax credit equals 30 per cent of the 'gross amount' (obtained by adding the tax credit to the net amount) and is thus equivalent to the basic rate of income tax for individuals. Shareholders due to pay higher rates of tax will have to include the gross amount of the dividend in their tax returns. Shareholders not liable to pay any tax will be entitled to reclaim the 'tax credit' from the Inland Revenue.[1]

When the new system of taxation was being drawn up, it was realised that many companies paying dividends to shareholders might in fact pay little or no corporation tax in the same year, owing to past losses or because they traded overseas and were able to set off overseas taxes against the UK corporation tax charge. The Government had no intention of restoring the position that applied in pre-corporation tax days before 1965, when a low income shareholder could reclaim from the Inland Revenue tax that had never been paid by the company in the first place. Accordingly, when a dividend is paid, companies are required to remit to the Revenue a sum equivalent to the total of the tax credits, and known as 'advance corporation tax' (ACT). Subject to the restriction noted below, the company can then deduct this advance payment from its subsequent liability for corporation tax on the income for the year during which the dividend was paid thus maintaining the principle that taking one year with another, payment of a dividend does not affect the total tax charge. The restriction built into the system is that for any accounting period the balance of corporation tax due after deducting advance corporation tax, known as the company's 'main stream liability', must never fall below a certain proportion of the total tax due before set-off (two-fifths while corporation tax is levied at 50 per cent, or one-quarter for small companies earning less than £15 000 profit in any year where the corporation tax rate is 40 per cent). Any ACT that cannot be set off owing to the above restriction can either be carried forward to be set off against future main stream liabilities, or carried back for set off in the two preceding accounting periods (but not prior to April 1973).[2] An Accounting Standard has now been issued.

---

[1] The figures quoted in this paragraph were applicable at the time of writing, but are likely to be varied in the Finance Act(s) subsequently brought into effect.
[2] Points to note in working out how much ACT can be set off are (i) only ACT on dividends paid *during* an accounting period are eligible for set off against corporation tax paid *for* that period; (ii) ACT cannot be set off against any corporation tax payable by a company on 'chargeable gains' as distinct from 'income'.

Value added tax   VAT is a tax on turnover, applying to both goods and services. Before the EEC decision to harmonise tax systems within the Common Market, various European countries had adopted turnover taxes but they were mostly what are known as 'cumulative cascade' types of turnover tax:

Importers:

to Manufacturers	sales of imported raw materials + turnover tax
to Wholesalers	sales of finished products + turnover tax
to Retailers	sales of finished products in depots + turnover tax
to General Public	sales of finished products in shops + turnover tax

Even if the rate of tax is low—say 5 per cent—the compounded effect of working out tax on tax at each level of manufacture and distribution can mean that the final tax borne by the ultimate consumer, the general public, is substantial. The main objection to this type of tax is the inequitable impact which it can have, hitting small firms who have to buy through the usual chain of distributors indicated above, and favouring large vertically organised concerns that can eliminate all the intermediate steps. Accordingly, in April 1967 an EEC directive was issued stating, *inter alia*, that all member states were to replace their existing systems of turnover taxes by a common system of tax on value added. The principle of this tax was defined as applying a general tax directly proportional to the price of goods and services concerned, irrespective of the number of steps in the production and distribution processes.

In the UK the decision to enter the Common Market was anticipated and VAT was first introduced in the 1972 Finance Act, to take effect from 1 April 1973, in replacement of *purchase tax* on goods and *selective employment tax* on services. Value added tax is to be charged on the supply of goods and services in the UK and on the importation of goods into the UK, and is to be under the care and management of the Commissioners of Customs and Excise. The standard rate of tax was fixed at 10 per cent in the 1973 Finance Act. Even if the UK had not joined the Common Market, VAT would have been introduced because of its advantages over the previous taxes. To mention just one example of these advantages relating to export sales: with VAT it is possible to eliminate all tax at all stages of production and distribution, whereas with purchase tax and SET it was never possible to eliminate the tax suffered on indirect expenses at earlier stages in the cycle.

At this point the question may be asked, why cannot the tax at 10 per cent be charged directly to the customer by the retailer, and then handed over to Customs and Excise? This would surely achieve the EEC objectives and would eliminate an enormous amount of administrative time and costs by 'exempting' the manufacturers and wholesalers from charging and paying over the tax? Unfortunately this apparently simple procedure would prove unworkable in practice because there would be too many opportunities for avoiding the tax, everyone would try to make out they were merely a link in the chain instead of admitting to being the 'ultimate consumer'. Further thought shows that the only way of avoiding large-scale evasion is to adopt the principle of value added tax advocated by the EEC, and that is to make everyone pay the tax at all stages in the chain of operations, and then to claim it back again if one is *not* an ultimate consumer. This is the underlying principle of our own system of VAT. To start the ball rolling an importer of raw materials, or a manufacturer importing goods himself, is charged with VAT on the value of the goods imported, although in practice the tax is not due until the goods are withdrawn from stock. (This is the one exception to the rule that the tax is paid over by the supplier of goods or services, and is of course necessary because the supplier of imported goods will be outside the UK tax jurisdiction.) When the importer sells the raw materials to the manufacturer, he will add to the invoice for the goods VAT at 10 per cent:

Importer		VAT			VAT
	£	£		£	£
Purchases (raw			Sales of raw materials		
materials imported)	1 000	100	to manfucturer	1 200	120
Wages ⎫ Added value	100	—			
⎬ £200					
Profit ⎭	100	—			
	1 200	100		1 200	120

Total VAT payable to Customs and Excise: £100 + £20.

The importer pays the £100 VAT on the materials he has imported, but because he is not an ultimate consumer, he is entitled to recover this from his customer, the manufacturer. In fact, he recovers £120 tax on his sales invoice, the additional £20 representing VAT at 10 per cent on the 'value' which he has added to the raw materials in making them available to the manufacturer, i.e. the £200 representing wages paid out and his own profit. Had he been able to sell the materials for £1 250, then the 'value added' would be £250 and so on.

The importer now balances his books by paying over the £20 to Customs and Excise, in addition to the £100 he has paid on the imported materials.

Turning now to the manufacturer in the above example, the only difference is that he does not have to make a direct payment to Customs and Excise on his raw materials, because this is charged to him by the importer on the purchase invoice. Also, it may be expected that in addition to wages and salaries, he incurs expenses on services etc. on which he also has to pay VAT. His Profit and Loss Account may look like this:

Manufacturer		VAT			VAT
	£	£		£	£
Purchases of raw			Sales to		
materials	1 200	120	wholesaler	2 700	270
Services	250	25			
Wages and ⎫ Added	⎧				
salaries ⎬ value	⎨ 900				
Profit ⎭ £1 250	⎩ 350				
	2 700	145		2 700	270
Balance of VAT due					
to Customs and Excise		£125			

Following on with the wholesaler and the retailer, the figures are:

Wholesaler		VAT			VAT
	£	£		£	£
Goods purchased from manufacturer	2 700	270	Sales to retailer	3 900	390
Services	300	30			
Wages and salaries ⎱ Added value £900	500				
Profit ⎰	400				
	3 900	300		3 900	390
Tax due to Customs and Excise		£90			

Retailer		VAT			VAT
	£	£		£	£
Goods purchased from wholesaler	3 900	390	Sales to customers	5 300	530
Services	450	45			
Wages and salaries ⎱ Added value £950	600				
Profit ⎰	350				
	5 300	435		5 300	530
Tax due to Customs and Excise		£95			

Looking now at the overall position:

		£
The importer, manufacturer, wholesaler and retailer paid over to Customs and Excise £100 + 20, 125, 90 and 95	=	430
The suppliers of services used in the above chain of operations would have to account to Customs and Excise for the tax which they added to their invoices £25, 30 and 45	=	100
Making a total paid over of		£530

—exactly equal to the tax charged to the ultimate consumers, the retailers' customers. Thus it will be seen that the tax ultimately payable is collected in instalments whenever goods are imported, goods change hands or services are performed and value has been added.

In practice it is not necessary to match sales of goods with the corresponding purchases; the tax charged by others on invoices for goods and services is added up, thus arriving at the total 'input tax', regardless of the nature of their inputs. For example, if capital expenditure on new machinery has been incurred, the VAT on this will be included in the total input tax. Similarly the VAT added to sales invoices for the period will be totalled, thus arriving at the total output tax. The difference between these two figures is then paid over to Customs and Excise (if output tax is larger) or recovered from them (if input tax is larger). For example, if the manufacturer in the above example had bought a machine for £2 000, then the position would be:

Manufacturer Taxable inputs		VAT	Taxable outputs		VAT
	£	£		£	£
Purchase of raw materials	1 200	120	Sales to wholesaler	2 700	270
Services	250	25			
Purchase of new machine	2 000	200			
		345			270
			VAT due from Customs and Excise		£75

Points to be noticed are that VAT is payable by 'taxable persons', who are defined as including individuals, partnerships and companies—and in certain circumstances, clubs and associations. However, it is only payable if the goods and service are supplied in the course of a business carried on by such taxable persons, and this explains why wages and salaries are not subject to VAT.

The wage earner and the salaried employee are providing a service to their employer, but it is not service in the 'course of a business carried on by them'. The word 'business' is used in a wide sense and includes professions and vocations.

Incidentally, the word 'supply' does not just refer to sales, but includes many other instances where goods change hands, such as goods hired out, goods given away or withdrawn from a business for personal use, or used elsewhere in the business.

Services given free are not charged to VAT, but otherwise all services provided within the UK are chargeable unless they are specifically exempted (see below).

Exceptions to the general rules

Non-deductible inputs

The Commissioners can issue regulations which prevent the VAT on certain items of expenditure being deducted from the VAT charged on sales etc. before arriving at the net tax due. For example, VAT payable on hotel bills incurred in travelling is deductible, as also is VAT payable on the entertainment of the firm's own staff or of overseas visitors. In other cases of entertainment, the VAT is non-deductible.

Another example relates to the purchase of motor cars for use in a business; VAT is non-deductible unless the cars are purchased for resale.

Zero rating

One of the principal advantages of the system of VAT introduced into the UK over the previous taxation methods of purchase tax and SET is the facility to eliminate *all* tax on goods exported. If this were not possible, Britain would be at a severe disadvantage in comparison with other EEC members when trying to build up export sales. The way in which this is achieved is to 'zero rate' all exported goods and also services to overseas traders, or for overseas purposes, as defined in Schedule 4 of the Act (Group 9).

Schedule 4 also specifies a number of other items which are to be regarded as zero rated and in 1973–74 these included foods bought in shops and taken away, water, fuel and power; books, newspapers and music, maps etc., newspaper advertisements; news services; drugs and medicines on prescription; construction of buildings, transport, residential caravans; gold and bank notes.

The borderline between standard rated and zero rated goods is illustrated by very detailed examples given in Schedule 4, complete with 'General items', 'Excepted items' and 'Items overriding the exceptions'. A very close study of these schedules is necessary before reaching a decision on the correct category. A well-known example quoted in the official *Scope and Coverage* booklet is fish and chips. If eaten in the café they attract VAT; if taken away to be eaten outside, they escape.

Whether goods are zero rated or standard rated does not alter the general principles of accounting for tax to Customs and Excise. A trading firm exporting everything, or selling in the UK only zero rated goods, will have no output tax to account for and will be able to reclaim all its input tax. A firm selling a proportion only of export goods or zero rated goods in the UK may find its output tax on its remaining sales of standard rated goods in the UK will be less than its input tax, and so this firm also will be able to reclaim the net balance of VAT suffered. Hence in either case the trading firm selling goods in the course of its business to its UK or overseas customers does not ultimately suffer any VAT itself.

Exempt services and associated goods

A rather different situation exists in the case of certain groups of services and goods associated with these services; these are listed in Schedule 5 to the Act and are regarded as 'Exempt supplies'. A person supplying only these exempt goods and services will have to pay VAT on any purchases he makes from his own suppliers, but apart from this, he can ignore VAT. He does not have to register, to add VAT to his invoices, or to pay over any VAT to Customs and Excise. This may sound attractive but when compared with someone selling zero rated goods, it will be seen that he is at a disadvantage as he is unable to reclaim any of his input tax.

Exempted services in 1973–74 were: interest in land; insurance; postal services; betting, gaming and lotteries; finance; education; medical and dental services etc.; burial and cremation. Here again the schedule has to be studied to find out from the examples given which items are exempt and which are standard rate. Burial services are exempted, but supplying a headstone is not.

Where a business deals partly in taxable supplies and partly in exempt supplies, there is again no need for registration for VAT if the amount of its annual turnover in taxable supplies brings it into the category of 'small trader' described below.

The small trader

If a trading firm is of the opinion that its annual turnover in taxable supplies of goods and services is likely to be £5 000 or less, there is no need to register for

VAT, and its position will then be similar to that of a firm providing only exempt services.

A firm deciding not to register for this reason will not have to add VAT to its sales invoices, and this would appear to give it an advantage in comparison with the larger firm. However, it will not be able to reclaim VAT payable on its own inputs, so it will have to allow for these in working out selling prices. Also, if it supplies goods to another *trader* rather than to an ultimate consumer, the customer will not be able to reclaim VAT, since the small firm has in effect included it in the selling price, and is not allowed to show it separately. One other disadvantage, all the firm's customers who are knowledgeable about VAT will know that turnover is less than £5 000 per annum.

A small trader may however register for VAT even if turnover is less than £5 000 per annum, provided that Customs and Excise agree.

The large trader selling exempt supplies

Where a firm sells more than £5 000 worth of taxable supplies and therefore needs to register, and also provides exempt services, etc. the input tax has to be apportioned; that part relating to exempt supplies cannot be deducted from the output tax on taxable supplies.

Registration

Registration is compulsory where taxable supplies for the preceding twelve months exceed £5 000, or where there are grounds for believing that the next twelve months' total will exceed £5 000. A firm is not allowed to wait until the end of the year before ascertaining the annual turnover and then finding out whether registration is necessary. Unless good reasons can be shown, registration is compulsory if taxable supplies for any quarter ended 31 March, 30 June etc., exceed £1 750, or for two quarters exceed £3 000, or for three quarters exceed £4 250.

Groups of companies may apply to be treated as a single unit for VAT (in which case inter-company supplies of goods or services are ignored for VAT purposes). A company carrying on business in separate divisions may apply to have each division treated as a separate company.

The tax invoice

The link which enables a business to reclaim VAT on goods and services obtained from its suppliers is the 'tax invoice' provided by the latter, in which the amount of VAT and other details prescribed is set out. This tax invoice has accordingly to be prepared for all sales to 'taxable persons', but is not necessary in other cases, such as retail sales to the general public. In addition to the usual details of names and addresses of supplier and customer, the invoice must contain an identifying number and date, the date of supply, and the supplier's VAT registration number. The invoice must also identify the type of supply, e.g. whether sale, hire etc.; give a description sufficient to identify the goods or service; show the quantity and amount payable for each description; the total amount payable excluding VAT; the rate of any cash discount offered; and finally the rate and amount of VAT charges.

There is an important exception to this rule applicable to retailers or other organisations having direct contact with the public, such as hotels, restaurants, etc. A tax invoice only has to be provided if it is asked for; and if the amount (including VAT) does not exceed £10, a shorter invoice is allowable, in which inter alia it is permissible to show the amount payable including VAT, with a note of the current rate of VAT. This short form of invoice which eliminates the necessity of showing VAT as a separate item, may not be used for zero rated or exempt supplies. In the full invoice these have to be totalled separately and indicated as bearing no tax.

Quarterly return

VAT has to be accounted for once a quarter, by completing the 'Return of value added tax'—see examples in Figs. 5.10.1–3. The tax as shown by the return is payable not later than the end of the following month (but less than £1 is treated as nil). Where a person finds that his input tax is always greater than his output tax, he is allowed to submit a return once a month. No prescribed form of bookkeeping or accounting is prescribed by the Act, but records must be retained for three years. A failure to keep records or supply information involves a fine of £100 plus £10 a day while the failure continues. Customs and Excise have far-reaching powers to enter and search premises etc.

Fig. 5.10.1
Extracts from H.M. Customs and Excise General Guide to Value Added Tax (Notice No. 700)

Appendix E (referred to in paragraph 112)

SPECIMEN VAT ACCOUNT FOR FULLY TAXABLE PERSONS

Period 1.1.74 to 31.3.74

TAX DEDUCTIBLE	£	£	TAX DUE	£	£
Input Tax			**Output Tax**		
January	8 096 20		January	9 827 80	
February	7 435 10		February	7 938 40	
March	8 118 30		March	8 556 90	
	Total	23 649 60		*Total*	26 323 10
			Tax due on imported goods and goods ex-warehouse:		
			January	432 10	
			February	240 60	
			March	301 70	
				Total	974 40
Overdeclarations and/or **overpayments** of tax in respect of previous periods:			**Underdeclarations** and/or **underpayments** of tax in respect of previous periods:		
(a) Notified by Customs and Excise	NIL		(a) Notified by Customs and Excise	NIL	
(b) Other	237 10		(b) Other	196 70	
	Total	237 10		*Total*	196 70
TOTAL TAX DEDUCTIBLE		23 886 70			
By Credit Transfer TAX PAYABLE		3 607 50			
		27 494 20	TOTAL TAX DUE		27 494 20

Fig. 5.10.2

Appendix C (referred to in paragraph 62)

SPECIMEN RETURN

Return of Value Added Tax

For the period

1 January 1974 to *31 March 1974*

H.M CUSTOMS
AND EXCISE

For official use

Registration No.	Period No.
912 3456 78	*012*

A. Wholesaler Ltd.

22 North Road,

London. N.12 4AN

The registered person named here must complete and return the form to VAT Central Unit, H.M. Customs and Excise, Alexander House, 21, Victoria Avenue, Southend-on-Sea X, SS99 1AB.

not later than.

30 April 1974

A pre-paid addressed envelope is enclosed
Any tax payable must be paid by the same date.

Before completing any item on this form please read the appropriate note; the paragraph numbers in the attached notes correspond to the numbers of the items on the form.

Note: A return which is incomplete or qualified in any way (e.g. marked "Provisional") does not satisfy the legal requirements. Failure to make a return or to pay the full amount of tax payable by the due date is an offence.

Fold here · Fold here

PART A. Account of tax payable or repayable

This part must be completed by all registered persons. Please complete all boxes, writing 'NONE' where there is no amount to be entered.

Tax due for this period:	Output tax	1	£ *26323*	*10*
	Tax on imported goods and goods ex-warehouse	2	£ *974*	*40*
Underdeclarations and/or underpayments of tax in respect of previous periods	Notified by Customs and Excise	3	£ *NONE*	
	Other	4	£ *196*	*70*
Total tax due:	Sum of boxes 1 to 4	5	£ *27494*	*20*
Deductible input tax for this period:	6 £ *23649* *60*			
Overdeclarations and/or overpayments of tax in respect of previous periods:	Notified by Customs and Excise	7	£ *NONE*	
	Other	8	£ *237*	*10*
Total tax deductible:	Sum of boxes 6 to 8	9	£ *23886*	*70*

Net tax payable or repayable
If the amount in box 5 is greater than that in box 9 tax is payable to Customs and Excise.
If the amount in box 9 is greater than that in box 5 tax is repayable by Customs and Excise.
(Please tick appropriate box).

Payable to Customs and Excise ✓
Repayable by Customs and Excise ☐

10	£ *3607*	*50*

Method of payment to Customs and Excise.
(Please tick appropriate box)

National Giro ✓   Bank Giro ☐   Remittance enclosed ☐

For Official Use

VAT 100   Sec. F.3790 (April, 1973)

Fig. 5.10.3

PART B. Value of outputs and inputs (excluding any tax)
This part must be completed by all registered persons. Please complete all the boxes, writing 'NONE' where there is no amount to be entered. Pence should be disregarded.

Outputs:			
	Outputs chargeable at the standard rate of tax	11	£ 269980
	Exports	12	£ 12842
	Other zero-rated taxable outputs	13	£ 21076
	Total taxable outputs (sum of boxes 11, 12 and 13)	14	£ 303898
	Exempt outputs	15	£ NONE
	Total outputs (sum of boxes 14 and 15)	16	£ 303898
Inputs:	Total taxable inputs including zero-rated inputs	17	£ 262421

PART C. Retailers' special schemes
This part must be completed by retailers who use any of the special schemes for the calculation of output tax described in Notice No. 707.

Enter in the box(es):
  1 if you have used scheme **1**
  2, 3 or **4** if you have used any of these schemes   18

PART D. Calculation of deductible input tax
Except as explained in the notes, this part must be completed by all partly exempt persons; it need NOT be completed by any other registered persons.

Enter **1, 2** or **3** in this box to show which method you have used	19	
Amount of any input tax wholly attributable to taxable supplies	20	£
Amount of input tax partly attributable to taxable supplies	21	£
Percentage used to attribute input tax $\frac{\text{box } 14 \times 100}{\text{box } 16}$ =	22	
That part of the amount in box 21 which is deductible for the period $\frac{\text{box } 21 \times \text{box } 22}{100}$ =	23	£
Total deductible input tax for the period (sum of boxes 20 and 23); this total should also be entered at box 6 overleaf	24	£

PART E. Declaration by the signatory
This part must be completed by or on behalf of all registered persons

I **ALAN NORMAN OTHER**
       (full name of signatory in BLOCK CAPITALS)

declare that (i) the information given in this return is true and complete in respect of all business or businesses carried on by the registered person except in so far as he is separately registered if so required and that, except as notified, none of the changes listed in Notice No. 700 has occurred during the period covered by the return.

      (ii) the amounts shown as deductible input tax in this return relate to tax which may be deducted by virtue of Section **3** of the Finance Act 1972 and regulations made under that Section, and I claim deduction of input tax accordingly,

      (iii) where I have used one of the retailers' special schemes I have complied with Notice No. 707.

Signed _____ *A.N.Other*
            (~~Proprietor, partner,~~ director, ~~secretary, responsible official, duly authorised to sign~~)

Date _____ **26/4/74**
*Delete as necessary

BEFORE RETURNING THIS FORM PLEASE DETACH THE NOTES

Special categories of traders

Special considerations apply to retailers, hotels and caterers, trade and professional bodies, charities, clubs and associations, local authorities, and to certain categories of goods—secondhand goods, antiques, etc., and full details will be found in the various explanatory booklets issued by Customs and Excise.

**The role of the
financial director**

Apart from policy decisions whether to register or not in the case of small traders, the primary role of the financial director vis-à-vis VAT will be to make sure that the accounting system is geared up to meet the new demands. In view of possible changes in the future to harmonise with EEC countries, he will want to make sure that if necessary four separate rates could be used for VAT calculations.

He will also probably wish to tighten up on the firm's credit control procedures, and make sure that customers pay up promptly. He will remember there is no relief obtainable for VAT on bad debts—it has to be accounted for whether or not the debt is paid.

Changes

The foregoing outline of the principle and practices of Value Added Tax has been included here, because of the recent date of introduction and because many managers (or students of management) may not have opportunity otherwise of becoming acquainted with the background and the procedure.

It must, however, be recognised that the outline is given in accordance with arrangements prevailing at the time of going to press, and that changes may subsequently be introduced which would vary the details set down in the foregoing pages.

An Accounting Standard on VAT has now been issued.

11 Control of financial resources

The newly appointed Financial Director introduced in chapter 1 has by now largely completed his survey of the various matters of principle likely to need his attention during his first year of office. He has examined the overall principles of control, and seen what needs to be done to introduce sound costing and budgetary control procedures. He has discussed with the Board and functional management the provision of suitable management information, and has taken part in setting up long-range planning and project evaluation procedures. All these aspects of his work may be described as providing a service to others, but he has also looked at matters which are more his own responsibility, such as office management and the implications of recent changes in taxation. His final task is to examine a subject of paramount importance to everyone in the business, the control of financial resources. He uses this term in its widest sense, to cover not only the control of financial assets such as cash and investments, but also the way in which finance is obtained from external sources. He also knows that under this heading he must advise the Board about the impact of inflation. Each of these main topics is now considered in turn.

Cash management

The Financial Director's main job here is to make sure that cash is available when it is needed for the business. Timing is the all-important factor. Knowing that cash will be available next month does not help pay today's wages if overdrafts are already stretched to the limit. The essential requirement is to identify clearly, first, the various sources of cash, and second, the various ways through which demands for cash will be channelled. Then if reliable forecasts can be built up of the probable volumes of cash inputs and cash outputs arising in each sector of the business it can be seen whether in total the situation will be in balance, or whether a number of peak requirements are likely to arise simultaneously, thus causing a severe strain on available supplies of cash.

Cash flow statement

The flows of cash into and out of a business will arise in many ways. Some of the cash payments will relate closely to the current day to day operations and activities of the business e.g. the payment of factory wages. Other payments may relate to operations and activities of previous periods, e.g. the payment to a supplier in March of goods supplied during January and February. Similarly, cash received from customers may relate to the current period if the goods were sold for cash, or to previous periods if the customer is granted credit facilities. It is clear from this that merely to summarise cash received and cash paid out during the year in respect of manufacturing and trading operations would be meaningless as a guide either to profitability or as a basis for forecasting future movements in the cash balance. Quite apart from these considerations the cash balance itself will be affected by a number of other transactions outside the normal operating activities, including the sale of investments, the issue of shares, the purchase of fixed assets and so on.

In view of the vital importance of keeping a constant watch on liquidity, an increasing number of companies are finding it essential to make a careful analysis of the different sources of cash inflows into the business, of the corresponding cash outflows, in such a way that conclusions can be drawn from a study of the figures presented. The usual practice is to analyse the cash flow in accordance with the diagram shown in Fig. 5.11.1.

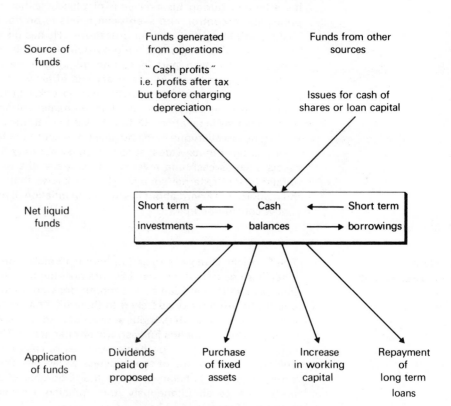

Fig. 5.11.1
Cash flow analysis

Points to note on examining this diagram are as follows:

● Actual cash balances can be increased or decreased overnight by short term financial transactions, such as calling in a deposit or borrowing sums from the bank to finance a shipment. The cash flow analysis is accordingly more meaningful if it is built up round the 'net liquid funds' of the business, i.e. cash balances plus short term investments, less short term borrowings.
● There is no need to analyse the 'cash profits' figure, since this can be obtained from the Profit and Loss statement, before deducting depreciation (which does not involve a flow of funds).

- Many public companies now include a statement of source and application of funds in their published accounts, and an example of the type of statement is given below.
- One of the key factors needing a close and continuous watch is the movement in overall working capital requirements, i.e. in stock plus debtors, less creditors. In an expanding business, the need to finance an additional volume of sales, combined with inflationary pressures on prices, can very quickly swallow up available cash balances. Drastic steps may then be necessary to tighten up on controls of stocks and debtors in an attempt to swing the balance the other way, and to increase liquid funds by releasing working capital.

In reviewing the effectiveness of an existing system of cash control, answers should be obtained to the following points:

- Is a cash flow statement prepared regularly?
- Does operating management prepare regular forecasts of future cash movements?
- Is there a positive policy of borrowing money when interest rates are low and of obtaining the highest possible rates consistent with safety when investing surplus funds?
- Are security arrangements adequate?
- Are stock control procedures adequate? What arrangements are made to speed up settlement of sales invoices?
- Is there an adequate control over capital expenditure?

Example

Source and application of funds

	This year £000	Last year £000
Net liquid funds (cash and short term investments less temporary borrowings) at end of year	161	
Net liquid funds at beginning of year	140	
Increase	21	

	£	
Source of funds		
Generated from operations		
Net profit for year	66	
Add back charges not requiring the use of funds:		
Depreciation of fixed assets	42	
Capitalised expenditure now written off	8	116
Funds from other sources		
Issue of shares	10	
Long term loans received	16	26
		142

Application of funds

Purchase of fixed assets		45
Increase in working capital:		
Stocks—increase	18	
Debtors—increase	12	
	30	
Less creditors—increase	10	20
Repayment of long term loans		3
Dividends to shareholders, paid and proposed		53	121
Net increase in funds as above			21

Cash flow statements are particularly important where there are a number of different companies or divisions making up a group in which the cash is centralised. In addition to the peaking effect referred to above, the cash flow in any business will be favourable in some years (input exceeds output) and unfavourable in others, but where several units are combined, there may well be a tendency for favourable trends in some units to offset unfavourable trends in others for years at a time. It is important to have a clear picture of this effect, so that if there is any likelihood of all the units reacting unfavourably at the same time, the full effect of this can be anticipated.

In April 1974 the Accounting Standards Steering Committee issued an Exposure Draft (ED/3) on the proposed standard accounting practice for Source and Application of Funds statements, with the object of establishing them as a part of audited accounts, and to lay down a minimum standard of disclosure in such statements.

Cash forecasts

Cash forecasting is a byproduct of long-range planning and annual budgeting. It is only when operating plans and capital expenditure proposals have been worked out in some detail that it becomes possible to form a view of the net inflow or outflow of cash from the activities or projects. With these as a starting point, financial management has to superimpose the forecasts for the inflow and outflow of associated financial transactions, such as investment income, expected taxation liabilities, projected dividend payments, etc.

Finally, it is necessary to allow for known or anticipated 'once off' or abnormal items, such as repayments of bank loans, sales of assets no longer required, gains or losses on foreign exchange transactions, share issues, and so on. When account has been taken of all these items, it becomes possible for the first time to quantify the net effect on cash balance at the end of each planning period, e.g. at the end of each of the next five years if five-year planning has been introduced, and more certainly, at the end of each quarter in the year ahead.

The ability to forecast cash movements in both long-range and short-range time scales, with reasonable accuracy, plays a vital role in running a business efficiently. Success is of course entirely dependent on the combined skills of each manager in the business in planning his own sphere of operations. The financial manager may frequently form a view that his colleagues on the operating side are unduly pessimistic or sometimes unduly optimistic; for example, it is a frequent occurrence to overestimate capital expenditure requirements in the year ahead: something always seems to happen to hold up the start of such projects. However it would be a rash financial manager who altered his colleagues' forecasts without first obtaining their agreement and, after all, this time they may be right.

However carefully the forecasts have been prepared, so many influences will be at work to affect the cash flows that it becomes essential to update the forecasts at frequent intervals—at least once a quarter. Before the figures are revised it will be helpful to insert the actual cash movements for the quarter just ended. Random fluctuations can of course occur from quarter to quarter without necessarily meaning that the year end forecast will be wide of the mark, but as soon as a definite trend appears to have set in it will be advisable to adjust the year-end figures. This will usually mean adjusting the longer range forecasts as well.

As experience is gained in cash forecasting, greater reliance will be placed on it, and it may become possible to plan more precisely the investment of surplus funds at economic rates of interest, e.g. by tying up funds for fixed periods of time rather than on a day-to-day basis. However, the most vital role of cash forecasting is to provide advance warning of future liquidity problems. If several major projects prove to be major misjudgments by management, and if they all flop at about the same time, liquidity can vanish at an alarming rate, and it is perhaps the Financial Director's most vital role to prevent this happening, if at all possible. Post-mortems held on the numerous cases of companies being forced into liquidation through lack of funds usually show that financial management was weak or non-existent. All business decisions involve the taking of risks, but the Financial Director must warn his Board when he thinks the risks will be too great. One danger to be avoided is being forced into a position where it becomes necessary to raise large sums of money at short notice at a time when interest rates are abnormally high.

If the cash forecasting system signals a future shortage of cash, as mentioned above, it is often possible to take avoiding action well in advance of the critical period, either by postponing capital expenditure or by eliminating the need for it, e.g. by renting a computer instead of buying it.

Economic use of money

Instances often occur where a company runs several bank accounts, and in these circumstances it is important that high interest charges are not being incurred on overdrafts while at the same time large sums are being held in other accounts earning little or no interest. If it becomes clear that there will be a temporary surplus of funds, advantage can be taken of the higher rates of interest obtainable on deposit accounts. If sums of £10 000 or over are available, very high rates of interest can be obtained by placing such sums with the London Money Market (through the firm's bankers) for stipulated periods of time such as a month or a year. In 1974 it was possible to obtain 15 per cent per annum in this way. Other outlets for surplus funds are provided by loans to local authorities at high rates of interest for a specified number of months or years. Full details are given in the financial press.

Security
arrangements

In view of the ease with which cash can be misappropriated, adequate arrangements are clearly essential to prevent losses of cash (whether in hand or at bank) through pilferage or fraud. The guiding principle is to avoid the situation where a single individual is in sole charge of cash transactions or cash balances. This means that there should always be at least two people present when the mail is opened, and not always the same two people. All cash and cheques received should be banked on the day of receipt, and not held over to meet payments. Cash required to pay wages should be drawn by cheque, and all cheques should bear the signatures of two responsible officials. Wages frauds are perhaps the easiest of all frauds to perpetrate, and suitable precautions must be taken to ensure that there are no 'dummy' names on the payroll. There should be a frequent reconciliation of cash book with bank statements to avoid the risk of hiding cash withdrawals by omitting them from the cash book. The firm's auditors are always ready to advise on improving the effectiveness of internal control procedures.

Stock control and
control of debtors

The recent inflationary trends that have caused many raw materials to double in price within a few months have brought home forcibly the need to keep a close watch on the cash required to finance stocks of raw materials and finished goods. In order to conserve finance it may be necessary to adopt a policy of buying materials as and when required, rather than building up substantial stocks. There may be a need to examine the firm's stock control procedures, to see whether it is possible to reduce stocks of finished goods held either in the factory or at depots, without running too much risk of being unable to supply customers' requirements.

The arrangements for supplying goods to customers on credit should be examined periodically to make sure that the terms are reasonable, and that adequate steps are taken to deal promptly with slow payers or potential bad debts. At the same time the credit facilities allowed by suppliers should be watched to make sure that full advantage is being taken and that cheques are not being sent out unnecessarily early.

Control of
capital
expenditure

The selection of suitable projects has been dealt with in chapter 10. Subsequent planning and control procedures should take care of the following points:

● Suitable warning must be given by operating management well in advance of the time that money will be needed to meet commitments.
● The Board as a whole should approve all capital projects before commitments are entered into with contractors or suppliers. A suitable way of obtaining this is to divide the procedure into two stages: (i) An outline proposal for the capital project is submitted at the time the annual budgets are prepared. This outline proposal will give the reasoning behind the project, the expected benefits, and an approximate estimate of the cost. If provisional approval is obtained at this stage, a more detailed proposal will be submitted shortly before it is desired to place the contract. (ii) When this is in turn approved, the contract can be placed.

● A control procedure is necessary to check that actual sums spent on capital items do not differ to any great extent from the sums authorised. Where it becomes apparent that the authorised total is going to be exceeded by a significant amount, arrangements should be made to review the whole project. A decision must then be taken whether to allow the overspending to proceed, or whether to cancel or defer the completion of the project. Much will of course depend on the financial strength of the company and the extent to which future profits will be penalised if the project does not go ahead.

Raising additional finance

Assuming that all possible steps have been taken to increase cash resources by tightening up on the control of working capital and capital expenditure, the point may be reached when it is necessary to look outside the business for additional finance. Some of the ways of doing this are outlined below:

Bank loans

An advance from the firm's bankers is one of the first avenues to be explored. The amount of the advance will depend on the security that can be provided and on the previous relationships built up between the bank and the company management. The bank will usually look for repayment of the advance within a short time.

Bills of exchange

A long established procedure for speeding up the cash flow is regularly used by firms engaged in importing or exporting goods, for example an overseas tea plantation company selling its annual tea crop for export and ultimate sale in the UK. The plantation company would draw up a bill of exchange for the amount involved, and the bill is accepted by the importing firm, or more usually by a bank or accepting house acting on behalf of this firm, payable at the end of say three months, by which time the tea would have been sold at auction in London. The accepted bill, together with the shipping documents that convey the title to the goods, is then discounted through the bill market at the current rate of interest (quoted in the financial press) and the plantation company gets the net proceeds at least three months earlier than they could otherwise have expected, but at the cost of the interest charge.

Factoring

There has been a considerable increase in the use of factoring in recent years to obtain an immediate improvement in cash resources, but this is a course of action not open to the smaller firm. The factor agrees to handle the whole of the debt collecting and credit control functions, and hands over immediately a substantial proportion, say 75 per cent, of the value of sales invoiced during the week or other period, with the remainder paid over only when the customer settles his account. Collection of debts can be with or without recourse, i.e. according to whether or not liability for bad debts is transferred. The remuneration received by the factor will include interest on the amounts outstanding as well as other charges.

Sale and leaseback

Many industrial firms have agreed with the idea that they are in business to convert raw materials to finished products and that they should not concern themselves with holding land and buildings as an investment. On the other hand, there are numerous financial institutions which are continually on the look-out for property investments that can be let at reasonable rentals to responsible tenants. As a result, there has been considerable growth in sale and leaseback arrangements, by which an industrial company may agree to sell the freehold of an office block in a provincial city, in exchange for leasing back the premises at an agreed rental. The financial institution gets its property investment and the industrial company not only gets a windfall in cash, but is likely to find its overall return on capital employed increased (since it should be able to earn far more on the cash released than the rental payable under the lease).

Raising
long-term loans

Generally speaking the larger and more successful the company, the easier it is for it to obtain further outside finance. The small family firm, with ambitions to grow in size and eventually hit the headlines, is the kind of business that will have to depend almost entirely in its early years on the finance that its founders can provide. This means that it is quite usual for a growing business of this kind to pay no dividends in its early years, but to retain all profits in the firm in order to finance expansion.

When a pattern of increasing profitability and growth has been built up, the first opportunity for obtaining outside long-term finance may arise from an application to the *Industrial and Commercial Finance Corporation*, a body sponsored by the clearing banks for this purpose. Loans may be granted for periods of between ten and twenty years, after a thorough survey of the company's status and resources has been carried out by one of the ICFC's investigating accountants.

Then there are the specialist 'venture capital' companies that are prepared to provide finance to a business that is expected to be sufficiently profitable in three to five years' time to be turned into a public company with a stock exchange quotation. The venture capital company will advance the funds required now on the understanding that it is allocated an agreed percentage of the ordinary share capital on favourable terms when the public issue is made.

Issue of shares
or debentures

When the time finally arrives for a business to turn public and be floated on the stock exchange, it has to consider the same kind of questions that existing public companies need to think about when raising additional finance, for example, what sort of capital structure should the company have, taking into account existing taxation requirements? The alternatives open to a company are to issue:

Debentures, carrying a fixed rate of interest, payable whether or not the company makes a profit, and redeemable on a specified date.

Preference shares, entitled to a dividend each year out of profits earned, up to a fixed maximum rate. If they are non-cumulative preference shares, then each year stands on its own and there is no question of making up this year for dividends passed in previous years however good this year's profits may be. If they are cumulative preference shares, then no dividend can be paid on ordinary shares until this year's and all previous years' preference dividends have been paid out of accumulated profits earned. Participating preference shares are entitled to share in the surplus profits with the ordinary shareholders after the fixed preference dividend has been paid. The conditions under which dividends may or may not be repaid will be specified in the company's Articles of Association.

Ordinary shares, known as equity capital, entitled to receive a dividend after all the prior charges (debentures and preference capital) have been satisfied. Ordinary shares are sometimes divided into preferred and deferred ordinary shares, or into voting and non-voting shares. Upon liquidation of a company, the assets available after repaying creditors will be distributed according to the regulations contained in the company's articles, but it is usual for the ordinary shareholders to receive the whole of the net assets after repaying the prior charges. Thus the ordinary shareholders are in the same position as the proprietors of a business, or the partners in a partnership when it comes to winding up a concern.

Convertible loan stock. A comparatively recent alternative for companies to consider is the issue of convertible loan stocks that carry a fixed rate of interest like a debenture but which also provide for conversion on specified terms into ordinary shares at specified future dates. They are particularly useful where there is likely to be a long development period before the company expects to make really spectacular profits.

Gearing

Before a decision can be taken on what kind of capital structure is needed (in the case of a new company) or in what form additional capital shall be raised (in the case of an existing company) a policy decision must be taken on the extent of gearing considered appropriate. For example, two companies had the following structure and each needed to increase total capital by £250 000 in order to finance expansion:

Company A	£	*Company B*	£
$8\frac{1}{2}$% Debentures	250 000	6% Preference capital	250 000
Ordinary capital	500 000	Ordinary capital	500 000

Company A decided to issue 500 000 additional £1 ordinary shares to existing shareholders, at par, on the basis of one new share for every one share held and to repay the debentures out of the proceeds.

Company B decided to issue £250 000 10 per cent debentures, at par, by inviting applications from existing preference and ordinary shareholders. The money was raised and the new capital structures were then:

Company A	£	*Company B*	£
		10% Debentures	250 000
		6% Preference capital	250 000
Ordinary capital	1 000 000	Ordinary capital	500 000
	£1 000 000		£1 000 000

Before the change in capital structure, both companies had equal gearing of 33 per cent. Since the change, Company A has eliminated all gearing, while Company B has increased the gearing element to 50 per cent. Assuming that both companies are at present earning 8 per cent on capital employed, ordinary shareholders in each company (ignoring taxation) will be earning 8 per cent on their shares (because the debenture holders and preference shareholders will also average 8 per cent between them). If next year profits fall to 4 per cent on capital employed, ordinary shareholders in A will receive 4 per cent, but nothing in Company B. If in the following year, profits rise to 12 per cent on capital employed the earnings for ordinary shareholders will be 12 per cent and 16 per cent respectively. Thus, gearing enhances the effect of movements in profits and will appeal to those who are optimistic about future growth.

Taxation considerations must normally be taken into account before deciding on the best way of raising additional funds, but as noted in chapter 10, there is no longer a taxation disadvantage in issuing preference shares.

Inflation

In the mid-1930s, the owners of a small private company, having found that the firm had accumulated £30 000 surplus funds, decided that it would be advisable to invest the money outside the business. Accordingly, the £30 000 was divided into three parts and dealt with as follows:
£10 000 was invested in freehold property;
£10 000 was placed on deposit with selected Building societies;
£10 000 was invested in $3\frac{1}{2}$ per cent War Loan at par, and accordingly purchased £10 000 stock.

Forty years later, the next generation of owners decided to realise these investments, as they wished to use the money in expanding the business.

	£
The freehold property realised	60 000
Amount withdrawn from Building Societies	10 000
The sale of £10 000 $3\frac{1}{2}$ per cent War Loan at 24 produced	2 400
	72 400

resulting in an apparent overall profit of £42 400. This would be a true picture of the outcome of the investments if money had held its value during the forty years, but unfortunately the value of money in the mid-70s, as measured by the goods and services it can buy, was only 16 per cent of its value in the mid-1930s. This means that in real terms the firm had lost money overall on its investments. It managed to break even on its investment in property—the £60 000 proceeds will probably just pay for the factory extension that could have been built for £10 000 in the mid-1930s. The £10 000 withdrawn from the Building societies will now buy only 16 per cent of what it would have purchased forty years before, so that in real terms the investment has lost 84 per cent of its value. The real disaster however has occurred with the investment in War Loan, where the proceeds in real terms represent only 4 per cent of the original outlay. This investment has suffered not only from the fall in the purchasing power of the pound, but also from the shrinkage in market prices for undated fixed interest securities, due to the steady rise in interest rates generally obtainable during the same period.

Inflation is therefore a vital factor that needs careful consideration by company managements. Every time new stocks of raw materials have to be bought, the purchase manager finds that he has to pay some 5 to 10 per cent more than on the previous occasion. Where is the money to come from to meet these higher charges? The problem of inflation is likely to have maximum impact when fixed assets need replacement. The sums accumulated in the business as the result of charging depreciation will do no more than cover the cost of replacement of a machine at the original price, which may now only represent 20 or 25 per cent of the new price.

Many companies have realised for some time that there is a need to allocate a sum out of profits each year to cover the extra cost of replacing stocks or fixed assets, and dividend payments will be restricted accordingly. However, very few companies have felt bold enough to regard this sum as a charge to be included before profits are struck. The great difficulty here is that for taxation purposes, profits have still to be calculated on the traditional basis. Any company which decided to adjust its annual accounts to eliminate the effect of inflation in this way would therefore not get a compensating reduction in the taxation charge, and would appear in an unfavourable light in comparison with its competitors, unless they also made the change. There are two possible solutions. The first is for the Government to agree to base corporation tax on the true 'inflation-proofed' profits rather than on reported profits. The second solution is for there to be a requirement that *all* companies adjust their accounts to an inflation-proof basis.

There are two basic methods of eliminating the effect of inflation: one is for each company to make its own calculations of the extent to which the prices of its raw materials and fixed assets have risen during the year as the result of inflation, and then to adjust the accounts on this basis; the other method, which is the one favoured by the Accounting Standards Steering Committee, is to make adjustments in the accounts by reference to the variations in the general purchasing power of money, as recorded in the official *Consumer Price Index*. A provisional Accounting Standard was issued in May 1974 (see page 716).

APPENDIX EXTRACTS FROM STATEMENTS BY THE ACCOUNTING STANDARDS STEERING COMMITTEE

This Appendix (No. 2) is for general guidance and does not form part of the Provisional Statement of Standard Accounting Practice.

EXAMPLE OF THE PRESENTATION OF A SUPPLEMENTARY CURRENT PURCHASING POWER STATEMENT

The example has been prepared in order to illustrate how the figures of a company might be presented in the supplementary current purchasing power statement. It should be emphasised that the following example is only one method of presenting the information required by the Standard and is not obligatory. Indeed it is desirable that companies should experiment with different methods of presentation during the early years of the use of this Standard.

SUMMARY OF RESULTS AND FINANCIAL POSITION
ADJUSTED FOR THE EFFECTS OF INFLATION (NOTE 1)

	Historical basis		Current purchasing power basis	
	£000 Last year (1)	£000 This year (2)	£000 This year (3)	£000 Last year (4)
RESULTS FOR THE YEAR				
Sales	1 920	2 110	2 190	2 134
Profit before taxation (see note 2)	205	215	175	195
Taxation	82	86	86	89
Profit after taxation	123	129	89	106
Dividends	60	60	61	65
Retained profit for the year	63	69	28	41
FINANCIAL POSITION AT END OF YEAR				
Net current assets	490	556	561	533
Fixed assets less depreciation	558	566	700	714
	1 048	1 122	1 261	1 247
Less: Loan capital (see note 3)	200	200	200	216
Deferred taxation	39	44	44	42
	239	244	244	258
Total equity interest	809	878	1 017	989
RATIOS				
Earnings per share (p) (based on 500 000 shares in issue)	24·6	25·8	17·8	21·2
Dividend cover (times)	2·1	2·2	1·5	1·6
Return on total equity interest (%)	15·2	14·7	8·8	10·7
Net assets per share (£)	1·6	1·8	2·0	2·0

Notes

1. The figures in the current purchasing power basis columns were arrived at by converting the corresponding figures in the historical basis columns by reference to the changes in a general price index between the dates of the original transactions and the end of 'this year'. The current purchasing power basis figures for both this and last year are measured in pounds of purchasing power at the end of 'this year'. The general price index used was that specified in Provisional Statement of Standard Accounting Practice No. 7. The Retail Price Index at the end of this year was 139·3 and at the end of last year was 129·0. Both figures are based on January 1974 = 100.

As the Inland Revenue do not at present accept CPP basis accounting, taxation liabilities are calculated by reference to profits on the historical basis and no adjustment therefore is made to the tax charge in the CPP basis column.

2. **Profit before taxation**
How the difference between profit on a historical basis and on a current purchasing power basis is made up.

	This Year £000	Last Year £000
PROFIT BEFORE TAXATION (historical basis)	215	205
Adjustment to convert to current purchasing power basis:		
STOCK		
Additional charge based on restating the cost of stock at the beginning and end of the year in pounds of current purchasing power, thus taking the inflationary element out of the profit on the sale of stocks	(37)	(25)
DEPRECIATION		
Additional depreciation based on cost, measured in pounds of current purchasing power, of fixed assets	(25)	(17)
MONETARY ITEMS		
Net gain in purchasing power resulting from the effects of inflation on the company's net monetary liabilities	12	10

SALES, PURCHASES AND ALL OTHER COSTS
These are increased by the change in the index between the average date at which
they occurred and the end of the year. The adjustment increases profit as sales
exceed the costs included in this heading

10		7	
	(40)		(25)

PROFIT BEFORE TAXATION
(Current purchasing power basis at end of year under review)

175		180

Adjustment required to update last year's profit from last year's pounds to this year's
pounds

	15

Profit before taxation
(Current purchasing power basis at end of this year)

175	195

3. The loan capital at the beginning of 'this year' amounted to £200 000. £200 000 at the beginning of this year is equivalent in purchasing power to £216 000 at the end of this year (because inflation has been 8 per cent during the year). As the company's liability to the providers of loan capital is fixed in money terms this liability has declined during the year in real terms from £216 000 to £200 000. This reduction of £16 000 in the company's obligation in terms of current purchasing power is included in the net gain on monetary items of £12 000 shown in note 2.

This Appendix (No. 3) is for general guidance and does not form part of the Provisional Statement of Standard Accounting Practice.

OUTLINE OF A METHOD* OF CONVERSION FROM BASIC ACCOUNTS TO SUPPLEMENTARY CURRENT PURCHASING POWER STATEMENTS

The method of conversion may be divided into four basic stages:

1. Figures for items in the balance sheet at the beginning of the year are converted into pounds of purchasing power at the beginning of the year as follows:
   (a) non-monetary items are adjusted for changes in the purchasing power of the pound since they were acquired or revalued;
   (b) monetary items are, by definition, already expressed in terms of pounds of purchasing power at the beginning of the year, and therefore require no conversion.

2. Figures for items in the balance sheet at the beginning of the year are then updated (see definition, paragraph 31), from pounds of purchasing power at the beginning of the year to pounds of purchasing power at the end of the year.

3. Figures for items in the balance sheet at the end of the year are converted into pounds of purchasing power at the end of the year as follows:
   (a) non-monetary items are adjusted for changes in the purchasing power of the pound since they were acquired or revalued;
   (b) monetary items are, by definition, already expressed in terms of pounds of purchasing power at the end of the year, and therefore require no conversion.

4. The difference between the total equity interest in the converted balance sheets at the beginning and end of the year (after allowing for dividends and the introduction of new capital), is the profit or loss for the year measured in pounds of purchasing power at the end of the year. This profit or loss can be analysed by producing a profit and loss account including figures expressed in pounds of

* There are other methods of conversion. Full details will be found in *Accounting for Inflation: A working guide to the accounting procedures*, published by The Trustees of Chartered Accountants' Trust for Education and Research of The Institute of Chartered Accountants in England and Wales.

purchasing power at the end of the year in the same detail as in the company's basic profit and loss account or in a more summarised form if desired. In addition to these items the converted profit and loss account should contain a figure for the net loss or gain in purchasing power resulting from the effects of inflation on the company's net monetary assets or liabilities.

Note

In stages 1 and 3 the figures for non-monetary items after conversion need to be reviewed, in the case of stocks, in the light of the test of lower of cost (in pounds of purchasing power at the respective balance sheet dates) and net realisable value, and in the case of fixed assets in the light of their estimated value to the business. It may then be necessary to make appropriate provisions against the converted figures. Consideration will also need to be given to the adequacy of the charge for depreciation on freehold and long leasehold property and whether it may be necessary to include in the deferred tax account in the supplementary statement an amount for the corporation tax on any chargeable gain which would arise on a sale of the assets at the date of the balance sheet at the amount shown in the supplementary statement (see paragraph 21).

This Appendix (No. 4) is for general guidance and does not form part of the Provisional Statement of Standard Accounting Practice.

AN INDEX OF PRICES OF CONSUMER GOODS AND SERVICES (JANUARY 1974 = 100)

Year	Index	Percentage increase (decrease) over the previous year	Factor*	Year	Index	Percentage increase (decrease) over the previous year	Factor*
1914	11·1		8·84	1946	29·4		3·34
1915	13·7	23	7·16	1947	31·4	6·8	3·12
1916	16·2	18	6·06	1948	33·8	7·6	2·90
1917	19·6	21	5·01	1949	34·6	2·4	2·84
1918	22·6	15	4·34	1950	35·6	2·9	2·76
1919	23·9	6	4·10	1951	38·8	9·0	2·53
1920	27·7	16	3·54	1952	41·2	6·2	2·38
1921	25·1	(9)	3·91	1953	41·9	1·7	2·34
1922	20·4	(19)	4·81	1954	42·6	1·7	2·30
1923	19·4	(5)	5·06	1955	44·1	3·5	2·22
1924	19·5	1	5·03	1956	46·0	4·3	2·13
1925	19·6	1	5·01	1957	47·5	3·3	2·07
1926	19·1	(2)	5·14	1958	48·8	2·7	2·01
1927	18·7	(2)	5·25	1959	49·1	0·6	2·00
1928	18·5	(1)	5·30	1960	49·6	1·0	1·98
1929	18·2	(1)	5·39	1961	51·0	2·8	1·92
1930	17·6	(4)	5·57	1962	53·0	3·9	1·85
1931	16·4	(7)	5·98	1963	54·0	1·9	1·82
1932	16·0	(3)	6·13	1964	55·8	3·3	1·76
1933	15·6	(3)	6·29	1965	58·4	4·7	1·68
1934	15·7	1	6·25	1966	60·7	3·9	1·62
1935	15·9	1	6·17	1967	62·3	2·6	1·57
1936	16·4	3	5·98	1968	65·2	4·7	1·50
1937	17·2	5	5·70	1969	68·7	5·4	1·43
1938	17·4	1	5·64	1970	73·1	6·4	1·34
				1971	80·0	9·4	1·23
				1972	85·7	7·1	1·14
				1973	93·5	9·1	1·05
				1973 (Dec. 31)	98·1		1·00

* The factor by which expenditure would have to be multiplied to convert it into pounds of current purchasing power at 31st December 1973.

Notes

1. Although the retail price index for a month relates to a point in time within the month, for all practical purposes it can also be taken as being the index at the end of the month.

2. It is not suggested that companies will need to analyse their expenditure on fixed assets as far back as 1914, but the index has been provided to assist those companies who may in exceptional circumstances require an index that far back.

3. If an index number is required for any month from January 1974 to date then use the relevant general index of retail prices (see paragraph 25 for sources of this index). For example the general index of retail prices for February 1974 is 101·7.

4. To ascertain the index number for any month prior to January 1974 divide the annual index for the relevant year given in this appendix by the average retail price index for the same year and multiply the result by the retail price index for the desired month. For example, to ascertain index for March 1960:

Annual index for 1960 (from this appendix) (January 1974 = 100)	49·6
Average retail price index for 1960 (from Method of Construction and Calculation of the index of retail prices) (17th January 1956 = 100)	110·6
Index of retail prices for March 1960	110
Therefore index for March 1960 (January 1974 = 100) (49·6 ÷ 110·6) × 110	49·3

12 Worked Example

Management Uses of Marginal and Standard Costing Combined with Budgetary Control

This worked example is based on ideas first developed in a training film, *Managing with Figures*, produced by Unilever Organisation Division for use in the Company's management training courses. The Author is grateful for permission to reproduce some of these ideas in this present context.

The Hotchpotch Manufacturing Co. is an old established business that for many years has manufactured products for sale to wholesalers in the consumer goods field. Each product is packaged and sold by weight, and Mr James Hotchpotch the chairman and managing director of the company has taken pride in maintaining a constant and uniform price for these products (£120 per tonne) over a period of several years. At present there are four products on the market, two of them (X1 and X2) being manufactured on 'Exeter' machines, and two others (Y1 and Y2) on the rather more modern 'Wyefield' machines.

Up to a year or so ago, James Hotchpotch ran the business himself, assisted by a factory manager and an accountant, but has eventually decided that if the business is to keep ahead of ever-increasing competition a board of experienced directors will be essential. He decides to make three appointments covering marketing, production and finance, and for the time being to continue to look after the personnel function himself.

Table 12.1
Sales trends

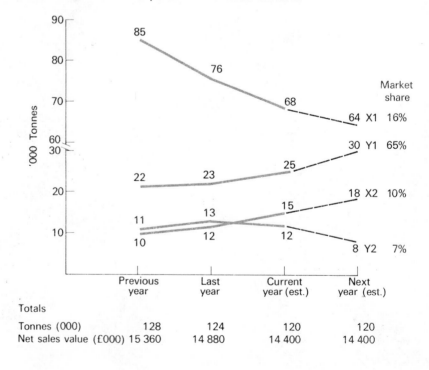

Totals	Previous year	Last year	Current year (est.)	Next year (est.)
Tonnes (000)	128	124	120	120
Net sales value (£000)	15 360	14 880	14 400	14 400

Peter Hornblower's first task on being appointed Marketing Director was to examine the sales trends of the four products over the last few years, and then to make careful estimates of the likely outcome of the current year. This would then lead on to a forecast of next year's sales, assuming that no changes are made in marketing policy or selling prices. At the same time he would obtain an assessment of the market share of each product, and of any other factors likely to affect future sales.

It is with some dismay that he finds that sales of the company's most important product X1 have been declining steadily for a number of years and that one other product Y2 has also begun to show the same tendency. Sales of X2 and Y1 are increasing each year, but so far these increases have not been sufficient to offset the decrease in sales of the other two products. Table 12.1 illustrates these trends in graphical form, including an estimate of next year's sales if no changes in marketing policies are made.

Planning for next year

Peter Hornblower takes this chart with him for a discussion with his newly appointed colleague John Sterling, the Financial Director. The latter then produces a statement which has just been handed to him by the firm's Accountant, giving an estimate of the current year's financial results, with a breakdown by products. The Accountant explains that it has been customary for this statement to show the profits and profit margins earned on each product after charging all factory expenses, and then to show administration, marketing and selling expenses as separate deductions from the total profit.

Table 12.2
Latest estimate
of results
and margins

Current year

		Total	X1	X2	Y1	Y2
Sales volume ('000 tonnes)		120	68	15	25	12
		£'000		£ per tonne		
Net sales value		14 400	120	120	120	120
Less cost of materials used	8 182					
factory direct expenses						
Labour and supervision	1 700					
Supplies	80					
Power	400	11 282	90	108	110	66
Maintenance and repairs	480					
Depreciation	440					
	3 110					
Gross profit		3 118	£30	£12	£10	£54
				Gross margins		
Less indirect expenses						
Factory	800					
Administration	820					
Marketing and selling	1 080	2 700				
Trading profit		418				

This statement (Table 12.2) is closely examined and it is calculated that after deducting tax at 50 per cent, the ratio of net profit to sales is only 1·5 per cent. There is general agreement that taking into account the prospect of sharply increased costs next year, a very serious position may well arise and urgent steps will need to be taken if the company is to remain viable.

Both directors agree that the Chairman will have to be approached with a view to obtaining his permission to a much more effective marketing policy in future, probably involving an extensive advertising campaign backed up with flexibility in fixing selling prices. At the same time they can see the need for urgent steps to reduce costs and before seeing the Chairman they decide to have a talk with the Production Director. Bill Plowright tells them that during his first tour of inspection of the factory he came to an immediate decision that there was considerable scope for improving performance and reducing costs, and he had already obtained the services of a work study engineer, so that methods can be improved, standards assessed and control procedures introduced.

Table 12.3

Estimated effect on sales of pricing and advertising alternatives

Product	Selling price per tonne	Advertising allocation £'000	Estimated sales '000 tonnes	Remarks
	£			
X1	120	Nil	64	This major product is faced with severe competition on a national basis and sales expected to continue to decline unless supported by advertising.
	120	160	70	
	120	480	80	
	120	900	90	
X2	120	—	18	This product also faced with national competition, but competitors' prices are mostly higher, so sales trend expected to continue rising.
	130	—	11	
	140	—	7	
	120	20	20	
	120	160	29	
	130	200	20	
Y1	120	—	30	Slight competition in some regions. Sales trend expected to continue to rise.
	130	—	23	
	140	—	18	
Y2	120	—	8	Product very attractively packaged. No national competition yet. A special sales effort would be put into the product combined with the substantial drop in price to reverse the declining trend and obtain the projected large increase in sales.
	100	—	25	
	80	—	45	
	70	—	60	

<table>
<tr><td>Assessment of
marketing
alternatives</td><td>The three directors then see the Chairman and obtain his approval to their working out plans for restoring the company to economic health. Peter Hornblower now turns his attention to next year's marketing plan and after considerable discussion with his Sales and Marketing Managers, eventually arrives at a series of estimates showing the effect on sales volume of changing selling prices, and of adopting an advertising programme for X1 and X2 products. He realises that it will be difficult to find the money to support an extensive advertising campaign and he considers that the most effective way of spending the money will be to allocate it solely to X products in the first instance. The results of his studies are shown in Table 12.3.</td></tr>
</table>

John Sterling discloses at this point that he is actively engaged in introducing a system of budgetary planning and standard costing that will tie in with the production director's standards and control records, and which will also enable him to provide marketing management with advance profitability figures for each of the company's four products. Peter Hornblower confirms that this will be much better than using historical costs and he looks forward to using these calculations for each of the alternatives set out in his table. He will then choose the course of action yielding the highest profit unless long term considerations suggest a different course.

While waiting for the new figures to be prepared, the two directors have a discussion with the Accountant to see whether it would be possible to use the latter's latest estimate of the current year's profit figures as a guide. This suggestion is rejected when it is realised that the profit figures per tonne disclosed by the statement are only relevant to the circumstances of the current year, i.e. sales volume, cost levels, etc., and that owing to the relatively high proportion of fixed costs, even if adjusted for changing cost levels, would be unlikely to provide a satisfactory guide to profitability next year if sales volumes are to alter materially. Accordingly a decision is taken to await new figures.

Preparation of
provisional
budgets and
standard costs
for next year

John Sterling can see very clearly that his colleague's marketing plan, when finally agreed, is going to be the key to the preparation of budgets for next year, but he is in some difficulty because, before he can calculate product costs and profit margins to help Peter Hornblower select the most profitable alternative, he needs to base his budgets on some level of sales, otherwise unit costs cannot be calculated. He realises he has two choices: to base his provisional budgets either on the current year's expected sales volume, or on the estimates prepared by marketing management for next year's volume of sales, if no changes in marketing policy or selling prices are made. He decides on the latter. Accordingly he is now able to draw up next year's provisional sales budget:

	Total	X1	X2	Y1	Y2
Sales volume ('000 tonnes)	120	64	18	30	8
Selling price per tonne (£)		120	120	120	120
Sales turnover (£000)	14 400	7 680	2 160	3 600	960

His next step is to consider the basis on which he will build up product costs from budgeted data and standards. Once again he is faced with several choices. He rejects the idea of including *all* factory costs in these product figures, because he knows that the main purpose in preparing them is to provide help in the assessment of alternatives, and the inclusion of large slices of fixed costs, e.g. factory rates, factory office costs etc., is going to create difficulties. At the same time he also knows that he may need to be able to calculate total factory costs per unit for stock valuation purposes when drawing up the firm's annual accounts. He decides his best course of action will be to draw up two sets of cost figures on a per unit basis:

1. Including only factory direct costs: raw materials, packaging materials, direct labour and direct expenses including such items as maintenance and depreciation of plant employed in manufacturing the firm's products. Factory indirect expenses would be excluded from the per unit calculations but would be included with administration, marketing and selling expenses as a separate deduction from total gross profits. This is in line with the firm's existing practice for preparing estimates of actual results.
2. Including only factory variable expenses, i.e. on a marginal costing basis and including raw materials, packaging materials and such proportion of factory direct expenses as can be regarded as varying directly with changes in the volume of production.

He can see that both these calculations will be necessary, the first set so that management can be sure that selling prices at least cover all direct expenses, and the second set as the most useful in assessing alternatives and identifying out-of-pocket costs of each product, ignoring standing charges.

The next question to be decided is the level of production in relation to the expected volume of sales, and after discussion with Bill Plowright it is decided for budgetary purposes to equate the two sets of figures. Having reached this

Table 12.4
Standard costs:
materials

Raw materials	Product X1		
Material formula		Price per tonne	Standard cost per tonne of product
Ingredient	Tonnes		
A	0·2	£84·60	£16·92
B	0·3	30·00	9·00
C	0·5	34·00	17·00
	1·0		42·92
Add standard process loss 2·5%	0·025		1·08
	1·025		£44·00

[Note. Standard costs for other products calculated in same way: X2 £60·00, Y1 £56·00, Y2 £20·00 per tonne]

Packaging materials
Estimated price of packaging material per specification   19·04
Add standard wastage allowance 5%   0·96

                   £20·00

[Note. Standard costs for other products calculated in same way: X2 £24·00, Y1 £16·00, Y2 £8·00 per tonne]

Table 12.5
Standard costs:
factory variable
costs

	Exeter plant (products X1 and X2)					Wyefield plant (products Y1 and Y2)
Physical standards per tonne				Rate		based on similar data
	M/c time	Operators per M/c	Labour time		Standard cost per tonne £	Standard cost per tonne £
Production labour	100 mins	5	500 mins			
Add change over allowance at 12%			60			
			560			
Equivalent to			$9\frac{1}{3}$ hours	£0·90 per hour	8·40	4·50
Packing labour			136 mins			
Add lost time allowance 10%			14			
			150			
Equivalent to			2·5 hours	£0·60	1·50	2·10
Supplies					0·60	0·50
Power	272 kilowatt hours			£1·25 per 100 kwh	3·40	2·50
Maintenance and repairs (variable proportion)					2·10	2·40
					16·00	12·00

decision, it is possible to build up the expense budgets on the two alternative methods agreed. The data from which these budgets are built up is contained in Tables 12.4 and 12.5, and the provisional budgets are shown in Tables 12.6 and 12.7. In Table 12.7 fixed costs are allocated on a factual basis to the Exeter and Wyefield plants, and then further subdivided by products, either factually or pro-rata to the maximum possible output of each product. (Y1 and Y2 charges are the same because the Wyefield plant is designed to produce equal quantities of each). The very severe fall in profits shown by the provisional budgets compared with the current year's results emphasises the vital need for changes in marketing policy.

Assessment of profitability aspects of marketing plan

The position has now been reached when the profitability aspects of the various marketing alternatives can be assessed. John Sterling discusses the schedule of marketing alternatives (Table 12.3) with Peter Hornblower and they decide to compare the results obtained by using (a) gross profit margins

Table 12.6
Provisional budget (based on allocating factory variable expenses)

	Total	X1		X2		Y1		Y2	
Sales volume ('000 tonnes)	120	64		18		30		8	
Selling price per tonne (£)		120		120		120		120	
Sales turnover (£'000)	14 400	7 680		2 160		3 600		960	
		Per tonne	£'000	*Per tonne*	£'000	*Per tonne*	£'000	*Per tonne*	£'000
Less	£'000								
Cost of production (at factory variable cost)									
Raw materials		44		60		56		20	
Packaging materials		20		24		16		8	
Direct labour—production		8·40		8·40		4·50		4·50	
—packaging		1·50		1·50		2·10		2·10	
Supplies		0·60		0·60		0·50		0·50	
Power		3·40		3·40		2·50		2·50	
Maintenance and repairs (ppn)		2·10		2·10		2·40		2·40	
Total		80·00	5 120	100·00	1 800	84·00	2 520	40·00	320
Add/Subtract stock adjustment*	—		—		—		—		—
			5 120		1 800		2 520		320
Variable profit margin	4 640	40·00	2 560	20·00	360	36·00	1 080	80·00	640
Less									
Factory direct expenses (fixed ppn)	1 720								
Factory indirect expenses	880								
Administration	860								
Marketing and selling expenses	1 140								
	4 600								
Trading profit	40								

* *Note.* Production volume has been budgeted at the same level as sales for each product. If budgeted production were to differ from budgeted sales, an appropriate adjustment would be made here to reflect the increase or decrease in stock level.

and (b) variable profit margins obtained from the two sets of provisional budgets. In using gross profit margins no attempt would be made to recalculate these for different sales levels, and in both sets of figures the margins would be varied simply by adding on or subtracting the proposed changes in selling prices. Arrows are used to mark the most favourable alternative in each case and it will be seen that in every case the 'best choice' obtained by using variable margins differs from that obtained from the use of gross margins. This illustration points out the danger of using unit costs or profit margins to assess alternative courses of action if the costs contain an allocation of fixed expenses. Each unit cost would need to be recalculated for each different level of sales, but it is of course much simpler to avoid this complication by excluding all fixed expenses from the unit costs, as in Table 12.9.

Table 12.7

Provisional budget (based on allocating factory direct expenses)

	Total	X1	X2	Y1	Y2
Sales volume ('000 tonnes)	120	64	18	30	8
Selling price per tonne (£)		120	120	120	120
Sales turnover (£'000)	14 400	7 680	2 160	3 600	960
Less					
Cost of production (at Factory direct cost)	£'000				
Control basis					
V Raw materials	5 736	2 816	1 080	1 680	160
V Packaging materials	2 256	1 280	432	480	64
V Direct labour—production	859	537	151	135	36
V —packaging	203	96	27	63	17
F Ancillary labour	520	190	50	140	140
F Supervision	360	126	34	100	100
V Supplies	68	38	11	15	4
V Power	374	218	61	75	20
F and V Maintenance and repairs V 264 ⎱ F 360 ⎰	624	135 ⎱ 190 ⎰ 325	38 ⎱ 50 ⎰ 88	72 ⎱ 60 ⎰ 132	19 ⎱ 60 ⎰ 79
F Depreciation	480	230	50	100	100
Total	11 480	5 856	1 984	2 920	720
Add/subtract stock adjustment*	—	—	—	—	—
	11 480	5 856	1 984	2 920	720
Gross profit	2 920	1 824	176	680	240
Gross margin		per tonne £28·50	per tonne £9·78	per tonne £22·66	per tonne £30·00
Less					
Factory indirect expenses	880				
Administration	860				
Marketing and selling expenses	1 140				
	2 880				
Trading profit	40				

* See note on Table 12.6.

Agreement on final marketing and production plans	Peter Hornblower can now see that his marketing plan should be based on the following decisions:

	Total sales volume ('000 *tonnes*)
X1 Leave selling price unchanged	
Allocate £480 000 for advertising	80
X2 Leave selling price unchanged	
Allocate £160 000 for advertising	29
Y1 Leave selling price unchanged	30
Y2 Reduce selling price to £80 or £70	45 or 60
(He decides on the maximum reduction to £70)	

Table 12.8
Estimated effect on profits of pricing and advertising alternatives (*a*) using gross profit margin

Product	Selling price per tonne £	Advertising allocation £'000	Estimated sales '000 tonne	Gross profit margin per tonne before advertising £	Gross profit before advertising £'000	Gross profit after advertising £'000
X1	120	Nil	64	28·5	1 824	1 824
	120	160	70	28·5	1 995	1 835 ←
	120	480	80	28·5	2 280	1 800
	120	900	90	28·5	2 565	1 665
X2	120	Nil	18	9·7	175	175
	130	Nil	11	19·7	217	217 ←
	140	Nil	7	29·7	208	208
	120	20	20	9·7	194	174
	120	160	29	9·7	281	121
	130	200	20	19·7	394	194
Y1	120	Nil	30	22·7	681	681
	130	Nil	23	32·7	752	752
	140	Nil	18	42·7	769	769 ←
Y2	120	Nil	8	30·0	240	240
	100	Nil	25	10·0	250	250 ←
	80	Nil	45	(10·0)	(450)	(450)
	70	Nil	60	(20·0)	(1 200)	(1 200)

Table 12.9
Estimated effect on profits of pricing and advertising alternatives (*b*) using variable profit (or contributory) margin

Product	Selling price per tonne £	Advertising allocation £'000	Estimated sales '000 tonne	Variable profit margin per tonne before advertising £	Variable profit before advertising £'000	Variable profit after advertising £'000
X1	120	Nil	64	40	2 560	2 560
	120	160	70	40	2 800	2 640
	120	480	80	40	3 200	2 720 ←
	120	900	90	40	3 600	2 700
X2	120	Nil	18	20	360	360
	130	Nil	11	30	330	330
	140	Nil	7	40	280	280
	120	20	20	20	400	380
	120	160	29	20	580	420 ←
	130	200	20	30	600	400
Y1	120	Nil	30	36	1 080	1 080 ←
	130	Nil	23	46	1 058	1 058
	140	Nil	18	56	1 008	1 008
Y2	120	Nil	8	80	640	640
	100	Nil	25	60	1 500	1 500
	80	Nil	45	40	1 800	1 800 ←
	70	Nil	60	30	1 800	1 800

At this point he goes to see Bill Plowright so that the latter can confirm that production of these quantities will cause no difficulties. John Sterling joins the meeting and before very long it becomes clear that some modification to the proposed programme for X1 and X2 may be necessary. The factor which now emerges from the discussions is that the concept of direct labour on the Exeter plant being a variable cost is correct up to a limit of 2 000 tonnes a week (100 000 tonnes p.a.)—the limit of single shift working. Above this limit it becomes necessary first to work overtime, then to go on to part-time shifts, until at a level of 140 000 tonnes p.a. the only solution is double-shift working (see Table 12.10). The proposal to produce 109 000 tonnes in all on the Exeter plant would result in an *additional* cost of around £40 000 per annum. Looking again at the position of X2, Peter Hornblower can see that this penalty will make the alternative approach of accepting a target level of 20 000 tonnes equally attractive, either by allocating £20 000 for advertising (profit £380 000) or by raising the selling price to £130 per tonne and spending £200 000 on advertising (profit £400 000). Taking into account the probable long term effects of an advertising campaign, he decides to back the latter alternative. Accordingly he asks John Sterling to prepare his final budgets after changing the decision on X2 to:

Raise selling price to £130 Allocate £200 000 for advertising	*Target sales* ('000 *tonnes*) 20

Table 12.10
Operating
alternatives: excess
cost over single shift
working 'X' products

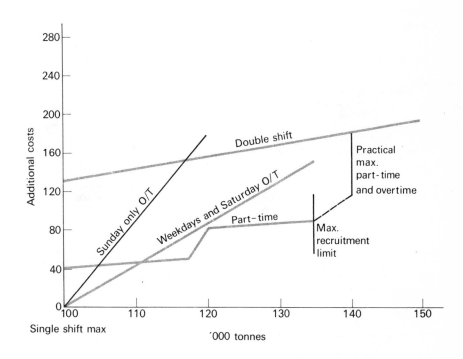

At the same time, he makes a note for future reference that in reaching these decisions they have assumed marketing and selling expenses (other than advertising and promotions) not to be affected by the increase in sales volume. As all products are at present sold ex works, the company does not have to pay for distribution costs. It is, however, possible that this policy may change, and, if in future years sales are made through depots, a proportion of the resulting distribution costs will have to be treated as 'variable costs' when evaluating various marketing alternatives.

Preparation and agreement of final budgets

John Sterling now makes the necessary alterations to the provisional budgets based on these decisions. In view of the greatly enlarged sales volume it is now hoped to achieve, a decision is taken by the Board to set up a "Development Unit", aimed at developing new products and new markets. Provision is made in the final budget for the agreed allocation of £460 000. The final budgets are shown in Tables 12.11 and 12. It will be seen that the final trading profit shown amounts to £940 000 compared with £40 000 shown in the provisional budgets. After allowing for tax at 50 per cent, this amounts to £470 000, equivalent to 2·35 per cent on sales turnover. The capital employed in the business (fixed assets and working capital) amounts to around £10 million, so that the return on capital employed works out at 4·7 per cent. These ratios are considered satisfactory in the short term, and it is hoped to improve both over the next few years. The budgets are discussed with all concerned and are eventually agreed by the Chairman.

Table 12.11

Final budget based on allocating factory variable expenses: for use by marketing management in evaluating alternative marketing policies

		Total	X1	X2	Y1	Y2
Sales volume ('000 tonnes)		190	80	20	30	60
Selling price per tonne (£)			120	130	120	70
Sales turnover (£'000)		20 000	9 600	2 600	3 600	4 200
Less						
Cost of production (at factory variable cost per tonne) as calculated for provisional budget			£80	£100	£84	£40
Amount (£000)		13 320	6 400	2 000	2 520	2 400
Add/subtract stock adjustment*		—	—	—	—	—
		13 320	6 400	2 000	2 520	2 400
Variable profit before advertising		6 680	3 200	600	1 080	1 800
Less advertising and promotions		680	480	200	—	—
		6 000	2 720	400	1 080	1 800
Less						
Factory direct expenses (fixed)	1 720					
Factory indirect expenses	880					
Administration	860					
Marketing selling and development	1 600					
		5 060				
Trading profit (£000)		940				

* See note on Table 12.6.

Table 12.12

Final budget based on allocating factory direct expenses: for use in calculating standard costs and gross margins

		Total	X1	X2	Y1	Y2
Sales volume ('000 tonnes)		190	80	20	30	60
Selling price per tonne (£)			120	130	120	70
Sales turnover (£'000)		20 000	9 600	2 600	3 600	4 200
Less						
Cost of production						
(at factory direct cost)						
Control basis						
V Raw materials		7 600	3 520	1 200	1 680	1 200
V Packaging materials		3 040	1 600	480	480	480
V Direct labour						
—production		1 245	672	168	135	270
—packaging		339	120	30	63	126
F Ancillary labour		520	190	50	140	140
F Supervision		360	126	34	100	100
V Supplies		105	48	12	15	30
V Power		565	272	68	75	150
F and V Maintenance and repairs	V 426 ⎱ F 360 ⎰	786	168 ⎱ 190 ⎰ 358	42 ⎱ 50 ⎰ 92	72 ⎱ 60 ⎰ 132	144 ⎱ 60 ⎰ 204
F Depreciation		480	230	50	100	100
Total		15 040	7 136 £89·20 per tonne	2 184 £109·20 per tonne	2 920 £97·34 per tonne	2 800 £46·67 per tonne
Standard costs						
Add/Subtract stock adjustment*		—	—	—	—	—
		15 040	7 136	2 184	2 920	2 800
Gross profit before advertising		4 960	2 464 £30·80 per tonne	416 £20·80 per tonne	680 £22·66 per tonne	1 400 £23·33 per tonne
Gross margins						
Less						
advertising and promotions		680	480	200		
Gross profit after advertising		4 280	1 984	216	680	1 400
Less						
Factory indirect expenses	880					
Administration	860					
Marketing selling and development	1 600	3 340				
Trading profit	(£000)	940				

* See note on Table 12.6.

Table 12.13
Phased sales budget

Product	X1 ('000 tonnes)	X2	Total £'000	Y1 ('000 tonnes)	Y2	Total £'000	Total £'000
Quarter 1	16	4	2 440	7	12	1 680	4 120
2	22	5	3 290	7	15	1 890	5 180
3	18	5	2 810	8	15	2 010	4 820
4	24	6	3 660	8	18	2 220	5 880
Total	80	20	12 200	30	60	7 800	20 000

Advertising and promotions—X1 and X2
£'000

Quarter 1	190
2	160
3	140
4	190
	680

Preparation of phased budgets

In order to provide a suitable basis for subsequent control, a supporting phased budget is prepared showing the phasing of sales tonnages and advertising allocations for each quarter of the year (Table 12.13).

Control of actual results

Marketing management maintains a set of statistical records that provides them with information about the level of sales, salesmen's performance and expenses control.

A number of daily and weekly physical controls are introduced in the factory covering all important aspects of the manufacture, such as machine utilisation, operator performance, material usage, etc. It is agreed that a series of financial statements are needed that will bring together and summarise the periodic results. A quarterly comparison of financial results with budgets and standard costs will be introduced in such a way that the nature of any variations from these targets can be readily seen.

John Sterling has to make a policy decision on what form these financial operating statements should take. On the factory side, he appreciates that the overall objective of manufacturing management, while maintaining quality standards, is to produce the required volume of goods at the minimum or target level of *cost per unit of product*. It is thus clear that volume of output and costs per unit must represent the key figures round which the summary operating statement for the factory will be designed. But on what basis should the unit costs be calculated? Factory variable expenses only, factory direct costs or an all-inclusive cost figure to include factory indirects and administration as well? There are pros and cons attaching to each of these approaches, but whereas the use of variable expenses (marginal costs) appears to have positive advantage in evaluating marketing alternatives, he concludes that for control of factory operations, the balance of advantage lies in basing the unit costs on factory direct expenses, including the appropriate allocation of fixed expenses such as depreciation. He thinks that only if this is done can the full impact of underutilisation of facilities be brought home to the departmental management concerned. It is true the impact would be even greater if indirect expenses were included in unit costs, but he considers that this is an unnecessary complication. After obtaining Bill Plowright's agreement to these ideas, the factory operating statement is drawn up accordingly.

On the sales side, he discusses the position with Peter Hornblower and agreement is reached on the need for a comparison of actual sales with budgeted sales in such a way that the reasons for variations can be seen. However, they also note that even if total sales are in line with budget, there is a possibility that actual profits may be less than expectation, due to an alteration in the sales mix and an increase in the proportion of less profitable lines. Another reason for lower profitability may be a reduction in the average net selling price obtained for each product, perhaps through carelessness in granting discounts. For these reasons, both directors agree on the importance of a comparison of actual profit margins and actual profits, with the corresponding budget figures, and accompanied by an analysis of variances. In calculating the actual profits and profit margins, it will be assumed that the factory has been able to produce the required output at standard cost per unit. Any variances relating to expenditure in the factory or due to fluctuation in the volume of throughput will be shown on the factory operating statement. They also note a need for a similar comparison of marketing and selling expenses, including advertising.

Finally, he agrees with Mr Hotchpotch that there should be a summary operating statement showing the overall results of the company's activities during the quarter. These three statements are shown in Tables 12.14–16 (see pages 854–6–7) are discussed in detail below.

Sales operating statement (Table 12.14)	Peter Hornblower takes an early opportunity of showing this statement to the chairman, and explaining some of its features. He points out that sales of X1 had fallen by 4 000 tonnes below the phased budget target and that this had been due to late delivery from production of a new pack required for X1 promotions. As a result, the marketing effort had to be switched at short notice to X2 promotions, which did not require a new pack. Unfortunately the margin of profit on X2 was very much less than on X1, so that despite the overall increase of 2 000 tonnes of X products, profits were no more than in line with target (target profit figures had been calculated by evaluating the phased budget sales volume at the budgeted gross profit margins). With regard to Y products, they had managed to hit target with Y1 at a higher than expected average selling price, but all stocks of this product had now been practically exhausted, as the factory output had fallen well below the planned figure. Bill Plowright had now reassured him on both points: ample stocks of the promotional packs for X1 had come through towards the end of the quarter, and the factory had caught up with Y1 production plans early in the following quarter.

So far as Y2 was concerned, Peter Hornblower reminded the chairman that as a result of cutting the selling price from £120 to £70 per tonne it had been hoped to boost sales from 8 000 to 60 000 per annum. He was still confident that this large increase would be obtained, but he now thinks they had been overoptimistic in fixing the target level of sales in the first quarter at 12 000 tonnes; the build-up would probably take place rather more slowly. The analysis of variances at the foot of the table summarises all these points.

Table 12.14

Sales Operating Statement—first quarter

Total tonnes '000			X1	X2	Total £'000	Y1	Y2	Total £'000	Total £'000
	Gross margins per tonne	Budget	£30·80	£20·80		£22·66	£23·33		
38 39	Sales	Actual Phased Budget	'000 tonnes 12 16	000 tonnes 10 4	£2 740 £2 440	'000 tonnes 7 7	'000 tonnes 9 12	£1 470 £1 680	£4 210 £4 120
	Gross profit	Actual Phased Budget	£'000 369·6 492·8	£'000 208·0 83·2	577·6 576·0	£'000 163·6 158·6	£'000 210·0 280·0	373·6 438·6	951·2 1 014·6
		Variance	(123·2)	124·8	1·6	5·0	(70·0)	(65·0)	(63·4)

Analysis of variances (£000)

	Turnover	Mix	Price
X1 and X2			
Change in sales mix—4 000 tonnes X2 instead of X1 at £10 per tonne		(40·0)	
less			
Net increase in sales—2 000 tonnes X2 at £20·80 per tonne	41·6		
Y1 and Y2			
Increased price of £1 per tonne on 5 000 tonnes Y1			5·0
Decrease in sales 3 000 tonnes Y2 at £23·33 per tonne	(70·0)		
NB. Unfavourable variances (in brackets)	(28·4)	(40·0)	(5·0)

Factory operating statement (Table 12.15)

This statement is very much a joint effort of the production and financial directors, and both of them go to see the chairman with it. The first point to be explained is the table of production output. The main differences between actual and phased budget output have already been pointed out to the chairman by the marketing director, and these are further discussed. Steps are being taken to make sure that there will be no hold-ups in turning out promotional packs in future; in this case the buyer had been at fault. Technical problems had accounted for the drop in production of product Y1, but these problems had now been overcome. The output targets relating to one-quarter of the annual budget have also been shown on this statement as a reminder of the fact that the product standard costs were linked to this rate of throughput (see Table 12.12). Any difference between actual output and these quarter-budget totals will automatically give rise to an over- or under-recovery of fixed expenses, and this will be reflected in the 'volume variance'.

In the main part of the statement, actual costs have been compared with the 'allowed' costs. For variable costs such as materials and direct labour, allowed costs are calculated by applying standard cost data to the actual output. The allowance for expenses such as maintenance and repairs which are partly variable and partly fixed are obtained either by reading off the allowance from a 'flexible budget', or by dividing up the expense into its fixed and variable parts, as has been done here. The allowance for fixed expenses is merely the budget figure.

In order to increase the usefulness of the statement as a management aid, variances have been analysed by causes. Some of these causes are within the control of management, and some are not. In the first quarter, raw material prices were much lower than anticipated due to factors quite outside the control of the company. On the other hand, the quality of some of these materials was not up to standard and this had given rise to increased work in the factory, resulting in unfavourable efficiency variances. Following a linear programming exercise, a change in formulation had been made which had resulted in a considerable gain for the company. The favourable variance in maintenance and repairs did not necessarily mean that this work had been carried out more efficiently, as some scheduled maintenance had been deferred until the next quarter.

As already indicated, the standard costs of the actual output have been calculated on the assumption that quarterly throughput equals one quarter of the annual target, and the overall shortfall of 8·5 tonnes in the quarter has given rise to an unfavourable volume variance. Details of the relevant figures are given below:

Quarter's budget	Actual output		Standard cost of actual output	Fixed costs over or (under) recovered
'000 tonnes			*£'000*	
20	18	X1	1 605·6	10% of 736 pa $\times \frac{1}{4}$ = (18·4)
5	6	X2	655·2	20% of 184 pa $\times \frac{1}{4}$ = 9·2
7·5	3	Y1	292·0	60% of 400 pa $\times \frac{1}{4}$ = (60·0)
15	12	Y2	560·0	20% of 400 pa $\times \frac{1}{4}$ = (20·0)
──	──		────	
47·5	39		3 112·8	Net under recovery (89·2)
──	──		────	────

Results for first quarter (Table 12.16)

This statement is circulated by John Sterling to his fellow directors, and is tabled for discussion at the board meeting held to review results for the quarter. He accompanies the statement with the operating statements illustrated in Tables 12.14 and 12.15 and with supporting schedules giving details of the factory indirect, administration, marketing, selling and development expenses. These are all thoroughly examined and discussed, and notes are made of any corrective action still required.

The feature of the summary statement which gives rise to the most discussion is the fact that although the final trading profit at £3 000 appears at first sight to be extremely disappointing, this in fact looks positively encouraging when compared with the target loss of £10 400 revealed by the phased budget. The reason for this peculiar result is discussed, and John Sterling points out that whereas the phased budget calls for 39 000 tonnes in the first quarter out of a total annual tonnage of 190 000 (20·5 per cent), a full 25 per cent of fixed expenses have been included, since these are not phased. The Board understands this explanation and looks forward to a bumper profit figure in the final quarter when phased budget sales will have risen to nearly 30 per cent of the annual total.

The Board meeting concludes with a resolution to set up a working team to make recommendations on extending the annual budgeting to longer range planning on a comprehensive basis to cover all aspects of the business.

Table 12.15

Factory Operating Statement: first quarter

Production ('000 tonnes)					
	X1	X2	Y1	Y2	Total
¼ Annual budget	20	5	7·50	15	47·50
Phased budget	16	4	7	12	39
Actual	18	6	3	12	39

	Actual (£000)	Allowed (£000)	Operating Variances				
			Total	Price and wage rates	Efficiency	Formulation	Other
Material costs							
Raw materials	1 480·0	1 560·0					
Packaging materials	600·0	648·0					
	2 080·0	2 208·0	128·0	118·2	(50·2	60·0	
Factory direct expenses							
Direct labour variable							
Production	287·4	269·0		9·8	(28·2)		
Packaging	77·0	67·6			(9·4)		
Ancillary labour and supervision	212·0	220·0			8·0		
Supplies	24·4	22·0			(2·4)		
Power	127·0	119·0			(8·0)		
Maintenance and repairs	160·2	176·4					16·2
Depreciation	120·0	120·0					
	1 008·0	994·0	(14·0)	9·8	(40·0)		16·2
Total costs	3 088·0	3 202·0	114·0	128·0	(90·2)	60·0	
Standard cost of actual output =		3 112·8					
Volume variance		(89·2)					

NB. Unfavourable variances in (brackets).

Table 12.16

Results for first quarter

	Actual		Quarter budget	Phased Budget
Tonnes sold ('000 tonnes)	38		47·5	39
Gross profit on budgeted sales (phased) (£000)	1 014·6			1 014·6
Less				
Net variances (volume, price, mix)	63·4			
Gross profit on actual sales (per sales operating statement)		951·2		
Less				
Advertising and promotions		136·0		190·0
Gross profit after advertising		815·2		824·6
Add				
Variances on factory direct expenses (per factory operating statement)				
Price and wage rates	128·0			
Efficiency etc. (90·2 − 16·2)	(74·0)			
Formulation	60·0			
Volume	(89·2)	24·8		
		840·0		
Less				
Indirect expenses				
Factory	210·0		220·0	
Administration	225·0		215·0	
Marketing selling and development	402·0	837·0	400·0	835·0
Trading profit (loss) (£000)		3·0		(10·4)

Conclusion   The above example has shown how budgets can be prepared, product costs predetermined and control statements issued which analyse variances from budgeted target figures or standard unit costs. In practice, budgets would be built up on a divisional or departmental basis as explained on page 693, and then summarised into company totals for inclusion in the Annual Plans. The determination of product costs and profit margins as illustrated in Tables 12.11 and 12.12 above would be carried out as a separate exercise, and top management would not need to see the detailed cost allocations shown in these tables.

Further reading

MERRETT, A. J. and SYKES, ALLEN, *The Finance and Analysis of Capital Projects,* Longmans, 1963.

RIVETT, PATRICK, *Principles of Model Building,* Wiley, 1972.

WESTWICK, C. A., *How to Use Management Ratios,* Gower Press, 1973.

WOOLF, E. H., *Internal Auditing,* 4th edn, HFL Publishers, 1973.

ANTHONY, ROBERT N., *Management Acounting: text and cases,* 4th edn, Homewood, Ill., Irwin, 1969.

BIGG, WALTER W., *Cost Accounts,* 9th edn, Macdonald & Evans, 1972.

SIZER, JOHN, *An Insight into Management Accounting,* Penguin Books, 1969.

WOOD, FRANK, *Business Accounting,* 2 vols, Longmans, 1973.

JONES, F. H., *Guide to Company Balance Sheets and Profit and Loss Accounts,* 7th edn, Heffer, 1970.

PARKER, R. H., *Understanding Company Financial Statements,* Penguin Books, 1972.

Survey of Published Accounts, Institute of Chartered Accountants in England and Wales, annual.

BOULTON, A. HARDING, *Handbook on Company Administration,* Jordan & Sons, 1972.

LONGMAN, H. H., *How to Cut Office Costs,* Anbar Publications, 1967.

DENYER, J. C., *Office Management,* Macdonald & Evans, 3rd edn, 1969.

STANDINGFORD, OLIVER, *Office,* British Broadcasting Corporation, 1972.

The Design of Forms in Government Departments, HMSO, 3rd edn, 1972.

Business Equipment Guide, BED Business Books in association with BETA, half-yearly.

ARGENTI, JOHN, *Corporate Planning,* Allen & Unwin, 1968.

HURSEY, D. E., *Introducing Corporate Planning,* Pergamon Press, 1971.

The Journal of the Society for Long-Range Planning, monthly.

CLARK, L. H., *Corporation Tax: the imputation system,* Institute of Chartered Accountants in England and Wales, 1973.

HUGHES, P. F. and GRAHAM, T. L. A. eds, *Key to Corporation Tax,* Taxation Publishing Co., 1971.

HUGHES, P. F. and TINGLEY, K. R., *Key to Value Added Tax,* Taxation Publishing Co., 1972.

RAY, E. E. and SHERRING, F. A., *Value Added Tax: a handbook for accountants and businessmen,* Institute of Chartered Accountants in England and Wales, 1973.

H.M. CUSTOMS AND EXCISE, *Value Added Tax: General Guide,* rev. edn, HMSO.

H.M. CUSTOMS AND EXCISE, *Value Added Tax: Scope and Coverage,* rev. edn, HMSO.

AYDON, CYRIL, *Financing Your Company,* BIM, 1972.

WRIGHT, M. C., *Financial Management,* McGraw-Hill, 1970.

Financial Times: topical articles on corporate finance.

SIZER, JOHN, *Case Studies in Management Accounting,* Longman, 1974.

BELEW, R. C., *How to Win Profit and Influence Bankers: the Art of Practical Projecting,* Van Nostrand Reinhold Co., 1973.

BROSTER, E. J., *Planning Profit Strategies,* Longman, 1970.

BROSTER, E. J., *Appraising Capital Works,* Longman, 1968.

AMEY, L. R. and EGGINGTON, D. A., *Management Accounting,* Longman, 1973.

PART SIX Computer management

by B. G. Maudsley

1 History and basic principles

Like machines in a factory the computer is a tool to be used and not an end in itself. Computing is here to stay and is already established as a valuable aid in science, industry and commerce. Its main attributes are not to be confused with any powers of reasoning; the machine merely has the ability to handle data, calculate and control automatically at an incredibly fast speed, and is capable of handling an extraordinarily wide range of different, and sometimes complex, applications. This is what distinguishes the modern electronic computer from all the mechanical aids to calculation developed since earliest times.

History

The first method of calculation used was the use of fingers, for which elaborate systems were developed. The word digit is derived from the Latin for finger.

The abacus was the first attempt to mechanise calculation. The early versions were boards covered with sand in which lines were drawn with the fingers and on which pebbles or counters could be used to indicate numbers. (Calculation comes from *Calcula*, the Latin word for stones.) The Chinese abacus of pierced beads on a wire counting frame is the best known form and is still widely used in the East for addition, subtraction, multiplication and division. The invention of logarithms by John Napier, Baron of Merchiston, in 1614, paved the way to relieving much of the drudgery of calculation and led to the development of the *slide rule* in the 1620s.

The first machine for doing the four fundamental operations of arithmetic, in money to six figures, was invented by Pascal in 1642, and later improved by Leibnitz in 1671, and recommended for use in the large volume of astronomical calculations required at that time. The machine was not all that reliable and it was not until the nineteenth century that satisfactory calculators appeared. These were forerunners to the electrically driven desk calculators widely used today for both commercial and scientific work.

The first analogue computers were derived from Kelvin's *Tidal Analyser* (1876), for predicting tides. Electronic analogue computers today are used principally in engineering applications. The first digital computer was conceived by Charles Babbage in 1833 and his 'analytical engine', as it was called, was built; although remarkable in conception it failed partly because of engineering limitations at that time. Work on a similar machine, the automatic sequence controlled calculator, was begun in America in 1939, at Harvard.

Punched cards, which were invented by the French textile engineer J. R. Jacquard (1752–1834) of Lyons to control weaving looms, were also used by Charles Babbage for his analytical engine for input and control. Hollerith used the same principle in the first punched card calculators and these were successfully developed and used extensively until the introduction of electronic computers into both scientific and commercial work in the late 1950s.

The need to compute artillery firing tables for the American army was met by Eckert and Mauchley in 1943 with a machine called ENIAC—*electronic number integrator computer*. Stemming from this work and the ideas of Von Neumann the world's first stored program computer EDSAC was built at Cambridge University. The first commercial stored program computer was UNIVAC 1 and was used by the American Bureau of Census from 1951 until quite recently.

Since the first office computer LEO (J. Lyons and Co. Electronic Office) was introduced in 1953 machines have increased in size, speed, reliability and now cover an extremely wide range of applications without any change in the fundamental principles.

Basic principles

It is important that the reader unfamiliar with computers should dispel any ideas he or she may have that there is any mystique about them. It may help future reading if this point is appreciated from the beginning.

There is a close parallel between the running of a large computer installation and the running of multipurpose machine tools in a production environment, and it is a submission that the overall techniques of production management are more appropriate to the successful running of computers than most line management disciplines. Unless manufacturing equipment enables the business to be profitable the equipment could be regarded as useless; the same statement is true of computing.

Fig. 6.1.1 shows the similarity between the operations of production and the running of a computer. The following comments on the various stages may be of value in helping to understand the parallel drawn and the philosophy implied.

Stage 1. Design drawing office compared with systems analyst functions

These are the common starting points and it is evident in both cases that most of the original thinking in terms of problem solving are embodied in the outputs of both functions.

Stage 2. Process planning compared with systems design/programming

The similarity of the two processes is marked. In the case of process planning for a piece part the planner first studies the drawing and other design information and proceeds to break the job down into operations according to the machines and established routines which are available and which act as local constraints. He then calculates operation times for machine loading and goes on to prepare a cost estimate based on his planning which is sent to the accounts department to form the basis of a comparison between estimated and actual batch costs for the part.

In a somewhat similar manner the systems programmer studies the flow diagram and job specification prepared by the Systems Analyst/Designer and proceeds to break the job down into computer operations according to the local constraints of the computer, peripherals and programming languages used, and ends up with a compiled and tested program together with run documentation. The programmer should also prepare an estimate of run times for computer loading purposes and from those times an estimate of run costs can be prepared and passed to the cost accounts department as a basis for checking the actual run cost.

Fig. 6.1.1
Production and
computer runs
compared

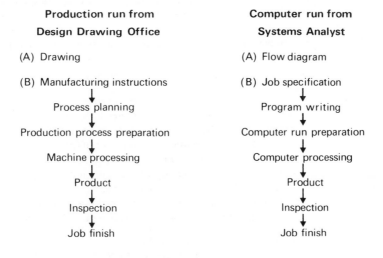

Production run from **Design Drawing Office**	Computer run from **Systems Analyst**
(A) Drawing	(A) Flow diagram
(B) Manufacturing instructions	(B) Job specification
↓ Process planning	↓ Program writing
↓ Production process preparation	↓ Computer run preparation
↓ Machine processing	↓ Computer processing
↓ Product	↓ Product
↓ Inspection	↓ Inspection
↓ Job finish	↓ Job finish

Stages 3 and 4.
Production
processing
compared with
computer processing

At these stages the analogy between production operations and computer operations is still very much in evidence. Whenever a batch of piece parts has to be made in production a batch route card is made out for the sequence of manufacturing operations and the estimated run times. A copy of the drawing of the part and raw material are given to the operator, who sets up his machine and makes the batch of piece parts. The actual material used and time taken for the batch are recorded and the batch cost is calculated on the usual basis of labour, material and overhead.

In the same way when a job is to be run on a computer the operator selects the appropriate job instructions and program, and the computer and peripherals are set up. Raw material in the form of punched cards or tape is fed into the machine and the process of computation is carried out according to the program instructions. The actual material used in the form of cards or tape, printer paper etc. and the actual run time on the machine and peripherals can be recorded and from this information the run cost is prepared on the basis of labour, plus material and overheads.

Stages 5 and 6.
Production
inspection
compared with
run check

The end product of a production run is a recognisable piece part which is checked and if found satisfactory is accepted. On the other hand the output from the computer run often results in a printout or video display or a magnetic tape. However, the final 'product' may be something less tangible in that the 'product' could consist of the process of updating a tape or disc file. As in the case of production these outputs are checked and if found to be satisfactory the computer run is deemed to be acceptable.

**Machine
down time**

Some of the causes of machine down time are:

- inadequate routine maintenance and inadequate preventive maintenance;
- breakdowns due to bad machine design;
- lack of standby units and facilities.

In this context one must distinguish between daily maintenance checks and routine preventive maintenance. The first category is carried out on a daily basis as a check of the functioning of the installation as a whole and most maintenance staff are quite conscientious in the carrying out of such checks. Similar parallels can be drawn in the case of maintenance whether daily checks or routine preventive maintenance to avoid breakdowns that may occur.

Machine loading

In a production environment good machine loading ensures that an even flow of work is available and helps highlight overload conditions in advance. The same philosophy should apply to a computer room. During production it is usual to load up to about 60 per cent of the theoretical shop capacity because time must be allowed for non-productive items. It is a well run workshop which can maintain a steady 60 to 70 per cent load capacity over a long period of time under batch production conditions.

A similar situation exists in a computer room as allowances for the following items have to be deducted from the total time available:

- daily maintenance checks
- machine and peripheral breakdowns
- abortive runs
- routine maintenance
- computer room staff on external courses
- holidays
- lateness
- tea breaks and personal allowances, etc.

Any attempt at systematic loading must proceed on the basis of actual time available after these allowances have been catered for, and these allowances can add up to a sizeable amount of time. Of the time remaining, priority for such key runs as payroll, financial accounting, inventory and stock control must take precedence.

Next, allowance has to be made for user departments not on a priority basis but for those who have a steady time booking. Finally, there are the requirements of the programmers and others working on program writing and program development. A further allocation of time should be held in reserve if the local top management is in the habit of demanding priority runs on an unscheduled basis, or to cover a situation which can arise whenever a major computer breakdown occurs. For these reasons it is desirable to have detailed run estimates covering both the main processor and the peripherals and to schedule long runs and development work over evenings and night shifts. Such a loading system can be run by the computer itself, with the advantage that rescheduling due to changing demand can be carried out immediately by the machine, which can indicate capacity scheduling, overloads, and late runs on an exception basis, and such a system should form an integral part of the data processing system of control.

**Why is a
computer needed?**

In reviewing the information needs of his company, a director or manager may come to the conclusion that it is not possible to meet these satisfactorily by existing methods. Where this is so, the use of a computer should be considered. Very broadly, a computer can do almost any work which involves information handling in a logical series of steps which can be laid down in advance. It can carry out mathematical calculations and can handle routine clerical operations, but it is clear that it will not always pay to put this type of work on to a computer.

Apart from mathematical and scientific work, the main use so far of computers in industry has been in the area of routine clerical work, often with the primary objective of saving money. Except in a few cases, where computer applications 'make money'—in other words, assist management to achieve better control, make better decisions, produce a better product and give customers a better service—they have only recently started to receive the attention they deserve. In many applications computers are essential, for example, where staff are not available and where a service is dependent on speedy processing of a large volume of data and many variables.

The stage has been reached where equipment considerations are no longer the limiting factor in the use of computers in business. The three major limitations which remain are: (i) the difficulty of providing explicit solutions to business problems; (ii) the shortage of trained people for such work; and (iii) the most important point, the inadequacy of management education in this field.

There are often real benefits to be gained from the use of a computer. Even where clerical savings cannot be shown to balance the costs, the estimated value of more useful, timely and accurate information may justify the adoption of a computer system. The need for specialist skills can frequently be reduced to a manageable level by ensuring that the system adopted and the equipment used are relatively simple, even where the detailed calculations to be carried out are voluminous and complicated. Moreover, it may well be easier to achieve the necessary disciplines in a mechanised system than in a manual system staffed by clerks of varying ability and intelligence. Although the computer must never be regarded as a means of avoiding problems of management, it should be given consideration as a means of meeting those problems more efficiently and effectively.

2 Hardware

Over the past few years, a very varied selection of computers has become available. They cost from, say, £5 000 for a unit about the size of a drawer to £5 million for a system occupying several rooms, and the range of facilities available shows a corresponding diversity.

Characteristics and disciplines

Basically a computer may be regarded as consisting of four elements—*input units*, through which data is presented for processing; *a central processing unit* to carry out the arithmetic and logical operations to be performed; *output units* for presenting the finished results; *storage devices* for holding data and files of information in a form usable by the processing units.

The following characteristics distinguish computers from other devices such as accounting machines or desk calculators:

- The data can be processed at high speeds in large volumes.
- The operation is controlled by a program of instructions held in the computer's store. The processing unit selects these instructions (each defining one basic operation) in sequence, so that a complete process may be carried out with little or no clerical intervention. Different programs may be used to enable the computer to perform different tasks.
- The basic operations available cover not only the arithmetic and data transfer functions, but the testing and comparison of numbers, characters or sequences of characters. According to the result of a test, the machine can be instructed to select one or another sequence of operations for execution, so that a computer can be given a predetermined program which allows for alternative actions to meet a variety of circumstances.
- Since the program of instructions defining the processing is followed automatically, the operation of the system is subject to a rigid discipline and the results of processing will be consistent.
- On the other hand, since a computer can do no more than follow the program, it has no power of improvisation. Thus the full range of alternatives must be foreseen and provided for in advance.
- Since the computer is carrying out a sustained sequence of operations on the data presented to it, failure to prepare the data accurately and in the proper form may invalidate the result of processing.

Some of the more important factors to be borne in mind in considering the use of a computer are:

- the implications for discipline in creating and handling the input data to be processed;

- the need for skilled people in the development and operation of systems;
- the necessity for management to retain effective control of the computer department; this will take management time and effort, as it is a responsibility that cannot be wholly delegated to specialists;
- since a computer application may involve appreciable development expenditure, estimated cash flows must be examined carefully to determine whether it is justified.

Mainframe computers

The top of the range of computers are known as mainframe computers, some of which are capable of handling very complex operations indeed. All of these mainframes have the characteristics previously described. Applications range from a conventional payroll or sales invoicing job to weather forecasting, banking transactions and space vehicle control. More recent commercial applications include company modelling and the forecasting of sales, production, profits and so on.

Some idea of the power of such machines can be obtained from typical file sizes and output speeds. One million stored records of 500 characters each, any one being available in less than $0 \cdot 1$ second is a common facility, while producing invoices at 3 000 per hour on a single printer is no problem for an average machine.

Minicomputers

The first minicomputers introduced just over ten years ago were used for aerospace and process control applications. Now there are dozens of different models and their estimated expansion in the next five years is enormous.

Minicomputers, usually stored program digital computers, can have certain advantages over mainframes as they offer very fast cycle times and fast input/output transfer rates in small, low cost units. This can be important in applications where high speed, but complex and perhaps dedicated processing, is needed. There is some doubt in fact as to where minicomputers begin in relation to mainframes, and sometimes they are used as part of a larger system handling scheduling and input/output tasks. Typical application areas are:

Process control
Numerical control of machine tools
Direct control of machines and production lines
Automated testing and inspection
Telemetry
Data acquisition and logging
Control and analysis of laboratory experiments
Analysis and interpretation of medical tests
Traffic control
Shipboard navigation control
Message switching
Communication controllers for larger computers
Communication line concentrators
Programmable communications terminals
Peripheral controllers for larger computers

Control of multistation key to disc systems
Display panel control
Computer aided design
Typesetting and photocomposition
Computer assisted instruction
Engineering and scientific computations

Forecasted growth trends of minicomputers, together with their decreasing cost means that they will soon make a more significant impact on business applications. For example, many machines are already installed for processing orders and producing invoices; this is the kind of job where a dedicated minicomputer working continuously on one application shows significant advantages over a much larger machine doing the same work in intermittent batches.

Visible record computers

The visible record computer (VRC) can be considered as the equipment that has bridged the gap between the conventional accounting machines and the larger computers. The essential feature is that the main files are stored on ledger cards. It has some of the features of the mainframe computer, including the ability to operate automatically under program control, storage devices to hold both program and data, and a range of input and output units. VRC's handle ledger cards which store information both visually and magnetically.

Although more limited than a computer since they often operate under a fixed program and have only a small store, the machines are easily handled and are as simple to operate as accounting machines. They may be more appropriate where the technical skills required for the design and implementation of a conventional computer system are not available, or where the volume of data processing is relatively small.

Like minicomputers, VRC's are often used in conjunction with large systems, either linked directly or by providing detailed information; for example, by production of a cassette tape with sales information, to be used as input for programs requiring a larger computer for more complex operations such as forecasting, sales analysis etc.

Data communications

Data communication systems can greatly facilitate the interchange of information between a central computer and its user; by enabling the user access to a data file in a remote computer, or to retrieve or update specific information at the time when it is needed.

Data communications can also allow the implementation of applications not practical by other means, for example, airline reservations and the enquiry procedure for the verification of bank balances, now available at the push of a button. The information on costs or accounts is stored in a large central computer, and may be accessed through terminals located virtually anywhere in the world.

Networks

A data communication system consists of three principal elements—the computer, the communication link and the terminals. Together these elements form a network, the simplest form being a central computer with one or more lines radiating from the centre to the remote terminals. This simple arrangement is often complicated by a second computer located next to the central machine. Their inputs and outputs are in parallel, and the machines are programmed so that if one should fail, the other takes over virtually instantaneously. By this means, a very high degree of reliability is obtained at the central installation.

More complex networks exist in which the terminals have access to more than one computer. This is the case where a user has access to a large computer from a simple teletypewriter terminal via the public telephone network. The connection is established by dialling, and access is controlled by the computer recognising the user's 'password'. Such a user may have passwords to several computers, and have the use of a different application program in each. He is charged according to his computer useage, plus the normal rate for the telephone (or telex) line. This type of operation is known as 'time sharing'.

Communication networks may also include computers whose sole purpose is for receiving, validating, storing and rerouting data or messages. Such a machine is called a 'message switching computer' and is normally used when a large number of terminals are making intensive use of a network containing one or more data processing computers. Only a computer is capable of handling the messages at the high speeds necessary; mechanical switching would be entirely inadequate. This type of system is being planned by the Post Office for providing a national data transmission service.

Terminals

Terminals can be of various types and may be intelligent or unintelligent, i.e. may be programmable or not. A programmable terminal is used to relieve the mainframe of trivial jobs, such as data validation, or for providing a range of different terminal applications.

Typewriter terminals

This is the most common type of terminal which, although slow (10–15 characters per second) and relatively cheap, provides a printed copy of both input and output data. They are generally not suitable for large volumes of data, but are used in areas where a small amount of input–output is to be transmitted and where complicated and lengthy computation is required. This is so in many time sharing applications.

Batch terminals

As the name implies these are mainly used where large batches of information are required to be transmitted. As the input volumes are considerable, typewriter terminals would be too slow and so other input/output media are used in the form of for example, punched cards, magnetic tape or punched paper tape. The speeds achieved range from 100 to 600 characters per second but could be higher in certain cases.

Cathode ray tube (CRT) terminal or visual display unit (VDU)

The basic VDU terminal includes a typewriter type keyboard for data input and a television type display screen for output. The VDU is a very high speed device capable of transmitting at several thousand characters per second. Information can be typed on the keyboard to appear on the screen, at which stage it can be checked and automatically edited and at the press of a button can be transmitted to the central computer. By this means it can be used as an enquiry terminal and the answer to the question transmitted can appear back on the screen very quickly.

Programmed
terminals

All the terminals described so far are unintelligent, in other words they can only transmit messages to the central computer and receive back information. Intelligent terminals (programmable terminals) can reduce the amount of data to be transmitted by performing some of the simple processing operations before sending information to the larger computer. In effect the situation is a computer talking to another computer. This reduces the turn-round time, for example, in a simple editing job that may be required before more complicated computation is needed and leaves the larger machine free for other work. Other specialised terminals for graphical output and plotters are available but not described here.

**Data entry
devices**

The original method of entering data into the computer was the punched card, and later paper and magnetic tape. However, with computer speeds increasing these are relatively slow speed input methods, especially as a great deal of data preparation and editing is required. It is logical therefore to look at devices capable of capturing data at its source and either entering it directly into a computer system or recording the data on an intermediate medium, for example a magnetic tape or disc, for subsequent direct entry to the system.

Optical character
recognition (OCR)

Optical character recognition devices read printed or handwritten alpha-numeric information from special size documents, journal tapes and also standard pages or forms; for example in banking, most cheques now have magnetic characters which are readable by the computer and also by humans. OCR applications are limited to those where it is difficult or expensive to convert the data to some other medium, and/or the volumes are very large. Typical examples are the reconciliation of national insurance postal drafts and the updating of Giro accounts, where there may be millions of documents each week.

There are two main kinds of paper transport, generally referred to as 'document' and 'page' transports. The former is a high speed machine (600 to 1 500 documents per minute) suitable for reading a single line of data on a small document such as a cheque. A page reader operates more slowly and handles large sheets containing many lines of print. The reading head, or scanner, is usually a cathode ray tube or a photocell array. Means are provided for registering the scanner over the area to be read, either manually or automatically.

Because of the complexity of the equipment and the nature of the medium, a high level of discipline is required in OCR systems for successful operation. Close control must be exercised over paper supplies, printing devices and the general organisation surrounding the system.

Optical mark readers (OMR)	Mark reading represents the simplest form of source data capture, the presence or absence of a handwritten or printed mark signifying one unit of data. A mark may mean yes or no, a number, or a sorting pocket, or can have any other significance according to the box in which it appears on the document. No special skill is required to enter marks and very little instruction is required to prepare acceptable documents. The main problem is usually the large area required by the marking boxes, especially if alphabetic information is to be entered. Imaginative form design will usually overcome this problem, rendering OMR a very powerful and economic technique of source data capture.

Typical applications are census forms, multiple choice examination papers, meter reading, billing, order forms, etc. It is usually economic for quite small volumes of data, say 500 documents a day using a hand fed documents reader, while the upper limit is determined only by the speed of the document transports available.

Key to disc	This is becoming a very popular form of data entry, making use of a number of techniques. Data is transcribed from the source document onto the screen of a VDU by a keyboard operator. Several VDU's are under the control of a minicomputer, which formats the data on the VDU screen and applies validation procedures simultaneously. Invalid data gives rise to screen messages, enabling the operator to make immediate corrections. Validated data is stored on a disc file. This is accumulated and transferred periodically to a magnetic tape by supervisor intervention. A completed batch of work on tape is finally taken to the mainframe computer for processing.

Key to disc operations generally have higher throughput rates than their card or paper tape equivalents and result in lower error rates. They are usually cost effective for anything over half a dozen operators. In the next few years they will probably overtake cards in terms of numbers of installations. An incidental benefit is the improvement in working conditions and reduced staff turnover.

Voice response	This is the technique of using computers to generate spoken replies taken from a prerecorded vocabulary. The concept is not new, having been demonstrated many years ago, but it has not so far been used as an output method. Interest has been revived recently, largely through the availability of the touch-tone telephone. This may be used as a very cheap computer terminal with a wide application potential. Data—i.e. simple enquiries—may be entered through the touch-tone keyboard, the ear piece being used for computer generated voice prompts and replies.

Applications at present are mainly limited to those where a relatively short, numeric answer is all that is needed, or where the main terminal function is for keying in data, the voice response is used for prompting. A typical example is in banking, answering teller queries on the status of customer accounts.

The corresponding technique of voice input is not yet a practical proposition.

Printers

The printer is the almost universal computer output device, providing a visible record of what the machine is doing, or displaying the contents of its store.

There are two main categories of machine:

Character printers print one character at a time in left to right sequence as on a typewriter. These are slow machines, operating in the range 10 to 200 characters per second.

Line printers print one line at a time, the characters within the line being printed in random order. Speeds range from 150 to 2 000 lines/minute, line width being from 80 to 160 characters. A line printer is always needed for anything more than small data volumes.

The choice of printer is normally based on throughput requirements and print quality, because as a general rule print quality deteriorates with increased speed.

Disc, drum and tape storage

Discs and drums fall into a general category called rotating memories; the three principal features serving to categorise this equipment are: the *medium, head arrangement* and the *media arrangement*. The medium is the component on which the magnetic patterns are recorded, it can be a flat disc or a drum-shaped cylinder with a single surface available for recording. Drums were the first computer storage media, however, discs that use a track to track recording density approach have become more popular. Looking at the two, a summary is:

- discs have the advantage in terms of capacity per unit volume;
- drums have the advantage for speed and shock resistance;
- fixed head arrangements have the advantage of speed;
- moving head arrangements have the advantage of cost and capacity;
- removable-media units have the advantage of unlimited offline storage capacity;
- fixed media units have the advantage of simplicity of design;
- rotating memories have the key advantage of flexibility.

Magnetic tape in common with discs and drums has the capability for information to be erased and rewritten without damaging the original medium. It is difficult to relate the use of magnetic tape and discs to specific data applications as it usually serves as an intermediate storage medium. The source of information, its use and its destination are of little significance except for the exchange of information between computers, where the tape provides a convenient high speed method for the transfer of data. Tapes are in the form of tape reels, as on a normal tape-recorder, or cassette tape, as described in a later application, whereby cassette tapes created on a computer run are fed into a mainframe for further processing. Tapes are of course one of the cheapest forms of intermediate storage.

Both tapes and discs can be used in data preparation, replacing punched cards. A video screen unit with keyboard can be used for data entry and validation and it provides a fast and versatile input medium to the computer.

3 Choosing a computer system

The Steering Committee

Included in any computer policy among many other subjects should be the structure of a Computer Steering Committee whose primary task is to select those projects most likely to achieve a high pay off or those that are essential for the efficient running of the business. The Committee should consist of top level management representing Finance, Marketing, Sales & Distribution, Production etc., and the Head of Computer Services. The Chairman in most cases should be the Board Member responsible for the data processing function. The objective is to ensure the involvement in some depth of all departments through senior management and to create an awareness of the kind of information that can be made available through the application of the computer and to aid management in the effective running of the business.

The terms of reference of the Computer Steering Committee depend on the organisation and structure of the company. It is necessary to consider the distinction between those decisions that can only be made by the data processing manager and his superior, i.e. which affect only the data processing department, and those decisions that must be made by the steering committee, i.e. which also affect interests outside the data processing department.

At the feasibility study stage the terms of reference should include:

- to appoint the team to carry out the feasibility study;
- to establish terms of reference for the study;
- to set a budget and method of cost control;
- to establish the time scale and completion date;
- to ensure the cooperation of departments likely to be affected by a decision to use a computer;
- to guide, monitor and participate in the study;
- to consider the report of the feasibility study team and take appropriate action.

Criteria for profitable applications

The Steering Committee has been set up and one of its first tasks is to assess those applications which have the best chance of helping to achieve business profitability.

Criteria for profitable computing have to be considered from two points of view: (a) those relating to the operations of the company overall; and (b) those concerned with the data processing systems or procedures handled by and within the computer. A representative selection of areas of benefit potential from both points of view is set out in Fig. 6.3.1, with indication of the degree of measurability. Bearing these points in mind, if it is felt a computer solution can help, a feasibility study should be set up to provide a detailed analysis of the potential areas to be considered.

(a) Company operations:

Fig. 6.3.1
Criteria for
profitable
computing

Area of benefit	Type of benefit	Measurability	Potential
Reduced company operating costs	Reduction in capital employed; reduction in staff; increased efficiency in use of resources	Some aspects measurable but others only assessible in conjunction with box below	Limited, since benefits are based on reduction of present levels
Increased operational effectiveness of company	Increased customer service; increased production flexibility; resources freed for other use	Difficult-must be measured in light of present and future market and trading conditions	Depends on circumstances of company, but can be very large
New company operational approaches	Ability to operate in ways not previously possible – e.g. use of LP's in oil industry Corporate modelling	Speculative-no firm basis of comparison with existing circumstances	Unlimited

Area of benefit	Type of benefit	Measurability	Potential
A. Reduction in data processing costs	Direct clerical savings	Good	May be large, but always limited, (by level of existing costs)
B. Increased data processing efficiency	Accuracy. Reliability. Timeliness. Presentation. Tending to more effective management operations and decisions	Qualitive-difficult to assess value	Significant in particular cases, but normally of minor value
C. Increased data processing capacity	Ability to meet increasing load at less than proportionate cost	Capacity usually measurable but future costs avoided may be difficult to define	Large where limits of present resources may be reached. Normally limited (as in A)

The feasibility study

If the decision is made to consider the use of a computer in the company the selection of a system to meet a particular company's needs is basically a two-stage procedure:

Stage 1. Preparation work aimed at determining what systems, including computer systems, can best meet company objectives—the so called 'feasibility study'.

Stage 2. The computer selection process itself.

A feasibility study having been preceded by a brief preliminary survey conducted by the steering committee, has determined that a full study, which may involve considerable time and effort, should be undertaken. The full study consists of five phases:

1. Background analysis
2. Identification of existing information processes
3. Management objectives and systems requirements
4. The development plan
5. Production of a feasibility study report.

1. Background analysis	The purpose of 'background analysis' is to gain an insight into the environment within which the company operates and an understanding of company policy and strategy within that environment. Both are essential to a proper understanding of the objectives to be met by information systems and their design. The analysis will cover such items as industry structure, industry technologies, government regulations and policies, company structure, policy and mode of operation within its environment, overall company performance, past, present and future, company forward plans in the major functional areas (marketing, sales, production, distribution, etc.).
2. Existing information processes and flows	A study of information processes or flows is usefully preceded by a study of the 'product' flow ('products' may be physical objects or services). Product and information flows are usually closely linked and should involve visits to factories, warehouses, depots and even customers' premises, to check on information suplied and to develop it to cover such supplementary items as trends, seasonal or cyclic variations. The result of the first phase will always include a chart of the product flow, with emphasis on those points where action is triggered off, e.g. when stock is ordered as a result of reaching a minimum stock level.

Similar visits should be undertaken in the information processing areas. Following the flow of information the investigator should record details of action requirements and actions in each area, noting at the same time:

- branches and conditions for information branch flows
- documents used, codes and field record sizes, etc.
- data on volumes, frequency of operations, error rates
- strengths and weaknesses of each process
- controls
- costs, including costs of system inadequacy and proneness to error.

Flow charts of information flow for each functional area or activity should be prepared.

3. Systems requirements and management objectives	Based on the knowledge gained so far, a view must now be taken about the suitability and cost effectiveness of the existing information processes. The criteria for judgment to be applied are those implied by management's objectives and a sound appreciation of what is good in the field of information technology. Questions to be answered are:

- Does the process provide timely, cost-effective and adequate results—or control information?
- For how long will the existing system continue to function adequately?
- Can it be improved without fundamental changes? If not, what changes are likely to be relevant?

4. Development plan

For functional areas where the introduction of computer methods is being considered it will be necessary to rethink the information processes, determining the information requirements and constraints, and the performance requirements in measurable terms as part of an overall systems development plan. Such a plan should be modular in approach and should set priorities. In addition, the methods available for processing (Service Bureaux, sharing computer facilities or acquiring a computer of one's own) should now be reviewed.

5. Presentation of the result of the feasibility study

The results of the feasibility study should include a report summary and oral presentation of terms of reference, conclusions and recommendations and costs and benefits to the company. In addition, the written report should cover: methods used and depth of study; existing systems, including costs and definition of problem areas; proposed new systems with an equipment plan, costs and benefit analysis, and mention of alternative systems considered. The report should also consider staffing problems, management and user education and a plan for introduction, implementation and control of the new system.

The selection process

Assuming the Steering Committee has accepted the results of the feasibility study so far, the next stage is to look at project and computer selection. The main objectives of project selection must relate to the values provided to the company overall or to the department concerned, and some criteria for selection in this context are the following:

- Cost saving
- Direct monetary gain
- Technical practicability
- Human factors
- Systems integration
- Research and development required
- Legal requirements
- Tangible and intangible benefits
- Impact on company operations

Projects will be selected after due consideration of both short-term and long-term advantages and will include both quantifiable and subjectively assessed benefits. In some cases different systems and projects should be integrated, if this increases profits and cash flow after taking into account all development and operating cost factors. The Steering Committee should authorise or reject the proposed projects on the basis of the criteria already outlined.

Computer selection

If, following approval of the projects by the Steering Committee and the Board, it has been decided to acquire an in-house computer, the first step is to prepare a short list of at least three potential suppliers who will be requested to propose equipment for the systems requirements.

Request for proposal

The request for proposal consists of two parts:
Part 1. An invitation to bid and a list of specific questions which the supplier must answer.
Part 2. A Systems Requirements Specification.

Part 1. Specific questions

Questions to be answered by suppliers should be posed in as uniform a manner as practical to permit easy comparison with other proposals and should be designed to clarify suppliers' positions in the following areas:

Background and experience of supplier
Equipment performance
Installation requirements
Financial considerations
Maintenance arrangements
Action in case of malfunction
Software (operating systems, compilers, utilities)
Personnel and training
Penalties acceptable for late delivery, failure to reach agreed standards, etc.

Part 2. Systems requirements specification

The systems requirements specification will be based on work done during the feasibility study (project selection) supplemented by additional work as necessary. It could specify for each project what the system is to provide by when, how and from what data it is to be produced. Estimated volumes should also, where appropriate, be given. It is important to provide the right level of detail, so that the supplier's proposal remains close to the envisaged system but is not, on the other hand, too constrained by detail to prevent a creative approach. Some indication of evaluation methods may have to be given at the same time if, for example, a 'bench-mark' test is to be constructed in which the supplier's help is requested.

Supplier's proposals

In addition to supplying detailed written answers to the questions asked in Part 1, the supplier should be expected to include the following items of information in the written response to the systems requirements specification:

- flow charts of all clerical and machine activities, showing input files and output files for each run;
- program content and run duration giving the basis of its calculation;
- data preparation effort required;
- frequency of each run;
- estimates of program and file sizes;
- restart and recovery procedures;
- control methods proposed;
- consideration of multiprogramming;
- a load schedule for each machine proposed.

In addition to information supplied in the request for proposal, suppliers should be given the opportunity to visit the potential customer's premises in order to supplement their knowledge of the business. Visits should be of a restricted nature. Any supplementary information supplied to one supplier should be issued formally to all other suppliers to ensure equality of treatment.

The proposal when completed should be followed by a formal presentation given by the supplier to provide an opportunity to discuss any points needing clarification.

Evaluation

Evaluation of proposals begins with visits to installations where equipment similar to that being proposed is in use. Two or three such visits based on a list of questions to evaluate user reaction to all aspects of training, implementation and operational running will usually provide a useful background to examination of the proposal itself.

Another aid to decision-making is bench-marking or similar tests; these can be of great help but are usually too demanding in effort to be worthwhile for a first time computer user. Other methods, such as simulation, will be of value in complicated large projects. Where such methods cannot be applied, a system of 'marking' proposals against a list of weighted, pre-determined criteria is usually adopted. This has the advantage of introducing a disciplined approach to the decision-making process.

Post evaluation procedure

Once a decision has been made, a formal proposal to the Board should be prepared to make the case for the choice and requesting permission to go ahead with the chosen solution. The approval of the Board may be followed by a 'letter of intent' designed to allow the supplier to allocate production resources to the customer's requirements. This will later be followed by a contractual arrangement for which legal advice should be obtained.

Planning

Implementation planning will begin at the latest when the proposal to acquire a computer has been approved by the Board. The use of bar graph networks such as PERT (Programme Evaluation and Review Technique) for this purpose is advisable (see page 384). Areas of planning include staffing and staff training, systems analysis and design, programming, testing of programs and systems, documentation, environmental planning, and acceptance procedures.

The role of consultants

Consultants often play an important role in computer selection, particularly where no previous computer experience is available inside the company or where consultants can supply specialised expertise.

Installation or outside service?

A company can of course install a computer on its own premises, but the use of an outside installation may be available and preferable.

When it is decided to install a computer, several courses are available: for example:

1. The equipment may be purchased outright from the supplier; in this case the supplier normally provides engineering maintenance in return for periodic payments.
2. The equipment may be rented from the supplier from year to year and the rental agreement includes maintenance.
3. The equipment may be acquired through a leasing company on a variety of bases by which the cost is spread over an agreed number of years.

Whichever way is selected, it is necessary to establish how far the costs of supporting services (programming, advice on systems etc.) are included in the agreed payments, and to what extent they are available and effective.

It may be found that the work to be done does not justify the cost of installing equipment, and it may be better to have the work carried out by making partial use of another machine. Computer service bureaux have been set up to provide such a service to outside users. Usually it will be found that a range of services is available; in addition to providing the computing facility for operating the job, the bureau will normally provide also the operating staff and may undertake data preparation and programming and system design work.

It may be possible to make an arrangement with another user who has spare capacity to share his equipment on an agreed basis. However, special problems may arise in respect of the relative priority of work and of increases in the work load of either or both companies beyond the capacity of the installation; and security is another consideration.

The nature of the user's responsibilities for the work will clearly vary with the basis selected and the terms agreed. Where the company installs its own equipment, it will be responsible for all aspects of the work. The use of a bureau may enable the user to avoid the problems associated with machine operation, data preparation, programming and some of the technical aspects of system design. But, however wide the agreement with the service bureau, some responsibilities must remain with the user. In particular there is the need to ensure that correct data is available at the right time, and, above all, that the true requirements are clearly defined and met.

Planning for use

If it has been agreed by the Steering Committee that a computer should be used, then terms of reference for the duties of the Committee should include:

● to formulate and review the policy for data processing in the company;
● to review both long-term and short-term plans for the data processing activity within the company;

- to plan and implement a company data processing education programme for all levels of management in departments likely to be affected by the use of the computer;
- to examine project proposals submitted to the committee and allocate priorities;
- to set up project teams to develop and implement individual projects;
- to approve the terms of reference for each project and to ensure that these terms of reference are adhered to and that co-operation is given by those departments concerned;
- to review the progress of each project;
- to review the costs and benefits of each operational system.

Some criteria for profitable computing in respect of the computer operations are shown in Fig. 6.3.1 (page 874).

4 Software: programming

Languages for
programming

While the first computer programmers were, of necessity, jacks-of-all-trades (they had to know machines, programming techniques and applications) programming soon generated its own sub-specialities. The first logical division of programming came with the distinction between 'applications programming' and 'systems programming'. Though there is and probably always will be an overlap, systems programmers write programs that run the computing equipment, while applications programmers write programs that put the computer to work on specific jobs.

An important subdivision of systems programming is programming language development: producing the Assemblers, Fortrans, Cobols and other translation programs. With programming languages, applications programmers can instruct a computer in a language closer to English and normal mathematical notation than the ones and zeros of machine language. Programming language development, then, is the creation of programs that permit the computer to translate a natural language statement into the numerical, machine-language instructions, or object programs, that actually operate the computer.

These areas of programming—systems programming, language development, and applications programming—are intrinsically interdependent, but the trends in programming will be clarified if we look at the evolution of each separately.

The development of programming languages began with the development of mnemonic techniques and macro-instructions to their numerical equivalents. Why, then, could they not be programmed to translate more general statements of mathematics and business calculations? They could and they were. From the base provided by the Assembler languages came high-level programming languages such as Fortran and Cobol:

Formula translation (Fortran) was an IBM development for scientific and engineering problems.
Common business orientated language (Cobol) was inspired by the USA Department of Defense as a machine independent language which would cut across the language boundaries of all computers.

Because earlier computers were designed primarily for either business or scientific computing, the programming languages that emerged during the 1950s and 1960s also reflected this specialisation. However, the difference between scientific and business computing has diminished. Traditionally, business computers were designed to handle a lot of data on which they performed a limited amount of calculation, while scientific computers performed a lot of computations on relatively small amounts of data. With the appearance of more sophisticated business problems, such as simulation of marketing plans and production facilities, business computers began to need the high-speed computing ability of scientific computers. Scientists and engineers, on the other hand, found that they could profitably use the commercial computer's talent in manipulating large data files for applications such as test data reduction. Some computers are designed for both business and scientific use and are prime examples of the way in which emerging computing requirements of business and science have affected computer design.

Current programming developments also show the trend toward multipurpose systems. One of the newer languages of importance is PL/1. A programmer can use this to write instructions for use in either scientific or business applications. However, Cobol and Fortran continue to be improved as programming languages. Figure 6.4.1 shows the relationship of other languages to PL/1 which is said to combine the best features from each.

Fig. 6.4.1
PL/1

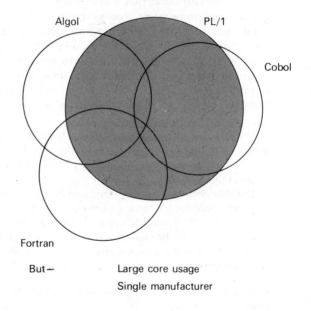

Comprehensive

Algol   PL/1

Cobol

Fortran

But—   Large core usage
              Single manufacturer

Systems programming/ operating systems

From the relatively straightforward job of creating little strings of instructions that directed a computer to read a card and write a tape record, systems programming has evolved into the most complex of programming tasks. The creation of input/output control systems set the direction. Faster and faster computers created the need for an even more efficient workflow. The computer became too fast to depend on human intervention to switch it from job to job, so programmers created monitor or executive programs to help the computer operator keep up with the workflow.

The first monitor program went into operation in 1960 on high-speed scientific computers. Under monitor control, a computer can run almost nonstop through an indefinite series of jobs stacked up in a waiting queue.

The development of a monitor control program, or operating system, played as important a part in the system design as did technical developments in electronics circuitry. Essentially, the operating system uses the decision-making speed of the computer to run routine tasks on the computer with a minimum of operator intervention. The computer is capable of 'looking' for a new job just as it 'looks' for a new instruction within the confines of a single program. The computer can also reallocate its own resources to meet the changing demands of each job.

A typical operating system is equipped with all the compilers—the language translation programs—and special programs that operate input/output equipment. The computer need not be halted to set up a certain compiler for one job and then another compiler for a subsequent job. The operating system controls all elements and calls them in when needed.

Operating systems add tremendous speed, flexibility and scope to computer-associated communications (teleprocessing) devices. Regardless of the work being performed by the computer at any given time, the operating system monitor can interrupt work in progress and execute programs needed to process incoming messages. When the message or inquiry has been completed, the monitor will then cause work to resume at the point where it was interrupted. In larger systems where the capacity is available, teleprocessing may be interleaved with other work.

| Applications programming | The programming developments that led to operating systems and high order programming languages had two major goals: to make computer programming and operation easier and more efficient. In essence, they are tools to produce and help execute the applications programs that do the actual computing jobs from writing payroll to simulating spacecraft. |

In the first years of commercial computing, manufacturers provided little in the way of direct application program assistance. It was felt that users would prefer to, and should, write their own applications programs to reflect their own particular needs or methods of doing business. This is still true to a large extent. Today, however, programmers are often able to start at some advanced point in their programming endeavours, thanks to applications programs supplied and proven by the manufacturer of the computer.

Certain broad data processing functions common to many companies—despite their individual differences—could be programmed and are applicable throughout industry, and customer companies and their programmers would welcome more specific programming assistance. Package applications proliferated: in banking, demand deposit accounting; in finance, portfolio selection; in aerospace, PERT; in metals manufacturing, numerical control of machine tools; in publishing, line justification; in education, class scheduling; in wholesale distribution, scientific inventory management. Applications programs for certain computers continue the trend. Many of them will operate under the control of operating systems.

Applications programs such as the Advanced Life Information System, Property and Liability Information System, Demand Deposit Accounting and

On-Line Teller Program are actually families of program modules which can be placed in auxiliary storage and called into use on an 'as needed' basis. The modularity of these programs makes them easier to tailor to specific jobs. Thus, the same kind of progress in the evolution of applications programming is found as in the evolution of systems programming.

5 Applications

Company Plans— Corporate Modelling

The use of computer based models in corporate planning and reporting within companies has greatly increased in the last few years and appears likely to grow even more rapidly in the near future. The five main fields of application of these models are:

Strategic planning
Five-year planning
Annual estimating
Monthly reporting
Updated forecasting

There seem to be two basic types of modelling systems, those suited to overall strategic planning for profit analysis and those suitable for monthly results, updated forecasts, and annual estimate calculations (Fig. 6.5.1). Strategic planning systems are not considered suitable for handling large volumes of data, and hence are not suited to annual estimating, monthly results or updated forecast calculations. They are best suited to strategic planning due to their flexibility, but may also be used for five-year planning; it must be noted that they lack the built-in framework considered useful for product hierarchy calculations.

Fig. 6.5.1
Basic types of modelling systems

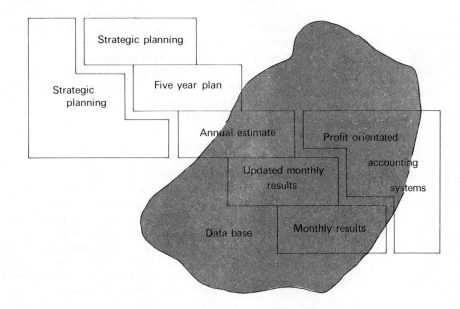

Profit oriented accounting systems

Profit as the deciding factor in management activities is a determinable quantity. Profit planning is thus an important part of comprehensive business planning. The difficulties arising from the planning process stem from the complexity of the firm on the one hand and the uncertainty of factors which must be taken into account on the other. A computerised accounting system can provide an excellent way of running quickly through the various alternatives encountered during the planning process. The function of such an accounting system could be to calculate future results for each line in the product range, taking into account all the expected costs, quantities and prices which could influence results at each level.

The profit estimates form the basis for managerial decisions, and allow comparisons between actual results as an aid to planning control, and permit the concept of 'management by exception'.

Financial aspects

Until quite recently, the computer has contributed more to the financial function than to other applications. The accountant who has a computer finds that he has access to a mass of data, and the benefits he derives are limited only by his ability to use the computer as an analytical tool. There are four major areas of interest to the accountant:

- management information retrieval, e.g. information about sales, production, finance, marketing, etc.;
- company modelling requiring information from him on costs and prices;
- financial reports;
- financial costing and control systems for the company and for the computer itself.

The Chief Accountant has the responsibility for coordinating annual budgets and the subsequent variance statements. The computer can be programmed to provide automatic generation of variance statements. The computer can also predict the cash flow for each period of the year and the consequences of change; for example credit restrictions and the effect of subsequent fall off in debtors receipts can be calculated almost instantly.

One of the most important functions of the Chief Accountant is measurement, particularly that of 'opportunity costs', i.e. the benefit the firm might have had if the resources available had been used in a different way. For example, the opportunity cost of a machine shop is not the added costs of labour, materials, depreciation allowance and overheads, but the revenue that could be obtained by using the production resources in the most advantageous way. It is the costing method which is relevant to short-term decision-making and it is an analytical tool which the computer has made into a practical and valuable reality by the use of modelling techniques. These are described briefly elsewhere and include, for example, use of linear programs for allocation problems such as vehicle or salesmen routing, or raw materials for manufacture of products. Another example is critical path methods (CPM) or network analysis used in the control of projects (see pages 384 and 802). Finally, there are more complex stochastic models which incorporate probability coefficients, for example deciding which project to invest money in by accounting for variables in which there is an element of chance, such as the possibility of import levies, or special taxes.

Business control
ratios

The references to 'interfirm comparison' in Part One (see page 76) and the details of accounting controls described in Part Five, chapters 4 and 5 (see pages 698 and 717) indicate that seven generally accepted ratios can provide key criteria for financial control:

1. Profit: sales
2. Profit: capital employed
3. Sales: capital employed
4. Sales: fixed assets
5. Sales: stocks
6. Sales: employees
7. Profit: employees

Overall financial aims are represented by the first three ratios which can be affected by all aspects of the business. If a comparison is made between similar companies in the UK and the USA, it shows that both profit and turnover related to capital employed are more than double for US companies, whereas profit on sales is only slightly higher in the USA. The rate of turnover of inventory in the USA is also about double that of the UK and it is highly probable that this latter factor contributes most to the higher return on capital employed in the USA. Lastly, for a given output an average American company employs less than half the people employed by an equivalent British company.

It is believed that the apparent superior performance of industry in the USA is due to four main factors: first, a better calibre of management, especially at second and lower levels, coupled with better company spirit and generally much better use of manpower and assets; second, recognition of the relative importance of the manufacturing function; third, more advanced production and stock control techniques; fourth, the successful use of computerisation, particularly of the manufacturing functions in the areas of bulk purchasing, scheduling, shop loadings, production control and stock control. It has been proved in many companies that computing used in this way helps to use operating assets much more effectively; to turn inventory over faster and achieve a more ordered (need-oriented) flow of materials from source, through production to customer; to enhance output, and sales per employee through, e.g., greater identification of management and employees at all levels with the objectives, improved team spirit and more effective work per man.

The effective application of computers in this way demands:

● a rigorous review of existing manual methods and systems, with the result in most cases of incidental exclusive benefits;
● specialised handling of computer output (quite different from accounting useage);
● onsite local computers with direct access storage facilities;
● specialised software and application packages;
● special data collection and data transmission facilities.

In more general terms, online computing can be applied in three major areas, all of which can have a marked effect on optimising control ratios:

1. Cost of product manufacturing
   production scheduling
   production control
   inventory management
   bill of materials
   labour recording
2. Increased revenues
   distribution systems
   online information retrieval and control systems
   scheduling all operations
   research/scientific computation
3. Management decisions
   financial planning
   market forecasting
   sales analysis

This can be illustrated by one example connected with supplying market forecasting. The current situation is that the market is expanding slowly, and a low growth rate is predicted; demand will increase much more slowly than costs. To hold profits the company needs increased turnover, which can be achieved by:

- increasing the number of buyers and exploring new markets;
- increasing quantity used by consumers;
- stealing from competition in existing or new sectors of the market;
- diversifying with new areas of markets or products.

In other words, revenue must be maximised by channelling the marketing effort into selling those items capable of generating profitable volume and, if appropriate investing idle funds to increase revenue. The sections dealing with marketing applications and sales forecasting describe the basic computer system features, which can assist with such a problem. Sales per employee and profits per employee can be improved in one way by the computer's ability to carry out simple repetitive tasks more accurately and reliably, and at lower cost; considerable staff reductions are normal when a computer is installed, particularly in clerical labour: for example, accounting, order entry and verification, invoice production, and sales and debtors ledger updating, and so on.

It appears from surveys that have been made of the usage of computers in consumer products industries that *live* as distinct from *planned* applications are predominantly financial. However, it is in those non-financial areas such as marketing, distribution and production, that the real need for computer assistance and real opportunities for profit lie. Typical applications in these areas successfully running in many companies, and the computer-based techniques currently in use, can be summarised in the following lists:

Use of computers | Order entry: invoicing
Sales accounting
Finished goods inventory accounting
Inventory forecasting

Payroll
Product scheduling: control
Raw materials accounting: control
Packing materials accounting: control
Sales forecasting: medium and long term
General: nominal ledger
Standard costing: budgetary control

Computer based techniques	Teleprocessing
	OCR
	Simulation
	Financial modelling
	Linear programming
	Critical path analysis (PERT)
	Vehicle scheduling

Marketing

The majority of marketing applications have been in short term operations, so that up to the present time it can be stated that

- vital ingredients are experience and intuition, and decisions are rarely based on analysis;
- marketing is hampered by imperfect information;
- the undoubted value of experience and intuition would be enhanced by objective measurements of markets, products and sales forces.

Areas in which computers can help certain marketing activities towards particular defined objectives are:

Marketing activities	Market potential evaluation
	Monitor competitors
	Sales forecasting
	Sales force effort
	Pricing
	Set optimum service level
	Advertising
	Promotion
	Launches
	Test marketing

Objectives	Increase market share/total market
	Enlarge and diversify product lines
	Maximise revenue
	Control and reduce selling costs and distribution costs

Interrelated
problems

Though the answers to problems often have a purely departmental aspect there is a need also to show the effects of problems across other functions in a company such as production, distribution, finance, personnel. For example, the effects of a sales promotion involve labour resources, raw material purchase, inventory levels, warehouse space, transport, and cash flow plans. The computer can help considerably in overcoming such problems as:

- too late and inaccurate sales statistics
- lack of basic data for resource planning
- poor sales forecasting
- preparation of the annual plan
- need for marketing models
- projection of the result of price changes
- recognition of promotion success
- interface with other functions

The basic structure for deciding system requirements to deal with these problems is shown in Fig. 6.5.2.

Fig. 6.5.2
Basic structures
for problem
solving

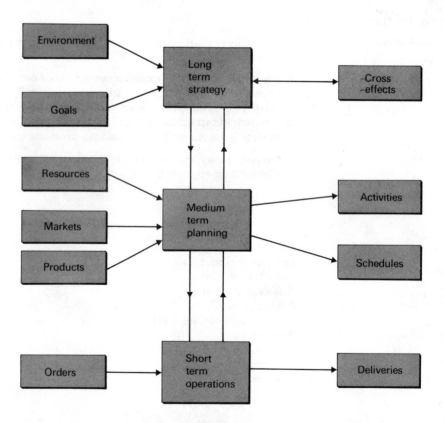

The most basic need is for the establishment and maintenance of a pool of data from both internal and external sources which is up to date and easily accessible and interpretable by management. This will enable fast evaluation and condensation of the following as decision-making aids:

Evaluation

- direct selling and merchandising effort
- above the line promotional activity
- below the line promotional activity (including the disturbance effect of special offers, packs, etc.

Product appraisal

- brand profitability
- pack contribution
- product launch
- brand competition

Fig. 6.5.3
Marketing model

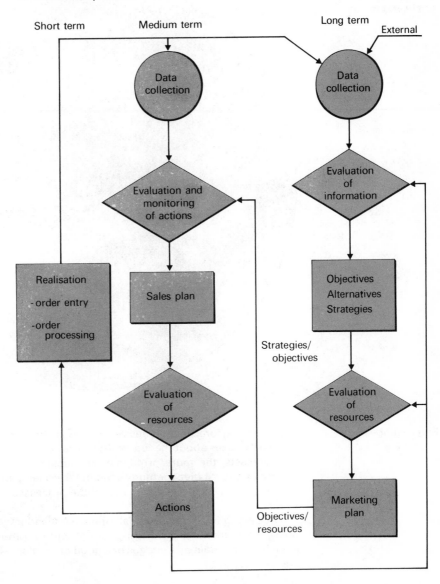

Market appraisal

● regions
● customers

Fig. 6.5.3 shows the way a marketing system looks from a computer's point of view, and has three main functions: data collection, evaluation, and preparation for management decisions. A related summary of marketing areas that can be computerised is shown in Fig. 6.5.4.

Fig. 6.5.4
Marketing
applications

Forecasting—
modelling

When making forecasts it is necessary to analyse information about the past to make inferences about the future. The more accurate, precise and quantitative our forecasts, the more profitable our business will be. There are a great variety of quantitative methods used in forecasting and they differ greatly in the extent to which they try to model the processes which determine future events.

Forecasting is a necessity in all branches of industry, it is used in deciding policy on marketing, advertising, stock control, production and personnel planning. The main advantages of a good computer sales forecasting system are:

Speed of response. Forecasts can be produced very quickly after the receipt of the latest set of demand figures.

Impartiality. The computer has no axe to grind and is neither optimistic nor pessimistic.

Presentation of results. Well arranged forecasts are given in both graphical and numerical form, and supported by adequate supplementary information and by warnings in the case of crisis or rapidly changing situations.

Convenience. Products can be grouped into classes or into sales areas with very little trouble.

Staff savings. Manual forecasting, especially of lines with a seasonal pattern, can be very time consuming.

Lower costs

In order to calculate a model, a sales history is required and also information about a number of sales periods in a year. This is used to calculate initial values and to look at simulation procedures.

The quality of the forecasts can be assessed by analysing the behaviour of the program in the period following the data used for calculating the initial model, including forecast error as well as demand and forecast and whether the demand is in the normal or fast-smoothing state.

In addition to printing period by period results during the simulation period, the computer can also print block diagrams of the forecast errors during the period and tables of mean and standard variation.

Forecasting must be one of the most profitable areas of computing today.

Distribution

Computers used for distribution purposes can provide typically the following information:

- Forecast *v.* actuals by product and depot
- Contribution of each product
- Profit variance
- Details of products for
  promotions
  multiples
  van sales
- Audit orders for
  credit-worthiness
  promotion validity
  cost of promotions
- Maximise orders validated before loading commences
- Accessible and accurate information on stocks, returns, shortages, in transits
- Forecast products by depot
- Forecast accurate scheduled costed deliveries: when, what, to, from, by . . .

● Proposed vehicle routes
● Fleet utilisation summaries

The problem of distribution as a bridge between production and marketing is compounded by the different operational time scales of these two functions. The trouble is that information is already available in the ordinary manual processing cycle, but is seldom accessible in the right form in the right place at the right time, and the computer can overcome these defects.

Problems

Some of the problem areas are:
Sales trends not known
Order details required
Credit discount policy out of control
Picking and loading
Stock information
Satisfy customer demand
Minimise distribution cost
Vehicle fleet costs

Fig. 6.5.5 shows how the distribution application areas fit into the functions of planning, execution, and monitoring of results within operating time scales. One computing solution to this achieves the following: collection and organisation of data; forecasts; definition of distribution strategy; planning of all transactions and monitoring them subsequently. Through these activities safety stock levels, depot grouping, delivery sequence, best alternative means of transport, optimum shipping quantities and possible direct deliveries can be achieved at the same time as minimising total cash in storage, transport and handling.

Sales administration, distribution and information (SADI)

Companies engaged in distributing finished goods to customers and stocks in warehouses or depots have to look at sales administration distribution and information (SADI). This assists the user in minimising his total distribution costs while maintaining stocks to supply his customers according to the most economic level for his business by using mathematical techniques that have been established as the most appropriate for forecasting demand and allocating goods to meet that demand economically. The system should be designed with the business user in mind and cater for many practical conditions that exist in the distribution of consumer packaged goods. It should also address the entire distribution area, in helping management to evaluate many alternative strategies and then, when a strategy has been selected, execute the necessary clerical procedure and monitor the transactions to ensure that the conditions on which the original strategy was based remain valid.

By reference to historical data, forecasts for the future demand for all products by distribution depot are made and assistance is given to the user in determining the most economic level of stocks required to meet that demand at each depot. SADI also enables the choice of the most economical way of supplying each depot from alternative factories and central warehouses, and the selection of the best types of transport. It then helps in choosing the best

Fig. 6.5.5
Distribution
application

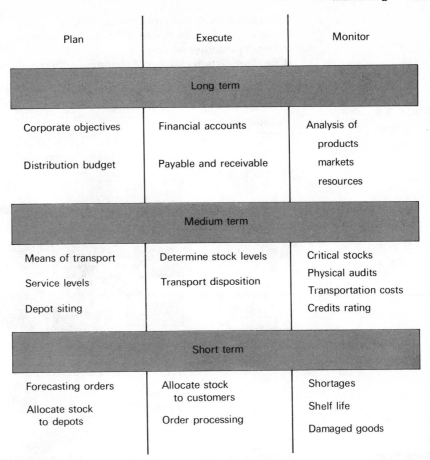

Plan	Execute	Monitor
Long term		
Corporate objectives	Financial accounts	Analysis of products
Distribution budget	Payable and receivable	markets resources
Medium term		
Means of transport	Determine stock levels	Critical stocks
Service levels	Transport disposition	Physical audits
		Transportation costs
Depot siting		Credits rating
Short term		
Forecasting orders	Allocate stock to customers	Shortages
Allocate stock to depots	Order processing	Shelf life
		Damaged goods

replenishment cycle and delivery quantity in each case. Many different distribution policies can be simulated, evaluated and implemented. Sales demand and the disposition of stock, using the selected distribution strategy as a basis for further optimisation, can recommend specific delivery instructions for each product and depot.

The short-term plan modifies the strategy on a short-term basis to meet special situations, such as lack of capacity in a depot, or to combine a direct customer delivery with replenishment of a depot. It keeps figures showing the cost effects of implementing the strategy or of deviating from it, and also monitors the demand to ensure that the conditions on which the strategy was based have not changed.

The period for which the short-term forecast is made can vary between a week and a month. The greatest benefits in stock savings are achieved, if this system is run at the beginning of each depot replenishment cycle, probably daily. Fig. 6.5.6 shows in one form a possible computer solution for a sales administration, distribution and information system for a medium to large size company with a network centre acting as a data base for all operational information. The advantages of such a system are:

● speedy transmission of data, leading to:
● better handling of stocks, vehicles, depot space;
● better customer service;
● flexible system capable of changing with company needs.

Fig. 6.5.6
SADI data
network

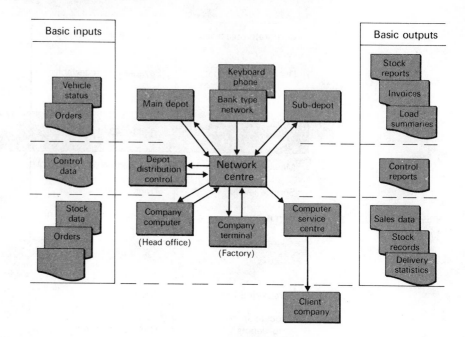

**Data base
management
system**

A data base management system (DBMS) is one of many techniques applied to a variety of information processing systems. It is intended to provide an interface between the actual processing programs and stored data in such a way that the programs are independent, irrespective of the different computer storage methods. The DBMS should be able to translate requests for information which are submitted in user terms into instructions for the computer to locate and select relevant data.

One example of the use of a Data Base system is in Communications Oriented Production Information and Control System (Fig. 6.5.7). The outstanding features of this system are that, in the area of production, valuable information can be provided by:

● a common data base for all of the manufacturing functions of a company;
● an integrated development plan for system design broken down into eight functional areas;
● a modular approach to the installation of applications;
● a clearly defined interface between each function showing how the flow of data reflects the organisation in the factory.

The basic requirements of such a system are that it should be able to change quickly, this being probably the most significant feature of industry today. To reduce delays in communications with all organisations, industry currently

Fig. 6.5.7
Data base system

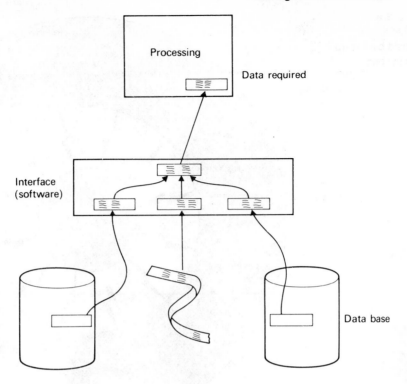

Processing

Data required

Interface
(software)

Data base

devotes a lot of time and money buffering itself against the lack of timely information: to meet management needs by providing such tools as simulated planning aids and controls and to ensure that application planning is based on the user department needs; also to expand applications into areas such as order entry, plant maintenance and cost planning and control, areas which have received less attention in the past. Figure 6.5.8 shows the twelve areas that can be covered in such a system. The system can pinpoint some solutions to these problems and looks at greater control in each area and the benefits both tangible and intangible that can be derived from such solutions.

**Management
information**

A revolution is taking place in commerce and industry which has produced new management techniques aimed at greater efficiency and better management control, which depends on the availability of information about company activity, about accounting, production, sales and service. The information is a normal product of a company's operations but to be of effective use must be collected, assimilated and interpreted as quickly as possible. Fig. 6.5.9 shows an example of various levels of management and some of their information requirements.

**Production and
process control**

Some of the problems of production which can be solved by computer information and control are shown in Fig. 6.5.10. They fall basically into three

Fig. 6.5.8
Twelve areas
covered by a data
base system

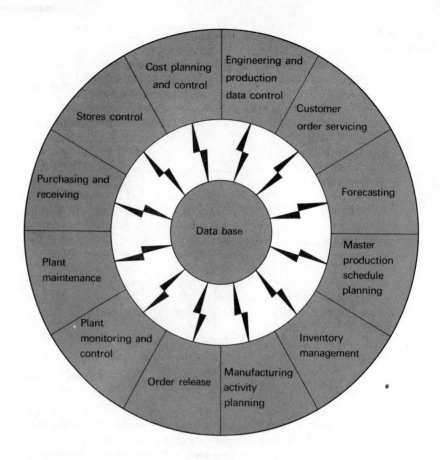

Fig. 6.5.9
Information
requirements by
management

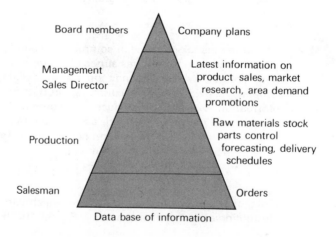

Fig. 6.5.10
Production
problems open to
computerisation

Problems	Information	Applications
Planning		
Long range planning	Marketing plan	Production planning
Capacity planning	Recipes	and intermediate
Intermediate planning	Standards	periods
interface with marketing	Wage forecasts	Products scheduling
and distribution	Resources availability	Purchasing
Scheduling	Demand	
Control		
Raw material packaging	Stock levels	Plant/machine status
Work in progress	Stock withdrawals	Materials control
Wastage	On-order position	
Weight control	Work in progress	
Quality contol	Operational reports	
Optimisation		
Plant efficiency	Maintenance reports	Plant control
Labour efficiency	Output by shift	Recipe optimisation (LP)
Yield	Output by machine	Plan vs actual
Costs	Standards	trend reporting
	Budgets	
	Operating costs	

groups, planning, control and optimisation which are all essentially tasks that management is unable to fulfil effectively if they do not have adequate and timely information. The information they require that can be supplied by the computer is shown in Fig. 6.5.11 together with applications which could be used to provide information needs for problem areas in production. The information necessary is normally already provided, but is either incomplete, too late or too inaccurate to assist in the solution of problems.

Fig. 6.5.12 shows an overall system and flow of applications in a computer materials control system, and Fig. 6.5.13 shows the various external systems that provide the necessary information to make a total system operate. Its main function is as a record keeping system which highlights exceptional conditions to management. The large number of records necessary to keep a proper control of stocks is shown in Fig. 6.5.13.

In contrast, a plant control system (Fig. 6.5.14) is primarily concerned with plant operations themselves. Its task is to acquire all information on plant operation and report out of order conditions, yields, by shift, by batch, within a day rather than weeks, as is normally the case. Initially the computer is concerned with direct acquisition of data as an aid to manual control. When this is successfully accomplished and a body of data acquired, then direct automatic control could be implemented (Fig. 6.5.15).

The computer's use in purchasing can liberate the buyer from routine control tasks and present him with facts or calculations relevant to any buying

Fig. 6.5.11
Production
information
available through
computers

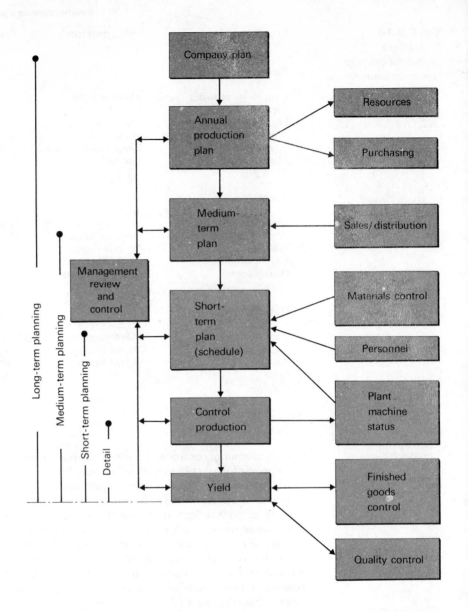

decision so that he can apply his skill to cutting the company purchasing bill. A typical scheme is shown in Fig. 6.5.16 and examples of output are given in Fig. 6.5.17 (= printed output illustration) and in Fig. 6.5.18 (= miscellaneous items).

Process control computers have also been used for many other applications, including online automation of warehouse operations in which the computer takes over the entire running of the warehouse.

Fig. 6.5.12
System and flow
of applications in a
computer program for
materials control

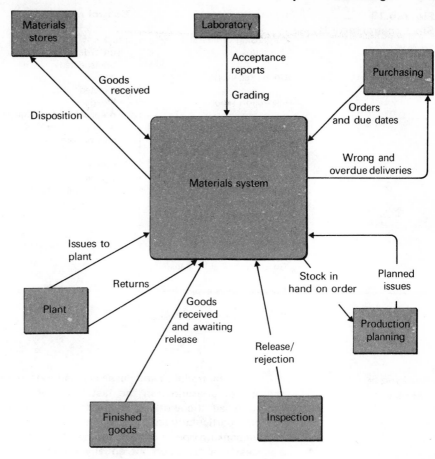

Computer aided design

Computer aided design (CAD) in its broadest interpretation includes simulation techniques, design of engineering components and even company modelling. It leads to three general benefits:

- improved design both technical and economic;
- improved coordination between design and production;
- shorter lead times.

CAD could also lead to new conceptual approaches to design, as manufacturing problems are more likely to be considered early in the design stage leading to cost savings. Design times can be reduced, with greater coordination between design and production giving shorter lead times and increased competitiveness. Lead times can be reduced by factors of 2 for pipe detailing, twenty for prestressed concrete beams, 30 for machine components, and 100 for hydrostatic bearing design. UK government statistics give the current value of the designing functions as £ 1000 millions per annum. The Department of Trade and Industry's CAD Centre has assessed the savings from using CAD in engineering design applications as 20 per cent, that is £200 million per annum, although it is thought that the savings could be even greater due to designs based on new concepts and improved manufacturing procedures.

Fig. 6.5.13
Stock control records

Inputs	Control records	Outputs
Purchasing orders and due dates	Stock on order uninspected passed rejected	Overdues Dispositions Below standard materials
Goods received		
Inspection reports	blends preprocessed awaiting tests issued to plant part packed	
Blend requirements		Planned vs actual availability
Planned requirements for processing packaging	Finished goods ageing awaiting inspection	
Issues to plant planned unplanned		Scheduled requirements shortfalls
Returns		Planned issues not taken up
Goods to be held for test		Issues overplan and returns
Goods to be released		
Goods to await reprocessing		

**Banking by
computer**

Banks were, by tradition and necessity, cautious in their attitude to changes in methods of operation. In the last ten years, however, computers have revolutionised the working methods of Britain's major banks and have reached a particularly advanced stage of development. The sheer overall size of many banking operations and their scattered nature posed many problems to successful automation but, equally, the benefits of better, faster and wider services for customers were seen to be enormous.

Among the many applications handled are the cheque sorting operations: up to one million cheques, drawn on accounts held, are stored and reconciled each working day. The cheques come in from other banks in random order. They are sorted into the appropriate sequence for subsequent account debiting by reading the magnetic ink characters along the bottom edge. Part of this sorting operation is carried out by optical character readers processing cheques at the rate of 50 000 per hour.

Setting up necessary links between the computer centres and the hundreds of branch offices throughout the country posed a major initial challenge. This challenge was met when the first online bank teleprocessing system in the UK to provide full output and enquiry facilities came into service.

To update central accounts instead of the tape being carried by special messenger to the central point as in the past, the tape can now be read into the terminal installed at the branch and transmitted over high-speed lines to the central computer. In addition, these terminals are fitted with keyboard printers, providing the branch with certain enquiry facilities. Operators at each branch can use the terminal to key in customer's transaction data directly into the central computer throughout the day, and the central files can be interrogated at any time for detailed information on any customer's account.

Fig. 6.5.14
Plant control
system

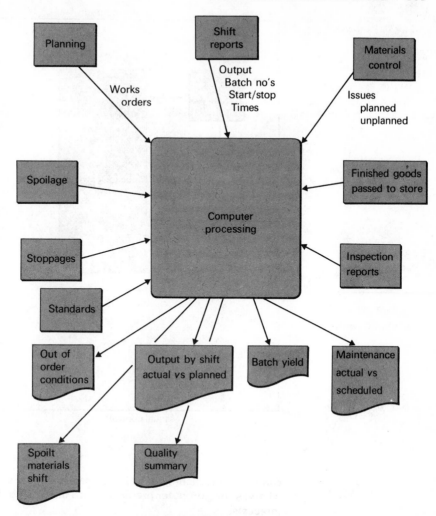

**Reservations:
airlines and hotels**

To give a faster and better service to customers is the prime objective of a computer-controlled reservations network. This is applied to both hotel bookings and airline seat reservations. The booking clerk, having a keyboard video terminal, can interrogate a central data base of information to determine, for example: whether a double room with bath is available in the Canary Islands or whether he can have a first-class flight to Tenerife that evening. These systems are valuable as an administrative network and normally result in cost savings because of the speed and availability of the information facilitating maximum bookings at all times.

Weather forecasting

Weather forecasting is at present a two-stage process; wind pressure and temperature distributions at some time in the future are predicted, and the weather is then deduced from them. The first stage is done to a large extent by computer. The United Kingdom Meteorological Office, for instance, uses

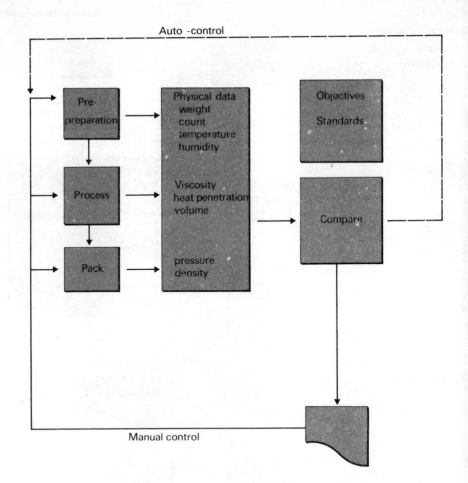

Fig. 6.5.15
Automatic control

computer forecasting for all its forecasts of upper air winds and temperatures, whereas the computer predictions are used as guidance only for the surface forecasts.

Observations of meteorological parameters are made at many places throughout the world, both at land stations and on ships. A fairly dense network of surface reports is supplemented by a less dense network of upper air reports, whilst information from satellites is becoming of increasing value to the forecaster. This raw data is transmitted through a communication network which is rapidly becoming automated, so that most of it is available in the main meteorological offices of the world within a few hours of the time of observation.

The network of observing stations is not regular, and the incoming data has to be analysed by computer in order to produce values at a regular grid of points for subsequent use in numerical weather prediction. Stringent quality control of the raw data is exercised, both for internal consistency and for compatibility in time and space.

The behaviour of atmospheric motions is an initial value problem, governed by a complicated non-linear set of partial differential equations in order to produce short, medium and long range forecasts and has made national

Fig. 6.5.16
Uses in purchasing

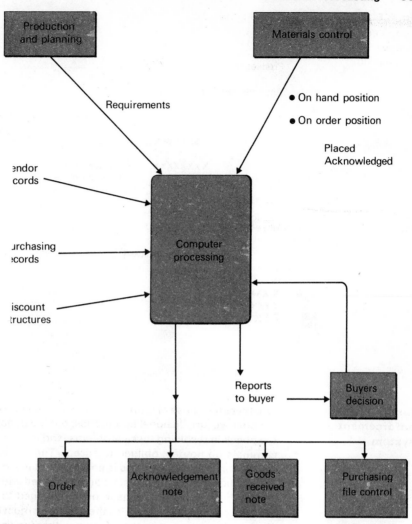

meteorological centres and research institutes customers for large 'number-crunching' computers.

Operational forecasts are made twice daily on a computer, using a ten-level model with a horizontal grid of 300 km which covers a large part of the Northern Hemisphere. A 72-hour forecast takes about 38 minutes; this time does not include that spent on preparing and analysing the raw data. Another limited area version of the model, with a much finer horizontal grid of 100 km and the capability of producing quantitative forecasts of rainfall amounts, is at present undergoing operational trials.

Fig. 6.5.17
Computer
printout
(purchasing)

For the buyer _____

Product required _____ X ____

Amounts required _____ A on $-/-/-$
                             B on $-/-/-$
                             C on $-/-/-$

Previously purchased from _____

X X X X X X X   A tonnes on $-/-/-$
Y Y Y Y Y Y Y   B tonnes on $-/-/-$
Z Z Z Z Z Z Z   C tonnes on $-/-/-$

Vendors for this product

	Indices				
	Quality	Delivery	Overall	Price	Discount group
V VVVVV V	—	—	—	—	—
W WWWWWW	—	—	—	—	—
X XXXXXX	—	—	—	—	—
Y YYYYYY	—	—	—	—	—
Z ZZZZZZ	—	—	—	—	—

City Police law enforcement system

Whatever the cause of crime, it is up to the police to cope with it. Criminals do not observe jurisdictional boundaries, but the police do. Computers can assist the police in resolving these problems, and in overcoming the handicaps that criminals do not feel obliged to accept. The challenge to develop computer systems in police operations is enormous. It is a dynamic operation in which information processing must be accomplished with great precision, accuracy, and high speed. Systems have been designed to reflect the real life of the criminal environment, in which the computer must be the servant of the officer on duty. Departmental policy demands that the computer must respond to a request for information within ten seconds. The system must function as an integral part of police operations rather than a computer environment into which the officer must be regimented.

The citizen's right to privacy is a most important factor in police information systems. In order to ensure confidentiality, the police department has established strict rules controlling the information recorded by the computer. Computers are used today to improve the quality of life, yet to some they symbolise the unresponsiveness and insensitivity of modern life. To others, computerised information systems represent the very latest form of pollution. It assumes that the general public will accept automated systems, once they have been assured that computer information systems have been designed to process and disseminate information in an ethical way. These systems are already used in America and are becoming more common in the UK, where computers are also used for such applications as fingerprint recognition, traffic control and even parking.

Fig. 6.5.18
Purchasing
information
(miscellaneous
items)

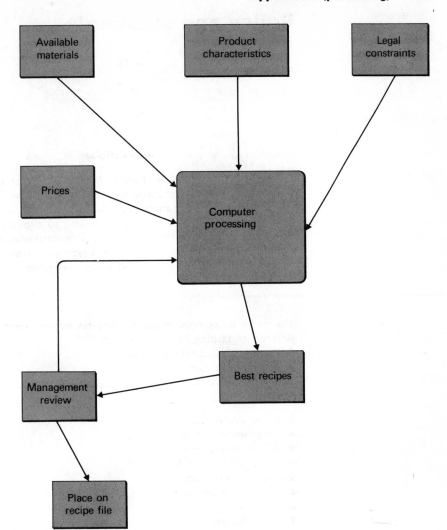

6 Policy and standards

Manuals

A policy and standards manual is necessary for any organisation using computers, whether it be a service bureau or an in-house machine. The objectives of such a manual are to lay down guidelines for the application and running of computers and systems and to provide a standard of recommended practice for the computer users, consultants, management and all technical staff concerned with the design or control of computing systems, including business systems and management services departments.

Policy objectives

The main objectives of policy may be summarised as follows, with some pointers regarding implementation:
1. Review and updating of policy
2. Policy implementation
3. Achievement of maximum profitability, efficiency, and effectiveness through:

- guidelines to best use
- maximise cost effectiveness
- use of experience
- management involvement
- avoidance of duplication
- assessment of needs and facilities
- formulating standards
- compatibility

Computer policy

Some important areas to be dealt with are:

- Organisation of computer affairs
- Application development
- Investment authorisation
- Compatibility
- Relationship with suppliers
- Software
- Hardware
- Data communication
- Time sharing
- Management education
- Personnel

- Information and communication
- Cost effectiveness
- Charging out
- Quality assurance
- Standard practices
- Security and insurance

All points of policy should be detailed in the standards manual, which should deal with both standard methods and performance standards.

Establishment of standard methods

These interpretations are closely related. The establishment of standard methods within a company or department will provide a basis for measurement of the performance of individuals or groups. As experience is gained it will be possible to set performance targets with increasing accuracy so that improved control of projects will be possible.

The main objectives of business systems and computing standards can be summarised as:

(a) to specify uniform methods and procedures for carrying out routine tasks so that the amount of time that professional staff can devote to professional work is maximised;

(b) to provide a formal mechanism for gathering and exchanging new and improved business systems concepts and techniques, so that all can benefit from the experience of others;

(c) to ensure complete and accurate documentation of all projects, thus allowing an orderly transfer of the completed system from a development group to one or more operations groups and facilitating system maintenance;

(d) to establish methods whereby management may control and participate in projects;

(e) to provide a basis for the training of all staff working in the business systems and computer areas;

(f) to provide flexibility by reducing dependence on individuals.

Plan of the manual

The manual is best written in modular form and can be arranged in several parts to include the following subjects:

- Management
- Application development
- Computer centre operations
- Typical documentation
- Data compatibility
- Systems techniques
- Programming techniques

Contents of the parts

Part I. Guidelines and principles for management concerned with the control of business systems and computer applications, and typical subjects are:

1. Introduction
2. The Computer Steering Committee
3. Consulting support
4. The Computer Feasibility Study
5. Project selection
6. Selection of computer facilities
7. Analysis of costs and benefits
8. Organisation and personnel
9. Project control
10. Security
11. Review of operational systems
12. Appraisal of computer centre.

Part II. Guidelines and principles for the conduct of a project until it has been accepted as a working system by the operational group or groups. It also includes systems maintenance, i.e. changes to an operational system. No attempt should be made to cover areas which are dependent on a particular manufacturer, machine type or programming language.

Part III. Guidelines and principles for operating a computer centre; as with Part II the subject matter should be independent of computer type and language.

Part IV. Typical forms which are useful for controlling and documenting projects and managing a computer centre.

Part V. Data compatibility techniques intended to enable transfer of data between companies.

Parts VI and VII. Material on techniques applicable to specific languages and computer types.

People, education and training

Training in the data processing field is particularly important because of the rapid changes that computer technology is undergoing. Areas to consider on a continuing basis are not only the correct selection of personnel who are suitable for specific jobs taking into account their experience, ability, creativity, education matched to company requirements, but also education and training of both the technical specialist and user management.

There is a serious danger that the need for specialisation could give rise to the computer men not being able to interface effectively with other members of the company and therefore training should be directed to helping them understand company problems and to communicate with non-computer personnel and to developing their specialist knowledge. On the other hand, user management must realise that the computer is a tool to aid them in their work and therefore they should be trained to use this tool.

Quality control and project evaluation

An essential requirement of any computer system is the continuing evaluation of projects to ascertain whether the original objectives of the system are being met. To determine whether the users are satisfied with the system and whether any operational improvements to the system need to or should be made, and lastly to provide feedback on system design, estimation, programming and planning, to the staff involved in the project. This post-implementation follow-up review should be initiated by the data processing manager and will of course involve the user management involved in the system.

Checklist for
Cyclic Review

The following points should be considered:

Does the system meet the requirements of user management?
Does the system meet the requirements of user operational staff?
Is the error rate in input within normal limits?
Is the error rate in output within normal limits?
Does the input reach data preparation section on time?
Does the input reach operations section on time?
Does the output reach the user on time?
Are the input documents and forms properly used?
Is the output properly used?
Are suitable facilities for the despatch or filing of output available?
Are the error routines satisfactory?
Are the clerical procedures properly understood and used?
Is any coding scheme properly used?
Is the user documentation complete, available and satisfactory?
Is the systems documentation complete, available and satisfactory?
Is the operations documentation complete, available and satisfactory?
Is the security copy of the documentation complete, available, properly stored
   and satisfactory?
Are adequate supplies of forms, etc. available? And is the re-ordering
   automatic?
Are the input and output volumes in accordance with predictions?
Are program running times as estimated?
Are the master files accurate?
Are the master files of the predicted size?
Do the programs meet the required standards?
Are the operational costs as predicted?
Were the development costs as predicted?
Have the envisaged savings been achieved?
Can improvements to the programs be made by recoding?
Is the division of the processing into programs satisfactory?
Is the division of programs into modules satisfactory?
Is core occupancy as predicted?
What problems have been encountered by the users?
What problems have been encountered by the data processing units?
Are security precautions adequate?
Is the audit trail (i.e. performance checking program) adequate?
Is the original purpose of the system still valid?
Is the original purpose of the system being met?
What other purposes is the system satisfying?
Could these purposes be met by alternative means?
What hardware feature now available could be utilised within the system?

Is the combination of programs practical and desirable?
Is reprogramming necessary?
What software features now available could be utilised within the system?
Has the documentation been updated with all modifications?

Computer information systems appraisals

Computing is a resource which needs careful review and control if it is going to make an effective contribution to the profitability of the company. Effective computing does not just happen, it must be planned, just as we plan for all other management tasks. To get the most out of our computer investments application development must be profit oriented and we should be monitoring the cost effectiveness of the resources employed. Techniques to evaluate the effectiveness in a limited way do exist, although true cost effectiveness is difficult to measure. However, a procedure for the appraisal of a computer unit has been developed successfully.

The appraisal should be carried out by a mixed team of house and outside staff to ensure an unbiased but acceptable view of the situation.

Areas to be considered

Among the most important areas for consideration are:

Critical application areas
Systems utilisation
Organisation
Documentation and standards
Computer room operations
Personnel
Software and hardware
Long-range plans

Their interrelation is illustrated in Fig. 6.6.1. As a result of such an appraisal immediate cost savings should be realised and should also act as a checkpoint and aid to the effective management of the computer system.

Performance measurements and predictions

Other measurement aids can be used to assess computer performance, the objectives being to provide a basis for assessing efficiency within units and as a means of evaluating any proposed extensions or changes in equipment that may be required. Monitors are used to look at both software and hardware performance, and also benchmark tests to assess throughput of systems using sample programs and simulation:

Performance measurements

● Hardware monitors
● Software monitors

Performance prediction measurements

● Speeds
● Instruction mixes

- Kernel programs
- Benchmarks
- Simulations
- Synthetic benchmarking.

Fig. 6.6.1
Computer
information
systems appraisals

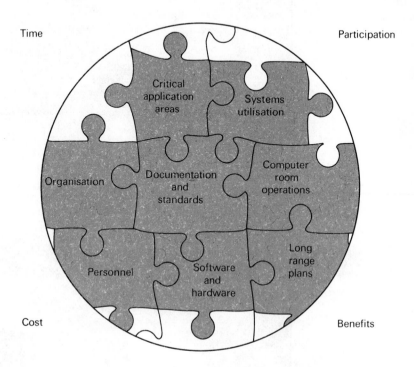

Security of computer and data

Data security can be defined as the protection of data from accidental or intentional disclosure to unauthorised persons and from unauthorised modification. Techniques for security include computer hardware features, programmed routines and manual procedures, as well as the usual physical means of safeguarding the environment.

Security is the responsibility of management, who must consider the risk involved in any environment. For example, a dishonest operator could copy a customer file during, say, a night shift and leave no visible trace. Magnetic tapes can be removed from the library. A program could be altered in such a way that it sabotages the company files, e.g. in financial forecasting a customer file used in a time-sharing system could be changed by a terminal operator interrogating the files.

The cost of complete security is enormous and so certain factors must be carefully considered. What is to be protected? What is it worth to the company? Therefore how much should be spent on security?

Whenever there is a mass of data, some highly confidential, there is always a certain degree of risk. Figure 6.6.2 shows in a simplified way some of the risk areas that need to be recognised.

Fig. 6.6.2
Examples of
security risks to
computer

Nature of risk	Accidental	Intentional
Inability to process	Equipment breakdown Fire Water Impact Power failure Air conditioning breakdown	Sabotage
Destruction of data	Erasure of data Loss of tapes,etc in transit Destruction of program library	Sabotage Theft
Alteration of data	Machine error wrong tape etc mounted	Fraud Sabotage
Compromise of data	Delivery or output to wrong individual	Theft By removal -detectable By copying -undetectable

Social implications   Apart from their scientific and business function, computers have a significant part to play in our social environment. For example, without them it would have been impossible for space research to have taken place, and this could be an important part of our evolution; and computers help in explaining new fields for our schools to influence the teaching of children in more advanced education than ever before. They help the world's transportation, not only in traffic control but in the design and control of our train and aircraft systems. Looking at nature and agriculture, computers are currently working on a problem looking at the feeding of the world's population, not only in the immediate future, but in the year 2000 when it is estimated there will be some six billion inhabitants. In medicine and construction, design and in many other field computers are playing their part in society.

Further reading

LAVER, MURRAY, *Introducing Computers*, HMSO 1973.

NATIONAL COMPUTING CENTRE, *Computers and the Year 2000*, 1972.

HOLLINGDALE, S. H. AND TOOTHILL, G. C., *Electronic Computers* (Penguin Books, 1970). Explains how computers work, how problems are presented to them, and what sort of jobs they can tackle.

GRINDLEY, K. AND HUMBLE, J., *The Effective Computer—A Management by Objectives Approach*, McGraw-Hill, 1973

BINGHAM, J. AND DAVIES, G., *A Handbook of Systems Analysis*, Macmillan, 1972.

STURT, H. AND YEARSLEY, R. (Editors), *Computers for Management*, Heinemann, 1969.

Marketing and Educational Publications on Computing Systems—available on request from most computer manufacturers and computer software companies.

SHERRILL, R. C. (Editor): *Dictionary of Inventory Control Terms and Production Control Terms* (plus related terms from Data Processing, Operations Research, Industrial Engineering, Cost Accounting). Third edition, 1970: American Production and Inventory Control Society.

ROSE, MICHAEL, *Computers, Managers and Society*, Pelican, 1969.

PART SEVEN Organisation planning and management development

by N. V. Terry and E. F. L. Brech

1 Introduction

The study of organisation structure in chapter 5 of Part One was related to current needs, to the framework of management action as currently carried out. In all undertakings, however, there are occasions when the needs of the future, both short-term and long-term, assume importance and demand attention. Forecasts of policy, of technical developments, of economic expansion, of changes in volume and range of trade and so on, are common features in the practice of sound and progressive management in the production, distribution and service industries. Such forecasts lead on to feasibility studies and provisional budgets for anticipated developments and new activities. These are necessarily in the form of guides which, closer to the time to which they relate, will be turned into specific plans and phased programmes for contemporary action. This forward thinking in terms of financial and physical activity needs to be matched both in terms of organisation structure and in terms of the provision of management competence required to meet the changed circumstances of the future when they are reached.

This juxtaposition of 'organisation structure' and 'management competence' is an essential relationship in looking to the future. Projected changes in the pattern of responsibilities which pay regard to future conditions have a meaning only in so far as they are directed to providing a framework for the management process which is better suited to the new conditions. They therefore provide a pointer to the future needs in terms of skilled management manpower. In this sense, the forward look at management responsibilities involves two closely interrelated topics which can usefully be labelled as 'organisation planning' and 'management development'.

It will be interesting for a moment to look at the circumstances from which the impetus for such a forward-looking approach may arise. In general terms, of course, the impetus will come from known or expected change: the era in which we live is one in which change is the most significant feature, whether in technological fields, economic conditions or social values. Some of the recent changes are, indeed, so dramatic as to justify use of the popular term 'explosion'. Such explosive effects of change are well exemplified by the measure of recent growth in two directions, both of which have exerted significant influences on management philosophies and practices.

Takeovers and mergers

The years spanned by the late 1960s and early 1970s have seen a remarkable growth in the number of financial deals which have resulted in takeovers or mergers of industrial and commercial enterprises. Fig. 7.1.1 (based on figures published in the *Financial Times*, 15 February 1973) shows a measure of this trend in the United Kingdom alone.

Fig. 7.1.1
Acquisitions
or mergers in
the UK, 1968–72

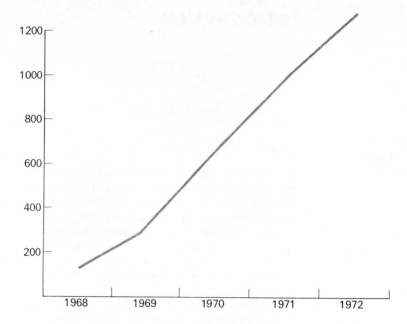

Assuming that each of the transactions which took place during this five-year period involved *only two* companies—the acquirer and the acquired—then the figures graphed indicate that several thousands of organisations were drastically affected by these deals. In fact, because more often than not several different enterprises were involved in each transaction, an even larger number of organisations have experienced the traumatic impact of this growing incidence of changes of ownership and consequent shifts of management responsibility and authority.

In the special context of this present Part, some of these effects have been farreaching and disruptive. Large numbers of managers who had never before been faced with these kinds of problems have been required urgently and critically to examine the organisation structures of separate enterprises which have, literally overnight, become joined together as one concern (in terms of ownership of their assets at any rate) and must henceforward share a common management direction and pursue mutually beneficial objectives. The special emphasis on problems of organisation planning and management development which stem from the effects of takeovers and mergers will be amply demonstrated by examples in later chapters.

Systems and
computers

During the same five-year period, managements in Britain and other major countries in Europe experienced another kind of 'explosion'—the upsurge in development and uses of automatic data processing systems based on electronic computer equipment. Fig. 7.1.2 (based on figures extracted from a European Economic Community policy memorandum[1]) gives some idea of

[1] *Industrial Policy of the Community*, Memorandum of the Commission to the Council, Brussels, 1970, Table 20.

Fig. 7.1.2
Requirements of
data processing
personnel
in UK

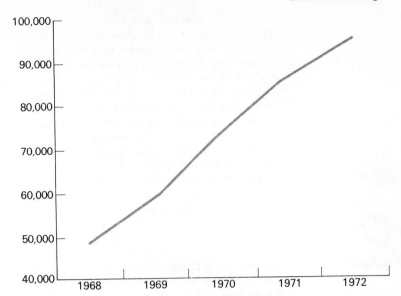

this rapid rate of growth as measured in terms of the numbers of trained personnel required to operate this specialised equipment and to interpret its output in language capable of being used for purposes of management.

Although the impact of this rapidly mounting use of data processing systems on forms of management organisation and patterns of delegated authority is unlikely to be as farreaching and revolutionary as many people at first believed, it undoubtedly has important implications, which will be examined in later pages.

Economic changes

Changes in economic and marketing situations which face industry and commerce are perhaps less spectacular; their effects are less readily discernible and more diffused. Nevertheless they too present managements with new situations and new challenges which place unusual strains and stresses on the ways in which they are organised and staffed. The shrinking of many hitherto established and 'safe' markets abroad has given way to opportunity for opening up new markets elsewhere. This has had special significance for the United Kingdom which, as a latecomer to the EEC, has been faced with particular problems in establishing its role in the Community. Coupled with shifting balances of trade, in both older and newer markets, there is developing a greater discrimination on the part of the consumer, imposing a greater emphasis on quality and variety of choice. At the same time the consumer tends to have more money to spend, while manipulation by the advertising media gives rise to a greater instability in his attitude and approach to spending it.

Change on this scale and in this wide variety of directions makes great demands on the capacity of management to adjust established organisations and practices. The impact leaves no aspect of management untouched. It brings into question existing policies, frameworks of responsibilities, technical resources, attitudes and abilities of existing managers. Above all, it heightens the demand and sharpens the evidence of need for personal competence. This fact is loudly echoed in the current cry of all industrial and commercial circles—the lament over the shortage of high-calibre professional managers and the seemingly meagre returns from incessant and expensive search. And yet, paradoxically, this constant quest for more and better ready-made managers (as manifested by page after page of costly display advertising in the 'quality' newspapers) tends simultaneously to highlight and to obscure organisational and other weaknesses within the companies concerned. For how many of these eye-catching advertisements, jostling each other to secure the services of unlikely paragons of all the management virtues, are spelling out confessions of failure on the part of existing managements to identify and get to grips with their own problems? How many of them represent pious hopes that solutions to these problems can be 'bought in' like raw materials or office stationery?

Social factors

Aside from such irony, other factors of a social kind are increasingly reinforcing emphasis on management competence; such factors as the increasing levels of education of the men and women employed, their growing awareness of personal and civic rights, and even the new strongly based position of the trade unions at national and local levels, claiming a responsible share in the affairs of industry and gaining the membership and allegiance of groups whose almost blind loyalty to management would have previously gone unquestioned. Also in recent times there has been some coalescing of public conscience about a number of seemingly unrelated matters concerned with the influences of industry, commerce and government on the social environment as a whole: matters such as preservation of the countryside, the control of pollution, the protection of the retail consumer, and more and better safeguards against misuses and abuses by monopolies of one kind or another.

It would seem that these significant shifts in social values and increasing public awareness are generally preceded by a good deal of well-intentioned resolution and even more lip service to the ideas they represent. But undoubtedly the writing is on the wall. This coming decade will see increasing loads of responsibility thrust on the shoulders of management for affairs which are not only those of industry and commerce as they have hitherto been understood, but for affairs which affect the community at large. And the higher the position of the manager in his own hierarchy, the fuller must be his responsibility, the greater his need for rounded professional competence. Also the clearer must be the lines through which he apportions and delegates parts of these complex responsibilities to others who in turn must be managerially competent as well as being socially aware.

Such wider issues aside, even in the context of a single enterprise, wisdom and prudence dictate investment for the future in two related fields: continuing development and adaptation of the organisational framework and the constant flow of qualified and experienced personnel effectively to conduct the processes of management through that framework.

2 Organisation planning

As defined in Part One, organisation is the *framework of management in action*. It is that aspect of planning which is concerned with determining and delineating the pattern of delegation of responsibilities by means of:

- dividing the total management responsibility and accountability between executive and specialist positions;
- defining the delegated responsibilities attaching to each position;
- establishing the formal relationships between the positions to ensure coordination of understanding and effort.

The overall pattern which emerges as the result of this delegation and sharing of responsibilities between the different executives and specialists is the *organisation structure,* the notional framework through which the declared purposes and the prescribed process of management are put into effect.

Existing structures

Since some form of organisation pattern, however simple or shortlived, is necessary whenever two or more people combine their efforts towards the same end, it follows that *every industrial and commercial undertaking already has an organisation structure.* But the extent to which this represents a pattern of delegated responsibilities which has been consciously planned and conscientiously promulgated by management is a matter for conjecture.

Before going on to examine the purposes and practices of organisation planning, it will be useful to consider a few of the virtually limitless number and variety of factors which could have contributed in some way or other towards determining the existing form of organisation of an industrial or commercial enterprise. Among the things most likely to have influenced its organisational development are:

- nature of the products or services being marketed; types of technology involved; relative intensities of materials, labour or capital content;
- numbers, sizes and locations of sites or premises in which operations are performed and the business is conducted;
- numbers and characteristics of the staff and operatives employed: ratios of professional, technical, skilled and unskilled workers;
- historical growth pattern of the undertaking itself: whether still basically the original single enterprise or now an amalgamation of two or more concerns;
- financial structure of the enterprise: whether privately owned, limited liability with restricted shareholdings or public company, whether wholly owned or partially owned subsidiary of another undertaking;

- past and present conditions of marketing: fluctuations in demand for labour required, materials consumed or products or services offered;
- extent to which general attitudes and behaviour have in the past been influenced by the personal traits and idiosyncracies of individual top managers;
- record of the chief executive and his senior departmental managers in constantly reviewing, planning, adapting and staffing an organisation structure suitable to the needs of the business.

Some inferences may be drawn from this list of 'likely factors'. First, because every organisation represents the results of an infinite number of interacting influences, no two organisation patterns (like fingerprints) can possibly be exactly identical. Even apparent similarities, viewed superficially, may be deceptive and misleading—a point to which reference will be made in a later section. Secondly, because so many of the contributing factors are subject to frequent, even random, movement, it follows that the organisation structure itself must to some degree be in a state of continual flux, albeit imperceptibly. After all, how could any arrangement which provides a framework for the activities of *people* remain completely static? Thirdly, and perhaps most important, it is evident from study of the likely factors that conscious and continuous management action represents only *one* of the complex of influences which may have determined the form, and indeed the effectiveness, of an organisation structure. Even where there is little discernible evidence of deliberate management action at all there is still a recognisable organisation structure. In short, organisations, like living organisms, tend to grow and develop untended.

Factors influencing structures

In the light of these comments, it would not be unreal to suggest that the form of organisation structure of almost any enterprise at any one time is to a large extent 'accidental' in nature. It may indeed be accidental in the fullest sense of the term, namely that nobody can recall when anybody gave any prolonged and serious thought to or took any deliberate decisions about the pattern of delegated responsibilities: that is to say, what exists today is what has emerged through custom and practice over the years, any decisions for change which *have* taken place being based on emergency, expediency or other purely short-term considerations.

Nevertheless, even assuming that the organisation structure has been thought about, has been planned and coordinated and staffed, it must still remain accidental to the extent that it reflects environmental features which are beyond the power of management to change immediately. For a simple example, suppose that the existing organisation structure of a manufacturing company is dominated (and fragmented) by the fact that its main activities are being conducted in half a dozen small and widely dispersed factories. It may be that there exists an agreed policy and a phased rationalisation programme for reducing the number of plants in the future. But in the meantime, the present organisation structure, with all its defects of splintered communication, coordination and control, must continue to operate as an expression of the realities.

A negative influence which may at first seem to be accidental (in the sense of being a matter of chance) is really an example of 'organisation planning by default'. This kind of situation not uncommonly occurs when the chief executive and other members of senior management become fully alive to some serious weakness or anomaly in the organisation arrangements, but then shy away from making any plans or taking any positive action to remedy matters. Their failure to act may be due to a number of reasons. It may be because the managers concerned simply do not know how to go about making the necessary organisation changes without risk of causing so much upset that the ailment would seem preferable to the cure. Or they may have persuaded themselves that, left undisturbed, the situation will work itself out and time alone will solve the problem. This latter course (which could be a perfectly proper decision) calls for brief comment. It will be emphasised later that the careful and judicious use of *time* is of the utmost importance in purposefully planning and implementing changes in an organisation structure. But time (or *timing*) must always be related to a reasoned forecast and a planned programme of change, no matter how crude this may be in concept or how frequently it may have to be revised in the light of subsequent events.

Most of the factors listed above, which might to some extent or other have combined to determine the existing pattern of organisation, could be generally described as 'environmental' in that they reflect the influences of external conditions and surroundings, past and present. Only one, the last mentioned, focuses on effects resulting from the exercise of conscious and positive *management planning and control* over the growth, shape and balance of the organisation structure. Of the two levels of management specifically mentioned (that is the chief executive or his senior departmental managers) it is generally found to be the latter—the specialist heads of the main groups into which the total operating responsibilities of management have been divided—who appear to exert more management influence (where it does occur) over shaping the form of the organisation structure.

Personal influences

A little consideration shows why this is not very surprising. It has been demonstrated that the essence of organisation is delegation. Once the total responsibility for management operations has been initially delegated and divided among a number of primary positions, then the manner in which these specialist functions subsequently develop tends largely to reflect the personalities and abilities of the holders of the key departmental appointments and, in course of time, those who for one reason or another succeed or replace them.

One of the most obvious personal responsibilities of the chief executive is that of *coordinating* the activities of the various departments and functions into which the total management task has been divided. That is to say, it is his responsibility, and his alone, to supervise all departmental activities and to ensure that they are being effectively discharged, balanced and coordinated towards achieving the total objectives of the organisation—a situation which he, and he alone, is in a position properly to judge.

A further responsibility of the chief executive, which is perhaps somewhat less obvious, is that of constantly and critically observing the *internal* organisation arrangements of the specialist departments and functions; this is to ensure that responsibilities are clearly defined and shared, and that departmental key positions are occupied by people who are competent and up-to-date in their specialised knowledge and experience. Assuming that this responsibility is acknowledged, the question might well be asked, how many chief executives are *qualified*, by training or experience, to make such critical reviews and judgments?

By common tradition the majority of managing directors or general managers have themselves graduated from being departmental heads in one or other of the specialised divisions of management, e.g. marketing, production, finance. Very few indeed have ever had any formal instruction or depth of experience within any other major function of management. Possession of specialised professional or technical competence in one area hardly equips a chief executive to judge whether or not all the other management functions for which he has become primarily responsible are, within themselves, properly organised and adequately staffed.

Thoughts expressed in the above paragraphs draw attention to a remarkable omission from the commonly accepted *lingua franca* or jargon of management as it is observed to operate in practice. The term 'organisation planning' is seldom encountered, except perhaps in the rarefied context of a giant industrial corporation or one of the nationalised industries. This lack of familiar usage of a term which defines a most significant aspect of the management process implies, surely, a lamentable neglect or sometimes total absence of the function itself. Thus, although a responsibility to ensure the continuing viability and effectiveness of the organisation structure falls squarely on every chief executive, there are substantial reasons for believing that more often than not this duty is honoured in the breach. It is fair to say, of course, that organisation planning is one of the few top management responsibilities which can never be wholly delegated to another person. Thus the managing director who appears to be neglecting this important duty may be doing so simply because he cannot find the time personally to attend to it. This problem and ways and means of overcoming it will be discussed in a later section.

Organisation studies

The foregoing pages were devoted to looking at some of the reasons why and the ways in which organisation structures originate and develop. It has been demonstrated that, by and large, the processes of change are engendered and conditioned more by environmental or personal factors than by conscious management intention and design.

It could be the case, of course, that when diagnosing and dealing with the endless problems and crises which seem to assail the average Managing Director and his senior colleagues, there emerges very little evidence even to suggest that any of their difficulties stem, directly or indirectly, from faults in the organisation structure. This would not be remarkable, because, unless they are of a really gross character, organisational weaknesses and shortcomings are not often readily apparent and recognisable as such; they tend to become overlaid and obscured by the effects of other kinds of management problems.

To examine and appraise an organisation structure with the object of identifying specific shortcomings under existing conditions (quite aside from discerning any changes which will have to be made to meet future conditions) calls for close and detailed observation of the structure *in action*. It involves the systematic collection, careful analysis and objective evaluation of factual information and personal opinions in order to arrive at worthwhile conclusions which in turn will lead to plans for improvement. Such an approach to the study of organisation in depth will be considered at length in later pages. Nevertheless, it is quite feasible to carry out a limited survey or rough 'health check' of an organisation by asking some pertinent questions. If such questions are answered thoughtfully and truthfully, the results could lead towards isolating and identifying weaknesses in the substance of an organisation structure: they could promote the further investigations and actions which would be necessary to deal with such weaknesses.

Organisation
checklist

A checklist of questions has been compiled to provide a basis for conducting such a survey. This questionnaire might at first give an impression of bringing scrutiny to bear on several seemingly diverse and unrelated aspects of the process of management in action. But it will become clear that they are all in fact directed towards finding the answer to a single question, a question which presents the ultimate test of every organisation structure: 'Is delegation clear in principle and effective in practice?' It will be expained how each one of the facets of management touched on by the questions represents and reflects to some extent the effectiveness or otherwise of the pattern of delegation of responsibilities, the organisational framework through which the processes of management are carried out. This list of management activities is grouped under the following broad headings:

- Organisation charts
- Management job descriptions
- Committees
- Communications
- Salary structures

The checklist should be studied and used in the light of the following remarks:

All the questions are designed to call for 'yes' or 'no' answers.
No attempt has been made to attach special significance or weighting to any single question or group of questions.
A 'no' response to a question *suggests the possibility* of a weakness or anomaly somewhere in the organisation structure.
The larger is the total number of 'no' responses, the greater is the need to carry out a critical study of the organisation structure in depth.

The checklist is followed by further explanation and discussion of the questions and their wider implications in the context of organisation structure.

Checklist:
(1) Organisation
charts

1. Does there exist an overall[1] organisation chart (supported where necessary by clearly related subsidiary or departmental charts) depicting all the managerial, senior specialist and supervisory positions?

[1] The term 'overall' is used here to indicate two distinct implications: it means that (i) the organisation structure being reviewed is 'self-contained' to the extent that ultimate responsibility for its operational activities as a unit devolve upon a single top executive, e.g. Managing Director, General Manager, Factory Manager, Departmental Head. In this sense, therefore, the 'overall organisation' could be the whole or any part of an undertaking which is capable of being separately studied as an operating group or unit; (ii) 'overall organisation' as used here also indicates at least the topmost *two* levels of management positions, i.e. those directly responsible to the top executive and the next level of positions appearing directly below.

2. Is there a single individual who is responsible for drafting and revising the *overall* organisation chart?
3. Have all the organisation charts been approved by the chief executive?
4. Have the charts been reviewed and updated within the last six months?
5. Have copies of the charts been circulated or made readily accessible to *all* the position holders whose names appear on them?
6. Does each 'position box' on the charts indicate clearly:
   the department or function?
   the position title?
   the name of the position holder?
7. Is the management structure, as depicted in the organisation charts, free from examples of :
   the holder of a position being apparently responsible to more than *one* superior?
   one position holder appearing to have direct responsibility for more than *six* interrelated managerial, specialist or supervisory positions?
   four or more 'levels' of management or supervision intervening between the chief executive and the point of actual operations?
8. Do the organisation charts reveal consistency in the uses of position titles? For example, do titles such as 'Manager', 'Superintendent', 'Section Leader', 'Foreman', in each case seem to embrace roughly similar allocations of responsibility and accountability?
9. Does the layout and form of presentation of the organisation charts appear to be free from attempts to ascribe special personal status to *some* position holders by use of such devices as enlarged 'boxes', thickened lines or heavier type-faces?
10. Is there reason to believe that *all* the holders of positions shown on the organisation charts are satisfied about the manner in which they and their departments are depicted?

Checklist:
(2) Management job descriptions

11. Do there exist management job descriptions relating to all the major positions (defined in item (ii) of the footnote on page 927) delineated on the organisation charts?
12. Is there a single individual who is responsible (on the chief executive's behalf) for initial drafting and ultimate circulation of management job descriptions?
13. Have the position holders and their immediate superiors actively participated in the preparation of their respective management job descriptions?
14. Have the management job descriptions been reviewed and updated within the last twelve months?
15. Do the contents of each management job description include:
    (a) definition of the position to which the job holder is directly accountable?
    (b) definition of the positions for which the job holder is directly responsible?
    (c) indication of positions with which the job holder will maintain essential co-operative relationships?
    (d) clear definition of the responsibilities allocated to the position?

Checklist:
(3) Committees

16. Have the purposes, terms of reference, constitutions and operating procedures of all 'management boards', committees, subcommittees, working parties (either permanently or temporarily established) been stated in writing and issued to members concerned?

17. Do the memberships of such committees seem to be in keeping with the overall organisation pattern and the allocation of management responsibilities?

18. Are the agenda and necessary working papers of committees issued far enough in advance for members to be able to prepare for meetings?

19. Are brief and accurate minutes of proceedings of committees issued promptly to members and other interested parties?

20. Have all the existing committees been reviewed by a single individual within the past twelve months in order to recommend whether they should be modified or discontinued?

Checklist:
(4) Communications

21. Do management distribution lists covering the issue of written communications (e.g. policy directives, organisation announcements and other kinds of instruction and information) conform to the pattern of delegated responsibilities which is jointly portrayed by the organisation charts and management job descriptions?

22. Is there a single individual who is responsible for issuing comprehensive and classified management distribution lists and for ensuring that they are kept up to date?

23. Does the cost centre system for preparation, authorisation and control of expenditure budgets (capital and revenue) clearly and manifestly conform to the visible pattern of organisation structure?

24. Do the procedures which provide control data for the review of management performances work smoothly and promptly?

25. Is there freedom from justifiable complaint by managers and supervisors about the distribution, timeliness and effectiveness of management communications?

Checklist:
(5) Salary structures

26. Is there a clearly defined salary structure and fringe benefits plan covering *all* managerial, senior specialist and supervisory positions?

27. Have the salary 'curve' and grade limits of the structure been established by systematic analysis and objective assessment of the positions included in the structure?

28. Is there a single person who is responsible to the chief executive for day-to-day administration of the management salary and remuneration plan?

29. Are there tangible and acceptable reasons for believing that:
    (a) payments and other benefits extended to management grades are compatible with those offered by other employers for positions carrying comparable responsibilities?
    (b) arrangements for the periodic review of senior salaries and fringe benefits are fair and equitable—and are manifestly seen to be so?

It was suggested at the beginning of this section that, if the foregoing questions are objectively asked and honestly answered, the results could represent a considerable movement towards recognising and remedying *organisational* weaknesses. Therefore it may at first seem surprising that the scope of some of the questions ranges well beyond those features of management which are customarily associated with the subject of organisation structure. But it must be remembered that organisation structure is itself a reality only in the sense of being a framework through which *all* the processes of management are carried out.

The most commonly recognised and generally understood way of expressing the existence of this management framework is by means of an organisation chart—or 'family tree' as it is often mistakenly called by those who, in so doing, betray their lack of understanding of the subject. Indeed, it is probably no exaggeration to say that for the majority of managers at all levels in most undertakings, large or small, the subject of organisation structure begins and ends with organisation charts. To many of them, directors, executives, even management consultants, a set of nicely presented, well proportioned and symmetrical diagrams denotes the existence of a well balanced and effective organisation in practice. This, of course, may be no less than the truth. Certainly, the good features of a soundly conceived organisational framework are bound to be to some extent reflected in the organisation charts. But the converse is by no means true. A seemingly acceptable, clear and tidy organisation chart may present something of a deceptive picture; it may be a mere gimmick, a glossy veneer below which the nature of the organisation structure as it actually operates leaves a very great deal to be desired.

Therefore, in order to achieve a proper perspective by referring to facts and opinions about the organisation *as it is operating in practice,* the checklist questions have been designed to probe into a number of different aspects of management in action. Each of these groups of management activity is to some extent a dynamic and tangible expression of the notional concept of organisation. Each provides some kinds of criteria by which the effectiveness of organisation can be assessed. To understand this more clearly, it will be useful to consider and comment on some of the underlying implications of questions posed under each of the functional group headings.

Notwithstanding the limitations just mentioned, organisation charts, properly used, are indispensable tools for the purposes of identifying, discussing and helping to secure widespread understanding of the pattern of delegated management responsibilities and the resultant interrelationships. It is a somewhat surprising fact that although organisation charts have been a familiar feature of the management scene for more than fifty years, there have not yet emerged any generally accepted standards of practice regarding their construction, contents and methods of use. Therefore the ten questions listed under the heading 'Organisation charts' are aimed towards highlighting the main essentials against which the form and practical uses of organisation charts can be evaluated: that is to say, what kind of information they contain, to whom they are circulated and what kind of anomalies they are likely to reveal. The last four questions in this group (nos. 7–10) are deliberately designed to seek out possible evidence of some of the more commonly encountered faults in organisation structure.[1]

Management job descriptions

The very existence of a set of properly conceived management job descriptions may be regarded as the hallmark of good organisation planning. For it is in the preparation and publication of management job descriptions that the purely conceptual idea of organisation structure as a notional framework comes closest to being translated into concrete terms. Lest the word 'hallmark' should seem extravagant in this context, let it be stressed that any top management which has even *recognised* the necessity for preparing and using job descriptions has taken the first major step towards securing a sound and balanced organisation structure through which to carry out its management processes. Accordingly, the initial question posed under the heading 'Management job descriptions' (no. 11) establishes whether or not this vital first step has been taken. The remaining questions are devoted to eliciting facts about how and where the management job descriptions originate and about the kind of information they contain. It will become apparent later that these questions, by their very nature, indicate the principles according to which management job descriptions should be devised and administered.

Committees

The forms and purposes of committees are considered and discussed at some length in chapter 8 of Part One of this volume, where the following sentences occur (see page 102):

'*Per se,* the committee forms a valuable *framework* for cooperative human effort'.
'In effect, a committee has the equivalent of a *management job description.*'

These two statements support the notion that, for practical purposes, the committee can be regarded as a component of organisation. It provides a *temporary* 'framework within a framework' for conducting some part of the process of management. The word 'temporary' is also a reminder that, like organisation structure, committees are abstract in character to the extent that they exist *only* when they are in session. Outside the committee meeting, members do not possess any special authority or responsibility by virtue of membership alone. This ephemeral nature of committees makes it all the more essential that they should be effectively constituted and properly conducted in a manner which accords with the wider framework of management: the organisation structure.

Experience has shown that for all practical purposes the establishment and operation of management boards and committees can sensibly be regarded as an aspect of the organisation planning function. It will be noted, therefore, that the tone of questions asked about committees (nos. 16–20) strikes the same keynote as those asked about other matters which plainly have to do with the organisation structure in action.

[1] More detailed checklists for examination of 'weaknesses' in organisation or 'criteria' for assessment will be found in E. F. L. Brech's *Organisation: the Framework of Management,* chapter 6 (page 157) and chapter 12 (page 447).

Communications

It seems quite logical to associate *communications* with *organisation*. For communication, the act of systematically imparting information, presupposes the existence of an orderly pattern of channels through which the information can be swiftly and accurately conveyed, and through which the required responses can be quickly sensed. It seems ironical that in this age of advanced methodology for reproducing and transmitting information, a high proportion of managerial misunderstandings, frustrations and failures can be clearly ascribed to breakdowns in communication. Out of the myriad causes of such breakdowns, human and mechanical, the questions listed under 'Communications' (nos. 21–25) isolate a few of those which signify *organisational* weaknesses of one kind or another. It may be regarded as axiomatic that an organisation structure which is in any way unbalanced or unclear cannot possibly support reliable systems of communication and control.

Salary structures

It was suggested above that mere existence of a set of well conceived management job descriptions is itself a sign of sound organisation. The main purpose of job schedules is, of course, to clarify the specific responsibilities and accountabilities which attach to each management position. They are impersonal in the sense that they define the *job only,* without reference to the *job holder.* But they do tell a great deal about the nature of the demands which are made on the job holder in terms of his capability to discharge the responsibilities of the position and (as will be seen later) they are used as a basis for preparing a *personal specification* of an individual suitable to hold the position. It is therefore reasonable to suggest that not only should the levels of *reward* for the job be commensurate with these personal demands, but they should be capable of being demonstrated to be so. This is to say there should be a cohesive salary structure within which every management position has been analysed, appraised and evaluated in terms which express the relative contribution it makes to performance of the total management task. When all the resultant valuations of individual jobs are compared with each other, the pattern of differentials which emerges should perceptibly conform to the general profile of the organisation structure. In this way senior salary planning may be regarded as a close concomitant of organisation planning. Certainly it is fair to say that a balanced and equitable remuneration structure simply cannot exist within an unbalanced and inequitable organisation structure.

Organisation responsibilities

It will be observed that the phrase 'Is there a single person who is responsible for . . . ?' appears repeatedly throughout the list of check questions. In light of the proposition that organisation is primarily concerned with the delegation and definition of responsibilities, *it is especially appropriate that responsibilities for the establishment and maintenance of organisation should be properly defined and specifically allocated.*

It was pointed out in an earlier passage that responsibility to ensure continuing effectiveness of organisation in its various facets falls squarely on the chief executive. It was also acknowledged that, because organisation completely permeates and deeply influences the *mores* of the total undertaking, this is one of the few top management responsibilities which can never be *wholly* delegated to others. Thus there arises something of a paradox.

Reflective scrutiny of replies made to the checklist questions will almost certainly reveal that the majority of the 'no' responses can be traced back to a common cause—the absence of a single individual who is responsible for that particular group of organisation-oriented activities; or to put it simply: 'Anything which is anybody's or everybody's business is at risk of becoming nobody's business.'

How, then, can a busy chief executive, who plainly cannot attend to the detail of such matters himself, take steps to ensure that these organisational responsibilities are defined and discharged? There is, of course, no single answer to such a question. There are a number of practical approaches to the problem and possible courses of action will vary widely according to the size and nature of the organisation. But since there is small doubt about the importance of the topic, chapter 8, under the heading 'Whose responsibility?', is devoted to discussing the subject in depth. Meanwhile, as and when it is necessary to make references in the text to a 'responsible individual' and to the tasks which he is required to carry out, the term *organisation planner* is used. It denotes a particular person who is directly accountable to the chief executive for the performance of these tasks: it does not in any other way indicate his position or personal status within the management structure.

Results of survey

Let it be assumed that, using the questioning method described in preceding pages, a rough 'health check' of an organisation in action has been carried out. This preliminary survey might have been undertaken by the chief executive himself or he could have delegated the task to the organisation planner. In either case, information and opinions would have been sought from other senior members of management and every possible effort would have been made to ensure that the questions were answered factually and frankly.

Now arises the need to assess the results of the survey and to draw useful conclusions from them. First let it be said that it is extremely unlikely that all, or even most, of the questions will have been answered in the affirmative. If in fact all the questions listed deserved truthfully to be answered with 'yes', there would be scant need to worry further about the effectiveness of the organisation structure. This is not to imply that the questionnaire frames a counsel of perfection, esoteric and unattainable. On the contrary, it is manifestly plain that these simple questions do not betoken anything which is outlandish or even unusual in character. What *would* be remarkable would be to find *all* these features of the management process being conducted, coordinated and controlled equally satisfactorily within a single undertaking. Certainly the co-authors of this text, who share a considerable length of experience in varied fields, both as consultants and as executives, have never encountered such a well integrated organisation.

Suppose, then, that the answers to the questionnaire have shown up a number of 'no' responses. Taking an objective and common sense look at the replies recorded within each group of questions could possibly have produced some interesting slants on the present degree of effectiveness of that particular aspect of organisation. Much more likely, however, it will have revealed how little relevant information there is available for making a proper assessment. In short, the results of this arbitrary spot check will not provide sufficient reliable evidence on which to base plans for organisation changes or developments of any real significance. The questionnaire represents no more than the first phase of a fact-finding procedure. In some ways it is analogous to the approach that a physician would make to a new patient who is suffering from some undiagnosed chronic complaint. The doctor would first carry out an overall routine examination in which, by questioning and observation, the whole of the patient's anatomy, major organs and bodily functions would be systematically checked. At the sign of any particular abnormality or malfunctioning, the doctor would proceed to carry out or to set in train much more detailed examinations of the affected parts or functions. These investigations could be quite lengthy and involve various kinds of measurements and tests, but they would be designed primarily towards diagnosing and quantifying the precise nature of the patient's disorder. Only after carefully evaluating the results of such a study in depth would the doctor prescribe an appropriate course of treatment.

So, let it be assumed that, by employing the checklist on organisation to make a preliminary diagnosis, enough doubts and uncertainties have been raised—or enough questions left unanswered—to convince the chief executive of the need to set in motion further investigations about the present state of the organisation structure.

3 Organisation study in depth

This chapter considers ways of assembling and analysing detailed information about an existing organisation structure. It discusses methods of presenting the relevant facts and opinions in such forms that they can be easily assimilated and objectively discussed.

Before proceeding with an organisation study there are certain formalities to be observed. The word 'formality' is used deliberately here as meaning 'etiquette or precision of manners'—for it will be seen that *successful* organisation planning constantly demands the employment of sensitivity and good manners. Thus a first courtesy would be to inform a number of people that an organisation study is about to take place, by whom it will be carried out and what purposes it is expected to achieve. Precisely who these people will be and how they will be informed depends largely on the size of the undertaking and the numbers involved. It is a reasonable rule-of-thumb, however, that the chief executive should personally speak about the matter to *all those who are directly responsible to him*. This verbal briefing should then be confirmed in writing with copies distributed fairly widely amongst those who are likely to become involved, directly or indirectly, in the fact finding part of the exercise. The memorandum reproduced below exemplifies the kind of tone which such an announcement ought to strike.

From: The Managing Director

Organisation Study

This is to confirm that I have asked Mr John Blank to carry out a study of our present Company organisation structure and to submit proposals as to how it might be developed to meet known future requirements.

Initially Mr Blank will be approaching you to seek facts and opinions. In due course he will discuss with you his findings and draft recommendations before presenting a final report to me.

Date: Signed...........................

This simple example of an introductory announcement calls for the following comments:

(*a*) It has been assumed that 'John Blank' (the organisation planner) would be known at least by name to all the recipients of the note. Supposing this was not so, the wording would have to be varied accordingly: for instance '...Mr John Blank, who recently joined the Company as...' In these circumstances Mr Blank would require to be introduced to people as he met them.

(b) The undertaking given in the final sentence that the organisation planner will 'discuss his findings and draft recommendations' may seem somewhat surprising. Recognising how delicate can be the topic of organisation and its repercussions on the status and personal images of individuals, any commitment to share discussions about possible changes would at first appear to be very rash indeed. It will become more and more apparent, however, that widespread and uninhibited consultations are essential features of effective organisation planning and its realistic implementation. Therefore the sooner conditions are created for such open consultations the better. It need hardly be stressed that these undertakings must not be given unless there are good reasons for believing that they can and will be observed.

(c) Generally speaking, responsibility for drafting the initial announcement about an organisation study can best be left to the organisation planner himself, even though it will *always* be approved and signed by the chief executive. The example quoted above is an extremely simple one: it could well be that more information requires to be imparted at this early stage (as a later example will show) and it is the job of the organisation planner, from the very outset, to create the atmosphere in which he is going to work; to set the stage for what will quite possibly be the first project of this kind to be carried out in the history of the enterprise.

(d) Distribution of notices advising the start of the organisation study also requires careful thought. Most executives become extremely touchy about being (in their view) unjustifiably omitted from such distribution lists. It is always better to 'overdo' the issue rather than run the risk of news about the impending investigation being spread by hearsay among those people who need to be informed that it is taking place. More often than not this question becomes simply a matter of forethought and good manners.

Assembling facts

The first part of the organisation study would be devoted to assembling the material required for preparation of an organisation chart (or charts) of the management structure under review. Ideally, this task of constructing organisation diagrams should be carried out *ab initio*—that is to say it should be a completely new exercise which does not require to make use of any existing organisation charts; the reason for exercising caution here is that information derived from existing charts (which were doubtless originally drafted in perfectly good faith) could prove to be positively misleading in the context of the present exercise. It would be necessary, then, to assemble a certain amount of personal data about all the members of management from the chief executive downwards. These facts would require to be tabulated under the following column headings:

Column
1. Department or function
2. Name

3. Appointment title
4. To whom directly responsible
5. Number directly supervised
6. Age
7. Length of service
8. Staff category
9. Annual salary
10. Comments

The significance of the column headings and ways of obtaining and presenting the required information are discussed below.

1. The heading *Department or function* would in the first instance represent the primary breakdown of responsibilities directly under the chief executive, e.g. Sales, Accounting, Manufacturing, Personnel, Purchasing. These categories might later become further subdivided e.g. Home Sales, Export Sales, Mail Order Sales.
2. The list of names to be included will depend on whether this first organisation study is to be fully comprehensive and to cover *the whole of the management structure,* or initially to 'skim off' the top management only. In the former case the names listed would exhaustively cover *every staff employee who is responsible for the work of others.* The alternative approach would call for use of some arbitrary criterion to signify membership of top management, such as a certain minimum salary level or pension grade. Criteria for recognising the higher levels of management will vary between different firms and forms of industrial and commercial activity, but it has been found that in most small and medium-sized companies, the category 'monthly paid staff' itself provides a reasonably accurate collective description of senior management personnel.
3. Under *Appointment title* would be entered the style by which the position holder is presently known or, to be more precise, the title above which he signs correspondence.
4. The entry *To whom directly responsible* is self-explanatory: it is also the most vital piece of information needed for constructing an organisation chart and must therefore be plain and unequivocal.
5. Under *Number directly supervised* would be entered the total number of staff or hourly-paid employees who are *immediately responsible* to the appointment holder.
6. *Age* would show the present age of the appointment holder within six months (e.g. 42).
7. *Length of service* would also be expressed in years to the nearest six months (e.g. 25).
8. Entries made under *Staff category* (or a similar heading) would relate to the locally accepted practice of grading or classifying staff employees. It could signify merely 'Weekly paid' or 'Monthly paid'. Or, where a formal salary structure exists, it could denote a particular staff grade or other mark of staff status.
9. *Annual salary* would be expressed as a total figure to the nearest £1, whether paid monthly or weekly. (The question of confidentiality is referred to below: see pages 940 and 1015).
10. The final *Comments* column would be left as spare for later entry of additional information or notes.

To ensure uniformity of presentation and to facilitate later study and analysis of this information, it would be advantageous to have prepared beforehand a supply of duplicated forms with the numbered column headings already shown.

**Collection
of data**

It would be extremely unlikely that all the information called for could be made available from any single source. This means that responsibility for mustering the data would almost certainly have to be delegated on a 'department or function' basis (see column 1). In other words, the manager or senior executive of each main division of the organisation would be required to cause the information to be assembled in respect of the managerial personnel within his own department or function. It is from this early starting point that the organisation planner should himself become closely involved in the exercise. He should seek opportunity to speak personally to each departmental head with the main objects of:

- explaining the purposes for which the information is required and how it will be used;
- handing over an adequate supply of blank 'data forms';
- accompanying these, where desirable, with a set of suitable explanatory notes (along the lines enumerated under items 1 to 10 above);
- offering to assist and explain further to those who are charged with the tasks of actually completing the forms;
- giving assurances that any departmental organisation charts which are drafted on the basis of information thus provided will be reviewed and discussed with the managers concerned before being finalised.

The assembly of part of the required information should be largely a straightforward matter of checking through personnel records or payrolls. Some of the facts called for, however, could pose problems, especially those items which precisely define *to whom* and *for whom* each individual member of management is responsible. It is possible that in some cases this particular information has never before been asked for, and some hard thinking may have to precede provision of the answers. It would always be advisable for the organisation planner to collect the completed forms personally. This would provide him with opportunity to check quickly over the various column entries, to query and clarify any obvious errors or omissions, also to discuss any problems which may have come up when compiling the information. Furthermore, these personal contacts and discussions would help towards cementing the basis of frank and informal relationship which must essentially develop between the organisation planner and all the key managers and executives in the organisation.

**Organisation
charts**
Preparation

The next task for the organisation planner would be to prepare a draft organisation chart or, more likely, a set of such charts. These would present in diagrammatic form all or most of the information which has been collected, so that it would be easier to assimilate the facts, to understand their significance and to discern the relationships between them. Two points must be made about the drafting of organisation charts at this stage of the study. First, all the information required for the preparation of accurate charts should be available from the completed forms. Second, the draft diagrams would be intended to serve no purpose beyond the one stated above, that is to facilitate understanding, further analysis and meaningful discussion.

The basic framework of an organisation may be constructed from information provided in columns 2 to 4 of the prescribed data collection forms. These entries show executives' names and appointment titles, and specify to whom they are directly responsible. The actual method of establishing the resultant organisation pattern is a somewhat empirical exercise. It consists of identifying the holder of the most senior appointment shown on a sheet (or set of departmental sheets) and then picking out the number and names of people who are shown as being directly responsible to him. Having thus determined the number (and occupants) of 'position boxes' which will appear directly under that particular appointment, these are roughly charted on a first draft diagram. The 'counting off' process is repeated at each level, working downwards, until all the names on the sheets have been accounted for and have been roughly mapped out on the draft chart. A simple illustration of this method of orienting a list of executive appointments into a discernable pattern of line relationships is shown in Fig. 7.3.1.

Fig. 7.3.1
Extract from
data form

Name	Appointment title	To whom responsible
2	3	4
A.Smith	General Manager	
B.Jones	Production Manager	A.Smith
J.Jenks	Press Shop Manager	B.Jones
K.Read	Assembly Manager	B.Jones
L.Lewis	Chief Inspector	B.Jones
E.White	Chief Engineer	A.Smith
M.Owen	Plant Engineer	E.White
P.Davis	Chief Draughtsman	E.White
R.Short	Production Engineer	E.White
C.Green	Commercial Manager	A.Smith
F.Black	Chief Accountant	C.Green
D.Brown	Production Controller	A.Smith
G.Blue	Senior Buyer	D.Brown
H.Robb	Stores Manager	D.Brown

Outline chart

The outline chart shown in Fig. 7.3.2 has been constructed from the above data. It will be noted that this empirical method of drafting a first diagram employs the *names* only of the appointment holders, rather than the appointment *titles*. Experience shows that, because there may be several appointments bearing the same title (e.g. Foreman), the 'personal name' approach provides the most practical and reliable way of establishing the pattern of relationships in the first instance.

Fig. 7.3.2
Outline chart

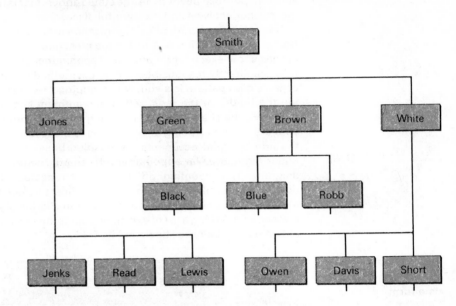

This kind of draft outline structure would now require to be refined and elaborated to display more information. Exactly how much personal data about individuals should be included in the charts would need to be decided. Perhaps the only item of personal information which could arouse doubts about being openly published on a chart would be salaries. The problem could easily be overcome by masking actual salary figures behind a simple coding system, the key to which would be available only to those who ought to know. Accordingly, on the assumption that *all* the information that had been collected would be embodied in the organisation charts, it would be necessary to devise some method of presenting the information in diagrammatic form. A way of doing this would be to record relevant data in the individual boxes relating to each management appointment, as shown in Fig. 7.3.3.

It was remarked earlier that there are as yet no generally accepted standards of practice regarding the construction, contents and methods of using organisation charts. Thus there is considerable scope for exercise of ingenuity and initiative in designing these pictorial presentations of a management organisation structure. This is aptly demonstrated by the bewildering variety of so-called 'family trees' of widely differing shapes and sizes which are to be seen—sometimes faded and yellow with age—displayed in managers' offices or to be found locked away, dusty and unused, in the drawers of their desks.

Guidelines

The serious organisation planner will find that at a very early stage in his activities it will be necessary to establish and observe some simple rules for the preparation of organisation charts. The more essential of these guidelines are discussed below under three headings: *clarity, consistency* and *courtesy*.

Fig. 7.3.3
Information
diagram

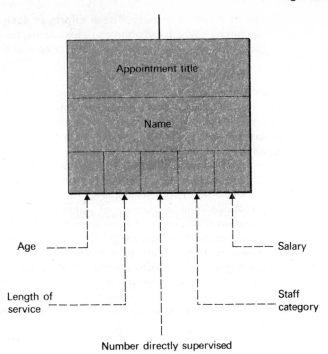

Organisation charts should be clear and unequivocal in what they are designed to convey. Two-dimensional diagrams, however artfully drawn, have their limitations and it is impossible to portray with precision a pattern of delegated responsibilities and resulting interrelationships on an organisation chart. It is therefore important to take good account of these limitations and studiously to avoid presenting information in any way that could be regarded as being obscure, confusing or ambiguous.[1] Some commonly encountered examples of departure from clarity are:

Clarity

- Showing a position holder to be apparently responsible to more than one person (usually by tentative addition of some faintly dotted lines!) without giving any explanation of this seemingly anomalous situation.
- Seeking to signify differences of status or personal importance between two position holders, both of whom answer directly to the same person. This is usually done by locating one 'position box' lower down that the other on the diagram: sometimes the effect is sought by varying the sizes of the boxes or the thickness of their frames.
- Crowding overmuch information on to a single chart, with the result that either the diagram becomes too big to handle comfortably or the details become too small to read easily.
- Attempting to illustrate any 'special relationships' that may be known to exist between position holders by the use of dotted lines or by connecting

[1] Charts are more fully considered in *Organisation: the Framework of Management*, page 430 and following.

lines of different colours. These efforts to spell out on a diagram inter-relationships which are often complex can be, perhaps more than anything else, the cause of an organisation chart becoming obscure and confusing.

Consistency

In addition to being clear and unambiguous, organisation charts should be consistent in their mode of presentation. That is to say, whoever produces them and for whatever purpose, all organisation charts issued within the same undertaking should follow a single style of presentation, layout and general appearance. Thus consistency of mode of presentation will gradually lead to the establishment of a kind of common sign language which everybody concerned has learned to read and to interpret quickly and easily. In spite of (or maybe because of) the widespread existence of organisation charts mentioned above, this uniformity of approach to the mechanics of drafting organisation charts is rarely encountered. On the contrary, frequent examples are to be seen of managers publishing purely departmental appointment announcements which are supported by 'attached diagrams'. These departmental organisation charts are often meticulously designed and beautifully reproduced—thus endowing them with an air of importance and authority. But they are as variegated in style of presentation as the number of departments whose internal appointment changes they are variously designed to support.

Courtesy

A reference has already been made to the importance of remembering to observe the common courtesies during the conduct of organisation planning activities. The need to extend thoughtful consideration to those people who might be affected is especially important in the preparation of organisation charts. It should be regarded as axiomatic that no diagram depicting the management structure of a department or function should ever be *published* (that is reproduced and circulated) until after it has been agreed by the head of that department and any of his subordinates whom he may wish to nominate. Much ill feeling is undoubtedly generated as a result of failure to observe this simple act of courtesy.

Uses of
organisation
charts

The foregoing guidelines would generally apply to the preparation of any kind of organisation chart, whatever purpose it was intended to serve. It must not be forgotten, however, that—notwithstanding their limitations—organisation charts are flexible management tools which can be used in various ways to achieve different ends. Such purposes would include:

1. Assisting towards gaining rapid understanding of the overall framework and salient features of an *existing* organisation. This refers to the kind of situation envisaged above, where overall study in depth of an organisation has been initiated. As may be seen later, these charts would be used primarily for communication and discussion purposes. It is possible that they would be reproduced for limited circulation.
2. Serving to illustrate some of the effects of likely changes arising out of tentative proposals for a *future* revised organisation structure and allocation of responsibilities. In this case the charts would have been drafted to

provide a basis *for exploratory discussions only.* Such consultations would almost certainly result in some amendments to the proposals and only a single copy of the chart would be drafted at this stage.

3. Supporting and illustrating the effects of authorised organisation and appointment changes. This kind of chart (which would be an attachment to a formal announcement) would be intended to *inform and instruct* the recipients about new organisation arrangements. Changes so announced could range between a single management appointment to a widespread company reorganisation: the number of charts circulated would vary accordingly.

4. Forming components of an overall 'Organisation Manual' or 'Organisation and Policy Manual'. Used in this way the charts would form a part of the permanent (and continually updated) formal records of the overall organisation arrangements of a total undertaking. Their purpose would be primarily *for information and reference* and they would be widely distributed amongst members of management.

Further mention (and some examples) of these different types of organisation charts appear in later pages.

Charting an existing organisation

One such example emerges from the situation described on p. 940. On that page is shown a rough outline sketch of part of an existing organisation (Fig. 7.3.2). The elementary diagram has been constructed from certain basic data and it now requires to be further refined and developed. It needs the addition of more information about individual appointments and it requires to be 'shaped' into a form suitable for presentation, and possibly also for reproduction of additional copies.

The organisation chart shown at Fig. 7.3.4 (overleaf) has been expanded and developed from the rough outline sketch. The chart serves to illustrate the *existing* management structure of a light engineering factory employing about 350 people. The plant, one of a number of subsidiaries of a company which supplies the automotive industry, fabricates large and small metal stampings. These, together with some bought-in items, are assembled to form major components of the company's products which are finally assembled and finished at other factories in the group. This plant, originally owner-managed, was acquired by the parent company about three years ago. All marketing and finance is now handled by a distant Group Headquarters, whence a certain amount of loosely defined functional direction and control extends to the plant, mainly in the areas of production engineering, production scheduling and industrial relations. The General Manager of the plant is responsible to the Group Director of Production.

Although it is not the intention to develop this situation fully as a comprehensive case study on organisation, these brief details of the background circumstances are sketched in to facilitate understanding of the notes and comments about Fig. 7.3.4 which follow:

Layout and presentation

It will be seen that twenty-six 'position boxes' have been plotted on the chart. These represent all the appointments in the plant which can be defined as

Fig. 7.3.4
Organisation
structure of a
light engineering
factory

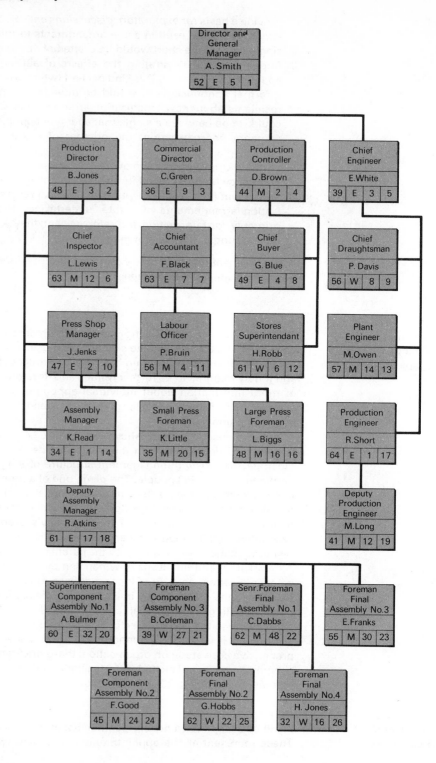

managerial or supervisory, i.e. are to any extent accountable for the work of others. Even showing this fairly large amount of information, the content of the organisation chart would be perfectly legible if it was reproduced on standard A4 size paper (i.e. 210 by 297 mm).

It will be noticed that no attempt has been made to follow what has become almost the traditional 'pyramid pattern' of layout, in which the descending order of management echelons are seen to widen out downwards from the pinnacle of the chief executive. This departure from the more usual style of presentation has two main advantages:

(*a*) substantially more information can be plotted on a single sheet without either overcrowding or wasting space;

(*b*) it becomes immediately obvious that seniority or status of an appointment is not necessarily signified by the 'level' at which it appears on the chart, thus avoiding the need to display a disclaimer of the kind that is often seen, such as: 'This chart is purely diagrammatic and shows lines of executive responsibility only. *It does not purport to indicate levels of status or authority.*'

Only one kind of relationship is illustrated on the organisation chart. This is the clear and unmistakable line of direct responsibility (and reciprocal accountability) which stems from the chief executive and should radiate to every employee in the undertaking. Attempts to reproduce other kinds of working relationships on an organisation chart are generally to be discouraged.

It will be noted that, as a simple but practical feature of layout, the 'position boxes' are uniformly in line when viewed horizontally. This consistent pattern greatly facilitates 'scanning' the chart for purposes of analysing information.

In this particular example of a draft organisation chart, information recorded in the 'position boxes' is codified as follows:

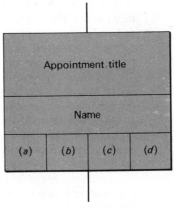

(*a*) = Age of appointment holder

(*b*) = Grade of staff: E, Executive;
                         M, Monthly;
                         W, Weekly

(*c*) = Number of people directly supervised

(*d*) = Serial number of position box
        (for ease of reference)
        reading the chart from left to right

Preliminary analysis and review

Turning again to the conduct of the organisation study, the next task of the organisation planner was to analyse and review the information now displayed on the draft chart (Fig. 7.3.4). He looked for any apparently anomalous situations and took note of any points which seemed to be of organisational significance or which would require further explanation. He then held personal consultations with the departmental heads and their senior subordinates, the latter always with the knowledge of the former. Using the draft organisation chart as a basis for discussion, he would first check the accuracy of the information as presented and then lead on into consideration and explanation of particular features of the organisation. A selection of matters which came up for review and discussion are briefly reported below, together with some generalised observations about their significance.

'One-over-one' positions

Any situation in which a manager or supervisor appears to be accountable for only one other person holding supervisory responsibilities (i.e. a 'one-over-one' position) should always be investigated and the reasons for it established. Four different examples of this kind of situation appear on Fig. 7.3.4, and further enquiries about them revealed the following explanations:

● Until the takeover of the factory by the parent company the Chief Accountant (7) had answered directly to the General Manager (1). Under the new regime an appointment of 'Commercial Director' was created. The Chief Accountant (then aged sixty) was not considered suitable for this new post. It was filled by a younger man from outside and the Chief Accountant became responsible to him.
● Since the time when it was established under wartime legislation, the post of Labour Officer (11) had been responsible to the Chief Accountant (7). Until recently the Labour Officer's duties had been of a somewhat elementary nature, e.g. maintaining statutory personnel records and supervising simple welfare matters. The position was now in course of being developed, however, as a functional outpost to represent the parent company's industrial relations policies and procedures.
● The position of Deputy Assembly Manager (18) had been created only a short time ago. This coincided with the creation of a new appointment of Assembly Manager (14) which was filled by a young man transferred from another factory in the Group. Until that time the present Deputy Assembly Manager (18) had been styled 'Senior Superintendent: Assembly' and had been directly responsible to the Production Director (2) for activities of the seven assembly shops.
● The appointment of Deputy Production Engineer (19) had been deliberately established a year ago to provide a position for the man chosen to succeed the present Production Engineer (17) who was now nearing retirement.

Without seeking to elaborate at this stage on reasons underlying the first three of the above one-over-one positions, it would seem on the face of it that only the fourth example (the deputy appointment specifically created to facilitate takeover of an impending vacancy) was well justified. In other words, from the organisational standpoint, one-over-one positions are to be avoided whenever possible. The appointment of deputy (except under 'planned succession' circumstances like those mentioned above) is a particularly unsatisfactory one, organisationally speaking, in spite of the frequency with which it appears in industrial and commercial undertakings. Reasons for this emerge later in dealing with management job descriptions (see page 955).

Staff grading

At an early stage in his investigations the organisation planner had discovered that the three-tier staff grading scheme (i.e. executive, monthly and weekly) bore little discernible relationship to the *staff salary structure* as such. When plotted on a scatter chart, the ranges of annual salaries currently being paid to members of the three staff grades revealed considerable overlapping, as illustrated by the diagram in Fig. 7.3.5 (overleaf): this demonstrates that not only were higher paid members of each grade being paid more than the lower paid members of the next grade above (a not unusual feature of a salary structure) *but certain weekly grade employees were actually receiving larger annual salaries than some of the executive grades.*

What did emerge from the organisation planner's enquiries, however, was that the grading system represented a kind of hierarchy within which there operated a long-standing tradition of perquisites, privileges and status symbols. Some of the more notable of these forms of class distinction were:

Executive grade   special dining room; free lunches and drinks
coffee served on trays in offices
membership of 'top-hat' pension scheme
personal private secretary
free car servicing
personal car parking bay
key to executive wash-room
first class travel arrangements
six months' termination notice

Monthly grade   special dining room; lunches and drinks on payment
free coffee served from trolleys in offices
share secretary
car parking facilities within factory perimeter
use of monthly grade wash-room
first class travel arrangements
one month's termination notice

Weekly grade   self-service canteen; lunches on payment (subsidised)
use of coffee dispensing machines
use of factory car park (outside perimeter)
second class tourist travel arrangements
one week's termination notice

The illogicality of some of these outdated customs and practices was highlighted when they were profiled against the management organisation structure as outlined at Fig. 7.3.4. For instance, there is a case in which *five* different levels of a single line of management share the same Grade status: they are:

General Manager (1)
Production Director (2)
Assembly Manager (14)

Fig. 7.3.5
Range of
salary grades

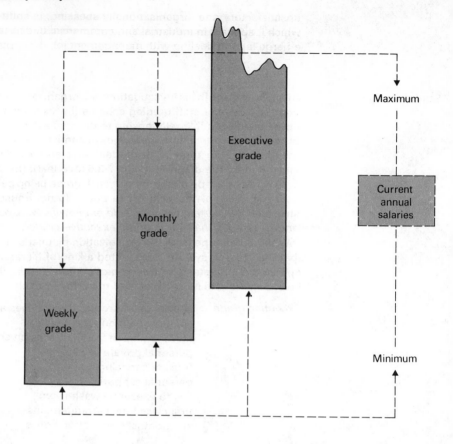

Deputy Assembly Manager (18)
Superintendent: Component Assembly 1 (20)

Another case shows an executive grade employee as being *responsible to* a monthly grade, viz: Production Controller (4) over Senior Buyer (8).

The overall imbalance of the distribution of management positions within the grading system may be diagrammatically demonstrated thus:

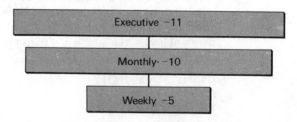

Ignoring for the moment any other effects caused by anomalies in the grading system, the balance of distribution of management positions in an organisation of this kind might have been expected to display something like the following proportions:

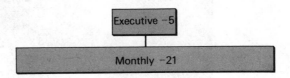

Age wastage

Analysis of the ages of managers and supervisors as charted on Fig. 7.3.4 shows that eight out of the total of twenty-six position holders are aged sixty years or upwards. This figure of 31 per cent, which to some extent reflects the growth pattern of the organisation over the past forty years, is almost double that which could be considered a normal expectation resulting from an even spread of ages. This is based on the following statistical reasoning:

Present overall average age = 50 years
Compulsory retirement age = 65 years
Overall 'age range' of management may thus be assumed
to be in the order of 15 + 15 = 30 years

Therefore number normally expected to be aged between
60–65 years in order of: $\dfrac{5}{30}$ = 16·5 per cent

Information given in Fig. 7.3.4 tends to suggest that in a single case only, i.e. planned replacement of the Production Engineer (17), was there any evidence of positive provision having been made to counter the effects of this excessively high rate of age wastage.

Titles

The various styles of appointment titles used in the organisation outlined in Fig. 7.3.4 are analysed and classified in Fig. 7.3.6 (overleaf), in respect of which the following observations are made:

● The three positions which carry the style of 'Director' are legacies from the days when the Managing Director and four senior executives of this small company were in fact members of its statutorily appointed Board of Directors. Since the takeover this Board has been dissolved and two of its members, the Managing Director and the Sales Director, have taken up appointments elsewhere in the Group. Three of them remain at this factory—still retaining as 'honorary titles' the style of Director.

Largely as a consequence of the spate of mergers and takeovers during recent years, the delicate matter of ex-directors' titles and their personal status has presented widespread problems throughout industry and commerce. For

Fig. 7.3.6
Analysis of
appointment titles
on organisation
chart

	Directors 3		Managers 3
Director and General Manager		Press Shop Manager	
Production Director		Assembly Manager	
Commercial Director		Deputy Assy. Manager	
Chief Inspector	'Chiefs' 5	Small Press Foreman	Foremen 8
Chief Engineer		Large Press Foreman	
Chief Accountant		Foreman Comp. Assy. 2	
Chief Draughtsman		Foreman Comp. Assy. 3	
Chief Buyer		Senior Foreman Final Assembly 1	
Store superintendent	Superin-tendents 2	Foreman Final Assembly 2	
Supt. Comp. Assy.		Foreman Final Assembly 3	
		Foreman Final Assembly 4	
Production Engineer	Engineers 3	Labour Officer	
Plant Engineer		Production Controller	
Deputy Production Engr.			

example, at the time of its formation a few years ago, one of the largest corporations in Britain had no fewer than 234 'directors' on its payroll—only *eight* of whom were truly directors in the sense that they were formally elected members of the statutory Board of the Corporation.

Unfortunately there are few signs of the existence of well thought out and consistently implemented policies aimed towards solving these problems. Most managements seem either to ignore them altogether (as being incapable of solution) or to tackle them in piecemeal fashion—sometimes with a crudity and lack of imagination which engender yet worse problems of resentment and insecurity. Nonetheless it is possible to devise ways and means of approaching these problems which, whilst being seen to be fair to those involved, are at the same time relatively 'painless' in their application.

An example of how one such policy was evolved and successfully carried out is documented at Appendix 7.1 (p. 1034). Study of this case history shows that its principle features were:

(a) detailed analysis and assessment of the problem accompanied by a carefully conceived policy and plan for implementation;

(b) widespread consultations before the plan was finally approved;

(c) consistent and unswerving adherence to the plan once it had been promulgated.

- Referring again to the organisation chart at Fig. 7.3.4 and the analysis in Fig. 7.3.6, it will be seen that there are five appointments with the word 'Chief' in their titles. Considering that four of them appear at the lowest level of management and these are each responsible for an average of fewer than eight people apiece, perhaps there is some justification for the quip 'too many Chiefs—too few Indians'. But undoubtedly the prefix 'Chief' has become a sadly overworked and frequently meaningless status symbol—especially in the engineering industries. There is on record a classic example of a very large firm in the Midlands where some years ago, out of twenty-two people who were directly responsible to the Engineering Director, no fewer than seventeen of them were entitled 'Chief' something or other.

- The appointment of 'Superintendent' appears twice in the organisation depicted at Fig. 7.3.4. In both cases it seems oddly out of key with the other titles. Enquiries revealed that the two present holders of these positions were very senior employees in the sense of being 'founder members' of the works staff. Therefore, although their current responsibilities were no heavier than those of the average Foreman, they had been given these titles as marks of esteem.

Many commercial and industrial enterprises, especially those which have grown out of acquisitions or mergers, have inherited the untidy consequences of past failures to control and to coordinate the uses of appointment titles. Not only can anomalies arise within single organisations (as witness the above examples) but when two or more organisations are involved the problems can become really complicated. For instance, it is common to find that by traditional usage the *same title* has taken on quite *different* meaning and significance in different companies within the *same industry*.

There are no quick and easy solutions to these problems. The only satisfactory course is to approach and tackle them along lines such as those indicated in Appendix 7.1. That is, carefully to marshal and analyse the facts of the matter, prepare a long-term improvement programme and thereafter *enforce it rigidly and consistently*.

Spans of control

Reference is made in Part One, chapter 5, to the phrase 'span of control': this has come to denote the number of people whose activities are directly supervised and coordinated by a single manager or supervisor. In this context, the distinction between *manager* and *supervisor* has certain significance. As a rule the term *supervisor* signifies the first line of management, the level at which responsibility is held for those who actually perform the manual operations or administrative tasks which collectively achieve the purposes of the undertaking. On the other hand, a *manager* is generally to be found responsible only for the work of other managers or supervisors. With these thoughts in mind, study of the spans of control which are depicted in Fig. 7.3.4 suggests two observations:

- Aside from the 'one-over-one' situation existing between the Assembly Manager (14) and the Deputy Assembly Manager (18)—which has already been discussed—the direct responsibility held by the latter for the heads of seven separate (but fairly obviously interrelated) assembly departments merits attention. On the face of it, this arrangement would appear to be unbalanced and unwieldy. After all, assembly work is clearly the most sizeable production area, engaging as it does the activities of more than four-fifths of the factory's manual workers.
- The number of manual employees supervised by a single superintendent or foreman is seen to average around twenty-four. But the Senior Foreman Final Assembly No. 1 (22) appears to be responsible for twice that number of workers. Enquiries revealed that there *had* been a second supervisor (Foreman) in this department. Although he had been transferred elsewhere in an emergency six months previously and had not been replaced, *the position was no longer formally recognised and shown as a vacant appointment.*

In introducing the foregoing notes and comments it was stated that they represented a selection of matters arising out of review of the draft organisation chart shown as Fig. 7.3.4. The main intention of these notes (which do not pretend to be exhaustive) is to demonstrate the kind of approach which would be made at this stage of an organisation study; to illustrate the kind of probing, questioning and reasoning which would begin to emerge from first scrutinies of a broad picture representing the basic elements of an existing organisation structure; to indicate that there is no established 'set-piece' pattern for conduct of such a study, but rather to suggest that most aspects of organisation are susceptible to an approach based on commonsense, perception, investigation and (surprisingly frequently) to some form of quantification.

Perhaps now is the appropriate time to confirm something which the reader probably already suspects. This is that the factory organisation on which the above illustrations are based does not and never did exist in reality. Nevertheless it would not be strictly accurate to describe the organisation as being completely fictitious. *All* its features, no matter how bizarre some of them may appear to be, have actually been encountered in real life situations at some time or other. To that extent, therefore, the organisation is a composite one, specially designed to act as a vehicle for embodying and demonstrating some of the more typical 'case situations' which arise in the field of organisation planning. The composite organisation will be used again in this role, as new aspects of the subject are developed in the following pages.

4 Responsibilities and relationships

Management job descriptions

The proposition was put forward in an earlier section that *organisation structure* represents the overall pattern or framework of management which emerges as the result of:

- dividing the total management responsibility and accountability among executive and specialist positions;
- defining the delegated responsibilities attaching to each position;
- establishing the formal relationships between positions to ensure coordination of understanding and effort.

Until now, when considering the sequence of tasks involved in carrying out an organisation study in depth, no reference has been made to the second and third items, namely *defining delegated responsibilities* and *establishing formal relationships.* Of course, a certain amount of information about what people are responsible for, what they do and how they relate to each other is self-evident from their appointment titles and the positions they occupy within the general framework of management as depicted on an organisation chart. But, as was stressed earlier, an organisation chart cannot by any means tell the whole story and may be positively misleading. This raises the subject of *management job descriptions*, in the preparation of which the conceptual ideas underlying organisation structure come closest to finding their expression in tangible and practical form.

It has been said that there exists a wide range of styles and methods of presenting organisation charts. But by comparison, the shapes, sizes and styles of management job descriptions are almost infinite in their variety. Indeed, it is only within recent years that the name by which they are called has become generally accepted and its abbreviation 'MJD' has achieved fairly wide recognition. Before then there was a bewildering array of 'position statements', 'job specifications', 'schedules of responsibilities', 'terms of reference', and so on. There is still no recognised standard form of layout and the *length* of an MJD can range anywhere between a single sentence and a four or five page document.[1]

A management job description should provide an understanding of the scope, content and objectives of a position. It should clearly define responsibilities, authority, accountability and the direct relationships by means of which these matters are delegated and discharged. Before going on to discuss

---

[1] As a matter of interest, the most closely detailed MJD with which the co-authors of this text are personally familiar is one which they drafted together in 1954. It spelt out the responsibilities of a District Manager in an Electricity Supply Board. Designed for a special purpose, it contained 110 clauses couched in more than 2 000 words and is reproduced as an Appendix to *Organisation: the Framework of Management* by E. F. L. Brech.

methods of preparing and using MJDs, however, it will be helpful to take a look at the sort of information they might be expected to contain and some of the ways in which this information could be presented.

Contents

As has already been indicated, there are very wide variations in the nature of the contents and the amount of detail to be found in existing examples of MJDs. Format and style, length and complexity will be governed not only by the purposes they are intended to serve and by the size of the organisation concerned, but also by the attitudes and personal whims of those who draft them. Nevertheless, there are certain essential items of information which must appear explicitly in any MJD worthy of the name. These basic elements, which serve mainly to orientate the position within the management framework, will specify:

- the title of the job or position;
- the title of the position *to which* the job holder is directly accountable;
- the titles of positions *for which* the job holder is responsible;
- the responsibilities *delegated* to the position.

Although management job descriptions are normally used in conjunction with (and in support of) organisation charts, it is interesting to observe that, if all the key appointments in an undertaking are defined in the above terms, the resultant related information will provide insight and understanding of the management structure *without need for use of organisation charts at all*. This is not to say, of course, that MJDs can sensibly serve as substitutes or obviate the need for organisation charts. It is no accident that *organisation structure* has, for most people, become synonymous with *organisation charts*, for it is undoubtedly easier in the first instance to grasp and understand the overall shape and major relationships of an organisation when the salient facts are presented in diagrammatic form.

Once the principle and practice of describing management jobs has been accepted, there seems to be virtually no limit to the amount of soul searching, analysis and recording of information that can be featured in them. As a consequence, perhaps the most valid criticism of many MJDs is that they are too long, too minutely detailed, too cumbersome for practical use as management tools. This also provides some justification for the frequently made assertion that overly detailed definitions of management responsibilities can actually *restrict and hamper* rather than assist in the exercise of dynamic management. It is with these thoughts in mind that the possible contents of management job descriptions are further reviewed and discussed below.

Titles

Three out of the four 'essential elements' of an MJD as listed above involve the use of specific job titles. Some pointers towards the kind of problems surrounding the uses of appointment titles in industry and commerce have already been highlighted in the case study relating to organisation analysis of a light engineering factory (refer to Fig. 7.3.4 on page 944). As will be seen later, the initial preparation of a set of interrelated MJDs represents both close-up and long-distance views of the total organisation; so, at this point some of the anomalies (and even the absurdities) of past titling practices become apparent. Each MJD makes reference to at least three different levels of management; first, that of the position holder; second, that of the one to whom he is responsible; and third, the level of those for whom he is responsible. Where organisational anomalies have developed such as 'one-over-one-over-one' situations (like those described in previous pages), all kinds of nomenclature devices may have crept in to sustain or to boost the 'hierarchical status' of some appointment holders. For instance, an extreme example of such status manipulation appeared recently in a Canadian newspaper announcing the appointment of Mr So-and-so as 'Associate Assistant Deputy Vice-President' of the Company!

Ernest Dale, a leading American writer on organisation and general management problems, has expressed some sobering thoughts about titles, as follows:

> Titles are obviously of great importance, but a sort of inflation is constantly eroding the status they confer. Sometimes titles are given as substitutes for pay increases or to sweeten smaller raises than the executives feel they deserve. Such titles may be cheap, they are easily given away, but the situation is comparable to printing money. Just as the value of money decreases as the supply increases relative to the goods and services available, so titles lose value when they do not go with comparable pay and responsibility. . . . Whilst it is impossible to arrive at a consistent titling plan for industry in general, it would be well to make the titling consistent within the company. Thus the titles 'director' and 'manager' should represent practically the same status and the same level in each division if possible. However, it may be wiser not to insist on this if some of those concerned will feel that a change in their titles would mean a real loss of status, and to work gradually towards uniformity.[1]

Functions and responsibilities

Although there is as yet little evidence of the emergence of a standard format for MJDs, it is becoming increasingly common practice to present the narrative part of the job description in two separate sections under such headings as 'Functions' and 'Responsibilities'.

Functions

This first section usually summarises the main sectors of responsibility and authority delegated to the position concerned and briefly states its objectives. It describes the primary purpose of the position and the outstanding elements which distinguish it from others. For example, this introductory section of the MJD for an Industrial Engineering Manager in a car component factory could read:

> 'Planning, directing and controlling the establishment of specifications, methods and competitive standards of measurement for the effective utilisation of staff, supervision, direct and indirect labour resources, and for the optimum utilisation of direct and indirect materials.'

Responsibilities

The second section of the MJD specifies in more detail the responsibility areas through which the function is performed. These are usually presented in itemised form and the functions of the Industrial Engineering Manager as quoted above could be followed by the list of 'responsibilities' shown below:

[1] Ernest Dale, *Organisation*, American Management Association, 1967.

1. Cooperating with Production Management in establishing capacity plans and capacity utilisation.
2. Investigating and recommending methods of improvement.
3. Assisting supervision in the efficient and effective manning of their operations.
4. Providing recommendations for cost improvements.
5. Developing, in conjunction with Plant Directors and Production Planning and Control, forward monthly operating programmes and forecasting the implications of those programmes.
6. Developing manning charts for direct, indirect and staff operations.
7. Assisting in the development of budgets and costs on a department-by-department basis.
8. Organising, budgeting, staffing and controlling resources of the Industrial Engineering Department adequately to meet these responsibilities.

Common responsibilities

Although the position of Industrial Engineering Manager as exemplified above is clearly a specialist appointment which maintains *functional* relationships with others, it will be noticed that the last item of the responsibilities listed (8) refers to *executive accountability* for the internal management of the Industrial Engineering Department.

This serves as a reminder that all managerial positions, whether *direct* or *functional* in nature, carry with them certain common (and inescapable) executive responsibilities. Notwithstanding all the policy guidance and staff support that might be available to him, *every* manager bears some degree of departmental or local accountability for such matters as:

● Performance of activities under his jurisdiction in fulfilment of objectives to required standards of effectiveness.
● Internal organisation; determination and delegation of individual responsibilities.
● Selection, training, development, discipline and (as necessary) replacement of staff.
● Determination of individual objectives, counselling, performance appraisal and salary review of subordinates.
● Preparation of departmental or sectional expense budgets; subsequent review of expenditure and cost control.
● Maintenance of two-way communications between superiors and subordinates.
● Conforming with the standards and practices of administration and financial control.

Generally speaking, there are three ways of dealing with this question of 'common responsibilities' in the field of management job descriptions. They can be (and frequently are) completely overlooked and remain unspecified. They can be included in every MJD for every position: this has the merit of spotlighting these executive responsibilities and ensuring their recognition, but tends to become clumsy and repetitious in practice. Or they can be drawn together and published as a separate document: this may then be issued as an adjunct or addendum to every manager's job description. An example of such a 'guide to common management responsibilities' is shown at Appendix 7.2 (p. 1038). The document is reproduced by kind permission of the British

Leyland Motor Corporation, one of the relatively few larger British companies which has extensively developed the use of MJDs as an integral part of its management policies and a day-to-day expression of its management practices.

Objectives

Another aspect of the contents of job descriptions concerns the manner in which the *objectives* of a management position are defined. A good deal has been said and written in the past few years about what is generally termed 'Management by objectives' or MbO. To its exponents MbO represents a new philosophy, a revolutionary approach to improving management performance by analysing and breaking down the total task of management and expressing it in terms of 'target objectives'. Each of these individual objectives is quantified in some way in order to record and measure the performance of the individual manager against predetermined standards. To its critics, on the other hand, MbO represents nothing more revolutionary than seeking to focus, simplify, codify and perhaps to energise those decision-taking and control processes which are already intrinsic to and inherent in every management situation. Whatever the merits or otherwise of this approach to the style of general management, considerable caution should be exercised in introducing the MbO concept of 'objectives' into management job descriptions, which are essentially an aspect of organisation—*the framework* of management. The two following extracts[1] from published MJDs will serve as a basis for illustrating and amplifying this point.

Extract 1
Amongst the items listed as 'Principal responsibilities' of a Divisional Manager of a company manufacturing and servicing consumer durable goods appear:

(*a*) Establish and maintain a company reputation for providing the highest quality of its value and services.

Measures for accountability	*Standards*
● Percent of served market	Percent
● Lapsed customers	Percent of total
● Percent selling cost	Budget-percent
● New accounts (number)	Percent of total

(*b*) Provide for mechanical maintenance to protect the investment, protect the quality of the service and assure optimum operating costs.

Measures for accountability	*Standards*
● Number of job failures	Number
● Operating equipment expenses	Budget
● Percentage of served market	Budget percentage
● Average life of equipment	Years

Extract 2
In the MJD of the Vice-President, Marketing, of a medium-sized company, the following items are listed under 'Standards of performance':

[1] Extract 1 is from Harold Stieglitz and Allen R. Janger, *Top Management Organisation in Divisionalised Companies*, National Industrial Conference Board Inc.,1965; Extract 2 is from Joseph J. Famularo, *Organisation Planning Manual*, American Management Association Inc., 1971.

- Sales volume for year: $00 000 000
- Share of market: 42 per cent Product A
                   9 per cent Product B
- Forecasts: Within 10 per cent accuracy in dollars
             Within 20 per cent accuracy in units
- Advertising enquiries: 750 per month
- Warranty claims: 2 per cent of sales by (date)

Comments

In citing the above two examples it is not the intention to be critical of the sense and purposes which they seek to convey: they must both be studied and assessed within their total settings as interesting examples of how two different companies approach their treatment and use of MJDs. But if the oft-repeated proposition that management job descriptions are a fundamental feature of *organisation structure* is to be taken seriously, then the following observations inevitably emerge:

- The quantified 'objectives' included in the above schedules signify planned *results* rather than *functions or responsibilities* of the positions being defined.
- All the 'personal performance' information which has been expressed in measured terms should be available through the established planning procedures, budgetary arrangements, control systems and communication channels of the undertaking.
- These management processes operate through and conform to the pattern of delegated responsibilities which is the *organisation structure*.
- Whereas the scheduled standards, budgets and targets for management performance are necessarily ephemeral and subject to short-term review and possible modification, the *organisation structure*, the framework of management, must be relatively stable and static.
- It follows, therefore, that specific short-term objectives have no rightful place in a management job description which purports to define a part of the *structure* through which the total processes of management are carried out.

Nevertheless, as has been pointed out in earlier pages, organisation structure itself tends to change (or be changed) with the passage of time. The best thought out management job descriptions can rapidly become historical documents. An essential feature, therefore, of every MJD should be some record of the date on which and by whom it was originally agreed. More will be said later about procedures for reviewing and up-dating MJDs.

Other relationships

In addition to determining those immediate and direct relationships which serve to orientate the position within the organisation (i.e. *to whom* and *for whom* the holder is responsible), it is sometimes necessary to specify other working relationships which are germane to the performance of the job. Some simple examples of these appear in the MJD for an Industrial Engineering Manager which was quoted earlier, namely:

Cooperating with Production Management in establishing capacity plans and capacity utilisation.

Developing in conjunction with Plant Directors and Production Planning and Control, forward monthly operating programmes and forecasting the implications of those programmes.

The choice of words (as italicised above) by which these operating relationships are defined is important. It is frequently a matter of some delicacy, calling for careful consideration of the commonly understood shades of meaning and precise use in the proper context of such 'action verbs' as:

advise	cooperate	facilitate
approve	counsel	guide
assist	check	initiate
concur	determine	participate
collaborate	develop	prescribe
control	devise	recommend
contribute	establish	suggest
coordinate	exercise	supervise

It is generally advisable to spell out these special relationships at the same time as the particular responsibilities with which they are associated—as shown in the above examples. This is more satisfactory than adding (as is sometimes the practice) a final 'blanket' clause to the MJD, such as: 'Will cooperate closely with Production Management, Plant Directors, Production Planning and Control and other affected departments in discharging the above responsibilities.'

Other information

Some other kinds of information which might, according to particular circumstances, form useful parts of the contents of a management job description could include:

Committees. Names of boards, committees or other bodies, internal or external, of which the job holder becomes a member by virtue of holding the position.
Deputy role. Where appropriate, indication of the circumstances under which the job holder will deputise for his superior.
Reservations. Any reservations or limitations on authority, as for example: 'The authority of the Plant Manager is final on all the above matters for which he is responsible, saving the extent to which he must adhere to the approved financial budgets and prescribed industrial relations policies of the Company.'

Preparation and presentation

Having discussed the probable contents of management job descriptions, it is now necessary to consider some of the ways in which this information can be prepared and presented for use as a management tool. Here again there appears a wide range of possible approaches. At one end of a spectrum is the practice of featuring abbreviated statements of responsibilities as supplementary information on organisation charts. At the other extreme are sophisticated routines for publishing and maintaining lengthy and detailed narrative statements in the form of handbooks or manuals. In between lies a variety of styles and methods of presentation, all of which will be influenced by needs, circumstances and time factors which will vary from one organisation to another. Nevertheless, despite what would seem to be a welter of different approaches and conflicting styles, it is suggested that some commonsense guidelines about ways of preparing and presenting management job descriptions may be derived from observation and experience. For instance, in any organisational situation where MJDs have never before been prepared, the initial exercise should ideally conform to the requirements spelt out below:

1. The method of approach should be kept very simple indeed, aiming at first to produce only broad outline sketches of the position responsibilities.
2. The exercise should start at the top and work downwards; that is to say, the most senior positions should be analysed and described first, these then to be followed by the definition of subordinate positions down to a predetermined cut-off level about which more will be said presently.

Note. It has been maintained by some people that when embarking for the first time on the task of producing MJDs, it is sensible to start at the lower levels and work upwards, thus automatically identifying and 'collecting' the principal responsibilities of the higher level positions. This method of approach, which has the superficial attraction of being easier to implement, really reveals a facile misunderstanding of the very nature of organisation. Throughout these pages it has been stressed that organisation represents the sharing and *delegation* of responsibilities. Therefore, in the sense that organisation is necessarily hierarchical, delegation denotes the allocation of responsibilities *downwards* through the management structure. Accordingly, as the act of preparing job descriptions is in effect giving tangible expression to the act of *delegation,* it follows that the order in which they are prepared, the direction of their flow, must be *downwards* from the uppermost level of authority and responsibility.

3. The results of the first exercise in producing management job descriptions should be capable of being easily related to and identified on organisation charts. Diagrams are, for most people, indispensable aids towards grasping the overall perspective, the total framework within which the management positions defined in MJDs relate one to another.
4. In making a start on MJDs, too much should not be attempted at once. It is much better to describe all the key management jobs in a single homogeneous area representing perhaps a relatively small (but preferably self-contained) part of the organisation than to produce a number of job descriptions which are not manifestly related, which may be scattered across the organisation and may appear to leave unfilled gaps between them.
5. Basic information required for the preparation of MJDs can be collected in a number of ways, two of which are most commonly encountered. The information can be assembled by means of carefully worded questionnaires, issued under suitable explanatory notes for completion and return by the job holders themselves. Or, more satisfactorily, it can be collected through personal interviews conducted by a job analyst (ordinarily the *organisation planner*) with the job holders, their own managers and others who might usefully contribute or have some interest in the results. Whichever method is used, the following courtesies should always be observed:

- The *job holder* should have first opportunity to say, in his own words, what he believes his responsibilities to be.
- The *organisation planner* should record this information, clear any points of doubt and write up the material in standardised form as a *first draft* job description.
- The first draft should then be discussed with the job holder, amended if necessary, and agreed with him. The process may call for considerable patience and should not be regarded as completed until agreement has been reached.
- The draft MJD should next be studied by, discussed and agreed with the *job holder's manager.*
- Where a list of general responsibilities includes reference to duties involving specialist or staff functions (e.g. finance, industrial relations, quality control), such references should be checked with the heads of the functional departments concerned.
- Depending on the levels and numbers of management job descriptions involved, it is generally desirable to ensure that all final drafts are approved by the local chief executive (e.g. Managing Director, General Manager, Branch Manager) before they are published.

6. Once management job descriptions have been drafted, agreed and approved, *a single person* should be made responsible for their publication and subsequent maintenance. This responsibility will include:

- ensuring that every MJD bears the date on which it was approved and indicates by whom it was issued;
- keeping a distribution list of names of those to whom copies of the MJDs were circulated;
- ensuring that, as and when subsequent changes in the content of MJDs are approved, the existing copies are either suitably amended or destroyed and replaced.

Experience all too often reveals the hoarding of undated and outdated organisation charts and management job descriptions. These frequently represent the relics of some previous upsurge of management zeal for organisation planning that has since faded and died for lack of continuing support and maintenance.

Further reference will be made to this matter of assuring the continuity of management action in chapter 8, 'Whose responsibility?'

Purposes

From what has been said up to now about management job descriptions it might possibly be inferred that their primary purpose, if not their only purpose, is to give tangible expression to the delegation of management responsibility and accountability; to make sure that there exists, in documentary form, some discernible evidence of that aspect of the planning element of management which is concerned with organisation structure. But, it could be argued, tens of thousands of organisations, industrial, commercial, social and otherwise, operate quite effectively without any written job descriptions at all. People occupy managerial positions and perform jobs by habit, custom, practice or personal idiosyncrasy, and there exist tacit understandings between them as to their duties, relationships and boundaries of responsibilities. Of course, there are few absolute standards by which the loose term 'operate quite effectively' may be assessed. It could be that *most* organisations would indeed enhance their effectiveness as a result of objective study and analysis of how they are structured and how their management responsibilities are delegated and discharged. However, be that as it may, it could be useful at this point to review in a rather wider perspective some of the purposes which might underlie a campaign to produce MJDs and to consider in detail a few of the practical benefits to be derived from conducting such an exercise.

Spin-off benefits

Even when the stated purpose behind the preparation of management job descriptions lies simply in the conduct of an organisational survey as described above, there is little doubt that spin-off benefits stem from the exercise itself. Indeed, it has been argued with force by some advocates of organisation planning that the very acts of having to question, to analyse, to define and to agree the content of management jobs represent the most salutary and beneficial aspects of the exercise: that the means are perhaps in some ways more important than the results. Certainly, participation in job analysis helps the person in the job better to understand the ramifications of his position: it obliges him to stand back and examine and assess the relative importance of everything for which he is accountable: it forces him to give some detached thought to the nature of the familiar day-to-day relationships through which he has to get results.

At the same time, of course, a number of people with whom the job holder has working relationships—including his own boss—will have been given cause to think about the position, about its responsibilities and the way it operates in practice. More often than not there emerge out of these discussions useful comments and suggestions which might otherwise have remained unspoken or passed unrecorded; comments about the impact of the job on others, suggestions for improvement where there appear to be gaps or overlaps in areas of responsibility, and so on.

Experience shows, however, that the most charitable and fairminded people seem to be quite incapable of remaining truly objective during the whole course of these discussions. The great majority (including even those who were trained in the scientific disciplines) appear unable to voice their comments and opinions about *the job* separately and distinctly from their attitudes and feelings towards *the job holder*. In consequence, the positive and constructive value of information obtained in this way will greatly depend on the patience, perception, detachment and sifting ability of the interviewer—*the organisation planner*.

Personal
specifications

The foregoing observations lead naturally towards consideration of another use for management job descriptions. Some first thoughts about this were raised in chapter 2 where, in the review of implications underlying the suggested 'Organisation checklist', the following passage appeared (p. 932):

> The main purpose of job schedules is, of course, to clarify the specific responsibilities and accountabilities which attach to each management

position. They are impersonal in the sense that they define the *job only,* without reference to the *job holder.* But they do tell a great deal about the nature of the demands which are made on the job holder in terms of his capability to discharge the responsibilities of the position and (as will be seen later) they are used as a basis for preparing a *personal specification* of an individual suitable to hold the position.

There are a number of possible uses for *personal specifications*, documents which are capable of providing assistance towards identifying and defining in quantifiable terms such factors as knowledge, experience and skills, educational standards, personality traits and other characteristics which appear to be required for the successful performance of particular jobs or groups of jobs. Potential applications of personal specifications would include such planning and development activities as:

Recruitment. Searching for, screening and identifying suitable candidates to fill existing or future management position vacancies.
Appraisal. Periodically assessing the performance of individuals against predetermined job standards; identifying personal strengths and weaknesses; determining training needs.
Training. Preparing and implementing programmes for the training and development of potential candidates or for existing holders of management positions.
Grading. Relating jobs one to another in rational terms within a grading structure: evaluating jobs accordingly for salary administration and other purposes.

Examples of the use of personal specifications derived from job descriptions appear in chapter 6, 'Management development'. Before leaving this topic, however, it should be noted that different kinds of specifications need to be devised to serve different purposes. In other words, to construct a *single* personal specification which is capable of reflecting, mirrorlike, *all* the job information required to meet the various purposes listed above is simply not practical. Where attempts have been made to produce such 'multipurpose' documents they have failed, in the opinion of the authors, because they have turned out to be either overcomplicated and confusing or oversimplified and superficial.

Announcement of changes

Perhaps the most widely encountered use of management job descriptions in some shape or other lies in the formal announcement of organisation and appointment changes. It is a matter of regret that it is not possible to phrase the latter part of this sentence as '. . . lies in the *formal development* and formal announcement of . . . etc. . . .' For very frequently these job descriptions, which are intended to explain the changes being made in the allocation of management responsibilities, have been hastily and amateurishly drafted and cursorily approved. Too often they bear signs of being a last-minute chore, quickly performed before belated issue of an announcement. Common though it may be, this sort of occurrence is unfortunate for a number of reasons. First, and perhaps most obviously, it fails to take best advantage of a rare opportunity to impart valuable management information in depth over a wide area. Because, among all the written communications which are normally circulated within industrial and commercial undertakings, *organisation and appointment announcements* always arouse interest, are usually studied with care and are often discussed with fervour.

Another and perhaps more cogent reason for devoting adequate time and thought to the 'job description' element of appointment notices lies within a remark made in a previous paragraph. This suggested that all the analysing, questioning and discussing that *should* precede final agreement of a management job description has a value in itself. There is little doubt that the quality of any MJD largely echoes the degree of understanding that emerges from widespread discussions beforehand.

Thus an experienced organisation planner brings into use, at the earliest possible stage of any significant developments, a 'cockshy' document which he uses as a working tool and which provides a common basis for all his consultations and discussions about proposed organisation changes. This document comprises the first draft outline of an announcement of the changes, usually supported by a rough organisation chart, but *always* spelling out the proposed job responsibilities attaching to key management positions which are involved in the changes. The document is termed a 'cockshy' because, apart from serving as a focus and a stimulus for participative thinking and exchanges of views, it usually emerges in final form, altered and amended, polished and refined but (most important) *understood and agreed* at least by those who will be immediately affected by the changes.

Examples of MJDs

The examples shown in Figs. 7.4.1, 2 and 3 have been chosen to illustrate and to develop further some of the points made in preceding pages about the purposes and presentation of management job descriptions.

Fig. 7.4.1 presents the use of MJDs in their most elementary form. By displaying highly abbreviated job descriptions in the setting of a simple organisation chart, there is produced a rapidly assimilable picture of the top management structure and delegation of major responsibilities within a medium sized manufacturing company. This style of presentation would obviously be of value in situations calling for a quick grasp and basic understanding of the overall functions of the organisation.

In Fig. 7.4.2 the *personnel* function as shown in the organisation in Fig. 7.4.1 is described in greater detail. Exactly the same method of diagrammatic presentation is used, and it is evident that if all the other main functions were similarly amplified, a substantial amount of cohesive information would have been made available. Because of its compact form and comparative ease of reference, this kind of presentation provides extremely useful basic material for discussion and development purposes.

Fig. 7.4.3 represents a straightforward example of an MJD in written form. It defines the relationships and the responsibilities of the Personnel Manager position which appears in the organisation shown in Figs. 7.4.1 and 7.4.2. It is interesting to observe that, when seeking to draft management job descriptions for the six positions directly responsible to the Personnel Manager, the introductory 'functions' sections of these MJDs could be lifted—almost without any change of wording—from the corresponding 'schedule of responsibilities' ascribed to the Personnel Manager himself.

Fig. 7.4.1
Allocation of
responsibilities
in a manufacturing
company

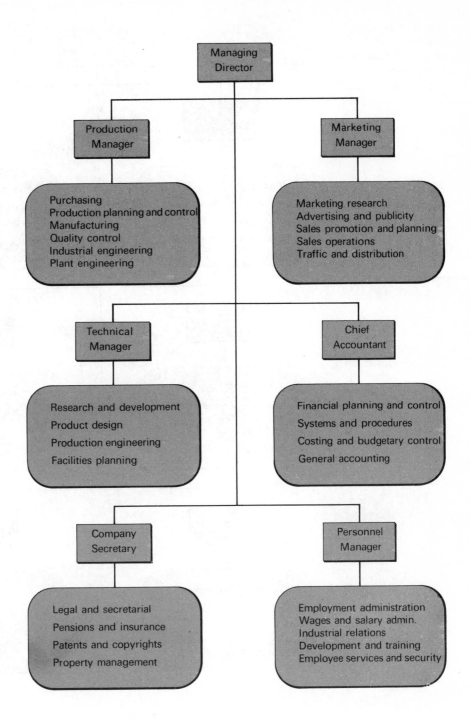

Fig. 7.4.2
Allocation of
responsibilities in
a Personnel
Department

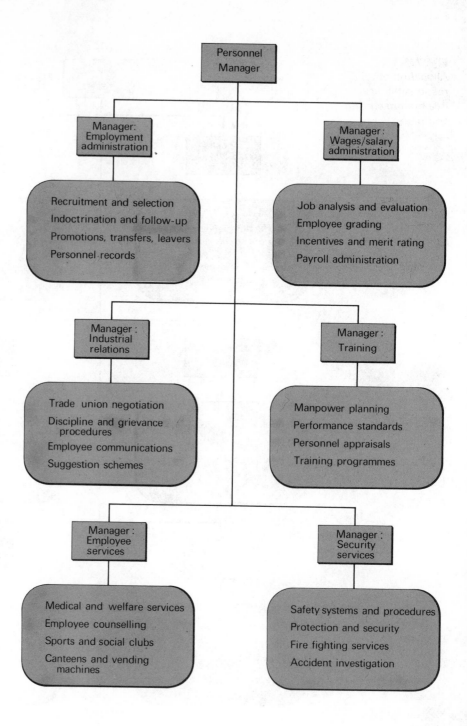

Fig. 7.4.3
Example of
management job
description

Position	Personnel Manager
Responsible to	Managing Director
Responsible for	Manager: Employment Administration
	Manager: Wages and Salary Administration
	Manager: Industrial Relations
	Manager: Training
	Manager: Employee Services
	Manager: Security Services

Functions

Developing (in accordance with Board policies) and ensuring proper achievement and administration of Company objectives, standards and procedures for the supply, deployment, compensation, training and development of salaried and hourly employees; for maintaining effective agreements and relationships with employees and their trade union representatives, and for the provision of employee benefits, security services and amenities.

Responsibilities

1. Maintaining liaison with all departments and keeping a register of budgeted and authorised employment vacancies. Searching for suitable applicants, conducting initial interviews and selection tests, investigating references. Seeing that new employees receive adequate indoctrination, training and information.

2. Cooperating in planning and coordinating the implementation of arrangements for promotion or transfer of existing employees to secure better utilisation of their capabilities. Supervising the termination arrangements of leavers and conducting exit interviews.

3. Preparing job descriptions and analyses for purposes of wage and salary determination; conducting job evaluations and developing rate scales; ensuring that each employee is assigned to a position within the approved salary structure or rate scales. Developing incentive and merit rating proposals, administering approved schemes and analysing results. Ensuring that all employees are correctly and promptly remunerated.

4. Ensuring effective observation and administration throughout the Company of procedure agreements with trade unions and representing the Company in relationships and negotiations with trade unions and the Employers' Federation at National level.

5. Making assessments and advising on the actual and potential effects on Company operations of plant, departmental or sectional proposals on industrial and staff relations matters, and concurring in such proposals as appropriate.

6. Developing and maintaining channels of communication for presenting information to employees; conducting attitude and opinion surveys; planning and administering the Company suggestion schemes.

7. Assisting in the determination of manpower standards and requirements that will most effectively and economically meet Company objectives; developing performance standards and methods of appraisal for key jobs.

8. Devising and coordinating the implementation of programmes for management, technical, supervisor and operator training and ensuring maximum assistance to departmental and plant managers so that training plans and objectives are realistically focused on the goals, problems and performance improvement needs of operating activities. Directing administration of the Company's apprentice training schemes.

9. Cooperating with the Medical Officer and his staff in administering programmes for prevention of diseases and physical ailments on the job. Ensuring the medical examination of applicants and certain employees; providing facilities for medical treatment and care as necessary.

10. Providing a personal and confidential counselling service for employees; operating employee welfare and transport arrangements. Representing the Company in organisation and operation of the Sports and Social Club and other recreational facilities. Supervising operation of the Company's catering and vending machine contracts.

11. Developing and maintaining adequate facilities and procedures for preventing on-the-job accidents; investigating and reporting on accidents; maintaining statistics. Taking suitable security precautions to protect the Company, its employees and property from theft, sabotage or other hazards. Organising and maintaining fire-prevention and fire-fighting services.

Reference No. P/1/5
August 1973

The spectrum
of MJDs

The three examples quoted above recall an earlier assertion that MJDs can range anywhere within a spectrum which has highly condensed summaries at one end and expansively detailed statements at the other. This effect is to some extent demonstrated above by the three different ways of describing the same job—that of the Personnel Manager. Study of the examples shows that this position was variously defined in the following numbers of words: Fig. 7.4.1. = 14 words; Fig. 7.4.2 = 86 words; Fig. 7.4.3 = 520 words.

While the factors governing economy of words at one end of the scale are fairly plain, what of the other extreme? Is it fanciful to ask if there is significance in the roughly sixfold rate of progression in numbers of words used? In short, could one expect to reach a stage where this particular MJD could find expression in more than 3 000 words? The answer to this question is 'No'. There are two principal factors which will determine the ultimate length of a management job description. The first of these is the use of ordinary commonsense judgment—deciding just when the division and subdivision of responsibility areas is becoming unnecessary or unrealistic. The second limiting factor, though also pragmatic, is somewhat more precise. It is possible to discern a point of fragmentation beyond which the concept of *responsibilities* begins to transform into *methods and procedures,* that is *the means by which responsibilities are carried out.* Scrutiny of the MJD shown at Fig. 7.4.3 reveals that it comes very close to this transformation point in several places. (Another viewpoint is, however, reflected in the footnote on page 953.)

A headquarters
appointment

The example of an MJD reproduced as Appendix 7.3 (see page 1040) is that of the head of Industrial Engineering, a position on the central headquarters staff of a group of engineering companies employing around 80 000 people in twenty-two factories. The plants are organised in divisions which operate under group direction, thus the chain of delegated responsibilities surrounding the industrial engineering function may be illustrated as in Fig. 7.4.4.

Fig. 7.4.4
Industrial
engineering
responsibilities

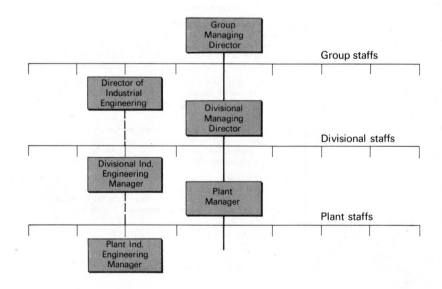

When the illustration at Appendix 7.3 is compared with an earlier example (p. 956) the resulting contrast in length and style of the two MJDs demonstrates yet another aspect of the spectrum effect of management job descriptions within the same organisation. For that earlier example (top of page 956) is in fact the MJD of the Plant Industrial Engineering Manager's position shown at the bottom level in Fig. 7.4.4.

The following observations emerge from comparative study of the two statements:

● The job description of the head of Industrial Engineering is detailed and comprehensive. It virtually represents a complete mandate for the introduction, operation and integration of all facets of the industrial engineering function across the group of companies. The responsibilities are largely directed towards policy-making, planning, communicating, coordinating and monitoring overall progress.

● The MJD of the Plant Industrial Engineering Manager is less detailed but is more sharply pointed towards specific courses of action. The responsibilities are narrowly aimed at securing maximum production with optimum utilisation of manpower and materials at factory level.

Consideration of these contrasts in style and presentation of job descriptions as applied to different *levels* of management raises a matter mentioned earlier, that is the question of determining the point below which it is unnecessary or unreal to devise and publish MJDs. To some extent the answer lies implicit within the examples and comments already presented. Although it could perhaps be argued that any job which is responsible for the work of others is a part of management and accordingly merits a management job description, this is not necessarily so in practice. Therefore the guidelines that have been suggested for determining *how long MJDs should be* could be adopted for deciding *how low MJDs should go*. These guidelines, it will be recalled, invoke commonsense recognition of the 'transformation point' beyond which definitions of management *responsibilities* have become so far delegated and fragmented that they begin to appear as descriptions of the *methods and procedures* through which responsibilities are carried out.

A proposed Quality Manager

Fig. 7.4.5 shows the outline management job description of a *proposed* senior position. It is in the form of a personal memorandum from the Managing Director of a medium-sized manufacturing concern to all the directors and senior executives of the company. The purposes of the memorandum are largely self-explanatory, but it is important to understand that declaring the intention to establish Quality Management as a completely new management function represented a policy decision of some significance in this particular undertaking at that time. Hitherto line inspection departments (answering to local factory managements) had been solely responsible for checking and reporting on product quality. Now the recently appointed Managing Director had observed that these arrangements were in many respects outdated and inadequate. After considerable consultation and discussion he had decided to prepare the way for introduction of more sophisticated concepts of 'total quality assurance' at all stages of design, development, production engineering and manufacture. The announcement shown as Fig. 7.4.5 represented the first step towards this objective. As a matter of

Fig. 7.4.5
Example of proposed management job description

To: Directors and   From: The Managing Director
    Senior Executives

PROPOSED APPOINTMENT OF CENTRAL QUALITY MANAGER

It has been decided to develop and gradually to establish a new appointment of Central Quality Manager. The holder of this position will become directly responsible to me and it is envisaged that in due course his responsibilities will broadly consist of:

1. Cooperating with the Engineering Design, Sales, Research and Development departments in the initial definition of specific commercial standards of quality and acceptable tolerances for all our products and industrial processes.

2. Ensuring that these predetermined quality standards and specifications are recorded, made known and properly understood at all the production planning, manufacturing and processing points throughout the Company.

3. Functionally cooperating with Factory Directors and their Senior Executives to ensure that local inspection and quality control organisations are adequately staffed, informed, equipped and empowered to maintain uniform quality standards at all stages of manufacture, i.e. from receipt of materials through to the finished product.

4. Constantly developing improved techniques and procedures for quality management (e.g. by means of statistical method, instrumentation, supplier quality assurance, data processing) and ensuring that these techniques are understood and used at factory level.

5. Investigating and reporting on cases of significant departure from predetermined quality standards which arise in the Company: ensuring that adjustments in manufacturing costs which result from approved changes in quality specifications are identified and taken into account commercially.

6. Representing the Company in top level discussions and negotiations with our customers' senior representatives on matters concerning the maintenance of agreed standards of product quality.

Because this is a new and important position which will require to be carefully developed, it is not expected that the appointment of Central Quality Manager will become operationally effective for some time ahead—probably in about twelve months time. In the meantime, Mr John Smith (presently Assistant to the Technical Director) has been assigned to prepare the necessary groundwork towards establishing this appointment. During these coming months Mr Smith will carry out an intensive development programme which will include:

(a) Studying in depth our methods and procedures for determining quality standards and their subsequent maintenance by local inspection and control systems throughout the manufacturing plants. This task will entail spending some time in the Central Services departments concerned and also at each of our factories.

(b) Investigating established and effective quality management systems which are known to be operating satisfactorily in the manufacturing companies similar to our own, both at home and overseas.

(c) Making an intensive study of any other worthwhile sources of information and modern techniques in the field of quality management.

At the end of this period of preparation and development, an appointment of Central Quality Manager will be made in accordance with the job description broadly outlined above.

Date: Managing Director fact, twelve months later John Smith, an energetic and enterprising young graduate chemist, was formally appointed as Central Quality Manager with an immediate staff of four people. His published responsibilities accorded closely with the cockshy job description which had appeared in the Managing Director's memorandum the previous year. These broad responsibilities were later spelt out in greater detail through the MJDs of his four assistants.

Commenting further on this actual case history, it is interesting to note that the Managing Director's introductory announcement was drafted by the organisation planner and was based on information which he obtained from a preliminary study of quality management within the company and from outside sources. The organisation planner was also responsible for informally testing opinions and seeking advice which resulted in John Smith being nominated to carry out further studies and to prepare for inception of the new function.

Line executive positions

The examples of management job descriptions quoted up to now have related to *functional staff* appointments and have been mainly associated with some aspect of manufacturing industry in the United Kingdom. The MJD which is reproduced as Appendix 7.4 is that of a *line executive* position in the agricultural industry, namely the appointment of Cultivation Manager on a large sugar estate in the West Indies (see page 1042).

It was pointed out (p. 956) that all managerial positions, whether *line* or *functional* in character, carry with them certain common and inescapable executive responsibilities which are mostly concerned with personnel administration and control of overhead costs. It was also suggested that these could best be drawn together and published as a separate document, and an example of such a 'guide to common management responsibilities' is given in Appendix 7.2. It will be observed, however, that in the Cultivation Manager's job description (Appendix 7.4) about one-third of all the responsibilities (i.e. most of those listed from item 12 onwards) are of this kind, that is to say they might be regarded as being incidental to *any* management position. The reason why they are spelt out in full detail in this MJD is that, notwithstanding advice or assistance that may be available from specialist departments (e.g. Labour Relations, Training, Welfare), this group of responsibilities represents the most onerous and time-consuming part of the Cultivation Manager's whole job: to have omitted them from the MJD would have been unrealistic. It is a sad truth that today these same remarks might be applied to the majority of line management jobs in those industrial or commercial undertakings which are labour intensive in nature, both in the United Kingdom and elsewhere.

A Divisional Manager

Appendix 7.5 (page 1045) provides another example of an operating (or line) MJD: it defines the delegated responsibilities of a Divisional Manager in a manufacturing organisation which has grown rapidly during recent years in one of the more advanced countries of East Asia. The activities of the company are carried out in three separate product divisions located on the same site. These are virtually independent of each other and the operating relationships between them are purely 'lateral': those of supplier and customer. However, haphazard and uncontrolled organisation development over the years has reflected the familiar growth pattern of the largest and oldest established of the manufacturing divisions continuing to have responsibility for providing functional staff and technical services to the other two divisions, without any clear definition of these responsibilities. Because of the peculiar supplier–customer relationships, this arrangement has inevitably given rise to conflicting loyalties, priority problems and similar strains between the executive and functional staffs concerned. After securing outside objective advice on the situation, the Board has formally expressed the intention to pursue a vigorous policy of decentralisation of both executive authority and functional and specialist activity; this to be directed towards making each manufacturing division of the company as far as possible managerially balanced and self-contained. A planned programme (which was preceded by lengthy and widespread consultations) has been designed to accelerate implementation of the decentralisation policy along practical lines. The Divisional Manager's job description reproduced as Appendix 7.5 signifies an important step in this programme. In effect it represents a mandate whereby a number of significant changes are given the formal stamp of authority. This accounts for its rather unusual format and for the manner in which some of the responsibilities are given special point and emphasis. The intention here is to leave no doubts about the newly granted freedom for enterprise and decision-taking compared with that which was previously permitted to the holder of this position.

In short, this example serves as a reminder that the content and tone of management job descriptions can be, indeed should be, honed and polished to serve as practical tools in the implementation of prescribed organisation policies and plans.

Organisation and appointment announcements

Some comments were made in earlier pages about the widely encountered use of organisation and *appointment announcements* as media for the publication of management job descriptions. It would be no exaggeration to say that, on several other counts, organisation and appointment announcements are the most important working documents used in the practice of organisation planning. As was implied in the earlier comments, it is probably equally true to say that their frequent amateurish and inadequate style shows a lamentable neglect of this very important facet of management administration. Of course, there could be many reasons for these inadequacies, not least of which stems from the comparative infrequency of such announcements and consequent absence of laid down patterns of procedure for preparing and issuing them. The following thoughts on the subject of organisation and appointment announcements could provide a possible basis for establishing such a systematic pattern.

Format

Ideally, the format and style of presentation of these announcements should remain uniformly consistent throughout an organisation. In the same way that the form and appearance of other management documents (e.g. budget proposals, control statements) are closely prescribed and leave little latitude for introducing the whims of individual managers, so also should organisation and appointment notices have an unmistakable style and appearance. Aside from other reasons, discussed below, such a standardised form in itself draws attention and lends weight and authority to a document which almost certainly is likely to be only one of a pile of papers which appears on a manager's desk.

Contents

Each announcement ought to be capable of standing as a self-sufficient and self-explanatory statement. To achieve this end its contents might be presented in the following sequence:

1. Main title heading, indicating the name of the organisation and of the branch, department or function concerned.
2. Clear indication of:
   (*a*) to whom the announcement is addressed
   (*b*) by whom it is being issued.
3. Introduction, giving brief explanation of reasons underlying organisation and/or appointment changes which follow: possibly cross-reference to previous announcement of other changes to which these are consequential or in some way related.
4. Reference to an attached organisation chart which, wherever possible, should be there to support, illustrate and assist in explaining any organisation announcement.
5. (*a*) Appointment title of each position affected, together with the name of person who will occupy it.
   (*b*) Name and appointment of the person to whom this position is directly accountable.
   (*c*) Brief description of the main responsibilities of the position.

   (The sequence 5(*a*) to (*c*) should be repeated for each affected position, these being grouped in descending order of seniority and capable of being easily identified on the supporting organisation chart.)

6. Concluding paragraph, if appropriate, recording brief final remarks about implications and effects of the announcement.
7. Personal signature and appointment title of the director or manager authorising the changes.
8. Date and reference number of the announcement.

A simple illustration of this style of presentation of an organisation and appointments notice appears as Appendix 7.6 (p.1049). The example is drawn from organisation changes in the engineering factory described in Fig. 7.3.4 (p. 944). It shows an announcement by the General Manager of one phase of a series of planned changes in the nature and delegation of responsibilities within this undertaking.

Consultations

The sequence of consultations and procedures to be undertaken before issuing organisation and appointment announcements is closely similar to that which was described on p. 960 as being a necessary preliminary to the authorisation and publication of management job descriptions. Here also the emphasis must be on consulting and advising *beforehand* all those who will be affected by the contents of the announcement. As a measure towards ensuring that these requirements are met, the following rule-of-thumb should invariably be applied:

No organisation and appointment announcement will be authorised and issued until the final draft has been studied by every position holder whose name appears on it.

Of course this simple rule is not exclusive: that is to say it does not by any means cover *all* the people who must be consulted or informed about an announcement. The total number of such people will include the *superiors* of the position holders who are named, at least up to the level below the manager who is signing the announcement. There are certain to be other 'interested parties' such as heads of specialist departments who may have some functional responsibilities for the affected appointments. What this amounts to is that a comprehensive list should be prepared, showing the names of all position holders who must be advised, either by right or as a matter of courtesy, before the general issue of *every* announcement concerning organisation and appointment changes. It is an important part of the organisation planner's task to compile this list and to take such action as will make it possible for him to assure the manager issuing the notice that everybody on the list has been informed and, where required, their approval or 'sign-off' has been obtained.

Distribution

Another practical aspect of organisation and appointment notices which calls for thoughtful planning and timing is concerned with actually issuing the documents after their approval. It will be recalled that in the Organisation checklist which was featured in an earlier section, Question 21 (p. 929) asked:

Do 'management distribution lists' covering the issue of written communications (e.g. policy directives, organisation announcements and other kinds of instruction and information) conform to the pattern of delegated responsibilities which is jointly portrayed by the organisation charts and management job descriptions?

As was suggested in the accompanying commentary on implications of the questionnaire, the answer to this question is frequently 'No', and the key to that answer is often to be found within Question 22:

Is there a single individual who is responsible for issuing comprehensive and classified management distribution lists and for ensuring that they are kept up to date?

Thoughts stimulated by these questions prompt the following observations about the distribution of organisation and appointment announcements:

● Experience shows that maintenance of classified management distribution lists, whether by a single individual or by a department, is relatively uncommon practice in the private sectors of industry and commerce. This is somewhat surprising, because it is frequently found to apply to quite sizeable undertakings where other aspects of internal administration and communication are adequate.

● A possible reason for this seeming neglect could be the fact that assembling and *maintaining* accurate and up-to-date lists of names and appointments, indexed and cross-indexed by managerial status, functions, locations, departments and so on, presents fiddling (and relatively costly) administrative problems, not the least of which are concerned with the continuing collection and correction of basic information. Since very few management payrolls have yet been fully computerised, this problem has not been greatly eased by the increases in availability of data processing resources: central management distribution lists still have to be maintained largely by means of legwork and handwork.

- Even assuming that such a centralised and comprehensive list of management personnel *was* available, it would require to be used very discreetly and discriminately for purposes of distributing an organisation and appointments announcement. In practice it is found that almost every such announcement really needs to be issued according to its own specially compiled distribution list.
- It will also be found that whatever may be the characteristics of an organisation, be it industrial or commercial, large or small, centralised or fragmented, it can invariably be broken down into readily recognisable sub-organisations (e.g. plants, branches, departments, sections, shops) within which there is at least one person who is familiar with the up-to-date management pattern and staffing arrangements. In many situations, of course, this person would quite properly be the local personnel manager or staff administration officer. But where no such appointment exists, there is always *somebody*; he may be an assistant to the local top executive; he may be (and not uncommonly is) the erstwhile Secretary of a small company which still retains its original organisational identity within a larger pattern of companies which have been merged.

Thus out of the foregoing observations there emerge the following conclusions:

1. It is to be recommended that the organisation planner should hold himself responsible for preparing and securing approval of a 'bespoke' distribution list for *every* organisation and appointment announcement. Even in those circumstances where he has not been greatly involved in preparation of the announcement (such as some notice of a relatively minor departmental change) the organisation planner's advice should always be sought on the question of distribution.
2. In planning for issue of the announcement, the organisation planner should obtain, perhaps partly from local people 'in the know' such as are mentioned above, names of current position holders to whom *in his opinion* it would be appropriate to send individual copies of the announcement.
3. Since experience proves it is no cynicism to say that the scope for administrative error and omission in carrying out such 'non routine' communication exercises seems to be almost limitless, it is a duty of the organisation planner personally to ensure that the organisation and appointment announcements do in fact find their way to the right people in the right order at the right time.

Many instances have been reported of carefully conceived, delicately negotiated and well documented organisation changes which have turned sour as the result of inadequate distribution of information and instructions. One example will suffice to illustrate the point. Some years ago a large company which operates several provincial factories from its London-based headquarters announced a number of significant organisation and personnel changes, including the appointment of a new Managing Director. Considerable resentment arose from the fact that first news of these important changes was gleaned by employees of the Scottish factory from reports in the national press. Hasty investigations revealed a torn and tattered package containing 300 copies of the organisation announcement, its address defaced and undecipherable, lying in the postal sorting room of the Scottish plant. It had been badly packed and smudgily addressed to the local Personnel Manager with a covering note *inside* requesting him to distribute the announcements at his discretion. This will be recognised as one of those pieces of careless and unimaginative administration which so often stem from failure *at senior management level* to check on important matters of detail.

5 Organisation planning as a management function

The main purport of previous pages has been to look at some of the ways and means—*the management tools*—through use of which organisation planning can be implemented. The studies have covered uses of organisation check-lists, methods of assembling, analysing and quantifying significant features of organisation structure, construction of organisation charts, development of management job descriptions, and ways of communicating information about organisation and appointment changes. Examples have been quoted to illustrate practical applications of all these organisation planning techniques under varying conditions and circumstances. It has now become necessary to pause and stand back, so to speak, in order to take a longer view of organisation planning and to discuss the place it occupies as a vital function of the total management process.

The phrase 'total management process' denotes, of course, what this book is all about. The greater part of the volume is devoted to examining in detail the different functions and activities into which the total responsibilities of management are divided and delegated and further subdivided. It will be acknowledged that most of these forms of division of the management task are to some extent arbitrary and determined by considerations of discretion and convenience. In other words, there are no immutable principles and practices which decree that, say, a manufacturing company shall be grouped for purposes of management into design, marketing, purchasing, production, personnel, accounting and secretarial functions. Yet this pattern of top management is sufficiently commonly encountered in this situation as to be regarded as almost standard practice—a pattern from which the organisation of *some companies* may appear to deviate for special reasons. Nevertheless, although the groupings into which management functions are divided and delegated may sometimes appear to be arbitrary, the necessity for existence of the functions themselves is in most cases clear and unequivocal. For instance, in the case of the manufacturing concern cited above, the question whether *Purchasing* should be separately identified as a top level function or should be embodied in the production activity is a matter which could conceivably be subject to argument. There can be no argument whatsoever about the need for *somebody* to be responsible for purchasing. By the same token, each one of the other basic functions mentioned has fairly obvious claims to existence in a medium-sized company engaged in designing, making and selling its products. These principal functions will be further divided and subdivided into related activities, each of which makes its contribution towards general management of the concern. For example, the main function of accounting may well be split into 'financial accounting' and 'cost accounting'; the latter could then be further subdivided into sections concerned with product costing, budget planning, labour cost control, and so on.

The point being stressed here is that the existence of the majority of these functions of management has been prescribed in the first instance *by obvious needs,* needs that are so clearly self-evident that it is difficult to envisage the organisation operating with any degree of success if they are not met in some way or other. It will be recalled, however, that for reasons which were examined in some depth and discussed at some length in the introductory pages to this subject, *there are no such obvious needs for the existence of the organisation planning function.*

This situation poses quite a problem. It raises the question of what practical steps can be taken to ensure that organisation planning really does (to quote from above) 'occupy its place as a vital function of the total management process'. This requires that organisation planning must be accepted and established as a continuous thread running through the weft and warp of the management fabric. It must become acknowledged as being a significant aspect of the regular planning and control elements of total management. It must cease to be regarded as an occasional management chore, an *ad hoc* job, hastily to be performed when an organisational emergency arises or a senior appointment suddenly falls vacant.

The first major step towards achieving these conditions is to appoint an *organisation planner.* Some thoughts about creating this role and deciding who shall fill it are considered in chapter 8, under the heading 'Whose responsibility?' Meanwhile, however, it will be useful to discuss in general terms the tasks which an organisation planner has to perform. It will be helpful to see how he fits in and how the performance of his duties can easily become a visible part of the ordinary processes of management planning, operations and control.

Feasibility studies

To strike the right keynote from the outset, the chief executive of the undertaking (to whom the organisation planner will normally be directly responsible) must make absolutely clear to everybody concerned that he will not consider any major organisation change proposals until they have been thoroughly discussed with the organisation planner. Moreover, the chief executive will require to be presented with 'feasibility studies' in support of such proposals. These situation reports, which the organisation planner will initiate and play an active part in preparing, should contain in summary form all the information required by the chief executive (and possibly also the Board) to arrive at informed decisions. Such summaries should include:

● Description of the present and proposed organisation structure, staffing arrangements and allocations of responsibilities.
● Exposition of the necessity for and the rationale underlying the proposals.
● Particulars of the present and the proposed staff salary and fringe benefit costs, together with any other relevant financial information about effect of the changes on capital or overhead expenditure.
● Assessment of the benefits that are expected to result, directly and indirectly, from the proposed organisation and staff changes, including a reasoned justification for any consequent increases in costs.

Because almost any organisation change or new appointment is generally accepted as being, by its very nature, something of an act of faith, the points raised in the last item very often tend to be overlooked or glossed over. But it is here that the organisation planner, with his strictly professional approach, will insist on using, so far as it is possible to do so, the mechanisms for scrutinising, authorising and controlling expenditure which are a normal feature of most of the other aspects of effective management.

Amongst the numerous satirical commentaries on modern management which have been published in recent years, one of the earliest, *Parkinson's Law*, scarcely hides a harsh ring of truth behind its lighthearted style[1]. Opening with the words: 'Work expands so as to fill the time available for its completion,' the author proceeds to prove the validity of what he describes as 'this recently discovered law' by means of a number of amusing allusions to the relentless growth of certain civil service departments. He identifies two 'motive forces' which he presents as 'almost axiomatic statements', thus: (1) 'An official wants to multiply subordinates, not rivals', and (2) 'Officials make work for each other'.

It must be admitted that Professor Parkinson was writing to amuse his readers; it must be agreed that his 'case material' was drawn mainly from civil service sources and statistics; it must be conceded that he probably selected and juxtaposed some of the facts to the point of ridicule. Nonetheless, a measured survey of the growth pattern of the staff departments of almost any industrial or commercial enterprise *relative to changes in its rate of output* can prove to be a very salutary exercise indeed. More often than not the results suggest that harsh truth really does lie behind Parkinson's gentle mockery.

The point emphasised by this aside is that the organisation planner, working in conjunction with finance staff and any other specialists who can assist, has a personal responsibility for vetting all organisation and staffing proposals to ensure that they are realistic and economical in the deployment of manpower, and that they are free from the self-expanding, empire-building tendencies which afflict so many organisations. In order to do this effectively, of course, the organisation planner will require to exercise a certain amount of special skill. Such expertise will come mainly from his familiarity with management job descriptions and his ability to assess their work content. But he will also develop other empirical methods of quantifying and measuring the various factors involved in setting up or modifying the staffing arrangements of a departmental organisation.

Aids to planning

Wherever possible, these methods of presenting relevant supporting information should involve liberal use of charts and diagrams, visual aids which offer considerable scope for ingenuity in condensing important facts and figures into simple form in order to convey their significance to individuals or to groups of people in a rapidly assimilable way. The experienced organisation planner will often equip himself with a set of these diagrams, specially designed to follow the sequence of a line of explanation and to support a logical argument.

Fig. 7.5.1 reproduces one of such a series of coordinated charts prepared for a particular organisation assignment. The project took place in a fairly large industrial undertaking which consisted of a parent factory and three branch

[1] C. Northcott Parkinson; *Parkinson's Law or the Pursuit of Progress*, J. Murray 1958.

Fig. 7.5.1
Factory overhead
expenses

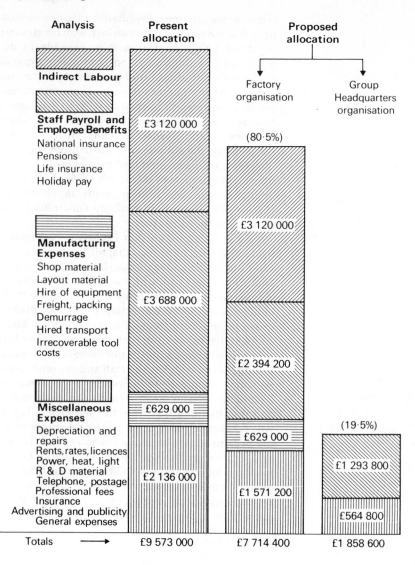

Analysis	Present allocation	Proposed allocation

Factory organisation   Group Headquarters organisation

Indirect Labour

Staff Payroll and Employee Benefits
National insurance
Pensions
Life insurance
Holiday pay

£3 120 000

(80·5%)

£3 120 000

Manufacturing Expenses
Shop material
Layout material
Hire of equipment
Freight, packing
Demurrage
Hired transport
Irrecoverable tool costs

£3 688 000

£2 394 200

Miscellaneous Expenses
Depreciation and repairs
Rents, rates, licences
Power, heat, light
R & D material
Telephone, postage
Professional fees
Insurance
Advertising and publicity
General expenses

£629 000

£629 000

(19·5%)

£1 293 800

£2 136 000

£1 571 200

£564 800

Totals ⟶   £9 573 000   £7 714 400   £1 858 600

factories. The three outlying plants had grown up over the previous ten years
and, because they were located in different parts of the country, each had
developed a representative range of staff functions, e.g. purchasing, accounting, personnel, production engineering, research and development. These
staff activities were *functionally* controlled by the respective departmental
heads back at the parent factory. Thus the specialist staffs at the parent plant
increasingly found themselves to be 'wearing two hats', that is to say,
performing in a coordinating and controlling 'group staff' role as well as
operating at factory level in the parent plant. This situation, charged as it was
with potential problems, was beginning to creak badly.
    Following preliminary investigations and discussions, the organisation

planner began to develop in detail a set of proposals designed towards improving the situation. In its effects this proposed solution was the fairly obvious one of organisationally separating out the 'group staffs' from the 'plant staffs' at the parent factory: a solution which might seem obvious in principle, but to those concerned was likely to appear difficult and disruptive to put into practice.

In developing justification for the proposed changes, the organisation planner made detailed analyses of the nature and methods of distributing overhead expenses under the existing organisation arrangements. Among the special set of charts he produced were some which demonstrated how disproportionate and unfair was the present allocation of overheads at the parent plant. This became particularly striking when the charges were expressed in terms of local production costs per unit of output as compared with the position at the branch factories. In purely accountancy terms, the solution to this particular aspect of the problem appeared to be simple: merely to separate out the true costs of overhead services rendered and to charge them accordingly to the 'users', wherever they may be in the group. But it is axiomatic to say that *no system of accounting which involves allocation of responsibility for expense budgets, cost centres, control procedures and the like can exist at all unless there is a clear organisational framework and pattern of delegation through which it can be operated.* In this case the overall organisation pattern of the company had failed to keep pace with changing needs and was now palpably incapable of accommodating an improved system for the allocation and control of overhead costs.

It must be understood, of course, that the organisation planner's investigations revealed that this difficulty concerning administration of overhead expenses represented only one of many management problems which could be attributed to faulty organisation structure and inadequate delegation. In order to provide a consistent basis for persuasive discussion of all these matters with the managers concerned, he prepared a set of ten sequential diagrams. Each of these served to illustrate and to quantify some aspect or other of the problems and to point towards their solution. The chart reproduced as Fig. 7.5.1 is one which appeared early in the sequence. It was designed to demonstrate diagrammatically:

- analysis of the parent factory's overheads by type of expense;
- present method of allocating these expenses within the existing organisation;
- proposed method of allocating the expenses within the suggested organisation.

It will be observed that maximum impact was secured by expressing significant figures in 'bar chart' form. This method of presentation enabled the organisation planner vividly to demonstrate, among other things, that irrespective of the way in which they might be allocated, the costs of 'non-productive' wages and salaries accounted for *nearly three-quarters* of the total overhead expenses. Indirect payroll proportions of this order are commonly encountered throughout manufacturing industry, a fact which frequently arouses surprise when it is first fully realised. It is also a fact which forcibly points the need for maintaining constant surveillance and control over departmental growth and staff increases. Clearly the organisation planner plays an active part towards the discharge of these responsibilities.

Short- and
long-term
planning

Activities of the organisation planner will generally fall into two categories: short-term and long-term projects. The former will be the sort of situation where the need for organisation study (and possibly change) is immediately apparent, or at least discernible to the organisation planner if to nobody else. This requires that the organisation planner should be privy to all policies and decisions which could conceivably give rise to effect on some part of the management structure and pattern of delegation. As will be seen later, this requirement virtually predetermines the position which the organisation planner must occupy within the hierarchy of management.

It may reasonably be assumed, of course, that in the area of short-term organisation planning the likelihood of structural or staffing changes arising out of management decisions or other causes will be fairly obvious to most of those concerned. What is important, however, is that the responsibility for pursuing, planning and proposing the changes should be vested in one person from the outset. Still more important, that this person should be, and should clearly be seen to be, personally independent and uninvolved; that is to say, not affected himself by any of the changes. This adds another requirement or dimension to the role of the organisation planner.

General information supported by typical examples has been given in previous pages to indicate how short-term organisation problems should be handled. It will have been observed that there is no prescribed or set piece method of approach. But it will have been gathered that investigation, analysis, consultation and discussion (followed where necessary by yet more investigation, analysis, consultation and discussion) will almost invariably produce an integrated and acceptable solution to a short-term organisation problem about which the facts are known.

But what of longer term organisational situations, where the future may be hazy and many of the facts unknown? It could be argued that every industrial and commercial organisation is eternally faced with this kind of problem. It might be said that, in order to plan ahead sensibly, those who are responsible for directing its affairs need to have some advance knowledge of the kind of management structure which will be required to meet its needs not only next year, but in five or ten years' time, or even fifteen to twenty years hence. Experience shows, however, that in this electronic age of space travel, when the forward planning of certain events can result in performances of almost incredible timing and precision, the long-term planning of industrial and commercial organisation structures continues to be a very pragmatic and pedestrian affair indeed.

Organisation
studies

It will be recalled that in the introductory passages to the subject of organisation planning some thought was given to what were described as 'just a few of the virtually limitless number and variety of factors which could have contributed in some way or other towards determining the existing form of an organisation'. When considering these possible influences it became evident that many of them were generated by circumstances and conditions over which *the management,* as such, had little or no control. In short, it was demonstrated that the organisation structure of almost any enterprise at any particular time is largely 'accidental' in nature. To cavil at this fact is to be unrealistic; to ignore it can be misleading. It points to one of the reasons why so much that has been written about the *principles* of organisation provides so little enlightenment or guidance to managers who are faced with the *practice* of organisation planning. Too many writers approach the subject with basic assumptions that are open to question. In some cases they seem vaguely to assume that a manager is starting off with a blank sheet of paper, so to speak, faced with the task of constructing an organisation where none has existed before. They fail to acknowledge that the probability of ever encountering such a basic situation in real life is so remote as to be almost academic. Other approaches, while recognising that an organisation already exists, postulate theories which could involve farreaching changes in its form and structure. These possibilities are discussed in a manner which suggests that management, given the required theoretical knowledge, already possesses the power to plan and implement sweeping changes in the shape and working methods of its organisation. In all these approaches to the study of organisation, two important factors tend to be either overlooked or underestimated. One of these is represented by failure to take sufficient account of the infinite number of *external* influences which contribute to shaping the pattern of an organisation. The other shortcoming is an apparent inability to bridge the gap that exists between expounding theory on the one hand and, on the other, tackling the practical problems of implementing changes *which are within the power of management to control.*

These criticisms are aptly illustrated by a book review which appeared in a recent British Institute of Management publication.[1] The reviewer comments in generally favourable terms on a book by an established and widely read author on the subject of organisation, but concludes his review with the following words:

> It helps us the more by repeated reading and may therefore be used as a practical reference book; but since the subject is far from trivial it also requires an element of abstract thought both to analyse one's organisation and to decide which options to choose in order to design an improved organisation. Having undertaken these two tasks, there remains a gulf before actual implementation in the real situation can be carried out; yet it is surely necessary to maintain this level of thinking. The Author more than competently helps us with the first two stages; it seems inevitable that the reader has to go it alone for the vital third stage. Let us hope we are up to it.

The foregoing criticisms and comments are *not* intended to imply that very little long-term organisation planning takes place simply because of lack of knowledge and advice about *how to do it.* It would be more realistic to acknowledge that very little long-term organisation planning takes place simply because of lack of information and material *with which to do it.*

Guide to planning

Any kind of planning which is to be of practical value in furnishing a guide to future management action has to meet at least three basic requirements. First, it must be founded on dependable data from which reasoned inferences can be drawn, likely needs can be foreseen, and planning proposals to meet those needs can be prepared. Second, when the plans have been approved and have become instruments of management policy they must be expressed in terms

[1] *Management Abstracts, Digests and Reviews,* **13,** no. 4, 1973.

of delegated responsibilities. Third, these responsibilities must be seen to be capable of being carried out by the executives to whom they are delegated.

How do the requirements of *long-term* organisation planning relate to these criteria? To begin, the question of 'dependable data' poses problems. It has been demonstrated in previous pages that, in comparison with most other aspects of management, *organisation structure* is an abstract affair. It is a notional pattern of interrelated responsibilities and accountabilities, a complex of intricate relationships, the substance of which can only partially be discerned and inadequately expressed in concrete terms by means of such devices as organisation charts, management job descriptions and formal appointment announcements. But no matter how inadequate these means of expressing organisation concepts may seem to be, in situations where they do not exist (or where they have been badly prepared or ill maintained) it follows that there is no 'dependable data from which reasoned inferences can be drawn'. In such circumstances no long-term organisation planning worthy of that description can take place. Even in those situations where dependable data *is* available, another problem arises.

This concerns the next stage of planning at which 'likely needs can be foreseen'. Basic information required for the conduct of long-term organisation planning is of two kinds. One part consists of knowledge of the *present* organisation structure coupled with an insight as to how effectively or otherwise it is operating under existing conditions. The other part consists of discernible knowledge about the *future* conduct and activity of the undertaking as a whole, together with an assessment of the impact that planned or foreseeable changes are likely to make on its organisational resources. But when this latter kind of information comes under scrutiny and discussion from a long-term organisation planning standpoint, its paucity and limitations quickly become apparent. However sophisticated may be the planning techniques from which the information is derived, doubts and uncertainties soon begin to be expressed in questions such as 'how really dependable is the data on which the forecasts are based?' or 'how long are these plans likely to hold good before they are significantly affected by unforeseen circumstances?' Of course such doubts and misgivings are not confined to wouldbe organisation planners: questions of this kind face all those who seek to plan ahead and make provision for anticipated change in any area of management. And obviously such questions are incapable of being answered: they merely signify the ultimate element of uncertainty which underlies all forms of forecasting and forward planning.

Assertions

The foregoing thoughts are not presented as a policy of despair. They are intended to serve as a prelude and introduction to the following set of assertions on the topic of long-term organisation planning—assertions which are drawn from practical experience in this particular problem area:

1. It has been found in practice to be virtually impossible to design long-term organisation plans to effect significant changes in organisation structure. In this context 'long-term' denotes any period reaching beyond two or three years into the future: 'significant changes' means changes affecting more than 10 to 15 per cent of management positions in an organisation or any

part thereof which is capable of being separately studied as an operating group or unit.

2. The reasons for this inability to plan ahead stem from the variety and unpredictability of factors likely to affect organisation structure. The 'likely factors' were examined and discussed at some length in the introduction to this subject (see pp. 924–6).

3. Short-term organisation planning should be conducted as a continuing activity. Here 'short-term' signifies organisation studies resulting in planned changes which could possibly take two to three years to implement: 'continuing activity' means under constant review and revision as circumstances require.

4. There should always be in existence an overall plan outlining the organisation structure as it is expected to be two to three years hence. Such an overall plan normally takes the form of a set of rough organisation charts supported by draft outline management job descriptions.

5. This continuous 'rolling plan' concept of *short-term organisation planning coupled with organisation control* disposes of the need for long-term organisation planning as such.

Organisation control

The newly introduced idea of *organisation control* calls for further explanation and comment.

The 'overall plan' mentioned at 4 above will not only show the 'target' organisation which it is intended to achieve in two to three years' time: it will show also some of the *stages* through which the organisation will pass as it is developed towards this target. The number of such 'intermediate phase' plans and their degree of detail will largely depend on the extent and importance of the organisation changes that are envisaged. If relatively little change has been planned for the next two to three years, twelve-monthly forecasts of the overall organisation pattern will probably suffice. But if plans have been made to effect significant or widespread organisation changes, then projections should be made to illustrate the anticipated results at stages which mark intervals of not more than five to seven months over the course of the following two to three years.

The practice of projecting and anticipating stages or steps in the implementation of organisation plans in itself activates the 'rolling plan' concept. For as each next stage is reached (in terms of elapsed time) it becomes necessary to project another foremost stage of the plan—as in the manner of maintaining a periodic moving average.

This 'continuous review' approach to organisation planning makes possible two other things. It ensures that the overall plan is frequently renewed and updated and (if it proves to be necessary) modified in the light of new circumstances or fresh thinking. It also provides the basis for producing tangible information from which timely progress reports can be prepared and departures from plan can be examined and explained. In other words, the managerial element of *control* (i.e. comparing performance with plan and identifying variances) can be exercised over the function of organisation planning. This provides practical means whereby organisation planning can, to quote what might earlier have seemed a somewhat fanciful phrase, 'become accepted and established as a continuous thread running through the weft and warp of the management fabric'.

It is of course obvious that the executive upon whom the responsibility for establishing and maintaining such a system of management controls is the organisation planner. What form his reports will take, how frequently they will be prepared and to whom they will be presented depends on the local style of management coordination and communication. In addition to statutory Board meetings (normally held monthly and often rather formally arid affairs) it is common enough for the chief executive of an undertaking to hold *operating management* meetings on a monthly, fortnightly, weekly or even daily basis. Assuming that such meetings are reasonably well organised and conducted, they will follow a previously issued agenda which in turn will be amplified and supported by factual information in the shape of performance figures, progress reports and statistical data to provide bases for review, discussion and decision-taking. Organisation should feature as a regular item on the agenda of such meetings and the organisation planner should be prepared to speak on his subject with the aid of suitable explanatory material. During discussion of other topics on the agenda the organisation planner must also be ready and able to make positive contribution on the organisational aspects and implications of any matter which arises. And, for the very reason that the *organisational* implications of management decisions can be so easily overlooked or neglected until unforeseen troubles begin to arise, this latter role of the organisation planner is especially important. How often do pressing management problems seem to be purely technical in nature? How frequently do the solutions appear to be solely concerned with improving performance of machinery or reliability of equipment or effectiveness of systems? Almost invariably management decisions made to tackle such problems will have organisational undertones; that is to say they will involve some change or shift of emphasis, temporarily or permanently, in the nature and delegation of responsibilities. And unless these new responsibilities are thought through and clarified from the outset, the chances of success of any corrective action will undoubtedly be put at risk.

Events which lie behind the memorandum reproduced as Fig. 7.5.2 serve usefully to illustrate this point. The background to the situation concerns a confectionery and processed foodstuffs firm with a wide range of product lines. One of these products is mechanically packaged in cartons, wrapped and labelled on high-speed automatic machines. Until recently the cartons and outer wrapping materials had been bought in from outside manufacturers, ready to be fed into the automatic machines. About six months ago, as the result of careful cost analysis and feasibility studies, it had been decided to install machinery and facilities for manufacturing the cartons, wrappings and printing the labels within the food processing plant. From the beginning unforeseen snags had arisen. Teething troubles, aggravated by unfamiliarity with the new equipment, had given rise to frequent breakdowns and output of this best-selling line of foodstuffs was suffering accordingly. Almost in despair the management hastily decided to call in a firm of consulting engineers who were known to possess specialised knowledge and experience of this type of equipment and its operation.

The matter had by this time become so pressingly urgent there is no doubt that, but for intervention of the organisation planner, the outside consulting engineers would have been moved in with 'dynamic' (and probably verbal) terms of reference such as 'take whatever action is necessary to get the job going as quickly as possible'. Maybe some kind of results would have been

Fig. 7.5.2
Memorandum
introducing firm
of consulting
engineers

To: All Executives and Supervisors

From: The Managing Director

MEATIMIX: PACKAGING MATERIAL OPERATIONS

You are aware that we have been encountering many 'teething troubles' on the recently installed line for manufacturing Meatimix packaging materials. Such problems were to be expected during the early days of pioneering this new and technically complex in-plant operation. Nevertheless, I believe that we have now reached the stage where we require the full-time support of experienced outside specialists to assist us in consolidating and further developing the production of packaging materials. Accordingly the following arrangements will become effective from Monday next, 27 January.

TEMPORARY MANAGEMENT

1. *Executive control*
   The firm of Kartoncups Design Limited (whose activities have been well known to us for several years) will take over complete executive and technical control of the carton assembly, wrapping materials and label printing equipment and ancillary services in the Meatmix Plant. It is anticipated that this temporary arrangement will last for about six months, i.e. until around next July.

2. *Organisation*
   The pattern of organisation and delegation of responsibilities through which these arrangements will operate is as follows:
   (a) Mr J. W. Brown of Kartoncups is appointed as Acting Production Manager: Packaging Materials. He will be directly responsible to Mr K. Johnson, Plant Manager, for all packaging material production and technical development activity.
   (b) Mr F. A. Green (Superintendent: Cartons) and Mr S. G. Blue (Superintendent: Wrapping and Printing) will both become directly responsible to Mr J. W. Brown. Their day-to-day duties for managing their respective plants will remain unchanged.
   (c) Mr A. B. Lewis (formerly Production Manager: Packaging Materials) is permanently appointed as Packaging Development Manager. For the duration of this assignment he will be responsible to Mr J. W. Brown and will provide him with the support of his extensive knowledge and experience of packaging technology. After the conclusion of this temporary arrangement Mr Lewis will become personally responsible to Mr K. Johnson and his terms of reference will be published at that time.

WORK PROGRAMME

The programme of work which will be carried out during this six months' intensive assignment is being discussed and agreed in detail with those who are closely concerned. In general terms, however, the main tasks ahead will be:

1. To identify and to eliminate engineering and technical problems affecting both prime machinery and ancillary equipment.

2. To develop and introduce planning, control and monitoring procedures necessary to ensure uninterrupted flow of quality production.

3. To assist in recruitment (where necessary) and to undertake the training of existing personnel: to establish an effective organisation suitable for future management and operation of our packaging material activity.

4. To arrange and conduct the phased withdrawal of Kartoncups Design personnel from executive management at the end of the assignment period.

CONCLUSION

I am firmly convinced that this course of action is necessary to overcome our packaging material production and development problems. But I am also aware that these temporary arrangements will call for a good deal of forbearance and cooperation on all sides. I feel sure that this cooperation will be forthcoming, but I would like to be kept closely informed of progress and about any difficulties that might possibly arise.

Date: *Managing Director*
Ref:

achieved through such an arrangement. But, on reflection, it was manifestly clear that here was a situation charged with high potential for sparking off personal frictions and misunderstandings, frustrations and recriminations. Those who may have in the past found themselves involved in similar circumstances will recall (perhaps with some bitterness) how rapidly such inflammatory situations are capable of developing, if the matter has not been thought through and planned beforehand.

In the event, the organisation planner, with the full approval and support of the Managing Director, carried out a series of prior consultations and explanations, both with local managers concerned and with staff of the consulting engineers. Agreements reached during these discussions were then confirmed by widespread distribution of the memorandum shown as Fig. 7.5.2.

Responsibilities

It now becomes necessary to recapitulate and to summarise the references which have appeared in previous pages to the organisation planner and the tasks he is required to perform. For it will by this time have become evident that the organisation planner represents both a focal point and a catalytic agent through whom all management-inspired organisation changes should be planned, implemented and controlled. Therefore a summary of the responsibilities attaching to this role will serve to bring organisation planning fully into perspective as a function of the total management process.

An organisation planner should be held accountable, directly or indirectly, for the performance of tasks which would include the following:

Information

1. Providing an information service to management on organisation structure, i.e. the pattern of activity which reflects the authorised division of tasks, delegation of responsibilities and the resultant working relationships.
2. Ensuring the orderly preparation, systematic maintenance and ready availability of such information by means of:
   (a) organisation policy and appointment announcements;
   (b) management job descriptions;
   (c) organisation charts, diagrams and graphs.

Investigation

1. Initiating, or following up requests for, the conduct of organisation studies that are warranted by actual or impending changes in operating conditions or other circumstances.
2. Collating, presenting and interpreting the results of these investigations so that their significance is capable of being easily understood.
3. Seeking to gain such understanding and recognition through consultations and discussions with managers concerned.

Recommendations

1. Encouraging, collecting and evaluating managers' own ideas or suggestions for organisational and appointment changes to meet new situations.
2. Developing specific recommendations for organisation changes: discussing these proposals (so far as it is feasible to do so) with people concerned

and modifying them accordingly, thus endeavouring wherever possible to arrive at integrated and mutually acceptable solutions to particular organisation problems or needs for change.

3. Ensuring that finally agreed proposals for organisation and appointment changes are 'signed off' by those managers whose approval should be obtained, whether as a matter of authority or as an act of courtesy.

Implementation

1. Planning, in close consultation with managers concerned, the implementation of authorised organisation changes: ensuring that those who will be affected by the changes are adequately briefed beforehand.

2. Drafting announcements of organisation and appointment changes supported, as appropriate, by management job descriptions, organisation charts and other explanatory aids.

3. Preparing suitable distribution lists for such announcements and supervising the administrative arrangements for their issue in an orderly and timely manner.

4. Following up and observing the effects of organisation and appointment changes: investigating and reporting on any problems which may have arisen: initiating action required to remove such difficulties.

Summary

It has been said that the primary purpose of this summary of responsibilities is to bring into sharper focus the range of organisation planning activity as it has been explained, by precept and example, in the preceding pages. But this list of main tasks of the organisation planner also serves another purpose. By its repeated references to consultation and communication, by its underlying insistence on the need for patience and understanding, it brings out with some force *the highly personal and subjective nature of the role of the organisation planner.*

This impression might at first seem to be at variance with frequent assertions that have been made about the necessity for detachment, impartiality and independence of judgment in the practice of organisation planning. But on reflection it will be recognised that the two ideas are not incompatible. Indeed, the one is complementary to the other because, first and foremost, the organisation planner must himself be *uninvolved*; he must be in a sense 'all things to all men' and accepted as standing outside their problems before he can even start to do his job. Thereafter his success will be in large part proportionate to the degree of rapport and confidence that he can inspire as a ready listener, a willing 'chopping block' for testing other people's ideas and a sympathetic adviser and helper on their organisation problems. No matter how well devised and logically presented a proposal for organisation change may be, it will stand little chance of becoming an effective working reality unless it has the support and understanding of the majority of the people who have to make it work.

In case it should be thought that these subjective aspects of the organisation planning function have been overstated (as indeed they could have been in the process of stressing their importance) a contrasting approach to definition of the function is provided in Appendix 7.7 (see page 1052). This shows the job description of the Organisation Planning Manager of a large British corporation. The exercise of organisation planning activity is well established within this company and it forms an important segment of the total personnel function. What makes this document interesting in the present context is the marked difference in style of presentation. Whereas the responsibilities identified add up to substantially the same as those listed above, they are couched in impersonal terms which seem remote, almost bureaucratic. Yet it is fair to say that very considerable effort is made by the management of this large undertaking to ensure that organisation planning activities are conducted on a widely consultative basis, with a warmth and understanding which is belied by the somewhat chilly tone of the job description.

While this subject of organisation planning has been dealt with in the present chapter as though a feature of management in its own right, this approach has been taken only for purposes of analysis and review. 'Organisation' is essentially the *framework* of the process and action of management, the medium by which managerial responsibilities are delegated and coordinated. It can, in fact, have no significance in its own right. 'Organisation planning', therefore, has specific objectives: the one that has been considered here as the provision for effective performance in managerial roles; the other, to which attention will now be turned, may be described as providing for the future continuance of effective performance by providing for the advancement of managerial competence.

6 Management development

In any and every business there is a process of management development automatically in action from the mere facts of the continuing conduct and progress of the firm. This is reflected in two aspects. In the first place, no arrangement of management staffing can remain static or undisturbed for very long. Any changes in these staffing arrangements is an instance of 'developing' management: promoting existing personnel to fill vacancies, or recruiting newcomers from outside; changes in responsibilities because of expansion or for rearrangement of delegation; the very development of vacancies by death, retirement or termination of service. All these are manifestations of the changing or developing process in the firm's management. The second aspect arises within the application of management itself by the influence that any manager exerts on his subordinates or colleagues. For good or ill, consciously or unconsciously, a manager is unavoidably exerting influence on his assistant managers, as well as on supervisors and other personnel working under his jurisdiction. And he is influencing, too, the attitudes and relations of other managers and supervisors alongside his own division or section. His exercise of delegated responsibility is thus an incidental process of management development.

Major contemporary interest

The trend of thinking over recent years has been advocating that this influence should be overtly recognised and should become both conscious and positive. Seen in perspective related to the inherent objectives of management, every manager carries within his own role a responsibility for bringing along in skill and competence the managers under his jurisdiction, and in particular, contributing to grooming a successor to his own position who, in the passing of time, will perform at the higher standard that changes will inevitably demand. This is a concept which is well understood and accepted by the armed services where, in peacetime, regular officers are required to be trained by their superiors to standards of performance higher than those essential to the rank they currently hold: this with the object of meeting, in times of emergency, the anticipated demands of rapid expansion and wastage.

It must be recognised, of course, that presentday tendencies towards greater size, specialisation and complexity of industrial and commercial organisations present certain challenges to this simple precept of individual responsibility for ensuring personal succession. Whereas in small, compact undertakings it is relatively easy for individual executives to assess their future staffing needs empirically and to plan accordingly, in larger concerns (particularly those which are rapidly expanding or developing new techniques) it becomes necessary to institute central procedures for the overall forecasting, planning and coordinating of management development processes. Nevertheless (and this point will be raised again in a later section) such systematic procedures must be so designed that they do not tend to absolve the individual manager or supervisor from his ultimate personal responsibility for training subordinates by coaching and example *on the job*. There is no substitute for this form of management development; all other training methods and development aids are merely adjuncts to it.

It is probably true to say that in recent years more words have been spoken and written on the subject of *management development* than any other single aspect of the management activity. It has figured prominently in seminars and conferences; it has been marketed in various 'package' forms by management consultants and specialist advisers. It has given rise to the mounting of innumerable courses of instruction at technical colleges, polytechnics and other centres of management training. It has supported a steady stream of books and pamphlets, all of them advocating policies and practices, recounting experiences and offering solutions to the problems of management development.

Training boards

The subject inevitably attracted considerable attention within the scope of the Industrial Training Boards in the earlier years of their activity. Virtually every ITB gave it specific attention, and several of them had for a time committees specialising on the study of their industries' needs. Comprehensively, on behalf of all ITBs, the Central Training Council had the subject under review for some two to three years through a broad-based committee composed of persons who had had some expert involvement in this field in the course of their professional career. It could be justifiably claimed that the subject of 'management development' was exhaustively studied through the deliberations of this body, and the findings published in two reports[1] will serve for a long time to come as a reliable guide to what is involved, what problems can be expected and what practical lines of action can usefully be pursued by individual firms, although it must be recognised the *form* of the reports is that of guide notes to the ITBs.

One of the astounding features of Britain's industrial and commercial scene is that, despite all this wealth of expert publication and discussion of the subject, the *practice* of management development appears to be scanty in the extreme, and as haphazard as it has always been. There is no evidence to suggest that any planned or systematic approach to management development has become accepted or adopted, or has secured the understanding and support of managements, thereby significantly influencing the 'continuous process' which has been going on. In other words, within the majority of individual firms, changes in organisation have taken place, vacancies have been filled, new appointments have been made, in the traditional customary way. All the evidence suggests that for every position which was filled as a consequence of intelligent forethought, careful planning and declared intention, considerably more appointments have continued to be made on a basis

[1] Central Training Council, Reports by the Management Training and Development Committee: *An Approach to the Training and Development of Managers*, HMSO (36–312), 1967; and *Training and Development of Managers: further proposals*, HMSO (865494), 1969.

of stopgap urgency or political expediency, or simply the unplanned drift of seniority as expressed by length of service and 'experience'.

Lagging practice

Why is this so? It is not the intention here to add much more to the mass of verbiage, to the spate of analyses, diagnoses and remedies which have hitherto marked the treatment of management development. Most of what has been said and written on this subject is sensible, sober stuff. Many of the reasons for failure of management development schemes seem to stem from failure to follow precepts and advice on the subject which are so readily available and in such quantity. Or is it just possible that the process of management development has become so overlain with information about manpower forecasting and planning, about development of systems and procedures, about techniques for selection and training, that the most likely cause of failure has become obscured and overlooked?

It will become increasingly apparent in the pages which follow that the principles and practices of management development are bound up inextricably with those that relate to organisation planning. And this close association starts at the beginning. That is to say, it starts at the point when the *need* for management development (like that of organisation planning) first becomes fully recognised as *an essential and integral part of the day-to-day management process*. But, it will be recalled from earlier chapters, the *need* for the organisation planning function is by no means always obvious. Some time was spent deliberating why it is so often difficult to relate the signs and symptoms of some managerial malady to what is probably its real root cause, namely ignorance or neglect of the organisation planning function. Precisely the same sort of circumstances surround the subject of management development. Like organisation, it represents a process of change which is constantly taking place, sometimes predictable but frequently random and unpremeditated. Because, as mentioned above, there is generally some sort of understanding, albeit vague and unspecific, that each individual manager is responsible for making provision for replacement or growth in his own area, the situation tends to diffuse into a condition similar to that described earlier about organisational matters, where 'something which is anybody's or everybody's business is at risk of becoming nobody's business'.

Top management lead

These thoughts suggest that the first requirement of an effective management development scheme must be clear and unequivocal recognition of *the need for it* by the senior executives of the undertaking, and in particular by the *chief executive*. Indeed, commonplace though it may be to assert that ultimate responsibility for *all* the activities of an enterprise falls squarely on the chief executive, so far as this activity is concerned it is absolutely essential that he should acknowledge, and be seen to acknowledge, the need to ensure continuity of succession and development of present and future managers on a planned and rational basis. And this amounts to considerably more than giving his blessing and lending his name to a suitable statement of policy on the matter. As will be demonstrated by example later, it means maintaining a lively interest and personally participating in the tasks of selecting and training managers.

But, it may well be asked, how can awareness of this need be aroused in a busy chief executive? By what means can a Managing Director, beset by more urgent 'practical problems', be persuaded that planned and organised management development is not just another passing fad, an esoteric refinement of something which, if left alone, will probably take care of itself anyhow?

The last few words are not used in any ironical sense. For the remarks really do bring into focus the point at which a considered decision should be made: a decision whether adequate resources of management talent *can* be expected to evolve 'naturally', so to speak, from within the various departments and functions: or whether foreseeable circumstances would appear to warrant the introduction of some form of centralised stimulus, planning and coordination. Like any other management decision, this one should be taken only after weighing and deliberating as many relevant facts as can reasonably be mustered beforehand. The assembly and presentation of such information can best be accomplished by means of a *management review*.

The people who studied this matter for the Central Training Council were in no doubt at all as to the unlikely outcome of adequate managerial talent from haphazard natural evolution, as the following passages confirm:

> Positive leadership, participation and example from those in the most senior positions is essential if the various techniques (for management development) are to be effective and not allowed to degenerate into mere routine.
>
> It must be the policy of the Board of Directors to see that the importance of management development is recognised throughout the company: it will be the particular responsibility of the senior executives to keep under review the training policies of the organisation as a whole. They need to understand the management process and the purpose which management education and training are designed to fulfil. Otherwise, they will find it difficult to guide and direct the development of their subordinates and are unlikely to be receptive to unfamiliar ideas and techniques.
>
> Against the background of rapid technological and social change, management training and development should be regarded as a continuous process applying to all managers, both as individuals and as members of a team.
>
> The existence of a statement of policy on management development makes clear to everyone in the business what the intentions of the Board of Directors are and it sets the context within which the detailed plans and techniques will fit. The preparation of such a policy statement compels top management and their specialist advisers to define their reasons for investing in systematic management development.[1]

Management review   A section of chapter 2 of this Part was devoted to describing a method of carrying out a rough 'health check' on an organisation structure by means of a specially devised questionnaire (see pp. 927–930). It was argued that well-considered answers to these precise questions would always produce clear indications as to whether further investigation and management action were desirable in this area. In much the same way it is possible to compile a list of questions, the collective answers to which will bring into perspective the likely *management development needs* of an undertaking and enable their

[1] *Training and Development of Managers*, 1969, paragraphs 14–16 and 25.

importance to be judged and evaluated against other demands on management time and resources.

The checklist of questions relating to organisation structure called for a 'yes' or 'no' answer to each question, and the number of negative replies gave a rough measure of organisational weaknesses or deficiencies. To carry out a management review a somewhat different approach has to be used. Here the aim is to classify and quantify known characteristics of managerial positions and of the people who occupy them; this with the object of making reasoned projections about future changes in management personnel and discerning likely requirements. In short, the primary purpose of the exercise is to accumulate information to use as a basis for speculation. To facilitate explanation of the exercise, each question is amplified by an accompanying comment, as follows:

Management categories

● What is the present total number of management positions in the organisation?

Comment. For this purpose 'management' can be taken to mean any position where the holder is responsible for the work of others.

● What are the categories by which these positions are customarily classified and listed?

Comment. If no 'customary categories' exist (such as specific title levels or executive salary gradings) or if, after scrutiny, such categories prove to be inadequate or irrational, then some suitable method of classifying management positions will have to be invented for purposes of a management review. In one case (the history of which will later be quoted in detail) all the managerial appointments were pragmatically placed within four groups, thus:

'Key' executive

Directors holding major executive positions and heads of main operating and functional departments (mostly Senior Executive grade) holding manifestly 'key' appointments in the Company.

'Secondary' managerial

Deputy and assistant heads of main departments; heads of secondary functional departments and sections.

Foremen

All Foremen (senior and junior) in charge of productive and non-productive works departments.

Chargehands

All chargehands and leading-hands—both staff and hourly paid—throughout the Company.

● How should these categories of management be further subdivided to identify main activities or functions?

Comment. Such subdivisions will probably relate to the major and specialised functions of the undertaking, e.g. design, sales, production, purchasing, personnel, accounting and secretarial.

● How many management positions of different categories fall within each functional subdivision?

Comment. This represents the first of what will probably be a series of analyses and cross-references, each designed to bring into sharp perspective information about the pattern of management posts and their occupants. Later it will be demonstrated how this information can effectively be presented in tabular or diagrammatic form.

Management movements

● What are the official retirement dates of all managers, by categories and functions, over the course of the next twenty years (or a shorter period, if particularly significant)?

Comment. Scrutiny of the resultant figures may show a fairly steady distribution of management vacancies arising annually from this cause. On the other hand, dependent on the historical growth pattern or other special features of the undertaking, it is not uncommon for such an investigation to reveal 'bulges' within which the annual average number of impending retirements increases alarmingly during certain periods, either overall or within particular groups or functions of management.

● What were the separation rates (for reasons other than retirement) of managers during the past five to seven years?

Comment. This information (which should be available from personnel records) will identify separations caused by deaths, resignations, dismissals, transfers to associated organisations, and so on. The figures must be expressed as annual percentages, thus:

$$\frac{\text{Number of separations} \times 100}{\text{Average numbers employed}} = \% \text{ Annual separation rate}$$

● What has been the rate of management expansion during the past five to seven years?

Comment. This refers to increases in the number of management positions (it being unlikely that the number has remained static and still less likely that it has decreased). These figures also should be expressed as annual percentages, thus:

$$\frac{\text{Year A: Increase in numbers} \times 100}{\text{Average number during year A–1}} = \text{Annual rate of increase}$$

● What are the estimated numbers and categories of management positions likely to be created within the different functions over the next two to three years?

Comment. This information should be derived from the current organisation plan, preparation and maintenance of which were fully described on pages 982 to 986.

Management requirements

By analysing, cross-analysing and compounding figures derived from the above sources, it will be possible to extrapolate reasoned forecasts of management requirements, both as replacements and as additions, over a period of years. The degree of sophistication and the amount of worthwhile information to be conveyed by these projections will depend on several factors, such as the size and complexity of the undertaking, the clarity of the organisation structure and the availability of detailed and accurate personnel records. The following example serves to illustrate what can be achieved through this method of approach. The example is based on an assignment carried out some years ago in a medium-sized manufacturing company and, as will be explained later, the results gave rise to a planned management development scheme which proved to be extremely successful. The findings of the initial management review were recorded in a fairly lengthy report supported by numerous appendices, charts and diagrams. For purposes of this illustration, only the most significant figures and the most cogent conclusions drawn from the report are summarised in the following tables and explanatory notes.

Example of management review

Numbers. Basic information about the relative numbers, categories, distribution and functional roles of management positions in this manufacturing organisation is summarised in Tables 7.6.1–4, with special aspects covered in Tables 7.6.5–7.

Table 7.6.1
Categories (totals)

Categories	Nos.	Proportion
'Key' executives	58	5·5%
'Secondary' managers	98	9·3%
Foremen	291	27·6%
Chargehands	607	57·6%
Total	1 054	100·0%

Table 7.6.2
Distribution
(factories)

Categories	Plant X	Plant Y	Plant Z
'Key' executives	47	5	6
'Secondary' managers	74	11	13
Foremen	234	39	18
Chargehands	400	145	62
Total	755	200	99

Table 7.6.3
Proportions of
total employees

Company employees	Nos.	Percentage
'Key' and 'secondary' managers	156	1
Foremen and chargehands	898	6
Other staff and hourly-paid	13 925	93
Total	14 979	100

Table 7.6.4
Distribution
(functions)

Function	'Key' executive	'Secondary' management	Total	Percentage
Commercial	8	6	14	9
Engineering	8	20	28	18
Accounting	6	18	24	15
Production	28	48	76	49
Administration	8	6	14	9
Total	58	98	156	100

Notes to
Tables
7.6.1–2–3–4

1. Figures in Tables 7.6.1 and 3 show that the appointments which, for purposes of this audit, had been classified as 'key' and 'secondary' accounted for only 14 per cent of all the management positions and represented *a mere one per cent of the total number of employees.* These ratios (the like of which are by no means uncommon in medium to large size industrial organisations) serve to bring into perspective the vital role played by a relatively tiny group of managers in planning, motivating, coordinating and controlling the activities of large numbers of people. Accordingly, this is the group of positions on which the efforts of management development must be concentrated primarily.
2. Table 7.6.2 shows the not unfamiliar pattern of three-quarters of the management positions being located at the parent factory (Plant X), the remainder being unevenly divided between two distant branch factories.
3. The breakdown of 'functions' shown in Table 7.6.4 may appear to be somewhat unorthodox. In fact it reflects the state of organisational development of the company at that time. Within 'Commercial' were grouped the activities of sales, purchasing, stores and transport: under 'Administration' came the secretarial, personnel and office management functions.
4. Since the majority of Foremen and Chargehands were production-oriented, Tables 7.6.1 and 4 illustrate the dominating influence of the Production function, which above accounted for over 90 per cent of all the management positions.

Retirements

Information about the predictable retirement pattern of people presently occupying key and secondary managerial positions is tabled below in highly condensed form. During the presentation and discussion phases of the actual exercise, the significance of this information was displayed more dramatically in a series of coloured bar charts, one of which is reproduced as an example at Appendix 7.8.

The scatter of retirement dates shown in Table 7.6.5 to some extent reflects the history and peculiar growth pattern of the undertaking. The company had originally been established in the late 1920s as a British subsidiary of a US owned corporation. At that time a group of promising young men of similar ages had been selected and trained by the team of American experts who were sent to establish and manage the venture. However, as US interests in the enterprise gradually diminished and withdrew, these local 'founder members' naturally gravitated to senior management positions.

At the time that this review was made, some hitherto unforeseen effects of the unusual growth pattern had begun to emerge. Two figures derived from Table 7.6.5 will suffice to demonstrate this point:

- Within the coming ten years, seventy-six top managers (almost exactly half the present total) will disappear as a consequence of retirement alone.
- The annual *rate* of management retirements, which had hitherto averaged around a fairly steady three or four per year, suddenly upsurged to an average of more than twelve per annum during the four-year period 1972–75.

Table 7.6.5
Retirements (functions)

| Year | Retirements at 65 years | | | | | Totals | |
	Commercial	Engineering	Accounts	Production	Administration	Year	Cumulative
1965	1					1	1
1966		1		1		2	3
1967				1		1	4
1968	2	2	1	4		9	13
1969				2	1	3	16
1970	1	1		4	1	7	23
1971	1		1	2		4	27
1972	1	3	1	10		15	42
1973		4	1	5	3	13	55
1974	1		3	7	1	12	67
1975			2	5	2	9	76
1976		1	1	1		3	79
1977		2		4		6	85
1978		1	3			4	89
1979		1	1	1	1	4	93
1980	1	2	1	3	1	8	101
1981		1		2	1	4	105
1982		1	2	5		8	113
1983		1		2		3	116
1984			2			2	118
1985 Onwards	6	7	5	17	3	38	156
Totals	14	28	24	76	14		156

Separations

Annual separation rates (for reasons other than retirement) among 'key' and 'secondary' managerial personnel over a preceding seven-year period, were found to have been as summarised in the second column of Table 7.6.6, indicating that losses of managers due to death, resignations, transfers, or dismissals, were likely to average about three or four per annum.

Table 7.6.6
Managerial separations and increases

| Year | Managers in post (average) | Separations | | Increases | |
		Numbers	Rate %	Numbers	Rate %
1	140	5	3·6	3	2·2
2	140	1	0·7	—	—
3	149	4	2·7	9	6·5
4	150	5	3·3	1	0·7
5	154	2	1·3	4	2·7
6	154	2	1·3	—	—
7	156	6	3·8	2	1·3
Average	149	3·6	2·4	2·7	1·8

Expansion

Over the same period, increases in numbers of top management positions were as shown in columns 4 and 5 of Table 7.6.6, not including *planned* additional positions. These latter were known to be four, seven and ten respectively for years 5, 6 and 7—a cumulative total of twenty-one extra managerial positions.

Results of management review

As was noted earlier, the detailed findings of the management review in this example were recorded in a lengthy report: the undoubted highlight of that document was the reasoned forecast that emerged regarding future requirements of top management manpower, that is to say, the numbers of qualified and experienced managers who would be needed to fill likely vacancies within the relatively small group of key and secondary executives who between them bore prime responsibility for running the business.

These projections were arrived at by analysing and compounding figures drawn from the various sources described above, by applying ordinary commonsense judgment to interpreting their significance and then presenting the collective results as a reasoned estimate of probable management requirements during the next ten years. The main features of this forecast are set out in Table 7.6.7. The estimates shown therein, representing as they did an amalgam of factual information and reasoned speculation, projected a truly alarming picture. The full significance of the forecasts was elaborated and illustrated in detail with the aid of charts and diagrams, but the following features alone serve to indicate some dimensions of the problems that had been revealed:

● The number of new managers who would be required over the next ten years was higher than the existing total strength of management personnel.
● More than 50 per cent of the impending vacancies would have to be filled within the following 5–10 years.
● The last four years of the ten-year period would see the draining away of nearly a third of existing management talent and experience—this the result of accelerated effects of retirement.

Table 7.6.7
Estimated management manpower requirements

| Year | Retirements | Other Separations | Additions | | Total | |
			Planned	Anticipated	Annual	Cumulative
1966	2	3	4	2	11	
1967	1	3	7	2	13	24
1968	9	3	10	2	24	48
1969	3	3	—	3	9	57
1970	7	3	—	3	13	70
1971	4	4	—	3	11	81
1972	15	4	—	3	22	103
1973	13	4	—	3	20	123
1974	12	4	—	3	19	142
1975	9	4	—	3	16	158
Total	75	35	21	27	158	—

Effects of
management
review

These revelations quickly produced some effects. The Managing Director, whose previous feelings of vague unease about the management succession situation had in the first place given rise to the investigation, took swift action. He immediately appointed a steering committee consisting of the Deputy Managing Director, the Finance Director, the Production Director and an outside specialist Consultant, with terms of reference clear and unequivocal, namely: 'To devise, plan and introduce a coordinated scheme of management development aimed towards meeting the Company's future needs for qualified and experienced executives, managers and supervisors'.

The Committee was required to submit regular progress reports to the Managing Director and the subject appeared as a permanent priority item on the agenda of the monthly Board meetings of the Company. This represented the beginning of what proved to be an extremely successful management development scheme.

Up to this point the case history has been used as an illustration to serve a single purpose. That is to demonstrate how, in a real life situation, the active support and understanding of top management generally (and the chief executive in particular) were secured as a direct consequence of carrying out a management review. Maybe not many of the forward pictures projected by surveys of this kind will reveal such a sorry state of affairs. But it is fair to say that almost any management review conducted along these lines, properly assembled and intelligently interpreted, is likely to produce some surprises—and will probably stimulate some actions.

Time and again experience has demonstrated that one thing about management development is certain: by whatever means it is achieved, the full understanding and manifest support of the chief executive is an absolutely vital prerequisite. Without it, the scheme is surely doomed to founder and to fail, and, where this happens, it can do a considerable amount of damage to management morale and vitality.

7 Planning for development

Essential features

Assuming that the necessary top management support and mandate are forthcoming, it must be made clear that there can be no standard method of approach to the task of developing managers in industrial and commercial undertakings. A well devised scheme which is working effectively in one organisation will not necessarily do so in another. The approach must be empirical, and each scheme, or part of a scheme, must be specially tailored to suit the conditions obtaining in the particular organisation. However, experience has proved that there are certain essential features which should appear, to some degree, in any systematic approach to long-term management development:

- Assignment of responsibility for planning and coordinating management development activities.
- Identification, classification and grouping of management positions.
- Preparation of management job descriptions.
- Preparation of personal specifications for the management positions.
- Forecast of probable future management needs.
- Appraisal of present and potential management performance.
- Establishment of search, selection and placement methods, and of promotion procedures.
- Determination of training and development programmes for individuals or for groups of managers.
- Development and maintenance of personal records.
- Implementation, coordination and control of management development programmes.
- Systematic structuring of salary scales for managerial positions and provision for periodical review.

The foregoing items have been arranged in a logical sequence, an order in which it may be expected they would be tackled under optimum conditions. It should be recognised, however, that planned management development might begin at any one of these stages, according to the particular conditions of urgency or acceptability or other determining factors within an organisation. Moreover, in some situations considerable emphasis might be placed on one or two of these features whereas others might receive only token recognition. These points are to some extent illustrated in the example which has already been quoted: those particular circumstances demanded initial concentration on classifying management positions somewhat arbitrarily, in order to establish a reasoned forecast of future needs in some depth. Although these two steps were not in the above sequence, they did in fact precipitate policies and plans for launching an organised management development scheme.

Following are some comments on the essential features of management development as listed above.[1]

Assignment of responsibility

Perhaps next in importance to securing solid support from top management is the need to assign to a suitable individual overall responsibility for planning and coordinating management development activities. But what is meant by 'a suitable individual'?

It was stated earlier that the principles and practice of management development are bound up inextricably with those that apply to organisation planning. Indeed, it might be said that the two activities are so closely related as to represent, in a sense, two aspects of a single management activity or process. *Organisation planning* is concerned with establishing the framework through which management responsibilities can be delegated and discharged; *management development* is concerned to ensure the availability of managers of suitable calibre and sufficient numbers actually to carry out those responsibilities. Thus it is not too fanciful to suggest that organisation structure and management development represent respectively the 'static' and the 'dynamic' elements of a single basic planning function.

Once this notion has been accepted, it follows naturally that the organisation planner should sensibly bear responsibility for overlooking and integrating the various activities which together add up to management development. Who can best occupy the position of organisation planner, and how the role can be fitted into the management team are matters which are deliberated at some length in chapter 8. In the meantime it will be assumed that some form of this appointment either exists or is created as the focal point of any worthwhile management development project.

Classifications of positions

In previous pages devoted to carrying out a management review some thought has been given to classifying management positions within categories designed to reflect both status and functional considerations. It will be recalled that in the example used to illustrate the conduct of a management review, the methods employed were acknowledged to be somewhat rough and ready, based largely on commonsense judgment. It should be understood that, in the absence of a recognised grading system, such a pragmatic approach is satisfactory, *provided all existing management positions are accounted for and included in one or other of the categories.* It is also necessary at this stage to classify (perhaps provisionally) any new management appointments which are anticipated and included in the forward calculations.

When all management positions have been initially identified and classified in this manner, they may be rearranged and grouped in different ways (e.g. by departments, by functions, by locations) in order to bring them into full

---

[1] These features reflect closely those portrayed in the Central Training Council Reports cited on p. 992 above. In that context they are fully reviewed in commentary at greater length than in the present pages, including also some reference to ways and means of practical implementation. Those two Reports were a highlight in the history of management progress in the British industrial scene and their content deserves close study in any review of management development.

perspective as the potential field for management development. Obviously, the scope and range of the managerial positions to be included must be determined and decided in the specific context of each firm individually, relative to its own organisation and setting. Yet, bearing in mind the purposes of management development, it can be legitimately argued in general that *all* positions having a bearing on the effective application of the management process should be included. This is readily understood in the context of operating (or 'line') positions, but it must also be valid for the major specialist ('staff' or 'functional') positions, like those of the Personnel Manager, the Financial Controller, the Chief Buyer or the Design Manager. In relation to the operating positions a particular problem may sometimes arise as to how far down to go; for instance, are 'supervisors' to be included? A general affirmative or negative could be very difficult to justify, whereas an individual firm could well be able to answer readily and justifiably for its own requirements. One significant requirement could be the relevance of the supervisory roles in that organisation as a source of candidates for promotion to managerial positions: if such promotion is a reasonably normal practice, then at least the senior supervisory roles should be included in the scope of the management development activities.

Management job descriptions

The purposes, types and methods of preparation of 'management job descriptions' (MJDs) have been covered in some detail in pp. 953–972 above and no recapitulation is called for here. The context there was that of pin-pointing the nature and extent of managerial responsibilities allocated by delegation to the various positions in the organisation and to their holders. This has long been an area of controversy; for many years there was a widespread opposition to the notion of 'defining managerial responsibilities', though how else any clear idea of the scope and extent of delegation could be given to the holders of the positions concerned was never explained or indicated by the opponents.

The Central Training Council's Reports brought this controversy to a head and at the same time effected a resolution of it—by putting the emphasis of advocacy for MJDs into the direction of requirements for the development of individual managerial competence.[1] Among the specific purposes they serve in this direction is that of determining the 'personal specifications' appropriate to the various management positions that form the organisation structure.

Personal specifications

It has been stated earlier that there are a number of different uses for personal specifications. It has also been emphasised that it is not possible to produce a 'multipurpose' type of personal specification to meet all those possible needs; different specifications have to be designed to serve the particular purposes for which they are required. In the context of management development these documents require to be drafted with the following principal objects, reflecting the scope and burden of the delegated responsibilities in the posts concerned:

[1] See *Training and Development of Managers*, 1969, paragraphs 27–32. A full analytical review of the subject of 'defining managerial responsibilities' will be found in *Organisation: the Framework of Management*, as already cited.

1. Producing 'checklists' of the main requirements of individuals best fitted to hold and discharge the management positions as defined in MJDs.
2. Providing guidance towards measuring or judging the extent and nature of the knowledge, experience, skills and personal qualities required in each appointment.
3. Indicating the areas within which training and guided experience will be required suitably to qualify future occupants of these positions.
4. Providing guidance for selection purposes when individual candidates are under consideration for appointment, by recruitment or by promotion, to specific managerial positions.

As in the case of management job descriptions, there is no generally accepted standard layout for personal specifications. Accordingly an appropriate outline form must be decided. To suit most situations this could take the shape of four main subject divisions, namely:

Personal data
Technical knowledge and experience
Managerial skills
Personal qualities

Some methods of collecting and recording the information called for under each of these headings are described in the following paragraphs.

Personal data

This initial part of the proposed personal specification might be subdivided into three desirable requirements: age group (at time of appointment); standard of general education and background; and standard of professional or technical education and qualifications.

At the time of first conducting this exercise it will usually be found that there is very little obvious information available towards determining desirable 'standards' or 'ranges' for these personal requirements in relation to the different types of appointments under consideration. Thus, in order to provide some guide to thinking and a basis for determination, it may be necessary:

● to study closely each MJD in order to discern pointers towards specification of at least the broad limits of these requirements;
● to examine and analyse the 'on appointment' ages, education and qualifications of employees who currently hold these positions;
● to conduct a fairly widespread 'opinion survey' on the subject amongst managers who have knowledge, direct or indirect, of the jobs under consideration.

From these three sources of information and suggestions it will normally be found possible to specify adequately and realistically the basic requirements listed under personal data.

Technical knowledge and experience

Provided the relevant management job descriptions have been carefully prepared, it should be possible to derive from each a list of all the purely 'technical' subjects about which the occupant of the appointment requires to have *some* knowledge and experience. It is necessary, however, to qualify each of these technical subjects according to the *degree* of actual knowledge required for practical purposes. This can be done by considering each subject carefully (possibly with the aid of an advisory panel) and assessing it under one of the following classifications:

Class A   requires specialised knowledge and experience sufficient to qualify the executive concerned as the main local source of information and advice on the subject.

Class B   requires sufficient knowledge and experience effectively to supervise, coordinate and check the performance of specialist subordinates in this field.

Class C   requires general background knowledge sufficient to promote balance of outlook in the appointment concerned and to ensure necessary degree of vertical and lateral coordination.

Without attempting, at this stage, to evaluate the *importance* of any one technical subject as compared with another, a summary of results of such an assessment will normally reveal that the higher an appointment appears in the organisational structure the wider in range and the less penetrating in depth become the evident requirements of technical knowledge.

Managerial skills

Some similar assessment needs to be made of the skills in management required for competently meeting the responsibilities of the positions concerned. Here, a much wider-ranging and more complex topic is raised, and one about which there are likely to be considerable differences of opinion. Nor is it easy to generalise, because of the different requirements that must inevitably arise in the many different positions constituting an organisation structure. In so far as a broad approach can be used, the grouping of five aspects of competence in management practice has been suggested as set out in Fig. 7.7.1. Variations of extent and emphasis will be found among these five groups, though some part of all of them is likely to figure in virtually any

Fig. 7.7.1
Aspects of
competence in
management
practice

(a) *Technology*—design, development, manufacturing, process planning, specifications: the skills of applying appropriate technical knowledge and standards to the phases of activity covered by the responsibility defined. In many commercial enterprises, or other organisations, this category would cover professional expertise rather than technological items.

(b) *Economic operating*—attaining and maintaining high standards of quality, performance, progress, costs and profitability: through the medium of techniques of analysis, evaluation, planning and control, with appropriate coordination.

(c) *Man management*—the appointment, training, motivation, command and control of the personnel required for the effective performance of operations and activities, and for the successful attainment of objectives in accordance with standards.

(d) *Cooperation*—promoting and reciprocating the degree of executive, technical and specialist cooperation essential to effective and economical performance and to progress in pursuit of profitable change.

(e) *Customer relations*—promoting and maintaining cooperative relationships with customers and potential customers effective to continuing profitable business; or (if more appropriate) with suppliers and other outside centres of service.

managerial position. Each of the five aspects would need to be specifically assessed.

1. Man management (or personnel management)

Class A requires knowledge, experience and manifest ability to exercise direct authority over and to be responsible for the motivation, direction, discipline, supervision and morale of large numbers of employees of all grades (e.g. 200 upwards) where the chain of delegated authority comprises upwards of three or four different levels of intermediate supervision.
Class B requires sufficient experience and skill to maintain similar executive authority over medium numbers of employees of all grades (e.g. 30 to 200) with one to three intermediate supervisory levels.
Class C requires experience necessary to handle and supervise the activities of a small number of employees (e.g. up to 30) mainly of fairly responsible staff grades.

2. Executive action

A more difficult assessment is posed in this aspect of the management process because of the interplay of techniques with personal skills and attitudes: and the availability of good or reliable techniques is not always a matter resting with the decision of an individual manager. It is through this facet of his role that the manager's skills in 'economic operating' (Fig. 7.7.1) are applied and his real performance judged as a 'manager in action'.

The broad scope of what is involved in everyday executive action is set out in chapter 7 of Part One (pp. 73–100), and in the present context those numerous and varied details can be usefully summarised into four major categories, for each of which the three-stage assessment approach can be used:

(a) *Planning.* Interpreting company policy and objectives into specific and practical plans for implementation *within his own area of executive control* and within the framework of the company's overall marketing programme. Explaining objectives, programme and plans to subordinates (delegation), and establishing and agreeing suitable standards of performance (e.g. target dates, sales budgets, output levels, and so on).
(b) *Control.* Using available control information and techniques (e.g. reports, statistics, cost and financial returns, performance indices) for the purposes of (i) constantly reviewing progress and comparing results against plans; (ii) investigating and following up variances from plan.
(c) *Coordination.* Ensuring that a proper balance is maintained between the different activities of subordinates and their staffs and seeing that their efforts are coordinated in pursuance of the common aims and plans.
(d) *Communication.* Establishing and maintaining adequate standards of communication practice, i.e. freely using every possible means and opportunity of circulating information, both within the immediate area of executive responsibility and also vertically and horizontally through the organisation structure (e.g. by personal contact, correspondence, formal and informal joint consultation, control statistics, visual aids).

Class A requires *a very high standard* of knowledge, experience and personal competence in the exercise of these skills.

Class B requires *an average standard* of knowledge, experience and ability.

Class C requires *comparatively little* knowledge and experience in this field.

This particular phase of preparing personal specifications lends itself very well to critical study and assessment on a consultative basis amongst a panel of senior executives who are familiar with the jobs concerned.

Personal qualities

In addition to determining the personal data, technical knowledge and managerial skills appropriate to each management position under review, it is necessary also to consider the purely *personal* qualities which are desirable in the occupant of the post. For practical purposes of drafting personal specifications it will normally suffice to outline briefly but specifically the personal qualities which common sense suggests as being appropriate to the majority of the management positions in the undertaking. Typical headings for such characteristics might be as follows:

Appearance and presence	Self-expression
Mental ability	Responsibility, judgment and stability
~~Self-confidence~~	Acceptability
Interest in individuals	Special personal qualities
Integrity and sincerity	

The question of identifying and quantifying the personal qualities or 'personality traits' to be desired in a good manager is a highly subjective matter. A great deal of experimental research has been carried out in this field (much of it superficial and pseudoscientific) and extravagant claims have been made about the effectiveness of some testing techniques for observing and measuring these characteristics. It seems to be a matter of common sense, however, that the most reliable evidence concerning personal qualities is to be discerned from the impact that an individual makes on other people in his working group *over a period of time.* Shrewd observation of these reactions and relationships is of more practical value than most psychology-oriented personality profiles.

Example of personal specification

By drawing together the information described in the preceding paragraphs a complete personal specification may be built up for each management position. An example of such a document, taken from the Electricity Supply industry, is shown at Appendix 7.9.

Forecast of future needs

The subject of forecasting probable future management needs has been discussed and illustrated in some detail in chapter 6, under 'Management Review'. Sufficient at this point, therefore, to reiterate that the results of a sensibly conducted survey of future requirements, both replacements and additions, almost invariably galvanise top management into action. It can also be added (not without a touch of cynicism) that although most managers, like the rest of us, are at heart resistant to change which promises to affect them personally and immediately, there is usually no difficulty in enlisting their willing support for this forward-looking aspect of a management development scheme. For this is a matter of planning for change *in the future*, change which is not likely to threaten anybody's immediate status or security. There is the added benefit that, within the framework of a planned management development scheme, selection for promotion can be in fact—and can be so seen—based upon objective criteria, thus removing the allegations of 'favouritism'.

Appraisal methods

The foregoing stages of approach to a possible scheme for the systematic development of managers have embraced the identification and definition of the management positions, the personal specifications and forecasting of anticipated requirements. The next logical step would be to conduct an appraisal of existing personnel against the standards established in these specifications. In short, having estimated the numbers and kinds of people required in managerial roles, it follows that a survey should be made amongst the existing employees in order to determine who will be actually or potentially available to meet those requirements.

The manner in which this appraisal should be carried out, especially when it is being carried out for the first time, is open to a wide range of choice and would vary according to the size and other circumstances prevailing in the undertaking. Broadly speaking there are three possible ways of approaching the problem, namely:

General. To carry out personal appraisals of *all* staff employees falling within certain predetermined limits of age, experience, salary, etc. (e.g. 'all male staff aged between twenty-five and forty-five years with more than three years' service and currently receiving a salary of £x upwards').
Nomination. To instruct line managers and departmental heads to *nominate* subordinate managers or other employees who meet specified requirements of age, etc., and who possess, in the opinion of the nominators, discernible potential for development and promotion.
Voluntary. To advertise internally (and perhaps also externally) for individual applications from staff members who meet certain prescribed basic standards and to *invite* them to be appraised with a view to being earmarked for special training and development.

Each of these methods of approach possesses advantages and disadvantages, but for purposes of illustration it will be assumed that the first or 'general' approach would be used, as the procedures employed would remain basically the same in all cases. In this approach *every* staff employee who falls within certain stated limits would be appraised by the manager to whom he was directly responsible.

Performance and potential

Before going on to consider possible methods and procedures for the conduct of appraisals, it is necessary to examine more closely the *purposes* of systematic appraisal schemes as they are used within the framework of organised management development. Broadly speaking, the purposes are twofold: that is to say they are aimed towards eliciting useful information about the present *performance* of an individual and also about his *potential* for further development. These two facets are aptly explained in the following extracts from the Central Training Council Report referred to above:

> *Appraisal of performance* measures the extent to which the manager has succeeded in attaining the objectives set out in his job description. It shows what he has or has not achieved, taking account of any factors outside his control or not foreseen when the objectives were originally decided. It has the immediate purpose of pointing to the areas where current performances could be improved, either immediately or after training.
>
> *Appraisal of potential* makes a judgment—necessarily in a broader and more subjective way—on what the manager may be capable of in the future, drawing on his past performance where relevant but looking particularly at his strengths and weaknesses and his capacity for development. In this way it would suggest answers to such questions as:
> —should he be transferred and if so where?
> —is he ready now for promotion?
> —is some form of training or guidance needed in order to fit him for transfer or promotion?
> —are there any personal factors such as bad health, unwillingness to move, etc. to be considered in planning his career?
> —what are his own ambitions and interests and how far are the company's plans for him consistent with them?
>
> Each of these requires a different approach. In *performance appraisal* it is the actual achievements of the man in his job which count. In *potential appraisal* an assessment has to be made which, although based on what he has done, must include an element of conjecture about how he might perform in changed circumstances. Although they involve separate considerations, performance and potential review may for convenience by conducted at the same time.
>
> Appraisal of performance and potential are both difficult, the latter particularly so because of the subjective element. Firms might find it advantageous to cover only appraisal of performance when they first set up their schemes and introduce appraisal of potential later. Appraisals also give the company the opportunity to consider its own activities in relation to its staff and thus to find out in what ways it is failing to sustain its personnel effectively.[1]

Attitudes to appraisal

Points made in the final paragraph of the passage quoted above call for some comment. There is no doubt that introducing appraisal is extremely difficult. In the eyes of many managers an appraisal scheme appears to be an excessively time-consuming source of drudgery, coupled with the risk of acute embarrassment. It represents a considerable load of paperwork in which (and this is the embarrassing part) intimate personal opinions about close subordinates have to be committed to writing and maybe even discussed with them. Too often this innate resistance to appraisal schemes tends to give rise to a safe, 'down-the-middle' approach to evaluations and ratings; and the recorded opinions then become as valueless as they are innocuous.

The observations suggest that the more readily apparent the *reasons* for conducting appraisals are, the easier it will be to overcome such inertia. And this immediately calls into question the idea that 'firms may find it advantageous to cover only appraisals of performance when they first set up their

[1] *Training and Development of Managers*, 1969, paras. 33–5.

schemes, and to introduce appraisal of potential later'. Mention was made earlier that it is generally not too difficult to secure understanding and to stir up interest and support—even enthusiasm—for the adoption of an organised management development project. It would therefore seem to be sensible to demonstrate from the outset that, useful though appraisal of *performance* may be, the appraisal of *potential* is one of the cornerstones of planned management development—and so take advantage of the momentum that an imaginatively launched management development scheme will engender.

To some extent there is a recurrent process of 'appraisal of performance' of managers and supervisors going all the time in the everyday exercise of management practice, in so far as a manager or senior manager is regularly supervising the exercise of responsibility by the men and women in the delegated positions under his jurisdiction. This informal appraisal is the more pertinent and the more realistic when systematic techniques of planning and control are in use within the firm: for example, a scheme of budgetary control, or a firmly framed marketing programme, or scheduling of production against predetermined standards. In these settings the data thrown up daily, weekly or monthly by the management information system form indicators to performance and reflect quite closely the exercise of responsibility by the supervisors and managers. In fact, modern techniques and systems of planning and control are specifically designed to line up with the patterns of delegation and so to pinpoint responsibility for performance in line with targets, plans and objectives. These indicators show the outcome of the application of managerial skill and, therefore, the informal reviews of actual performance thereby provided will correctly contribute to the assessments made in the more formal periodic appraisal. This aspect of appraisal is also included in the guidenotes from the Central Training Council cited above.

Appraisal forms

Introduction of an appraisal scheme must be preceded by a good deal of careful preparation and widespread consultation. The layout and content of the form which is actually used for recording information about the individuals concerned will to a large extent set the keynote of the project. And the range of possibilities in this matter is very wide indeed. At its most simple and straightforward the outline shape of the personal appraisal form could directly reflect the pattern of the personal specification as described above (see pages 1005–8). In effect it could be so designed that the relevant facts and the considered opinions could be recorded about each individual being appraised under the following headings:

Personal data
  Name
  Age
  Present appointment
  Previous appointments
  Education
  Training
  Qualifications
Technical knowledge and experience
Managerial experience and performance
Personal qualities
General comments

Guidance would be given to the assessors towards completing the technical, managerial and personal qualities sections of the appraisals by issuing and explaining a choice of 'graded evaluations' similar to the different classifications used in the preparation of personal specifications.

In the final part of the appraisal (under General comments) the assessor could be invited to comment freely and constructively on such matters as:

1. The individual's general suitability for further training and development in any particular field.
2. Any outstanding qualities or special aptitudes displayed by the individual during the course of his duties.
3. Any noteworthy weaknesses or defects which might be remedied as the result of specific training or planned and guided experience.

An example of a more closely detailed and sophisticated Performance and Potential Appraisal form is shown at Appendix 7.10. It will be noted that this form is designed for completion by two 'reviewers' and it comprises six parts, viz:

   I. Personal data[1]
  II. Performance review
 III. Performance rating overall
 IV. Training and development recommendations
  V. Forecast of potential
 VI. Performance rating code (for use when completing Part II of the appraisal).

A somewhat different approach to the design of a Performance and Potential Appraisal form is illustrated at Appendix 7.11. It will be seen that this form has been designed for completion at the time of salary review, thus making use of the fact that this is a time when every manager is required to reflect and to marshal his thoughts about the performances of his subordinates. The design of the form and the factors selected as guides to appraisal represent an endeavour to reflect significant aspects of the managerial roles. The 'two grade' form of assessment necessitates (even compels) serious consideration before an entry is made, especially if there are 'weak' ratings to be recorded.

Pilot runs

Before introducing a staff appraisal system of any kind on a widespread basis throughout an undertaking, it is advisable to carry out limited 'pilot runs' (with the full knowledge and cooperation of those being appraised) in order to give guidance and practice to the assessors, but more particularly to gain experience of the administrative procedures involved. These arrangements need to be well thought out and efficiently implemented; poor administration can bring the best of appraisal plans rapidly into disrepute. This is one of the most cogent reasons why a simple approach is to be recommended. Probably, appraisal schemes have failed more as the result of becoming bogged down in an administrative morass than for any other reason![2]

---

[1] As the information was the same as that called for in the previous example, Part I has not been reproduced in the layout at Appendix 7.10.

[2] A fuller commentary on appraising performance and of the contribution from management development programmes will be found in *Managing for Revival*, by E. F. L. Brech, Management Publications, 1972, pp. 241–54.

Selection for development

On completion of the initial survey, all the personal appraisal forms would be checked and analysed. By careful sifting and intelligent interpretation of the facts and opinions recorded, it should be possible roughly to grade all the staff employees concerned in terms of their relative potential for development. Closer scrutiny would then be made of, say, the most promising 20 per cent and from amongst those would be finally screened and selected an appropriate number for planned training and development towards filling future management vacancies.

Here again, procedures through which the process of screening and selection is carried out will vary according to local circumstances and needs. It is not proposed to dwell here on alternative methods of approach, but one aspect must be strongly emphasised: that is the importance of conducting the whole exercise on a footing which is as frank and open as possible. This attitude would include, for instance, taking some pains courteously to explain to all unsuccessful candidates the reasons why they have not been chosen at this particular time. One of the most commonly encountered objections to any organised and publicised scheme of management development is the assertion that it gives rise to what is sneeringly termed the 'blue-eyed boy' situation. Although the risk is often exaggerated (and sometimes shelters excuses for doing nothing at all) there is a danger of its arising. The most sensible safeguards against it lie within the spirit and letter of the scheme: ensuring that the selection methods are rational and fair, that they are as objective as possible, that they are honestly and sympathetically administered—and that all these things are seen by everybody concerned to be manifestly true.

Preparation of development programmes

With this activity the main feature of management development is reached, the core of the objective of the policy and of its application. This is where the practical steps will be established for contributing towards the strengthening and/or upgrading of the managerial competence and performance in the firm's organisation. In this context the outcome of the appraisal activity needs to be looked at from three different (though interrelated) aspects:

1. Providing for the systematic development, by training and planned experience, of that 20 per cent or so who have been identified as showing promise of potential. This cadre of staff will emerge when a systematic appraisal procedure is applied and carried through for the first time; thereafter, in subsequent years (say) there will be incidental additional members of staff selected for potential promotion.
2. Providing for further development of the firm's managers and supervisors in accordance with the deficiencies or needs identified from the appraisals; again, there may be a widespread requirement brought to light here the first time a systematic appraisal is undertaken; once appraisal is operating regularly the needs identified will be more specific and individual, and will be related more closely to the planned or known developments in the firm's activities and organisation for which the further or higher managerial positions and responsibilities are required.
3. Providing the special development programmes and facilities for the small selected group of existing managers who are deemed to show potential for advancement to the senior managerial positions within the foreseeable future.

*Management
trainee*

The development programmes for each of these three categories have their specific importance, but it is clear that the second and third must be highly individual, whereas the first may have several more generalised features. It is only in respect of this first category that the term 'management trainee' may be used.

For the selected personnel in this first category it may be possible to assume that the particular function or department for which each candidate is to be groomed can be identified: then his current personal appraisal should be reviewed against the standards and requirements prescribed in the personal specifications of the supervisory or managerial appointments in that particular function or department. The resultant comparison would broadly reveal, under the headings of technical knowledge, managerial skills and personal qualities, the attributes in which the employee concerned is at present weak or deficient. Suitably compiled, with appropriate explanatory notes and comments, this information would provide a training profile on which an individual development programme could be first sketched out and then built up.

Methods of training and personal development which could be embodied in an individual programme include such features as:

- Planned movement or job rotation
- Special project assignments
- Personal assistant or temporary understudy appointments
- Attendance at selected internal and external courses
- Facilities for part-time or sandwich course technical studies.

It will not generally be found possible, even if it were considered desirable, to plan firm development programmes in detail for long periods ahead. Progress at any one stage will have depended largely on the individual's response to training as well as to other imponderable factors such as those governing opportunities for movement. Nevertheless, there should always be in existence a broad outline programme in respect of each selected employee covering the next two to three years' planned development. Not only should this personal programme be reviewed frequently and altered in detail as the necessity arises, but it should form a part (along with the programmes of all the other management trainees) of the organisation planner's fund of knowledge, the pool of material from which he draws when reviewing the 'dynamic' aspects of detailed proposals for organisation change.

Consideration of development and training programmes for existing managers will be dealt with in a later section.

Personal records

What kind of personal records should be kept about management trainees' progress and by whom should these be maintained? The sources of information for such records are obvious: periodic appraisals (along the lines already described) together with factual records of movements, performance reports on specific tasks, projects or courses completed; results of personal counselling interviews; all these and many more things will provide material for personal dossiers which will accumulate about each trainee as the time passes. Two points require to be stressed concerning this matter. First, the records must be comprehensive, accurate and reliable—otherwise they will be worthless. Should this appear to be a somewhat trite statement, let it be noted that wide experience has demonstrated *most* personnel records encountered in industrial and commercial undertakings *to be in some way or other out of date, and thus inaccurate.*

The second point concerns *confidentiality.* Contents of personal records should, on the face of it, be made accessible to those who properly require them, but there may be some conflict between this and the need for confidentiality of some of the information they contain. It has been found possible to overcome this difficulty by making one person (perhaps the organisation planner) responsible for the maintenance and custody of management trainees' personal records, with discretion as to how much of the information should be made available to people other than the chief executive.

Development programmes

The effort and care exerted in the periodic or occasional reviews of individual performance and progress in managerial prowess and practice will have been all in vain, unless serious attention is given to taking positive and effective action in terms indicated by the outcome of the appraisals. Clearly, such action will have to be determined and initiated in closely individual terms, reflecting the assessed needs of individual managers and aspirant managers. The appraisals may at times throw up what appears to be a more general need: for instance, a commonly encountered deficiency in planning and control techniques or in information for decision. This kind of deficiency is, manifestly, not individual, and it could be corrected through a broadly based approach such as a training programme or a specialist consultant assignment, covering all or many of the firm's sections and managers. More significant are pointers highlighting deficiencies or needs of the managers individually, especially those for whom there appears on other grounds to be evidence of suitability for advancement to major responsibilities in the top echelons of the organisation.

This is where the main task of management development emerges and, therefore, where the chief executive and other senior managers can benefit from the advice and assistance of a knowledgeable specialist as to how to interpret the training needs into 'training action' and what facilities are available, or can be made available, to provide what is needed. Quoting the Central Training Council's Report again:

> In principle the training needs of each individual may be discerned by comparing the requirements of his job (position) with an appraisal of his performance in that job, but in practice this is not a simple matter. Sometimes the emphasis will need to be on remedying deficiencies in the knowledge and skill of the manager or bringing him up to date with new developments; in other cases, training may be aimed at consolidating and developing his strong points. But it is often intrinsically difficult to make an accurate assessment of individual needs and, even when the best assessment has been made it is not always easy to translate this into actual programmes of training.[1]

Some guidelines on this matter are offered in a later section (see p. 1018).

[1] *Training and Development of Managers,* 1969, para. 100.

Coordination and administration

From the foregoing pages it will have become clear that management development on a systematic basis must inevitably entail some burden of planning and oversight, for which a responsibility has to be allocated at a senior level. There are also a number of incidental administrative tasks. Both these needs will emerge, even when the policy is to be applied on only a limited scale, but in no firm should the serious pursuit of directed management development be foregone just because certain burdens are inevitably involved. The tasks and the burdens and the costs of the man-hours taken up by them should be seen as an investment in the betterment of the managerial calibre of the firm and, therefore, in the provision for the improvement of its overall performance and profitability.

As has been stressed, the focal responsibility for the implementation must rest with the Managing Director (as chief executive), closely supported by his senior managers. It will have been he who formed the policy and brought it before the Board of Directors for approval and issue; again, here, it is to be hoped that he would have the support and cooperation of his senior managers in framing the policy and in formulating the overall strategy or programme for its implementation. The tasks and details of application can therefore be seen rightly as done on behalf of the chief executive, whoever it is that actually carries them out. This latter point will be looked at later in the following chapter (see page 1022) in the context of examining how the expert assistance can be given to the chief executive and senior managers and whose role is best placed to be the source of such knowledge and expertise.

In terms of the details of application, the tasks entailed have been sketched out among the foregoing pages of examination of the stages of management development and they can be briefly recapitulated as follows:

- Reviewing and updating forecasts of the company's probable future management needs.
- Initiating and conducting the procedure for the personal appraisal of potential managers at the periods laid down.
- Consulting with (senior) managers for identification, screening and nomination of individuals selected as suitable for development, and obtaining broad guidance as to their training needs.
- Planning and preparing individual development programmes.
- Reviewing and recording progress of individuals within the programmes established.
- Consulting and negotiating with managers and functional specialists concerning the use of internal facilities for development, such as selective appointments, temporary transfers, personal assistants, investigation projects.
- Investigating available external facilities for study of technical, professional, managerial and 'human relations' subjects.
- Planning arrangement of suitable courses for individuals, and supervising the effective carry-through of arrangements.
- Ensuring that a performance appraisal record is obtained from the attendances.
- Planning, organising and conducting study groups, seminars and outside visits for individuals undergoing management training.
- Providing 'personal counsellor' facilities on any aspect of management development as and when the need arises.

● Answering to the chief executive for the progress of management development (i.e. for performance of the various activities and procedures, and for
the efficacy of the results being achieved).

While these various tasks are straightforward in themselves, the practical
difficulty to which they give rise stems from the fact that they touch on various
sections of any firm's organisation. Differences of opinion could arise (and
have arisen in many firms in point of fact) as to 'whose jurisdiction' should take
the role as the main focus. A lot of opinion already favours the Personnel
Manager, because of his obvious functional involvement in matters of
training, selection, promotion and human resources generally. For the effective accomplishment of management development this issue is significant
enough to warrant further consideration in depth, and forms the subject-
matter of chapter 8.

Training and development

Forming individual programmes for improvement, whether to overcome
deficiencies disclosed or to add prowess in expectation of advancement, is an
aspect of management development practice wherein a good deal of realistic
and reliable knowledge is called for, as well as the expertise to be able to
interpret and translate the disclosed 'needs' into the ways and means of
improvement. General guidance on this matter is not easy to offer and it could
be unwise if allowed to become the substitute for expert assistance. It is also
important that the programmes for development, whether by training (learning) or by other means, should allow for and encourage the self-help efforts of
the individual managers and personnel concerned. There is a great deal to be
gained from this factor in improving competence.

There is major benefit to be gained, too, from wise counselling by an older
and senior manager; this is particularly true when the improvements called for
lie in the direction of personal attitude, of behaviour towards colleagues and
subordinates, or of judgment and decision. Such counselling should not occur
only at the periodic appraisal reviews, but should rather be a feature of the
everyday exercise of the managerial role. Accumulation of this incidental
appreciation of performance and conduct can form a valuable foundation and
background for the more formal periodic appraisal. How the incidental review
is made must depend on the routines and mechanics of management practice
in the firm, and on the information systems in use. Managerial roles carried
out in the up-to-date systematic forms called for, when a comprehensive
marketing programme and integrated management information system are
being operated, afford an excellent milieu for such incidental appraisal to be
both factual and reliable.

Outcome of review

Bringing together the incidental and the formal reviews means that there is
available a reliable estimate of the strengths and weaknesses of individual
managers and supervisors, as well as of the managerial team overall.
Reflections on the organisation structure as the framework of delegation and
on the data procedures or systems by which planning and control of operations and expenditure are applied will also have been thrown up. This material

has to be interpreted and translated into the programmes of action for individual betterment, by learning, by training, or by other means, and involving the contributions of self-development from the individual and of guidance from his superior. The more these aids to betterment can be generated and applied within the environment of the firm's own operations the better: to provide, as it were, the opportunity for 'improvement by doing'. This last observation is not in any way intended to negate the value of training through study courses, including the personal benefits stemming from the interplay of deliberation and discussion among the members (from different firms and organisations) attending the courses. Some aspects of management improvement can best be attained through courses. This is particularly true, for instance, where the need is for improvement of knowledge of management techniques and practices, though there is also the consequential requirement of application to real situations—in other words, the opportunity for the practical experience of what has been learned in theory or in principle.

Where the need for improvement relates to behaviour and human relations, courses have a less realistic contribution to offer. Some benefit *can* be obtained from suitably selected participatory seminars or group sessions, but far more is to be gained from wise counselling and from guided self-development. It is in this respect that the mature and experienced senior manager can be of the greatest benefit. There are numerous instances also where guidance and counselling of this kind have been given by consultants, when they are involved within a firm in the introduction and application of management development. Some benefit in the improvement of skills of consultation and cooperation is nearly always obtained from training and experience in diagnostic techniques like work study or O and M (organisation and method)—because the success of those techniques depends essentially on effective communication together with winning the active support of the personnel whose operations are under study.

There are occasions when the training need is for supplementary knowledge in technological subjects, or in branches of professional expertise. A manager, for example, promoted to head a new department, or to take over an additional sector of activity, might well benefit from brushing up technical or professional expertise long since rusted through lack of use, or from acquiring up-to-date knowledge of subjects contiguous to his own field hitherto.

Objectives

All these various aspects of advancement in management skills and competence have to be taken into account in forming the individual programmes in line with the assessments made through the personal appraisals, having also taken into consideration what has been gained from the recurrent incidental observation. The determination of requirements needs to be related to the characteristics of the person under appraisal—age, educational standard, original professional qualification, channel of service in the firm so far, progress over recent years, present position and length of service in it, previous exposure to techniques and systems, personal calibre, mental capacity for acquiring advanced knowledge, assessed potential for progress to greater responsibilities. This complex scope of factors explains the 'difficulty of formulating individual programmes' referred to in the extract above (p.1015) from the Central Training Council's second Report. What such programmes are seeking to prescribe may be summarised in three aspects:

- Improving the abilities of all managers and supervisors in the firm, so as to promote overall effectiveness; and, similarly, extending the abilities of personnel selected for initial development with supervisory or managerial roles.
- Providing special help to betterment for those managers who are deemed potentially suitable for promotion in due course to the major responsibilities of senior management.
- By such means, ensuring that the firm has available within itself a cadre of men and women well prepared to assume positions of responsibility newly arising from expansion of business, from diversification of activity, or from acquisitions of other enterprises.

Put together, these three aspects add up to being the 'management development programme' of the firm as a whole. The objectives then can be summarised as follows:

1. To provide the opportunity for increasing knowledge according to the requirements in the present position or to line up with the intended promotion or development in responsibility. In a number of cases the knowledge required may be technological, in the sense of updating knowledge gained at qualification stage or making special studies of new developments in materials, processes and such like. In other cases, the knowledge may be of management techniques in planning and control, financial analysis, marketing studies and the like. For most managers there could be the requirement of a wider range of management knowledge, particularly in human relations, coping with change and other matters covered by the behavioural sciences.

2. To improve judgment and decision in the exercise of a managerial role. This can come far less from studies than from the guidance exerted by the superior manager in the course of his own direction of his management team. _Decision_ is the most important skill that the younger manager has to acquire, and the one for which his senior's support can be of the utmost value. The guidance is given not by taking decisions for him, but by closely collaborating with him in a review of his reasoning and an evaluation of his assumptions. Perhaps more educational still is the patient and sympathetic review of the 'what' and the 'why' when a particular decision has proved to be a wrong one. To some extent, improvement of judgment and decision can be fostered through project studies, especially those having a significant evaluation factor in them.

3. The development of all mental talents through variety of experiences and the challenge of new opportunities: this is best achieved through tours of duty in _management services_, after specialist training or by participation in other temporary roles, as has already been described. Here, of course, the bigger firm has advantages, because of the likely greater resort to management services of various kinds, and also because of the greater flexibility inherent in the larger number of managers employed. (This point is further considered in the next chapter: see page 1025.)

4. An overall growth in capacity to deal skilfully with human problems and human situations: this could be a byproduct of the stages of development in the foregoing items. Some benefit can undoubtedly be gained from a serious study of the factors involved in conflict and cooperation, so that acquiring knowledge through courses does have a contribution to make

here. Again, however, more substantial benefit should have come from the guidance given by the superior manager: invariably there will be human problems in the course of day-to-day working. Further, many of the project studies or activities undertaken as variety of experience will pose challenges in winning the cooperation of people, in settings with which the manager may not previously have been concerned, and thus will present excellent opportunities for improving skills in communication and consultation.

5. All through the stages of development, emphasis will have been laid on the nexus of cooperation in which every manager and supervisor is inevitably involved, so that capacity to play a part as a cooperative member of a management team will be considerably strengthened.

6. One special requirement should be built in to the programme for every manager, namely, to increase his concern for the improvement of operating performance, the advancement of productivity, the pursuit of market development, and the betterment of the firm's profitability. To some extent, valuable contributions will be gained here from a selective programme of studies, and several of the projected tours of duty could be directed to this objective. Yet, once again, it will be the example and lead given by the senior managers that will be the main factors. From everything in the firm's managerial activities, younger managers (and all other personnel as well for that matter) should constantly be learning by example the significance of the "three Ps" in the roles of management and supervision. It will be recalled that this was strongly emphasised in Part One as an essential feature of management practice (see, for example, page 32).

Development strategy

It can be felt at times, when the activities of some companies are being aired at seminars and conferences, that management development is being pursued just for the sake of having those activities on the go, with the accompanying impression that no senior manager in those companies has any real sympathy with what is going on or places any reliability in it. Nor would such impressions always be erroneous. The simple fact needs recurrently to be emphasised that policies and practices of management development have their objective *only* in the improvement of the prowess, the performance, the productivity and the profitability of the firm, as attained by the actions and attitudes of the firm's managers and directors. And this is the only reason why the realistic involvement of directors and managers is so strongly stressed; also why there must be a starting point in a defined policy and in a focus of responsibility centred in the chief executive, the Managing Director forming the immediate link of Board and Executive, policy into practice.

If this broad objective is to be fully reflected in the firm's programmes of action, there is a strong case for seeing 'management development' in a wider setting than the conventional approach that has been followed thus far in these pages, namely, concerned specifically and only with the managers as persons and with individuals selected for advancement to management responsibilities. This approach should better be seen as just one facet, with three others that have an equally important contribution to make:

1. Contributing to the advancement of the managerial calibre and attitude of the men and women charged with technical and business responsibilities in the various positions forming the organisation structure.

2. Pursuing opportunities for improving management techniques and practices, which are applied in the control of day-to-day operations and in forming business decisions.
3. Reviewing and pursuing opportunities for commercial advancement through technological development, through diversification of activity, or through increase of market potential.
4. Determining (and bringing into being) patterns of organisation for the delegation of management responsibilities, in line with changes in marketing objectives or in the character and scale of the company's operations.

Performance and profitability

Seen this way, there is an altogether more vital interpretation of 'development' in which all managers are participating. That participation will be in two streams: the one as a natural corollary to each manager's own delegated responsibilities, the other as his special involvement in contributing to the firm's advancement by self-development, whether for his own skills or for his departmental practices. This participation stems, of course, from the inherent purpose of the management process, as analysed in Part One, to attain effective and efficient performance of the activities and personnel over which jurisdiction is held by delegation. A rider was added in that context which is very pertinent in this present one: that a management position holds an inherent obligation for improvement of performance, the 'job improvement' aspect that is the natural element in all managerial objectives.

In terms of this philosophy it makes sense to interrelate the above four aspects within an integrated framework of 'development', so that all four can be given attention appropriate to their potential contribution to the firm's improvement of overall performance and profitability. The policy will need to be defined and stated in this form; organisational arrangements may also be effected because of the bearing that this wider approach will have on where responsibility for the twofold expert and administrative role should be focused. This wider interpretation makes the logic for the interrelation of *management services* with management development in the conventional sense, as suggested above. Those management services are likely to be the major source of the firm's advancement in the other three aspects of development, because they afford the expert media by which the opportunities for potential betterment can be identified and pursued.

Smaller firms

In the main in this present Part, the analysis and illustration of organisation planning and management development have been presented in settings drawn from medium-sized and larger firms; but it would be gravely mistaken to conclude that these are aspects of effective management pertinent only to the larger enterprises. That is far from true. The approaches and the practices can be more readily seen and were emphatically demonstrated in the context of the larger organisation. Of course, some aspects are more appropriate there. Yet, what organisation planning and management development, systematically applied, can give to the smaller firm is every bit as significant to its continuing vitality and progress. The smaller scale and scope of the management structure and team means only that simpler lines of approach and practices are used; but virtually everything that these past two or three chapters have covered is as relevant to the smaller firms as to the larger ones.

8 Whose responsibility?

Whose responsibility? The first answer to this question is the obvious and simple one: *all managers*, for the improvement of performance and profitability is an inherent objective in the management process. And *that* is precisely what 'management development' is all about. To each manager falls, in one way or another, responsibility for contributing to the four aspects summarised on the preceding page, a responsibility that he has professionally or functionally to exercise along three different but interrelated paths:

● in relation to his own skills and competence in the exercise of his own role, the personal and individual improvement of management performance;
● in the direction and guidance given to subordinate managers, supervisors and other responsible personnel for their advancement in competence, performance and attitude; here, he will also be participating in the firm's programmes for management development;
● in contributing to the improvement or innovation of techniques of organisation or of business development in the interests of the firm overall.

Within a firm's framework of management many individuals will be active along these three paths, and it at once becomes obvious that there *must* be clear and known coordination if the true potential benefit of such activity is to be realised. The primary focus of coordination lies in the normal role of the chief executive, as has already been stressed, and he can best and most effectively discharge and fulfil that responsibility by having it as a *normal* facet of business progress, rather than a seemingly extraneous and separate exercise. Naturally, that approach cannot be taken at the outset, when a policy for systematic management development is being first introduced in a firm. Yet, if the intention is to pursue these objectives seriously, then that new policy will be defined by the Board of Directors and made known to all managers as *a permanent feature* of the firm's activities: from that foundation the transition to being a normal facet of management practice and progress can be simply and speedily attained, given the continuing sincerity and good intention of the Managing Director and his senior manager team.

The marketing programme

One very effective way to attain this transition and to maintain the 'normality' of management development is to interrelate it within the firm's marketing programme; this is, of course, where it really belongs when seen in proper perspective. All economic activity (and that is only another way of identifying a nation's industry and commerce) rests on the motivation of the consumer. If the nation's citizens do not perform actively as consumers by buying goods and services, economic activity must flag: the decline is made manifest by the flagging of the business activities of firms. *Business has no meaning except to serve and satisfy customers profitably*: the firm's marketing programme is but the statement of how it intends to fulfil that objective in its own area of activity—in other words, how it intends to take up and apply its own part in the overall economic activity of the community. Good performance and profitability are inherent in those intentions: why not, then, make them explicit? Why not have all four aspects of management development recurrently before the eyes of the managerial team, as they periodically form their plans and as they day-by-day carry them into effect? In what better way can their essential responsibility for performance and profitability be highlighted and fulfilled? This approach also resolves in the most effective way the problem of coordination. A marketing programme represents the integration of the activities of the firm's management team, under the guidance and supervision of the chief executive, and the framework of coordination for development and progress is thereby automatically presented.[1] That some of the procedures for management are occasional (e.g. annual) rather than routine is not significant—other aspects of a marketing programme share this feature (for example, review of product performance via market research).

| Specialist assistance | Granted, then, that policy and a known marketing programme provide for the chief executive and all his managers a foundation and a framework for exercising their shared responsibility for the practice of management development, thereby is provided an effective first answer. But the question 'Whose responsibility?' still requires a supplementary answer. Neither the chief executive nor the members of his managerial team can normally be expected to have the expertise to carry out in depth the requirements of planning and supervision for management development; nor are they likely through the year to have the time available to devote to many of the requisite mechanics. Moreover, there will be wisdom in avoiding the dangers of disparate lines of activity among the several members of the management team. So the supplementary answer recommends that there should be an individual to serve as adviser and assistant in this field to the chief executive and to the other managers. One basic feature needs to be stressed as soon as mention is made of such specialist assistance: it does not and cannot relieve either the chief executive or the other managers of their *inherent responsibility* for the practice and application of management development. An assistant can guide them, advise them, inform them, and relieve them of burdens of detailed mechanics and chores—but never relieve them of the responsibility for active and effective contribution. His responsibilities will stem from expertise; he must be the firm's focus of knowledge, information and advice on all that management entails. And because this process lies embedded in the foundation of the firm's top management, he must himself be accredited at that level in the organisation, preferably reporting directly to the chief executive. |

In organisational terms, whatever his own status of character, his role is 'staff', never 'line'. He may in larger enterprises have a small team of specialist personnel to assist in many of the practicalities, and thereby acquire the

---

[1] See Part One (p. 27) and Part Two (p. 235) for further reference to the role of the marketing programme. A fuller treatment is also to be found in *Managing for Revival*, chapter 3.

normal 'line' responsibility of command of his own subordinates; yet, even were his team to be the size of a department under his jurisdiction (which Heaven forfend!), his role and relationships to the organisation in general remain 'staff'; in another form of jargon he is a 'functional specialist'. By status he may be himself a senior manager in the firm, or he may be a member of the Board of Directors, or with an independent standing he may be a consultant accredited to the firm on a retainer. The differences of status do not and cannot affect his role and responsibility, apart from minor or marginal variations; nor do they affect his attachment to the chief executive and his close cooperative relations with the (senior) managerial team. In the main, the role will call for a man or woman on full-time service, though there are known instances in medium-sized firms where an adequately timed part-time service has proven effective and successful. Mostly, the status has then been that of consultant; in a few instances the expert professional has served the firm in the role of 'outside director', a member of the Board of Directors on part-time service, taking up the top-line advisory responsibility for management development in addition to sharing the normal corporate responsibility of the other directors. It is natural enough to expect, in these part-time cases, that the top line specialist from outside will have somebody nominated inside to undertake for him the incidental practicalities and procedures: this may well be the Personnel Manager.

Scope of role

Pursuing for the moment the assumption that this top functional specialist is on full-time service in the firm, with status of senior manager responsible to the chief executive, the third question then comes in the form: What should his overall role cover? As has already been noted, there would be a fairly widespread tendency to cast the mould in terms of the customary top level 'personnel' services; and even to argue that this role should be taken by the Personnel Manager among his other specialist human resources activities. There is a logic to support this point of view, but its weakness is exposed in practice if the broad-based approach to management development is required: in other words, if the effective pursuit of overall performance and profitability is posed as the true objective rather than just the development of the skills, prowess and attitudes of individual managers.

Two other lines of approach have at times been advocated. One has been the importance of associating management development with forward planning of organisation structure, as reviewed in depth in the earlier text of this Part: in this case the role would be formed and held as part of the responsibility of the 'organisation planner'. The other would recommend the full integrated approach to development in all the four aspects listed above (see p. 1020), and the role would then be held in a senior managerial position also embracing 'management services'. These two approaches merit some further consideration.

The notion and role of an organisation planner has been used in the earlier section of this Part, though it has not been intended that this is necessarily a recommended title; if wider responsibilities are to be assumed in this role, a firm may wish to choose another title. For the present context the style of 'organisation planner' will be continued, and it is suggested that the MJD for the position could include the coordinating services of management development on the Managing Director's behalf. His role has already been represented as a focal point and catalytic agent through which organisational changes can be planned and implemented, including the coordination and supervision to ensure effective and successful accomplishment. He would thus be exercising a comparable role in regard to management development—a natural and logical extension—and the functions allocated to his role in the MJD can be summarised as follows (see page 988):

Information. Maintaining suitable records and providing an information service on matters concerned with current organisation structure and management staffing arrangements.

Investigation. Conducting studies to determine future organisation needs and forecasts of likely managerial requirements.

Recommendation. Collating and developing specific proposals for organisation structure and related management appointment changes; preparing plans for the selection and development of future managers; preparing plans and programmes for the training and development of managers and aspirant managers.

Implementation. Assisting in the introduction and administration of agreed changes in organisation structure and staffing arrangements; ensuring continuity and supervising the conduct of management development programmes; arranging for and supervising the carrying out of plans and programmes for management training and development.

Consultation. Consulting and cooperating closely with senior managers, and in particular with the Personnel Manager, in all aspects of the responsibilities allocated for organisation development, managerial staffing, and management development.

Management services

The alternative approach suggested above extends the roles of organisation planning and management development by associating it intimately with the application of management services, thereby accrediting to the chief executive and the top managerial team a specialist adviser-cum-assistant embracing all four aspects of development in an interrelated form. 'Management services' is a loosely used label and it will be found to have different connotations in different organisations; but they all concur in designating the combination of specialist skills directed to the advancement of business and management performance, through methods, planning, and systems data. Most of the services involve some form of investigation or diagnosis; and they all call for the rigour of systematic approach, with constructively critical insight. By and large what is covered by these services and skills can be summarised as specialist activities particularly directed to the betterment of operations and of business progress; they can be summarised into four categories, although there is inevitably a certain amount of overlap among them and a good deal of interrelationship in action:

1. *Diagnostic.* Activities directed primarily to collating, reviewing and assessing the facts of a situation in order to determine basic arrangements, to improve methods, to design systems, to measure work loads, to formulate standards. For example: work study; O and M; operations research; systems analysis; capacity assessment; layout and flow studies (handling).

2. *Intelligence*. Activities directed to appraising economic and market conditions as the basis for the formulation of commercial and development policy, the determination and financial appraisal of plans and programmes, and guidance for management decisions. For example: economic intelligence, market research; profit projections; simulation studies in forecasting; linear programming; project appraisals.

3. *Control*. Data procedures or similar techniques which afford to management the means of assessing 'actual' against plan or target, thereby aiding decisions in regard to continuing/amending operations or plans. For example: production control; budgetary control; ADP systems; programme evaluations; product-profitability analysis; management accounting.

4. *Development*. Activities directed to future orientation of operations or management with particular reference to vitality of progress. For example: technical research and development; long-term economic forecasting; factory location studies; diversification studies; organisation planning; management development.

There could not, of course, be the slightest expectation that a man or woman could be found knowledgeable or experienced in all these different techniques: nor is anything like that required. The senior manager or specialist who would head this combined role could be expected to have understanding of the scope and purpose of the techniques, himself to have personal training and experience in some of them, and to be intelligently competent to supervise the development and application (by expert personnel) of those outside of his personal acquaintance. Candidates with that capacity may not be easy to find, but they are in this day and age certainly numerous. Moreover, in the course of time the necessary flow of such competent men or women can be developed within the firm.

Development opportunities

The practice now being advocated is that a spell of service in training and application of one or more of the management services, techniques or systems should figure as part of the management development programmes for most, if not all, of the up-and-coming managers in any firm that really sees itself as progressive and seeks to take seriously its development of performance and profitability. Which services are selected for which aspirant managers, how and where the training is conducted, what periods of experience are to be allotted—these and many other points are to be determined in the context of the development programmes, as referred to in chapter 7 above (see page 1013). These are matters in which the head of the development planning activity will give his specialist attention on behalf of and in consultation with the firm's senior managers and chief executive.

The scope and level of responsibility delegated to this functional specialist are certainly farreaching, as shown by the two illustrative MJDs in Fig. 7.8.1, parts (a) and (b): see pp. 1028–9.[1] It could be argued that the responsibility should be thought of as roving rather than static—in the sense that the incumbent holding it should be changed every four or five years. The role

[1] These schedules of responsibilities are extracted from a set appearing as illustrative matter in chapter 13 of *Organisation: the Framework of Management*, wherein the concept of the combined role is more fully considered. See also *Managing for Revival*, chapter 7.

would be held as the prelude to promotion to general management or chief executive positions, and would be an excellent breeding ground for high-level management performance. Just as the spread and deepening of managerial proficiency can be gained from the recurrent involvement of up-and-coming managers in the realistic application of management services, so at this more senior level an important topping-up could be gained by men and women who are at the edge of stepping into the very high rank of overall managerial responsibility. The spell of duty in charge of this combined range of specialist activities directed overtly to productivity prowess and progress cannot fail to inbue the incumbent with a sense of vitality that will permanently redound to the advancement of the firm, as well as of the man himself.

There are also personal factors involved in the exercise of this responsibility which cannot fail to add to the value of the experience in influencing the growth of calibre, understanding and competence. Of its very nature, as reflected in the outline MJD (see p. 1025), this responsibility will call for high qualities in personal make-up as conditional for its successful accomplishment. In turn, these features point to the calibre and prowess to be sought when candidates are under assessment for selection. This role cannot be effectively exercised, if indeed exercised at all, unless the incumbent is able to command:

- a comprehensive and realistic understanding of the objectives, policies and philosophy of the firm in which he is serving;
- a thoroughgoing knowledge of the firm's structure, operations, procedures, systems and techniques by means of which the management process is delegated and activated;
- ready access to the chief executive and to all managers, with the assurance of personal and functional acceptance by them;
- well developed ability to diagnose organisation and staffing problems with sensitivity and objectivity, supported upon unquestioned personal integrity;
- capacity to assess needs for development and to diagnose underlying opportunities or obstacles, so as to draw recommendations effectively matching potential with facilities;
- ability to exercise a flexible, imaginative and pragmatic approach to the planning and administration of organisation and management, areas in which there exist few recognised principles and virtually no guidelines capable of general application.

Finding the specialist

For many readers of the foregoing requirements the first reaction could be one of scepticism that any such paragon of human virtue and perfection could ever be found. Not indeed an unreasonable reaction, if reliance is being placed only on finding the article readymade. At the outset of a new development like this, going out to the marketplace may indeed be the only practical way of finding the man to head the initiation. In the course of time, however, it will be possible to generate the expertise and the calibre from within; this can be made easier if the start is restricted to the first two of the new activities, namely, organisation planning and the simpler phases of management development. Expertise could be brought to bear by part-time assistance from outside, for example, through professional consultant service or through the medium of a suitably qualified independent director.

Fig. 7.8.1a
MJD for
overall
development
responsibility

Title: Senior Manager, Development and Planning

Responsible to: The Managing Director

Functions

(a) To serve as 'forward looking' unit serving the Company as a whole through the Managing Director.
(b) To establish and maintain effective market intelligence services providing relevant data for guidance in formulation of policy and growth programmes.
(c) To afford facilities for new product search and to maintain effective progress control in respect of new product development.
(d) To give guidance to all Divisions and/or Departments on:

(i) the formulation of long-term programmes of activity for growth;
(ii) the sound operation of planning and control procedures;
(iii) the preparation of yearly plans of trading activity and profitability;
(iv) the application of data and statistical techniques.

(e) To maintain and apply diagnostic services directed to determining opportunities for improvements in efficiency and economy through methods, equipment, layout, standards, systems, organisation, and other aspects of the Company's operations.
(f) To advise and assist the Managing Director and the Divisional Senior Managers in the application of a management development programme.
(g) To be a focus of responsibility for keeping abreast of development in all spheres of management practice which can contribute to the Company's advancement.

Responsibilities

1. By consultation with the Managing Director, ensuring that he is currently informed as to the Company's objectives and policies, with particular reference to expectations for growth and to factors bearing on the formulation of the Five Year Plans (= the marketing programme).
2. Maintaining appropriate contact with Divisional Senior Managers to assist their effective application of the specialist services available.
3. Directing and/or advising the specialist managers under his jurisdiction in regard to the promotion of their own areas of responsibility, and in particular as to requirements for keeping available services in line with contemporary advances in practice.
4. On the basis of guidance from the specialist managers, determining ways and means of using the available services as a medium of contribution to the management development programme.
5. Frequently consulting with the Senior Manager of Marketing Division in regard to the effectiveness of the economic and marketing intelligence services, and to their utilisation in the preparation of sales forecasts.
6. Periodically consulting with the Divisional Senior Managers and Department Heads to check:

(a) effective application of the diagnostic services in the interests of pursuing all opportunities of improving the efficiency and economy of operations and methods;
(b) the correct working of planning and control systems, taking heed of pointers for the betterment of the systems.

7. Establishing and managing library and information services competent to assist Managers in keeping up-to-date with advancements in management thought and practice.

Special responsibilities

The Senior Manager of Development and Planning is specifically responsible for formulating and applying programmes of 'management development' on behalf of the Managing Director and in consultation with the Divisional Senior Managers. (The functions and responsibilities appropriate to this role are set out in the appended Schedule.)

Subordinates

Market Statistics Officer
Methods and Systems Adviser
Product Research Manager.

Limitations

The role of the Senior Manager of Development and Planning is essentially one of guidance and coordination in the application of specialist services, with emphasis on the advisory assistance to the Managing Director. He has no jurisdiction over any of the Divisional Senior Managers or Department Heads.

His executive responsibilities are limited to the three specialist Managers accredited as his subordinates, with any personnel operating under their jurisdiction as permanent or temporary members.

Fig. 7.8.1b
MJD for
advisory role
in management
development

Title: The Management Development Adviser

Responsible to: The Managing Director

Functions

To serve as the focal source of advice and assistance to the Managing Director and Divisional Senior Managers in respect of:

(a) the formulation of policy and programmes for the review and development of potential managerial ability;

(b) the application of appraisal procedures for managerial, supervisory and senior specialist personnel in relation to promotion or other advancement;

(c) the planning and conducting of training schemes for management development, including use of external facilities;

(d) the arrangement of salary gradings for managerial and other senior personnel;

(e) the clarification of respective responsibilities and relationships within the organisation structure;

(f) keeping the Company abreast of developments in practice and technique relative to the advancement of management competence.

Responsibilities

1. Advising the Managing Director on items for recommendation to the Board of Directors where modifications or extensions of policy are required relative to management selection, promotion, training, remuneration or terms of service.

2. Advising and assisting the Divisional Senior Managers in the application of the personnel appraisal procedures and in discussion of difficulties of appraisal or other cases of management personnel problems.

3. Ensuring that reliable records of individual development progress are maintained for the guidance of decisions on promotions, transfers, etc.

4. Objectively advising the Managing Director and Divisional Senior Managers in regard to selection for promotion when specific vacancies occur.

5. Undertaking selection procedure and interviewing for management recruitment from outside, when this is deemed desirable as alternative or supplement to internal candidates.

6. In consultation with the Managing Director and the Divisional Senior Managers, preparing forward programmes of attendance at selected courses in line with individual needs in the interest of development of management competence.

7. In consultation with Divisional Senior Managers, organising and/or conducting:

   (a) appropriate training courses for supervisory personnel or for junior technical personnel in responsible positions;

   (b) internal development seminars for selected junior or middle-level managers, in line with agreed Company programmes.

8. Assisting the Managing Director and the Divisional Senior Managers in review of personnel whose cases suggest that all interests are best served by planned termination of service.

9. Advising and assisting the Managing Director and Divisional Senior Managers in regard to keeping effective the definitions of responsibilities and position specifications covering the Company's organisation structure.

10. On the Company's behalf keeping abreast of and ensuring that the Managing Director and Divisional Senior Managers are appropriately informed of:

    (a) New developments in management practice;

    (b) progress in management facilities;

    (c) sources of management development information.

11. Consulting with the Methods and Systems Adviser in regard to the utilisation of special duties or assignments as contributions to individual advancement in management practice and experience; recommending to the Managing Director and Divisional Senior Managers how available opportunities of such special duties should be exploited.

12. Advising the Managing Director in regard to patterns of remuneration for management personnel in line with good contemporary practice elsewhere.

13. Preparing each year for the Managing Director's approval a budget of expenditure covering the proposed Management Development Programme for the ensuing year; watching expenditure to keep within approved budget or to seek authorisation for justifiable addition.

Special responsibilities

(i) Serving as secretary to the Management Appraisal Panel.

(ii) Appropriate consultation with the Methods and Systems Adviser to provide for trial application or internal development of new techniques arising from contemporary practice and management research elsewhere.

(iii) On behalf of the Managing Director and Divisional Senior Managers keeping a 'second watch' for possibilities of under-utilisation of or deployment of potential managerial talent.

(iv) Consulting with the Personnel Officer in regard to coordinating of practices and administrative procedures, as relevant.

This practical problem of having available the man to get the process started and under way in a firm is one reason why much of the specialist work in this field in the past ten or fifteen years has stemmed from consultant assignments, often undertaken under brand names, such as 'management by objectives' or 'improving managerial performance'. Not that there has been any great deal of real accomplishment in practical form even from this stimulus. How little active interest has been taken in the organisational aspects is reflected from an informal survey maintained on one occasion over a twelve-month period, during which every advertisement in one of the main Sunday media was scrutinised. There were over 7 000 executive-type advertisements in the year: among these *only one* was found calling for specialist service in organisation planning, and as a matter of interest it is reproduced as Fig. 7.8.2, with the identity of the advertiser masked. It will be noted that even here reference is made to the support of professional consultants.

Fig. 7.8.2
Advertisement for
organisation planner

Manager—Organisation Planning

A. & B. Company Limited is embarked on a total organisation development effort at its manufacturing plant and head office situated at H............ T............ in South Yorkshire. The wide-ranging programme has the full commitment of top management and is supported by access to external consultants.

A. & B. seek a person to plan and to manage this programme. Apart from being fully conversant with organisation theory, the successful applicant will have the personality, integrity and consultative skills which will enable him to win and retain the respect and confidence of busy line managers. He will also possess the intelligence and sensitivity required to diagnose the need for organisation change, together with a practical approach to change processes to ensure that these are in line with the objectives of the organisation. He will also be intimately concerned with the implementation of plans which are presently being developed to ensure a steady flow of additional and replacement managers as dictated by needs of the organisation programme and other causes.

Salary is negotiable, depending on qualifications and experience, but would be in the region of £5 500 to £6 000 per annum. Please write, etc....

That the professional consultants have played the leading part in recent times in the initiation of systematic organisation planning, management development and management services is a natural reflection of the trend of industrial progress in Britain in the past twenty to thirty years. There has been keen interest in new techniques, but no previous history of their application, at least outside the larger firms. Many of the very large organisations have been able to design and support their own innovation of management improvement, though even among these there have been several instances of consultant support. Among the medium-sized firms such support has been the common feature, to the extent that any number of firms have taken up this innovation; the number is still, relatively speaking, quite small. The service of the consultant in this field has the merit of underlining the independence and objectivity of approach, because the consultant is by definition an 'outsider'. He has, of course, the initial handicap of not knowing the firm's activities, personalities and characteristics, and has therefore to spend time in familiarisation. Yet, this period is an investment of time, because it is coincidental with the collection of information, the diagnosis of situations and the assessment of problems—all taken objectively by critical appraisal. Benefit comes in the construction phases, because the consultant's expertise and experience facilitate the speedy translation of diagnosis into recommendation for improvement.

Implementation

It is at the implementation stage that the consultant approach may bring disadvantage: implementation of any thorough changes in organisation or management practice usually requires time to accomplish effectively—it is not at all unusual for major changes to require some two to three years to carry through successfully. The steady maturing of changeover on extended period has often been the reason for successful accomplishment, especially in firms which have long-standing traditional practices and attitudes, seldom experiencing the incidence of change. For consultant service to be available over such long periods of gestation and implementation can well prove too expensive for many firms. It will then be essential for an inside man to be alongside the consultant from quite an early stage, so that he can look after the continuing implementation when the time has come for the consultant to pull out. This inside man would hold the role of *organisation planner* or *management development adviser*. There have been known cases of the consultant (by agreement with his own professional partners) taking up service with the client firm in this role as permanent employment. There is also at least one known instance of a consultant staying on in that role in his independent capacity over a long period of implementation and consolidation: a total of fifteen years, from first assignment.

For the medium-sized and smaller firms, the required expertise and the objectivity of guidance has in a number of instances been provided by an 'outside director', serving as a member of the Board of Directors on a part-time formula. Obviously the amount of time called for in this management development service will be appreciably more than if he were serving only as a member of the Board: in the early stages of diagnosis and initiation some two days per week may be required in a firm having fifteen to thirty managers and Directors. And there must in time also be found and established one manager to be the internal head of the services and programmes. Provided an adequately expert individual can be found at the outside director level, this approach can be for many firms every bit as good and as successful as the retention of professional consultant service. There is, of course, the obvious compromise that a consultant can be retained part-time whether or not as an outside director, to provide the expert knowhow and supervision.

In passing, it may be noted that an outside Director can bring other benefits to a firm, especially if it is one wherein elections to the Board of Directors have always come from 'the family' or from within the firm. It has been argued that much of the weakness of Britain's industry and commerce stem from such habitual inbreeding. The Confederation of British Industry has strongly advocated the wider adoption of the practice of electing an outside Director 'to bring to bear independent, objective and detached approach to policy matters; and to give the benefits of knowledge and experience in other areas'.[1]

[1] CBI, *Report on a New Look at the Responsibilities of the British Public Company*, 1973.

9 Conclusion

The topics under review in this final Part go right to the heart of a firm's progress, and in turn they touch on the contribution that each and any firm can make to the wellbeing and progress of the nation's economy. These topics are all concerned with change, directed to improvement of performance: the one aspect (organisation planning) relates to the structure or framework of the management process; the other two (management development and management services) relate to the persons and the methods through which that process is exercised.

Certain bedrock principles underlie these topics, as delineated in the consideration of the management process in Part One. Any firm operating in industry or commerce is a microcosm of economic activity involved in and contributing to the economic macrocosm of the nation, and, indeed of the world overall. While its own immediate objectives may seem to be primarily concerned with its marketing programme and the return on the capital invested by its shareholders, yet, by its very operations it is enmeshed with the wider activities and influences of the wider economy. It has no freedom of choice whether to be so involved or not: the involvement is a simple fact of economic life, as firms in Britain have been painfully learning during recent years.

Recognition of this view adds to the role of directors and managers a new dimension, for their judgment and decisions are seen to bear not only on the affairs of their firm for good or ill, but also on the progress of the national economy and of the community's standard of living. A firm operating at a high level of management performance and profitability is automatically contributing to national wellbeing and progress; a firm running in mediocre fashion or inefficiently is wasting the community's resources and hindering its headway. By their *professional role*, directors and managers acquire this economic and social mandate. Fortunately they can discharge it by the normal exercise of their everyday responsibilities, provided they have recognised the significance of an *attitude of vitality*. The professional objective of management lies in performance and profitability, the effective utilisation of the resources of materials, machines, manpower and money put at their disposal in the constitution of the firm.

This attitude of vitality calls for unceasing vigilance towards progress—a genuine professional concern for the advancement of performance; three specialist aids to this objective will be found in organisation planning, in systematic mangement development and in the effective use of management services. One thing that these three aids, interrelated as they are, have in common is their emphasis on the team factor in effective management.

There is still a widespread acclaim for the high-riding successful entrepreneur, the one-man boss who drives his business from the seat of his pants, with the intuitive judgment of his entrepreneurial flair. Somehow, a mythology has gained ascendancy in Britain that this is the only recipe for profitable success. Nothing in real life could be further from truth. For every tycoon who successfully runs his firm, there are a thousand other firms that have no such luxury available to them. Nor will the tycoon himself go on for ever. Continuity of success for the majority of firms in any economy must depend on the succession of managers with better calibre and competence than those they succeed.

Progress stems from advancement and this automatically spells the increase of standards: today's manager cannot be good enough for tomorrow's situation. Unless there is an upward spiral of advancement in the nation's managerial talent, the economic future must be bleak indeed. And the motive power of the spiral can be found only in conscious management development: improvement of performance because the directors and managers themselves have recognised and accepted their professional obligation, and have put their minds and efforts to its systematic fulfilment. They have a ready criterion of accomplishment, for they may obtain success if the men and women who follow on after them are manifestly of better calibre and competence in management, by reason of what they have provided in policy and practice.

Appendix 7.1 Reducing 'Executive Directors'

The documents reproduced in this Appendix record the policy and plan for reducing the number of Executive Directors' titles in a large engineering company. This was a real situation and the events actually took place. Only the names of companies involved in the case have been changed. The documents comprise:

(a) A memorandum submitted by the Director of Organisation to the Managing Director of an engineering company with seven factories employing around 32 000 people. The existing organisation had resulted from the merger of five firms four years previously.

(b) A personal letter from the Chairman of the Board of Directors to all executive directors of the Company spelling out future policy regarding the reduction in number of directors' appointments.

(c) A memorandum submitted to the Managing Director by the Manager of Organisation Planning recording the situation three years later.

(a) The initial memorandum

Letcombe Manufacturing Company Limited
Internal memorandum

To: The Managing Director   From: Director, Organisation

Executive Directors' Appointments

I. *Purposes*

The purposes of this memorandum are briefly:

(a) to consider the present numbers and categories of executive directors within Letcombe Manufacturing Company;

(b) to examine and discuss executive posts in LMC which are presently established as 'divisional directors' appointments and to note certain anomalies;

(c) to review past and anticipated future rate of terminations of executive directors;

(d) to propose a policy and plan for reducing the number of executive directors in LMC.

II. *Present Position*

  A. Categories and grades

    At the present time there are 30 executive directors employed in LMC—an average of 1 per 1 060 employees. Full particulars of the directorate are shown in the appended schedule and the appointment categories and staff grades are classified thus:

LMC Board Directors	(Salary Grade MSA)	8
Local Directors	(Salary Grade MSA)	3
Divisional Directors	(Salary Grade MSB)	19

B. Divisional directors

The following section considers some facts relating to LMC *divisional* directors only.

1. *Origins*

Analysis of current LMC divisional directorships indicates that their executive appointments originated within subsidiary companies as follows:

ex-William Letcombe Ltd	10
ex-Acme Pressings Ltd	4
ex-John Bassett Ltd	1
ex-Cranfield Ltd	1
ex-Dalby Automotive Ltd	3
	19

2. *Executive appointments*

Executive appointments in LMC which are presently 'established' as divisional directors' posts are summarised thus:

Factory Managers	7
Engineering Departmental Heads	4
Divisional Personnel Managers	2
Director/Deputy Director of Research	2
Deputy Divisional General Manager	1
Works Director	1
Deputy Company Secretary	1
Director of Tooling	1
	19

The word 'established' is used above in a very loose sense: the appointments range between those which were objectively and organisationally planned (e.g. Factory Managers, Divisional Personnel Managers) and those which were more subjectively personal in origin (e.g. Director of Tooling, Deputy Company Secretary).

III. *Anomalous grade MSC appointments*

A. Staff appointment grades

The LMC staff grading scheme which classifies senior salary ranges and general employment conditions of senior employees is outlined below:

	Grade
Board and Local Directors	MSA
Divisional Directors	MSB
Senior Executives	MSC
Executives and Senior Specialists	MSD
Junior Executives and Specialists	MSE

B. 'Special list'

At the present time there exists a 'special list' of marginal Grade MSC appointments, i.e. six senior executives whose *salaries* fall within the MSB (divisional directors) range, but who are treated for all other purposes as Grade MSC (senior executive) employees.

This is an anomalous situation which will undoubtedly worsen:

(*a*) as additional highly paid executives and specialists are recruited from outside;

(*b*) as fringe benefits which have hitherto been confined to LMC divisional directors (such as provision of company cars) are increasingly made available in associated companies on a salary-oriented basis.

IV. *Terminations of Directors*

A. Past wastage rate

During the past four years (i.e. since formation of the present Company) eighteen people have terminated their employment with LMC as executive directors. This reflects a recent past average wastage rate of 15 per cent per annum.

B. Reasons

Reasons for these separations are analysed as follows:

Early retirements	7
Transfers to associated companies	5
Resignations	3
Retirements at 65 years	3
	—
	18
	—

C. Future age wastage

Age spread of the oldest ten members of the present LMC executive directorate reveals the following pattern over the next four years:

Will have retired at 65 years	3
Will have reached 65th year	3
Will have reached 64th year	2
Will have reached 63rd year	2
	—
	10
	—

D. Anticipated wastage (all reasons)

Against the background of the foregoing figures it is anticipated that the overall annual wastage rate of LMC directors over the next few years is likely to be in the order of 10–15 per cent per annum.

V. *Proposed policy*

In view of the generally acknowledged need to reduce the present number of LMC executive directors, and bearing in mind the above facts, the following policy is proposed:

1. To confine all future new appointments of executive directors to membership of the statutory Board of the Company as vacancies arise.
2. To abolish gradually the appointment of 'divisional director' and to replace it with a new staff category of 'divisional executive'.

A course of action for implementation of this policy has been drafted. The Managing Director will discuss the matter with the Chairman and seek his agreement to bring this up for consideration by the Board of Directors. The Chairman will then send out a personal letter. This policy will result in the number of LMC executive directors being reduced from 30 to around 8–10 within the next five years or so.

Date:...............   *Signed:*...............

(*b*) The chairman's letter

Letcombe Manufacturing Company Limited

Personal   *From the Chairman*
                                                Date:...............

Dear

For some time past the Managing Director and I have been considering the fact that we have in this Company too many executive posts carrying the title and style of 'director'. This situation is to some extent historical, arising from the growth of our present integrated organisation out of several different companies and product divisions. The fact is that today no fewer than thirty executive posts carry the title 'director'.

On bringing this matter before the Board of Directors recently, there was unanimous agreement that the time has now come to lay down a policy enabling us, over a period of time, to reduce the number of these 'director' appointments to a more appropriate level. I am therefore addressing this personal letter to you (and to all those concerned) to give you advance information as to this policy and how it will be implemented.

Firstly, let me say that nobody at present holding a 'director' appointment will be adversely affected. Moreover, he will not, under ordinary circumstances, be asked in the future to fill any other appointment which does not carry at least the equivalent status and more properly the title of 'director'.

Next, the Board propose to pursue a policy that all future new appointments of directors will be confined to membership of the Company's main Board, the body which is statutorily responsible for the Company's affairs.

This means that henceforward no individuals will be freshly appointed as 'divisional' directors. Instead, when divisional directors' posts fall vacant, they will be re-designated and filled by 'divisional executives'. This new senior staff grade will carry exactly the same status, salary range and fringe benefits as those currently extended to divisional directors. Thus, for some time to come, we shall have a mixture of 'divisional executives' and 'divisional directors' operating at the same level of management.

By taking advantage of retirements and other changes, we anticipate that this policy will result in reducing our present complement of directors by about one third over the next 3–4 years—without loss of status or hardship to anybody. Thereafter the rate of reduction will accelerate.

Although I am addressing this policy letter to you personally, I do not want you to regard it as being confidential. Indeed, I would like you to use your own discretion as to how far you will impart its contents to those of your more promising senior executives who could at present regard a divisional directorship as a proper target for their ambitions.

In the meantime, should you have any particular comments or queries about this policy and its implications, I shall be pleased to hear from you and, if you wish, to discuss the matter further.

Signed:...............

(c) Memorandum
three years later

Letcombe Manufacturing Company Limited

Internal Memorandum

To: The Managing Director   From: Manager, Organisation Planning

Reduction of 'Director' Titles

With reference to our conversation on the above subject today, it is confirmed that, since the issue of the Chairman's policy letter three years ago this month, the number of appointments bearing the title of 'director' within the Company has come down by thirteen—a reduction of 43 per cent.

During this period eleven 'divisional executive' appointments were created, each carrying the same status and privileges which have hitherto applied to divisional directors. In no single case did a nominee hesitate to accept the post without the 'director' title.

Date:...............   *Signed*...............

Appendix 7.2 Common personnel and administration functions

Extract from the Organisation and Policy Manual of the British Leyland Motor Corporation Ltd
(Reproduced with permission)

PERSONNEL AND ADMINISTRATIVE FUNCTIONS COMMON TO ALL MANAGERS AND SUPERVISORS IN BRITISH LEYLAND MOTOR CORPORATION

The following paragraphs attempt to define certain functions common to all managers and supervisors throughout the Corporation. These responsibilities, because they are held in common, are not normally spelt out in individual Statements of Functions throughout the Organisation and Policy Manual. It is however of great importance that every executive accepts his individual responsibility for these tasks as an essential element of good and effective management, and that he assesses and counsels his supervisory staff on these aspects of their overall performance.

1. Develop within the framework of Corporate, Group or Division policies and practices an operating pattern and organisation structure for his assigned area of responsibility that is effective, flexible and clearly understood.
2. Ensure that operating, budgetary and other objectives of his activity are established and clearly stated, that his employees are committed to achieving them and that they are reviewed when the need arises in the light of changing conditions and circumstances.
3. Develop a forward operating plan for achieving his assigned objectives on a basis that will ensure the most efficient utilisation of employees, facilities and other resources and full contribution to maximising corporate profit.
4. Provide direction, assistance and supervision to the individuals in his activity on a continuing basis to ensure that:

   - Subordinates are fully aware of the functions for which they are responsible and against which their performance will be appraised.
   - Problems are properly analysed, causal factors are accurately identified and effective solutions are implemented.
   - Working relationships and services are established and maintained in the context of the stated Line and Staff principles of the Corporation.
   - Effective operating systems and procedures are established within his activity and are continually reviewed for improvement.
   - A proper level of budget and performance awareness is fostered among responsible subordinates.

5. Recommend re-examination or revision of policies and programmes outside his immediate area of responsibility wherever this would appear to result in more effective accomplishment of objectives.
6. Ensure that his activity is staffed with competent individuals and that capable replacements are identified, trained and developed.
7. Encourage and motivate each employee to develop and realise his true performance potential and actively assist him by counselling him periodically on his performance against objectives and by recommending appropriate training and personal development plans.
8. Represent his subordinates to Management and provide an effective 'two-way' channel of communication for the dissemination of information on Corporate and local policies and objectives and for the reporting and solution of subordinates' problems and grievances.
9. Apply consistently and fairly agreed personnel policies and standards, including those for the remuneration and reward of personnel, for personnel administration and discipline, and for participation in fringe benefits, employee services schemes and other privileges to which employees may be entitled.
10. Promote the understanding and observance of policies and agreements with Trade Unions, maintain relationships with designated employees' representatives and ensure the prompt resolution of disputes and grievances through implementation of agreed procedure.
11. Provide periodic and special reports on the personnel management of his activities as are required.

Organisation Planning
November 1971

Appendix 7.3 Example of a management job description in a manufacturing company

Position: Head of Industrial Engineering (Director)

Responsible to: Group Managing Director

Functions

Planning and directing the Group Industrial Engineering staff in formulating and coordinating Group policy, standards and practices relating to industrial engineering, including the establishment of direct and indirect labour standards, material utilisation and method improvement; and in providing guidance to Divisional and Plant activities in their application and operation. Giving appropriate assistance in other areas of the Group on industrial engineering matters, with particular responsibility for scrutinising and advising on the industrial engineering aspects of all draft agreements for new or revised payment systems.

Responsibilities

1. Formulating, developing, publishing and ensuring the implementation of Group policies, procedures and practices relating to industrial engineering, including direct and indirect labour standards, non-production material utilisation standards, method improvement, manning levels and the work standards aspects of sourcing and capacity planning.
2. Advising and assisting the Manufacturing Divisions and other Group activities in the consistent application of required industrial engineering procedures and methods; in administering improvement programmes, establishing labour standards and analysing and eliminating off-standard conditions.
3. Performing periodic and special audits and surveys of operating activities, work standards, associated data and related practices: ensuring compliance with Group Industrial Engineering policy and procedures and ascertaining the effectiveness of industrial engineering operations throughout the Group.
4. Evaluating new industrial engineering methods and techniques and providing technical advice and assistance to the Manufacturing Divisions on such matters; assisting in those areas of business activity where industrial engineering can make a contribution to maximising operating effectiveness.
5. Reviewing the industrial engineering aspects of Divisional and Plant projects, including programmes and implementation: monitoring progress and recommending any action towards achieving objectives. Working closely with appropriate activities on the industrial engineering

implications of the manufacturing sources of new parts, taking into consideration the objectives of maximum long run utilisation of Group facilities.

6. Reviewing, in conjunction with Group Finance, labour standard hours incorporated in labour budgets, off-standard conditions and relevant forward cost proposals stemming from the Manufacturing Divisions; coordinating closely with Group Finance with regard to variable design cost estimating for new product programmes as regards the labour content: assisting in interdivisional pricing matters in so far as labour and indirect material standards are concerned.

7. Ensuring that agreements made between management and representative bodies of employees are compatible with the implementation of Group Industrial Engineering practices and procedures. Assisting Group Personnel and Field Personnel activities, to the extent required, in discussions and negotiations regarding the acceptance and implementation of work standards and related industrial engineering requirements.

8. Planning and developing required training programmes and ensuring that they are conducted in such a way that all affected management personnel, particularly plant supervision, acquire the relevant understanding of industrial engineering principles and practices, with special regard to the introduction and operation of revised payment systems. Additionally, planning, developing and conducting training programmes to ensure that industrial engineers are familiar with management organisation, practices and procedures.

9. Conducting special studies and assignments, as and when required, on matters relating to the improvement of operating effectiveness such as the utilisation of non-production stores, development and repair standards, appraisal of labour and material content of employee suggestions.

10. Reviewing and concurring in the role and organisation of industrial engineering activities throughout the Group and in the selection, change in assignment and training of key industrial engineering personnel.

HGB/243
January 1973

Appendix 7.4 A management job description on a West Indian sugar estate

Position: Cultivation Manager

Responsible to: The General Manager

Functions

Planting, cultivating and reaping sugar cane and bananas at satisfactory levels of quality, quantity and cost.

Responsibilities

1. Conducting research and experimental projects in soil improvement, seed varieties, irrigation methods, uses of fertilizers, herbicides, etc (in close collaboration with the Sugar Manufacturers' Association Research Centre); reporting on the findings of such trials and experiments and applying the results in practice.
2. Planning, organising and carrying out initial land preparation, planting (by predetermined cycles), tending, irrigating and weeding crops of sugar cane and bananas.
3. Planning and conducting crop season reaping programmes designed to ensure (as far as weather conditions permit) a round-the-clock flow of freshly harvested sugar cane in adequate quantities to meet the processing capacity of the Factory.
4. Continually checking quantities harvested against predetermined reaping plans and taking any action necessary to achieve those plans.
5. Issuing orders for subcontract cane farmers to deliver canes on daily quota: ensuring that such canes are delivered in clean condition and of quality fit for the manufacture of sugar. Preparing forward estimates of farmers' canes and inspecting and recommending loans in accordance with Company policy.
6. Examining all causes of delay or stoppage in cultivation or reaping activities and initiating any necessary action: taking appropriate steps to ascertain and (where possible) permanently remove such causes of delay or breakdown.
7. Determining appropriate stock levels of all expendable items of material and equipment used in the Cultivation Department; ensuring that these are properly accounted for and that adequate arrangements exist for their ordering, receipt, storage and issue.
8. Establishing and maintaining satisfactory standards of labour performance for all operations carried out within the Cultivation Department.
9. Ensuring close coordination and cooperation with the Tractors and

Transport Manager and his staff in the planning and day-to-day operation of tractors and agricultural implements employed by the Cultivation Department.

10. Ensuring that necessary statutory and contractual records in respect of the Cultivation Department's activities are properly maintained and that routine internal records, statistics and returns approved by the General Manager are prepared and produced promptly.

11. Preparing and submitting to the General Manager such special reports or forecasts in regard to Cultivation Department activities as may be called for.

12. Keeping all Cultivation Department activities and costs under continuous observation with a view to reporting to the General Manager any current or expected deviation from normal or anticipated costs.

13. Authorising (in consultation with the General Manager) any increases in personnel under his control and finally selecting, training, transferring, promoting, suspending or dismissing all supervisory, skilled and un-skilled personnel employed in the Cultivation Department.

14. Ensuring that the provisions of labour agreements entered into by the Company are properly and faithfully implemented in regard to all Cultivation Department employees.

15. Investigating all labour disputes, grievances or claims at the appropriate levels: conducting department-level negotiations with trade union officials and delegates: collaborating with the Labour Relations Officer in the handling of labour matters at General Manager level.

16. Applying the Company's personnel and welfare policies throughout all branches of the Cultivation Department and promoting a high level of morale amongst all the Department's employees.

17. Ensuring that planned facilities are made available for the further training and development of Cultivation Department supervisory staff.

18. Maintaining in proper order and condition all Cultivation Department buildings and compounds, including adequate provision for repairs, renewals, decorations, etc.

Special responsibilities

1. Preparing annual budget estimates for capital and revenue expenditure within the Cultivation Department.

2. Making suitable arrangements, as required by the General Manager, for the conducted tour of individual visitors or parties around the cultivation areas.

Immediate subordinates

The Section Manager (North)
The Section Manager (South)
The Section Manager (West)
The Research Officer
The Surveyor

Main functional contacts

The Superintending Engineer

The Commercial Manager
The Factory Manager
The Tractor and Transport Manager
The Civil and Hydraulic Engineer
The Labour Relations Officer

Ref: CD/1
Date:

Appendix 7.5 A management job description for a divisional manager of an East Asian company

Position: Divisional Manager

Responsible to: The Managing Director

Responsible for:

1. *Policy*

   (*a*) Advising the Managing Director on management policies to be followed within the Division: referring matters where it appears advisable to sanction departure from prescribed Company policies.
   (*b*) Receiving policy directives from the Managing Director: ensuring that such directives are properly interpreted as *instructions* which are made known to and carried into effect by his subordinates.

2. *Manufacturing programmes*

   Formulating (in consultation with other officers concerned, e.g. Controller of Accounts) and submitting to the Managing Director, forward manufacturing programmes based on:

   (*a*) known sales requirements of the Division's products;
   (*b*) anticipated manufacturing resources, e.g. buildings, services, tools, equipment, staff and labour;
   (*c*) known availability of materials (direct and indirect).

3. *Production planning and control*

   Breaking down approved manufacturing programmes and preparing, issuing and encouraging compliance with schedules of labour, materials, facilities, instructions and all additional items required to complete manufacturing orders so that they will be available when and where required. This will include:

   (*a*) specifying the most practicable combination of where and when to perform every activity required to complete an order;
   (*b*) supplying as and when needed all direct and indirect materials, facilities, jigs, tools, etc. required;
   (*c*) aiding manufacturing departments to follow the schedules established by the above production planning function;
   (*d*) frequently being advised of production progress relative to instructions issued.

4. *Purchasing*

Securing when required, and at minimum cost, the quantity and quality of materials, supplies, services and equipment required to operate the Division: seeing that purchased items and services arrive as promised by suppliers.

5. *Storekeeping*

Receiving, safeguarding, issuing and accounting for items required to manufacture a product, perform a service or operate the Division.

6. *Industrial engineering*

Planning the utilisation of labour, facilities, tools, jigs and fixtures to attain the desired quantity and quality of output at minimum cost. This will include:

(a) establishing the best methods of performing necessary direct and indirect production tasks;
(b) establishing the best physical arrangement of facilities, utilities and work areas in the shops of the division;
(c) establishing time standards for performing necessary direct and indirect production tasks: calculating numbers of operators required according to these established standards.

7. *Quality control (inspection)*

(a) Establishing quality standards and acceptable limits of variation in the attributes of the Division's products at all stages of manufacture.
(b) Conducting quality control measurements and analyses; rejecting unsuitable products; halting substandard production processes and notifying those affected.
(c) Establishing ways of preventing or limiting production of unacceptable parts, subassemblies or products; investigating customer complaints.

8. *Plant maintenance*

(a) Maintaining buildings, facilities and utility services within the Division in safe operating condition: establishing a system of planned maintenance.
(b) Specifying or approving all Divisional factory and office equipment and buildings and ensuring their proper installation.
(c) Ensuring the provision of all electricity, compressed air, heat, water and similar services needed by the Division.
(d) Maintaining specification and location records of all capitalised equipment in the Division.

9. *Product development*

Reappraising and redesigning the Division's existing products with respect to materials, appearance, performance and manufacturing requirements, to reduce costs and to improve quality.

10. *Cost accounting*

Planning, directing and measuring the monetary results of the Division's operations by means of:

(a) preparing (in consultation with the Controller of Accounts) planned budgets, performance standards or target costs for all the Division's activities;

(b) recording costs incurred in relation to work performed;

(c) measuring the actual results against budgets, standards and targets: analysing and accounting for variances;

(d) investigating the causes of variances, reporting these to the Managing Director and taking the necessary corrective action.

11. *Personnel administration (establishments)*

(a) Ensuring Divisional compliance with the legal, statutory and Company policy requirements in regard to the employment of staff and labour.

(b) Ensuring that all positions are filled by competent personnel at reasonable cost and that all employees are fairly and equitably rewarded.

(c) Ensuring that the internal organisation structure and allocation of authority and responsibility within the Division is balanced and adequate to meet its needs.

(d) Ensuring that all executive, specialist and supervisory appointments are properly defined and published.

(e) Maintaining the general welfare of employees on the job and assisting them with problems relating to their security and personal well-being.

(f) Investigating labour disputes and taking action towards maintaining sound and harmonious Company–trade union relationships.

12. *Reports*

Submitting to the Managing Director such regular reports, returns or other information as he may call for about the Division's operations and costs.

13. *General*

Ensuring that all management and supervisory decisions and actions taken within the Division are consistent with the approved policies and practices which are being exercised throughout the Company and the Group of which it forms a part. Seeking advice or direction from the Managing Director on any points of information or doubt about these matters.

Senior staff

To support and assist him in discharge of the foregoing responsibilities the Divisional Manager's senior staff officers will comprise:

1. Works Manager
2. Production Controller

6. Divisional Chief Inspector
7. Divisional Maintenance Engineer

3. Divisional Purchasing Officer
4. Divisional Stores Officer
5. Divisional Industrial Engineer

8. Divisional Development Engineer
9. Divisional Cost Accountant
10. Divisional Establishments Officer

H. K. Subbrayam
Group Organisation
Date:

Appendix 7.6 An organisation and appointments announcement in a light engineering company

To: All Directors, Executives   From: The General Manager
     and Monthly Staff

Production Planning and Control Services—Organisation:
Following the redesignation of Mr D. Brown's appointment as Manager: Production Planning and Control Services (as specified in Organisation Memo No. 24 of 6 October last), the following new appointments become effective immediately:

New Products Coordinator: *Mr J. Woods*

Mr Woods is appointed New Products Coordinator responsible to Mr D Brown for:

1. Preparing and monitoring primary programmes for the coordination and introduction of new models, products or major modifications. This will entail very close consultation with sales/customers' product planning, design engineering, tool administration, facilities planning, presswork and assembly managements and other departments concerned.
2. Up-dating programmes as necessary and modifying plans as dictated by changing requirements or deviations from progress targets.
3. Developing and maintaining the use of network analysis as a medium for preparing, monitoring and modifying 'new model' programmes.
4. Coordinating the introduction of approved modifications in close conjunction with factory executives, customers' representatives and Group Modification Liaison sections.
5. Assisting in the preparation of agenda and performing other secretarial duties in connection with the New Products Committee Meetings.
6. Planning and organising such coordination meetings as may be necessary during the various development stages of productionising a new model or major modification. Attending, chairing or acting as secretary of such meetings; reporting results to the New Products Committee and taking appropriate action in connection with programmes.
7. Developing improved production planning and control procedures for introduction of new models in close consultation with systems specialists and factory managements.

In addition to discharging the foregoing responsibilities, Mr Woods will deputise for Mr D. Brown in the latter's absence.

Production Controller (Press Shops)   *Mr B. Wilson*

As Production Controller (Press Shops), Mr Wilson will answer to Mr D. Brown and his responsibilities will include:

1. Coordinating with factory managements and specialist departments in the development of new production control techniques within the press shops. Ensuring that there is sufficient commonality of procedure to enable overall press shop capacity accurately to be determined.
2. Advising on large and small press run sizes in relation to press capacities and pallet and storage availability.
3. Maintaining records of press shop achievement so that ¬·ailable capacity data can be constantly updated.
4. Carrying out press studies to determine forward press shop loads in relation to available capacity and to provide information for the calculation of pallet and storage requirements: in conjunction with Production Engineering, carrying out those studies required for the determination of future press shop developments.
5. Planning tryout press requirements in close cooperation with tool administration and press shop managements.
6. Allocating presswork within the press shops and coordinating the interdepartmental movement of large and small pressings.

Production Controller (Assembly Shops)   *Mr W. Banks*

Mr Banks (who has hitherto answered to Mr R. Atkins, Deputy Assembly Manager) now becomes responsible to Mr D. Brown for:

1. translating customers' schedules into detailed manufacturing programmes on a component and final assembly basis;
2. maintaining data on available assembly capacities based on both facilities and manpower;
3. monitoring production performances against programmes and preparing management returns as required: preparing, maintaining and publishing assembly production statistics on a weekly accounting period basis;
4. liaising with customers' and suppliers' production and material control departments in regard to production performance with particular reference to disputes, stoppages, shortages or other interruptions in supply;
5. determining, in conjunction with departmental managers concerned, desirable pressings and components stock levels and where necessary liaising with transport contractors in connection with the supply of trailer storage facilities.

Pallet Controller   *Mr S. Harris*

Mr Harris (who has also answered hitherto to Mr R. Atkins, Deputy Assembly Manager) becomes responsible to Mr D. Brown for:

1. determining future pallet requirements on a type-by-type and department-by-department basis: this in close collaboration with the press shops and assembly shops Production Controllers and with Pallet Officers at departmental level;

2. checking and controlling the movements of pallets to ensure that these are available in the right place at the right time, this with due regard to the requirement to minimise transportation costs of moving empties;
3. progressing and expediting the return of pallets from locations outside the factory.

A further announcement regarding additional responsibilities of the newly formed Production Planning and Control Services function will be issued shortly.

A. Smith
Director and General Manager

Date:
O/M No. 27

Appendix 7.7 Job description for an organisation planning manager

Position: Manager, Organisation Planning

Responsible to: The Managing Director

Function

The Manager, Organisation Planning is responsible to the Managing Director for making recommendations on the organisational concepts, structures and relationships which will most effectively assist the achievement of the Corporation's business objectives: for functionally supervising, reviewing and providing consultancy assistance to the Staffs and Operations of the Corporation on organisation matters: and for providing an information service to the management of the Corporation on organisation matters, management appointments and statements of overall corporate policy.

Responsibilities

1. Develop and recommend for approval basic concepts, plans, policies, procedures and standards relating to the current and forward organisation of the Corporation, its committees and constituent organisation components.
2. Recommend organisation plans for newly established activities and provide advice and assistance on the organisation, policy and management control aspects of new business plans and programmes.
3. Conduct or participate in studies of current organisation in any area of the Corporation as requested and propose to line management organisation changes to improve operating effectiveness, to optimise spans of control and levels of supervision, to simplify responsibilities and relationships and to reduce operating costs.
4. Advise line management and staff activities on operating and forward planning problems considered to have organisation and related policy implications and develop organisation proposals as appropriate.
5. Develop procedures for the development and submission of major organisation change proposals by operating Groups, Divisions and other activities and review requests for the establishment, elimination or restructuring of organisational components. Guide decentralised Personnel activities in local organisation planning administration and in development of local organisation proposals. Coordinate the implementation of proposed changes to ensure orderly execution.

6. Represent the Corporation in studies of operating relationships with affiliated or otherwise related activities, in policy revisions and in delegations of authority. Participate in developing intra-Corporation working relationship agreements and secure approvals.

7. Advise on the delegation of management approval authorities and assist in developing for assigned areas effective patterns of approval responsibilities.

8. Participate in formulating overall statements of corporate policy on matters of major operating significance which have organisational implications; presenting proposals for management approval.

9. Undertake research into advanced organisation and related management control concepts and practice, including contemporary and forward trends in business management theory, the organisational aspects of personnel and behavioural research and operating practices in competitor and comparator companies.

10. Develop and present for approval plans for the long range corporate organisation of the Corporation and advise management of environmental factors which may influence organisation requirements.

11. Administer directly, or functionally control, the commitment of organisation change by means of the announcement procedure, participate in drafting announcements as required, and assure prior Central Staff visibility of all announcements of major organisation changes that are to be issued in any Group or Division of the Corporation.

12. Publish and maintain the Corporate Organisation and Policy Manual and provide an information service on all organisation, personnel assignments and authorities matters.

13. Provide a total organisation planning service directly to those staff and field activities of the Corporation which have no local Personnel or Staff Relations activity. Functionally control local organisation planning activity in all other areas of the Corporation.

Organisation Planning
Date:

Chart showing pattern of future retirements at 65 years

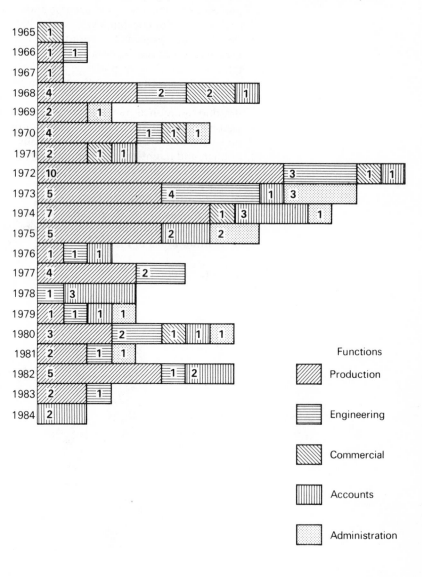

Chart showing pattern of future retirements at 65 years

Appendix 7.9 Personal specification

Position: Chief Engineer Electricity Supply (Distribution) Board

I. *Personal data*

   A. *Age group:*
   Normally 40 to 50 years

   B. *Education:*
     1. General:
      Grammar School/Public School
     2. Technical:
      University/Technical College

   C. *Qualifications:*
   Science Degree (Engineering). Normally, Associate membership of the Institution of Electrical Engineers and of the British Institute of Management.

II. *Technical knowledge and experience*
(To be studied in conjunction with Schedule of Responsibilities of the Chief Engineer)

   A. *General*
   Requires knowledge and experience sufficient to enable him effectively to plan, coordinate, supervise and check the performance of specialist subordinates in the field of:
     1. Distribution Planning
     2. Carrying out Capital Works
     3. Conduct of Operations (System Control)
     4. Distribution System Maintenance
     5. Distribution System Communications
     6. Meters
     7. Safety Arrangements
     8. Electrical Research
     9. Planning, Erection, Modification, Maintenance of Non-Operational Buildings
     10. Provision, Employment and Maintenance of Transport

   B. *Background*
   Requires general background knowledge sufficient to promote balance of outlook and to ensure the necessary degree of vertical and lateral coordination in matters concerning:
     1. Publicity arrangements

2. Sales development (energy)
3. Sales development (appliances, etc.)
4. Sales administration
5. Tariffs
6. Contracting
7. Street lighting
8. Preparation of accounts
9. Collection of accounts
10. Banking
11. Payment of accounts
12. Costing procedures
13. Preparation and use of statistics
14. Salaries and wages
15. Income tax
16. Superannuation
17. Financial accounts
18. Insurance
19. Security
20. Audit arrangements
21. Organisation and methods
22. Personnel Administration
23. National wage and salary agreements
24. Welfare
25. Training
26. Joint consultation
27. Trade unions
28. Legal matters
29. Office Administration
30. Purchasing arrangements
31. Purchasing (certain contracts)
32. Stock Identification and control
33. Operational research

III. *Managerial skills*

A. *Personnel management*
Requires knowledge, experience and manifest ability to exercise direct authority over and be responsible for the handling, discipline and morale of large numbers of employees of all grades, where the chain of delegated authority comprises upwards of 3–4 different levels of intermediate supervision.

B. *Executive ability*
Requires a high standard of knowledge, experience and personal competence in the use of the following executive skills:
1. *Planning*
Interpreting Board policy (as expressed in Standing Instructions and other prescribed procedures) and translating this into specific and practical plans for implementation *within his own field of executive control*. Explaining these plans to subordinates (delegation) and establishing and agreeing suitable standards of performance (e.g. target dates, sales budgets, cost allocations, etc.)

2. *Control*

   Using all available 'control information' (e.g. reports, statistics, cost and financial returns, etc.) for the purposes of: constantly reviewing progress and comparing results against plans; investigating and following up variances and departures from plan.

3. *Coordination*

   Ensuring that a proper balance is maintained between the different activities of his subordinates and their staffs and seeing that their efforts are coordinated in pursuance of the common plan.

4. *Communications*

   Establishing and maintaining high standards of communication practice, i.e. freely using every possible means of circulating information, both within his own area of executive control and also vertically and laterally through the Board's organisation structure (e.g. by personal contact correspondence, meetings, formal and informal joint consultation).

C. *Public relations*

   Requires disposition for and experience in positively pursuing public relations activities over a wide field, for example:

   1. Public speaking and discussions; delivering addresses and papers; staging and presenting demonstrations and exhibitions.
   2. Participating in technical conferences and meetings, organised sports and social functions, etc., both within and outside the Board's sphere of operations.
   3. Holding office and/or Committee membership of professional, technical, commercial and social corporate bodies.

IV. *Personal qualities*

   A. *Appearance and presence*

   Should habitually present a neat and tidy appearance (e.g. quiet mode of dress, fastidious personal grooming, etc.) and should have an easy, approachable manner.

   B. *Mental ability*

   Should be above average intelligence as evidenced by ability readily to grasp and comprehend the essential facts of a situation; to relate and coordinate these in an orderly way to arrive at a reasoned and balanced conclusion (e.g. suitable course of action).

   C. *Self-confidence*

   Should constantly display (and express in action) a quiet self-confidence, without being overbearing.

   D. *Interest in individuals*

   Should show a lively interest in the understanding of individuals and should manifest readiness and ability to see the points of view of others.

   E. *Integrity and sincerity*

   Should possess an unquestioned reputation for moral and material integrity (honesty) and should display a degree of sincerity which will earn the implicit trust of others.

   F. *Self-expression*

   Should be capable of expressing his thoughts clearly and briefly, both in speech and in writing.

G. *Responsibility, judgment and stability*
Should have displayed an active and above-average readiness to accept responsibility and to take decisions, tempered by desirable degrees of mature judgment and personal stability.

H. *Acceptability*
Should be readily acceptable, as an individual, to superiors, colleagues, subordinates and consumers.

Appendix 7.10 Performance and potential appraisal form

Name.................... *Department*....................

Performance review
A. *General performance*

Specific examples of important strengths and needs

Quantity of work
Speed and consistency in producing required results
Quality of work
Extent to which results meet requirements of accuracy and thoroughness
Knowledge of job
Grasp of technical (or professional) knowledge and practical knowhow required for the job
Attitude to job
Extent of enthusiasm, cooperation and initiative
Adaptability
Ability to anticipate changing conditions and willingness to perform a variety of tasks within scope of accountabilities
Innovation
Ability and willingness to introduce new ideas and methods

RATING:

B. *Personal characteristics*
   (in relation to the job)
Problem solving
Ability to grasp and apply new methods and to deal with unfamiliar problems or situations

Effectiveness in communication

(*a*) Oral: at meetings, discussions, interviews
(*b*) Written: reports, memoranda, letters
(*c*) Keeping superiors and subordinates well
informed

Acceptability

Relationships with senior and junior staff and
colleagues

Manner and appearance

Suitability of these characteristics in relation
to the job

RATING:

C. *Supervisory/Managerial ability*

(to be completed only for those having responsibility for the work of subordinates)

Planning

Anticipating needs, devising programmes,
budgets, schedules as required

Organising and delegating

Dividing, distributing and assigning responsibility for work

Controlling and coordinating

Keeping unit working towards objectives,
measuring performance, interpreting results, initiating corrective action

Leading

Securing full and willing response from subordinates individually and as a team

Training and developing

Selecting, developing and training staff
effectively; showing concern about their future and accepting counselling responsibilities

RATING:

Performance rating overall

RATING:

....
signed [First Reviewer]

I confirm: ....
signed [Confirming Reviewer]

Training and development
What specific job objectives, training courses or other developmental plans are recommended to:
1. *Improve performance in present job*

2. *Develop potential*

Forecast of potential
Having discussed the individual in relation to his present job performance, the reviewers should jointly decide on answers to the following questions:
1. *Promotability*
   (*a*) General: Is he capable of doing a bigger job?

   YES   NO   NOT YET

If the answer is 'NO' or 'NOT YET' state the reason
(*b*) Specific: Is there a likely promotion in the Department/Section?

   YES   NO   DON'T KNOW

If 'YES' to what job?

How would you assess his promotability in relation to that job?

   READY NOW   WITHIN 12 MONTHS   WITHIN 2 YEARS

2. *Transferability*
   Which jobs in other departments or sections could he perform at the same level?

3. *Potential*

What is the highest job level (e.g. Factory Manager, Departmental Head, Shop Superintendent, etc) at which you can envisage this person operating satisfactorily within the next five years?

What particular strengths will help him?

What needs must be met if he is to achieve this?

Performance rating code

(For use when completing Parts II and III)

Outstanding: 'O' Performance is consistently distinguished in almost every respect. It is attainable by very few people, but they may be at any level in the organisation. This performance would normally indicate a promotion need.

Excellent: 'E' Performance is marked by initiative and high quality of work. Valuable contributions are made in excess of the requirements of the position and consistently sound judgment is evident. This level of assessment normally indicates that promotion can be considered.

Superior: 'S' Performance is noticeably better than acceptable; the accountabilities of the job are being exceeded. This performance may indicate promotion potential.

Acceptable: 'A' Performance is fully acceptable; the accountability for the job is being fully achieved.

Fair: 'F' Performance comes close to being acceptable, but further development is needed to make it fully satisfactory.

Marginal: 'M' Inexperienced newcomer to job, or one whose performance is below an acceptable level. Performance is required to improve.

Unsatisfactory: 'U' Performance is consistently unacceptable: must improve considerably if job is to be held.

Appendix 7.11 **Personal assessment form**

Strictly Confidential

Appraisal at: .... Name: ....

Department: .... Age: .... years

Position: .... Service: .... years

Held since: ....

Qualifications:

Present remuneration		Recommendation		Reached top of Grade?
Grade	Salary	Increase	Grade	
	£	£		Yes/No

Assessment made by: ....

Length of acquaintance: one year/Less than one year/ .... years

Scrutinised and countersigned by: .... Controller

Notes:
  (i) This form is designed for completion by Senior Managers on the basis of personal knowledge of the individual who is being rated.
 (ii) The assessor is invited to complete the appraisal with the utmost objectivity, not influenced by an occasional incident.
(iii) Comments are invited/encouraged as freely as possible, and should *always* be expressed when a 'weak' rating is recorded.
(iv) No provision is made in the present context for discussion of the appraisal with the individual manager or staff member concerned; it is intended that that step should be introduced into the procedure later.

Personal assessment	Rating		
	Good	Weak	Comments
Characteristics General assessment of personality Attention to his duties Discipline and timekeeping General behaviour and attitude			

Mental calibre
Is he quick to grasp essentials?
Can he penetrate to underlying facets?
Are his responses and reactions to
    problems pertinent?
    —and prompt?
Is he open-minded to new ideas and
    other people's thoughts?
Does he show maturity of judgment?			

Initiative Does he show good self-confidence? Are there signs of over-confidence? Does he get action started? Is he a source of new ideas?			
Cooperation Is he respected by his colleagues? —and subordinates? Does he work in easily with others? Does he make himself easily understood? How do you enjoy working with him?			
Responsibility Is he a stable personality? Does he have a good sense of responsibility? Do others rely on his judgment? Is he a man of mental integrity?			

In what respects has he 'grown as a
    person' since the last appraisal
    (or since you have known him)?
What personal deficiencies are marked?
    Have these been pointed out to him?

Proficiency: Technical
Is his technical knowledge up to date with requirements of position?   Yes/No
Has he added to *technical* competence in past year?   Yes/No
    In what ways?

What technical deficiencies does he still show:
—in knowledge?
—in experience?
What steps should be taken to overcome these?

Proficiency: Management   *Rating*

	Good	Weak	Comments
Does he understand his responsibilities? And discharge them? What is his ability in planning: —his own activities? —of his subordinates? Are his instructions to subordinates clearly given? What is his competence in: —controlling subordinates? —conforming with budgets? —implementing changes? —written communication? Does he persist in progress in spite of difficulties? Has he a commercial awareness? Is he contributing to development of subordinates?			

What deficiencies does he still show as a manager?

When were these last discussed with him?

What recommendations were given to him to overcome them?

Development potential

Taking an *overall assessment* how would you rate him in relation to performance in his *present position*?

Tick item(s) applicable.

—a highly competent manager?..
—a satisfactory manager?..
—room for considerable improvement?...
—a good scientist but not a manager?..
—little potential discernible? ....

What *further experience* would you *recommend* for him in relation to better performance in present position?

Is he ready for some development/promotion now?   Yes/No

In *what directions* do you see his *best potential* for advancement:
—short-term promotion?
—longer-term development?

What *management studies* would you recommend for him?

Further reading

BRECH, E. F. L., *Organisation—the Framework of Management*, Longmans, 1965.

BARNES, M. C. et al., *Company Organisation: Theory and Practice*, Allen & Unwin, 1970.

SADLER, P. J. AND BARRY, B. A., *Organisational Development*, Longman, 1970.

BROWN, WILFRED (Lord), *Organisation*, Heinemann, 1971.

STEWART, ROSEMARY, *The Reality of Organisations*, Macmillan, 1970.

REVANS, R. W., *Developing Effective Managers*, Longman, 1971.

RAPOPORT, R. N., *Mid-career Development*, Tavistock Publications, 1970.

ARGYRIS, C., *Interpersonal Competence and Organisational Effectiveness*, Tavistock Publications, 1962.

MANT, A., *The Experienced Manager*, British Institute of Management, 1969.

NEWMAN, A. D., *Organisation Design*, Arnold, 1973.

JOHANNSEN, H. (Ed.), *Company Organisation Structure*, British Institute of Management, 1970.

BUSINESS GRADUATES ASSOCIATION, *The Graduate in British Industry*, London, 1973.

HUMBLE, JOHN, *Improving Performance of the Experienced Manager*, McGraw-Hill, 1973

HAGUE, H., *Executive Self-development*, Macmillan, 1974.

BRECH, E. F. L., *Managing for Revival*, British Institute of Management, 1972.

SINGER, E. J., *Effective Management Coaching*, Institute of Personnel Management, 1974.

Index